THE BOOK OF LIEDER

The Book of Lieder

The original texts of over 1000 songs

Chosen, translated and introduced by RICHARD STOKES

Foreword by IAN BOSTRIDGE

faber and faber

First published in 2005
by Faber and Faber Limited
3 Queen Square London WC1N 3AU

Typeset in Minion by Faber and Faber Limited
Printed in England by The Bath Press, Bath

A CIP record for this book
is available from the British Library

ISBN 0–571–22439–3

10 9 8 7 6 5 4 3 2 1

For Tabitha and Hannah

Nimm sie hin denn, diese Lieder

Contents

Foreword

I fell in love with Lieder in one of my earliest German lessons, at the age of fourteen. My teacher was Richard Stokes, and the catalyst was a recording of 'Erlkönig' performed by Dietrich Fischer-Dieskau and Gerald Moore. There was something a little miraculous about it, as with so many musical epiphanies. It wasn't as if I hadn't heard a Schubert song before – in fact, as a treble, I'd sung 'The Shepherd on the Rock' ('Der Hirt auf dem Felsen'), in execrable German, only a couple of years before. And what's more, the thing that is supposed to be so special about the Lied, the intermeshing of music and text, was in some sense lost on me because, in my first or second lesson, I obviously didn't understand German beyond the odd word. All I knew was the outline of the story: boy riding through forest with father, lured and destroyed by an evil spirit. It's a powerful, archetypal narrative with all the psychoanalytic resonance of the fairy tale. The picture I had in my head was familiar, something like the cover of C. S. Lewis's *Prince Caspian*, all darkness and urgency; and what I heard through the medium of incomprehensible, talismanic syllables, and pounding, swelling piano, was the energy of the ride, the sense of foreboding. By some sort of alchemy, the music embodied the story.

The question that presented itself fairly quickly to my adolescent mind, so keen to categorize and define, was: what is the Lied? The question is a tricky one. The German word 'Lied' means song, often synonymous with *Gesang*. There is, indeed, another virtual synonym which, yoking the two words together, evokes a sort of generic grandeur, *Liedgesang*. 'Lied' is a word which, because of the cultural dissemination of Romantic German song, has passed into the fringes of many European languages, at the same time as inspiring radical departures in national song traditions in France, Italy, Spain, even eventually in England, that notorious 'land without music'. In America, the term for this sort of music is 'art song' and that captures, if slightly awkwardly, what is at issue here: the ambition of the genre and its seriousness of purpose.

A Lied tends to set pre-existing literary texts: sometimes lyric poems which, in typical Romantic fashion, were half conceived to be sung (the poems of Wilhelm Müller, poet of *Die schöne Müllerin*, *Die Winterreise* and two-thirds of 'Der Hirt auf dem Felsen' spring to mind); sometimes, at the other extreme, poems with the metaphysical grandeur of Goethe's *Grenzen der Menschheit*. Some of the most famous Lieder come from novels where one of the characters is supposed to sing the poem in the course of the narrative (Goethe's Bildungsroman *Wilhelm Meister* gives us the songs of Mignon and the Harper, famously set by Schubert, Schumann and Wolf); others come from plays.

While the idea of the Romantic lyric calls a guitar to mind – a miller-boy playing by the brook – the essential technological progenitor of the Lied as we know it was the piano. The invention and domestic triumph of the piano changed the rules of the game for keyboard-accompanied song, and the story could be told as a historical-materialist one in which technical developments drive aesthetic change. Certainly it was the piano's increasing volume, colour palette and suppleness that pushed the Lied into areas of dramatic autonomy and psychological subtlety. One of the things that distinguishes the Lieder recital to this day is its recognition of the absolute centrality of the piano's so-called accompaniment.

This leads me to the other big mystery for my adolescent self: why does everyone say that Schubert invented the Lied? How can he, however peerless as a songwriter, have invented song, the Lied, itself? Something new was certainly going on with Schubert: reviewers of the time found much of his Lieder output difficult to understand, railing against 'the unwarrantably strong inclination to modulate again and again, with neither rest or respite'. Schubert, according to this critic, writing in the *Leipziger Allgemeine Musikalische Zeitung* in 1824, 'seeks to make up for the want of inner unity, order and regularity by eccentricities which are hardly or not at all justified and by often rather wild goings-on'. Turn all this on its head, and you have the reasons for the newness of the Schubert Lied; it is the wild goings-on which in fact supply much of the inner unity. An early critic of 'Erlkönig' understood this well:

> In the greatest work by our composer, the 'Erl King', it is neither the melodic expression nor the succession of notes in the voice part which gives organic unity to the whole, but rather the harmonic expression, the tone, imparted to the work by the accompaniment. This is the foundation ... on which the tone-picture is laid.*

Schubert is famous as a great melodist and the reputation is a just one. But the resources of the piano encouraged him to produce songs of great harmonic complexity – from which, of course, a stunning simplicity can more tellingly emerge – in which the so-called accompanying instrument became more often than not the equal of the vocal soloist. This is clear not only from the evidence of the notes on the page. Schubert himself wrote of the new performing style his songs entailed:

> The manner in which Vogl sings and I accompany, the way in which we seem, at such a moment, to become *one*, is something quite new and unheard of for these people.

This, then, is truly vocal chamber music in its Romantic incarnation, music with the transcendental ambitions, the urge to sublimity of the piano sonata or the string quartet. We're an age away from the condescension of the Enlightenment, usefully embodied in Jean-Jacques Rousseau's determinedly casual definition of song from his *Dictionary of Music*:

* Friedrich von Hentl in the *Wiener Zeitschrift für Kunst*, 23 March 1822, 'A Glance at Schubert's Songs, Opp. 1–7'.

A type of short lyrical poem, usually on a pleasant topic, to which a tune is added, to be sung at homely occasions such as at table, with one's friends, with one's mistress, or even alone, to while away some moments of boredom if one is rich, or to alleviate one's misery and fatigue if one is poor.

The sheer volume of Schubert's songs, around six hundred, is testament to the dedication of this extraordinary musical mind to moving beyond such an impoverished notion of song. The titanic cycle *Winterreise* was a confident assertion of the centrality of the Lied form to the most progressive music of the 1820s. It was influential not only in establishing the artistic credibility of the Lied as a significant art form, but also in helping to legitimate a new Romantic aesthetic in which the juxtaposition of small forms, such as songs, could have great expressive power. Following the emotional contours of the text, *Winterreise* unfolds with an affective logic which leaves behind the formal musical structures inherited from the eighteenth century. The alliance with text was, paradoxically, a liberation, and one revelled in by that most literary of composers, Robert Schumann, starting with the piano pieces of the 1830s and culminating in the songs of 1840.

Yet it is 1814, Schubert's eighteenth year, which stands out as a watershed in the history of song. One song of that year, 'Gretchen am Spinnrade' is what one might call the *Urlied*, the *fons et origo*. It allows us to talk about the invention of the Lied, in the sense of a world-conquering genre which forms to this day a central part of the classical repertoire. It preempts the only work by an older composer which could claim to be part of the new current of song, Beethoven's rather un-Beethovenian *An die ferne Geliebte*; it sets a poem by the master poet of the German language, the challenge of whose verse remained at the centre of song composition for over a hundred years; it is grounded in the textures and rhythmic impulse of the piano; and it possesses an ineffable psychological penetration and formal unity. 'Erlkönig' followed in 1815. Not every song of Schubert's possesses the same extraordinary focus; many glanced back to models of the past. But as we perform each Schubert song in recital, even the most backward-looking, we do so in the light of his transformation of the genre; and it is Schubert's example that made song a matter of moment for Schumann, Brahms, Wolf, Gustav Mahler, for Berlioz, Fauré, Duparc, Debussy, for Benjamin Britten and for Francis Poulenc.

Around 1800 there was an aesthetic conundrum to be solved: the Romantic coalescence of music and the poetic impulse. It's interesting to see that two composers, born within a year of each other, Schubert and Carl Loewe, were obsessed by the same problem, both producing a massive body of Lieder. Schubert's preeminence returns me to my first paragraph. Loewe is diligent, ingenious, even masterly in solving the problems which the Lied presents; but his music does not soar to the heights of Schubert. It isn't simply that the music of Schubert's songs, considered separately, is greater; of course this is what we would expect of the composer of the quintet, the 'Unfinished' Symphony and the late piano sonatas. It is that curious quality which seized me in that German lesson, the capacity to bring language alive through and in music, regardless of whether the language itself is understood or not, to crystallize and realize the movement and emotion of a text, to grasp and present it.

The irony is that it should have been Goethe who provoked Schubert's breakthrough: Goethe, the universal genius, the master-spirit of modern German literature, a man well aware of the revolution in musical possibility at the end of the eighteenth century but unable to accept the seeming appropriation, or even overwhelming, of the poetic text which the Schubertian Lied might represent. Schubert's settings were sent to Goethe on two occasions and, famously, he never replied. His views on musical setting were conservative; his preferred composer was his friend, Johann Friedrich Reichardt. Yet if Goethe's poetry lives for a non-German-speaking audience at the beginning of the twenty-first century, it is thanks to the universal appeal of Schubert's songs.

This universality or, more measurably, the exportability of the Lieder of Schubert, Schumann, Brahms, Wolf and others is astonishing for a form rooted in the least familiar major European language. The popularity of the Lied in German-speaking countries is hardly surprising: a recent commentator, Edward Kravitt, has estimated that Berlin could support twenty such concerts a week, mostly sold-out, in the years immediately before the First World War. As for Vienna, the multinational capital of German musical culture, by the late 1880s, Hugo Wolf, writing as a critic, could describe Lieder recitals as an 'epidemic'.

German history might also have impeded the progress of such a German art form. If, for liberal Germans, the Lied spoke the language of Goethe, Schiller and Heine, for the more nationalistically-minded it expressed the superiority of German values, of *Kultur* over *Zivilisation*. Such a point of view is overtly embodied in a painting hanging in the National Gallery in Berlin. In his *Quarters at a Base outside Paris*, painted in 1894 but set in 1871, Anton von Werner depicts a muddy, manly Prussian officer singing Schumann's 'Mondnacht' to piano accompaniment in an effete French drawing room. Without the Nazi associations which Wagner's operas acquired in the twentieth century, Lieder could nevertheless become attached to dispiriting moments in the history of Germany over the period 1871 to 1945, even if in more consolatory than triumphalist vein. A sentimental Second World War movie has Elizabeth Schwarzkopf singing 'Mondnacht' as the bombs fall in late 1942; and a gruesome fascination attaches to the 1945 recording of *Winterreise* by the tenor Peter Anders, made in the ruins of Berlin.

Despite such impoverished appropriations, and such horrific associations, the impact of the Lied on European-wide musical culture has been intense, and long-lasting. The Germanness of the Lied did not inhibit the success of Schwarzkopf or Fischer-Dieskau recitals in the 1950s and 1960s, indeed, they saw themselves as cultural ambassadors for a repentant Germany. Much more recently, the Song-makers' Almanac and the Wigmore Hall have carried forward the peculiar rooted-ness of Lied performance in London.

The particularity of the Lied has nevertheless remained a problem for some. For those emerging from what they saw as hypocritical, stale Victorianism in the 1920s, Lieder were sentimental effusions which could only embarrass. Stravinsky's friend Lord Berners composed a mocking Heine *Liederkreis* in which 'Du bist wie eine Blume' was supposedly sung in honour of a deliciously lovely white pig. Ingmar Bergman's *Fanny and Alexander* and his disciple Woody Allen's *Midsummer Night's Sex Comedy* both feature excrutiatingly embarrassing scenes of domestic Lieder performances (of 'Du Ring an meinem Finger' and 'Ich grolle nicht' respec-tively). With more of a political edge, writing in 1982, the distinguished American historian of Germany Gordon Craig expressed distaste for the Romantic nihilism which he saw embedded in the whole Lied thing. He wrote of something

> undeniably . . . unhealthy about the Romantics' preoccupation with a world that lay beyond the confines of our own, in which good and evil spirits moved and in which all the real answers and solutions were to be found. It denoted, if nothing else, an abdication of responsibility for the problems of actual exis-tence. And even more troubling was the fascination with death that was so pronounced among the first Romantic generation.

To underline that last point, he cited *Die schöne Müllerin*, *Winterreise*, and Goethe on Classic healthiness versus Romantic sickness. Setting aside the whole historical debate about the German *Sonderweg* – the special path to the *Nazizeit*, the putative contribution of German culture to the German 'problem' – in the modern period, one detects a feeling that Lieder wallow in a psychologically unhealthy obsessive-ness with death and nothingness.

There is something Freudian here, a view of art as pathological. Freud himself was uninterested in music, a striking fact for a Moravian-born Jewish intellectual living in Vienna. As he wrote at the beginning of *Moses and Michelangelo*, as far as works of art were concerned he liked

> to explain to myself what their effect is due to. Wherever I cannot do this, as for instance with music, I am almost incapable of obtaining any pleasure. Some rationalistic, or perhaps analytic turn of mind in me rebels against being moved by a thing without knowing why I am thus affected and what it is that affects me.

As his nephew Harry put it, more bluntly, 'he despised music and considered it solely as an intrusion.' Nonetheless there is something in Freud's notion of 'being moved by a thing without knowing why' which is very true to everyone's experi-ence of music and which, moreover, hints at how the Lied achieves its broader power, beyond being an apt or accomplished setting of a worthy text. It is what goes on in the Lied which we do not understand that gives the Lied its power. The form, at its best, is inspired by the totality of a poetic vision, and will even attend to some expressive details of that poem. But what makes for the power of the genre is the sense that more is going on than is being said. In fact, one might see many of the Lieder of Schubert and his successors, as anticipations and analogues of the Freudian theory of the mind, with (crudely) voice as conscious being following, escaping, or transcending the dictates of the pianistic unconscious. This is complicated, of course, by the frequent assumption by the piano of an imitative role in which it represents nature or material reality: a spinning wheel; a galloping horse; a whispering forest. It is a material reality, however, that is suffused with feeling and modulated by neurotic response; no more so than in *Winterreise*, where even nature seems to conspire against the protagonist.

This precocious psychoanalytic dimension enhances the archetypal quality of much of the Lied repertoire. Another concept that might clarify the power of German Romantic song is performance itself, the intensity of performance which is enabled and required by this art-form. In the concentration on word, as if the Lied were the literary musician's high-minded answer to the vulgar charade of opera, we forget the theatrical power of song. The drama of the Lied is very different from that of opera – its extreme concentration, its single voice, its eschewing of baubles and greasepaint – but it is dramatic nonetheless. Leopold Sonnleithner, one of the more high-minded and respectable of Schubert's circle, was an early critic of this notion of Lied as theatre:

> One of the chief merits of Schubert's songs lies in the altogether noble, charming and expressive melody; with him this is always the most important thing and, interesting as the writing of the accompaniment usually is, it nevertheless always plays a merely supporting role . . . Schubert, therefore, demanded above all that his songs should not be so much declaimed as sung flowingly, that the proper vocal timbre should be given to every note, to the complete exclusion of the unmusical speaking voice, and that by this means the musical idea should be displayed in its purity.

This seems to me to be a thoroughgoing misunderstanding of Schubert's invention of the Lied, from the fetishization of melody to the denial of declamation. Different sorts of song, different passages within a song, demand a different balance between lyrical and dramatic, legato and declamation. Sonnleithner specifically criticized the Schubert style of Schubert's closest musical collaborator, Johann Michael Vogl, setting up an opposition between the supposed theatrical excesses of that style and the cultivated, refined, melodic amateurism of Schönstein, the dedicatee of *Die schöne Müllerin*. The preference for some sort of melodically grounded simplicity persists in some quarters to this day, but Josef von

Spaun, Schubert's most loyal friend, the companion of his schooldays, seems closer to the mark. He defended Vogl, declaring that his theatricality 'heightened the effect in a great many songs', remembering how the superannuated opera singer 'sang with almost no voice more movingly than all the vocally gifted singers of those days, with the single exception of Freiherr von Schönstein who, aided by a quite magnificent voice and many-sided culture, had taken Vogl's manner of performance as a model'. This seems much truer to the composer whom Mayrhofer, the most gifted poet of the Schubert circle, perceived in the *Winterreise*: 'The poet's irony, rooted in despair, appealed to him: he expressed it in cutting tones.'

One of the great mysteries for singers as well as for audiences is how the weakest of verse – Craigher's feeble 'Totengräbers Heimweh', for instance, Chamisso's glutinous *Frauenliebe und -leben* cycle, or Collin's bizarre 'Der Zwerg' – can lie at the heart of some of the most extraordinary and inspiriting music ever written. Something like the suspension of disbelief, a concept the philosophically minded reader of Greek, Johann Michael Vogl would have well understood, is surely at work. The Lied should be understood as theatre, as psychodrama. An immersion in the whole work of art, the poetic idea transformed and sublimated through its musical and dramatic re-enactment: this is the heart of the matter, and the key to the invention of the Lied.

Ian Bostridge, February 2005

Introduction

This volume contains, in parallel translation, over a thousand of the most frequently performed Lieder – piano-accompanied, instrumental and orchestral – from C. P. E. Bach to Hanns Eisler. Composers have been listed alphabetically, and their songs appear under poet in chronological order of composition – thus allowing the reader to engage in depth with a particular poet and also to follow, in Wolf's Eichendorff settings, say, the composer's development from the early 'Nacht' (1880) to the mature Lieder of late 1888. In the case of song-cycles or Liederreihen that contain poems by a variety of poets – such as Schumann's *Myrten* and *Liederalbum für die Jugend* – the poems have been printed in the published order, and not separately under poet. Every effort has been made to print the correct date, usually that of the final version – so that Beethoven's 'Der Kuß', though sketched in 1798 and published in 1825, is dated 1822, the year of its composition. When known, the actual day of each composition is recorded, enabling the reader to see that on 5 July 1815, for example, Schubert composed no fewer than three masterpieces: 'Wandrers Nachtlied I', 'Der Fischer' and 'Erster Verlust'.

The composers and poets represented here are introduced by notes or short essays, and where possible I have quoted their actual words in German (with English translations) when they comment on their approach to poetry or Lieder composition. I have supplied footnotes when such information seemed important for an understanding of a poem – Wolf's setting of Goethe's 'St Nepomuk's Vorabend', for example, is only comprehensible when we know that Nepomuk received a martyr's death through drowning, after he had refused to disclose the sins confessed to him by Queen Johanna of Bohemia; stars were said to have shone around his body as it floated down the Vltava (Moldau).

When the same poem has been set by a variety of composers, their names appear in parenthesis at the foot of a poem, in the hope that singers and pianists will explore less well-known settings – not always piano-accompanied solo songs, but also duets, trios, choral or orchestral versions. It should be pointed out that poems are often altered in different ways by different composers: the text of Schumann's 'Der Sänger', for example, differs significantly from Schubert's setting; while Loewe, Mendelssohn, Schumann and Wolf all used a different translation for Byron's 'Sun of the sleepless'. And sometimes a composer will change the name of a poem. Goethe's 'Ein gleiches', for example, was renamed 'Wandrers Nachtlied' by Schubert, 'Nachtlied' by Schumann and 'Ilmenau' by Charles Ives. Long strophic songs have very occasionally, for lack of space, been reduced in length – Schubert's settings of Jacobi's 'Litanei auf das Fest aller Seelen' and Claudius's 'Das Lied vom Reifen' have, for example, been cut respectively from nine stanzas to three, and fifteen to four. When the poem forms part of a Novelle, novel or play, the provenance has been printed after a song's title.

A special feature of this volume is the attempt to print the *sung* version, while retaining the punctuation and layout of the original poem – something that has not always been done before. Karl Henckell's 'Ruhe, meine Seele!' is printed, for example, not as three four-line stanzas but as a single verse of twenty-four short lines, whose shape clearly inspired Richard Strauss in his depiction of a stifling hot summer's day:

Nicht ein Lüftchen
Regt sich leise,
Sanft entschlummert
Ruht der Hain;
Durch der Blätter
Dunkle Hülle
Stiehlt sich lichter
Sonnenschein [. . .]

And Schubert's setting of Leitner's 'Die Sterne', instead of being printed as four stanzas of lengthy lines, is now allowed to sparkle in its original versification – the following comparison shows the importance of such accuracy for a full enjoyment of Lieder:

Wie blitzen die Sterne so hell durch die Nacht!
Bin oft schon darüber vom Schlummer erwacht.

Wie blitzen
Die Sterne
So hell durch die Nacht!
Bin oft schon
Darüber
Vom Schlummer erwacht.

Refrains have not usually been included, except when they form part of the original poem, as in Schumann's setting of 'Rose, Meer und Sonne'; composers' word repetitions have likewise been omitted. In order to preserve the aesthetic pleasure of looking at a poem as the poet wished, I have tried to retain the original punctuation of the edition used by the composer, even when the published score, for no apparent reason, alters that punctuation: italics and indents have been restored, superfluous exclamation marks excised.

I have been greatly helped in this quest for poetic authenticity by such volumes as Kurt E. Schürmann's *Ludwig van Beethoven – Alle vertonten und musikalisch bearbeiteten Texte* (Aschendorff Münster, 1980); Maximilian and Lilly Schocow's two-volume *Franz Schubert – Die Texte seiner einstimmig und mehrstimmig komponierten Lieder und ihre Dichter* (Georg Olms Verlag, 1974); Helmut Schanze's

Robert Schumann – Literarische Vorlagen der ein- und mehrstimmigen Lieder, Gesänge und Deklamationen (Schott, 2002), Eric Sams's *The Songs of Johannes Brahms* (Yale University Press, 2000) and Reinhold Schlötterer's *Die Texte der Lieder von Richard Strauss* (W. Ludwig Verlag, 1988). Extensive research in German, Austrian, English and American libraries has made it possible to print the authentic version of almost every poem. Archaic orthography has, however, been modernized, so that Goethe's 'Gränzen der Menschheit', 'Wonne der Wehmuth', 'Trost in Thränen' and 'Ueber allen Gipfeln ist Ruh'', for example, become 'Grenzen der Menschheit', 'Wonne der Wehmut', 'Trost in Tränen' and 'Über allen Gipfeln ist Ruh''. For the section on Schubert's songs (pp. 288–426) I have, in general, used the Gesamtausgabe, edited by Eusebius Mandyczewski.

There are a few poems, however, which do not exist in any authentic published form, or are extremely difficult to trace. Those in the first category include *An die ferne Geliebte* by Alois Jeitteles, whose poems were never printed; Schober's 'An die Musik', which does not appear in *Gedichte* (1842) or the revised and enlarged edition of 1865; and the anonymous 'Wiegenlied' which, though attributed by Schubert on the title-page to Matthias Claudius, has never been discovered in the *Sämtliche Werke* of Claudius or elsewhere. Some poems, such as Jacobi's 'An Chloe', do exist in printed form but are notoriously elusive. Absent from Jacobi's *Sämtliche Werke* and *Iris*, the journal he edited (8 volumes, 1774–6), 'An Chloe' can only be found in an almanach of fabled rarity, the *Göttinger Musenalmanach* of 1785. Mozart, who used four of Jacobi's thirteen stanzas, actually wrote the poem into a special notebook, as we learn from Constanze's letter to Breitkopf & Härtel of 27 November 1799, where she refers to a 'Sammlung eigenhändig geschriebener schöner Lieder, so wie sie ihm in die Hände kamen, um sie gelegentlich zu komponieren' ('a collection of handwritten poems, written out as he received them, to be composed perhaps at some time in the future').

Assigning songs to one composer in preference to another has been an invidious task. All of Goethe's *Wilhelm Meister* poems have been listed under Wolf, which does no justice to Schubert and others; to Schubert, on the other hand, go 'Ganymed' and 'Prometheus'. Brahms, and not Schubert, is honoured with Hölty's 'Minnelied', while Chamisso's *Frauenliebe und -leben* is printed under Schumann instead of Loewe. When the German song is a translation of an English text, I have translated the German as it stands, which means that Shakespeare, Sir Walter Scott, Christina Rossetti, Byron and Colley Cibber, for example, do not look quite as we know them.

'In der Beschränkung zeigt sich erst der Meister' ('Only in limitation is mastery revealed') wrote Goethe in his late sonnet 'Natur und Kunst' – a statement that makes little sense to anyone given the impossible task of compiling a concise anthology of Lieder. My selection attempts to do justice not only to the great Lieder composers like Schubert, Schumann, Brahms and Wolf, but also to honour neglected figures such as C. P. E. Bach, Reichardt, Schulz and Zumsteeg who played an important part in the development of the Lied and wrote some beautiful songs. In such a short survey, however, there are inevitably many sins of omission. Prominent absentees from the nineteenth century include Abt, Burgmüller, Fuchs, Humperdinck, Jensen, Josephine Lang, Marschner, Nicolai, Luise Reichardt and Vesque von Püttlingen; and another volume needs to focus on the Lied in the twentieth century, featuring the songs of Blacher, Dessau, von Einem, Graener, Henze, Killmayer, Knab, Krenek, Lothar, Pepping, Reimann, Reutter, Rihm, von Schillings, Schreker, Schwarz-Schilling, Stephan, Ullmann, Weill, Wolf-Ferrari and Wolpe. Other significant non-German Lieder composers – apart from Britten, Busoni, Grieg and Meyerbeer – include Delius, Griffes, Ives, Kilpinen, Lange-Müller, MacDowell, Peterson-Berger, Rubinstein, Sibelius and Maude Valérie White.

Some readers will be startled to see composers such as Kreutzer, Lachner, Medtner, Mittler, Salmhofer, Schulz, Tomášek and Zelter rubbing shoulders with Beethoven, Schubert, Schumann, Wolf and other giants of the genre, and there has perhaps been some positive discrimination in my wish to encourage the revival of songs that are not sung often enough. As W. H. Auden wrote in *The Poet's Tongue* (1937): 'We do not want to read 'great' poetry all the time, and a good anthology should contain poems for every mood.' Nor do we wish to hear 'great' Lieder all the time – a performance of, say, Franz Mittler's setting of Rilke's 'Volksweise' can, on certain occasions, be as moving as a rendering of Schubert's 'Nähe des Geliebten'. I only regret that lack of space has made it impossible to include other unknown gems such as Christian Friedrich Schubart's 'Weihnachtswiegenlied' and Friedrich Glück's wonderful setting of Eichendorff's 'Das zerbrochene Ringlein'.

Richard Stokes

ACKNOWLEDGEMENTS

I should like to thank the Institute of Germanic Studies in Russell Square for unearthing first editions of little-known poems; Eva and Wolfgang Holzmair, Brigitte and Waldemar Weinheimer for valuable discussions on thorny textual problems; Kate Ward for being the most meticulous, patient and imaginative of production editors; and Graham Johnson, that great accompanist and scholar, who has shared with me his vast knowledge of Lieder with typical enthusiasm and generosity.

The author wishes to thank Suhrkamp Verlag for permission to reproduce five poems by Hermann Hesse ('Beim Schlafengehen', 'September', 'Frühling', 'Ravenna', 'Im Nebel', and three poems by Bertolt Brecht ('Über den Selbstmord', 'Die Flucht' and 'Ostersonntag').

Carl Philipp Emanuel Bach (1714–88)

Der tiefsinnigste Harmonist
Vereinte die Neuheit mit der Schönheit,
War groß
In der vom Worte geleiteten,
Noch größer
In der kühnen sprachlosen Musik.

(The most profound harmonist
United novelty and beauty,
Was great
In the setting of words,
Still greater
In bold and wordless music)

This epitaph, written by Klopstock in the year of C. P. E Bach's death (1788) for a commemorative monument in Hamburg's Michaeliskirche, pays homage to Bach who composed some 300 songs. His earliest collection, *Herr Professor Gellerts geistliche Oden und Lieder* (1758), comprised fifty-four settings of Gellert's sacred poems, thus representing one of the first serious attempts by a Lieder composer to engage in depth with a particular poet – anticipating the Schubert-Goethe, Schumann-Heine, Wolf-Mörike volumes of the following century, and exercising an undoubted influence on Beethoven's own *Gellert-Lieder*, especially in the way Bach's music is meticulously moulded to the nuances of Gellert's verse. Bach's next collection, *Herr Doctor Cramers übersetzte Psalmen mit Melodien zum Singen bey dem Claviere* (1774) was published by the composer himself as a companion volume to the Gellert songs. It met with less success, due partly to the rather sentimental moralizing of Cramer's rhymed verse, and partly to Bach's wish, as he explained in the Preface, to appeal to 'Liebhaber von verschiedenen Fähigkeiten' ('amateurs of varying degrees of ability'), and write uncomplicated music for domestic music making. Bach's third substantial collection, *Aus Sturms geistlichen Liedern* (1780), contains biblical Lieder and songs that are designed to encourage a religious contemplation of nature, as we see in 'Der Frühling'. Bach's best songs reveal an engagement with the text that is years ahead of its time – such as the recitative-like and chromatic portrayal of Christ's agony in 'Jesus in Gethsemane', the dark blurred harmonies of 'Über die Finsternis kurz vor dem Tode Jesu', or the startlingly realistic vision of the Last Judgement in 'Der Tag des Weltgerichts'.

Christoph Christian Sturm (1740–86)

Principal pastor at St Peter's Church in Hamburg, where he was also a school inspector. Celebrated as a writer of hymns, Sturm's *Betrachtungen über die Werke Gottes im Reiche der Natur und der Vorsehung auf alle Tage des Jahres* ('Reflections on the works of God in the realm of Nature and Providence for every day of the year') was greatly admired by Beethoven.

1780 Der Frühling / Spring Wq 197

Erwacht zum neuen Leben
Steht vor mir die Natur;
Und sanfte Lüfte wehen
Durch die beschneite Flur.
Empor aus seiner Hülle
Drängt sich der junge Halm;
Der Wälder öde Stille
Belebt der Vögel Psalm.

O Vater, deine Milde
Fühlt Berg und Tal und Au.
Es grünen die Gefilde,
Beperlt vom Morgentau.
Der Blumenweid entgegen
Blökt schon die Herd im Tal;
Und in dem Staube regen
Sich Würmer ohne Zahl.

Lobsing ihm, meine Seele,
Dem Gott, der Freuden schafft!
Lobsing ihm und erzähle
Die Werke seiner Kraft!
Hier, von dem Blütenhügel
Bis zu der Sterne Bahn,
Steig auf der Andacht Flügel
Dein Loblied himmelan.
(*Mozart, Reichardt*)

Awakened to new life,
Spring stands before me,
And gentle breezes blow
Through snow-covered fields.
Young blades of grass
Shoot up from the earth;
The hymn of birds brings to life
The forests' desolate silence.

O Father, Thy kindness is felt
By mountain, vale and meadow.
The fields are growing green
In the pearls of morning dew.
The lowing herd in the valley
Draws near the flowering meadow;
And worms without number
Are teeming in the dust.

Sing praises, O my soul,
To God who creates such joy!
Sing praises and recount
The creations of His might!
From this hill of blossoms
To the Milky Way,
Let your song of praise
Wing heavenward in devotion.

Ludwig van Beethoven (1770–1827)

Beethoven was the first great Lieder composer: most of his eighty or so solo songs were composed before Schubert's, and in them he used all the main song types – simple strophic, *durchkomponiert* and the cycle – that his successors were to employ. Beethoven, moreover, seems to have been the first composer in the history of German song to coin the word 'Liederkreis'; in an undated letter from 1816 to his publisher S. A. Steiner he wrote: „Ich bitte Sie um die letzte Korrektur von dem Liederkreise an die Entfernte ..." ('Please send me the final proofs of the Distant Beloved song cycle ...') On the nine occasions (excluding 'An die Freude') that Beethoven and Schubert set the same text, Beethoven six times composed the more successful version – Matthisson's 'Adelaide' and 'Andenken', Goethe's 'Sehnsucht' ('Was zieht mir das Herz so'), 'Wonne der Wehmut' and 'Freudvoll und leidvoll', and Stoll's 'An die Geliebte' – while his settings of 'Kennst du das Land', 'Der Wachtelschlag' and 'Klage' are certainly not inferior to Schubert's versions of the same poems. Although the style of 'Adelaide' and other Lieder ('Mit einem gemalten Band' and 'Neue Liebe, neues Leben', for example) is that of the eighteenth rather than the nineteenth century, with numerous florid word repetitions, Beethoven also composed songs such as 'Ich liebe dich' which, in their unaffected simplicity and sincerity, anticipate the most lyrical songs of Schubert. The songs also reveal another side of Beethoven that is often ignored: he was not always high-minded and heroic, and there are among the Lieder delicious examples of his wit, such as 'Der Kuß', 'Marmotte' and 'Selbstgespräch'. Beethoven, as a Lieder composer, differed in two important respects from many of his predecessors: he had a passion for poetry, and often chose his texts as a medium for highly personal confession: 'Seufzer eines Ungeliebten' and 'Gegenliebe', for example, express his fear of rejection and his longing for a woman's love; the *Sechs Lieder von Gellert* Op. 48 (1802) inspired him to reveal the spiritual aspect of his nature, while many early songs treat the theme of the distant loved-one long before *An die ferne Geliebte* Op. 98 (1816) and his celebrated letter to 'The Immortal Beloved' (July 1812).

Gottfried August Bürger (1747–94)

See Strauss

1794–95 *Seufzer eines Ungeliebten; Gegenliebe* / The sigh of one unloved; Requited love* **WoO 118**

---

* The melody of 'Gegenliebe' was later used in the Choral Fantasia, Op. 80 and the Ninth Symphony.

1

Seufzer eines Ungeliebten / The sigh of one unloved

Hast du nicht Liebe zugemessen
Dem Leben jeder Kreatur?
Warum bin ich allein vergessen,
Auch meine Mutter, du! Natur?

Wo lebte wohl in Forst und Hürde
Und wo in Luft und Meer ein Tier,
Das nimmermehr geliebet würde?
Geliebt wird alles außer mir!

Wenngleich im Hain, auf Flur und Matten
Sich Baum und Staude, Moos und Kraut
Durch Lieb' und Gegenliebe gatten;
Vermählt sich mir doch keine Braut.

Mir wächst vom süßesten der Triebe
Nie Honigfrucht zur Lust heran.
Denn ach! mir mangelt Gegenliebe,
Die Eine nur gewähren kann.

Have you not accorded love
To every living creature?
Why am I alone forgotten,
O Nature, you my mother too?

Where in forest or fold,
Where in the air and sea,
Was a creature that was never loved?
All things are loved but me!

Though in grove and field and meadow,
Tree and shrub, moss and herb
Are united by love and love requited –
No bride ever marries me.

The sweetest of passions never ripen for me
Into honeyed fruits of happiness,
For alas! I lack that requited love
Which only one woman can grant me.

2

Gegenliebe / Requited love

Wüßt' ich, wüßt' ich, daß du mich
Lieb und wert ein bißchen hieltest
Und von dem, was ich für dich,
Nur ein Hundertteilchen fühltest;

Daß dein Dank hübsch meinem Gruß
Halben Wegs entgegenkäme,
Und dein Mund den Wechselkuß
Gerne gäb' und wieder nähme:

Dann, o Himmel, außer sich,
Würde ganz mein Herz zerlodern!
Leib und Leben könnt' ich dich
Nicht vergebens lassen fodern!

Gegengunst erhöhet Gunst,
Liebe nähret Gegenliebe
Und entflammt zur Feuersbrunst,
Was ein Aschenfünkchen bliebe.
(*Haydn*)

If I knew, if I knew that you
Loved and valued me a little,
And felt but a hundredth part
Of what I feel for you;

Knew that you, in sweet gratitude,
Would meet my greeting half-way,
And your lips would gladly kiss
And receive my kiss in return:

Then, O Heaven, my whole heart
Would perish utterly in flames!
I would not let you ask in vain
For my body and my life!

A favour returned increases favour,
Love nurtures requited love,
And what would else be but a spark
Becomes a mighty conflagration.

Giuseppe Carpani (1752–1825)

Best known as a poet and playwright, he also wrote an important book on Haydn, and accompanied Rossini on his visit to Beethoven in 1822. 'In questa tomba oscura' was composed in response to a competition organized by the publishing house of Mollo in Vienna. Carpani's text was set sixty-three times by a total of forty-six composers, including Cherubini, Salieri and Zingarelli. Beethoven's was the final setting of this strange collection, which was dedicated by the publisher to Prince Lobkowitz, one of Beethoven's most important patrons.

1806–07 In questa tomba oscura / In this dark tomb WoO 133

In questa tomba oscura	In this dark tomb
Lasciami riposar;	Let me rest;
Quando vivevo, ingrata,	While I still lived, O faithless one,
Dovevi a me pensar.	You should have thought of me.
Lascia che l'ombre ignude	Allow, at least, a naked shade
Godansi pace almen,	To enjoy its peace,
E non bagnar mie ceneri	And do not bathe my ashes
D'inutile velen.	In useless venom.

Christian Fürchtegott Gellert (1715–69)

An important figure in the German Enlightenment, Gellert wrote a great deal of poetry, including the *Geistliche Oden und Lieder* which have remained popular since their publication in 1757. Apart from C. P. E. Bach's fifty-five settings, there are four Haydn songs from the late 1790s, and several by Loewe and Tchaikovsky. The theme of much of his writing (plays, novels, poems, stories) was contentment with one's lot and the curbing of passions.

c.1801 Sechs Lieder nach Gedichten von Gellert / Six songs by Gellert **Op. 48**

1

Bitten / Supplication

Gott, deine Güte reicht so weit,	Thy goodness, Lord, extends so far,
So weit die Wolken gehen;	As far as clouds drift;
Du krönst uns mit Barmherzigkeit,	Thou dost crown us with mercy,
Und eilst, uns beizustehen.	And art quick to succour us.
Herr, meine Burg, mein Fels, mein Hort,	Lord, my fortress, rock and refuge,
Vernimm mein Flehn, merk' auf mein Wort;	Hear my entreaty, hearken to my words,
Denn ich will vor dir beten!	For I would pray to Thee!
(*C. P. E. Bach*)	

2
Die Liebe des Nächsten / Love of one's neighbour

So jemand spricht: Ich liebe Gott,
Und haßt doch seine Brüder,
Der treibt mit Gottes Wahrheit Spott,
Und reißt sie ganz darnieder.
Gott ist die Lieb' und will, daß ich
Den Nächsten liebe, gleich als mich.

If a man say: I love God!
And yet hates his brother,
He mocks God's truth
And utterly abases it.
God is love, and wishes me
To love my neighbour as myself.

3
Vom Tode / Of death

Meine Lebenszeit verstreicht,
Stündlich eil' ich zu dem Grabe,
Und was ist's, das ich vielleicht,
Das ich noch zu leben habe?
Denk, o Mensch! an deinen Tod.
Säume nicht; denn Eins ist not.

My days on earth slip by,
Hour by hour I hasten to the grave;
And how long do I perhaps
Still have to live?
Think, O man, upon your death.
Do not delay; for one thing is needful.

4
Die Ehre Gottes aus der Natur / The glory of God in nature

Die Himmel rühmen des Ewigen Ehre,
Ihr Schall pflanzt seinen Namen fort.
Ihn rühmt der Erdkreis, ihn preisen die Meere;
Vernimm, o Mensch, ihr göttlich Wort!

The heavens extol the glory of God,
Their sound propagates His name.
The earth extols, the seas praise Him;
Hearken, O man, to their godly word!

Wer trägt der Himmel unzählbare Sterne?
Wer führt die Sonn aus ihrem Zelt?
Sie kömmt und leuchtet und lacht uns von
    ferne,
Und läuft den Weg, gleich als ein Held.
(*C. P. E. Bach*)

Who supports the heaven's countless stars?
Who leads the sun from its tabernacle?
It comes and gleams and smiles on us from
    afar,
And like a hero runs its course.

5
Gottes Macht und Vorsehung / God's might and providence

Gott ist mein Lied!
Er ist der Gott der Stärke;
Hehr ist sein Nam' und groß sind seine Werke,
Und alle Himmel sein Gebiet.
(*Loewe*)

God is my song!
He is the God of strength;
Exalted is His name, and great are His works,
And all the heavens His domain.

An dir allein, an dir hab' ich gesündigt,
  Und übel oft vor dir getan.
Du siehst die Schuld, die mir den Fluch
  verkündigt;
  Sieh, Gott, auch meinen Jammer an.

Dir ist mein Flehn, mein Seufzen nicht ver-
  borgen,
  Und meine Tränen sind vor dir.
Ach Gott, mein Gott, wie lange soll ich sorgen?
  Wie lang entfernst du dich von mir?

Herr, handle nicht mit mir nach meinen
  Sünden,
  Vergilt mir nicht nach meiner Schuld.
Ich suche dich; laß mich dein Antlitz finden,
  Du Gott der Langmut und Geduld.

Früh woll'st du mich mit deiner Gnade füllen,
  Gott, Vater der Barmherzigeit.
Erfreue mich um deines Namens willen;
  Du bist ein Gott, der gern erfreut.

Laß deinen Weg mich wieder freudig wallen,
  Und lehre mich dein heilig Recht.
Mich täglich tun nach deinem Wohlgefallen;
  Du bist mein Gott, ich bin dein Knecht.

Herr, eile du, mein Schutz, mir beizustehen,
  Und leite mich auf ebner Bahn.
Er hört mein Schrein, der Herr erhört mein
  Flehen,
  Und nimmt sich meiner Seelen an.
(C.P. E. Bach)

Against Thee, Thee alone have I sinned,
  And done evil often in Thy sight.
Thou dost see the sin, which calls Thy curse
  on me;
  O God, see also my distress.

From Thee my prayers, my sighs are not
  hid,
  And my tears are shed in Thy sight.
Ah God, my God, how long am I to grieve?
  How long wilt Thou forsake me?

Lord, treat me not according to my sins,
  Reward me not according to my guilt.
It is Thee I seek. Grant that I see Thy counte-
  nance,
  God of patience and forbearance.

Pray, fill me with Thy grace betimes,
  God, Father of Mercy.
For Thy name's sake comfort me;
  Thou art the God who gladly brings joy.

Let me again walk cheerfully in Thy path,
  Teach me Thy holy law,
To act each day according to Thy will;
  Thou art my God, and I Thy servant.

Lord, my shield, hasten to my aid,
  And guide me along an even path.
He hears my cries, the Lord heeds my
  entreaty,
  And takes my soul into His care.

Johann Wilhelm Ludwig Gleim (1719–1803)

He was an Anacreontic poet, who wrote a great number of stylized and unsensual poems in praise of love, wine and song. 'Wir, die wir von Wein und Liebe gesungen, aber wenig getrunken und wenig geliebt haben' ('We, who sang of love and wine, drank little and loved little') Gleim once confided to Ewald von Kleist, and this feeling of artificiality is evident in Beethoven's playful and rococo setting of 'Selbstgespräch', full of trills, repetitions and vocal doubling of the accompaniment.

Ich, der mit flatterndem Sinn
Bisher ein Feind der Liebe bin
Und es so gern beständig bliebe,
Ich! ach! ich glaube, daß ich liebe.

Der ich sonst Hymen* angeschwärzt
Und mit der Liebe nur gescherzt,
Der ich im Wankelmut mich übe,
Ich glaube, daß ich Doris liebe.

Denn ach! seitdem ich sie gesehn,
Ist mir kein' andre Schöne schön.
Ach, die Tyrannin meiner Triebe,
Ich glaube gar, daß ich sie liebe.

I who, fickle of mind,
Have till now been an enemy of love
And would always like to remain so,
I, alas, I think I'm in love!

I who used to slander Hymen
And merely made fun of love,
I who practise inconstancy,
Believe I'm in love with Doris.

For ah! since seeing her,
I find no other beauty fair.
Ah, that tyrant who rules my desires,
I do indeed think I love her.

Heinrich Goeble (dates unknown)

1820 Abendlied unterm gestirnten Himmel / Evening song beneath a starry sky WoO 150

Wenn die Sonne niedersinket,
Und der Tag zur Ruh sich neigt,
Luna freundlich leise winket,
Und die Nacht herniedersteigt;
Wenn die Sterne prächtig schimmern,
Tausend Sonnenstraßen flimmern:
Fühlt die Seele sich so groß,
Windet sich vom Staube los.

When the sun sinks down
And day draws to its peaceful close,
When the moon beckons gently and kindly,
And night descends;
When the stars shine in splendour
And a thousand suns blaze in their path:
The soul feels so immense,
It rises from the dust.

Schaut so gern nach jenen Sternen,
Wie zurück ins Vaterland,
Hin nach jenen lichten Fernen,
Und vergißt der Erde Tand;
Will nur ringen, will nur streben,
Ihrer Hülle zu entschweben:
Erde ist ihr eng und klein,
Auf den Sternen möcht sie sein.

It loves to gaze up at those stars,
As if back to its native land,
To gaze at those distant lights,
Forgetting earth's vain trumpery;
It only seeks to struggle, strive,
To float free of its mortal frame:
Earth's too narrow to contain it,
It longs to be among the stars.

Ob der Erde Stürme toben,
Falsches Glück den Bösen lohnt:
Hoffend blicket sie nach oben,
Wo der Sternenrichter thront.
Keine Furcht kann sie mehr quälen,
Keine Macht kann ihr befehlen;
Mit verklärtem Angesicht
Schwingt sie sich zum Himmelslicht.

Whether earth's tempests rage
Or false fortune rewards the wicked,
Full of hope it looks aloft
To the Judge enthroned among the stars.
Fear can no longer torment it,
No power can command it;
With transfigured countenance
It soars aloft to Heaven's light.

* Hymenaeus or Hymen, the god of marriage among the Greeks.

Eine leise Ahnung schauert	A faint presentiment from those worlds
Mich aus jenen Welten an;	Instils in me a sense of awe;
Lange, lange nicht mehr dauert	My pilgrimage on earth
Meine Erdenpilgerbahn;	Will not now last much longer;
Bald hab ich das Ziel errungen,	Soon I shall have reached the goal,
Bald zu euch mich aufgeschwungen,	Soon I shall have risen to you,
Ernte bald an Gottes Thron	Soon I shall reap before God's throne
Meiner Leiden schönen Lohn.	My suffering's sweet reward.

Johann Wolfgang von Goethe (1749–1832)

See Brahms, Hensel, Loewe, Mendelssohn, Mozart, Reichardt, Schubert, Strauss, Wolf, Zelter

Early Goethe, middle Goethe, late Goethe; lyric, philosophical, epic, epigrammatic, occasional verse; plays, novels, Singspiele – everything he wrote had a musical quality about it. In his autobiography *Dichtung und Wahrheit*, he describes how he would wake up in the middle of the night and rush to his desk in order to write down poems such as 'Der Musensohn' that were already fully formed in his brain; and how he preferred to use a pencil, since the scratching of the quill would disturb his 'somnambulistic writing'. Many of the early love poems, such as 'Mailied', flame with the passion of requited love. The stress in the first verse falls forcefully on the pronoun 'mir': the poet is concerned with the intensity of his own love, and like in so many of these exultant early poems, the girl is hardly described at all. As his excitement mounts, the verbs vanish, the ellipses increase, each line flows into the next and new words are coined to express new feelings: ellipsis, neologism and enjambement are the technical hallmarks of many of these highly charged love poems – typical of the *Sturm und Drang* movement which expressed a reaction against rationalism, a reliance on individuality and an exaltation of freedom that we see in such celebrated poems as 'Prometheus' and 'An Schwager Kronos' (Schubert).

When Beethoven wrote to Goethe on 12 April 1811, he received a lukewarm reply, and their first encounter only took place on 19 July 1812 in Teplitz. For reliable evidence of that meeting we must turn to their letters, in which both poet and composer express themselves unequivocally. Goethe, in a letter to Zelter dated 2 September 1812, wrote:

Sein Talent hat mich in Erstaunen gesetzt; allein er ist leider eine ganz unge-
bändigte Persönlichkeit, die zwar gar nicht unrecht hat, wenn sie die Welt
detestabel findet, aber sie freilich dadurch weder für sich noch für andere
genußreicher macht.

His talent astonished me, but he is unfortunately an utterly uncontrolled
personality; although he is not wrong to find the world detestable, that does
not help to make it a more pleasant place either for himself or others.

And Beethoven was equally damning, when he wrote to Breitkopf & Härtel on 9 August 1812:

Goethe behagt die Hofluft zu sehr, mehr als es einem Dichter ziemt. Es ist nicht viel mehr über die Lächerlichkeiten der Virtuosen hier zu reden, wenn Dichter, die als die ersten Lehrer der Nation anzusehen sein sollten, über diesem Schimmer alles andere vergessen können.

Goethe appreciates the Court air too much, more than is proper for a poet. There is nothing more ridiculous than when poets, who should be regarded as the first teachers of the nation, forget all else when faced with such glitter.

Despite these reservations, Goethe remained for Beethoven a creative god, and his settings of Goethe's poems – there are about a dozen – all testify to his admiration, and have remained permanently in the repertoire.

Early 1790s Marmotte / Marmotte Op. 52, no. 7
FROM *Das Jahrmarktsfest zu Plundersweilern*

Ich komme schon durch manches Land	*I've travelled already through many lands*
Avecque la marmotte,	Avecque la marmotte,
Und immer was zu essen fand	*And always found something to eat*
Avecque la marmotte,	Avecque la marmotte,
Avecque si, avecque la,	Avecque si, avecque la,
Avecque la marmotte.	Avecque la marmotte.

c.1793 Maigesang (Mailied) / May song Op. 52, no. 4

Wie herrlich leuchtet	How gloriously
Mir die Natur!	Nature gleams for me!
Wie glänzt die Sonne!	How the sun sparkles!
Wie lacht die Flur!	How the field laughs!
Es dringen Blüten	Blossoms burst
Aus jedem Zweig	From every bough
Und tausend Stimmen	And a thousand voices
Aus dem Gesträuch	From every bush
Und Freud und Wonne	And delight and rapture
Aus jeder Brust.	From every breast.
O Erd, o Sonne!	O earth, O sun!
O Glück, o Lust!	O joy, O bliss!
O Lieb, o Liebe!	O love, O love!
So golden schön,	So golden fair
Wie Morgenwolken	As morning clouds
Auf jenen Höhn!	On yonder hills!

Du segnest herrlich
Das frische Feld,
Im Blütendampfe
Die volle Welt.

O Mädchen, Mädchen,
Wie lieb ich dich!
Wie blickt dein Auge!
Wie liebst du mich!

So liebt die Lerche
Gesang und Luft,
Und Morgenblumen
Den Himmelsduft,

Wie ich dich liebe
Mit warmem Blut,
Die du mir Jugend
Und Freud und Mut

Zu neuen Liedern
Und Tänzen gibst.
Sei ewig glücklich,
Wie du mich liebst!
(*Franz, Hensel, Knab, Loewe, Pfitzner,
Reichardt, Schoeck, Tomášek*)

You bless with glory
The fresh field,
In a mist of blossom
The teeming world.

O maiden, maiden,
How I love you!
How you look at me!
How you love me!

The skylark loves
Song and air,
And morning flowers
The hazy sky,

As I with warm blood
Love you,
Who give me youth
And joy and heart

For new songs
And new dances.
Be happy always
As in your love for me!

1809 Neue Liebe, Neues Leben / New love, new life Op. 75, no. 2

Herz, mein Herz, was soll das geben?
Was bedränget dich so sehr?
Welch ein fremdes, neues Leben!
Ich erkenne dich nicht mehr.
Weg ist alles, was du liebtest,
Weg, warum du dich betrübtest,
Weg dein Fleiß und deine Ruh –
Ach, wie kamst du nur dazu!

Fesselt dich die Jugendblüte,
Diese liebliche Gestalt,
Dieser Blick voll Treu und Güte
Mit unendlicher Gewalt?
Will ich rasch mich ihr entziehen,
Mich ermannen, ihr entfliehen,
Führet mich im Augenblick,
Ach, mein Weg zu ihr zurück.

Und an diesem Zauberfädchen,
Das sich nicht zerreißen läßt,
Hält das liebe, lose Mädchen

Heart, my heart, what can this mean?
What is it that besets you so?
What a strange and new existence!
I do not know you any more.
Fled is all you used to love,
Fled is all that used to grieve you,
Fled your work and peace of mind –
Ah, how can this have come about!

Does the bloom of youth ensnare you,
This dear figure full of charm,
These eyes so kind and faithful
With inexorable power?
When I try to hasten from her,
Control myself, escape her,
In a moment I am led,
Ah, back to her again.

And by this magic little thread
That cannot be severed,
The sweet and playful girl

Mich so wider Willen fest;	Holds me fast against my will;
Muß in ihrem Zauberkreise	In her enchanted realm
Leben nun auf ihre Weise.	I must now live as she dictates.
Die Verändrung, ach, wie groß!	Ah, what a monstrous change!
Liebe! Liebe! laß mich los!	Love! Love! Let me free!
(*Hensel, Reichardt, Spohr, Zelter*)	

1809 Lied des Mephistopheles in Auerbachs Keller (Mephistos Flohlied) / Mephisto's song of the flea Op. 75, no. 3
FROM *Faust*

Es war einmal ein König,	There was once a king
Der hatt' einen großen Floh,	Who had a large flea,
Den liebt' er gar nicht wenig,	Whom he loved not a little,
Als wie seinen eig'nen Sohn.	Just like his own son.
Da rief er seinen Schneider,	He summoned his tailor,
Der Schneider kam heran:	The tailor appeared:
„Da, miß dem Junker Kleider	'Here – make robes for this knight
Und miß ihm Hosen an!"	And make him breeches too!'
In Sammet und in Seide	In silk and satin
War er nun angetan,	The flea was now attired,
Hatte Bänder auf dem Kleide,	With ribbons on his coat,
Hatt' auch ein Kreuz daran,	And a medal too,
Und war sogleich Minister,	And became a minister straightaway
Und hatt einen großen Stern.	And wore an enormous star.
Da wurden seine Geschwister	His brothers and his sisters
Bei Hof auch große Herrn.	Became grand at court as well.
Und Herrn und Frau'n am Hofe,	And courtly lords and ladies
Die waren sehr geplagt,	Were most grievously plagued,
Die Königin und die Zofe	Queen and maid-in-waiting
Gestochen und genagt,	Were bitten and were stung,
Und durften sie nicht knicken,	Yet they were not allowed
Und weg sie jucken nicht. –	To squash or scratch them away. –
Wir knicken und ersticken	We bow and scrape and suffocate,
Doch gleich, wenn einer sticht.	As soon as any bite.
(*Berlioz, Busoni, Mussorgsky, Wagner*)	

Klärchens Lieder I und II / Klärchen's songs I and II
FROM *Egmont*

1809–10 Die Trommel gerühret / Bang the drum Op. 84

Die Trommel gerühret!	Bang the drum!
Das Pfeifchen gespielt!	Sound the fife!
Mein Liebster gewaffnet	My lover in armour

Dem Haufen befiehlt,	Commands the throng,
Die Lanze hoch führet,	With his spear raised high
Die Leute regieret.	He rules the people.
Wie klopft mir das Herz!	How my heart throbs!
Wie wallt mir das Blut!	How my blood races!
O hätt' ich ein Wämslein	Ah, would that *I* had a doublet
Und Hosen und Hut!	And breeches and helmet!
Ich folgt' ihm zum Tor' naus	I'd follow him out of the gate
Mit mutigem Schritt,	With valiant stride,
Ging' durch die Provinzen,	I'd march through the provinces,
Ging' überall mit.	Wherever he went.
Die Feinde schon weichen,	The foe retreats,
Wir schießen dadrein;	We fire into their ranks!
Welch' Glück sondergleichen,	What joy without compare
Ein Mannsbild zu sein!	To be a man!
(*Reichardt*)	

1809–10 Freudvoll und leidvoll / Full of joy and full of sorrow Op. 84

Freudvoll	Full of joy,
Und leidvoll,	And full of sorrow,
Gedankenvoll sein;	Full of thoughts;
Langen	Yearning
Und bangen	And trembling
In schwebender Pein;	In uncertain anguish;
Himmelhoch jauchzend,	Exulting to heaven,
Zum Tode betrübt –	Cast down unto death –
Glücklich allein	Happy alone
Ist die Seele, die liebt.	Is the soul that loves.
(*Liszt, Reichardt, Rubinstein, Schubert, Zelter*)	

1810 Wonne der Wehmut / Delight in sadness Op. 83, no. 1

Trocknet nicht, trocknet nicht,	Grow not dry, grow not dry,
Tränen der ewigen Liebe!	Tears of lasting love!
Ach, nur dem halbgetrockneten Auge	Ah, to the merely half-dry eye
Wie öde, wie tot die Welt ihm erscheint!	How bleak, how dead the world appears!
Trocknet nicht, trocknet nicht,	Grow not dry, grow not dry,
Tränen unglücklicher Liebe!	Tears of unhappy love!
(*Adolf Busch, Franz, Hensel, Reichardt,*	
Salmhofer, Schubert, Tomášek, Zelter, Zillig)	

1810 Sehnsucht / Longing Op. 83, no. 2

Was zieht mir das Herz so?	What pulls at my heart so?
Was zieht mich hinaus?	What draws me outside?
Und windet und schraubt mich	And wrenches and wrests me

Aus Zimmer und Haus?	From room and house?
Wie dort sich die Wolken	How the clouds disperse
Um Felsen verziehn!	About those cliffs!
Da möcht ich hinüber,	That's where I'd like to be,
Da möcht ich wohl hin!	That's where I'd like to go!
Nun wiegt sich der Raben	The gregarious ravens
Geselliger Flug;	Wing through the air;
Ich mische mich drunter	I mingle with them
Und folge dem Zug.	And follow their flight.
Und Berg und Gemäuer	We flutter around
Umfittichen wir;	Mountains and ruins:
Sie weilet da drunten;	Her home's in the valley,
Ich spähe nach ihr.	I look out for her.
Da kommt sie und wandelt!	Suddenly I see her walking!
Ich eile sobald,	I hasten at once,
Ein singender Vogel,	Singing like a bird,
Zum buschigen Wald.	To the bushy woods.
Sie weilet und horchet	She lingers and listens
Und lächelt mit sich:	And smiles to herself:
„Er singet so lieblich	'He sings so sweetly
Und singt es an mich."	And he sings for me.'
Die scheidende Sonne	The setting sun
Vergüldet die Höhn;	Turns the mountains gold;
Die sinnende Schöne,	My sweetheart muses
Sie läßt es geschehn.	And gives it no thought.
Sie wandelt am Bache	She walks by the stream
Die Wiesen entlang,	Across the meadows,
Und finster und finstrer	The winding path
Umschlingt sich der Gang.	Grows dark and darker.
Auf einmal erschein' ich,	All at once I appear,
Ein blinkender Stern.	A glittering star.
„Was glänzet da droben,	'What's shining up there
So nah und so fern?"	So near and so far?'
Und hast du mit Staunen	And when, astonished,
Das Leuchten erblickt:	You've caught sight of the gleam –
Ich lieg dir zu Füßen,	I'll be lying at your feet,
Da bin ich beglückt!	Filled with delight!
(*Hensel, Reichardt, Schubert, Wolf*)	

1810 Mit einem gemalten Band / To accompany a painted ribbon Op. 83, no. 3

Kleine Blumen, kleine Blätter	Little flowers, little leaves
Streuen mir mit leichter Hand	Are delicately strewn
Gute junge Frühlingsgötter	By kindly young spring gods
Tändelnd auf ein luftig Band.	Playfully on an airy ribbon.

Zephyr, nimm's auf deine Flügel,	Take it, West Wind, on your wings,
Schling's um meiner Liebsten Kleid;	Wind it round my loved one's dress;
Und so tritt sie vor den Spiegel	Then she'll step before the mirror
All in ihrer Munterkeit.	In all her lively charm.
Sieht mit Rosen sich umgeben,	Will see herself girdled by roses,
Selbst wie eine Rose jung.	She herself as young as a rose.
Einen Blick, geliebtes Leben!	Give me a single glance, my love,
Und ich bin belohnt genung.	And I'll be rewarded well enough!
Fühle, was dies Herz empfindet,	Feel what this heart is feeling,
Reiche frei mir deine Hand,	Freely give your hand to me,
Und das Band, das uns verbindet,	And may the bond that binds us both
Sei kein schwaches Rosenband!	Be no frail ribbon of roses!
(*Knab, Lehár, Pepping, Reichardt, Schoeck,*	
Tomášek)	

Paul von Haugwitz (1791–1856)

He enjoyed a successful career in the army, which he left with the rank of lieutenant-colonel. An occasional poet, he also translated Wordsworth, Byron and Thomas Moore.

1817 Resignation / Resignation WoO 149

Lisch aus, mein Licht!	Go out, my light!
Was dir gebricht,	What you lack
Das ist nun fort,	Is now departed,
An diesem Ort	In this place
Kannst du's nicht wieder finden!	You shall never find it again!
Du mußt nun los dich binden.	You must now break free.
Sonst hast du lustig aufgebrannt,	Once you burned brightly,
Nun hat man dir die Luft entwandt;	Now you've been deprived of air;
Wenn diese fort gewehet,	When that has blown away,
Die Flamme irregehet –	The flame splutters –
Sucht – findet nicht –	Seeks – fails to find –
Lisch aus, mein Licht!	Go out, my light!

Karl Friedrich Herrosee (1754–1821)

A pastor and poet from Züllichau. Beethoven's first version of 'Zärtliche Liebe' (*c.*1797) contained five verses; revising the song around 1800, he reduced the song to the second stanza of the original poem, added the second half of the third verse ('Drum Gottes Segen über dir. . .') and renamed the song 'Ich liebe dich'.

Ich liebe dich, so wie du mich,
Am Abend und am Morgen,
Noch war kein Tag, wo du und ich
Nicht teilten unsre Sorgen.
Auch waren sie für dich und mich
Geteilt, leicht zu ertragen;
Du tröstetest im Kummer mich,
Ich weint' in deine Klagen.

Drum Gottes Segen über dir,
Du, meines Lebens Freude.
Gott schütze dich, erhalt' dich mir,
Schütz und erhalt' uns beide.

I love you as you love me,
At evening and at morning,
No day there was when you and I
Did not share our sorrows.
And for me and you they were,
When shared, an easy burden;
You comforted me in my distress,
I wept when you lamented.

May God then bless you,
You, my life's delight.
God protect and keep you for me,
Protect and keep us both.

Alois Jeitteles (1794–1858)

Alois Jeitteles came from a literary family – his cousin Ignaz's *Bacchus* was considered by Beethoven as a potential opera in 1822 – and his poems, which were never published in book form, appeared in such journals as *Selam* and the *Wiener Zeitschrift für Kunst, Literatur, Theater und Mode,* the source for a number of Schubert's songs. Some of his plays were produced at the Burgtheater, and with Ignaz he founded a Jewish weekly, *Siona,* which enjoyed a short-lived success in 1819. Jeitteles must have met Beethoven in Vienna while finishing his medical studies; he became a well-respected doctor in Brno, greatly admired for his selfless devotion to his patients in the cholera epidemics of 1831 and 1836.

1816 *An die ferne Geliebte / To the distant beloved* Op. 98

1

Auf dem Hügel sitz ich, spähend
In das blaue Nebelland,
Nach den fernen Triften sehend,
Wo ich dich, Geliebte, fand.
Weit bin ich von dir geschieden,
Trennend liegen Berg und Tal
Zwischen uns und unserm Frieden,
Unserm Glück und unsrer Qual.
Ach, den Blick kannst du nicht sehen,
Der zu dir so glühend eilt,
Und die Seufzer, sie verwehen
In dem Raume, der uns teilt.
Will denn nichts mehr zu dir dringen,
Nichts der Liebe Bote sein?
Singen will ich, Lieder singen,

I sit on the hill, gazing
Into the misty blue countryside,
Towards the distant meadows
Where, my love, I first found you.
Now I'm far away from you,
Mountain and valley intervene
Between us and our peace,
Our happiness and our pain.
Ah, you cannot see the fiery gaze
That wings its way towards you,
And my sighs are lost
In the space that comes between us.
Will nothing ever reach you again?
Will nothing be love's messenger?
I shall sing, sing songs

Die dir klagen meine Pein!
Denn vor Liedesklang entweichet
Jeder Raum und jede Zeit,
Und ein liebend Herz erreichet
Was ein liebend Herz geweiht!

2

Wo die Berge so blau
Aus dem nebligen Grau
Schauen herein,
Wo die Sonne verglüht,
Wo die Wolke umzieht,
Möchte ich sein!
Dort im ruhigen Tal
Schweigen Schmerzen und Qual.
Wo im Gestein
Still die Primel dort sinnt,
Weht so leise der Wind,
Möchte ich sein!
Hin zum sinnigen Wald
Drängt mich Liebesgewalt,
Innere Pein.
Ach, mich zög's nicht von hier,
Könnt ich, Traute, bei dir
Ewiglich sein!

3

Leichte Segler in den Höhen
Und du Bächlein, klein und schmal,
Könnt mein Liebchen ihr erspähen,
Grüßt sie mir viel tausendmal.
Seht ihr, Wolken, sie dann gehen
Sinnend in dem stillen Tal,
Laßt mein Bild vor ihr entstehen
In dem luft'gen Himmelssaal.
Wird sie an den Büschen stehen,
Die nun herbstlich falb und kahl,
Klagt ihr, wie mir ist geschehen,
Klagt ihr, Vöglein, meine Qual.
Stille Weste, bringt im Wehen
Hin zu meiner Herzenswahl
Meine Seufzer, die vergehen
Wie der Sonne letzter Strahl.
Flüstr' ihr zu mein Liebesflehen,
Laß sie, Bächlein klein und schmal,
Treu in deinen Wogen sehen
Meine Tränen ohne Zahl!

That speak to you of my distress!
For sounds of singing put to flight
All space and all time;
And a loving heart is reached
By what a loving heart has hallowed!

Where the blue mountains
From the misty grey
Look out towards me,
Where the sun's glow fades,
Where the clouds scud by –
There would I be!
There, in the peaceful valley,
Pain and torment cease.
Where among the rocks
The primrose meditates in silence,
And the wind blows so softly –
There would I be!
I am driven to the musing wood
By the power of love,
Inner pain.
Ah, nothing could tempt me from here,
If I were able, my love,
To be with you eternally!

Light clouds sailing on high,
And you, narrow little brook,
If you catch sight of my love,
Greet her a thousand times.
If, clouds, you see her walking
Thoughtful in the silent valley,
Let my image loom before her
In the airy vaults of heaven.
If she be standing by the bushes
Autumn has turned fallow and bare,
Pour out to her my fate,
Pour out, you birds, my torment.
Soft west winds, waft my sighs
To her my heart has chosen –
Sighs that fade away
Like the sun's last ray.
Whisper to her my entreaties,
Let her, narrow little brook,
Truly see in your ripples
My never-ending tears!

4

Diese Wolken in den Höhen,	These clouds on high,
Dieser Vöglein muntrer Zug	This cheerful flight of birds
Werden dich, o Huldin, sehen.	Will see you, O gracious one.
Nehmt mich mit im leichten Flug!	Take me lightly winging too!
Diese Weste werden spielen	These west winds will playfully
Scherzend dir um Wang' und Brust,	Blow about your cheeks and breast,
In den seidnen Locken wühlen. –	Will ruffle your silken tresses. –
Teilt ich mit euch diese Lust!	Would I might share that joy!
Hin zu dir von jenen Hügeln	This brooklet hastens eagerly
Emsig dieses Bächlein eilt.	To you from those hills.
Wird ihr Bild sich in dir spiegeln,	If she's reflected in you,
Fließ zurück dann unverweilt!	Flow directly back to me!

5

Es kehret der Maien,	May returns,
Es blühet die Au,	The meadow blooms.
Die Lüfte, sie wehen	The breezes blow
So milde, so lau,	So gentle, so mild,
Geschwätzig die Bäche nun rinnen.	The babbling brooks flow again,
Die Schwalbe, die kehret	The swallow returns
Zum wirtlichen Dach,	To its rooftop home,
Sie baut sich so emsig	And eagerly builds
Ihr bräutlich Gemach,	Her bridal chamber,
Die Liebe soll wohnen da drinnen.	Where love shall dwell.
Sie bringt sich geschäftig	She busily brings
Von Kreuz und von Quer	From every direction
Manch weicheres Stück	Many soft scraps
Zu dem Brautbett hieher,	For the bridal bed,
Manch wärmendes Stück für die Kleinen.	Many warm scraps for her young.
Nun wohnen die Gatten	Now the pair lives
Beisammen so treu,	Faithfully together,
Was Winter geschieden,	What winter parted,
Verband nun der Mai,	May has joined,
Was liebet, das weiß er zu einen.	For May can unite all who love.
Es kehret der Maien,	May returns,
Es blühet die Au,	The meadow blooms.
Die Lüfte, sie wehen	The breezes blow
So milde, so lau;	So gentle, so mild;
Nur ich kann nicht ziehen von hinnen.	I alone cannot move on.
Wenn alles, was liebet,	When spring unites
Der Frühling vereint,	All lovers,
Nur unserer Liebe	Our love alone
Kein Frühling erscheint,	Knows no spring,
Und Tränen sind all ihr Gewinnen.	And tears are its only gain.

Nimm sie hin denn, diese Lieder,	Accept, then, these songs
Die ich dir, Geliebte, sang,	I sang for you, beloved;
Singe sie dann abends wieder	Sing them again at evening
Zu der Laute süßem Klang!	To the lute's sweet sound!
Wenn das Dämmrungsrot dann ziehet	As the red light of evening draws
Nach dem stillen blauen See,	Toward the calm blue lake,
Und sein letzter Strahl verglühet	And its last rays fade
Hinter jener Bergeshöh;	Behind those mountain heights;
Und du singst, was ich gesungen,	And you sing what I sang
Was mir aus der vollen Brust	From a full heart
Ohne Kunstgepräng erklungen,	With no display of art,
Nur der Sehnsucht sich bewußt:	Aware only of longing:
Dann vor diesen Liedern weichet	Then, at these songs,
Was geschieden uns so weit,	The distance that parted us shall recede,
Und ein liebend Herz erreichet,	And a loving heart be reached
Was ein liebend Herz geweiht!	By what a loving heart has hallowed!

Friedrich von Matthisson (1761–1831)

See Schubert

In 1800, four years after the composition of 'Adelaide', Beethoven sent the song to Friedrich von Matthisson, the author of the poem which had enjoyed enormous popularity as soon as it was published. The second paragraph of the accompanying letter begins:

Zwar auch jetzt schicke ich Ihnen die *Adelaide* mit Ängstlichkeit. Sie wissen selbst, was einige Jahre bei einem Künstler, der immer weiter geht, für eine Veränderung hervorbringen; je größere Fortschritte in der Kunst man macht, desto weniger befriedigen einen seine älteren Werke. Mein größester Wunsch ist befriedigt, wenn Ihnen die musikalische Komposition Ihrer himmlischen *Adelaide* nicht ganz mißfällt . . .

Even now, I send you my *Adelaide* with some apprehension. You yourself are aware what difference a few years can make in a composer who continues to develop: the greater the progress one makes in art, the less satisfactory one's early works become. My greatest wish will have been fulfilled if my musical setting of your heavenly *Adelaide* does not entirely displease you . . .

When the song was mentioned to Beethoven many years later, he contented himself with the lapidary reply, „Das Gedicht ist sehr schön" ('The poem is very beautiful').

Einsam wandelt dein Freund im Frühlings-
 garten,
Mild vom lieblichen Zauberlicht umflossen,
Das durch wankende Blütenzweige zittert,
Adelaide!

In der spiegelnden Flut, im Schnee der Alpen,
In des sinkenden Tages Goldgewölken,
Im Gefilde der Sterne strahlt dein Bildnis,
Adelaide!

Abendlüftchen im zarten Laube flüstern,
Silberglöckchen des Mais im Grase säuseln,
Wellen rauschen und Nachtigallen flöten:
Adelaide!

Einst, o Wunder! entblüht auf meinem Grabe
Eine Blume der Asche meines Herzens;
Deutlich schimmert auf jedem Purpur-
 blättchen:
Adelaide!
(*Schubert*)

Your friend wanders lonely in the spring
 garden,
Gently bathed in the magical sweet light
That shimmers through swaying boughs in bloom,
Adelaide!

In the mirroring waves, in the Alpine snows,
In the golden clouds of the dying day,
In the fields of stars your image shines,
Adelaide!

Evening breezes whisper in the tender leaves,
The silvery bells of May rustle in the grass,
Waves murmur and nightingales sing:
Adelaide!

One day, O miracle! there shall bloom on my
 grave
A flower from the ashes of my heart;
On every purple leaf shall clearly shimmer:
Adelaide!

1809 Andenken / Remembrance WoO 136

Ich denke dein,
Wenn durch den Hain
Der Nachtigallen
Akkorde schallen!
Wann denkst du mein?

Ich denke dein
Im Dämmerschein
Der Abendhelle
Am Schattenquelle!
Wo denkst du mein?

Ich denke dein
Mit süßer Pein,
Mit bangem Sehnen
Und heißen Tränen!
Wie denkst du mein?

O denke mein,
Bis zum Verein
Auf besserm Sterne!
In jeder Ferne
Denk' ich nur dein!
(*Ries, Schubert, Weber, Wolf, Zumsteeg*)

I think of you
When through the grove
The nightingales'
Songs resound!
When do you think of me?

I think of you
In the twilight
Of evening
By the shadowed spring!
Where do you think of me?

I think of you
In sweet agony,
With fearful longing
And passionate tears!
How do you think of me?

O think of me
Until we are united
On a better star!
However far away,
I think only of you!

Christian Ludwig Reissig (1783–1822)

A minor poet and soldier who was wounded in battle in 1809 and discharged from the army. He persuaded many composers to set his verse, and Beethoven obliged with seven songs.

1809 Lied aus der Ferne / Song from afar WoO 137

Als mir noch die Träne der Sehnsucht nicht floß,
Und neidisch die Ferne nicht Liebchen verschloß,
Wie glich da mein Leben dem blühenden Kranz,
Dem Nachtigallwäldchen, voll Spiel und voll Tanz!

Before my tears of longing flowed,
And envious distance kept my beloved from me,
How my life resembled the blossoming wreath,
The nightingale wood, full of play and dancing!

Nun treibt mich oft Sehnsucht hinaus auf die Höhn,
Den Wunsch meines Herzens wo lächeln zu seh'n!
Hier sucht in der Gegend mein schmachtender Blick,
Doch kehret er nimmer befriedigt zurück.

Now longing often drives me out to the hills
To see where my heart's desire is smiling!
My yearning gaze searches all around,
But never returns contented to me.

Wie klopft es im Busen, als wärst du mir nah,
O komm, meine Holde, dein Jüngling ist da!
Ich opfre dir alles, was Gott mir verlieh,
Denn wie ich dich liebe, so liebt' ich noch nie!

How my heart pounds, as if you were near;
O come, my sweetest, your beloved is here!
I'll offer you all that God has granted me,
For I was never in love, the way I love you!

O Teure, komm eilig zum bräutlichen Tanz!
Ich pflege schon Rosen und Myrten zum Kranz.
Komm, zaubre mein Hüttchen zum Tempel der Ruh,
Zum Tempel der Wonne, die Göttin sei du!

O sweetest, come quickly to your bridal dance!
I've roses and myrtles for your wreath.
Come, make my hut a magic temple of peace,
A temple of rapture, and be its goddess!

Johann Ludwig Stoll (1778–1815)

The son of a doctor, Stoll travelled widely throughout Europe and, having settled in Weimar, wrote comedies for the court theatre. In 1808, he founded with Baron Leo Seckendorf the journal *Prometheus* which published poems by Goethe, Wieland and the Schlegel brothers. On Goethe's recommendation, he was appointed resident dramatist at the Burgtheater in Vienna; having lost his job there, he spent the rest of his life in poverty.

O daß ich dir vom stillen Auge
In seinem liebevollen Schein
Die Träne von der Wange sauge,
Eh sie die Erde trinket ein!

Ah, that from your tranquil eyes
With their loving light,
And from your cheeks I might drink the tear,
Before the earth consumes it!

Wohl hält sie zögernd auf der Wange
Und will sich heiß der Treue weihn.
Nun ich sie so im Kuß empfange,
Nun sind auch deine Schmerzen mein!
(*Schubert*)

It lingers trembling on your cheek,
An ardent witness to true love;
Now when I capture it in a kiss,
Your sorrows too are mine!

Christoph August Tiedge (1752–1841)

Poet and translator, whose philosophical *Urania: über Gott, Unsterblichkeit und Freiheit* (1801) supplied Beethoven with the text of 'An die Hoffnung' and was frequently reprinted in the first half of the nineteenth century. Tiedge and Beethoven met in Teplitz in 1811, and a warm friendship developed. Schubert also set one of his poems: 'An die Sonne', D272.

An die Hoffnung / To Hope
FIRST VERSION: 1804–5, OP. 32; SECOND VERSION: C.1813–15, OP. 94

Ob ein Gott sei? Ob er einst erfülle,
Was die Sehnsucht weinend sich verspricht?
Ob, vor irgendeinem Weltgericht,
Sich dies rätselhafte Sein enthülle?
Hoffen soll der Mensch! Er frage nicht!

Does a God exist? Will He one day grant
What tearful longing promises?
Will, at some Last Judgment,
This mysterious being reveal itself?
Man should hope! Not question!

Die du so gern in heil'gen Nächten feierst
Und sanft und weich den Gram verschleierst,
Der eine zarte Seele quält,
O Hoffnung! laß, durch dich emporgehoben,
Den Dulder ahnen, daß dort oben
Ein Engel seine Tränen zählt!

You who so gladly celebrate on sacred nights,
And softly and gently veil the grief
Which torments a tender soul,
O Hope! Uplifted by you,
Let the sufferer sense that there on high
An angel is counting his tears!

Wenn, längst verhallt, geliebte Stimmen
schweigen;
Wenn unter ausgestorbnen Zweigen
Verödet die Erinn'rung sitzt:
Dann nahe dich, wo dein Verlaßner trauert,
Und, von der Mitternacht umschauert,
Sich auf versunkne Urnen stützt.

When, long since hushed, beloved voices are
silent;
When, beneath dead branches
Memory sits in desolation –
Then draw near to where your forsaken one mourns,
And, enveloped in eerie midnight,
Leans against sunken urns.

Und blickt er auf, das Schicksal anzuklagen,
Wenn scheidend über seinen Tagen
Die letzten Strahlen untergehn:

And should he look up to accuse fate,
When the last departing rays
Set on his days:

Dann laß ihn um den Rand des Erdentraumes	Then, around the rim of this earthly dream,
Das Leuchten eines Wolkensaumes	Let him see the hem of a cloud
Von einer nahen Sonne sehn!	Glowing in the light of a nearby sun!

Georg Friedrich Treitschke (1776–1842)

Poet and playwright who worked in Vienna, mostly at the Kärtnertor Theater. When *Fidelio* was revived there in 1814, Beethoven asked him to revise the libretto. He wrote a number of Singspiele, including *Die gute Nachricht* and *Die Ehrenpforten* for which Beethoven composed an aria each: 'Germania' (WoO 94) and 'Es ist vollbracht' (WoO 97).

1816 Ruf vom Berge / Call from the mountains WoO 147

Wenn ich ein Vöglein wär'	If I were a little bird,
Und auch zwei Flüglein hätt',	And had two little wings,
Flög' ich zu dir!	I'd fly to you!
Weil's aber nicht kann sein,	But since it cannot be,
Bleib ich allhier.	I shall stay right here.

Wenn ich ein Sternlein wär'	If I were a little star
Und auch viel Strahlen hätt',	And had many beams,
Strahlt' ich dich an.	I'd beam on you.
Und du sähst freundlich auf,	And you would raise your kindly gaze
Grüßtest hinan.	And greet me.

Wenn ich ein Bächlein wär'	If I were a little stream,
Und auch viel Wellen hätt',	And had many ripples,
Rauscht' ich durch's Grün.	I'd murmur through green fields.
Nahte dem kleinen Fuß,	Draw close to your little foot
Küßte wohl ihn.	And perhaps even kiss it.

Würd' ich zur Abendluft,	If I were the evening breeze,
Nähm' ich mir Blütenduft,	I'd breathe the scent
Hauchte dir zu.	Of flowers on you.
Weilend auf Brust und Mund,	Lingering on your breast and lips,
Fänd' ich dort Ruh'.	I'd find peace.

Geht doch kein' Stund' der Nacht,	Not an hour of night goes by
Ohn' daß mein Herz erwacht	Without my heart awakening
Und an dich denkt.	And thinking of you,
Wie du mir tausendmal	And of how a thousand times
Dein Herz geschenkt.	You've given me your heart.

Wohl dringen Bach und Stern,	Though stream and star,
Lüftlein und Vöglein fern,	Breeze and bird
Kommen zu dir.	Approach you from afar,
Ich nur bin festgebannt,	I alone am rooted to this spot,
Weine allhier.	And shed my tears.

Christian Felix Weiße (1726–1804)

See Mozart

Weiße was the son of a headmaster in Leipzig, where he rubbed shoulders with literary figures such as Lessing, Gottsched and Gellert. Having tried his hand as a private tutor, he became a tax-collector and the well-respected author of several volumes of verse and lengthy tragedies in prose. 'Der Kuß' is in his anacreontic vein, and clearly captivated Beethoven, who indicates on the score that it should be sung 'scherzend', i.e. 'playfully'. The song is one of several that were composed when Beethoven was a young man, and not published until decades later: it was sketched in 1798, composed in 1822 and only published in 1825.

1822 Der Kuß / The kiss Op. 128

Ich war bei Chloen ganz allein,	I was with Chloe all alone,
Und küssen wollt ich sie:	And wished to kiss her:
Jedoch sie sprach, sie würde schrein,	But she said she would scream,
Es sei vergebne Müh.	That it would be in vain.
Ich wagt es doch und küßte sie,	But I dared to and kissed her,
Trotz ihrer Gegenwehr.	Despite her resistance.
Und schrie sie nicht? Jawohl, sie schrie,	And did she scream? Oh yes, she screamed,
Doch lange hinterher.	But not until long after.
(*Bohm*)	

Alban Berg (1885–1935)

When in 1904 an advertisement appeared in the 'Neue musikalische Presse', inviting professional musicians and serious amateurs to take part in a music course given by Arnold Schoenberg and other teachers, Alban Berg submitted a not inconsiderable number of juvenilia, and Schoenberg, immediately recognizing the young composer's talent, accepted him as a private pupil. Berg began to study with Schoenberg in the autumn of 1904, and his teacher's influence can be clearly seen in the four songs of Op. 2. Although Berg gives the first three key signatures – D minor, E flat minor and A flat minor – tonality is beginning to lose its hold, and in the fourth song, 'Warm die Lüfte', is finally abandoned. It is Berg's first 'atonal' piece and a wonderfully expressive setting of Mombert's impressionistic poem, the only one of the four that does not have sleep as its theme.

It is not known how many songs Berg composed during his student years, for he destroyed many of them, and all remained unpublished during his lifetime – all, that is, except the *Sieben frühe Lieder,* which appeared in 1928. The reason for their publication was the enormous triumph of his opera *Wozzeck,* and Berg's wish to produce another successful vocal work of more modest proportions, without embarking on an entirely new project. The songs all have love as their theme, and the influence of Schubert, Brahms and Wolf is not difficult to detect. There are anticipations of atonality ('Nacht' uses whole-tone harmony, and 'Im Zimmer' delays its tonic chord to the very end), but these seven songs with their expressive melodic lines are typical products of the late-Romantic style – particularly in the orchestral version, where 'Nacht' and 'Sommertage' are lushly scored for large orchestra. After *Wozzeck,* Berg composed only one more song (he called *Der Wein* a 'concert aria'), a setting of Theodor Storm's 'Schließe mir die Augen beide' (1925), a reworking of the text he had first set in 1907, both of which he now dedicated to Emil Hertzkas of Universal Edition to symbolize the way in which Hertzkas had been, as he stated in the *Die Musik* journal of 1930, the only publisher to have supported both tonal and twelve-note music during the twenty-five years of Universal Edition's existence.

Friedrich Hebbel (1813–63) and Alfred Mombert (1872–1942)

1910 *Vier Lieder / Four songs* Op. 2

Hebbel, though best known for his dramas (*Julia, Maria Magdalena, Herodes und Mariamne, Michel Angelo* [dedicated to Schumann], *Agnes Bernauer, Gyges und sein Ring*), is a more considerable poet, and his poems have been set by a select group of composers, including Brahms, Cornelius, Liszt, Pfitzner, Reger, Schoeck,

Schumann, Rudi Stephan and Wolf. His collected verse, published in 1857, included a cycle of eleven poems, called 'Dem Schmerz sein Recht', which express Hebbel's vulnerability to isolation and despair, and his longing for escape. Suffering as the consuming force of life was a theme dear to Georg Büchner (born in the same year as Hebbel), whose *Wozzeck* obsessed Berg when he first saw the play in 1914. Alfred Mombert was interested in the occult and the doctrine of the transmigration of souls. As a Jew, he was dismissed from the Prussian Academy, lived on in Germany and was sent to a concentration camp in 1940. Rescued by a friend, he was allowed into Switzerland, the country of his birth. Berg chose three of his poems from 'Der Glühende' (1896).

1

Schlafen, Schlafen / Sleep, sleep
FRIEDRICH HEBBEL

Schlafen, Schlafen, nichts als Schlafen!	Sleep, sleep, nothing but sleep!
Kein Erwachen, keinen Traum!	No awakening, no dream!
Jener Wehen, die mich trafen,	Of the pains I had to bear
Leisestes Erinnern kaum.	Scarce the faintest memory –
Daß ich, wenn des Lebens Fülle	So that when life's plenitude
Nieder klingt in meine Ruh',	Echoes down to where I rest,
Nur noch tiefer mich verhülle,	I enshroud myself more deeply still,
Fester zu die Augen tu'!	Press my eyes more tightly shut!
(*Schoeck*)	

2

Schlafend trägt man mich / I am borne in sleep
ALFRED MOMBERT

Schlafend trägt man mich	I am borne in sleep
in mein Heimatland.	to my homeland.
Ferne komm' ich her,	I come from afar,
über Gipfel, über Schlünde,	over peaks, over gorges,
über ein dunkles Meer	over a dark sea
in mein Heimatland.	to my homeland.
(*Knab, Marx, Szymanowski*)	

3

Nun ich der Riesen Stärksten überwand / Now I've conquered the strongest of giants
ALFRED MOMBERT

Nun ich der Riesen Stärksten überwand,	Now I've conquered the strongest of giants,
mich aus dem dunkelsten Land	and from the darkest land
heimfand	have found my way home
an einer weißen Märchenhand –	guided by a white faerie hand –

Hallen schwer die Glocken.
Und ich wanke durch die Gassen
schlafbefangen.

The bells sound heavily.
And I stagger through the streets,
drunk with sleep.

4
Warm die Lüfte / Warm the breezes
ALFRED MOMBERT

Warm die Lüfte,
es sprießt Gras auf sonnigen Wiesen.
Horch! –
Horch, es flötet die Nachtigall . . .
Ich will singen:

Warm the breezes,
grass grows on sunlit meadows.
Listen! –
Listen, the nightingale is singing . . .
I shall sing:

Droben hoch im düstern Bergforst,
es schmilzt und glitzert kalter Schnee,
ein Mädchen in grauem Kleide
lehnt an feuchtem Eichstamm,
krank sind ihre zarten Wangen,
die grauen Augen fiebern
durch Düsterriesenstämme.
„Er kommt noch nicht. Er läßt mich warten"
. . .

High in the gloomy mountain forest,
cold snow melts and glitters,
a girl dressed in grey
leans against the damp trunk of an oak,
her tender cheeks are sick,
her grey eyes stare feverishly
through the gloom of giant trunks.
'Still he does not come. He keeps me waiting'
. . .

Stirb!
Der Eine stirbt, daneben der Andere lebt:
Das macht die Welt so tiefschön.

Die!
One dies, while another lives:
That makes the world so profoundly beautiful.

Theodor Storm (1817–88)

See Brahms

A North German poet, celebrated above all for his Novellen and lyric poetry. Of his more than fifty Novellen, the best known are 'Der Schimmelreiter' (1888) and 'Immensee' (1851) which, as with Mörike's 'Maler Nolten', integrates poetry and narrative. Like Mörike, with whom he corresponded, Storm defies all classification as a poet; he belonged to no movement but wrote exquisite poems about love, the transience of life and the North Sea coastal region around Husum, where he was born and lived. He once wrote to Keller that a poet could only succeed „höchstens ein halbes, allerhöchstens ein ganzes Dutzend Mal" ('at most half a dozen, at the very most a dozen times') to write a perfect poem. 'Schließe mir die Augen beide' is one such example. Others include 'Über die Heide' (Brahms), 'Nelken' (Reger), 'Hyazinthen' (Hermann Reutter) and 'Wohl fühl ich, wie das Leben rinnt' (Schreker).

Schließe mir die Augen beide / Close both my eyes
FIRST VERSION 1907; SECOND VERSION 1925

Schließe mir die Augen beide
Mit den lieben Händen zu!
Geht doch alles, was ich leide,
Unter deiner Hand zur Ruh.

Und wie leise sich der Schmerz
Well' um Welle schlafen leget,
Wie der letzte Schlag sich reget,
Füllest du mein ganzes Herz.
(*Goetz, Hessenberg, Marx*)

Close both my eyes
With your dear hands!
For all my suffering is soothed
Beneath your hands.

While wave after wave of anguish
Gently ebbs away,
And while the last pang quivers,
You fill my entire heart.

Sieben frühe Lieder / Seven Early Songs
1905–08; REVISED AND ORCHESTRATED 1928

1

Nacht / Night
CARL HAUPTMANN (1858–1921)

Dämmern Wolken über Nacht und Tal.
Nebel schweben. Wasser rauschen sacht.
Nun entschleiert sich's mit einem Mal.
O gib acht! gib acht!

Weites Wunderland ist aufgetan,
Silbern ragen Berge traumhaft groß,
Stille Pfade silberlicht talan
Aus verborg'nem Schoß.

Und die hehre Welt so traumhaft rein.
Stummer Buchenbaum am Wege steht
Schattenschwarz – ein Hauch vom fernen Hain
Einsam leise weht.

Und aus tiefen Grundes Düsterheit
Blinken Lichter auf in stummer Nacht.
Trinke Seele! trinke Einsamkeit!
O gib acht! gib acht!

Clouds loom over night and valley.
Mists hover, waters softly murmur.
Now at once all is unveiled.
O take heed! take heed!

A vast wonderland opens up,
Silvery mountains soar dreamlike tall,
Silent paths climb silver-bright valleywards
From a hidden womb.

And the glorious world so dreamlike pure.
A silent beech-tree stands by the wayside
Shadow-black – a breath from the distant grove
Blows solitary soft.

And from the deep valley's gloom
Lights twinkle in the silent night.
Drink soul! drink solitude!
O take heed! take heed!

2

Schilflied / Reed song
NIKOLAUS LENAU (1802–50)

Auf geheimem Waldespfade
Schleich' ich gern im Abendschein
An das öde Schilfgestade,
Mädchen, und gedenke dein!

Along a secret forest path
I love to steal in the evening light
To the desolate reedy shore
And think, my girl, of you!

Wenn sich dann der Busch verdüstert,
Rauscht das Rohr geheimnisvoll,
Und es klaget und es flüstert,
Daß ich weinen, weinen soll.

Und ich mein', ich höre wehen
Leise deiner Stimme Klang,
Und im Weiher untergehen
Deinen lieblichen Gesang.
(*Claussen, Franz, Griffes, Marteau, Pfitzner, Schoeck*)

When the bushes then grow dark,
The reeds pipe mysteriously,
Lamenting and whispering,
That I must weep, must weep.

And I seem to hear the soft sound
Of your voice,
And your lovely singing
Drowning in the pond.

3

Die Nachtigall / The nightingale
THEODOR STORM (1817–88), FROM *Hinzelmeier*

Das macht, es hat die Nachtigall
Die ganze Nacht gesungen;
Da sind von ihrem süßen Schall,
Da sind in Hall und Widerhall
Die Rosen aufgesprungen.

It is because the nightingale
Has sung throughout the night,
That from the sweet sound
Of her echoing song
The roses have sprung up.

Sie war doch sonst ein wildes Blut,
Nun geht sie tief in Sinnen;
Trägt in der Hand den Sommerhut
Und duldet still der Sonne Glut
Und weiß nicht, was beginnen.

She was once a wild creature,
Now she wanders deep in thought;
In her hand a summer hat,
Bearing in silence the sun's heat,
Not knowing what to do.

Das macht, es hat die Nachtigall
Die ganze Nacht gesungen;
Da sind von ihrem süßen Schall,
Da sind in Hall und Widerhall
Die Rosen aufgesprungen.
(*Ernest Vietor*)

It is because the nightingale
Has sung throughout the night,
That from the sweet sound
Of her echoing song
The roses have sprung up.

4

Traumgekrönt / Crowned with dreams
RAINER MARIA RILKE (1875–1926)

Das war der Tag der weißen Chrysanthemen, –
mir bangte fast vor seiner Pracht . . .
Und dann, dann kamst du mir die Seele
    nehmen
tief in der Nacht.

That was the day of the white chrysanthe-
    mums –
Its brilliance almost frightened me . . .
And then, then you came to take my soul
at the dead of night.

Mir war so bang, und du kamst lieb und
    leise, –
ich hatte grad im Traum an dich gedacht.
Du kamst, und leis wie eine Märchenweise
erklang die Nacht . . .

I was so frightened, and you came sweetly
    and gently,
I had been thinking of you in my dreams.
You came, and soft as a fairy tune
the night rang out . . .

5

Im Zimmer / In the room
JOHANNES SCHLAF (1862–1941)

Herbstsonnenschein.
Der liebe Abend blickt so still herein.
Ein Feuerlein rot
Knistert im Ofenloch und loht.

So! – Mein Kopf auf deinen Knie'n. –
So ist mir gut;
Wenn mein Auge so in deinem ruht.

Wie leise die Minuten ziehn! . . .

Autumn sunshine.
The lovely evening looks in so silently.
A little red fire
Crackles and blazes in the hearth.

Like this! – With my head on your knees. –
Like this I am content;
When my eyes rest in yours like this.

How gently the minutes pass! . . .

6

Liebesode / Ode to love
OTTO ERICH HARTLEBEN (1864–1905)

Im Arm der Liebe schliefen wir selig ein.
Am offnen Fenster lauschte der Sommerwind,
und unsrer Atemzüge Frieden
trug er hinaus in die helle Mondnacht. –

Und aus dem Garten tastete zagend sich
ein Rosenduft an unserer Liebe Bett
und gab uns wundervolle Träume,
Träume des Rausches – so reich an Sehnsucht!
(*Marx, Reger*)

In love's arms we fell blissfully asleep.
The summer wind listened at the open window,
and carried the peace of our breathing
out into the moon-bright night. –

And from the garden a scent of roses
came timidly to our bed of love
and gave us wonderful dreams,
ecstatic dreams – so rich in longing!

7

Sommertage / Summer days
PAUL HOHENBERG (dates unknown)

Nun ziehen Tage über die Welt,
gesandt aus blauer Ewigkeit,
im Sommerwind verweht die Zeit.
Nun windet nächtens der Herr
Sternenkränze mit seliger Hand
über Wander- und Wunderland.

O Herz, was kann in diesen Tagen
dein hellstes Wanderlied denn sagen
von deiner tiefen, tiefen Lust:
Im Wiesensang verstummt die Brust,
nun schweigt das Wort, wo Bild um Bild
zu dir zieht und dich ganz erfüllt.

Days, sent from blue eternity,
journey now across the world,
time drifts away in the summer wind.
The Lord at night now garlands
star-chains with his blessed hand
across lands of wandering and wonder.

In these days, O heart, what can
your brightest travel-song say
of your deep, deep joy?
The heart falls silent in the meadows' song,
words now cease when image after image
comes to you and fills you utterly.

Johannes Brahms (1833–97)

Much of the verse selected by Brahms for his Lieder was written by minor poets such as Georg Daumer, whose sentimental poetry (including translations) inspired no fewer than nineteen Lieder, and some forty more songs set as duets and quartets. Brahms's preference for second-rate verse has led some commentators to assert that he failed to appreciate the likes of Goethe (a mere five settings), Eichendorff (six), Heine (six), Keller (three), Mörike (two) and Storm (one). Such statistics are misleading. Brahms's knowledge of German literature was considerable, and throughout his life he was an ardent collector of poetry; but as he confided to Georg Henschel in *Personal Recollections of Johannes Brahms* (1907), he felt that a poem should not be perfect, like many of Goethe's, but should provide the composer with the possibility of creating a song that is greater than the original. In another volume, *Musings and Memoirs of a Musician* (1918), Henschel quotes Brahms on his method of composition:

> [...] when I, for instance, have found the first phrase of a song [...] I might shut the book there and then, go for a walk, do some other work and perhaps not think of it for months. Nothing however is lost. If afterwards I approach the subject again, it is sure to have taken shape.

The inference is that Brahms was a master of absolute music, which explains, perhaps, why so many passages from his songs re-appear in his instrumental works: 'Komm bald' and 'Wie Melodien zieht es mir' (Violin Sonata no. 2), 'Todessehnen' and 'Immer leiser wird mein Schlummer' (Piano Concerto no. 2), 'Ständchen' (Academic Festival Overture), 'Regenlied' (G major Violin Sonata). And yet he could respond to the verbal detail of a poem as imaginatively as any of the great Lieder composers, nowhere more memorably than in the third of the *Vier ernste Gesänge*, where the harsh closed vowels of 'O Tod, wie bitter bist du' yield to the soft alliteration and open-vowelled assonance of 'O Tod, wie wohl tust du', and Brahms, in a magical modulation from minor to major, finds one of his sweetest melodies to depict the power of death's assuagement.

Brahms's choice of texts betrays his own essentially melancholy nature and often reflects the impossibility of sustaining successful emotional relationships with the women in his life, such as Clara Schumann and Agathe von Siebold. Although he felt passionately about them, he feared too close a union and eventually shied away from both. An extraordinary number of poems have loneliness as their subject ('Waldeinsamkeit', 'Feldeinsamkeit') or deal with isolation ('Es hing der Reif'), lamentation ('Klage') and nostalgia ('O wüßt ich doch den Weg zurück') – themes which merge in his only cycle, *Die schöne Magelone*, and prompted Nietzsche, in an unkind and unfair phrase, to describe Brahms's music as 'Die Melancholie des Unvermögens' ('the melancholy of inability'), a view passionately shared by Hugo Wolf. Arnold Schoenberg, however, hailed Brahms as a great progressive, a great innovator in the realm of musical language.

Schumann once complained in a letter to Clara that he found it difficult 'für das Volk zu schreiben' ('to write for the people'). Not so Brahms; he was a man of the people and found no difficulty in absorbing popular music. The Volkslied, indeed, was more important to Brahms than any of the other great Lieder composers. Many of his own songs have a folksong feel about them, and throughout his composing career he made several arrangements of Volkslieder: the *14 Volks-Kinderlieder*, for example, of 1857–8, or the *28 Volkslieder* of the same period. He also adapted folksongs of Persian, Arabian, Russian, Lithuanian, Turkish, Polish, Moravian, Slovakian and Bohemian origin; finally in 1894, as an old man, he found the time to compose/arrange the seven books of his greatest folksong collection: *49 deutsche Volkslieder*.

Anonymous

c.1860 Sonntag / Sunday Op. 47, no. 3
ED. LUDWIG UHLAND (1787–1862)

So hab ich doch die ganze Woche
Mein feines Liebchen nicht gesehn,
Ich sah es an einem Sonntag
Wohl vor der Türe stehn:
Das tausendschöne Jungfräulein,
Das tausendschöne Herzelein,
Wollte Gott, ich wär heute bei ihr!

So will mir doch die ganze Woche
Das Lachen nicht vergehn,
Ich sah es an einem Sonntag
Wohl in die Kirche gehn:
Das tausendschöne Jungfräulein,
Das tausendschöne Herzelein,
Wollte Gott, ich wär heute bei ihr!
(*Reger*)

For a whole week now
I haven't seen my love,
I saw her on a Sunday,
Standing at her door:
My loveliest girl,
My loveliest sweet,
Would to God I were with her today!

So I'll still be able
To laugh all week,
I saw her on a Sunday,
As she went to church:
My loveliest girl,
My loveliest sweet,
Would to God I were with her today!

by 1868 Der Gang zum Liebchen / The walk to the beloved Op. 48, no. 1
CZECH, TRANSLATED BY JOSEPH WENZIG (1807–76)

Es glänzt der Mond nieder,
Ich sollte doch wieder
Zu meinem Liebchen,
Wie mag es ihr gehn?

The moon shines down,
So I should set out
Again to my love,
How is she, I wonder?

Ach weh, sie verzaget	Alas, she's despairing
Und klaget, und klaget,	And lamenting, lamenting
Daß sie mich nimmer	She'll never see
Im Leben wird sehn!	Me again in her life!
Es ging der Mond unter,	The moon went down,
Ich eilte doch munter,	But I hurried off happily,
Und eilte, daß keiner	Hurried so that no one
Mein Liebchen entführt.	Should steal my love.
Ihr Täubchen, o girret,	Keep cooing, you doves,
Ihr Lüftchen, o schwirret,	Keep whispering, you breezes,
Daß keiner mein Liebchen,	So that no one
Mein Liebchen entführt!	Should steal my love!

*c.*1878 Vergebliches Ständchen / Vain serenade Op. 84, no. 4

(ER)	(HE)
Guten Abend, mein Schatz,	Good evening, my sweetheart,
Guten Abend, mein Kind!	Good evening, my child!
Ich komm aus Lieb zu dir,	I come because I love you,
Ach, mach mir auf die Tür,	Ah! open up your door to me,
Mach mir auf die Tür!	Open up your door!
(SIE)	(SHE)
Mein Tür ist verschlossen,	My door's locked,
Ich laß dich nicht ein;	I won't let you in;
Mutter, die rät mir klug,	Mother gave me good advice,
Wärst du herein mit Fug,	If you were allowed in,
Wär's mit mir vorbei!	All would be over with me!
(ER)	(HE)
So kalt ist die Nacht,	The night's so cold,
So eisig der Wind,	The wind's so icy,
Daß mir das Herz erfriert,	My heart is freezing,
Mein Lieb erlöschen wird;	My love will go out;
Öffne mir, mein Kind!	Open up, my child!
(SIE)	(SHE)
Löschet dein Lieb,	If your love goes out,
Laß sie löschen nur!	Then let it go out!
Löschet sie immerzu,	If it keeps going out,
Geh heim zu Bett, zur Ruh,	Then go home to bed and go to sleep,
Gute Nacht, mein Knab!	Good night, my lad!

*c.*1883 **Vorschneller Schwur / Overhasty vow Op. 95, no. 5**
SERBIAN, TRANSLATED BY SIEGFRIED KAPPER (1821–79)

Schwor ein junges Mädchen
Blumen nie zu tragen;
Blumen nie zu tragen,
Niemals Wein zu trinken;
Niemals Wein zu trinken,
Knaben nie zu küssen.

A young girl vowed
Never to wear flowers;
Never to wear flowers,
Never to drink wine;
Never to drink wine,
Never to kiss boys.

Gestern schwor das Mädchen –
Heute schon bereut es:
„Wenn ich Blumen trüge
Wär' ich doch noch schöner!
Wenn ich Rotwein tränke
Wär' ich doch noch froher!
Wenn den Liebsten küßte,
Wär' mir doch noch wohler!"

That's what she vowed yesterday –
Today she regrets it:
'If I wore flowers,
I'd be even prettier!
If I drank red wine,
I'd be even merrier!
If I kissed my sweetheart,
I'd be even happier!'

by 1885 Trennung / Separation Op. 97, no. 6

Da unten im Tale
Läuft's Wasser so trüb,
Und i kann dir's net sagen,
I hab di so lieb.

Down there in the valley
The water runs so bleakly,
And I cannot say
How much I love you.

Sprichst allweil von Liebe,
Sprichst allweil von Treu,
Und a bissele Falschheit
Is auch wohl dabei.

You speak only of love,
Speak only of constancy,
And a bit of falsehood
Goes with it too.

Und wenn i dir's zehnmal sag,
Daß i di lieb und mag,
Und du willst nit verstehn,
Muß i halt weiter gehn.

And if I tell you ten times
That I love you,
And you refuse to understand –
I shall have to go on my way.

Für die Zeit, wo du g'liebt mi hast,
Da dank i dir schön,
Und i wünsch, daß dir's anderswo
Besser mag gehn.

For the time that you loved me,
I thank you so much,
And wish that elsewhere
You might fare better.

Hermann Allmers (1821–1902)

A native of Friesland, Allmers was a respected farmer in Rechtenflet, and also a minor poet and dramatist who did much to encourage the local *Heimatkunst*. Today he is remembered only for his 'Feldeinsamkeit' and his unfortunate response to Brahms's music. Brahms was so pleased with his setting that he instructed the baritone Karl Reinthaler to perform the song to the poet. Allmers was unimpressed and wrote to Praeger and Meier, the Bremen music publishers, that Brahms's 'artificial melody' wholly failed to express the mood of the poem; and he concluded the same letter by awarding the palm for the best setting of his poem to a long-forgotten composer who rejoiced in the name of Focken [*sic*].

c.1879 Feldeinsamkeit / Alone in fields Op. 86, no. 2

Ich ruhe still im hohen grünen Gras
Und sende lange meinen Blick nach oben,
Von Grillen rings umschwirrt ohn' Unterlaß,
Von Himmelsbläue wundersam umwoben.

Die schönen weißen Wolken ziehn dahin
Durchs tiefe Blau, wie schöne stille Träume; –
Mir ist, als ob ich längst gestorben bin,
Und ziehe selig mit durch ew'ge Räume.
(*Ives*)

I rest at peace in tall green grass
And gaze steadily aloft,
Surrounded by unceasing crickets,
Wondrously interwoven with blue sky.

The lovely white clouds go drifting by
Through the deep blue, like lovely silent dreams;
I feel as if I have long been dead,
Drifting happily with them through eternal
	space.

Clemens Brentano (1778–1842)

An important figure in German Romanticism, Brentano is remembered for a number of short stories (*Geschichte vom braven Kasperl und dem schönen Annerl*), lyrical poems and *Des Knaben Wunderhorn*, the three volumes of folk poetry which he collected, edited and partially wrote with Achim von Arnim. Brentano was a regular guest at the house of Privy Councillor von Stägemann in Berlin, where the charades took place that led to the creation of Wilhelm Müller's *Die schöne Müllerin*. It was during these evenings that he fell in love with the eighteen-year-old Luise Hensel (sister of Wilhelm, soon to marry Fanny Mendelssohn), who had also attracted the attentions of Wilhelm Müller. Brentano proposed to her and was refused; Müller poured out his infatuation in the poems of *Die schöne Müllerin* (see p. 350).

c.1877 O kühler Wald / O cool forest Op. 72, no. 3

O kühler Wald,
Wo rauschest du,
In dem mein Liebchen geht?
O Widerhall,
Wo lauschest du,
Der gern mein Lied versteht?

Im Herzen tief,
Da rauscht der Wald,
In dem mein Liebchen geht,
In Schmerzen schlief

O cool forest,
In which my beloved walks,
Where are you murmuring?
O echo,
Where are you listening,
Who love to understand my song?

Deep in my heart
Is where the forest murmurs,
In which my beloved walks,
The echo

Der Widerhall,
Die Lieder sind verweht.
(*Marschner*)

Fell asleep in sorrow,
The songs have blown away.

Karl Candidus (1817–72)

A priest and minor poet; Brahms set seven of his poems, including the duet 'Jäger-lied'. This distinguished theologian and professor belonged to an old Alsatian family of clerics, but always wrote in German. Schumann set his 'Husarenabzug'.

c.1876 Alte Liebe / Old love Op. 72, no. 1

Es kehrt die dunkle Schwalbe
Aus fernem Land zurück,
Die frommen Störche kehren
Und bringen neues Glück.

The dark swallow returns
From a distant land,
The pious storks return
And bring new happiness.

An diesem Frühlingsmorgen,
So trüb verhängt und warm,
Ist mir, als fänd ich wieder
Den alten Liebesharm.

On this Spring morning,
So bleakly veiled and warm,
I seem to rediscover
Love's grief of old.

Es ist, als ob mich leise
Wer auf die Schulter schlug,
Als ob ich säuseln hörte,
Wie einer Taube Flug.

It is as if someone
Tapped me on the shoulder,
As if I heard a whirring,
Like a dove in flight.

Es klopft an meine Türe
Und ist doch niemand draus;
Ich atme Jasmindüfte,
Und habe keinen Strauß.

There's a knock at my door,
Yet no one stands outside;
I breathe the scent of jasmine,
Yet have no bouquet.

Es ruft mir aus der Ferne,
Ein Auge sieht mich an,
Ein alter Traum erfaßt mich
Und führt mich seine Bahn.

Someone calls me from afar,
Eyes are watching me,
An old dream takes hold of me
And leads me on its path.

1877 Tambourliedchen / Drummer's ditty Op. 69, no. 5

Den Wirbel schlag ich gar so stark,
Daß euch erzittert Bein und Mark!
Drum denk ich ans schön Schätzelein.
Blaugrau,
Blau,
Blaugrau,
Blau
Ist seiner Augen Schein.

I play my drum-roll so violently
That it thrills right through you!
That's why I think of my beautiful love.
Blue-grey,
Blue,
Blue-grey,
Blue
Is the colour of her eyes.

Und denk ich an den Schein so hell,

And when I think of that bright glow,

Von selber dämpft das Trommelfell	The drum muffles of its own accord
Den wilden Ton, klingt hell und rein,	Its fierce tone, and sounds bright and clear.
Blaugrau,	Blue-grey,
Blau,	Blue,
Blaugrau,	Blue-grey,
Blau	Blue
Sind Liebchens Äugelein.	Is the glow of my sweetheart's eyes.

Hugo Conrat (dates unknown)

Hugo Conrat was a cultured Viennese, whose daughter Ilse sculpted the marble monument to Brahms in the Vienna Zentralfriedhof. The *Zigeunerlieder*, Hungarian folksongs with piano accompaniments by Zoltán Nagy, were translated by Conrat with the help of Fräulein Witzl, a young Hungarian woman who worked as nanny in the house of Ignaz and Marie Brüll, where the first performance of Brahms's version for vocal quartet and four hands took place.

Zigeunerlieder / Gipsy songs Op. 103, nos. 1–8
FIRST VERSION (SATB SOLI, 1–11): 1887
SECOND VERSION (SOLO VOICE, 1–7 AND 11): 1887–8

1

Hej te cigány

He, Zigeuner, greife in den Saiten ein!	Hey, gipsy, sound your strings!
Spiel das Lied vom ungetreuen Mägdelein!	Play the song of the faithless girl!
Laß die Saiten weinen, klagen, traurig bange,	Make the strings weep and moan in sad despair
Bis die heiße Träne netzet diese Wange!	Till hot tears moisten these cheeks!

2

Mély a Rima

Hochgetürmte Rimaflut, wie bist du so trüb,	Rima, how troubled your towering waters are;
An dem Ufer klag ich laut nach dir, mein Lieb!	I'll lament for you loudly on its banks, my love!
Wellen fliehen, Wellen strömen,	Waves rush by, waves stream past,
Rauschen an den Strand heran zu mir;	Roaring towards me on the shore;
An dem Rimaufer laßt mich ewig weinen	On the banks of the Rima let me weep for her
nach ihr!	eternally!

3

Akktor szép a kis lány

Wißt ihr, wann mein Kindchen	Do you know when my little girl
Am allerschönsten ist?	Is at her loveliest?
Wenn ihr süßes Mündchen	When her sweet little mouth
Scherzt und lacht und küßt.	Jokes and laughs and kisses.

Mägdelein,	Little girl,
Du bist mein,	You are mine,
Inniglich	Tenderly
Küß ich dich,	I kiss you,
Dich erschuf der liebe Himmel	Dear heaven made you
Einzig nur für mich!	For me alone!

Wißt ihr wann mein Liebster	Do you know when my beloved
Am besten mir gefällt?	Pleases me most?
Wenn in seinen Armen	When he holds me
Er mich umschlungen hält.	In his arms' embrace.
Schätzelein,	Sweetheart,
Du bist mein,	You are mine,
Inniglich	Tenderly
Küß ich dich,	I kiss you,
Dich erschuf der liebe Himmel	Dear heaven made you
Einzig nur für mich!	For me alone!

4

Isten tudja hányszor meg nem bántam

Lieber Gott, du weißt, wie oft bereut ich hab,	Dear God, you know how often I've regretted
Daß ich meinem Liebsten einst ein Küßchen gab.	That little kiss I once gave my dearest.
Herz gebot, daß ich ihn küssen muß,	My heart decreed I had to kiss him,
Denk so lang ich leb an diesen ersten Kuß.	As long as I live I'll think of that first kiss.

Lieber Gott, du weißt, wie oft in stiller Nacht	Dear God, you know how often in silent nights
Ich in Lust und Leid an meinen Schatz gedacht.	I've thought of my love in joy and pain.
Lieb ist süß, wenn bitter auch die Reu,	Love is sweet, however bitter the regret,
Armes Herze bleibt ihm ewig, ewig treu.	My poor heart will ever be faithful to him.

5

Barna legény tánczra viszi

Brauner Bursche führt zum Tanze	A swarthy lad leads his lovely
Sein blauäugig schönes Kind,	Blue-eyed lass to the dance,
Schlägt die Sporen keck zusammen,	Boldly clashes his spurs together,
Czardas-Melodie beginnt,	A csardas melody begins,
Küßt und herzt sein süßes Täubchen,	He kisses and hugs his sweet little dove,
Dreht sie, führt sie, jauchzt und springt;	Turns her, leads her, exults and leaps;
Wirft drei blanke Silbergulden	Throws three shining silver florins
Auf das Cimbal, daß es klingt.	That make the cimbalom ring.

6

Három rózsa egy sorjában

| Röslein dreie in der Reihe blühn so rot, | Three little red roses bloom side by side, |
| Daß der Bursch zum Mädel geht, ist kein Verbot! | It's no crime for a lad to visit his lass! |

Lieber Gott, wenn das verboten wär,
Ständ die schöne weite Welt schon längst
   nicht mehr,
Ledig bleiben Sünde wär!

Schönstes Städtchen in Alföld* ist
   Ketschkemet†,
Dort gibt es gar viele Mädchen schmuck und
   nett!
Freunde, sucht euch dort ein Bräutchen aus,
Freit um ihre Hand und gründet euer Haus,
Freudenbecher leeret aus!

Dear God, if that were a crime,
This fair wide world would long ago have
   ceased to exist,
Staying single would be a sin!

The loveliest town in Alföld is
   Kecskemét,
Where many smart and nice girls live!
Friends, find yourselves a young bride
   there,
Win her hand and set up house,
Drain beakers of joy!

7
Jut e néha

Kommt dir manchmal in den Sinn,
Mein süßes Lieb,
Was du einst mit heilgem Eide
Mir gelobt?
Täusch mich nicht, verlaß mich nicht,
Du weißt nicht wie lieb ich dich hab,
Lieb du mich, wie ich dich,
Dann strömt Gottes Huld auf dich herab!

Do you sometimes recall,
My sweetest,
What you once pledged to me
With a sacred oath?
Do not deceive me, do not leave me,
You do not know how much I love you,
Love me as I love you,
And God's grace will pour down on you!

8
Esti hajnal az ég alján

Rote Abendwolken ziehn
Am Firmament,
Sehnsuchtsvoll nach dir, mein Lieb,
Das Herze brennt;
Himmel strahlt in glühnder Pracht
Und ich träum bei Tag und Nacht
Nur allein von dem süßen Liebchen mein.

Red evening clouds drift
Across the sky,
My heart burns longingly
For you, my love;
The sky's ablaze in glowing glory
And night and day I dream
Solely of my sweet love.

Georg Daumer (1800–75)

Best known to non-musicians as the philanthropic schoolmaster who undertook the earliest education of Kaspar Hauser, Daumer was a student of comparative religion and a gifted linguist who translated a great number of poems from a variety of languages, including Persian. There is a sweetness about much of his verse that makes him the ideal translator of Hafiz, the fourteenth-century Persian poet, who was aptly named 'Sugar-lip' by his contemporaries. Daumer also wrote much

* Alföld, or Pusztas, is the great plain of mid-Hungary, stretching from the Danube to the Carpathians.
† Hungarian town SSE of Budapest.

original verse, often mildly erotic, as in 'Von waldbekränzter Höhe' and 'Unbewegte laue Luft'. Max Kalbeck, in volume II, pp. 137–38 of his *Johannes Brahms*, tells how the composer set out one day for Würzburg to express his gratitude to Daumer, who had provided him with so many song texts.

[Er] fand nach vieler Mühe Straße und Haus, und war überrascht, als sich ihm ein verschrumpftes Männchen als der deutsche Hafis vorstellte. Brahms, der im Laufe des Gespräches merkte, daß Daumer nichts von ihm und seinen Liedern wußte, erkundigte sich scherzhaft nach seinen vielen Schätzen, womit er die so glühend besungenen Frauenbilder meinte. Da lächelte der Alte still vor sich hin und rief aus der anstoßenden Kammer ein ebenso altes, kleines und verhutzeltes Weiblein herein, indem er sagte: „Ich habe nie eine andere geliebt als diese meine Frau."

After some trouble he found the street and the house, and was astonished when a little shrivelled old man introduced himself as the German Hafiz. Brahms, who in the course of the conversation realized that Daumer knew nothing of him and his songs, inquired jokingly after the many lovers of whom Daumer had painted such glowing portraits in his poems. The old man smiled quietly and summoned from the adjoining room a little woman, as old, as tiny and as wizened as himself, saying: 'This is the only woman I've ever loved – my wife.'

September 1864 **Nicht mehr zu dir zu gehen / Never to go to you again** Op. 32, no. 2
FROM THE MOLDAVIAN

Nicht mehr zu dir zu gehen,	Never to go to you again,
Beschloß ich und beschwor ich,	So I decided and so I vowed,
Und gehe jeden Abend,	And go each evening,
Denn jede Kraft und jeden Halt verlor ich.	For I've lost all strength and all resolve.
Ich möchte nicht mehr leben,	I wish to live no more,
Möcht augenblicks verderben,	Would sooner die at once,
Und möchte doch auch leben	And yet would sooner live
Für dich, mit dir, und nimmer, nimmer sterben.	For you, with you, and never, never die.
Ach rede, sprich ein Wort nur,	Ah! speak, say but a word,
Ein einziges, ein klares;	A single one, a clear one;
Gib Leben oder Tod mir,	Give me life or death,
Nur dein Gefühl enthülle mir, dein wahres!	But show me how you really feel!

September 1864 **Bitteres zu sagen denkst du / You mean to say bitter things** Op. 32, no. 7
AFTER HAFIZ (C.1327–90)

Bitteres zu sagen denkst du;	You mean to say bitter things,
Aber nun und nimmer kränkst du,	But neither now nor ever do you hurt me,

Ob du noch so böse bist.
Deine herben Redetaten
Scheitern an korallner Klippe,
Werden all zu reinen Gnaden,
Denn sie müssen, um zu schaden,
Schiffen über eine Lippe,
Die die Süße selber ist.

However angry you may be.
Your bitter recriminations
Founder on a coral reef,
Become pure graciousness,
For, in order to inflict damage,
They must sail over lips
That are sweetness itself.

September 1864 So stehn wir / So here we stand Op. 32, no. 8
AFTER HAFIZ (C.1327–90)

So stehn wir, ich und meine Weide,
So leider mit einander beide:

So here we stand, I and my heart's desire,
At loggerheads with each other:

Nie kann ich ihr was tun zu Liebe,
Nie kann sie mir was tun zu Leide.

I can never please her,
She can never hurt me.

Sie kränket es, wenn ich die Stirn ihr
Mit einem Diadem bekleide;

It offends her, when I set a diadem
On her brow;

Ich danke selbst, wie für ein Lächeln
Der Huld, für ihre Zornbescheide.

I even thank her, as I would for a gracious
Smile, for her outbursts of anger.

September 1864 Wie bist du, meine Königin / How blissful, my queen, you are Op. 32, no. 9
AFTER HAFIZ (C.1327–90)

Wie bist du, meine Königin,
Durch sanfte Güte wonnevoll!
Du lächle nur – Lenzdüfte wehn
Durch mein Gemüte wonnevoll!

How blissful, my queen, you are,
By reason of your gentle kindness!
You merely smile, and springtime fragrance
Wafts through my soul blissfully!

Frisch aufgeblühter Rosen Glanz
Vergleich ich ihn dem deinigen?
Ach, über alles was da blüht,
Ist deine Blüte, wonnevoll!

Shall I compare the radiance
Of freshly blown roses to yours?
Ah! more blissful than all that blooms
Is your blissful bloom!

Durch tote Wüsten wandle hin,
Und grüne Schatten breiten sich,
Ob fürchterliche Schwüle dort
Ohn Ende brüte, wonnevoll.

Roam through desert wastes,
And green shade will spring up –
Though fearful sultriness broods
Endlessly there – blissfully.

Laß mich vergehn in deinem Arm!
Es ist in ihm ja selbst der Tod,
Ob auch die herbste Todesqual
Die Brust durchwüte, wonnevoll.

Let me perish in your arms!
Death in your embrace will be –
Though bitterest mortal agony rage
Through my breast – blissful.

1867 Wenn du nur zuweilen lächelst / If you will only sometimes smile Op. 57, no. 2
AFTER HAFIZ (C.1327–90)

Wenn du nur zuweilen lächelst,	If you only sometimes smile,
Nur zuweilen Kühle fächelst	Only sometimes fan coolness
Dieser ungemeßnen Glut –	On this infinite ardour,
In Geduld will ich mich fassen	I shall compose myself in patience
Und dich Alles treiben lassen,	And let you do all those things
Was der Liebe wehe tut.	That inflict pain on love.

by 1868 Botschaft / A message Op. 47, no. 1
AFTER HAFIZ (C.1327–90)

Wehe, Lüftchen, lind und lieblich	Blow breeze, gently and sweetly
Um die Wange der Geliebten,	About the cheek of my beloved,
Spiele zart in ihrer Locke,	Play softly with her tresses,
Eile nicht, hinwegzufliehn!	Make no haste to fly away!
Tut sie dann vielleicht die Frage,	Then if she should chance to ask
Wie es um mich Armen stehe,	How things are with wretched me,
Sprich: „Unendlich war sein Wehe,	Say: 'His sorrow's been unending,
Höchst bedenklich seine Lage;	His condition most grave;
Aber jetzo kann er hoffen	But now he can hope
Wieder herrlich aufzuleben,	To revel in life once more,
Denn du, Holde, denkst an ihn."	For you, fair one, think of him.'

1871 Von waldbekränzter Höhe / From forest-wreathed heights Op. 57, no. 1

Von waldbekränzter Höhe	From forest-wreathed heights
Werf ich den heißen Blick	I turn the passionate gaze
Der liebefeuchten Sehe	Of my love-moistened eyes
Zur Flur, die dich umgrünt, zurück.	To the green fields about you.
Ich senk ihn auf die Quelle,	I lower my gaze to the stream,
Vermöcht ich, ach, mit ihr	Ah! if only I could flow
Zu fließen, eine Welle,	With it, as a wave,
Zurück, o Freund, zu dir, zu dir!	Back, O friend, to you!
Ich richt ihn auf die Züge	I lift my gaze to the scudding
Der Wolken über mir,	Clouds above me,
Ach, flög ich ihre Flüge,	Ah! if only I could follow their flight
Zurück, o Freund, zu dir, zu dir!	Back, O friend, to you!
Wie wollt ich dich umstricken,	How I would ensnare you,
Mein Heil und meine Pein,	My anguish and salvation,
Mit Lippen und mit Blicken,	With my lips and my glances,
Mit Busen, Herz und Seele dein!	With my bosom, heart and soul all yours!

1871 Es träumte mir / I dreamed Op. 57, no. 3
FROM THE SPANISH

Es träumte mir,	I dreamed
Ich sei dir teuer;	I was dear to you;
Doch zu erwachen	But I scarcely needed
Bedurft ich kaum.	To awaken.
Denn schon im Traume	For even in my dreams
Bereits empfand ich,	I felt
Es sei ein Traum.	It was a dream.

1871 Unbewegte laue Luft / Motionless mild air Op. 57, no. 8

Unbewegte laue Luft,	Motionless mild air,
Tiefe Ruhe der Natur;	Nature deep at rest;
Durch die stille Gartennacht	Through the still garden night
Plätschert die Fontäne nur;	Only the fountain plashes;
Aber im Gemüte schwillt	But my soul swells
Heißere Begierde mir;	With a more ardent desire;
Aber in der Ader quillt	Life surges in my veins
Leben und verlangt nach Leben.	And yearns for life.
Sollten nicht auch deine Brust	Should not your breast too
Sehnlichere Wünsche heben?	Heave with more passionate longing?
Sollte meiner Seele Ruf	Should not the cry of my soul
Nicht die deine tief durchbeben?	Quiver deeply through your own?
Leise mit dem Ätherfuß	Softly on ethereal feet
Säume nicht, daher zu schweben!	Glide to me, do not delay!
Komm, o komm, damit wir uns	Come, ah! come, that we might
Himmlische Genüge geben!	Give each other heavenly satisfaction!

1873 Eine gute, gute Nacht / A good, good night Op. 59, no. 6

Eine gute, gute Nacht	A good good night
Pflegst du mir zu sagen –	You are wont to bid me –
Über dieses eitle Wort,	Those idle words,
O wie muß ich klagen!	Oh how I bewail them!
Daß du meiner Seele Glut	If only you would not so cruelly
Nicht so grausam nährtest!	Fuel the fire in my soul;
„Eine gute, gute Nacht",	A good good-night,
Daß du sie gewährtest!	If only you would grant it!

c.1884 Wir wandelten / We were walking Op. 96, no. 2
FROM THE MAGYAR

Wir wandelten, wir zwei zusammen;	We were walking, we two together;
Ich war so still und du so stille;	I so silent and you so silent;
Ich gäbe viel, um zu erfahren,	I would give much to know
Was du gedacht in jenem Fall.	What you were thinking then.

Was ich gedacht – unausgesprochen	What I was thinking – let it remain
Verbleibe das! Nur Eines sag' ich:	Unspoken! One thing only I shall say:
So schön war Alles, was ich dachte,	All my thoughts were so beautiful,
So himmlisch=heiter war es all.	So heavenly and serene.
In meinem Haupte die Gedanken	The thoughts in my mind
Sie läuteten, wie goldne Glöckchen;	Chimed like golden bells:
So wundersüß, so wunderlieblich	So wondrously sweet and lovely
Ist in der Welt kein andrer Hall.	Is no other sound on earth.

Paul Flem[m]ing (1609–40)

Poetry in the Baroque often spoke with two voices: publicly, it proclaimed the majesty of God and exalted truths about existence, spoke about transience and vanity, and recommended stoical resignation to cope with life's reverses; privately, it would sing of man's joys and sorrows, of human love, true and false, and human beauty, as in Fleming's 'O liebliche Wangen' and 'An die Stolze'. His earliest poems were versions of the psalms; he also wrote much pietistic verse, including 'Geistliches Lied', which Brahms set as his Op. 30 for mixed chorus with organ.

by 1868 O liebliche Wangen / O charming cheeks Op. 47, no. 4

O liebliche Wangen,	O charming cheeks,
Ihr macht mir Verlangen,	You fill me with longing
Dies Rote, dies Weiße	To gaze persistently
Zu schauen mit Fleiße.	At this red and this white.
Und dies nur alleine	And nor is this all
Ist's nicht, was ich meine,	That I mean,
Zu schauen, zu grüßen,	To gaze, to greet,
Zu rühren, zu küssen.	To touch, to kiss.
Ihr macht mir Verlangen,	You fill me with longing,
O liebliche Wangen!	O charming cheeks!
O Sonne der Wonne!	O rapturous sun!
O Wonne der Sonne!	O sunny rapture!
O Augen, so saugen	O eyes that drink
Das Licht meiner Augen.	The light of mine.
O englische Sinnen,	O angelic thoughts,
O himmlisch Beginnen!	O heavenly beginning!
O Himmel auf Erden!	O heaven on earth!
Magst du mir nicht werden,	Won't you be mine,
O Wonne der Sonne,	O sunny rapture,
O Sonne der Wonne!	O rapturous sun!
O Schönste der Schönen!	O fairest of the fair!
Benimm mir dies Sehnen.	Free me from this longing.
Komm, eile, komm, komme,	Come quickly, come, come,

Du Süße, du Fromme;	Sweet innocent one;
Ach, Schwester, ich sterbe,	Ah, sister, I'm dying,
Ich sterb, ich verderbe,	I'm dying, I perish,
Komm, komme, komm eile,	Come, come, come quickly,
Komm, komme, komm eile,	Come, come, come quickly,
Benimm mir dies Sehnen,	Free me from this longing,
O Schönste der Schönen!	O fairest of the fair!

Emanuel Geibel (1815–84)

See Wolf

1883–84 Mein Herz ist schwer / My heart is heavy Op. 94, no. 3

Mein Herz ist schwer, mein Auge wacht,	My heart is heavy, my eyes keep watch,
Der Wind fährt seufzend durch die Nacht;	The wind goes sighing through the night;
Die Wipfel rauschen weit und breit,	The tree-tops murmur far and wide,
Sie rauschen von vergangner Zeit.	Murmuring of times now past.
Sie rauschen von vergangner Zeit,	Murmuring of times now past,
Von großem Glück und Herzeleid,	Of great happiness and heartache,
Vom Schloß und von der Jungfrau drin –	Of the castle and the maiden within –
Wo ist das alles, alles hin?	Where has all this, all this fled?
Wo ist das alles, alles hin,	Where has all this, all this fled,
Leid, Lieb und Lust und Jugendsinn?	Grief, love and joy and youth?
Der Wind fährt seufzend durch die Nacht,	The wind goes sighing through the night,
Mein Herz ist schwer, mein Auge wacht.	My heart is heavy, my eyes keep watch.

Johann Wolfgang von Goethe (1749–1832)

See Beethoven, Hensel, Loewe, Mendelssohn, Mozart, Reichardt, Schubert, Strauss, Wolf, Zelter

„Das Auge war vor allen anderen das Organ, womit ich die Welt erfasste" ('It was through the visual, above all other senses, that I comprehended the world'), wrote Goethe in his autobiography, *Dichtung und Wahrheit* – a statement which seems to be confirmed by his indefatigable study of natural phenomena and his delight in art and architecture, in seeing. Lynceus's line at the end of *Faust*, „Zum Sehen geboren, zum Schauen bestellt" ('I was born for seeing, employed to watch') (see LOEWE, p. 175) has an unmistakably autobiographical ring. Whereas Eichendorff was susceptible to the sounds of nature, Goethe was, above all, a visual being, an *Augenmensch*. No other poem of Goethe's illustrates this as powerfully as 'Dämmrung senkte sich von oben', which describes the gradual approach of dusk, apprehended through the eye. It is strange that Brahms was tempted to set this perfect poem of Goethe's old age (1827), for, as he confided to Georg Henschel (*Personal recollections of Johannes Brahms* [1907]), he felt that a poem should not be perfect, like many of Goethe's: 'They are all so finished, there is nothing one can do to them with music' – which explains, perhaps, why Brahms set only five.

1873 Dämmrung senkte sich von oben / Dusk has fallen from on high Op. 59, no. 1

Dämmrung senkte sich von oben,	Dusk has fallen from on high,
Schon ist alle Nähe fern;	All that was near now is distant;
Doch zuerst emporgehoben	But first the evening star appears
Holden Lichts der Abendstern!	Shining with its lovely light!
Alles schwankt ins Ungewisse,	All becomes an uncertain blur,
Nebel schleichen in die Höh';	The mists creep up the sky;
Schwarzvertiefte Finsternisse	Ever blacker depths of darkness
Widerspiegelnd ruht der See.	Are mirrored in the silent lake.
Nun am östlichen Bereiche	Now in the eastern reaches
Ahn' ich Mondenglanz und -glut,	I sense the moon's light and glow,
Schlanker Weiden Haargezweige	The branching hair of slender willows
Scherzen auf der nächsten Flut.	Frolics on the nearby water.
Durch bewegter Schatten Spiele	Through the play of moving shadows,
Zittert Lunas Zauberschein,	The moon's magic light quivers down,
Und durchs Auge schleicht die Kühle	And coolness steals through the eye
Sänftigend ins Herz hinein.	Soothingly into the heart.
(*Hensel, Schoeck*)	

1876 Serenade: Liebliches Kind / Serenade: Lovely child Op. 70, no. 3
FROM *Claudine von Villa Bella*

Liebliches Kind,	Lovely child,
Kannst du mir sagen,	Can you tell me,
Sagen warum	Tell me why,
Einsam und stumm	Lonely and silent,
Zärtliche Seelen	Sensitive souls
Immer sich quälen,	Always agonise,
Selbst sich betrüben	Always grieve,
Und ihr Vergnügen	And feel they'd be happier
Immer nur ahnen	Anywhere than where
Da, wo sie nicht sind;	They actually are;
Kannst du mir's sagen,	Can you tell me,
Liebliches Kind?	Lovely child?
(*Bruch, Medtner, Neef, Reichardt*)	

1876 Unüberwindlich / Invincible Op. 72, no. 5

Hab ich tausendmal geschworen	A thousand times I've vowed
Dieser Flasche nicht zu trauen,	Not to trust this bottle,
Bin ich doch wie neugeboren,	Yet I feel as if new-born,
Läßt mein Schenke fern sie schauen.	When my cup-bearer shows it me from afar.

Alles ist an ihr zu loben,	Everything about it merits praise,
Glaskristall und Purpurwein.	Crystal glass and crimson wine;
Wird der Pfropf herausgehoben –	Once the cork is drawn,
Sie ist leer und ich nicht mein.	It's empty and I've no control.
Hab ich tausendmal geschworen	A thousand times I've vowed
Dieser Falschen nicht zu trauen,	Not to trust this traitress,
Und doch bin ich neugeboren,	And yet I feel as if new-born,
Läßt sie sich ins Auge schauen.	When she lets me gaze in her eyes.
Mag sie doch mit mir verfahren,	Let her treat me
Wie's dem stärksten Mann geschah:	Like the strongest man was treated –
Deine Scher' in meinen Haaren,	Set your scissors to my hair,
Allerliebste Delila!	Adorable Delilah!

Klaus Groth (1819–99)

Groth was born in Dithmarschen, the North German district from which Brahms's family also hailed. He and Brahms had much in common, including an admiration of each other's work, and similar moods of melancholy and nostalgia. They became close friends. Groth's *Musikalische Erlebnisse* include a most touching description of Schumann's funeral, which Brahms also attended, and his *Erinnerungen an Johannes Brahms* contain a great deal of domestic detail about the times Brahms and Groth spent together. Groth's literary fame rests on his Plattdeutsch or Low German poetry, collected in *Quickborn* (1853). The poems of Brahms's fourteen Groth songs, including two duets and 'Im Herbst' for unaccompanied mixed chorus, all written in High German, were taken from *Hundert Blätter*, a signed copy of which, inscribed with the 'Regenlied' poem ('Regentropfen aus den Bäumen'), was given by Groth to the composer in 1856. Brahms returned the compliment by presenting Groth with a handwritten copy of the song in the summer of 1872.

1873 Regenlied / Rain song Op. 59, no. 3

Walle, Regen, walle nieder,	Cascade, rain, cascade down,
Wecke mir die Träume wieder,	Wake for me those dreams again
Die ich in der Kindheit träumte,	That I dreamed in childhood,
Wenn das Naß im Sande schäumte!	When water foamed on the sand!
Wenn die matte Sommerschwüle	When oppressive summer heat
Läßig stritt mit frischer Kühle,	Contended idly with cool freshness,
Und die blanken Blätter tauten	And shiny leaves dripped with dew
Und die Saaten dunkler blauten,	And crops turned a darker blue,
Welche Wonne, in dem Fließen	How blissful then it was to stand
Dann zu stehn mit nackten Füßen!	With naked feet in the flow!
An dem Grase hinzustreifen	Or to brush against the grass
Und den Schaum mit Händen greifen,	Or grasp the foam in both hands,

Oder mit den heißen Wangen	Or to catch the cold drops
Kalte Tropfen aufzufangen,	On my glowing cheeks,
Und den neu erwachten Düften	And to bare my boyish breast
Seine Kinderbrust zu lüften!	To fresh-awakened scents!

Wie die Kelche, die da troffen,	Like the dripping chalices,
Stand die Seele atmend offen,	My breathing soul stood open,
Wie die Blumen, düftetrunken	Like the flowers drunk with fragrance,
In den Himmelstau versunken.	Drowned in heaven's dew.

Schauernd kühlte jeder Tropfen	Each shuddering drop seeped through
Tief bis an des Herzens Klopfen,	And cooled my beating heart,
Und der Schöpfung heilig Weben	And creation's sacred weaving
Drang bis ins verborgne Leben. –	Penetrated our secret lives. –

Walle, Regen, walle nieder,	Cascade, rain, cascade down,
Wecke meine alten Lieder,	Wake in me those old songs
Die wir in der Türe sangen,	That we sang in the doorway
Wenn die Tropfen draußen klangen!	When outside the drops resounded!

Möchte ihnen wieder lauschen,	I'd love again to listen
Ihrem süßen, feuchten Rauschen,	To their sweet moist murmuring,
Meine Seele sanft betauen	And softly bedew my soul
Mit dem frommen Kindergrauen.	With innocent childlike awe.

1873 Nachklang / Distant echo Op. 59, no. 4

Regentropfen aus den Bäumen	Raindrops from the trees
Fallen in das grüne Gras,	Fall into the green grass,
Tränen meiner trüben Augen	Tears from my sad eyes
Machen mir die Wange naß.	Moisten my cheeks.

Wenn die Sonne wieder scheinet,	When the sun shines again,
Wird der Rasen doppelt grün:	The grass gleams twice as green:
Doppelt wird auf meinen Wangen	Twice as ardently on my cheeks
Mir die heiße Träne glühn.	My scalding tears will glow.

1873 Mein wundes Herz / My wounded heart Op. 59, no. 7

Mein wundes Herz verlangt nach milder Ruh,	My wounded heart craves gentle peace,
O hauche sie ihm ein!	Oh! breathe such peace into it!
Es fliegt dir weinend, bange schlagend zu –	It flies to you, weeping and beating anxiously –
O hülle du es ein!	Oh! enfold it in your arms!

Wie wenn ein Strahl durch schwere Wolken bricht,	As when a sunbeam pierces heavy cloud,
So winkest du ihm zu:	So you beckon to my heart:
O lächle fort mit deinem milden Licht!	Oh! let your gentle light shine on!
Mein Pol, mein Stern bist du!	You are my pole, you are my star!

1873 Dein blaues Auge / Your blue eyes Op. 59, no. 8

Dein blaues Auge hält so still,	Your blue eyes stay so still,
Ich blicke bis zum Grund.	I look into their depths.
Du fragst mich, was ich sehen will?	You ask me what I seek to see?
Ich sehe mich gesund.	Myself restored to health.
Es brannte mich ein glühend Paar,	A pair of ardent eyes have burnt me,
Noch schmerzt das Nachgefühl:	The pain of it still throbs:
Das deine ist wie See so klar	Your eyes are limpid as a lake,
Und wie ein See so kühl.	And like a lake as cool.

1874 Heimweh II: O wüßt ich doch den Weg zurück / Longing for home II: Ah! if I but knew the way back Op. 63, no. 8

O wüßt ich doch den Weg zurück,	Ah! if I but knew the way back,
Den lieben Weg zum Kinderland!	The sweet way back to childhood's land!
O warum sucht ich nach dem Glück	Ah! why did I seek my fortune
Und ließ der Mutter Hand?	And let go my mother's hand?
O wie mich sehnet auszuruhn,	Ah! how I long for utter rest,
Von keinem Streben aufgeweckt,	Immune from any striving,
Die müden Augen zuzutun,	Long to close my weary eyes,
Von Liebe sanft bedeckt!	Gently shrouded by love!
Und nichts zu forschen, nichts zu spähn,	And search for nothing, watch for nothing,
Und nur zu träumen leicht und lind,	Dream only light and gentle dreams,
Der Zeiten Wandel nicht zu sehn,	Not to see the times change,
Zum zweiten Mal ein Kind!	To be a child a second time!
O zeigt mir doch den Weg zurück,	Ah! show me that way back,
Den lieben Weg zum Kinderland!	The sweet way back to childhood's land!
Vergebens such ich nach dem Glück –	I seek happiness in vain –
Ringsum ist öder Strand!	Ringed round by barren shores!

1885 Komm bald! / Come soon! Op. 97, no. 5

Warum denn warten	Why then wait
Von Tag zu Tag?	From day to day?
Es blüht im Garten	Everything in the garden blooms
Was blühen mag.	That wishes to bloom.
Wer kommt und zählt es,	Who will come and count
Was blüht so schön?	All that lovely blossoming?
An Augen fehlt es,	Where are the eyes
Es anzusehn.	To look at it all?
Die meinen wandern	My own eyes wander
Vom Strauch zum Baum –	From bush to tree –
Mir scheint, auch andern	I think others too
Wär's wie ein Traum.	Would find it like a dream.

Und von den Lieben,
Die mir getreu
Und mir geblieben,
Wärst du dabei.

And among the dear friends
Still true to me
And still alive –
I wish that you were one of them.

1886 Wie Melodien / Like melodies Op. 105, no. 1

Wie Melodien zieht es
Mir leise durch den Sinn,
Wie Frühlingsblumen blüht es
Und schwebt wie Duft dahin.

Thoughts, like melodies,
Steal softly through my mind,
Like spring flowers they blossom
And drift away like fragrance.

Doch kommt das Wort und faßt es
Und führt es vor das Aug',
Wie Nebelgrau erblaßt es
Und schwindet wie ein Hauch.

Yet when words come and capture them
And bring them before my eyes,
They turn pale like grey mist
And vanish like a breath.

Und dennoch ruht im Reime
Verborgen wohl ein Duft,
Den mild aus stillem Keime
Ein feuchtes Auge ruft.
(*Ives*)

Yet surely in rhyme
A fragrance lies hidden,
Summoned by moist eyes
From the silent seed.

1888 Es hing der Reif / Hoarfrost hung from the linden tree Op. 106, no. 3

Es hing der Reif im Lindenbaum,
Wodurch das Licht wie Silber floß;
Ich sah dein Haus, wie hell im Traum
Ein blitzend Feenschloß.

Hoarfrost hung from the linden tree,
Through which light flowed like silver;
I saw your house, bright as in a dream,
A gleaming fairy castle.

Und offen stand das Fenster dein,
Ich konnte dir ins Zimmer sehn –
Da tratst du in den Sonnenschein,
Du dunkelste der Feen!

And your window was open wide,
I could look into your room –
You then stepped into the sunshine,
You the darkest of fairies!

Ich bebt, in seligem Genuß,
So frühlingswarm und wunderbar:
Da merkt ich gleich an deinem Gruß,
Daß Frost und Winter war.

I trembled in blissful pleasure,
Filled with springtime warmth and wonder:
Then I saw at once from your greeting
That frost had set in and winter.

Otto Gruppe (1804–76)

Gruppe's poem, the fifth of an eleven-poem cycle entitled *Das Mädchen spricht*, was published in *Gedichte* (1835).

1886 Das Mädchen spricht / The girl speaks Op. 107, no. 3

Schwalbe, sag mir an,
Ist's dein alter Mann,

Tell me, swallow,
Is it last year's mate

Mit dem du's Nest gebaut,	You've built your nest with,
Oder hast du jüngst erst	Or are you
Dich ihm vertraut?	But recently betrothed?
Sag, was zwitschert ihr,	Say, what are you twittering,
Sag, was flüstert ihr	Say, what are you whispering
Des Morgens so vertraut?	So intimately in the morning?
Gelt, du bist wohl auch noch	Am I right, you haven't long
Nicht lange Braut?	Been married either?

Friedrich Halm (1806–71)

Friedrich Halm was the pseudonym of Eligius Franz Joseph, Freiherr von Münch-Bellinghausen, whose family moved in 1811 from Cracow to Vienna, where Münch was educated at the same school, the Schottengymnasium, as Nikolaus Lenau. Famous in his day as a dramatist (his plays were regularly produced at the Burgtheater), he was Intendant of both the Burgtheater and the Oper from 1867 to 1870. His poetry was published in *Gedichte* (1850), and *Neue Gedichte* (1864). Brahms was attracted by the gentle melancholy of his verse and set six of his poems. 'Kein Haus, Keine Heimat' comes from the dramatic poem *In der Südsee*.

1883–84 Steig auf, geliebter Schatten / Rise up, beloved shade Op. 94, no. 2

Steig auf, geliebter Schatten,	Rise up before me, beloved shade,
Vor mir in toter Nacht	At the dead of night,
Und lab mich Todesmatten	And revive me, wearied to death,
Mit deiner Nähe Macht!	By the power of your presence!
Du hast's gekonnt im Leben,	You could do it in life,
Du kannst es auch im Tod,	You can in death as well,
Sich nicht dem Schmerz ergeben,	Never yield to sorrow,
War immer dein Gebot.	Was always your command.
So komm! Still' meine Tränen,	Come then! Dry my tears,
Gib meiner Seele Schwung,	Exhilarate my soul
Und Kraft den welken Sehnen,	And strengthen my shrivelled limbs
Und mach' mich wieder jung.	And make me young again.

c.1883 Der Jäger / The huntsman Op. 95, no. 4

Mein Lieb ist ein Jäger,	My love's a huntsman,
Und grün ist sein Kleid,	And he dresses in green,
Und blau ist sein Auge,	And his eyes are blue,
Nur sein Herz ist zu weit.	But his heart's too open.
Mein Lieb ist ein Jäger,	My love's a huntsman,
Trifft immer in's Ziel,	Never misses his mark,

| Und Mädchen berückt er, | And he bewitches girls, |
| So viel er nur will. | As many as he will. |

Mein Lieb ist ein Jäger,	My love's a huntsman,
Kennt Wege und Spur,	Knows tracks and trails,
Zu mir aber kommt er	But he'll only come to me
Durch die Kirchtüre nur.	Through the church door.

1884 or 1884 Kein Haus, keine Heimat / No house, no homeland Op. 94, no. 5

Kein Haus, keine Heimat,	No house, no homeland,
Kein Weib und kein Kind,	No wife and no child,
So wirbl' ich, ein Strohhalm,*	Thus I'm whirled, a wisp of straw,
In Wetter und Wind!	In storm and wind!

Well' auf und Well' nieder,	Tossed on the waves,
Bald dort und bald hier;	Here one moment, there the next;
Welt, fragst du nach mir nicht,	If you, world, don't ask about me,
Was frag ich nach dir?	Why should I ask about you?

Heinrich Heine (1797–1856)

See Mendelssohn, Robert Schumann, Wolf

Brahms intended to express his admiration for Heine by setting four of his poems – 'Der Tod, das ist die kühle Nacht', 'Es schauen die Blumen', 'Meerfahrt' and 'Wie der Mond sich leuchtend drängend' – as Op. 96, but the last song was destroyed by the composer after Elisabet von Herzogenburg had criticized it. Despite Brahms's admiration for Heine, he set only five of his poems, all from the *Buch der Lieder*, except 'Es schauen die Blumen' which was published posthumously.

1877 Es liebt sich so lieblich im Lenze / How lovely to love in Spring Op. 71, no. 1

Die Wellen blinken und fließen dahin –	The waves glisten and flow away –
Es liebt sich so lieblich im Lenze!	How lovely to love in Spring!
Am Flusse sitzet die Schäferin	The shepherdess sits by the river
Und windet die zärtlichsten Kränze.	Weaving most delicate garlands.

Das knospet und quillt und duftet und blüht –	There's budding and swelling and fragrance and blossom –
Es liebt sich so lieblich im Lenze!	How lovely to love in Spring!
Die Schäferin seufzt aus tiefer Brust:	The shepherdess sighs from the depths of her heart:
„Wem geb ich meine Kränze?"	'To whom shall I give my garlands?'

* A pun on the poet's name.

Ein Reiter reitet den Fluß entlang;   Along the river a horseman rides;
Er grüßet so blühenden Mutes!   He greets her in youthful high spirits!
Die Schäferin schaut ihm nach so bang,   She anxiously watches him go on his way,
Fern flattert die Feder des Hutes.   The plume in his hat flutters afar.

Sie weinet und wirft in den gleitenden   She weeps, and into the waves she
   Fluß   flings
Die schönen Blumenkränze.   Her beautiful garlands of flowers.
Die Nachtigall singt von Lieb und Kuß –   The nightingale sings of loving and kissing –
Es liebt sich so lieblich im Lenze!   How lovely to love in Spring!
(*Franz*)

1878 Sommerabend / Summer evening Op. 85, no. 1

Dämmernd liegt der Sommerabend   Summer evening twilight lies
Über Wald und grünen Wiesen;   Over forest and green meadows;
Goldner Mond im blauen Himmel   A golden moon in the blue sky
Strahlt herunter, duftig labend.   Shines down in a soothing haze.

An dem Bache zirpt die Grille,   By the brook the cricket chirps
Und es regt sich in dem Wasser,   And the waters stir,
Und der Wandrer hört ein Plätschern   And the traveller hears a plashing
Und ein Atmen in der Stille.   And a breathing in the stillness.

Dorten, an dem Bach alleine,   Over there by the brook, alone,
Badet sich die schöne Elfe;   A lovely water-nymph is bathing;
Arm und Nacken, weiß und lieblich,   Arms and neck, white and comely,
Schimmern in dem Mondenscheine.   Shimmer in the moonlight.
(*Lachner, Schoeck*)

1878 Mondenschein / Moonlight Op. 85, no. 2

Nacht liegt auf den fremden Wegen,   Night lies over unknown pathways,
Krankes Herz und müde Glieder, –   Sick heart and tired limbs, –
Ach, da fließt, wie stiller Segen,   Then, sweet moon, like a silent blessing,
Süßer Mond, dein Licht hernieder;   Your radiance streams down;

Süßer Mond, mit deinen Strahlen   With your beams, sweet moon,
Scheuchest du das nächtge Grauen;   You dispel nocturnal terrors;
Es zerrinnen meine Qualen   All my torments melt away
Und die Augen übertauen.   And my eyes brim over.
(*Griffes, Hensel, Lachner*)

c.1884 Der Tod, das ist die kühle Nacht / Death is cool night Op. 96, no. 1

Der Tod, das ist die kühle Nacht,   Death is cool night,
Das Leben ist der schwüle Tag.   Life is sultry day.
Es dunkelt schon, mich schläfert,   Dusk falls now, I feel drowsy,
Der Tag hat mich müd gemacht.   The day has wearied me.

Über mein Bett erhebt sich ein Baum,
Drin singt die junge Nachtigall;
Sie singt von lauter Liebe,
Ich hör es sogar im Traum.
(*Cornelius, Reger*)

Over my bed rises a tree,
In which the young nightingale sings;
She sings of nothing but love,
I hear it even in my dreams.

c.1884 Es schauen die Blumen / The flowers all turn their faces Op. 96, no. 3

Es schauen die Blumen alle
Zur leuchtenden Sonne hinauf;
Es nehmen die Ströme alle
Zum leuchtenden Meere den Lauf.

The flowers all turn their faces
Up to the radiant sun,
The rivers all run their course
Down to the radiant sea.

Es flattern die Lieder alle
Zu meinem leuchtenden Lieb;
Nehmt mit meine Tränen und Seufzer,
Ihr Lieder wehmütig und trüb!

My songs all flutter their way
To my radiant love;
Take with you my tears and sighs,
O wistful and gloomy songs!

c.1884 Meerfahrt / Sea voyage Op. 96, no. 4

Mein Liebchen, wir saßen beisammen
Traulich im leichten Kahn.
Die Nacht war still und wir schwammen
Auf weiter Wasserbahn.

My sweetest, we sat together,
Lovingly in our light boat.
The night was still, and we drifted
Along a wide waterway.

Die Geisterinsel, die schöne,
Lag dämmrig im Mondenglanz;
Dort klangen liebe Töne
Und wogte der Nebeltanz.

The beautiful haunted island
Lay dimly in the moon's light;
Sweet music was sounding there,
And dancing mists were swirling.

Dort klang es lieb und lieber
Und wogt es hin und her;
Wir aber schwammen vorüber
Trostlos auf weitem Meer.
(*Franz, MacDowell, Ropartz, Wolf*)

The sounds grew sweeter and sweeter,
The mists swirled this way and that;
We, however, drifted past,
Desolate on the wide sea.

Paul Heyse (1830–1914)

See Wolf

c.1887 Mädchenlied / A young girl's song Op. 107, no. 5

Auf die Nacht in der Spinnstub'n,
Da singen die Mädchen,
Da lachen die Dorfbub'n,
Wie flink gehn die Rädchen!

At night in the spinning-room,
The girls are singing,
The village lads are laughing,
How swiftly the wheels go round!

Spinnt Jedes am Brautschatz,	Each girl spins for her trousseau
Daß der Liebste sich freut.	To please her lover.
Nicht lange, so gibt es	It won't be long
Ein Hochzeitgeläut.	Before wedding-bells sound.
Kein Mensch, der mir gut ist,	No man who cares for me
Will nach mir fragen;	Will ask after me;
Wie bang mir zu Mut ist,	How anxious I feel,
Wem soll ich's klagen?	To whom shall I tell my sorrow?
Die Tränen rinnen	The tears go coursing
Mir übers Gesicht –	Down my cheeks –
Wofür soll ich spinnen?	What am I spinning for?
Ich weiß es nicht!	I don't know!
(*Jensen*)	

Hoffmann von Fallersleben (1798–1874)

Christened August Heinrich Hoffman, he added the Fallersleben (his birthplace) to lend distinction to his name. He expressed his support of German unity in his *Unpolitische Lieder* (1840) which led to dismissal from his post as Professor of German language and literature at Breslau University. His 'Deutschland, Deutschland über alles' dates from 1841 and was often sung as a patriotic hymn before it became the official national anthem. 'Von ewiger Liebe' (Brahms's title) was taken from *Gedichte* (1837). Its relevance to Brahms's emotional impasse vis-à-vis Clara cannot have escaped the thirty-one-year-old composer – a supposition strengthened by Kalbeck, who records how Brahms had confided to Hermann Deiters, a long-standing friend, how Clara had reacted to hearing the song: „Da sagte er [Brahms], als er das Lied bei der Schumann vorgespielt, habe sie auch stumm dagesessen, und als er auf sie hingesehen, sei sie in Tränen zerflossen gewesen." ('Then Brahms described, when he had played the song to Frau Schumann, how she had sat there in silence, and how, when he looked at her, he had seen that her face was bathed in tears.') [Kalbeck II, 300]

July 1853 Wie die Wolke nach der Sonne / As the cloud strays after the sun Op. 6, no. 5

Wie die Wolke nach der Sonne	As the cloud strays after the sun,
Voll Verlangen irrt und bangt,	Filled with longing and fear,
Und durchglüht von Himmelswonne	And glowing with heavenly bliss
Sterbend ihr am Busen hangt:	Hangs dying on her breast:
Wie die Sonnenblume richtet	As the sunflower turns
Auf die Sonn ihr Angesicht	Its face towards the sun
Und nicht eh'r auf sie verzichtet,	And only fails to do so
Bis ihr eignes Auge bricht:	When its own eyes close in death:

Wie der Aar auf Wolkenpfade	As the eagle on its cloudy path
Sehnend steigt ins Himmelszelt	Soars yearningly into heaven's vault
Und berauscht vom Sonnenbade	And intoxicated from its sun-bath
Blind zur Erde niederfällt:	Falls blindly back to earth:
So auch muß ich schmachten, bangen,	So I too must languish, tremble,
Spähn und trachten, dich zu sehn,	Gaze and strive to see you,
Will an deinen Blicken hangen,	I too wish to hang on your gaze
Und an ihrem Glanz vergehn.	And perish in its radiance.

July 1853 Nachtigallen schwingen / Nightingales flutter Op. 6, no. 6

Nachtigallen schwingen	Nightingales joyfully
Lustig ihr Gefieder,	Flutter their feathers,
Nachtigallen singen	Nightingales sing
Ihre alten Lieder,	Their old songs,
Und die Blumen alle,	And the flowers
Sie erwachen wieder	Wake again
Bei dem Klang und Schalle	At the tones and sounds
Aller dieser Lieder.	Of all these songs.
Und meine Sehnsucht wird zur Nachtigall	And my longing becomes a nightingale
Und fliegt in die blühende Welt hinein,	And flies out into the blossoming world,
Und fragt bei den Blumen überall,	And asks everywhere of every flower,
Wo mag doch mein, mein Blümchen sein?	Where might my own floweret be?
Und die Nachtigallen	And the nightingales
Schwingen ihren Reigen	Flutter their dances
Unter Laubeshallen	Beneath leafy arbours
Zwischen Blütenzweigen,	Among blossoming boughs,
Vor den Blumen allen	But I must keep silent
Aber ich muß schweigen,	About all the flowers,
Unter ihnen steh ich	I stand among them
Traurig sinnend still;	Sadly lost in silent thought;
Eine Blume seh ich,	I see a flower
Die nicht blühen will.	That does not wish to bloom.

1864 Von ewiger Liebe / Eternal love Op. 43, no. 1

Dunkel, wie dunkel in Wald und in Feld!	Dark, how dark in forest and field!
Abend schon ist es, nun schweiget die Welt.	Evening already, and the world is silent.
Nirgend noch Licht und nirgend noch Rauch,	Nowhere a light and nowhere smoke,
Ja, und die Lerche sie schweiget nun auch.	And even the lark is silent now too.
Kommt aus dem Dorfe der Bursche heraus,	Out of the village there comes a lad,
Gibt das Geleit der Geliebten nach Haus,	Escorting his sweetheart home,
Führt sie am Weidengebüsche vorbei,	He leads her past the willow-copse,
Redet so viel und so mancherlei:	Talking so much and of so many things:

„Leidest du Schmach und betrübest du dich,	'If you suffer sorrow and suffer shame,
Leidest du Schmach von andern um mich,	Shame for what others think of me,
Werde die Liebe getrennt so geschwind,	Then let our love be severed as swiftly,
Schnell wie wir früher vereiniget sind.	As swiftly as once we two were plighted.
Scheide mit Regen und scheide mit Wind,	Let us depart in rain and depart in wind,
Schnell wie wir früher vereiniget sind."	As swiftly as once we two were plighted.'
Spricht das Mägdelein, Mägdelein spricht:	The girl speaks, the girl says:
„Unsere Liebe, sie trennet sich nicht!	'Our love cannot be severed!
Fest ist der Stahl und das Eisen gar sehr,	Steel is strong, and so is iron,
Unsere Liebe ist fester noch mehr:	Our love is even stronger still:
Eisen und Stahl, man schmiedet sie um,	Iron and steel can both be reforged,
Unsere Liebe, wer wandelt sie um?	But our love, who shall change it?
Eisen und Stahl, sie können zergehn,	Iron and steel can be melted down,
Unsere Liebe muß ewig bestehn!"	Our love must endure for ever!'

Ludwig Hölty (1748–76)

See Schubert

Brahms was greatly attracted to the gentle melancholy of Hölty's verse, as he reveals in a letter to Adolph Schubring, dated February 1869:

> Welches sind denn meine 'verschossenen' Liedertexte? Doch hoffentlich nicht mein lieber Hölty, für dessen schöne, warme Worte mir nur meine Musik nicht stark genug ist, sonst würdest Du seine Verse öfter bei mir sehn.

> Which "fustian" texts do you mean? I hope you don't mean my beloved Hölty, for whose lovely warm words my music is not sufficiently strong, otherwise you'd find me setting more of them.

1866 Die Mainacht / May night Op. 43, no. 2

Wann der silberne Mond durch die Gesträuche blinkt	When the silvery moon gleams through the bushes,
Und sein schlummerndes Licht über den Rasen streut,	And sheds its slumbering light on the grass,
Und die Nachtigall flötet,	And the nightingale is fluting,
Wandl' ich traurig von Busch zu Busch.	I wander sadly from bush to bush.
Überhüllet vom Laub, girret ein Taubenpaar	Covered by leaves, a pair of doves
Sein Entzücken mir vor; aber ich wende mich,	Coo to me their ecstasy; but I turn away,
Suche dunklere Schatten,	Seek darker shadows,
Und die einsame Träne rinnt.	And the lonely tear flows down.

Wann, o lächelndes Bild, welches wie Morgenrot	When, O smiling vision, that shines through my soul
Durch die Seele mir strahlt, find' ich auf Erden dich?	Like the red of dawn, shall I find you here on earth?
Und die einsame Träne	And the lonely tear
Bebt mir heißer die Wang' herab.	Quivers more ardently down my cheek.
(*Hensel, Schubert*)	

1868 An die Nachtigall / To the nightingale Op. 46, no. 4

Geuß nicht so laut der liebentflammten Lieder Tonreichen Schall	Do not pour so loudly the full-throated sounds Of your love-kindled songs
Vom Blütenast des Apfelbaums hernieder, O Nachtigall!	Down from the blossoming boughs of the apple-tree O nightingale!
Du tönest mir mit deiner süßen Kehle Die Liebe wach;	The tones of your sweet throat Awaken love in me;
Denn schon durchbebt die Tiefen meiner Seele Dein schmelzend Ach.	For the depths of my soul already quiver With your melting lament.
Dann flieht der Schlaf von neuem dieses Lager, Ich starre dann	Sleep once more forsakes this couch, And I stare
Mit nassem Blick' und totenbleich und hager Den Himmel an.	Moist-eyed, haggard and deathly pale At the heavens.
Fleuch, Nachtigall, in grüne Finsternisse, Ins Haingesträuch,	Fly, nightingale, to the green darkness, To the bushes of the grove,
Und spend' im Nest der treuen Gattin Küsse; Entfleuch, entfleuch!	And there in the nest kiss your faithful mate; Fly away, fly away!
(*Schubert*)	

1868 An ein Veilchen / To a violet Op. 49, no. 2

Birg, o Veilchen, in deinem blauen Kelche,	Hide, O violet, in your blue calyx,
Birg die Tränen der Wehmut, bis mein Liebchen	Hide the tears of sorrow, till my beloved
Diese Quelle besucht! Entpflückt sie lächelnd	Visits this spring! Should she then with a smile
Dich dem Rasen, die Brust mit dir zu schmücken;	Pluck you from the grass to adorn her breast;
O, dann schmiege dich ihr ans Herz, und sag' ihr,	Ah, then nestle close to her heart and tell her
Daß die Tropfen in deinem blauen Kelche	That the drops in your blue calyx
Aus der Seele des treusten Jünglings flossen,	Were shed from the soul of her most faithful young lover,
Der sein Leben verweinet, und den Tod wünscht!	Who weeps away his life and longs for death!

1877 Minnelied / Love song Op. 71, no. 5

Holder klingt der Vogelsang,
  Wenn die Engelreine,
Die mein Jünglingsherz bezwang,
  Wandelt durch die Haine.

Röter blühen Tal und Au,
  Grüner wird der Wasen,
Wo die Finger meiner Frau
  Maienblumen lasen.

Ohne sie ist Alles tot,
  Welk sind Blüt und Kräuter,
Und kein Frühlingsabendrot
  Dünkt mir schön und heiter.

Traute, minnigliche Frau,
  Wollest nimmer fliehen;
Daß mein Herz, gleich dieser Au,
  Mög' in Wonne blühen!
(*Ives, Mendelssohn, Schubert*)

Birdsong sounds more beautiful
  When the pure angel
Who has won my young heart
  Wanders through the woods.

Valley and meadow bloom redder,
  The grass grows greener,
Where my lady's fingers
  Gathered Maytime flowers.

Without her all is dead,
  Flowers and herbs are withered,
And the spring sunset
  Seems neither radiant nor fair.

Gentle, charming lady,
  Do not ever leave me;
That my heart, like this meadow,
  Might bloom in bliss!

Max Kalbeck (1850–1921)

A music critic, whose close friendship with Brahms makes his eight-volume biography of the composer essential and mostly reliable reading. Kalbeck tells us that in January 1875 he gave the text of 'Nachtwandler' to Brahms, who then copied it into a notebook, a frequent occurrence with texts he was considering for composition. According to Kalbeck, Brahms would then carry the notebook around with him and wait for inspiration – a habit that tallies with Georg Henschel's description of Brahms's method in *Musings and Memoirs of a Musician* (1918). 'Nachtwandler' was eventually composed in 1877.

c.1877 Nachtwandler / Sleepwalker Op. 86, no. 3

Störe nicht den leisen Schlummer
Dess, den lind ein Traum umfangen!
Laß ihm seinen süßen Kummer!
Ihm sein schmerzliches Verlangen!

Sorgen und Gefahren drohen,
Aber keine wird ihn schrecken,
Kommst du nicht, den Schlafesfrohen
Durch ein hartes Wort zu wecken.

Do not disturb the gentle slumber
Of one whom dreams have softly embraced!
Leave him to his sweet grief!
To his painful longing!

Though cares and dangers threaten,
None of them will frighten him,
Unless you with harsh words
Rouse him from his happy sleep.

Still in seinen Traum versunken	Silently immersed in his dream,
Geht er über Abgrundtiefen	He passes over deep abysses,
Wie vom Licht des Vollmonds trunken,	As though drunk with the full moon's light,
Weh den Lippen, die ihn riefen!	Woe to the lips that would call him!

Franz Kugler (1808–58)

Kugler was an art historian, poet and composer who wrote a *Frauenliebe und -leben* before either Schumann or Loewe. He knew Eichendorff well and was a friend of Robert Reinick with whom he published a *Liederbuch für deutsche Künstler* (1833). He was also a talented draughtsman and illustrated his own *Skizzenbuch* (1830) from which 'Ständchen' is taken. The song contains a cryptic reference to Agathe von Siebold by incorporating her name (GADE) into the opening melody.

*c.*1888 Ständchen / Serenade Op. 106, no. 1

Der Mond steht über dem Berge,	The moon shines over the mountain,
So recht für verliebte Leut;	Just right for people in love;
Im Garten rieselt ein Brunnen,	A fountain purls in the garden –
Sonst Stille weit und breit.	Otherwise silence far and wide.
Neben der Mauer, im Schatten,	By the wall in the shadows,
Da stehn der Studenten drei	Three students stand
Mit Flöt' und Geig' und Zither,	With flute and fiddle and zither,
Und singen und spielen dabei.	And sing and play.
Die Klänge schleichen der Schönsten	The sounds steal softly into the dreams
Sacht in den Traum hinein,	Of the loveliest of girls,
Sie schaut den blonden Geliebten	She sees her fair-headed lover
Und lispelt: „Vergiß nicht mein."	And whispers 'Remember me.'

Karl Lemcke (1831–1913)

No other Lieder composer, apart from Abt, Jensen and Rubinstein, seems to have set Lemcke's poetry. Although Brahms might have turned to him out of geographical loyalty – Lemcke's *Lieder und Gedichte* (1861) were published in Hamburg, where Brahms was born – it was the theme of doomed love that caused the composer to set him seven times. There are also four settings of Lemcke's patriotic lyrics for four-part male chorus (Op. 41, nos. 2–5).

1877 Über die See / Across the sea Op. 69, no. 7

Über die See,	Across the sea,
Fern über die See	Far across the sea
Ist mein Schatz gezogen,	My sweetheart travelled,
Ist ihm mein Herz	And my heart,

Voll Ach und Weh,
Bang ihm nachgeflogen.

Brauset das Meer,
Wild brauset das Meer,
Stürme dunkel jagen,
Sinket die Sonn',
Die Welt wird leer –
Muß mein Herz verzagen.

Bin ich allein,
Ach' immer allein,
Meine Kräfte schwinden.
Muß ich zurück
In matter Pein,
Kann dich nimmer finden.

Full of anguish and pain,
Has flown anxiously after him.

The ocean roars,
The ocean roars wildly,
Dark storms race on,
The sun sinks,
The world becomes empty –
My heart must despair.

I am alone,
Ah, ever alone,
My strength is failing.
I must return,
Weak with grief,
I can no longer find you.

1877 Verzagen / Despair Op. 72, no. 4

Ich sitz' am Strande der rauschenden See
Und suche dort nach Ruh',
Ich schaue dem Treiben der Wogen
Mit dumpfer Ergebung zu.

Die Wogen rauschen zum Strande hin,
Sie schäumen und vergeh'n,
Die Wolken, die Winde darüber,
Die kommen und verweh'n.

Du ungestümes Herz sei still
Und gib dich doch zur Ruh;
Du sollst mit Winden und Wogen
Dich trösten, – was weinest du?

I sit by the shore of the raging sea
Searching there for rest,
I gaze at the waves' motion
In numb resignation.

The waves crash on the shore,
They foam and vanish,
The clouds, the winds above,
They come and go.

You, unruly heart, be silent
And surrender yourself to rest;
You should find comfort
In winds and waves, – why are you weeping?

1878 In Waldeseinsamkeit / In woodland solitude Op. 85, no. 6

Ich saß zu deinen Füßen
In Waldeseinsamkeit;
Windesatmen, Sehnen
Ging durch die Wipfel breit.

In stummem Ringen senkt' ich
Das Haupt in deinen Schoß
Und meine bebenden Hände
Um deine Knie ich schloß.

Die Sonne ging hinunter,
Der Tag verglühte all,
Ferne, ferne, ferne
Sang eine Nachtigall.

I sat at your feet
In woodland solitude;
A breath of wind, a yearning,
Moved through the broad tree-tops.

I lowered in silent struggle
My head into your lap,
And clasped my trembling hands
Around your knees.

The sun went down,
All daylight faded,
Far, far, far away
A nightingale sang.

1886 Verrat / Betrayal Op. 105, no. 5

Ich stand in einer lauen Nacht
An einer grünen Linde,
Der Mond schien hell, der Wind ging sacht,
Der Gießbach floß geschwinde.

Die Linde stand vor Liebchens Haus,
Die Türe hört ich knarren,
Mein Schatz ließ sacht ein Mannsbild 'raus:
„Laß morgen mich nicht harren.

Laß mich nicht harren, süßer Mann,
Wie hab ich dich so gerne!
Ans Fenster klopfe leise an,
Mein Schatz ist in der Ferne."

Laß ab von Druck und Kuß, Feinslieb,
Du Schöner im Sammetkleide,
Nun spute dich, du feiner Dieb,
Ein Mann harrt auf der Heide.

Der Mond scheint hell, der Rasen grün
Ist gut zu uns'rem Begegnen,
Du trägst ein Schwert und nickst so kühn,
Dein' Liebschaft will ich segnen! –

Und als erschien der lichte Tag,
Was fand er auf der Heide?
Ein Toter in den Blumen lag
Zu einer Falschen Leide.

One mild night I was standing
By a green linden tree,
The moon shone brightly, the wind blew softly,
And swiftly flowed the torrent.

The linden tree stood before my love's house,
I heard the door creak,
Cautiously my love let a man out:
'Don't keep me waiting tomorrow.

Don't keep me waiting, sweet man,
I love you so very dearly!
Tap gently against the window-pane,
My sweetheart's far away.'

Leave your cuddling and kissing, my dear,
And you, you handsome man in velvet,
Make haste, you cunning thief,
A man awaits you on the moor.

The moon shines bright, the green turf
Is fit for our encounter,
You wear a sword and nod so boldly,
I shall bless your liaison! –

And when the light of dawn appeared,
What did it find on the moor?
A dead man lay among the flowers,
To a false woman's sorrow.

1888 Salamander / Salamander Op. 107, no. 2

Es saß ein Salamander
Auf einem kühlen Stein,
Da warf ein böses Mädchen
In's Feuer ihn hinein.

Sie meint', er soll verbrennen,
Ihm war erst wohl zu Mut,
Wohl wie mir kühlem Teufel
Die heiße Liebe tut.

A salamander was sitting
On a cool stone,
When suddenly a bad girl
Threw it into the fire.

She thought it would burn up,
But it felt even more at ease,
Just as hot love
Suits a cool devil like me.

Detlev von Liliencron (1844–1909)

Brahms came across 'Auf dem Kirchhofe' and 'Maienkätzchen' in *Adjutantenritte und andere Gedichte* (1883) that Liliencron had posted to the composer. Brahms replied in a letter dated December 1886 that, though he had tried, he had not succeeded in setting any of the poems to music. Two years later, however, both 'Maienkätzchen' and 'Auf dem Kirchhofe' had been composed, and Brahms sent Liliencron, via Klaus Groth, the music of Op. 105. Liliencron's reaction was to dash off a euphoric letter to his friend Wilhelm Friedrich:

> Eben hatte ich eine *unermeßliche* Freude: Klaus Groth schickt mir, von *Johannes Brahms! schreibe J-o-h-a-n-n-e-s B-r-a-h-m-s! von ihm!!!* Op. 105, erschienen bei Simrock in Berlin: darin: 'Auf dem Kirchhofe' von Detlev von Liliencron. *Das* ist mir die höchste *Auszeichnung.*

> I have just been overwhelmed with huge happiness: Klaus Groth has sent me Opus 105 by *Johannes Brahms! can you believe it J-o-h-a-n-n-e-s B-r-a-h-m-s!*, published by Simrock in Berlin, which includes 'Auf dem Kirchhofe' by Detlev von Liliencron. *That* for me is the greatest *honour.*

Liliencron was one of the first to recognize the genius of Hugo Wolf (see p. 578) – a fact that would not have endeared him to Brahms. He served with distinction in the Austro-Prussian and Franco-Prussian wars, and wrote short stories, novels, plays and poems, the best of which have a freshness and a way of capturing the fleeting moment that commended him to the Naturalists.

*c.*1887 Maienkätzchen / May catkins Op. 107, no. 4

Maienkätzchen, erster Gruß,	May catkins, first greeting,
Ich breche euch und stecke euch	I pick you and pin you
An meinen alten Hut.	On my old hat.
Maienkätzchen, erster Gruß,	May catkins, first greeting,
Einst brach ich euch und steckte euch	Once I picked and pinned you
Der Liebsten an den Hut.	On my sweetheart's hat.
(*Berg, Zemlinsky*)	

*c.*1888 Auf dem Kirchhofe / In the churchyard Op. 105, no. 4

Der Tag ging regenschwer und sturmbewegt,	The day was heavy with rain and storms,
Ich war an manch vergeßnem Grab gewesen.	I had stood by many a forgotten grave.
Verwittert Stein und Kreuz, die Kränze alt,	Weathered stones and crosses, faded wreaths,
Die Namen überwachsen, kaum zu lesen.	The names overgrown, scarcely to be read.
Der Tag ging sturmbewegt und regenschwer,	The day was heavy with storms and rains,
Auf allen Gräbern fror das Wort: Gewesen.	On each grave froze the word: Deceased.
Wie sturmestot die Särge	How the coffins slumbered, dead to the
schlummerten –	storm –
Auf allen Gräbern taute still: Genesen.	Silent dew on each grave proclaimed: Released.

Hermann Lingg (1820–1905)

He resigned his commission as a medical officer in the Bavarian army in 1846 and became, like Geibel and Heyse, a member of the 'Münchner Dichterkreis'. He published six volumes of poems, but few composers, apart from Brahms, Pfitzner, Reger and Schoenberg, have set any of them to music.

1886 Immer leiser wird mein Schlummer / My sleep grows ever quieter Op. 105, no. 2

Immer leiser wird mein Schlummer,
Nur wie Schleier liegt mein Kummer
   Zitternd über mir.
Oft im Traume hör' ich dich
Rufen draus vor meiner Tür,
Niemand wacht und öffnet dir,
   Ich erwach' und weine bitterlich.

My sleep grows ever quieter,
Only my grief, like a veil,
   Lies trembling over me.
I often hear you in my dreams
Calling outside my door,
No one keeps watch and lets you in,
   I awake and weep bitterly.

Ja, ich werde sterben müssen,
Eine andre wirst du küssen,
   Wenn ich bleich und kalt.
Eh die Maienlüfte wehn,
Eh die Drossel singt im Wald;
Willst du mich noch einmal sehn,
   Komm, o komme bald!
(*Hiller, Kienzl, Orff, Pfitzner, Thuille*)

Yes, I shall have to die,
You will kiss another
   When I am pale and cold.
Before May breezes blow,
Before the thrush sings in the wood;
If you would see me once again,
   Come soon, come soon!

Martin Luther (1483–1546)

'Hier stehe ich. Ich kann nicht anders. Gott helfe mir.' ('Here I stand. I can do no other. May God help me.') These famous words, uttered at the Diet of Worms in 1521, enshrine a confidence in the power of individual feeling that was to inspire the Sturm und Drang movement in Germany, and subsequently the Romantic writers. The free-thinking Brahms loved the directness and power of Luther's German, which he set, not just in the *Vier ernste Gesänge*, but in *Ein deutsches Requiem* and many other choral works such as the first of the *Three Motets*, Op. 110 ('Ich aber bin elend'), the third of the *Fest- und Denksprüche*, Op. 109 ('Wo ist ein so herrlich Volk'), the first of the *Two Motets*, Op. 74 ('Warum ist das Licht gegeben') etc.

1896 *Vier ernste Gesänge / Four Serious Songs* Op. 121, nos. 1–4

1

Denn es gehet dem Menschen / For that which befalleth the sons of men
ECCLESIASTES 3: 19–22

Denn es gehet dem Menschen wie dem Vieh, wie dies stirbt, so stirbt er auch, und haben alle einerlei Odem; und der Mensch hat nichts mehr denn das Vieh; denn es ist alles eitel.

Es fährt alles an einen Ort; es ist alles von Staub gemacht, und wird wieder zu Staub.

Wer weiß, ob der Geist des Menschen aufwärts fahre, und der Odem des Viehes unterwärts unter die Erde fahre?

Darum sahe ich, daß nichts bessers ist, denn daß der Mensch fröhlich sei in seiner Arbeit; denn das ist sein Teil. Denn wer will ihn dahin bringen, daß er sehe, was nach ihm geschehen wird?

For that which befalleth the sons of men befalleth beasts; [. . .] as the one dieth, so dieth the other; yea, they have all one breath; so that a man hath no pre-eminence above a beast; for all is vanity.

All go unto one place; all are of dust, and all turn to dust again.

Who knoweth the spirit of man [. . .] goeth upward and the spirit of the beast that goeth downward to the earth?

Wherefore I perceive that there is nothing better, than that a man should rejoice in his own works, for that is his portion. For who shall bring him to see what shall happen after him?

2
Ich wandte mich / So I returned
ECCLESIASTES 4: 1–3

Ich wandte mich, und sahe an alle, die Unrecht leiden unter der Sonne; und siehe, da waren Tränen derer, die Unrecht litten und hatten keinen Tröster, und die ihnen Unrecht täten, waren zu mächtig, daß sie keinen Tröster haben konnten.

Da lobte ich die Toten, die schon gestorben waren, mehr als die Lebendigen, die noch das Leben hatten;

Und der noch nicht ist, ist besser als alle beide, und des Bösen nicht inne wird, das unter der Sonne geschieht.

So I returned, and considered all the oppressions that are done under the sun; and behold the tears of such as were oppressed, and they had no comforter; and on the side of their oppressors there was power; but they had no comforter.

Wherefore I praised the dead which are already dead more than the living which are yet alive.

Yea, better is he than both they, which hath not yet been, who hath not seen the evil work that is done under the sun.

3
O Tod / O death
ECCLESIASTICUS 41: 1–2

O Tod, wie bitter bist du, wenn an dich gedenket ein Mensch, der gute Tage und genug hat und ohne Sorge lebet; und dem es wohl geht in allen Dingen und noch wohl essen mag!

O Tod, wie wohl tust du dem Dürftigen, der da schwach und alt ist, der in allen Sorgen steckt, und nichts Bessers zu hoffen, noch zu erwarten hat!

O death, how bitter is the remembrance of thee to a man that liveth at rest in his possessions, unto the man that hath nothing to vex him, and that hath prosperity in all things; yea, unto him that is yet able to receive meat!

O death, acceptable is thy sentence unto the needy and unto him whose strength faileth, that is now in the last age, and is vexed with all things, and to him that despaireth, and hath lost patience!

4

Wenn ich mit Menschen / Though I speak with the tongues of men
I CORINTHIANS 13: 1–3, 12–13

Wenn ich mit Menschen- und mit Engelzungen redete, und hätte der Liebe nicht, so wär ich ein tönend Erz, oder eine klingende Schelle.

Und wenn ich weissagen könnte und wüßte alle Geheimnisse und alle Erkenntnis, und hätte allen Glauben, also, daß ich Berge versetzte, und hätte der Liebe nicht, so wäre ich nichts.

Und wenn ich alle meine Habe den Armen gäbe, und ließe meinen Leib brennen, und hätte der Liebe nicht, so wäre mirs nichts nütze.

Wir sehen jetzt durch einen Spiegel in einem dunkeln Worte, dann aber von Angesicht zu Angesichte. Jetzt erkenne ichs stückweise, dann aber werd ichs erkennen, gleichwie ich erkennet bin.

Nun aber bleibet Glaube, Hoffnung, Liebe, diese drei; aber die Liebe ist die größeste unter ihnen.

Though I speak with the tongues of men and of angels, and have not charity, I am become as sounding brass or a tinkling cymbal.

And though I have the gift of prophecy, and understand all mysteries, and all knowledge; and though I have all faith, so that I could remove mountains, and have not charity, I am nothing.

And though I bestow all my goods to feed the poor, and though I give my body to be burned, it profiteth me nothing . . .

For now we see through a glass, darkly; but then face to face: now I know in part, but then shall I know even as also I am known.

And now abideth faith, hope, charity, these three; but the greatest of these is charity.

August von Platen (1796–1835)

Platen, in full Karl August Georg Maximilian, Graf von Platen-Hallermünde, suffered from a sense of isolation throughout his short life. A nobleman, he served as an officer in the army from 1814 to 1818 – a career quite unsuitable for a gay and eccentric dreamer. Having left the army, he studied literature and language at university, sought success as a playwright, failed, and then turned his back on Germany and spent the rest of his life in voluntary exile in Italy. His finest poetry (he published *Ghaselen* in 1821 and *Sonette aus Venedig* in 1824) deserves a place in any anthology of German verse. Brahms set five of his poems in Op. 32. Other composers attracted to his poetry include Cornelius, Loewe ('Der Pilgrim von St Just'), Marx and, of course, Schubert ('Die Liebe hat gelogen' and 'Du liebst mich nicht').

September 1864 Wie rafft ich mich auf in der Nacht / How I leapt up in the night Op. 32, no. 1

Wie rafft ich mich auf in der Nacht, in der Nacht,	How I leapt up in the night, in the night,
Und fühlte mich fürder gezogen,	And felt myself drawn onward,
Die Gassen verließ ich, vom Wächter bewacht,	I left the streets, patrolled by the watch,

Durchwandelte sacht
In der Nacht, in der Nacht
Das Tor mit dem gotischen Bogen.

Der Mühlbach rauschte durch felsigen
    Schacht,
Ich lehnte mich über die Brücke,
Tief unter mir nahm ich der Wogen in Acht,
Die wallten so sacht
In der Nacht, in der Nacht,
Doch wallte nicht eine zurücke.

Es drehte sich oben, unzählig entfacht
Melodischer Wandel der Sterne,
Mit ihnen der Mond in beruhigter Pracht,
Sie funkelten sacht
In der Nacht, in der Nacht,
Durch täuschend entlegene Ferne.

Ich blickte hinauf in der Nacht, in der Nacht,
Und blickte hinunter aufs neue;
O wehe, wie hast du die Tage verbracht,
Nun stille du sacht,
In der Nacht, in der Nacht,
Im pochenden Herzen die Reue!

Quietly walked on
In the night, in the night,
Through the gate with the Gothic arch.

The millstream rushed through the rocky
    gorge,
I leaned over the bridge,
Far below me I watched the waves
That flowed so quietly
In the night, in the night,
But not a single wave ever flowed back.

The countless, kindled stars above
Went on their melodious way,
With them the moon in tranquil splendour –
They glittered quietly
In the night, in the night,
Through deceptively distant space.

I gazed aloft in the night, in the night,
And gazed down again once more;
Oh how have you spent your days, alas,
Now quietly silence
In the night, in the night,
The remorse that pounds in your heart!

September 1864 Ich schleich umher / I creep about Op. 32, no. 3

Ich schleich umher
Betrübt und stumm,
Du fragst, o frage
Mich nicht, warum?
Das Herz erschüttert
So manche Pein!
Und könnt ich je
Zu düster sein?

Der Baum verdorrt,
Der Duft vergeht,
Die Blätter liegen
So gelb im Beet,
Es stürmt ein Schauer
Mit Macht herein,
Und könnt ich je
Zu düster sein?
(*Burgmüller*)

I creep about,
Troubled and silent,
You ask me – oh, ask
Me not – why?
My heart is shaken
By so much pain!
And could I ever
Be too gloomy?

The tree withers,
Fragrance fades,
Leaves lie so yellow
In the flowerbed.
A heavy shower
Comes storming up,
And could I ever
Be too gloomy?

September 1864 Der Strom, der neben mir verrauschte / The river that rushed by me Op. 32, no. 4

Der Strom, der neben mir verrauschte, wo ist
  er nun?
Der Vogel, dessen Lied ich lauschte, wo ist er
  nun?
Wo ist die Rose, die die Freundin am Herzen
  trug,
Und jener Kuß, der mich berauschte, wo ist
  er nun?
Und jener Mensch, der ich gewesen, und den
  ich längst
Mit einem andern Ich vertauschte, wo ist er
  nun?

The river that rushed by me, where is it
  now?
The bird whose song I listened to, where is it
  now?
Where is the rose my love wore on her
  heart,
And that kiss which entranced me, where is it
  now?
And that man I used to be, and whom I long
  ago
Exchanged for another self, where is he
  now?

September 1864 Wehe, so willst du mich wieder / Alas, would you once again Op. 32, no. 5

Wehe, so willst du mich wieder,
Hemmende Fessel, umfangen?
Auf, und hinaus in die Luft!
Ströme der Seele Verlangen,
Ström es in brausende Lieder,
Saugend ätherischen Duft!

Strebe dem Wind nur entgegen,
Daß er die Wange dir kühle,
Grüße den Himmel mit Lust!
Werden sich bange Gefühle
Im Unermesslichen regen?
Atme den Feind aus der Brust!
(Lang)

Alas, would you once again
Enchain me, restraining fetters?
Up and out into the open!
Pour out the soul's longing,
Pour it into impassioned songs,
Absorbing ethereal fragrance!

Struggle into the teeth of the wind,
That it may cool your cheeks,
Greet the heavens with joy!
Can you feel anxiety,
When confronted by the infinite universe?
Breathe out the foe from your breast!

September 1864 Du sprichst, daß ich mich täuschte / You tell me I was mistaken Op. 32, no. 6

Du sprichst, daß ich mich täuschte,
Beschworst es hoch und hehr,
Ich weiß ja doch, du liebtest,
Allein du liebst nicht mehr!

Dein schönes Auge brannte,
Die Küsse brannten sehr,
Du liebtest mich, bekenn es,
Allein du liebst nicht mehr!

Ich zähle nicht auf neue,
Getreue Wiederkehr;

You tell me I was mistaken,
You swore it by all you hold dear,
Yet I know you loved me once,
But no longer love me now!

Your beautiful eyes smouldered,
Your kisses even more,
You loved me once, confess it,
But no longer love me now!

I do not ever expect you
To love me faithfully again;

Gesteh nur, daß du liebtest,	Just confess you loved me once
Und liebe mich nicht mehr!	And no longer love me now!

Christian Reinhold (1813–56)

The pseudonym of Christian Köstlin, an occasional poet whose daughter, Marie Fellinger, was a famous photographer who made many portraits of Brahms in his old age. It was she who drew his attention to her father's poems, of which Brahms set four. The melody of 'Nachtigall' had originally been composed for another Reinhold song, 'Der Wanderer'; Brahms then slightly adapted the text of 'Nachtigall' in order to accommodate the same tune.

c.1885 Nachtigall / Nightingale Op. 97, no. 1

O Nachtigall,	O nightingale,
Dein süßer Schall,	Your sweet voice
Er dringet mir durch Mark und Bein.	Pierces me to the marrow.
Nein, trauter Vogel, nein!	No, dear bird, no!
Was in mir schafft so süße Pein,	What causes me such sweet pain
Das ist nicht dein, –	Is not your notes, –
Das ist von andern, himmelschönen,	But others, of heavenly beauty,
Nun längst für mich verklungenen Tönen,	Long since vanished for me,
In deinem Lied ein leiser Widerhall.	A gentle echo in your song.

Robert Reinick (1805–52)

See Robert Schumann, Wolf

April 1852 Juchhe! / Hurrah! Op. 6, no. 4

Wie ist doch die Erde so schön, so schön!	How fair, how fair the earth is!
Das wissen die Vögelein:	The little birds know this:
Sie heben ihr leicht Gefieder,	They flutter their light feathers
Und singen so fröhliche Lieder	And sing such happy songs
In den blauen Himmel hinein.	Into the blue sky above.
Wie ist doch die Erde so schön, so schön!	How fair, how fair the earth is!
Das wissen die Flüss' und Seen:	The rivers and lakes know this;
Sie malen im klaren Spiegel	In their clear mirrors they paint
Die Gärten und Städt' und Hügel,	The gardens and towns and hills,
Und die Wolken, die drüber gehn!	And the clouds that pass overhead!
Und Sänger und Maler wissen es,	And poets and painters know it,
Und es wissen's viel andre Leut',	And many other folk as well,
Und wers nicht malt, der singt es,	And those who don't paint it, sing it,
Und wers nicht singt, dem klingt es	And those who don't sing it, can hear it

Im Herzen vor lauter Freud'!
(*Kienzl, Marschner*)

Sound in their hearts for sheer joy!

January 1853 Liebestreu / True love Op. 3, no. 1

„O versenk, o versenk dein Leid, mein Kind,
In die See, in die tiefe See!" –
Ein Stein wohl bleibt auf des Meeres Grund,
Mein Leid kommt stets in die Höh'. –

'Oh drown, oh drown your grief, my child,
In the sea, the fathomless sea!' –
A stone may stay on the ocean bed,
My grief will always surface. –

„Und die Lieb', die du im Herzen trägst,
Brich sie ab, brich sie ab, mein Kind!" –
Ob die Blum' auch stirbt, wenn man sie bricht:
Treue Lieb' nicht so geschwind. –

'And the love you bear in your heart,
Pluck it out, pluck it out, my child!' –
Though a flower will die when it is plucked:
Faithful love will not fade so fast. –

„Und die Treu, und die Treu, 's war nur ein
  Wort,
In den Wind damit hinaus!" –
O Mutter, und splittert der Fels auch im Wind,
Meine Treue, die hält ihn aus. –

'Faithful, faithful – is but a word,
Away with it to the winds!' –
Though a rock, O mother, will split in the
  wind,
My faithful love will withstand it. –

Friedrich Rückert (1788–1866)

See Mahler, Robert Schumann

c.1883 Mit vierzig Jahren / At forty Op. 94, no. 1

Mit vierzig Jahren ist der Berg erstiegen,
  Wir stehen still und schaun zurück;
  Dort sehen wir der Kindheit stilles liegen
  Und dort der Jugend lautes Glück.
Noch einmal schau, und dann gekräftigt weiter
  Erhebe deinen Wanderstab!
  Hindehnt ein Bergesrücken sich, ein breiter,
  Und hier nicht, drüben gehts hinab.
Nicht atmend aufwärts brauchst du mehr zu
  steigen,
  Die Ebne zieht von selbst dich fort;
  Dann wird sie sich mit dir unmerklich
  neigen,
  Und eh' du's denkst, bist du im Port.

At forty the mountain has been climbed,
  We stand in silence and look back;
  There we see childhood's silent joys
  And the strident joys of youth.
Take one more look and then, strengthened,
  Take up your walking staff!
  A broad mountain ridge stretches far away,
  And the descent lies not here but the other side.
You no longer need to gasp your way
  upwards,
  The plain draws you on of its own accord;
  Imperceptibly, then, it will descend with
  you,
  And before you know, you will be in port.

c.1884 Gestillte Sehnsucht / Assuaged longing Op. 91, no. 1

In goldnen Abendschein getauchet,
  Wie feierlich die Wälder stehn!
  In leise Stimmen der Vöglein hauchet
  Des Abendwindes leises Wehn.

Bathed in golden evening light,
  How solemnly the forests stand!
  The evening winds mingle softly
  With the soft voices of the birds.

Was lispeln die Winde, die Vögelein?	What do the winds, the birds whisper?
Sie lispeln die Welt in Schlummer ein.	They whisper the world to sleep.
Ihr Wünsche, die ihr stets euch reget	But you, my desires, ever stirring
Im Herzen sonder Rast und Ruh!	In my heart without respite!
Du Sehnen, das die Brust beweget,	You, my longing, that agitates my breast –
Wann ruhest du, wann schlummerst du?	When will you rest, when will you sleep?
Beim Lispeln der Winde, der Vögelein,	The winds and the birds whisper,
Ihr sehnenden Wünsche, wann schlaft ihr ein?	But when will you, yearning desires, slumber?
Ach, wenn nicht mehr in goldne Fernen	Ah! when my spirit no longer hastens
Mein Geist auf Traumgefieder eilt,	On wings of dreams into golden distances,
Nicht mehr an ewig fernen Sternen	When my eyes no longer dwell yearningly
Mit sehnendem Blick mein Auge weilt;	On eternally remote stars;
Dann lispeln die Winde, die Vögelein,	Then shall the winds, the birds whisper
Mit meinem Sehnen mein Leben ein.	My life – and my longing – to sleep.

Adolf Friedrich von Schack (1815–94)

See Strauss

1867 Abenddämmerung / Dusk Op. 49, no. 5

Sei willkommen, Zwielichtstunde	I bid you welcome, twilight hour
Dich vor allen lieb' ich längst,	Long have I loved you best of all,
Die du, lindernd jede Wunde,	You who, soothing every wound,
Unsre Seele mild umfängst.	Tenderly enfold our soul.
Hin durch deine Dämmerhelle	There amid your dusky brightness,
In den Lüften, abendfeucht,	In the breezes moist with evening,
Schweben Bilder, die der grelle	Hover visions that were banished
Schein des lauten Tags gescheucht.	By the garish light of loud day.
Träume und Erinnerungen	Dreams and memories
Nahen aus der Kinderzeit,	Draw near from childhood days,
Flüstern mit den Geisterzungen	Whispering with ghostly tongues
Von vergangner Seligkeit.	Of vanished rapture.
Und zu Jugendlust-Genossen	And we return to our paternal home
Kehren wir ins Vaterhaus;	And youthful joy's companions;
Arme, die uns einst umschlossen,	Arms that once embraced us
Breiten neu sich nach uns aus.	Reach out to us again.
Nach dem Trennungsschmerz, dem langen,	After the long pain of parting
Dürfen wir noch einmal nun	We can now, once more,
Denen, die dahingegangen,	Rest on the beloved hearts
Am geliebten Herzen ruhn,	Of those who have passed away,
Und, indes zum Augenlide	And, while sleep flows softly
Sanft der Schlummer niederrint,	Down into our eyes,

| Sinkt auf uns ein sel'ger Friede | A blessed peace descends on us |
| Aus dem Land, wo Jene sind. | From that land where they abide. |

1867 Herbstgefühl / Autumn feeling Op. 48, no. 7

Wie wenn im frost'gen Windhauch tödlich	As when summer's last flower
Des Sommers letzte Blüte krankt,	Falls fatally ill in the freezing wind,
Und hier und da nur, gelb und rötlich,	And only here and there, yellow and reddish,
Ein einzles Blatt im Windhauch schwankt:	A solitary leaf stirs in that breeze:

So schauert über mein Leben	So there shudders over my life
Ein nächtig trüber, kalter Tag;	A darkly cold and sombre day;
Warum noch vor dem Tode beben,	Why do you still tremble at the thought of death,
O Herz, mit deinem ew'gen Schlag!	O heart, with your eternal beating!

Sieh rings entblättert das Gestäude!	See the shrubs all stripped of leaves!
Was spielst du, wie der Wind am Strauch,	Why still trifle, like the wind in the bushes,
Noch mit der letzten, welken Freude?	With the withered happiness that remains?
Gib dich zur Ruh'! bald stirbt sie auch.	Surrender to rest! soon that happiness too will die.

Max von Schenkendorf (1783–1817)

Schenkendorf began to write the patriotic poems for which he became famous in the summer of 1806, when Prussia was isolated in Europe. In 1813 he joined the campaign against Napoleon, but did not fight because of an injury to his hand; instead, he wrote a series of poems that expressed a German rather than a Prussian patriotism. Brahms, as an ardent supporter of Bismarck, admired Schenkendorf's work, but set only those poems that expressed his Romantic side. There are five of them; no other Lieder composer, apart from Weber and Josefine Lang, seems to have set his poems.

1878 Todessehnen / Yearning for death Op. 86, no. 6

Ach, wer nimmt von meiner Seele	Ah, who will relieve my soul
Die geheime, schwere Last,	Of its secret, heavy burden,
Die, je mehr ich sie verhehle,	Which, the more I conceal it,
Immer mächtiger mich faßt?	Presses ever more powerfully?

Möchtest du nur endlich brechen,	If only you would break at last,
Mein gequältes, banges Herz!	Tormented, fearful heart!
Findest hier mit deinen Schwächen,	All you find here, with your failings
Deiner Liebe, nichts als Schmerz.	And your love, is pain.

Dort nur wirst du ganz genesen,	Only there will you recover completely,
Wo der Sehnsucht nichts mehr fehlt,	Where your yearning lacks nothing,
Wo das schwesterliche Wesen	Where that sister-being
Deinem Wesen sich vermählt.	Is united with your own.

Hör es, Vater in der Höhe,	Hear me, Father on high,
Aus der Fremde fleht dein Kind:	Your child implores you from afar,
Gib, daß er mich bald umwehe,	Grant it may soon blow about me,
Deines Todes Lebenswind.	Your life-giving wind of death.
Daß er zu dem Stern mich hebe,	That it may raise me to the star
Wo man keine Trennung kennt,	Where parting is unknown,
Wo die Geistersprache Leben	Where the language of spirits
Mit der Liebe Namen nennt.	Calls life by the name of love.

Georg Scherer (1828–1909)

Celebrated as an anthologist – he compiled such collections as *Illustriertes Deutsches Kinderbuch* (1849), *Deutsche Volkslieder* (1851) and *Die schönsten deutschen Volkslieder* (1868) – Scherer is best known as the author of the second verse (the first is anonymous) of Brahms's 'Wiegenlied', although Brahms – unlike Ives – rewrote Scherer's final couplet, which did not fit his melody.

1868 Wiegenlied / Lullaby Op. 49, no. 4

Guten Abend, gut' Nacht,	Good evening, good night,
Mit Rosen bedacht,	Canopied with roses,
Mit Näglein besteckt	Bedecked with carnations,
Schlupf' unter die Deck'.	Slip beneath the coverlet.
Morgen früh, wenn Gott will,	Tomorrow morning, if God wills,
Wirst du wieder geweckt.	You shall be woken again.
Guten Abend, gut' Nacht,	Good evening, good night,
Von Englein bewacht!	Watched over by angels!
Die zeigen im Traum	In your dreams they'll show you
Dir Christkindleins Baum:	The Christmas Tree:
Schlaf' nun selig und süß,	Sleep sweetly now and blissfully,
Schau im Traum's Paradies.	Behold Paradise in your dreams.
(*Ives*)	

Hans Schmidt (1856–1923)

Schmidt lived in Vienna, where he worked as a tutor in the house of the violinist Josef Joachim. When Joachim, suspecting too close a relationship with his wife Amalie, dismissed Schmidt in the summer of 1881, the poet sent Brahms a copy of his *Gedichte und Übersetzungen* and received a charming letter, praising his poetry. Brahms had in the past also aroused Joachim's jealousy, so understood the young man's plight.

Rosen brach ich nachts mir am dunklen
  Hage,
Süßer hauchten Duft sie, als je am Tage;
Doch verstreuten reich die bewegten Äste
  Tau, der mich näßte.

Auch der Küsse Duft mich wie nie berückte,
Die ich nachts vom Strauch deiner Lippen
  pflückte;
Doch auch dir, bewegt im Gemüt gleich jenen,
  Tauten die Tränen.

I gathered roses from the dark hedge by night,
The fragrance they breathed was sweeter
  than by day;
But when I moved the branches, they showered
  Me with dew.

And the fragrant kisses thrilled me as never before,
When I gathered them from your rose-bush
  lips by night;
But you too, moved in your heart like those roses,
  Shed the dew of tears!

Felix Schumann (1854–79)

Felix, the youngest son of Robert and Clara Schumann, was born in 1854, when Schumann had already been confined to a mental home. On 17 September 1873, Clara wrote Brahms a touching letter in which she described how Felix was recuperating from an attack of the lung disease that would soon kill him. She also enclosed poems that Felix had written:

Ich sende Dir [...] seine Gedichte, und wäre es mir lieb, wenn Du sie ’mal durchsähest und an die, welche Dir etwas gefallen, ein Zeichen machtest. Einige davon sind doch recht hübsch, er hat oft sinnige Gedanken und Humor. [...] Sage mir o f f e n, was Du davon denkst – glaube nicht, daß ich als schwache Mutter an ein Genie bei ihm dächte, im Gegenteil, ich habe eine solche Angst vor Überschätzung der Talente seiner Kinder, daß ich vielleicht manchmal zu viel verlange von ihnen.

(I enclose his poems [...], and would be grateful if you could cast an eye over them and mark any you happen to like. Some of them are really very pretty, his thoughts are often clever and humorous. [...] Tell me *honestly* what you think of them, and don’t for a moment think that I, as a weak mother, consider him to be a genius. On the contrary I’m so frightened of overestimating the talents of one’s children, that I sometimes perhaps ask too much of them.

Brahms was clearly touched by Clara’s request and immediately set about composing ‘Meine Liebe ist grün’, a manuscript copy of which reached the Schumann’s Berlin home in time for Christmas. The only other poems of his godson that Brahms set were ‘Wenn um den Hollunder’ and ‘Versunken’. Felix never published his verse.

1873 Meine Liebe ist grün / My love's as green   Op. 63, no. 5

Meine Liebe ist grün wie der Fliederbusch
Und mein Lieb ist schön wie die Sonne;
Die glänzt wohl herab auf den Fliederbusch
Und füllt ihn mit Duft und mit Wonne.

My love's as green as the lilac bush,
And my sweetheart's as fair as the sun;
The sun shines down on the lilac bush,
Fills it with delight and fragrance.

Meine Seele hat Schwingen der Nachtigall
Und wiegt sich in blühendem Flieder,
Und jauchzet und singet vom Duft berauscht
Viel liebestrunkene Lieder.

My soul has a nightingale's wings
And sways in the blossoming lilac,
And, drunk with fragrance, exults and sings
Many a love-drunk song.

Karl Simrock (1802–76)

Karl Simrock was the uncle of Brahms's publisher and friend Fritz Simrock. Best known for his translations from Old German, he was a passionate collector of folksongs, and Brahms, as well as setting two of Simrock's original poems ('Auf dem See' and 'An den Mond'), also composed 'Vor dem Fenster', Op. 14, no. 1, from Simrock's *Die deutschen Volkslieder* (1851).

1873 Auf dem See / On the lake   Op. 59, no. 2

Blauer Himmel, blaue Wogen,
Rebenhügel um den See,
Drüber blauer Berge Bogen
Schimmernd weiß im reinen Schnee.

Blue sky, blue waves,
Vine-clad hills around the lake,
An arc of blue mountains beyond,
Shimmering white in pure snow.

Wie der Kahn uns hebt und wieget,
Leichter Nebel steigt und fällt,
Süßer Himmelsfriede lieget
Über der beglänzten Welt.

As the boat lifts and rocks us,
Light mist rises and falls,
The sweet peace of heaven
Lies over the radiant world.

Stürmend Herz, tu auf die Augen,
Sieh umher und werde mild;
Glück und Frieden magst du saugen
Aus des Doppelhimmels Bild.

Pounding heart, open your eyes,
Look about you and be appeased;
You can absorb happiness and peace
From this double image of heaven.

Spiegelnd sieh die Flut erwidern
Turm und Hügel, Busch und Stadt,
Also spiegle du in Liedern
Was die Erde Schönstes hat.

See how the waters reflect
Tower and hill, woodland and town,
Likewise in your songs reflect
The fairest that earth has to offer.

Theodor Storm (1817–88)

See Berg

Storm was a great admirer of Brahms's music, and in a letter to Emil Kuh tells of the pleasure he derived from playing Brahms duets with his niece (21 August 1873); another letter, dated 26 October 1873, describes how his choir was busy rehearsing Brahms's *Liebeslieder*.

c.1877 **Über die Heide / Over the heath** Op. 86, no. 4

Über die Heide hallet mein Schritt;	Over the heath my steps resound;
Dumpf aus der Erde wandert es mit.	Muffled sounds from the earth wander with me.
Herbst ist gekommen, Frühling ist weit,	Autumn has come, Spring is far distant,
Gab es denn einmal selige Zeit?	Did rapture once really exist?
Brauende Nebel geisten umher,	Swirling mists ghost about,
Schwarz ist das Kraut und der Himmel so leer.	The heather is black and the sky so empty.
Wär ich nur hier nicht gegangen im Mai!	Had I never wandered here in May!
Leben und Liebe – wie flog es vorbei!	Life and love – how they flew by!

Ludwig Tieck (1773–1853)

Despite Tieck's original contributions to early German Romanticism, in particular his short stories and fairy tales, it is as a translator and editor of Shakespeare's plays that he is best known today. Brahms's Op. 33 probably started life as an old Provençal poem. The earliest extant version seems to be a fourteenth century French novel of chivalry, entitled *La Belle Maguelonne, princesse de Naples, et le comte Pierre de Provence,* and by the end of the fifteenth century it had been printed in five French editions and translated into numerous other languages. Lope de Vega fashioned from it his drama *The Three Diamonds,* and in Germany it became extremely popular as a prose narrative. Tieck's version of the story was published in 1796, and a second, slightly altered edition followed in 1812. He shortened the narrative, gave greater psychological depth to the characterization and couched the tale in a florid language that brimmed with poetic nature description. And he inserted into each of the eighteen chapters a verse romance, of which Brahms chose fifteen when he started to compose the cycle in 1861.

Romanzen aus L. Tiecks Magelone / *Romances from L. Tieck's* Magelone [Die schöne Magelone] Op. 33, nos. 1–15

1

July 1861 **Keinen hat es noch gereut / No man yet has rued**

Keinen hat es noch gereut,	No man yet has rued
Der das Roß bestiegen,	Mounting his steed
Um in frischer Jugendzeit	In the first flush of youth
Durch die Welt zu fliegen.	To fly through the world.
Berge und Auen,	Mountains and meadows,
Einsamer Wald,	Lonely forest,
Mädchen und Frauen	Maidens and ladies
Prächtig im Kleide,	Resplendent in robes,
Golden Geschmeide,	Golden jewellery,
Alles erfreut ihn mit schöner Gestalt.	All that is beautiful charms him.
Wunderlich fliehen	Strange visions
Gestalten dahin,	Flit past,
Schwärmerisch glühen	Passionate desire
Wünsche in jugendlich trunkenem Sinn.	Burns in the heady emotions of youth.
Ruhm streut ihm Rosen	Fame strews roses
Schnell in die Bahn,	Swiftly in his path,
Lieben und Kosen,	Love and caresses,
Lorbeer und Rosen	Laurel and roses
Führen ihn höher und höher hinan.	Lead him higher and ever higher.
Rund um ihn Freuden,	Joys surround him,
Feinde beneiden,	Enemies envy the hero,
Erliegend, den Held –	Even as they fall,
Dann wählt er bescheiden	Then he modestly chooses
Das Fräulein, das ihm nur vor allen gefällt.	The maiden who pleases him most.
Und Berge und Felder	And back he rides,
Und einsame Wälder	Leaving mountains and fields
Mißt er zurück.	And lonely forests behind.
Die Eltern in Tränen,	His parents weep,
Ach alle ihr Sehnen –	Their longing, ah! now ended –
Sie alle vereinigt das lieblichste Glück.	Dearest delight unites them all.
Sind Jahre verschwunden,	When years have passed,
Erzählt er dem Sohn	He recounts all to his son
In traulichen Stunden	As they sit close together,
Und zeigt seine Wunden,	And shows his scars,
Der Tapferkeit Lohn.	The reward of valour.
So bleibt das Alter selbst noch jung,	Thus old age itself stays young,
Ein Lichtstrahl in der Dämmerung.	A ray of sunshine in the twilight.

2

July 1861 Traun! Bogen und Pfeil / In truth! bow and arrow

Traun! Bogen und Pfeil	In truth! bow and arrow
Sind gut für den Feind,	Are fit for the foe,
Hülflos alleweil	Helplessly

Der Elende weint;	The wretched will always weep;
Dem Edlen blüht Heil,	A noble soul will flourish
Wo Sonne nur scheint,	Wherever the sun shines,
Die Felsen sind steil,	The cliffs are steep,
Doch Glück ist sein Freund.	But fortune is his friend.

3

July 1861 Sind es Schmerzen / Are these sorrows

Sind es Schmerzen, sind es Freuden,	Are these sorrows, are these joys
Die durch meinen Busen ziehn?	That steal through my heart?
Alle alten Wünsche scheiden,	All my old desires depart,
Tausend neue Blumen blühn.	A thousand new flowers blossom.
Durch die Dämmerung der Tränen	Through the twilight of my tears
Seh ich ferne Sonnen stehn –	I can see distant suns –
Welches Schmachten! Welches Sehnen!	What yearning! What longing!
Wag ich's? Soll ich näher gehn?	Dare I? Shall I draw near?
Ach, und fällt die Träne nieder,	Ah! and when my tears fall,
Ist es dunkel um mich her;	There is darkness all around me;
Dennoch kömmt kein Wunsch mir wieder,	Yet if no desires return,
Zukunft ist von Hoffnung leer.	The future is void of hope.
So schlage denn, strebendes Herz,	So beat then, ambitious heart,
So fließet denn, Tränen, herab,	So flow then, tears, down my cheek,
Ach, Lust ist nur tieferer Schmerz,	Ah! pleasure is but deeper pain,
Leben ist dunkles Grab. –	Life a dark grave.
Ohne Verschulden	Must I suffer
Soll ich erdulden?	Without deserving?
Wie ist's, daß mir im Traum	How is it that in my dreams
Alle Gedanken	All my thoughts
Auf und nieder schwanken!	Drift up and down!
Ich kenne mich noch kaum.	I hardly recognize myself.
O hört mich, ihr gütigen Sterne,	Oh hear me, kindly stars,
O höre mich, grünende Flur,	Oh hear me, greening meadow,
Du, Liebe, den heiligen Schwur;	Hear, O Love, my sacred vow;
Bleib ich ihr ferne,	If I remain far from her,
Sterb ich gerne.	I shall gladly die.
Ach! nur im Licht von ihrem Blick	Ah! only in the light of her eyes
Wohnt Leben und Hoffnung und Glück!	Dwell life and hope and happiness!
(*Weber*)	

4

July 1861 Liebe kam aus fernen Landen / Love came from far-off lands

Liebe kam aus fernen Landen	Love came from far-off lands
Und kein Wesen folgte ihr,	And no one followed her,

Und die Göttin winkte mir,	And the goddess beckoned me,
Schlang mich ein mit süßen Banden.	Binding me in sweet bonds.
Da begann ich Schmerz zu fühlen,	Then I began to feel pain,
Tränen dämmerten den Blick:	Tears dimmed my eyes:
„Ach! was ist der Liebe Glück,"	'Ah! what is love's happiness',
Klagt ich, „wozu dieses Spielen?"	'I lamented, why this dallying?'
„Keinen hab ich weit gefunden,"	'Far and wide no man I've found,'
Sagte lieblich die Gestalt,	Said the vision lovingly,
„Fühle du nun die Gewalt,	'Now you shall feel the force
Die die Herzen sonst gebunden."	That once bound heart to heart.'
Alle meine Wünsche flogen	All my desires flew
In der Lüfte blauen Raum,	Into the blue realm of breezes,
Ruhm schien mir ein Morgentraum,	Fame seemed but a morning dream,
Nur ein Klang der Meereswogen.	The sound of ocean waves.
Ach! wer löst nun meine Ketten?	Ah! who shall now loosen my chains?
Denn gefesselt ist der Arm,	For my arms are fettered,
Mich umfleugt der Sorgen Schwarm;	Sorrows swarm all around me;
Keiner, keiner will mich retten?	Will no one, no one rescue me?
Darf ich in den Spiegel schauen,	Dare I look into the mirror
Den die Hoffnung vor mir hält?	That hope holds up before me?
Ach, wie trügend ist die Welt!	Ah! how deceptive is the world!
Nein, ich kann ihr nicht vertrauen.	No, I cannot trust it.
O und dennoch laß nicht wanken,	And yet, do not allow
Was dir nur noch Stärke gibt,	Your sole source of strength to falter,
Wenn die Einzge dich nicht liebt,	If·your only love does not love you,
Bleibt nur bittrer Tod dem Kranken.	For the sick only bitter death remains.

5

May 1862 So willst du des Armen / So you'll kindly pity a poor man

So willst du des Armen	So you'll kindly pity
Dich gnädig erbarmen?	A poor man?
So ist es kein Traum?	Is it, then, no dream?
Wie rieseln die Quellen,	How the streams ripple,
Wie tönen die Wellen,	How the waves resound,
Wie rauschet der Baum!	How the tree rustles!
Tief lag ich in bangen	I lay imprisoned
Gemäuern gefangen,	Deep within fearful walls,
Nun grüßt mich das Licht;	Now daylight greets me;
Wie spielen die Strahlen!	How the sunbeams flicker!
Sie blenden und malen	They dazzle and colour
Mein schüchtern Gesicht.	My timid face.

Und soll ich es glauben?
Wird keiner mir rauben
    Den köstlichen Wahn?
Doch Träume entschweben,
Nur lieben heißt leben:
    Willkommene Bahn!

Wie frei und wie heiter!
Nicht eile nun weiter,
    Den Pilgerstab fort!
Du hast überwunden,
Du hast ihn gefunden,
    Den seligsten Ort!
(*Hensel*)

And shall I believe it?
Will no one rob me
    Of this precious illusion?
Yet dreams disappear,
Only loving is living:
    A welcome path!

How free, how serene!
Hasten now no further,
    Discard your pilgrim's staff!
You have conquered,
You have found
    The most blissful place of all!

6

May 1862 Wie soll ich die Freude / How then shall I bear the joy

Wie soll ich die Freude,
Die Wonne denn tragen?
Daß unter dem Schlagen
Des Herzens die Seele nicht scheide?

Und wenn nun die Stunden
Der Liebe verschwunden,
Wozu das Gelüste,
In trauriger Wüste
Noch weiter ein lustleeres Leben zu ziehn,
Wenn nirgend dem Ufer mehr Blumen
    erblühn?

Wie geht mit bleibehangnen Füßen
Die Zeit bedächtig Schritt vor Schritt!
Und wenn ich werde scheiden müssen,
Wie federleicht fliegt dann ihr Tritt!

Schlage, sehnsüchtige Gewalt,
In tiefer treuer Brust!
Wie Lautenton vorüberhallt,
Entflieht des Lebens schönste Lust.
Ach, wie bald
Bin ich der Wonne mir kaum noch bewußt.

Rausche, rausche weiter fort,
Tiefer Strom der Zeit,
Wandelst bald aus Morgen Heut,
Gehst von Ort zu Ort;
Hast du mich bisher getragen,
Lustig bald, dann still,

How, then, shall I bear the joy
And how the bliss?
So that, beneath the pulsing
Of my heart, my soul will not escape?

And should the hours
Of love now vanish,
Why crave
In a dreary desert
To prolong a life devoid of pleasure,
When flowers no longer bloom on the
    shore?

How time passes on leaden feet,
Step by deliberate step!
And when I must leave,
How feather-light its tread then flits!

Beat, O powerful longing,
Deep in my faithful heart!
Like the lute's dying strains,
The sweetest pleasures of life fade.
Ah, how soon
Till I'm scarcely aware of such bliss.

Flow onward, ever onward,
Deep river of time,
You soon turn tomorrow into today,
You move from place to place;
Since you have carried me thus far,
Now cheerful, now silent,

Will es nun auch weiter wagen,
Wie es werden will.

Darf mich doch nicht elend achten,
Da die Einzge winkt,
Liebe läßt mich nicht verschmachten,
Bis dies Leben sinkt!
Nein, der Strom wird immer breiter,
Himmel bleibt mir immer heiter,
Fröhlichen Ruderschlags fahr ich hinab,
Bring Liebe und Leben zugleich an das Grab.

I shall venture further,
Come what may.

For I must not count myself wretched,
Since my beloved beckons me,
Love shall never let me languish,
Until this life is done!
No, the river grows ever broader,
The sky for me stays ever clear,
With happy strokes I row on down,
Bring love and life together to the grave.

7
1869 War es dir / Was it for you

War es dir, dem diese Lippen bebten,
Dir der dargebotne süße Kuß?
Gibt ein irdisch Leben so Genuß?
Ha! wie Licht und Glanz vor meinen Augen
     schwebten,
Alle Sinne nach den Lippen strebten!

Was it for you these lips quivered,
For you, that sweetly proffered kiss?
Can earthly life give such joy?
Ah! how light and radiance floated before my
     eyes,
All my senses yearned for those lips!

In den klaren Augen blinkte
Sehnsucht, die mir zärtlich winkte,
Alles klang im Herzen wider,
Meine Blicke sanken nieder,
Und die Lüfte tönten Liebeslieder!

In those clear eyes gleamed
A longing that tenderly beckoned me,
Everything echoed in my heart,
I lowered my gaze,
And the breezes resounded with songs of love!

Wie ein Sternenpaar
Glänzten die Augen, die Wangen
Wiegten das goldene Haar,
Blick und Lächeln schwangen
Flügel, und die süßen Worte gar
Weckten das tiefste Verlangen:
O Kuß! wie war dein Mund so brennend rot!
Da starb ich, fand ein Leben erst im schön-
     sten Tod.

Like twin stars
Her eyes shone, her cheeks
Cradled her golden hair,
Her looks and smiles took
Wing, and her sweet words
Awoke deepest longing:
O kiss, how your red lips burned!
There I died, and first found life in sweetest
     death.

8
1869 Wir müssen uns trennen / We must part

Wir müssen uns trennen,
Geliebtes Saitenspiel,
Zeit ist es, zu rennen
Nach dem fernen erwünschten Ziel.

We must part,
Beloved lute,
It is time to race
Toward the distant, longed-for goal.

Ich ziehe zum Streite,
Zum Raube hinaus,
Und hab ich die Beute,
Dann flieg ich nach Haus.

I set out for battle,
For spoils,
And with my booty,
I'll speed back home.

Im rötlichen Glanze
Entflieh ich mit ihr,
Es schützt uns die Lanze,
Der Stahlharnisch hier.

Kommt, liebe Waffenstücke,
Zum Scherz oft angetan,
Beschirmet jetzt mein Glücke
Auf dieser neuen Bahn!

Ich werfe mich rasch in die Wogen,
Ich grüße den herrlichen Lauf,
Schon mancher ward niedergezogen,
Der tapfere Schwimmer bleibt oben auf.

Ha! Lust zu vergeuden
Das edele Blut!
Zu schützen die Freuden,
Mein köstliches Gut!
Nicht Hohn zu erleiden,
Wem fehlt es an Mut?

Senke die Zügel,
Glückliche Nacht!
Spanne die Flügel,
Daß über ferne Hügel
Uns schon der Morgen lacht!

In the reddish glow
I'll escape with her,
This lance shall protect us,
And this steel armour.

Come, dear weapons,
Often donned in sport,
Protect now my happiness
On this new path!

I'll hurl myself into the waves,
I'll welcome their glorious surge,
Many have been dragged under,
The bold swimmer remains on the surface.

Ha! What pleasure
To shed noble blood!
To protect joy,
My treasured possession!
To suffer no scorn,
Who lacks courage for that?

Slacken your reins,
Happy night!
Spread your wings,
So that over distant hills
Dawn shall soon smile on us!

9

1869 Ruhe, Süßliebchen / Rest, my sweetheart

Ruhe, Süßliebchen, im Schatten
    Der grünen, dämmernden Nacht;
Es säuselt das Gras auf den Matten,
Es fächelt und kühlt dich der Schatten,
    Und treue Liebe wacht.
    Schlafe, schlaf ein,
    Leiser rauscht der Hain –
    Ewig bin ich dein.

Schweigt, ihr versteckten Gesänge,
    Und stört nicht die süßeste Ruh!
Es lauscht der Vögel Gedränge,
Es ruhen die lauten Gesänge,
    Schließ, Liebchen, dein Auge zu.
    Schlafe, schlaf ein,
    Im dämmernden Schein,
    Ich will dein Wächter sein.

Rest, my sweetheart, in the shadow
    Of this green, fading night;
The grass rustles on the meadows,
The shadow fans and cools you,
    And faithful love keeps watch.
    Sleep, go to sleep,
    The grove rustles more gently now,
    I am yours for evermore.

Hush, you hidden songsters,
    And do not disturb her sweetest rest!
The thronging birds listen,
The noisy songs are stilled,
    Close your eyes, my love.
    Sleep, go to sleep,
    In the fading light
    I shall watch over you.

Murmelt fort, ihr Melodien,
    Rausche nur, du stiller Bach,
Schöne Liebesphantasien
Sprechen in den Melodien,
    Zarte Träume schwimmen nach.
Durch den flüsternden Hain
Schwärmen goldene Bienelein
Und summen zum Schlummer dich ein.
(*Franz, Hensel, Lachner, Louise Reichardt,
Spohr*)

Murmur on, you melodies,
    Babble on, quiet brook,
Fair fantasies of love
Speak in those melodies,
    Tender dreams float after them.
Through the whispering grove
Golden bees are swarming
And humming you to sleep.

10

by 1869 Verzweiflung / Despair

So tönet denn, schäumende Wellen,
Und windet euch rund um mich her!
Mag Unglück doch laut um mich bellen,
Erbost sein das grausame Meer!

Resound, then, foaming waves,
And coil yourselves around me!
Let misfortune rage loud around me,
And let the cruel sea roar!

Ich lache den stürmenden Wettern,
Verachte den Zorngrimm der Flut,
O mögen mich Felsen zerschmettern!
Denn nimmer wird es gut.

I scoff at the raging gales,
Scorn the fury of the flood,
If only rocks would dash me to pieces!
For I shall never thrive.

Nicht klag ich, und mag ich nun scheitern,
In wäßrigen Tiefen vergehn!
Mein Blick wird sich nie mehr erheitern,
Den Stern meiner Liebe zu sehn.

I shall not complain, though I now founder,
And perish in watery depths!
Nevermore shall my gaze be cheered
By the sight of my love's star.

So wälzt euch bergab mit Gewittern,
Und raset, ihr Stürme, mich an,
Daß Felsen an Felsen zersplittern!
Ich bin ein verlorener Mann.

So thunder down the mountainside,
And rage at me, you storms,
So that rock shatters on rock!
I am a lost man.

11

1869 Wie schnell verschwindet / How soon they vanish

Wie schnell verschwindet
So Licht als Glanz,
Der Morgen findet
Verwelkt den Kranz,

How soon they vanish,
Radiance and light,
Morning finds
The garland withered

Der gestern glühte
In aller Pracht,
Denn er verblühte
In dunkler Nacht.

That yesterday glowed
In such splendour,
For its flowers faded
In dark night.

Es schwimmt die Welle
Des Lebens hin,

The wave of life
Rolls onwards,

Und färbt sich helle,
Hat's nicht Gewinn;

Die Sonne neiget,
Die Röte flieht,
Der Schatten steiget
Und Dunkel zieht:

So schwimmt die Liebe
Zu Wüsten ab,
Ach, daß sie bliebe
Bis an das Grab!

Doch wir erwachen
Zu tiefer Qual:
Es bricht der Nachen,
Es löscht der Strahl,

Vom schönen Lande
Weit weggebracht
Zum öden Strande
Wo um uns Nacht.

Though bright its hue,
It profits nothing.

The sun sets,
The red glow departs,
The shadows rise
And darkness draws on:

So love drifts away
Into deserts,
Ah! would it endure
Until the grave!

But we awake
To deep torment:
The boat is wrecked,
The light extinguished,

We are borne far away
From our beautiful land
To a desolate shore,
Surrounded by night.

12

by 1869   Muß es eine Trennung geben? / Must there be a parting?

Muß es eine Trennung geben,
Die das treue Herz zerbricht?
Nein, dies nenne ich nicht leben,
Sterben ist so bitter nicht.

Hör ich eines Schäfers Flöte,
Härme ich mich inniglich,
Seh ich in die Abendröte,
Denk ich brünstiglich an dich.

Gibt es denn kein wahres Lieben?
Muß denn Schmerz und Trennung sein?
Wär ich ungeliebt geblieben,
Hätt ich doch noch Hoffnungsschein.

Aber so muß ich nun klagen:
Wo ist Hoffnung, als das Grab?
Fern muß ich mein Elend tragen,
Heimlich bricht das Herz mir ab.

Must there be a parting
That breaks the faithful heart?
No, I cannot call this living,
Dying is not so bitter.

When I hear a shepherd's pipe,
I suffer endless anguish,
When I see the setting sun,
I think ardently of you.

Does true love then not exist?
Must there be pain and parting?
Had I remained unloved,
I should still have a gleam of hope.

But this must now be my lament:
Where is hope but in the grave?
I must bear my grief far away,
Secretly my heart is breaking.

13

May 1862 Sulima / Sulima

Geliebter, wo zaudert	Where, my love, do you tarry
Dein irrender Fuß?	And stray?
Die Nachtigall plaudert	The nightingale tells
Von Sehnsucht und Kuß.	Of longing and kisses.
Es flüstern die Bäume	The trees whisper
Im goldenen Schein,	In golden light,
Es schlüpfen mir Träume	Dreams steal in
Zum Fenster herein.	Through my window.
Ach! kennst du das Schmachten	Ah! do you know the yearning
Der klopfenden Brust?	Of a pounding heart?
Dies Sinnen und Trachten	This musing and striving
Voll Qual und voll Lust?	Full of torment and joy?
Beflügle die Eile	Give wings to your haste
Und rette mich dir,	And rescue me,
Bei nächtlicher Weile	Under cover of night
Entfliehn wir von hier.	We'll steal away.
Die Segel, sie schwellen,	The sails are swelling,
Die Furcht ist nur Tand:	Your fear is but vain:
Dort, jenseit der Wellen	There beyond the waves
Ist väterlich Land.	Is your fatherland.
Die Heimat entfliehet,	My homeland recedes,
So fahre sie hin!	So let it go!
Die Liebe, sie ziehet	The power of love
Gewaltig den Sinn.	Draws me on.
Horch! wohllüstig klingen	Listen! How seductively
Die Wellen im Meer,	The waves ring out,
Sie hüpfen und springen	They bound and leap
Mutwillig einher,	Playfully around us,
Und sollten sie klagen?	And why should they grieve?
Sie rufen nach dir!	They are summoning you!
Sie wissen, sie tragen	They know they are taking
Die Liebe von hier.	Love from here.
(*Louise Reichardt*)	

14

May 1869 **Wie froh und frisch / How briskly and brightly**

Wie froh und frisch mein Sinn sich hebt,	How briskly and brightly my spirits soar,
Zurückbleibt alles Bangen,	All fear is left behind,
Die Brust mit neuem Mute strebt,	My heart strives with fresh courage,
Erwacht ein neu Verlangen.	Fresh longing awakes.

Die Sterne spiegeln sich im Meer,	The stars are mirrored in the sea,
Und golden glänzt die Flut. –	And the waves gleam with gold.
Ich rannte taumelnd hin und her,	I ran reeling this way and that,
Und war nicht schlimm, nicht gut.	And was neither bad nor good.
Doch niedergezogen	But doubts and misgivings
Sind Zweifel und wankender Sinn,	Are now laid low;
O tragt mich, ihr schaukelnden Wogen,	Oh, carry me, you pitching waves,
Zur längst ersehnten Heimat hin.	To the homeland I've long desired.
In lieber, dämmernder Ferne,	In the dear, darkening distance
Dort rufen heimische Lieder,	The songs of home are calling,
Aus jeglichem Sterne	From every star
Blickt sie mit sanftem Auge nieder.	She gazes gently down.
Ebne dich, du treue Welle,	Be calmed, O trusty waves,
Führe mich auf fernen Wegen	Lead me along distant paths
Zu der vielgeliebten Schwelle,	To the much-loved threshold,
Endlich meinem Glück entgegen!	To happiness at last!

15

1869 Treue Liebe dauert lange / True love abides

Treue Liebe dauert lange,	True love abides,
Überlebet manche Stund,	Outlives many an hour,
Und kein Zweifel macht sie bange,	And no doubts can make it fearful,
Immer bleibt ihr Mut gesund.	Its courage is always steadfast and sound.
Dräuen gleich in dichten Scharen,	Though death and disaster threaten,
Fordern gleich zum Wankelmut	Encouraging inconstancy,
Sturm und Tod, setzt den Gefahren	As they throng together – Love pits
Lieb entgegen treues Blut.	Loyal blood against such perils.
Und wie Nebel stürzt zurücke,	And whatever held the spirit captive
Was den Sinn gefangen hält,	Then recedes like mist,
Und dem heitern Frühlingsblicke	And the wide world opens its doors
Öffnet sich die weite Welt.	To the cheerful gaze of spring.
Errungen,	Happiness
Bezwungen	Is achieved,
Von Lieb ist das Glück,	Is compelled by love,
Verschwunden	Vanished
Die Stunden,	Those hours,
Sie fliehen zurück:	They fly away;
Und selige Lust,	And blissful delight
Sie stillet	Stills,
Erfüllet	Fulfils
Die trunkene, wonneklopfende Brust;	The ecstatic breast that throbs with delight,
Sie scheide	May it part
Von Leide	From sorrow

Auf immer,	For ever,
Und nimmer	And never
Entschwinde die liebliche, selige, himmlische	Fade, this lovely, blissful, heavenly
Lust!	delight!

Thibault de Champagne (1201–53)

King of Navarre and patron of men of letters, he took part in the crusade against the Albigenses. Much of his poetry was said to have been inspired by the regent Blanche de Castille.

1858 Ein Sonett / A sonnet Op. 14, no. 4
TRANSLATED BY JOHANN HERDER (1744–1803)

Ach könnt ich, könnte vergessen sie,	Ah, could I, could I forget her,
Ihr schönes, liebes, liebliches Wesen,	Her fine, loving, lovely nature,
Den Blick, die freundliche Lippe, die!	Her look, her friendly lips, ah them!
Vielleicht ich möchte genesen!	I might perhaps be healed!
Doch ach, mein Herz, mein Herz kann es nie!	Yet ah, my heart, my heart can never!
Und doch ists Wahnsinn zu hoffen sie!	And yet to hope for her is madness!
Und um sie schweben	And to hover round her
Gibt Mut und Leben	Gives zest and courage
Zu weichen nie.	To waver never.
Und denn, wie kann ich vergessen sie,	And then, how can I forget her,
Ihr schönes, liebes, liebliches Wesen,	Her fine, loving, lovely nature,
Den Blick, die freundliche Lippe, die?	Her look, her friendly lips, ah them!
Viel lieber nimmer genesen!	Much better never to be healed!
(*Hensel, Zelter*)	

Ludwig Uhland (1787–1862)

See Kreutzer

May 1851 Heimkehr / Homecoming Op. 7, no. 6

O brich nicht, Steg, du zitterst sehr,	O footbridge, do not break, you tremble so,
O stürz nicht, Fels, du dräuest schwer;	O do not crumble, cliffs, you threaten to;
Welt, geh nicht unter, Himmel, fall nicht ein,	World, do not end, sky, do not fall in,
Bis ich mag bei der Liebsten sein!	Until I'm by my beloved's side!
(*Curschmann, Kreutzer*)	

May 1859 Der Schmied / The blacksmith Op. 19, no. 4

Ich hör meinen Schatz,	I hear my sweetheart
Den Hammer er schwinget,	Swinging his hammer,

Das rauschet, das klinget,
Das dringt in die Weite
Wie Glockengeläute,
Durch Gassen und Platz.

Am schwarzen Kamin,
Da sitzet mein Lieber,
Doch, geh ich vorüber,
Die Bälge dann sausen,
Die Flammen aufbrausen
Und lodern um ihn.
(*Jensen, Schumann*)

It sounds, it resounds,
It peals out afar
Like ringing bells
Through alleys and square.

By the black forge
My love is sitting,
But if I go past,
The bellows start blowing,
The flames flare up
And blaze all about him.

Benjamin Britten (1913–76)

Throughout his songwriting career, Britten – despite his fondness for Aldeburgh and East Anglia – continually reached out to other cultures and languages. While still at school, and not yet fifteen, he composed his *Four French Songs* to poems by Hugo and Verlaine (1928). *Les Illuminations* followed in 1939, astonishing tour-de-force settings of Rimbaud; the florid *Seven Sonnets of Michelangelo* appeared a year later, the first of Britten's song-cycles written for the voice of Peter Pears; then, in 1957, came the *Songs from the Chinese*, brief, concise and aphoristic. In 1958, he turned to German, and composed the *Sechs Hölderlin-Fragmente* which he dedicated to Prince Ludwig of Hessen, a great admirer of Hölderlin's poetry. *The Poet's Echo*, settings of six Pushkin poems, dates from 1965.

Friedrich Hölderlin (1770–1843)

See Eisler, Fortner

One of Germany's greatest poets, Hölderlin sought to amalgamate the spiritual strength of Greek civilization with the ideals of German nationhood and the Christian religion. Like Schiller, who lamented the lost beauty of the Hellenic world in 'Die Götter Griechenlands' ('Schöne Welt, wo bist du?'), Hölderlin believed passionately in his mission of regenerating Germany in what he regarded to be an unspiritual age. Like Mayrhofer (see SCHUBERT), he felt tragically unable to fulfil the task. Much of his early verse is modelled on Schiller, who acquired for him the post of tutor to the son of Charlotte von Kalb, who had cured Schiller's own melancholy in 1784. When Schiller, influenced by Goethe's negative criticism, suddenly lost interest in his work, Hölderlin's confidence collapsed. Having obtained the post of tutor to the children of a wealthy Frankfurt businessman, he fell in love with his employer's wife, Susette Gontard, whom he revered as Diotima, the heroine of Plato's *Symposion* who taught Socrates the art of love. He idolized her in his poetry and in his novel *Hyperion*. When she died in 1802, he gradually became deranged and spent the final years of his life, from 1807 to 1843, in the care of a local master carpenter, named Zimmer. He would rise early and, unable to follow any consecutive train of thought, walk up and down the garden, plucking blades of grass and talking unintelligibly to himself; at other times he would sit at his piano and repeat a phrase for hours on end, or walk to and fro indoors, reading aloud from *Hyperion* and other of his works (Mörike's description of the red hat bobbing up and down in 'Der Feuerreiter' is said to have been inspired by the sight of Hölderlin pacing up and down in his room in a white cap.)

Zimmer wrote to Hölderlin's mother on 19 April 1812:

Sein dichterischer Geist zeigt Sich noch immer thätig, so sah Er bey mir eine Zeichnung von einem Tempel. Er sagte mir ich solte einen von Holz machen, ich versetzte Ihm drauf daß ich um Brot arbeiten müßte, ich sey nicht so glüklich so in Philosofischer ruhe zu leben wie Er, gleich versetzte Er, Ach ich bin doch ein armer Mensch, und in der nehmlichen Minute schrieb Er mir folgenden Vers mit Bleistift auf ein Brett: 'Die Linien des Lebens sind Verschieden...'

His poetic spirit still shows itself to be active; in my house, for instance, he saw the drawing of a temple and told me to make one out of wood, I replied that I had to work for my living, that I was not fortunate enough to live in philosophic calm like him, immediately he replied: 'Ah, I am a wretched creature' and in the same minute he wrote the following verses on a wooden board with his pencil: 'Die Linien des Lebens sind verschieden...'

Hölderlin titled the poem 'An Zimmern'.

1958 Sechs Hölderlin-Fragmente / Six Hölderlin Fragments Op. 61

1
Menschenbeifall / Applause of men

Ist nicht heilig mein Herz, schöneren Lebens voll,	Is my heart not hallowed, filled with a fairer life,
Seit ich liebe? warum achtetet ihr mich mehr,	Now that I love? Why did you prize me more
Da ich stolzer und wilder,	When I was prouder and wilder,
Wortereicher und leerer war?	More full of words and emptier?
Ach! der Menge gefällt, was auf den Marktplatz taugt,	Ah, the mob likes what sells in the marketplace,
Und es ehret der Knecht nur den Gewaltsamen;	And the slavish revere none but the violent;
An das Göttliche glauben	Things divine are believed in
Die allein, die es selber sind.	Only by those who themselves are divine.

2
Die Heimat / Homeland

Froh kehrt der Schiffer heim an den stillen Strom	Happily the sailor comes home to the quiet river
Von fernen Inseln, wo er geerntet hat;	From distant isles, where he has harvested;
Wohl möcht' auch ich zur Heimat wieder;	I too should like to come home again;
Aber was hab' ich, wie Leid, geerntet? –	But what have I harvested but suffering? –
Ihr holden Ufer, die ihr mich auferzogt,	Dear river-banks, you that brought me up,
Stillt ihr der Liebe Leiden? ach! gebt ihr mir,	Will you soothe the sufferings of love? Ah, will you give me,
Ihr Wälder meiner Kindheit, wann ich	will you give me,

Komme, die Ruhe noch einmal wieder?
(*Eisler, Hauer*)

O forests of my childhood, when I
Return, peacefulness once more?

3
Sokrates und Alcibiades* / Socrates and Alcibiades

„Warum huldigest du, heiliger Sokrates,
  Diesem Jünglinge stets? kennest du
Größers nicht?
  Warum siehet mit Liebe,
  Wie auf Götter, dein Aug auf ihn?"

'Why, holy Socrates, do you always pay homage
  To this young man? Are not greater things
known to you?
  Why do you look upon him with love,
  As you would look upon gods?'

Wer das Tiefste gedacht, liebt das
  Lebendigste,
  Hohe Tugend versteht, wer in die Welt
geblickt,
  Und es neigen die Weisen
  Oft am Ende zu Schönem sich.

He who has pondered deepest, loves what is
  most alive,
  He who has seen the world, understands
true virtue,
  And in the end the wise
  Will often yield to Beauty.

4
Die Jugend / Youth

Da ich ein Knabe war,
  Rettet' ein Gott mich oft
  Vom Geschrei und der Rute der Menschen,
  Da spielt' ich sicher und gut
  Mit den Blumen des Hains,
  Und die Lüftchen des Himmels
    Spielten mit mir.

When I was a boy,
  A god often saved me
  From the screams and the rod of mankind,
  Then safe and innocent I played
  With the woodland flowers,
  And the breezes of Heaven
    Played with me.

Und wie du das Herz
Der Pflanzen erfreust,
Wenn sie entgegen dir
Die zarten Arme strecken,

And as you delight
The hearts of plants,
When they stretch out to you
Their delicate arms,

So hast du mein Herz erfreut,
Vater Helios! und, wie Endymion,†
War ich dein Liebling,
Heilige Luna!

So you delighted my heart,
Father Helios! and, like Endymion,
I was your darling,
Sacred Luna!

O all ihr treuen
Freundlichen Götter!
Daß ihr wüßtet,
Wie euch meine Seele geliebt!

O all you faithful
And kindly gods!
Would that you knew
How my soul loved you!

---

* An impetuous Athenian general, whose wildness was checked for a while by his teacher Socrates. He died, aged forty-six, in 404 BC.
† A shepherd, son of Aethlius and Calyce. Diana, seeing Endymion naked as he slept on Mount Latmos, came down each night from heaven to enjoy his company.

Mich erzog der Wohllaut
Des säuselnden Hains
Und lieben lernt' ich
Unter den Blumen.

Im Arme der Götter wuchs ich groß.

I was raised by the melodious sound
Of the rustling grove
And I learned to love
Among the flowers.

I grew up in the arms of the gods.

5
Hälfte des Lebens / The middle of life

Mit gelben Birnen hänget
Und voll mit wilden Rosen
Das Land in den See,
Ihr holden Schwäne,
Und trunken von Küssen
Tunkt ihr das Haupt
Ins heilignüchterne Wasser.

The land with yellow pears
And wild roses hangs
Down into the lake,
You gracious swans,
And drunk with kisses
You dip your heads
Into the sacredly sober water.

Weh mir, wo nehm' ich, wenn
Es Winter ist, die Blumen, und wo
Den Sonnenschein
Und Schatten der Erde?
Die Mauern stehn
Sprachlos und kalt, im Winde
Klirren die Fahnen.
(*Rihm, Wolpe*)

Alas, where shall I, when
It is winter, find the flowers, and where
The sunshine
And shadows of the earth?
The walls stand
Speechless and cold, in the wind
The weather-vanes clatter.

6
Die Linien des Lebens / The lines of life

Die Linien des Lebens sind verschieden
Wie Wege sind, und wie der Berge Grenzen.
Was hier wir sind, kann dort ein Gott ergänzen
Mit Harmonien und ewigem Lohn und Frieden.

The lines of life are various
As paths are, and the mountains' boundaries.
What here we are, can there by a god be completed
With harmonies and eternal recompense and peace.

Ferruccio Busoni (1866–1924)

In the final five years of his life Busoni composed six songs to texts by Goethe, one of which, 'Die Bekehrte' (for soprano), had already been set by Hugo Wolf. All of them were composed at a time when Busoni was working on his opera *Doktor Faust*, and two were actually taken from Goethe's play. 'Lied des Brander' is a crude student's song ('Brandfuchs' is slang for a second-year university student) sung in 'Auerbachs Keller', while 'Lied des Mephistopheles', familiar to us from Beethoven's and Mussorgsky's settings, satirizes court life – Busoni rewrote this song in G minor for tenor and incorporated it into his opera, where it is sung by Mephistopheles, as he announces the death of the Duchess of Parma. 'Lied des Unmuts' is part of the 'Buch des Unmuts' from the *West-östlicher Divan*, and 'Zigeunerlied' was written by Goethe to open Act V of the first version of his play *Götz von Berlichingen*.

Johann Wolfgang von Goethe (1749–1832)

See Beethoven, Brahms, Hensel, Loewe, Mendelssohn, Mozart, Reichardt, Schubert, Strauss, Wolf, Zelter

1919–24 *Cinque Lieder su testi di Goethe*

1

Lied des Brander / Brander's song
FROM *Faust*

Es war eine Ratt im Kellernest,	Once in a cellar there lived a rat,
Lebte nur von Fett und Butter,	Ate nothing but fat and butter,
Hatte sich ein Ränzlein angemäst't,	Until his paunch became as fat
Als wie der Doktor Luther.	As that of Doctor Luther.
Die Köchin hatt' ihr Gift gestellt,	The cook she laid some poison down,
Da ward's so eng ihr in der Welt,	Then the world closed in about her,
Als hätt' sie Lieb im Leibe.	As though she had love inside her.
Sie fuhr herum, sie fuhr heraus,	She scurried here, she scurried there,
Und soff aus allen Pfützen,	And drank from every puddle,
Zernagt', zerkratzt' das ganze Haus,	She scratched and gnawed throughout the house,
Wollte nichts ihr Wüten nützen;	Though her fury was in vain;
Sie tät gar manchen Ängstesprung,	She leapt great leaps in mortal fear,
Bald hatte das arme Tier genung,	The poor beast soon had had enough,
Als hätt' es Lieb im Leibe.	As though she had love inside her.
Sie kam für Angst am hellen Tag	In broad daylight, out of fear,
Der Küche zugelaufen,	She ran towards the kitchen,
Fiel an den Herd und zuckt' und lag,	Fell down by the range, quivered and lay
Und tät erbärmlich schnaufen.	And struggled for breath most wretchedly.
Da lachte die Vergift'rin noch:	The cook, who'd poisoned her, now laughed:

„Ha, sie pfeift auf dem letzten Loch,
Als hätt' sie Lieb im Leibe".
(*Wagner*)

'Ha! she's on her last legs,
As though she she had love inside her.'

2
Lied des Mephistopheles / Mephistopheles' song
FROM *Faust*
See Beethoven, p. 12

3
Lied des Unmuts / Song of ill humour

Keinen Reimer wird man finden,
Der sich nicht den besten hielte,
Keinen Fiedler, der nicht lieber
Eigne Melodien spielte.

You'll never find a rhymester
Who doesn't think he's best,
Nor fiddler who'd not rather
Play melodies of his own.

Und ich konnte sie nicht tadeln;
Wenn wir andern Ehre geben,
Müssen wir uns selbst entadeln;
Lebt man denn, wenn andre leben?

And neither could I blame them;
In honouring others,
We deprive ourselves of honour;
For are we alive when others live?

Und so fand ich's denn auch juste
In gewissen Antichambern,
Wo man nicht zu sondern wußte
Mäusedreck von Koriandern.

And that's what I've recently found
In certain ante-chambers,
Where no one could distinguish
Mouse droppings from coriander.

Das Gewesne wollte hassen
Solche rüstige neue Besen,
Diese dann nicht gelten lassen,
Was sonst Besen war gewesen.

The has-beens were wont to hate
Such vigorous new brooms,
Who in turn would not recognize
Those who formerly were brooms.

Und wo sich die Völker trennen
Gegenseitig im Verachten,
Keins von beiden wird je bekennen,
Daß sie nach demselben trachten.

And where two nations separate
In mutually held contempt,
Neither will ever admit
They're striving for the same goal.

Und das grobe Selbstempfinden
Haben Leute hart gescholten,
Die am wenigsten verwinden,
Wenn die andern was gegolten.
(*Schoeck*)

And this vulgar self-esteem
Has been condemned outright by those
Who are slowest to recover
When others have made their mark.

4
Schlechter Trost / Small comfort

Mitternachts weint und schluchzt ich,
Weil ich dein entbehrte.
Da kamen Nachtgespenster,

At midnight I wept and sobbed,
Because I was missing you.
Then nocturnal ghosts appeared,

Und ich schämte mich.
„Nachtgespenster", sagt ich,
„Schluchzend und weinend
Findet ihr mich, dem ihr sonst
Schlafendem vorüberzogt.
Große Güter vermiß ich.
Denkt nicht schlimmer von mir,
Den ihr sonst weise nanntet,
Großes Übel betrifft ihn!" –
Und die Nachtgespenster
Mit langen Gesichtern
Zogen vorbei,
Ob ich weise oder törig,
Völlig unbekümmert.
(*Pepping*)

And I felt ashamed.
'Nocturnal ghosts,' I said,
'You find me sobbing and weeping,
Whom you have always passed by
And left sleeping.
I pine for great things dear to me.
Do not think less of me,
Whom you once called wise,
Great ill afflicts him!' –
And the nocturnal ghosts
With long faces
Flitted by,
Whether I was wise or foolish
Concerned them not at all.

5

Zigeunerlied / Gypsy song
FROM *Gottfried von Berlichingen*

Im Nebelgeriesel, im tiefen Schnee,
Im wilden Wald, in der Winternacht,
Ich hörte der Wölfe Hungergeheul,
Ich hörte der Eulen Geschrei.
   Wille wau wau wau!
   Wille wo wo wo!
   Wito hu!

In drizzle and mist, in deep snow,
In the wild forest, in the winter night,
I heard the ravening howl of the wolves,
I heard the screeching of the owls.
   Wille wau wau wau!
   Wille wo wo wo!
   Wito hu!

Ich schoß einmal eine Katz am Zaun,
Der Anne, der Hex, ihre schwarze liebe Katz.
Da kamen des Nachts sieben Werwölf zu mir,
Waren sieben sieben Weiber vom Dorf.
   Wille wau wau wau!
   Wille wo wo wo!
   Wito hu!

I once shot a cat beside the fence,
Annie the witch's, her dear black cat.
And at night seven werewolves came to me,
Seven seven wenches from the village.
   Wille wau wau wau!
   Wille wo wo wo!
   Wito hu!

Ich kannte sie alle, ich kannte sie wohl,
Die Anne, die Ursel, die Käth,
Die Liese, die Barbe, die Ev, die Beth,
Sie heulten im Kreise mich an.
   Wille wau wau wau!
   Wille wo wo wo!
   Wito hu!

I knew them all, I knew them well,
Annie, Ursula, Cath,
Lizzie, Babs, Eve and Beth;
They stood in a circle howling at me.
   Wille wau wau wau!
   Wille wo wo wo!
   Wito hu!

Da nannt ich sie alle bei Namen laut:
Was willst du, Anne? was willst du, Beth?
Da rüttelten sie sich, da schüttelten sie sich,
Und liefen und heulten davon.

And I called them all by their names out loud:
'What is it, Annie? what is it, Beth?'
Then they quivered, and then they shook,
And howling, they ran away.

Wille wau wau wau!   Wille wau wau wau!
Wille wo wo wo!   Wille wo wo wo!
Wito hu!*   Wito hu!
(*Spohr*)

* The song is sung by the marksman who, in verse two, shot Annie the witch's cat. The other witches now turn themselves into werewolves to wreak revenge on the marksman – but by calling them all by name, he is able to keep them at bay.

Peter Cornelius (1824–74)

Peter Cornelius, like Schumann, grew up in a literary environment and shared the same enthusiasm for poets such as Heine, Eichendorff, Hebbel and Rückert. In 1852 he became secretary in Weimar to Franz Liszt, who mounted a production of Cornelius's opera *Der Barbier von Bagdad*. Having met Wagner in Vienna in 1861 he was allowed to participate in the preparations for *Tristan*; Cornelius coached the singers in their roles and probably attended every one of the seventy-seven rehearsals. He fell under Wagner's spell, and Wagner clearly loved him. When Cornelius broke ties with him, Wagner pleaded:

> Freund, Du mußt zu mir ziehen, ein für allemal! . . . Versteh mich recht, Du treibst, was Du kannst, und ich tu's; aber immer wie zwei Menschen, die eigentlich, wie ein Ehepaar, zusammengehören.

> Friend, you must come to me once and for all! . . . Don't misunderstand me; you shall go about your ways, and I shall go about mine; but always as two people who, like a married couple, really belong together.

Following Wagner's example, he wrote the texts to many of his own works, and like Wagner's, his vocal line often approaches recitative – 'Ein Ton', for example, is written on a single note. Though almost all of Cornelius's Lieder are settings of his own verse, his duets set poems by other writers, such as Friedrich Hebbel with whom he enjoyed a close friendship.

1854 *Trauer und Trost / Grief and comfort* Op. 3

1
Trauer / Grief

Ich wandle einsam,	I wander lonely,
Mein Weg ist lang,	My way is long,
Zum Himmel schau ich	I gaze up to heaven
Hinauf so bang.	So fearfully.
Kein Stern von oben	No star above
Blickt niederwärts,	Looks down,
Glanzlos der Himmel,	The sky is dull,
Dunkel mein Herz.	My heart dark.
Mein Herz und der Himmel	My heart and the sky
Hat gleiche Not,	Share one distress,
Sein Glanz ist erloschen,	Its gleam is gone,
Mein Lieb ist tot.	My love is dead.

2

Angedenken / Memento

Von stillem Ort,
Von kühler Statt
Nahm ich mit fort
Ein Efeublatt.

Ein Requiem
Tönt leis und matt,
So oft ich nehm
Zur Hand das Blatt.

Wenn aller Schmerz
Geendet hat,
Legt mir auf's Herz
Das Efeublatt.

From a quiet
And cool place
I took away
An ivy leaf.

A requiem sounds
Faint and dim
Each time I pick
Up that leaf.

When all agony
Is over,
Lay the ivy leaf
On my heart.

3

Ein Ton / One tone

Mir klingt ein Ton so wunderbar
In Herz und Sinnen immerdar,
Ist es der Hauch, der Dir entschwebt,
Als einmal noch Dein Mund gebebt?
Ist es des Glöckleins trüber Klang,
Der Dir gefolgt den Weg entlang?
Mir klingt der Ton so voll und rein,
Als schlöß er Deine Seele ein.
Als stiegest liebend nieder Du
Und sängest meinen Schmerz in Ruh.
(*Ives*)

One sound keeps ringing wondrously
In my mind and heart,
Is it the breath that escaped you,
When once your lips were trembling?
Is it the sad note of the bell
That followed you on your way?
The sound to me is so full and clear,
As if it enclosed your soul.
As if you came down to me with love
And sang my sorrow to rest.

4

An den Traum / To dreams

Öffne mir die goldne Pforte,
Traum, zu deinem Wunderhain,
Was mir blühte und verdorrte,
Laß mir blühend neu gedeihn.
Zeige mir die heil'gen Orte
Meiner Wonne, meiner Pein,
Laß mich lauschen holdem Worte,
Liebesstrahlen saugen ein.
Öffne mir die goldne Pforte,
Traum, o laß mich glücklich sein!

Open up the golden gate,
O dream, to your magic glade,
Let whatever bloomed and faded
Flourish for me and bloom again.
Reveal to me those sacred places
Of my rapture and my pain,
Let me listen to sweet words
And drink in the beams of love.
Open up the golden gate,
O dream, and grant me happiness!

5
Treue / Faithfulness

Dein Gedenken lebt in Liedern fort,
Lieder, die der tiefsten Brust entwallen,
Sagen mir: Du lebst in ihnen allen,
Und gewiß, die Lieder halten Wort.

Dein Gedenken blüht in Tränen fort,
Tränen, aus des Herzens Heiligtume,
Nähren tauend der Erinnrung Blume,
In dem Tau blüht Dein Gedenken fort.

Dein Gedenken lebt in Träumen fort,
Träume, die Dein Bild verklärt mir zeigen,
Sagen: daß Du ewig bist mein eigen,
Und gewiß, die Träume halten Wort.

Your memory lives on in songs,
Songs from the depth of my heart
Tell me: you dwell in all of them,
And songs most certainly keep their word.

Your memory blossoms on in tears,
Tears from the heart's sanctuary
Bedew and nourish memory's flower,
Your memory blossoms on in that dew.

Your memory lives on in dreams,
Dreams, which show me you transfigured,
Say that you are mine forever,
And dreams most certainly keep their word.

6
Trost / Comfort

Der Glückes Fülle mir verlieh'n
    Und Hochgesang,
Nun auch in Schmerzen preis' ich ihn
    Mein Leben lang.
Mir sei ein sichres Himmelspfand,
    Was ich verlor,
Mich führt der Schmerz an starker Hand
    Zu ihm empor.
Wenn ich in Wonnen bang beklagt
    Den Flug der Zeit,
In Schmerzen hat mir hell getagt
    Unsterblichkeit.

He who granted me abundant joy
    And exalted song,
I shall praise Him, even in grief,
    My whole life long.
Let what I lost
    Assure me a place in heaven;
Grief leads me strongly by the hand
    To Him above.
If, in bliss, I anxiously lamented
    The flight of time,
Immortality dawned brightly for me
    In grief.

1854 Komm, wir wandeln zusammen / Come, we'll walk together Op. 4, no. 2

Komm, wir wandeln zusammen im Mond-
    schein!
So zaubrisch glänzt jedes Blatt,
Vielleicht steht auf einem geschrieben,
Wie lieb mein Herz Dich hat.

Komm, wir wandeln zusammen im Mond-
    schein!
Der Mond strahlt aus Wellen bewegt,
Vielleicht, daß Du ahnest, wie selig
Mein Herz Dein Bildnis hegt.

Come, we'll walk together in the moon-
    light!
Each leaf gleams so magically,
On one perhaps is written
How dearly my heart adores you.

Come, we'll walk together in the moon-
    light!
The moon ripples from the waves,
Moved perhaps that you will sense
With what rapture I hold you in my heart.

Komm, wir wandeln zusammen im Mond- schein! Der Mond will ein königlich Kleid Aus goldenen Strahlen Dir weben, Daß Du wandelst in Herrlichkeit!	Come, we'll walk together in the moon- light! The moon will weave you a regal robe From golden beams, That you may walk in majesty!

1856 *Weihnachtslieder / Christmas songs* Op. 8

1

Christbaum / The Christmas tree

Wie schön geschmückt der festliche Raum! Die Lichter funkeln am Weihnachtsbaum! O fröhliche Zeit, o seliger Traum! Die Mutter sitzt in der Kinder Kreis, Nun schweiget alles auf ihr Geheiß, Sie singet des Christkinds Lob und Preis, Und rings vom Weihnachtsbaum erhellt Ist schön in Bildern aufgestellt Des heiligen Buches Palmenwelt. Die Kinder schauen der Bilder Pracht, Und haben wohl des Singens Acht, Das tönt so süß in der Weihenacht. O glücklicher Kreis im festlichen Raum, O gold'ne Lichter am Weihnachtsbaum, O fröhliche Zeit, o seliger Traum!	How lovely the festive room looks! The candles glitter on the Christmas tree! O joyful time, O blissful vision! Mother sits with her children around her, All are now silent at her bidding, She sings the Christ-child's praise and glory, Lit all around by the Christmas tree Beautifully displayed in pictures – The palm-tree world of the Holy Book. The children gaze at the pictures' splendour, And listen attentively to the singing That sounds so sweet in the Christmas night. O happy circle in the festive room, O golden candles on the Christmas tree, O joyful time, O blissful vision!

2

Die Hirten / The shepherds

Hirten wachen im Feld,
Nacht ist rings auf der Welt,
Wach sind die Hirten alleine
    Im Haine.
	Shepherds keep watch in the field,
	Night lies on the world around,
	Only the shepherds are awake
	    In the grove.

Und ein Engel so licht
Grüßet die Hirten und spricht:
„Christ, das Heil aller Frommen,
    Ist kommen!"
	And an angel so bright
	Greets the shepherds, saying:
	'Christ, the Saviour of the pious,
	    Is come!'

Engel singen umher:
„Gott im Himmel sei Ehr'!
Und den Menschen hienieden
    Sei Frieden!"
	Angels sing all around:
	'Glory be to God on high,
	And to men on earth
	    Be peace!'

Eilen die Hirten fort,
Eilen zum heil'gen Ort,
Beten an in den Windlein
    Das Kindlein.
	The shepherds hasten away,
	Hasten to the holy place,
	To adore the infant
	    In his swaddling clothes.

3
Die Könige / The kings

Drei Kön'ge wandern aus Morgenland,	Three kings journey from the East,
Ein Sternlein führt sie zum Jordanstrand,	A little star leads them to Jordan's banks,
In Juda fragen und forschen die Drei,	In Judaea the three of them seek and inquire
Wo der neugeborene König sei?	Where the new-born king might be.
Sie wollen Weihrauch, Myrrhen und Gold	They wish to make offerings to the child:
Dem Kinde spenden zum Opfersold.	Gold, frankincense and myrrh.
Und hell erglänzet des Sternes Schein,	And brightly shines the light of the star,
Zum Stalle gehen die Kön'ge ein,	The three kings enter the stable,
Das Knäblein schauen sie wonniglich,	They gaze in rapture at the child,
Anbetend neigen die Kön'ge sich,	Bowing low in adoration,
Sie bringen Weihrauch, Myrrhen und Gold	Gold, frankincense and myrrh
Zum Opfer dar dem Knäblein hold.	They bring to the child as offering.
O Menschenkind! halte treulich Schritt,	O child of man! Follow them faithfully,
Die Kön'ge wandern, o wandre mit!	The kings are journeying, O journey too!
Der Stern der Liebe, der Gnade Stern	Let the star of love, the star of grace,
Erhelle dein Ziel, so du suchst den Herrn,	Light your way as you seek the Lord,
Und fehlen Weihrauch, Myrrhen und Gold,	And if you lack frankincense, myrrh and gold,
Schenke dein Herz dem Knäblein hold!	Give your heart to that sweet child!

4
Simeon* / Simeon

Das Knäblein nach acht Tagen	After eight days the child
Ward gen Jerusalem	Was taken to the temple
Zum Gotteshaus getragen	In Jerusalem
Vom Stall in Bethlehem.	From the Bethlehem stable.
Da kommt ein Greis geschritten,	An aged man steps forth,
Der fromme Simeon,	The pious Simeon,
Er nimmt in Tempels Mitten	And in the temple takes
Vom Mutterarm den Sohn.	The son from his mother's arms.
Vom Angesicht des Alten	The old man's face
Ein Strahl der Freude bricht,	Beams with joy,
Er preiset Gottes Walten	He praises God's might,
Weissagungsvoll und spricht:	Prophesying and saying:
„Nun lässest du in Frieden,	'Lord, now lettest Thou Thy servant
Herr, Deinen Diener gehn,	Depart in peace,

* The first-born child of every Jewish family had to be presented within the temple at Jerusalem forty days after birth. Simeon, a devout Jew, welcomed them with the words that form part of the evening offices of the Christian Church as the *Nunc Dimittis*.

Da Du mir noch beschieden,
Den Heiland anzusehn,
Den du zur Welt gesendet,
Daß er dem Heidentum
Des Lichtes Helle spendet
Zu deines Volkes Ruhm!"
Mit froh erstaunten Sinnen
Vernimmt's der Eltern Paar,
Dann tragen sie von hinnen
Das Knäblein wunderbar.

For Thou hast permitted me
To see the Saviour,
Whom Thou hast sent into the world
That He may bring light
To the Gentiles
For the glory of Thy people!'
In joy and astonishment
The parents listen,
Then they depart
With the wondrous child.

5
Christus der Kinderfreund / Christ, the children's friend

Das zarte Knäblein ward ein Mann,
Erlöst uns von der Sünde Bann,
Doch neigt er freundlich immerdar
Und liebend sich zur Kinderschar.
Habt ihr den Ruf des Herrn vernommen,
Des Heilands Stimme mild und weich?
„Lasset die Kleinen zu mir kommen,
Denn ihrer ist das Himmelreich!"

The tender child became a man,
Redeemed us from the curse of sin,
But ever friendly and full of love,
He helps little children everywhere.
Have you heard what our Lord said,
The mild sweet voice of the Saviour?
'Suffer little children to come unto me,
For their's is the Kingdom of Heaven!'

Mich aber mahnt die Weihnachtszeit
An Träume der Vergangenheit;
Erinnrungsodem hauchet mild
Den Schleier von der Kindheit Bild;
Da Lichter hell am Baum erglommen,
Ist mir, als würd' ich Kindern gleich,
Als dürft' ich mit Euch Kleinen kommen,
Zu teilen Euer Himmelreich.

But Christmastide recalls to me
Dreams of bygone days;
The breath of memory wafts away
The veil from childhood scenes;
When candles gleam brightly on the tree,
I feel I am a child once more,
As if I might come with you children
To share your Kingdom of Heaven.

6
Christkind / The Christ-child

Das einst ein Kind auf Erden war,
Christkindlein kommt noch jedes Jahr.

Once a baby on this earth,
The Christ-child still returns each year.

Kommet vom hohen Sternenzelt,
Freut und beglücket alle Welt.

He comes from the firmament on high,
Filling all the world with gladness and joy.

Mit Kindern feiert's froh den Tag,
Wo Christkind in der Krippe lag.

He joins the children in honouring the day
When the Christ-child lay in the manger.

Den Christbaum zündet's überall,
Weckt Orgelklang und Glockenschall.

He lights Christmas trees everywhere,
Makes organs peal and bells ring.

Christkindlein kommt zu Arm und Reich,
Die Guten sind ihm alle gleich.

Danket ihm denn und grüßt es fein,
Auch euch beglückte Christkindlein.

The Christ-child comes to both rich and poor,
The virtuous to Him are all alike.

So give Him thanks and greet Him well,
The Christ-child has made you happy too.

Hanns Eisler (1898–1962)

Eisler, who studied with Schoenberg in Vienna from 1919 to 1923, composed over 250 songs in a variety of styles. The six atonal songs of Op. 2, on poems by Claudius, Klabund and a Bethge translation from the Japanese, betray the influence of his teacher, as do the *Palmström Lieder* of Op. 5, which were composed at Schoenberg's suggestion and premiered in a concert which also featured *Pierrot lunaire*. Having joined the German Communist Party in 1926, Eisler composed a number of *Massenlieder* (*Songs for the masses*) which reached a much wider audience than any of his previous songs. It was this type of music – simple and rhythmic – that led the East German government to ask Eisler in 1949 to compose the music to Becher's 'Auferstanden aus Ruinen', which became the national anthem of the German Democratic Republic.

With the rise of the Nazis, Eisler fled Germany and began his life of exile, ending up in Los Angeles, like a great number of other German intellectuals, including Otto Klemperer, Bruno Walter, Schoenberg, Max Reinhardt, Fritz Lang, Alfred Döblin, Thomas and Heinrich Mann, and Franz Werfel. It was during the early thirties that he began to work with Brecht – a collaboration which yielded some 150 Lieder and cabaret songs and climaxed in the *Hollywood Songbook*, a collection of forty-six songs (of which twenty-eight were to poems by Brecht, six by Hölderlin, five by Mörike, two by Pascal, one from the Bible and one each by Goethe, Eichendorff, Eisler and Berthold Viertel). The presence of Goethe, Eichendorff, Hölderlin and Mörike relates to the conflict between the culture of Hollywood and that of the Lieder tradition which had developed in Germany – 'Über den Selbstmord' quotes the opening bars of *Winterreise*, 'Erinnerung an Eichendorff und Schumann' sets the first verse of 'In der Fremde' ('Aus der Heimat hinter den Blitzen rot') and 'An eine Stadt' is dedicated to Franz Schubert. This multi-faceted collection – five Hölderlin *Fragmente* and three Brecht songs are printed here – contains poems that deal with such themes as exile, suffering, evil, hope, courage in adversity, poetry, suicide. Brecht was thrilled with his friend's settings of his verse, and noted in his diary that Eisler had read his poems 'mit enormer Genauigkeit' – with enormous precision. In a sketch for a foreword to the Songbook, Eisler wrote: „In einer Gesellschaft, die ein solches Liederbuch versteht und liebt, wird es sich gut und gefahrlos leben lassen. Im Vertrauen auf eine solche sind diese Stücke geschrieben." ('In a society that understands and loves such a songbook, life will be lived well and without danger. These pieces have been written with such a society in mind.')

Bertolt Brecht (1898–1956)

Brecht was fifth on the Nazi black list, and a glance at his works tells us why. The Nazis not only hated what they perceived to be the 'entartete' ('degenerate') world of *Mahagonny*, *Happy End* and *Die Dreigroschenoper*; they also feared Brecht's incessant and explicit criticism of their regime in his poetry. Brecht spent his exile fleeing the Nazis, moving from Switzerland to Denmark, to Finland, to Russia and, finally, to California, 'öfter als die Schuhe die Länder wechselnd' ('changing countries more often than shoes') as he put it in the celebrated 'An die Nachgeborenen' ('To Posterity'), an extract of which was set by Eisler as 'An die Überlebenden'. 'Die Flucht' and 'Ostersonntag' belong to Brecht's *Steffinische Sammlung*, a series of poems written in memory of Margarete Steffin, a friend whom he had been forced to abandon in a Russian hospital, as he fled; she had collaborated with him on many projects, including *Die Maßnahme* and *Die Mutter*. 'Über den Selbstmord' is spoken by Shen Te in scene 3 of *Der gute Mensch von Sezuan*. Though Brecht's reputation rests mainly on his plays, he is arguably a finer poet, and there are echoes in his lyrically didactic verse of Heine, Goethe and Martin Luther's Bible.

1943 from *Das Hollywooder Liederbuch* / *The Hollywood Songbook*

Über den Selbstmord / On suicide

In diesem Lande und in dieser Zeit
Dürfte es trübe Abende nicht geben
Auch hohe Brücken über die Flüsse
Selbst die Stunden zwischen Nacht und Morgen
Und die ganze Winterzeit dazu, das ist
  gefährlich.
Denn angesichts dieses Elends
Werfen die Menschen
In einem Augenblick
Ihr unerträgliches Leben fort.

In this country and in these times
Gloomy evenings should not be allowed
Nor high bridges over rivers
Even the hours between night and morning
And the whole winter season too, they are
  dangerous.
For faced with this misery
It only takes a moment
For people to throw
Away their unbearable lives.

Die Flucht / Escape

Auf der Flucht vor meinen Landsleuten
Bin ich nun nach Finnland gelangt. Freunde,
Die ich gestern nicht kannte, stellten uns Betten
In saubere Zimmer. Im Lautsprecher
Höre ich die Siegesmeldungen des
  Abschaums.* Neugierig
Betrachte ich die Karte. Hoch oben in Lapp-
land

Fleeing from my countrymen
I have now reached Finland. Friends,
Who till yesterday were strangers, brought us
  beds
Into clean rooms. On the wireless
I hear the victory announcements of the scum.
  Eagerly
I scour the map. In the far north in Lapland,

* 'Scum' – Brecht's pejorative term for the Nazis

| Nach dem nördlichen Eismeer zu | Towards the Arctic Circle, |
| Sehe ich noch eine kleine Tür. | I see one more tiny door. |

Ostersonntag / Easter Sunday

Heute, Ostersonntag früh	Today, Easter Sunday morning
Ging ein plötzlicher Schneesturm über die Insel.	A sudden snow-storm swept the island.
Zwischen den grünenden Hecken lag Schnee.	Snow was lying between greening hedges.
Mein junger Sohn	My young son
Holte mich zu einem Aprikosenbäumchen	Dragged me to a little apricot tree
an der Hausmauer	by the house wall
Von einem Verse weg, in dem ich auf diejen-	Away from a poem in which I accused those
igen mit dem Finger deutete	Who were preparing this war, which will
Die diesen Krieg vorbereiteten, der	destroy
Diesen Kontinent, diese Insel, mein Volk,	This continent, this island, my people, my
und meine Familie und mich	family and me.
Vertilgen muß. Schweigend	Silently
Legten wir einen Sack	We placed a sack
Um den frierenden Baum.	Around the freezing tree.

Friedrich Hölderlin (1770–1843)

See Britten, Fortner

An die Hoffnung / To Hope

O Hoffnung! holde! gütiggeschäftige!	O Hope! Gracious one! Active and kind!
Die du das Haus der Trauernden nicht ver-	Who does not disdain the house of those
schmähst,	who mourn,
Und gerne dienend zwischen den Sterblichen	And gladly serves among mortals:
waltest:	
	Where are you? Little have I lived; yet the
Wo bist du? wenig lebt' ich; doch atmet kalt	breath
Mein Abend schon. Und stille, den Schatten	Of my evening is already cold. And silent, like
gleich,	shades,
Bin ich schon hier; und schon gesanglos	I am already here; and already without song
Schlummert das schaudernde Herz.	My shuddering heart is sleeping.
(*Reger*)	

Andenken / Remembrance

Der Nordost weht,	The north-easterly blows,
Der liebste unter den Winden	The dearest of all winds
Dir, weil er gute Fahrt verheißet.	To you, because it promises a fair voyage.
Geh aber nun, grüße	But go now, greet
Die schöne Garonne,*	The lovely Garonne

* French river which rises on the Spanish side of the Pyrenees and is known below Bordeaux as the Gironde

Und die Gärten von Bordeaux
Dort, wo am scharfen Ufer
Hingehet der Steg und in den Strom
Tief fällt der Bach, darüber aber
Hinschauet ein edel Paar
Von Eichen und Silberpappeln;

　　An Feiertagen gehn
Die braunen Frauen daselbst
Auf seidnen Boden,
Zur Märzenzeit,
Wenn gleich ist Tag und Nacht,
Und über langsamen Stegen,
Von goldenen Träumen schwer,
Einwiegende Lüfte ziehn.

And the gardens of Bordeaux,
Where along the rugged bank
The path extends, and the brook
Falls deep into the river, above which, however,
A noble pair of oaks
And silver poplars gaze;

　　That is where on holidays
Dusky women walk
On a silken ground,
In March,
When night and day are equal,
And over slow paths,
Heavy with golden dreams,
Gently rocking breezes waft.

Elegie 1943 / Elegy 1943

Wie wenn die alten Wasser
... In andern Zorn,
In schrecklichern verwandelt,
　　Wieder kämen,

So gärt' und wuchs und wogte von Jahr
　　zu Jahr
Die unerhörte Schlacht, daß weit
　　hüllt
In Dunkel und Blässe das Haupt der
　　Menschen.

Wer brachte den Fluch? von heut
　　Ist er nicht und nicht von gestern, und die
　　zuerst
Das Maß verloren, unsre Väter
　　Wußten es nicht.

Zu lang, zu lang schon treten die Sterblichen
　　Sich gern aufs Haupt,
　　Den Nachbar fürchtend.

Und unstet, irren und wirren, dem Chaos
　　gleich,
Dem gärenden Geschlecht die Wünsche nach
Und wild ist und unverzagt und kalt von
Sorgen das Leben.

As though ancient waters, transformed
... into another,
Fiercer rage returned
　　Once more,

Thus billowed and grew and raged from year
　　to year
The unheard-of battle, so that far and
　　wide
The heads of men were shrouded in
　　darkness and pallor.

Who brought this curse? It is not
Today's or yesterday's, and they who
　　first
Overstepped the bounds, our fathers
Knew it not.

Too long, too long have mortals trodden
　　Gleefully on others' heads,
　　Fearing their neighbour.

And chaotically, confused and inconstant,
　　The desires of this turbulent race roam,
And life is savage and despairing and
　　cold
And fearful.

An eine Stadt* (Franz Schubert gewidmet) / To a town (dedicated to Franz Schubert)

Lange lieb ich dich schon, möchte dich, mir
    zur Lust,
Mutter nennen, und dir schenken ein kunst-
    loses Lied,
    Du, der Vaterlandsstädte
    Ländlichschönste, so viel ich sah.

Long have I loved you, would like, for my
    delight,
To call you mother and give you an artless
    song,
    You, of the towns in my native land,
    The most rurally fair I ever saw.

Wie der Vogel des Walds über die Gipfel fliegt,
Schwingt sich über den Strom, wo er vorbei
    dir glänzt,
    Leicht und kräftig die Brücke,
    Die von Wagen und Menschen tönt.

Like a forest bird skimming over mountains,
The bridge, rumbling with carts and
    men,
    Lightly and strongly vaults over the river
    That runs gleaming past you.

Da ich vorüberging, fesselt' der Zauber auch
    mich,
Und herein in die Berge
    Mir die reizende Ferne schien.

As I passed by, I too was spell-
    bound,
And deep into the mountains
    The ravishing distance shone.

Du hast dem Flüchtigen
Kühlenden Schatten geschenkt, und die Ge-
    stade
Sahen ihm alle nach, und es tönte
    Aus den Wellen das liebliche Bild.

You gave the fugitive
Cooling shadows, and your shores
    All watched him as he passed, and the
    lovely picture
    Resounded from the waves.

Sträucher blühten herab, bis wo im heiteren
    Tal,
An den Hügel gelehnt, oder dem Ufer hold,
    Deine fröhlichen Gassen
    Unter duftenden Gärten ruhn.

Shrubs ran blossoming down to where in the
    cheerful valley,
Leaning against the hillside or the graceful shore,
    Your happy streets
    Repose among fragrant gardens.

Erinnerung / Remembrance

O heilig Herz der Völker, o Vaterland!
    Allduldend, gleich der schweigenden Mut-
    ter Erd,
    Und allverkannt, wenn schon aus deiner
    Tiefe die Fremden ihr Bestes haben!

O sacred heart of nations, O Fatherland!
    Enduring all, like silent mother earth,
    And wholly misunderstood, even though
    from your
    Depths strangers have gleaned what is best!

Sie ernten den Gedanken, den Geist von dir,
    Sie pflücken gern die Traube, doch höhnen
    sie
    Dich, ungestalte Rebe! daß du
    Schwankend den Boden und wild umirrst.

They harvest thoughts and spirits from you,
    They are happy to pick grapes, but they
    scorn
    You, shapeless vine! that you
    Sway and trail wildly along the ground.

Doch magst du manches Schöne nicht
    bergen mir;

But some beautiful things you cannot con-
    ceal from me;

* Heidelberg

Oft stand ich überschauend das sanfte
Grün,
Den weiten Garten hoch in deinen
Lüften auf hellem Gebirg und sah dich.

Und an den Ufern sah ich die Städte blühn,
Die Edlen, wo der Fleiß in der Werkstatt
schweigt,
Die Wissenschaft, wo deine Sonne
Milde dem Künstler zum Ernste leuchtet.

I often stood gazing over the gentle green,
The extensive garden high in
Your skies on your bright mountain, and
saw you.

And by your shores I saw the cities bloom,
The noble cities, where industry keeps
silent in the workplace,
Saw knowledge, where your sun
Gently enlightens the artist to be earnest.

Wolfgang Fortner (1907–87)

Vocal music looms large in the work-list of this professor of theory and composition at Heidelberg, where Hans Werner Henze was his pupil. There are five operas, of which the best known is *Blood Wedding* (García Lorca), several cantatas, a *Deutsche Liedmesse*, a number of choral works and some thirty songs. Fortner, like Benjamin Britten, preferred to set poems in their original language rather than in translation, and composed a series of impressive songs on poems by Petrarch, Shakespeare and Neruda. His *Vier Gesänge* to poems by Hölderlin (1934) represent, like Britten's *Sechs Hölderlin-Fragmente*, some of the finest settings of this great poet. Fortner is one of the very few composers to have successfully set the poetry of Hugo von Hofmannsthal – *Terzinen* for male voice and piano appeared in 1966.

Friedrich Hölderlin (1770–1843)

See Britten, Eisler

Referring to the poem 'An die Parzen', Hölderlin wrote to his mother on 8 July 1799:

Das Gedichtchen hätte Sie nicht beunruhigen sollen, teuerste Mutter! Es sollte nichts weiter heißen, als wie sehr ich wünsche einmal eine ruhige Zeit zu haben, um das zu erfüllen, wozu mich die Natur bestimmt zu haben schien.

The little poem ought not to have caused you anxiety, dearest Mother! It should have meant no more than how much I wished to have for once a period of quiet, in order to fulfil that for which Nature seemed to have intended me.

1934 *Vier Gesänge / Four songs*

1
An die Parzen / To the fates

Nur einen Sommer gönnt, ihr Gewaltigen!	Grant me but a single summer, Almighty Ones!
Und einen Herbst zu reifem Gesange mir,	And one autumn for mellow song,
Daß williger mein Herz, vom süßen	That, surfeited with sweet playing,
Spiele gesättiget, dann mir sterbe.	My heart might die more willingly.
Die Seele, der im Leben ihr göttlich Recht	The soul, whose divine right was withheld on earth,
Nicht ward, sie ruht auch drunten im Orkus* nicht;	Does not rest in Orcus either;
Doch ist mir einst das Heilige, das am	Yet if but once that sacred thing,
Herzen mir liegt, das Gedicht gelungen,	The poem, so close to my heart, succeed,

* Orcus, one of the names for the god of hell. The word usually refers to the infernal regions.

Willkommen dann, o Stille der Schattenwelt!
    Zufrieden bin ich, wenn auch mein
    Saitenspiel
        Mich nicht hinab geleitet: *Einmal*
        Lebt ich, wie Götter, und mehr bedarfs
        nicht.
(*Hauer, Hindemith, Reutter*)

Then welcome, O silent world of shades!
    I shall be content, even though my lyre
    Does not descend with me; *once*
    I lived as the gods lived, and no more is
    needed.

2

Hyperions* Schicksalslied / Hyperion's song of Fate
FROM *Hyperion, oder Der Eremit in Griechenland*

Ihr wandelt droben im Licht
    Auf weichem Boden, selige Genien!
        Glänzende Götterlüfte
        Rühren euch leicht,
            Wie die Finger der Künstlerin
            Heilige Saiten.

Schicksallos, wie der schlafende
    Säugling, atmen die Himmlischen;
        Keusch bewahrt
        In bescheidener Knospe,
        Blühet ewig
            Ihnen der Geist,
            Und die seligen Augen
            Blicken in stiller
            Ewiger Klarheit.

Doch uns ist gegeben,
    Auf keiner Stätte zu ruhn,
    Es schwinden, es fallen
    Die leidenden Menschen
    Blindlings von einer
    Stunde zur andern,
        Wie Wasser von Klippe
        Zu Klippe geworfen,
            Jahrlang ins Ungewisse hinab.
(*Brahms, Hauer*)

You wander above in light
    On yielding ground, blessed Genii!
        Divine and gleaming breezes
        Caress you lightly,
            As an artist's fingers
            Caress her sacred strings.

Fateless, like sleeping
    Infants, the Celestial breathe;
        Chastely preserved
        In modest bud,
        Their spirits
            Bloom eternally,
            And their blissful eyes
            Gaze in tranquil
            Eternal clearness.

But we are destined
    To find no resting place,
    Suffering mortals
    Vanish and fall
    Blindly from one
    Hour to the next,
        As water hurled
        From crag to crag
            For years into the unknown.

3
Abbitte / Plea for forgiveness

Heilig Wesen! gestört hab ich die goldene
    Götterruhe dir oft, und der geheimeren,

Holy being! I have often disturbed your golden
    God's repose, and you have learnt

---

* Hyperion in Hölderlin's novel is a Greek youth who yearns to free his country from Turkish occupation.
This poem, which he addresses to the 'blessed Genii', is presented in the form of a cataract in which
human life is dashed from rock to rock.

Tiefern Schmerzen des Lebens
Hast du manche gelernt von mir.

O vergiß es, vergib! gleich dem Gewölke dort
Vor dem friedlichen Mond, geh ich dahin,
und du
Ruhst und glänzest in deiner
Schöne wieder, du süßes Licht!
(*Hauer, Pfitzner*)

4
Geh unter, schöne Sonne / Descend, fair sun

Geh unter, schöne Sonne, sie achteten
Nur wenig dein, sie kannten dich, Heil'ge,
nicht,
Denn mühelos und stille bist du
Über den Mühsamen aufgegangen.

Mir gehst du freundlich unter und auf, o Licht!
Und wohl erkennt mein Auge dich, Herr-
liches!
Denn göttlich stille ehren lernt' ich,
Da Diotima* den Sinn mir heilte.

O du des Himmels Botin! wie lauscht ich dir!
Dir, Diotima! Liebe! wie sah von dir
Zum goldnen Tage dieses Auge
Glänzend und dankend empor. Da
rauschten

Lebendiger die Quellen, es atmeten
Der dunkeln Erde Blüten mich liebend an,
Und lächelnd über Silberwolken
Neigte sich segnend herab der Äther.

Some of life's deeper, more secret
Agonies from me.

O forget, forgive! Like those clouds up there
Drifting past the peaceful moon,
I too shall pass, and you will rest and
gleam
In your beauty once more, sweet light!

Descend, fair sun, they heeded you
But little, nor knew your worth, O Holy
One,
Since you rose effortlessly
Above those in toil.

For me you rise and set like a friend,
O light!
To my eyes your glory is manifest!
For godlike, I learned silent reverence,
When Diotima healed my senses.

O Heaven's messenger, how I listened to you!
To you, Diotima! Love! How my eyes
Would turn from you
To greet the golden day
Gleaming and grateful. The springs

Then purled more brightly, the dark earth's blossom
Breathed on me lovingly,
And smiling above silver clouds,
The sky bent low to me in blessing.

* Diotima, the priestess in Plato's *Symposium*, is the name used by Hölderlin to describe the woman he loved, Susette Gontard.

Robert Franz (1815–92)

This prolific Lieder composer led a sheltered existence in Halle, where he was Director of the Academy of Music until deafness forced him to retire in 1841. He was content to compose almost nothing but songs, and it is on these – there are over three hundred – that his reputation rests. His favourite poets were Heine (sixty-seven settings), Osterwald (fifty-one), Lenau (eighteen), Eichendorff and Geibel (thirteen). There are also seven Goethe Lieder – 'Gleich und gleich' (see WOLF), composed in 1870, and the six songs of Op. 33 (1864), which include not only 'Wonne der Wehmut' and 'Mailied' (see BEETHOVEN), but 'Rastlose Liebe' and 'Schweizerlied', already set by Schubert. Championed by Elisabeth Schumann, his Lieder are now rarely heard on the concert platform, possibly because his melodies are considered too foursquare and the keyrelationships too unadventurous. In a letter to Liszt, written in 1855, Franz wrote: „Meine Lieder sollen nicht erregen, sie sollen Frieden und Versöhnung geben." ('My Lieder are not meant to arouse, but create peace and reconciliation') – something which the more successful songs undoubtedly achieve. He was greatly admired by Schumann, while Brahms urged Julius Stockhausen, the finest Lieder singer of the era, to include Franz's songs in his recitals.

Ferdinand von Freiligrath (1810–76)

See Liszt

1860 Mutter, o sing mich zur Ruh / Mother, oh sing me to sleep Op. 10, no. 3

Mutter, o sing mich zur Ruh,	Mother, oh sing me to sleep,
Wie noch in schöneren Stunden,	As you did in more beautiful times,
Sing meinem Herzen, dem wunden,	Sing to my heart, my wounded heart,
Tröstende Lieder sing du!	Sing your comforting songs!
Drücke die Augen mir zu!	Close my eyes!
Blumen die Häupter jetzt neigen;	Flowers are now drooping their heads;
Trauernde rasten und schweigen,	Those who grieve now rest and fall silent,
Mutter, o sing mich zur Ruh!	Mother, oh sing me to sleep!
Bette dein Vögelchen du!	Put your fledgling to bed,
Stürme, ach! haben's entfiedert;	Storms, alas, have unfeathered it;
Liebe, sie drückt unerwidert;	Love, unrequited, oppresses it;
Mutter, o sing mich zur Ruh!	Mother, oh sing me to sleep!

Heinrich Heine (1797–1856)

See Mendelssohn, Robert Schumann, Wolf

1845 Aus meinen großen Schmerzen / Out of my great sorrows Op. 5, no. 1

Aus meinen großen Schmerzen
Mach' ich die kleinen Lieder;
Die heben ihr klingend Gefieder
Und flattern nach ihrem Herzen.

Sie fanden den Weg zur Trauten,
Doch kommen sie wieder und klagen,
Und klagen, und wollen nicht sagen,
Was sie im Herzen schauten.
(*Lachner, Wolf*)

Out of my great sorrows
I make little songs;
They raise their resonant wings
And flutter to her heart.

They found their way to my dear one,
But they come back and lament,
Lament, and will not tell me
What they saw in her heart.

1862 Auf dem Meere / On the sea Op. 36, no. 1

Das Meer hat seine Perlen,
Der Himmel hat seine Sterne,
Aber mein Herz, mein Herz,
Mein Herz hat seine Liebe.

Groß ist das Meer und der Himmel,
Doch größer ist mein Herz,
Und schöner als Perlen und Sterne
Leuchtet und strahlt meine Liebe.

The sea has its pearls,
The heavens have their stars,
But my heart, my heart,
My heart has its love.

Great are the sea and the heavens,
But greater is my heart,
And fairer than pearls and stars
Is the radiant light of my love.

Nikolaus Lenau (1802–50)

See Robert Schumann

c.1860 Bitte / Entreaty Op. 9, no. 3

Weil' auf mir, du dunkles Auge,
Übe deine ganze Macht,
Ernste, milde, träumerische,
Unergründlich süße Nacht!

Nimm mit deinem Zauberdunkel
Diese Welt von hinnen mir,
Daß du über meinem Leben
Einsam schwebest für und für.
(*Hensel, Ives, Loewe, Orff, Reger, Vesque von Püttlingen*)

Linger on me, O dark eyes,
Exert the whole of your power,
Solemn, gentle, dreamy,
Unfathomably sweet night!

Take this world away from me
With your magic darkness,
So that you alone shall hover
Over my life for evermore.

Christoph Willibald Gluck (1714–87)

Gluck's contribution to German song – the only music he composed to German texts – is no more than a slim volume of seven short pieces, entitled *Klopstocks Oden und Lieder*. Written in the early 1770s between the composition of two reform operas (*Paride ed Elena* and *Iphigénie en Aulide*), these settings all remain true to the principle that Gluck had applied to his operas: that music should be an obedient servant to the poetry, renouncing all coloratura extravagancies, playful frills and paralysing repetitions of words, in favour of a concise musical line. No song illustrates this concept better than 'Die frühen Gräber', which Klopstock, who had become a close friend of the composer, once asked Gluck's adopted niece Marianne to sing. 'Das kann sie noch nicht!' ('She's not yet able to!'), Gluck exclaimed, and proceeded to sing the beautiful melody 'mit seiner rauhen Stimme, aber allerdings mit unnachahmlichem Vortrag ('with a rough voice but inimitable delivery') [Anton Schmid: *Gluck*, Leipzig 1854]. Like Mozart a decade later, Gluck at the end of his life felt a need to set his own language to music, as we see from a letter he wrote in 1780 to Herzog Karl-August von Sachsen-Weimar:

> Ich bin nun einmal sehr alt geworden, und habe der französischen Nation die mehreste Kräfte meines Geistes verschleudert, dessen ungeachtet empfinde ich in mir einen innerlichen Trieb Etwas vor meine Nation zu verfertigen.

> I have now grown very old, and have squandered the greatest part of my intellect on the French nation; nonetheless I feel an inner impulse to compose something for my own nation.

Friedrich Gottlieb Klopstock (1724–1803)

See Schubert

?1775 Die frühen Gräber / The early graves

Willkommen, o silberner Mond,	Welcome, O silver moon,
Schöner, stiller Gefährt der Nacht!	Lovely, tranquil companion of night!

Du entfliehst? Eile nicht, bleibe, Gedanken-
    freund!
	You flee? Do not hasten away, stay, friend to
	    thought!

Sehet, er bleibt, das Gewölk wallte nur hin.	Look, she stays, the clouds alone moved on.
Des Maies Erwachen ist nur	Only May's awakening
Schöner noch wie die Sommernacht,	Is lovelier still than the summer night,

Wenn ihm Tau, hell wie Licht, aus der Locke
    träuft,
	When dew, bright as light, drips from his
	    locks,

Und zu dem Hügel herauf rötlich er kommt.	As he rises red above the hill.

Ihr Edleren, ach, es bewächst	You nobler spirits, alas, gloomy moss
Eure Male schon ernstes Moos!	Already grows on your monuments!
O, wie war glücklich ich, als ich noch mit euch	Ah, how happy I was when, still with you, I could
Sahe sich röten den Tag, schimmern die Nacht.	Watch the day dawn and the night shimmer.
(*Hensel, Krenek, Schubert*)	

?1775 Die Sommernacht* / The summer night

Wenn der Schimmer von dem Monde nun herab	When the shimmering moon sheds its light
In die Wälder sich ergießt und Gerüche	Down into the woods, and fragrances
Mit den Düften von der Linde	And lime tree scents
In den Kühlungen wehn;	Float through the coolness;
So umschatten mich Gedanken an das Grab	Thoughts of my beloved's grave cast a shadow
Der Geliebten, und ich seh in dem Walde	Round me, and I merely see the woods
Nur es dämmern, und es weht mir	Darken, and no blossom
Von der Blüte nicht her.	Blows in my direction.
Ich genoß einst, o ihr Toten, es mit euch!	Once, O dead ones, I enjoyed this with you!
Wie umwehten uns der Duft und die Kühlung,	How the fragrance and coolness wafted round us,
Wie verschönt warst von dem Monde	How the moon increased your loveliness,
Du, o schöne Natur!	Lovely nature!
(*Hensel, Schubert*)	

* The poem was written in memory of Klopstock's wife, Meta Moller, who died in childbirth in 1758.

Edvard Grieg (1843–1907)

The songs of Edvard Grieg – there are some 180 of them, set for the most part to Norwegian, Danish and German texts – were all written for the composer's wife Nina, whose style of singing, according to the Danish baritone Julius Steenberg, resembled that of 'animated dramatic recitative'. As Grieg himself put it in a letter, dated 17 July 1900, to his American biographer Henry T. Finck:

> I don't think I have a greater talent for composing songs than for any other musical genre. Why, then, have songs played such a prominent role in my music? Quite simply because I, like other mortals, was (to use Goethe's phrase) once in my life endowed with *Genie*. And that flash of genius was: love. I loved a young woman with a marvellous voice and an equally marvellous gift as an interpreter. This woman became my wife and has remained my life's companion to this day. She has been, I can truly say, the only true interpreter of my songs . . . My songs came to life naturally and through a necessity like that of a natural law, and all of them were written for her.

The six songs of Op. 48 were published in 1889, the first time since the Op. 4 songs of 1864 that Grieg had used German texts.

1884–1889 *Seks Sange / Six songs* **Op. 48**

1
Gruß / Greeting
See Mendelssohn, p. 229

2
Dereinst, Gedanke mein / One day, my thoughts
See Wolf, p. 674

3
Lauf der Welt / The way of the world
LUDWIG UHLAND (1787–1862)

An jedem Abend geh' ich aus,	Every evening I go out,
Hinauf den Wiesensteg.	Up the meadow path.
Sie schaut aus ihrem Gartenhaus,	She looks out from her summer house,
Es stehet hart am Weg.	Which stands close by the road.
Wir haben uns noch nie bestellt,	We've never planned a rendezvous,
Es ist nur so der Lauf der Welt.	It's just the way of the world.
Ich weiß nicht, wie es so geschah,	I don't know how it came about,
Seit lange küss' ich sie,	For a long time I've been kissing her,
Ich bitte nicht, sie sagt nicht: ja!	I don't ask, she doesn't say yes!

Doch sagt sie: nein! auch nie.
Wenn Lippe gern auf Lippe ruht,
Wir hindern's nicht, uns dünkt es gut.

Das Lüftchen mit der Rose spielt,
Es fragt nicht: hast mich lieb?
Das Röschen sich am Taue kühlt,
Es sagt nicht lange: gib!
Ich liebe sie, sie liebet mich,
Doch keines sagt: ich liebe dich!
(*Hensel*)

But neither does she ever say no!
When lips are pleased to rest on lips,
We don't prevent it, it just seems good.

The little breeze plays with the rose,
It doesn't ask: do you love me?
The rose cools itself with dew,
It doesn't dream of saying: give!
I love her, she loves me,
But neither says: I love you!

4

Die verschwiegene Nachtigall / The secretive nightingale
WALTHER VON DER VOGELWEIDE (1170–*c*.1230)

Unter den Linden,
An der Haide,
Wo ich mit meinem Trauten saß,
Da mögt ihr finden,
Wie wir beide
Die Blumen brachen und das Gras.
Vor dem Wald mit süßem Schall,
Tandaradei!
Sang im Tal die Nachtigall.

Under the lime trees
By the heath
Where I sat with my beloved,
There you may find
How both of us
Crushed the flowers and grass.
Outside the wood, with a sweet sound,
Tandaradei!
The nightingale sang in the valley.

Ich kam gegangen
Zu der Aue,
Mein Liebster kam vor mir dahin.
Ich ward empfangen
Als hehre Fraue,
Daß ich noch immer selig bin.
Ob er mir auch Küsse bot?
Tandaradei!
Seht, wie ist mein Mund so rot!

I came walking
To the meadow,
My beloved arrived before me.
I was received
As a noble lady,
Which still fills me with bliss.
Did he offer me kisses?
Tandaradei!
See how red my mouth is!

Wie ich da ruhte,
Wüßt' es einer,
Behüte Gott, ich schämte mich.
Wie mich der Gute
Herzte, keiner
Erfahre das als er und ich –
Und ein kleines Vögelein,
Tandaradei!
Das wird wohl verschwiegen sein.
(*Burgmüller, Busoni, Kienzl, Pfitzner*)

If anyone knew
How I lay there,
God forbid, I'd be ashamed.
How my darling hugged me,
No one shall know
But he and I –
And a little bird,
Tandaradei!
Who certainly won't say a word.

5

Zur Rosenzeit / Time of roses
JOHANN WOLFGANG VON GOETHE (1749–1832), FROM *Erwin und Elmire*

Ihr verblühet, süße Rosen,
Meine Liebe trug euch nicht;
Blühet, ach! dem Hoffnungslosen,
Dem der Gram die Seele bricht!

Jener Tage denk' ich trauernd,
Als ich, Engel, an dir hing,
Auf das erste Knöspchen lauernd
Früh zu meinem Garten ging;

Alle Blüten, alle Früchte
Noch zu deinen Füßen trug
Und vor deinem Angesichte
Hoffnung in dem Herzen schlug.

Ihr verblühet, süße Rosen,
Meine Liebe trug euch nicht;
Blühet, ach! dem Hoffnungslosen,
Dem der Gram die Seele bricht!
(*Hensel, Kayser, Knab, Reichardt, Schoeck*)

You fade, sweet roses,
My love did not wear you;
Ah! you bloom for one bereft of hope,
Whose soul now breaks with grief!

Sorrowfully I think of those days,
When I, my angel, set my heart on you,
And waiting for the first little bud,
Went early to my garden;

Laid all the blossoms, all the fruits
At your very feet,
With hope beating in my heart,
When you looked on me.

You fade, sweet roses,
My love did not wear you;
Ah! you bloom for one bereft of hope,
Whose soul now breaks with grief!

6

Ein Traum / A dream
FRIEDRICH VON BODENSTEDT (1819–1892)

Mir träumte einst ein schöner Traum:
Mich liebte eine blonde Maid;
Es war am grünen Waldesraum,
Es war zur warmen Frühlingszeit:

Die Knospe sprang, der Waldbach schwoll,
Fern aus dem Dorfe scholl Geläut –
Wir waren ganzer Wonne voll,
Versunken ganz in Seligkeit.

Und schöner noch als einst der Traum
Begab es sich in Wirklichkeit –
Es war am grünen Waldesraum,
Es war zur warmen Frühlingszeit:

Der Waldbach schwoll, die Knospe sprang,
Geläut erscholl vom Dorfe her –
Ich hielt dich fest, ich hielt dich lang
Und lasse dich nun nimmermehr!

I once dreamed a beautiful dream:
A blond maiden loved me,
It was in the green woodland glade,
It was in the warm springtime:

The buds bloomed, the forest stream swelled,
From the distant village came the sound of bells –
We were so full of bliss,
So lost in happiness.

And more beautiful yet than the dream,
It happened in reality,
It was in the green woodland glade,
It was in the warm springtime:

The forest stream swelled, the buds bloomed,
From the village came the sound of bells;
I held you fast, I held you long,
And now shall never let you go!

O frühlingsgrüner Waldesraum!
Du lebst in mir durch alle Zeit –
Dort ward die Wirklichkeit zum Traum,
Dort ward der Traum zur Wirklichkeit!

O woodland glade so green with spring!
You shall live in me for evermore –
There reality became a dream,
There dream became reality!

Joseph Haydn (1732–1809)

Despite Haydn's lyrical gift, the court of Esterháza hardly encouraged him to compose Lieder. Eighteenth-century musical life was dominated socially by the nobility, who commissioned operas and instrumental music, and the church, which encouraged the composition of masses and cantatas. And since contemporary movements in poetry, which so affected the Berlin school of composers such as Reichardt and Zelter, passed Haydn by, it is not surprising that he wrote so few songs. He nonetheless composed some fifty in German and English, possessed an impressive voice, and more than once sang compositions at royal parties in London.

The first volume of *Lieder für das Clavier* (1781) was criticized in 1796 by Reichardt in the 'Berliner Musikalischer Almanach' for its feeble texts: „Es ist kaum begreiflich, wie dieser große Künstler sich zur Bearbeitung solcher Reimereien herablassen konnte." ('It is scarcely conceivable how this great artist could stoop to setting such doggerel.') His seeming lack of interest in literature meant that he relied on the advice of his literary mentor, Hofrat von Greiner, who chose many of the texts that Haydn set.

Despite Haydn's alleged indifference to poetry, he expressed clear views on word setting, as a letter to his publisher Artaria, of 23 June 1781, makes clear: „Dan es fügt sich daß mancher Text eine wahre Antipatie wider den Compositor oder Compositor wider den Text hat." ('For it can happen that there exists a real antipathy between text and composer, or between composer and text.') In another letter to Artaria, dated 20 July 1781, we read:

> Diese drei Lieder sind von herrn Capellmeister Hofmann (unter uns) elendig componirt; und eben weil der Prahlhans glaubt, den Parnaß aleinig getragen zu haben, und mich bey einer gewissen großen Weld in allen Fällen zu unterdrücken sucht, hab ich die nemblichen 3 Lieder um der nemblich groß sin wolenden Weld den Unterschied zu zeigen, in die Musik gesetzt.

> These three songs ['Eine sehr gewöhnliche Geschichte', 'An Thyrsis' and 'Trost unglücklicher Liebe'] have already been set wretchedly (between ourselves) by Kapellmeister Hofmann; and since the braggart deems himself the sole conqueror of Parnassus, and seeks at every turn to diminish me in the eyes of society, I have set the same three songs to music, to let that same society hear the difference.

Haydn's greatest contribution to the history of the Lied was in the realm of comic song: 'Lob der Faulheit', 'Die zu späte Ankunft der Mutter' and 'Eine sehr gewöhnliche Geschichte' remain three of the wittiest songs in the repertoire.

Johann Wilhelm Ludwig Gleim (1719–1803)

See Beethoven

?1781 Das Leben ist ein Traum / Life is a dream Hob. XXVIa/21

Das Leben ist ein Traum!
Wir schlüpfen in die Welt und schweben
Mit jungem Zahn
Und frischem Gaum
Auf ihrem Wahn
Und ihrem Schaum,
Bis wir nicht mehr an Erde kleben:
Und dann, was ist's, was ist das Leben?
Das Leben ist ein Traum!

Das Leben ist ein Traum:
Wir lieben, uns're Herzen schlagen,
Und Herz an Herz
Gefüget kaum,
Ist Lieb' und Scherz
Ein leerer Schaum,
Ist hingeschwunden, weggetragen!
Was ist das Leben? hör' ich fragen:
Das Leben ist ein Traum!

Life is a dream!
We slip into the world and float
With young teeth
And fresh palate
On its illusions
And froth,
Till we can cling to earth no more:
And then – what is this life?
Life is a dream!

Life is a dream:
We love, our hearts throb,
And hardly has heart
Joined heart,
When love and jest,
Turn to empty bubbles,
Vanish and are borne away!
What, I hear you ask, is life?
Life is a dream!

Lorenz Leopold Haschka (1749–1827)

As Napoleon threatened Vienna, Graf von Sarau commissioned an Austrian National Anthem to rival the 'Marseillaise' that was inspiring the French troops. Haschka, a Professor of Theology, was entrusted with the task and Haydn wrote the music which received its first performance on 12 February 1797 at the Hoftheater, during the first interval in Dittersdorf's *Doctor und Apotheker*. The song was sung as the Emperor entered his box, after which the entire audience, who had received copies of it in advance, reprised it with enormous enthusiasm – to the visible discomfort of Kaiser Franz, who hated such demonstrations. Hoffmann von Fallersleben's poem, 'Deutschland, Deutschland über Alles', which later became the German national anthem, was written in 1841.

?1796–97 Gott, erhalte Franz den Kaiser / God save Franz, the Emperor Hob. XXVIa/43

Gott, erhalte Franz den Kaiser,
Unsern guten Kaiser Franz!
Lange lebe Franz der Kaiser
In des Glückes hellstem Glanz!

God save Franz the Emperor,
Our good Emperor Franz!
Long live Franz the Emperor,
May the best of fortune shine on him!

Ihm erblühen Lorbeerreiser,	Wheresoever he might tread,
Wo Er geht, zum Ehrenkranz!	Let laurels spring up as garlands!
Gott, erhalte Franz den Kaiser,	God save Franz the Emperor,
Unsern guten Kaiser Franz!	Our good Emperor Franz!
Laß von Seiner Fahnen Spitzen	Let victory and fecundity
Strahlen Sieg und Fruchtbarkeit!	Flow from his banners!
Laß in Seinem Rate sitzen	Let wisdom, shrewdness and honesty
Weisheit, Klugheit, Redlichkeit;	Dwell in his council chamber;
Und mit Seiner Hoheit Blitzen	And let justice alone hold sway
Schalten nur Gerechtigkeit!	In his Majesty's glittering presence!
Gott, erhalte Franz den Kaiser,	God save Franz the Emperor,
Unsern guten Kaiser Franz!	Our good Emperor Franz!
Ströme deiner Gaben Fülle	Pour Thy abundant gifts
Über Ihn, Sein Haus und Reich!	Over him, his dynasty and realm!
Brich der Bosheit Macht, enthülle	End the power of evil, bring to light
Jeden Schelm- und Buben-Streich!	All knavery and villainy!
Dein Gesetz sei stets Sein Wille,	May Thy law be his will,
Dieser uns Gesetzen gleich!	His will like law to us!
Gott, erhalte Franz den Kaiser,	God save Franz the Emperor,
Unsern guten Kaiser Franz!	Our good Emperor Franz!
Froh erleb Er Seinem Lande,	May he bear happy witness
Seiner Völker höchsten Flor!	To his nations in their prime,
Seh sie, Eins durch Bruder-Bande,	May he see them, united through brotherhood,
Ragen allen andern vor,	Tower above all other nations,
Und vernehme noch am Rande	And later hear beside his tomb
Später Gruft der Enkel Chor!	The choir of grandchildren sing!
Gott, erhalte Franz den Kaiser,	God save Franz the Emperor,
Unsern guten Kaiser Franz!	Our good Emperor Franz!

Gotthold Ephraim Lessing (1729–81)

Dramatist, critic and one of the sharpest minds of the Aufklärung (Enlightenment), his *Laokoon* (1766) and *Hamburgische Dramaturgie* (1767–8) had a profound influence on aesthetics. Despite Lessing's celebrated disclaimer „Ich bin weder Schauspieler noch Dichter" ('I am neither an actor nor a poet'), he wrote a number of important plays, the finest of which are *Minna von Barnhelm* (1763), *Emilia Galotti* (1772) and, above all, *Nathan der Weise* (1779), in which the character of Nathan is based on that of Moses Mendelssohn, the grandfather of Felix. Apart from Beethoven's 'Die Liebe', Haydn's 'Lob der Faulheit', Georg Henschel's 'Du Diebin mit der Rosenwange' and Karg-Elert's *Zehn Epigramme von Lessing*, his poetry has attracted no Lieder composers.

1784 Lob der Faulheit / In praise of sloth Hob. XXVIa/22

Faulheit, endlich muß ich dir
Auch ein kleines Loblied singen. –
O – – wie sau – – er – – wird es mir, – –
Dich – – nach Würden – – zu besingen!
Doch, ich will mein Bestes tun,
Nach der Arbeit ist gut ruhn.

Höchstes Gut! wer dich nur hat,
Dessen ungestörtes Leben – –
Ach! – – ich – – gähn' – – ich – – werde matt – –
Nun – – so – – magst du – – mir's vergeben,
Daß ich dich nicht singen kann;
Du verhinderst mich ja dran.

Sloth, now at last I must sing
A short hymn of praise to you. –
Oh – – how – – tir – – ing I find it, – –
To – – extol you – – as you deserve!
Still, I shall do my best,
After labour, rest is sweet.

Highest boon! Whoever has you,
His untroubled life – –
Ah! – – I – – yawn – – I – – grow weary – –
Well – – please – – forgive me – – then,
If I cannot sing your praises;
You are, you see, preventing me.

Christian Felix Weiße (1726–1804)

See Beethoven

1781 Die zu späte Ankunft der Mutter / Mother's tardy arrival Hob. XXVIa/12

Beschattet von blühenden Ästen,
Gekühlet von spielenden Westen,
Lag Rosilis am Bache hier
Und Hylas neben ihr.

Sie sangen sich scherzende Lieder,
Sie warf ihn mit Blumen, er wieder;
Sie neckte ihn, er neckte sie,
Wer weiß wie lang und wie.

Von Lenz und von Liebe gerühret,
Ward Hylas zum Küssen verführet:
Er küßte sie, er drückte sie,
Daß sie um Hülfe schrie.

Die Mutter kam eilend und fragte,
Was Hylas für Frevel hier wagte;
Die Tochter rief: Es ist geschehn!
Ihr könnt nun wieder gehn.

Shaded by blossoming branches,
Cooled by playful west winds,
Rosalis lay here by the brook
With Hylas by her side.

Playfully, they sang to each other,
Showering each other with blossom;
She teased him, he teased her,
Who knows how long or how?

Moved by love and springtime,
Hylas was tempted to steal a kiss;
He kissed her, he hugged her,
So that she cried for help.

Her mother ran up and asked
What crime Hylas was committing there;
The daughter cried out: it's all over now!
You can go away again.

1781 Eine sehr gewöhnliche Geschichte / An exceedingly common story Hob. XXVIa/4

Philint stand jüngst vor Babets Tür,
Und klopft', und rief: Ist niemand hier?
Ich bin Philint! laßt mich hinein!
Sie kam und sprach: Nein, nein!

Philint stood lately at Babette's door,
Knocking and calling: 'Is no one there?
It's me! Philint! Let me in!'
She came and answered: 'No, no!'

Er seufzt', und bat recht jämmerlich.
Nein, sagte sie, ich fürchte dich:
Es ist schon Nacht, ich bin allein;
Philint, es kann nicht sein!

Bekümmert will er wieder gehn,
Da hört er schnell den Schlüssel drehn;
Er hört: „Auf einen Augenblick!
Doch geh auch gleich zurück!"

Die Nachbarn plagt' die Neugier sehr:
Sie warteten der Wiederkehr;
Er kam auch, doch erst Morgens früh.
Ei, ei, wie lachten sie!

He sighed and pleaded most wretchedly.
'No,' said she, 'I'm afraid of you:
It's already night, I'm alone;
Philint, this cannot be!'

Distressed, he makes to go away,
But suddenly hears the key in the lock;
And a voice saying: 'Just for a moment!
Then back you go again!'

Curiosity plagued the neighbours sore:
They watched for him to reappear;
Which he did, but not till dawn,
Oh, oh, and how they laughed!

Fanny Hensel (1805–47)

Although she composed more than 250 Lieder, few of them were known during her lifetime. Both her father and brother discouraged her from publishing music, and six songs actually appeared as her brother's (Op. 8, nos. 2, 3, 12; and Op. 9, nos. 7, 10, 12). The nineteenth-century view that it was inappropriate for women of her station to write music is vividly illustrated by an anecdote told by Mendelssohn in a letter to his mother (1841): when asked by Queen Victoria to give her one of his songs to sing, Mendelssohn produced 'Italien', which the Queen, with a few wrong notes, sang 'ganz allerliebst rein, streng im Takt und recht nett im Vortrag' ('quite charmingly in strict time and tune'). When she had finished, Mendelssohn confessed that the song was by his sister. The texts to many of her songs are still, rather unfairly, better known in settings by other composers: 'Mainacht' (Brahms), 'Übern Garten durch die Lüfte' (Schumann), 'Bitte' (Franz), and 'Die frühen Gräber' (Gluck and Schubert). Perhaps her finest achievement in song are the five Lieder of Op. 10, which Felix helped to publish posthumously, possibly due to his guilt at not encouraging her sufficiently while she was alive. The final song of Op. 10, 'Bergeslust', was written one day before her untimely death, and the final two lines are inscribed on her tombstone. The quality of many of her Lieder is only now being recognized; Goethe was the poet she most favoured, but there are also many settings of Eichendorff, Heine, Hölty, Klopstock, Lenau, Tieck and Uhland.

Joseph von Eichendorff (1788–1857)

See Pfitzner, Robert Schumann, Wolf

Fanny Hensel's 'Bergeslust' sets the second half of Eichendorff's 'Durch Feld und Buchenhallen', a poem set in full by Schoeck and Reinhard Schwarz-Schilling, one of the finest composers of Eichendorff songs, in his Liederreihe, *Der wandernde Musikant*.

1847 Bergeslust / Bergeslust Op. 10, no. 5

O Lust, vom Berg zu schauen	Ah, the joy of gazing from the mountain
Weit über Wald und Strom,	Far over wood and river,
Hoch über sich den blauen	With the blue, pellucid vault of heaven
Tiefklaren Himmelsdom!	Arching overhead!
Vom Berge Vöglein fliegen	Little birds and clouds
Und Wolken so geschwind,	Fly so swiftly from the mountain,
Gedanken überfliegen	Thoughts skim past
Die Vögel und den Wind.	The birds and the wind.

Die Wolken ziehn hernieder,
Das Vöglein senkt sich gleich,
Gedanken gehn und Lieder
Fort bis ins Himmelreich.
(*Schoeck, Schwarz-Schilling*)

The clouds drift down,
The little bird plummets,
Thoughts and songs go winging on
Till they reach the kingdom of heaven.

Johann Wolfgang von Goethe (1749–1832)

See Beethoven, Brahms, Loewe, Mendelssohn, Mozart, Reichardt, Schubert, Strauss, Wolf, Zelter

Fanny, like all her family, revered the great man of German letters, and after a meeting between Goethe and the Mendelssohns in 1822, Lea Mendelssohn wrote:

> Auch gegen Fanny war er sehr gütig und herablassend; sie mußte ihm viel Bach spielen und seine von ihr komponierten Lieder gefielen ihm außerordentlich.

> He was also very kind and gracious to Fanny; she had to play him much Bach, and her own songs to his poems pleased him enormously.

When some years later in 1827 Goethe discovered through Felix that Fanny could find no poems suitable for setting to music, he sent her, via her teacher Zelter, the manuscript of 'An die Entfernte' ('Wenn ich mir in stiller Seele'), which she then set to music the following year. 'Wanderlied' is the second song of her Op. I, a setting of Goethe's poem that had appeared in the first version of *Wilhelm Meisters Wanderjahre*.

1837 Wanderlied / Song of travel Op. 1, no. 2
FROM *Wilhelm Meisters Wanderjahre*

Von den Bergen zu den Hügeln,
Niederab das Tal entlang,
Da erklingt es wie von Flügeln,
Da bewegt sich's wie Gesang.
Und dem unbedingten Triebe
Folget Freude, folget Rat,
Und dein Streben, sei's in Liebe
Und dein Leben sei die Tat.

From the mountains to the hills,
And down along the valley,
There's a sound as of wings,
A stirring as of song.
And such unconfined urges
Give rise to joy and counsel:
And may your striving be in love,
And may your life be one of deeds.

Bleibe nicht am Boden heften,
Frisch gewagt und frisch hinaus!
Kopf und Arm mit heitern Kräften,
Überall sind wir zu Haus.
Wo wir uns der Sonne freuen,
Sind wir jede Sorge los,
Daß wir uns in ihr zerstreuen,
Darum ist die Welt so groß.

Do not remain earth-bound here,
Be full of venture and explore!
With a serene mind and strong arm
We shall always find a home.
Wherever we enjoy the sun,
We are free of every care,
That we amuse ourselves on earth
Makes the world so very great.

Franz Grillparzer (1791–1872)

Austrian poet and dramatist whose plays – *Die Ahnfrau* (1817), *Sappho* (1818), *Das goldene Vließ* (1821), *König Ottokars Glück und Ende* (1825), *Ein treuer Diener seines Herrn* (1828), *Der Traum ein Leben* (1831), *Weh dem, der lügt!* (1838), *Ein Bruderzwist in Habsburg* (1850) and *Die Jüdin von Toledo* (1851) – are stilled performed today. To music lovers, Grillparzer is best known for the speech he wrote for Beethoven's funeral, the text to Schubert's delectable 'Ständchen' for solo voice and women's chorus (D920/1), and the inscription on the funeral monument at Schubert's grave: „Die Tonkunst begrub hier einen reichen Besitz, aber noch viel schönere Hoffnungen" ('The art of music has buried here a rich treasure and still far richer promise'). In 1823 Grillparzer wrote *Melusina* as a libretto for Beethoven, whom he greatly admired. Beethoven did not pursue the project, and the libretto was eventually set to music by Conradin Kreutzer.

24 August 1825 Italien / Italy Op. 8, no. 3

Schöner und schöner	The plain grows
Schmückt sich der Plan,	More and more beautiful,
Schmeichelnde Lüfte	Flattering breezes
Wehen mich an;	Blow in my face;
Fort aus der Prosa	Away from all
Lasten und Müh,	The burdens of prose,
Zieh' ich zum Lande	I fly to the land
Der Poesie;	Of poetry;
Goldner die Sonne,	The sun's more golden,
Blauer die Luft,	The air's more blue,
Grüner die Grüne,	Greens are greener,
Würz'ger der Duft.	Scents more spicy.
Dort an dem Maishalm,	There by the corn-stalk,
Schwellend von Saft,	Swelling with sap,
Sträubt sich der Aloe	The aloe bristles
Störrische Kraft.	With stubborn strength.
Ölbaum, Cypresse,	Olive-tree, cypress,
Blond du, du braun,	Now blond, now brown,
Nickt ihr wie zierliche,	Do you greet us
Grüßende Fraun?	Like graceful ladies?
Was glänzt im Laube,	What gleams among leaves,
Funkelnd wie Gold?	Sparkling like gold?
Ha, Pomeranze,	Ah, pomegranate,
Birgst du dich hold!	How sweetly you hide!

Trotz'ger Poseidon,*
Warest du dies,
Der unten scherzt und
Murmelt so süß?

Und dies halb Wiese, halb
Äther zu schaun,
Es war des Meeres
Furchtbares Graun?

Hier will ich wohnen!
Göttliche, du,
Bringst du, Parthenope,†
Wogen zur Ruh?

Nun dann versuch es,
Eden der Lust,
Ebne die Wogen
Auch dieser Brust!

Defiant Neptune,
Was it you who,
Joking below,
Murmured so sweetly?

And this, half meadow
And half ether to the eye,
Was this the ocean's
Fearsome horror?

Here is where I wish to dwell!
Divine Parthenope,
Can you lull
Waves to rest?

Try then now,
O Eden of delight,
To smooth the waves
Of this breast too!

* Greek God of the sea.
† One of the Sirens.

Paul Hindemith (1895–1963)

The setting of words occupied Hindemith throughout his artistic life. Between 1919 and 1922 he composed the three early one-act 'anti-operas' (*Mörder, Hoffnung der Frauen; Das Nusch-Nuschi* and *Sancta Susanna*). The eight *Lieder* of Op. 18 date from 1920, and the *Nine English Songs* from 1942: settings of Herrick, Shelley, Blake, Whitman, composed in exile after the Nazis had taken exception to his anti-totalitarian *Mathis der Maler* (1934) and branded his music 'degenerate'. For a long time it was assumed that he composed no Lieder in the late twenties and thirties, but a large number of songs were found after his death, including six Hölderlin settings: 'Sonnenuntergang', 'Ehemals und jetzt', 'Des Morgens', 'Abendphantasie', 'Fragment' and 'An die Parzen'. The best-known of Hindemith's eighty Lieder are the two cycles, *Die junge Magd*, to poems by Georg Trakl, and *Das Marienleben*, which sets Rilke's work on the life of the Virgin. *Die junge Magd*, which describes how a brutal blacksmith's apprentice seduces a young farm maid who dies as she gives birth to his child, was composed in four days in 1922, and is scored for alto, flute, clarinet and string quartet (Hindemith was a fine viola player and gave the first performance of William Walton's viola concerto in 1929). The first song with its instrumental introduction is the last piece in Hindemith's œuvre which has a key signature. A year later he had moved further away from traditional tonality when he composed *Das Marienleben* – the original version, with its taxingly low tessitura for the soprano, never satisfied the composer, who continued to revise the cycle. In 1938 he made an orchestral version of 'Geburt Mariä', 'Argwohn Josephs', 'Geburt Christi' and 'Rast auf der Flucht nach Ägypten'; and in 1948, twenty-four years after the original version, he completely revised the work in an attempt to make it less 'atonal' and more singable. Only one song, 'Stillung Mariä mit dem Auferstandenen' was left untouched. In the preface to the new edition he explained what he called his 'System tonal-emotioneller-gedanklicher Bezogenheiten' ('system of tonal-emotional-intellectual relations': the tonality of E denotes Christ, the Virgin is depicted by the dominant tonality B, while the subdominant tonality A represents the divine.

Rainer Maria Rilke (1875–1926)

Rilke's first volume of poetry, *Leben und Lieder* appeared in 1894, followed by *Larenopfer* (1896) and *Traumgekrönt* (1897). *Die Weise von Liebe und Tod des Cornets Christoph Rilke* (1903) – set by Frank Martin and Viktor Ullmann – describes the death in action of Cornet Rilke of Langenau, from whose ancestral line Rilke claimed he was descended. With Lou Andreas-Salomé he undertook two journeys to Russia, where he was greatly impressed by the spirituality and simplicity of the

Russian people – a mood captured in *Das Stunden-Buch*, purportedly written by a Russian monk. Rilke hoped to capture the spiritual essence of Russian life in Worpswede, where from 1900–1902 he joined a colony of artists. His marriage to Clara Westhoff proved a failure but enabled him to meet her teacher, Auguste Rodin, with whom he stayed for a great part of the period between 1902 to 1906, and on whom he wrote a monograph. The sentimentality of *Das Stunden-Buch* is largely absent from *Das Buch der Bilder* (1902) which contains such celebrated poems as 'Herbsttag' and 'Herbst' (both beautifully set by the Swiss composer Conrad Beck), and had vanished completely by the time he published the two volumes of *Neue Gedichte* (1907–08), a work which, following the example of Rodin, shows a wonderful unity of form and content. Supported financially by friends and well-wishers, Rilke spent some time in Scandinavia, Spain and at Duino Castle in Dalmatia, where in 1912 he began his most famous work, the *Duineser Elegien* (published 1923). It was also at Duino, in January 1912, that he wrote with great rapidity most of *Das Marien-Leben*, the idea for which had been provided by the Worpswede painter, Heinrich Vogeler, who had shown him sketches of an *Annunciation* and a *Rest on the Flight into Egypt* which inspired the first two *Marien-Leben* poems that Rilke wrote. The fifteen poems of the cycle represent those moments in the life of the Virgin that are traditionally represented in painting. When in 1922 a Swiss patron placed Muzot Castle at Rilke's disposal, the poet moved in and wrote within three weeks the two groups of *Die Sonette an Orpheus* and the remaining five *Duineser Elegien*.

1922–23 *Das Marienleben / The life of the Virgin Mary* Op. 27
REVISED 1936–48

1

Geburt Mariae / Birth of Mary

O was muß es die Engel gekostet haben,
nicht aufzusingen plötzlich, wie man aufweint,
da sie doch wußten: in dieser Nacht wird
    dem Knaben
die Mutter geboren, dem Einen, der bald
    erscheint.

Schwingend verschwiegen sie sich und
    zeigten die Richtung,
wo, allein, das Gehöft lag des Joachim,
ach, sie fühlten in sich und im Raum die
    reine Verdichtung,
aber es durfte keiner nieder zu ihm.

Denn die beiden waren schon so außer sich
    vor Getue.

Oh, what must it have cost the angels
not suddenly to burst out singing, as one
    bursts into tears,
knowing that: this night the mother would
    be born
for the boy, for Him now soon to appear.

Soaring, they kept silent and showed the
    direction,
where, alone, Joachim's farm was to be found,
ah, they felt within them and in space the
    pure creation,
but not one of them could descend to him.

For the two were quite beside themselves
    with commotion.

Eine Nachbarin kam und klugte und wußte
   nicht wie,
und der Alte, vorsichtig, ging und verhielt
   das Gemuhe
einer dunkelen Kuh. Denn so war es noch
   nie.

A neighbour came and acted wise but had no
   idea,
and the old man cautiously went and
   restrained the mooing
of a dark cow. For things had never been like
   this.

2

Die Darstellung Mariae im Tempel / Presentation of Mary in the Temple

Um zu begreifen, wie sie damals war,
mußt du dich erst an eine Stelle rufen,
wo Säulen in dir wirken; wo du Stufen
nachfühlen kannst; wo Bogen voll Gefahr
den Abgrund eines Raumes überbrücken,
der in dir blieb, weil er aus solchen Stücken
getürmt war, daß du sie nicht mehr aus dir
ausheben kannst: du rissest dich denn ein.
Bist du so weit, ist alles in dir Stein,
Wand, Aufgang, Durchblick, Wölbung –, so
   probier
den großen Vorhang, den du vor dir hast,
ein wenig wegzuzerrn mit beiden Händen:
da glänzt es von ganz hohen Gegenständen
und übertrifft dir Atem und Getast.
Hinauf, hinab, Palast steht auf Palast,
Geländer strömen breiter aus Geländern
und tauchen oben auf an solchen Rändern,
daß dich, wie du sie siehst, der Schwindel
   faßt.
Dabei macht ein Gewölk aus Räucherstän-
   dern
die Nähe trüb; aber das Fernste zielt
in dich hinein mit seinen graden Strahlen –,
und wenn jetzt Schein aus klaren Flammen-
   schalen
auf langsam nahenden Gewändern spielt:
wie hältst du's aus?

Sie aber kam und hob
den Blick, um dieses alles anzuschauen.
(Ein Kind, ein kleines Mädchen zwischen
   Frauen.)
Dann stieg sie ruhig, voller Selbstvertrauen,
dem Aufwand zu, der sich verwöhnt verschob:
So sehr war alles, was die Menschen bauen,
schon überwogen von dem Lob
in ihrem Herzen. Von der Lust

To understand how she was at that time,
you must first summon yourself to a place
where columns work within you; where you
can feel steps; where arches full of danger
span the chasm of a space
which remained in you, because it towered up
from fragments you could no longer
lift: unless you collapsed in ruins.
With this achieved, when all in you is stone,
wall, stairway, vista, vaulting – try
with both hands to pull aside a little
the great curtain before your eyes:
a radiance now falls from highly exalted objects,
overwhelming your breathing and sense of
   touch.
Above and below, palace sees palace,
balustrades stream broader out of balustrades
and re-emerge above on such ledges
that you, in beholding them, are seized with
   vertigo.
Clouds from incense-burners meanwhile
dim the foreground; but what is furthest
   directs
at you its unswerving rays –
and if now the gleam from bowls of bright
   torches
plays on dresses that gradually draw near:
how can you endure it?

She, however, came and raised
her eyes to take in all this scene.
(A child, a small girl among women.)
Then she ascended calmly, fully confident,
towards the pomp which, pampered, moved
   aside:
so very much was all that men build
already outweighed by the praise
in her heart. By her longing

sich hinzugeben an die innern Zeichen:
Die Eltern meinten, sie hinaufzureichen,
der Drohende mit der Juwelenbrust
empfing sie scheinbar: Doch sie ging durch alle,
klein wie sie war, aus jeder Hand hinaus
und in ihr Los, das, höher als die Halle,
schon fertig war, und schwerer als das Haus.

to surrender herself to the inner signs:
her parents thought they were presenting her,
the threatening one with the jewelled breast
apparently received her: yet she walked
    through all,
small as she was, away from every hand
and into her destiny which, loftier than the hall,
already was prepared, and heavier than the
    house.

3
Mariae Verkündigung / The Annunciation

Nicht daß ein Engel eintrat (das erkenn),
erschreckte sie. Sowenig andre, wenn
ein Sonnenstrahl oder der Mond bei Nacht
in ihrem Zimmer sich zu schaffen macht,
auffahren –, pflegte sie an der Gestalt,
in der ein Engel ging, sich zu entrüsten;
sie ahnte kaum, daß dieser Aufenthalt
mühsam für Engel ist. (O wenn wir wüßten,
wie rein sie war. Hat eine Hirschkuh nicht,
die, liegend, einmal sie im Wald eräugte,
sich so in sie versehn, daß sich in ihr,
ganz ohne Paarigen, das Einhorn zeugte,
das Tier aus Licht, das reine Tier –.)
Nicht, daß er eintrat, aber daß er dicht,
der Engel, eines Jünglings Angesicht
so zu ihr neigte; daß sein Blick und der,
mit dem sie aufsah, so zusammenschlugen
als wäre draußen plötzlich alles leer
und, was Millionen schauten, trieben, trugen,
hineingedrängt in sie: nur sie und er;
Schaun und Geschautes, Aug und Augenweide
sonst nirgends als an dieser Stelle – : sieh,
dieses erschreckt. Und sie erschraken beide.

Dann sang der Engel seine Melodie.

It wasn't an angel entering (understand),
that frightened her. No more than others start,
when sunbeam at night or moon
flit about their room, was she wont to be
    shocked
at the shape which an angel had assumed;
little did she suspect that dwelling on earth
is difficult for angels. (Oh, if we knew
how pure she was. Did not a hind,
lying recumbent and seeing her once in a wood,
become so rapt in beholding her,
that, quite without mate, the unicorn was born,
that creature of light and of purity?)
No, not the angel's entering, but rather
because the angel's youthful countenance
inclined so close; that his gaze and hers,
as she looked up, so mingled,
as though all things outside were suddenly void
and, that which millions see and do,
was compressed into them: only he and she;
beholder and beheld, eye and eye's delight,
nowhere else but in this place – O see,
it is this that terrifies. And both were terrified.

Then the angel sang his melody.

4
Mariae Heimsuchung / Visitation of the Virgin

Noch erging sie's leicht im Anbeginne,
doch im Steigen manchmal ward sie schon
ihres wunderbaren Leibes inne, –
und dann stand sie, atmend, auf den hohn

She still walked easily at first,
yet sometimes, climbing, she became
aware of her wondrous body –
and then, pausing for breath, she stood on
    the high

Judenbergen. Aber nicht das Land,
ihre Fülle war um sie gebreitet;
gehend fühlte sie: man überschreitet
nie die Größe, die sie jetzt empfand.

Und es drängte sie, die Hand zu legen
auf den andern Leib, der weiter war.
Und die Frauen schwankten sich entgegen
und berührten sich Gewand und Haar.

Jede, voll von ihrem Heiligtume,
schützte sich mit der Gevatterin.
Ach der Heiland in ihr war noch Blume,
doch den Täufer in dem Schooß der Muhme
riß die Freude schon zum Hüpfen hin.

5

Argwohn Josephs / Joseph's mistrust

Und der Engel sprach und gab sich Müh
an dem Mann, der seine Fäuste ballte:
Aber siehst du nicht an jeder Falte,
daß sie kühl ist wie die Gottesfrüh.

Doch der andre sah ihn finster an,
murmelnd nur: Was hat sie so verwandelt?
Doch da schrie der Engel: Zimmermann,
merkst du's noch nicht, daß der Herrgott
  handelt?

Weil du Bretter machst, in deinem Stolze,
willst du wirklich *den* zu Rede stelln,
der bescheiden aus dem gleichen Holze
Blätter treiben macht und Knospen schwelln?

Er begriff. Und wie er jetzt die Blicke,
recht erschrocken, zu dem Engel hob,
war der fort. Da schob er seine dicke
Mütze langsam ab. Dann sang er lob.

6

Verkündigung über den Hirten / Annunciation over the shepherds

Seht auf, ihr Männer. Männer dort am Feuer,
die ihr den grenzenlosen Himmel kennt,
Sterndeuter, hierher! Seht, ich bin ein neuer
steigender Stern. Mein ganzes Wesen brennt
und strahlt so stark und ist so ungeheuer
voll Licht, daß mir das tiefe Firmament

hills of Judea. But it was not the land
that spread around her, but her fullness;
walking, she felt: the greatness
she now knew would never be surpassed.

And she felt the need to lay her hand
on the other body that was further.
And the women swayed to one another
and touched each other's dress and hair.

Each one, filled with what was sacred to her,
used her kinswoman as a shield.
Ah, the Saviour in her was still a bud,
but the Baptist was so transported
that he leapt in her cousin's womb.

And the angel spoke and took pains
with the man who clenched his fists:
but can you not tell by every fold
that she is as fresh as God's dawn?

But the other looked at him darkly,
and merely murmured: what changed her
  so?
But at that the angel cried: carpenter,
can you still not detect the hand of God?

Because you fashion planks, in your pride,
will you really take *Him* to task,
who modestly from that same wood
causes leaves to grow and buds to swell?

He understood. And as he now lifted up
to the angel his truly frightened gaze,
the angel was gone. Slowly he shoved
the hat from his head. Then he sang praise.

Look up, you men, you men round the fire,
who are acquainted with the boundless sky,
astrologers, look this way! Behold, I am a new
rising star. My whole being burns
and shines forth so strongly and is filled
with such vast light, that the deep firmament

nicht mehr genügt. Laßt meinen Glanz hinein
in euer Dasein: Oh, die dunklen Blicke,
die dunklen Herzen, nächtige Geschicke
die euch erfüllen. Hirten, wie allein
bin ich in euch. Auf einmal wird mir Raum.
Stauntet ihr nicht: der große Brotfruchtbaum
warf einen Schatten. Ja, das kam von mir.
Ihr Unerschrockenen, o wüßtet ihr,
wie jetzt auf eurem schauenden Gesichte
die Zukunft scheint. In diesem starken Lichte
wird viel geschehen. Euch vertrau ichs, denn
ihr seid verschwiegen; euch Gradgläubigen
redet hier alles. Glut und Regen spricht,
der Vögel Zug, der Wind und was ihr seid,
keins überwiegt und wächst zur Eitelkeit
sich mästend an. Ihr haltet nicht
die Dinge auf im Zwischenraum der Brust
um sie zu quälen. So wie seine Lust
durch einen Engel strömt, so treibt durch euch
das Irdische. Und wenn ein Dorngesträuch
aufflammte plötzlich, dürfte noch aus ihm
der Ewige euch rufen, Cherubim,
wenn sie geruhten neben eurer Herde
einherzuschreiten, wunderten euch nicht:
ihr stürztet euch auf euer Angesicht,
betetet an und nenntet dies die Erde.

Doch dieses war. Nun soll ein Neues sein,
von dem der Erdkreis ringender sich weitet.
Was ist ein Dörnicht uns: Gott fühlt sich ein
in einer Jungfrau Schooß. Ich bin der Schein
von ihrer Innigkeit, der euch geleitet.

suffices me no more. Let my radiance
enter your existence: ah, the dark glances,
the dark hearts, nocturnal fates
that fill you. Shepherds, how solitary
I am in you. Suddenly I have space.
You did not marvel: the great bread-fruit tree
cast a shadow. Yes, that came from me.
You fearless ones, if only you knew
how on your gazing faces
the future now shines. Much will happen
in this powerful light. I confide this to you, for
you are discreet; everyone here
speaks to you upright believers. Heat and rain speak,
birds in flight, the wind and what you are,
none prevails or, glutting themselves,
grows vain. You do not hold
things back in the breast's interstice
in order to torment them. Just as his rapture
streams through an angel, so earthly things
rush through you. And if a thorn-bush
were suddenly to flare, the Eternal One might still
summon you; cherubim, if they deigned
to walk beside your flock, would not surprise
    you:
you would fall on your faces,
worship and call this earth.

But this has been. Now new things shall be,
by which the world will strive to spread wider wings.
What is a thorn-bush to us: God feels His way
into a virgin's womb. I am the gleam
of her inwardness, which leads you on.

7

Geburt Christi / Birth of Christ

Hättest du der Einfalt nicht, wie sollte
dir geschehn, was jetzt die Nacht erhellt?
Sieh, der Gott, der über Völkern grollte,
macht sich mild und kommt in dir zur Welt.

Hast du dir ihn größer vorgestellt?

Was ist Größe? Quer durch alle Maße,
die er durchstreicht, geht sein grades Los.
Denn ein Stern hat keine solche Straße.
Siehst du, diese Könige sind groß,

und sie schleppen dir vor deinen Schooß

Had you not been simple, how could this
have befallen you, which now illumines the night?
Behold, God who vented his wrath on nations,
grows mild and descends, in you, to the world.

Did you imagine Him greater?

What is greatness? Across all dimensions
runs His unswerving destiny.
Even a star treads no such path.
Behold, these kings are great,

and they drag treasures and place them

Schätze, die sie für die größten halten,
und du staunst vielleicht bei dieser Gift – :
aber schau in deines Tuches Falten,
wie er jetzt schon alles übertrifft.

Aller Amber, den man weit verschifft,

jeder Goldschmuck und das Luftgewürze,
das sich trübend in die Sinne streut:
alles dieses war von rascher Kürze,
und am Ende hat man es bereut.

Aber (du wirst sehen): Er erfreut.

in your lap, the greatest treasures they know,
and you maybe marvel at these gifts –
but see how, in the folds of your shawl,
he already surpasses all.

All the amber shipped afar,

all gold ornaments and aromatic spices,
that blur and daze the mind:
all this was of brief duration,
and in the end a matter of regret.

But he (as you shall see): brings joy.

8

Rast auf der Flucht in Ägypten / Rest on the flight into Egypt

Diese, die noch eben atemlos
flohen mitten aus dem Kindermorden:
o wie waren sie unmerklich groß
über ihrer Wanderschaft geworden.

Kaum noch daß im scheuen Rückwärtsschauen
ihres Schreckens Not zergangen war,
und schon brachten sie auf ihrem grauen
Maultier ganze Städte in Gefahr;

denn so wie sie, klein im großen Land,
– fast ein Nichts – den starken Tempeln
    nahten,
platzten alle Götzen wie verraten
und verloren völlig den Verstand.

Ist es denkbar, daß von ihrem Gange
alles so verzweifelt sich erbost?
und sie wurden vor sich selber bange,
nur das Kind war namenlos getrost.

Immerhin, sie mußten sich darüber
eine Weile setzen. Doch da ging –
sieh: der Baum, der still sie überhing,
wie ein Dienender zu ihnen über:

er verneigte sich. Derselbe Baum,
dessen Kränze toten Pharaonen
für das Ewige die Stirnen schonen,
neigte sich. Er fühlte neue Kronen
blühen. Und sie saßen wie im Traum.

These who, breathless, even now
were fleeing from the massacre of children:
ah, how imperceptibly great
they had grown on their journey.

Scarcely had their timid looking back
dissolved their horror's worst extremity,
than they brought, on their grey
mule, danger to entire cities;

for when they, small in the vast region,
– nothing almost – came near the strong
    temples,
all idols burst, as if betrayed,
and wholly lost their reason.

Is it conceivable that, as they passed,
all were so desperately enraged?
And they grew afraid of themselves,
the child alone being ineffably at ease.

Nonetheless, they had to sit
and ponder this. But then –
see: the tree that silently bent over them,
went up to them like a serving man:

bowed low. The same tree,
whose wreaths protect the brows
of dead pharaohs everlastingly,
bowed low. Felt new crowns
bloom. And they sat as in a dream.

Von der Hochzeit zu Kana / Of the marriage at Cana

Konnte sie denn anders, als auf ihn
stolz sein, der ihr Schlichtestes verschönte?
War nicht selbst die hohe, großgewöhnte
Nacht wie außer sich, da er erschien?

Ging nicht auch, daß er sich einst verloren,
unerhört zu seiner Glorie aus?
Hatten nicht die Weisesten die Ohren
mit dem Mund vertauscht? Und war das Haus

nicht wie neu von seiner Stimme? Ach
sicher hatte sie zu hundert Malen
ihre Freude an ihm auszustrahlen
sich verwehrt. Sie ging ihm staunend nach.

Aber da bei jenem Hochzeitsfeste,
als es unversehns an Wein gebrach, –
sah sie hin und bat um eine Geste
und begriff nicht, daß er widersprach.

Und dann tat er's. Sie verstand es später,
wie sie ihn in seinen Weg gedrängt:
denn jetzt war er wirklich Wundertäter,
und das ganze Opfer war verhängt,

unaufhaltsam. Ja, es stand geschrieben.
Aber war es damals schon bereit?
Sie: sie hatte es herbeigetrieben
in der Blindheit ihrer Eitelkeit.

An dem Tisch voll Früchten und Gemüsen
freute sie sich mit und sah nicht ein,
daß das Wasser ihrer Tränendrüsen
Blut geworden war mit diesem Wein.

Could she be other than proud of him,
who beautified all that was simplest in her?
Was not the lovely, vast-accustomed night
as though beside itself when he appeared?

That he had once lost himself, did that not add
unprecedentedly to his renown?
And did not the wisest change ears
into mouths? And did the house

not seem new, as his voice rang out? Ah,
certainly a hundred times
she must have kept her joy in him
from shining forth. Marvelling, she followed him.

But then at the marriage feast,
when unexpectedly the wine ran out –
she looked and begged for a sign
and did not understand that he protested.

And then he did it. She understood later
how she had thrust him on his way:
for now he'd become a true miracle-maker,
and the whole sacrifice was pre-ordained

unalterably. Yes, it was written.
But was it at that time prepared already?
It was she who had driven on the deed
in the blindness of her vanity.

At the table, heaped with fruits and vegetables,
she shared the joy and was not aware
that the water from her own tear-ducts
had with this wine been turned to blood.

10

Vor der Passion / Before the Passion

O hast du dies gewollt, du hättest nicht
durch eines Weibes Leib entspringen dürfen:
Heilande muß man in den Bergen schürfen,
wo man das Harte aus dem Harten bricht.

Tut dirs nicht selber leid, dein liebes Tal
so zu verwüsten? Siehe meine Schwäche;
ich habe nichts als Milch- und Tränenbäche,
und du warst immer in der Überzahl.

Oh, had this been your will, you would not
have sprung from a woman's body.
Men should quarry saviours from the mountains
where they hew the hard from the hard.

Does it not make you sad to ravage
your own dear valley? See how weak I am;
I have nothing but streams of milk and tears,
and you were always there excessively.

Mit solchem Aufwand wardst du mir verheißen.
Was tratst du nicht gleich wild aus mir hinaus?
Wenn du nur Tiger brauchst, dich zu zerreißen,
warum erzog man mich im Frauenhaus,

ein weiches reines Kleid für dich zu weben,
darin nicht einmal die geringste Spur
von Naht dich drückt – : so war mein ganzes
    Leben,
und jetzt verkehrst du plötzlich die Natur.

You were promised me with such pomp.
Why did you not run wild from me at once?
If all you need is tigers to tear you apart,
why was I reared in the woman's house,

to weave for you a soft and pure dress,
with not so much as a trace of seam
to press on you –: such was my whole
    life,
and nature is suddenly overthrown by you.

11
Pietà / Pietà

Jetzt wird mein Elend voll, und namenlos
erfüllt es mich. Ich starre wie des Steins
Inneres starrt.
Hart wie ich bin, weiß ich nur Eins:
Du wurdest groß –
...... und wurdest groß,
um als zu großer Schmerz
ganz über meines Herzens Fassung
hinauszustehn.
Jetzt liegst du quer durch meinen Schooß,
jetzt kann ich dich nicht mehr
gebären.

Now is my misery complete, and namelessly
it fills me. I stare as a stone's
essence stares.
Hard as I am, I know but one thing:
you grew –
...... and grew,
in order to stand out
as too much pain
and quite beyond my heart's composure.
Now straight across my lap you lie,
now I can no longer
give you birth.

12
Stillung Mariae mit dem Auferstandenen / Consolation of Mary with the risen Christ

Was sie damals empfanden: ist es nicht
vor allen Geheimnissen süß
und immer noch irdisch:
da er, ein wenig blaß noch vom Grab,
erleichtert zu ihr trat:
an allen Stellen erstanden.
O zu ihr zuerst. Wie waren sie da
unaussprechlich in Heilung.
Ja sie heilten, das war's. Sie hatten nicht nötig,
sich stark zu berühren.
Er legte ihr eine Sekunde
kaum seine nächstens
ewige Hand an die frauliche Schulter.
Und sie begannen
still wie die Bäume im Frühling,
unendlich zugleich,
diese Jahreszeit
ihres äußersten Umgangs.

What they perceived then: is it not
sweet above all secrets
and still of this earth:
when he, still a little pale from the grave,
came to her with diminished suffering:
risen in all places.
Oh, first to her. How ineffable
they were in healing.
Yes, they were healing, that was it. They had
    no need
to touch each other firmly.
For a second he laid,
but only just, his soon to be eternal hand
on the woman's shoulder.
And they began,
still as trees in Spring,
endlessly together,
this season of their extremest communing.

Vom Tode Mariae

DREI STÜCKE / THREE PIECES

i

Derselbe große Engel, welcher einst	The same mighty angel, who had once
ihr der Gebärung Botschaft niederbrachte,	descended with tidings of her birth,
stand da, abwartend daß sie ihn beachte,	stood there, waiting for her to notice him,
und sprach: Jetzt wird es Zeit, daß du erscheinst.	and spake: Now it is time for you to appear.
Und sie erschrak wie damals und erwies	And she, as then, was terrified and was once again
sich wieder als die Magd, ihn tief bejahend.	the maid, giving profound assent.
Er aber strahlte und, unendlich nahend,	But he shone forth and, infinitely drawing near,
schwand er wie in ihr Angesicht – und hieß	vanished as though into her countenance – and called
die weithin ausgegangenen Bekehrer	the evangelists, who had gone far away,
zusammenkommen in das Haus am Hang,	to gather in the house on the hillside,
das Haus des Abendmahls. Sie kamen schwerer	the house of the Last Supper. With heavier
und traten bange ein: Da lag, entlang	step they came
die schmale Bettstatt, die in Untergang	and entered fearfully: she lay along
und Auserwählung rätselhaft Getauchte,	the narrow bedstead, bemusedly immersed
ganz unversehrt, wie eine Ungebrauchte,	in her decline and being chosen,
und achtete auf englischen Gesang.	utterly inviolate, like one unused,
Nun da sie alle hinter ihren Kerzen	and listened to the angelic song.
abwarten sah, riß sie vom Übermaß	But when she saw them all waiting
der Stimmen sich und schenkte noch von	behind their candles, she tore herself away
Herzen	from the excess of voices and, from her heart,
die beiden Kleider fort, die sie besaß,	gave as gifts the two dresses she possessed,
und hob ihr Antlitz auf zu dem und dem . . .	and lifted up her face to him and him . . .
(O Ursprung namenloser Tränen-Bäche).	(O origin of nameless streams of tears).

Sie aber legte sich in ihre Schwäche	But she now laid back in her frailty
und zog die Himmel an Jerusalem	and drew the heavens so near Jerusalem
so nah heran, daß ihre Seele nur,	that her soul needed now, for its departure,
austretend, sich ein wenig strecken mußte:	only to reach out a little further:
schon hob er sie, der alles von ihr wußte,	already he, who knew all things about her,
hinein in ihre göttliche Natur.	was lifting her into her god-like nature.

ii

Wer hat bedacht, daß bis zu ihrem Kommen	Who has considered that before her assumption
der viele Himmel unvollständig war?	manifold heaven remained incomplete?
Der Auferstandne hatte Platz genommen,	The Risen One had taken his place,
doch neben ihm, durch vierundzwanzig Jahr,	but next to him for four and twenty years
war leer der Sitz. Und sie begannen schon	the seat had been vacant. And they had begun
sich an die reine Lücke zu gewöhnen,	to grow accustomed to the pure gap,
die wie verheilt war, denn mit seinem schönen	which was as though healed, for with his fair
Hinüberscheinen füllte sie der Sohn.	radiance the Son had filled it.

So ging auch sie, die in die Himmel trat,	So, entering heaven, even she, great though
nicht auf ihn zu, so sehr es sie verlangte;	her longing was, did not go up to him;

dort war kein Platz, nur *Er* war dort und
   prangte
mit einer Strahlung, die ihr wehe tat.
Doch da sie jetzt, die rührende Gestalt,
sich zu den neuen Seligen gesellte
und unauffällig, licht zu licht, sich stellte,
da brach aus ihrem Sein ein Hinterhalt
von solchem Glanz, daß der von ihr erhellte
Engel geblendet aufschrie: Wer ist die?
Ein Staunen war. Dann sahn sie alle, wie
Gott-Vater oben unsern Herrn verhielt,
so daß, von milder Dämmerung umspielt
die leere Stelle wie ein wenig Leid
sich zeigte, eine Spur von Einsamkeit,
wie etwas, was er noch ertrug, ein Rest
irdischer Zeit, ein trockenes Gebrest – .
Man sah nach ihr; sie schaute ängstlich hin,
weit vorgeneigt, als fühlte sie: *ich bin*
sein längster Schmerz –: und stürzte plötzlich
   vor.
Die Engel aber nahmen sie zu sich
und stützten sie und sangen seliglich
und trugen sie das letzte Stück empor.

no place was there, only *He* whose glow
was so bright that it hurt her.
But when she now, that touching figure,
went and joined those who had been newly
   blessed,
and stood there unnoticed, light next to light,
a withheld glory broke from her
with such brilliance that the angel, lit by her,
cried out, dazzled: Who is she?
They marvelled. They all now saw how,
on high, God the Father restrained our Lord,
so that, lapped around by gentle twilight,
like a little sorrow, the vacant place
was revealed, a trace of solitude,
like something he still endured, a residue
of earthly time, a sere affliction –.
They looked at her: she watched anxiously,
leaning far forward, as though she felt: *I am*
his longest agony – : and suddenly fell for-
   wards.
But the angels took her to themselves
and supported her and sang blissfully
and for the remaining distance bore her up.

   iii

Doch vor dem Apostel Thomas, der
kam, da es zu spät war, trat der schnelle
längst darauf gefaßte Engel her
und befahl an der Begräbnisstelle:

Dräng den Stein beiseite. Willst du wissen,
wo die ist, die dir das Herz bewegt:
Sieh: sie ward wie ein Lavendelkissen
eine Weile da hineingelegt,

daß die Erde künftig nach ihr rieche
in den Falten wie ein feines Tuch.
Alles Tote (fühlst du), alles Sieche
ist betäubt von ihrem Wohl-Geruch.

Schau den Leinwand: wo ist eine Bleiche,
wo er blendend wird und geht nicht ein?
Dieses Licht aus dieser reinen Leiche
war ihm klärender als Sonnenschein.

Staunst du nicht, wie sanft sie ihm entging?
Fast als wär sie's noch, nichts ist verschoben.
Doch die Himmel sind erschüttert oben:
Mann, knie hin und sieh mir nach und sing.

But in front of Thomas the Apostle,
who came too late, there swiftly stepped the angel
long since prepared for this,
and commanded at the burial place:

push the stone aside. If you would know
where she is, who has moved your heart:
see: she was like a lavender pillow
laid down here for a while,

that the earth might in future bear her scent,
as a fine cloth might do in its folds.
All dead things (you feel!), all that are sick
she benumbs with her fragrance.

Look at the winding-sheet: where is the bleachery,
where it could dazzle and yet not shrink?
This light from this pure corpse
was more dazzling to it than sunshine.

Are you not amazed at how softly she took her leave?
As if she were still there, all is in place.
Yet the heavens above are shaken:
O man, kneel down, look on me and sing.

Georg Trakl (1887–1914)

Trakl came from a comfortable middle-class Salzburg family, studied in Vienna, and trained as a pharmacist. It was as a chemist that he joined the Austrian army medical corps at the outbreak of the First World War; tending an excessive number of wounded at the battle of Grodek in Galicia inspired his most famous poem 'Grodek', but also led to a nervous breakdown. He was sent to hospital in Cracow, where he died of an overdose of cocaine. *Die junge Magd* is an early poem, dedicated to Ludwig von Ficker, who published much of his friend's early verse in his periodical *Der Brenner*. Trakl's profoundly melancholy poems also inspired Anton Webern in 'Ein Winterabend' from Op. 13 and the *Sechs Lieder nach Gedichten von Georg Trakl*, Op. 14, for voice, clarinet, bass clarinet, violin and cello.

1922 *Die junge Magd / The young farm maid* Op. 23b

1

Oft am Brunnen, wenn es dämmert,
Sieht man sie verzaubert stehen
Wasser schöpfen, wenn es dämmert.
Eimer auf und nieder gehen.

In den Buchen Dohlen flattern
Und sie gleichet einem Schatten.
Ihre gelben Haare flattern
Und im Hofe schrein die Ratten.

Und umschmeichelt von Verfalle
Senkt sie die entzundenen Lider.
Dürres Gras neigt im Verfalle
Sich zu ihren Füßen nieder.

Often, when dusk is falling,
you can see her spellbound at the well,
Drawing water, when dusk is falling.
Pails go up and down.

Jackdaws in the beech-trees flutter,
And she resembles a shadow.
Her yellow locks flutter,
And rats squeal in the yard.

And wooed all round by decay,
She lowers her inflamed eyelids.
Dry grasses that decay
Droop at her feet.

2

Stille schafft sie in der Kammer
Und der Hof liegt längst verödet.
Im Holunder vor der Kammer
Kläglich eine Amsel flötet.

Silbern schaut ihr Bild im Spiegel
Fremd sie an im Zwielichtscheine
Und verdämmert fahl im Spiegel
Und ihr graut vor seiner Reine.

Traumhaft singt ein Knecht im Dunkel
Und sie starrt von Schmerz geschüttelt.
Röte träufelt durch das Dunkel.
Jäh am Tor der Südwind rüttelt.

She toils away quietly in the room,
The yard has long been deserted.
In the elder tree outside the room
A blackbird sings plaintively.

Her face, silver in the mirror,
Stares back at her strangely in the twilight
And fades pallidly in the mirror,
She shudders at its purity.

A farm-hand sings dreamily in the darkness,
And she stares ahead, shaken with grief.
Red light trickles through the darkness.
The gusting south wind rattles the gate.

3

Nächtens übern kahlen Anger	At night across the bare meadow
Gaukelt sie in Fieberträumen.	She floats in feverish dreams.
Mürrisch greint der Wind im Anger	The surly wind moans in the meadow,
Und der Mond lauscht aus den Bäumen.	And the moon listens from the trees.

Balde rings die Sterne bleichen	The stars all around soon turn pale,
Und ermattet von Beschwerde	And worn out with worries,
Wächsern ihre Wangen bleichen.	Her waxen cheeks turn pale,
Fäulnis wittert aus der Erde.	The earth reeks of putrescence.

Traurig rauscht das Rohr im Tümpel	The reeds rustle sadly in the pool,
Und sie friert in sich gekauert.	And freezing, she crouches in the cold.
Fern ein Hahn kräht. Übern Tümpel	A cock crows from afar. Across the pool
Hart und grau der Morgen schauert.	The morning shudders hard and grey.

4

In der Schmiede dröhnt der Hammer	In the smithy booms the hammer
Und sie huscht am Tor vorüber.	And she flits by past the gate.
Glührot schwingt der Knecht den Hammer	The farm-hand swings the red-hot hammer,
Und sie schaut wie tot hinüber.	And she looks on as though she were dead.

Wie im Traum trifft sie ein Lachen;	As in a dream she hears laughter;
Und sie taumelt in die Schmiede,	And she staggers into the smithy,
Scheu geduckt vor seinem Lachen,	Nervously cowers before his laughter,
Wie der Hammer hart und rüde.	Hard and brutal like the hammer.

Hell versprühn im Raum die Funken	The smithy's full of flying sparks,
Und mit hilfloser Geberde	And with a helpless gesture
Hascht sie nach den wilden Funken	She snatches at the wild sparks
Und sie stürzt betäubt zur Erde.	And, stunned, collapses on the ground.

5

Schmächtig hingestreckt im Bette	With her frail form stretched out in bed,
Wacht sie auf voll süßem Bangen	She wakes filled with sweet trepidation,
Und sie sieht ihr schmutzig Bette	And she sees her soiled bed
Ganz von goldnem Licht verhangen,	Shrouded in golden light,

Die Reseden dort am Fenster	Sees the mignonettes there at the window
Und den bläulich hellen Himmel.	And the shining bluish sky.
Manchmal trägt der Wind ans Fenster	Sometimes the wind bears to the window
Einer Glocke zag Gebimmel.	The timid ringing of a bell.

Schatten gleiten übers Kissen,	Shadows flit across her pillow,
Langsam schlägt die Mittagsstunde	Slowly a bell announces noon,
Und sie atmet schwer im Kissen	And she breathes heavily on her pillow,
Und ihr Mund gleicht einer Wunde.	And her mouth resembles a wound.

6

Abends schweben blutige Linnen,
Wolken über stummen Wäldern,
Die gehüllt in schwarze Linnen.
Spatzen lärmen auf den Feldern.

Und sie liegt ganz weiß im Dunkel.
Unterm Dach verhaucht ein Girren.
Wie ein Aas in Busch und Dunkel
Fliegen ihren Mund umschwirren.

Traumhaft klingt im braunen Weiler
Nach ein Klang von Tanz und Geigen,
Schwebt ihr Antlitz durch den Weiler,
Weht ihr Haar in kahlen Zweigen.

Strips of cloud-like bloodstained linen
Float in the evening over silent woods,
Enveloped in black linen.
Sparrows clamour in the fields.

All white she lies in the dark.
The cooing fades beneath the roof.
Like carrion in the bushes and dark,
Her mouth is seething with flies.

Dream-like in the dark hamlet
Dancing and fiddling can be heard,
Her face floats through the hamlet,
Her hair waves in bare branches.

Erich Wolfgang Korngold (1897–1957)

In a poll conducted by *Das Neue Wiener Tageblatt* in 1928, the two greatest living composers were deemed to be Erich Korngold and Arnold Schoenberg. Korngold's fame, having waned in the post-war years, is now once more in the ascendancy. He first attracted attention as a composer of one-act operas, such as *Der Ring des Polykrates* and *Violanta* (1916), and then four years later achieved international renown with *Die tote Stadt*, the first German opera performed at the Metropolitan Opera after the First World War. Max Reinhardt, with whom he had collaborated on several stage projects, took him to Hollywood in 1934, and it was there that he settled after the Anschluß. Almost every Viennese composer of his era left behind a fair corpus of Lieder, and Korngold was no exception – well over fifty, including the unpublished and occasional songs he composed for film and theatre.

Among his juvenilia is a remarkable cycle of twelve Eichendorff songs, composed at the age of fourteen; two of the poems are better known in other settings (Wolf's 'Das Ständchen' and Schoeck's 'Waldeinsamkeit'), but the remainder are unfamiliar – all twelve are fine examples of a child prodigy's remarkable feel for song. Korngold's first published songs were the *Einfache Lieder* of Op. 9, which, in 'Liebesbriefchen', contains one of the loveliest melodies he ever composed. Four years later in 1915 he wrote 'Österreichischer Soldatenabschied' which was frequently performed in war relief charities during 1917. In 1919 Korngold asked the poet Ernst Lothar to write a new text for the song: the resultant 'Gefaßter Abschied' then became one of the *Vier Lieder des Abschieds*, Op. 14. These four songs, characterized by wide intervals, chromatic harmonies and vocal glissandi, were inspired by the enormous loss of life during the Great War. The five songs of Op. 38 (1948) were composed in America, most of them being re-workings of music he had written for films: 'Glückwunsch', for example, to a text by Richard Dehmel, was based on a melody he had composed in 1943 for *Devotion*, a film about the Brontë family. Korngold's final song, 'Sonett für Wien' dates from 1948, a sort of epilogue for all those Viennese composers, such as Schoenberg, Schreker, Zemlinsky and Korngold himself who were driven into exile by the Nazis and for whom the Austrian capital remained their spiritual home.

Richard Dehmel (1863–1920)

See Schoenberg

1947 Glückwunsch / Congratulation Op. 38, no. 1

Ich wünsche dir Glück.	I wish you happiness.
Ich bring' dir die Sonne in meinem Blick.	I bring you the sun in my gaze.

Ich fühle dein Herz in meiner Brust;	I feel your heart beat in my breast;
es wünscht dir mehr als eitel Lust.	it wishes you more than mere pleasure.
Es fühlt und wünscht: die Sonne scheint,	It feels and hopes: the sun shines,
auch wenn dein Blick zu brechen meint.	even when your eyes think to close in death.
Es wünscht dir Blicke so sehnsuchtslos,	It wishes your eyes to be as free of yearning,
als trügest du die Welt im Schoß.	as if you carried the world in your womb.
Es wünscht dir Blicke so voll Begehren,	It wishes your eyes to be as full of desire,
als sei die Erde neu zu gebären.	as if the earth were to be born again.
Es wünscht dir Blicke voll der Kraft,	It wishes your eyes to be full of the strength
die aus Winter sich Frühling schafft.	that fashions spring from winter.
Und täglich leuchte durch dein Haus	And may your house be daily lit
aller Liebe Blumenstrauß!	by the gleaming bouquet of love!

Elisabeth Honold (dates unknown)

1913 Liebesbriefchen / Billet-doux Op. 9, no. 4

Fern von dir	Far from you
Denk' ich dein,	I think of you,
Kindelein.	Dear child.
Einsam bin ich,	I am lonely,
Doch mir blieb	But my love
Treue Lieb'.	Has stayed true.
Was ich denk',	I think
Bist nur du,	Only of you,
Herzensruh.	O peace of my heart.
Sehe stets	I always see,
Hold und licht	Fair and bright,
Dein Gesicht.	Your face.
Und in mir	And you sound
Immerzu	Within me
Tönest du.	Always.
Bist's allein,	It is you alone
Die die Welt	Who brightens
Mir erhellt.	For me the world.
Ich bin dein,	I am yours,
Liebchen fein,	My sweetest,
Denke mein!	Think of me!

Hans Kaltneker (1895–1919)

Poet, short-story writer and dramatist, Kaltneker was one of the main exponents of Austrian expressionism. He wrote *Die Heilige*, which Hans Müller adapted for the libretto of *Das Wunder der Heliane*. Kaltneker also wrote the three poems of Korngold's Op. 18.

1948 Sonett für Wien / Sonnet for Vienna Op. 41

Du Stadt, du Psalm, aus Gottes Mund er-
klungen
Und Stein geworden, Marmor, Park und
Garten,
Gedicht und Lied der liebsten Engelszungen,
Die lange deiner goldnen Kirchen harrten,

Drin alle Heil'gen, wunderlich bezwungen
Von ihrer hohen Form, zu Glanz erstarrten!
Stadt der Fontänen, altem Stein entsprungen,
Barocker Bauten, gnädiger Standarten,

Die über hohen Prozessionen schweben!
Du Stadt, darin der Klang vergangner Zeiten
Noch klingt, darin das alte Gold noch
leuchtet,

Darin die dunklen, frommen Bilder leben
Und Gottes Auge aus den grünen Weiten
Der Berge strahlt, von Wehmut sanft
befeuchtet.

O city, O psalm, resounding from the mouth
of God
And made into stone, marble, park and garden,
Poem and song from tongues of sweetest
angels,
Who long awaited your golden churches,

In which all saints, wondrously subdued
By their lofty form, were petrified into glory!
City of fountains, sprung from ancient stone,
Baroque buildings, gracious banners

That flutter above grand processions!
O city, where the sound of bygone ages
Still lingers, where ancient gold still
gleams,

Where dark, devout pictures live,
And the eye of God shines from the green
expanses
Of mountains, gently moistened by melancholy.

1920–21 *Vier Lieder des Abschieds / Four songs of farewell* Op. 14

Sterbelied / Requiem

CHRISTINA ROSSETTI (1830–1904), TRANSLATED BY ALFRED KERR (1867–1948)

Laß, Liebste, wenn ich tot bin,
Laß du von Klagen ab.
Statt Rosen und Cypressen
Wächst Gras auf meinem Grab.

Ich schlafe still im Zwielichtschein
In schwerer Dämmernis.
Und wenn du willst, gedenke mein,
Und wenn du willst, vergiß.

Ich fühle nicht den Regen,
Ich seh' nicht, ob es tagt,
Ich höre nicht die Nachtigall,
Die in den Büschen klagt.

When I am dead, my dearest,
Do not lament.
Instead of roses and cypress,
Grass shall cover my grave.

I shall sleep quietly in the twilight,
In the heavy dusk.
And if you will, remember,
And if you will, forget.

I shall not feel the rain,
I shall not see the dawn,
I shall not hear the nightingale
Lamenting in the trees.

Vom Schlaf erweckt mich keiner,
Die Erdenwelt verblich.
Vielleicht gedenk ich deiner,
Vielleicht vergaß ich dich.

No one shall ever wake me,
All the world has vanished.
Perhaps I shall remember you,
Perhaps I'll have forgotten you.

Dies eine kann mein Sehnen nimmer fassen / This one thing my longing can never grasp
EDITH RONSPERGER

Dies eine kann mein Sehnen nimmer fassen,
Daß nun von mir zu dir kein Weg mehr führ',
Daß du vorübergehst an meiner Türe
In ferne, stumme, ungekannte Gassen.

This one thing my longing can never grasp,
That now no path leads me to you,
That you walk past my door
Into distant, silent, unknown streets.

Wär' es mein Wunsch, daß mir dein Bild
    erbleiche,
Wie Sonnenglanz, von Nebeln aufgetrunken,
Wie einer Landschaft frohes Bild, versunken
Im glatten Spiegel abendlicher
    Teiche?

Could it be my wish that you should fade
    away,
Like the sun's brilliance engulfed in mist,
Like a landscape's happy reflection,
Sunk in the smooth mirror of evening
    ponds?

Der Regen fällt. Die müden Bäume triefen.
Wie welkes Laub verweh'n viel Sonnenstunden.
Noch hab' ich in mein Los mich nicht gefunden
Und seines Dunkels uferlose Tiefen.
(Schreker)

The rain falls. The tired trees drip.
Many hours of sun fade like withered leaves.
I have not yet come to terms with my fate
And the boundless depths of its darkness.

Mond, so gehst du wieder auf / Moon, thus you rise once more
ERNST LOTHAR (1890–1974)

Mond, so gehst du wieder auf
Über'm dunklen Tal der ungeweinten Tränen!
Lehr, so lehr's mich doch, mich nicht nach
    ihr zu sehnen,
Blaß zu machen Blutes Lauf,
Dies Leid nicht zu erleiden,
Aus zweier Menschen Scheiden.

Moon, thus you rise once more
Over the dark valley of unwept
    tears!
Teach, teach me not to yearn for her,
To make my blood run pale,
Not to suffer this sorrow,
Caused when two souls part.

Sieh', in Nebel hüllst du dich.
Doch verfinstern kannst du nicht den Glanz
    der Bilder,
Die mir weher jede Nacht erweckt und wilder.
Ach! Im Tiefsten fühle ich:
Das Herz, das sich mußt' trennen,
Wird ohne Ende brennen.

See, you shroud yourself in mist.
Yet you cannot darken the bright images
That the night arouses in me with wilder and
    fiercer pain.
Ah! I feel in the depths of my being:
The heart that has suffered separation
Will burn eternally.

Gefaßter Abschied / Resigned farewell

ERNST LOTHAR (1890–1974)

Weine nicht, daß ich jetzt gehe,
Heiter laß dich von mir küssen.
Blüht das Glück nicht aus der Nähe,
Von ferne wird's dich keuscher grüßen.

Nimm diese Blumen, die ich pflückte,
Monatsrosen rot und Nelken,
Laß die Trauer, die dich drückte,
Herzens Blume kann nicht welken.

Lächle nicht mit bitter'm Lächeln,
Stoße mich nicht stumm zur Seite.
Linde Luft wird bald dich wieder fächeln,
Bald ist Liebe dein Geleite!

Gib deine Hand mir ohne Zittern,
Letztem Kuß gib alle Wonne.
Bang' vor Sturm nicht: aus Gewittern
Geht strahlender auf die Sonne.

So schau zuletzt noch die schöne Linde,
Drunter uns kein Auge je erspähte.
Glaub, o glaub, daß ich dich wiederfinde,
Denn ernten wird, wer Liebe lächelnd
    säte.

Do not weep that I am now going,
Be cheerful and let me kiss you.
If joy does not bloom when we are near,
It will greet you more chastely from afar.

Take these flowers that I have picked,
Red China roses and carnations,
Shake off the sorrow that oppressed you,
The heart's blossom cannot wither.

Do not smile a bitter smile,
Do not push me aside in silence.
A soft breeze will soon fan you once more,
Love will soon escort you!

Give me your hand without trembling,
Give all your rapture to this last kiss.
Be not afraid of tempests: after storms
The sun rises more resplendently.

So, take one last look at the lovely lime-tree,
Beneath which no eye ever saw us.
Believe, O believe, I shall find you again,
For they who sowed love with a smile shall
    reap its harvest.

Conradin Kreutzer (1780–1849)

A composer of some thirty operas, three piano concertos, two oratorios, numerous part-songs and over 150 Lieder, Kreutzer's music has never been entirely forgotten: *Das Nachtlager in Granada* is still occasionally performed in Germany, and his incidental music to Raimund's *Der Verschwender* is regularly played in Austrian theatres. His *Neun Wander-Lieder von Uhland*, composed a decade before *Winterreise* in 1818, almost certainly influenced Schubert. Uhland's sixth poem is entitled 'Winterreise'; both Müller and Uhland use similar imagery (frozen landscapes, darkened suns, cold winds, falling leaves, deserted pathways); and both protagonists set out on journeys. Spaun in his memoirs told an anecdote of how Schubert reacted to Kreutzer's *Wanderlieder*.

> Wir trafen ihn einmal die eben erschienenen 'Wanderlieder' von Kreutzer durchspielen. Einer seiner Freunde [Hüttenbrenner] sagte: 'Lasse das Zeug und singe uns ein paar Lieder von dir', worauf er kurz erwiderte: 'Ihr seid doch ungerecht, die Lieder sind sehr schön, und ich möchte sie geschrieben haben.'

> We once found him playing through Kreutzer's *Wanderlieder*, which had just been published. One of his friends said: 'Leave that rubbish and sing us a few of your own songs', whereupon he replied tersely: 'But you are unjust, the songs are very beautiful and I wish I had written them.'

Ludwig Uhland (1787–1862)

A lawyer by training, he was appointed Professor of German Language and Literature at Tübingen University, and became a Liberal member of the Württemberg Parliament. He published a volume of political poems ('Vaterländische Gedichte', 1817) and a number of unsuccessful plays, but it was his 'Gedichte' (1815) that made his reputation as a poet.

1818 *Neun Wander-Lieder von Uhland* / *Nine Wander-Lieder by Uhland* Op. 34

1
Lebewohl / Farewell

Lebe wohl, lebe wohl, mein Lieb!	Farewell, farewell, my love!
Muß noch heute scheiden.	I must leave you today.
Einen Kuß, einen Kuß mir gib!	A kiss, give me a kiss!
Muß dich ewig meiden.	I must leave you forever.
Eine Blüt', eine Blüt' mir brich	A flower, pick me a flower
Von dem Baum im Garten!	From the tree in the garden!

Keine Frucht, keine Frucht für mich!
Darf sie nicht erwarten.
(*Schoeck*)

No fruit, no fruit for me!
I cannot expect that.

2
Scheiden und Meiden / Farewell and parting

So soll ich nun dich meiden,
Du, meines Lebens Lust!
Du küssest mich zum Scheiden,
Ich drücke dich an die Brust.

So I must now leave you,
Joy of my life!
You kiss me in parting,
I press you to my breast.

Ach, Liebchen! heißt das meiden,
Wenn man sich herzt und küßt?
Ach, Liebchen! heißt das scheiden,
Wenn man sich fest umschließt?
(*Brahms, Burgmüller, Cornelius, Schoeck*)

Ah, beloved, can this be parting,
This caressing and kissing?
Ah, beloved, can this be farewell,
This tight embrace?

3
In der Ferne / In the distance

Will ruhen unter den Bäumen hier,
Die Vöglein hör' ich so gerne.
Wie singet ihr so zum Herzen mir!
Von unsrer Liebe was wisset ihr
In dieser weiten Ferne?

I'll rest beneath the trees here,
I love listening to the birds.
How your singing pierces my heart!
What do you know of our love
In this far distant land?

Will ruhen hier an des Baches Rand,
Wo duftige Blümlein sprießen.
Wer hat euch, Blümlein, hieher gesandt?
Seid ihr ein herzliches Liebespfand
Aus der Ferne von meiner Süßen?
(*Brahms, Burgmüller*)

I'll rest here by the banks of the stream,
Where fragrant little flowers spring up.
Who sent you here, little flowers?
Are you a fond token of love
From my sweetheart far away?

4
Morgenlied / Morning song

Noch ahnt man kaum der Sonne Licht,
Noch sind die Morgenglocken nicht
Im finstern Tal erklungen.

Hardly a sign yet of the sun's light,
The morning bells have not yet rung,
Down in the dark valley.

Wie still des Waldes weiter Raum!
Die Vöglein zwitschern nur im Traum,
Kein Sang hat sich erschwungen.

How silent the vast forest!
Just the twittering of dreaming birds,
No song can yet be heard.

Ich hab' mich längst ins Feld gemacht
Und habe schon dies Lied erdacht
Und hab' es laut gesungen.
(*Curschmann, Rubinstein*)

I've long been up and in the fields,
And thought up this song
And sung it out loud.

5
Nachtreise / Night journey

Ich reit' ins finstre Land hinein,
Nicht Mond noch Sterne geben Schein,
Die kalten Winde tosen.
Oft hab' ich diesen Weg gemacht,
Wann goldner Sonnenschein gelacht,
Bei lauer Lüfte Kosen.

Ich reit' am finstern Garten hin,
Die dürren Bäume sausen drin,
Die welken Blätter fallen.
Hier pflegt' ich in der Rosenzeit,
Wann alles sich der Liebe weiht,
Mit meinem Lieb zu wallen.

Erloschen ist der Sonne Strahl,
Verwelkt die Rosen allzumal,
Mein Lieb zu Grab' getragen.
Ich reit' ins finstre Land hinein
Im Wintersturm, ohn' allen Schein,
Den Mantel umgeschlagen.
(*Bohm, Burgmüller, Fuchs*)

I ride out into the dark land,
Neither moon nor stars are shining,
The cold winds rage.
I've often been this way
When golden sunshine laughed,
And mild, caressing breezes blew.

I ride past the dark garden,
The withered trees are rustling,
The dead leaves fall.
Here, when roses bloomed
And all things devote themselves to love,
I used to walk with my beloved.

The sun is now extinguished,
The roses are all wilted,
My love is buried.
I ride out into the dark land
Through winter storms, devoid of light,
Wrapped up in my coat.

6
Winterreise / Winter journey

Bei diesem kalten Wehen
Sind alle Straßen leer,
Die Wasser stille stehen,
Ich aber schweif' umher.

Die Sonne scheint so trübe,
Muß früh hinuntergehn,
Erloschen ist die Liebe,
Die Lust kann nicht bestehn.

Nun geht der Wald zu Ende,
Im Dorfe mach' ich halt,
Da wärm' ich mir die Hände,
Bleibt auch das Herze kalt.
(*Burgmüller, Strauss*)

In this cold wind
All streets are empty,
The river stands still,
But I wander up and down.

The sun shines so pale,
Will soon set,
Love is extinguished,
Pleasure cannot last.

Now the forest opens out,
I'll stop in the village,
There I warm my hands,
Though my heart remains cold.

7
Abreise / Departure

So hab' ich nun die Stadt verlassen,
Wo ich gelebet lange Zeit;

Finally I've left the town
Where I lived a long time;

Ich ziehe rüstig meiner Straßen,
Es gibt mir niemand das Geleit.

Man hat mir nicht den Rock zerrissen,
Es wär' auch schade für das Kleid!
Noch in die Wange mich gebissen
Vor übergroßem Herzeleid.

Auch keinem hat's den Schlaf vertrieben,
Daß ich am Morgen weitergeh';
Sie konnten's halten nach Belieben,
Von *Einer* aber tut mir's weh.
(*Burgmüller, Vesque von Püttlingen*)

I go briskly on my way,
No one walks by my side.

They have not torn my coat to shreds,
It's too good for that!
Nor have they bitten my cheeks
With overwhelming sorrow.

And no one has lost any sleep
That I left in the morning;
They could do as they liked,
But there's *one* who makes me suffer.

8
Einkehr / At the inn

Bei einem Wirte, wundermild,
Da war ich jüngst zu Gaste;
Ein goldner Apfel war sein Schild
An einem langen Aste.

Es war der gute Apfelbaum,
Bei dem ich eingekehrt;
Mit süßer Kost und frischem Schaum
Hat er mich wohl genährt.

Es kamen in sein grünes Haus
Viel leichtbeschwingte Gäste;
Sie sprangen frei und hielten Schmaus
Und sangen auf das beste.

Ich fand ein Bett zu süßer Ruh'
Auf weichen, grünen Matten;
Der Wirt, er deckte selbst mich zu
Mit seinem kühlen Schatten.

Nun fragt' ich nach der Schuldigkeit,
Da schüttelt' er den Wipfel.
Gesegnet sei er allezeit
Von der Wurzel bis zum Gipfel!
(*Burgmüller, Schoeck, Strauss*)

I was recently the guest
Of such a gentle host;
His inn-sign was a golden apple
At the end of a long branch.

The host who put me up
Was the worthy apple tree;
He nourished me well
With sweet fare and fresh juice.

Many light-hearted guests
Came to his verdant house;
Wildly they danced and feasted well
And sang for all their worth.

I found a bed for sweet rest
On soft and verdant meadows;
Mine host himself covered me
With his cool shadow.

When I asked how much I owed,
He just shook his head.
May he be blest for evermore,
From his roots to his crest!

9
Heimkehr / Homecoming
See Brahms, p. 88

Franz Lachner (1803–90)

Despite Busoni's satirical depiction of Lachner as a risible figure of mediocrity (see 'Aus der klassischen Walpurgisnacht'), Lachner was a considerable composer of some six operas, eight symphonies, six string quartets, much chamber music and over two hundred songs, and he was at one time extremely close to Schubert. In a letter to Johann Friedrich David Dingelstedt, dated 17 June 1854, he reminisced:

> Wir waren allerdings die intimsten Freunde, spielten einander des Vormittags unsere Kompositionen vor und tauschten unsere Ansichten darüber mit größter Offenheit aus, wobei wir beide lernten.

> We were intimate friends, played each other our own music in the mornings and exchanged our opinions with great openness to our mutual benefit.

Sir George Grove recounted in his *Dictionary of Music and Musicians* that Lachner told him that 'he had taken half a dozen of the *Winterreise* songs to Haslinger and brought back half a dozen gulden – each gulden being then worth a franc ...'. Lachner composed his *Sängerfahrt*, a sequence of sixteen Heine Lieder, in 1831 and 1832, while courting Julie Royko, who later became his wife.

Heinrich Heine (1797–1856)

See Brahms, Mendelssohn, Robert Schumann, Wolf

1831–32 *Sängerfahrt / Minstrel's journey* Op. 33

1
Die badende Elfe / The bathing water-nymph
See Brahms, p. 53 [Sommerabend]

2
An den Mond / To the moon
See Brahms, p. 53 [Mondenschein]

3
Der Winterabend / The winter evening

Mädchen mit dem roten Mündchen,
Mit den Äuglein süß und klar,
Du mein liebes, kleines Mädchen,
Deiner denk' ich immerdar.

Lang ist heut der Winterabend,
Und ich möchte bei dir sein,

Maiden with the rosy lips
And with eyes so sweet and clear,
You my sweet little maiden,
I think of you incessantly.

This winter evening passes slowly,
And I would like to be with you,

Bei dir sitzen, mit dir schwatzen,
Im vertrauten Kämmerlein.

An die Lippen wollt' ich pressen
Deine kleine, weiße Hand,
Und mit Tränen sie benetzen,
Deine kleine, weiße Hand.
(*Franz, Wolf*)

Sit with you, and talk with you
In your cosy little room.

I'd love to press against my lips
Your tiny white hand,
And moisten it with my tears,
Your tiny white hand.

4
Die Bergstimme / The voice of the mountains

Ein Reiter durch das Bergtal zieht,
Im traurig stillen Trab:
Ach! zieh' ich jetzt wohl in Liebchens Arm
Oder zieh' ich ins dunkle Grab?
Die Bergstimm' Antwort gab:
Ins dunkle Grab!

A horseman rides through the mountain valley
At a sad, silent trot:
Ah! do I ride into my beloved's arms,
Or into the dark grave?
The mountain's voice replied:
Into the dark grave!

Und weiter reitet der Reitersmann,
Und seufzet schwer dazu:
So zieh ich denn hin ins Grab so früh –
Wohlan, im Grab ist Ruh!
Die Stimme sprach dazu:
Im Grab ist Ruh!

And onwards still the horseman rides,
Sighing deeply all the while:
If I go to the grave so soon –
So be it, in the grave is peace!
To which the voice replied:
In the grave is peace!

Dem Reitersmann eine Träne rollt
Von der Wange bleich und kummervoll:
Und ist nur im Grabe die Ruhe für mich –
So ist mir im Grabe wohl!
Die Stimm' erwidert hohl:
Im Grabe wohl!
(*Medtner, Schulz*)

A tear rolls down the horseman's cheek,
Pale and woebegone:
If peace can be found but in the grave –
I shall be happy in the grave!
With a hollow sound the voice replied:
Happy in the grave!

5
Der wunde Ritter / The wounded knight

Ich weiß eine alte Kunde,
Die hallet dumpf und trüb:
Ein Ritter lag liebeswunde,
Doch treulos ist sein Lieb.

I know an ancient story –
Muffled and sad it sounds –
The knight lies smitten with love,
But his loved-one's unfaithful.

Als treulos muß er verachten
Die eigne Herzliebste sein,
Als schimpflich muß er betrachten
Die eigne Liebespein.

He must despise his own beloved
For being unfaithful to him,
He must regard it as shameful,
The love that tortures him.

Er möcht in die Schranken reiten
Und rufen die Ritter zum Streit:

He would like to enter the lists
And challenge the knights to a duel:

Der mag sich zum Kampfe bereiten,
Wer mein Lieb eines Makels zeiht!

    Da würden wohl Alle schweigen,
Nur nicht sein eigner Schmerz;
Da müßt er die Lanze neigen
Wider's eigne klagende Herz.

He who declares my love is sullied,
Must prepare himself to fight.

    All might then be silent,
But not his own great pain,
He would then have to point his spear
At his own lamenting heart.

6
Im Mai / In May
See Schumann, p. 468 ['Im wunderschönen Monat Mai']

7
Eine Liebe / A love
See Schumann, p. 469 ['Die Rose, die Lilie']

8
Die Meerfrau / The water-sprite

    Der Abend kommt gezogen,
Der Nebel bedeckt die See;
Geheimnisvoll rauschen die Wogen,
Da steigt es weiß in die Höh'.

    Die Meerfrau steigt aus den Wellen,
Und setzt sich zu mir, am Strand;
Die weißen Brüste quellen
Hervor aus dem Schleiergewand.

    Sie drückt mich und sie preßt mich
Und tut mir fast ein Weh; –
Du drückst ja viel zu fest mich,
Du schöne Wasserfee!

    „Ich presse dich in meinen Armen,
Und drücke dich mit Gewalt;
Ich will bei dir erwarmen,
Der Abend ist so kalt."

    Der Mond schaut immer blasser
Aus dämmriger Wolkenhöh'; –
Dein Auge wird trüber und nasser,
Du schöne Wasserfee!

    „Es wird nicht trüber und nasser,
Mein Aug ist naß und trüb,
Weil, als ich stieg aus dem Wasser,
Ein Tropfen im Auge blieb."

    Evening draws on,
Mist hides the sea from view;
The waves roar mysteriously,
Something white looms up.

    The water-sprite rises from the waves
And sits down by me on the shore;
Her white breasts billow
From the veil she wears.

    She clasps me and she clutches me,
And almost causes me pain;
You clasp me much too tightly,
You lovely water-sprite!

    'I clasp you in my arms
And clutch you with all my might;
I want to warm myself on you,
The evening is so cold.'

    The moon gleams ever paler
Through a twilit bank of clouds;
Your eyes grow dimmer and wetter,
You lovely water-sprite!

    'It does not grow dimmer and wetter,
My eyes are dim and wet,
Because, when I rose from the water,
My eyes stayed moist from the waves.'

Die Möwen schrillen kläglich,	The mournful gulls are shrilling,
Es grollt und brandet die See; –	The sea breaks angrily on the shore –
Dein Herz pocht wild beweglich,	Your heart is throbbing wildly,
Du schöne Wasserfee!	You lovely water-sprite!
„Mein Herz pocht wild beweglich,	'My heart is throbbing wildly,
Es pocht beweglich wild,	Wildly it is throbbing,
Weil ich dich liebe unsäglich,	Because I love you past all telling,
Du liebes Menschenbild! –"	My beloved mortal child!'

9
Wasserfahrt / Sea voyage

Ich stand gelehnet an den Mast,	I stood leaning against the mast
Und zählte jede Welle.	And counted every wave.
Leb' wohl, mein schönes Vaterland!	Farewell, my lovely fatherland!
Mein Schiff, das segelt schnelle!	My ship speeds swiftly on!
Ich kam schön Liebchens Haus vorbei,	I passed before my sweetheart's house,
Die Fensterscheiben blinken;	The windows were shining bright;
Ich schau' mir fast die Augen aus,	I almost stare my eyes out,
Doch will mir niemand winken.	But no one makes a sign.
Ihr Tränen, bleibt mir aus dem Aug',	Be gone, you tears, from my eyes,
Daß ich nicht dunkel sehe.	So that I'm not blinded.
Mein krankes Herze, brich mir nicht	My sick heart, O do not break
Vor allzu großem Weh'.	From excessive grief.
(*Franz, Pfitzner, Mendelssohn*)	

10
Das Fischermädchen / The fishermaiden
See Schubert, p. 323

11
Liebessehnen / Love's yearning
See Schumann, p. 475 ['Lehn' deine Wang']

12
Ein Traumbild / A vision

Ich lag und schlief, und schlief recht mild,	I lay and slept in sweet repose,
Verscheucht war Gram und Leid;	Grief and pain were banished;
Da kam zu mir ein Traumgebild',	In a vision there came to me
Die allerschönste Maid.	The loveliest of maids.
Sie war wie Marmelstein so bleich,	She was as pale as marble,
Und heimlich, wunderbar;	Secretive and wonderful;

Im Auge schwamm es perlengleich,	Pearls seemed to swim in her eyes,
Gar seltsam wallt' ihr Haar.	Her hair flowed strangely down.
Und leise, leise sich bewegt	And noiselessly she begins to move,
Die marmorblasse Maid,	That pale and marble maid,
Und an mein Herz sich niederlegt	And lays herself upon my heart,
Die marmorblasse Maid.	That pale and marble maid.
Wie bebt und pocht vor Weh und Lust	How my heart thrills and throbs,
Mein Herz und brennt so heiß!	Burning with pain and joy!
Nicht bebt, nicht pocht der Schönen Brust,	The fair one's breast neither thrills nor throbs,
Die ist so kalt wie Eis.	It is as cold as ice.
„Nicht bebt, nicht pocht wohl meine Brust,	'My heart neither thrills nor throbs,
Die ist wie Eis so kalt;	It is as cold as ice;
Doch kenn' auch ich der Liebe Lust,	And yet I know the joy of love,
Der Liebe Allgewalt.	The mighty power of love.
Mir blüht kein Rot auf Mund und Wang',	Red does not bloom on my lips or cheeks,
Mein Herz durchströmt kein Blut;	No blood flows through my heart;
Doch sträube dich nicht schauernd bang,	But do not resist in uneasy fear,
Ich bin dir hold und gut."	I love and cherish you.'
Und wilder noch umschlang sie mich,	And wilder still she clung to me,
Und tat mir bald ein Leid,	And soon caused me pain;
Da kräht der Hahn – und stumm entwich	The cock then crowed – and silently
Die marmorblasse Maid.	The pale and marble maiden fled.

13
Die einsame Träne / The solitary tear
See Schumann, p. 514

14
Ihr Bildnis / Her likeness
See Schubert, p. 323

15
Mein Traum / My dream
See Schumann, p. 472 ['Ich hab' im Traum geweinet']

16
Die Liebesboten / Messengers of love
See Franz, p. 113 ['Aus meinen großen Schmerzen']

Franz Liszt (1811–86)

Over a third of Liszt's Lieder exists in two or more versions – the final revision being frequently occasioned by the collected edition organised in 1860. Liszt generally preferred the later versions, as he explained in a letter to Josef Dessauer, written in the early 1850s: „Meine früheren Lieder sind meistens zu aufgebläht sentimental, und häufig zu vollgepropft in der Begleitung." ('My earlier songs are often too inflatedly sentimental, and frequently too overladen in the accompaniment'). The later versions tend to be more austere, and the vocal line makes greater attempts to match the rhythms of the verse, but the earlier settings, such as 'Lorelei', though they often explode the simplicity and integrity of the poems, are wonderfully expressive, abounding in sforzandi, smorzandi and repeated phrases, displaying truly virtuosic accompaniments – which reminds us that Liszt came to song by way of the piano and wrote his first Lieder soon after he had made piano transcriptions of Schubert's *Schwanengesang* and *Winterreise* in 1838–39. At least two of the songs are musically prophetic: 'Glocken von Marling' (1874) anticipates twentieth-century departures from accepted tonality; while 'Ich möchte hingehn' (1845) foreshadows the '*Tristan* motif' (which also occurs in 'Die Lorelei'), a decade before Wagner composed the music to *Tristan und Isolde*.

Ferdinand Freiligrath (1810–76)

Freiligrath's *Gedichte* (1838) contained some of his most exotic poems, which, like Victor Hugo's *Les Orientales* (1829), soon established his reputation, which meant that he could abandon his career in the bank and devote himself to writing. Following the publication of his political poems, *Ein Glaubensbekenntnis* (1844), he was exposed to political persecution and emigrated first to Belgium and then to Switzerland. He returned to Germany in 1848 and contributed regularly to the *Neue Rheinische Zeitung*, edited by Karl Marx. Fearing further persecution, he fled to London in 1851 where he remained for seventeen years. In 1868 he returned again to Germany, where he spent the last years of his life. 'O lieb, so lang du lieben kannst!' was written on the death of his father.

*c.*1845 O lieb, so lang du lieben kannst! / O love as long as you can! Searle 298

O lieb, so lang du lieben kannst!	O love as long as you can!
O lieb, so lang du lieben magst!	O love as long as you may!
Die Stunde kommt, die Stunde kommt,	The hour will come, the hour will come
Wo du an Gräbern stehst und klagst!	When you will stand by graves and mourn!
Und sorge, daß dein Herze glüht	And be sure that your heart glows,
Und Liebe hegt und Liebe trägt,	And nourishes and harbours love,

So lang ihm noch ein ander Herz
In Liebe warm entgegenschlägt!

Und wer dir seine Brust erschließt,
O tu ihm, was du kannst, zulieb!
Und mach ihm jede Stunde froh,
Und mach ihm keine Stunde trüb!

Und hüte deine Zunge wohl,
Bald ist ein böses Wort gesagt!
O Gott, es war nicht bös gemeint, –
Der andre aber geht und klagt.

As long as another heart
Beats lovingly in reply!

And whoever opens his heart to you,
O do all you can to love him!
Make him happy at every moment,
And at no moment make him sad!

And take good care of what you say,
It's easy to utter an angry word!
O God, though you meant no harm –
The other departs and grieves.

Friedrich Hebbel (1813–63)

See Berg

c.1860 Blume und Duft / Flower and scent Searle 324

In Frühlings Heiligtume,
    Wenn dir ein Duft ans Tiefste rührt,
Da suche nicht die Blume,
    Der ihn ein Hauch entführt.

Der Duft läßt Ew'ges ahnen,
    Von unbegrenztem Leben voll;
Die Blume kann nur mahnen,
    Wie schnell sie welken soll.

In the sanctuary of spring,
    When some fragrance moves you deeply,
Do not seek the flower
    From which some breeze has borne it.

Fragrance is a foretaste of the eternal,
    Full of infinite life;
The flower can but remind
    How quickly it shall fade.

Heinrich Heine (1797–1856)

See Brahms, Mendelssohn, Robert Schumann, Wolf

1860 Ein Fichtenbaum steht einsam / A spruce tree stands lonely Searle 309
FIRST SETTING: *c*.1855, SEARLE 309; SECOND SETTING: *c*.1860 RAABE 399B

    Ein Fichtenbaum steht einsam
Im Norden auf kahler Höh'.
Ihn schläfert; mit weißer Decke
Umhüllen ihn Eis und Schnee.

    Er träumt von einer Palme,
Die, fern im Morgenland,
Einsam und schweigend trauert
Auf brennender Felsenwand.
(*Franz, Grieg, Hensel, Hummel, Kempff,
Marx, Medtner, Pfitzner, Rimsky-Korsakov,
Stenhammar, Vesque von Püttlingen*)

    A spruce tree stands lonely,
Naked on a northern height.
And drowses; a white blanket
Enshrouds it in ice and snow.

    It dreams of a palm tree,
Which, far away in the east,
Grieves lonely and silent
On a blazing wall of rock.

1842 Vergiftet sind meine Lieder / My songs are filled with poison Searle 289

Vergiftet sind meine Lieder; –	My songs are filled with poison –
Wie könnt' es anders sein?	How could it be otherwise?
Du hast mir ja Gift gegossen	For you have poured poison
Ins blühende Leben hinein.	Into my blossoming life.
Vergiftet sind meine Lieder; –	My songs are filled with poison –
Wie könnt' es anders sein?	How could it be otherwise?
Ich trage im Herzen viel Schlangen,	Many serpents dwell in my heart,
Und dich, Geliebte mein.	And you, beloved, too.
(*Borodin, Glazunov, Schoeck*)	

Georg Herwegh (1817–75)

A polemical, socialist, anti-clerical poet whose *Gedichte eines Lebendigen* (1841), much admired by King Friedrich Wilhelm of Prussia, established his reputation. When he fell out of favour with the King, he was expelled from Prussia and moved to Paris. Having led an abortive invasion of Baden-Baden in 1848, he fled to Switzerland, but returned to Baden-Baden at the end of his life. He translated the works of Lamartine and seven of Shakespeare's plays.

c.1845 Ich möchte hingehn / I should like to pass away Searle 296

Ich möchte hingehn wie das Abendrot	I should like to pass away like the setting sun
Und wie der Tag mit seinen letzten Gluten –	Or like the day with its final rays –
O leichter, sanfter, ungefühlter Tod! –	O easy, gentle, imperceptible death! –
Mich in den Schoß des Ewigen verbluten.	To bleed away in the Eternal's lap.
Ich möchte hingehn wie der heitre Stern,	I should like to pass away like the bright star,
Im vollsten Glanz, in ungeschwächtem Blinken;	In its fullest, undiminished radiance;
So still und schmerzlos möchte gern	To sink as silently and painlessly
Ich in des Himmels blaue Tiefe sinken!	Into the blue depths of heaven!
Ich möchte hingehn wie der Blume Duft,	I should like to pass away like the flower's scent
Der freudig sich dem schönen Kelch entringet	That rises joyfully from the lovely calyx
Und auf dem Fittich blütenschwangrer Luft	And soars on blossom-laden air
Als Weihrauch auf des Herrn Altar sich schwinget.	Like incense to the altar of the Lord.
Ich möchte hingehn wie der Tau im Tal,	I should like to pass away like dew in the valley,
Wenn durstig ihm des Morgens Feuer winken;	When summoned by dawn's thirsty fires;
O, wollte Gott, wie ihn der Sonnenstrahl,	O would God drink my life-weary soul,
Auch meine lebensmüde Seele trinken!	As the sunshine drinks the dew!
Ich möchte hingehn wie der bange Ton,	I should like to pass away like the timid sound
Der aus den Saiten einer Harfe dringet,	The strings of a harp emit,

| Und, kaum dem irdischen Metall entflohn, | Which, scarcely released from the earthly metal, |
| Als Wohllaut in des Schöpfers Brust verklinget. | Fades as harmony in the Creator's breast. |

Du wirst nicht hingehn wie das Abendrot,	You will not pass away like the setting sun,
Du wirst nicht stille wie der Stern versinken,	You will not sink in silence like the star,
Du stirbst nicht einer Blume leichten Tod,	You will not die a flower's easy death,
Kein Morgenstrahl wird deine Seele trinken.	No morning ray will drink in your soul.

Wohl wirst du hingehn, hingehn ohne Spur,	You will indeed pass away, pass away without trace,
Doch wird das Elend deine Kraft erst schwächen;	But misery first will sap your strength;
Sanft stirbt es einzig sich in der Natur,	Only in nature does death come gently,
Das arme Menschenherz muß stückweis brechen.	Mankind's heart must break into fragments.

Emil Kuh (1828–76)

Despite a career in business and administration, Kuh became increasingly drawn to literature. He was a close friend of Friedrich Hebbel, whose works he edited.

1874 Ihr Glocken von Marling* / Bells of Marling Searle 328

Ihr Glocken von Marling,	Bells of Marling,
Wie brauset ihr so hell;	How brightly you chime;
Ein wohliges Lauten,	A pleasing sound
Als sänge der Quell.	Like a babbling spring.

Ihr Glocken von Marling,	Bells of Marling,
Ein heil'ger Gesang	A sacred song
Umwallet wie schützend	Embraces and protects
Den weltlichen Klang.	The sounds of this earth.

Nehmt mich in die Mitte	Take me to the heart
Der tönenden Flut,	Of your resounding flood,
Ihr Glocken von Marling,	Bells of Marling,
Behütet mich gut!	Watch over me well!

Nikolaus Lenau (1802–50)

See Schumann

1860 Die drei Zigeuner / The three gipsies Searle 320

| Drei Zigeuner fand ich einmal | I once saw three gipsies |
| Liegen an einer Weide, | Lying against a willow, |

* A town southwest of Merano in South Tyrol, where Kuh spent the last years of his life.

Als mein Fuhrwerk mit müder Qual	As my carriage with weary groans
Schlich durch sandige Heide.	Crept across a sandy heath.
Hielt der eine für sich allein	One of them, sitting apart,
In den Händen die Fiedel,	Held a fiddle in his hands,
Spielt, umglüht vom Abendschein,	And, glowing in the evening sun,
Sich ein lustiges Liedel.	Played himself a merry song.
Hielt der zweite die Pfeif' im Mund,	The second with a pipe in his mouth
Blickte nach seinem Rauche,	Gazed contentedly after the smoke,
Froh, als ob er vom Erdenrund	As if he needed nothing more
Nichts zum Glücke mehr brauche.	For happiness on earth.
Und der dritte behaglich schlief,	And the third slept peacefully,
Und sein Zimbal am Baum hing,	His cimbalom hanging from a tree,
Über die Saiten der Windhauch lief,	A breeze swept over its strings,
Über sein Herz ein Traum ging.	A dream passed over his heart.
An den Kleidern trugen die drei	All three of them had clothes
Löcher und bunte Flicken,	Of holes and motley patches;
Aber sie boten trotzig frei	But defiant and free they scoffed
Spott den Erdengeschicken.	At what fate on earth might have in store.
Dreifach haben sie mir gezeigt,	In three ways they showed me how,
Wenn das Leben uns nachtet,	When life for us turns dark,
Wie man's verschläft, verraucht, vergeigt	To sleep it, smoke it, fiddle it away,
Und es dreimal verachtet.	And three ways of disdaining it.
Nach den Zigeunern lang noch schaun	As I drove past the gipsies
Mußt' ich im Weiterfahren,	I had to look at them a long time,
Nach den Gesichtern dunkelbraun,	With their dark brown faces
Den schwarzlockigen Haaren.	And their curly black hair.
(*Hiller, Rubinstein, Schoeck*)	

Oskar von Redwitz (1823–91)

The success of his narrative poem *Amaranth* (1849) persuaded him to leave the legal profession and devote himself to politics and literature. Wrote a number of successful plays and a three-volume epic novel of family life called *Hermann Stark, deutsches Leben*. A cycle of 450 sonnets, *Das Lied vom neuen deutschen Reich* (1871) earned him a short-lived success after the Franco-Prussian War.

1857 Es muß ein Wunderbares sein / How wondrous it must be Searle 314

Es muß ein Wunderbares sein	How wondrous it must be
Ums Lieben zweier Seelen,	When two souls love each other,
Sich schließen ganz einander ein,	Locking each other wholly in,
Sich nie ein Wort verhehlen,	Never concealing a single word,
Und Freud und Leid und Glück und Not	And sharing with each other

So mit einander tragen;
Vom ersten Kuß bis in den Tod
Sich nur von Liebe sagen.
(*Bohm, Lachner*)

Joy and sorrow, weal and woe;
Talking only of love
From the first kiss unto death.

Ludwig Uhland (1787–1862)

See Kreutzer

c.1849 Hohe Liebe / Exalted love Searle 307

In Liebesarmen ruht ihr trunken,
Des Lebens Früchte winken euch;
Ein Blick nur ist auf mich gesunken,
Doch bin ich vor euch allen reich.

In love's embrace you lie enraptured,
The fruits of life beckon you;
One glance alone has fallen on me,
Yet I am richer than all of you.

Das Glück der Erde miss' ich gerne
Und blick', ein Märtyrer, hinan,
Denn über mir in goldner Ferne
Hat sich der Himmel aufgetan.

I gladly forego earth's happiness
And gaze aloft like a martyr,
For above in the golden distance
Heaven has opened up to me.

c.1849 Gestorben war ich / I lay dead Searle 308

Gestorben war ich
Vor Liebeswonne;
Begraben lag ich
In ihren Armen;
Erwecket ward ich
Von ihren Küssen;
Den Himmel sah ich
In ihren Augen.
(*Rimsky-Korsakov*)

I lay dead
From love's bliss;
I lay buried
In her arms;
I was wakened
By her kisses;
I saw heaven
In her eyes.

Carl Loewe (1796–1869)

Carl Loewe, apart from a few rarely heard operas, oratorios and piano music, composed virtually nothing but songs – some four hundred in all. Known best for his popular ballads, this pupil of Reichardt also wrote a few of the most bewitching lyrical songs in the repertoire, a number of cycles, including a *Frauenliebe* that bears comparison with Schumann's, and a remarkable number of those rare phenomena, witty art songs – a realm in which he and Wolf stand head and shoulders above all other Lieder composers. Wolf who, according to many friends, sang Loewe's ballads 'with compelling intensity', was not the only composer to admire the 'North German Schubert', as contemporaries allegedly called him. Schumann, who knew him in Dresden, wrote as early as 1835 a glowing tribute in his *Zeitschrift für Musik*, in which he not only praised the ballads, but also expressed his admiration for the tenderness of his Lieder. Liszt, having played the third Lynceus song ('Zum Sehen geboren, zum Schauen bestellt'), exclaimed in astonishment: „So etwas vermag nur das wirkliche Genie zu schaffen" ('Only a true genius can create something like that.') And Wagner not only preferred Loewe's 'Erlkönig' to Schubert's, but considered 'Herr Oluf', especially in its use of the leitmotif, to be 'one of the most important works of musical literature'.

Adelbert von Chamisso (1781–1838)

See Robert Schumann

Following the success of his first volume of poetry, Chamisso wrote with pride:

> Das Volk singt meine Lieder, man singt sie in den Salons, die Componisten reißen sich danach, die Jungen declamiren sie in den Schulen, mein Portrait erscheint nach Goethe, Tieck und Schlegel als das vierte in der Reihe der gleichzeitigen deutschen Dichter und schöne Damen drücken mir fromm die Hand.

> The people sing my songs, they are sung in salons, composers vie with each other to set them, boys recite them in school, my portrait appears after those of Goethe, Tieck and Schlegel as the fourth in the ranks of contemporary German poets, and beautiful ladies squeeze my hand with devotion.

Frauenliebe / A woman's love

See Schumann for nos. 1–8

1836 Traum der eignen Tage / Dream of my own days Op. 60, no. 9

Traum der eignen Tage,
  Die nun ferne sind,
Tochter meiner Tochter,
  Du mein süßes Kind,
Nimm, bevor die Müde
  Deckt das Leichentuch,
Nimm ins frische Leben
  Meinen Segensspruch.

Siehst mich grau von Haaren,
  Abgezehrt und bleich,
Bin, wie du, gewesen
  Jung und wonnereich,
Liebte, so wie du liebst,
  Ward, wie du, auch Braut,
Und auch du wirst altern,
  So wie ich ergraut.

Laß die Zeit im Fluge
  Wandeln fort und fort,
Nur beständig wahre
  Deines Busens Hort;
Hab' ich's einst gesprochen,
  Nehm' ich's nicht zurück:
Glück ist nur die Liebe,
  Liebe nur ist Glück.

Als ich, den ich liebte,
  In das Grab gelegt,
Hab' ich meine Liebe
  Treu in mir gehegt;
War mein Herz gebrochen,
  Blieb mir fest der Mut,
Und des Alters Asche
  Wahrt die heil'ge Glut.

Nimm, bevor die Müde
  Deckt das Leichentuch,
Nimm ins frische Leben
  Meinen Segensspruch:
Muß das Herz dir brechen,
  Bleibe fest dein Mut,
Sei der Schmerz der Liebe
  Dann dein höchstes Gut.

Dream of my own days,
  That now are distant,
Daughter of my daughter,
  You sweet child of mine,
Take, before the weary one
  Is covered by a shroud,
Take into your young life
  My own blessing.

You see me grey-haired,
  Emaciated and pale,
Once I was like you,
  Young and blissful,
I loved, as you now love,
  Became, like you, a bride,
And you too will grow old,
  And your hair, like mine, turn grey.

Let time fly past
  And keep on changing,
But preserve for ever
  The treasure of your heart;
What I once said,
  I shall not take back:
Happiness alone is love,
  Love alone is happiness.

When I buried
  The man I loved,
I cherished my love
  In my faithful heart:
Though my heart was broken,
  My courage stood firm,
And the ashes of old age
  Preserve the sacred glow.

Take, before the weary one
  Is covered by a shroud,
Take into your young life
  My own blessing:
If your heart must break,
  May your courage stand firm,
May love's sorrow then be
  Your dearest possession.

Theodor Fontane (1819–98)

Best known as a novelist – *Irrungen Wirrungen* (1888), *Frau Jenny Treibel* (1893), *Effi Briest* (1895), *Die Poggenpuhls* (1896), *Der Stechlin* (1898) – Fontane portrayed the social life of Berlin with gentle irony and compassion. His first volumes of poetry appeared in 1850, and his fame soon spread as one of the most accomplished ballad writers of the nineteenth century. 'Archibald Douglas' describes an incident in Scottish history concerning the feud between James V and the Douglas clan, related by Walter Scott in *The Lady of the Lake* and *Tales of a Grandfather*. Scott's source was Hume of Godscroft, according to whom Archibald of Kilspindie was not pardoned but sent back in exile to France, where he died of a broken heart. 'Tom der Reimer' is based on the legend of Thomas Ercildoune, a thirteenth-century bard who owed his gift of prophecy to his sojourn with the fairy queen. The poem appears in Fontane's *Jenseits des Tweed* (1860).

1857 Archibald Douglas / Archibald Douglas Op. 128

„Ich hab' es getragen sieben Jahr',
Und ich kann es nicht tragen mehr,
Wo immer die Welt am schönsten war,
Da war sie öd' und leer.

'I have borne it for seven years,
And can bear it no longer!
Wherever the world was loveliest,
To me it was void and drear.

Ich will hintreten vor sein Gesicht
In dieser Knechtsgestalt,
Er kann meine Bitte versagen nicht,
Ich bin ja worden so alt.

I shall step right up to him,
Clad in this vassal's clothes,
He cannot now refuse my plea,
For I have become so old.

Und trüg' er noch den alten Groll
Frisch wie am ersten Tag,
So komme, was da kommen soll,
Und komme, was da mag."

And if he still bears the ancient grudge,
Fresh as on that first day,
Then happen what must,
Then come what may.'

Graf Douglas spricht's. Am Weg ein Stein
Lud ihn zu harter Ruh,
Er sah in Wald und Feld hinein,
Die Augen fielen ihm zu.

So spake Lord Douglas. A wayside rock
Invited him to stony rest,
He looked across at forest and field,
And his eyelids closed.

Er trug einen Harnisch, rostig und schwer,
Darüber ein Pilgerkleid –
Da horch, vom Waldrand scholl es her
Wie von Hörnern und Jagdgeleit.

He wore a rusty and heavy armour
And over it a pilgrim's cloak. –
But hark! from the forest's edge,
There came the sounds of bugle and hunt.

Und Kies und Staub aufwirbelte dicht,
Herjagte Meut' und Mann,
Und ehe der Graf sich aufgericht't,
Waren Roß und Reiter heran.

Gravel and dust went whirling thick,
Huntsmen and hounds came bounding up,
And before Lord Douglas could rise,
Horses and riders were by his side.

König Jakob saß auf hohem Roß,
Graf Douglas grüßte tief,
Dem König das Blut in die Wangen schoß,
Der Douglas aber rief:

„König Jakob, schaue mich gnädig an
Und höre mich in Geduld!
Was meine Brüder dir angetan,
Es war nicht meine Schuld.

Denk nicht an den alten Douglas-Neid,
Der trotzig dich bekriegt,
Denk lieber an deine Kinderzeit,
Wo ich dich auf Knieen gewiegt.

Denk lieber zurück an Stirling-Schloß,
Wo ich Spielzeug dir geschnitzt,
Dich gehoben auf deines Vaters Roß
Und Pfeile dir zugespitzt.

Denk lieber zurück an Linlithgow,
An den See und den Vogelherd,
Wo ich dich fischen und jagen froh
Und schwimmen und springen gelehrt.

Und denk an alles, was einstens war,
Und sänftige deinen Sinn,
Ich hab' es getragen sieben Jahr',
Daß ich ein Douglas bin."

„Ich seh' dich nicht, Graf Archibald,
Ich hör' deine Stimme nicht,
Mir ist, als ob ein Rauschen im Wald
Von alten Zeiten spricht.

Mir klingt das Rauschen süß und traut,
Ich lausch' ihm immer noch,
Dazwischen aber klingt es laut:
Er ist ein Douglas doch.

Ich seh' dich nicht, ich hör' dich nicht,
Das ist alles, was ich kann,
Ein Douglas vor meinem Angesicht
Wär' ein verlor'ner Mann."

König Jakob gab seinem Roß den Sporn,
Bergan ging jetzt sein Ritt,
Graf Douglas faßte den Zügel vorn
Und hielt mit dem Könige Schritt.

Der Weg war steil, und die Sonne stach,
Sein Panzerhemd war schwer,

King James sat high upon his horse,
Lord Douglas bowed down low;
Blood flushed into the King's face,
Douglas, however, cried:

'King James, look on me in mercy,
And in patience hear me out!
What my brothers did to you
Was no fault of mine.

Think not of the old Douglas envy
That defiantly wars against you,
Think rather of your childhood days
When I rocked you on my knee.

Think rather back to Stirling Castle,
Where I used to carve you toys,
Lifted you onto your father's horse
And sharpened arrows for you.

Think rather back to Linlithgow,
To the loch and the fowling-floor,
Where I taught you to fish and hunt,
And how to swim and jump.

O think of all that used to be,
And let your heart relent –
I have borne it for seven years
That I am of Douglas blood.'

'I see you not, Lord Archibald,
I do not hear your voice,
It is as though the rustling woods
Spoke to me of days gone by.

That rustling sounds sweetly in my ear,
And still I listen to it,
Yet all the while I hear the cry:
He is a Douglas still.

I see you not, I hear you not,
That is as much as I can do –
A Douglas who came within my sight
He were as good as dead.'

King James put spur to his horse
And rode away uphill,
Lord Douglas seized the horse's reins
And kept pace with the king.

The way was steep, the sun burned,
His mail shirt weighed him down,

| Doch ob er schier zusammenbrach, | But though his body almost broke, |
| Er lief doch nebenher. | Still he ran alongside. |

„König Jakob, ich war dein Seneschall,	'King James, I was your seneschal,
Ich will es nicht fürder sein,	That I will be no more,
Ich will nur tränken dein Roß im Stall	I only wish to water your horse
Und ihm schütten die Körner ein.	And pour the oats for his feed.

Ich will ihm selber machen die Streu	I myself will put out his straw
Und es tränken mit eigner Hand,	And fetch his drink with my own hand,
Nur laß mich atmen wieder aufs neu	Only let me breathe once more
Die Luft im Vaterland.	The air of my native land.

Und willst du nicht, so hab einen Mut,	If you will not, then dare the deed,
Und ich will es danken dir,	And I shall thank you for it,
Und zieh dein Schwert und triff mich gut	And draw your sword and strike me down
Und laß mich sterben hier."	And let me perish here.'

König Jakob sprang herab vom Pferd,	King James leapt down from his horse,
Hell leuchtete sein Gesicht,	His face was shining bright,
Aus der Scheide zog er sein breites Schwert,	From the scabbard he drew his sword,
Aber fallen ließ er es nicht.	But did not let it fall.

„Nimm's hin, nimm's hin und trag es aufs neu	'Take it, take it, and wear it again,
Und bewache mir meine Ruh!	And guard my peace of mind!
Der ist in tiefster Seele treu,	For he is loyal in heart and soul
Wer die Heimat so liebt wie du.	Who loves his homeland as you.

Zu Roß, wir reiten nach Linlithgow,	To horse! We shall ride to Linlithgow,
Und du reitest an meiner Seit',	And you will ride at my side,
Da wollen wir fischen und jagen froh	There we shall happily fish and hunt,
Als wie in alter Zeit."	As we did in days gone by.'

1860 Tom der Reimer / Thomas Rhymer Op. 135a
TRANSLATED BY FONTANE FROM AN 18TH-CENTURY SCOTTISH BALLAD

Der Reimer Thomas lag am Bach,	Thomas Rhymer lay by the burn,
Am Kieselbach bei Huntly Schloß,	The pebble burn by Huntly Castle,
Da sah er eine blonde Frau,	When he beheld a fair lady
Die saß auf einem weißen Roß.	Sitting on a white steed.

Sie saß auf einem weißen Roß,	She was sitting on a white steed
Die Mähne war geflochten fein,	Whose mane was finely braided,
Und hell an jeder Flechte hing	And brightly shining from each braid
Ein silberblankes Glöckelein.	There hung a tiny silver bell.

Und Tom der Reimer zog den Hut	And Thomas Rhymer doffed his hat
Und fiel aufs Knie; – er grüßt und spricht:	And dropped on one knee, and greets her thus:
„Du bist die Himmelskönigin!	'You must be the Queen of Heaven!
Du bist von dieser Erde nicht."	You are not of this earth.'

Die blonde Frau hält an ihr Roß:	The fair lady reins in her steed:
„Ich will dir sagen, wer ich bin,	'I shall tell you who I am;
Ich bin die Himmelsjungfrau nicht,	I am not the Queen of Heaven,
Ich bin die Elfenkönigin.	I am the Queen of the Elves.
Nimm deine Harf' und spiel' und sing	Take up your harp and play and sing
Und laß dein bestes Lied erschalln,	And let your finest song be heard,
Doch wenn du meine Lippe küßt,	But if you ever kiss my lips,
Bist du mir sieben Jahr verfalln."	You shall serve me for seven years.'
„Wohl! Sieben Jahr, o Königin,	'To serve you, O queen, for seven years,
Zu dienen dir, es schreckt mich kaum!"	Shall scarcely frighten me!'
Er küßte sie, sie küßte ihn,	He kissed her, she kissed him,
Ein Vogel sang im Eschenbaum.	A bird sang in the ash-tree.
„Nun bist du mein, nun zieh mit mir,	'Now you are mine, now come with me,
Nun bist du mein auf sieben Jahr'";	Now you are mine for seven years!'
Sie ritten durch den grünen Wald,	They rode through the green wood,
Wie glücklich da der Reimer war.	How happy now the Rhymer was.
Sie ritten durch den grünen Wald	They rode through the green wood,
Bei Vogelsang und Sonnenschein,	The birds sang, the sun shone,
Und wenn sie leicht am Zügel zog,	And when she lightly pulled the reins,
So klangen hell die Glöckelein.	The little bells rang brightly.

Johann Wolfgang von Goethe (1749–1832)

See Beethoven, Brahms, Hensel, Mendelssohn, Mozart, Reichardt, Schubert, Strauss, Wolf, Zelter

Goethe, whom Loewe set more than fifty times, was the composer's favourite poet. His 'Erlkönig', composed some two years after Schubert's, is arguably truer to the original poem, and Wagner preferred it; the pity is that when Loewe met Goethe in Jena to talk about balladry, there was no piano on which he could accompany himself. In Loewe's diary, however, there are tantalizing snippets of their conversation:

Goethe war außerordentlich gütig. Während er mit mir im Salon auf- und niederging, unterhielt er sich mit mir über das Wesen der Ballade – Noch stand der Diener immer auf der Schwelle, und erst als das Gespräch schon eine geraume Zeit gedauert hatte, winkte Goethe und wir blieben allein. – Ich sagte ihm, wie ich die Ballade vor allen andern Dichtungsformen liebe, wie die volksthümliche Sage seines Erlkönig in dem großartig romantischen Gewande seiner Dichtung mich ganz hingenommen; so hingenommen, daß ich diesen Erlkönig habe componiren müssen: „Ich hielte schon deshalb den Erlkönig für die beste deutsche Ballade, weil die Personen alle redend eingeführt seien." „Da haben Sie Recht," sagte Goethe.

Goethe was extraordinarily gracious. As he walked with me up and down the drawing room, we conversed about the nature of balladry. The servant was still standing by the door, and it was only when we had been talking for some time that Goethe gestured to him – and we were alone. I told him how I loved the ballad more than any other literary genre, how the traditional legend of the Erlking in the superbly romantic guise of his poem had so completely bowled me over, that I simply had to set this Erlking to music: 'I consider the Erlking to be the best German ballad, because each character is introduced through speech.' 'You are right,' said Goethe.

1832 Der Zauberlehrling / The sorcerer's apprentice Op. 20, no. 2

Hat der alte Hexenmeister	The old sorcerer
Sich doch einmal wegbegeben!	Has finally gone away!
Und nun sollen seine Geister	Now the spirits he controls
Auch nach meinem Willen leben.	Shall obey my commands.
Seine Wort' und Werke	I've noted his method,
Merkt' ich und den Brauch,	What he says and does,
Und mit Geistesstärke	And with strength of spirit,
Tu' ich Wunder auch.	I shall work wonders too.

Walle! walle	Wander! Wander
Manche Strecke,	On and on,
Daß zum Zwecke	So that water
Wasser fließe	Might flow,
Und mit reichem, vollem Schwalle	And gush abundantly
Zu dem Bade sich ergieße.	And fill the bath.

Und nun komm, du alter Besen!	So come along, you old broomstick!
Nimm die schlechten Lumpenhüllen!	Dress yourself in rotten rags!
Bist schon lange Knecht gewesen;	You've long been a servant;
Nun erfülle meinen Willen!	Obey my orders now!
Auf zwei Beinen stehe,	Stand up on two legs,
Oben sei ein Kopf,	Let's give you a head on top,
Eile nun und gehe	Make haste now and off you go
Mit dem Wassertopf!	With the water-jug!

Walle! walle	Wander! Wander
Manche Strecke,	On and on,
Daß zum Zwecke	So that water
Wasser fließe	Might flow,
Und mit reichem, vollem Schwalle	And gush abundantly
Zu dem Bade sich ergieße.	And fill the bath.

Seht, er läuft zum Ufer nieder;	Look, he's running down to the bank;
Wahrlich! ist schon an dem Flusse,	In truth! He's already reached the river,
Und mit Blitzesschnelle wieder	And back he comes as quick as lightning
Ist er hier mit raschem Gusse.	And swiftly pours it all out.

Schon zum zweiten Male!
Wie das Becken schwillt!
Wie sich jede Schale
Voll mit Wasser füllt!

    Stehe! stehe!
    Denn wir haben
    Deiner Gaben
    Vollgemessen! –
    Ach, ich merk es! Wehe! wehe!
    Hab' ich doch das Wort vergessen!

Ach, das Wort, worauf am Ende
Er das wird, was er gewesen.
Ach, er läuft und bringt behende!
Wärst du doch der alte Besen!
Immer neue Güsse
Bringt er schnell herein,
Ach! und hundert Flüsse
Stürzen auf mich ein.

    Nein, nicht länger
    Kann ich's lassen;
    Will ihn fassen.
    Das ist Tücke!
    Ach! nun wird mir immer bänger!
    Welche Miene! welche Blicke!

O du Ausgeburt der Hölle!
Soll das ganze Haus ersaufen?
Seh' ich über jede Schwelle
Doch schon Wasserströme laufen.
Du verruchter Besen,
Der nicht hören will!
Stock, der du gewesen,
Steh doch wieder still!

    Willst's am Ende
    Gar nicht lassen?
    Will dich fassen,
    Will dich halten
    Will das alte Holz behende
    Mit dem scharfen Beile spalten.

Seht, da kommt er schleppend wieder!
Wie ich mich nur auf dich werfe,
Gleich, o Kobold, liegst du nieder;
Krachend trifft die glatte Schärfe.
Wahrlich! brav getroffen!
Seht, er ist entzwei!

Here he comes a second time!
Look how the tub is filling!
Look how every basin
Fills to overflowing!

    Stand still, stand still!
    Because we
    Have had our fill
    Of all your gifts! –
    Alas! Alas! I realize now:
    I've forgotten the magic word!

The word, alas, that turns him back
Into what he once was.
Alas! speedily he runs and fetches!
If only you were a broom as before!
He keeps rushing in
With more and more water,
Alas! a hundred rivers
Pour down on my head!

    No, I won't permit it
    A moment longer;
    I shall seize him.
    Oh, the spiteful brute!
    Ah, now I'm getting really scared!
    What a face! And what a look!

O, you creature from hell!
Shall the entire house be drowned?
I can see streams of water
Pouring through every door.
A despicable broom
Not to listen!
You who were once a stick –
Will you once again stand still!

    Will you never
    Ever stop?
    I'll catch you,
    I'll hold you,
    And swiftly split this old wood
    With this sharp hatchet.

Look, once more he comes, dragging pails!
Wait till I get to grips with you,
Then, O goblin, I'll knock you flat;
The smooth blade crashes down on him.
A fine blow, in truth!
Look – he's split in two!

| Und nun darf ich hoffen, | There's hope for me now, |
| Und ich atme frei! | I can breathe freely again! |

Wehe! wehe!	Alas! alas!
Beide Teile	Both halves
Stehn in Eile	Stand up at once,
Schon als Knechte	A pair of servants,
Völlig fertig in die Höhe!	Ready for action!
Helft mir, ach! ihr hohen Mächte!	Ah, help me, you powers on high!

Und sie laufen! Naß und nässer	And off they run! Hall and steps
Wird's im Saal und auf den Stufen.	Get wetter and wetter.
Welch entsetzliches Gewässer!	What a ghastly inundation!
Herr und Meister! hör mich rufen! –	Lord and master, hear my cries! –
Ach, da kommt der Meister!	Ah, my master comes at last!
Herr, die Not ist groß!	Sir, I'm in desperate straits!
Die ich rief, die Geister,	The spirits I summoned –
Werd' ich nun nicht los.	I can't get rid of them.

„In die Ecke,	'Into the corner,
Besen! Besen!	Brooms! Brooms –
Seid's gewesen!	Have done!
Denn als Geister	Only your old master
Ruft euch nur, zu seinem Zwecke,	Can call you forth
Erst hervor der alte Meister."	As spirits.'

(*Zelter, Zumsteeg*)

1832 Die wandelnde Glocke / The walking bell Op. 20, no. 3

Es war ein Kind, das wollte nie	A child there was who never would
Zur Kirche sich bequemen,	Agree to go to church,
Und sonntags fand es stets ein Wie,	And every Sunday would find a way
Den Weg ins Feld zu nehmen.	Of escaping to the fields.

Die Mutter sprach: „Die Glocke tönt,	His mother said: the church bell's ringing,
Und so ist dir's befohlen,	And so you are commanded,
Und hast du dich nicht hingewöhnt,	And if you don't make a habit of going,
Sie kommt und wird dich holen."	The bell will come and fetch you.

Das Kind, es denkt: Die Glocke hängt	The child thinks, the bell's hanging
Da droben auf dem Stuhle.	Up there in the belfry.
Schon hat's den Weg ins Feld gelenkt,	And already he's heading for the fields,
Als lief' es aus der Schule.	As though running out of school.

Die Glocke, Glocke tönt nicht mehr,	The bell, the bell no longer rings,
Die Mutter hat gefackelt.	Mother was telling lies.
Doch welch ein Schrecken hinterher!	But what a fright – behind the child
Die Glocke kommt gewackelt.	The bell comes waddling after him.

| Sie wackelt schnell, man glaubt es kaum; | It waddles fast, it's beyond belief; |
| Das arme Kind im Schrecken, | The poor child, in his terror, |

Es läuft, es kommt als wie im Traum:	Runs as though he's in a dream;
Die Glocke wird es decken.	The bell will smother him.

Doch nimmt es richtig seinen Husch,	But he runs in the right direction,
Und mit gewandter Schnelle	And swiftly and with agility
Eilt es durch Anger, Feld und Busch	Hurries across field and mead and bush
Zur Kirche, zur Kapelle.	To the church and to the chapel.

Und jeden Sonn- und Feiertag	And every Sunday and feast day
Gedenkt es an den Schaden,	He remembers the misadventure,
Läßt durch den ersten Glockenschlag,	Obeys the first stroke of the bell,
Nicht in Person sich laden.	Without waiting to be summoned.
(*Robert Schumann*)	

1833 *Drei Lieder des Turmwächters Lynceus / Three Songs of Watchman Lynceus*
Op. 9, VIII
FROM *Faust*, PART II

1

Turmwächter Lynceus, zu den Füßen der Helena / Watchman Lynceus at Helena's feet

Laß mich knieen, laß mich schauen,	Let me kneel, let me gaze,
Laß mich sterben, laß mich leben!	Let me die, let me live!
Denn schon bin ich hingegeben	For I am already pledged
Dieser gottgegebnen Frauen!	To this God-given woman!

Harrend auf des Morgens Wonne,	Waiting for the morning's rapture,
Östlich spähend ihren Lauf,	Gazing eastward for its rays,
Ging auf einmal mir die Sonne	Suddenly I saw the sun
Wunderbar im Süden auf,	Rise wondrously in the south,

Zog den Blick nach jener Seite,	Turned my gaze in that direction,
Statt der Schluchten, statt der Höh'n,	Not at ravines or mountain heights,
Statt der Erd- und Himmelsweite,	Not at the earth or the wide heavens,
Sie, die Einzige, zu spähn.	But simply to behold her.

Augenstrahl ist mir verliehen	Piercing vision I was granted,
Wie dem Luchs auf höchstem Baum;	Like the lynx on the highest tree,
Doch nun mußt' ich mich bemühen	But now I had to exert myself,
Wie im allertiefsten Traum.	As in the deepest of all dreams.

Wüßt' ich irgend mich zu finden?	Could I discover where I am?
Zinne? Turm? Geschloßnes Tor?	Battlements? Tower? A closed gate?
Nebel schwanken, Nebel schwinden:	Mists swirl, mists vanish:
Solche Göttin tritt hervor!	Such a goddess now steps forth!

Aug' und Brust ihr zugewendet,	With eyes and heart fixed on her,
Sog ich an den milden Glanz;	I imbibed her gentle radiance;
Diese Schönheit, wie sie blendet,	How this dazzling beauty
Blendete mich Armen ganz.	Dazzled poor me entirely.

Ich vergaß des Wächters Pflichten,	I forgot the watchman's duties,
Völlig das beschworne Horn. –	Forgot my vow to blow the horn:
Drohe nur, mich zu vernichten!	Though you threaten to destroy me,
Schönheit bändigt allen Zorn.	Beauty quells all anger.

2

Lynceus, der Helena seine Schätze anbietend / Lynceus, offering Helena his treasures

Du siehst mich, Königin, zurück!	You see me, Queen, back home again!
Der Reiche bettelt einen Blick:	The rich man begs a glance,
Er sieht dich an und fühlt sogleich	He looks at you, and feels at once
Sich bettelarm und fürstenreich.	He's a pauper and a prince!

Was war ich erst? Was bin ich nun?	What was I once? What am I now?
Was ist zu wollen? Was zu tun?	What should I want? What should I do?
Was hilft der Augen schärfster Blitz?	What do the eyes' keenest gaze accomplish?
Er prallt zurück an deinem Sitz.	My eyes gaze back to where you sit.

Von Osten kamen wir heran,	We came here from the East,
Und um den Westen war's getan;	The West was already overrun;
Ein lang' und breites Volksgewicht,	A long and seething mass of people,
Der erste wußte vom letzten nicht.	The first knew nothing of the last.

Der erste fiel, der zweite stand,	The first fell, the second stood,
Des dritten Lanze war zur Hand –	The third man's lance was ready to throw –
Ein jeder hundertfach gestärkt,	A hundred reinforcements for every man,
Erschlagne Tausend unbemerkt.	Thousands slain went unnoticed.

Wir drängten fort, wir stürmten fort,	We pressed on, we stormed on,
Wir waren Herrn von Ort zu Ort;	We were masters of every town;
Und wo ich herrisch heut befahl,	And where I barked out orders today,
Ein andrer morgen raubt' und stahl.	Another robbed and stole tomorrow.

Wir schauten, – eilig war die Schau:	We looked, – but we looked in haste:
Der griff die allerschönste Frau,	One man seized the fairest of women,
Der griff den Stier von festem Tritt,	Another the sturdy oxen,
Die Pferde mußten alle mit.	And the horses had to come with us.

Ich aber liebte zu erspähn	But I loved to feast my eyes
Das Seltenste, was man gesehn,	On the rarest thing to be seen,
Und was ein andrer auch besaß,	And whatever others possessed,
Das war für mich gedörrtes Gras.	Was for me but withered grass.

Den Schätzen war ich auf der Spur,	I tracked down treasures,
Den scharfen Blicken folgt' ich nur;	I followed where sharp sight led me,
In alle Taschen blickt' ich ein,	I looked into every purse,
Durchsichtig war mir jeder Schrein.	I could see through every casket.

Und Haufen Goldes waren mein,	And heaps of gold belonged to me,
Am herrlichsten der Edelstein:	Finest of all were precious stones;
Nun der Smaragd allein verdient,	Only this emerald is worthy
Daß er an deinem Herzen grünt.	To shed its green on your breast.

Nun schwanke zwischen Ohr und Mund	Let the raindrop pearl from the ocean's depths
Das Tropfenei aus Meeresgrund!	Quiver between ear and mouth!
Rubinen werden gar verscheucht:	Rubies are dismissed:
Das Wangenrot sie niederbleicht.	Red cheeks cause them to pale.
Und so den allergrößten Schatz	And so I set the greatest treasure
Versetz' ich hier auf deinen Platz;	Here where you are sitting;
Zu deinen Füßen sei gebracht	May the spoils of bloody battles
Die Ernte mancher blut'gen Schlacht.	Be placed here at your feet.
So viele Kisten schlepp' ich her,	No matter how many iron chests I bring,
Der Eisenkisten hab' ich mehr;	I still have many more;
Erlaube mich auf deiner Bahn,	Allow me to escort you,
Und Schatzgewölbe füll' ich an.	And I shall fill your treasuries.
Denn du bestiegest kaum den Thron,	For you had hardly ascended the throne
So neigen schon, so beugen schon	When understanding, wealth and power
Verstand und Reichtum und Gewalt	Inclined their heads and bowed
Sich vor der einzigen Gestalt.	Before your matchless form.
Das alles hielt ich fest und mein,	All that belonged to me, was mine,
Nun aber, lose, wird es dein!	Is now yours, since I loosen my grasp!
Ich glaubt' es würdig, hoch und bar,	I believed it was worthy, noble and pure,
Nun seh' ich, daß es nichtig war.	But now I see it was nothing.
Verschwunden ist, was ich besaß,	What I possessed has vanished,
Ein abgemähtes, welkes Gras:	Like mown and withered grass.
O gib mit einem heitern Blick	O give it back its whole value
Ihm seinen ganzen Wert zurück!	With a radiant glance!

3

Lynceus*, der Türmer, auf Faust's Sternwarte singend / Lynceus, the watchman, singing on Faust's observatory

Zum Sehen geboren,	I am born for seeing,
Zum Schauen bestellt,	Employed to watch,
Dem Turme geschworen,	Sworn to the tower,
Gefällt mir die Welt.	I delight in the world.
Ich blick' in die Ferne,	I see what is far,
Ich seh' in der Näh'	I see what is near,
Den Mond und die Sterne,	The moon and the stars,
Den Wald und das Reh.	The wood and the deer.
So seh' ich in allen	In all these I see
Die ewige Zier,	Eternal beauty,
Und wie mir's gefallen,	And as it has pleased me,
Gefall' ich auch mir.	I'm pleasing to myself.

* The name of the hero who served the Argonauts as lookout and watchman. The name is derived from the same source as 'lynx'. Goethe's Lynceus of Faust, Act V, stands on a 'Warte', an observation tower and announces all that he sees; he also acts as Faust's conscience.

Ihr glücklichen Augen,	O happy eyes,
Was je ihr gesehn,	Whatever you have seen,
Es sei, wie es wolle,	Let it be as it may,
Es war doch so schön!	How fair it has been!
(*Schumann*)	

1833 Mädchenwünsche / What a girl desires Op. 9, VIII

O fände für mich	Oh, if only a husband
Ein Bräutigam sich!	Could be found for me!
Wie schön wär es da:	How good it would be
Man nennt uns Mama;	To be called Mama;
Da braucht man zum Nähen,	There'd be no need for school
Zur Schul' nicht zu gehen;	In order to sew;
Da kann man befehlen,	I'd snap out orders,
Hat Mägde, darf schmälen,	Have maids and rebuke them,
Man wählt sich die Kleider,	Choose my own clothes
Nach Gusto den Schneider;	And a dressmaker I liked;
Da läßt man spazieren,	I'd be taken out walking
Auf Bälle sich führen,	Or taken to dances,
Und fragt nicht erst lange	Without having to ask
Papa und Mama.	Papa and Mama.
(*Bernhard Theodor Breitkopf*)	

1833 Gutmann und Gutweib / Goodman and goodwife Op. 9, VIII
TRANSLATION BY GOETHE OF TRADITIONAL SCOTTISH BALLAD

Und morgen fällt St. Martins Fest,	It is Saint Martinmas eve,
Gutweib liebt ihren Mann;	Goodwife loves her husband;
Da knetet sie ihm Puddings ein	She's been preparing him puddings
Und bäckt sie in der Pfann'.	And now cooks them in the pan.

Im Bette liegen beide nun,	Both of them now lie in bed,
Da saust ein wilder West;	A furious west wind starts to blow;
Und Gutmann spricht zur guten Frau:	And Goodman says to his good wife:
„Du riegle die Türe fest."	'Get up and bar the door.'

„Bin kaum erholt und halb erwarmt,	'I've hardly had time to warm myself,
Wie käm' ich da zur Ruh;	How would I ever get to sleep;
Und klapperte sie einhundert Jahr,	And though it banged for a hundred years,
Ich riegelte sie nicht zu."	I would never bar that door.'

Drauf eine Wette schlossen sie	Whereupon they whispered a bet
Ganz leise sich ins Ohr:	Into each other's ear:
So wer das erste Wörtlein spräch',	Let him who speaks the first word
Der schöbe den Riegel vor.	Get up and bar the door.

Zwei Wanderer kommen um Mitternacht	Two travellers arrive as midnight strikes,
Und wissen nicht, wo sie stehn,	Without knowing where they were,

| Die Lampe losch, der Herd verglomm, | The lamp went out, the coals burned low, |
| Zu hören ist nichts, zu sehn. | There was neither light nor sound. |

„Was ist das für ein Hexenort?	'What kind of haunted place is this?
Da bricht uns die Geduld!"	Our patience is at an end!'
Doch hörten sie kein Sterbenswort,	But there was not a word in reply,
Des war die Türe schuld.	For that the door was to blame.

Den weißen Pudding speisten sie,	And first they ate the white pudding,
Den schwarzen ganz vertraut;	And then they ate the black;
Und Gutweib sagt sich selber viel,	And Goodwife says much to herself,
Doch keine Silbe laut.	But not a word out loud.

Zu diesem sprach der eine dann:	One traveller now said to the other:
„Wie trocken ist mir der Hals!	'My throat's so parched and dry!
Der Schrank, der klafft, und geistig riecht's,	The cupboard's wide open, it smells of spirits,
Da findet sich's allenfalls.	That'll be where they keep it.

„Ein Fläschchen Schnaps ergreif' ich da,	I'll grab a bottle of Schnapps,
Das trifft sich doch geschickt!	Just what the doctor ordered!
Ich bring' es dir, du bringst es mir,	I'll serve you and you'll serve me,
Und bald sind wir erquickt."	And soon we'll be refreshed.'

Doch Gutmann sprang so heftig auf	But Goodman leapt wildly to his feet,
Und fuhr sie drohend an:	And bellowed in their face:
„Bezahlen soll mit teurem Geld,	'Whoever's wasted my own Schnapps
Wer mir den Schnaps vertan!"	Shall pay for it in cash!'

Und Gutweib sprang auch froh heran,	At which our Goodwife started up
Drei Sprüng', als wär' sie reich:	And skipped about with glee:
„Du Gutmann sprachst das erste Wort,	'Goodman, you've spoken first,
Nun riegle die Türe gleich!"	Get up and bar the door!'
(*Wolf*)	

1835 Canzonette / Canzonetta WoO

War schöner als der schönste Tag,	She was lovelier than the loveliest day,
Drum muß man mir verzeihen,	And so I must be forgiven
Daß ich sie nicht vergessen mag,	That I cannot forget her,
Am wenigsten im Freien.	Especially out of doors.
Im Garten war's, sie trat heran,	It was in the garden, she drew near
Mir ihre Gunst zu zeigen;	To offer me her favours;
Das fühl' ich noch und denke dran	I feel it still and think of it
Und bleib' ihr ganz zu eigen.	And am wholly hers.

Johann Gottfried Herder (1744–1803)

Herder was one of the first intellectuals to formulate the view that history is a process of organic growth, and thus exercised a huge influence on literature, music, aesthetics and politics. *Stimmen der Völker in Liedern* (1807) contained Herder's German versions of European lyrics and ballads, including 'Edward', 'Erlkönigs Tochter' and 'Elvershöh' – all of which were set by Loewe. This seminal anthology of verse introduced Goethe to Shakespeare and folk poetry. It was also in *Stimmen der Völker in Liedern* that Goethe first encountered the Danish Erlking legend.

1824 Edward Op. 1, no. 1
TRANSLATION BY HERDER FROM AN 18TH-CENTURY SCOTS BALLAD

Dein Schwert, wie ist's von Blut so rot?
   Edward, Edward!
Dein Schwert, wie ist's von Blut so rot,
   Und gehst so traurig da? – Oh!
Ich hab' geschlagen meinen Geier tot,
   Mutter, Mutter!
Ich hab' geschlagen meinen Geier tot,
   Und das, das geht mir nah – Oh!

Deines Geiers Blut ist nicht so rot,
   Edward, Edward!
Deines Geiers Blut ist nicht so rot,
   Mein Sohn, bekenn mir frei – Oh!
Ich hab' geschlagen mein Rotroß tot,
   Mutter, Mutter!
Ich hab' geschlagen mein Rotroß tot,
   Und's war so stolz und treu – Oh!

Dein Roß war alt und hast's nicht not,
   Edward, Edward!
Dein Roß war alt und hast's nicht not,
   Dich drückt ein andrer Schmerz – Oh!
Ich hab' geschlagen meinen Vater tot,
   Mutter, Mutter!
Ich hab' geschlagen meinen Vater tot,
   Und das, das quält mein Herz – Oh!

Und was wirst du nun an dir tun?
   Edward, Edward!
Und was wirst du nun an dir tun?
   Mein Sohn, das sage mir – Oh!
Auf Erden soll mein Fuß nicht ruhn!
   Mutter, Mutter!
Auf Erden soll mein Fuß nicht ruhn!
   Will wandern übers Meer – Oh!

Und was soll werden dein Hof und Hall?
   Edward, Edward!
Und was soll werden aus Hof und Hall?

Why is your sword so red with blood?
   Edward, Edward!
Why is your sword so red with blood,
   And why do you walk so sadly? – O!
I have struck my falcon dead,
   Mother, mother!
I have struck my falcon dead,
   And that's what makes me sad – O!

Your falcon's blood is not so red,
   Edward, Edward!
Your falcon's blood is not so red,
   My son, confess the truth – O!
I have struck my red roan dead,
   Mother, mother!
I have struck my red roan dead,
   And it was so proud and true – O!

Your steed was old and you need it not,
   Edward, Edward!
Your steed was old and you need it not,
   Some other grief afflicts you– O!
I have struck my father dead,
   Mother, mother!
I have struck my father dead,
   And that torments my heart – O!

And what penance will you now do?
   Edward, Edward!
And what penance will you now do?
   Tell me that, my son – O!
My feet will never rest on earth,
   Mother, mother!
My feet will never rest on earth,
   I'll fare across the sea – O!

And what shall become of your house and home?
   Edward, Edward!
And what shall become of your house and home?

So herrlich sonst, so schön – Oh!
Ach immer steh's und sink und fall!
    Mutter, Mutter!
Ach immer steh's und sink und fall!
    Ich werd' es nimmer sehn – Oh!

Und was soll werden aus Weib und Kind?
    Edward, Edward!
Und was soll werden aus Weib und Kind,
    Wann du gehst übers Meer? – Oh!
Die Welt ist groß, laß sie betteln drin,
    Mutter, Mutter!
Die Welt ist groß, laß sie betteln drin,
    Ich seh' sie nimmermehr – Oh!

Und was soll deine Mutter tun?
    Edward, Edward!
Und was soll deine Mutter tun?
    Mein Sohn, das sage mir – Oh!
Der Fluch der Hölle soll auf Euch ruhn,
    Mutter, Mutter!
Der Fluch der Hölle soll auf Euch ruhn,
    Denn Ihr, Ihr rietet's mir! – Oh!
(*Brahms, Schubert, Tchaikovsky*)

Till now so lordly and fair – O!
Let them stand till down they fall,
    Mother, mother!
Let them stand till down they fall,
    I shall see them nevermore – O!

And what shall become of your wife and child?
    Edward, Edward?
And what shall become of your wife and child?
    When you go across the sea? – O!
The world is wide, let them beg through life,
    Mother, mother!
The world is wide, let them beg through life,
    I shall see them nevermore! – O!

And what is your mother now to do?
    Edward, Edward?
And what is your mother now to do?
    Tell me that, my son!
The curse of hell shall fall on you,
    Mother, mother!
The curse of hell shall fall on you,
    For it was you who counselled me! – O!

1821 Herr Oluf / Sir Oluf Op. 2, no. 2

Herr Oluf reitet spät und weit,
Zu bieten auf seine Hochzeitleut.

Da tanzen die Elfen auf grünem Strand,
Erlkönigs Tochter reicht ihm die Hand:

„Willkommen, Herr Oluf, komm tanze mit mir,
Zwei goldene Sporen schenke ich dir."

„Ich darf nicht tanzen, nicht tanzen ich mag,
Denn morgen ist mein Hochzeittag."

„Tritt näher, Herr Oluf, komm tanze mit mir,
Ein Hemd von Seide schenke ich dir,

Ein Hemd von Seide, so weiß und fein,
Meine Mutter bleicht's mit Mondenschein."

„Ich darf nicht tanzen, nicht tanzen ich mag,
Denn morgen ist mein Hochzeittag."

„Tritt näher, Herr Oluf, komm tanze mit mir,
Einen Haufen Goldes schenke ich dir."

Sir Oluf rode far through the night
Inviting his friends to his wedding;

Elves were dancing on the green shore,
Erlking's daughter holds out her hand.

'Welcome, Sir Oluf, come, dance with me,
Two golden spurs I'll give to thee.'

'I must not dance, I will not dance,
For tomorrow is my wedding day.'

'Come closer, Sir Oluf, come dance with me,
A silken shirt I'll give to thee,

A silken shirt so white and fine,
My mother bleached it with moonshine.'

'I must not dance, I will not dance,
For tomorrow is my wedding day.'

'Come closer, Sir Oluf, come, dance with me,
A heap of gold I'll give to thee.'

„Einen Haufen Goldes nähme ich wohl;
Doch tanzen ich nicht darf noch soll."

'I'd gladly take a heap of gold,
But I may not and must not dance.'

„Und willst du, Herr Oluf, nicht tanzen mit mir,
Soll Seuch und Krankheit folgen dir."

'And if, Sir Oluf, you'll not dance with me,
Disease and sickness shall follow thee.'

Sie tät ihm geben einen Schlag auf's Herz,
Sein Lebtag fühlt er nicht solchen Schmerz.

She struck her hand across his heart,
Never in his life did he feel such pain.

Drauf tät sie ihn heben auf sein Pferd:
„Reit hin zu deinem Fräulein wert!"

She lifted him up onto his steed:
'Ride back home to your worthy bride.'

Und als er kam vor Hauses Tür,
Seine Mutter zitternd stand dafür.

And when at last he reached his home,
His mother stood trembling outside the door.

„Sag an, mein Sohn, und sag mir gleich,
Wovon du bist so blaß und bleich?"

'Tell me, my son, tell me at once,
Why are you so pale and wan?'

„Und sollt ich nicht sein blaß und bleich,
Ich kam in Erlenkönigs Reich."

'And should I not be pale and wan?
I set foot in the Erlking's realm.'

„Sag an, mein Sohn, so lieb und traut,
Was soll ich sagen deiner Braut?"

'Tell me, my son, so beloved and dear,
What shall I say to your bride-to-be?'

„Sagt ihr, ich ritt in den Wald zur Stund
Zu proben allda mein Roß und Hund."

'Tell her I rode just now to the wood,
There to try my horse and hound.'

Frühmorgens, als der Tag kaum war,
Da kam die Braut mit der Hochzeitschar.

At early morn, when day had scarce dawned,
His bride arrived with the wedding throng.

Sie schenkten Met, sie schenkten Wein;
„Wo ist Herr Oluf, der Bräutgam mein?"

They poured the mead, they poured the wine,
'Where is Sir Oluf, my husband-to-be?'

„Herr Oluf ritt in den Wald zur Stund,
Zu proben allda sein Roß und Hund."

'Sir Oluf rode just now to the wood,
There to try his horse and hound.'

Die Braut hob auf den Scharlach rot:
Da lag Herr Oluf und war tot.
(*Pfitzner*)

The bride raised up the scarlet cloth,
There lay Sir Oluf, and was dead.

Friedrich Rückert (1788–1866)

See Robert Schumann

1837 Süßes Begräbnis / Loving burial Op. 62, no. 4

Schäferin, ach, wie haben
  Sie dich so süß begraben!
Alle Lüfte haben getönet,
  Maienglocken zu Grab dir getönet.
  Glühwurm wollte die Fackel tragen,
  Stern ihm selbst es tät versagen.

Shepherdess, O how sweetly
  Have they buried you!
All the breezes broke out sighing,
  Lilies-of-the-valley rang their bells,
  The glow-worm wished to bear the torch,
  But the star would not allow it.

Nacht ging schwarz in Trauerflören,	Night wore black in deep mourning,
Und all ihre Schatten gingen in Chören.	And all its shadows formed a choir.
Die Tränen wird dir das Morgenrot weinen,	Dawn will shed its tears for you,
Und den Segen die Sonn' aufs Grab dir scheinen.	And the sun shine its blessing on your grave.
Schäferin, ach, wie haben	Shepherdess, O how sweetly
Sie dich so süß begraben!	Have they buried you!

1837 Hinkende Jamben / Limping iambics Op. 62, no. 5

Ein Liebchen hatt' ich, das auf einem Aug' schielte;	I had a sweetheart who squinted with one eye;
Weil sie mir schön schien, schien ihr Schielen auch Schönheit.	Because I found her lovely, her squint was lovely too.
Eins hatt' ich, das beim Sprechen mit der Zung' anstieß;	Another I had who lisped when she spoke;
Mir war's kein Anstoß, stieß sie an und sprach: Liebster!	I took no umbrage when she lisped: Sweetheart!
Jetzt hab' ich eines, das auf einem Fuß hinket;	Now I have one who limps with one foot;
Ja freilich, sprech' ich, hinkt sie, doch sie hinkt zierlich.	Yes indeed, say I, she limps, but limps most gracefully.

1838 Kleiner Haushalt / A little home Op. 71

Einen Haushalt klein und fein	I've set up
Hab' ich angestellt;	A little home;
Der soll mein Gast sein,	He who likes it well
Dem er wohlgefällt.	Shall be my guest.
Der Specht, der Holz mit dem Schnabel haut,	The wood-pecking woodpecker
Hat das Haus mir aufgebaut;	Built it for me;
Daß das Haus beworfen sei,	The swallow provided
Trug die Schwalbe Mörtel bei,	The plastering,
Und als Dach hat sich zuletzt	And finally for the roof
Obendrauf ein Schwamm gesetzt.	A mushroom sat on top.
Drinnen die Kammern	The rooms within,
Und die Gemächer,	And the apartments,
Schränke und Fächer,	Cupboards and shelves
Flimmern und flammen;	Shine and sparkle;
Alles hat mir unbezahlt	The butterfly, free of charge,
Schmetterling mit Duft bemalt.	Painted and scented everything.
O wie rüstig in dem Haus	Oh how briskly about the house
Geht die Wirtschaft ein und aus.	My managers go in and out.
Wasserjüngferchen, das flinke,	The nimble dragonfly
Holt mir Wasser, das ich trinke;	Fetches me water to drink;
Biene muß mir Essen holen,	The bee's task is to bring my food,
Frage nicht, wo sie's gestohlen.	I don't ask where she's filched it from.
Schüsseln sind die Eichelnäpfchen,	Acorn-cups are dishes,
Und die Krüge Tannenzäpfchen,	Fir-cones are jugs,

Messer, Gabel,
Rosendorn und Vogelschnabel.
　Storch im Haus ist Kinderwärter,
Maulwurf Gärtner,
Und Beschließerin im Häuslein
Ist das Mäuslein.
　Aber die Grille
Singt in der Stille,
Sie ist das Heimchen, ist immer daheim,
Und weiß nichts, als den einen Reim.
　Doch im ganzen Haus das Beste
Schläft noch feste.
　In dem Winkel, in dem Bettchen,
Zwischen zweien Rosenblättchen,
Schläft das Schätzchen Tausendschönchen,
Ihr zu Fuß ein Kaiserkrönchen.
Hüter ist Vergißmeinnicht,
Der vom Bette wanket nicht;
Glühwurm mit dem Kerzenschimmer
Hellt das Zimmer.
　Die Wachtel wacht
Die ganze Nacht,
Und wenn der Tag beginnt,
Ruft sie: Kind! Kind!
Wach auf geschwind.
　Wenn die Liebe wachet auf,
Geht das Leben raschen Lauf.
　In seidnen Gewändern,
Gewebt aus Sommerfaden,
In flatternden Bändern,
Von Sorgen unbeladen,
Lustig aus dem engen Haus
Lustig auf die Flur hinaus.
　Schönen Wagen
Hab' ich bestellt,
Uns zu tragen
Durch die Welt.
　Vier Heupferdchen sollen ihn
Als vier Apfelschimmel ziehn;
Sie sind wohl ein gut Gespann,
Das mit Rossen sich messen kann;
Sie haben Flügel,
Sie leiden nicht Zügel,
Sie kennen alle Blumen der Au',
Und alle Tränken von Tau genau.
　Es geht nicht im Schritt;
Kind, kannst du mit?
Es geht im Trott!

Knife and fork –
A rose's thorn, a bird's beak.
　The stork acts as nanny,
The mole as gardener,
And a little mouse
Runs the house.
　But the cricket
Sings in the silence,
The house cricket is always at home
And only knows the same old tune.
　But the best thing in all the house
Is still sound asleep.
　In the corner, in the cot,
Between two rose-petals,
The darling daisy is sleeping,
A crown-imperial at her feet.
Forget-me-not watches over her,
Never leaves her bedside;
The glow-worm with his candles
Lights the room.
　The quail keeps watch
All night long,
And when day dawns,
Cries: Child! Child!
Wake up at once.
　When my dear child wakes,
Then our life proceeds apace.
　In silken garments
Of gossamer weave,
In streaming ribbons,
Unburdened by care,
We cheerfully leave our cramped house,
Out into the field.
　I've ordered
A beautiful coach
To convey us
Through the world.
　Four grasshoppers shall draw it,
Like four dapple-greys;
A fine team, to be sure,
A match for any steed;
They have wings,
They can't stand reins,
Each meadow flower's known to them
And every dewy watering-place.
　We don't move slowly;
Child, can you keep up?
We go at a trot!

Nur zu mit Gott!	Onwards in God's name!
Laß du sie uns tragen	Let them carry us
Nach ihrem Behagen;	Just as they please;
Und wenn sie uns werfen vom Wagen herab,	And if they fling us from the coach,
So finden wir unter Blumen ein Grab.	We'll find a flowery grave.

Johann Nepomuk Vogl (1802–66)

Austrian poet whose *Balladen und Romanzen* (1835–41) and *Bilder aus dem Soldatenleben* (1852) once enjoyed great popularity. The historical model for 'Heinrich der Vogler' was Heinrich I, Duke of Saxony and German Emperor – the König Heinrich of Wagner's *Lohengrin*.

1836 Heinrich der Vogler / Henry the Fowler Op. 56, no. 1

Herr Heinrich sitzt am Vogelherd,	Lord Henry sits by his fowling-floor,
Recht froh und wohlgemut;	Happily and full of cheer;
Aus tausend Perlen blinkt und blitzt	The glow of dawn glistens
Der Morgenröte Glut.	From a thousand dewy pearls.

In Wies und Feld, in Wald und Au,	In field and meadow, wood and glade –
Horch, welch ein süßer Schall!	Just listen to those sweet sounds!
Der Lerche Sang, der Wachtel Schlag,	The lark's song, the quail's call,
Die süße Nachtigall!	The sweet voice of the nightingale!

Herr Heinrich schaut so fröhlich drein:	Lord Henry looks on cheerfully:
Wie schön ist heut die Welt!	The world seems so fair today!
Was gilt's, heut gibt's 'nen guten Fang!	The catch, I wager, will be good!
Er schaut zum Himmelszelt.	He looks up at the sky.

Er lauscht und streicht sich von der Stirn	He listens and brushes from his brow
Das blondgelockte Haar ...	His blond and curly hair ...
Ei doch! was sprengt denn dort herauf	But ah! what horsemen are these
Für eine Reiterschar?	Galloping up so fast?

Der Staub wallt auf, der Hufschlag dröhnt,	Dust billows, hooves drum,
Es naht der Waffen Klang;	The clank of arms draws near;
Daß Gott! die Herrn verderben mir	Great God, these men will wreck
Den ganzen Vogelfang!	The whole of this day's hunt!

Ei nun! was gibt's? Es hält der Troß	But what is this? All at once
Vorm Herzog plötzlich an,	The troop pulls up before the duke,
Herr Heinrich tritt hervor und spricht:	Lord Henry steps forward and says:
Wen sucht ihr Herrn? Sagt an!	Tell me, good sirs, who is it you seek?

Da schwenken sie die Fähnlein bunt	At that, they wave their bright flags,
Und jauchzen: Unsern Herrn!	And rejoicing cry: 'Our Master!
Hoch lebe Kaiser Heinrich, hoch!	Long may Emperor Henry live,
Des Sachsenlandes Stern!	Long live the star of Saxony!'

Sich neigend knien sie vor ihm hin,
Und huldigen ihm still,
Und rufen, als er staunend fragt:
's ist deutschen Reiches Will!

Da blickt Herr Heinrich tief bewegt
Hinauf zum Himmelszelt:
Du gabst mir einen guten Fang!
Herr Gott, wie dir's gefällt!

They bow and kneel before him
And pay him silent homage,
And to his astonished question, roar:
'The German Empire wills it!'

Deeply moved, Lord Henry looks up
To the heavens above:
'Thou hast granted me a good catch,
Lord God, as it pleaseth Thee!'

Alma Mahler (1879–1964)

Although Alma Mahler, according to her own testimony, wrote more than a hundred Lieder, only fourteen survive. Most of them were written after Zemlinsky became her composition teacher in 1897; following a passionate affair with him, she married Gustav Mahler who, in a celebrated letter, discouraged her from composing: „Ist es Dir möglich, von nun an *meine* Musik als die *Deine* anzusehen?" ('Is it possible for you from now on to regard *my* music as *yours*?') It was only after nine years of marriage that Mahler expressed an interest in Alma's songs and urged her to have them published. But it was too late: „Zehn Jahre verlorene Entwicklung sind nicht mehr nachzuholen. Es war ein galvanisierter Leichnam, den er neu beleben wollte." ('Ten years of wasted development cannot be made up any more. It was a galvanized corpse that he wanted to resurrect.') However, in the summer of 1910, Mahler selected five Lieder, composed by Alma in 1900–01, and had them published by Universal, at the same time as his own Eighth Symphony, which he dedicated to her. Universal published another five songs in 1915, while Weinberger of Leipzig published four more in 1924, including 'Der Erkennende', composed in the autumn of 1915 to a text by Franz Werfel. She fell under Werfel's spell, and they eventually married in 1929, fleeing from Nazi-occupied Austria to New York. It was to Alma that Alban Berg dedicated *Wozzeck* in 1922.

Rainer Maria Rilke (1875–1926)

See Hindemith

1900–01 Bei dir ist es traut / I feel warm and close with you

Bei dir ist es traut:	I feel warm and close with you:
Zage Uhren schlagen	clocks strike hesitantly,
wie aus weiten Tagen.	like they did in distant days.
Komm mir ein Liebes sagen –	Say something loving to me –
aber nur nicht laut.	but not aloud.
Ein Tor geht irgendwo	A gate opens somewhere
draußen im Blütentreiben.	out in the burgeoning.
Der Abend horcht an den Scheiben.	Evening listens at the window-panes.
Laß uns leise bleiben:	Let us stay quiet,
Keiner weiß uns so.	no one knows us thus.

Gustav Mahler (1860–1911)

Gustav Mahler is the only important Lieder composer never to have set in his piano-accompanied songs a single poem by one of the great poets of German literature, and this has in some quarters encouraged an erroneous view of him as being insensitive to lyric poetry; the fact, moreover, that many of his songs were either used in symphonies or have a symphonic feel to them has led some commentators to assert that he was a symphonist at heart, with scant regard for the subtleties of word-setting. Little could be further from the truth, although there is an orchestral quality inherent in virtually all his songs, even the piano-accompanied originals.

Mahler's approach to song-composition is recorded, somewhat vaingloriously, in *Gustav Mahler in den Erinnerungen von Natalie Bauer-Lechner*. Referring to his own songs, he asked her:

> Hast du bemerkt, daß bei mir immer die Melodie vom Worte ausgeht, das sich jene gleichsam schafft, nie umgekehrt! So ist es bei Beethoven und Wagner. Und nur so ist es aus einem Gusse, ist das, was man die Identität von Wort und Ton nennen möchte, vorhanden. Das Entgegengesetzte, wo irgendwelche Worte willkürlich zu einer Melodie sich fügen müssen, ist eine konventionelle Verbindung, aber keine organische Verschmelzung beider.

> Have you noticed that, with me, the melody always grows out of the words, that the words, so to speak, create the melody, never vice versa. That is the way it is with Beethoven and Wagner. And only in this way is the song a perfect whole, only in this way is achieved what one might call the identity of note and word. The opposite process, in which some words or other have to fit a melody arbitrarily, is the conventional relationship, but not an organic fusion of both elements.

And referring to Carl Loewe, Mahler told Bauer-Lechner:

> Auch kann er sich von der alten Form noch nicht befreien, wiederholt die einzelnen Strophen, während ich ein ewiges Weiterlaufen mit dem Inhalt des Liedes, das Durchkomponieren, als das wahre Prinzip der Musik erkenne. Bei mir findest du von allem Anfang an keine Wiederholung bei wechselnden Strophen mehr, eben weil in der Musik das Gesetz ewigen Werdens, ewiger Entwicklung liegt.

> He cannot free himself from the old style, he repeats the individual stanzas, whereas I recognize a perpetual evolution of the song's content, i.e. through-composition, as the true principle of music. In my writing, from the very beginning, you will no longer find any repetition from stanza to stanza, for the reason that music is governed by the law of eternal evolution, eternal development.

Des Knaben Wunderhorn

Almost half of Mahler's forty or so solo songs are settings of poems from *Des Knaben Wunderhorn*, a volume of folk verses collected by Achim von Arnim and Clemens Brentano, the first part of which was published in 1805 and dedicated to Goethe. The title refers to the figure of a boy on horseback brandishing a horn, an illustration of 'Das Wunderhorn', the anthology's opening poem. The source for many of the poems was oral, but the editors made frequent amendments in accordance with their own tastes. The poems have a childlike naivety but often enshrine profound wisdom in their unpolished, unarty verses. Many of Mahler's settings deal with military life, and in the piano accompaniment we frequently hear the beat of horses' hooves, fanfares, drums and marches. Mahler spent much of his childhood in the Moravian garrison town of Jihlava, and it is reliably reported that as a young boy he knew hundreds of military tunes by heart.

There are three different groups of *Wunderhorn* settings. The first nine, written for voice and piano, date from 1887–91, and were published in February 1892 by Schott, together with five earlier songs to texts by Leander, Mahler and Tirso de Molina, as *Lieder und Gesänge für eine Singstimme und Clavier*. The publishers later added the words 'aus der Jugendzeit' to distinguish these songs from the later *Wunderhorn* settings, *Kindertotenlieder* and the other Rückert songs. The *Ten orchestral songs from* Des Knaben Wunderhorn (1892–98) were published by Josef Weinberger in 1900; and these were followed by the final two *Wunderhorn* songs, 'Revelge' and 'Der Tamboursg'sell'' which date from 1899 and 1901 respectively.

From *Lieder und Gesänge für eine Singstimme mit Clavier*, c.1887–91

Um schlimme Kinder artig zu machen / How to make naughty children behave

Es kam ein Herr zum Schlösseli	A gentleman came to the castle,
Auf einem schönen Rösseli,	Riding on a fine horse,
Ku-kukuk, ku-kukuk, ku-kukuk!	Cu-cuckoo, cu-cuckoo, cu-cuckoo!
Da lugt die Frau zum Fenster aus	The lady looked out of the window
Und sagt: „der Mann ist nicht zu Haus	And said: 'My husband's out,
Und niemand heim als meine Kind,	And no one's home but the children,
Unds Mädchen ist auf der Wäschewind!"	And the maid's wringing out the washing!'
Der Herr auf seinem Rösseli	The gentleman on his horse
Sagt zu der Frau im Schlösseli:	Says to the lady of the castle:
Ku-kukuk, ku-kukuk, ku-kukuk!	Cu-cuckoo, cu-cuckoo, cu-cuckoo!
„Sinds gute Kind, sinds böse Kind?	'Are the children good or naughty?
Ach, liebe Frau, ach sagt geschwind",	Come, dear lady, tell me quickly',
Ku-kukuk, ku-kukuk, ku-kukuk!	Cu-cuckoo, cu-cuckoo, cu-cuckoo!
„In meiner Tasch für folgsam Kind,	'For children who are good

Da hab ich manche Angebind",
Ku-kukuk, ku-kukuk, ku-kukuk!

Die Frau die sagt: „sehr böse Kind!,
Sie folgen Muttern nicht geschwind,
Sind böse!"

Da sagt der Herr: „So reit ich heim,
Der gleichen Kinder brauch ich kein!"
Ku-kukuk, ku-kukuk, ku-kukuk!
Und reit auf seinem Rösseli
Weit entweg vom Schlösseli!
Ku-kukuk, ku-kukuk, ku-kukuk!
(*Theodor Streicher*)

I've many presents in my pocket,'
Cu-cuckoo, cu-cuckoo, cu-cuckoo!

The lady says: 'Very naughty children!
They don't obey their mother promptly,
They are naughty!'

The gentleman says: 'Then I'll ride home,
I've no need of children like that!'
Cu-cuckoo, cu-cuckoo, cu-cuckoo!
And he rides away on his horse,
Far away from the castle!
Cu-cuckoo, cu-cuckoo, cu-cuckoo!

Ich ging mit Lust durch einen grünen Wald / I walked joyfully though a green wood

Ich ging mit Lust durch einen grünen Wald,
Ich hört die Vöglein singen.
Sie sangen so jung, sie sangen so alt,
Die kleinen Waldvögelein im grünen Wald!
Wie gern hört ich sie singen, ja singen!

Nun sing, nun sing, Frau Nachtigall!
Sing du's bei meinem Feinsliebchen:
'Komm schier, komm schier, wenns finster ist,
Wenn niemand auf der Gasse ist,
Dann komm zu mir, dann komm zu mir!
Herein will ich dich lassen, ja lassen!'

Der Tag verging, die Nacht brach an,
Er kam zu Feinsliebchen gegangen;
Er klopft so leis' wohl an den Ring,
„Ei, schläfst du oder wachst, mein Kind?
Ich hab so lang gestanden!"

Es schaut der Mond durchs Fensterlein
Zum holden, süßen Lieben,
Die Nachtigall sang die ganze Nacht.
Du schlafselig Mägdelein, nimm dich in Acht!
Wo ist dein Herzliebster geblieben?

I walked joyfully through a green wood,
I heard the little birds sing.
They sang so young, they sang so old,
Those woodland birds in the green wood!
How gladly I heard them sing, yes sing!

Please sing, please sing, Mrs Nightingale!
Sing this at my beloved's house:
'Come quick, come quick, when darkness falls,
When not a soul is in the street,
Then come to me, then come to me!
And I will let you in, yes in!'

The day departed, night fell,
He went to his beloved;
He tapped so softly with the knocker,
'Are you asleep or awake, my child?
I've been standing here so long!'

The moon looks through the window,
Saw the charming, sweet caresses,
The nightingale sang all night long.
Sleepy little maid, take care!
Where is your sweetheart now?

Aus! Aus! / Out! Out!

Heute marschieren wir,
Juchhe, juchhe, im grünen Mai!
Morgen marschieren wir
Zu dem hohen Tor hinaus! Aus!

Reist du denn schon fort?

Today we'll march,
Hurrah, hurrah, in the green May!
Tomorrow we'll march
Out through the high gate! Out!

Are you already leaving?

Je, je! Mein Liebster!
Kommst niemals wieder heim?
Je, je! Mein Liebster!

Heute marschieren wir,
Juchhe, juchhe im grünen Mai!
Ei, du schwarzbrauns Mägdelein,
Unsre Lieb ist noch nicht aus!

Trink du ein Gläschen Wein
Zur Gesundheit dein und mein!
Siehst du diesen Strauß am Hut?
Jetzo heißt's marschieren gut!
Nimm das Tüchlein aus der Tasch,
Deine Tränlein mit abwasch!

Heute marschieren wir,
Juchhe, juchhe, im grünen Mai!

Ich will ins Kloster gehn,
Weil mein Schatz davon geht!
Wo gehts denn hin, mein Schatz?
Gehst du fort, heut schon fort?
Und kommst nimmer wieder?
Ach! wie wirds traurig sein
Hier in dem Städtchen!
Wie bald vergißt du mein!
Ich! armes Mädchen!

Morgen marschieren wir,
Juchhe, juchhe, im grünen Mai!
Tröst dich, mein lieber Schatz,
Im Mai blühn gar viel Blümelein!
Die Lieb ist noch nicht aus! Aus! Aus!'

Alas! Alas, my love!
Will you never come back home?
Alas! Alas, my love!

Today we'll march,
Hurrah, hurrah, in the green May!
Hey, my dark-haired girl,
Our love's not yet played out!

Come, drink a glass of wine
To your health and mine!
Do you see the flowers on my hat?
It means: the time has come to march!
Take your kerchief from your pocket
To wipe away your tears!

Today we'll march,
Hurrah, hurrah, in the green May!

'I shall enter a convent,
Since my love's going away!
Where are you going to, my love?
Are you going already today?
And will you never return?
Ah, how sad it will be
Here in the town!
How soon you'll forget me!
Poor girl that I am!'

Tomorrow we'll march,
Hurrah, hurrah in the green May!
Console yourself, my darling love,
Many flowers bloom in May!
Our love's not yet played out! Out! Out!

Starke Einbildungskraft / Vivid imagination

MÄDCHEN
  Hast gesagt, du willst mich nehmen,
Sobald der Sommer kommt!
Der Sommer ist gekommen, ja kommen,
Du hast mich nicht genommen, ja nommen!
Geh, Büble, geh nehm mich! Gelt, ja?
Du nimmst mich noch?

BÜBLE
  Wie soll ich dich denn nehmen,
Dieweil ich dich schon hab?
Und wenn ich halt an dich gedenk,
So mein ich alleweile:
Ich wär schon bei dir!

GIRL
  You said you'd take me
As soon as summer comes!
Summer has come, has come,
You've yet to take me, take me!
Come, my lad, come take me now!
Surely you will?

BOY
  But how can I take you,
When I already have you?
And whenever I think of you,
I feel all the time:
I'm with you already!

Zu Straßburg auf der Schanz / At Strasbourg on the ramparts

Zu Straßburg auf der Schanz,
Da ging mein Trauern an,
Das Alphorn hört ich drüben wohl anstimmen,
Ins Vaterland mußt ich hinüber schwimmen;
Das ging ja nicht an.

Ein' Stund in der Nacht
Sie haben mich gebracht;
Sie führten mich gleich vor des Hauptmanns
    Haus,
Ach Gott, sie fischten mich im Strome aus,
Mit mir ist es aus.

Früh morgens um zehn Uhr
Stellt man mich vors Regiment;
Ich soll da bitten um Pardon,
Und ich bekomm doch meinen Lohn,
Das weiß ich schon.

Ihr Brüder allzumal,
Heut seht ihr mich zum letztenmal;
Der Hirtenbub ist nur schuld daran,
Das Alphorn hat mir's angetan,
Das klag ich an.

At Strasbourg on the ramparts
My troubles began;
I heard the alpine horn over there,
I had to swim across to my fatherland;
And that was not allowed.

In the middle of the night
They brought me back;
They took me at once to the captain's
    house,
They fished me out of the water, my God!
I'm done for now.

In the early morning at ten o'clock
They'll stand me before the regiment;
I'll have to beg for pardon,
Yet I shall get my due reward,
That much I know.

You comrades, everywhere,
You'll see me today for the last time;
The shepherd boy's alone to blame,
I could not resist the alpine horn,
That's what I accuse.

Ablösung im Sommer / The changing of the summer guard

Kukuk hat sich zu Tode gefallen,
An einer grünen Weiden,
Kukuk ist tot, hat sich zu Tod gefallen!
Wer soll uns denn den Sommer lang
Die Zeit und Weil vertreiben?

Ei das soll tun Frau Nachtigall,
Die sitzt auf grünem Zweige;
Die kleine, feine Nachtigall,
Die liebe, süße Nachtigall.
Sie singt und springt, ist allzeit froh,
Wenn andre Vögel schweigen.

Wir warten auf Frau Nachtigall;
Die wohnt im grünen Hage,
Und wenn der Kukuk zu Ende ist,
Dann fängt sie an zu schlagen.
(*Hessenberg*)

The cuckoo's sung himself to death
On a green willow.
Cuckoo is dead, has sung himself to death!
Who shall now all summer long
While away the time for us?

Ah! Mrs Nightingale shall do that,
She sits on the green branch,
That small and graceful nightingale,
That sweet and lovely nightingale.
She hops and sings, is always joyous,
When other birds are silent.

We'll wait for Mrs Nightingale;
She lives in the green grove,
And when the cuckoo's time is up,
She will start to sing.

Scheiden und Meiden / Farewell and parting

Es ritten drei Reiter zum Tore hinaus!
  Ade!
Fein's Liebchen, das schaute zum Fenster hinaus,
  Ade!
Und wenn es denn soll geschieden sein,
So reich mir dein goldenes Ringelein,
    Ade! Ade!
Ja, Scheiden und Meiden tut weh, tut weh!

Es scheidet das Kind schon in der Wieg!
  Ade!
Wann werd ich mein Schätzel wohl kriegen?
  Ade!
Und ist es nicht morgen, ach, wär es doch heut,
Es machte uns Beiden wohl grosse Freud,
    Ade! Ade! Ade!
Ja, Scheiden und Meiden tut weh.

Three horsemen rode out through the gate!
  Farewell!
The beloved looked out of the window,
  Farewell!
And if it's time for us to part,
Then give me your little gold ring,
    Farewell! Farewell!
Yes, farewell and parting bring pain!

The child departs in the cradle even!
  Farewell!
When shall my loved one at last be mine?
  Farewell!
And if it be not tomorrow, ah, were it today,
That would give us both such joy!
    Farewell! Farewell! Farewell!
Yes, farewell and parting bring pain.

Nicht wiedersehen! / Never to meet again!

Und nun ade, mein herzallerliebster Schatz,
Jetzt muß ich wohl scheiden von dir,
Bis auf den andern Sommer,
Dann komm ich wieder zu dir! Ade!

Und als der junge Knab heimkam,
Von seiner Liebsten fing er an,
„Wo ist meine Herzallerliebste,
Die ich verlassen hab?"

„Auf dem Kirchhof liegt sie begraben,
Heut ists der dritte Tag,
Das Trauern und das Weinen
Hat sie zum Tod gebracht."

Jetzt will ich auf den Kirchhof gehn,
Will suchen meiner Liebsten Grab,
Will ihr all'weile rufen,
Bis daß sie mir Antwort gab!

Ei du mein allerherzliebster Schatz,
Mach auf dein tiefes Grab!
Du hörst kein Glöcklein läuten,
Du hörst kein Vöglein pfeifen,
Du siehst weder Sonne noch Mond!
Ade, mein herzallerliebster Schatz! Ade!

And now farewell, my dearest love!
Now must I be parted from you
Till summer comes again,
When I'll return to you! Farewell!

And when the young man came home again,
He enquired after his love:
'Where is my dearest love,
She whom I left behind?'

'In the churchyard she lies buried,
Today is the third day,
The mourning and the weeping
Brought about her death.'

Then I'll go to the churchyard,
To look for my beloved's grave,
And I'll never cease calling her,
Until she answers me!

O you, my dearest love,
Open up your deep grave!
You cannot hear the bells ringing,
You cannot hear the birds singing,
You can see neither sun nor moon!
Farewell, my dearest love! Farewell!

Selbstgefühl / Self-assurance

Ich weiß nicht, wie mir ist,
Ich bin nicht krank und nicht gesund,
Ich bin blessirt und hab kein Wund.

Ich weiß nicht, wie mir ist!
Ich tät gern essen und schmeckt mir nichts,
Ich hab ein Geld und gilt mir nichts.

Ich weiß nicht, wie mir ist,
Ich hab sogar kein Schnupftabak,
Und hab kein Kreuzer Geld im Sack.

Ich weiß nicht, wie mir ist,
Heiraten tät ich auch schon gern,
Kann aber Kinderschrein nicht hörn.

Ich weiß nicht, wie mir ist,
Ich hab erst heut den Doktor gefragt,
Der hat mirs ins Gesicht gesagt.

Ich weiß wohl, was dir ist:
Ein Narr bist du gewiß;
Nun weiß ich wie mir ist!

I don't know what's wrong with me,
I'm not ill and I'm not well.
I'm wounded and have no wound.

I don't know what's wrong with me,
I'd like to eat but nothing tastes,
I've got money but it's worth nothing.

I don't know what's wrong with me,
I haven't even a pinch of snuff
And not a penny in my purse.

I don't know what's wrong with me,
I'd really like to get married,
But can't bear the sound of crying kids.

I don't know what's wrong with me,
Only today I asked the doctor,
He told me straight to my face.

I know what's wrong with you,
You're quite clearly a fool;
Now I know what's wrong with me!

1892–98 *Ten Orchestral Songs from* Des Knaben Wunderhorn

Der Schildwache Nachtlied / The sentinel's night song

„Ich kann und mag nicht fröhlich sein,
Wenn alle Leute schlafen,
So muß ich wachen,
Muß traurig sein."

„Lieb Knabe, du mußt nicht traurig sein,
Will deiner warten
Im Rosengarten,
Im grünen Klee."

„Zum grünen Klee, da geh ich nicht,
Zum Waffengarten
Voll Helleparten
Bin ich gestellt."

„Stehst du im Feld, so helf dir Gott!
An Gottes Segen
Ist alles gelegen,
Wers glauben tut."

'I can't and won't be cheerful,
When folk are asleep,
I must keep watch,
Must be sad.'

'Dear boy, you must not be sad,
I'll wait for you
In the rose-garden,
In the green clover.'

'I cannot go to the green clover,
To the battle-field
Where halberds are thick
Is where I'm ordered.'

'When you stand in battle, may God help you!
All depends
On God's blessing,
For him with faith.'

„Wers glauben tut, ist weit davon,
Er ist ein König,
Er ist ein Kaiser,
Er führt den Krieg."

Halt! Wer da? Rund! Bleib mir vom Leib!
Wer sang es hier? Wer sang zur Stund?
Verlorne Feldwacht
Sang es um Mitternacht!
Mitternacht! Mitternacht! Feldwacht!
(*Theodor Streicher*)

'He who has faith is far from here,
He is a king.
He is an emperor.
He wages war.'

Halt! Who goes there? Patrol! Keep away!
Who was singing here! Who sang just now?
A forlorn sentinel
Sang his song at midnight!
Midnight! Midnight! Sentinel!

Verlorne Müh / Wasted effort

SIE
  Büble, wir wollen ausse gehe,
Wollen wir? Unsere Lämmer besehe,
Komm, liebs Büberle,
Komm, ich bitt.

SHE
  Hey laddie, shall we go walking,
Shall we see to our lambs?
Come, dear laddie,
Come, I beg you.

ER
  Närrisches Dinterle,
Ich geh dir halt nit.

HE
  Foolish girl,
I'll not go with you.

SIE
  Willst vielleicht a Bissel nasche,
Hol dir was aus meiner Tasch;
Hol, liebs Büberle,
Hol, ich bitt.

SHE
  Perhaps you'd like a little nibble,
Take a morsel from my pack;
Take it, dear lad,
Take something, I beg you.

ER
  Närrisches Dinterle,
Ich nasch dir halt nit.

HE
  Foolish girl,
I'll take no nibbles from you.

SIE
  Gelt, ich soll mein Herz dir schenke,
Immer willst an mich gedenke;
Nimms, liebs Büberle!
Nimms, ich bitt.

SHE
  I'll offer you my heart, then,
So you'll always think of me;
Take it, dear laddie!
Take it, I beg you.

ER
  Närrisches Dinterle,
Ich mag es halt nit!

HE
  Foolish girl,
I'll have none of it!

Trost im Unglück / Consolation in sorrow

HUSAR
  Wohlan die Zeit ist kommen,
Mein Pferd das muß gesattelt sein,
Ich hab mirs vorgenommen,

HUSAR
  So be it! The time has come,
My horse must now be saddled,
I have decided,

Geritten muß es sein.
Geh du nur hin, ich hab mein Teil,
Ich lieb dich nur aus Narretei;
Ohn dich kann ich wohl leben;
Ohn dich kann ich wohl sein.

  So setz ich mich aufs Pferdchen,
Und trink ein Gläschen kühlen Wein,
Und schwör bei meinem Bärtchen,
Dir ewig treu zu sein.

MÄDCHEN
  Du glaubst, du bist der Schönste
Wohl auf der ganzen weiten Welt,
Und auch der Angenehmste,
Ist aber weit, weit gefehlt.

  In meines Vaters Garten
Wächst eine Blume drin,
So lang will ich noch warten,
Bis die noch größer ist.

  Und geh' du nur hin, ich hab mein Teil,
Ich lieb dich nur aus Narretei;
Ohn dich kann ich wohl leben;
Ohn dich kann ich wohl sein.

HUSAR
  Du denkst ich werd dich nehmen,
Das hab ich lang noch nicht im Sinn,
Ich muß mich deiner schämen,
Wenn ich in Gesellschaft bin.

I must to horse.
Away with you, I've had my fill,
I love you but from foolishness;
I can live without you,
I can exist without you.

  And so I mount my horse,
And drink a glass of cool wine,
And swear by my beard
To be faithful to you forever.

GIRL
  You think you are the handsomest man
In all the wide world,
The most agreeable as well,
But you are very much mistaken.

  In my father's garden
There blooms a lovely flower,
And I am only waiting
Till it has grown taller.

  Away with you, I've had my fill,
I love you but from foolishness;
I can live without you,
I can exist without you.

HUSAR
  You think I'd take you,
That's very far from my mind,
I'd be ashamed of you,
When in company.

Wer hat dies Liedlein erdacht? / Who made up this little song?

  Dort oben am Berg in dem hohen Haus
Da gucket ein fein's, lieb's Mädel heraus,
Es ist nicht dort daheime,
Es ist des Wirts sein Töchterlein,
Es wohnet auf grüner Heide.

  Mein Herzle ist wund,
Komm, Schätzle, machs gsund.
Dein schwarzbraune Äuglein,
Die habn mich verwundt.
Dein rosiger Mund
Macht Herzen gesund,
Macht Jugend verständig,
Macht Tote lebendig,
Macht Kranke gesund.

  High in the mountain stands a house,
From it a sweet pretty maid looks out.
But that is not her home,
She's the innkeeper's young daughter.
She lives on the green moor.

  My heart is sick.
Come, my love, and cure it.
Your dark brown eyes
Have wounded me.
Your rosy lips
Can cure sick hearts,
Make young men wise,
Make dead men live,
Can cure the sick.

Wer hat denn das schöne Liedlein erdacht?
Es habens drei Gäns übers Wasser gebracht,
Zwei graue und eine weiße;
Und wer das Liedlein nicht singen kann,
Dem wollen sie es pfeifen. Ja!

Who made up this pretty little song?
Three geese brought it across the water.
Two grey ones and a white one;
And for those who can't sing this song,
They will pipe it to them. They will!

Das irdische Leben / Life on earth

Mutter, ach Mutter! es hungert mich,
Gib mir Brot, sonst sterbe ich.
    Warte nur mein liebes Kind!
    Morgen wollen wir ernten geschwind.

Mother, ah mother, I am starving.
Give me bread or I shall die.
    Wait, only wait, my beloved child!
    Tomorrow the reaping will be swiftly done.

Und als das Korn geerntet war,
Rief das Kind noch immerdar:
Mutter, ach Mutter! es hungert mich,
Gib mir Brot, sonst sterbe ich.
    Warte nur mein liebes Kind!
    Morgen wollen wir dreschen geschwind.

And when at last the corn was reaped,
Still the child kept on crying:
Mother, ah mother, I am starving,
Give me bread or I shall die.
    Wait, only wait, my beloved child!
    Tomorrow the threshing will be swiftly done.

Und als das Korn gedroschen war,
Rief das Kind noch immerdar:
Mutter, ach Mutter! es hungert mich,
Gib mir Brot, sonst sterbe ich.
    Warte nur mein liebes Kind!
    Morgen wollen wir backen geschwind.
Und als das Brot gebacken war,
Lag das Kind auf der Totenbahr.

And when at last the corn was threshed,
Still the child kept on crying:
Mother, ah mother, I am starving.
Give me bread or I shall die.
    Wait, only wait, my beloved child!
    Tomorrow the baking will be swiftly done.
And when at last the bread was baked,
The child lay dead upon the bier.

Des Antonius von Padua Fischpredigt / Antony of Padua's sermon to the fishes

Antonius zur Predigt
Die Kirche findt ledig,
Er geht zu den Flüssen
Und predigt den Fischen;
    Sie schlagn mit den Schwänzen,
    Im Sonnenschein glänzen.

Antony finds the church
Empty for his sermon,
He goes to the river
To preach to the fishes;
    They all flick their tails
    And glint in the sun.

Die Karpfen mit Rogen
Sind all hierher zogen,
Habn d'Mäuler aufrissen,
Sich Zuhörns beflissen:
    Kein Predigt niemalen
    Den Fischen so gfallen.

The carp, fat with roe,
Have all come along,
Their mouths open wide,
Attentive and rapt:
    No sermon was ever
    So pleasing to fish.

Spitzgoschete Hechte,
Die immerzu fechten,
Sind eilends herschwommen
Zu hören den Frommen.

Sharp-snouted pike,
Perpetually fighting,
Swam swiftly along
To hear this devout.

Auch jene Phantasten,
Die immerzu fasten,
Die Stockfisch ich meine,
Zur Predigt erscheinen.
  Kein Predigt niemalen
  Den Stockfisch so gfallen.

Gut Aale und Hausen
Die Vornehme schmausen,
Die selbst sich bequemen,
Die Predigt vernehmen.
Auch Krebse, Schildkroten,
Sonst langsame Boten,
Steigen eilig vom Grund,
Zu hören diesen Mund:
  Kein Predigt niemalen
  Den Krebsen so gfallen.

Fisch große, Fisch kleine,
Vornehm und gemeine,
Erheben die Köpfe
Wie verständge Geschöpfe:
  Auf Gottes Begehren,
  Die Predigt anhören.

Die Predigt geendet,
Ein Jeder sich wendet,
Die Hechte bleiben Diebe,
Die Aale viel lieben.
  Die Predigt hat gfallen,
  Sie bleiben wie allen.

Die Krebs gehn zurücke,
Die Stockfisch bleibn dicke,
Die Karpfen viel fressen,
Die Predigt vergessen.
  Die Predigt hat gfallen,
  Sie bleiben wie allen.

Those strange creatures even,
Perpetually fasting,
It's the cod I refer to,
Appear for the sermon.
  No sermon was ever
  So pleasing to cod.

Good eels and sturgeon,
Prized by the wealthy,
Even they condescend
To hear the sermon.
Even crabs, even turtles,
Slow-coaches at most times,
Shoot up from below
To hear the address:
  No sermon was ever
  So pleasing to crabs.

Large fish and small fish,
High-born and low-born,
They all lift their heads up
Like intelligent creatures:
  At God's behest
  They give ear to the sermon.

The sermon concluded,
They all swim away,
The pike remain thieves,
The eels remain lechers.
  The sermon was pleasing,
  All stay as they were.

The crabs still go backwards,
The cod are still bloated,
The carp are still gorging,
The sermon's forgotten.
  The sermon was pleasing,
  All stay as they were.

Rheinlegendchen / Little Rhine legend

Bald gras ich am Neckar,
Bald gras ich am Rhein,
Bald hab ich ein Schätzel,
Bald bin ich allein.

Was hilft mir das Grasen,
Wenn d'Sichel nicht schneidt,
Was hilft mir ein Schätzel,
Wenn's bei mir nicht bleibt.

I mow by the Neckar,
I mow by the Rhine;
At times I've a sweetheart,
At times I'm alone.

What use is mowing,
If the sickle won't cut,
What use is a sweetheart,
If she'll not stay.

So soll ich denn grasen	So if I'm to mow
Am Neckar, am Rhein,	By the Neckar, and Rhine,
So werf ich mein goldenes	I'll throw in their waters
Ringlein hinein.	My little gold ring.
Es fließet im Neckar	It'll flow in the Neckar
Und fließet im Rhein,	And flow in the Rhine,
Soll schwimmen hinunter	And float right away
Ins Meer tief hinein.	To the depths of the sea.
Und schwimmt es das Ringlein,	And floating, the ring
So frißt es ein Fisch,	Will be gulped by a fish,
Das Fischlein soll kommen	The fish will be served
Aufs Königs sein Tisch.	At the King's own table.
Der König tät fragen,	The King will enquire
Wems Ringlein sollt sein?	Whose ring it might be;
Da tät mein Schatz sagen,	My sweetheart will say
Das Ringlein g'hört mein.	The ring belongs to me.
Mein Schätzlein tät springen,	My sweetheart will bound
Berg auf und Berg ein,	Over hill, over dale,
Tät mir wiedrum bringen	And bring back to me
Das Goldringlein fein.	My little gold ring.
Kannst grasen am Neckar,	You can mow by the Neckar,
Kannst grasen am Rhein,	And mow by the Rhine,
Wirf du mir nur immer	If you'll always keep throwing
Dein Ringlein hinein.	Your ring in for me.

Lied des Verfolgten im Turm / Song of the prisoner in the tower

DER GEFANGENE	THE PRISONER
Die Gedanken sind frei,	Thoughts are free,
Wer kann sie erraten;	Who can guess them;
Sie rauschen vorbei	They flit past
Wie nächtliche Schatten.	Like nocturnal shadows.
Kein Mensch kann sie wissen,	No one can know them,
Kein Jäger sie schießen;	No hunter shoot them down;
Es bleibet dabei,	So shall it always be,
Die Gedanken sind frei.	Thoughts are free.
DAS MÄDCHEN	THE GIRL
Im Sommer ist gut lustig sein,	In summer it's good to make merry
Auf hohen, wilden Bergen,	On wild mountain heights,
Dort findet man grün Plätzelein,	Many green glades can be found,
Mein herzverliebtes Schätzelein,	My dearest love,
Von dir mag ich nicht scheiden.	I never wish to part from you.
DER GEFANGENE	THE PRISONER
Und sperrt man mich ein	And though they lock me

In finstere Kerker,	In a gloomy cell,
Dies alles sind nur	All such measures
Vergebliche Werke;	Are in vain;
Denn meine Gedanken	For my thoughts
Zerreißen die Schranken	Can shatter the bars
Und Mauern entzwei,	And the walls in two,
Die Gedanken sind frei.	Thoughts are free.

DAS MÄDCHEN / THE GIRL

Im Sommer ist gut lustig sein,	In summer it's good to make merry,
Auf hohen wilden Bergen,	On wild mountain heights;
Man ist da ewig ganz allein,	There you can be quite alone
Auf hohen, wilden Bergen,	On the wild mountain heights,
Man hört da gar kein Kindergeschrei,	There you hear no children cry,
Die Luft mag einem da werden.	The air is good up there.

DER GEFANGENE / THE PRISONER

So seis wie es will,	Then so let it be,
Und wenn es sich schicket,	And whatever should befall,
Nur alles sei in der Stille,	May it be done in secret,
Mein Wunsch und Begehren,	My wishes and longings
Niemand kann's wehren;	None can restrain;
Es bleibt dabei,	So shall it always be,
Die Gedanken sind frei.	Thoughts are free.

DAS MÄDCHEN / THE GIRL

Mein Schatz, du singst so fröhlich hier,	My love, you sing so happily here,
Wies Vögelein im Grase;	Like the small bird in the grass;
Ich steh so traurig bei Kerkertür,	I stand forlorn at the prison gate,
Wär ich doch tot, wär ich bei dir,	Would I were dead or at your side,
Ach muß ich immer denn klagen?	Ah, must my weeping never end?

DER GEFANGENE / THE PRISONER

Und weil du so klagst,	And since you weep so,
Der Lieb ich entsage,	I foreswear your love,
Und ist es gewagt,	And once that's done,
So kann mich nichts plagen,	Nothing can harm me,
So kann ich im Herzen	From now in my heart
Stets lachen und scherzen.	I'll laugh and I'll jest.
Es bleibet dabei,	So shall it always be,
Die Gedanken sind frei.	Thoughts are free.

Wo die schönen Trompeten blasen / Where the splendid trumpets sound

Wer ist denn draußen und wer klopfet an,	Who stands outside and knocks at my door,
Der mich so leise wecken kann?	Waking me so gently?
Das ist der Herzallerliebste dein,	It is your own true dearest love,
Steh auf und laß mich zu dir ein.	Arise, and let me in.

Was soll ich hier nun länger stehn?	Why leave me longer waiting here?
Ich seh die Morgenröt aufgehn,	I see the rosy dawn appear,
Die Morgenröt, zwei helle Stern,	The rosy dawn and two bright stars.
Bei meinem Schatz da wär ich gern,	I long to be beside my love,
Bei meinem Herzallerliebe.	Beside my dearest love.
Das Mädchen stand auf, und ließ ihn ein,	The girl arose and let him in,
Sie heißt ihn auch willkommen sein.	She bids him welcome too.
Willkommen, lieber Knabe mein,	O welcome, dearest love of mine,
So lang hast du gestanden.	Too long have you been waiting.
Sie reicht ihm auch die schneeweiße Hand.	She gives to him her snow-white hand,
Von Ferne sang die Nachtigall,	From far off sang the nightingale,
Das Mädchen fing zu weinen an.	The girl began to weep.
Ach weine nicht, du Liebste mein,	Ah, do not weep, my dearest love,
Aufs Jahr sollst du mein eigen sein;	Within a year you shall be mine,
Mein eigen sollst du werden gewiß,	You shall be mine most certainly,
Wies keine sonst auf Erden ist.	As no one else on earth.
O Lieb auf grüner Erden.	O love upon the green earth.
Ich zieh' in Krieg auf grüne Haid',	I'm going to war, to the green heath,
Die grüne Haide, die ist so weit.	The green heath so far away.
Allwo dort die schönen Trompeten blasen,	There where the splendid trumpets sound,
Da ist mein Haus von grünem Rasen.	There is my home of green turf.

Lob des hohen Verstandes / In praise of high intellect

Einstmal in einem tiefen Tal	Once upon a time in a deep valley
Kukuk und Nachtigall	The cuckoo and the nightingale
Täten ein Wett anschlagen,	Between them made a wager:
Zu singen um das Meisterstück:	Whoever sang the finer song,
„Gewinn es Kunst, gewinn es Glück,	Whoever won by skill or luck,
Dank soll er davon tragen."	Should carry off the prize.
Der Kukuk sprach: So dirs gefällt,	The cuckoo said: I have, so please you,
Hab ich den Richter wählt,	Already chosen the judge.
Und tät gleich den Esel ernennen,	And named the donkey straightaway,
Denn weil er hat zwei Ohren groß,	Because with his two large ears
So kann er hören desto bos,	He'll hear much clearer what is bad,
Und was recht ist, kennen.	And also know what's good.
Sie flogen vor den Richter bald,	So they soon flew before the judge,
Wie dem die Sache ward erzählt,	When he was told how matters stood,
Schuf er, sie sollten singen.	He commanded them to sing.
Die Nachtigall sang lieblich aus,	The nightingale sang beautifully,
Der Esel sprach, du machst mirs kraus.	The donkey said, you're confusing me.
Du machst mir's kraus. Ija! Ija!	You're confusing me. Hee-haw! Hee-haw!
Ich kanns in Kopf nicht bringen.	I just can't understand it.

Der Kukuk drauf fing an geschwind	Whereat the cuckoo quickly sang
Sein Sang durch Terz und Quart und Quint.	His song through thirds and fourths and fifths.
Dem Esel gfiels, er sprach nur: Wart,	The donkey liked it, merely said: wait,
Dein Urteil will ich sprechen.	Wait while I give my verdict.

Wohl sungen hast du Nachtigall,	Nightingale, you sang well,
Aber Kukuk singst gut Choral,	But you, cuckoo, sing a fine hymn
Und hältst den Takt fein innen;	And keep the strictest measure;
Das sprech ich nach mein' hohn Verstand,	My high intellect pronounces this,
Und kost es gleich ein ganzes Land,	And though it cost a whole country,
So laß ichs dich gewinnen.	I declare you now the winner.
Kukuk, Kukuk, Ija!	Cuckoo, cuckoo, hee-haw!

1899 *Two Orchestral Wunderhorn Songs*

Revelge / Reveille

Des Morgens zwischen drein und vieren,	Between three and four of a morning,
Da müssen wir Soldaten marschieren	We soldiers have to march
Das Gäßlein auf und ab;	Up and down the alleyway;
Tralali, tralaley, tralalera,	Tralalee, tralalay, tralala,
Mein Schätzel sieht herab.	My love looks at me from her window.

„Ach Bruder, jetzt bin ich geschossen,	'O comrade, I've been shot,
Die Kugel hat mich schwer getroffen,	The bullet's wounded me badly,
Trag mich in mein Quartier.	Carry me back to the camp,
Tralali, tralaley, tralalera,	Tralalee, tralalay, tralala,
Es ist nicht weit von hier."	It isn't far from here.'

„Ach Bruder, ich kann dich nicht tragen,	'O comrade, I cannot carry you,
Die Feinde haben uns geschlagen,	The enemy have routed us,
Helf dir der liebe Gott;	May dear God help you;
Tralali, tralaley, tralalera,	Tralalee, tralalay, tralala,
Ich muß marschieren bis in Tod."	I must march on to meet my death.'

„Ach Brüder, ihr geht ja mir vorüber,	'Ah, comrades, you pass me by,
Als wärs mit mir vorbei,	As though I were done for,
Tralali, tralaley, tralalera,	Tralalee, tralalay, tralala,
Ihr tretet mir zu nah."	You march too close to where I lie.

„Ich muß wohl meine Trommel rühren,	I must now start to beat my drum,
Tralali, tralaley, tralali, tralaley,	Tralalee, tralalay, tralala,
Sonst werd' ich mich verlieren,	Or else I'll be lost forever,
Tralali, tralaley, tralala,	Tralalee, tralalay, tralala,
Die Brüder dick gesät,	My comrades strewn so thick
Sie liegen wie gemäht."	Lie like mown grass on the ground.

| Er schlägt die Trommel auf und nieder, | Up and down he beats his drum, |
| Er wecket seine stillen Brüder, | He wakes his silent comrades, |

Tralali, tralaley, tralali, tralaley,
Sie schlagen ihren Feind,
Tralali, tralaley, tralalera,
Ein Schrecken schlägt den Feind.

Er schlägt die Trommel auf und nieder,
Da sind sie vor dem Nachtquartier schon
  wieder,
Tralali, tralaley, tralali, tralaley,
Ins Gäßlein hell hinaus,
Sie ziehn vor Schätzeleins Haus,
Tralali, tralaley, tralali, tralaley, tralalera,
Sie ziehn vor Schätzeleins Haus.

Des Morgens stehen da die Gebeine,
In Reih und Glied, sie stehn wie Leichensteine,
Die Trommel steht voran,
Daß sie ihn sehen kann,
Tralali, tralaley, tralali, tralaley, tralalera,
Daß sie ihn sehen kann.
(*Knab*)

Tralalee, tralalay, tralala,
They fall upon their foe,
Tralalee, tralalay, tralala,
And terror strikes the foe.

Up and down he beats his drum,
Soon they're all back at camp,
Tralalee, tralalay, tralala,
Out into the bright street
They pass before his sweetheart's
  house,
Tralalee, tralalay, tralala,
They pass before his sweetheart's house.

There in the morning lie their bones,
In rank and file like tombstones,
At their head the drummer-boy
That she may see him there,
Tralalee, tralalay, tralala,
That she may see him there.

1901 Der Tamboursg'sell / The drummer-boy

Ich armer Tamboursg'sell.
Man führt mich aus dem G'wölb,
Wär ich ein Tambour blieben,
Dürft ich nicht gefangen liegen.

O Galgen, du hohes Haus,
Du siehst so furchtbar aus,
Ich schau dich nicht mehr an,
Weil i weiß, daß i g'hör dran.

Wenn Soldaten vorbeimarschiern,
Bei mir nit einquartiern,
Wenn sie fragen wer i g'wesen bin:
Tambour von der Leibkompanie.

Gute Nacht, ihr Marmelstein,
    Ihr Berg und Hügelein,
    Gute Nacht, ihr Offizier,
Korporal und Musketier,
    Gute Nacht, ihr Offizier,
    Korporal und Grenadier,
Ich schrei mit heller Stimm,
    Von euch ich Urlaub nimm,
    Gute Nacht.

Woe is me, poor drummer-boy.
They lead me from my cell,
Had I remained a drummer,
I'd not have been in prison.

O gallows, you lofty house,
How grim you seem to me,
I'll look at you no more,
For I know you're meant for me.

When the soldiers march past
To quarters other than mine,
And when they ask who I was:
Drummer to the King's Bodyguard.

Good night, you stones of marble,
    You mountains and you hills,
    Good night, you officers,
Corporals and musketeers.
    Good night, You officers,
    Corporals and grenadiers,
I cry out loud and clear:
    I take my leave of you,
    Good night.

Richard Leander (1830–89)

The pseudonym of Richard von Volkmann, who as a surgeon served with distinction in the wars of 1866 and 1870/1. Published several volumes of short stories and verse: *Aus der Burschenzeit* (1876), *Gedichte* (1878), *Kleine Geschichten* (1885), *Alte und neue Troubador-Lieder* (1889). 'Frühlingsmorgen' and 'Erinnerung' come from *Kleine Lieder* (1854–6). Mahler often declared that he was loath to set great poetry, since it was already self-sufficient. It was, he said, as if a sculptor had chiselled a statue from marble and a painter came along and coloured it.

Frühlingsmorgen / Spring morning

Es klopft an das Fenster der Lindenbaum
Mit Zweigen, blütenbehangen:
Was liegst du im Traum?
Steh' auf! Steh' auf!
Die Sonn' ist aufgegangen!

The linden tree taps at the window
With blossom-laden boughs:
Why do you lie dreaming?
Get up! Get up!
The sun has risen!

Die Lerche ist wach, die Büsche weh'n,
Die Bienen summen und Käfer;
Und dein munteres Lieb hab' ich auch schon
    geseh'n, –
Steh' auf, Langschläfer, Langschläfer!

The lark's awake, the bushes are stirring,
The bees are humming and beetles too;
And I've already seen your cheery
    lover, –
Get up, sleepy-head, sleepy-head!

Erinnerung / Recollection

Es wecket meine Liebe
Die Lieder immer wieder;
Es wecken meine Lieder
Die Liebe immer wieder.

My love inspires songs
Again and again;
My songs inspire love
Again and again.

Die Lippen, die da träumen
Von deinen heißen Küssen,
In Sang und Liedesweisen
Von dir sie tönen müssen.

The lips that dream
Of your ardent kisses
Must sing of you
In melody and song.

Und wollen die Gedanken
Der Liebe sich entschlagen,
So kommen meine Lieder
Zu mir mit Liebesklagen!

And if my thoughts
Seek to banish love,
My songs return,
Lamenting love!

So halten mich in Banden
Die beiden immer wieder:
Es weckt das Lied die Liebe,
Die Liebe weckt die Lieder.

So both hold me captive
Again and again:
Songs inspire love,
Love inspires songs.

Gustav Mahler (1860–1911)

Mahler wrote his own poems for an early song, 'Hans und Grete', and the *Lieder eines fahrenden Gesellen*. The cycle originally contained six poems, as we learn from Mahler's letter of 1 January 1885 to his friend Fritz Löhr, in which he speaks of his obsession for Johanna Richter, a soprano at the Kassel Opera House where Mahler was chorus master. She was the inspiration behind this passionate outpouring, though Mahler does not mention to Löhr that the first song borrows substantially from a *Knaben Wunderhorn* poem, which begins:

> Wann mein Schatz Hochzeit macht,
> Hab ich einen traurigen Tag:
> Geh ich in mein Kämmerlein,
> Wein um meinen Schatz.
>
> Blümlein blau, verdorre nicht,
> Du stehst auf grüner Heide;
> Des Abends, wenn ich schlafen geh,
> So denk ich an das Lieben.

1883–5? *Lieder eines fahrenden Gesellen / Songs of a wayfarer*

1

Wenn mein Schatz Hochzeit macht,	When my love has her wedding-day,
Fröhliche Hochzeit macht,	Her joyous wedding-day,
Hab' ich meinen traurigen Tag!	I have my day of mourning!
Geh' ich in mein Kämmerlein,	I go into my little room,
Dunkles Kämmerlein!	My dark little room!
Weine! wein'! Um meinen Schatz,	I weep, weep! For my love,
Um meinen lieben Schatz!	My dearest love!
Blümlein blau! Blümlein blau!	Blue little flower! Blue little flower!
Verdorre nicht, verdorre nicht!	Do not wither, do not wither!
Vöglein süß! Vöglein süß!	Sweet little bird! Sweet little bird!
Du singst auf grüner Heide!	Singing on the green heath!
„Ach! wie ist die Welt so schön!	'Ah, how fair the world is!
Ziküth! Ziküth!"	Jug-jug! Jug-jug!'
Singet nicht! Blühet nicht!	Do not sing! Do not bloom!
Lenz ist ja vorbei!	For spring is over!
Alles Singen ist nun aus!	All singing now is done!
Des Abends, wenn ich schlafen geh',	At night, when I go to rest,
Denk' ich an mein Leid!	I think of my sorrow!
An mein Leide!	My sorrow!

2

Ging heut' Morgen über's Feld,
Tau noch auf den Gräsern hing,
Sprach zu mir der lust'ge Fink:
„Ei, du! Gelt?
Guten Morgen! Ei, Gelt? Du!
Wird's nicht eine schöne Welt?
Zink! Zink! Schön und flink!
Wie mir doch die Welt gefällt!"

Auch die Glockenblum' am Feld
Hat mir lustig, guter Ding',
Mit den Glöckchen, klinge, kling,
Ihren Morgengruß geschellt:
„Wird's nicht eine schöne Welt?
Kling! Kling! Schönes Ding!
Wie mir doch die Welt gefällt!"

Und da fing im Sonnenschein
Gleich die Welt zu funkeln an;
Alles, Alles, Ton und Farbe gewann!
Im Sonnenschein!
Blum' und Vogel, groß und klein!
„Guten Tag! Guten Tag!
Ist's nicht eine schöne Welt?
Ei, du! Gelt? Schöne Welt!"

Nun fängt auch mein Glück wohl an?
Nein! Nein! Das ich mein',
Mir nimmer, nimmer blühen kann!

3

Ich hab' ein glühend Messer,
Ein Messer in meiner Brust,
O weh! O weh!
Das schneid't so tief
In jede Freud' und jede Lust,
So tief! so tief!
Es schneid't so weh und tief!

Ach, was ist das für ein böser Gast!
Nimmer hält er Ruh',
Nimmer hält er Rast!
Nicht bei Tag,
Nicht bei Nacht, wenn ich schlief!
O weh! O weh! O weh!

Wenn ich in den Himmel seh',
Seh' ich zwei blaue Augen steh'n!
O weh! O weh!

I walked across the fields this morning,
Dew still hung on the grass,
The merry finch said to me:
'You there, hey –
Good morning! Hey, you there!
Isn't it a lovely world?
Tweet! Tweet! Bright and sweet!
O how I love the world!'

And the harebell at the field's edge,
Merrily and in good spirits,
Ding-ding with its tiny bell
Rang out its morning greeting:
'Isn't it a lovely world?
Ding-ding! Beautiful thing!
O how I love the world!'

And then in the gleaming sun
The world at once began to sparkle;
All things gained in tone and colour!
In the sunshine!
Flower and bird, great and small.
'Good day! Good day!
Isn't it a lovely world?
Hey, you there!? A lovely world!'

Will my happiness now begin?
No! No! The happiness I mean
Can never never bloom for me!

I've a gleaming knife,
A knife in my breast,
Alas! Alas!
It cuts so deep
Into every joy and every bliss,
So deep, so deep!
It cuts so sharp and deep!

Ah, what a cruel guest it is!
Never at peace,
Never at rest!
Neither by day
Nor by night, when I'd sleep!
Alas! Alas! Alas!

When I look into the sky,
I see two blue eyes!
Alas! Alas!

Wenn ich im gelben Felde geh',	When I walk in the yellow field,
Seh' ich von fern das blonde Haar	I see from afar her golden hair
Im Winde weh'n! O weh! O weh!	Blowing in the wind! Alas! Alas!
Wenn ich aus dem Traum auffahr'	When I wake with a jolt from my dream
Und höre klingen ihr silbern Lachen,	And hear her silvery laugh,
O weh! O weh!	Alas! Alas!
Ich wollt', ich läg' auf der schwarzen Bahr',	I wish I were lying on the black bier,
Könnt' nimmer die Augen aufmachen!	And might never open my eyes again!

4

Die zwei blauen Augen von meinem Schatz,	The two blue eyes of my love
Die haben mich in die weite Welt geschickt.	Have sent me into the wide world.
Da mußt' ich Abschied nehmen	I had to bid farewell
Vom allerliebsten Platz!	To the place I loved most!
O Augen blau, warum habt ihr mich angeblickt?	O blue eyes, why did you look on me?
Nun hab' ich ewig Leid und Grämen!	Grief and sorrow shall now be mine forever!

Ich bin ausgegangen in stiller Nacht,	I set out in the still night,
Wohl über die dunkle Heide.	Across the dark heath.
Hat mir niemand Ade gesagt, Ade!	No one bade me farewell, farewell!
Mein Gesell' war Lieb' und Leide!	My companions were love and sorrow!

Auf der Straße stand ein Lindenbaum,	A lime tree stood by the roadside,
Da hab' ich zum ersten Mal im Schlaf geruht!	Where I first found peace in sleep!
Unter dem Lindenbaum,	Under the lime tree
Der hat seine Blüten über mich geschneit,	Which snowed its blossom on me,
Da wußt' ich nicht, wie das Leben tut,	I was not aware of how life hurts,
War alles, alles wieder gut!	And all, all was well once more!
Alles! Alles!	All! All!
Lieb' und Leid, und Welt und Traum!	Love and sorrow, and world and dream!

Tirso de Molina (?1583–1648)

Spanish dramatist, whose real name was Fray Gabriel Téllez. Tirso wrote some four hundred plays on religious, historical and social themes, of which over eighty survive.

1880–87 Serenade / Serenade
FROM *El burlador de Sevilla o el convidado de piedra*, TRANSLATED BY L. BRAUNFELS

Ist's dein Wille, süße Maid,	If it's your will, sweet maiden,
Meinem heißen Liebesstreben	Only to yield in death
Erst im Tode Raum zu geben,	To my passionate pleading,
O, da wart' ich lange Zeit!	Ah, I'll have long to wait!

Soll ich deine Gunst genießen	If I'm to enjoy your favours
Erst nach meinem Erdengange,	Only when my life is over,
Währt mein Leben allzulange!	Then my life is far too long!

Mag es gleich im Nu zerfließen! | Let it melt away at once!

Ist's dein Wille, süße, Maid, | If it's your will, sweet maiden,
Meinem heißen Liebesstreben | Only to yield in death
Erst im Tode Raum zu geben, | To my passionate pleading,
O das ist gar lange Zeit! | Ah, I'll have long to wait!

1880–87 Phantasie / Fantasy
FROM *El burlador de Sevilla o el convidado de piedra*, TRANSLATED BY L. BRAUNFELS

Das Mägdlein trat aus dem Fischerhaus, | The girl stepped from the fisherman's hut,
Die Netze warf sie in's Meer hinaus! | She cast her nets out into the sea!
Und wenn kein Fisch in das Netz ihr ging, | And even if she caught no fish,
Die Fischerin doch die Herzen fing! | The fisher-girl trapped hearts!

Die Winde streifen so kühl umher, | The breezes blow cool about her,
Erzählen leis' eine alte Mär'! | Whispering an old fairy tale!
Die See erglühet im Abendrot, | The sea glows red in the sunset,
Die Fischerin fühlt nicht Liebesnot | The fisher-girl feels no pangs of love
Im Herzen! | In her heart!

Friedrich Rückert (1788–1866)

See Robert Schumann

Mahler's *Fünf Lieder nach Rückert* were written in the first two years of the twentieth century and later published with 'Revelge' and 'Der Tamboursg'sell'' as *Sieben Lieder aus letzter Zeit*. The songs are uninfluenced by folksong which had dominated his earlier Lieder.

1901–02 *Fünf Lieder nach Rückert* / Five Rückert songs

1
Ich atmet' einen linden Duft / I breathed a gentle fragrance

Ich atmet' einen linden Duft. | I breathed a gentle fragrance.
  Im Zimmer stand | In the room stood
  Ein Zweig der Linde, | A spray of lime,
  Ein Angebinde | A gift
  Von lieber Hand; | From a dear hand;
  Wie lieblich war der Lindenduft! | How lovely the fragrance of lime was!
Wie lieblich ist der Lindenduft! | How lovely the fragrance of lime is!
  Das Lindenreis | The spray of lime
  Brachst du gelinde; | Was gently plucked by you;
  Ich atme leis | Softly I breathe
  Im Duft der Linde | In the fragrance of lime
  Der Liebe linden Duft. | The gentle fragrance of love.

2
Blicke mir nicht in die Lieder! / Do not look into my songs!

Blicke mir nicht in die Lieder!
 Meine Augen schlag' ich nieder,
 Wie ertappt auf böser Tat;
Selber darf ich nicht getrauen,
 Ihrem Wachsen zuzuschauen:
 Deine Neugier ist Verrat!
Bienen, wenn sie Zellen bauen,
 Lassen auch nicht zu sich schauen,
 Schauen selbst auch nicht zu.
Wenn die reichen Honigwaben
 Sie zu Tag befördert haben,
 Dann vor allen nasche du!

Do not look into my songs!
 I lower my gaze,
 As if caught in the act;
I cannot even dare
 To watch them growing:
 Your curiosity is treason!
Bees, when they build cells,
 Let no one watch either,
 And do not even watch themselves.
When the rich honeycombs
 Have been brought to daylight,
 You shall be the first to taste!

3
Ich bin der Welt abhanden gekommen / I am lost to the world

Ich bin der Welt abhanden gekommen,
 Mit der ich sonst viele Zeit verdorben.
 Sie hat so lange nichts von mir vernommen,
 Sie mag wohl glauben, ich sei gestorben.
Es ist mir auch gar nichts daran gelegen,
 Ob sie mich für gestorben hält.
 Ich kann auch gar nichts sagen dagegen,
 Denn wirklich bin ich gestorben der Welt.
Ich bin gestorben dem Weltgetümmel,
 Und ruh' in einem stillen Gebiet.
 Ich leb' allein in meinem Himmel,
 In meinem Lieben, in meinem Lied.

I am lost to the world
 With which I used to waste much time;
 It has for so long heard nothing of me,
 It may well believe that I am dead.
Nor am I at all concerned
 If it should think me dead.
 Nor can I deny it,
 For truly I am dead to the world.
I am dead to the world's tumult
 And rest in a quiet realm.
 I live alone in my heaven,
 In my loving, in my song.

4
Um Mitternacht / At midnight

Um Mitternacht hab' ich gewacht
 Und aufgeblickt zum Himmel; kein Stern
 vom Sterngewimmel
Hat mir gelacht um Mitternacht.
Um Mitternacht hab' ich gedacht
 Hinaus in dunkle Schranken; es hat kein
 Lichtgedanken
Mir Trost gebracht um Mitternacht.
Um Mitternacht nahm ich in acht
 Die Schläge meines Herzens; ein einz'ger
 Puls des Schmerzens
War angefacht um Mitternacht.
Um Mitternacht kämpft' ich die Schlacht,

At midnight I kept watch
 And looked up to heaven; not a star in the
 galaxy
Smiled on me at midnight.
At midnight my thoughts went out
 To the dark reaches of space; no shining
 thought
Brought me comfort at midnight.
At midnight I paid heed
 To the beating of my heart; a single pulse of
 pain
Was set alight at midnight.
At midnight I fought the fight,

O Menschheit, deiner Leiden; nicht konnt'
  ich sie entscheiden
Mit meiner Macht um Mitternacht.
Um Mitternacht hab' ich die Macht
In deine Hand gegeben: Herr über Tod und
  Leben,
Du hältst die Wacht um Mitternacht.
(*Reutter*)

O Mankind, of your afflictions; I could not
  gain victory
By my own strength at midnight.
At midnight I gave my strength
Into Thy hands: Lord over life and
  death,
Thou keepest watch at midnight.

5
Liebst du um Schönheit / If you love for beauty

Liebst du um Schönheit,
  O nicht mich liebe!
  Liebe die Sonne,
  Sie trägt ein goldnes Haar.
Liebst du um Jugend,
  O nicht mich liebe!
  Liebe den Frühling,
  Der jung ist jedes Jahr.
Liebst du um Schätze,
  O nicht mich liebe!
  Liebe die Meerfrau,
  Sie hat viel Perlen klar.
Liebst du um Liebe,
  O ja mich liebe!
  Liebe mich immer,
  Dich lieb' ich immerdar.
(*Reutter, Clara Schumann*)

If you love for beauty,
  O love not me!
  Love the sun,
  She has golden hair.
If you love for youth,
  O love not me!
  Love the spring
  Which is young each year.
If you love for riches,
  O love not me!
  Love the mermaid
  Who has many shining pearls.
If you love for love,
  Ah yes, love me!
  Love me always,
  I shall love you ever more.

1901–04 *Kindertotenlieder / Songs on the death of children*

Kindertotenlieder, like *Lieder eines fahrenden Gesellen*, was originally written for piano and voice, and only orchestrated later. Mahler wrote the first two songs in the summer of 1901 while at work on his Fifth Symphony, choosing the poems from a volume of verse by Friedrich Rückert entitled 'Kindertotenlieder', which contained four hundred and twenty-eight poems on the theme of the death of infants. Rückert had written these poems in 1834 after losing his two youngest children in a scarlet fever epidemic (Joseph von Eichendorff was at the very same time pouring his grief into a similar but smaller cycle of ten poems, 'Auf meines Kindes Tod', one of which Othmar Schoeck later set to music as part of his Op. 20). Mahler was still a bachelor in 1901, but in the following year he married Alma Maria Schindler and soon became a father. His second daughter was born in 1904 and it was during the summer of that year, while at work on the Sixth Symphony, that he composed the last three songs of the cycle. They were published and premiered in

1905. Although it has often been asked how Mahler could have been so morbid as to compose such songs when his own children were happy and healthy, it should be remembered that he was simply completing a work that had been begun in 1901. Tragically, however, as if he had been tempting providence, Mahler lost his eldest daughter two years later.

1

Nun will die Sonn' so hell aufgehn,
  Als sei kein Unglück die Nacht geschehn.

Das Unglück geschah nur mir allein,
  Die Sonne, sie scheinet allgemein.

Du mußt nicht die Nacht in dir ver-
  schränken,
  Mußt sie ins ew'ge Licht versenken.

Ein Lämplein verlosch in meinem Zelt,
  Heil sei dem Freudenlicht der Welt!

Now the sun will rise as bright,
  As though no misfortune had befallen in
  the night.

The misfortune befell me alone,
  The sun, it shines on all mankind.

You must not enclose the night within you,
  You must immerse it in eternal light.

A little lamp went out in my firmament,
  Hail to the joyful light of the world!

2

Nun seh' ich wohl, warum so dunkle Flammen
  Ihr sprühet mir in manchem Augenblicke,
  O Augen, gleichsam, um voll in einem
  Blicke
  Zu drängen eure ganze Macht zusammen.

Dort ahnt' ich nicht, weil Nebel mich
  umschwammen,
  Gewoben vom verblendenden Geschicke,
  Daß sich der Strahl bereits zur Heimkehr
  schicke
  Dorthin, von wannen alle Strahlen stammen.

Ihr wolltet mir mit eurem Leuchten sagen:
  Wir möchten nah dir bleiben gerne,
  Doch ist uns das vom Schicksal abgeschlagen.

Sieh' uns nur an, denn bald sind wir dir ferne.
  Was dir nur Augen sind in diesen Tagen,
  In künft'gen Nächten sind es dir nur Sterne.

Now I see clearly why you so often
  Flash such dark flames at me,
  O eyes, to compress, as it were, all your
  power
  Into a single glance.

Yet I could not guess, for mists surrounded
  me,
  Woven by fate to dazzle me,
  That your brightness was already making
  for home,
  Towards that place whence all light comes.

With your shining light you wished to tell me:
  We'd love to stay here by your side,
  But this our destiny denies us.

Look at us well, for soon we shall be far away.
  What now are merely eyes to you,
  In nights to come shall be merely stars.

3

Wenn dein Mütterlein
  Tritt zur Tür herein,
  Und den Kopf ich drehe,
  Ihr entgegen sehe,
  Fällt auf ihr Gesicht
  Erst der Blick mir nicht,

When your dear mother
  Comes in through the door
  And I turn my head
  To look at her,
  My gaze falls first,
  Not on her face,

Sondern auf die Stelle,
Näher nach der Schwelle,
Dort, wo würde dein
Lieb Gesichtchen sein,
Wenn du freudenhelle
Trätest mit herein,
Wie sonst, mein Töchterlein.

Wenn dein Mütterlein
Tritt zur Tür herein
Mit der Kerze Schimmer,
Ist es mir, als immer
Kämst du mit herein,
Huschtest hinterdrein,
Als wie sonst in's Zimmer.
O du, des Vaters Zelle,
Ach, zu schnelle
Erlosch'ner Freudenschein!

But on that place
Nearer the threshold
Where your
Dear little face would be,
If you, bright-eyed,
Were entering with her,
As you used, my daughter.

When your dear mother
Comes in through the door
With the flickering candle,
I always think
You are coming too,
Stealing in behind her,
As you used.
O you, the joyful light,
Ah, too soon extinguished,
Of your father's flesh and blood!

4

Oft denk' ich, sie sind nur ausgegangen,
Bald werden sie wieder nach Hause gelangen,
Der Tag ist schön, o sei nicht bang,
Sie machen nur einen weiten Gang.

Ja wohl, sie sind nur ausgegangen,
Und werden jetzt nach Hause gelangen,
O sei nicht bang, der Tag ist schön,
Sie machen nur den Gang zu jenen Höhn.

Sie sind uns nur voraus gegangen
Und werden nicht wieder nach Haus
verlangen.
Wir holen sie ein auf jenen Höhn
Im Sonnenschein, der Tag ist schön auf
jenen Höhn.

I often think they have only gone out,
They will soon be coming home again,
It is a beautiful day, ah do not be afraid,
They have only gone for a long walk.

Yes, they have only gone out
And will now be coming home again,
Do not be afraid, it is a beautiful day,
They are only walking to those hills.

They have merely gone on ahead of us
And will not ask to come home
again,
We shall overtake them on those hills
In the sunshine, the day is beautiful on
those hills.

5

In diesem Wetter, in diesem Braus,
Nie hätt' ich gesendet die Kinder hinaus;
Man hat sie getragen, getragen hinaus,
Ich durfte nichts dazu sagen.

In diesem Wetter, in diesem Saus,
Nie hätt' ich gelassen die Kinder hinaus,
Ich fürchtete, sie erkranken,
Das sind nun eitle Gedanken.

In diesem Wetter, in diesem Graus,

In this weather, this raging storm,
I'd never have sent the children out;
They were carried, carried from the house,
There was nothing I could say.

In this weather, this howling gale,
I'd never have let the children out,
I feared that they would fall ill,
These are now but idle thoughts.

In this weather, this dreadful blast,

Nie hätt' ich gelassen die Kinder hinaus,	I'd never have let the children out,
Ich sorgte, sie stürben morgen,	I feared they might die next day,
Das ist nun nicht zu besorgen.	There is no cause for such fears now.
In diesem Wetter, in diesem Graus,	In this weather, this dreadful blast,
Nie hätt' ich gesendet die Kinder hinaus,	I'd never have sent the children out.
Man hat sie hinaus getragen;	They were carried from the house;
Ich durfte nichts dazu sagen.	There was nothing I could say.
In diesem Wetter, in diesem Saus, in diesem Braus,	In this weather, this howling gale, this raging storm,
Sie ruhn, als wie in der Mutter Haus,	They rest, as if in their mother's house,
Von keinem Sturm erschrecket,	Frightened by no storm,
Von Gottes Hand bedecket,	Protected by God's hand,
Sie ruhn wie in der Mutter Haus.	They rest, as if in their mother's house.

1907–08 *Das Lied von der Erde* / *The song of the earth*

TRANSLATED FROM THE CHINESE BY HANS BETHGE (1876–1946)

1

Das Trinklied vom Jammer der Erde / Drinking song of the earth's sorrow

AFTER LI-TAI-PO (702–63)

Schon winkt der Wein im gold'nen Pokale, –	The wine now beckons in the golden goblet, –
Doch trinkt noch nicht, erst sing' ich euch ein Lied!	But drink not yet, first I'll sing you a song!
Das Lied vom Kummer	The song of sorrow
Soll auflachend in die Seele euch klingen.	Shall resound through your soul in gusts of laughter.
Wenn der Kummer naht,	When sorrow draws near,
Liegen wüst die Gärten der Seele,	The gardens of the soul lie wasted,
Welkt hin und stirbt die Freude, der Gesang.	Joy and singing wither and die.
Dunkel ist das Leben, ist der Tod.	Dark is life, is death.
Herr dieses Hauses!	Master of this house!
Dein Keller birgt die Fülle des goldenen Weins!	Your cellar is filled with golden wine!
Hier, diese Laute nenn' ich mein!	I name this lute here my own!
Die Laute schlagen und die Gläser leeren,	Striking the lute and draining beakers,
Das sind die Dinge, die zusammenpassen!	These are things that go well together!
Ein voller Becher Weins zur rechten Zeit	A full beaker of wine at the right time
Ist mehr wert als alle Reiche dieser Erde.	Is worth more than all the kingdoms of this earth.
Dunkel ist das Leben, ist der Tod!	Dark is life, is death!
Das Firmament blaut ewig, und die Erde	The firmament is forever blue, and the earth
Wird lange fest stehn und aufblühn im Lenz.	Will long stand firm and blossom in spring.
Du aber, Mensch, wie lang lebst denn du?	But you, O man, how long do you live?
Nicht hundert Jahre darfst du dich ergötzen	Not even a hundred years can you delight
An all dem morschen Tande dieser Erde.	In all the brittle trumpery of this earth.

Seht dort hinab! Im Mondschein auf den
    Gräbern
Hockt eine wild-gespenstische Gestalt.
Ein Aff' ist's! Hört ihr, wie sein Heulen
Hinausgellt in den süßen Duft des Lebens!
Jetzt nehmt den Wein! Jetzt ist es Zeit,
    Genossen!
Leert eure goldnen Becher zu Grund.
Dunkel ist das Leben, ist der Tod.

Look down there! On the moonlit
    graves
A wild ghostly form is squatting.
It is an ape! Hear him howl
And screech at life's sweet fragrance!
Now take up the wine! Now, friends, is the
    time!
Drain your golden beakers to the dregs.
Dark is life, is death.

2

Der Einsame im Herbst / The lonely one in autumn
AFTER TSCHANG-TSI (*fl.* 800)

Herbstnebel wallen bläulich überm See,
Vom Reif bezogen stehen alle Gräser,
Man meint, ein Künstler habe Staub von Jade
Über die feinen Blüten ausgestreut.

Bluish autumn mists drift over the lake,
Each blade of grass is covered with rime,
As though an artist had strewn jade-dust
Over the delicate blossoms.

Der süße Duft der Blumen ist verflogen,
Ein kalter Wind beugt ihre Stengel nieder;
Bald werden die verwelkten, goldnen Blätter
Der Lotosblüten auf dem Wasser ziehn.

The sweet fragrance of the flowers has faded,
A cold wind bends low their stems;
Soon the withered golden petals
Of the lotus-flowers will drift on the water.

Mein Herz ist müde. Meine kleine Lampe
Erlosch mit Knistern, es gemahnt mich an
    den Schlaf.
Ich komm' zu dir, traute Ruhestätte, –
Ja, gib mir Ruh, ich hab Erquickung not!

My heart is weary. My little lamp
Guttered with a hiss, it summons me to
    sleep.
I come to you, beloved resting-place, –
Yes, give me rest, I need to be refreshed!

Ich weine viel in meinen Einsamkeiten,
Der Herbst in meinem Herzen währt zu lange;
Sonne der Liebe, willst du nie mehr scheinen,
Um meine bittern Tränen mild aufzutrocknen?

I weep much in my loneliness,
The autumn in my heart persists too long;
Sun of love, will you never shine again
And dry up tenderly my bitter tears?

3

Von der Jugend / Of youth
AFTER LI-TAI-PO (702–63)

Mitten in dem kleinen Teiche
Steht ein Pavillon aus grünem
Und aus weißem Porzellan.

In the middle of the little pool
Stands a pavilion of green
And white porcelain.

Wie der Rücken eines Tigers
Wölbt die Brücke sich aus Jade
Zu dem Pavillon hinüber.

Like a tiger's back
The jade bridge arches
Over to the pavilion.

In dem Häuschen sitzen Freunde,
Schön gekleidet, trinken, plaudern, –
Manche schreiben Verse nieder.

Friends sit in the little house,
Beautifully dressed, drinking, chatting, –
Several are writing verses.

Ihre seidnen Ärmel gleiten	Their silken sleeves slip
Rückwärts, ihre seidnen Mützen	Back, their silken caps
Hocken lustig tief im Nacken.	Fall cheerfully onto their necks.

Ihre seidnen Ärmel gleiten
Rückwärts, ihre seidnen Mützen
Hocken lustig tief im Nacken.

Auf des kleinen Teiches stiller
Wasserfläche zeigt sich alles
Wunderlich im Spiegelbilde:

Alles auf dem Kopfe stehend,
In dem Pavillon aus grünem
Und aus weißem Porzellan.

Wie ein Halbmond steht die Brücke,
Umgekehrt der Bogen. Freunde,
Schön gekleidet, trinken, plaudern.

Their silken sleeves slip
Back, their silken caps
Fall cheerfully onto their necks.

On the little pool's still
Surface everything is
Strangely mirrored:

Everything stands on its head
In the pavilion of green
And white porcelain.

The bridge seems like a half-moon,
Its arch inverted. Friends,
Beautifully dressed, are drinking, chatting.

4

Von der Schönheit / Of beauty
AFTER LI-TAI-PO (702–63)

Junge Mädchen pflücken Blumen,
Pflücken Lotosblumen an dem Uferrande.
Zwischen Büschen und Blättern sitzen sie,
Sammeln Blüten in den Schoß und rufen
Sich einander Neckereien zu.

Goldne Sonne webt um die Gestalten,
Spiegelt sie im blanken Wasser wider,
Sonne spiegelt ihre schlanken Glieder,
Ihre süßen Augen wider,
Und der Zephir hebt mit Schmeichelkosen
Das Gewebe ihrer Ärmel auf, führt den Zauber
Ihrer Wohlgerüche durch die Luft.

O sieh, was tummeln sich für schöne Knaben
Dort an dem Uferrand auf mut'gen Rossen?
Weithin glänzend wie die Sonnenstrahlen;
Schon zwischen dem Geäst der grünen Wei-
den
Trabt das jungfrische Volk einher.
Das Roß des einen wiehert fröhlich auf,
Und scheut, und saust dahin,
Über Blumen, Gräser wanken hin die Hufe,
Sie zerstampfen jäh im Sturm die hinge-
sunk'nen Blüten.
Hei! wie flattern im Taumel seine Mähnen,
Dampfen heiß die Nüstern!
Gold'ne Sonne webt um die Gestalten,
Spiegelt sie im blanken Wasser wider.

Young girls are picking flowers,
Lotus-flowers by the river's edge.
They sit among bushes and leaves,
Gather blossoms into their laps and call
To each other teasingly.

Golden sunlight weaves round their forms,
Mirrors them in the shining water,
Sunlight mirrors their slender limbs
And their sweet eyes,
And the breeze lifts with its caresses
The fabric of their sleeves, wafts the magic
Of their fragrance through the air.

O look, what handsome boys are these, riding
Friskily along the bank on spirited horses?
Shining afar, like the sun's rays;
Now they canter between green willow
branches,
These lads in the flush of youth.
The horse of one whinnies happily,
And shies and races off,
Its hooves fly over flowers and grass,
Trampling the fallen blossoms as they storm
past.
Look how its mane flutters in its frenzy,
Look how the nostrils steam!
Golden sunlight weaves round their forms,
Mirrors them in the shining water.

Und die schönste von den Jungfraun sendet	And the loveliest of the girls
Lange Blicke ihm der Sehnsucht nach.	Shoots him long yearning glances.
Ihre stolze Haltung ist nur Verstellung:	Her proud bearing is mere pretence:
In dem Funkeln ihrer großen Augen,	In the flashing of her large eyes,
In dem Dunkel ihres heißen Blicks	In the darkness of her ardent gaze
Schwingt klagend noch die Erregung ihres	Her agitated heart still throbs and grieves for
Herzens nach.	him.

5

Der Trunkene im Frühling / The drunkard in spring
AFTER LI-TAI-PO (702–63)

Wenn nur ein Traum das Leben ist,	If life is but a dream,
Warum denn Müh und Plag?	Why should there be toil and torment?
Ich trinke, bis ich nicht mehr kann,	I drink till I can drink no longer,
Den ganzen lieben Tag.	The whole day through.
Und wenn ich nicht mehr trinken kann,	And when I can drink no longer,
Weil Kehl und Seele voll,	Since throat and soul are full,
So tauml ich bis zu meiner Tür	I stagger to my door
Und schlafe wundervoll!	And sleep stupendously!
Was hör' ich beim Erwachen? Horch,	What do I hear when I wake? Listen!
Ein Vogel singt im Baum.	A bird sings in the tree.
Ich frag ihn, ob schon Frühling sei, –	I ask him if spring has come, –
Mir ist als wie im Traum.	It all seems like a dream.
Der Vogel zwitschert: ja, der Lenz	The bird twitters: yes, spring
Ist da, sei kommen über Nacht, –	Is here, it came overnight!
Aus tiefstem Schauen lausch' ich auf,	In deepest contemplation I listened,
Der Vogel singt und lacht.	The bird sings and laughs.
Ich fülle mir den Becher neu	I fill my beaker again
Und leer ihn bis zum Grund	And drain it to the dregs
Und singe, bis der Mond erglänzt	And sing until the moon shines bright
Am schwarzen Firmament.	In the black firmament.
Und wenn ich nicht mehr singen kann,	And when I can sing no longer,
So schlaf ich wieder ein.	I fall asleep again.
Was geht mich denn der Frühling an!?	For what has spring to do with me!?
Laßt mich betrunken sein!	Let me be drunk!

6

Der Abschied / The farewell
AFTER MONG-KAO-JEN (*fl.* 8TH CENTURY)

Die Sonne scheidet hinter dem Gebirge,	The sun sinks behind the mountains,
In alle Täler steigt der Abend nieder	Evening falls in every valley
Mit seinen Schatten, die voll Kühlung sind.	With its shadows full of coolness.

O sieh! wie eine Silberbarke schwebt
Der Mond am blauen Himmelssee herauf.
Ich spüre eines feinen Windes Wehn
Hinter den dunklen Fichten!

O look! like a silver bark
The moon floats up the sky's blue lake.
I feel a gentle breeze stir
Behind the dark spruces!

Der Bach singt voller Wohllaut durch das
  Dunkel,
Die Blumen blassen im Dämmerschein.
Die Erde atmet voll von Ruh und Schlaf.

The brook sings melodiously through the
  dark,
The flowers grow pale in the twilight.
The earth breathes full of peace and sleep.

Alle Sehnsucht will nun träumen,
Die müden Menschen gehn heimwärts,
Um im Schlaf vergessnes Glück
Und Jugend neu zu lernen.
Die Vögel hocken still in ihren Zweigen,
Die Welt schläft ein.

All desire now turns to dreaming,
Weary mortals make for home,
To recapture in sleep
Forgotten happiness and youth.
Birds huddle silently on their branches,
The world falls asleep.

Es wehet kühl im Schatten meiner Fichten,
Ich stehe hier und harre meines Freundes;
Ich harre sein zum letzten Lebewohl.
Ich sehne mich, O Freund, an deiner Seite
Die Schönheit dieses Abends zu genießen.
Wo bleibst du? Du läßt mich lang allein!

A cool wind blows in the shadow of my spruces,
I stand here and wait for my friend;
I wait to bid him a final farewell.
I long, O friend, to enjoy
The beauty of this evening by your side.
Where can you be? You have left me alone so long!

Ich wandle auf und nieder mit meiner Laute
Auf Wegen, die von weichem Grase
  schwellen.
O Schönheit! O ewigen Liebens, Lebens
  trunk'ne Welt!

I wander up and down with my lute
On pathways rippling with soft grass.
O beauty! O world drunk with eternal love
  and life!

AFTER WANG-WEI (*fl.* 8TH CENTURY)

Er stieg vom Pferd und reichte ihm den Trunk
Des Abschieds dar. Er fragte ihn, wohin er führe
Und auch warum es müßte sein.
Er sprach, seine Stimme war umflort: Du,
  mein Freund,
Mir war auf dieser Welt das Glück nicht hold.

He dismounted and handed him the stirrup-
  cup.
He asked him where he was going
And also why it had to be.
He spoke, his voice was veiled: my friend,
Fortune was not kind to me on earth.

Wohin ich geh? Ich geh, ich wandre in die
  Berge,
Ich suche Ruhe für mein einsam Herz.
Ich wandle nach der Heimat, meiner Stätte!
Ich werde niemals in die Ferne schweifen, –
Still ist mein Herz und harret seiner Stunde!

Where am I going? I go into the mountains,
I seek peace for my lonely heart.
I am making for home, my resting-place!
I shall never roam abroad again –
My heart is still and awaits its hour!

Die liebe Erde allüberall
Blüht auf im Lenz und grünt aufs neu!
Allüberall und ewig blauen licht die Fernen!
Ewig ... Ewig ...

Everywhere the dear earth
Blossoms in spring and grows green again!
Everywhere and forever the distance shines
  bright and blue!
Forever ... Forever ...

Frank Martin (1890–1974)

Though French was this Swiss composer's mother tongue, three of his most successful vocal works were written in German: *Die Weise von Liebe und Tod des Cornets Christoph Rilke*, *Drey Minnlieder* and *Sechs Monologe aus* Jedermann (1943). Martin chose six monologues from Hofmannsthal's play in order to 'summarize the psychological and spiritual evolution of the central character, from his animal-like terror of death to his total acceptance of it, in the knowledge that he would be pardoned [. . .], and describe his gradual indifference to worldly goods, and his ascension, through anguish and suffering, to the world of the spirit.' Though tempted to write an opera on the theme, Martin contented himself with orchestrating the songs in 1949; the first performance of this second version was given the same year in Venice.

Hugo von Hofmannsthal (1874–1929)

Austrian playwright and poet, who published his first poetry at the age of sixteen under the pseudonym of Loris; his early plays and poems, written at the start of the 1890s, are characterized by a *fin de siècle* melancholy. Though his extremely musical verse has found little favour with Lieder composers, Hofmannsthal's libretti were eagerly seized on by Richard Strauss who, having rejected *Der Triumph der Zeit* for a proposed ballet in 1900, subsequently set to music no fewer than seven of his works: *Elektra* (1909), *Der Rosenkavalier* (1911), *Ariadne auf Naxos* (1912), *Die Frau ohne Schatten* (1919), *Die Ägyptische Helena* (1928), *Arabella* (1933) and the ballet *Josephslegende* (1912). The religious parable *Jedermann* was published in 1911 and soon became popular throughout Germany; it is known to European audiences through the performances given each year at the Salzburg Festival, where it received its first performance in August 1920.

1943 *Sechs Monologe aus* Jedermann / *Six monologues from* Jedermann

1

Ist alls zu End das Freudenmahl	Is the banquet now all over,
Und alle fort aus meinem Saal?	Has everyone left my hall?
Bleibt mir keine andere Hilfe dann,	Is there no other help for me,
Bin ich denn ein verlorner Mann?	Am I a lost soul?
Und ganz alleinig in der Welt,	And am I quite alone in the world?
Ist es schon so um mich bestellt,	Has my fate already been sealed,
Hat mich Der schon dazu gemacht,	Has He reduced me to this state,
Ganz nackend und ohn alle Macht,	Quite naked and deprived of power,
Als läg ich schon in meinem Grab,	As if I were already in my grave,
Wo ich doch mein warm Blut noch hab	Even though my blood's still warm

Und Knecht mir noch gehorsam sein
Und Häuser viel und Schätze mein.
Auf! Schlagt die Feuerglocken drein!
Ihr Knecht nicht lungert in dem Haus,
Kommt allesamt zu mir heraus!

Ich muß schnell eine Reise tun
Und das zu Fuß und nit zu Wagen,
Gesamte Knecht, die sollen mit
Und meine große Geldtruhen,
Die sollen sie herbeitragen.
Die Reis wird wie ein Kriegszug scharf,
Daß ich der Schätze sehr bedarf.

2

Ach Gott, wie graust mir vor dem Tod,
Der Angstschweiß bricht mir aus vor Not;
Kann der die Seel im Leib uns morden?
Was ist denn jählings aus mir worden?
Hab immer doch in bösen Stunden
Mir irgend einen Trost ausgefunden,
War nie verlassen ganz und gar,
Nie kein erbärmlich armer Narr.
War immer wo doch noch ein Halt
Und habs gewendet mit Gewalt.
Sind all denn meine Kräft dahin
Und alls verworren schon mein Sinn,
Daß ich kaum mehr besinnen kann,
Wer bin ich denn: der Jedermann,
Der reiche Jedermann allzeit.
Das ist mein Hand, das ist mein Kleid
Und was da steht auf diesem Platz,
Das ist mein Geld, das ist mein Schatz,
Durch den ich jederzeit mit Macht
Hab alles spielend vor mich bracht.
Nun wird mir wohl, daß ich den seh
Recht bei der Hand in meiner Näh.
Wenn ich bei dem verharren kann
Geht mich kein Graus und Ängsten an.
Weh aber, ich muß ja dorthin,
Das kommt mir jählings in den Sinn.
Der Bot war da, die Ladung ist beschehn.
Nun heißt es auf und dorthin gehn.
Nit ohne dich, du mußt mit mir,
Laß dich um alles nit hinter mir.
Du mußt jetzt in ein andres Haus
Drum auf mit dir und schnell heraus!

And my servants still obedient
And my houses and wealth still mine?
Get up! Sound the fire-bell!
Servants, stop idling about the house,
Come out to me, each one of you!

I've a journey to make without delay,
On foot, though, and not by carriage,
All my servants shall come with me,
And they shall bring out
My vast treasure chests.
This journey will be as harsh as a battle,
So I shall have great need of my treasure.

O God, how scared I am of death,
I break out in a cold sweat;
Can death kill the body's soul?
What has suddenly become of me?
In times of trouble I was always able
To find some kind of solace.
I was never totally forsaken,
Never a poor and wretched fool.
Some support was always to be found
And I always applied it with force.
Now all my strength is spent
And my senses so bewildered
That I can scarcely recall
Who I am: Everyman,
Still the wealthy Everyman.
This is my hand, this is my cloak,
And that which I see before me,
That is my money, that is my treasure,
Through which I've always had the power
To fulfil with ease all my wishes.
My spirits now rise when I see
My treasure near at hand.
As long as it's safe by my side,
I shall not feel terror or fear.
But alas, I must go to that place –
It suddenly flashes through my mind.
The Messenger came, the summons arrived,
I must now set out for that place.
But not without you, you must come with me,
On no account shall I leave you here.
You must now go to another house,
So up you get and quickly leave!

3

Ist als wenn eins gerufen hätt,
Die Stimme war schwach und doch recht klar,
Hilf Gott, daß es nit meine Mutter war.
Ist gar ein alt, gebrechlich Weib,
Möcht, daß der Anblick erspart ihr bleib.
O nur soviel erbarm dich mein,
Laß das nit meine Mutter sein!

It's as if someone had called,
The voice was faint and yet quite clear,
I pray to God it was not my mother.
She's such an old and frail woman,
I should like her to be spared this sight.
O show me this much mercy,
May it not be my mother!

4

So wollt ich ganz zernichtet sein,
Wie an dem ganzen Wesen mein
Nit eine Fiber jetzt nit schreit
Vor tiefer Reu und wildem Leid.

I wish to be utterly destroyed
Just as in my whole being
There's not one fibre that does not scream,
Deeply repentent and wild with grief.

Zurück! Und kann nit! Noch einmal!
Und kommt nit wieder! Graus und Qual!
Hie wird kein zweites Mal gelebt!
Nun weiß die aufgerissne Brust,
Als sie es nie zuvor gewußt,
Was dieses Wort bedeuten mag:
Lieg hin und stirb, hie ist dein Tag!

Go away! I cannot bear it! Not again!
And don't come back! Horror and grief!
Life's not lived a second time here!
The gaping, wounded breast now knows,
As it has never known before,
The meaning of these words:
Lie down and die, your day is come!

5

Ja! Ich glaub: Solches hat er vollbracht,
Des Vaters Zorn zunicht gemacht,
Der Menschheit ewig Heil erworben
Und ist dafür am Kreuz verstorben.
Doch weiß ich, solches kommt zugut,
Nur dem, der heilig ist und gut:
Durch gute Werk und Frommheit eben
Erkauft er sich ein ewig Leben.
Da sieh, so stehts um meine Werk:
Von Sünden hab ich einen Berg
So überschwer auf mich geladen,
Daß mich Gott gar nit kann begnaden,
Als er der Höchstgerechte ist.

Yes, I believe that Christ has done this,
Has appeased his Father's wrath,
Brought mankind eternal salvation
Through dying on the cross.
Yet I know, only he partakes of this,
Whose soul is good and holy:
Through good deeds and piety,
He shall gain eternal life.
But look at the state of my deeds:
I have weighed myself down
With such a mountain of sins
That God, the most righteous of all,
Could never grant me mercy.

6

O ewiger Gott! O göttliches Gesicht!
O rechter Weg! O himmlisches Licht!
Hier schrei ich zu dir in letzter Stund,
Ein Klageruf geht aus meinem Mund.
O mein Erlöser, den Schöpfer erbitt,
Daß er beim Ende mir gnädig sei,
Wenn der höllische Feind sich drängt herbei,
Und der Tod mir grausam die Kehle
    zuschnürt,

O eternal God! O divine countenance!
O path of righteousness! O heavenly light!
I cry to Thee in my final hour,
My lips utter a plaintive cry.
O my Redeemer, beseech my Maker
That He show me grace when my end is
    nigh,
When the hellish foe gathers near
And Death cruelly tightens the noose,

Daß er meine Seel dann hinaufführt.
Und, Heiland, mach durch deine Fürbitt,
Daß ich zu seiner Rechten hintritt,
In seine Glorie mit ihm zu gehn.
Laß dir dies mein Gebet anstehn,
Um willen, daß du am Kreuz bist gestorben
Und hast all unsre Seelen erworben.

May He lead my soul to Heaven.
And Thou, my Saviour, intercede for me
That I might sit at His right hand,
That I might walk with Him in glory,
Mayest Thou hear my prayer,
Since Thou didst die upon the cross
And didst redeem all our souls.

Joseph Marx (1882–1964)

Born a year before Webern and eight years after Schoenberg, Marx wrote music that remained, like Strauss's, firmly rooted in tonality. He wrote over a hundred songs, composed mostly between 1906 and 1916, many of which (including both songs printed here) he orchestrated. The beautiful melody of 'Hat dich die Liebe berührt' is marked 'langsam und ausdrucksvoll', and Marx, aware that singers might maul his vocal line, was wise enough to add a parenthetical 'doch nicht schleppend' ('but not dragging'). 'Venezianisches Wiegenlied', the seventeenth and final song of Marx's *Italienisches Liederbuch*, in which he set poems by Heyse which Wolf had omitted, is a delightful lullaby that can be sung, according to the composer's note on the score, either by the man to his sweetheart, or – with the appropriate textual changes – by the girl to her lover.

Paul Heyse (1830–1914)

See Wolf

1908 Hat dich die Liebe berührt / If Love has touched you

Hat dich die Liebe berührt,	If Love has touched you
Still unter lärmendem Volke,	Softly amid noisy mankind,
Gehst du in gold'ner Wolke,	You will walk on a cloud of gold,
Sicher von Gott geführt.	Led safely by God.
Nur wie verloren umher	You gaze about you
Lässest die Blicke du wandern,	As though you are lost,
Gönnst ihre Freuden den andern,	You do not begrudge others their happiness,
Trägst nur nach Einem Begehr.	Only one thing do you desire.
Scheu in dich selber verzückt,	In shy and rapt introspection,
Möchtest du leugnen vergebens,	You deny in vain
Daß nun die Krone des Lebens	That life's gleaming crown
Strahlend die Stirn dir schmückt.	Now adorns your brow.

1912 Venezianisches Wiegenlied / Venetian cradle-song

Nina ninana will ich dir singen.	I shall sing you a lullaby.
Um Mitternacht hörst du ein Glöckchen klingen,	At midnight you'll hear a little bell ring,
Nicht mein ist diese Glocke, die wir hören,	The bell we shall hear is not mine,
Santa Lucia wird sie wohl gehören.	But belongs, I think, to Santa Lucia.
Santa Lucia gab dir ihre Augen,	Santa Lucia gave you her eyes,
Die Magdalena ihre blonden Flechten,	Magdalena her golden tresses,

Die Engel schenkten ihre Farben, Kindchen,	The Angels, child, their pretty colours, Saint
Die heil'ge Martha ihr holdsel'ges Mündchen,	Martha her lovely mouth,
Ihr Mündchen süß von Florentiner Schnitte;	Her sweet mouth with its Florentine curve;
O sag, wie fängt die Liebe an, ich bitte!	O tell me how love starts, I pray!
Sie fängt wohl mit Musik und Geigen an,	It starts, I guess, with violins and music
Und endigt mit den kleinen Kindern dann;	And then ends with little children;
Sie fängt wohl an mit Singen und mit Sehnen,	It starts I guess with singing and yearning,
Und hört dann auf mit Jammern und mit	And ceases then with grieving and
Tränen.	tears.

Nikolai Medtner (1880–1951)

Since Medtner's parents were of German descent, it is not surprising he was drawn to the world of Lieder. Although his compositions are almost exclusively for the piano, his hundred or so songs, described in *New Grove* as some of 'the finest songs of the twentieth century', contain many wonderful settings of Pushkin and Goethe. There are three sets of Goethe songs: nine from Op. 6 (1904), twelve from Op. 15 (1908) and six from Op. 18 (1908). Songs such as 'An die Türen will ich schleichen', 'Meeresstille', 'Nähe des Geliebten', 'Der du von dem Himmel bist', 'Über allen Gipfeln', 'Gefunden', 'Liebliches Kind', 'Erster Verlust', 'Das Veilchen', 'Die Spröde', 'Die Bekehrte', 'Jägers Abendlied', 'Gleich und gleich' and 'Mignon' are more familiar to us in settings by other composers, but Medtner's versions make fascinating comparisons.

Johann Wolfgang von Goethe (1749–1832)

See Beethoven, Brahms, Hensel, Loewe, Mendelssohn, Reichardt, Schubert, Strauss, Wolf, Zelter

1908 Vor Gericht / In court Op. 15, no. 6

Von wem ich es habe, das sag ich euch nicht,	I shall not tell you the father's name
Das Kind in meinem Leib.	Of the child I bear in my womb.
„Pfui!" speit ihr aus: „die Hure da!"	'Shame on the strumpet!' I hear you spit.
Bin doch ein ehrlich Weib.	Yet I'm an honest woman.
Mit wem ich mich traute, das sag ich euch nicht.	I shall not say to whom I'm wedded.
Mein Schatz ist lieb und gut,	My love is good and kind,
Trägt er eine goldene Kett am Hals,	Whether he wears a gold chain round his neck,
Trägt er einen strohernen Hut.	Or wears a hat of straw.
Soll Spott und Hohn getragen sein,	If scorn and sneers must be endured,
Trag ich allein den Hohn.	I'll bear the scorn alone.
Ich kenn ihn wohl, er kennt mich wohl,	I know him well, he knows me well,
Und Gott weiß auch davon.	And God knows about us too.
Herr Pfarrer und Herr Amtmann ihr,	Mr Parson and Mr Magistrate,
Ich bitte, laßt mich in Ruh!	I pray you, leave me in peace!
Es ist mein Kind, es bleibt mein Kind,	It is my child, and will remain my child,
Ihr gebt mir ja nichts dazu.	And you do nothing to help.

1908 Glückliche Fahrt* / Prosperous voyage Op. 15, no. 8

Die Nebel zerreißen,	The mists disperse,
Der Himmel ist helle,	The sky is bright,
Und Äolus† löset	And Aeolus loosens
Das ängstliche Band.	The fearful knot.
Es säuseln die Winde,	The winds are blowing,
Es rührt sich der Schiffer.	The sailor's alert.
Geschwinde! Geschwinde!	Make haste! Make haste!
Es teilt sich die Welle,	The waves are parting,
Es naht sich die Ferne;	The distance approaches;
Schon seh' ich das Land!	I already see land!
(*Beethoven, Reichardt, Tomášek*)	

* Published in Goethe's *Collected Works* as a companion piece to 'Meeres Stille' (See Schubert, p. 307).
Mendelssohn's overture 'Meeresstille und glückliche Fahrt', op. 27, dates from 1828.
† Aeolus, the king of storms and winds.

Felix Mendelssohn (1809–47)

Almost a third of Mendelssohn's seventy-eight published songs (some forty more still await publication) contain the word 'Gesang' or 'Lied' in the title, and there is a melodic immediacy about his Lieder that is striking. His best-known song, 'Auf Flügeln des Gesanges', (1833), reflects accurately what its poet, Heinrich Heine, felt a song should be, when a decade earlier he wrote in an essay, 'Das deutsche Lied': „Wahrlich, man kann jene Componisten nicht genug ehren, welche uns Lieder-Melodien geben, die von der Art sind, daß sie sich Eingang bei dem Volke verschaffen und echte Lebenslust und wahren Frohsinn verbreiten." ('Indeed, one can scarcely praise those composers enough, who create such song-melodies, which find their way into the hearts of the people and disseminate true zest for life and genuine joy.'). This simplicity of utterance in so many of Mendelssohn's songs, most of which are modified strophic, has led some commentators to denigrate his Lieder and compare them unfavourably with Schubert's. He is criticized for following the example of his composition teacher Zelter and the ideals of the Berlin School, which favoured simple accompaniments that would not distract the listener from the poem; he is condemned for rarely plumbing the depths of a poem, the inference being that his privileged lifestyle – he was wealthy, at home in high society and had access to an orchestra that played his own music – encouraged superficiality. The truth is that the beauty of Mendelssohn's melodies in 'Schilflied', 'Nachtlied', 'Scheidend' and 'Der Mond', for example, actually deepens the emotion expressed in the poem. Mendelssohn also had an astonishing capacity for creating a vivid sense of atmosphere – songs such as 'Neue Liebe' and 'Hexenlied' conjure up the world of the piano scherzo from Op. 16 and *A Midsummer Night's Dream* – like almost no other Lieder composer.

Anonymous

24 September 1821 Der Verlassene / The forsaken one WoO

Nacht ist um mich her, im Mondenscheine
Feiert rings die blühende Natur.
Schwarz bedecket ruht die junge Flur,
Philomelens Lied erstarb im Haine.

Alles ruht so süß! Ich Armer nur
Stehe traurig auf der Flur und weine,
Suche überall nur sie, die eine,
Ach, und finde nirgends ihre Spur.

Night envelops me, in the moonlight
Blossoming nature rejoices all around.
The young field rests beneath its black cover,
The nightingale's song has died in the grove.

All rests so sweetly! My poor self alone
Stands sadly in the field and weeps,
Searching everywhere for her alone,
And finding, alas, not a single trace.

Wie die Blumen hier nach neuer Sonne	As the flowers here crave a new sun
An den goldnen Strahlen zu erwarmen	To warm themselves in the golden rays,
Mit gesenktem Haupt sich innig sehnen,	And incline their heads,
So erträum ich mir in meinen Tränen	So I dream, as I weep tears,
Jene neidenswerte Himmelswonne,	Of that divine and desirable joy
Die Verlorne wieder zu umarmen.	Of embracing once more she whom I lost.

Lord Byron (1788–1824)

Gooch-Thatcher's bibliography lists no fewer than 1287 compositions based on Byron's works – hardly surprising, since Byron was arguably the most influential poet in nineteenth-century Europe. His lyric verse has attracted a huge number of composers, including Henry Bishop, Busoni, David Diamond, Annette von Droste-Hülshoff, Hans Florey, Ives, Loewe, Mussorgsky, Ferdinand Ries, Rimsky-Korsakov, Schumann and Wolf. Loewe, Mendelssohn, Rimsky-Korsakov, Schumann and Wolf all set different translations of these two poems.

Zwei Romanzen von Lord Byron / Two Romances by Lord Byron

?1833 Keine von der Erde Schönen / None of earth's beauties WoO
TRANSLATED BY ?MENDELSSOHN

Keine von der Erde Schönen	None of earth's beauties
Waltet zaubernd gleich dir;	Works its magic like you;
Auf der Flut ein Silbertönen	Your voice sounds to me
Dünkt deine Stimme mir.	Like silver music on the waves.
Leiser wird des Meeres Rauschen,	The sea hushes its murmuring
Entzückt dir zu lauschen,	To listen to you in rapture,
Legt sich der Wogen Schäumen,	When foaming waves subside,
Alle die Winde träumen.	All the winds start dreaming.
Golden webt der Mond auf Wellen	The moon weaves its web of gold
Sein Netz, sanft scheint die Flut	On the waves, the sea's full breast
Die volle Brust zu schwellen,	Seems gently to heave,
Wie ein Kind schlummernd ruht.	Like a slumbering child:
So sink' ich zu deinen Füßen,	Thus I prostrate myself at your feet
Anbetend dich zu grüßen;	To greet you and adore you;
Wie die See von West beweget,	Like the west wind ruffled sea,
Voll und sanft in mir sich's regt.	My full heart gently stirs.
(*Hensel, Wolf*)	

TRANSLATED BY MENDELSSOHN (1809–47)

Schlafloser Augen Leuchte, trüber Stern,
Dess' tränengleicher Schein, unendlich fern,
Das Dunkel nicht erhellt, nur mehr es zeigt,
O wie dir ganz des Glücks Erinnerung gleicht!
So leuchtet längst vergangner Tage Licht:
Es scheint, doch wärmt sein matter Schimmer
   nicht,
Dem wachen Gram erglänzt die Luftgestalt,
Hell, aber fern, klar, aber ach, wie kalt!
(*Isaac Nathan, Nietzsche, Rimsky-Korsakov,
Schumann, Wolf*)

Light of sleepless eyes, dim star,
Whose eternally distant tearful glow
Cannot illumine but only increases the
   dark,
Ah, how the memory of bliss resembles you!
Thus the light of days long past now shines:
It glows, but faintly and gives no warmth,
The mirage gleams on sorrow's insomnia,
Distinct but distant, clear but, ah, how cold!

Joseph von Eichendorff (1788–1857)

See Pfitzner, Robert Schumann, Wolf

?1835 Pagenlied / Page's song WoO

Wenn die Sonne lieblich schiene
Wie in Welschland lau und blau,
Ging' ich mit der Mandoline
Durch die überglänzte Au'.

In der Nacht das Liebchen lauschte
An dem Fenster süß verwacht,
Wünschte mir und ihr, uns beiden,
Heimlich eine schöne Nacht.

Wenn die Sonne lieblich schiene
Wie in Welschland lau und blau,
Ging' ich mit der Mandoline
Durch die überglänzte Au'.
(*Hiller, Schwarz-Schilling, Trunk*)

If the sun were to shine gently
As in Italy, from warm, blue skies,
I would go with my mandoline
Through the sun-drenched meadow.

In the night my love would listen
From her window, sweetly awake,
And she would wish both of us,
In secret, a lovely night.

If the sun were to shine gently
As in Italy, from warm, blue skies,
I would go with my mandoline
Through the sun-drenched meadow.

1 Oct 1847 Nachtlied / Night song Op. 71, no. 6

Vergangen ist der lichte Tag,
Von ferne kommt der Glocken Schlag;
So reist die Zeit die ganze Nacht,
Nimmt manchen mit, der's nicht gedacht.

Wo ist nun hin die bunte Lust,
Des Freundes Trost und treue Brust,
Der Liebsten süßer Augenschein?
Will keiner mit mir munter sein?

Daylight has departed,
The sound of bells comes from afar;
Thus time moves on throughout the night,
Taking many an unwitting soul.

Where now is all the garish joy,
The comforting breast of a faithful friend,
The sweet light of the loved one's eyes?
Will no one stay awake with me?

Frisch auf denn, liebe Nachtigall,	Strike up then, dear nightingale,
Du Wasserfall mit hellem Schall!	You cascade of bright sound!
G o t t loben wollen wir vereint,	Together we shall praise *God*,
Bis daß der lichte Morgen scheint!	Until the light of morning dawns!
(*Curschmann, Klein, Schoeck*)	

Ernst Freiherr von Feuchtersleben (1806–49)

Studied medicine in Vienna where he also read philosophy and literature. Became a lecturer in psychiatry in 1844 and contributed articles to several medical journals. His *Collected Poems* (1851–53) were edited by Friedrich Hebbel and once enjoyed a considerable vogue; only 'Gottes Rat und Scheiden' ('Es ist bestimmt in Gottes Rat') has stood the test of time. He was on close terms with Bauernfeld, Grillparzer and Moritz von Schwind, and supplied the latter with poems which von Schwind then illustrated.

18 April 1839 Volkslied / Folk song Op. 47, no. 4

Es ist bestimmt in Gottes Rat,	It is decreed in God's law
Daß man, vom Liebsten, was man hat,	That we must part
Muß scheiden;	From what we hold most dear;
Wiewohl doch nichts im Lauf der Welt	Although nothing in the world
Dem Herzen ach! so sauer fällt,	Is so bitter to the heart
Als Scheiden! ja, Scheiden!	As parting! yes, parting!
So dir geschenkt ein Knösplein was,	If you have been given a little bud,
So tu es in ein Wasserglas,	Put it in a glass of water,
Doch wisse:	But remember:
Blüht morgen dir ein Röslein auf,	Though a little rose will bloom by morning,
Es welkt wohl schon die Nacht darauf;	It will wither when night falls,
Das wisse! ja, wisse!	Remember! yes, remember!
Und hat dir Gott ein Lieb beschert,	And if God has granted you a sweetheart,
Und hältst du sie recht innig wert,	And if you love your dearest
Die Deine –	Most tenderly,
Es wird nur wenig Zeit wohl sein,	It might not be long
Da läßt sie dich so gar allein,	Before she leaves you bereft,
Dann weine! ja, weine!	Then weep! yes, weep!
Nun mußt du mich auch recht verstehn,	You must now understand me well,
Ja recht verstehn!	Yes, understand me well!
Wenn Menschen auseinander gehn,	When humans part from each other,
So sagen sie: Auf Wiedersehn,	They say: farewell,
Auf Wiedersehn!	Farewell!
(*Busoni, Kreutzer, Schoeck, Robert Schumann, Wagner*)	

Emanuel Geibel (1815–84)

See Wolf

1851 Der Mond / The moon Op. 86, no. 5

Mein Herz ist wie die dunkle Nacht,
Wenn alle Wipfel rauschen;
Da steigt der Mond in voller Pracht
Aus Wolken sacht,
Und sieh! der Wald verstummt in tiefem
    Lauschen.

Der Mond, der lichte Mond bist du:
In deiner Liebesfülle
Wirf einen, einen Blick mir zu
Voll Himmelsruh',
Und sieh! dies ungestüme Herz wird stille.
(*Griffes, Lassen, Marschner, Pfitzner*)

My heart is like the dark night,
When all the tree-tops rustle;
The moon rises in full splendour
Gently from the clouds – and see!
The wood falls silent, raptly
    listening.

You are the moon, the shining moon:
In the fullness of your love,
Throw me one, one single glance
Of brimming heavenly peace – and see!
This tempestuous heart is soothed.

Johann Wolfgang von Goethe (1749–1832)

See Beethoven, Brahms, Hensel, Loewe, Mozart, Reichardt, Schubert, Strauss, Wolf, Zelter

Mendelssohn was taken by Zelter to visit Goethe in Weimar during November 1821, and in the following years their relationship developed into one of deep friendship. Although Mendelssohn paid Goethe no fewer than five substantial visits between 1821 and 1830, he composed very few Lieder to Goethe's poems: two Suleika songs, 'Lied einer Freundin', 'Erster Verlust' and 'Die Liebende schreibt', one of his loveliest songs, set to a sonnet in which the fifty-eight-year-old poet was almost certainly expressing his obsession for Wilhelmine (Minchen) Herzlieb, the eighteen-year-old foster daughter of his publisher friend Karl Friedrich Ernst Frommann.

10 August 1831 Die Liebende schreibt / The beloved writes Op. 86, no. 3

Ein Blick von deinen Augen in die meinen,
Ein Kuß von deinem Mund auf meinem
    Munde,
Wer davon hat, wie ich, gewisse Kunde,
Mag dem was anders wohl erfreulich scheinen?

Entfernt von dir, entfremdet von den Meinen,
Da führ ich die Gedanken in die Runde,
Und immer treffen sie auf jene Stunde,
Die einzige; da fang ich an zu weinen.

One glance from your eyes into mine,
One kiss from your mouth onto my
    mouth,
Who, like me, is assured of these,
Can he take pleasure in anything else?

Far from you, estranged from my family,
I let my thoughts rove constantly,
And always they fix on that hour,
That precious hour; and I begin to weep.

Die Träne trocknet wieder unversehens:	Suddenly my tears grow dry again:
Er liebt ja, denk ich, her in diese Stille,	His love, I think, he sends into this silence,
Und solltest du nicht in die Ferne reichen?	And should you not reach out into the distance?
Vernimm das Lispeln dieses Liebewehens;	Receive the murmurs of this loving sigh;
Mein einzig Glück auf Erden ist dein Wille,	Your will is my sole happiness on earth,
Dein freundlicher, zu mir; gib mir ein Zeichen!	Your kind will; give me a sign!
(*Brahms, Schubert*)	

Heinrich Heine (1797–1856)

See Schumann, Wolf

Although Mendelssohn fails to understand the poem – Heine mocks his own romantic longing, knows he has been jilted and knows the dream to be a lie – 'Auf Flügeln des Gesanges', with its beautiful A flat major melody and exquisite harmony, has become one of the world's most popular art songs. Mendelssohn might miss Heine's irony – the condescending diminutive ('Herzliebchen') and the ghastly rhyme ('Ganges' with the genitive 'Gesanges') is worthy of Ogden Nash – but this setting has indeed 'found its way into the hearts of the people' and Heine would have admired it.

?1834 Neue Liebe / New love Op. 19a, no. 4

In dem Mondenschein im Walde	In the moonlight of the forest
Sah ich jüngst die Elfen reiten,	I saw of late the elves riding,
Ihre Hörner hört' ich klingen,	I heard their horns resounding,
Ihre Glöcklein hört' ich läuten.	I heard their little bells ring.
Ihre weißen Rößlein trugen	Their little white horses
Gold'nes Hirschgeweih' und flogen	Had golden antlers and flew
Rasch dahin; wie wilde Schwäne	Quickly past; like wild swans
Kam es durch die Luft gezogen.	They came through the air.
Lächelnd nickte mir die Kön'gin,	With a smile the queen nodded to me,
Lächelnd im Vorüberreiten,	With a smile she rode quickly by,
Galt das meiner neuen Liebe?	Was it to herald a new love?
Oder soll es Tod bedeuten?	Or does it signify death?

?1834 Gruß / Greeting Op. 19a, no. 5

Leise zieht durch mein Gemüt	A sweet sound of bells
Liebliches Geläute.	Peals gently through my soul.
Klinge, kleines Frühlingslied,	Ring out, little song of spring,
Kling hinaus ins Weite.	Ring out far and wide.

Zieh hinaus, bis an das Haus,	Ring out till you reach the house
Wo die Veilchen sprießen.	Where violets are blooming.
Wenn du eine Rose schaust,	And if you should see a rose,
Sag, ich lass' sie grüßen.	Send to her my greeting.
(*Franz, Grieg, Ives, Lachner, Rubinstein,*	
Schulz)	

?1836 Auf Flügeln des Gesanges / On wings of song Op. 34, no. 2

Auf Flügeln des Gesanges,	On wings of song
Herzliebchen, trag' ich dich fort,	I'll bear you, beloved, away,
Fort nach den Fluren des Ganges,	Away to the fields by the Ganges
Dort weiß ich den schönsten Ort.	Where I know the loveliest spot.
Dort liegt ein rotblühender Garten	A red-blossoming garden lies there
Im stillen Mondenschein;	In the quiet light of the moon;
Die Lotosblumen erwarten	The lotus flowers await
Ihr trautes Schwesterlein.	Their dear little sister.
Die Veilchen kichern und kosen	The violets titter and flirt
Und schaun nach den Sternen empor;	And gaze up at the stars;
Heimlich erzählen die Rosen	Secretly the roses whisper
Sich duftende Märchen ins Ohr.	Fragrant tales to each other.
Es hüpfen herbei und lauschen	The knowing and innocent gazelles
Die frommen, klugen Gazell'n;	Come leaping up to listen;
Und in der Ferne rauschen	And in the distance murmur
Des heiligen Stromes Well'n.	The waves of the sacred stream.
Dort wollen wir niedersinken	Let us lie down by its banks
Unter dem Palmenbaum,	Underneath the palm,
Und Liebe und Ruhe trinken,	And drink in love and peace
Und träumen seligen Traum.	And dream a blissful dream.
(*Lachner*)	

?1836 Reiselied / Song of travel Op. 34, no. 6

Der Herbstwind rüttelt die Bäume,	The autumn wind shakes the trees,
Die Nacht ist feucht und kalt;	The night is damp and cold;
Gehüllt im grauen Mantel,	Wrapped in a grey cloak,
Reite ich einsam im Wald.	I ride in the forest alone.
Und wie ich reite, so reiten	And as I ride, so my thoughts
Mir die Gedanken voraus;	Ride on ahead of me;
Sie tragen mich leicht und luftig	They carry me light as air
Nach meiner Liebsten Haus.	To my beloved's house.
Die Hunde bellen, die Diener	The dogs bark, the servants appear
Erscheinen mit Kerzengeflirr;	With flickering candlelight;
Die Wendeltreppe stürm' ich	I dash up the spiral staircase
Hinauf mit Sporengeklirr.	To the sound of clattering spurs.

Im leuchtenden Teppichgemache,	There in her brightly tapestried room,
Da ist es so duftig und warm,	With its fragrance and warmth,
Da harret meiner die Holde –	My loved one is waiting for me –
Ich fliege in ihren Arm.	I fly into her arms.
Es säuselt der Wind in den Blättern,	The wind rustles in the leaves,
Es spricht der Eichenbaum:	The oak-tree says:
„Was willst du, törichter Reiter,	Foolish rider, what do you want
Mit deinem törichten Traum?"	With your foolish dream?

?1840 **Morgengruß / Morning greeting** Op. 47, no. 2

Über die Berge steigt schon die Sonne,	The sun is rising over the mountains,
Die Lämmerherde läutet von fern;	The flock of sheep can be heard from afar;
Mein Liebchen, mein Lamm, meine Sonne und Wonne,	My dearest, my lamb, my sun and my joy,
Noch einmal säh' ich dich gar zu gern!	How I should love to see you again!
Ich schaue hinauf mit spähender Miene –	I raise my eyes expectantly –
Leb' wohl, mein Kind, ich wandre von hier!	Farewell, my child, I'm going away!
Vergebens! Es regt sich keine Gardine;	In vain! The curtain does not move;
Sie liegt noch und schläft – und träumt von mir?	She's still asleep – and dreaming of me?

Ludwig Hölty (1748–76)

See Brahms, Schubert

?1828 **Hexenlied (Andres Maienlied) / Witches' song (Another kind of May song)** Op. 8, no. 8

Die Schwalbe fliegt,	Swallows are flying,
Der Frühling siegt,	Spring's triumphant,
Und spendet uns Blumen zum Kranze!	Dispensing flowers for wreaths!
Bald huschen wir	Soon we'll flit
Leis' aus der Tür,	Quietly outside,
Und fliegen zum prächtigen Tanze!	And fly to the splendid dance!
Ein schwarzer Bock,	A black goat,
Ein Besenstock,	A broomstick,
Die Ofengabel, der Wocken,	The furnace rake, the distaff
Reißt uns geschwind,	Whisk us on our way,
Wie Blitz und Wind,	Like lightning and wind,
Durch sausende Lüfte zum Brocken!*	Through whistling gales to the Brocken!
Um Beelzebub	Our coven dances
Tanzt unser Trupp,	Round Beelzebub
Und küßt ihm die kralligen Hände!	And kisses his claw-like hands!

* The highest mountain in the Harz, where a witches' sabbath was said to be held each 'Walpurgisnacht' – the night of 30 April / 1 May.

Ein Geisterschwarm	A ghostly throng
Faßt uns beim Arm,	Seizes our arms,
Und schwinget im Tanzen die Brände!	Waving firebrands as they dance!
Und Beelzebub	And Beelzebub
Verheißt dem Trupp	Pledges the throng
Der Tanzenden Gaben auf Gaben:	Of dancers gift after gift:
Sie sollen schön	They shall be dressed
In Seide gehn	In beautiful silk
Und Töpfe voll Goldes sich graben!	And dig themselves pots full of gold!
Ein Feuerdrach'	A fiery dragon
Umflieget das Dach	Flies round the roof
Und bringet uns Butter und Eier:	And brings us butter and eggs:
Die Nachbarn dann sehn	The neighbours catch sight
Die Funken wehn,	Of the flying sparks,
Und schlagen ein Kreuz vor dem Feuer.	And cross themselves for fear of the fire.
Die Schwalbe fliegt,	Swallows are flying,
Der Frühling siegt,	Spring's triumphant,
Die Blumen erblühen zum Kranze.	Flowers are blooming for wreaths.
Bald huschen wir	Soon we'll flit
Leis' aus der Tür,	Quietly outside –
Juchheisa! zum prächtigen Tanze!	Tally-ho to the splendid dance!

Karl Klingemann (1798–1862)

Klingemann was a native of Hamburg and a fine amateur musician. Though ten years older than Mendelssohn, he became the composer's closest friend and was sorely missed when he left for England in 1827 as a diplomat. During Mendelssohn's 1829 visit to England, Klingemann introduced him to English society and they toured Scotland together. Mendelssohn composed more songs to Klingemann's texts than those of any other poet; he also wrote two of his stage works on libretti by Klingemann: *Die Hochzeit des Camach* (1825) and *Die Heimkehr aus der Fremde* (1829).

?1836 Frühlingslied / Spring song Op. 34, no. 3

Es brechen im schallenden Reigen	In resounding roundelays
Die Frühlingsstimmen los,	The voices of spring break out,
Sie können's nicht länger verschweigen,	They can no longer be silent,
Die Wonne ist gar zu groß!	Their joy is far too great!
Wohin, sie ahnen es selber kaum,	Whither, they scarcely know themselves,
Es rührt sie ein alter, ein süßer Traum!	They're touched by an old, sweet dream!
Die Knospen schwellen und glühen	The buds swell and glow
Und drängen sich an das Licht,	And press towards the light,

Und warten in sehnendem Blühen,
Daß liebende Hand sie bricht.
Wohin, sie ahnen es selber kaum,
Es rührt sie ein alter, ein süßer Traum!

Und Frühlingsgeister, sie steigen
Hinab in der Menschen Brust,
Und regen da drinnen den Reigen
Der ew'gen Jugendlust.
Wohin, wir ahnen es selber kaum,
Es rührt uns ein alter, ein süßer Traum!

And wait in burgeoning desire
To be picked by a loving hand.
Whither, they scarcely know themselves,
They're touched by an old, sweet dream!

And spirits of spring descend
Into the breasts of men,
And stir within it the roundelay
Of youth's eternal joy.
Whither, we scarcely know ourselves,
We're touched by an old, sweet dream!

?1840 Bei der Wiege / Beside the cradle Op. 47, no. 6

Schlummre und träume von kommender Zeit,
Die sich dir bald muß entfalten,
Träume, mein Kind, von Freud' und Leid,
Träume von lieben Gestalten!
Mögen auch viele noch kommen und gehen,
Müssen dir neue doch wieder erstehen,
Bleibe nur fein geduldig!

Slumber and dream of times to come
That will soon unfold for you,
Dream, my child, of joy and sorrow,
Dream of the people you love!
However many may come and go,
There will always be new ones to follow,
Be patient!

Schlummre und träume von Frühlingsgewalt
Schau all das Blühen und Werden,
Horch, wie im Hain der Vogelsang schallt,
Liebe im Himmel, auf Erden!
Heut zieht's vorüber und kann dich nicht
    kümmern,
Doch wird dein Frühling auch blühn und
    schimmern.
Bleibe nur fein geduldig!

Slumber and dream of spring's great might,
See how everything blossoms and grows,
Listen how birdsong resounds in the grove –
Love in heaven and love on earth!
Today spring passes and does not concern
    you,
But your own spring will one day bloom for
    you.
Be patient!

Nikolaus Lenau (1802–50)

See Schumann

17 April 1839 Frühlingslied / Spring song Op. 47, no. 3

Durch den Wald, den dunkeln, geht
Holde Frühlingsmorgenstunde,
Durch den Wald vom Himmel weht
Eine leise Liebeskunde.

Spring's glorious morning hour
Passes through the dark wood,
A gentle message of love
Blows from heaven through the wood.

Selig lauscht der grüne Baum,
Und er taucht mit allen Zweigen
In den schönen Frühlingstraum,
In den vollen Lebensreigen.

The green tree listens in rapture
And dips all its boughs
Into the beautiful spring dream,
Into the full dance of life.

Blüht ein Blümlein irgendwo,	Wherever a small flower blooms,
Wird's vom hellen Tau getränket,	It is watered by the bright dew,
Das Versteckte zittert froh,	The hidden flower quivers with joy
Daß der Himmel sein gedenket.	That heaven has remembered it.
In geheimer Laubesnacht	In the secret darkness of the leaves
Wird des Vogels Herz getroffen	The bird's heart is struck
Von der Liebe Zaubermacht,	By the magic power of love,
Und er singt ein süßes Hoffen.	And it sings of its sweet hope.
All das frohe Lenzgeschick	All these joyful spring messages
Nicht ein Wort des Himmels kündet;	Speak not a single word of heaven;
Nur sein stummer, warmer Blick	Only its silent and ardent glance
Hat die Seligkeit entzündet;	Has kindled happiness.
Also in den Winterharm,	Thus in this grim winter,
Der die Seele hielt bezwungen,	Which kept my soul subdued,
Ist ein Blick mir, still und warm,	A quiet and ardent glance
Frühlingsmächtig eingedrungen.	Has pierced me with the power of spring.
(*Franz, Schoeck*)	

3 November 1842 Schilflied / Reed song Op. 71, no. 4

Auf dem Teich, dem regungslosen,	On the pond, the motionless pond,
Weilt des Mondes holder Glanz,	The moon's fair radiance lingers,
Flechtend seine bleichen Rosen	Weaving its pale roses
In des Schilfes grünen Kranz.	Into the reeds' green garland.
Hirsche wandeln dort am Hügel,	Red deer wander there on the hill,
Blicken durch die Nacht empor;	Looking upwards through the night;
Manchmal regt sich das Geflügel	Dreamily in thick reeds
Träumerisch im tiefen Rohr.	Birds will sometimes stir.
Weinend muß mein Blick sich senken;	I must lower my tearful gaze;
Durch die tiefste Seele geht	Through the very depths of my soul
Mir ein süßes Deingedenken,	Sweet thoughts of you pass
Wie ein stilles Nachtgebet!	Like a quiet evening prayer!
(*Franz, Griffes, Henri Marteau*)	

27 July 1847 Auf der Wanderschaft / On the road Op. 71, no. 5

Ich wandre fort ins ferne Land;	I travel to a distant land;
Noch einmal blickt' ich um, bewegt,	Once more I looked back, moved,
Und sah, wie sie den Mund geregt	And saw how her mouth quivered,
Und wie gewinket ihre Hand.	And how she waved her hand.
Wohl rief sie noch ein freundlich Wort	I guess she uttered a friendly word
Mir nach auf meinem trüben Gang,	To me on my sad journey,
Doch hört' ich nicht den liebsten Klang,	But I did not hear that loveliest of sounds,
Weil ihn der Wind getragen fort.	Because the wind bore it away.

Daß ich mein Glück verlassen muß,	I must leave my bliss behind,
Du rauher, kalter Windeshauch,	You cold, raw breath of wind –
Ist's nicht genug, daß du mir auch	Is that not enough? Must you also
Entreißest ihren letzten Gruß?	Deny me her final greeting?
(*Franz, Griffes, Schoeck*)	

22 September 1847 An die Entfernte / To the distant beloved Op. 71, no. 3

Diese Rose pflück' ich hier	I pluck this rose here
In der weiten Ferne,	Far away from you;
Liebes Mädchen, dir, ach dir,	Dear girl, how I should love
Brächt' ich sie so gerne!	To bring it you!
Doch bis ich zu dir mag zieh'n	Yet long before I could reach you,
Viele weite Meilen,	From so many miles away,
Ist die Rose längst dahin;	The rose would have withered;
Denn die Rosen eilen.	For roses hurry through life.
Nie soll weiter sich ins Land	Lovers should never venture
Lieb' von Liebe wagen,	Further apart
Als sich blühend in der Hand	Than a hand can carry
Läßt die Rose tragen;	A blossoming rose;
Oder als die Nachtigall	Or further than the nightingale
Halme bringt zum Neste,	Fetches straw for the nest,
Oder als ihr süßer Schall	Or further than her sweet song
Wandert mit dem Weste.	Can be borne on the West Wind.
(*Josefine Lang, Marschner, Schoeck, Vesque*	
von Püttlingen)	

Friedrich Spee von Langenfeld (1591–1635)

Having entered the Society of Jesus in 1610, Spee became involved with the re-establishment of Roman Catholicism in Westphalia and the Rhineland, and was wounded by a religious opponent who made an attempt on his life in 1629. His *Cautio criminalis* (1631), written in the wake of his experiences in preparing witches for death, was critical of the way in which they were treated by the Law. Spee, whose verse, mostly religious in nature, is filled with a love for all God's creatures, died of the plague while tending the sick at Trier; his most famous poem is probably 'In stiller Nacht', set by Brahms in his *49 Deutsche Volkslieder* of 1894. Mendelssohn changed the final verse of 'Der trübe Winter ist vorbei' to reflect his own melancholy mood in this, his final song.

8 October 1847 Altdeutsches Frühlingslied / Old German Spring song Op. 86, no. 6

Der trübe Winter ist vorbei	The sombre winter is past,
Die Schwalben wiederkehren;	The swallows return;

Nun reget sich alles wieder neu,	Everything now stirs again,
Die Quellen sich vermehren:	The springs multiply:
Laub allgemach	Fresh leaves softly
Nun schleicht an Tag,	Emerge into daylight,
Die Blümlein nun sich melden,	The flowers announce their arrival;
Wie Schlänglein krumm	Like little snakes,
Gehn lächlend um	The cool streams
Die Bächlein kühl in Wäldern.	Laugh their way through woods.
Wo man nur schaut, fast alle Welt	Wherever one looks, nearly all the world
Zur Freuden sich tut rüsten:	Participates in this joy;
Zum Scherzen alles ist gestellt,	Everyone is happy,
Schwebt alles fast in Lüsten.	Wallowing almost in pleasure.
Nur ich allein,	Only I alone
Ich leide Pein,	Suffer agony,
Ohn Ende werd ich leiden,	I shall suffer without end:
Seit du von mir,	Ever since
Und ich von dir,	You and I,
O Liebste, mußte scheiden.	O dearest, had to part.

J. N. Voss [J. G. Droysen] (1808–84)

Mendelssohn's father hired Droysen to tutor his son, and according to Fanny in a letter to Klingemann dated 27 December 1828, Droysen possessed 'knowledge far in advance of his age'. He became a lifelong friend of the composer. The first edition of Op. 9 stated that two of the poems, 'Frage' and 'Scheidend', were by H. Voss – and it was for many years thought that this was a pseudonym for Mendelssohn himself.

1830 Scheidend / Separation Op. 9, no. 6

Wie so gelinde die Flut bewegt!	How gently the tide flows!
Wie sie so ruhig den Nachen trägt!	How tranquilly it bears the boat!
Fern liegt das Leben, das Jugendland!	Far away life and the land of my youth!
Fern liegt der Schmerz, der dort mich band,	Far away the pain, which bound me there.
Sanft tragt mich, Fluten, zum fernen Land!	Bear me gently away, O tide, to the far-off land!
Droben der Sterne stiller Ort,	The stars dwell silently above me,
Unten der Strom fließt fort und fort.	Below me the current flows on and on,
Wohl warst du reich, mein Jugendland!	You were indeed rich, land of my youth!
Wohl war es süß, was dort mich band,	What bound me there was sweet indeed,
Sanft tragt mich, Fluten, zum fernen Land!	Bear me gently away, O tide, to the far-off land!

Giacomo Meyerbeer (1791–1864)

Heinrich Heine wrote to Meyerbeer on 28 May 1842: „In der Tat, um Ihren Namen dreht sich die ganze Geschichte der Musik seit 10 Jahren." ('In truth, the whole history of music in the last ten years revolves around your name.') Despite Heine's hyperbole, Meyerbeer's fame was indeed at its zenith around 1831, when *Robert le Diable* received its first performance. Although his star has long since been on the wane, there are gems to be enjoyed among his ninety or so songs, composed to French, German and Italian texts. Due perhaps to his enormous international reputation, the mélodies were translated into German by Ignaz Castelli and Ludwig Rellstab, and the Lieder into French. Of the thirty-five or so Lieder, there are charming settings of Heine, Rückert and Marianne von Willemer better known in versions by Schubert and Schumann ('Komm' ['Das Fischermädchen'], 'Sie und ich' ['Daß sie hier gewesen'], 'Hör ich das Liedchen klingen', 'Die Rose, die Lilie' and 'Suleika' ['Wie mit innigstem Behagen']. Meyerbeer also composed twenty Lieder from Auerbach's *Schwarzwälder Dorfgeschichten* and a handful of songs to texts by Müller and Rellstab.

Michael Beer (1800–33)

Meyerbeer's youngest brother experienced his greatest literary triumph in 1824 when Goethe staged a performance in Weimar of *Der Paria*, a one-act play in support of Jewish emancipation that had been premiered the previous year. Two tragedies *Klytämnestra* (1819) and *Struensee* (1829) were also well received, especially the latter for which Meyerbeer composed incidental music.

Menschenfeindlich / The misanthrope

Gegen mich selber in Haß entbrannt,
Von Vielen gemieden, von Allen verkannt,
So sitz' ich den lieben, den sonnigen Tag
Und lausche des Herzens unwilligem Schlag.
So sitz' ich bei Mondes vertraulichem Schein
Und starr' in die leuchtende Nacht hinein,
Allein, allein, allein!

Nie gönnt mein Herz der Liebe Raum;
Ich hasse die Wirklichkeit, hasse den Traum,
Den Sommer, den Winter, die Frühlingszeit.
Was gestern ich hasste, das hass' ich auch heut'.
So sitz' ich bei Mondes vertraulichem Schein
Und starr' in die leuchtende Nacht hinein,
Allein, allein, allein!

Consumed with hatred against myself,
Shunned by many, misunderstood by all,
I sit all sunny day long
And listen to my heart's reluctant beating.
So I sit in the moon's intimate light,
And stare into the shimmering night,
Alone, alone, alone!

My heart never makes room for love;
I hate reality, I hate illusion,
Summer, winter and springtime too.
What I hated yesterday, I still hate today.
So I sit in the moon's intimate light,
And stare into the shimmering night,
Alone, alone, alone!

Franz Mittler (1893–1970)

Mittler came from a family of Austrian entrepreneurs of Jewish descent and, following military service in the First World War, he settled in Vienna as pianist, accompanist and composer. During a concert tour of Holland in 1939, he was warned not to return to Vienna, and eventually emigrated to America, where he worked as principal arranger for Columbia and wrote music, including the *One-Finger Polka* for the index finger of Chico Marx. He composed an opera (*Raffaella*), piano and chamber music and a large number of songs, which include settings of poems by Mörike, Morgenstern, Wilhelm Busch, Rilke and Karl Kraus. His most popular composition was 'Volksweise' (from Rilke's early collection 'Larenopfer'), the second number of his song-cycle for medium voice and piano; it was published in 1911 by Universal Edition, who reprinted it in 1925 and 1952 under the title 'Böhmisches Lied'. The song, greatly admired by Bruno Walter, was often performed on prestigious occasions – as, for example, at a White House concert in 1940 in honour of the Roosevelts.

Rainer Maria Rilke (1875–1926)

See Hindemith

1911 Volksweise / Folk song

Mich rührt so sehr	I am so moved
böhmischen Volkes Weise,	by a Bohemian folksong,
schleicht sie ins Herz sich leise,	which, stealing into my heart,
macht sie es schwer.	weighs it down.
Wenn ein Kind sacht	When a child sings softly
singt beim Kartoffeljäten,	while weeding potatoes,
klingt dir sein Lied im späten	you'll still hear his song
Traum noch der Nacht.	in a dream late at night.
Magst du auch sein	Even though you've travelled
weit über Land gefahren,	far overland,
fällt es dir doch nach Jahren	you'll hear it years later
stets wieder ein.	again and again.

Wolfgang Amadeus Mozart (1756–91)

Although Mozart cannot be considered to be one of the founders of the Lied, he was fully aware of the need to create a German genre in both song and opera. In a revealing letter to Professor Anton Klein, dated 21 March 1785, he expressed the hope that one day a German Opera House might be founded, and exclaimed with mock horror:

> Das wäre Ja ein Ewiger Schandfleck für teutschland, wenn wir teutsche einmal mit Ernst anfiengen teutsch zu denken – teutsch zu handeln – teutsch zu reden, und gar teutsch – zu Singen!!!

> And it would be to Germany's eternal shame if we Germans should one day seriously set about thinking in German, acting in German, speaking in German and even singing in German!!!

Seven of his stage works were composed to German libretti, and he wrote over thirty songs to German texts during every period of his creative life, of which thirteen were published in his lifetime. Far from being 'crumbs from the table of his operas and instrumental works' (Einstein), they are serious works in their own right and reveal in their variety the complexity of Mozart's own character, including a sensuality which in at least one song, 'An Chloe', turns unequivocally lubricious. Like Schubert and Wolf, he was capable of composing several songs a day: three on 7 May 1785 (K472–74) and three on 14 January 1791 (K596–98).

Anonymous

Conceived of as a bass aria for an *opera buffa* and sketched for strings, two oboes and two horns, 'Warnung' was left incomplete at Mozart's death. He called it 'Arie des Wahrmond' ('Truemouth's aria'), and it was included in the 'Œuvres complettes' of 1799 in a piano reduction by A. E. Müller.

?1783 Warnung / Warning K433

Männer suchen stets zu naschen,	Men always try to nibble,
Läßt man sie allein;	If they're left alone,
Leicht sind Mädchen zu erhaschen,	Girls can easily be caught,
Weiß man sie zu überraschen,	If you take them by surprise.
Soll das zu verwundern sein?	Is that to be wondered at?
Mädchen haben frisches Blut,	Girls have fresh young blood,
Und das Naschen schmeckt so gut.	And nibbling is so pleasant.

Doch das Naschen vor dem Essen	But nibbling before meals
Nimmt den Appetit,	Takes away the appetite.
Manche kam, die das vergessen,	Many a girl who's forgotten that
Um den Schatz, den sie besessen	Has lost the treasure she possessed,
Und um ihren Liebsten mit.	And with it her beloved.
Väter, laßt euch's Warnung sein,	Fathers, let this be a warning,
Sperrt die Zuckerplätzchen ein,	Lock your sugar-drops away,
Sperrt die jungen Mädchen ein.	Lock young girls away.
(*Marx, Reger*)	

Gabriele von Baumberg (1768–1839)

A member of the Mozart-Jacquin circle, her *Sämmtliche Gedichte* were not published till 1800. Mozart's source for 'Als Luise . . .' was the *Wiener Musenalmanach* for 1786. Her husband was the Hungarian poet Janos Bacsányi who, during the French occupation of Vienna in 1809, translated into Hungarian Napoleon's proclamation of 15 May, summoning all Hungarians to rebel against the Austrians. As a consequence, he was later obliged to leave Austria. He eventually settled in Linz where he lived with Gabriele in reduced circumstances. Having once played a prominent part in Viennese literary society (Schubert set five of her poems), Gabriele spent the rest of her life largely forgotten.

26 May 1787 Als Luise die Briefe ihres ungetreuen Liebhabers verbrannte / When Luise burnt her unfaithful lover's letters K520

Erzeugt von heißer Phantasie,	Begotten by ardent fantasy,
In einer schwärmerischen Stunde	Born in
Zur Welt gebrachte! – geht zu Grunde!	An emotional moment! Perish,
Ihr Kinder der Melancholie!	Ye children of melancholy!
Ihr danket Flammen euer Sein:	You owe your existence to flames,
Ich geb' euch nun den Flammen wieder,	To flames I now return you
Und all die schwärmerischen Lieder;	And all those passionate songs;
Denn ach! er sang nicht mir allein.	For ah! he did not sing for me alone.
Ihr brennet nun, und bald, ihr Lieben,	Now you are burning, and soon, my dears,
Ist keine Spur von euch mehr hier:	Not a trace of you will remain:
Doch ach! der Mann, der euch geschrieben,	But ah! the man who wrote you
Brennt lange noch vielleicht in mir.	May smoulder long yet in my heart.

Joachim Heinrich Campe (1746–1818)

Employed as a tutor by the Humboldt family, Campe devoted his life to education. 'Abendempfindung' was published by Gräffer (1781) in 'Dichter-Manuskripte', an extremely rare volume, edited by Johann Friedrich Schink. Campe's authorship of the poem should therefore not be disputed.

4 June 1787 Abendempfindung / Evening thoughts K523

Abend ist's, die Sonne ist verschwunden,
Und der Mond strahlt Silberglanz;
So entflieh'n des Lebens schönste Stunden,
Flieh'n vorüber wie im Tanz!

It is evening, the sun has vanished,
And the moon sheds its silver light;
So life's sweetest hours speed by,
Flit by as in a dance!

Bald entflieht des Lebens bunte Szene,
Und der Vorhang rollt herab.
Aus ist unser Spiel! Des Freundes Träne
Fließet schon auf unser Grab.

Soon life's bright pageant will be over,
And the curtain will fall.
Our play is ended! Tears wept by a friend
Flow already on our grave.

Bald vielleicht mir weht, wie Westwind leise,
Eine stille Ahnung zu –
Schließ' ich dieses Lebens Pilgerreise,
Fliege in das Land der Ruh'.

Soon perhaps, like a gentle zephyr,
A silent presentiment will reach me,
And I shall end this earthly pilgrimage,
Fly to the land of rest.

Werdet ihr dann an meinem Grabe weinen,
Trauernd meine Asche seh'n,
Dann, o Freunde, will ich euch erscheinen
Und will Himmel auf euch weh'n.

If you then weep by my grave
And gaze mourning on my ashes,
Then, dear friends, I shall appear to you
Bringing a breath of heaven.

Schenk' auch du ein Tränchen mir
Und pflücke mir ein Veilchen auf mein Grab;
Und mit deinem seelenvollen Blicke
Sieh' dann sanft auf mich herab.

May you too shed a tear for me
And pluck a violet for my grave;
And let your compassionate gaze
Look tenderly down on me.

Weih' mir eine Träne und ach!
Schäme dich nur nicht, sie mir zu weih'n,
O sie wird in meinem Diademe
Dann die schönste Perle sein.

Consecrate a tear to me and ah!
Be not ashamed to do so;
In my diadem it shall become
The fairest pearl of all.

Johann Wolfgang von Goethe (1749–1832)

See Beethoven, Brahms, Hensel, Loewe, Mendelssohn, Mozart, Reichardt, Schubert, Strauss, Wolf, Zelter

The overwhelming musical experience of Goethe's youth was the visit to Frankfurt in 1763 of the six-year-old Mozart. The fourteen-year-old Goethe was smitten, and his adoration lasted until he died some sixty years later. As Director of the

Hoftheater in Weimar from 1791 to 1817, Goethe championed the operas of Mozart, when it was not entirely fashionable to do so: *Figaro* received twenty performances, *Die Entführung* forty-nine, *Don Giovanni* sixty-eight and *Die Zauberflöte* eighty-two. The text of 'Das Veilchen' comes from Goethe's Singspiel *Erwin und Elmire* (1775), where it is sung retrospectively by Elmire, who bitterly regrets the way she had trifled with Erwin's affections.

8 June 1785 Das Veilchen / The violet K476
FROM *Erwin und Elmire*

Ein Veilchen auf der Wiese stand,
Gebückt in sich und unbekannt;
Es war ein herzigs Veilchen.
Da kam ein' junge Schäferin
Mit leichtem Schritt und munterm Sinn
Daher, daher,
Die Wiese her, und sang.

A violet was growing in the meadow,
Unnoticed and with bowed head;
It was a dear sweet violet.
Along came a young shepherdess,
Light of step and happy of heart,
Along, along
Through the meadow, and sang.

Ach! denkt das Veilchen, wär' ich nur
Die schönste Blume der Natur,
Ach, nur ein kleines Weilchen,
Bis mich das Liebchen abgepflückt
Und an dem Busen matt gedrückt!
Ach nur, ach nur
Ein Viertelstündchen lang!

Ah! thinks the violet, if I were only
The loveliest flower in all Nature,
Ah! for only a little while,
Till my darling had picked me
And crushed me against her bosom!
Ah only, ah only
For a single quarter hour!

Ach! aber ach! das Mädchen kam
Und nicht in acht das Veilchen nahm,
Ertrat das arme Veilchen.
Es sank und starb und freut' sich noch:
Und sterb' ich denn, so sterb' ich doch
Durch sie, durch sie,
Zu ihren Füßen doch.
Das arme Veilchen!
Es war ein herzigs Veilchen!
(*Amalie, Herzogin von Sachsen-Weimar,*
Johann André, Kayser, Medtner, Reichardt,
Schoeck, Clara Schumann, Tomášek)

But alas, alas, the girl drew near
And took no heed of the violet,
Trampled the poor violet.
It sank and died, yet still rejoiced:
And if I die, at least I die
Through her, through her
And at her feet.
The poor violet!
It was a dear sweet violet!

Friedrich von Hagedorn (1708–54)

Known in his day as 'the German Horace', Hagedorn's elegant, rococo verse was much prized in the eighteenth century. He was a man of private means and spent some time in London as secretary to the Danish Minister.

18 May 1787 Die Alte / The old woman K517

Zu meiner Zeit
Bestand noch Recht und Billigkeit.
Da wurden auch aus Kindern Leute;
Aus tugendhaften Mädchen Bräute:
Doch alles mit Bescheidenheit.
    O gute Zeit!
Es ward kein Jüngling zum Verräter,
Und unsre Jungfern freiten später:
Sie reizten nicht der Mutter Neid.
    O gute Zeit!

    Zu meiner Zeit
Ward Pflicht und Ordnung nicht entweiht.
Der Mann ward, wie es sich gebühret,
Von einer lieben Frau regieret,
Trotz seiner stolzen Männlichkeit!
    O gute Zeit!
Die Fromme herrschte nur gelinder!
Uns blieb der Hut und ihm die Kinder.
Das war die Mode weit und breit.
    O gute Zeit!

    Zu meiner Zeit
War noch in Ehen Einigkeit.
Jetzt darf der Mann uns fast gebieten,
Uns widersprechen und uns hüten,
Wo man mit Freunden sich erfreut.
    O schlimme Zeit!
Mit dieser Neuerung im Lande,
Mit diesem Fluch im Ehestande
Hat ein Comet uns längst bedräut.
    O schlimme Zeit!

In my day,
Right and justice still prevailed.
Boys grew up to be men,
Virtuous girls became brides –
But always with moderation.
    O happy days!
Young men were never unfaithful,
And our young women courted later:
They never provoked a mother's envy.
    O happy days!

In my day,
Duty and order were not abused:
A man, as is right and proper,
Was ruled by his dear wife,
Despite his proud manliness!
    O happy days!
The good wife's rule was more gentle!
We wore the trousers, he had the children.
That was the fashion, far and wide.
    O happy days!

In my day,
Marriage still meant harmony.
Nowadays a man can almost dragoon us,
Contradict us and prevent us
Enjoying ourselves with friends.
    O evil days!
A comet has long been threatening us
With these changes in the land,
With this blight on the married state.
    O evil days!

Johann Georg Jacobi (1740–1814)

See Schubert

4 June 1787 An Chloe / To Chloe K524

Wenn die Lieb' aus deinen blauen,
Hellen, offnen Augen sieht,
Und vor Lust, hineinzuschauen,
Mir's im Herzen klopft und glüht;

Und ich halte dich und küsse
Deine Rosenwangen warm,

When love looks out of your blue,
Bright and open eyes,
And the joy of gazing into them
Causes my heart to throb and glow;

And I hold you and kiss
Your rosy cheeks warm,

| Liebes Mädchen, und ich schließe | Sweet girl, and clasp |
| Zitternd dich in meinen Arm, | You trembling in my arms, |

Mädchen, Mädchen, und ich drücke — Sweet girl, sweet girl, and press
Dich an meinen Busen fest, — You firmly to my breast,
Der im letzten Augenblicke — Where until my dying moment
Sterbend nur dich von sich läßt; — I shall hold you tight –

Den berauschten Blick umschattet — My ecstatic gaze is blurred
Eine düst're Wolke mir; — By a sombre cloud;
Und ich sitze dann ermattet, — And I sit then exhausted,
Aber selig neben dir. — But blissful, by your side.

Christian Adolf Overbeck (1755–1821)

After studies in Göttingen, Overbeck became a lawyer in Lübeck where he eventually rose to mayor and president of the upper court. His *Sammlung vermischter Gedichte* were published simultaneously in Lübeck and Leipzig in 1794. His publications also include translations of Anacreon and Sappho.

14 January 1791 Sehnsucht nach dem Frühlinge / Longing for spring K596

Komm, lieber Mai, und mache — Come, sweet May, and turn
Die Bäume wieder grün, — The trees green again,
Und laß mir an dem Bache — And make the little violets
Die kleinen Veilchen blüh'n! — Bloom for me by the brook!
Wie möcht' ich doch so gerne — I'd love so very much
Ein Veilchen wieder seh'n! — To see a violet again!
Ach, lieber Mai, wie gerne — Ah, sweet May, I'd love so much
Einmal spazieren geh'n! — To go out for a walk!

Zwar Wintertage haben — Winter days, it's true,
Wohl auch der Freuden viel; — Have many pleasures as well;
Man kann im Schnee eins traben — You can tramp through the snow
Und treibt manch' Abendspiel; — And play games in the evening;
Baut Häuserchen von Karten, — Build houses of cards,
Spielt Blindekuh und Pfand; — Play blindman's-buff and forfeits;
Auch gibt's wohl Schlittenfahrten — And there are also sleigh-rides
Aufs liebe freie Land. — Into the pleasant open country.

Doch wenn die Vögelein singen, — But when the birds sing
Und wir dann froh und flink — And we skip happily and nimbly
Auf grünen Rasen springen, — Over the green lawn,
Das ist ein ander Ding! — That's quite a different thing!
Jetzt muß mein Steckenpferdchen — Now my little hobby-horse
Dort in dem Winkel steh'n, — Must stand in the corner there,
Denn draußen in dem Gärtchen — For outside in the garden
Kann man vor Kot nicht geh'n. — You cannot walk for mud.

Am meisten aber dauert
Mich Lottchens Herzeleid.
Das arme Mädchen lauert
Recht auf die Blumenzeit!
Umsonst hol' ich ihr Spielchen
Zum Zeitvertreib herbei:
Sie sitzt in ihrem Stühlchen
Wie's Hühnchen auf dem Ei.

Ach, wenn's doch erst gelinder
Und grüner draußen wär'!
Komm, lieber Mai, wir Kinder,
Wir bitten dich gar sehr!
O komm und bring vor allen
Uns viele Veilchen mit!
Bring' auch viel Nachtigallen
Und schöne Kuckucks mit.
(*Robert Schumann*)

But most of all I'm sorry
For Lottie's misery;
The poor girl's watching out
For flowers to bloom again!
In vain I bring her games
To while away the time:
She sits on her little chair
Like a hen on its egg.

Ah, if only it were milder
And greener out of doors!
Come, sweet May, we children
Are begging you to come!
O come, and above all bring
Us lots of violets!
Bring many nightingales as well
And lovely cuckoos too!

Christian Felix Weiße (1726–1804)

See Beethoven

Mozart owned Weiße's *Kleine lyrische Gedichte* (Leipzig, 1772), from which these four poems are taken.

7 May 1785 Der Zauberer / The magician K472

Ihr Mädchen, flieht Damöten ja!
Als ich zum ersten Mal ihn sah,
Da fühlt' ich – so was fühlt' ich nie;
Mir ward – mir ward – ich weiß nicht wie:
Ich seufzte, zitterte, und schien mich doch zu
  freun:
Glaubt mir, er muß ein Zaub'rer sein!

Sah ich ihn an, so ward mir heiß.
Bald ward ich rot, bald ward ich weiß;
Zuletzt nahm er mich bei der Hand:
Wer sagt mir, was ich da empfand?
Ich sah, ich hörte nicht, sprach nichts als Ja
  und Nein –
Glaubt mir, er muß ein Zaub'rer sein!

Er führte mich in dies Gesträuch;
Ich wollt' ihn fliehn, und folgt' ihm gleich.
Er setzte sich, ich setzte mich;
Er sprach – nur Silben stammelt' ich;

Girls, keep well clear of Damötas!
The first time I saw him,
I felt – as I'd never felt before;
It was like – was like – I know not what:
I sighed, trembled and yet seemed over-
  joyed:
Believe me, he must be a magician!

When I looked at him I went hot all over,
Now blushing red, now turning pale,
Finally he took me by the hand:
Words cannot say how I felt then!
I saw nothing, heard nothing,
Could only stammer Yes and No:
Believe me, he must be a magician!

He led me into these bushes,
I wanted to flee, but followed at once:
He sat down, I sat down:
He spoke – but I could only stammer;

Die Augen starrten ihm, die meinen wurden
    klein:
Glaubt mir, er muß ein Zaub'rer sein!

His eyes bulged, my own
    shrank:
Believe me, he must be a magician!

Entbrannt drückt' er mich an sein Herz.
Was fühlt' ich! welch ein süßer Schmerz!
Ich schluchzt', ich atmete sehr schwer;
Da kam zum Glück die Mutter her:
Was würd', o Götter, sonst nach so viel
    Zauberein
Aus mir zuletzt geworden sein!

He pressed me passionately to his heart.
What a sensation! Such sweet agony!
I sobbed, I could hardly breathe!
Then, thank goodness, mother came
    along:
Otherwise, O gods, after so much magic,
What would have become of me!

7 May 1785 Die Zufriedenheit / Contentment K473

Wie sanft, wie ruhig fühl' ich hier
Des Lebens Freuden ohne Sorgen!
Und sonder Ahnung leuchtet mir
Willkommen jeder Morgen.

How gently, how peacefully I feel here
Life's joys without its troubles,
And every bright new morning
Welcomes me without foreboding.

Mein frohes, mein zufriednes Herz
Tanzt nach der Melodie der Haine,
Und angenehm ist selbst mein Schmerz,
Wenn ich vor Liebe weine.

My happy, my contented heart
Dances to the music of the groves,
And even my pain is pleasant
When I weep for love.

Wie sehr lach' ich die Großen aus,
Die Blutvergießer, Helden, Prinzen!
Denn mich beglückt ein kleines Haus,
Sie nicht einmal Provinzen.

How I laugh at the great and grand,
Those shedders of blood, heroes, princes!
For I am content with a little house,
They not even with provinces.

Wie wüten sie nicht wider sich,
Die göttergleichen Herrn der Erden;
Doch brauchen sie mehr Raum als ich,
Wenn sie begraben werden?

How they rage at one another,
These god-like masters of the earth;
But will they need more room than I
When they come to be buried?

7 May 1785 Die betrogene Welt / The deluded world K474

Der reiche Tor, mit Gold geschmücket,
Zieht Selimenens Augen an:
Der wackre Mann wird fortgeschicket,
Den Stutzer wählt sie sich zum Mann;
Es wird ein prächtig Fest vollzogen:
Bald hinkt die Reue hinterdrein.
Die Welt will ja betrogen sein:
Drum werde sie betrogen!

The rich fool, bedecked with gold,
Catches Selina's eye:
The worthy man is sent packing,
She chooses the dandy for husband.
Repentance soon limps along
In the wake of the splendid wedding feast.
For the world wants to be deceived:
Therefore let it be deceived!

Beate, die vor wenig Tagen
Der Buhlerinnen Krone war,
Fängt an sich violett zu tragen,
Und kleidet Kanzel und Altar.
Dem äußerlichen Schein gewogen,

Beate, who not many days before,
Was the queen of all wantons,
Begins to wear penitential purple,
And decorates pulpit and altar.
Swayed by outward appearances,

Hält mancher sie für engelrein.	Many think her pure as an angel.
Die Welt will ja betrogen sein:	For the world wants to be deceived:
Drum werde sie betrogen!	Therefore let it be deceived!

Wenn ich mein Carolinchen küsse,	When I kiss my little Caroline,
Schwör' ich ihr zärtlich ew'ge Treu';	I tenderly vow to be true for ever;
Sie stellt sich, als ob sie nicht wisse,	She pretends not to know
Daß außer mir ein Jüngling sei.	Any other young man but me.
Einst, als mich Chloe weggezogen,	Once, when Chloe had lured me away,
Nahm meine Stelle Damis ein.	Damis took my place.
Soll alle Welt betrogen sein:	If all the world can be deceived:
So werd' auch ich betrogen!	I too can be deceived!

1787 Die Verschweigung / Keeping mum K518

Sobald Damötas Chloen sieht,	As soon as Damötas sees Chloe,
So sucht er mit beredten Blicken	He strives with eloquent glances
Ihr seine Klagen auszudrücken,	To tell her of his sorrowful state,
Und ihre Wange glüht.	And her cheeks glow.
Sie scheinet seine stillen Klagen	She seems more than half
Mehr als zur Hälfte zu verstehn;	To understand his silent sorrows;
Und er ist jung, und sie ist schön:	And he is young, and she is fair:
Ich will nichts weiter sagen.	I need say nothing more.

Vermißt er Chloen auf der Flur,	When he misses Chloe in the fields,
Betrübt wird er von dannen scheiden,	He goes saddened on his way,
Dann aber hüpft er voller Freuden,	But then he jumps for joy
Entdeckt er Chloen nur.	As soon as he discovers her.
Er küßt ihr unter tausend Fragen	Asking a thousand questions, he kisses
Die Hand, und Chloe läßt's geschehn;	Her hand, and Chloe lets it happen;
Und er ist jung, und sie ist schön:	And he is young, and she is fair:
Ich will nichts weiter sagen.	I need say nothing more.

Sie hat an Blumen ihre Lust:	She takes delight in flowers:
Er stillet täglich ihr Verlangen;	Each day he satisfies her craving;
Sie klopft ihn schmeichelnd auf die Wangen,	She gives his cheeks a flattering pat,
Und steckt sie vor die Brust.	And wears them on her breast.
Der Busen bläht sich, sie zu tragen,	Her bosom swells to wear them,
Er triumphirt, sie hier zu sehn;	He rejoices to see them there;
Und er ist jung, und sie ist schön:	And he is young, and she is fair:
Ich will nichts weiter sagen.	I need say nothing more.

Wenn sie ein kühler heitrer Bach,	When a cool babbling brook,
Beschützt von Büschen, eingeladen,	Hidden by bushes, invites her
In seinen Wellen sich zu baden:	To bathe in its waters,
So schleicht er listig nach.	He cunningly steals after her.
In diesen schwülen Sommertagen	On these sultry summer days
Hat er ihr oftmals zugesehn;	He has often gazed at her;
Und er ist jung, und sie ist schön:	And he is young, and she is fair:
Ich will nichts weiter sagen.	I need say nothing more.

Hans Pfitzner (1869–1949)

A conservative both in politics and musical aesthetics, Pfitzner reacted violently against such composers as Schoenberg and Busoni who sought rational explanations for the way music worked, and responded to their arguments by writing an essay, *The New Aesthetic of Musical Impotence*, full of incandescent rage. Alban Berg responded with an essay of his own in which he cited the first ten measures of Pfitzner's song 'Nacht' as an example of the potency of the new music. In later life Pfitzner resumed his attack on the New German theorists, and in two important books, *Impotenz* and *Inspiration*, outlined three methods of Lieder composition, rejecting the first two, and espousing the last: 'The more attention [. . .] a composer pays to the text [. . .] the more he is bound to neglect [. . .] the purely musical organization of his songs, which, as a consequence, often becomes musical nonsense – despite declamation.' Declamation was not Pfitzner's only target. He objected in particular to the way in which 'the composer shapes his melodies [. . .] as if they were instrumental [. . .], later adjusting the text so that it more or less fits the music.' And the ideal way of approaching Lieder composition? 'There are times [. . .] when, from two different springs, the same spirit flows together in word and tone [. . .] into one channel like the tones of a perfect interval.' For this to happen, the music 'must come from its own sphere and evoke the same mood as that of the poem; this can occur *wholly* independently, *before* the composer has any knowledge of the poem.' Best known in Germany for his opera *Palestrina* (1917) and the romantic cantata *Von deutscher Seele* (1922), Pfitzner composed over one hundred Lieder, from Op. 2 in 1888 to the late songs of 1931.

Adelbert von Chamisso (1781–1838)

See Loewe, Robert Schumann

1907 Tragische Geschichte / A tragic tale Op. 22, no. 2

's war einer, dem's zu Herzen ging,
Daß ihm der Zopf nach hinten hing,
Er wollt es anders haben.

There was a man who took to heart
His pigtail dangled down his back,
He wished that things were different.

Da denkt er denn, wie fang ich's an?
Ich dreh' mich 'rum, so ist's getan,
Der Zopf, der hängt ihm hinten.

And then he thinks, what shall I do?
I'll turn around and that will be that –
The pigtail dangles down his back.

Da hat er flink sich umgedreht,
Und wie es stund, es annoch steht:
Der Zopf, der hängt ihm hinten.

Nimbly he turned round again,
And things still stand as they were:
The pigtail dangles down his back.

Da dreht er schnell sich anders 'rum,	So he swiftly turns the other way,
's wird aber noch nicht besser drum,	But that didn't improve things either –
Der Zopf, der hängt ihm hinten.	The pigtail dangles down his back.
Er dreht sich links, er dreht sich rechts,	He turns to the left, he turns to the right,
Er tut nichts Guts, er tut nichts Schlechts,	He does no good, he does no harm –
Der Zopf, der hängt ihm hinten.	The pigtail dangles down his back.
Er dreht sich wie ein Kreisel fort,	He turns round like a spinning-top,
Es hilft zu nichts, mit einem Wort –	But it's no use, in a word –
Der Zopf, der hängt ihm hinten.	The pigtail dangles down his back.
Und seht, er dreht sich immer noch	And look, still he's turning round and round,
Und denkt, es hilft am Ende doch,	Thinking it will help in the end –
Der Zopf, der hängt ihm hinten.	The pigtail dangles down his back.
(*Vesque von Püttlingen*)	

Richard Dehmel (1863–1920)

See Schoenberg

1922 Die stille Stadt / The silent town Op. 29, no. 4

Liegt eine Stadt im Tale,	A town lies in the valley,
ein blasser Tag vergeht;	a pale day is fading;
es wird nicht lange dauern mehr,	it will not be long
bis weder Mond noch Sterne,	before neither moon nor stars
nur Nacht am Himmel steht.	but night alone will deck the skies.
Von allen Bergen drücken	From every mountain
Nebel auf die Stadt;	mists weigh on the town;
es dringt kein Dach, nicht Hof noch Haus,	no roof, no courtyard, no house,
kein Laut aus ihrem Rauch heraus,	no sound can penetrate the smoke,
kaum Türme noch und Brücken.	scarcely towers and bridges even.
Doch als den Wandrer graute,	But as fear seized the traveller,
da ging ein Lichtlein auf im Grund;	a gleam appeared in the valley;
und durch den Rauch und Nebel	and through the smoke and mist
begann ein leiser Lobgesang,	came a faint song of praise
aus Kindermund.	from a child's lips.
(*Alma Mahler, Sibelius*)	

Joseph von Eichendorff (1788–1857)

See Robert Schumann, Wolf

Joseph, Freiherr von Eichendorff spent an idyllic childhood on the family estate at
Schloss Lubowitz in Silesia, surrounded by wooded mountains high above the

Oder valley. He was educated by private tutors, but later attended a Catholic school in Breslau; he remained there until 1805, when he and his devoted brother Wilhelm went to Halle University to study Law. In 1807 he moved to Heidelberg, where he was much influenced by Arnim and Brentano's *Des Knaben Wunderhorn*, a rich source of German Romantic folk poems, published between 1805 and 1808. Having left university, the brothers embarked on a Grand Tour, which took in Paris, Nuremberg and Vienna, before they returned home to help manage the declining family estate. By this time Eichendorff had already written his first poems that were soon to feature in every anthology of German poetry. While working on the family estate, he fell in love with the daughter of a neighbouring landowner, Aloysia von Larisch, who later became his wife.

In 1809 Eichendorff visited Berlin, where he met Arnim, Brentano and Kleist, and the following year he moved to Vienna to study for his civil service exams and came into frequent contact with Friedrich Schlegel. In 1813, fired by Friedrich Wilhelm's appeal to the Prussian people, he enlisted as a volunteer in the War of Liberation and stayed in the army till Napoleon's defeat in 1815, the year which saw the publication of his first novel, *Ahnung und Gegenwart*, and his marriage to Aloysia, who bore him four children and lived with him till her death in 1855. From 1816 for the next twenty-eight years he held a number of positions in the civil service until his early retirement in 1844. He now withdrew from all public life, took no part in the 1848 revolution, which he bitterly criticized, devoted his time to literature and, when his wife fell ill, moved to Neisse to live with his daughter's family. After Aloysia's death, he began to write his memoirs, but fell ill with a cold in early November 1857, which finally led to pneumonia. He died on 26 November, and was buried four days later by the side of his wife.

Eichendorff's verse is to a quite unusual degree musical, which probably accounts for the astonishing frequency with which composers have set his poetry. According to Fischer-Dieskau in his *Töne sprechen, Worte klingen* (DVA/Piper), the final sixty-seven years of the nineteenth century produced well over five thousand Eichendorff settings. His poems – unlike those of Goethe, who was more an *Augenmensch* – are peppered with references to horns, bells, lutes, mandolins and other musical instruments; and no other German poet wrote so many poems about minstrels, musicians or the sounds of nature. Two themes predominate: beauty of landscape and religious faith. The beauty of God is manifested in nature, and Eichendorff – although, unlike the early Romantic writers, he never theorized about his ideas – attempted in his verse to free man's spirit from the routine of everyday life. Many of his five hundred or so poems are variations on these themes, but his range is wider than is usually believed. He grouped his poems into eight sections: *Wanderlieder, Sängerleben, Zeitlieder, Frühling und Liebe, Totenopfer, Geistliche Gedichte, Romanzen* and *Aus dem Spanischen*.

Hörst du nicht die Bäume rauschen
Draußen durch die stille Rund?
Lockts dich nicht, hinabzulauschen
Von dem Söller in den Grund,
Wo die vielen Bäche gehen
Wunderbar im Mondenschein,
Wo die stillen Schlösser sehen
In den Fluß vom hohen Stein?

Kennst du noch die irren Lieder
Aus der alten, schönen Zeit?
Sie erwachen alle wieder
Nachts in Waldeseinsamkeit,
Wenn die Bäume träumend lauschen
Und der Flieder duftet schwül
Und im Fluß die Nixen rauschen –
Komm herab, hier ist's so kühl.
(*Hensel*)

Can you not hear the murmuring trees
Out there in the surrounding silence?
Are you not tempted from your balcony
To listen down there in the valley
Where countless streams meander
Wondrously in the moonlight,
Where silent castles from rocky heights
Gaze down into the river?

Do you remember the wonderful songs
From the lovely days of old?
They all awake again at night
In the forest solitude,
When the dreaming trees all listen
And lilacs shed their sultry fragrance
And mermaids whisper in the river –
Come down to us, where the water's so cool.

1888–89 *Fünf Lieder/ Five songs* Op. 9

1

Der Gärtner / The gardener

Wohin ich geh' und schaue,
In Feld und Wald und Tal,
Vom Berg hinab in die Aue:
Viel schöne, hohe Fraue,
Grüß' ich dich tausendmal.

In meinem Garten find' ich
Viel' Blumen, schön und fein,
Viel' Kränze wohl draus wind' ich
Und tausend Gedanken bind' ich
Und Grüße mit darein.

I h r darf ich keinen reichen,
Sie ist zu hoch und schön,
Sie müssen alle verbleichen,
Die Liebe nur ohnegleichen
Bleibt ewig im Herzen stehn.

Ich schein' wohl froher Dinge
Und schaffe auf und ab,
Und, ob das Herz zerspringe,
Ich grabe fort und singe
Und grab' mir bald mein Grab.
(*Franz, Knab, Mendelssohn, Schoeck*)

Wherever I walk and gaze,
Through valley, wood and field,
From mountaintop to meadow:
I, lovely gracious lady,
Greet you a thousand times.

I seek out in my garden
Many fine and lovely flowers,
Weaving many garlands,
Binding a thousand thoughts
And greetings with them too.

I cannot give *her* a garland,
She is too noble and lovely,
They would all perish,
But love without compare
Remains forever in my heart.

I appear to be of good cheer,
And continue busily my work,
And though my heart may break,
I shall dig away and sing
And shortly dig my grave.

2
Die Einsame / The lonely woman

Wär's dunkel, ich läg' im Walde,
Im Walde rauscht's so sacht,
Mit ihrem Sternenmantel
Bedeckt mich da die Nacht,
Da kommen die Bächlein gegangen:
Ob ich schon schlafen tu?
Ich schlaf' nicht, ich hör' noch lang
Den Nachtigallen zu,
Wenn die Wipfel über mir schwanken,
Das klingt die ganze Nacht,
Das sind im Herzen die Gedanken,
Die singen, wenn niemand wacht.
(*Schoeck*)

Were it dark, I'd lie in the forest,
The forest murmurs so softly,
With her cloak of stars
The night covers me there,
The brooklets steal up and ask:
If I'm already asleep.
I do not sleep, for long yet I'll listen
To the nightingales,
When the treetops sway above me,
They sound the whole night through,
They are the heart's own thoughts
That sing when no one's awake.

3
Im Herbst / In autumn

Der Wald wird falb, die Blätter fallen,
Wie öd und still der Raum!
Die Bächlein nur gehn durch die Buchenhallen
Lind rauschend wie im Traum.
Und Abendglocken schallen
Fern von des Waldes Saum.

The wood turns fallow, the leaves fall,
Such silence, such desolation!
Only the streams still flow through the beeches,
Gently murmuring as in dreams.
And evening bells ring out
Far beyond the forest's edge.

Was wollt ihr mich so wild verlocken,
Hier in der Einsamkeit?
Wie in der Heimat klingen diese Glocken
Aus stiller Kinderzeit –
Ich wende mich erschrocken,
Ach, was mich liebt, ist weit!

Why entice me so wildly
In this solitude?
These bells sound as once in gentle childhood
In my native land –
I turn round in horror,
Ah! those who love me are far away!

So brecht hervor nur, alte Lieder,
Und brecht das Herz mir ab!
Noch einmal grüß ich aus der Ferne wieder,
Was ich nur Liebes hab.
Mich aber zieht es nieder
Vor Wehmut wie ins Grab.
(*Hensel, Lassen*)

So break out again, old songs,
And in doing so break my heart!
Once more I greet from afar
All those I love.
But sadness drags me down,
As though into my grave.

4
Der Kühne / The brave man

Und wo noch kein Wandrer gegangen,
Hoch über Jäger und Roß

Where no wanderer has ever been,
High above huntsman and horse,

Die Felsen im Abendrot hangen
Als wie ein Wolkenschloß.

Dort, zwischen Zinnen und Spitzen
Von wilden Nelken umblüht,
Die schönen Waldfrauen sitzen
Und singen im Winde ihr Lied.

Der Jäger schaut nach dem Schlosse:
„Die droben, das ist mein Lieb",
Er sprengt von dem scheuenden Rosse –
Weiß keiner, wo er blieb.
(*Franz*)

5
Abschied / Farewell

Abendlich schon rauscht der Wald
Aus den tiefen Gründen,
Droben wird der Herr nun bald
An die Sternlein zünden,
Wie so stille in den Schlünden,
Abendlich nur rauscht der Wald.

Alles geht zu seiner Ruh,
Wald und Welt versausen,
Schauernd hört der Wandrer zu,
Sehnt sich recht nach Hause,
Hier in Waldes grüner Klause,
Herz, geh endlich auch zur Ruh!
(*Franz, Hensel, Schoeck*)

1901 Zum Abschied meiner Tochter / A farewell to my daughter Op. 10, no. 3

Der Herbstwind schüttelt die Linde,
Wie geht die Welt so geschwinde!
Halte dein Kindelein warm.
Der Sommer ist hingefahren,
Da wir zusammen waren –
Ach, die sich lieben, wie arm!

Wie arm, die sich lieben und scheiden!
Das haben erfahren wir beiden,
Mir graut vor dem stillen Haus.
Dein Tüchlein läßt du noch wehen,
Ich kann's vor Tränen kaum sehen,
Schau' still in die Gasse hinaus.

The cliffs at sunset are suspended
Like a castle of cloud.

There, between spires and battlements,
Ringed by wild carnations in bloom,
The lovely forest women sit,
Singing their songs in the wind.

The hunter looks at the castle:
That's my sweetheart up there! –
He leaps from his shying horse,
No one knows where he has gone.

The forest murmurs at dusk
From the deep valleys,
God on high will very soon
Begin to light the stars,
How softly in the chasms
The forest murmurs only at dusk.

Every creature goes to rest,
World and forest cease to stir,
Quivering, the wanderer listens,
Longing now to be at home,
Here in the forest's green retreat,
You too, my heart, go at last to rest!

The autumn wind shakes the lime tree,
How swiftly the world goes by!
Keep your little child warm.
The summer is gone
When we were together –
Ah, how wretched are they who love!

How wretched are they who love and part!
This we have both discovered,
The silent house fills me with dread.
Still you wave your handkerchief,
I can hardly see it for tears,
As silently I gaze into the street.

Die Gassen schauen noch nächtig,
Es rasselt der Wagen bedächtig –
Nun plötzlich rascher der Trott
Durchs Tor in die Stille der Felder,
Da grüßen so mutig die Wälder,
Lieb Töchterlein, fahre mit Gott!

1904 Zorn / Anger Op. 15, no. 2

Seh' ich im verfallnen, dunklen
Haus die alten Waffen hangen,
Zornig aus dem Roste funkeln,
Wenn der Morgen aufgegangen,

Und den letzten Klang verflogen,
Wo im wilden Zug der Wetter,
Aufs gekreuzte Schwert gebogen,
Einst gehaust des Landes Retter;

Und ein neu Geschlecht von Zwergen
Schwindelnd um die Felsen klettern,
Frech, wenn's sonnig auf den Bergen,
Feige krümmend sich in Wettern,

Ihres Heilands Blut und Tränen
Spottend noch einmal verkaufen,
Ohne Klage, Wunsch und Sehnen
In der Zeiten Strom ersaufen;

Denk' ich dann, wie du gestanden
Treu, da niemand treu geblieben:
Möcht' ich über unsre Schande
Tiefentbrannt in zorn'gem Lieben,

Wurzeln in der Felsen Marke,
Und empor zu Himmels Lichten
Stumm anstrebend, wie die starke
Riesentanne, mich aufrichten.

1904 Sonst / In other times Op. 15, no. 4

Es glänzt der Tulpenflor, durchschnitten
von Alleen,
Wo zwischen Taxus still die weißen Statuen
stehn,
Mit goldnen Kugeln spielt die Wasserkunst
im Becken,
Im Laube lauert Sphinx, anmutig zu
erschrecken.

The streets are still wreathed in night,
Slowly the carriage rattles along –
Then suddenly accelerates
Out through the gate into silent fields,
Where the woods give spirited welcome,
Dearest daughter, go with God!

When I see the old weapons hanging
In the dark and gloomy house,
Flashing angry in their rust,
When day has dawned,

And the last sound has died away,
Where, as the wild storm blew,
The country's saviour once dwelt,
Bowed over his crossed sword;

When I see a new race of dwarfs
Clamber dizzily about the rocks,
Audacious, when the mountain's sunny,
Cowardly cringing in storms,

Selling and mocking once again
Their Saviour's blood and tears,
Drowning desire and wishes without grievance
In the river of time;

If I then think how you once stood,
True, when no one else stayed true:
Then, deeply enraged at our shame,
And angered in my love, I would

Take root in the rock itself,
And, mutely striving,
Reach up to the clear light of heaven,
Like the mighty, giant pine.

The tulips gleam, cut through by
avenues,
Where white statues stand among yew
trees,
The fountain in the basin plays with golden
balls,
A Sphinx lurks in the arbour, causing sweet
alarm.

Die schöne Chloe heut spaziert in dem
Garten,
Zur Seit' ein Kavalier, ihr höflich aufzuwarten,
Und hinter ihnen leis Cupido kommt gezogen,
Bald duckend sich im Grün, bald zielend mit
dem Bogen.

Es neigt der Kavalier sich in galantem Kosen,
Mit ihrem Fächer schlägt sie manchmal nach
dem Losen,
Es rauscht der taftne Rock, es blitzen seine
Schnallen,
Dazwischen hört man oft ein art'ges Lachen
schallen.

Jetzt aber hebt vom Schloß, da sich's im
West will röten,
Die Spieluhr schmachtend an, ein Menuett
zu flöten,
Die Laube ist so still, er wirft sein Tuch zur
Erde
Und stürzet auf ein Knie mit zärtlicher
Gebärde.

„Wie wird mir, ach, ach, ach, es fängt schon
an zu dunkeln,
So angenehmer nur seh' ich zwei Sterne
funkeln –"
„Verwegner Kavalier!" – „Ha, Chloe, darf ich
hoffen?" –
Da schießt Cupido los und hat sie gut getrof-
fen.

Lovely Chloe walks today in the garden,
A nobleman on her arm in polite
attendance,
And Cupid steals up behind them,
Now hiding in the bushes, now aiming his
bow.

The gallant nobleman bends down to caress
her,
Several times she strikes the rogue with her
fan,
Her taffeta rustles, his buckles flash,
Between times a pretty laugh rings
out.

But now from the château, in the westering
sun,
A musical clock plays a pining
minuet,
The arbour's so still, he throws his kerchief
down,
And falls to one knee with a tender
gesture.

'I feel, ah! ah! it's already growing
dark,
All the better to see two sparkling
stars –'
'What temerity!' – 'Ah, Chloe, may I
hope?' –
Then Cupid fires and hits his targets
well.

1907 In Danzig / In Danzig Op. 22, no. 1

Dunkle Giebel, hohe Fenster,
Türme tief aus Nebeln sehn,
Bleiche Statuen wie Gespenster
Lautlos an den Türen stehn.

Träumerisch der Mond drauf scheinet,
Dem die Stadt gar wohl gefällt,
Als läg' zauberhaft versteinet
Drunten eine Märchenwelt.

Ringsher durch das tiefe Lauschen,
Über alle Häuser weit,
Nur des Meeres fernes Rauschen –
Wunderbare Einsamkeit!

Dark gables, high windows,
Towers looming from thick mist,
Pale spectre-like statues
Stand at doors without a sound.

Dreamingly the moon shines on
The town it so favours,
As if magically turned to stone,
A fairy world dwelt below.

All around in utter silence,
Far across the houses,
Only the distant roar of the sea –
Wondrous solitude!

255

Und der Türmer wie vor Jahren	And the watchman, as of yore,
Singet ein uraltes Lied:	Sings an ancient song:
Wolle Gott den Schiffer wahren,	Grant that God protect the sailor
Der bei Nacht vorüberzieht!	Who sails by in the night!

1916 Nachts / At night Op. 26, no. 2

Ich stehe in Waldesschatten	I stand in the forest's shadow
Wie an des Lebens Rand,	As on the brink of life,
Die Länder wie dämmernde Matten,	The landscape like dusky meadows,
Der Strom wie ein silbern Band.	The stream like a silver ribbon.

Von fern nur schlagen die Glocken	No sound but the distant bells
Über die Wälder herein,	Ringing out across the woods,
Ein Reh hebt den Kopf erschrocken	A startled deer lifts its head
Und schlummert gleich wieder ein.	And returns at once to slumber.

Der Wald aber rühret die Wipfel	But the forest stirs the treetops
Im Traum von der Felsenwand.	On the rock-face as they dream.
Denn der Herr geht über die Gipfel	For the Lord is passing over the peaks
Und segnet das stille Land.	And blesses the silent land.

Gottfried Keller (1819–90)

See Schoeck, Wolf (for nos. 3-5, 7-8, p. 613-16)

1923 *Alte Weisen / Old saws* Op. 33, nos. 1, 2, 6

1

Mir glänzen die Augen	My eyes sparkle
Wie der Himmel so klar;	As bright as the sky;
Heran und vorüber,	Come on and come by,
Du schlanker Husar!	You lean hussar!

Heran und vorüber	Come on and come by
Und wieder zürück!	And back again!
Vielleicht kann's geschehen,	Perhaps you'll find
Du findest dein Glück!	Your happiness!

Was weidet dein Rapp mir	Why does your black horse
Den Reseda dort ab?	Munch my mignonettes?
Soll das nun der Dank sein	Is that the thanks
Für die Lieb, so ich gab?	For the love I gave?

Was richten deine Sporen	Why are your spurs
Mein Spinngarn zugrund?	Tangling my yarn?
Was hängt mir am Hage	Why does your bright tunic
Deine Jacke so bunt?	Hang there on my hedge?

Troll nur dich von hinnen
Auf deinem groben Tier
Und laß meine freudigen
Sternaugen mir!
(*Hans Sommer*)

Clear off from here
On your crude horse,
And leave my radiant
Bright eyes alone!

2

Ich fürcht nit Gespenster,
Keine Hexen und Feen,
Und lieb's, in ihre tiefen
Glühaugen zu sehn.

I fear no ghosts,
No witches, no fairies,
And love gazing into
Their deep glowing eyes.

Im Wald in dem grünen
Unheimlichen See,
Da wohnet ein Nachtweib,
Das ist weiß wie der Schnee.

In the wood
In the green, eerie lake,
A night-witch lives
As white as snow.

Es haßt meiner Schönheit
Unschuldige Zier;
Wenn ich spät noch vorbeigeh,
So zankt es mit mir.

She hates my beauty's
Innocent grace;
When I pass by late,
She rants at me.

Jüngst, als ich im Mondschein
Am Waldwasser stand,
Fuhr sie auf ohne Schleier,
Ohne alles Gewand.

When recently I stood in the moonlight
By the woodland lake,
She rose up without a veil,
With no garments on at all.

Es schwammmen ihre Glieder
In der taghellen Nacht;
Der Himmel war trunken
Von der höllischen Pracht.

Her limbs were bathed
In the day-bright night;
The heavens were drunk
With the hellish splendour.

Aber ich hab entblößt
Meine lebendige Brust;
Da hat sie mit Schande
Versinken gemußt!
(*Felix Weingartner*)

But I laid bare
My living breast;
Which forced her for shame
To sink out of sight!

6

Röschen biß den Apfel an,
Und zu ihrem Schrecken
Brach und blieb ein Perlenzahn
In dem Butzen stecken.

Rosie bit into the apple,
And to her horror
A pearly tooth broke
And stuck in the core.

Und das gute Kind vergaß
Seine Morgenlieder;
Tränen ohne Unterlaß
Perlten nun hernieder.

And the good child forgot
Her morning songs;
Tears without end
Came pearling down.

Conrad Ferdinand Meyer (1825–98)

Meyer – with Gottfried Keller the greatest nineteenth-century Swiss poet – suffered intermittently from mental illness and spent the last six years of his life in a state of complete derangement. His Novellen are filled with violence and ruthless characters, as though he wished to project his own unfulfilled longings onto heroes from the Middle Ages, Renaissance, Reformation and Counter-Reformation – his favourite periods. „Großer Stil, große Kunst – all mein Gedanken und Träumen liegt darin" ('Great style, great art – the basis of all my thoughts and dreams') was how he once described his literary ambitions. He was brought up on French literature and wrote almost exclusively in French until the Franco-Prussian War of 1870 seemed to make him conscious of his German blood. Apart from Pfitzner, Richard Strauss and Schoeck, few song composers have shown an interest in his work; but despite Theodor Storm's denunciation („Ein Lyriker ist er nicht" – 'He is no lyric poet'), it is on Meyer's poetry rather than his Novellen that his reputation now rests. He took enormous trouble over the presentation of his poems, some of which underwent countless alterations of detail, being recast three or four times. Many of his poems are based on things seen – such as architecture, statues and painting – and thus anticipate the 'Dinggedicht' of the twentieth century.

1923 *Vier Lieder für Bariton oder Bass / Four songs for baritone or bass* Op. 32

1

Hussens Kerker* / Hus's dungeon

Es geht mit mir zu Ende,	My end draws near,
Mein Sach und Spruch ist schon	My case and sentence have passed
Hoch über Menschenhände gerückt vor Gottes Thron,	Out of human hands To the lofty throne of God,
Schon schwebt auf einer Wolke,	Already the Son of Man,
Umringt von seinem Volke,	Surrounded by his Host,
Entgegen mir des Menschen Sohn.	Draws near on a cloud.
Den Kerker will ich preisen,	I shall praise my dungeon,
Der Kerker, der ist gut!	My dungeon is good!
Das Fensterkreuz von Eisen	My cross-bar window
Blickt auf die frische Flut,	Looks onto the cool tide,
Und zwischen seinen Stäben	And between its bars
Seh ich ein Segel schweben,	I see a fluttering sail,
Darob im Blau die Firne ruht.	And snow above it against the blue.
Wie nah die Flut ich fühle,	How close I feel the waters,

---

* Condemned to death as a heretic by the Council of Constance, Jan Hus (*c.*1373–1415) faced burning at the stake by steadfastly accepting his fate and acknowledging God's will.

Als läg ich drein versenkt,
Mit wundersamer Kühle
Wird mir der Leib getränkt –
Auch seh ich eine Traube
Mit einem roten Laube,
Die tief herab ins Fenster hängt.

Es ist die Zeit zu feiern!
Es kommt die große Ruh!
Dort lenkt ein Zug von Reihern
Dem ewigen Lenze zu,
Sie wissen Pfad und Stege,
Sie kennen ihre Wege –
Was, meine Seele, fürchtest du?

2
Säerspruch / Sower's saying

Bemeßt den Schritt! Bemeßt den Schwung!
Die Erde bleibt noch lange jung!
Dort fällt ein Korn, das stirbt und ruht.
Die Ruh ist süß. Es hat es gut.

Hier eins, das durch die Scholle bricht.
Es hat es gut. Süß ist das Licht.
Und keines fällt aus dieser Welt
Und jedes fällt, wies Gott gefällt.

3
Eingelegte Ruder / Shipped oars

Meine eingelegten Ruder triefen,
Tropfen fallen langsam in die Tiefen.

Nichts, das mich verdroß! Nichts, das mich
    freute!
Niederrinnt ein schmerzenloses Heute!

Unter mir – ach, aus dem Licht verschwunden –
Träumen schon die schönern meiner Stunden.

Aus der blauen Tiefe ruft das Gestern:
Sind im Licht noch manche meiner Schwest-
    ern?
(Behn)

As though I lay immersed,
My body is steeped
In its wondrous coolness –
I also see a cluster of grapes
Hanging from their red foliage
Into the window.

It is time to celebrate!
Great peace is now at hand!
A flight of herons up there
Leads to eternal spring,
They know all the paths,
They know their way –
What, O soul, do you fear?

Measure your stride! Measure your swing!
The earth will stay young for a long time yet!
One grain will fall and die and rest.
Rest is sweet. That grain is content.

Another grain breaks through the soil.
It too is content. The light is sweet.
And neither will vanish from this world
And each falls according to God's will.

My shipped oars are dripping,
Drops fall slowly into the deep.

Nothing to distress me! Nothing to gladden
    me!
A day devoid of pain is trickling down!

Below me – ah, vanished from the light –
The finer of my hours already dream.

Yesterday cries from the blue depths:
Are there more of my sisters up there in the
    light?

4
Laß scharren deiner Rosse Huf! / Let your horses paw the ground!

Geh nicht, die Gott für mich erschuf!
Laß scharren deiner Rosse Huf
   Den Reiseruf!

Du willst von meinem Herde fliehn?
Und weißt ja nicht, wohin, wohin
   Dich deine Rosse ziehn!

Die Stunde rinnt! das Leben jagt!
Wir haben uns noch nichts gesagt –
   Bleib, bis es tagt!

Du darfst aus meinen Armen fliehn?
Und weißt ja nicht, wohin, wohin
   Dich deine Rosse ziehn ...
(*Behn*)

Do not go, you whom God created for me!
Let your horses paw the ground
   With their parting call!

You wish to flee my hearth?
And yet do not know where, where
   Your horses will draw you!

Time passes! Life rushes by!
We have yet to speak to each other –
   Stay, till day dawns!

You must flee my arms?
And yet do not know where, where
   Your horses will draw you ...

Max Reger (1873–1916)

Only a few of his three hundred or so songs have remained in the repertoire. Influenced in his youth by Schumann and Brahms, Reger fell under the spell of Wagner's chromaticism and the songs of Hugo Wolf, to whom the *Zwölf Lieder* Op. 52 are dedicated, and several of whose songs he orchestrated. He also admired the songs of Richard Strauss, some of which he arranged for piano solo. No fewer than fourteen of his own songs were to the same texts that Strauss had chosen: 'Hat gesagt, bleibt's nicht dabei', 'Du meines Herzens Krönelein', 'All mein Gedanken', 'Glückes genug', 'Meinem Kinde', 'Wiegenlied' ('Bienchen, Bienchen'), 'Waldseligkeit', 'Wiegenlied' ('Träume, träume'), 'Morgen!', 'Ich schwebe', 'Nachtgang', 'Traum durch die Dämmerung', 'Freundliche Vision' and 'Leise Lieder . . .'. Many of these Strauss songs are among his most popular Lieder, but Reger does not always lose out in comparison. Much of his output, however, suffers from his predilection for peppering scores with accidentals, expression marks, awkward chromatic shifts and fine rhythmic distinctions that do not encourage accessibility. Yet many of his songs are much simpler and deserve to be better known – such as the *Geistliche Lieder*, Op. 137, which form a religious counterpart to the *Schlichte Weisen* (1903–12), and such gems as 'Waldeinsamkeit' and 'Mariä Wiegenlied' that Elisabeth Schumann made famous in Reger's own orchestrated version.

Anonymous

Waldeinsamkeit / Woodland solitude Op. 76, no. 3

Gestern abend in der stillen Ruh'	Last evening in the peaceful quiet
Sah ich im Wald einer Amsel zu;	I observed a blackbird in the
Als ich da so saß,	wood;
Meiner ganz vergaß,	As I was sitting there,
Kommt mein Schatz und schleichet sich um mich	Quite obliviously,
	My beloved steals up
Und küßet mich.	And kisses me.
So viel Laub als an der Linden ist	She gave me many thousands of kisses,
Und so viel tausendmal hat mich mein Schatz geküsst;	As many as there are leaves on the lime;
	For I must admit;
Denn ich muß gestehn	No one saw,
Es hats niemand gesehn,	And the blackbird shall be my witness –
Und die Amsel soll mein Zeuge sein:	We were alone.
Wir war'n allein.	

1914 Uns ist geboren ein Kindelein / To us is born a little child Op. 137, no. 3

Uns ist geboren ein Kindelein,	To us is born a little child,
Ist klarer denn die Sonne,	Brighter than the sun,
Das soll der Welt ein Heiland sein,	He shall be the world's Saviour,
Dazu der Engel Wonne.	And the delight of angels.
Hätt ich Flügel von Seraphim,	If I had angels' wings,
Wie fröhlich wollt ich fliegen	How happily I would fly
Mit den Engeln schön dahin	With the angels
Zu Jesu meinem Geliebten.	To my beloved Jesus.

1914 Christleins Wiegenlied / The Christ-child's lullaby Op. 137, no. 10

Laßt uns das Kindlein wiegen,	Let us rock the little child,
Das Herz zum Kripplein biegen!	Incline our hearts to the crib!
Laßt uns im Geist erfreuen,	Let us be glad in spirit,
Das Kindlein benedeien!	And bless the little child!
O Jesulein süß, o Jesulein süß!	O sweet little Jesus!
Laßt uns dem Kindlein neigen,	Let us bow to the little child,
Um Lieb und Dienst erzeigen!	Show him love and service!
Laßt uns doch jubilieren	Let us be joyful
Und geistlich triumphieren!	And triumph in spirit!
O Jesulein süß, o Jesulein süß!	O sweet little Jesus!
Laßt unser Stimmlein schallen,	Let our small voices ring out,
Es wird dem Kindlein g'fallen.	It will please the little child.
Laßt ihm ein Freudlein machen,	Make him happy,
Das Kindlein wird eins lachen.	The little child will laugh.
O Jesulein süß, o Jesulein süß!	O sweet little Jesus!

Martin Boelitz (1874–1918)

The son of a parson, Boelitz spent a period in London (1899–1901) where he co-edited *Stimmen der Gegenwart*; he was also the director of the E. Nieter publishing house in Nuremberg. His many publications of verse include *Aus Traum und Leben* (1896), *Lieder des Lebens* (1900), *London* (1901), *Frohe Ernte* (1905), *Fünfzig Melodien zu alten Kinderliedern* (1906) and *Hundert Gedichte* (1922).

1911–12 Mariä Wiegenlied / Mary's lullaby Op. 76, no. 52

Maria sitzt am Rosenhag	Mary sits by the rose bower
Und wiegt ihr Jesuskind,	And rocks her little Jesus,
Durch die Blätter leise	Softly through the leaves
Weht der warme Sommerwind.	The warm wind of summer blows.

Zu ihren Füßen singt
Ein buntes Vögelein:
Schlaf, Kindlein, süße,
Schlaf nun ein!

Hold ist dein Lächeln,
Holder deines Schlummers Lust,
Leg dein müdes Köpfchen
Fest an deiner Mutter Brust!
Schlaf, Kindlein, süße,
Schlaf nun ein!

A brightly coloured bird
Sings at her feet:
Go to sleep, sweet child,
It's time to go to sleep!

Your smile is lovely,
Your happy sleep lovelier still,
Lay your tired little head
Against your mother's breast!
Go to sleep, sweet child,
It's time to go to sleep!

Johann Friedrich Reichardt (1752–1814)

Perhaps the most prolific of all Lieder composers, Reichardt wrote more than 1,500 songs (at least twice as many as Schubert) to texts by 125 different poets over a period of forty years (1773–1811). Like Wolf, he almost always set verse of quality (Claudius, Kleist, Hagedorn, Gleim, Matthisson, Hölty, Schiller, Herder loom large), and his output includes 140 songs to the poetry of Goethe, which he published between 1809 and 1811 in four volumes entitled *Göthes Lieder, Oden, Balladen und Romanzen*. Goethe in 1823 called these songs 'Das Unvergleichlichste, was ich in dieser Art kenne.' ('The most incomparable that I know of their kind') – an understandable response, since Reichardt's songs often fulfil those requirements that Goethe deemed essential in Lieder composition: that the accompaniment should be subservient to the poem and should not seek to illustrate its imagery (see SCHUBERT). But not all of Reichardt's songs conform to this model – many, such as 'Gott', 'Rhapsodie', 'Einziger Augenblick' and 'Feiger Gedanken', are characterized by a kind of free declamation, thus preparing the way for the Lieder of Schubert's generation. The range of subject matter in his songs is as impressive as the quantity: *Gesänge für das schöne Geschlecht, Frohe Lieder für deutsche Männer, Lieder für Kinder, Lieder für die Jugend, Wiegenlieder für gute deutsche Mütter, Lieder geselliger Freunde* and *Gesänge der Klage und des Trostes* – titles which conformed to the taste and aesthetics of the Berlin School which encouraged folksong-like Lieder of strophic simplicity. Few of these songs are available or performed today, but Reichardt's finest Lieder, usually to great poetry, are with their melodic beauty and faithful declamation of the text among the best of all pre-Schubert songs.

Johann Wolfgang von Goethe (1749–1832)

See Beethoven, Brahms, Hensel, Loewe, Mendelssohn, Mozart, Schubert, Strauss, Wolf, Zelter

From 29 November to 19 December 1777 Goethe undertook a journey at the behest of Duke Carl August across the Harz mountains. On 1 December he noted in his diary: „. . . gegen Mittag in Elbingerode. Felsen und Bergwerk. Gelindes Wetter. Leiser Regen. Dem Geier gleich." ('In Elbingerode towards noon. Cliffs and mines. Mild weather. Gentle rain. Vulture-like.'). The purpose of the journey was threefold: to inspect the state of the copper mines; to climb the Brocken; and to visit a man named Friedrich Viktor Lebrecht Plessing, who had been plunged into depression by reading *Werther*. The poem, 'Harzreise im Winter', begins with the celebrated image, 'Dem Geier gleich', the phrase that Goethe had entered in his diary. Brahms, in his *Alto Rhapsody* (the complete text of which is printed below), used only verses 5–7 of Goethe's eleven stanzas, while Reichardt merely set 6–7. Goethe's theme here is Plessing's melancholy and suffering, although the very next verse (not set by either Reichardt or Brahms) clearly deals with Goethe's own loneliness.

?1809 Die schöne Nacht / The beautiful night

Nun verlaß ich diese Hütte,
Meiner Liebsten Aufenthalt,
Wandle mit verhülltem Schritte
Durch den öden, finstern Wald:
Luna bricht durch Busch und Eichen,
Zephyr meldet ihren Lauf,
Und die Birken streun mit Neigen
Ihr den süßten Weihrauch auf.

Now I leave this hut,
Where my beloved dwells,
Walk with muffled steps
Through the desolate dark wood:
The moon breaks through bush and oak-trees,
The West Wind announces her presence,
And the bowing birch-trees strew
Sweetest incense in her path.

Wie ergötz ich mich im Kühlen
Dieser schönen Sommernacht!
O wie still ist hier zu fühlen,
Was die Seele glücklich macht!
Läßt sich kaum die Wonne fassen;
Und doch wollt ich, Himmel, dir
Tausend solcher Nächte lassen,
Gäb mein Mädchen *eine* mir.
(*Ries*)

How exquisite is the coolness
Of this beautiful summer night!
O how I feel in this silence
What fills the heart with happiness!
Its rapture can scarcely be grasped;
And yet, O heaven, I would forego
A thousand such nights,
If my beloved would grant me *one*.

?1794 Rhapsodie / Rhapsody
FROM *Harzreise im Winter*

[Aber abseits wer ist's?
Ins Gebüsch verliert sich sein Pfad,
Hinter ihm schlagen
Die Sträuche zusammen,
Das Gras steht wieder auf,
Die Öde verschlingt ihn.]

[But who is this who has turned aside?
His trail is lost in undergrowth,
The bushes close up
Behind him,
The grass springs up again,
Desolation devours him.]

Ach, wer heilet die Schmerzen
Des, dem Balsam zu Gift ward?
Der sich Menschenhaß
Aus der Fülle der Liebe trank?
Erst verachtet, nun ein Verächter,
Zehrt er heimlich auf
Seinen eignen Wert
In ungnügender Selbstsucht.

Ah, who shall heal this man's pain,
For whom balm turned to poison?
Who drank hatred of mankind
From abundance of love?
First scorned, now scorning,
He secretly consumes
His own worth
In unsatisfying selfishness.

Ist auf deinem Psalter,
Vater der Liebe, ein Ton
Seinem Ohre vernehmlich,
So erquicke sein Herz!
Öffne den umwölkten Blick

If there be in your psaltery,
Father of Love, a sound
Perceptible to his ear,
Then refresh his heart!
Open his clouded gaze

Über die tausend Quellen
Neben dem Dürstenden
In der Wüste!

To the thousand springs around him,
As he stands thirsting
In the wilderness!

?1809 Aus *Euphrosyne** / From *Euphrosyne*

Tiefer liegt die Nacht um mich her; die
   stürzenden Wasser
Brausen gewaltiger nun neben dem
   schlüpfrigen Pfad.
Unbezwingliche Trauer befällt mich, entkräf-
   tender Jammer,
Und ein moosiger Fels stützet den Sinkenden
   nur.
Wehmut reißt durch die Saiten der Brust; die
   nächtlichen Tränen
Fließen, und über dem Wald kündet der
   Morgen sich an.

Night deepens around me, the plunging
   waters
Now roar more fiercely beside the slippery
   path.
An uncontrollable sadness seizes me, an
   enervating grief,
And only a mossy rock supports me as I
   swoon;
Melancholy tears at the strings of my heart; I
   weep
At night, and dawn announces its approach
   above the forest.

* Written by Goethe (Reichardt sets only the final six lines of this long poem) to commemmorate the death of a young Weimar actress, Christiane Becker. Euphrosyne was one of the Three Graces, a role Christiane had acted in Joseph Weigl's *Das Petermännchen* shortly before her death.

Franz Salmhofer (1900–75)

Austrian conductor who studied composition with Schreker and Franz Schmidt. He conducted at the Burgtheater (where he wrote music for over three hundred stage works), and then became director of the Staatsoper (1945–55) and Volksoper (1955–63). Apart from his incidental music to plays, he composed a number of operas and ballets, trumpet, cello and violin concertos, six string quartets, instrumental and chamber music. Amongst his many songs, which include settings of Eichendorff and Heine, it is his *Heiteres Herbarium*, the German equivalent of Milhaud's *Catalogue de fleurs*, that stands out. Salmhofer chose twenty-three of Karl Heinrich Waggerl's flower poems – each of which ends with a witty moral – set them to elegant and, at times, tender music, and ends the collection with a letter from the poet to the reader, signing off Karl Heinrich Waggerl. A largely unknown masterpiece, despite Patzak's recording with the composer at the piano, *Heiteres Herbarium* awaits rediscovery.

Karl Heinrich Waggerl (1897–1973)

Austrian novelist and short-story writer. *Heiteres Herbarium* was published in 1950.

1951 Kamille / Camomile
FROM *Heiteres Herbarium*

Die Kraft, das Weh im Leib zu stillen, verlieh der Schöpfer den Kamillen.	The Lord gave camomile the properties to cure the pain in human bellies.
Sie blühn und warten unverzagt auf jemand, den das Bauchweh plagt.	It blossoms and waits undaunted– make no mistake – for someone plagued with stomach-ache.
Der Mensch jedoch in seiner Pein glaubt nicht an das, was allgemein	Man, however, though wracked with pain, does not trust nature's Medicine.
zu haben ist. Er schreit nach Pillen. Verschont mich, sagt er, mit Kamillen, um Gotteswillen!	He screams for pills. Spare me camomile for my ills – that's not, for God's sake, what God wills!

Othmar Schoeck (1886–1957)

Hermann Hesse, Schoeck's Swiss compatriot, put his finger on a crucial aspect of his song-writing genius when he wrote in a 1931 essay on the composer:

> In Schoecks Vertonungen [of Hesse's own 'Ravenna' and 'Im Kreuzgang von St. Stefano'] ist nirgends das leiseste Mißverständnis des Textes, nirgends fehlt das zarteste Gefühl für die Nuancen, und überall ist mit fast erschreckender Sicherheit der Finger auf das Zentrum gelegt, auf jenen Punkt, wo um ein Wort oder um die Schwingung zwischen zwei Worten sich das Erlebnis des Gedichtes gesammelt hat. Gerade dies Erfühlen der Keimzelle in jedem Gedicht war mir stets das sicherste Kennzeichen für Schoecks Genialität.

> Nowhere in Schoeck's settings is there the slightest misunderstanding of the words; nowhere can we fail to note the most sensitive feeling for light and shade; and everywhere he puts his finger with almost frightening certainty on the central point where the experience of the poet has become crystallized in a word or in the vibrations between two words. It is the way he thus penetrates to the germinal cell of each poem that to me has always been the surest indication of Schoeck's genius.

More than any other Lieder composer, Schoeck composed collections of songs to the verse of a single poet. He wrote over four hundred Lieder which are, to a large extent, grouped together in *Liederreihen*, devoted to some of the greatest names in German poetry: Claudius, Eichendorff, Goethe, Hebbel, Heine, Hesse, Keller, Lenau, Meyer, Mörike and Uhland. The best-known cycles are *Wanderung im Gebirge* (nine poems by Lenau), *Das Wandsbecker Liederbuch* (seventeen by Matthias Claudius), *Unter Sternen* (twenty-five by Keller), *Das stille Leuchten* (twenty-eight by Conrad Ferdinand Meyer), *Das holde Bescheiden* (forty by Mörike), and *Notturno*, a cycle for baritone and string quartet to twenty-four poems by Lenau and Eichendorff. There are also three orchestral cycles, of which *Lebendig begraben* (fourteen songs to poems by Gottfried Keller) is the most frequently performed. Schoeck is one of the most literary of Lieder composers, and it was his practice to live with a poem for many years before setting it to music. This humility towards his chosen texts is expressed again and again in Werner Vogel's *Othmar Schoeck im Gespräch* (Atlantis-Verlag Zurich, 1965), where Schoeck defines a song as the poem in another shape: 'The poem is as it were the chrysalis, in which the miracle of metamorphosis takes place and from which the butterfly, like the song, then escapes.'

Joseph von Eichendorff (1788–1857)

See Robert Schumann and Pfitzner

Auf meines Kindes Tod was Eichendorff's title for a sequence of ten poems, written in March 1832, after the death of his two-year-old daughter Anna. 'Von fern die Uhren schlagen' is the eighth of the cycle.

1914 Nachruf / In memoriam Op. 20, no. 14

Du liebe, treue Laute,	Dear faithful lute,
Wie manche Sommernacht,	How many a summer night
Bis daß der Morgen graute,	Till day-break
Hab' ich mit dir durchwacht!	Have I watched with you!
Die Täler wieder nachten,	Again the valleys darken,
Kaum spielt noch Abendrot,	The twilight's nearly spent,
Doch die sonst mit uns wachten,	But they who once watched with us
Die liegen lange tot.	Perished long ago.
Was wollen wir nun singen	Why should we want to sing
Hier in der Einsamkeit,	Here in solitude,
Wenn alle von uns gingen,	When all have gone
Die unser Lied erfreut?	Who delighted in our song?
Wir wollen dennoch singen!	Nonetheless, we shall sing!
So still ist's auf der Welt;	The world is so still;
Wer weiß, die Lieder dringen	Who knows, songs may reach
Vielleicht zum Sternenzelt.	As far as the stars.
Wer weiß, die da gestorben,	Who knows, those who died
Sie hören droben mich,	May hear me up there,
Und öffnen leis die Pforten	And quietly open the gates,
Und nehmen uns zu sich.	And take us to them.
(*Wolf*)	

1914 Auf meines Kindes Tod / On the death of my child Op. 20, no. 8

Von fern die Uhren schlagen,	The clocks ring out from afar,
Es ist schon tiefe Nacht,	It is already deep night,
Die Lampe brennt so düster,	The lamp burns so dimly,
Dein Bettlein ist gemacht.	Your little bed is made.
Die Winde nur noch gehen	Only the winds still blow
Wehklagend um das Haus,	Wailing round the house,
Wir sitzen einsam drinne	We sit lonely inside
Und lauschen oft hinaus.	And often listen out.
Es ist, als müßtest leise	It is as though you were about

Du klopfen an die Tür,	To tap gently on the door,
Du hätt'st dich nur verirret,	As though you had only lost your way,
Und kämst nun müd' zurück.	And were now returning tired.
Wir armen, armen Toren!	We poor, poor fools!
Wir irren ja im Graus	It is we who still wander
Des Dunkels noch verloren –	Lost in darkness and horror –
Du fandst dich längst nach Haus.	Long ago you found your way home.

4 October 1918 Waldeinsamkeit! / Woodland solitude! Op. 30, no. 1
FROM *Dichter und ihre Gesellen*

Waldeinsamkeit!	Woodland solitude!
Du grünes Revier,	You verdant realm,
Wie liegt so weit	How far from here
Die Welt von hier!	The world lies!
Schlaf nur, wie bald	Sleep on, beautiful evening
Kommt der Abend schön,	Will soon be here,
Durch den stillen Wald	Through the silent wood
Die Quellen gehn,	The streams are running,
Die Mutter Gottes wacht,	The Mother of God keeps watch,
Mit ihrem Sternenkleid	With her starry raiment
Bedeckt sie dich sacht	She gently shrouds you
In der Waldeinsamkeit,	In woodland solitude,
Gute Nacht, gute Nacht! –	Good night, good night! –
(*Rubinstein*)	

Johann Wolfgang von Goethe (1749–1832)

See Beethoven, Brahms, Hensel, Loewe, Mendelssohn, Mozart, Reichardt, Schubert, Strauss, Wolf, Zelter

5 August 1909 Herbstgefühl / Autumn mood Op. 19a, no. 1

Fetter grüne, du Laub,	Grow more lushly, you leaves,
Am Rebengeländer	On the vine-trellis
Hier mein Fenster herauf!	Up to my window here!
Gedrängter quellet,	Swell more densely,
Zwillingsbeeren, und reifet	Twin-born clusters, and ripen
Schneller und glänzend voller!	Swifter and gleam more richly!
Euch brütet der Mutter Sonne	You are warmed by Mother sun's
Scheideblick; euch umsäuselt	Farewell glance; round you rustles
Des holden Himmels	Gracious heavens'
Fruchtende Fülle;	Fruit-bearing fullness;
Euch kühlet des Mondes	You are cooled by the moonlight's
Freundlicher Zauberhauch,	Friendly magical breath,
Und euch betauen, ach!	And you are bedewed, ah!

Aus diesen Augen
Der ewig belebenden Liebe
Vollschwellende Tränen.
(*Reichardt*)

By the full-flowing tears
Of the eternally life-giving love
These eyes have shed.

Hermann Hesse (1877–1962)

Awarded the Nobel Prize for Literature in 1946 and celebrated as a novelist – *Peter Camenzind* (1904), *Unterm Rad* (1906), *Gertrud* (1910), *Roßhalde* (1913), *Siddhartha* (1922), *Der Steppenwolf* (1927), *Narziß und Goldmund* (1930), *Das Glasperlenspiel* (1943) – Hesse's poetry has gained in popularity over the years and has been set more often than that of any other twentieth-century German poet. It is through Richard Strauss's 'Beim Schlafengehen', 'Frühling' and 'September' from the *Vier letzte Lieder* that Hesse is best known, but there are numerous other settings, including those by Mark Lothar and Gottfried von Einem. Writing in June 1950 to the composer Hermann Wetzel, Hesse guessed that there were 'probably some two thousand settings of my poems'. Schoeck's first Hesse songs date from 1906 ('Elisabeth', 'Aus zwei Tälern', 'Auskunft' and 'Jahrestag'), and it was not long before poet and composer were to become lifelong friends and collaborators. Although two opera libretti, *Der verkaufte Ehemann* and *Bianca* (1910–11) were not to Schoeck's liking, the composer always responded eagerly to Hesse's poetry.

6 May 1913 Ravenna / Ravenna Op. 24b, no. 9

Ich bin auch in Ravenna gewesen.
Ist eine kleine tote Stadt,
Die Kirchen und viel Ruinen hat,
Man kann davon in den Büchern lesen.

I too have been to Ravenna.
It is a small dead town
With churches and many ruins,
You can read about it in books.

Du gehst hindurch und schaust dich um,
Die Straßen sind so trüb und naß
Und sind so tausendjährig stumm
Und überall wächst Moos und Gras.

You walk through it and look around,
The streets are so gloomy and wet
And so silent with their thousand years,
And moss and grass grow everywhere.

Das ist wie alte Lieder sind –
Man hört sie an und keiner lacht
Und jeder lauscht und jeder sinnt
Hernach daran bis in die Nacht.

That is what old songs are like –
You listen to them and no one laughs,
And everyone listens and everyone ponders
Them thereafter into the night.

1952 Im Nebel / In the mist Op. post.

Seltsam, im Nebel zu wandern!
Einsam steht jeder Busch und Stein,
Kein Baum sieht den andern,
Jeder ist allein.

Strange, to wander in the mist!
Each bush and stone is solitary,
No tree sees the other,
Each is alone.

Voll von Freunden war mir die Welt,	The world to me was full of friends,
Als noch mein Leben licht war;	When my life still shone brightly;
Nun, da der Nebel fällt,	Now that the mist is falling,
Ist keiner mehr sichtbar.	There's not one in sight.
Wahrlich, keiner ist weise,	Truly, no man is wise
Der nicht das Dunkel kennt,	Who does not know the dark,
Das unentrinnbar und leise	Which softly, inescapably
Von allem ihn trennt.	Divides him from all.
Seltsam, im Nebel zu wandern!	Strange, to wander in the mist!
Leben ist Einsamsein.	Life is solitude.
Kein Mensch kennt den andern,	No one knows the other,
Jeder ist allein.	Each is alone.
(*Von Einem*)	

Gottfried Keller (1819–1890)

See Wolf

Swiss novelist, poet and short-story writer. His fame rests on *Der grüne Heinrich*, a long, autobiographical novel that exists in two versions (1854–5 and 1879–80), a collection of Novellen *Die Leute von Seldwyla* (1856) and his poems, which first appeared in *Gedichte* (1846) and were finally collected in *Gesammelte Gedichte* (1883). Keller's own life was tinged with personal sadness: his proposals of marriage (by letter) to Luise Rieter and Joanna Kapp were both declined, he was too shy to declare his love for Betty Tendering, and lived first with his mother and, after her death, with his sister, who kept house for him. Yet his poetry, like Goethe's, is generally life-affirming and hymns the beauty and goodness of the everyday world, as 'Abendlied' exemplifies. Schoeck was greatly attracted to his compatriot's verse: *Unter Sternen*, from which 'Abendlied' and 'Ein Tagewerk' are taken, contains twenty-five poems, *Gaselen* ten and the orchestral cycle *Lebendig begraben* fourteen. Few other composers, apart from Wolf, Pfitzner, Brahms and Schoenberg, have been attracted to his verse; the most popular Keller-inspired composition remains Delius's opera *A Village Romeo and Juliet*, based on *Romeo und Julia auf dem Dorfe*, a Novelle first published in 1856.

1941–43 Abendlied / Evening song Op. 55, no. 12

Augen, meine lieben Fensterlein,	Eyes, my beloved little windows,
Gebt mir schon so lange holden Schein,	For so long you've given me wondrous light,
Lasset freundlich Bild um Bild herein:	Letting image after image in:
Einmal werdet ihr verdunkelt sein!	The time will come when you'll be darkened!

Fallen einst die müden Lider zu,
Löscht ihr aus, dann hat die Seele Ruh';
Tastend streift sie ab die Wanderschuh',
Legt sich auch in ihre finstre Truh'.

Noch zwei Fünklein sieht sie glimmend stehn
Wie zwei Sternlein, innerlich zu sehn,
Bis sie schwanken und dann auch vergehn,
Wie von eines Falters Flügelwehn.

Doch noch wandl' ich auf dem Abendfeld,
Nur dem sinkenden Gestirn gesellt;
Trinkt, o Augen, was die Wimper hält,
Von dem goldnen Überfluß der Welt!
(*Wilhelm Kempff*)

When your weary eyelids close
And you are extinguished, the soul will be at rest;
Haltingly, it will slip off its walking-boots
And lay down too in its dark coffin.

It still sees two tiny sparks gleaming,
Like two little stars inwardly visible,
Until they flicker and go out,
As if snuffed by a moth's wing.

But still I walk in the evening field,
The setting sun my sole companion;
Drink, O eyes, all that your lashes can hold
Of this world's golden profusion!

1941–43 aus: Ein Tagewerk / from: One day's work Op. 55, no. 23

1

Vom Lager stand ich mit dem Frühlicht auf
Und nahm hinaus ins Freie meinen Lauf,
Wo duftiggrau die Morgendämmrung lag,
Umflorend noch den rosenroten Tag;
Mich einmal satt zu gehn in Busch und Feldern
Vom Morgen früh bis in die späte Nacht,
Und auch ein Lied zu holen in den Wäldern,
Hatt ich zum festen Vorsatz mir gemacht.

Rein war der Himmel, bald zum Tag erhellt,
Der volle Lebenspuls schlug durch die Welt;
Die Lüfte wehten und der Vogel sang,
Die Eichen wuchsen und die Quelle sprang.
Die Blumen blühten und die Früchte reiften,
Ein jeglich Gras tat seinen Atemzug;
Die Berge standen und die Wolken schweiften
In gleicher Luft, die meinen Odem trug.

Ich schlenderte den lieben Tag entlang,
Im Herzen regte sich der Hochgesang;
Es brach sich Bahn der Wachtel heller Schlag,
Jedoch mein Lied – es rang sich nicht zu Tag.
Der Mittag kam, ich lag an Silberflüssen,
Die Sonne sucht ich in der klaren Flut
Und durfte nicht von Angesicht sie grüßen,
Der ich allein in all dem Drang geruht.

Die Sonne sank und ließ die Welt der Ruh,
Die Abendnebel gingen ab und zu;
Ich lag auf Bergeshöhen matt und müd,
Tief in der Brust das ungesungne Lied.

I rose at first light from my bed
And made my way out into the open,
Where the dawn lay grey and hazy,
Still veiling the rose-red day;
To walk my fill in wood and field,
From morning till late at night,
And to draw from the woods a song –
That had been my firm intent.

The sky was clear, soon brightening into day,
Life's full pulse was beating through the world;
Breezes blew and birds sang,
Oak trees grew and fountains gushed.
Flowers bloomed and fruits ripened,
Each blade of grass was drawing breath;
Mountains stood firm and clouds drifted
In that same air that bore my breath.

I sauntered on throughout the day,
High exultation stirring in my heart;
The quail's bright song sounded forth,
But my own song – did not succeed.
Midday came, I lay by silver streams,
I sought the sun in the clear water
And dared not greet it face to face,
I who in all this teeming alone took rest.

The sun set and left the world to peace,
The evening mists came and went;
I lay on mountain peaks, faint and weary,
My unsung song deep in my breast.

2

Aber ein kleiner goldener Stern	But one small golden star
Sang und klang mir in die Ohren:	Sang and rang in my ears:
„Tröste dich nur, dein Lied ist fern,	'Be comforted, your song is far,
Fern bei uns und nicht verloren!	Far away with us and not lost!
Findest du nicht oft einen Klang,	Do you not often find a note
Wie zu früh herüber geklungen?	Reaches you as if too soon?
Also hat sich heut dein Sang	So today has your own song
Heimlich zu uns hinüber geschwungen!	Winged its way secretly to us!
Dort, im donnernden Weltgesang,	There, in the world's thunderous melody,
Wirst du ein leises Lied erkennen,	You will recognize a gentle song
Das dir, wie fernster Glockenklang,	Which, like far distant bells,
Diesen Sommertag wird nennen.	Shall name for you this summer's day.
Denn die Ewigkeit ist nur	For eternity is only
Hin und her ein tönendes Weben;	A resonant stirring to and fro;
Vorwärts, rückwärts wird die Spur	Your footprints will reverberate
Deiner Schritte klingend erbeben,	Forwards and backwards
Deiner Schritte durch das All,	Throughout the universe,
Bis, wie eine singende Schlange,	Until, like a singing serpent,
Einst dein Leben den vollen Schall	Your life shall one day find
Findet im Zusammenhange."	Its full coherent sound.'

Conrad Ferdinand Meyer (1825–1898)

See Pfitzner

Schoeck composed the twenty-eight songs of *Das stille Leuchten* in the early spring of 1946 and divided the collection into two groups, 'Geheimnis und Gleichnis' ('Mystery and symbol') and 'Berg und See' ('Mountain and lake'). The title of the collection, meaning 'The gentle radiance', is taken from a line of Meyer's patriotic poem 'Firnelicht'.

1946 Liederseelen / Song-souls Op. 60, no. 2

In der Nacht, die die Bäume mit Blüten deckt,	In the night that decks the trees with blossom,
Ward ich von süßen Gespenstern erschreckt.	I was frightened by sweet phantoms.
Ein Reigen schwang im Garten sich,	Dancers whirled about the garden
Den ich mit leisem Fuß beschlich;	Where I entered on tiptoe;
Wie zarter Elfen Chor im Ring	A white and living gleam passed by,
Ein weißer lebendiger Schimmer ging.	Like a throng of dainty elves in a ring.
Die Schemen hab ich keck befragt:	Boldly I asked these shadowy figures:
„Wer seid ihr, luftige Wesen? Sagt!"	'Who are you, airy creatures? Speak!'
„Ich bin ein Wölkchen, gespiegelt im See."	'I'm a lake-reflected cloud.'

„Ich bin eine Reihe von Stapfen im Schnee."
„Ich bin ein Seufzer gen Himmel empor!"
„Ich bin ein Geheimnis, geflüstert ins Ohr!"
„Ich bin ein frommes, gestorbenes Kind."
„Ich bin ein üppiges Blumengewind –"
„Und die du wählst, und ders beschied,
Die Gunst der Stunde, die wird ein Lied."
(*Hermann Behn, Wilhelm Kempff*)

'I'm a row of steps in the snow.'
'I'm a sigh rising to heaven!'
'I'm a secret whispered in your ear!'
'I'm an innocent, departed child.'
'I'm a sumptuous garland of flowers –'
'And the one you choose and the hour
Favours, will grow into a song.'

1946 Reisephantasie / A travel fantasy Op. 60, no. 3

Mittagsruhe haltend auf den Matten
In der morschen Burg gezacktem Schatten,
Vor dem Türmchen eppichübersponnen,
Hab ich einen Sommerwunsch gesonnen,
Während ich ein Eidechsschwänzchen blitzen
Sah und, husch, verschwinden durch die
   Ritzen …
Wenn es lauschte … wenn es meiner harrte …
Wenn – das Pförtchen in der Mauer knarrte …
Dem Geräusche folgend einer Schleppe,
Fänd ich eine schmale Wendeltreppe
Und, von leiser Hand emporgeleitet,
Droben einen Becher Wein bereitet …
Dann im Erker säßen wir alleine,
Plauderten von nichts im Dämmerscheine,
Bis der Pendel stünde, der da tickte,
Und ein blondes Haupt entschlummernd
   nickte,
Unter seines Lides dünner Hülle
Regte sich des blauen Quelles Fülle …
Und das unbekannte Antlitz trüge
Ähnlichkeiten und Geschwisterzüge
Alles Schönen, was mir je entgegen
Trat auf allen meinen Erdenwegen …
Was ich Tiefstes, Zartestes empfunden,
Wär an dieses blonde Haupt gebunden.
Und in eine Schlummernde vereinigt,
Was mich je beseligt und gepeinigt …
Dringend hätt es mich emporgerufen
Dieser Wendeltreppe Trümmerstufen,
Daß ich einem ganzen vollen Glücke
Stillen Kuß auf stumme Lippen drücke …
Einmal nur in einem Menschenleben –
Aber nimmer wird es sich begeben!

Resting at midday on the meadow
In the decaying castle's jagged shadow,
I thought up a summer wish
By the ivy-covered turret,
As I saw a lizard's tail flash
And quickly vanish through crevices …
Suppose it were listening … waiting for me …
Suppose – the door in the wall were to
   creak …
Following the rustle of a train,
I'd find a narrow spiral staircase
And, guided upstairs by a gentle hand,
A goblet of wine waiting for me there …
Then we'd sit in the bay-window together,
Talk of sweet nothings in the dark,
Till the pendulum clock stopped its ticking,
And a blond head nodded off into sleep,
And beneath its lightly-veiling lids
The full blueness of the well would stir …
And that unknown countenance would bear
The likeness and sibling features
Of all the beauty I ever encountered
On my earthly journey …
All the deepest, most tender things I ever
   felt
Would be attached to that blond head
And united in one slumbering woman,
All that had ever enraptured or tormented me …
I would be urgently summoned to climb
The crumbling steps of that spiral staircase,
So that I might press a secret kiss
Of utter happiness on silent lips …
Just once in my mortal life –
But that will never come to pass!

1946 Der römische Brunnen / The fountain in Rome Op. 60, no. 14

Aufsteigt der Strahl und fallend gießt	Up soars the jet and falling fills
Er voll der Marmorschale Rund,	The marble basin's curving rim,
Die, sich verschleiernd, überfließt	Which, clouding over, spills
In einer zweiten Schale Grund;	To reach a second basin's brim;
Die zweite gibt, sie wird zu reich,	The second, overflowing, sheds
Der dritten wallend ihre Flut,	Its flood into the third,
Und jede nimmt und gibt zugleich	And each one takes and gives as well
Und strömt und ruht.	And rests and flows.

1946 Das Ende des Festes / The end of the feast Op. 60, no. 15

Da mit Sokrates die Freunde tranken	When friends were drinking with Socrates
Und die Häupter auf die Polster sanken,	And heads were sinking onto cushions,
Kam ein Jüngling, kann ich mich entsinnen,	A young man came, I can recall,
Mit zwei schlanken Flötenbläserinnen.	With two slender flute-playing girls.
Aus den Kelchen schütten wir die Neigen,	We shake the dregs from our goblets,
Die gesprächesmüden Lippen schweigen,	Weary with talk our lips fall silent,
Um die welken Kränze zieht ein Singen ...	Singing is heard around faded wreaths ...
Still! Des Todes Schlummerflöten klingen!	Hush! The slumber flutes of death are sounding!
(*Wilhelm Kempff*)	

1946 Jetzt rede du! / Now you speak! Op. 60, no. 28

Du warest mir ein täglich Wanderziel,	You were my daily destination,
Viellieber Wald, in dumpfen Jugendtagen,	Much loved wood, in my apathetic youth,
Ich hatte dir geträumten Glücks so viel	I had so much to tell you of dreamt delights
Anzuvertraun, so wahren Schmerz zu klagen.	And to complain of real sorrow.
Und wieder such ich dich, du dunkler Hort,	Once more I seek you out, O dark refuge,
Und deines Wipfelmeers gewaltig Rauschen –	And the mighty roaring of your tree-
Jetzt rede du! Ich lasse dir das Wort!	tops –
Verstummt ist Klag und Jubel. Ich will	Now you speak! I give way to you!
lauschen.	Lament and joy are stilled. I listen.
(*Hermann Behn, Wilhelm Kienzl*)	

Eduard Mörike (1804–75)

See Wolf

The forty songs of Schoeck's *Das holde Bescheiden* were written between 1947–49 and premiered by the composer and his wife Hilde. The title of the collection is taken from Mörike's poem 'Gebet' (see WOLF).

1909 Peregrina II* / Peregrina II Op. 17, no. 4

Ein Irrsal kam in die Mondscheingärten	A disturbance broke into the moonlit gardens
Einer einst heiligen Liebe.	Of a once sacred love.
Schaudernd entdeckt' ich verjährten Betrug.	With horror I discovered a betrayal of years ago.
Und mit weinendem Blick, doch grausam,	And tearfully, yet cruelly,
Hieß ich das schlanke,	I banished the slender,
Zauberhafte Mädchen	Enchanting girl
Ferne gehen von mir.	Far from my presence.
Ach, ihre hohe Stirn	Alas, her noble forehead
War gesenkt, denn sie liebte mich;	Was bowed, for she loved me;
Aber sie zog mit Schweigen	But she went in silence
Fort in die graue	Out into the grey
Welt hinaus.	World.
Krank seitdem,	My heart since then
Wund ist und wehe mein Herz.	Has been sick, wounded and sore.
Nimmer wird es genesen!	Never will it heal!
Als ginge, luftgesponnen, ein Zauberfaden	As if, spun from air, there were a magic thread
Von ihr zu mir, ein ängstig Band,	Between her and me, a fearful bond,
So zieht es, zieht mich schmachtend ihr nach!	I am drawn, drawn to her in longing!
– Wie? Wenn ich eines Tags auf meiner Schwelle	– What if I were to find her one day
Sie sitzen fände, wie einst, im Morgen-Zwielicht,	Sitting outside my door, as once I did in the dawn,
Das Wanderbündel neben ihr,	Her bundle by her side,
Und ihr Auge, treuherzig zu mir aufschauend,	And her eyes, gazing faithfully up at me,
Sagte: da bin ich wieder	Were to say: Here I am again,
Hergekommen aus weiter Welt!	Back from the wide world!

1948–49 Peregrina / Peregrina Op. 62, no. 14

Aufgeschmückt ist der Freudensaal.	The festive room is adorned and ready.
Lichterhell, bunt, in laulicher Sommernacht	Brightly lit with many-coloured lamps, the garden pavilion
Stehet das offene Gartengezelte.	Stands open in the mild summer night.
Säulengleich steigen, gepaart,	Rising column-like, in pairs,
Grün-umranket, eherne Schlangen,	Wreathed in green, twelve bronze serpents,
Zwölf mit verschlungenen Hälsen,	With necks intertwined,
Tragend und stützend das	Bear and support the lightly latticed roof.
Leicht gegitterte Dach.	
Aber die Braut noch wartet verborgen	But the bride still waits, hidden
In dem Kämmerlein ihres Hauses.	In the house, in her little room.
Endlich bewegt sich der Zug der Hochzeit,	At last the wedding procession sets off,
Fackeln tragend,	Bearing torches,

---

* The poem describes the background to the Maria Meyer episode in Mörike's life. See WOLF, p. 619.

Feierlich stumm.	Solemn and silent.
Und in der Mitte,	And in its midst,
Mich an der rechten Hand,	Myself at her right hand,
Schwarz gekleidet, geht einfach die Braut;	Dressed in simple black, the bride walks;
Schön gefaltet ein Scharlachtuch	A scarlet cloth, in lovely folds,
Liegt um den zierlichen Kopf geschlagen.	Is wound about her dainty head.
Lächelnd geht sie dahin; das Mahl schon duftet.	She walks with a smile; the feast already wafts its fragrance.

Feierlich stumm.
Und in der Mitte,
Mich an der rechten Hand,
Schwarz gekleidet, geht einfach die Braut;
Schön gefaltet ein Scharlachtuch
Liegt um den zierlichen Kopf geschlagen.
Lächelnd geht sie dahin; das Mahl schon
    duftet.

Später im Lärmen des Fests
Stahlen wir seitwärts uns beide
Weg, nach den Schatten des Gartens wandelnd,
Wo im Gebüsche die Rosen brannten,
Wo der Mondstrahl um Lilien zuckte,
Wo die Weymouthsfichte mit schwarzem Haar
Den Spiegel des Teiches halb verhängt.

Auf seidnem Rasen dort, ach, Herz am
    Herzen,
Wie verschlangen, erstickten meine Küsse
    den scheueren Kuß!
Indes der Springquell, unteilnehmend
An überschwenglicher Liebe Geflüster,
Sich ewig des eignenen Plätscherns freute;
Uns aber neckten von fern und lockten
Freundliche Stimmen,
Flöten und Saiten umsonst.

Ermüdet lag, zu bald für mein Verlangen,
Das leichte, liebe Haupt auf meinem Schoß.
Spielender Weise mein Aug auf ihres drückend,
Fühlt ich ein Weilchen die langen Wimpern,
Bis der Schlaf sie stellte,
Wie Schmetterlingsgefieder auf und nieder
    gehn.

Eh das Frührot schien,
Eh das Lämpchen erlosch im
    Brautgemache,
Weckt ich die Schläferin,
Führte das seltsame Kind in mein Haus ein.

Solemn and silent.
And in its midst,
Myself at her right hand,
Dressed in simple black, the bride walks;
A scarlet cloth, in lovely folds,
Is wound about her dainty head.
She walks with a smile; the feast already wafts
    its fragrance.

Later, amid the noisy feast,
Both of us stole
Away, walking towards the shaded garden,
Where roses flamed in the bushes,
Where moonlight flickered on lilies,
Where the white pine with its black hair
Half shrouds the surface of the pond.

There on the silky lawn, ah, heart against
    heart,
How my kisses devoured and smothered her
    more timid kiss!
While the fountain, ignoring the whispers of
    wild love,
Took delight in its own eternal murmuring;
In the distance, friendly voices, flutes and
    strings
Teased and lured us in vain.

Too soon fatigued for my desire,
Her dear head lay lightly on my lap.
Playfully pressing my eyes on hers,
I felt for a while her long lashes,
Till sleep closed them,
Rise and fall like butterfly
    wings.

Before dawn broke,
Before the lamp went out in the bridal
    chamber,
I woke the sleeping girl,
Led the strange child into my house.

Ludwig Uhland (1787–1862)

See Schubert

This is the earliest of all Schoeck's published songs, composed in the summer of 1903.

Wann im letzten Abendstrahl
Goldne Wolkenberge steigen
Und wie Alpen sich erzeigen,
Frag' ich oft mit Tränen:
Liegt wohl zwischen jenen
Mein ersehntes Ruhetal?
(*Hensel*)

When in the last rays of evening
Golden cloud-banks climb the sky
And appear like mountains,
I often ask as I weep:
'Might the tranquil valley I crave
Lie somewhere in their midst?'

Arnold Schoenberg (1874–1951)

Schoenberg began his career by writing songs and the lyrical impulse always remained with him, culminating during different periods of his life in such master-pieces as *Erwartung* (1909), *Das Buch der hängenden Gärten* (1909), *Gurrelieder* (1911), *Pierrot lunaire* (1912) and the opera *Moses und Aron* (1932). Between 1898 and 1900 he composed a large number of Lieder, twelve of which he published as his Op. 1, Op. 2 and Op. 3. Although they clearly belong to the great tradition of nineteenth-century German Song – the scores, for example, are scattered with such markings as 'leidenschaftlich bewegt' (with passionate emotion), 'sehr zart' (very gently) and 'sehr innig' (very tenderly) – there is in some of them a rhythmic freedom independent of the bar line and passages in which tonality is obscured. By 1908, when he composed most of *Das Buch der hängenden Gärten*, he had virtually abandoned the old system of major/minor keys, and fully expected the public to react with hostility. In a programme note for the first performance of the cycle, he wrote:

> In the George Lieder I have succeeded for the first time in approaching an ideal of expression and form that had hovered before me for some years. Hitherto, I had not sufficient strength and sureness to realize that ideal. Now, however, that I have definitely set out on my journey, I may confess to having broken through the barriers of an outlived aesthetic; and if I am striving toward a goal that seems to me to be certain, nevertheless I already feel the opposition that I shall overcome.

Schoenberg later modified his statement that he had 'broken through the barriers of an outlived aesthetic', by writing in *My Evolution*: 'This music is distinctly a product of evolution, no more revolutionary than any other development in the history of music.' There is indeed something traditional about *Das Buch der hängenden Gärten*; despite the partial break with tonality, the absence of recurring themes and word-painting, the rigorous independence of accompaniment and voice, and the presence of 'dissonant' chords, the cycle follows the tradition of the great nineteenth-century song-cycles such as *An die ferne Geliebte, Die schöne Müllerin, Winterreise* and *Dichterliebe*. There is a discernible narrative to the poems, which deal with a doomed relationship, and a performance of these songs can be as moving as any performance of the Schubert or Schumann cycles. As Schoenberg himself wrote: 'I warn you of the danger lurking in the die-hard reaction against Romanticism. The old Romanticism is dead; long live the new!'

Richard Dehmel (1863–1920)

The son of a gamekeeper, Dehmel retained throughout his life a spirit of independence and compassion for the underdog. He was a co-founder of the Berliner Volksbühne (1890), whose aim was to put on good modern plays at moderate prices for the working-classes. He was the most influential of the Haus Nyland group of young poets who regarded modern industry, technical inventions and social problems to be the true subject-matter of poetry. Dehmel's notoriety, his verse on sexual liberation and attacks on puritanical contemporaries resulted in a trial on charges of obscenity, and made him a cult figure among the younger generation. Richard Strauss was attracted to Dehmel's socialistic verse ('Lied an meinen Sohn' and 'Der Arbeitsmann'), and Schoenberg, in a letter to the poet dated 13 December 1912, wrote:

Ihre Gedichte haben auf meine musikalische Entwicklung entscheidenden Einfluß ausgeübt. Durch sie war ich zum ersten Mal genötigt, einen neuen Ton in der Lyrik zu suchen. Das heißt, ich fand ihn ungesucht, indem ich musikalisch widerspiegelte, was Ihre Verse in mir aufwühlten.

Your poems have had a decisive influence on my development as a composer. They caused me to look for a new tone when setting poetry. That's to say, it came to me unbidden, as I mirrored in my music the feelings your poetry aroused in me.

In the early years of the twentieth century, at a time when Rilke was considered to be a mere aesthete and George deliberately avoided the public eye, Dehmel was widely regarded as Germany's leading contemporary poet.

August 1899 Erwartung / Expectation Op. 2, no. 1

Aus dem meergrünen Teiche	From the sea-green pond
neben der roten Villa	near the red villa
unter der toten Eiche	beneath the dead oak
scheint der Mond.	the moon is shining.
Wo ihr dunkles Abbild	Where its dark image
durch das Wasser greift,	gleams through the water,
steht ein Mann und streift	a man stands, and draws
einen Ring von seiner Hand.	a ring from his hand.
Drei Opale blinken;	Three opals glimmer;
durch die bleichen Steine	through the pale stones
schwimmen rot und grüne	red and green sparks float
Funken und versinken.	and sink.
Und er küßt sie, und	And he kisses them, and
seine Augen leuchten	his eyes gleam
wie der meergrüne Grund:	like the sea-green depths:
ein Fenster tut sich auf.	a window opens.

Aus der roten Villa	From the red villa
neben der toten Eiche	near the dead oak
winkt ihm eine bleiche	a woman's pale hand
Frauenhand ...	waves to him ...

?1899 Jesus bettelt / Jesus begs Op. 2, no. 2

Schenk mir deinen goldenen Kamm;	Give me your golden comb;
jeder Morgen soll dich mahnen,	every morning shall remind you
daß du mir die Haare küßtest.	that you kissed my hair.
Schenk mir deinen seidnen Schwamm;	Give me your silken sponge;
jeden Abend will ich ahnen,	every evening I want to sense
wem du dich im Bade rüstest –	for whom you prepare yourself in the bath –
oh, Maria!	oh, Maria!

Schenk mir Alles, was du hast;	Give me everything you have;
meine Seele ist nicht eitel,	my soul is not vain,
stolz empfang ich deinen Segen.	proudly I receive your blessing.
Schenk mir deine schwerste Last:	Give me your heaviest burden:
willst du nicht auf meinen Scheitel	will you not lay on my head
auch dein Herz, dein Herz noch legen –	your heart too, your heart –
Magdalena?	Magdalena?

November 1899 Erhebung / Exaltation Op. 2, no. 3

Gieb mir nur die Hand,	Give me your hand only,
nur den Finger, dann	only a finger, then
seh ich diesen ganzen Erdkreis	I shall see this whole round earth
als mein Eigen an!	as my own!

O, wie blüht mein Land!	Oh, how my country blossoms!
Sieh dir's doch nur an,	Just look at it,
daß ich mit dir über die Wolken	ah! to go with you above the clouds
in die Sonne kann!	into the sun!

Stefan George (1868–1933)

1908–09 *Fünfzehn Gedichte aus 'Das Buch der hängenden Gärten' / Fifteen poems from 'The Book of the Hanging Gardens'* Op. 15

1

Unterm schutz von dichten blättergründen	Protected by dense leafy thickets
Wo von sternen feine flocken schneien	Where fine flakes snow from stars ·
Sachte stimmen ihre leiden künden ·	Where gentle voices proclaim their agonies ·
Fabeltiere aus den braunen schlünden	Where fabled creatures from brown jaws
Strahlen in die marmorbecken speien ·	Spew jets of water into marble basins ·
Draus die kleinen bäche klagend eilen:	From which lamenting the little brooks rush:

Kamen kerzen das gesträuch entzünden ·
Weisse formen das gewässer teilen.

Candles came to illuminate the bushes ·
White forms divide the waters.

2

Hain in diesen paradiesen
Wechselt ab mit blütenwiesen
Hallen · buntbemalten fliesen.
Schlanker störche schnäbel kräuseln
Teiche die von fischen schillern ·
Vögel-reihen matten scheines
Auf den schiefen firsten trillern
Und die goldnen binsen säuseln –
Doch mein traum verfolgt nur eines.

Groves in these paradises
Alternate with flowery meadows
Porticos and coloured tiles.
Beaks of slender storks ruffle
Pools that iridesce with fish ·
Rows of faintly gleaming birds
Trill on the sloping gables
And the golden rushes murmur –
But my dream pursues one thing alone.

3

Als neuling trat ich ein in dein gehege
Kein staunen war vorher in meinen mienen ·
Kein wunsch in mir eh ich dich blickte rege.
Der jungen hände faltung sieh mit huld ·
Erwähle mich zu denen die dir dienen
Und schone mit erbarmender geduld
Den der noch strauchelt auf so fremdem
   stege.

As a novice I entered your preserve
Before no wonder showed in my face ·
No wish stirred in me before I saw you.
Look with favour on these young folded
   hands ·
Choose me to be among your servants
And spare with merciful patience
One who still stumbles on so strange a path.

4

Da meine lippen reglos sind und brennen
Beacht ich erst wohin mein fuss geriet:
In andrer herren prächtiges gebiet.
Noch war vielleicht mir möglich mich zu
   trennen ·
Da schien es dass durch hohe gitterstäbe
Der blick vor dem ich ohne lass gekniet
Mich fragend suchte oder zeichen gäbe.

Only now that my lips are motionless and
   burning
Do I notice where my steps have strayed:
Into the sumptuous realm of other masters.
Still I might have broken free ·
Then it seemed that through high trellises
The glance before which I had ceaselessly knelt
Looked quizzically at me or gave me a sign.

5

Saget mir auf welchem pfade
Heute sie vorüberschreite –
Dass ich aus der reichsten lade
Zarte seidenweben hole ·
Rose pflücke und viole ·
Dass ich meine wange breite ·
Schemel unter ihrer sohle.

Tell me on which path
She will pass today –
That I from the richest shrine
Might fetch finely woven silks ·
Might gather roses and violets ·
That I might fashion from my cheek ·
A stool for her feet.

6

Jedem werke bin ich fürder tot.
Dich mir nahzurufen mit den sinnen ·
Neue reden mit dir auszuspinnen ·
Dienst und lohn gewährung und verbot ·

To all labours I am henceforth lost.
To summon you to me with all my senses ·
To devise new discourses with you ·
Service and reward permission and denial ·

Von allen dingen ist nur dieses not
Und weinen dass die bilder immer fliehen
Die in schöner finsternis gediehen –
Wann der kalte klare morgen droht.

This alone is needful
And to weep because images always take flight
That flourished in fair darkness –
When the cold clear morning looms.

7

Angst und hoffen wechselnd mich beklem-
    men ·
Meine worte sich in seufzer dehnen ·
Mich bedrängt so ungestümes sehnen
Dass ich mich an rast und schlaf nicht kehre
Dass mein lager tränen schwemmen
Dass ich jede freude von mir wehre
Dass ich keines freundes trost begehre.

Fear and hope in turn depress me ·
My words lengthen into sighs ·
Such violent yearning besets me
That I turn no more to rest and
    sleep
That tears drench my couch
That I repel every pleasure
That I crave no friend's comfort.

8

Wenn ich heut nicht deinen leib berühre
Wird der faden meiner seele reissen
Wie zu sehr gespannte sehne.
Liebe zeichen seien trauerflöre
Mir der leidet seit ich dir gehöre.
Richte ob mir solche qual gebühre ·
Kühlung sprenge mir dem fieberheissen
Der ich wankend draussen lehne.

If today I do not touch your body
The thread of my soul will break
Like a bowstring stretched too tight.
Let love tokens be veils of sorrow
For me who suffers since I belong to you.
Judge yourself if I deserve such torment ·
Drip coolness on my hot fever
As I falter and lean outside your door.

9

Streng ist uns das glück und spröde ·
Was vermocht ein kurzer kuss?
Eines regentropfens guss
Auf gesengter bleicher öde
Die ihn ungenossen schlingt ·
Neue labung missen muss
Und vor neuen gluten springt.

Fortune is severe and coy with us ·
What could one short kiss achieve?
It is like a single drop of rain
On a parched pale desert
That swallows it unslaked ·
That lacking new refreshment
Cracks with renewed heat.

10

Das schöne beet betracht ich mir im harren ·
Es ist umzäunt mit purpurn-schwarzem
    dorne
Drin ragen kelche mit geflecktem sporne
Und sammtgefiederte geneigte farren
Und flockenbüschel wassergrün und rund
Und in der mitte glocken weiss und mild –
Von einem odem ist ihr feuchter mund
Wie süsse frucht vom himmlischen gefild.

I look at the lovely flower bed as I wait ·
It is hedged with purple-black thorn
From which calyxes rise with speckled spurs
And velvet-feathered inclining ferns
And cornflower clusters water-green and round
And in the middle bell-flowers white and
    gentle –
Their moist mouths breathing fragrance
Like sweet fruit from the fields of heaven.

11

Als wir hinter dem beblümten tore
Endlich nur das eigne hauchen spürten

When we beyond the garlanded gate
Felt at last no breathing but our own

Warden uns erdachte seligkeiten?
Ich erinnere dass wie schwache rohre
Beide stumm zu beben wir begannen
Wenn wir leis nur an uns rührten
Und dass unsre augen rannen –
So verbliebest du mir lang zu seiten.

Did we then sense imagined raptures?
I recall that like fragile reeds
We both began silently to tremble
At the merest touch
And that our eyes welled with tears –
Long thus at my side you remained.

12

Wenn sich bei heilger ruh in tiefen matten
Um unsre schläfen unsre hände schmiegen ·
Verehrung lindert unsrer glieder brand:
So denke nicht der ungestalten schatten
Die an der wand sich auf und unter wiegen ·
Der wächter nicht die rasch uns scheiden dürfen
Und nicht dass vor der stadt der weisse sand
Bereit ist unser warmes blut zu schlürfen.

When in the blest repose of deep meadows
Our hands twine round our temples ·
When reverence soothes the fire in our limbs:
Do not then think of the misshapen shadows
That move up and down on the wall ·
Nor of the guards who may swiftly part us
And nor of the white sand beyond the town
Ready to drink in our warm blood.

13

Du lehnest wider eine silberweide
Am ufer · mit des fächers starren spitzen
Umschirmest du das haupt dir wie mit blitzen
Und rollst als ob du spieltest dein geschmeide.
Ich bin im boot das laubgewölbe wahren
In das ich dich vergeblich lud zu steigen ·
Die weiden seh ich die sich tiefer neigen
Und blumen die verstreut im wasser fahren.

You lean against a silver willow
By the river bank · with your fan's stiff slats
You shield your head as if with lightning flashes
And play with your jewels as if with toys.
I am in the boat that leafy vaults conceal
Into which I vainly bade you step ·
I see the willows bending lower
And scattered flowers drifting on the waters.

14

Sprich nicht immer
Von dem laub ·
Windes raub ·
Vom zerschellen
Reifer quitten ·
Von den tritten
Der vernichter
Spät im jahr.
Von dem zittern
Der libellen
In gewittern
Und der lichter
Deren flimmer
Wandelbar.

Speak not always
Of the leaves ·
The wind's plunder ·
Of the dashing
Of ripe quinces ·
Of the steps
Of the destroyers
Late in the year ·
Of the dragonflies
Quivering
In storms
And of the lights
Whose glimmer
Is inconstant.

15

Wir bevölkerten die abend-düstern
Lauben · lichten tempel · pfad und beet
Freudig – sie mit lächeln ich mit flüstern –
Nun ist wahr dass sie für immer geht.
Hohe blumen blassen oder brechen ·
Es erblasst und bricht der weiher glas
Und ich trete fehl im morschen gras ·
Palmen mit den spitzen fingern stechen.
Mürber blätter zischendes gewühl
Jagen ruckweis unsichtbare hände
Draussen um des edens fahle wände.
Die nacht ist überwölkt und schwül.

We peopled the evening-dusky
Arbours · bright temples · paths and flower-beds
Joyfully – she with a smile I with whispers –
Now it is true she will leave forever.
Tall flowers grow pale or break ·
Glassy ponds pale and break
And I stumble in decaying grass ·
Palms prick with sharp fingers.
Hissing throngs of brittle leaves
Are gusted away by invisible hands
Outside around Eden's ashen walls.
The night is sultry and overcast.

Gottfried Keller (1819–90)

See Wolf

November 1899–1900 Die Aufgeregten / Flustered creatures Op. 3, no. 2

Welche tief bewegten Lebensläufchen,
Welche Leidenschaft, welch wilder Schmerz!
Eine Bachwelle und ein Sandhäuschen
Brachen gegenseitig sich das Herz!

What deeply disturbed little lives,
What passion, what fierce torment!
A ripple in the brook and a little heap of sand
Broke each other's heart!

Eine Biene summte hohl und stieß
Ihren Stachel in ein Rosendüftchen,
Und ein holder Schmetterling zerriß
Den azurnen Frack im Sturm der
    Mailüftchen!

A bee buzzed and pierced
A little fragrant rose with its sting,
And a lovely butterfly tore
Its blue dress in the storm of a little May
    breeze!

Und die Blume schloß ihr Heiligtümchen
Sterbend über dem verspritzten Tau!

And the flower, dying, closed its tiny sanctuary
Over the spilled dew!

September–November 1899–1900 Geübtes Herz / Practised heart Op. 3, no. 5

Weise nicht von dir mein schlichtes Herz,
Weil es schon so viel geliebet!
Einer Geige gleicht es, die geübet
Lang ein Meister unter Lust und Schmerz.

Do not reject my simple heart,
Because it has loved so much already!
It is like a violin, practised on for years
By a master in joy and sorrow.

Und je länger er darauf gespielt,
Stieg ihr Wert zum höchsten Preise;
Denn sie tönt mit sichrer Kraft die
    Weise,
Die ein Kund'ger ihren Saiten stiehlt.

And the longer he played on it
Its value rose to the greatest price;
Because it plays with confident strength the
    tune
An expert steals from its strings.

Also spielte manche Meisterin
In mein Herz die rechte Seele,
Nun ist's wert, daß man es dir empfehle,
Lasse nicht den köstlichen Gewinn!
(*Felix Weingartner*)

Thus did many a master craftswoman play
A true soul into my heart,
Now it is worthy to be commended you,
Do not forego the exquisite prize!

Franz Schubert (1797–1828)

If Reichardt, Zelter, Mozart and Beethoven laid the foundations of the German Lied, Schubert was the first, in songs such as 'Gretchen am Spinnrade' and 'Erlkönig', to deepen the psychological importance of the accompaniment. He and the baritone Johann Michael Vogl also created the *Liederabend* when in 1825 they toured Upper Austria with a programme of songs that included the recently composed Sir Walter Scott settings from *The Lady of the Lake*. Schubert described to his brother Ferdinand the impact made by these performances on the audience: 'Die Art und Weise, wie Vogl singt und ich accompagniere, wie wir in einem solchen Augenblicke *Eins* zu sein scheinen, ist diesen Leuten etwas ganz Neues, Unerhörtes.' ('The manner in which Vogl sings and I accompany, the way in which we seem, at such a moment, to become *one*, is something quite new and unheard-of for these people.')

The overwhelming majority of Schubert's songs are settings of verse by poets who were his contemporaries. Despite the wealth of fine poetry from the past, Schubert concentrated almost exclusively on contemporary poetry and, to a large extent, the dilettante or minor verse of his closest friends. That should not surprise us. Although great poetry inspired him – there are, after all, many masterpieces among the Goethe, Schiller and Heine settings – it was not necessarily a poet's pedigree that attracted him. In the heady artistic ambience of Biedermeier Vienna, where so many of Schubert's friends were poets, painters or composers, it was entirely natural that he should treat his poet friends as seriously as they treated him; indeed, the success of the Schubertiads depended on such mutual respect. If Schubert composed some 150 songs to the second-rank verse of his friends and acquaintances, that does not imply a lack of literary awareness, but rather a gift for friendship.

Schubert, like Beethoven, often chose his texts for their autobiographical relevance, and the theme of friendship appears with some frequency; but unlike the older composer, Schubert was rarely tempted to set religious poetry, despite the success of songs such as 'Ave Maria', 'Die junge Nonne', 'Die Allmacht' and 'Dem Unendlichen'. An extraordinary number of his songs, however, deal with death, not because it was fashionable, but because much of Schubert's life was lived in death's shadow: seven of his brothers and sisters died before he was born, and two more – Josef and Aloisia Magdalena – while he was still an infant.

Schubert was the first Lieder composer of significance, *pace* C. P. E Bach, Reichardt and Zelter, to explore in depth a particular poet's work. Goethe inspired seventy-four songs, Mayrhofer forty-seven, Müller forty-five, Schiller forty-four, Matthisson twenty-nine, Hölty twenty-three and Kosegarten twenty-one. And like Liszt, Schubert would often set a text several times before he felt he had done justice to a poem: there are, for example, six settings of 'Nur wer die Sehnsucht kennt', four of 'So laßt mich scheinen', three of 'Der Jüngling am Bache', 'Des Mädchens Klage' and 'Der Geistertanz' – indeed, over 120 of his songs and partsongs exist in more than one version. The revisions are often radical, and it is not always easy, as in 'Der Jüngling am Bache' and Goethe's 'An den Mond', to decide which is the more successful song. Schubert's obsessive immersion in a single poet anticipates Wolf, and both were capable of composing several songs a day. Schubert was on three occasions even more prolific than Wolf: seven songs were written both on 15 and 19 October 1815, while five Goethe settings ('Heidenröslein', 'Der Schatzgräber', 'Bundeslied', 'An den Mond' and 'Der Rattenfänger') belong to 19 August of the same year.

It is a hallmark of musical genius that a composer is able to give each major work – or in Schubert's case, poet – an unmistakable style or timbre. Schubert, like Wolf, found an entirely different voice for poets as varied as Goethe, Heine, Hölty, Mayrhofer, Müller, Platen, Rellstab and Rückert; and he was equally at home in setting epic, lyric, comic, epigrammatic, religious, tragic or dramatic verse. It is only surprising that a composer who could write such dramatic and theatrical songs such as 'Erlkönig', 'Gretchen am Spinnrade', 'Gruppe aus dem Tartarus', 'Der Zwerg', 'Die junge Nonne', 'Dem Unendlichen', and reveal such mastery of declamation and recitative in, for example, 'Prometheus', 'Szene aus *Faust*', 'Grenzen der Menschheit', 'Der Doppelgänger' and 'An die Leier', should fail to write a single opera (despite over ten attempts) capable of retaining its place in the repertoire.

Anonymous

The autograph gives Matthias Claudius as the poet of 'Wiegenlied', but there is no poem of that title in his Collected Works. The autograph of 'Der Strom' contains the remark 'Zum Andenken für Herrn Stadler' – 'In memory of Herr Stadler' – a schoolfriend of Schubert's who provided the composer with the libretto of *Fernando* (D220). Although Deutsch suggests that Schubert might have written the poem, it is possible that Stadler, a minor composer and poet, was himself the author.

November 1816 Wiegenlied / Cradle song D498

Schlafe, holder, süßer Knabe,	Sleep now, you dear sweet boy,
Leise wiegt dich deiner Mutter Hand;	Your mother's hand rocks you gently;
Sanfte Ruhe, milde Labe	This swaying cradle strap
Bringt dir schwebend dieses Wiegenband.	Brings you tender peace and comfort.
Schlafe in dem süßen Grabe,	Sleep in the sweet grave,
Noch beschützt dich deiner Mutter Arm,	Your mother's arms still protect you,
Alle Wünsche, alle Habe	All her wishes, all she holds dear,
Faßt sie liebend, alle liebewarm.	She lovingly embraces in warm love.

Schlafe in der Flaumen Schoße,
Noch umtönt dich lauter Liebeston,
Eine Lilie, eine Rose,
Nach dem Schlafe werd' sie dir zum Lohn.

Sleep in her down-soft lap,
Love's pure music still echoes round you.
You shall be rewarded when you wake
With a lily and a rose.

?1817 Der Strom / The river D565

Mein Leben wälzt sich murrend fort,
Es steigt und fällt in krausen Wogen,
Hier bäumt es sich, jagt nieder dort,
In wilden Zügen, hohen Bogen.

My life rolls grumbling onwards,
Rising and falling in furrowed waves,
Here it rears up, there plunges down,
Leaping wildly in soaring curves.

Das stille Tal, das grüne Feld
Durchrauscht es nun mit leisem Beben,
Sich Ruh' ersehnend, ruhige Welt,
Ergötzt es sich am ruhigen Leben.

Gently rippling, it hurries through
The silent valley and green fields,
Longing for peace, a tranquil world,
Delighting in a peaceful life.

Doch nimmer findend, was es sucht,
Und immer sehnend tost es weiter,
Unmutig rollt's auf steter Flucht,
Wird nimmer froh, wird nimmer heiter.

Yet never finding what it seeks,
It surges on in endless longing,
Vexed, it rolls on in endless flight,
Never happy, never content.

Franz von Bruchmann (1798–1867)

Bruchmann certainly knew Schubert by the early twenties, for both were present at Johann Senn's, when the police raided the latter's lodgings in March 1820. Schubertiads were held at the Bruchmann home between 1822–4, and he attended some of the reading parties. Schubert set five of Bruchmann's poems, all from manuscript, since his poems were never published. When his sister Justina became engaged to Schober, Bruchmann and his family urged her to break off the relationship – which led to a severing of all contact with Schubert, who took Schober's side. Having reacted as a young man against his Catholic upbringing, he eventually rejoined the Catholic church and in 1833 became a redemptorist priest. Bruchmann wrote 'Schwestergruß' in 1820 after the death of his sister Sybilla.

?1822–3 An die Leier / To the lyre D737

Ich will von Atreus'* Söhnen,
Von Kadmus† will ich singen!
Doch meine Saiten tönen
Nur Liebe im Erklingen.
Ich tauschte um die Saiten,
Die Leier möcht' ich tauschen,

I would sing of Atreus's sons,
And of Cadmus too!
But my strings sound
Forth nothing but love.
I have changed the strings,
I would gladly change the lyre,

* Atreus was father to Agamemnon and Menelaus.
† Cadmus laid the foundations of Thebes.

Alcidens* Siegesschreiten	Let Alcides' victory march
Sollt' ihrer Macht entrauschen!	Thunder from its mighty heart!
Doch auch die Saiten tönen	But these strings too sound
Nur Liebe im Erklingen.	Forth nothing but love.
So lebt denn wohl, Heroen,	Farewell, then, heroes,
Denn meine Saiten tönen,	For my strings,
Statt Heldensang zu drohen,	Instead of threatening with heroic song,
Nur Liebe im Erklingen.	Sound forth nothing but love.

November 1822 Schwestergruß / Sister's greeting D762

Im Mondenschein	In the moonlight
Wall' ich auf und ab,	I wander up and down,
Seh' Totenbein'	See the bones of the dead
Und stilles Grab.	And a silent grave.
Im Geisterhauch	In the ghostly breeze
Vorüber schwebt's,	A form floats past,
Wie Flamm' und Rauch	Quivering
Vorüber bebt's;	Like flame and smoke;
Aus Nebeltrug	From deceptive mists
Steigt eine Gestalt,	A figure looms,
Ohn' Sünd' und Lug	Without sin or falsehood,
Vorüber wallt,	And drifts past,
Das Aug' so blau,	With such blue eyes
Der Blick so groß	And staring gaze,
Wie in Himmelsau,	As in the fields of heaven,
Wie in Gottes Schoß;	As in the lap of God;
Ein weiß Gewand	A white garment
Bedeckt das Bild,	Clothes the vision,
In zarter Hand	A lily springs
Eine Lilie quillt,	From its delicate hand,
In Geisterhauch	In a ghostly whisper
Sie zu mir spricht:	She speaks to me:
„Ich wand're schon	'Already I walk
Im reinen Licht,	In pure light,
Seh' Mond und Sonn'	See the moon and sun
Zu meinem Fuß	Below me
Und leb' in Wonn',	And live in bliss,
In Engelkuß;	Kissed by angels;
Und all' die Lust,	And your heart,
Die ich empfind',	O child of man,

* Alcides, a name for Hercules, from his grandfather Alcaeus.

Nicht deine Brust	Cannot know all the joy
Kennt, Menschenkind!	I feel,

Wenn du nicht läßt	Unless you abandon
Den Erdengott,	The gods of this world,
Bevor dich faßt	Before you are seized
Der grause Tod."	By fearful death.'

So tönt die Luft,	The air resounds,
So saust der Wind,	The wind moans,
Zu den Sternen ruft	The child of heaven
Das Himmelskind,	Calls to the stars,

Und eh' sie flieht,	And before she flees,
Die weiß' Gestalt,	Her white form
In frischer Blüt'	Is folded
Sie sich entfalt':	In fresh flowers:

In reiner Flamm'	She floats aloft
Schwebt sie empor,	In pure flame,
Ohne Schmerz und Harm,	Without pain or grief
Zu der Engel Chor.	To the angels' choir.

Die Nacht verhüllt	Night obscures
Den heil'gen Ort,	The holy place,
Von Gott erfüllt	Filled with God,
Sing' ich das Wort.	I sing the word.

Matthias Claudius (1740–1815)

Matthias Claudius, whom Herder described in a letter as 'das größte Genie' ('the greatest genius'), was set by Schubert thirteen times. Like Mörike, he resists any attempt at categorization, and was hardly influenced by the literary movements of his age. Many of his poems celebrate nature and simple piety, and the gentle didacticism of much of his work reveals his belief in Enlightenment and education. He published his stories, letters, reviews, reflections and poems in the *Wandsbecker Bote*, a journal that he edited and to which he was the chief contributor. His verse, which can also be humorous, has inspired many composers, including Beethoven ('Urians Reise um die Welt'), Loewe ('Der Zahn'), Reichardt, Othmar Schoeck in the seventeen songs of his *Wandsbecker Bote*, and Zelter.

November 1816 An die Nachtigall / To the nightingale D497

Er liegt und schläft an meinem Herzen,	He lies and slumbers on my heart,
Mein guter Schutzgeist sang ihn ein;	My guardian angel sang him to sleep;
Und ich kann fröhlich sein und scherzen,	And I can make merry and jest,
Kann jeder Blum' und jedes Blatts mich freun.	Delight in every flower and leaf.

Nachtigall, ach! Nachtigall, ach!
Sing mir den Amor nicht wach!

Oh! when Christmas comes along,
Do not wake Cupid with your song!

4 November 1816 Am Grabe Anselmos* / By Anselm's grave D504

Daß ich dich verloren habe,
Daß du nicht mehr bist,
Ach! daß hier in diesem Grabe
Mein A n s e l m o i s t,
Das ist mein Schmerz! Das ist mein Schmerz!!!
Seht, wie liebten wir uns beide,
Und so lang' ich bin, kommt Freude
Niemals wieder in mein Herz.

That I have lost you,
That you are no more,
Ah! that here in this grave
My *Anselm* lies buried,
That is my grief! That is my grief!!!
See, we loved each other so,
And as long as I live, joy
Shall never return to my heart.

February 1817 Der Tod und das Mädchen / Death and the Maiden D531

DAS MÄDCHEN
Vorüber! Ach, vorüber!
Geh, wilder Knochenmann!
Ich bin noch jung, geh Lieber!
Und rühre mich nicht an.

THE MAIDEN
Away! Ah, away!
Away, fierce man of bones!
I am still young, go, please go!
And do not touch me.

DER TOD
Gib deine Hand, du schön und zart Gebild!
Bin Freund, und komme nicht, zu strafen.
Sei gutes Muts! ich bin nicht wild,
Sollst sanft in meinen Armen schlafen!

DEATH
Give me your hand, you lovely, tender creature!
I am a friend, and do not come to punish.
Be not afraid! I am not fierce,
You shall sleep softly in my arms!

February 1817 Das Lied vom Reifen / Song of the hoar-frost D532

Seht meine lieben Bäume an,
  Wie sie so herrlich stehn,
Auf allen Zweigen angetan
  Mit Reifen wunderschön!

Just look at my beloved trees,
  Standing there so splendidly,
With each branch clad
  In frosty beauty!

Von unten an bis oben 'naus
  Auf allen Zweigelein
Hängt's weiß und zierlich, zart und kraus,
  Und kann nicht schöner sein;

From foot to crown
  Each twig is hung
With crisp, fragile, delicate white,
  And could not be more beautiful;

Ein Engel Gottes geht bei Nacht,
  Streut heimlich hier und dort,
Und wenn der Bauersmann erwacht,
  Ist er schon wieder fort.

An angel of God comes at night,
  Sprinkling secretly here and there,
And when the farmer wakens,
  The angel has gone again.

Du Engel, der so gütig ist,
  Wir sagen Dank und Preis.

O angel, you who are so good,
  We give you thanks and praise.

* Anselmo was the name of Claudius's first child; born on 30 September 1772, he lived only a few hours.

O mach uns doch zum heil'gen Christ
Die Bäume wieder weiß!

Oh! when Christmas comes along,
Make our trees white again!

Matthäus von Collin (1779–1824)

Having qualified as a lawyer at the University of Vienna, Collin became Professor
of Philosophy at Cracow and later in Vienna, where he also worked in the ministry of finance. He wrote a number of libretti and historical plays, but had more
success as a literary critic. His poems, which were eventually collected by Baron
Hammer-Purgstall and published as *Nachgelassene Gedichte* in 1827, inspired three
of Schubert's finest songs and his most beautiful duet ('Licht und Liebe').

?November 1822 Der Zwerg / The dwarf D771

Im trüben Licht verschwinden schon die Berge,
Es schwebt das Schiff auf glatten
   Meereswogen,
Worauf die Königin mit ihrem Zwerge.

The mountains already fade in the
   gloom,
The ship drifts on the sea's smooth swell,
With the queen and her dwarf on board.

Sie schaut empor zum hochgewölbten Bogen,
Hinauf zur lichtdurchwirkten blauen Ferne,
Die mit der Milch des Himmels blaß durchzogen.

She gazes up at the high arching
   vault,
At the distant blue woven with light,
Streaked by the pale Milky Way.

Nie habt ihr mir gelogen noch, ihr Sterne,
So ruft sie aus, bald werd' ich nun
   entschwinden,
Ihr sagt es mir, doch sterb' ich wahrlich gerne.

'Never, stars, have you lied to me yet,'
She cries, 'Soon I shall be no more,
You tell me so, yet truly I shall gladly
   die.'

Da tritt der Zwerg zur Königin, mag binden
Um ihren Hals die Schur von roter Seide,
Und weint, als wollt er schnell vor Gram
   erblinden.

The dwarf then steps up to the queen,
To tie the red silk cord about her neck,
And weeps, as though he'd go blind with
   grief.

Er spricht: Du selbst bist schuld an diesem
   Leide,
Weil um den König du mich hast verlassen,
Jetzt weckt dein Sterben einzig mir noch
   Freude.

He speaks: 'You yourself are to blame for
   this torment,
Because you forsook me for the
   king,
Your death alone can gladden me.

Zwar werd ich ewiglich mich selber hassen,
Der dir mit dieser Hand den Tod gegeben,
Doch mußt zum frühen Grab du nun
   erblassen.

Though I shall always hate myself
For killing you with this hand,
You must now perish, go early to your
   grave.'

Sie legt die Hand auf's Herz voll jungem
   Leben,
Und aus dem Aug' die schweren Tränen rinnen,
Das sie zum Himmel betend will erheben.

She lays her hand on her young
   heart,
And heavy tears stream from her eyes,
She now raises to heaven in prayer.

„Mögst du nicht Schmerz durch meinen Tod
    gewinnen!"
Sie sagt's, da küßt der Zwerg die bleichen
    Wangen,
Drauf alsobald vergehen ihr die Sinnen.

Der Zwerg schaut an die Frau vom Tod
    befangen,
Er senkt sie tief in's Meer mit eignen Handen.
Ihm brennt nach ihr das Herz so voll Verlangen.
An keiner Küste wird er je mehr landen.

'May you suffer no anguish through my
    death!'
She says; the dwarf then kisses her pale
    cheeks,
And forthwith she falls unconscious.

The dwarf looks down at his dying lady,
Lowers her with his hands deep into the
    sea.
His heart burns for her with such desire.
He will never again set foot on shore.

?1822 Nacht und Träume / Night and dreams D827

Heil'ge Nacht, du sinkest nieder;
Nieder wallen auch die Träume,
Wie dein Mondlicht durch die Räume,
Durch der Menschen stille Brust.
Die belauschen sie mit Lust,
Rufen, wenn der Tag erwacht:
Kehre wieder, heil'ge Nacht!
Holde Träume, kehret wieder!

Holy night, you float down;
Dreams too drift down,
Like your moonlight through space,
Through the silent hearts of men.
They listen to them with delight,
Cry out when day awakes:
Come back, holy night!
Sweet dreams, come back again!

November 1822 Wehmut / Melancholy D772

Wenn ich durch Wald und Fluren geh,
Es wird mir dann so wohl und weh
In unruhvoller Brust.
So wohl, so weh, wenn ich die Au
In ihrer Schönheit Fülle schau',
Und all die Frühlingslust.

When I walk through forest and field,
I feel so happy and sad
In my restless heart.
So happy and so sad when I see
The meadow in all its beauty,
And all the joy of spring.

Denn was im Winde tönend weht,
Was aufgetürmt gen Himmel steht,
Und auch der Mensch, so hold vertraut
Mit all der Schönheit, die er schaut,
Entschwindet, und vergeht.

For all that blows and echoes in the wind,
All that towers up to heaven,
And man himself, so fondly bound
To all the beauty he beholds,
Shall vanish and pass away.

Jacob Nicolaus Craigher de Jachelutta (1797–1855)

Italian businessman, translator and poet. The dilettante nature of this remarkable
man is suggested by the title of his collected verse, *Poetische Betrachtungen in
freyen Stunden*. Born in Friuli, he settled in Vienna where his erudition was great-
ly appreciated in literary circles. He had an astonishing knowledge of European
languages, and was contracted to supply Schubert with German translations of
English, French, Spanish and Italian poems, in the metres of the originals, which
Schubert then planned to set and publish with the German and original texts –

clearly with an eye on the foreign market. The incentive for such an agreement was probably the success of Colley Cibber's 'The blind boy', which Schubert had set in early 1825, and which can indeed be sung – with some questionable stresses – to Schubert's music.

1824–25 Die junge Nonne / The young nun D828

Wie braust durch die Wipfel der heulende Sturm!
Es klirren die Balken – es zittert das Haus!
Es rollet der Donner – es leuchtet der Blitz! –
Und finster die Nacht, wie das Grab! – – –
    Immerhin, immerhin!

So tobt' es auch jüngst noch in mir!
Es brauste das Leben, wie jetzo der Sturm!
Es bebten die Glieder, wie jetzo das Haus!
Es flammte die Liebe, wie jetzo der Blitz! –
Und finster die Brust, wie das Grab! –

Nun tobe du wilder, gewaltiger Sturm!
Im Herzen ist Friede, im Herzen ist Ruh! –
Des Bräutigams harret die liebende Braut,
    Gereinigt in prüfender Glut –
    Der ewigen Liebe getraut. –

Ich harre, mein Heiland, mit sehnendem Blick;
Komm, himmlischer Bräutigam! hole die Braut!
Erlöse die Seele von irdischer Haft! –
Horch! friedlich ertönet das Glöcklein vom Turm;
    Es lockt mich das süße Getön
    Allmächtig zu ewigen Höhn –
    „Alleluja!"

How the raging storm howls through the treetops!
The rafters groan – the house shudders!
The thunder rolls – the lightning flashes! –
And the night is dark as the tomb! – – –
    So be it, so be it!

Not long ago a storm still raged in me!
My life raged like the storm now!
My limbs quaked like the house now!
Love flashed like the lightning now! –
And my heart was as dark as the tomb! –

Rage on, you wild and mighty storm!
In my heart is peace, in my heart is calm! –
The loving bride awaits the bridegroom,
    Purified by testing fire –
    Wedded to eternal love. –

I wait, my Saviour, with longing gaze;
Come, heavenly bridegroom! claim your bride!
Deliver her soul from earthly bonds! –
Hark! the bell tolls peacefully from the tower;
    The sweet sound lures me
    All-powerfully to eternal heights –
    Halleluja!'

1825 Der blinde Knabe / The blind boy D833
AFTER COLLEY CIBBER (1671–1757), TRANSLATED BY CRAIGHER

O sagt, ihr Lieben, mir einmal,
Welch Ding ist's, Licht genannt?
Was sind des Sehens Freuden all,
Die niemals ich gekannt?

Die Sonne, die so hell ihr seht,
Mir Armen scheint sie nie,
Ihr sagt, sie auf und nieder geht,
Ich weiß nicht wann noch wie.

O tell me, dear friends,
What is that thing called light?
What are all these joys of seeing
I have never known?

The sun that you see so bright,
It never shines for me, poor boy,
It rises and it sets, you say,
Yet I don't know when or how.

Ich mach mir selbst so Tag und Nacht,
Dieweil ich schlaf und spiel;
Mein innres Leben schön mir lacht,
Ich hab der Freuden viel.

Zwar kenn ich nicht, was euch erfreut,
Doch drückt mich keine Schuld,
Drum freu ich mich in meinem Leid,
Und trag es mit Geduld.

Ich bin so glücklich, bin so reich
Mit dem, was Gott mir gab,
Bin wie ein König froh, obgleich
Ein armer blinder Knab'.

I make my own day and night,
While I sleep and play,
My inner life is full of smiles,
And many are my joys.

Though I don't know what gladdens you,
No guilt weighs me down,
So I rejoice in my pain
And bear it patiently.

I am so happy and so rich
With what God has given to me,
I am as joyful as a king,
Though only a poor blind boy.

April 1825 Totengräbers Heimwehe / Gravedigger's longing D842

O Menschheit – o Leben! –
Was soll's – o was soll's?! –
Grabe aus – scharre zu!
Tag und Nacht keine Ruh! –
Das Treiben, das Drängen –
Wohin! – o wohin?! – –
„Ins Grab – tief hinab!" –

O Schicksal – o traurige Pflicht –
Ich trag's länger nicht! – –
Wann wirst du mir schlagen,
O Stunde der Ruh?! –
O Tod! komm und drücke
Die Augen mir zu! – –
Im Leben da ist's ach! so schwül! –
Im Grabe – so friedlich, so kühl!
Doch ach, wer legt mich hinein? –
Ich stehe allein! – so ganz allein!! –

Von allen verlassen
Dem Tod nur verwandt,
Verweil' ich am Rande –
Das Kreuz in der Hand,
Und starre mit sehnendem Blick,
Hinab – ins tiefe Grab! –

O Heimat des Friedens,
Der Seligen Land!
An dich knüpft die Seele
Ein magisches Band. –
Du winkst mir von Ferne,
Du ewiges Licht: –
Es schwinden die Sterne –

O mankind – O life! –
To what end – oh what end?! –
Digging out – filling in!
Day and night no rest! –
The urgency, the haste –
Where does it lead! – ah where?! – –
'Deep down – into the grave!' –

O fate – O sad duty –
I can bear it no more! – –
When will you toll for me,
O hour of peace?! –
O death! come
And close my eyes! – –
Life, alas, is so oppressive! –
The grave so peaceful, so cool! –
But ah! who will lay me there? –
I stand alone! – so utterly alone!! –

Abandoned by all,
With death my only kin,
I linger on the edge –
Cross in hand,
And stare longingly
Down – into the deep grave! –

O homeland of peace,
Land of the blessed!
A magic bond
Binds my soul to you. –
Eternal light,
You beckon me from afar: –
The stars vanish –

Das Auge schon bricht! – –	My eyes close in death! – –
Ich sinke – ich sinke! – Ihr Lieben –	I am sinking – I am sinking! – Loved ones –
Ich komme! – – –	I come! – – –

Johann Wolfgang von Goethe (1749–1832)

See Beethoven, Brahms, Hensel, Loewe, Mendelssohn, Mozart, Reichardt, Strauss, Wolf, Zelter

Schubert's obsession with Goethe, which was to yield over seventy songs, began on 19 October 1814 with the composition of 'Gretchen am Spinnrade'. By the end of 1815 he had set over thirty-four Goethe poems, five of which were composed on August 19. On 17 April 1816, Josef von Spaun sent the poet on Schubert's behalf a parcel of sixteen of his friend's Goethe settings, including 'Wandrers Nachtlied' ('Der du von dem Himmel bist'), 'Der Fischer', 'Rastlose Liebe', 'Schäfers Klagelied', 'Erster Verlust', 'Nähe des Geliebten' and 'Erlkönig'. Goethe never replied, and the parcel was returned without acknowledgement. Nine years later, in May 1825, Schubert again approached the poet, sending him through his publisher, Anton Diabelli, two copies of three songs printed on satinated paper with gold borders: 'An Schwager Kronos', 'An Mignon' and 'Ganymed'. The parcel arrived and Goethe's secretary, C. F. John, entered in the diary – presumably at Goethe's dictation – 'Sendung von Schubart [*sic*] aus Wien: Von meinen Liedern Compositionen.' ('Consignment from Schubart from Vienna: settings of my poems.').

Many reasons have been adduced for Goethe's failure to respond to these wonderful songs. Were they actually performed for him? And if so, was the performance adequate? Spaun, at the end of his accompanying letter, stated that „[. . .] es dem Klavierspieler [. . .] an Fertigkeit und Ausdruck nicht fehlen dürfe" ('the pianist must not lack facility or expression'). Perhaps no such pianist could be found. Or did the songs arrive at a time when Goethe was unusually busy? After all, he enjoyed a huge international reputation and received a daily deluge of letters and visits. The most likely explanation for Goethe's silence, however, must be sought elsewhere. He was not unmusical, but his concept of what constituted a song was profoundly different from Schubert's. Isolated in Weimar, he relied very much on Carl Friedrich von Zelter to keep him informed about the musical world of Berlin and beyond, and Zelter was essentially a conservative. In a letter to him, dated 2 May 1820, Goethe expounds his belief that the accompaniment should not seek to illustrate the imagery of a poem:

Die reinste und höchste Malerei in der Musik ist die, welche du auch ausübst, es kommt darauf an, den Hörer in die Stimmung zu versetzen, welche das Gedicht angibt [. . .]. Töne durch Töne zu malen: zu donnern, zu schmettern, zu plätschern und zu patschen ist detestabel.

The purest and noblest form of painting in music is the one which you also practise – it's a question of transporting the listener into the mood of the poem. To depict sounds by sounds: to thunder, warble, ripple and splash is abominable.

And in the *Annals* of 1801 he makes it clear that through-composed songs can lose their lyrical character by what he calls a 'falsche Teilnahme am Einzelnen' ('a misplaced concern with detail').

And yet Goethe, contrary to received opinion, was intensely musical. While Director of the Weimar Hoftheater from 1791 to 1817, he mounted productions by an astonishing variety of composers, including Mozart, Gluck, Beethoven, Dittersdorf, Paisiello, Cimarosa, Cherubini, Boieldieu, Paër and Spontini. And his voluminous correspondence with Zelter reveals his genuine interest in art song. In a letter dated 21 December 1809, he praises Zelter's settings of some Schiller ballads, and adds: 'Die Komposition suppliert sie, wie eigentlich das Lied durch jede Komposition erst vollständig werden soll.' ('Your composition adds to the ballads, just as any poem can only be complete when set to music.') The letters also make it quite clear that he was not implacably opposed to through-composed songs. He admired, for example, Reichardt's stormy setting of 'Rastlose Liebe' and remained a devotee all his life of Zelter's 'Um Mitternacht' (see p. 694), which is far from purely strophic.

19 October 1814 Gretchen am Spinnrade / Gretchen at the spinning-wheel D118
FROM *Faust*

Meine Ruh ist hin,	My peace is gone,
Mein Herz ist schwer;	My heart is heavy;
Ich finde sie nimmer	I shall never
Und nimmermehr.	Ever find peace again.
Wo ich ihn nicht hab'	When he's not with me,
Ist mir das Grab,	Life's like the grave;
Die ganze Welt	The whole world
Ist mir vergällt.	Is turned to gall.
Mein armer Kopf	My poor head
Ist mir verrückt,	Is crazed,
Mein armer Sinn	My poor mind
Ist mir zerstückt.	Shattered.
Meine Ruh ist hin,	My peace is gone,
Mein Herz ist schwer;	My heart is heavy;
Ich finde sie nimmer	I shall never
Und nimmermehr.	Ever find peace again.
Nach ihm nur schau ich	It's only for him

Zum Fenster hinaus,	I gaze from the window,
Nach ihm nur geh' ich	It's only for him
Aus dem Haus.	I leave the house.
Sein hoher Gang,	His proud bearing,
Sein' edle Gestalt,	His noble form,
Seines Mundes Lächeln,	The smile on his lips,
Seiner Augen Gewalt,	The power of his eyes,
Und seiner Rede	And the magic flow
Zauberfluß,	Of his words,
Sein Händedruck,	The touch of his hand,
Und ach, sein Kuß!	And ah, his kiss!
Meine Ruh ist hin,	My peace is gone,
Mein Herz ist schwer;	My heart is heavy;
Ich finde sie nimmer	I shall never
Und nimmermehr.	Ever find peace again.
Mein Busen drängt	My bosom
Sich nach ihm hin.	Yearns for him.
Ach dürft' ich fassen	Ah! if I could clasp
Und halten ihn,	And hold him,
Und küssen ihn	And kiss him
So wie ich wollt',	To my heart's content,
An seinen Küssen	And in his kisses
Vergehen sollt'!	Perish!
(*Loewe, Spohr, Verdi, Wagner*)	

30 November 1814 Nachtgesang / Night song D119

O gib, vom weichen Pfühle,	O lend from your soft pillow,
Träumend, ein halb Gehör!	Dreaming, half an ear!
Bei meinem Saitenspiele	As I pluck the strings
Schlafe! was willst du mehr?	Sleep! what more can you desire?
Bei meinem Saitenspiele	As I pluck the strings,
Segnet der Sterne Heer	The starry throng blesses
Die ewigen Gefühle;	Eternal feelings;
Schlafe! was willst du mehr?	Sleep! what more can you desire?
Die ewigen Gefühle	Eternal feelings
Heben mich, hoch und hehr,	Raise me sublimely aloft,
Aus irdischem Gewühle;	Above all earthly turmoil;
Schlafe! was willst du mehr?	Sleep! what more can you desire?
Vom irdischen Gewühle	From all earthly turmoil
Trennst du mich nur zu sehr,	You detach me only too well,
Bannst mich in diese Kühle;	Hold me spellbound in this coolness;
Schlafe! was willst du mehr?	Sleep! what more can you desire?

Bannst mich in diese Kühle,
Gibst nur im Traum Gehör.
Ach, auf dem weichen Pfühle
Schlafe! was willst du mehr?
(*Loewe, Reichardt, Zelter*)

Hold me spellbound in this coolness,
Lending ear but in your dreams.
Ah! on your soft pillow
Sleep! what more can you desire?

30 November 1814 Trost in Tränen / Consolation in tears D120

Wie kommt's, daß du so traurig bist,
Da alles froh erscheint?
Man sieht dir's an den Augen an,
Gewiß du hast geweint.

How is it that you're so sad,
When everyone is happy?
I can see from your eyes,
I'm sure that you've been weeping.

„Und hab' ich einsam auch geweint,
So ist's mein eigner Schmerz,
Und Tränen fließen gar so süß,
Erleichtern mir das Herz."

'If I have wept in solitude,
The grief is mine alone,
And tears flow so sweetly,
Comforting my heart.'

Die frohen Freunde laden dich,
O! komm an unsre Brust!
Und was du auch verloren hast,
Vertraue* den Verlust.

Your happy friends invite you,
O come, then, to our breast!
And whatever you have lost,
Confide to us the loss.

„Ihr lärmt und rauscht und ahnet nicht,
Was mich den Armen quält.
Ach nein! Verloren hab' ich's nicht,
So sehr es mir auch fehlt."

'You make merry and revel, unaware
What tortures this poor man.
Alas! I have sustained no loss,
Though I sorely feel its lack.'

So raffe denn dich eilig auf,
Du bist ein junges Blut.
In deinen Jahren hat man Kraft
Und zum Erwerben Mut.

Then quickly pull yourself together,
You are young in years.
At your age one has the strength
To achieve what one desires.

„Ach nein! Erwerben kann ich's nicht,
Es steht mir gar zu fern.
Es weilt so hoch, es blinkt so schön,
Wie droben jener Stern."

'Alas! I cannot achieve my aim,
It lies too far away.
It dwells as high, it gleams as bright
As that star up there.'

Die Sterne, die begehrt man nicht,
Man freut sich ihrer Pracht,
Und mit Entzücken blickt man auf
In jeder heitern Nacht.

One should not desire the stars,
But revel in their splendour,
And gaze up with delight
On each unclouded night.

„Und mit Entzücken blick 'ich auf
So manchen lieben Tag;
Verweinen laßt die Nächte mich,
So lang' ich weinen mag."
(*Brahms, Cornelius, Loewe, Reichardt,
Tomášek, Zelter*)

'I have gazed up with delight
For many days on end;
Leave me to weep away my nights,
As long as I wish to weep.'

* The Friedlaender edition has 'Vertraure' = 'mourn'

Da droben auf jenem Berge	On that mountain over there
Da steh' ich tausendmal	I've stood a thousand times,
An meinem Stabe hingebogen	Leaning on my shepherd's staff
Und sehe hinab in das Tal.	Gazing into the valley below.
Dann folg' ich der weidenden Herde,	I follow then the grazing flock
Mein Hündchen bewahret mir sie.	My sheepdog guards for me.
Ich bin herunter gekommen	I've come down to the valley
Und weiß doch selber nicht wie.	And do not myself know how.
Da steht von schönen Blumen	The whole meadow is blooming,
Die ganze Wiese so voll.	Thronged with beautiful flowers.
Ich breche sie, ohne zu wissen,	I pick them without knowing
Wem ich sie geben soll.	Who to give them to.
Und Regen, Sturm und Gewitter	In rain and storm and tempest
Verpaß ich unter dem Baum.	I shelter beneath the tree.
Die Türe dort bleibet verschlossen;	The door over there stays locked;
Und alles ist leider ein Traum.	And all, alas, is a dream.
Es stehet ein Regenbogen	A rainbow arches
Wohl über jenem Haus!	Over that house!
Sie aber ist fortgezogen,	But she has gone away,
Gar weit in das Land hinaus.	Far away to distant parts.
Hinaus in das Land und weiter,	To distant parts and further,
Vielleicht gar über die See.	Perhaps even over the sea.
Vorüber, ihr Schafe, nur vorüber!	Move on, O sheep, move on!
Dem Schäfer ist gar so weh.	Your shepherd feels so sad.
(*Reichardt, Tomášek, Zelter*)	

12 December 1814 Szene aus *Faust* / Scene from *Faust* D126

(CATHEDRAL. ORGAN AND SINGING DURING THE SERVICE. GRETCHEN SURROUNDED BY THE
CONGREGATION. EVIL SPIRIT BEHIND GRETCHEN.)

BÖSER GEIST	EVIL SPIRIT
Wie anders, Gretchen, war dir's,	How differently you felt, Gretchen,
Als du noch voll Unschuld	When you, still full of innocence,
Hier zum Altar trat'st,	Stepped up to the altar here,
Aus dem vergriff'nen Büchelchen	Murmuring prayers
Gebete lalltest,	From your well-thumbed book,
Halb Kinderspiele,	Your heart half full of children's games,
Halb Gott im Herzen!	And half of God!
Gretchen!	Gretchen!
Wo steht dein Kopf?	What are you thinking of?
In deinem Herzen,	What misdeed
Welche Missetat?	Is lodged in your heart?

* This was the first Schubert song to be performed in public (on 28 February 1819)

Bet'st du für deiner Mutter* Seele, die
Durch dich zur langen, langen Pein hinüber-
 schlief?
Auf deiner Schwelle wessen Blut?†
– Und unter deinem Herzen
Regt sich's nicht quillend schon,
Und ängstigt dich und sich
Mit ahnungsvoller Gegenwart?

GRETCHEN
Weh! Weh!
Wär'ich der Gedanken los,
Die mir herüber und hinüber gehen
Wider mich!

CHOR
Dies irae, dies illa,
Solvet saeclum in favilla.
(*Orgelton*)

BÖSER GEIST
Grimm faßt dich!
Die Posaune tönt!
Die Gräber beben!
Und dein Herz,
Aus Aschenruh
Zu Flammenqualen
Wieder aufgeschaffen,
Bebt auf!

GRETCHEN
Wär' ich hier weg!
Mir ist, als ob die Orgel mir
Den Atem versetzte,
Gesang mein Herz
Im Tiefsten lös'te.

CHOR
Judex ergo cum sedebit,
Quidquid latet adparebit,
Nil inultum remanebit.

GRETCHEN
Mir wird so eng!
Die Mauerpfeiler
Befangen mich!
Das Gewölbe
Drängt mich! – Luft!

Do you pray for your mother's soul, who
Through your doing, passed over into long,
 long torment?
Whose blood stains your doorstep?
Does something not stir and swell
Beneath your heart,
Filling you and it
With fear and foreboding?

GRETCHEN
Alas! Alas!
Were I but free of the thoughts
That teem in my mind,
Despite myself!

CHOIR
Day of wrath, on that day
The century shall crumble to ashes.
(*The organ plays*)

EVIL SPIRIT
The wrath of God seizes
 you!
The trump sounds!
Sepulchres quake!
And your heart,
Fanned from ashen sleep
To fiery torment,
Trembles!

GRETCHEN
If only I could escape!
The organ seems
To stifle my breath,
The chanting voices
Pierce my heart.

CHOIR
For when the judge shall hold court,
All that is hidden shall be revealed,
Nothing shall remain unavenged.

GRETCHEN
I feel trapped!
The pillars in the walls
Crowd in on me!
The vaulted roof
Bears down on me! – Air!

* Gretchen, before sleeping with Faust, gave her mother a sleeping potion which killed her.
† Refers to the death of her brother Valentin, killed by Faust.

BÖSER GEIST	EVIL SPIRIT
Verbirg dich! Sünd' und Schande	You think you can hide! Sin and shame
Bleibt nicht verborgen.	Will not stay hidden.
Luft? Licht?	Air? Light?
Wehe dir!	Woe to you!

CHOR	CHOIR
Quid sum miser tunc dicturus?	What am I, wretched one, to say?
Quem patronum rogaturus?	What patron am I to implore,
Cum vix justus sit securus.	When scarcely the just man is secure?

BÖSER GEIST	EVIL SPIRIT
Ihr Antlitz wenden	Transfigured souls
Verklärte von dir ab.	Recoil from you.
Die Hände dir zu reichen,	The pure in heart shudder
Schauert's den Reinen.	At the thought of helping you.
Weh!	Woe!

CHOR	CHOIR
Quid sum miser tunc dicturus?	What am I, wretched one, to say?
Quem patronum rogaturus?	What patron am I to implore?

?1815 Geistes-Gruß / Ghostly greeting D142

Hoch auf dem alten Turme steht	High on the ancient turret
Des Helden edler Geist,	Stands the hero's noble shade,
Der, wie das Schiff vorüber geht,	And bids the passing ship
Es wohl zu fahren heißt.	A safe voyage.

„Sieh, diese Senne war so stark,	'See, these sinews were so strong,
Dies Herz so fest und wild,	This heart so wild and steadfast,
Die Knochen voll von Rittermark,	These limbs full of knightly valour,
Der Becher angefüllt;	This goblet filled to the brim;

Mein halbes Leben stürmt' ich fort,	For half my life I ventured forth,
Verdehnt' die Hälft' in Ruh,	In peace the other half stretched out,
Und du, du Menschen-Schifflein dort,	And you, little ship of mankind,
Fahr' immer, immer zu!"	Sail onward, ever onward!'
(*Medtner, Reichardt, Tomášek, Zelter*)	

Am Flusse / By the river
FIRST VERSION: D160 (27 FEBRUARY 1815)
SECOND VERSION: D766 (DECEMBER 1822)

Verfließet, vielgeliebte Lieder,	Flow on, songs I loved so well,
Zum Meere der Vergessenheit!	To the ocean of oblivion!
Kein Knabe sing' entzückt euch wieder,	Let no youth sing you again,
Kein Mädchen in der Blütenzeit.	Or maiden in the spring of life.

Ihr sanget nur von meiner Lieben;	You sang solely of my beloved;

Nun spricht sie meiner Treue Hohn.
Ihr wart in's Wasser eingeschrieben;
So fließt denn auch mit ihm davon.
(*Hensel, Reichardt, Tomášek*)

She now scorns my constancy.
You were written in water;
So with the water flow away.

27 February 1815 An Mignon / To Mignon D161

Über Tal und Fluß getragen
Ziehet rein der Sonne Wagen.
Ach! sie regt in ihrem Lauf,
So wie deine, meine Schmerzen,
Tief im Herzen,
Immer morgens wieder auf.

Over valley and stream
The sun's chariot moves chastely along.
Ah! it wakens in its course
Your agonies and mine,
Deep in our hearts,
Each new morning.

Kaum will mir die Nacht noch frommen,
Denn die Träume selber kommen
Nun in trauriger Gestalt,
Und ich fühle dieser Schmerzen,
Still im Herzen,
Heimlich bildende Gewalt.

Night brings but scant relief,
For dreams themselves now come
In melancholy guise,
And silently in my heart
I feel the secret might
Of those agonies grow in my heart.

Schon seit manchen schönen Jahren
Seh' ich unten Schiffe fahren;
Jedes kommt an seinen Ort;
Aber ach! die steten Schmerzen,
Fest im Herzen,
Schwimmen nicht im Strome fort.

For many a long year
I have watched the ships sail below;
Each one reaches its haven;
But ah! the constant agonies
Deep in my heart,
Are not borne away in the river.

Schön in Kleidern muß ich kommen,
Aus dem Schrank sind sie genommen,
Weil es heute Festtag ist;
Niemand ahnet, daß von Schmerzen
Herz im Herzen,
Grimmig mir zerrissen ist.

I must come in fine clothing,
Taken from the closet,
For today's a holiday;
No one suspects
That in my inmost heart
I'm racked by savage pain.

Heimlich muß ich immer weinen,
Aber freundlich kann ich scheinen
Und sogar gesund und rot;
Wären tödlich diese Schmerzen
Meinem Herzen,
Ach! schon lange wär' ich tot.
(*Reichardt, Spohr, Zelter, Zumsteeg*)

Secretly I must keep weeping,
Yet outwardly I can seem cheerful,
Even ruddy and well;
If these agonies
Were fatal to my heart,
Ah! I would long ago have died.

27 February 1815 Nähe des Geliebten / Nearness of the beloved D162

Ich denke dein, wenn mir der Sonne Schimmer
    Vom Meere strahlt;
Ich denke dein, wenn sich des Mondes Flimmer
    In Quellen malt.

I think of you, when the shimmering sun
    Streams from the sea;
I think of you, when the glittering moon
    Is mirrored in springs.

Ich sehe dich, wenn auf dem fernen Wege
    Der Staub sich hebt;
In tiefer Nacht, wenn auf dem schmalen Stege
    Der Wandrer bebt.

Ich höre dich, wenn dort mit dumpfem
    Rauschen
    Die Welle steigt.
Im stillen Hain, da geh' ich oft zu lauschen,
    Wenn alles schweigt.

Ich bin bei dir, du seist auch noch so ferne,
    Du bist mir nah!
Die Sonne sinkt, bald leuchten mir die Sterne.
    O wärst du da!
(*Burgmüller, Hensel, Hindemith, Kreutzer,
Josephine Lang, Loewe, Medtner, Reichardt,
Schumann, Tomášek, Zelter, Zillig*)

I see you, when on distant paths
    The dust rises;
In deep night, when on the narrow bridge,
    The traveller trembles.

I hear you, when with muffled
    roar
    The waves surge.
I often listen in the quiet grove,
    When all is silent.

I am with you, however far you be,
    You are by my side!
The sun sets, soon the stars will shine on me.
    O that you were here!

19 May 1815 Rastlose Liebe / Restless love D138

Dem Schnee, dem Regen,
Dem Wind entgegen,
Im Dampf der Klüfte,
Durch Nebeldüfte,
Immer zu! Immer zu!
Ohne Rast und Ruh!

Lieber durch Leiden
Wollt'ich mich schlagen,
Als so viel Freuden
Des Lebens ertragen.
Alle das Neigen
Von Herzen zu Herzen,
Ach wie so eigen
Schaffet es Schmerzen!

Wie soll ich flieh'n?
Wälderwärts zieh'n?
Alles vergebens!
Krone des Lebens,
Glück ohne Ruh,
Liebe, bist du.
(*Franz, Raff, Reichardt, Schoeck, Schumann,
Tomášek, Zelter*)

Into snow, into rain,
Into wind,
Through steaming ravines,
Through mist and haze,
On and on!
Without respite!

I'd rather fight
My way through affliction
Than endure so many
Of life's joys.
All this attraction
Of heart to heart,
Ah, what special
Anguish it brings!

How shall I flee?
Fly to the forest?
All in vain!
Crown of life,
Joy without rest –
This, Love, is you.

Jägers Abendlied / Huntsman's evening song
FIRST VERSION: D215 (20 JUNE 1815)
SECOND VERSION: D368 (EARLY 1816)

Im Felde schleich' ich still und wild,
Gespannt mein Feuerrohr,
Da schwebt so licht dein liebes Bild,
Dein süßes Bild mir vor.

I creep through fields, silent and fierce,
My firearm at the ready,
Your dear image suddenly looms
So bright and sweet before me.

Du wandelst jetzt wohl still und mild
Durch Feld und liebes Tal,
Und ach, mein schnell verrauschend Bild,
Stellt sich dir's nicht einmal?

You no doubt walk gently now
Silent through fields and dear valley,
And ah, does my fast fading image
Not even appear to you?

Des Menschen, der die Welt durchstreift
Voll Unmut und Verdruß,
Nach Osten und nach Westen schweift,
Weil er dich lassen muß.

The image of one who roves the world,
Ill-humoured and morose,
Roaming eastward and roaming westward,
Because he must part from you.

Mir ist es, denk' ich nur an dich,
Als in den Mond zu sehn;
Ein stiller Friede kommt auf mich,
Weiß nicht wie mir geschehn.
(*Hensel, Kayser, Medtner, Reichardt, Tomášek,
Zelter*)

If I but only think of you,
I seem to gaze into the moon;
A silent peace steals over me,
But how, I cannot tell.

Meeres Stille / Calm sea
FIRST VERSION: D215A (20 JUNE 1815)
SECOND VERSION: D216 (21 JUNE 1815)

Tiefe Stille herrscht im Wasser,
Ohne Regung ruht das Meer,
Und bekümmert sieht der Schiffer
Glatte Fläche rings umher.
Keine Luft von keiner Seite!
Todesstille fürchterlich!
In der ungeheuern Weite
Reget keine Welle sich.
(*Beethoven, Griffes, MacDowell, Medtner,
Reichardt*)

Deep silence weighs on the water,
Motionless the sea rests,
And the fearful boatman sees
A glassy surface all around.
No breeze from any quarter!
Fearful, deadly silence!
In all that vast expanse
Not a single ripple stirs.

5 July 1815 Wandrers Nachtlied I / Wanderer's nightsong I D224

Der du von dem Himmel bist,
Alles Leid und Schmerzen stillst,
Den, der doppelt elend ist,
Doppelt mit Entzückung füllst,
Ach, ich bin des Treibens müde!
Was soll all der Schmerz und Lust?

You who come from heaven,
Soothing all pain and sorrow,
Filling the doubly wretched
Doubly with delight,
Ah, I am weary of this restlessness!
What use is all this joy and pain?

Süßer Friede!
Komm, ach komm in meine Brust!
(*Hensel, Kayser, Liszt, Loewe, Marx, Medtner,*
Pfitzner, Tomášek, Wolf, Zelter, Zemlinsky)

Sweet peace!
Come, ah come into my breast!

5 July 1815 Der Fischer / The angler D225

Das Wasser rauscht', das Wasser schwoll,
Ein Fischer saß daran,
Sah nach der Angel ruhevoll,
Kühl bis ans Herz hinan.
Und wie er sitzt und wie er lauscht,
Teilt sich die Flut empor;
Aus dem bewegten Wasser rauscht
Ein feuchtes Weib hervor.

The water rushed, the water rose,
An angler on the bank
Sat gazing calmly at his line,
Cool to his very heart.
And as he sits and listens,
The waters surge and part;
And from the water's churning swell
A water-nymph arose.

Sie sang zu ihm, sie sprach zu ihm:
Was lockst du meine Brut,
Mit Menschenwitz und Menschenlist,
Hinauf in Todesglut?
Ach! wüßtest du, wie's Fischlein ist
So wohlig auf dem Grund,
Du stiegst herunter, wie du bist,
Und würdest erst gesund.

She sang to him, she spoke to him:
Why lure my brood away
With human wit and human guile
To the deadly blaze of day?
Ah! if you but knew how blithe and free
The fish all thrive below,
You'd descend, just as you are,
And only then feel whole.

Labt sich die liebe Sonne nicht,
Der Mond sich nicht im Meer?
Kehrt wellenatmend ihr Gesicht
Nicht doppelt schöner her?
Lockt dich der tiefe Himmel nicht,
Das feuchtverklärte Blau?
Lockt dich dein eigen Angesicht
Nicht her in ew'gen Tau?

Does not the dear sun refresh itself,
The moon too in the sea?
Do not their faces, breathing waves,
Return here doubly fair?
Are you not enticed by this deep sky,
This moist transfigured blue?
Does not your own face draw you down
Into this eternal dew?

Das Wasser rauscht', das Wasser schwoll,
Netzt' ihm den nackten Fuß;
Sein Herz wuchs ihm so sehnsuchtsvoll,
Wie bei der Liebsten Gruß.
Sie sprach zu ihm, sie sang zu ihm;
Da war's um ihn geschehn:
Halb zog sie ihn, halb sank er hin,
Und ward nicht mehr gesehn.
(*Hensel, Loewe, Reichardt, Robert Schumann,*
Strauss, Tomášek, Vesque von Püttlingen, Wolf,
Zelter)

The water rushed, the water rose
And wet his naked feet;
He felt such longing in his heart,
As though his love were calling.
She spoke to him, she sang to him;
And then his fate was sealed:
Half dragged, half willing, down he sank,
And was not seen again.

5 July 1815 Erster Verlust / First loss D226
FROM *Die ungleichen Hausgenossen*

Ach, wer bringt die schönen Tage,
Jene Tage der ersten Liebe,
Ach, wer bringt nur eine Stunde
Jener holden Zeit zurück!

Einsam nähr' ich meine Wunde,
Und mit stets erneuter Klage
Traur' ich um's verlorne Glück.

Ach, wer bringt die schönen Tage,
Wer jene holde Zeit zurück!
(*Berg, Hensel, Knab, Medtner, Mendelssohn,
Reichardt, Schoeck, Tomášek, Zelter*)

Ah, who will bring the fair days back,
Those days of first love,
Ah, who will bring but one hour back
Of that radiant time!

In my loneliness I feed my wound,
And with ever renewed lament
Mourn the happiness I lost.

Ah, who will bring the fair days back,
Who that radiant time!

August 1815 Die Spinnerin / The spinster D247

Als ich still und ruhig spann,
Ohne nur zu stocken,
Trat ein schöner junger Mann
Nahe mir zum Rocken.

Lobte, was zu loben war:
Sollte das was schaden?
Mein dem Flachse gleiches Haar,
Und den gleichen Faden.

Ruhig war er nicht dabei,
Ließ es nicht beim Alten;
Und der Faden riß entzwei,
Den ich lang' erhalten.

Und des Flachses Steingewicht
Gab noch viele Zahlen;
Aber, ach, ich konnte nicht
Mehr mit ihnen prahlen.

Als ich sie zum Weber trug,
Fühlt' ich was sich regen,
Und mein armes Herze schlug
Mit geschwindern Schlägen.

Nun, beim heißen Sonnenstich,
Bring' ich's auf die Bleiche,
Und mit Mühe bück' ich mich
Nach dem nächsten Teiche.

Was ich in dem Kämmerlein
Still und fein gesponnen,

As I kept spinning on and on,
Quietly without stopping,
A young and handsome gentleman
Approached me at the staff.

He duly complimented me –
How could that do harm? –
On my hair resembling flax
And the flaxen thread.

He was anything but calm,
Would not let things be;
And the thread I'd held so long
Suddenly snapped in two.

And the distaff's weight of stone
Still spun many threads;
But ah, I could no longer
Proudly show them off.

When I took them to the weaver,
I felt something stir,
And my poor heart began to pound
With much quicker beats.

Now, beneath the scorching sun,
I bring them to the bleachery,
And with effort I bend down
By the nearest pool.

What I've so secretly spun
In my little room

Kommt – wie kann es anders sein –
Endlich an die Sonnen.
(*Reichardt, Ries, Tomášek*)

Will – how could it otherwise? –
Be discovered in the end.

19 August 1815 Heidenröslein / The little wild rose D257

Sah ein Knab ein Röslein stehn,
Röslein auf der Heiden,
War so jung und morgenschön,
Lief er schnell es nah zu sehn,
Sah's mit vielen Freuden.
Röslein, Röslein, Röslein rot,
Röslein auf der Heiden.

A boy once saw a wild rose growing,
Wild rose on the heath,
It was so young and morning-fair,
He ran to look more closely,
Looked on it with great delight.
Wild rose, wild rose, wild rose red,
Wild rose on the heath.

Knabe sprach: Ich breche dich,
Röslein auf der Heiden!
Röslein sprach: Ich steche dich,
Daß du ewig denkst an mich,
Und ich will's nicht leiden.
Röslein, Röslein, Röslein rot,
Röslein auf der Heiden.

I shall pluck you, said the boy,
Wild rose on the heath!
I shall prick you, said the rose,
That you'll ever think of me,
I shall not let you do it.
Wild rose, wild rose, wild rose red,
Wild rose on the heath.

Und der wilde Knabe brach
's Röslein auf der Heiden;
Röslein wehrte sich und stach,
Half ihm doch kein Weh und Ach,
Mußt' es eben leiden.
Röslein, Röslein, Röslein rot,
Röslein auf der Heiden.
(*Brahms, Lehár, Reichardt, Reissiger, Robert
Schumann, Tomášek*)

And the rough boy plucked the rose,
Wild rose on the heath;
In defence the rose then pricked,
Sighs and cries were all in vain,
She had to suffer after all.
Wild rose, wild rose, wild rose red,
Wild rose on the heath.

An den Mond / To the moon
FIRST VERSION: 19 AUGUST 1815 (D259)
SECOND VERSION: ? 1819 (D296)

Füllest wieder Busch und Tal
Still mit Nebelglanz,
Lösest endlich auch einmal
Meine Seele ganz;

Once more you fill wood and vale
Silently with radiant mist,
And at last
Set my soul quite free;

Breitest über mein Gefild
Lindernd deinen Blick,
Wie des Freundes Auge mild
Über mein Geschick.

Soothingly you spread your gaze
Over my domain,
Like a gentle friend
Watching over my fate.

Jeden Nachklang fühlt mein Herz
Froh- und trüber Zeit,
Wandle zwischen Freud' und Schmerz
In der Einsamkeit.

My heart feels every echo
Of happy times and sad,
I drift between joy and pain
In my loneliness.

Fließe, fließe, lieber Fluß!	Flow, flow on, beloved river!
Nimmer werd' ich froh,	Never shall I be happy,
So verrauschte Scherz und Kuß,	This was how they streamed away,
Und die Treue so.	Kisses, laughter, faithfulness.
Ich besaß es doch einmal,	Yet I once possessed
Was so köstlich ist!	What is so precious!
Daß man doch zu seiner Qual	Ah, the torment
Nimmer es vergißt!	Of never forgetting it!
Rausche, Fluß, das Tal entlang,	Murmur, river, along the valley,
Ohne Rast und ohne Ruh,	Ever onward without cease,
Rausche, flüstre meinem Sang	Murmur, whisper for my songs
Melodien zu,	Your melodies,
Wenn du in der Winternacht	As when on winter nights
Wütend überschwillst,	You rage and break your banks,
Oder um die Frühlingspracht	Or when you bathe the springtime splendour
Junger Knospen quillst.	Of burgeoning young buds.
Selig, wer sich vor der Welt	Happy are they who, without hate,
Ohne Haß verschließt,	Withdraw from the world,
Einen Freund am Busen hält	Holding to their heart one friend
Und mit dem genießt,	And with him enjoy
Was von Menschen nicht gewußt	What, unknown to human kind,
Oder nicht bedacht,	Or not even pondered,
Durch das Labyrinth der Brust	Drifts through the heart's
Wandelt in der Nacht.	Labyrinth at night.
(*Hensel, Pfitzner, Reichardt, Tomášek, Zelter*)	

October 1815 Erlkönig* / Erlking D328
FROM *Die Fischerin*

Wer reitet so spät durch Nacht und Wind?	Who rides so late through night and wind?
Es ist der Vater mit seinem Kind;	It is the father with his child;
Er hat den Knaben wohl in dem Arm,	He has the boy safe in his arms,
Er faßt ihn sicher, er hält ihn warm.	He holds him close, he keeps him warm.
„Mein Sohn, was birgst du so bang dein Gesicht?"	'My son, why hide your face in fear?'
„Siehst, Vater, du den Erlkönig nicht?	'Can't you see the Erlking, father?
Den Erlenkönig mit Kron' und Schweif?"	The Erlking with his crown and robe?'
„Mein Sohn, es ist ein Nebelstreif."	'My son, it is a streak of mist.'
„Du liebes Kind, komm, geh mit mir!	'You sweetest child, come go with me!
Gar schöne Spiele spiel' ich mit dir;	Wondrous games I'll play with you;
Manch' bunte Blumen sind an dem Strand;	Many bright flowers grow on the shore;
Meine Mutter hat manch gülden Gewand."	My mother has many a garment of gold.'

* There is also a simplified version in duple quavers, not triplets, that Schubert himself was said to have used.

„Mein Vater, mein Vater, und hörest du nicht,	'Father, O father, can't you hear
Was Erlenkönig mir leise verspricht?"	The Erlking's whispered promises?'
„Sei ruhig, bleibe ruhig, mein Kind;	'Be calm, stay calm, my child,
In dürren Blättern säuselt der Wind."	The wind is rustling in withered leaves.'

„Willst, feiner Knabe, du mit mir gehn?	'Won't you come with me, fine boy?
Meine Töchter sollen dich warten schön;	My daughters shall take good care of you;
Meine Töchter führen den nächtlichen Reihn,	My daughters lead the nightly dance,
Und wiegen und tanzen und singen dich ein."	And will rock and dance and sing you to sleep.'

„Mein Vater, mein Vater, und siehst du nicht dort	'Father, O father, can't you see
Erlkönigs Töchter am düstern Ort?"	The Erlking's daughters there in the gloom?'
„Mein Sohn, mein Sohn, ich seh' es genau;	'My son, my son, I can see quite clearly:
Es scheinen die alten Weiden so grau."	It's the old willows gleaming so grey.'

„Ich liebe dich, mich reizt deine schöne Gestalt;	'I love you. Your beautiful figure excites me;
Und bist du nicht willig, so brauch' ich Gewalt."	And if you're not willing, I'll take you by force.'
„Mein Vater, mein Vater, jetzt faßt er mich an!	'Father, O father, he's seizing me now!
Erlkönig hat mir ein Leids getan!"	The Erlking's done me harm!'

Dem Vater grauset's, er reitet geschwind,	The father shudders, swiftly he rides,
Er hält in Armen das ächzende Kind,	With the groaning child in his arms,
Erreicht den Hof mit Müh' und Not;	With a final effort he reaches home;
In seinen Armen das Kind war tot.	The child lay dead in his arms.
(*Beethoven [sketch], Loewe, Reichardt, Corona Schröter, Spohr, Tomášek, Zelter*)	

1816 Der König in Thule* / The king in Thule D367
FROM *Faust*

Es war ein König in Thule	There was a king in Thule,
Gar treu bis an das Grab,	Faithful to the grave,
Dem sterbend seine Buhle	To whom his mistress, as she died,
Einen goldnen Becher gab.	Gave a golden beaker.

Es ging ihm nichts darüber,	He valued nothing higher,
Er leert' ihn jeden Schmaus;	He drained it at every feast,
Die Augen gingen ihm über,	And each time he drank from it,
So oft er trank daraus.	His eyes would fill with tears.

Und als er kam zu sterben,	And when he came to die,
Zählt' er seine Städt' im Reich,	He counted the cities of his realm,
Gönnt' alles seinen Erben,	Gave all he had to his heirs,
Den Becher nicht zugleich.	The beaker though excepted.

Er saß beim Königsmahle,	He sat at the royal banquet,
Die Ritter um ihn her,	Surrounded by his knights,

---

* An unidentified island in the North Sea, called 'Ultima' by the ancients, because of its great distance from the continent.

Auf hohem Vätersaale,	There in the lofty ancestral hall,
Dort auf dem Schloß am Meer.	In the castle by the sea.
Dort stand der alte Zecher,	There he stood, that old toper,
Trank letzte Lebensglut,	Drank his life's last glow,
Und warf den heil'gen Becher	And hurled the sacred beaker
Hinunter in die Flut.	Into the waves below.
Er sah ihn stürzen, trinken	He saw it fall and fill
Und sinken tief ins Meer.	And sink deep into the sea.
Die Augen täten ihm sinken;	His eyes closed;
Trank nie einen Tropfen mehr.	He never drank another drop.
(*Berlioz, Liszt, Marschner, Reichardt, Silcher,*	
Tomášek, Zelter)	

?1816 An Schwager Kronos* / To Coachman Chronos D369

Spute dich, Kronos!	Make haste, Chronos!
Fort den rasselnden Trott!	Away at a rattling trot!
Bergab gleitet der Weg;	The road runs downhill;
Ekles Schwindeln zögert	I grow nauseous and giddy
Mir vor die Stirne dein Zaudern.	At your dawdling.
Frisch, holpert es gleich,	Quick, though the road is rough,
Über Stock und Steine den Trott	Speed past hedge and ditch
Rasch in's Leben hinein!	Headlong into life!
Nun schon wieder	Now once more
Den eratmenden Schritt	You toil uphill
Mühsam Berg hinauf!	Out of breath!
Auf denn, nicht träge denn,	Up then, don't be sluggish,
Strebend und hoffend hinan!	Upwards, striving, hoping!
Weit, hoch, herrlich rings den Blick	Wide, high, glorious
Ins Leben hinein;	The view all around into life;
Vom Gebirg' zum Gebirg'	From mountain range to mountain range
Schwebet der ewige Geist,	The eternal spirit soars,
Ewigen Lebens ahndevoll.	Presaging eternal life.
Seitwärts des Überdachs Schatten	A shade-giving roof
Zieht dich an	Draws you aside
Und ein Frischung verheißender Blick	And the girl's gaze
Auf der Schwelle des Mädchens da.	Promises refreshment on the step.
Labe dich – Mir auch, Mädchen,	Take comfort – give me too, lass,
Diesen schäumenden Trank,	This foaming draught,
Diesen frischen Gesundheitsblick!	This fresh, health-giving look!
Ab denn, rascher hinab!	Downhill, then, faster down!
Sieh, die Sonne sinkt!	See, the sun is sinking!

* The Greek name of Saturn, or time.

Eh' sie sinkt, eh' mich Greisen
Ergreift im Moore Nebelduft,
Entzahnte Kiefern schnattern
Und das schlotternde Gebein –

Trunknen vom letzten Strahl
Reiß mich, ein Feuermeer
Mir im schäumenden Aug',
Mich geblendeten Taumelnden
In der Hölle nächtliches Tor.

Töne, Schwager, ins Horn,
Raßle den schallenden Trab,
Daß der Orkus vernehme: wir kommen,
Daß gleich an der Tür
Der Wirt uns freundlich empfange.

Before it sinks and I, an old man,
Am trapped on the misty moor,
With toothless jaws chattering
And limbs shaking –

Snatch me, still drunk
With its last rays, a fiery sea
Glinting in my eyes,
Dazzled and reeling
Into Hell's night gate.

Coachman, sound your horn,
Clatter resoundingly on,
Let Orcus know: we're coming,
So mine host will be there
To greet us at the gate.

?March 1817 Auf dem See / On the lake D543

Und frische Nahrung, neues Blut
Saug' ich aus freier Welt;
Wie ist Natur so hold und gut,
Die mich am Busen hält!
Die Welle wieget unsern Kahn
Im Rudertakt hinauf,
Und Berge, wolkig himmelan,
Begegnen unserm Lauf.

And fresh nourishment, new blood
I suck from these open spaces;
How sweet and kindly Nature is,
Who holds me to her breast!
The waves cradle our boat
To the rhythm of the oars,
And mountains, soaring skywards in cloud,
Meet us in our path.

Aug', mein Aug', was sinkst du nieder?
Goldne Träume, kommt ihr wieder?
Weg, du Traum! so gold du bist;
Hier auch Lieb' und Leben ist.

Why, my eyes, do you look down?
Golden dreams, will you return?
Away, O dream, however golden;
Here too is love and life.

Auf der Welle blinken
Tausend schwebende Sterne,
Weiche Nebel trinken
Rings die türmende Ferne;
Morgenwind umflügelt
Die beschattete Bucht,
Und im See bespiegelt
Sich die reifende Frucht.
(*Loewe, Medtner, Reichardt, Tomášek, Wolf*)

Stars in their thousands
Drift and glitter on the waves,
Gentle mists drink in
The towering skyline;
Morning breezes flutter
Round the shaded bay,
And the ripening fruit
Is reflected in the lake.

March 1817 Ganymed* / Ganymede D544

Wie im Morgenglanze
Du rings mich anglühst,
Frühling, Geliebter!

How in the morning radiance
You glow at me from all sides,
Spring, beloved!

* Son of Tros, taken up to Heaven to serve as cup-bearer to the gods.

Mit tausendfacher Liebeswonne
Sich an mein Herze drängt
Deiner ewigen Wärme
Heilig Gefühl,
Unendliche Schöne!

Daß ich dich fassen möcht'
In diesen Arm!

Ach an deinem Busen
Lieg' ich und schmachte,
Und deine Blumen, dein Gras
Drängen sich an mein Herz.
Du kühlst den brennenden
Durst meines Busens,
Lieblicher Morgenwind!
Ruft drein die Nachtigall
Liebend nach mir aus dem Nebeltal.

Ich komm', ich komme!
Ach wohin, wohin?

Hinauf strebt's, hinauf!
Es schweben die Wolken
Abwärts, die Wolken
Neigen sich der sehnenden Liebe.
Mir! Mir!
In eurem Schoße
Aufwärts!
Umfangend umfangen!
Aufwärts an deinen Busen,
Alliebender Vater!
(*Loewe, Reichardt, Wolf*)

With thousandfold delights of love,
The sacred feeling
Of your eternal warmth
Presses against my heart,
Beauty without end!

To clasp you
In these arms!

Ah, on your breast,
I lie and languish,
And your flowers, your grass
Press against my heart.
You cool the burning
Thirst of my breast,
Sweet morning breeze!
The nightingale calls out to me
Longingly from the misty valley.

I come, I come!
Where? Ah, where?

Upwards! Upwards I'm driven!
The clouds float
Down, the clouds
Bow to yearning love.
To me! To me!
Enveloped by you
Upwards!
Embraced and embracing!
Upwards to your bosom,
All-loving Father!

May 1817 Liebhaber in allen Gestalten / A lover in all disguises D558

Ich wollt', ich wär' ein Fisch,
So hurtig und frisch;
Und kämst du zu angeln,
Ich würde nicht mangeln.
Ich wollt', ich wär' ein Fisch,
So hurtig und frisch.

Ich wollt', ich wär' ein Pferd,
Da wär' ich dir wert.
O wär' ich ein Wagen,
Bequem dich zu tragen.
Ich wollt', ich wär' ein Pferd!
Da wär' ich dir wert.

I wish I were a fish,
So brisk and quick;
And if you came with your rod,
I'd not fail to bite.
I wish I were a fish,
So brisk and quick.

I wish I were a horse,
You'd value me then.
O if I were a coach,
I'd carry you in comfort.
I wish I were a horse,
You'd value me then.

Ich wollt', ich wäre Gold!	I wish I were gold!
Dir immer im Sold;	Always at your service;
Und tätst du was kaufen,	And if you bought something,
Käm' ich gelaufen.	I'd come running again.
Ich wollt', ich wäre Gold!	I wish I were gold!
Dir immer im Sold.	Always at your service.
Doch bin ich wie ich bin,	But I am as I am,
Und nimm mich nur hin!	Just take me as such!
Willst beßre besitzen,	If you want someone better,
So laß dir sie schnitzen.	Have someone better made.
Ich bin nun wie ich bin;	I am as I am;
So nimm mich nur hin!	Just take me as such!
(*Zelter*)	

May 1817 Gretchens Bitte / Gretchen's prayer D564
FROM *Faust*

Ach neige,	Ah, incline your countenance,
Du Schmerzenreiche,	You who are full of sorrow,
Dein Antlitz gnädig meiner Not!	To my distress!
Das Schwert im Herzen,	With the sword in your heart,
Mit tausend Schmerzen	And a thousand griefs,
Blickst auf zu deines Sohnes Tod.	You look up at your dying son.
Zum Vater blickst du,	You gaze up to the Father
Und Seufzer schickst du	And utter sighs
Hinauf um sein' und deine Not.	For His affliction and your own.
Wer fühlet,	Who can feel
Wie wühlet	How the pain
Der Schmerz mir im Gebein?	Churns in my bones?
Was mein armes Herz hier banget,	What my poor heart dreads,
Was es zittert, was verlanget,	Why it quakes, what it craves,
Weißt nur du, nur du allein!	Only you, only you can know!
Wohin ich immer gehe,	Wherever I go,
Wie weh, wie weh, wie wehe	How it throbs, it throbs, it throbs
Wird mir im Busen hier!	Here in my breast!
Ich bin ach kaum alleine,	Alas, as soon as I'm alone,
Ich wein', ich wein', ich weine,	I weep, I weep, I weep,
Das Herz zerbricht in mir.	My heart breaks.
(*Loewe, Verdi, Wagner, Wolf*)	

? Autumn 1819 Hoffnung / Hope D295

Schaff', das Tagwerk meiner Hände,	Grant, O Fortune, that my hands
Hohes Glück, daß ich's vollende!	Might fulfil their daily task!
Laß, o laß mich nicht ermatten!	Let, O let me not grow weary!

Nein, es sind nicht leere Träume:　　　No, these are not empty dreams:
Jetzt nur Stangen, diese Bäume　　　　These trees, now mere shafts,
Geben einst noch Frucht und Schatten.　Will one day yield fruit and shade.

October 1819　Prometheus* / Prometheus　D674

Bedecke deinen Himmel, Zeus,　　　　Cover your heaven, Zeus,
Mit Wolkendunst,　　　　　　　　　　With cloudy vapours,
Und übe, dem Knaben gleich,　　　　　And test your strength, like a boy
Der Disteln köpft,　　　　　　　　　Beheading thistles,
An Eichen dich und Bergeshöhn;　　　On oaks and mountain peaks;
Mußt mir meine Erde　　　　　　　　Yet you must leave
Doch lassen stehn,　　　　　　　　　My earth alone,
Und meine Hütte, die du nicht gebaut,　And my hut you did not build,
Und meinen Herd,　　　　　　　　　And my hearth,
Um dessen Glut　　　　　　　　　　Whose fire
Du mich beneidest.　　　　　　　　You envy me.

Ich kenne nichts Ärmeres　　　　　I know nothing more paltry
Unter der Sonn' als euch, Götter!　Beneath the sun than you, gods!
Ihr nährt kümmerlich　　　　　　Meagrely you nourish
Vom Opfersteuern　　　　　　　Your majesty
Und Gebetshauch　　　　　　　On levied offerings
Eure Majestät,　　　　　　　　And the breath of prayer,
Und darbtet, wären　　　　　　And would starve, were
Nicht Kinder und Bettler　　　Not children and beggars
Hoffnungsvolle Toren.　　　　Optimistic fools.

Da ich ein Kind war,　　　　　When I was a child,
Nicht wußte, wo aus noch ein,　Not knowing which way to turn,
Kehrt' ich mein verirrtes Auge　I raised my misguided eyes
Zur Sonne, als wenn drüber wär'　To the sun, as if above it there were
Ein Ohr, zu hören meine Klage,　An ear to hear my lament,
Ein Herz, wie mein's,　　　　　A heart like mine,
Sich des Bedrängten zu erbarmen.　To pity me in my anguish.

Wer half mir　　　　　　　　Who helped me
Wider der Titanen Übermut?　Withstand the Titans' insolence?
Wer rettete vom Tode mich,　Who saved me from death
Von Sklaverei?　　　　　　　And slavery?
Hast du nicht alles selbst　Did you not accomplish all this yourself,
　vollendet,　　　　　　　　Sacred glowing heart?
Heilig glühend Herz?　　　　And did you not – young, innocent,
Und glühtest jung und gut,　Deceived – glow with gratitude for your
Betrogen, Rettungsdank　　　　deliverance
Dem Schlafenden da droben?　To that slumberer in the skies?

* Prometheus was punished by Jupiter for stealing fire from the chariot of the sun; he was tied to a rock,
where for 30,000 years a vulture was to feed on his liver.

Ich dich ehren! Wofür?
Hast du die Schmerzen gelindert
Je des Beladenen?
Hast du die Tränen gestillet
Je des Geängsteten?
Hat mich nicht zum Manne geschmiedet
Die allmächtige Zeit
Und das ewige Schicksal,
Meine Herrn und deine?

Wähntest du etwa,
Ich sollte das Leben hassen,
In Wüsten fliehen,
Weil nicht alle
Blütenträume reiften?

Hier sitz' ich, forme Menschen
Nach meinem Bilde,
Ein Geschlecht, das mir gleich sei,
Zu leiden, zu weinen,
Zu genießen und zu freuen sich,
Und dein nicht zu achten,
Wie ich!
(*Reichardt, Wolf*)

I honour you? Why?
Did you ever soothe the anguish
That weighed me down?
Did you ever dry my tears
When I was terrified?
Was I not forged into manhood
By all-powerful Time
And everlasting Fate,
My masters and yours?

Did you suppose
I should hate life,
Flee into the wilderness,
Because not all
My blossoming dreams bore fruit?

Here I sit, making men
In my own image,
A race that shall be like me,
That shall suffer, weep,
Know joy and delight,
And ignore you,
As I do!

February 1821 Versunken / Immersed D715

Voll Locken kraus ein Haupt so rund! –
Und darf ich dann in solchen reichen
    Haaren
Mit vollen Händen hin und wieder fahren,
Da fühl' ich mich von Herzensgrund gesund.
Und küß ich Stirne, Bogen, Auge, Mund,
Dann bin ich frisch und immer wieder wund.
Der fünfzackte Kamm, wo sollt' er
    stocken?
Er kehrt schon wieder zu den Locken.
Das Ohr versagt sich nicht dem Spiel,
So zart zum Scherz, so liebeviel!
Doch wie man auf dem Köpfchen kraut,
Man wird in solchen reichen Haaren
Für ewig auf und nieder fahren.

Such a round head, such a tangle of curls! –
And when she lets me run my fingers
To and fro in these thick locks
The depths of my heart are healed.
And when I kiss forehead, eyebrows, eyes,
    mouth,
I'm repeatedly stricken afresh.
Where shall this five-fingered comb stop?
Already it returns to her hair.
Her ear too joins in the game,
So delicate for dalliance, so rich in
    love!
But he who tousles this little head
Will run his hands up and down
These thick locks forever.

March 1821 Grenzen der Menschheit / Limitations of mankind D716

Wenn der uralte
Heilige Vater
Mit gelassener Hand
Aus rollenden Wolken

When the ancient of days,
The holy father
With a serene hand
From rolling clouds

Segnende Blitze	Scatters beneficent lightning
Über die Erde sät,	Over the earth,
Küss' ich den letzten	I kiss the extreme
Saum seines Kleides,	Hem of his garment,
Kindliche Schauer	Childlike awe
Tief in der Brust.	Deep in my breast.
Denn mit Göttern	For no man
Soll sich nicht messen	Should measure himself
Irgend ein Mensch.	Against the gods.
Hebt er sich aufwärts,	If he reaches up
Und berührt	And touches
Mit dem Scheitel die Sterne,	The stars with his head,
Nirgends haften dann	His uncertain feet
Die unsichern Sohlen,	Lose their hold,
Und mit ihm spielen	And clouds and winds
Wolken und Winde.	Make sport of him.
Steht er mit festen,	If he stands with firm,
Markigen Knochen	Sturdy limbs
Auf der wohlgegründeten,	On the solid
Dauernden Erde,	Enduring earth,
Reicht er nicht auf,	He cannot even reach up
Nur mit der Eiche	To compare himself
Oder der Rebe	With the oak
Sich zu vergleichen.	Or vine.
Was unterscheidet	What distinguishes
Götter von Menschen?	Gods from men?
Daß viele Wellen	Before them
Vor jenen wandeln,	Many waves roll onwards,
Ein ewiger Strom:	An eternal river:
Uns hebt die Welle,	We are tossed by the wave,
Verschlingt die Welle,	Engulfed by the wave,
Und wir versinken.	And we founder.
Ein kleiner Ring	A little ring
Begrenzt unser Leben,	Bounds our life,
Und viele Geschlechter	And many generations
Reihen sich dauernd	Constantly succeed each other
An ihres Daseins	Like links in the endless chain
Unendliche Kette.	Of existence.
(*Berg, Wolf*)	

March 1821 Geheimes / A secret D719

Über meines Liebchens Äugeln	The way my beloved makes eyes
Stehn verwundert alle Leute;	Causes everyone to wonder;
Ich, der Wissende, dagegen,	But I, the knowing one,
Weiß recht gut was das bedeute.	Am well aware of what she means.

Denn es heißt: ich liebe diesen,
Und nicht etwa den und jenen.
Lasset nur ihr guten Leute
Euer Wundern, euer Sehnen!

For she's saying: It's him I love,
And not, for instance, him or him.
So no more wondering, good people,
And no more longing either!

Ja, mit ungeheuren Mächten
Blicket sie wohl in die Runde;
Doch sie sucht nur zu verkünden
Ihm die nächste süße Stunde.

Though she looks about her
With infinite fervour,
She only seeks to tell him
Of their next sweet hour together.

December 1822 Der Musensohn / The son of the Muses D764

Durch Feld und Wald zu schweifen,
Mein Liedchen wegzupfeifen,
So gehts von Ort zu Ort!
Und nach dem Takte reget,
Und nach dem Maß beweget
Sich alles an mir fort.

Roaming through fields and woods,
Whistling out my song,
Is how I go from place to place!
And the whole world keeps time
And moves in rhythm`
With me.

Ich kann sie kaum erwarten
Die erste Blum' im Garten,
Die erste Blüt' am Baum.
Sie grüßen meine Lieder,
Und kommt der Winter wieder,
Sing' ich noch jenen Traum.

I can scarcely wait for them,
The first flower in the garden,
The first blossom on the tree.
My songs greet them,
And when winter returns,
I still sing of my dream.

Ich sing' ihn in der Weite,
Auf Eises Läng' und Breite,
Da blüht der Winter schön!
Auch diese Blüte schwindet
Und neue Freude findet
Sich auf bebauten Höhn.

I sing it far and wide,
Throughout the icy realm,
Then winter blossoms in beauty!
This blossoming also passes
And new joys are discovered
On the villages on the hills.

Denn wie ich bei der Linde
Das junge Völkchen finde,
Sogleich erreg' ich sie.
Der stumpfe Bursche bläht sich,
Das steife Mädchen dreht sich
Nach meiner Melodie.

For as soon as I see
Young folk by the lime tree,
I rouse them in a trice.
The bumpkin puffs his chest out,
The prim girl pirouettes
In time to my melody.

Ihr gebt den Sohlen Flügel
Und treibt, durch Tal und Hügel
Den Liebling weit von Haus.
Ihr lieben holden Musen,
Wann ruh' ich ihr am Busen
Auch endlich wieder aus?
(*Reichardt, Zelter*)

You lend my feet wings
And drive over hill and dale
Your favourite far from home.
Dear, gracious Muses,
When shall I at last find rest
In my beloved's embrace?

December 1822 An die Entfernte / To the distant beloved D765

So hab' ich wirklich dich verloren?
Bist du, o Schöne, mir entflohn?
Noch klingt in den gewohnten Ohren
Ein jedes Wort, ein jeder Ton.

Have I, then, truly lost you?
Are you, my fairest, fled from me?
I still hear ringing in my ears
Your every inflection, your every word.

So wie des Wandrers Blick am Morgen
Vergebens in die Lüfte dringt,
Wenn, in dem blauen Raum verborgen,
Hoch über ihm die Lerche singt:

As the wanderer's gaze at daybreak
Attempts in vain to pierce the skies,
When, concealed in the blue firmament,
The lark sings high above him:

So dringet ängstlich hin und wieder
Durch Feld und Busch und Wald mein Blick;
Dich rufen alle meine Lieder;
O komm, Geliebte, mir zurück!
(*Hensel, Reichardt, Tomášek, Zelter*)

So I gaze anxiously to and fro
Through fields and thickets and woods;
All my songs call out to you;
O come back to me, my love!

December 1822 Willkommen und Abschied / Greeting and farewell D767

Es schlug mein Herz, geschwind zu Pferde!
Es war getan fast eh' gedacht;
Der Abend wiegte schon die Erde
Und an den Bergen hing die Nacht;
Schon stand im Nebelkleid die Eiche,
Ein aufgetürmter Riese, da,
Wo Finsternis aus dem Gesträuche
Mit hundert schwarzen Augen sah.

My heart pounded, quick, to horse!
No sooner thought than done;
Evening already cradled the earth,
And night clung to the hills;
The oak-tree loomed in its misty cloak,
Towering like a giant, there,
Where darkness peered from bushes
With a hundred jet-black eyes.

Der Mond von einem Wolkenhügel
Sah kläglich aus dem Duft hervor,
Die Winde schwangen leise Flügel,
Umsausten schauerlich mein Ohr;
Die Nacht schuf tausend Ungeheuer;
Doch frisch und fröhlich war mein Mut:
In meinen Adern welches Feuer!
In meinem Herzen welche Glut!

The moon gazed from a bank of cloud
Mournfully through the haze,
The winds softly beat their wings,
Whirred eerily about my ears;
Night brought forth a thousand monsters,
Yet I was buoyant and bright:
What fire in my veins!
What ardour in my heart!

Dich sah ich, und die milde Freude
Floß von dem süßen Blick auf mich;
Ganz war mein Herz an deiner Seite
Und jeder Atemzug für dich.
Ein rosenfarbnes Frühlingswetter
Umgab das liebliche Gesicht,
Und Zärtlichkeit für mich – ihr Götter!
Ich hofft' es, ich verdient' es nicht!

I saw you, felt the gentle joy
Of your sweet eyes flood over me;
My heart was wholly at your side
And every breath I took for you.
A rose-red light of spring
Framed her lovely face,
And tenderness for me – O gods!
This I had hoped but never deserved!

Doch ach! schon mit der Morgensonne
Verengt der Abschied mir das Herz:
In deinen Küssen, welche Wonne!

But alas, with the morning sun,
Parting now constricts my heart:
In your kisses what delight!

In deinem Auge, welcher Schmerz!
Ich ging, du standst und sahst zur Erden,
Und sahst mir nach mit nassem Blick:
Und doch, welch Glück geliebt zu werden!
Und lieben, Götter, welch ein Glück!
(*Pfitzner, Reichardt*)

In your eyes what pain!
I went, you stood there gazing down,
And gazed moist-eyed after me:
And yet, what joy to be loved!
And to be in love, O gods, what joy!

?December 1822 Wandrers Nachtlied II / Wanderer's nightsong II D768

Über allen Gipfeln
Ist Ruh',
In allen Wipfeln
Spürest Du
Kaum einen Hauch;
Die Vöglein schweigen im Walde.
Warte nur, balde
Ruhest du auch.
(*Hensel, Ives, Liszt, Loewe, Medtner, Pepping,
Reger, Robert Schumann, Tomášek, Zelter*)

Over every mountain-top
Lies peace,
In every tree-top
You scarcely feel
A breath of wind;
The little birds are hushed in the wood.
Wait, soon you too
Will be at peace.

Heinrich Heine (1797–1856)

See Mendelssohn, Robert Schumann, Wolf

These six poems were first published in Vol. 1 of Heine's *Reisebilder* (1826), and later incorporated into the *Buch der Lieder*. Tobias Haslinger published Schubert's settings posthumously as part of *Schwanengesang* (see RELLSTAB and SEIDL).

August 1828 Der Atlas / Atlas D957/8
FROM *Schwanengesang*

Ich unglücksel'ger Atlas! eine Welt,
Die ganze Welt der Schmerzen, muß ich
    tragen,
Ich trage Unerträgliches, und brechen
Will mir das Herz im Leibe.

Du stolzes Herz! du hast es ja gewollt!
Du wolltest glücklich sein, unendlich glück-
    lich,
Oder unendlich elend, stolzes Herz,
Und jetzo bist du elend.

I, unfortunate Atlas! a world,
The whole world of sorrow I must bear,
I bear what cannot be borne, and my
    heart
Would break in my body.

You proud heart! you willed it so!
You wished to be happy, endlessly
    happy,
Or endlessly wretched, proud heart,
And now you are wretched.

August 1828 Ihr Bild / Her likeness D957/9
FROM *Schwanengesang*

Ich stand in dunkeln Träumen,
Und starrt' ihr Bildnis an,
Und das geliebte Antlitz
Heimlich zu leben begann.

Um ihre Lippen zog sich
Ein Lächeln wunderbar,
Und wie von Wehmutstränen
Erglänzte ihr Augenpaar.

Auch meine Tränen flossen
Mir von den Wangen herab –
Und ach, ich kann es nicht glauben,
Daß ich dich verloren hab'!
(*Grieg, Lachner, Clara Schumann, Wolf*)

I stood in dark dreams,
And gazed at her likeness,
And that beloved face
Sprang mysteriously to life.

A wonderful smile played
About her lips,
And her eyes glistened,
As though with sad tears.

My tears too
Streamed down my cheeks –
And ah, I cannot believe
I have lost you!

August 1828 Das Fischermädchen / The fishermaiden D957/10
FROM *Schwanengesang*

Du schönes Fischermädchen,
Treibe den Kahn ans Land;
Komm zu mir und setze dich nieder,
Wir kosen Hand in Hand.

Leg' an mein Herz dein Köpfchen,
Und fürchte dich nicht zu sehr;
Vertraust du dich doch sorglos
Täglich dem wilden Meer.

Mein Herz gleicht ganz dem Meere,
Hat Sturm und Ebb' und Flut,
Und manche schöne Perle
In seiner Tiefe ruht.
(*Borodin, Lachner, Loewe, Meyerbeer*)

You lovely fishermaiden,
Row your boat ashore;
Come and sit down by my side,
Hand in hand we'll cuddle.

Lay your little head on my heart
And don't be too afraid;
Each day, after all, you trust yourself
Fearlessly to the raging sea.

My heart's just like the sea,
It storms and ebbs and floods,
And many lovely pearls
Are resting in its depths.

August 1828 Die Stadt / The town D957/11
FROM *Schwanengesang*

Am fernen Horizonte
Erscheint, wie ein Nebelbild,
Die Stadt mit ihren Türmen
In Abenddämmrung gehüllt.

Ein feuchter Windzug kräuselt
Die graue Wasserbahn;
Mit traurigem Takte rudert
Der Schiffer in meinem Kahn.

On the distant horizon
The town with its turrets
Looms like a misty vision,
Veiled in evening light.

A dank breeze ruffles
The gloomy waterway;
With sad and measured strokes
The boatman rows my boat.

Die Sonne hebt sich noch einmal
Leuchtend vom Boden empor,
Und zeigt mir jene Stelle,
Wo ich das Liebste verlor.
(*Franz*)

The sun rises once again,
Gleaming from the earth,
And shows me that place
Where I lost what I loved most.

August 1828 Am Meer / By the sea D957/12
FROM *Schwanengesang*

Das Meer erglänzte weit hinaus
Im letzten Abendscheine;
Wir saßen am einsamen Fischerhaus,
Wir saßen stumm und alleine.

The sea gleamed far and wide
In the last evening light;
We sat by the fisherman's lonely hut,
We sat in silence and alone.

Der Nebel stieg, das Wasser schwoll,
Die Möwe flog hin und wieder;
Aus deinen Augen liebevoll
Fielen die Tränen nieder.

The mist lifted, the water rose,
The gull flew to and fro;
From your loving eyes
The tears began to fall.

Ich sah sie fallen auf deine Hand,
Und bin aufs Knie gesunken;
Ich hab' von deiner weißen Hand
Die Tränen fortgetrunken.

I watched them fall on your hand,
And sank upon my knee;
From your white hand
I drank away the tears.

Seit jener Stunde verzehrt sich mein Leib,
Die Seele stirbt vor Sehnen; –
Mich hat das unglücksel'ge Weib
Vergiftet mit ihren Tränen.
(*Hensel*)

Since that hour my body wastes,
My soul expires with longing;
That unhappy woman
Has poisoned me with her tears.

August 1828 Der Doppelgänger / The wraith D957/13
FROM *Schwanengesang*

Still ist die Nacht, es ruhen die Gassen,
In diesem Hause wohnte mein Schatz;
Sie hat schon längst die Stadt verlassen,
Doch steht noch das Haus auf demselben
    Platz.

The night is still, the streets are at rest,
This is the house where my loved-one lived;
She left the town long ago,
But the house still stands in the same
    place.

Da steht auch ein Mensch und starrt in
    die Höhe,
Und ringt die Hände, vor Schmerzensgewalt;
Mir graust es, wenn ich sein Antlitz sehe, –
Der Mond zeigt mir meine eigne Gestalt.

A man stands there too, and stares up,
Wracked with pain, he wrings his
    hands;
I shudder when I see his face –
The moon shows me my own form.

Du Doppelgänger! du bleicher Geselle!
Was äffst du nach mein Liebesleid,
Das mich gequält auf dieser Stelle,
So manche Nacht, in alter Zeit?
(*Vesque von Püttlingen*)

You wraith! You pale companion!
Why do you ape the pain of love
That tormented me on this same spot,
So many nights in times gone by?

Ludwig Hölty (1748–1776)

See Brahms

Hölty, who died of tuberculosis at the age of twenty-seven, was a founder member of the Göttinger Hainbund, a group of young poets devoted to a cult of friendship and sensibility that was created spontaneously during a moonlit woodland walk in September 1772 when those present, inspired by the beauty of the night, danced round an oak tree. They championed the emotional and apparently spontaneous poetry of Klopstock, and met regularly to recite their poems on nature, friendship and love. Something of the group's touching ingenuousness is caught by Schubert in many of his twenty-three settings of the poet, especially those composed in 1816. Johann Heinrich Voss, who had been present on that evening in 1772, was elected leader of the group and after Hölty's death published his friend's poems with many editorial 'improvements'. It was this edition that Schubert and Brahms used for their settings.

17 May 1815 An den Mond / To the moon D193

Geuß, lieber Mond, geuß deine Silberflimmer	Shed your silver light, dear moon,
Durch dieses Buchengrün,	Through these green beeches,
Wo Phantasien und Traumgestalten immer	Where fancies and dream-like visions
Vor mir vorüber fliehn!	Forever flit by me!
Enthülle dich, daß ich die Stätte finde,	Unveil yourself, that I might find the place
Wo oft mein Mädchen saß,	Where my sweetheart often sat,
Und oft, im Wehn des Buchbaums und der Linde,	And where, to the rustle of beech and lime,
Der goldnen Stadt vergaß!	I often forgot the gilded town!
Enthülle dich, daß ich des Strauchs mich freue,	Unveil yourself, that I might enjoy The murmuring bushes that cooled her,
Der Kühlung ihr gerauscht,	
Und einen Kranz auf jeden Anger streue,	And lay a wreath on every meadow,
Wo sie den Bach belauscht!	Where she once listened to the brook!
Dann, lieber Mond, dann nimm den Schleier wieder,	Then, dear moon, veil yourself once more
Und traur' um deinen Freund,	And mourn your friend,
Und weine durch den Wolkenflor hernieder,	And weep through hazy clouds,
Wie dein Verlaßner weint.	Just like I, forsaken, weep.

13 May 1816 Frühlingslied / Spring song D243

Die Luft ist blau, das Tal ist grün,	The sky's blue, the valley's green,
Die kleinen Maienglocken blühn,	Little lilies-of-the-valley bloom

Und Schlüsselblumen drunter;
　　Der Wiesengrund
　　Ist schon so bunt,
Und malt sich täglich bunter.

Drum komme, wem der Mai gefällt,
Und schaue froh die schöne Welt
Und Gottes Vatergüte,
　　Die solche Pracht
　　Hervorgebracht,
Den Baum und seine Blüte.

With cowslips mixed among them;
　　The meadow,
　　So bright with colour,
Grows brighter every day.

Draw near, then, if you love May,
Feast your eyes on the fair world
And the goodness of God the Father,
　　Who created
　　Such splendour,
The trees and all their blossom.

13 May 1816 Die Knabenzeit / Boyhood D400

Wie glücklich, wem das Knabenkleid
　　Noch um die Schultern fliegt!
Nie lästert er der bösen Zeit,
　　Stets munter und vergnügt.

Das hölzerne Husarenschwert
　　Belustiget ihn itzt,
Der Kreisel, und das Steckenpferd,
　　Auf dem er herrisch sitzt.

Und schwinget er durch blaue Luft
　　Den buntgestreiften Ball;
So achtet er nicht Blütenduft,
　　Nicht Lerch' und Nachtigall.

Nichts trübt ihm, nichts in weiter Welt
　　Sein heitres Angesicht,
Als wenn sein Ball ins Wasser fällt,
　　Als wenn sein Schwert zerbricht.

O Knabe, spiel' und laufe nur,
　　Den lieben langen Tag,
Durch Garten und durch grüne Flur
　　Den Schmetterlingen nach.

Bald schwitzest du, nicht immer froh,
　　Im engen Kämmerlein,
Und lernst vom dicken Cicero
　　Verschimmeltes Latein!

Happy the boy, whose coat
　　Still trails about his shoulders!
He never curses the bad times,
　　Is always cheerful and content.

The soldier's wooden sword
　　Is what delights him now,
The spinning-top, the hobby-horse,
　　Which he rides like a lord.

And when he throws the ball
　　With bright stripes through the blue sky,
He pays no heed to scented flowers,
　　Or lark or nightingale.

Nothing in the whole wide world
　　Can cloud his happy face,
Unless his ball fall into water,
　　Or his sword break.

Play, O child, and run about
　　Throughout the livelong day,
Through the garden and green field,
　　Chasing butterflies.

Soon you'll sweat, not always happy,
　　In your cramped little room,
Learning from a fat tome of Cicero
　　Fusty, mouldy Latin!

13 May 1816 Winterlied / Winter song D401

Keine Blumen blühn,
Nur das Wintergrün
Blickt durch Silberhüllen;
Nur das Fenster füllen

No flowers bloom,
Only winter-green
Peeps through its silver canopy;
Only tiny red and white flowers,

Blumen, rot und weiß,
Aufgeblüht aus Eis.

   Ach! kein Vogelsang
Tönt mit frohem Klang;
Nur die Winterweise
Jener kleinen Meise,
Die am Fenster schwirrt,
Und um Futter girrt.

   Minne flieht den Hain,
Wo die Vögelein,
Sonst im grünen Schatten
Ihre Nester hatten;
Minne flieht den Hain,
Kehrt ins Zimmer ein.

   Kalter Januar,
Hier werd' ich fürwahr
Unter Minnespielen
Deinen Frost nicht fühlen!
Walte immerdar,
Kalter Januar!
(*Reichardt*)

Blossoming from ice,
Fill the window.

   Ah! no birdsong
Rings out joyfully;
Only the titmouse's
Wintry strains,
Fluttering at the window,
Chirping for food.

   Love flees the grove
Where little birds
Used to nest
In the green shade;
Love flees the grove
And comes indoors.

   Cold January,
Here, in truth,
In loving banter,
I shall not feel your frost!
May you reign forever,
Cold January!

May 1816 Blumenlied / Flower song D431

Es ist ein halbes Himmelreich,
Wenn, Paradiesesblumen gleich,
Aus Klee die Blumen dringen;
Und wenn die Vögel silberhell
Im Garten hier, und dort am Quell,
Auf Blütenbäumen singen.

   Doch holder blüht ein edles Weib,
Von Seele gut, und schön von Leib,
In frischer Jugendblüte.
Wir lassen alle Blumen stehn,
Das liebe Weibchen anzusehn,
Und freun uns ihrer Güte.

It's half a kingdom of heaven
When, like blooms of Paradise,
Flowers spring up from the clover,
And when birds with silvery voice,
Now in the garden, now by the stream,
Sing from blossom-laden boughs.

   But a noble lady blooms lovelier still,
Sweet of soul and fair of form
In the flush of youth.
We pay no heed to any flowers,
But gaze at the beloved lady
And delight in her goodness.

May 1816 Seligkeit / Bliss D433

Freuden sonder Zahl
Blühn im Himmelssaal
Engeln und Verklärten,
Wie die Väter lehrten.
O da möcht' ich sein,
Und mich ewig freun!

Joys without number
Bloom in the halls of Heaven
For angels and transfigured souls,
As our fathers taught us.
How I'd love to be there
And rejoice eternally!

Jedem lächelt traut	A heavenly bride smiles
Eine Himmelsbraut;	Sweetly on everyone;
Harf' und Psalter klinget,	Harp and psalter resound,
Und man tanzt und singet.	And there's dancing and singing.
O da möcht' ich sein,	How I'd love to be there
Und mich ewig freun!	And rejoice eternally!
Lieber bleib' ich hier,	I'd sooner stay here
Lächelt Laura mir	If Laura smiles on me
Einen Blick, der saget,	With a look that says
Daß ich ausgeklaget.	I've to grieve no more.
Selig dann mit ihr,	Blissfully then with her
Bleib' ich ewig hier!	I'd stay forever here!

May 1816 Erntelied / Harvest song D434

Sicheln schallen;	Sickles ring out;
Ähren fallen	Ears of corn fall
Unter Sichelschall;	To the sickle's ring;
Auf den Mädchenhüten	Blue flowers quiver
Zittern blaue Blüten;	On girls' bonnets;
Freud' ist überall.	Joy is everywhere.
Sicheln klingen;	Sickles resound;
Mädchen singen	Girls sing
Unter Sichelklang;	To the sickle's sound,
Bis, vom Mond beschimmert,	Till, bathed in moonlight,
Rings die Stoppel flimmert,	The stubble shimmers all around,
Tönt der Erntesang.	And the harvest song rings out.
Alles springet,	Everyone's dancing,
Alles singet,	Everyone with a voice
Was nur lallen kann.	Sings out.
Bei dem Erntemahle	At the harvest feast
Ißt aus einer Schale	Farmer and labourer
Knecht und Bauersmann.	Eat from the same bowl.
Jeder scherzet,	Everyone jests,
Jeder herzet	Everyone then hugs
Dann sein Liebelein.	His sweetheart.
Nach geleerten Kannen	When the tankards are empty,
Gehen sie von dannen,	They go on their way,
Singen und juchhein!	Singing and shouting with joy!

12 May 1816 Klage an den Mond / Lament to the moon D436

Dein Silber schien	Your silvery light
Durch Eichengrün,	Shone down on me
Das Kühlung gab,	Through the green oaks

Auf mich herab,	That gave cool shade,
O Mond, und lachte Ruh	O moon, and shed smiling peace
Mir frohen Knaben zu.	On this happy boy.
Wenn jetzt dein Licht	When now your light
Durch's Fenster bricht,	Streams through my window,
Lacht's keine Ruh	It sheds no smiling peace
Mir Jüngling zu.	On this young man.
Sieht's meine Wange blaß,	It sees my cheeks pale,
Mein Auge tränennaß.	My eyes moist with tears.
Bald, lieber Freund,	Soon, dear friend,
Ach, bald bescheint	Ah soon! your silvery light
Dein Silberschein	Will shine
Den Leichenstein,	On the tombstone
Der meine Asche birgt,	That hides my ashes,
Des Jünglings Asche birgt!	The young man's ashes!
(Beethoven, Hensel, Zumsteeg)	

Johann Georg Jacobi (1740–1814)

Professor of philosophy, poet, translator and editor of the literary quarterly *Iris*, in which a number of Goethe poems first appeared. Jacobi wrote poems that were published in four collections: *Poetische Versuche* (1764), *Abschied an den Amor* (1769), *Die Winterreise* (1769) and *Die Sommerreise* (1770). Of Schubert's seven Jacobi songs composed in 1816, only 'Litanei auf das Fest aller Seelen' has a firm place in the repertoire. The first edition printed just three of Jacobi's nine verses, the first, third and sixth; the *Gesamtausgabe* published all nine, explaining there was no proof that it was Schubert who selected these three verses.

August 1816 Litanei auf des Fest aller Seelen* / Litany for the Feast of All Souls D343

Ruhn in Frieden alle Seelen,	May all souls rest in peace,
Die vollbracht ein banges Quälen,	Those whose fearful agony is ended,
Die vollendet süßen Traum,	Those whose sweet dreams are over,
Lebenssatt, geboren kaum,	Those who, weary of life, scarcely born,
Aus der Welt hinüber schieden:	Have departed the world:
Alle Seelen ruhn in Frieden!	May all souls rest in peace!
Liebevoller Mädchen Seelen,	The souls of girls in love,
Deren Tränen nicht zu zählen,	Whose tears are without number,
Die ein falscher Freund verließ,	Who, abandoned by a faithless lover,
Und die blinde Welt verstieß:	Were rejected by a blind world:
Alle, die von hinnen schieden,	All who have departed hence,
Alle Seelen ruhn in Frieden!	May all souls rest in peace!

* The feast of All Souls falls on 2 November, when Catholics seek through prayer and almsgiving to alleviate the suffering of souls in purgatory. See also Strauss's 'Allerseelen', p. 550.

Und die nie der Sonne lachten,	And those who never smiled at the sun,
Unterm Mond auf Dornen wachten,	Lay awake on thorns beneath the moon,
Gott, im reinen Himmels-Licht,	So that one day they might see God,
Einst zu sehn von Angesicht:	Face to face in Heaven's pure light:
Alle, die von hinnen schieden,	All who have departed hence,
Alle Seelen ruhn in Frieden!	May all souls rest in peace!

Friedrich Gottlieb Klopstock (1724–1803)

The young Goethe admired Klopstock, as he explains in *Dichtung und Wahrheit* Part I, Book II, for the way he liberated German verse from the tyranny of rhyme, especially in the twenty cantos of his religious epic *Der Messias* (1748–1773), which Goethe and his sister were compelled to read clandestinely in order to avoid their father's wrath. Goethe also admired the personal and emotional tone of the *Oden*, revered by Hölty and the Göttinger Hain who used to recite Klopstock's poetry at their meetings. 'An Schwager Kronos' (see p. 313), Goethe tells us, was written as a revolt against stagnation after a visit to the doyen of German poetry on 10 October 1774: he had seen a poet in decline, devoid of that energy which had characterized the poetry he knew so well and loved. 'Das Rosenband', a poem sketched by Beethoven and composed by Richard Strauss, celebrates Klopstock's love for his wife, Meta Moller, the Cidli of several Schubert settings. She died in childbirth in 1758, and Klopstock expressed his grief in 'Die Sommernacht' (see GLUCK). Klopstock himself was an amateur musician, and has been much set by composers – he approached several personally – such as C. P. E. Bach, Beethoven, Gluck, Mahler, Meyerbeer, Robert Schumann and Richard Strauss. Schubert set thirteen of his poems.

September 1815 Das Rosenband / The rose garland D280

Im Frühlingsgarten fand ich sie;	I found her in the spring garden;
Da band ich sie mit Rosenbändern:	I bound her fast with a rose garland:
Sie fühlt' es nicht und schlummerte.	Oblivious, she slumbered on.
Ich sah sie an; mein Leben hing	I gazed on her; with that gaze
Mit diesem Blick an ihrem Leben:	My life became entwined with hers:
Ich fühlt' es wohl, und wußt' es nicht.	This I sensed, and did not know.
Doch lispelt' ich ihr leise zu,	I murmured softly to her
Und rauschte mit den Rosenbändern:	And rustled the garland of roses:
Da wachte sie vom Schlummer auf.	Then she woke from slumber.
Sie sah mich an; ihr Leben hing	She gazed on me; with that gaze
Mit diesem Blick an meinem Leben,	Her life became entwined with mine,
Und um uns ward Elysium.	And Paradise bloomed about us.
(*MacDowell, Strauss, Zemlinsky, Zelter*)	

Wie erhebt sich das Herz, wenn es dich,
Unendlicher, denkt! wie sinkt es,
Wenn es auf sich herunterschaut!
Elend schauts wehklagend dann, und Nacht
    und Tod!

Allein du rufst mich aus meiner Nacht, der
    im Elend, der im Tode hilft!
Dann denk ich es ganz, daß du ewig mich
    schufst,
Herrlicher! den kein Preis, unten am Grab',
    oben am Thron,
Herr Gott! den, dankend entflammt, kein
    Jubel genug besingt.

Weht, Bäume des Lebens, ins Harfengetön!
Rausche mit ihnen ins Harfengetön, kristall-
    ner Strom!
Ihr lispelt, und rauscht, und Harfen, ihr tönt
Nie es ganz! Gott ist es, den ihr preist!

Welten, donnert in feierlichem Gang, Welten
    donnert in der Posaunen Chor!
Tönt, all' ihr Sonnen auf der Straße voll
    Glanz,
In der Posaunen Chor!

Ihr Welten, ihr donnert,
Du, der Posaunen Chor, hallest
Nie es ganz: Gott, nie es ganz, Gott,
Gott, Gott ist es, den ihr preist!

How the heart leaps, whenever,
Infinite One, it thinks of you! how it sinks,
When it gazes on itself!
Lamenting, it sees but misery then, and night
    and death!

You alone summon me from my night, suc-
    cour me in misery and death!
Then I remember that you created me for
    eternity,
Glorious One, for whom no praise – in the
    grave below or by your throne –
Lord God, no grateful hymn of praise can
    sufficiently extol.

Sway, trees of life, to the harp's sound!
Murmur to the harp's sound, crystal river!
You whisper and murmur, and, harps, you play,
But never wholly satisfy! It is God whom you
    praise!

Thunder forth, you worlds in solemn
    motion, to the chorus of trumpets!
Resound all you suns on your resplendent
    course,
To the chorus of trumpets!

You worlds thunder
And you trumpet choirs ring out,
But never fully. It is God,
God whom you praise!

Theodor Körner (1791–1813)

Although Körner first attracted attention in *Knospen* (1810), it was his patriotic poetry, published posthumously by his father under the title *Leyer und Schwert* ('Lyre and Sword') which made a great impression on the young Schubert and his contemporaries. Körner was appointed resident dramatist at the Burgtheater in January 1813, but enlisted two months later in Adolf Lützow's Free Corps to fight against Napoleon. He was killed at the battle of Gadebusch. Schubert, who was introduced to the poet by Josef von Spaun, set fourteen of Körner's poems, and composed *Der vierjährige Posten* to one of his libretti.

Hoch auf dem Gipfel
Deiner Gebirge
Steh' ich und staun' ich,
Glühend begeistert,
Heilige Koppe,
Himmelsanstürmerin!

High on the summit
Of your mountains
I stand and marvel,
Glowing with rapture,
Sacred,
Heaven-storming peak!

Weit in die Ferne
Schweifen die trunknen
Freudigen Blicke,
Überall Leben,
Üppiges Streben,
Überall Sonnenschein.

My joyful,
Intoxicated gaze
Ranges far into the distance,
Everywhere is life,
Luxuriant growth,
Everywhere sunshine.

Blühende Fluren,
Schimmernde Städte,
Dreier Könige
Glückliche Länder
Schau' ich begeistert,
Schau' ich mit hoher
Inniger Lust.

Blossoming fields,
Shimmering towns,
The happy kingdoms
Of three monarchs
I behold with ardour,
With sublime,
Heartfelt delight.

Auch meines Vaterlands
Grenze erblick' ich,
Wo mich das Leben
Freundlich begrüßte,
Wo mich der Liebe
Heilige Sehnsucht
Glühend ergriff.

I see the frontiers
Of my homeland too,
Where life bade me
A friendly welcome,
Where love's
Sacred longing
Seized me with its fire.

Sei mir gesegnet
Hier in der Ferne,
Liebliche Heimat!
Sei mir gesegnet
Land meiner Träume!
Kreis meiner Lieben,
Sei mir gegrüßt!

Accept my blessing
From afar,
Lovely homeland!
Accept my blessing,
Land of my dreams!
Loved ones,
I greet you!

Ludwig Theobul Kosegarten (1758–1818)

This professor of theology wrote largely conventional verse which made a profound impression on the young Schubert, who set twenty-one of his poems including a recently identified *Liederspiel*. Seven of them were composed on 19 October 1815.

* The Riesengebirge is a mountain range not far from Körner's native Dresden.

Sonne du sinkst!	Sun, you are setting!
Sonne du sinkst!	Sun, you are setting!
Sink' in Frieden, o Sonne!	Set in peace, O sun!

Still und ruhig ist deines Scheidens Gang,
Rührend und feierlich deines Scheidens
  Schweigen.
Wehmut lächelt dein freundliches Auge,
Tränen entträufeln den goldenen Wimpern,
Segnungen strömst du der duftenden Erde.
    Immer tiefer,
    Immer leiser,
Immer ernster, feierlicher
Sinkest du den Äther hinab.

Your parting is calm and tranquil,
Your silent parting touching and solemn.
Your smiling eyes radiate sadness,
Tears fall from your golden lashes,
You rain down blessings on the fragrant
  earth.
    Ever deeper,
    Ever softer,
Ever more serious and solemn
You slip down the sky.

    Sonne du sinkst! / Sun, you are setting!
    Sonne du sinkst! / Sun, you are setting!
    Sink' in Frieden, o Sonne! / Set in peace, O sun!

Es segnen die Völker,
Es säuseln die Lüfte,
Es räuchern die dampfenden Wiesen dir nach;
Winde durchrieseln dein lockiges Haar;
Wogen kühlen die brennende Wange;
Weit auf tut sich dein Wasserbett –
    Ruh' in Frieden!
    Ruh' in Wonne!
Die Nachtigall flötet dir Schlummergesang.

Nations bless you,
Breezes murmur,
Steaming meadows follow in your wake;
Winds ripple through your curly hair;
Waves cool your burning cheeks;
Your watery bed opens wide –
    Rest in peace!
    Rest in joy!
The nightingale's song sings you to sleep.

    Sonne du sinkst! / Sun, you are setting!
    Sonne du sinkst! / Sun, you are setting!
    Sink' in Frieden, o Sonne! / Set in peace, O sun!

Karl Lappe (1773–1843)

A schoolmaster in Stralsund, Lappe eventually turned to farming. His poems were published in *Gedichte* (1801), *Sämmtliche poetische Werke* (1836), *Blüte des Alters* (1841) and *Blätter* (1824), Schubert's source for 'Im Abendrot' and 'Der Einsame'.

?January 1825 Im Abendrot / Sunset glow D799

O wie schön ist deine Welt,
Vater, wenn sie golden strahlet!
Wenn dein Glanz herniederfällt,
Und den Staub mit Schimmer malet;

Ah, how lovely is your world,
Father, when it gleams with gold!
When your radiance descends,
And paints the dust with glitter;

Wenn das Rot, das in der Wolke blinkt,
In mein stilles Fenster sinkt!

Könnt' ich klagen, könnt' ich zagen?
Irre sein an dir und mir?
Nein, ich will im Busen tragen
Deinen Himmel schon allhier.
Und dies Herz, eh' es zusammenbricht,
Trinkt noch Glut und schlürft noch Licht.

When the red that glows from the clouds
Sinks into my quiet window!

Could I complain, could I lose heart?
Despair of you and me?
No, I shall bear your heaven
Here within this breast.
And this heart, before it breaks,
Shall still drink fire and savour light.

?January 1825 Der Einsame / The recluse D800

Wenn meine Grillen schwirren,
Bei Nacht, am spät erwärmten Herd,
Dann sitz' ich, mit vergnügtem Sinn,
Vertraulich zu der Flamme hin,
So leicht, so unbeschwert.

When my crickets chirrup at night
By the late-burning hearth,
I sit contentedly in my chair,
Confiding to the flame,
So light-heartedly, so at ease.

Ein trautes stilles Stündchen
Bleibt man noch gern am Feuer wach.
Man schürt, wenn sich die Lohe senkt,
Die Funken auf, und sinnt und denkt:
Nun abermal ein Tag!

For one more sweet and peaceful hour
It's good to linger by the fire,
Stirring the embers when the blaze dies down,
Musing and thinking:
Well, that's another day!

Was Liebes oder Leides
Sein Lauf für uns daher gebracht,
Es geht noch einmal durch den Sinn;
Allein das Böse wirft man hin.
Es störe nicht die Nacht.

Whatever joy or sorrow
It has brought us,
Runs once more through the mind;
But the bad is cast aside,
So as not to spoil the night.

Zu einem frohen Traume
Bereitet man gemach sich zu.
Wenn sorgelos ein holdes Bild
Mit sanfter Lust die Seele füllt,
Ergibt man sich der Ruh.

We gently prepare ourselves
For pleasant dreams.
When a lovely image fills the soul
With carefree, tender joy,
We succumb to sleep.

O wie ich mir gefalle
In meiner stillen Ländlichkeit!
Was in dem Schwarm der lauten Welt
Das irre Herz gefesselt hält,
Gibt nicht Zufriedenheit.

Oh, how I love
My quiet rustic life!
What holds the wayward heart captive
In the bustle of the noisy world,
Cannot bring contentment.

Zirpt immer, liebe Heimchen,
In meiner Klause, eng und klein.
Ich duld' euch gern: ihr stört mich nicht.
Wenn euer Lied das Schweigen bricht,
Bin ich nicht ganz allein.

Chirp away, friendly house crickets
In my narrow little room.
I gladly put up with you: you're no trouble.
When your song breaks the silence,
I'm no longer all alone.

Karl Gottfried Ritter von Leitner (1800–90)

Karl Gottfried von Leitner, a teacher and poet from Styria, was allegedly known as the 'Austrian Uhland' – a flattering accolade that ignores the somewhat saccharine nature of many of his poems. Yet they inspired Schubert to eleven songs, two of which, 'Die Sterne' and 'Der Winterabend', are undisputed masterpieces. Leitner played a leading role in the cultural life of Graz, where he published his first volume of poems, *Gedichte*, in 1825. Schubert was given a copy by Marie Pachler when he visited Graz in the summer of 1827.

November 1827 Der Kreuzzug / The crusade D932

Ein Münich steht in seiner Zell'	A monk is standing in his cell
Am Fenstergitter grau,	At the grey iron-bars,
Viel Rittersleut' in Waffen hell	Many knights in shining armour
Die reiten durch die Au'.	Come riding through the meadow.
Sie singen Lieder frommer Art	They are singing holy songs
Im schönen, ernsten Chor,	In a fine and solemn chorus,
Inmitten fliegt, von Seide zart,	The Crusaders' flag of softest silk
Die Kreuzesfahn' empor.	Streams above them in their midst.
Sie steigen an dem Seegestad'	At the water's edge they step
Das hohe Schiff hinan.	Aboard the lofty ship.
Es läuft hinweg auf grünem Pfad,	It sails away on its green path,
Ist bald nur wie ein Schwan.	And soon looks like a swan.
Der Münich steht am Fenster noch,	The monk still stands at the bars,
Schaut ihnen nach hinaus:	And gazes after them:
„Ich bin, wie ihr, ein Pilger doch	'I am a pilgrim just like you,
„Und bleib' ich gleich zu Haus'.	Although I stay at home.
„Des Lebens Fahrt durch Wellentrug	'Life's journey through treacherous waves
„Und heißen Wüstensand,	And burning desert sand,
„Es ist ja auch ein Kreuzeszug	Is, after all, a crusade too
„In das gelobte Land."	Into the Promised Land.'

January 1828 Der Winterabend / The winter evening D938

Es ist so still, so heimlich um mich,	It is so still and homely around me,
Die Sonn' ist unter, der Tag entwich,	The sun has set, the day is done,
Wie schnell nun heran der Abend graut! –	How swiftly the evening now grows grey!
Mir ist es recht, sonst ist mir's zu laut.	That suits me well, day is too loud.
Jetzt aber ist's ruhig, es hämmert kein Schmied,	But now all is quiet, blacksmith and plumber Hammer no more, people are tired, have
Kein Klempner, das Volk verlief und ist müd;	gone back home;
Und selbst, daß nicht raßle der Wagen Lauf,	And the snow has even draped the streets,
Zog Decken der Schnee durch die Gassen auf.	Lest carts should rattle as they pass.

Wie tut mir so wohl der selige Frieden!	This blissful peace is so good for me!
Da sitz' ich im Dunkeln, ganz abgeschieden,	I sit in the darkness, quite secluded,
So ganz für mich; – nur der Mondenschein	Quite self-contained; only the moonlight
Kommt leise zu mir in's Gemach.	Softly enters my room.
Er kennt mich schon und läßt mich schweigen.	It knows me and leaves me to my silence,
Nimmt nur seine Arbeit, die Spindel, das Gold,	Just gets down to work with spindle and gold,
Und spinnet stille, webt und lächelt hold,	Spins silently, weaves and smiles a sweet smile,
Und hängt dann sein schimmerndes Schleiertuch	And then drapes its shimmering veil
Ringsum an Gerät und Wänden aus.	Over the chattels and walls around me.
Ist gar ein stiller, ein lieber Besuch,	The moon's a silent and much-loved guest,
Macht mir gar keine Unruh' im Haus'.	Who does not disturb the house at all.
Will er bleiben, so hat er Ort,	If it wishes to stay, there's room enough,
Freut's ihn nimmer, so geht er fort.	If the pleasure palls, it can move on.
Ich sitze dann stumm im Fenster gern',	Then I like to sit quietly by the window,
Und schaue hinauf in Gewölk und Stern.	And gaze up at the clouds and stars,
Denke zurück, ach weit, gar weit,	Think back, so far, ah! so far
In eine schöne, verschwund'ne Zeit.	To the lovely vanished past.
Denk' an sie, an das Glück der Minne,	Think of her and love's happiness,
Seufze still, und sinne und sinne. –	Sigh in silence, and muse and muse.

January 1828 Die Sterne / The stars D939

Wie blitzen	How brightly
Die Sterne	The stars
So hell durch die Nacht!	Shine through the night!
Bin oft schon	They've often
Darüber	Roused me
Vom Schlummer erwacht.	From slumber.
Doch schelt' ich	But I don't blame
Die lichten	Those shining
Gebilde d'rum nicht,	Folk for that,
Sie üben	They secretly
Im Stillen	Perform
Manch heilsame Pflicht.	Many a healing task.
Sie wallen	They wander
Hoch oben	Like angels
In Engelgestalt,	High above,
Sie leuchten	And light
Dem Pilger	The pilgrim
Durch Heiden und Wald.	Through heath and wood.
Sie schweben	Like harbingers
Als Boten	Of love
Der Liebe umher,	They hover above,
Und tragen	And often

Oft Küsse	Carry kisses
Weit über das Meer.	Across the sea.
Sie blicken	Tenderly
Dem Dulder	They gaze
Recht mild in's Gesicht,	On the sufferer's face,
Und säumen	And fringe
Die Tränen	His tears
Mit silbernem Licht.	With silver light.
Und weisen	Kind and consoling,
Von Gräbern	They direct
Gar tröstlich und hold	Us away
Uns hinter	From the grave
Das Blaue	To beyond the blue
Mit Fingern von Gold.	With fingers of gold.
So sei denn	Blessings, then,
Gesegnet	Upon you,
Du strahlige Schar!	O shining throng!
Und leuchte	And long
Mir lange	May you shine on me,
Noch freundlich und klar.	Kind and clear.
Und wenn ich	And if one day
Einst liebe,	I fall in love,
Seid hold dem Verein,	Smile on the union,
Und euer	And let your
Geflimmer	Twinkling
Laßt Segen uns sein.	Be a blessing on us.

Friedrich von Matthisson (1761–1831)

See Beethoven

The son of a clergyman, Matthisson was ennobled in 1809, having worked as a private tutor for Princess Luise von Anhalt-Dessau and King Friedrich I of Württemberg. His slightly melancholy poetry, first published in 1781, was admired by Schubert: over half of the twenty-nine settings were composed between 1812 and 1814, including this third version of 'Der Geistertanz', written just three days before 'Gretchen am Spinnrade'.

14 October 1814 Der Geistertanz / Ghost dance D116
FIRST VERSION: *c.*1812 (D15); SECOND VERSION: *c.*1812 (D15); THIRD VERSION: 14 OCTOBER 1814 (D116)

Die bretterne Kammer	The boarded chamber
Der Toten erbebt,	Of the dead trembles,

Wenn zwölfmal den Hammer	When midnight twelve times
Die Mitternacht hebt.	Raises its hammer.
Rasch tanzen um Gräber	Swiftly round graves
Und morsches Gebein	And mouldering bones,
Wir luftigen Schweber	We airy spirits
Den sausenden Reihn.	Whirl and dance.
Was winseln die Hunde	Why do the dogs whine
Beim schlafenden Herrn?	As their master sleeps?
Sie wittern die Runde	They scent from afar
Der Geister von fern.	The spirits' dance.
Die Raben entflattern	Ravens flutter up
Der wüsten Abtei,	From the ruined abbey,
Und fliehn an den Gattern	And fly off
Des Kirchhofs vorbei.	Past the graveyard gates.
Wir gaukeln und scherzen	Up and down
Hinab und empor,	We tumble and jest,
Gleich irrenden Kerzen	Like will-o'-the-wisps
Im dunstigen Moor.	On the misty moor.
O Herz! dessen Zauber	O heart! whose magic
Zur Marter uns ward,	Became our martyrdom,
Du ruhst nun, in tauber	You now lie at rest,
Verdumpfung erstarrt.	Frozen in numb stupor.
Tief bargst du im düstern	In the deep, dark chamber
Gemach unser Weh;	You have buried our grief;
Wir Glücklichen flüstern	Happily we whisper you
Dir fröhlich: Ade!	A cheerful farewell!
(Suppé)	

Johann Baptist Mayrhofer (1787–1836)

Mayrhofer's poetry was not published until 1824, by which time Schubert had already set forty-three of his friend's poems – mostly from manuscript: 'Die Tinte noch naß!' as Beckmesser was later to exclaim. The final number of forty-seven means that Mayrhofer, with the exception of Goethe, was Schubert's preferred poet for Lieder composition. He worked in Vienna as a book censor and shared lodgings with Schubert for a while, from the autumn of 1818 until the winter of 1820. They drifted apart in the following years, and Schubert's name was absent from the subscription list that accompanied the publication of Mayrhofer's poems in 1824. Whatever the reasons for this cooling of relations, Mayrhofer's influence on Schubert cannot be underestimated, and the poems printed here paint a vivid picture of this melancholic poet who committed suicide in 1836, after a failed attempt in 1831, by hurling himself from a third-floor window of the office where he worked.

'Geheimnis' (1816), which Mayrhofer subtitled 'To F. Schubert', was probably written by Mayrhofer out of gratitude for the eight songs Schubert had already composed to his own poems, including 'Abschied', and for the way in which Schubert's music could rescue him from 'trüber Gegenwart' ('the gloomy present'). His inherent pessimism is reflected in 'Auflösung', an ecstatic vision of final dissolution; 'Fahrt zum Hades' describes the torments of Hell, while 'Nachtstück' depicts death as Mayrhofer would wish it, a gentle and imperceptible transition into 'den langen Schlummer' ('the long sleep'). 'Rückweg' refers to the oppressive nature of Metternich's Vienna; 'Sehnsucht' speaks of the impossibility of living up to ideals on earth; 'Auf der Donau' laments human ephemerality; 'Abendstern' and 'Der Sieg' make veiled references to his homosexuality and, prophetically, his suicide. Optimistic poems such as 'Der Schiffer', which enjoins man to embrace his fate, or nature poems, like 'Nach einem Gewitter', that rejoice in earth's beauty, are rare within his œuvre. Mayrhofer also wrote the libretti to two of Schubert's stage works: *Die Freunde von Salamanca* and *Adrast*.

September 1816 Abschied. Nach einer Wallfahrtsarie / Farewell. Based on a pilgrims' song D475

Über die Berge	Over the mountains
Zieht ihr fort;	You go on your way;
Kommt an manchen	Come to many
Grünen Ort,	A green place,
Muß zurücke	I must return
Ganz allein;	All alone;
Lebet wohl!	Farewell!
Es muß so sein.	It must be so.
Scheiden,	Parting,
Meiden,	Leaving
Was man liebt,	Those we love,
Ach wie wird	Ah, how that
Das Herz betrübt!	Saddens the heart!
O Seenspiegel,	Glassy lakes,
Wald und Hügel –	Woods and hills –
Schwinden all';	All vanish;
Hör' verschwimmen	I hear
Eurer Stimmen	Your voices' echo
Widerhall.	Fade away.
Lebt wohl! klingt klagevoll,	Farewell! sounds plaintive,
Ach wie wird	Ah, how that
Das Herz betrübt!	Saddens the heart!
Scheiden,	Parting,
Meiden,	Leaving
Was man liebt!	Those we love!

September 1816 Rückweg / The return D476

Zum Donaustrom, zur Kaiserstadt
Geh' ich in Bangigkeit:
Denn was das Leben Schönes hat,
Entweichet weit und weit.

Die Berge schwinden allgemach,
Mit ihnen Wald und Fluß;
Der Kühe Glocken läuten nach,
Und Hütten nicken Gruß.

Was starrt dein Auge tränenfeucht
Hinaus in blaue Fern'?
Ach, dorten weilt ich, unerreicht,
Frei unter Freien gern!

Wo Liebe noch und Treue gilt,
Da öffnet sich das Herz;
Die Frucht an ihren Strahlen schwillt,
Und strebet himmelwärts.

I approach with apprehension
The river Danube, the imperial city:
For all that is beautiful in life
Dwindles more and more.

The mountains gradually disappear,
With them forests and rivers;
The sound of cowbells follows us,
And chalets nod in greeting.

Why do your eyes, wet with tears,
Stare into the distant blue?
Ah! there I lived a secluded life,
Free and happy among free men!

Where love and loyalty still count,
The heart will open out;
Fruit will ripen in their rays
And reach up to heaven.

October 1816 Geheimnis (An Franz Schubert) / A secret (To Franz Schubert) D491

Sag an, wer lehrt dich Lieder,
So schmeichelnd und so zart?
Sie rufen einen Himmel
Aus trüber Gegenwart.
Erst lag das Land, verschleiert,
Im Nebel vor uns da –
Du singst – und Sonnen leuchten,
Und Frühling ist uns nah.

Den schilfbekränzten Alten,
Der seine Urne gießt,
Erblickst du nicht, nur Wasser,
Wie's durch die Wiesen fließt.
So geht es auch dem Sänger,
Er singt, er staunt in sich;
Was still ein Gott bereitet,
Befremdet ihn, wie dich.

Who teaches you, O say, to sing
Such tender, honeyed songs?
They conjure up a heaven
Out of troubled times.
Before, the land lay veiled
In mist before our eyes –
You sing – and suns gleam
And spring draws near.

You have no eyes for the reed-crowned
Ancient who empties his urn,
Water flowing through the meadows
Is all you see.
Thus it is with the singer,
He sings, he marvels inwardly;
That which God quietly creates
Astonishes both him and you.

January 1817 Der Alpenjäger / The alpine huntsman D524

Auf hohem Bergesrücken,
Wo frischer Alles grünt,
In's Land hinabzublicken,
Das nebelleicht zerrinnt –
Erfreut den Alpenjäger.

High up on the mountain ridge,
Where everything's more fresh and green,
The alpine huntsman delights
In looking down through drifting mist
Onto the land below.

Je steiler und je schräger
Die Pfade sich verwinden,
Je mehr Gefahr aus Schlünden,
So freier schlägt die Brust.

The more steeply the paths
Wind across the hill,
The greater the ravine's danger –
The more his heart exults.

Er ist der fernen Lieben,
Die ihm daheim geblieben,
Sich seliger bewußt.

He's more blissfully aware
Of his distant beloved,
Who remains at home.

Und ist er nun am Ziele:
So drängt sich in der Stille
Ein süßes Bild ihm vor.
Der Sonne goldne Strahlen,
Sie weben und sie malen,
Die er im Tal erkor.

And once he has reached his goal:
A sweet image in the silence
Appears before him.
The golden sunbeams
Weave and paint the portrait
Of his chosen one in the valley.

January 1817 Fahrt zum Hades / Journey to Hades D526

Der Nachen dröhnt, Cypressen flüstern –
Horch, Geister reden schaurig drein;
Bald werd' ich am Gestad', dem düstern,
Weit von der schönen Erde sein.

The boat creaks, cypresses whisper –
Hark, spirits utter their chilling cries;
Soon I shall reach the gloomy shore,
Far from the lovely world.

Da leuchten Sonne nicht, noch Sterne,
Da tönt kein Lied, da ist kein Freund.
Empfang die letzte Träne, o Ferne!
Die dieses müde Auge weint.

Neither sun nor stars shine there,
No song is heard, no friend is found.
O distant earth, accept this last tear
Shed by my weary eyes.

Schon schau' ich die blassen Danaiden,*
Den fluchbeladnen Tantalus;†
Es murmelt todesschwangern Frieden,
Vergessenheit, dein alter Fluß.

Already I see the pale Danaides,
And curse-laden Tantalus;
Your ancient river, O Oblivion,
Murmurs of death-swollen peace.

Vergessen nenn' ich zwiefach Sterben.
Was ich mit höchster Kraft gewann,
Verlieren – wieder es erwerben –
Wann enden diese Qualen? wann?

Oblivion to me is a double death.
To lose that which needed all my strength
To win, and to strive for it once more –
When will these torments cease? When?

January 1817 Schlaflied / Lullaby D527

Es mahnt der Wald, es ruft der Strom:
„Du liebes Bübchen zu uns komm!"
Der Knabe kommt und staunend weilt,
Und ist von jedem Schmerz geheilt.

The forest entreats, the river cries:
'Sweet child, come to us!'
The boy draws near, marvels and stays,
And is cured of every pain.

Aus Büschen flötet Wachtelschlag,
Mit irren Farben spielt der Tag;

The song of the quail sounds from the bushes,
The daylight plays with shimmering colours;

* The Danaides were the fifty daughters of Danaus, king of Argos, all but one of whom murdered their husbands-to-be by order of their father. They were punished for their crime by being dispatched to hell.
† King of Lydia, who suffered insatiable thirst in hell.

Auf Blümchen rot, auf Blümchen blau
Erglänzt des Himmels feuchter Tau.

Ins frische Gras legt er sich hin:
Läßt über sich die Wolken zieh'n –
An seine Mutter angeschmiegt,
Hat ihn der Traumgott eingewiegt.

The moist dew of heaven glistens
On little red and blue flowers.

He lies down in the cool grass:
Lets the clouds drift over him –
As he nestled up close to his mother,
The god of dreams lulled him to sleep.

Spring 1817 Sehnsucht / Longing D516

Der Lerche wolkennahe Lieder
Erschmettern zu des Winters Flucht.
Die Erde hüllt in Samt die Glieder,
Und Blüten bilden rote Frucht.
Nur du, o sturmbewegte Seele,
Bist blütenlos, in dich gekehrt,
Und wirst in goldner Frühlingshelle
Von tiefer Sehnsucht aufgezehrt.

Nie wird, was du verlangst, entkeimen
Dem Boden, Idealen fremd;
Der trotzig deinen schönsten Träumen
Die rohe Kraft entgegen stemmt.
Du ringst dich matt mit seiner Härte,
Vom Wunsche heftiger entbrannt:
Mit Kranichen ein strebender Gefährte
Zu wandern in ein milder Land.

The songs of the cloud-soaring lark
Ring out as winter flees,
The earth is clad in velvet,
And blossoms burst into red fruit.
You alone, O storm-tossed soul,
Do not bloom – turned in on yourself,
You are consumed by deep longing
In the golden radiance of spring.

What you crave will never burgeon
From this earth which, averse to ideals,
Defiantly opposes its raw strength
To your finest dreams.
Your struggle with its harshness wearies you,
Increasingly inflamed by the desire,
As the cranes' aspiring companion,
To migrate to a kinder land.

?1817 Der Schiffer / The boatman D536

Im Winde, im Sturme befahr' ich den Fluß,
Die Kleider durchweicht der Regen im Guß;
Ich peitsche die Wellen mit mächtigem Schlag,
Erhoffend, erhoffend mir heiteren Tag.

Die Wellen, sie jagen das ächzende Schiff,
Es drohet der Strudel, es drohet das Riff,
Gesteine entkollern den felsigen Höh'n,
Und Tannen erseufzen wie Geistergestöh'n.

So mußte es kommen – ich hab es gewollt,
Ich hasse ein Leben behaglich entrollt;
Und schlängen die Wellen den ächzenden
    Kahn,
Ich priese doch immer die eigene Bahn.

Drum tose des Wassers ohnmächtiger Zorn,
Dem Herzen entquillet ein seliger Born,
Die Nerven erfrischend – o himmlische Lust!
Dem Sturme zu trotzen mit männlicher Brust.

I ply the river in wind and storm,
My garments soaked by teeming rain;
I lash the waves with powerful strokes,
Filled with hopes for a bright day.

The waves drive on the creaking boat,
Whirlpool and reef loom threateningly,
Rocks roll down the towering cliffs,
And fir-trees sigh like groaning ghosts.

It had to come – I willed it so,
I hate a snugly unfolding life;
And were waves to engulf the creaking
    boat,
I should still extol my chosen course.

So – let waters roar in impotent rage,
A fountain of bliss spurts from my breast,
Renewing my courage, O heavenly joy!
To brave the storm with a manly heart.

March 1817 Am Strome / By the river D539

Ist mir's doch, als sei mein Leben
An den schönen Strom gebunden.
Hab' ich Frohes nicht an seinem Ufer,
Und Betrübtes hier empfunden?

Ja, du gleichest meiner Seele;
Manchmal grün, und glatt gestaltet,
Und zu Zeiten – herrschen Stürme –
Schäumend, unruhvoll, gefaltet!

Fließest zu dem fernen Meere,
Darfst allda nicht heimisch werden.
Mich drängt's auch in mildre Lande –
Finde nicht das Glück auf Erden.

I feel as if my life
Were bound to the beautiful river.
Have I not known joy
And sorrow on its banks?

Yes, you resemble my soul;
Sometimes green and tranquil,
And sometimes – when storms blow –
Foaming, restless, furrowed!

You flow away to the distant sea,
Where you fail to find your home.
I too yearn for kinder shores –
Can find no happiness on earth.

March 1817 Memnon* / Memnon D541

Den Tag hindurch nur einmal mag ich
    sprechen,
Gewohnt zu schweigen immer, und zu trauern:
Wenn durch die nachtgebornen Nebelmauern
Aurorens Purpurstrahlen liebend brechen.

Für Menschenohren sind es Harmonien.
Weil ich die Klage selbst melodisch künde,
Und durch der Dichtung Glut das Rauhe
    ründe,
Vermuten sie in mir ein selig Blühen.

In mir – nach dem des Todes Arme langen,
In dessen tiefstem Herzen Schlangen wühlen;
Genährt von meinen schmerzlichen
    Gefühlen –
Fast wütend durch ein ungestillt Verlangen:

Mit dir, des Morgens Göttin, mich zu einen,
Und weit von diesem nichtigen Getriebe,
Aus Sphären edler Freiheit, aus Sphären rein-
    er Liebe,
Ein stiller, bleicher Stern herab zu scheinen.

The whole day long I may speak but
    once,
Eternal silence and sorrow being my wont:
When Aurora's purple rays break lovingly
Through the night-born walls of mist.

To the ears of man it is music.
Since I voice my lament in melody
And smooth its harshness in poetry's
    fire,
They think that rapture blooms in me.

In me – to whom death stretches out his arms,
While serpents writhe in the depths of my
    heart;
Nourished by my anguished feelings –
Almost maddened with unappeased desire:

To be united with you, goddess of dawn,
And far from this futile commotion to shine
    down
From spheres of noble liberty and pure love,
As a pale and silent star.

* Memnon was the son of Aurora (Dawn). Having slain Antilochus in Troy, he in turn was killed by
Achilles; and when Aurora beseeched Zeus to resuscitate her son, he agreed to wake him at dawn each day
with the rays of the rising sun – which drew from Memnon a sad wailing.

April 1817 Auf der Donau / On the Danube D553

Auf der Wellen Spiegel	The boat glides
Schwimmt der Kahn.	On the waves' surface.
Alte Burgen ragen	Old castles soar
Himmelan;	Heavenward;
Tannenwälder rauschen	Pine-forests stir
Geistergleich –	Like ghosts –
Und das Herz im Busen	And our hearts grow
Wird uns weich.	Faint within us.
Denn der Menschen Werke	For the works of man
Sinken all';	All perish;
Wo ist Turm, wo Pforte,	Where are towers, where gates,
Wo der Wall,	Where ramparts,
Wo sie selbst, die Starken?	Where are the mighty themselves?
Erzgeschirmt,	Who clad in bronze armour,
Die in Krieg und Jagden	Stormed
Hingestürmt.	Into wars and hunts.
Trauriges Gesträppe	Melancholy briars
Wuchert fort,	Grow rank and rampant,
Während frommer Sage	While the power
Kraft verdorrt.	Of pious myth withers.
Und im kleinen Kahne	And in our small boat
Wird uns bang –	We grow afraid –
Wellen droh'n, wie Zeiten,	Waves, like time, threaten
Untergang.	Destruction.

May 1817 Nach einem Gewitter / After a thunderstorm D561

Auf den Blumen flimmern Perlen,	Pearls glisten on the flowers,
Philomelens Klagen fließen;	Philomel's* lament pours forth;
Mutiger nun dunkle Erlen	Dark alders shoot up more bravely
In die reinen Lüfte sprießen.	Into the pure air.
Und dem Tale, so erblichen,	A lovely redness now returns
Kehret holde Röte wieder,	To the pale valley,
In der Blüten Wohlgerüchen	Birds bathe their plumage
Baden Vögel ihr Gefieder.	In the fragrant flowers.
Hat die Brust sich ausgewittert,	When the heart's storm is ended,
Seitwärts lehnt der Gott den Bogen –	God tilts his bow sideways –
Und sein golden Antlitz zittert	And his golden countenance quivers
Reiner auf versöhnten Wogen.	More purely on appeased waves.

* A poetic name for the nightingale.

September 1817 Erlafsee* / Lake Erlaf D586

Mir ist so wohl, so weh
Am stillen Erlafsee.
Heilig Schweigen
In Fichtenzweigen.
Regungslos
Der blaue Schoß;
Nur der Wolken Schatten flieh'n
Überm dunklen Spiegel hin.

 Frische Winde
 Kräuseln linde
 Das Gewässer;
 Und der Sonne
 Goldne Krone
 Flimmert blässer.

Mir ist so wohl, so weh
Am stillen Erlafsee.

I feel so happy, so sad
By quiet Lake Erlaf :
Sacred silence
In the pine branches.
Motionless
The blue depths;
Only cloud shadows flit
Across the glassy surface.

 Fresh breezes
 Gently ruffle
 The water;
 And the sun's
 Golden crown
 Grows paler.

I feel so happy, so sad
By quiet Lake Erlaf.

October 1819 Nachtstück / Nocturne D672

Wenn über Berge sich der Nebel breitet,
Und Luna mit Gewölken kämpft,
So nimmt der Alte seine Harfe, und schreitet,
Und singt waldeinwärts und gedämpft:
 „Du heil'ge Nacht!
 „Bald ist's vollbracht.
 „Bald schlaf' ich ihn
 „Den langen Schlummer,
 „Der mich erlöst
 „Von allem Kummer."

 „Die grünen Bäume rauschen dann,
 „Schlaf süß, du guter alter Mann;
 „Die Gräser lispeln wankend fort,
 „Wir decken seinen Ruheort;
 „Und mancher liebe Vogel ruft,
 „O laß ihn ruh'n in Rasengruft!" –

Der Alte horcht, der Alte schweigt –
Der Tod hat sich zu ihm geneigt.

When mist spreads over the mountains,
And Luna battles with the clouds,
The old man takes up his harp, and steps
Into the forest, singing softly:
 'O holy night!
 Soon it shall be done.
 Soon I shall sleep
 The long sleep,
 That shall free me
 From all affliction.'

 'Then the green trees will rustle:
 Sleep well, good old man;
 The swaying grass will whisper:
 We will cover his resting-place;
 And many a sweet bird will call:
 O let him rest in his grassy grave!' –

The old man listens, the old man is silent –
Death has inclined towards him.

?September 1820 Freiwilliges Versinken / Voluntary descent D700

Wohin, o Helios? In kühlen Fluten
Will ich den Flammenleib versenken,

Whither, O Helios? In cool waters
I shall immerse my burning body,

* A lake in Lower Austria.

Gewiß im Innern, neue Gluten
Der Erde Feuerreich zu schenken.

Ich nehme nicht, ich pflege nur zu geben;
Und wie verschwenderisch mein Leben,
Umhüllt mein Scheiden goldne Pracht,
Ich scheide herrlich, naht die Nacht.

Wie blaß der Mond, wie matt die Sterne!
So lang ich kräftig mich bewege,
Erst wenn ich auf die Berge meine Krone lege,
Gewinnen sie an Mut und Kraft in weiter
    Ferne.

Inwardly certain that I can bestow
New warmth upon the earth's fires.

I do not take, accustomed only to giving;
And however prodigal my life has been,
My parting is bathed in golden splendour,
I depart in glory, when night approaches.

How pale the moon, how faint the stars,
As long as I am powerfully in motion,
Only when I lay my crown on the mountains
Do they, far off, gain in heart and strength.

April 1822 Nachtviolen / Dame's violets D752

Nachtviolen, Nachtviolen!
Dunkle Augen, Seelenvolle, –
Selig ist es, sich versenken
In dem sammtnen Blau.

Dame's violets, dame's violets,
Dark, soulful eyes –
How blissful to immerse myself
In your velvet blue.

Grüne Blätter streben freudig
Euch zu hellen, euch zu schmücken;
Doch ihr blicket ernst und schweigend
In die laue Frühlingsluft.

Green leaves strive cheerfully
To brighten and adorn you;
But you gaze out stern and silent
Into the mild spring air.

Mit erhabnen Wehmutsstrahlen
Trafet ihr mein treues Herz.
Und nun blüht in stummen Nächten
Fort die heilige Verbindung.

With sublime shafts of melancholy
You have pierced my faithful heart,
And now in silent nights
Our sacred union blossoms.

April 1822 Aus Heliopolis* I / From Heliopolis I D753

Im kalten, rauhen Norden
Ist Kunde mir geworden
Von einer Stadt, der Sonnenstadt.
Wo weilt das Schiff, wo ist der Pfad,
Die mich zu jenen Hallen tragen?
Von Menschen konnt' ich nichts erfragen, –
In Zwiespalt waren sie verloren.
Zur Blume, die sich H e l i o s erkoren,
Die ewig in sein Antlitz blickt,
Wandt' ich mich nun, – und ward entzückt:
    „Wende, so wie ich, zur Sonne
    Deine Augen! Dort ist Wonne,
    Dort ist Leben;
    Treu ergeben,
    Pilg're zu, und zweifle nicht:

In the cold, raw north
I heard tell
Of a city, the city, of the sun.
Where is the ship, where is the path
That will take me to those halls?
Men could tell me nothing,
Confused as they were in strife.
To that flower, chosen by *Helios*
For himself, which forever gazes at his face,
I now turned – and was enchanted:
    'Turn, like I do, your eyes
    To the sun! There is bliss,
    There is life;
    In true devotion
    Pilgrim on towards it, and do not doubt:

* A city in Lower Egypt, where there was a temple sacred to the sun.

Ruhe findest du im Licht;
Licht erzeuget alle Gluten, –
Hoffnungspflanzen, Tatenfluten!"

You shall find peace in light;
Light engenders all ardour,
Flowers of hope, torrents of deeds!'

April 1822 Aus Heliopolis II / From Heliopolis II D754

Fels auf Felsen hingewälzet,
Fester Grund und treuer Halt;
Wasserfälle, Windesschauer,
Unbegriffene Gewalt –
Einsam auf Gebirges Zinne
Kloster- wie auch Burg-Ruine:
Grab' sie der Erinn'rung ein!
Denn der Dichter lebt vom Sein.
Atme du den heil'gen Äther,
Schling' die Arme um die Welt;
Nur dem Würdigen, dem Großen
Bleibe mutig zugesellt.
Laß die Leidenschaften sausen
Im metallenen Accord;
Wenn die starken Stürme brausen,
Findest du das rechte Wort.

Rock piled on rock,
Solid ground and firm foothold;
Waterfalls, blasts of wind,
Uncomprehended power –
Lonely on the mountain peak,
Ruined monastery and castle:
Etch them in the memory!
For the poet lives from Being.
Breathe in the hallowed ether,
Fling your arms around the world;
Have courage and consort only
With the great and worthy.
Let passions seethe
In brazen harmony;
When fierce tempests rage,
You shall find the right word.

?1822 Lied eines Schiffers an die Dioskuren* / Seafarer's song to the Dioscuri D360

Dioskuren, Zwillingssterne,
Die ihr leuchtet meinem Nachen,
Mich beruhigt auf dem Meere
Eure Milde, euer Wachen.

Dioscuri, twin stars,
You who light my vessel's way,
Your gentle vigilance
Consoles me on the seas.

Wer auch, fest in sich begründet,
Unverzagt dem Sturm begegnet;
Fühlt sich doch in euren Strahlen
Doppelt mutig und gesegnet.

Though a man, full of confidence,
Stands intrepid against the storm,
He feels doubly valiant and blessed
When you shine on him.

Dieses Ruder, das ich schwinge,
Meeresfluten zu zerteilen;
Hänge ich, so ich geborgen,
Auf an eures Tempels Säulen.

This oar that I ply
To part the ocean's waves,
I shall hang on your temple's pillar,
Once I am safely ashore.

March 1824 Der Sieg / The victory D805

O unbewölktes Leben!
So rein und tief und klar.
Uralte Träume schweben
Auf Blumen wunderbar.

O unclouded life!
So pure and deep and clear.
Age-old dreams hover
Wondrously over flowers.

---

* Dioscuri, or *sons of Jupiter*, was a name given to Castor and Pollux.

Der Geist zerbrach die Schranken,	The spirit broke through the bonds
Des Körpers träges Blei;	Of the body's leaden weight;
Er waltet groß und frei.	Great and free, it now prevails.
Es laben die Gedanken	Thoughts are refreshed
An Edens Früchten sich;	By the fruits of Paradise;
Der alte Fluch entwich.	The ancient curse is lifted.
Was ich auch je gelitten,	Whatever I may have suffered,
Die Palme ist erstritten,	The victor's palm is won,
Gestillet mein Verlangen.	My longing stilled.
Die Musen selber sangen	The Muses themselves sang
Die Sphinx in Todesschlaf,	The sphinx to sleep and death,
Und meine Hand – sie traf.	And my hand – it struck the blow.
O unbewölktes Leben!	O unclouded life!
So rein und tief und klar.	So pure and deep and clear.
Uralte Träume schweben	Age-old dreams hover
Auf Blumen wunderbar.	Wondrously over flowers.

March 1824 Abendstern / Evening star D806

Was weilst du einsam an dem Himmel,	Why do you linger lonely in the sky,
O schöner Stern? und bist so mild;	O lovely star? and are yet so gentle;
Warum entfernt das funkelnde Gewimmel	Why do all your glittering brothers
Der Brüder sich von deinem Bild?	Shun your sight?
„Ich bin der Liebe treuer Stern,	'I am the faithful star of love,
„Sie halten sich von Liebe fern."	They keep aloof from love.'
So solltest du zu ihnen gehen,	If you are love's messenger,
Bist du der Liebe, zaudre nicht!	You should seek them out, do not delay!
Wer möchte denn dir widerstehen?	For who could resist you,
Du süßes eigensinnig Licht.	O sweet and wayward light.
„Ich säe, schaue keinen Keim,	'I sow no seed, I see no fruit,
„Und bleibe trauernd still daheim."	And in silent sorrow stay at home.'
(*Zemlinsky*)	

March 1824 Auflösung / Dissolution D807

Verbirg dich, Sonne,	Conceal yourself, sun,
Denn die Gluten der Wonne	For the fires of rapture
Versengen mein Gebein;	Scorch my whole being;
Verstummet Töne,	Fall silent, sounds,
Frühlings Schöne	Spring beauty,
Flüchte dich, und laß mich allein!	Flee, and leave me to myself!
Quillen doch aus allen Falten	For sweet powers well up
Meiner Seele liebliche Gewalten;	From every recess of my soul,
Die mich umschlingen,	And envelop me
Himmlisch singen –	With celestial song –

Geh' unter Welt, und störe	Dissolve, world, and never more
Nimmer die süßen ätherischen Chöre!	Disturb the sweet ethereal choirs!

March 1824 Gondelfahrer / The gondolier D808

Es tanzen Mond und Sterne	Moon and stars are dancing
Den flücht'gen Geisterreih'n:	The fleeting spirits' round:
Wer wird von Erdensorgen	Who would be forever fettered
Befangen immer sein!	By earthly cares!
Du kannst in Mondesstrahlen	Now, my boat, you can drift
Nun, meine Barke, wallen;	In the moonlight;
Und aller Schranken los,	And freed from all restraints,
Wiegt dich des Meeres Schoß.	Be rocked by the lapping sea.
Vom Markusturme* tönte	From the tower of St Mark's
Der Spruch der Mitternacht:	Midnight's decree tolled forth:
Sie schlummern friedlich Alle,	Everyone sleeps in peace,
Und nur der Schiffer wacht.	And only the boatman's awake.

Wilhelm Müller (1794–1827)

Wilhelm Müller (1794–1827), the son of a master tailor, was the friend of many of the Romantic writers, including Arnim and Brentano. He fought in the Greek Wars of Liberation, and his *Lieder der Griechen* (1821–4) earned him the nickname 'Griechen-Müller'. He translated Marlowe's *Dr Faustus*, but it is through Schubert's song-cycles and 'Der Hirt auf dem Felsen' that he is still known to us today. *Die schöne Müllerin* appeared in *Siebenundsiebzig Gedichte aus den hinterlassenen Papieren eines reisenden Waldhornisten* ('*77 poems from the posthumous papers of a travelling horn player*'), the first volume of which was dedicated to Ludwig Tieck, the poet of Brahms's *Die schöne Magelone*. Heine admired Müller's poetry and set him above Uhland in his *Romantische Schule*; he also wrote him this glowing letter to accompany a volume of his own *Reisebilder*:

> [...] aber ich glaube in Ihren Liedern den reinen Klang und die wahre Einfachheit, wonach ich immer strebte, gefunden zu haben. Wie rein, wie klar sind Ihre Lieder, und sämmtlich sind es Volkslieder.

> [...] but I think that it was in your songs that I discovered the pure tone and the true simplicity for which I was always striving. How pure and clear your songs are – folksongs every one of them.

He relished the simplicity of Müller's writing and those passages of romantic irony, of which Heine himself was such as master.

* St Mark's in Venice.

In the winter of 1816/17 Privy Councillor Friedrich August von Stägemann and his wife Elisabeth, both of whom were published poets, organized in their Berlin home evenings of literary charades, to entertain their adolescent children, August and the sixteen-year-old daughter Hedwig, the original 'schöne Müllerin'. Among their guests were Clemens Brentano, the twenty-two-year-old Wilhelm Hensel, who was soon to marry Fanny Mendelssohn, his eighteen-year-old sister Luise Hensel, Ludwig Rellstab and of course Wilhelm Müller, then aged twenty-three. The charades must have been emotionally fraught, since both Brentano and Müller were in love with Luise. Brentano actually proposed marriage to her (unsuccessfully, as it turned out), but the younger Müller, shy like *Die schöne Müllerin*'s hero, confided his own passion to his diary from October 1815 to December 1816: he is tortured by the thought that she might not return his love, he expresses his delight at Luise's gift of a songbook, he shows her his own poetry and favourite pieces by other writers, he worries about her health, and often ends an entry with the words 'Gute Nacht, Luise!' – a phrase that was to provide the title to the opening poem of *Die Winterreise* that Schubert later adapted for his own *Winterreise*.

1823 *Die schöne Müllerin / The beautiful maid of the mill* D795/1–20

1

Das Wandern / Journeying

Das Wandern ist des Müllers Lust,	To journey is the miller's joy,
Das Wandern!	To journey!
Das muß ein schlechter Müller sein,	A wretched miller he must be
Dem niemals fiel das Wandern ein,	Who never thought of journeying,
Das Wandern.	Of journeying.
Vom Wasser haben wir's gelernt,	We've learnt this from the water,
Vom Wasser!	The water!
Das hat nicht Rast bei Tag und Nacht,	It never rests by day or night,
Ist stets auf Wanderschaft bedacht,	But always thinks of journeying,
Das Wasser.	The water.
Das sehn wir auch den Rädern ab,	We've learnt it from the mill-wheels too,
Den Rädern!	The mill-wheels!
Die gar nicht gerne stille stehn,	They don't like standing still at all,
Die sich mein Tag nicht müde drehn,	And will never, ever tire,
Die Räder.	The mill-wheels.
Die Steine selbst, so schwer sie sind,	Even the mill-stones, heavy as they are,
Die Steine!	The mill-stones!
Sie tanzen mit den muntern Reihn	They join in the merry dance
Und wollen gar noch schneller sein,	And long to move even faster,
Die Steine.	The mill-stones.

| O Wandern, Wandern, meine Lust,
    O Wandern!
Herr Meister und Frau Meisterin,
Laßt mich in Frieden weiter ziehn
    Und wandern.
(*Marschner, Nicolai*) | O journeying, journeying, my joy,
    O journeying!
Master and mistress,
Let me go my way in peace,
    And journey. |

2
Wohin? / Where to?

Ich hört' ein Bächlein rauschen Wohl aus dem Felsenquell, Hinab zum Tale rauschen So frisch und wunderhell.	I heard a brooklet murmuring From its rocky source, Murmuring down into the valley, So bright and wondrous clear.
Ich weiß nicht, wie mir wurde, Nicht, wer den Rat mir gab, Ich mußte auch hinunter Mit meinem Wanderstab.	I do not know what seized me, Or who prompted me, I too had to journey down With my wanderer's staff.
Hinunter und immer weiter, Und immer dem Bache nach, Und immer frischer rauschte Und immer heller der Bach.	Down and ever onwards, Always following the stream, As it murmured ever brighter And murmured ever clearer.
Ist das denn meine Straße? O Bächlein, sprich, wohin? Du hast mit deinem Rauschen Mir ganz berauscht den Sinn.	Is this, then, my path? O brooklet, say where it leads? You have with your murmuring Quite bemused my mind.
Was sag' ich denn vom Rauschen? Das kann kein Rauschen sein: Es singen wohl die Nixen Tief unten ihren Reihn.	Why do I speak of murmuring? That's no murmuring I hear: It must be the water nymphs Singing and dancing below.
Laß singen, Gesell, laß rauschen, Und wandre fröhlich nach! Es gehn ja Mühlenräder In jedem klaren Bach!	Let them sing, let the stream murmur, And follow it cheerfully! For mill-wheels turn In every clear stream!

3
Halt! / Halt!

| Eine Mühle seh' ich blinken
Aus den Erlen heraus,
Durch Rauschen und Singen
Bricht Rädergebraus. | I see a mill gleaming
Among the alder trees,
The roar of mill-wheels is heard
Through the murmuring and singing. |
| Ei willkommen, ei willkommen,
Süßer Mühlengesang! | Welcome, O welcome,
Sweet song of the mill! |

Und das Haus, wie so traulich!   And how inviting the house looks!
Und die Fenster, wie blank!   And how the windows gleam!

    Und die Sonne, wie helle   And the sun, how brightly
Vom Himmel sie scheint!   It shines from the sky!
Ei, Bächlein, liebes Bächlein,   O brooklet, dear brooklet,
War es also gemeint?   Is this what you meant?

4

Danksagung an den Bach / Thanksgiving to the brook

War es also gemeint,   Is this what you meant,
Mein rauschender Freund,   My murmuring friend,
Dein Singen, dein Klingen,   Your singing, your ringing,
War es also gemeint?   Is this what you meant?

    Zur Müllerin hin!   To the maid of the mill!
So lautet der Sinn.   That is what you wish to say.
Gelt, hab' ich's verstanden?   Have I understood you?
Zur Müllerin hin!   To the maid of the mill!

    Hat s i e dich geschickt?   Was it *she* who sent you?
Oder hast mich berückt?   Or have you bewitched me?
Das möcht' ich noch wissen,   I should dearly like to know,
Ob s i e dich geschickt.   Whether *she* it was who sent you.

    Nun wie's auch mag sein,   Well, however it may be,
Ich gebe mich drein: I accept my fate:
Was ich such', hab' ich funden,   What I seek, I've found,
Wie's immer mag sein.   However it may be.

    Nach Arbeit ich frug,   I asked for work,
Nun hab' ich genug,   Now I have enough,
Für die Hände, für's Herze   For my hands, for my heart,
Vollauf genug!   More than enough!
(*Curschmann*)

5

Am Feierabend / When work is over

Hätt' ich tausend   If only I'd a thousand
Arme zu rühren!   Arms to work with!
Könnt' ich brausend   If only I could keep
Die Räder führen!   The mill-wheels roaring!
Könnt' ich wehen   If only I could whirl
Durch alle Haine,   Through every wood,
Könnt' ich drehen   If only I could turn
Alle Steine!   Every mill-stone!
Daß die schöne Müllerin   That the beautiful maid of the mill
Merkte meinen treuen Sinn!   Might see my faithful love!

Ach, wie ist mein Arm so schwach!
Was ich hebe, was ich trage,
Was ich schneide, was ich schlage,
Jeder Knappe tut mir's nach.
Und da sitz' ich in der großen Runde,
In der stillen kühlen Feierstunde,
Und der Meister spricht zu Allen:
Euer Werk hat mir gefallen;
Und das liebe Mädchen sagt
Allen eine gute Nacht.

But my arm, alas, is so weak!
Whatever I lift, whatever I carry,
Whatever I cut, whatever I hammer,
Any apprentice could do as much.
And there I sit with them in a circle,
When work is over, in the cool and quiet,
And the master says to all of us:
'I am pleased with your work.'
And the sweet girl wishes
Us all a good night.

6
Der Neugierige / The inquisitive one

Ich frage keine Blume,
Ich frage keinen Stern,
Sie können mir alle nicht sagen,
Was ich erführ' so gern.

I ask no flower,
I ask no star,
None of them can tell me
What I'd so love to hear.

Ich bin ja auch kein Gärtner,
Die Sterne stehn zu hoch;
Mein Bächlein will ich fragen,
Ob mich mein Herz belog.

After all, I'm no gardener,
And the stars are too high;
I shall ask my brooklet
If my heart deceived me.

O Bächlein meiner Liebe,
Wie bist du heut' so stumm!
Will ja nur Eines wissen,
E i n Wörtchen um und um.

O brooklet of my love,
How silent you are today!
Just one thing I wish to hear,
One word repeatedly.

Ja, heißt das eine Wörtchen,
Das andre heißet Nein,
Die beiden Wörtchen schließen
Die ganze Welt mir ein.

One little word is 'yes',
The other is 'no',
By these two little words
My whole world is bounded.

O Bächlein meiner Liebe,
Was bist du wunderlich!
Will's ja nicht weiter sagen,
Sag', Bächlein, liebt sie mich?
(*Hensel*)

O brooklet of my love,
How strange you are!
I'll let it go no further –
Tell me, brooklet, does she love me?

7
Ungeduld / Impatience

Ich schnitt' es gern in alle Rinden ein,
Ich grüb' es gern in jeden Kieselstein,
Ich möcht' es sä'n auf jedes frische Beet
Mit Kressensamen, der es schnell verrät,
Auf jeden weißen Zettel möcht' ich's schreiben:
Dein ist mein Herz, und soll es ewig bleiben.

I'd like to carve it on every tree,
Engrave it on every pebble,
Sow it on every fresh plot
With cress-seed that would soon reveal it,
Write it on every scrap of white paper:
My heart is yours, and shall be forever!

Ich möcht' mir ziehen einen jungen Star,
Bis daß er spräch' die Worte rein und klar,
Bis er sie spräch' mit meines Mundes Klang,
Mit meines Herzens vollem heißem Drang;
Dann säng' er hell durch ihre Fensterscheiben:
Dein ist mein Herz, und soll es ewig bleiben.

Den Morgenwinden möcht' ich's hauchen ein,
Ich möcht' es säuseln durch den regen Hain;
O, leuchtet' es aus jedem Blumenstern!
Trüg' es der Duft zu ihr von nah und fern!
Ihr Wogen, könnt ihr nichts als Räder treiben?
Dein ist mein Herz, und soll es ewig bleiben.

Ich meint', es müßt' in meinen Augen stehn,
Auf meinen Wangen müßt' man's brennen
    sehn,
Zu lesen wär's auf meinem stummen Mund,
Ein jeder Atemzug gäb's laut ihr kund;
Und sie merkt nichts von all' dem bangen
    Treiben:
Dein ist mein Herz, und soll es ewig bleiben!
(*Curschmann, Spohr*)

I'd like to train a young starling
To say the words pure and plain,
To say them with my voice's sound,
With my heart's full urgent passion;
Then he'd sing brightly through her window:
My heart is yours, and shall be forever.

I'd like to breathe it to the morning breeze,
Murmur it through the quivering trees;
If it could shine from every flower!
If their scent could bring it her from near and far!
O water, are mill-wheels all you can move?
My heart is yours, and shall be forever.

I'd have thought it must show in my eyes,
Could be seen on my burning cheeks,
Could be read on my silent lips,
I'd have thought every breath proclaimed it
    loud;
And she sees nothing of this anxious
    pleading:
My heart is yours, and shall be forever!

8
Morgengruß / Morning greeting

Guten Morgen, schöne Müllerin!
Wo steckst du gleich das Köpfchen hin,
Als wär' dir was geschehen?
Verdrießt dich denn mein Gruß so schwer?
Verstört dich denn mein Blick so sehr?
So muß ich wieder gehen.

    O laß mich nur von ferne stehn,
Nach deinem lieben Fenster sehn,
Von ferne, ganz von ferne!
Du blondes Köpfchen, komm hervor!
Hervor aus eurem runden Tor,
Ihr blauen Morgensterne!

    Ihr schlummertrunknen Äugelein,
Ihr taubetrübten Blümelein,
Was scheuet ihr die Sonne?
Hat es die Nacht so gut gemeint,
Daß ihr euch schließt und bückt und weint,
Nach ihrer stillen Wonne?

    Nun schüttelt ab der Träume Flor,
Und hebt euch frisch und frei empor

Good morning, beautiful maid of the mill!
Why do you dart your head back in,
As though something were troubling you?
Does my greeting so displease you?
Does my gaze so disturb you?
Then I must be on my way.

    Oh, just let me stand from afar
And watch your dear window
From afar, from afar!
Little blond head, come out!
Gaze out from your round gates,
Blue morning stars!

    Little sleep-drunk eyes,
Dew-afflicted little flowers,
Why do you fear the sun?
Was night so good to you
That you close and bow and weep
For its silent bliss?

    Shake off now the veil of dreams,
And look up gladly and freely

In Gottes hellen Morgen!
Die Lerche wirbelt in der Luft,
Und aus dem tiefen Herzen ruft
Die Liebe Leid und Sorgen.
(*Marschner*)

At God's bright morning!
The lark is warbling in the sky,
And from the heart's depths
Love draws pain and sorrow.

9
Des Müllers Blumen / The miller's flowers

Am Bach viel kleine Blumen stehn,
Aus hellen blauen Augen sehn;
Der Bach der ist des Müllers Freund,
Und hellblau Liebchens Auge scheint,
Drum sind es meine Blumen.

Many little flowers grow by the brook,
Gazing out of bright blue eyes;
The brooklet is the miller's friend,
And my sweetheart's eyes are brightest blue,
Therefore they are my flowers.

Dicht unter ihrem Fensterlein
Da will ich pflanzen die Blumen ein,
Da ruft ihr zu, wenn alles schweigt,
Wenn sich ihr Haupt zum Schlummer neigt,
Ihr wißt ja, was ich meine.

Close beneath her little window
I shall plant my flowers,
Call up to her when all is silent,
When she lays down her head to sleep,
For you know what I mean to say.

Und wenn sie tät die Äuglein zu,
Und schläft in süßer, süßer Ruh',
Dann lispelt als ein Traumgesicht
Ihr zu: Vergiß, vergiß mein nicht!
Das ist es, was ich meine.

And when she closes her little eyes,
And sleeps in sweet, sweet repose,
Then whisper as a dream:
'Forget, forget me not!'
That is what I mean to say.

Und schließt sie früh die Laden auf,
Dann schaut mit Liebesblick hinauf:
Der Tau in euren Äugelein,
Das sollen meine Tränen sein,
Die will ich auf euch weinen.
(*Hensel*)

And when in the morning she opens the shutters,
Gaze up at her with a loving look:
The dew in your little eyes
Shall be my tears,
The tears I'll weep on you.

10
Tränenregen / Rain of tears

Wir saßen so traulich beisammen
Im kühlen Erlendach,
Wir schauten so traulich zusammen
Hinab in den rieselnden Bach.

We sat so closely together
Beneath the cool alder roof,
We gazed so closely together
Into the rippling brook.

Der Mond war auch gekommen,
Die Sternlein hinterdrein,
Und schauten so traulich zusammen
In den silbernen Spiegel hinein.

The moon had also appeared,
Followed by little stars,
And they gazed so closely together
Into the silvery mirror.

Ich sah nach keinem Monde,
Nach keinem Sternenschein,

I did not look at the moon,
I did not look at the stars,

Ich schaute nach ihrem Bilde,
Nach ihren Augen allein.

    Und sahe sie nicken und blicken
Herauf aus dem seligen Bach,
Die Blümlein am Ufer, die blauen,
Sie nickten und blickten ihr nach.

    Und in den Bach versunken
Der ganze Himmel schien,
Und wollte mich mit hinunter
In seine Tiefe ziehn.

    Und über den Wolken und Sternen
Da rieselte munter der Bach,
Und rief mit Singen und Klingen:
Geselle, Geselle, mir nach.

    Da gingen die Augen mir über,
Da ward es im Spiegel so kraus:
Sie sprach: Es kommt ein Regen,
Ade, ich geh' nach Haus.

I gazed only at her reflection,
Only at her eyes.

    I saw them nodding and gazing
Up from the blissful brook,
The little blue flowers on the bank
Were nodding and glancing at her.

    And the whole sky seemed
Sunk beneath the brook,
And wanted to draw me down
Into its depths.

    And over the clouds and stars
The brook rippled merrily on,
And called with singing and ringing:
'Friend, friend, follow me.'

    At that my eyes brimmed over,
The brook's surface blurred:
She said: 'it's about to rain,
Goodbye, I'm going home.'

11
Mein! / Mine!

Bächlein, laß dein Rauschen sein!
Räder, stellt eur Brausen ein!
All' ihr muntern Waldvögelein,
Groß und klein,
Endet eure Melodein!
Durch den Hain
Aus und ein
Schalle heut' e i n Reim allein:
Die geliebte Müllerin ist m e i n !
M e i n !
Frühling, sind das alle deine Blümelein?
Sonne, hast du keinen hellern Schein?
Ach, so muß ich ganz allein,
Mit dem seligen Worte m e i n ,
Unverstanden in der weiten Schöpfung sein.
(*Curschmann*)

Brooklet, cease your murmuring!
Mill-wheels, stop your roaring!
All you merry woodland birds,
Large and small,
Put an end to your songs!
Throughout the wood,
In and out,
Let *one* rhyme ring out today:
The maid of the mill I love is *mine!*
Mine!
Spring, have you no more flowers?
Sun, can't you shine more brightly?
Ah, then I must be all alone
With that blissful word *mine*,
Understood nowhere in all creation.

12
Pause / Pause

Meine Laute hab' ich gehängt an die Wand,
Hab' sie umschlungen mit einem grünen
    Band –

I've hung my lute on the wall,
Have wound a green ribbon round
    it –

Ich kann nicht mehr singen, mein Herz ist zu
    voll,
Weiß nicht, wie ich's in Reime zwingen soll.
Meiner Sehnsucht allerheißesten Schmerz
Durft' ich aushauchen in Liederscherz,
Und wie ich klagte so süß und fein,
Glaubt' ich doch, mein Leiden wär' nicht klein:
Ei, wie groß ist wohl meines Glückes Last,
Daß kein Klang auf Erden es in sich faßt?

    Nun, liebe Laute, ruh' an dem Nagel hier!
Und weht ein Lüftchen über die Saiten dir,
Und streift eine Biene mit ihren Flügeln dich,
Da wird mir so bange und es durchschauert
    mich.
Warum ließ ich das Band auch hängen so lang'?
Oft fliegt's um die Saiten mit seufzendem Klang.
Ist es der Nachklang meiner Liebespein?
Soll es das Vorspiel neuer Lieder sein?

I can sing no more, my heart's too
    full,
I don't know how to force it to rhyme.
The most ardent pangs of my longing
I could express in playful song,
And as I lamented, so sweetly and tenderly,
I still thought my sorrows heavy enough:
Ah, how my happiness must weigh on me
That no sound on earth can contain it.

    Rest now, dear lute, here on this nail!
And if a breeze move across your strings
Or a bee brush you with its wings,
I feel so afraid and shudder.
Why did I let the ribbon hang so low?
Often it trails across the strings with a
    sighing sound.
Is this the echo of my love's torment?
Or the prelude to new songs?

13

Mit dem grünen Lautenbande / To accompany the lute's green ribbon

„Schad' um das schöne grüne Band,
„Daß es verbleicht hier an der Wand,
„Ich hab' das Grün so gern!"
So sprachst du, Liebchen, heut' zu mir;
Gleich knüpf' ich's ab und send' es dir:
Nun hab' das Grüne gern!

    Ist auch dein ganzer Liebster weiß,
Soll Grün doch haben seinen Preis,
Und ich auch hab' es gern.
Weil unsre Lieb' ist immergrün,
Weil grün der Hoffnung Fernen blühn,
Drum haben wir es gern.

    Nun schlinge in die Locken dein
Das grüne Band gefällig ein,
Du hast ja 's Grün so gern.
Dann weiß ich, wo die Hoffnung wohnt,
Dann weiß ich, wo die Liebe thront,
Dann hab' ich's Grün erst gern.

'A pity this lovely green ribbon
Should fade here on the wall,
I'm so fond of green!'
So, my love, you told me today;
I untie it at once and send it you:
Now be fond of green!

    Though he you love be dressed all in white,
Green too deserves praise,
And I too am fond of it.
Because our love is evergreen,
Because distant hope blossoms green,
That's why we're fond of it.

    Now twine the green ribbon
Prettily in your hair,
Since you're so fond of green.
Then I'll know where hope dwells,
Then I'll know where love reigns,
Then I'll be truly fond of green.

14

Der Jäger / The hunter

Was sucht denn der Jäger am Mühlbach hier?
Bleib', trotziger Jäger, in deinem Revier!

What does the hunter want here by the millstream?
Keep, haughty hunter, to your own preserve!

Hier gibt es kein Wild zu jagen für dich,
Hier wohnt nur ein Rehlein, ein zahmes, für
  mich.
Und willst du das zärtliche Rehlein sehn,
So laß deine Büchsen im Walde stehn,
Und laß deine klaffenden Hunde zu Haus,
Und laß auf dem Horne den Saus und Braus,
Und schere vom Kinne das struppige Haar,
Sonst scheut sich im Garten das Rehlein für-
  wahr.

Doch besser, du bliebest im Walde dazu,
Und ließest die Mühlen und Müller in Ruh'.
Was taugen die Fischlein im grünen
  Gezweig?
Was will denn das Eichhorn im bläulichen
  Teich?
Drum bleibe, du trotziger Jäger, im Hain,
Und laß mich mit meinen drei Rädern allein;
Und willst meinem Schätzchen dich machen
  beliebt,
So wisse, mein Freund, was ihr Herzchen
  betrübt:
Die Eber, die kommen zu Nacht aus dem Hain,
Und brechen in ihren Kohlgarten ein,
Und treten und wühlen herum in dem Feld:
Die Eber, die schieße, du Jägerheld!

There's no game here for you to hunt,
Only one doe, a tame one, lives here for
  me.
And if you would see that gentle doe,
Then leave your guns in the forest,
And leave your yapping hounds at home,
And leave off blowing your blaring horn,
And shave that scraggy beard from your
  chin,
Or the doe will take fright in her garden.

But better by far if you stayed in the forest,
And left both millers and mills in peace.
What good are fish among green
  branches?
What can the squirrel want in the bluish
  pond?
So, haughty hunter, keep to the wood,
And leave me alone with my three wheels;
And if you want to win my love's favour,
Then know, my friend, what's troubling her
  heart:
The wild boar that come by night from the
  wood
And break into her cabbage patch,
And trample and root about in the field:
Shoot the wild boar, you big bold hunter!

15
Eifersucht und Stolz / Jealousy and pride

Wohin so schnell, so kraus und wild, mein
  lieber Bach?
Eilst du voll Zorn dem frechen Bruder Jäger
  nach?
Kehr' um, kehr' um, und schilt erst deine
  Müllerin,
Für ihren leichten, losen, kleinen Flattersinn.
Sahst du sie gestern abend nicht am Tore
  stehn,
Mit langem Halse nach der großen Straße
  sehn?
Wenn von dem Fang der Jäger lustig zieht
  nach Haus,
Da steckt kein sittsam Kind den Kopf zum
  Fenster 'naus.
Geh', Bächlein, hin und sag' ihr das, doch sag'
  ihr nicht,

Where are you bound, dear brook, so fast,
  so furrowed, so wild?
Are you dashing angrily after our insolent
  huntsman friend?
Turn back, turn back, and scold first your
  maid of the mill
For her frivolous, wanton and fickle ways.
Didn't you see her last night by the
  gate,
Craning her neck to watch the wide
  road?
When a huntsman returns happy from the
  kill,
Nice girls don't peer from their
  window.
Go tell her that, my brooklet, but don't
  say

Hörst du, kein Wort, von meinem traurigen
   Gesicht;
Sag' ihr: Er schnitzt bei mir sich eine Pfeif'
   aus Rohr,
Er bläst den Kindern schöne Tänz' und
   Lieder vor.

A word, do you hear, about my unhappy
   face;
Tell her: he's with me, cutting reed
   pipes,
And piping pretty dances and songs for the
   children.

16
Die liebe Farbe / The beloved colour

In Grün will ich mich kleiden,
In grüne Tränenweiden,
Mein Schatz hat's Grün so gern.
Will suchen einen Zypressenhain,
Eine Heide von grünem Rosmarein,
Mein Schatz hat's Grün so gern.

I'll clothe myself in green,
In green weeping willow,
My love's so fond of green.
I'll seek out a cypress grove,
A heath full of green rosemary,
My love's so fond of green.

   Wohlauf zum fröhlichen Jagen!
Wohlauf durch Heid' und Hagen!
Mein Schatz hat's Jagen so gern.
Das Wild, das ich jage, das ist der Tod,
Die Heide, die heiß ich die Liebesnot,
Mein Schatz hat's Jagen so gern.

   Up, away to the merry hunt!
Away over thicket and heath!
My love's so fond of hunting.
The game I hunt is called Death,
I call the heath Love's Anguish,
My love's so fond of hunting.

   Grabt mir ein Grab im Wasen,
Deckt mich mit grünem Rasen,
Mein Schatz hat's Grün so gern.
Kein Kreuzlein schwarz, kein Blümlein bunt,
Grün, alles grün so rings und rund!
Mein Schatz hat's Grün so gern.
(*Hensel*)

   Dig me a grave in the turf,
Cover me with green grass,
My love's so fond of green.
No black cross, no bright flowers,
Nothing but green all around!
My love's so fond of green.

17
Die böse Farbe / The hateful colour

Ich möchte ziehn in die Welt hinaus,
Hinaus in die weite Welt,
Wenn's nur so grün, so grün nicht wär'
Da draußen in Wald und Feld!

I'd like to go out into the world,
Into the wide world,
If only it weren't so green
Out there in wood and field!

   Ich möchte die grünen Blätter all'
Pflücken von jedem Zweig,
Ich möchte die grünen Gräser all'
Weinen ganz totenbleich.

   I'd like to pluck the green leaves
From every single branch,
I'd like to weep the green grass
As pale as death with my tears.

   Ach Grün, du böse Farbe du,
Was siehst mich immer an,
So stolz, so keck, so schadenfroh,
Mich armen weißen Mann?

   Ah, green, you hateful colour,
Why must you always stare
So proud, so bold, so gloating
At me, a poor white miller?

Ich möchte liegen vor ihrer Tür,
Im Sturm und Regen und Schnee,
Und singen ganz leise bei Tag und Nacht
Das eine Wörtchen Ade!

   Horch, wenn im Wald ein Jagdhorn schallt,
Da klingt ihr Fensterlein,
Und schaut sie auch nach mir nicht aus,
Darf ich doch schauen hinein.

   O binde von der Stirn dir ab
Das grüne, grüne Band,
Ade, Ade! und reiche mir
Zum Abschied deine Hand!

I'd like to lie outside her door
In storm and rain and snow,
And sing softly all day and night
The single word: Farewell!

   When a horn sounds in the wood,
Listen – I hear her window open,
And though it's not for me she looks out,
Yet I can look in at her.

   O untie from your forehead
The green green ribbon,
Farewell, farewell! and give me
Your hand in parting!

18
Trockne Blumen / Withered flowers

Ihr Blümlein alle,
Die sie mir gab,
Euch soll man legen
Mit mir ins Grab.

   Wie seht ihr alle
Mich an so weh,
Als ob ihr wüßtet,
Wie mir gescheh'?

   Ihr Blümlein alle,
Wie welk, wie blaß?
Ihr Blümlein alle
Wovon so naß?

   Ach, Tränen machen
Nicht maiengrün,
Machen tote Liebe
Nicht wieder blühn.

   Und Lenz wird kommen,
Und Winter wird gehn,
Und Blümlein werden
Im Grase stehn,

   Und Blümlein liegen
In meinem Grab,
Die Blümlein alle,
Die sie mir gab.

   Und wenn sie wandelt
Am Hügel vorbei,

All you flowers
She gave me,
You shall be laid
With me in my grave.

   How sadly
You all gaze at me,
As if you knew
Of my fate!

   All you flowers,
Why faded, why pale,
All you flowers,
What makes you so wet?

   Ah, tears do not bring back
The green of May,
Nor cause dead love
To bloom again.

   And spring will come
And winter will go,
And little flowers
Spring up in the grass,

   And little flowers
Will lie in my grave,
All the flowers
She gave me.

   And when she wanders
By the mound

Und denkt im Herzen:	And thinks in her heart:
D e r meint' es treu!	*His* feelings were true!
Dann Blümlein alle,	Then, all you flowers,
Heraus, heraus!	Spring up, spring up!
Der Mai ist kommen,	May has come,
Der Winter ist aus.	Winter is past.

19

Der Müller und der Bach / The miller and the brook

DER MÜLLER	THE MILLER
Wo ein treues Herze	Where a true heart
In Liebe vergeht,	Dies of love,
Da welken die Lilien	Then lilies wither
Auf jedem Beet.	In every bed.
Da muß in die Wolken	The full moon then
Der Vollmond gehn,	Slips behind clouds,
Damit seine Tränen	So that mortals
Die Menschen nicht sehn;	Don't see its tears;
Da halten die Englein	Then little angels
Die Augen sich zu,	Cover their eyes
Und schluchzen und singen	And sob and sing
Die Seele zur Ruh'.	The soul to rest.
DER BACH	THE BROOK
Und wenn sich die Liebe	And whenever love
Dem Schmerz entringt,	Breaks free from sorrow,
Ein Sternlein, ein neues,	A tiny new star
Am Himmel erblinkt.	Shines in the sky.
Da springen drei Rosen,	Then three roses spring up,
Halb rot und halb weiß,	Half red and half white,
Die welken nicht wieder,	From branches of thorn,
Aus Dornenreis.	And wither no more.
Und die Engelein schneiden	And the little angels
Die Flügel sich ab,	Clip off their wings,
Und gehn alle Morgen	And every morning
Zur Erde herab.	Descend to earth.
DER MÜLLER	THE MILLER
Ach, Bächlein, liebes Bächlein,	Ah, brooklet, dear brooklet,
Du meinst es so gut:	You mean so well:
Ach, Bächlein, aber weißt du,	Ah, brooklet, but do you know
Wie Liebe tut?	What love can do?
Ach, unten, da unten,	Ah, there, down there,
Die kühle Ruh'!	Is cool repose!

Ach, Bächlein, liebes Bächlein,
So singe nur zu.
(*Nicolai*)

Ah, brooklet, dear brooklet,
Sing on, sing on.

20
Des Baches Wiegenlied / The brook's lullaby

Gute Ruh', gute Ruh'!
Tu' die Augen zu!
Wandrer, du müder, du bist zu Haus.
Die Treu' ist hier,
Sollst liegen bei mir,
Bis das Meer will trinken die Bächlein aus.

Rest well, rest well!
Close your eyes!
Weary wanderer, you are home.
There is constancy here,
You shall lie with me
Till the sea drinks all the brooklets dry.

Will betten dich kühl,
Auf weichen Pfühl,
In dem blauen kristallenen Kämmerlein.
Heran, heran,
Was wiegen kann,
Woget und wieget den Knaben mir ein!

I shall bed you down
On a cool soft pillow
In my little blue crystal chamber.
Draw near, draw near,
Whoever can rock,
Flow about him and rock my boy to sleep!

Wenn ein Jagdhorn schallt
Aus dem grünen Wald,
Will ich sausen und brausen wohl um dich her.
Blickt nicht herein,
Blaue Blümelein!
Ihr macht meinem Schläfer die Träume so
    schwer.

When a hunting horn brays
From the green forest,
I shall surge about you and roar.
Do not look in,
Little blue flowers!
You'll give my sleeper such bad
    dreams.

Hinweg, hinweg
Von dem Mühlensteg,
Böses Mägdelein, daß ihn dein Schatten
    nicht weckt!
Wirf mir herein
Dein Tüchlein fein,
Daß ich die Augen ihm halte bedeckt!

Away, away
From the mill-bridge,
Wicked maid,
Lest your shadow wake him!
Throw in to me
Your fine shawl
That I may cover his eyes!

Gute Nacht, gute Nacht!
Bis alles wacht,
Schlaf' aus deine Freude, schlaf' aus dein Leid!
Der Vollmond steigt,
Der Nebel weicht,
Und der Himmel da oben, wie ist er so weit!
(*Marschner*)

Good night, good night!
Till all the world wakes,
Rest from your joy, rest from your sorrow!
The full moon is rising,
The mists are parting,
And the heavens up there stretch on and on!

1

Gute Nacht / Good night

Fremd bin ich eingezogen,
Fremd zieh' ich wieder aus.
Der Mai war mir gewogen
Mit manchem Blumenstrauß.
Das Mädchen sprach von Liebe,
Die Mutter gar von Eh' –
Nun ist die Welt so trübe,
Der Weg gehüllt in Schnee.

A stranger I came,
A stranger I depart.
The month of May favoured me
With many bouquets of flowers.
The girl spoke of love,
Her mother of marriage even –
And now the world's so bleak
The road concealed in snow.

Ich kann zu meiner Reisen
Nicht wählen mit der Zeit:
Muß selbst den Weg mir weisen
In dieser Dunkelheit.
Es zieht ein Mondenschatten
Als mein Gefährte mit,
Und auf den weißen Matten
Such' ich des Wildes Tritt.

I cannot choose the time
For my journey:
I must find my own way
In this darkness.
A shadow in the moonlight
Keeps me company,
And on the white meadows
I seek the tracks of deer.

Was soll ich länger weilen,
Daß man mich trieb' hinaus?
Laß irre Hunde heulen
Vor ihres Herren Haus!
Die Liebe liebt das Wandern, –
Gott hat sie so gemacht –
Von einem zu dem andern –
Fein Liebchen, gute Nacht!

Why should I wait any longer
For them to drive me out?
Let stray dogs howl
Before their master's house!
Love loves to wander –
God has made it so –
From one to another –
My sweetest love, good night!

Will dich im Traum nicht stören,
Wär' schad' um deine Ruh',
Sollst meinen Tritt nicht hören –
Sacht, sacht die Türe zu!
Schreib' im Vorübergehen
An's Tor dir gute Nacht,
Damit du mögest sehen,
An dich hab' ich gedacht.

I'll not disturb your dreams,
A shame to spoil your rest!
You shall not hear my footsteps –
As I softly close the door!
I'll write 'Good night' on your gate,
As I pass,
So that you may see
I've thought of you.

2

Die Wetterfahne / The weather-vane

Der Wind spielt mit der Wetterfahne
Auf meines schönen Liebchens Haus.
Da dacht' ich schon in meinem Wahne,
Sie pfiff' den armen Flüchtling aus.

The wind plays with the weather-vane
On my beloved's house.
In my folly I thought it mocked
The wretched fugitive.

Er hätt' es eher bemerken sollen, He should have noticed it sooner,
Des Hauses aufgestecktes Schild, This sign fixed on the house,
So hätt' er nimmer suchen wollen He'd never then have thought to find
Im Haus ein treues Frauenbild. A faithful woman there.

Der Wind spielt drinnen mit den Herzen, The wind plays with hearts inside,
Wie auf dem Dach, nur nicht so laut. Though less loudly than on the roof.
Was fragen sie nach meinen Schmerzen? What is my torment to them?
Ihr Kind ist eine reiche Braut. Their child's a rich bride.

3
Gefrorne Tränen / Frozen tears

Gefrorne Tropfen fallen Frozen drops fall
Von meinen Wangen ab: From my cheeks:
Ob es mir denn entgangen, Did I, then, not notice
Daß ich geweinet hab'? I've been weeping?

Ei Tränen, meine Tränen, Ah tears, my tears,
Und seid ihr gar so lau, Are you so tepid
Daß ihr erstarrt zu Eise, That you turn to ice
Wie kühler Morgentau? Like cool morning dew?

Und dringt doch aus der Quelle And yet you spring from my heart
Der Brust so glühend heiß, With such fierce heat,
Als wolltet ihr zerschmelzen As if you would melt
Des ganzen Winters Eis. All the winter's ice.

4
Erstarrung / Numbness

Ich such' im Schnee vergebens In vain I seek
Nach ihrer Tritte Spur, Her steps in the snow,
Wo sie an meinem Arme Where we walked arm in arm
Durchstrich die grüne Flur. Through the green field.

Ich will den Boden küssen, I shall kiss the ground,
Durchdringen Eis und Schnee Pierce ice and snow
Mit meinen heißen Tränen, With my hot tears,
Bis ich die Erde seh'. Till I see the earth.

Wo find' ich eine Blüte, Where shall I find a flower,
Wo find' ich grünes Gras? Where shall I find green grass?
Die Blumen sind erstorben, The flowers have withered,
Der Rasen sieht so blaß. The grass looks so pale.

Soll denn kein Angedenken Is there no keepsake, then,
Ich nehmen mit von hier? For me to take from here?
Wenn meine Schmerzen schweigen, Who, when my grief is silent,
Wer sagt mir dann von ihr? Will speak to me of her?

Mein Herz ist wie erstorben,
Kalt starrt ihr Bild darin:
Schmilzt je das Herz mir wieder,
Fließt auch ihr Bild dahin.

My heart seems dead,
Her cold image numb within:
Should my heart ever thaw,
Her image too will melt.

5
Der Lindenbaum / The linden tree

Am Brunnen vor dem Tore
Da steht ein Lindenbaum:
Ich träumt' in seinem Schatten
So manchen süßen Traum.

By the well, before the gate,
Stands a linden tree:
I used to dream in its shade
So many a sweet dream.

Ich schnitt in seine Rinde
So manches liebe Wort;
Es zog in Freud' und Leide
Zu ihm mich immer fort.

I used to carve in its bark
So many a word of love;
In joy and in sorrow
I felt ever drawn to it.

Ich mußt' auch heute wandern
Vorbei in tiefer Nacht,
Da hab' ich noch im Dunkel
Die Augen zugemacht.

I had to pass it again
Today at dead of night,
And even in the dark,
I closed my eyes.

Und seine Zweige rauschten,
Als riefen sie mir zu:
Komm her zu mir, Geselle,
Hier findst du deine Ruh'!

And its branches rustled,
As though calling me:
Come to me, my friend,
Here you shall find rest!

Die kalten Winde bliesen
Mir grad' in's Angesicht,
Der Hut flog mir vom Kopfe,
Ich wendete mich nicht.

The cold winds blew
Full into my face,
My hat flew from my head,
I did not turn back.

Nun bin ich manche Stunde
Entfernt von jenem Ort,
Und immer hör' ich's rauschen:
Du fändest Ruhe dort!
(*Kreutzer, Silcher*)

Many hours have passed
Since I left that place,
Yet still I hear the rustling:
There shall you find rest!

6
Wasserflut / Flood

Manche Trän' aus meinen Augen
Ist gefallen in den Schnee;
Seine kalten Flocken saugen
Durstig ein das heiße Weh.

Many a tear from my eyes
Has fallen into the snow;
The cold flakes thirstily drink
My burning anguish.

Wenn die Gräser sprossen wollen,
Weht daher ein lauer Wind,

When grass is ready to grow,
A warm wind blows,

Und das Eis zerspringt in Schollen,
Und der weiche Schnee zerrinnt.

Schnee, du weißt von meinem Sehnen:
Sag', wohin doch geht dein Lauf?
Folge nach nur meinen Tränen,
Nimmt dich bald das Bächlein auf.

Wirst mit ihm die Stadt durchziehen,
Muntre Straßen ein und aus:
Fühlst du meine Tränen glühen,
Da ist meiner Liebsten Haus.

And the ice breaks into fragments,
And the soft snow melts.

Snow, you know of my longing:
Tell me where your path leads?
You've only to follow my tears
And the stream will bear you away.

It will carry you through the town,
In and out of busy streets:
When you feel my tears burning,
That will be my loved-one's house.

7
Auf dem Flusse / On the river

Der du so lustig rauschtest,
Du heller, wilder Fluß,
Wie still bist du geworden,
Gibst keinen Scheidegruß.

Mit harter, starrer Rinde
Hast du dich überdeckt,
Liegst kalt und unbeweglich
Im Sande ausgestreckt.

In deine Decke grab' ich
Mit einem spitzen Stein
Den Namen meiner Liebsten
Und Stund' und Tag hinein:

Den Tag des ersten Grußes,
Den Tag, an dem ich ging,
Um Nam' und Zahlen windet
Sich ein zerbrochner Ring.

Mein Herz, in diesem Bache
Erkennst du nun dein Bild?
Ob's unter seiner Rinde
Wohl auch so reißend schwillt?

You who murmured so merrily,
You clear, raging stream,
How silent you've become,
You bid me no farewell.

You've covered yourself
With a hard stiff crust,
You lie cold and motionless,
Stretched out in the sand.

With a sharp stone
I carve on your surface
The name of my beloved,
And the hour and the day:

The day of our first greeting,
The day I went away,
Around the name and figure
Is wound a broken ring.

My heart, do you now see
Your own likeness in this stream?
Is there such a raging torrent
Beneath its surface too?

8
Rückblick / A backward glance

Es brennt mir unter beiden Sohlen,
Tret' ich auch schon auf Eis und Schnee.
Ich möcht' nicht wieder Atem holen,
Bis ich nicht mehr die Türme seh'.

Hab' mich an jeden Stein gestoßen,
So eilt' ich zu der Stadt hinaus;

The ground blazes beneath my feet,
Though I walk on ice and snow.
I shall not pause for breath again,
Till the towers are out of sight.

I've stumbled over every stone
In my haste to leave the town;

Die Krähen warfen Bäll’ und Schloßen
Auf meinen Hut von jedem Haus.

Wie anders hast du mich empfangen,
Du Stadt der Unbeständigkeit!
An deinen blanken Fenstern sangen
Die Lerch’ und Nachtigall im Streit.

Die runden Lindenbäume blühten,
Die klaren Rinnen rauschten hell,
Und ach, zwei Mädchenaugen glühten! –
Da war’s geschehn um dich, Gesell!

Kömmt mir der Tag in die Gedanken,
Möcht’ ich noch einmal rückwärts sehn,
Möcht’ ich zurücke wieder wanken,
Vor i h r e m Hause stille stehn.

The crows shied snow and hailstones
Onto my hat from every roof.

How differently you welcomed me,
City of inconstancy!
Lark and nightingale vied in song
At your gleaming windows.

The rounded linden trees blossomed,
The clear fountains murmured brightly,
And ah! the girl’s eyes flashed fire! –
And your fate, my friend, was sealed!

When I think of that day,
I long to look back once more,
Long to stumble back again,
Stand silently before *her* house.

9
Irrlicht / Will-o’-the-wisp

In die tiefsten Felsengründe
Lockte mich ein Irrlicht hin:
Wie ich einen Ausgang finde,
Liegt nicht schwer mir in dem Sinn.

Bin gewohnt das Irregehen,
’S führt ja jeder Weg zum Ziel:
Unsre Freuden, unsre Leiden,
Alles eines Irrlichts Spiel!

Durch des Bergstroms trockne Rinnen
Wind’ ich ruhig mich hinab –
Jeder Strom wird’s Meer gewinnen,
Jedes Leiden auch sein Grab.

A will-o’-the-wisp lured me
Into the deepest rocky chasm:
How to find a way out
Does not greatly concern me.

I’m used to going astray,
Every path leads to one goal:
Our joys, our sorrows
Are all a will-o’-the-wisp’s game!

Through the dry bed of a mountain stream
I calmly make my way down –
Every river will reach the sea,
Every sorrow find its grave.

10
Rast / Rest

Nun merk’ ich erst, wie müd’ ich bin,
Da ich zur Ruh’ mich lege;
Das Wandern hielt mich munter hin
Auf unwirtbarem Wege.

Die Füße frugen nicht nach Rast,
Es war zu kalt zum Stehen,
Der Rücken fühlte keine Last,
Der Sturm half fort mich wehen.

In eines Köhlers engem Haus
Hab’ Obdach ich gefunden;

Only now as I lie down to rest,
Do I notice how tired I am;
Walking had kept me cheerful
On the desolate road.

My feet demanded no rest,
It was too cold for standing still,
My back felt no burden,
The storm helped to drive me on.

I have found shelter
In a charcoal-burner’s cramped hut;

Doch meine Glieder ruhn nicht aus:
So brennen ihre Wunden.

Auch du, mein Herz, in Kampf und Sturm
So wild und so verwegen,
Fühlst in der Still' erst deinen Wurm
Mit heißem Stich sich regen!

But my sores hurt so much
That my limbs cannot rest.

You too, my heart, in storm and strife
So audacious and so wild,
You feel stirring in this stillness
The fierce pangs of anguish!

11
Frühlingstraum / Dream of Spring

Ich träumte von bunten Blumen,
So wie sie wohl blühen im Mai,
Ich träumte von grünen Wiesen,
Von lustigem Vogelgeschrei.

Und als die Hähne krähten,
Da ward mein Auge wach;
Da war es kalt und finster,
Es schrieen die Raben vom Dach.

Doch an den Fensterscheiben
Wer malte die Blätter da?
Ihr lacht wohl über den Träumer,
Der Blumen im Winter sah?

Ich träumte von Lieb' um Liebe,
Von einer schönen Maid,
Von Herzen und von Küssen,
Von Wonne und Seligkeit.

Und als die Hähne krähten,
Da ward mein Herze wach;
Nun sitz' ich hier alleine
Und denke dem Traume nach.

Die Augen schließ' ich wieder,
Noch schlägt das Herz so warm.
Wann grünt ihr Blätter am Fenster?
Wann halt' ich mein Liebchen im Arm?
(*Kreutzer*)

I dreamt of colourful flowers,
Such as might bloom in May,
I dreamt of green meadows
And happy singing of birds.

And when the cocks crowed,
My eyes awoke;
It was dark and cold,
The ravens screamed from the roof.

But who painted those leaves
On the window-panes?
Are you mocking the dreamer
Who saw flowers in winter?

I dreamt of love requited,
Dreamt of a beautiful girl,
Of caressing and of kissing,
Of rapture and of joy.

And when the cocks crowed,
My heart awoke;
Now I sit here alone,
And think about the dream.

I close my eyes again,
My heart still beats so warm.
Leaves on my window, when will you turn green?
When shall I hold my love in my arms?

12
Einsamkeit / Loneliness

Wie eine trübe Wolke
Durch heitre Lüfte geht,
Wenn in der Tanne Wipfel
Ein mattes Lüftchen weht:

Like a dark cloud
Drifting across clear skies,
When a faint breeze
Blows through the fir-tops:

So zieh' ich meine Straße
Dahin mit trägem Fuß,
Durch helles, frohes Leben,
Einsam und ohne Gruß.

Ach, daß die Luft so ruhig!
Ach, daß die Welt so licht!
Als noch die Stürme tobten,
War ich so elend nicht.

I go on my way
With dragging steps,
Through life's bright joys,
Lonely and ignored.

Alas, why is the air so calm!
Alas, why is the world so bright!
While storms were still raging,
I was not so wretched.

13
Die Post / The mail-coach

Von der Straße her ein Posthorn klingt.
Was hat es, daß es so hoch aufspringt,
　　Mein Herz?

Die Post bringt keinen Brief für dich:
Was drängst du denn so wunderlich,
　　Mein Herz?

Nun ja, die Post kommt aus der Stadt,
Wo ich ein liebes Liebchen hatt',
　　Mein Herz!

Willst wohl einmal hinübersehn,
Und fragen, wie es dort mag gehn,
　　Mein Herz?
(*Kreutzer*)

A post-horn sounds from the road.
Why do you surge so wildly,
　　My heart?

There will be no letter for you:
Why do you throb so strangely,
　　My heart?

Because the post comes from the town,
Where once I had a beloved,
　　My heart!

I suppose you'd like to look in
And ask how things are there,
　　My heart?

14
Der greise Kopf / The hoary head

Der Reif einen weißen Schein
Mir über's Haar gestreuet.
Da glaubt' ich schon ein Greis zu sein,
Und hab' mich sehr gefreuet.

Doch bald ist er hinweggetaut,
Hab' wieder schwarze Haare,
Daß mir's vor meiner Jugend graut –
Wie weit noch bis zur Bahre!

Vom Abendrot zum Morgenlicht
Ward mancher Kopf zum Greise.
Wer glaubt's? Und meiner ward es nicht
Auf dieser ganzen Reise!

The frost has sprinkled a white sheen
On my hair.
I believed I was an old man
And was overjoyed.

But soon it melted,
My hair is black again,
So that I shudder at my youth –
How far still to the grave!

Between dusk and dawn,
Many a head has turned grey.
Yet mine, would you believe it, has not,
Throughout this whole journey!

15
Die Krähe / The crow

Eine Krähe war mit mir
Aus der Stadt gezogen,
Ist bis heute für und für
Um mein Haupt geflogen.

Krähe, wunderliches Tier,
Willst mich nicht verlassen?
Meinst wohl bald als Beute hier
Meinen Leib zu fassen?

Nun, es wird nicht weit mehr gehn
An dem Wanderstabe.
Krähe, laß mich endlich sehn
Treue bis zum Grabe!

One crow came with me
From the town,
And to this day
Has steadily circled my head.

O crow, strange creature,
Do you not wish to leave me?
Do you intend soon
To seize my body as prey?

Well, I've not much further
To journey with my staff.
O crow, let me at last see
Faithfulness unto death!

16
Letzte Hoffnung / Last hope

Hie und da ist an den Bäumen
Manches bunte Blatt zu sehn,
Und ich bleibe vor den Bäumen
Oftmals in Gedanken stehn.

Schaue nach dem einen Blatte,
Hänge meine Hoffnung dran;
Spielt der Wind mit meinem Blatte,
Zittr' ich, was ich zittern kann.

Ach, und fällt das Blatt zu Boden,
Fällt mit ihm die Hoffnung ab,
Fall' ich selber mit zu Boden,
Wein' auf meiner Hoffnung Grab.

Here and there on the trees
Many bright leaves can be seen,
And by those trees
I often stand lost in thought.

I look at the one remaining leaf,
And hang my hopes on it;
If the wind plays with my leaf,
I tremble in every limb.

Ah, and if the leaf falls to the ground,
My hope falls with it,
I too fall to the ground,
Weep on my hope's grave.

17
Im Dorfe / In the village

Es bellen die Hunde, es rasseln die Ketten.
Es schlafen die Menschen in ihren Betten,
Träumen sich Manches, was sie nicht haben,
Tun sich im Guten und Argen erlaben:
Und morgen früh ist Alles zerflossen. –
Je nun, sie haben ihr Teil genossen,
Und hoffen, was sie noch übrig ließen,
Doch wieder zu finden auf ihren Kissen.

Bellt mich nur fort, ihr wachen Hunde,
Laßt mich nicht ruhn in der Schlummer-
stunde!

Dogs bark, chains rattle.
People are asleep in bed,
Dreaming of much they do not possess,
Delighting in good things and bad:
And by morning all will have vanished. –
Still, they've enjoyed their share
And hope to find on their pillows
What is still left to enjoy.

Bark me on my way, watchful dogs,
Give me no rest in this hour of
sleep!

Ich bin zu Ende mit allen Träumen –
Was will ich unter den Schläfern säumen?

I'm finished with all dreaming –
Why should I linger among slumberers?

18
Der stürmische Morgen / The stormy morning

Wie hat der Sturm zerrissen
Des Himmels graues Kleid!
Die Wolkenfetzen flattern
Umher in mattem Streit.

How the storm has rent
The grey garment of the sky!
Ragged clouds flit about
In weary strife.

    Und rote Feuerflammen
Ziehn zwischen ihnen hin.
Das nenn' ich einen Morgen
So recht nach meinem Sinn!

    And red streaks of lightning
Flash between them.
That's what I call a morning
After my own heart!

    Mein Herz sieht an dem Himmel
Gemalt sein eignes Bild –
Es ist nichts als der Winter,
Der Winter kalt und wild!

    My heart sees its own likeness
Painted on the sky –
It's nothing but winter,
Winter cold and wild!

19
Täuschung / Delusion

Ein Licht tanzt freundlich vor mir her;
Ich folg' ihm nach die Kreuz und Quer;
Ich folg' ihm gern und seh's ihm an,
Daß es verlockt den Wandersmann.
Ach, wer wie ich so elend ist,
Gibt gern sich hin der bunten List,
Die hinter Eis und Nacht und Graus
Ihm weist ein helles, warmes Haus,
Und eine liebe Seele drin –
Nur Täuschung ist für mich Gewinn!

A friendly light dances before me,
I follow it this way and that,
I follow it willingly, and see
That it lures the wanderer from his path.
Ah, any man as wretched as I
Gladly yields to such garish guile,
That shows him beyond ice and night and terror
A bright warm house,
And a loving soul within –
Delusion is all I profit from!

20
Der Wegweiser / The signpost

Was vermeid' ich denn die Wege,
Wo die andern Wandrer gehn,
Suche mir versteckte Stege
Durch verschneite Felsenhöhn?

Why do I avoid the paths
That other wanderers tread,
Seek out hidden ways
Through snow-bound rocky heights?

    Habe ja doch nichts begangen,
Daß ich Menschen sollte scheun –
Welch ein törichtes Verlangen
Treibt mich in die Wüstenein?

    I have, after all, done no wrong,
That I should shun mankind –
What foolish desire
Drives me into the wilderness?

    Weiser stehen auf den Wegen,
Weisen auf die Städte zu,

    Signposts stand along the way,
Pointing to the towns,

Und ich wandre sonder Maßen,
Ohne Ruh', und suche Ruh'.

    Einen Weiser seh' ich stehen
Unverrückt vor meinem Blick;
Eine Straße muß ich gehen,
Die noch Keiner ging zurück.

And I wander on and on
Restlessly in search of rest.

    One signpost I see standing,
Firmly before my eyes;
One road I must travel
From which no man has ever returned.

21

Das Wirtshaus / The inn

Auf einen Totenacker
Hat mich mein Weg gebracht.
Allhier will ich einkehren:
Hab' ich bei mir gedacht.

    Ihr grünen Totenkränze
Könnt wohl die Zeichen sein,
Die müde Wandrer laden
In's kühle Wirtshaus ein.

    Sind denn in diesem Hause
Die Kammern all' besetzt?
Bin matt zum Niedersinken,
Bin tödlich schwer verletzt.

    O unbarmherz'ge Schenke,
Doch weisest du mich ab?
Nun weiter denn, nur weiter,
Mein treuer Wanderstab!

My journey has brought me
To a graveyard.
Here, I thought, is where
I shall rest for the night.

    You green funeral wreaths
Must be the signs
That invite weary travellers
Inside the cool inn.

    Are all the rooms, then,
Taken in this house?
I am weary, ready to sink,
Wounded unto death.

    O pitiless inn,
Yet you turn me away?
On, then, ever onwards,
My trusty staff!

22

Mut! / Courage!

Fliegt der Schnee mir in's Gesicht,
Schüttl' ich ihn herunter.
Wenn mein Herz im Busen spricht,
Sing' ich hell und munter.

    Höre nicht, was es mir sagt,
Habe keine Ohren,
Fühle nicht, was es mir klagt,
Klagen ist für Toren.

    Lustig in die Welt hinein
Gegen Wind und Wetter!
Will kein Gott auf Erden sein,
Sind wir selber Götter.

If snow drives into my face,
I shake it off.
If my heart speaks in my breast,
I sing loud and merrily.

    I don't hear what it tells me,
I have no ears,
I don't feel what it laments,
Lamenting is for fools.

    Cheerfully out into the world
Against wind and weather!
If there's no god on earth,
Then we ourselves are gods.

23

Die Nebensonnen / Phantom suns

Drei Sonnen sah ich am Himmel stehn,	I saw three suns in the sky,
Hab' lang' und fest sie angesehn;	Long and hard I stared at them;
Und sie auch standen da so stier,	And they too stood there so fixedly,
Als wollten sie nicht weg von mir.	As though they'd never leave me.
Ach, m e i n e Sonnen seid ihr nicht!	Alas, you are not *my* suns!
Schaut Andern doch in's Angesicht!	You gaze into other faces!
Ja, neulich hatt' ich auch wohl drei:	Lately, yes, I did have three:
Nun sind hinab die besten zwei.	But the best two now are down.
Ging' nur die dritt' erst hinterdrein!	If only the third would follow!
Im Dunkeln wird mir wohler sein.	I'd fare better in the dark.

24

Der Leiermann / The organ-grinder

Drüben hinter'm Dorfe	There, beyond the village,
Steht ein Leiermann,	An organ-grinder stands,
Und mit starren Fingern	And with numb fingers
Dreht er was er kann.	Plays as best he can.
Barfuß auf dem Eise	Barefoot on the ice
Wankt er hin und her;	He staggers to and fro;
Und sein kleiner Teller	And his little plate
Bleibt ihm immer leer.	Is always empty.
Keiner mag ihn hören,	No one cares to listen,
Keiner sieht ihn an;	No one looks at him;
Und die Hunde knurren	And the dogs snarl
Um den alten Mann.	Around the old man.
Und er läßt es gehen,	And he lets it all happen,
Alles, wie es will,	Happen as it will,
Dreht, und seine Leier	He turns the handle,
Steht ihm nimmer still.	His hurdy-gurdy's never still.
Wunderlicher Alter,	Strange old man!
Soll ich mit dir gehn?	Shall I go with you?
Willst zu meinen Liedern	Will you grind your hurdy-gurdy
Deine Leier drehn?	To my songs?
(*Wilhelm Kienzl*)	

1828 Der Hirt auf dem Felsen / The shepherd on the rock D965
[STANZAS 5 AND 6 BY HELMINA VON CHÉZY?]

Wenn auf dem höchsten Fels ich steh',	When I stand on the highest rock,
In's tiefe Tal hernieder seh',	Look down into the deep valley
Und singe,	And sing,

Fern aus dem tiefen dunkeln Tal	From far away in the deep dark valley
Schwingt sich empor der Widerhall	The echo from the ravines
Der Klüfte.	Rises up.
Je weiter meine Stimme dringt,	The further my voice carries,
Je heller sie mir wieder klingt	The clearer it echoes back to me
Von unten.	From below.
Mein Liebchen wohnt so weit von mir,	My sweetheart lives so far from me,
Drum sehn' ich mich so heiß nach ihr	Therefore I long so to be with her
Hinüber.	Over there.
In tiefem Gram verzehr ich mich,	Deep grief consumes me,
Mir ist die Freude hin,	My joy has fled,
Auf Erden mir die Hoffnung wich,	All earthly hope has vanished,
Ich hier so einsam bin.	I am so lonely here.
So sehnend klang im Wald das Lied,	The song rang out so longingly through the wo⟨
So sehnend klang es durch die Nacht,	Rang out so longingly through the night,
Die Herzen es zum Himmel zieht	That it draws hearts to heaven
Mit wunderbarer Macht.	With wondrous power.
Der Frühling will kommen,	Spring is coming,
Der Frühling, meine Freud',	Spring, my joy,
Nun mach' ich mich fertig	I shall now make ready
Zum Wandern bereit.	To journey.
(*Kreutzer*)	

Novalis (1772–1801)

The pseudonym (the poet placed the stress on the first syllable) of Friedrich Leopold von Hardenberg, the finest poet of the first Romantic school. He met Schiller in 1791 while studying at Jena, and the young Friedrich Schlegel in Leipzig; but it was the death of his twelve-year old fiancée Sophie von Kühn in March 1797 that released his poetic powers. Her death led to a religious crisis and the writing of the mystical *Hymnen an die Nacht*, four of which were set by Schubert in 1819. The *Hymns to Night* were completed in his final years, when he also wrote the *Geistliche Lieder* and *Heinrich von Ofterdingen*, an unfinished novel written partly as a reaction against the worldliness of Goethe's *Wilhelm Meisters Lehrjahre*; 'eine hohe lichtblaue Blume' appears to Heinrich in a dream – the blue flower which quickly became a widely recognized symbol of Romantic longing. He died of tuberculosis, the disease that had killed Sophie.

?May 1819 Marie / Mary D658

Ich sehe dich in tausend Bildern,	I see you in a thousand pictures,
Maria, lieblich ausgedrückt,	Mary, sweetly portrayed,

Doch keins von allen kann dich schildern,	Yet none of them can show you,
Wie meine Seele dich erblickt.	As my soul sees you.
Ich weiß nur, daß der Welt Getümmel	I only know that the world's tumult
Seitdem mir wie ein Traum verweht,	Has since vanished like a dream,
Und ein unnennbar süßer Himmel	And an ineffably sweet heaven
Mir ewig im Gemüte steht.	Is forever in my heart.
(*Marx, Reger, Louise Reichardt, Schoeck*)	

August Graf von Platen (1796–1835)

See Brahms

Schubert was introduced to the poetry of Platen through Franz von Bruchmann, who met the poet in 1821 and in a letter dated 2 August of the same year mentioned to him 'einige Goethische Gedichte, von Schubert herrlich gesetzt' ('some wonderful settings of Goethe poems by Schubert').

March/April 1822 Die Liebe hat gelogen / Love has lied D751

Die Liebe hat gelogen,	Love has lied,
Die Sorge lastet schwer,	Sorrow oppresses me,
Betrogen, ach, betrogen	I am betrayed, ah, betrayed
Hat alles mich umher!	By all around!
Es rinnen heiße Tropfen	Hot tears keep flowing
Die Wange stets herab,	Down my cheeks,
Laß ab, mein Herz, zu klopfen,	Beat no more, my heart,
Du armes Herz, laß ab!	Wretched heart, beat no more!

1822 Du liebst mich nicht / You do not love me D756

Mein Herz ist zerrissen, du liebst mich nicht!	My heart is broken, you do not love me!
Du ließest mich's wissen, du liebst mich nicht!	You let me know you do not love me!
Wiewohl ich dir flehend und werbend erschien,	Though I wooed you and beseeched you
Und liebebeflissen, du liebst mich nicht!	With devotion, you do not love me!
Du hast es gesprochen, mit Worten gesagt,	You told me so, you said it in words,
Mit allzugewissen, du liebst mich nicht!	All too clearly, you do not love me!
So soll ich die Sterne, so soll ich den Mond,	So must I forgo the stars, forgo the moon
Die Sonne vermissen? du liebst mich nicht!	And the sun? You do not love me!
Was blüht mir die Rose? was blüht der Jasmin?	Why does the rose bloom? Why the jasmine?
Was blühn die Narzissen? du liebst mich	Why the narcissus? You do not love
nicht!	me!

Adolf von Pratobevera (1806–75)

A government official in Vienna, who became minister of justice and governor of Lower Austria. He was also an occasional poet, and 'Abschied von der Erde' was written as an epilogue to his dramatic poem, 'Der Falke', where it is spoken by Mechthild while her father-in-law lies dying. Pratobevera asked Schubert to compose a piano accompaniment to the speech for a performance of the play to celebrate his father's birthday on 17 February 1826. It is the only example of melodrama in Schubert's songs.

February 1826 Abschied von der Erde / Farewell to the earth D829

Leb' wohl, du schöne Erde!
Kann dich erst jetzt verstehn,
Wo Freude und wo Kummer
An uns vorüber wehn.

Farewell, beautiful earth!
Only now do I understand you,
When joy and sorrow
Pass away from us.

Leb' wohl du Meister Kummer!
Dank dir mit nassem Blick!
Mit mir nehm' ich die Freude,
Dich lass' ich hier zurück.

Farewell, Master Sorrow!
I thank you with tearful eyes!
I take joy with me,
You I leave behind.

Sei nur ein milder Lehrer,
Führ alle hin zu Gott,
Zeig' in den trübsten Nächten
Ein Streiflein Morgenrot!

Try to be a kindly teacher,
Lead all men to God,
Reveal in the darkest of nights
A little streak of dawn!

Lasse sie Liebe ahnen,
So danken sie dir noch,
Der früher und der später,
Sie danken weinend doch.

Let them sense what love is,
And they will thank you for it,
Some sooner, some later,
All will thank you with tears.

Dann glänzt das Leben heiter,
Mild lächelt jeder Schmerz,
Die Freude hält umfangen
Das ruh'ge klare Herz.

Life will then be radiant,
All sorrows will gently smile,
Joy will hold in its embrace
The pure and tranquil heart.

Johann Ladislaus Pyrker von Oberwart (1772–1847)

A poet, dramatist and priest of Hungarian origin who became Patriarch of Venice in 1820 and Archbishop of Erlau in 1827. Schubert first met him at the house of Matthäus von Collin in c.1820 and dedicated to him the three songs of Op. 4. 'Die Allmacht', an extract from a long poem in blank verse, *Elisa in zwei Gesängen*, was composed in August 1825, after Schubert had met Pyrker again at Gastein. The song was sung by Vogl at Schubert's concert on 26 March 1828, and was also performed at the two memorial concerts in 1829.

Groß ist Jehova, der Herr! denn Himmel und Erde verkünden	Great is Jehovah, the Lord! for heaven and earth proclaim
Seine Macht! – Du hörst sie im brausenden Sturm, in des Waldstroms	His might! – You hear it in the roaring storm, in the forest river's
Lautaufrauschendem Ruf, in des grünenden Waldes Gesäusel;	Loud uplifted cry, in the greenwood's murmuring;
Siehst sie in wogender Saaten Gold, in lieblicher Blumen	You see it in the gold of waving corn, in the radiant lustre
Glühendem Schmelz, im Glanz des sternebesaeten Himmels!	Of lovely flowers, in the gleam of the starstrewn sky!
Furchtbar tönt sie im Donnergeroll, und flammt in des Blitzes	It rings out awesomely in the thunder's roll, and flares in the lightning's
Schnellhinzuckendem Flug; doch kündet das pochende Herz dir	Swift and jagged flight; but your pounding heart will reveal
Fühlbarer noch Jehova's Macht, des ewigen Gottes,	More palpably the power of Jehovah, the eternal God,
Blickst du flehend empor, und hoffst auf Huld und Erbarmen!	If you gaze up in prayer and hope for grace and mercy!

Johann Anton Friedrich Reil (1773–1843)

Actor and writer who was a member of the Burgtheater from 1809–31, where he met with particular success as Miller in Schiller's *Kabale und Liebe* and Nathan in Lessing's *Nathan der Weise*. He was an occasional poet and also wrote two additional stanzas for Diabelli's edition of 'Ständchen' ('Horch, horch! Die Lerch' im Ätherblau'). He provided Conradin Kreutzer with the libretto for *Fridolin, oder der Gang nach dem Eisenhammer*.

June 1827 Das Lied im Grünen / Song of the open air D917

Ins Grüne, ins Grüne!	Into the open, the open!
Da lockt uns der Frühling der liebliche Knabe,	Spring, that sweet youth, invites us,
Und führt uns am blumenumwundenen Stabe,	And leads us with his flower-twined staff
Hinaus, wo die Lerchen und Amseln so wach,	To where larks and blackbirds are wide-awake,
In Wälder, auf Felder, auf Hügel, zum Bach,	To woods and fields, over hills to the brook,
Ins Grüne, ins Grüne.	Into the open, the open.
Im Grünen, im Grünen!	In the open, the open!
Da lebt es sich wonnig, da wandeln wir gerne,	Life is blissful, we love to roam there,
Und heften die Augen dahin schon von ferne;	We fix our eyes there even from afar;
Und wie wir so wandeln mit heiterer Brust,	And on our way with cheerful hearts,
Umwallet uns immer die kindliche Lust,	A childlike joy envelops us,
Im Grünen, im Grünen.	In the open, the open.

Im Grünen, im Grünen,
Da ruht man so wohl, empfindet so Schönes,
Und denket behaglich an Dieses und Jenes,
Und zaubert von hinnen, ach! was uns
    bedrückt,
Und alles herbei, was den Busen entzückt,
Im Grünen, im Grünen.

Im Grünen, im Grünen,
Da werden die Sterne so klar, die die Weisen
Der Vorwelt zur Leitung des Lebens uns
    preisen.
Da streichen die Wölkchen so zart uns dahin,
Da heitern die Herzen, da klärt sich der Sinn,
Im Grünen, im Grünen.

Im Grünen, im Grünen,
Da wurde manch Plänchen auf Flügeln
    getragen,
Die Zukunft der grämlichen Ansicht
    entschlagen.
Da stärkt sich das Auge, da labt sich der Blick,
Sanft wiegen die Wünsche sich hin und zurück,
Im Grünen, im Grünen.

Im Grünen, im Grünen,
Am Morgen, am Abend, in traulicher Stille,
Entkeimet manch Liedchen und manche
    Idylle
Und Hymen oft kränzt den poetischen Scherz.
Denn leicht ist die Lockung, empfänglich das
    Herz
Im Grünen, im Grünen.

O gerne im Grünen
Bin ich schon als Knabe und Jüngling gewesen,
Und habe gelernt, und geschrieben, gelesen,
Im Horaz und Plato, dann Wieland und Kant,
Und glühendes Herzens mich selig genannt,
Im Grünen, im Grünen.

Ins Grüne, ins Grüne!
Laßt heiter uns folgen dem freundlichen
    Knaben!
Grünt einst uns das Leben nicht fürder, so
    haben
Wir klüglich die grünende Zeit nicht versäumt
Und, wann es gegolten, doch glücklich
    geträumt,
Im Grünen, im Grünen.

In the open, the open,
We find such peace, sense such
    beauty,
We gently muse on this and that,
And conjure away, ah! all our troubles,
And conjure up our heart's delight,
In the open, the open.

In the open, the open,
How brightly shine the stars, which the wise
    men
Of old commend for life's guidance.
Gossamer clouds drift gently by,
Our hearts grow light, our senses clear,
In the open, the open.

In the open, the open,
Many a little scheme took wing
And the future was stripped of its gloomy
    aspect.
Our eye is strengthened, our gaze
    refreshed,
Our desires sway gently to and fro,
In the open, the open.

In the open, the open,
In the morning and evening in intimate quiet,
Many songs and idylls burgeon,
And Hymen often crowns the poetic
    flirtation.
For enticement is easy, receptive the
    heart
In the open, the open.

I loved, as a boy and youth,
To be in the open
Where I learnt and wrote and read
Horace and Plato, then Wieland and Kant,
And with glowing heart counted myself happy,
In the open, the open.

Into the open, the open
Let us happily follow
The friendly youth!
When life one day is no longer green,
    wisely
We'll not have missed the verdant years,
And will, when it mattered, have happily
    dreamed,
In the open, the open.

Ludwig Rellstab (1799–1860)

Ludwig Rellstab, two years younger than Schubert, was active in Berlin as literary critic, dramatist, novelist, poet and librettist. He had originally offered his poems to Beethoven, who died before he could set them to music, but not before studying the poems in detail, as this extract from Rellstab's memoirs makes clear:

> Einige waren mit Bleistiftzeichen versehen, von Beethovens eigener Hand; es waren diejenigen, welche ihm am besten gefielen und die er damals an Schubert zur Komposition gegeben, weil er selbst sich zu unwohl fühlte ... Mit Rührung empfing ich die Blättchen zurück, die einen so eigentümlichen, aber der Kunst fruchtbar gewordenen Weg gemacht hatten, bis sie wieder zu mir zurückkehrten.

> A few had been marked with pencil, in Beethoven's own hand – those which he liked best and had then passed on to Schubert to set, since he himself felt too ill ... It was a moving experience to receive back the manuscripts which had travelled a route so strange, yet so fruitful for Art, before they returned to me.

Schubert's source, then, for these songs was almost certainly the annotated manuscript that Beethoven's secretary, Anton Schindler, had provided for him after Beethoven's death. If Schubert had not immortalized Rellstab in these poems and three others not included in *Schwanengesang* ('Herbst', 'Lebensmut' and 'Auf dem Strom'), his name, *pace* Franz Liszt and his three settings, would now be little known. His poems were published in 1827, the same year as Heine's *Buch der Lieder*.

March 1828 Auf dem Strom / On the river D943

Nimm die letzten Abschiedsküsse,	Take these final farewell kisses
Und die wehenden, die Grüße,	And the greetings I wave to you,
Die ich noch ans Ufer sende,	As you stand on the shore,
Eh' Dein Fuß sich scheidend wende!	Before turning to leave!
Schon wird von des Stromes Wogen	The river's swift current
Rasch der Nachen fortgezogen,	Already bears the boat away,
Doch den tränendunklen Blick	But my tear-dimmed gaze
Zieht die Sehnsucht stets zurück!	Is constantly drawn back by longing!
Und so trägt mich denn die Welle	And so the waves bear me away
Fort mit unerflehter Schnelle.	With unwelcome speed.
Ach, schon ist die Flur verschwunden,	Ah, the field where I joyously,
Wo ich selig S i e gefunden!	Once found *her*, has disappeared!
Ewig hin, ihr Wonnetage!	You days of bliss have gone forever!
Hoffnungsleer verhallt die Klage	My lament echoes forlornly
Um das schöne Heimatland,	For that fair homeland,
Wo ich i h r e Liebe fand.	Where I found *her* love.

379

Sieh, wie flieht der Strand vorüber,	See how the shore rushes past,
Und wie drängt es mich hinüber,	And how, with ineffable bonds,
Zieht mit unnennbaren Banden,	I am drawn
An der Hütte dort zu landen,	To land by that little house,
In der Laube dort zu weilen;	To linger in that arbour;
Doch des Stromes Wellen eilen	But the river rushes on
Weiter ohne Rast und Ruh,	Without respite,
Führen mich dem Weltmeer zu!	Bearing me off to the ocean!
Ach, vor jener dunklen Wüste,	Ah, how I shudder with horror
Fern von jeder heitern Küste,	At that dark wilderness,
Wo kein Eiland zu erschauen,	Far from every friendly coast,
O, wie faßt mich zitternd Grauen!	Where no island can be seen!
Wehmutstränen sanft zu bringen,	No song can bring me from the shore
Kann kein Lied vom Ufer dringen;	Gentle tears of sadness;
Nur der Sturm weht kalt daher	Only the storm blows cold
Durch das grau gehobne Meer!	Across the angry grey sea!
Kann des Auges sehnend Schweifen	When my longing, roaming eyes
Keine Ufer mehr ergreifen,	Can no longer make out the shore,
Nun so schau' ich zu den Sternen	I shall gaze up to the stars
Auf in jenen heil'gen Fernen!	In those remote and sacred regions!
Ach, bei i h r e m milden Scheine	Ah, it was beneath *their* soft light
Nannt' ich s i e zuerst die Meine;	That I first called *her* mine;
Dort vielleicht, o tröstend Glück!	Maybe there, consoling fate!
Dort begegn' ich i h r e m Blick.	There I'll meet *her* gaze again.

April 1828 Herbst / Autumn D945

Es rauschen die Winde	The winds are blowing
So herbstlich und kalt;	So autumnal and cold;
Verödet die Fluren,	The fields are barren,
Entblättert der Wald.	Leafless the woods.
Ihr blumigen Auen!	You blossoming meadows!
Du sonniges Grün!	You sunlit green!
So welken die Blüten	Thus do life's blossoms
Des Lebens dahin.	Wither away.
Es ziehen die Wolken	The clouds drift by
So finster und grau;	So sombre and grey;
Verschwunden die Sterne	The stars have faded
Am himmlischen Blau!	From the heavenly blue!
Ach, wie die Gestirne	Ah, as the stars
Am Himmel entfliehn,	Flee from the sky,
So sinket die Hoffnung	Thus does life's hope
Des Lebens dahin!	Fade away!
Ihr Tage des Lenzes	You days of spring
Mit Rosen geschmückt,	Adorned with roses,

Wo ich die Geliebte	When I pressed my beloved
Ans Herze gedrückt!	Against my heart!
Kalt über den Hügel	Howl on, chill winds,
Rauscht, Winde, dahin!	Across the hills!
So sterben die Rosen	Thus do love's roses
Der Liebe dahin.	Die away.
(*Lachner, Liszt*)	

1828 Liebesbotschaft / Love's message D957/1
FROM *Schwanengesang*

Rauschendes Bächlein,	Murmuring brooklet,
So silbern und hell,	So silver and bright,
Eilst zur Geliebten	Is it to my love
So munter und schnell?	You rush with such glee?
Ach, trautes Bächlein,	Ah, be my messenger,
Mein Bote sei Du;	Beloved brooklet;
Bringe die Grüße	Bring her greetings
Des Fernen ihr zu.	From her distant love.
All' ihre Blumen	All the flowers
Im Garten gepflegt,	She tends in her garden,
Die sie so lieblich	And wears with such grace
Am Busen trägt,	On her breast,
Und ihre Rosen	And her roses
In purpurner Glut,	In their crimson glow –
Bächlein, erquicke	Brooklet, refresh them
Mit kühlender Flut.	With your cooling waves.
Wenn sie am Ufer,	When on your bank,
In Träume versenkt,	Lost in dreams,
Meiner gedenkend	She inclines her head
Das Köpfchen hängt;	As she thinks of me –
Tröste die Süße	Comfort my sweetest
Mit freundlichem Blick,	With a kindly look,
Denn der Geliebte	For her lover
Kehrt bald zurück.	Will soon return.
Neigt sich die Sonne	And when the sun sets
Mit rötlichem Schein,	In a reddish glow,
Wiege das Liebchen	Rock my sweetheart
In Schlummer ein.	Into slumber.
Rausche sie murmelnd	Murmur her
In süße Ruh,	Into sweet repose,
Flüstre ihr Träume	Whisper her
Der Liebe zu.	Dreams of love.

1828 Kriegers Ahnung / Warrior's foreboding D957/2
FROM *Schwanengesang*

In tiefer Ruh liegt um mich her
Der Waffenbrüder Kreis;
Mir ist das Herz so bang und schwer,
Von Sehnsucht mir so heiß.

    Wie hab' ich oft so süß geträumt
An ihrem Busen warm!
Wie freundlich schien des Herdes Glut,
Lag sie in meinem Arm!

    Hier, wo der Flammen düstrer Schein
Ach! nur auf Waffen spielt,
Hier fühlt die Brust sich ganz allein,
Der Wehmut Träne quillt.

    Herz! Daß der Trost Dich nicht verläßt!
Es ruft noch manche Schlacht.
Bald ruh' ich wohl und schlafe fest,
Herzliebste – Gute Nacht!

In deep repose my brothers-in-arms
Lie round me in a circle;
My heart's so heavy and afraid,
So afire with longing.

    How often have I dreamt sweet dreams,
Resting on her warm breast!
How welcoming the fire's glow seemed,
When she lay in my arms!

    Here, where the flames' sombre glow
Plays merely, alas, on weapons,
Here the heart feels quite alone,
A tear of sadness wells.

    O heart, may comfort not abandon you!
Many a battle still calls.
I shall soon be at rest and fast asleep,
Sweetest love – good night!

1828 Frühlings-Sehnsucht / Spring longing D957/3
FROM *Schwanengesang*

Säuselnde Lüfte
Wehend so mild,
Blumiger Düfte
Atmend erfüllt!
Wie haucht ihr mich wonnig begrüßend an!
Wie habt ihr dem pochenden Herzen getan?
Es möchte Euch folgen auf luftiger Bahn!
Wohin?

    Bächlein, so munter
Rauschend zumal,
Wollen hinunter
Silbern ins Tal.
Die schwebende Welle, dort eilt sie dahin!
Tief spiegeln sich Fluren und Himmel darin.
Was ziehst Du mich, sehnend verlangender
    Sinn,
Hinab?

    Grüßender Sonne
Spielendes Gold,
Hoffende Wonne
Bringest Du hold.

Whispering breezes
Blowing so gently,
Filled with the fragrant
Breath of flowers!
How blissfully you greet me and breathe on me!
What have you done to my pounding heart?
It yearns to follow your airy path!
But where?

    Silvery brooklets,
Murmuring so bright,
Cascade down
To the valley below!
The ripples glide swiftly that way,
Reflecting fields and sky in their
    depths.
Why, longing desire, do you draw
Me down?

    The welcoming sun's
Glittering gold,
The bliss of hope
All this you sweetly bring.

Wie labt mich Dein selig begrüßendes Bild! | How your rapturous greeting refreshes me!
Es lächelt am tiefblauen Himmel so mild | It smiles so gently in the deep blue sky
Und hat mir das Auge mit Tränen gefüllt! | And has filled my eyes with tears!
Warum? | But why?

    Grünend umkränzet | The woods and hills
Wälder und Höh'! | Are wreathed in green!
Schimmernd erglänzet | The snowy blossom
Blütenschnee! | Shimmers and gleams!
So dränget sich Alles zum bräutlichen Licht; | All things reach out to the bridal light;
Es schwellen die Keime, die Knospe bricht; | Seeds are swelling, buds are bursting;
Sie haben gefunden was ihnen gebricht: | They have found what they once lacked:
Und Du? | And you?

    Rastloses Sehnen! | Restless longing!
Wünschendes Herz, | Yearning heart,
Immer nur Tränen, | Nothing but tears,
Klage und Schmerz? | Complaints and pain?
Auch ich bin mir schwellender Triebe bewußt! | I too am aware of rising passion!
Wer stillet mir endlich die drängende Lust? | Who shall finally quell my longing?
Nur Du befreist den Lenz in der Brust, | Only *you* can set free the spring in my heart,
Nur Du! | Only you!
(*Marschner*)

1828 Ständchen / Serenade D957/4
FROM *Schwanengesang*

Leise flehen meine Lieder | Softly my songs implore you
Durch die Nacht zu Dir; | Through the night;
In den stillen Hain hernieder, | Come down to me, my love,
Liebchen, komm' zu mir! | Into the silent grove!

    Flüsternd schlanke Wipfel rauschen | Slender tree-tops whisper
In des Mondes Licht; | And murmur in the moonlight;
Des Verräters feindlich Lauschen | Do not fear, my sweetest,
Fürchte, Holde, nicht. | Any eavesdropping enemy.

    Hörst die Nachtigallen schlagen? | Can you hear the nightingales call?
Ach! sie flehen Dich, | Ah! they are imploring you,
Mit der Töne süßen Klagen | With their sweet and plaintive songs
Flehen sie für mich. | They are imploring for me.

    Sie verstehn des Busens Sehnen, | They understand the heart's longing,
Kennen Liebesschmerz, | They know the pain of love,
Rühren mit den Silbertönen | They touch with their silver notes
Jedes weiche Herz. | Every tender heart.

Laß auch Di r die Brust bewegen, | Let *your* heart too be moved,
Liebchen, höre mich! | Listen to me, my love!

Bebend harr' ich Dir entgegen!
Komm', beglücke mich!
(*Lachner*)

Quivering, I wait for you!
Come – make me happy!

1828 Aufenthalt / Resting place D957/5
FROM *Schwanengesang*

Rauschender Strom,
Brausender Wald,
Starrender Fels
Mein Aufenthalt.

Thundering river,
Raging forest,
Unyielding rock,
My resting place.

   Wie sich die Welle
An Welle reiht,
Fließen die Tränen
Mir ewig erneut.

   As wave
Follows wave,
So my tears
Flow on and on.

   Hoch in den Kronen
Wogend sich's regt,
So unaufhörlich
Mein Herze schlägt.

   As the high tree-tops
Stir and bend,
So my heart pounds
Without respite.

   Und wie des Felsen
Uraltes Erz,
Ewig derselbe
Bleibet mein Schmerz.

   Like the rock's
Age-old ore,
My grief remains
Forever the same.

   Rauschender Strom,
Brausender Wald,
Starrender Fels
Mein Aufenthalt.
(*Marschner*)

   Thundering river,
Raging forest,
Unyielding rock,
My resting place.

1828 In der Ferne / Far away D957/6
FROM *Schwanengesang*

Wehe dem Fliehenden
Welt hinaus ziehenden! –
Fremde durchmessenden,
Heimat vergessenden,
Mutterhaus hassenden,
Freunde verlassenden
Folget kein Segen, ach!
Auf ihren Wegen nach!

Woe to the fugitive,
Who sets out into the world! –
Who roams foreign parts,
Who forgets his fatherland,
Who hates his family home,
Who forsakes his friends –
Alas, no blessing follows him
On his way!

   Herze, das sehnende,
Auge, das tränende,
Sehnsucht, nie endende,
Heimwärts sich wendende!
Busen, der wallende,

   The yearning heart,
The weeping eyes,
The endless longing,
The turning for home!
The swelling breast,

Klage, verhallende,
Abendstern, blinkender,
Hoffnungslos sinkender!

Lüfte, ihr säuselnden,
Wellen sanft kräuselnden,
Sonnenstrahl, eilender,
Nirgend verweilender:
Die mir mit Schmerze, ach!
Dies treue Herze brach, –
Grüßt von dem Fliehenden
Welt hinaus ziehenden!

The fading lament,
The glittering evening star,
Sinking without hope!

You whispering breezes,
You gently ruffled waves,
You fleeting sunbeams,
You who never linger:
Ah! send greetings to her who broke
This faithful heart with pain –
From the fugitive,
From one who sets out into the world!

1828 Abschied / Farewell D957/7
FROM *Schwanengesang*

Ade, Du muntre, Du fröhliche Stadt, Ade!
Schon scharret mein Rösslein mit lustigem Fuß;
Jetzt nimm noch den letzten, den scheiden-
den Gruß.
Du hast mich wohl niemals noch traurig
gesehn,
So kann es auch jetzt nicht beim Abschied
geschehn.
Ade, du muntre, u.s.w.

Ade, ihr Bäume, ihr Gärten so grün, Ade!
Nun reit’ ich am silbernen Strome entlang,
Weit schallend ertönet mein Abschiedsgesang;
Nie habt ihr ein trauriges Lied gehört,
So wird euch auch keines beim Scheiden
beschert.
Ade, ihr Bäume u.s.w.

Ade, ihr freundlichen Mägdlein dort, Ade!
Was schaut ihr aus blumenumduftetem
Haus
Mit schelmischen, lockenden Blicken heraus?
Wie sonst, so grüß’ ich und schaue mich um,
Doch nimmer wend’ ich mein Rösslein um.
Ade, ihr freundlichen u.s.w.

Ade, liebe Sonne, so gehst Du zur Ruh’, Ade!
Nun schimmert der blinkenden Sterne Gold.
Wie bin ich euch Sternlein am Himmel so
hold;
Durchziehn wir die Welt auch weit und breit,
Ihr gebt überall uns das treue Geleit.
Ade, liebe Sonne u.s.w.

Farewell, lively, cheerful town,
farewell!
My horse is happily pawing the
ground;
Accept now my final farewell.
Never yet have you seen me sad,
Nor shall you now at parting.
Farewell, you lively etc.

Farewell, trees and gardens so green,
farewell!
Now I ride by the silvery stream,
My farewell song echoes far and wide;
You’ve never heard a sad song yet,
Nor shall you now I’m leaving.
Farewell, trees etc.

Farewell, you friendly maidens there,
farewell!
Why do you gaze from flower-fragrant
houses
With such roguish and enticing eyes?
I greet you as always and turn my head,
But never again shall I turn back my horse.
Farewell, you friendly etc.

Farewell, dear sun, as you sink to rest,
farewell!
The stars now glitter in shimmering gold.
How I love you, little stars in the sky;
Though we travel the whole world far and wide,
You always serve us as faithful guides.
Farewell, dear sun etc.

Ade, Du schimmerndes Fensterlein hell, Ade!	Farewell, gleaming little window so bright, farewell!
Du glänzest so traulich mit dämmerndem Schein	Your faint light has such a homely gleam,
Und ladest so freundlich ins Hüttchen uns ein.	Which kindly invites us into the cottage.
Vorüber, ach, ritt ich so manches Mal	Ah, I've ridden past so many a time,
Und wär' es denn heute zum letzten Mal?	And might it today then be the last?
Ade, du schimmerndes u.s.w.	Farewell, gleaming etc.

Ade, ihr Sterne, verhüllet Euch grau! Ade!	Farewell, stars, veil yourself in grey! Farewell!
Des Fensterlein trübes, verschimmerndes Licht	You countless stars cannot replace The little window's fading light;
Ersetzt ihr unzähligen Sterne mir nicht;	
Darf ich h i e r nicht weilen, muß h i e r vorbei,	If I can't linger *here*, if I have to ride on,
Was hilft es, folgt ihr mir noch so treu!	What use are you, however faithfully you follow!
Ade, ihr Sterne, verhüllet euch grau! Ade!	Farewell, stars, veil yourself in grey! Farewell!

Johann Friedrich Rochlitz (1769–1842)

Rochlitz first met Schubert in 1822 during a visit to Vienna and soon became an admirer of his work – to such an extent that he wrote him a long letter in November 1827, describing in detail the outline for the setting of one of his poems. Although Schubert's reply was cool, the composer thought highly enough of this poet, playwright and critic to dedicate to him both 'Alinde' and 'An die Laute'. Schubert's setting of Rochlitz's 'Klagelied' (1812) is one of the first true Lieder he ever composed.

January 1827 An die Laute / To the lute D905

Leiser, leiser, kleine Laute,	Play more softly, little lute,
Flüstre, was ich dir vertraute,	Whisper what I confided to you
Dort zu jenem Fenster hin!	In at that window there!
Wie die Wellen sanfter Lüfte,	Like the ripple of gentle breezes,
Mondenglanz und Blumendüfte,	Like moonlight and the scent of flowers,
Send' es der Gebieterin!	Send the message to my mistress!

Neidisch sind des Nachbars Söhne,	All my neighbour's sons are jealous,
Und im Fenster jener Schöne	And in that beauty's window
Flimmert noch ein einsam Licht.	A solitary lamp still burns.
Drum noch leiser, kleine Laute:	So play more softly, little lute:
Dich vernehme die Vertraute,	That you be heard by my love,
Nachbarn aber – Nachbarn nicht!	But not – ah, not – the neighbours!

Friedrich Rückert (1788–1866)

See Robert Schumann

1822 Sei mir gegrüßt! / I greet you! D741

O du Entriß'ne mir und meinem Kusse!
Sei mir gegrüßt!
Sei mir geküßt!
Erreichbar nur meinem Sehnsuchtsgruße!
Sei mir gegrüßt!
Sei mir geküßt!

Du von der Hand der Liebe diesem Herzen
Gegeb'ne! du
Von dieser Brust
Genomm'ne mir! mit diesem Tränengusse
Sei mir gegrüßt!
Sei mir geküßt!

Zum Trotz der Ferne, die sich, feindlich trennend,
Hat zwischen mich
Und dich gestellt;
Dem Neid der Schicksalsmächte zum Verdrusse
Sei mir gegrüßt!
Sei mir geküßt!

Wie du mir je im schönsten Lenz der Liebe
Mit Gruß und Kuß
Entgegen kamst,
Mit meiner Seele glühendstem Ergusse
Sei mir gegrüßt!
Sei mir geküßt!

Ein Hauch der Liebe tilget Räum' und Zeiten,
Ich bin bei dir,
Du bist bei mir,
Ich halte dich in dieses Arms Umschlusse,
Sei mir gegrüßt!
Sei mir geküßt!

O you who were snatched from me and my
   kiss!
I greet you!
I kiss you!
O you reached only by my longing greeting!
I greet you!
I kiss you!

You who were given this heart by the hand
Of love! You
Who were taken
From this heart! – in a flood of tears
I greet you!
I kiss you!

To defy the distance that, hostile and dividing,
Has come
Between you and me;
To spite envious powers of fate,
I greet you!
I kiss you!

As in love's fairest spring
You once came to me
With kisses and greetings,
So with my soul's most ardent outpouring
I greet you!
I kiss you!

One breath of love effaces time and space,
I am with you,
You are with me,
I hold you closely in my arms,
I greet you!
I kiss you!

?1822 Daß sie hier gewesen / That she was here D775

Daß der Ostwind Düfte
Hauchet in die Lüfte,
Dadurch tut er kund,
Daß du hier gewesen.

By breathing fragrance
Into the air,
The East Wind makes known
That you were here.

Daß hier Tränen rinnen,
Dadurch wirst du innen,
Wär's dir sonst nicht kund,
Daß ich hier gewesen.

Schönheit oder Liebe,
Ob versteckt sie bliebe?
Düfte tun es und
Tränen kund,
Daß sie hier gewesen.
(*Meyerbeer*)

Because tears fall here,
You will know,
Though you were not told,
That I was here.

Beauty or love,
Can they remain concealed?
Fragrance and tears
Will make known
That she was here.

1823 Du bist die Ruh / You are repose D776

Du bist die Ruh,
  Der Friede mild,
  Die Sehnsucht du,
  Und was sie stillt.
Ich weihe dir
  Voll Lust und Schmerz
  Zur Wohnung hier
  Mein Aug' und Herz.
Kehr ein bei mir,
  Und schließe du
  Still hinter dir
  Die Pforten zu.
Treib andern Schmerz
  Aus dieser Brust.
  Voll sei dies Herz
  Von deiner Lust.
Dies Augenzelt
  Von deinem Glanz
  Allein erhellt,
  O füll es ganz.
(*Curschmann, Hensel, Lachner*)

You are repose
  And gentle peace,
  You are longing
  And what stills it.
I pledge to you
  Full of joy and pain
  As a dwelling here
  My eyes and heart.
Come in to me,
  And softly close
  The gate
  Behind you.
Drive other pain
  From this breast!
  Let my heart be filled
  With your joy.
This temple of my eyes
  Is lit
  By your radiance alone,
  O fill it utterly.

?1823 Lachen und Weinen / Laughter and tears D777

Lachen und Weinen zu jeglicher Stunde
  Ruht bei der Lieb' auf so mancherlei Grunde.
  Morgens lacht' ich vor Lust;
  Und warum ich nun weine
  Bei des Abendes Scheine,
  Ist mir selb' nicht bewußt.
Weinen und Lachen zu jeglicher Stunde
  Ruht bei der Lieb' auf so mancherlei Grunde.
  Abends weint' ich vor Schmerz;
  Und warum du erwachen

Laughter and tears at any hour
  Arise in love from so many different causes.
  In the morning I laughed with joy;
  And why I now weep
  In the evening light,
  Is unknown even to me.
Tears and laughter at any hour
  Arise in love from so many different causes.
  In the evening I wept with grief;
  And why you can wake

Kannst am Morgen mit Lachen,
Muß ich dich fragen, o Herz.

In the morning with laughter,
I must ask you, my heart.

?1823 Greisengesang / Old man's song D778

Der Frost hat mir bereifet
Des Hauses Dach;
Doch warm ist mir's geblieben
Im Wohngemach.

The rime has frosted
The roof of my house;
But I've kept warm
In the parlour.

Der Winter hat die Scheitel
Mir weiß gedeckt.
Doch fließt das Blut, das rote
Durch's Herzgemach.

Winter has whitened
The top of my head.
But the blood flows red
Through my heart.

Der Jugendflor der Wangen,
Die Rosen sind
Gegangen, all' gegangen
Einander nach.

The flush of youth in my cheeks,
The roses
All have gone,
One by one.

Wo sind sie hingegangen?
In's Herz hinab.
Da blühn sie nach Verlangen,
Wie vor so nach.

Where have they gone?
Down into my heart.
There they blossom as desired,
Now as before.

Sind alle Freudenströme
Der Welt versiegt?
Noch fließt mir durch den Busen
Ein stiller Bach.

Have all this world's rivers
Of joy run dry?
A quiet stream
Still flows through my breast.

Sind alle Nachtigallen
Der Flur verstummt?
Noch ist bei mir im Stillen
Hier eine wach.

Have all the field's nightingales
Fallen silent?
Inside me, secretly,
One still stirs.

Sie singet: Herr des Hauses!
Verschleuß dein Tor,
Daß nicht die Welt, die kalte,
Dring' in's Gemach.

It sings: Master of the house!
Lock your door,
Lest the cold world
Penetrate the parlour.

Schleuß aus den rauhen Odem
Der Wirklichkeit,
Und nur dem Duft der Träume
Gib Dach und Fach.
(*Strauss*)

Shut out the harsh breath
Of reality,
Offer shelter only
To the fragrance of dreams.

Johann Gaudenz von Salis-Seewis (1762–1834)

Johann Gaudenz von Salis-Seewis was a Swiss poet who lived in Paris during the French Revolution and met Goethe, Herder and Schiller on a tour of Germany.

Schubert set thirteen of his songs, all from *Gedichte*, originally published by Matthisson in 1793 and subsequently enlarged.

?1815 Der Jüngling an der Quelle / The youth by the brook D300

Leise, rieselnder Quell, ihr wallenden,
   flispernden Pappeln,
Euer Schlummergeräusch wecket die Liebe
   nur auf.
Linderung sucht' ich bei euch, und sie zu
   vergessen, die Spröde;
Ach! und Blätter und Bach seufzen:
   Louise, dir nach!

Hush! you rippling brook, you waving,
   whispering poplars,
Your sleepy murmurings awaken only
   love.
I sought comfort by your side to forget the
   prudish girl;
But alas, leaves and brook both sigh,
   Louise, for you!

November 1816 Herbstlied / Autumn song D502

Bunt sind schon die Wälder;
Gelb die Stoppelfelder,
Und der Herbst beginnt.
Rote Blätter fallen,
Graue Nebel wallen,
Kühler weht der Wind.

The woods are bright with colour;
The fields of stubble yellow,
And autumn now begins.
Red leaves fall,
Grey mists swirl,
Colder blows the wind.

Wie die volle Traube,
Aus dem Rebenlaube,
Purpurfarbig strahlt;
Am Geländer reifen
Pfirsiche mit Streifen
Rot und weiß bemalt.

How the plump grapes
Shine purple
From the vine leaves;
Peaches, streaked with red and white,
Ripen
On the trellises.

Sieh! Wie hier die Dirne
Emsig Pflaum' und Birne
In ihr Körbchen legt;
Dort, mit leichten Schritten,
Jene, goldne Quitten
In den Landhof trägt!

See how this girl
Busily fills her basket
With plums and pears;
And how that girl
Carries golden quinces
With light steps into the house!

Flinke Träger springen,
Und die Mädchen singen,
Alles jubelt froh!
Bunte Bänder schweben,
Zwischen hohen Reben,
Auf dem Hut von Stroh!

The lads dance nimbly,
And the girls sing,
Everyone rejoices!
Coloured ribbons
On straw hats
Flutter among tall vines!

Geige tönt und Flöte
Bei der Abendröte
Und im Mondenglanz;
Junge Winzerinnen

Fiddles and flutes
Play in the evening glow
And by the light of the moon;
Young grape-gathering girls

Winken und beginnen
Deutschen Ringeltanz.
(*Reichardt*)

Beckon each other to join
A German round-dance.

Samuel Friedrich Sauter (1766–1846)

A village schoolmaster whose naïve, somewhat saccharine and unintentionally comic verses received the 'Stuffed Owl' treatment from L. Eichrodt and A. Hussmaul in the Munich weekly *Fliegende Blätter*, which published his poetry as the work of 'the Swabian schoolmaster Gottlieb Biedermaier [*sic*] and his friend Horatius Treuherz', thus coining the pejorative term 'Biedermeier'. Beethoven's setting, which influenced Schubert's, dates from 1803.

?1822 Der Wachtelschlag / The quail's cry D742

Ach! mir schallt's dorten so lieblich hervor;
   Fürchte Gott!
   Fürchte Gott!
Ruft mir die Wachtel in's Ohr!
Sitzend im Grünen, von Halmen umhüllt,
Mahnt sie den Horcher im Saatengefild:
   Liebe Gott!
   Liebe Gott!
Er ist so gütig, so mild.

Wieder bedeutet ihr hüpfender Schlag:
   Lobe Gott!
   Lobe Gott!
Der dich zu lohnen vermag.
Siehst du die herrlichen Früchte im Feld,
Nimm es zu Herzen, Bewohner der Welt!
   Danke Gott!
   Danke Gott!
Der dich ernährt und erhält.

Schreckt dich im Wetter der Herr der Natur,
   Bitte Gott!
   Bitte Gott!
Ruft sie, er schonet die Flur.
Machen Gefahren der Krieger dir bang:
   Traue Gott!
   Traue Gott!
Sieh, er verziehet nicht lang.
(*Beethoven*)

Ah! how sweet that sound from yonder;
   Fear the Lord!
   Fear the Lord!
The quail calls out to me!
In the open, surrounded by corn,
It exhorts the listener in the field:
   Love the Lord!
   Love the Lord!
He's so good, so kind.

Again its leaping call enjoins us:
   Praise the Lord!
   Praise the Lord!
Who can reward you.
When you see the wonderful fruits of the field,
Ponder them well, you dwellers on earth!
   Thank the Lord!
   Thank the Lord!
Who nourishes and sustains you.

If the Lord of Nature scares you in the storm,
   Pray to God!
   Pray to God!
It cries, He spares the fields.
If you fear the dangers of waging war,
   Trust in God!
   Trust in God!
See, He does not tarry long.

Friedrich Schiller (1759–1805)

Schiller's plays have attracted many opera composers, in particular Verdi: *Giovanna d'Arco* (*Die Jungfrau von Orleans*), *I masnadieri* (*Die Räuber*), *Luisa Miller* (*Kabale und Liebe*) and *Don Carlos*. His poetry, though there are settings by Brahms, Bruch, Liszt, Mendelssohn, Pfitzner, Schubert, Schumann and others, has not proved so popular. Schubert's interest in Schiller predates his first Goethe song by three years, and although Goethe was to become his favourite poet, he continued to be fascinated by Germany's most celebrated playwright and set him no fewer than forty-four times. Two of these songs form part of plays ('Des Mädchens Klage' from *Die Piccolomini* and 'Amalia' from *Die Räuber*). Among the early songs are a number of unwieldy and unsuccessful ballads – inspired by Zumsteeg and a wish to master operatic form in miniature – that have given Schubert's Schiller settings an unjustifiably bad name. It is not only, however, such gargantuan ballads as 'Leichenfantasie' (1811), 'Der Taucher' (1813), 'Die Bürgschaft' (1815), 'Klage der Ceres' (1815–16), 'Die vier Weltalter' (1816), 'Ritter Toggenburg' (1816) and 'Der Graf von Habsburg' (1818) that enthused Schubert, but also Schiller's shorter, more intellectual verse for which he found his own musical language. Songs such as 'Hoffnung', 'Sehnsucht', 'Thekla', 'Das Geheimnis', 'Die Götter Griechenlands' and 'Gruppe aus dem Tartarus' show us another side of Schubert's genius, and the fact that he set many of them twice or even three times testifies to the care he lavished on them. 'Der Jüngling am Bache' is the first setting of a true lyric by Schubert, who till then had been almost exclusively concerned with Gothic ballads. The song is dated 24 September 1812.

Des Mädchens Klage / The girl's lament
FROM *Die Piccolomini*
FIRST VERSION: ?1811 (D6)
SECOND VERSION: 15 MAY 1815 (D191)
THIRD VERSION: MARCH 1816 (D389)

Der Eichwald braust, die Wolken ziehn,	The oak wood roars, the clouds race by,
Das Mägdlein sitzt an Ufers Grün,	The girl sits by the grassy shore,
Es bricht sich die Welle mit Macht, mit Macht,	The breakers crash with all their might,
Und sie seufzt hinaus in die finst're Nacht,	And she sighs into the dark night,
Das Auge von Weinen getrübet.	Her eyes bedimmed with weeping.
„Das Herz ist gestorben, die Welt ist leer,	'My heart is dead, the world is void
Und weiter gibt sie dem Wunsche nichts mehr,	And no longer yields to my desires,
Du Heilige, rufe dein Kind zurück,	Holy Mother, call back your child,
Ich habe genossen das irdische Glück,	I have enjoyed earthly bliss,
Ich habe gelebt und geliebet!"	I have lived and loved!'
Es rinnet der Tränen vergeblicher Lauf,	In vain the tears pour down her cheek,
Die Klage, sie wecket die Toten nicht auf;	No lament of hers can wake the dead;

Doch nenne, was tröstet und heilet die Brust
Nach der süßen Liebe verschwundener Lust,
Ich, die Himmlische, will's nicht versagen.

„Laß rinnen der Tränen vergeblichen Lauf,
Es wecke die Klage die Toten nicht auf!
Das süßeste Glück für die trauernde Brust,
Nach der schönen Liebe verschwundener Lust,
Sind der Liebe Schmerzen und Klagen."
(*Glinka, Hensel, Krufft, Mendelssohn, Zelter,
Zumsteeg*)

But say, what heals and comforts the heart,
When the joy of sweet love has vanished –
I, the Heavenly Maid, shall not refuse it.

'Let my tears pour down in vain,
Let my lament not wake the dead!
The sweetest joy for a grieving heart,
When the pleasures of love have vanished,
Is love's sorrow and lament.'

Der Jüngling am Bache / The young man by the brook
FIRST VERSION: 24 SEPTEMBER 1812 (D30)
SECOND VERSION: 15 MAY 1815 (D192)
THIRD VERSION: APRIL 1819 (D638)

An der Quelle saß der Knabe,
　　Blumen wand er sich zum Kranz,
Und er sah sie fortgerissen,
　　Treiben in der Wellen Tanz: –
Und so fliehen meine Tage
　　Wie die Quelle rastlos hin!
Und so bleichet meine Jugend,
　　Wie die Kränze schnell verblühn.

By the spring a young man sat,
　　Twining flowers to make a wreath,
And he saw them snatched away,
　　Drifting on the dancing waves –
So too my days speed away,
　　Like the brook without respite!
So too my youth fades away,
　　As swiftly as the wreathes wilt.

Fraget nicht, warum ich traure
　　In des Lebens Blütenzeit!
Alles freuet sich und hoffet,
　　Wenn der Frühling sich erneut.
Aber diese tausend Stimmen
　　Der erwachenden Natur
Wecken in dem tiefen Busen
　　Mir den schweren Kummer nur.

Do not ask why I mourn
　　When my life's in fullest bloom!
All creatures are glad and full of hope,
　　When spring renews itself once more.
But the thousand voices
　　Of awakening nature
Merely kindle grievous sorrow
　　Deep within my heart.

Was soll mir die Freude frommen,
　　Die der schöne Lenz mir beut?
Eine nur ist's, die ich suche,
　　Sie ist nah und ewig weit.
Sehnend breit' ich meine Arme
　　Nach dem teuren Schattenbild,
Ach, ich kann es nicht erreichen,
　　Und das Herz bleibt ungestillt!

What shall the joys
　　Of lovely spring avail me?
There is only one I seek,
　　She is near, yet ever far.
I open wide my yearning arms
　　To clasp her dear shadowy form,
But I, alas, cannot reach her,
　　And my heart remains unstilled!

Komm herab, du schöne Holde,
　　Und verlaß dein stolzes Schloß!
Blumen, die der Lenz geboren,
　　Streu' ich dir in deinen Schoß.

Come down to me, my fairest one,
　　And leave your haughty castle!
Flowers, which the spring created,
　　I shall strew into your lap.

Horch, der Hain erschallt von Liedern,
   Und die Quelle rieselt klar!
Raum ist in der kleinsten Hütte
   Für ein glücklich liebend Paar.
(*Reichardt, Tomášek*)

Hark, the grove resounds with song,
   And the spring ripples brightly!
The smallest hut has room enough
   For a happy loving pair.

Sehnsucht / Longing
FIRST VERSION: 15–17 APRIL 1813 (D52)
SECOND VERSION: 1821 (D636)

Ach, aus dieses Tales Gründen,
   Die der kalte Nebel drückt,
Könnt' ich doch den Ausgang finden,
   Ach wie fühlt' ich mich beglückt!
Dort erblick' ich schöne Hügel,
   Ewig jung und ewig grün!
Hätt' ich Schwingen, hätt' ich Flügel,
   Nach den Hügeln zög' ich hin.

Could I but find the way out
   From the depths of this valley,
Where cold mist presses down,
   Ah, how happy I would feel!
I see lovely hills out there,
   Ever young and ever green!
If I had pinions, if I had wings,
   I would soar up to those hills.

Harmonien hör' ich klingen,
   Töne süßer Himmelsruh,
Und die leichten Winde bringen
   Mir der Düfte Balsam zu,
Goldne Früchte seh' ich glühen,
   Winkend zwischen dunkelm Laub,
Und die Blumen, die dort blühen,
   Werden keines Winters Raub.

I hear harmonious sounds
   Of sweet, heavenly peace,
And balmy scents are borne
   To me on the breeze,
I see the glow of golden fruits
   Beckoning from dark leaves,
And the flowers that bloom there
   Shall never perish as winter's prey.

Ach wie schön muß sich's ergehen
   Dort im ew'gen Sonnenschein,
Und die Luft auf jenen Höhen,
   O wie labend muß sie sein!
Doch mir wehrt des Stromes Toben,
   Der ergrimmt dazwischen braust,
Seine Wellen sind gehoben,
   Daß die Seele mir ergraust.

Ah, how lovely it must be
   To wander there in eternal sun,
And the air on those heights,
   How refreshing it must be!
But the raging torrent thwarts me,
   Foaming angrily between us,
Its waves rise up so high
   That my soul is filled with dread.

Einen Nachen seh' ich schwanken,
   Aber ach! der Fährmann fehlt.
Frisch hinein und ohne Wanken!
   Seine Segel sind beseelt.
Du mußt glauben, du mußt wagen,
   Denn die Götter leihn kein Pfand,
Nur ein Wunder kann dich tragen
   In das schöne Wunderland.
(*Hensel, Kreutzer, Reichardt, Silcher, Tomášek,
Zumsteeg*)

I can see a small boat pitching,
   Without a ferryman, alas!
Quick, jump in without delay!
   Its sails are billowing.
You must believe, you must venture,
   For the gods grant no pledge,
Only a wonder can transport you
   To that fair and wondrous land.

Thekla*: Eine Geisterstimme / Thekla: a phantom voice

FIRST VERSION: 22-23 AUGUST 1813 (D73)
SECOND VERSION: NOVEMBER 1817 (D595)

Wo ich sei, und wo mich hingewendet,
Als mein flücht'ger Schatte dir entschwebt?
Hab' ich nicht beschlossen und geendet,
Hab' ich nicht geliebet und gelebt?

Willst du nach den Nachtigallen fragen,
Die mit seelenvoller Melodie
Dich entzückten in des Lenzes Tagen?
Nur so lang' sie liebten, waren sie.

Ob ich den Verlorenen gefunden?
Glaube mir, ich bin mit ihm vereint,
Wo sich nicht mehr trennt, was sich verbunden,
Dort, wo keine Träne wird geweint.

Dorten wirst auch du uns wieder finden,
Wenn dein Lieben unserm Lieben gleicht;
Dort ist auch der Vater frei von Sünden,
Den der blut'ge Mord nicht mehr erreicht.

Und er fühlt, daß ihn kein Wahn betrogen,
Als er aufwärts zu den Sternen sah;
Denn wie jeder wägt, wird ihm gewogen,
Wer es glaubt, dem ist das Heil'ge nah.

Wort gehalten wird in jenen Räumen
Jedem schönen gläubigen Gefühl;
Wage du, zu irren und zu träumen;
Hoher Sinn liegt oft in kind'schem Spiel.
(Reichardt, Tomášek)

Where am I, you ask, and where did I go,
When my fleeting shadow drifted from you?
Have I not finished and reached my end,
Have I not loved and lived?

Do you ask where the nightingales are,
Who with their soulful melodies
Once delighted you in spring?
They lived only as long as they loved.

You ask if I found my lost beloved?
Believe me, I am united with him
Where our bonds can never be severed,
And where no tears are shed.

There you too shall find us again,
When your love resembles ours;
Our father too is there, free from sin,
Whom bloody murder can no longer strike.

And he knows that he was not deceived,
When he gazed up at the stars;
For as a man judges, so shall he be judged,
Whoever believes this is close to holiness.

In those realms each fine, devout feeling
Will be fulfilled;
Venture to err and venture to dream:
Deep meaning often accompanies childish
    play.

1815 An die Freude / To joy D189

Freude, schöner Götterfunken,
Tochter aus Elysium,
Wir betreten feuertrunken,
Himmlische, dein Heiligtum!
Deine Zauber binden wieder,
Was die Mode streng geteilt;
Alle Menschen werden Brüder,
Wo dein sanfter Flügel weilt.
Seid umschlungen, Millionen!
Diesen Kuß der ganzen Welt!
Brüder, überm Sternenzelt
Muß ein lieber Vater wohnen.

Joy, fair divine spark,
Daughter of Elysium,
We enter your sanctuary,
Heavenly one, drunk with ardour!
Your magic powers reunite
What harsh custom has set apart;
All men become brothers,
Where your gentle wings hover.
Accept this embrace, you millions!
This kiss is for all the world!
Brothers, a loving father must dwell
Above the starry firmament.

* Thekla was the daughter of Wallenstein, the hero of Schiller's trilogy.

Wem der große Wurf gelungen,	He who has had the great good fortune
Eines Freundes Freund zu sein,	To be a friend's friend,
Wer ein holdes Weib errungen,	He who has won a loving wife,
Mische seinen Jubel ein!	Let him join in and rejoice!
Ja – wer auch nur *eine* Seele	Yes – even he who on earth
Sein nennt auf dem Erdenrund!	Calls but *one* soul his own!
Und wers nie gekonnt, der stehle	And he who never could – let him steal
Weinend sich aus diesem Bund.	Weeping from this brotherhood.
Was den großen Ring bewohnet,	Whoever inhabits this great globe,
Huldige der Sympathie!	Let them pay homage to sympathy!
Zu den Sternen leitet sie,	It leads to the stars,
Wo der Unbekannte thronet!	Where the Unknown is enthroned!
Freude trinken alle Wesen	All creatures drink joy
An den Brüsten der Natur,	From nature's breast,
Alle Guten, alle Bösen	All good men, all bad men
Folgen ihrer Rosenspur.	Follow her rosy trail.
Küsse gab sie uns und Reben,	She gave us kisses and grapes,
Einen Freund, geprüft im Tod.	And a friend, tried in death.
Wollust ward dem Wurm gegeben,	The worm was endowed with lust,
Und der Cherub steht vor Gott.	And the Cherub stands before God.
Ihr stürzt nieder, Millionen?	Do you fall to your knees, O millions?
Ahnest du den Schöpfer, Welt?	Do you sense, O world, the Creator?
Such ihn überm Sternenzelt!	Seek Him above the firmament!
Über Sternen muß er wohnen.	He must dwell above the stars.
(*Beethoven, Zumsteeg*)	

Das Geheimnis / The secret
FIRST VERSION: 7 AUGUST 1815 (D250)
SECOND VERSION: MAY 1823 (D793)

Sie konnte mir kein Wörtchen sagen,	She could not speak one word to me,
Zu viele Lauscher waren wach,	Too many ears were listening there,
Den Blick nur durft' ich schüchtern fragen,	I could only shyly question her eyes,
Und wohl verstand ich, was er sprach.	And I grasped well what they meant.
Leis' komm ich her in deine Stille,	Softly I come to enter the stillness
Du schön belaubtes Buchenzelt,	Of your lovely beech-tree canopy,
Verbirg in deiner grünen Hülle	Conceal beneath your green cloak
Die Liebenden dem Aug der Welt!	Those who love from the eyes of the world!
Von ferne mit verworrnem Sausen	Far away, with chaotic roar,
Arbeitet der geschäft'ge Tag,	The bustling day is at work,
Und durch der Stimmen hohles Brausen	And through the hollow hum of voices
Erkenn' ich schwerer Hämmer Schlag.	I hear the beat of heavy hammers.
So sauer ringt die kargen Lose	So men struggle to wrest
Der Mensch dem harten Himmel ab,	Their meagre destiny from a harsh heaven,
Doch leicht erworben aus dem Schoße	Yet happiness is easily won,
Der Götter fällt das Glück herab.	When it falls from the lap of the gods.

Daß ja die Menschen nie es hören,
  Wie treue Lieb' uns still beglückt!
Sie können nur die Freude stören,
  Weil Freude nie sie selbst entzückt.
Die Welt wird nie das Glück erlauben,
  Als Beute nur wird es gehascht,
Entwenden mußt du's oder rauben,
  Eh' dich die Mißgunst überrascht.

Leis' auf den Zehen kommt's geschlichen,
  Die Stille liebt es und die Nacht,
Mit schnellen Füßen ist's entwichen,
  Wo des Verräters Auge wacht.
O schlinge dich, du sanfte Quelle,
  Ein breiter Strom um uns herum,
Und drohend mit empörter Welle
  Verteidige dies Heiligtum!
(*Reichardt, Tomášek*)

May no one ever discover
  How happy true love makes us!
They can only mar our joy
  Since they've never delighted in joy.
The world will never grant happiness,
  It can only be snatched as prey;
You must either purloin or steal it,
  Before envy takes you unawares.

It comes on tiptoe, approaches softly,
  Cherishing silence and the night,
And fleet of foot, it vanishes
  When a traitor lurks nearby.
O gentle source, envelop us,
  Engulfing us like a mighty river,
And with the threat of angry waves
  Defend this sanctuary!

Hoffnung / Hope
FIRST VERSION: 7 AUGUST 1815 (D251)
SECOND VERSION: ?1817 (D637)

Es reden und träumen die Menschen viel
  Von bessern künftigen Tagen,
Nach einem glücklichen goldenen Ziel
  Sieht man sie rennen und jagen;
Die Welt wird alt und wird wieder jung,
Doch der Mensch hofft immer Verbesserung.

Die Hoffnung führt ihn ins Leben ein,
  Sie umflattert den fröhlichen Knaben,
Den Jüngling begeistert ihr Zauberschein,
  Sie wird mit dem Greis nicht begraben;
Denn beschließt er im Grabe den müden Lauf,
Noch am Grabe pflanzt er – die Hoffnung auf.

Es ist kein leerer, kein schmeichelnder Wahn,
  Erzeugt im Gehirne des Toren,
Im Herzen kündet es laut sich an:
  Zu was Besserm sind wir geboren!
Und was die innere Stimme spricht,
Das täuscht die hoffende Seele nicht.
(*Krufft, Lachner, Reichardt*)

Men talk and dream a great amount
  Of better days to come,
We see them chasing and running
  After a golden, happy goal;
The world grows old, grows young again,
But man always hopes for better things.

Hope brings man into the world,
  It hovers round the happy boy,
Its magic radiance inspires youth,
  Nor is it buried with old age;
For though his tired life ends in the grave,
By that grave he sows seeds of hope.

Hope is no vain, flattering illusion,
  Begotten in the foolish mind,
Loud it proclaims in the hearts of men:
  We are born for better things!
And what the inner voice declares
Does not deceive the hopeful soul.

Gruppe aus dem Tartarus / Scene from Hades
FIRST VERSION: MARCH 1816 (D396)
SECOND VERSION: SEPTEMBER 1817 (D583)

Horch – wie Murmeln des empörten Meeres,
Wie durch hohler Felsen Becken weint ein Bach,
Stöhnt dort dumpfigtief ein schweres, leeres,
    Qualerpreßtes Ach!

    Schmerz verzerret
Ihr Gesicht, Verzweiflung sperret
    Ihren Rachen fluchend auf.
Hohl sind ihre Augen – ihre Blicke
Spähen bang nach des Cocytus* Brücke,
    Folgen tränend seinem Trauerlauf.

Fragen sich einander ängstlich leise,
Ob noch nicht Vollendung sei? –
Ewigkeit schwingt über ihnen Kreise,
    Bricht die Sense des Saturns† entzwei.

Hark! – like the angered ocean's murmuring,
Like a brook weeping through rocky hollows,
There rises up, dank and deep, a heavy, empty
    Tormented cry!

    Pain distorts
Their faces, despair opens
    Wide their jaws in imprecation.
Their eyes are hollow – their gaze
Fixes fearfully on Cocytus Bridge,
    Weeping they follow the river's doleful course.

Anxiously, softly, they ask each other
If the end is nigh? –
Eternity sweeps in circles above them,
    Breaks Saturn's scythe asunder.

November 1819 Die Götter Griechenlands / The gods of Greece D677

Schöne Welt, wo bist du? Kehre wieder,
Holdes Blütenalter der Natur!
Ach, nur in dem Feenland der Lieder
Lebt noch deine fabelhafte Spur.
Ausgestorben trauert das Gefilde,
Keine Gottheit zeigt sich meinem Blick,
Ach, von jenem lebenwarmen Bilde
Blieb der Schatten nur zurück.

Beautiful world, where are you? Come again,
Fair springtime of nature!
Ah, only in the enchanted land of song
Does your fabled memory still live on.
The fields, deserted, mourn,
No god appears before my eyes,
Ah, of all that living warmth
Only the shadow have remained.

?1824 Dithyrambe/ Dithyramb D801

Nimmer, das glaubt mir, erscheinen die Götter,
Nimmer allein.
Kaum daß ich Bacchus, den lustigen, habe,
Kommt auch schon Amor, der lächelnde Knabe,
Phöbus der herrliche findet sich ein.
    Sie nahen, sie kommen, die Himmlischen
    alle,
    Mit Göttern erfüllt sich die irdische Halle.

Sagt, wie bewirt' ich, der Erdegeborne,
Himmlischen Chor?

Never, believe me, never, do the gods appear
Alone.
No sooner is merry Bacchus to hand,
Than Cupid comes too, the smiling boy,
Glorious Phoebus also drops by.
    The Immortals are coming, one and
    all,
    This earthly abode is filled with gods.

Say, how shall I, born of this earth,
Entertain the heavenly choir?

* A river of Epirus. The word is derived from the Greek word *to lament*; because of its vicinity to the Acheron, it is often called one of the rivers of hell.
† Roman deity, identified with the Greek Kronos (Time)

Schenket mir euer unsterbliches Leben,	Grant me your immortal life,
Götter! was kann euch der Sterbliche geben?	Ye gods! What can a mere mortal give you?
Hebet zu eurem Olymp mich empor!	Raise me up to your Olympus!
Die Freude, sie wohnt nur in Jupiters Saale,	Joy dwells only in Jupiter's hall,
O füllet mit Nektar, o reicht mir die Schale!	O pour me some nectar, O hand me the cup!
Reich' ihm die Schale! O schenke dem Dichter,	Pass him the cup! O fill the poet's cup,
Hebe*, nur ein!	Hebe, fill!
Netz' ihm die Augen mit himmlischem Taue,	Moisten his eyes with heavenly dew,
Daß er den Styx, den verhaßten, nicht schaue,	So he does not see the hated Styx,
Einer der Unsern sich dünke zu sein.	And think himself as one of us.
Sie rauschet, sie perlet, die himmlische Quelle,	The heavenly spring murmurs and sparkles,
Der Busen wird ruhig, das Auge wird helle.	The heart grows calm, the eye grows bright.

(*Kreutzer, Reichardt*)

Franz Xaver von Schlechta (1796–1875)

Baron von Schlechta met Schubert when they were both students at the Imperial College, and soon became a close friend and devoted admirer. Three weeks after Schubert's death, he published a touching commemorative epitaph in the *Wiener Zeitschrift für Kunst* :

> Die Muse weint; ein Liebling folgt dem andern:
>   Warum so jung, so hoffnungsreich auch du?
>
> Der Winter herrscht, die Nachtigallen wandern
>   Dem Frühling eines schön'ren Landes zu!

A civil servant who became head of a department in the Ministry of Finance, Schlechta wrote poems, plays and theatre reviews, including those on two of Schubert's stage works: *Die Zwillingsbrüder* and *Die Zauberharfe*. His poems, of which Schubert set seven, were published in *Dichtungen* (1824).

?1819 Widerschein / Reflection D949

Harrt ein Fischer auf der Brücke,	A fisherman waits on the bridge,
Die Geliebte säumt,	His beloved is late,
Schmollend taucht er seine Blicke	Sullenly he stares
In den Bach – und träumt.	Into the stream – and dreams.
Doch die lauscht im nahen Flieder,	But she's listening in the nearby lilac,
Und ihr Bildchen strahlt	And now her face,
Jetzt aus klaren Wellen wider	Never more truly portrayed,
Treuer nie gemalt.	Is reflected in the clear water.

* The goddess of youth and cup-bearer to all the gods.

Und er sieht's, und er kennt die Bänder,	And he sees it, and he knows those ribbons,
Kennt den süßen Schein:	Knows her sweet radiance:
Und er hält sich am Geländer	And he holds on to the railing,
Sonst – zieht's ihn hinein.	For fear of falling in.

?March 1826 Fischerweise / Fisherman's song D881

Den Fischer fechten Sorgen	The fisherman's not bothered
Und Gram und Leid nicht an,	By cares or grief or sorrow,
Er löst am frühen Morgen	With a light heart he unties his boat
Mit leichtem Sinn den Kahn.	In the early morning.

Da lagert rings noch Friede	Peace still lies all around
Auf Wald und Flur und Bach,	Over forest, field and stream,
Er ruft mit seinem Liede	His singing causes
Die gold'ne Sonne wach.	The golden sun to wake.

Er singt zu seinem Werke	He sings while he's working
Aus voller frischer Brust,	With a lusty, cheerful voice,
Die Arbeit gibt ihm Stärke,	His work gives him vigour,
Die Stärke Lebenslust!	His vigour – a love of life!

Bald wird ein bunt Gewimmel	Soon a colourful throng
In allen Tiefen laut,	Can be heard deep down below,
Und plätschert durch den Himmel	Splashing through the sky
Der sich im Wasser baut –	Reflected in the water.

Doch wer ein Netz will stellen	Yet he who wants to cast a net
Braucht Augen klar und gut,	Needs a pair of good clear eyes,
Muß heiter gleich den Wellen	He must be as cheerful as the waves
Und frei sein wie die Flut;	And as free as the tide.

Dort angelt auf der Brücke	Up there on the bridge the shepherdess
Die Hirtin – schlauer Wicht,	Fishes – sly minx,
Gib auf nur deine Tücke,	Give up your tricks,
Den Fisch betrügst du nicht!	This is a fish you'll never catch!

Friedrich von Schlegel (1772–1829)

With his brother August Wilhelm von Schlegel, Friedrich founded *Das Athenaeum*, the principal journal of the Romantic movement. Having spent several years lecturing in Jena, he moved to Vienna in 1808, as an administrator in the Austrian civil service. With his wife Dorothea Veit, the daughter of Moses Mendelssohn, he held soirées at his home which became a much frequented meeting-place amongst Vienna's intellectual elite. Best known for his lectures, aphorisms and critical writings, he wrote some fine poems, sixteen of which were set to music by Schubert, including ten from *Abendröte*, which Schlegel had written between 1800 and 1801.

The pantheism of the cycle is suggested by the titles of individual poems: 'Die Berge', 'Die Vögel', 'Der Fluß', 'Der Hirt', 'Die Rose', 'Der Schmetterling', 'Die Sonne', 'Die Lüfte', 'Der Mond', 'Der Wasserfall', 'Die Blumen', 'Die Sterne', 'Gebüsche' and so on. The Romantic view of the unity of man and nature is expressed in such songs as 'Abendröte', 'Die Gebüsche' and 'Die Sterne'; and though 'Im Walde' does not form part of the *Abendröte* cycle, Schlegel's espousal of pantheism glows from every bar of this astonishing song. He later converted to a rigid Catholicism.

?February 1819 Der Wanderer / The wanderer D649

Wie deutlich des Mondes Licht	How clearly the moon's light
Zu mir spricht,	Speaks to me,
Mich beseelend zu der Reise:	Encouraging me to journey:
„Folge treu dem alten Gleise,	'Faithfully do what you've always done.
Wähle keine Heimat nicht.	Choose nowhere as your home.
Ew'ge Plage	Hard times will otherwise
Bringen sonst die schweren Tage;	Bring lasting worry;
Fort zu andern	You must move, must journey
Sollst du wechseln, sollst du wandern,	To other places,
Leicht entfliehend jeder Klage."	Lightly casting off all complaints.'
Sanfte Ebb' und hohe Flut,	My soul, deep within me,
Tief im Mut,	Gently ebbs and breaks its banks,
Wandr' ich so im Dunkeln weiter,	Thus I walk on in the darkness,
Steige mutig, singe heiter,	Climbing boldly, singing cheerfully,
Und die Welt erscheint mir gut.	And the world seems good to me.
Alles reine	I see all things clearly,
Seh' ich mild im Widerscheine,	Gently reflected,
Nichts verworren	With nothing distorted
In des Tages Glut verdorren:	Or withered in the heat of day:
Froh umgeben, doch alleine.	Happily surrounded, yet alone.

February 1819 Das Mädchen / The maiden D652

Wie so innig, möcht' ich sagen,	How fondly, I should like to say,
Sich der Meine mir ergibt,	My lover gives himself to me,
Um zu lindern meine Klagen,	To quieten my complaints
Daß er nicht so innig liebt.	That he does not love so fondly.
Will ich's sagen, so entschwebt es;	If I try to say it, the words escape;
Wären Töne mir verliehen,	If music were granted me,
Flöss' es hin in Harmonien,	I should pour it out in harmony,
Denn in jenen Tönen lebt es;	For it dwells in music;
Nur die Nachtigall kann sagen,	Only the nightingale can say
Wie er innig sich mir gibt,	How fondly he gives himself to me,
Um zu lindern meine Klagen,	To quieten my complaints
Daß er nicht so innig liebt.	That he does not love so fondly.

?March 1820 Der Schmetterling / The butterfly D633

Wie soll ich nicht tanzen?
Es macht keine Mühe,
Und reizende Farben
Schimmern hier im Grünen.
Immer schöner glänzen
Meine bunten Flügel,
Immer süßer hauchen
Alle kleinen Blüten.
Ich nasche die Blüten,
Ihr könnt sie nicht hüten.

Wie groß ist die Freude,
Sei's spät oder frühe,
Leichtsinnig zu schweben
Über Tal und Hügel.
Wenn der Abend säuselt
Seht ihr Wolken glühen;
Wenn die Lüfte golden
Scheint die Wiese grüner.
Ich nasche die Blüten,
Ihr könnt sie nicht hüten.

Why shouldn't I dance?
It costs me no effort,
And enchanting colours
Shimmer here in the open.
My colourful wings
Gleam ever more brightly,
Each tiny flower's scent
Grows ever sweeter.
I feast on the flowers,
You cannot protect them.

What a joy it is,
Either early or late,
To flit so carefree
Over hill and dale.
When the evening murmurs,
You see the clouds glow;
When the light's golden,
The meadows are greener.
I feast on the flowers,
You cannot protect them.

?1820 Die Sterne / The stars D684

Du staunest, o Mensch, was heilig wir
    strahlen,
O folgest du nur den himmlischen Winken,
Vernähmest du besser, was freundlich wir
    blinken,
Wie wären verschwunden die irdischen Qualen!
Dann flösse die Liebe aus ewigen Schalen,
Es atmeten alle in reinen Azuren,
Das lichtblaue Meer umschwebte die Fluren,
Und funkelten Sterne auf den heimischen
    Talen.

    Aus göttlicher Quelle sind alle genommen,
Ist jegliches Wesen nicht eines im Chore?
Nun sind ja geöffnet die himmlischen Tore,
Was soll denn das bange Verzagen noch
    frommen?
O wäret ihr schon zur Tiefe geklommen,
So sähet das Haupt ihr von Sternen umflogen
Und spielend um's Herz die kindlichen Wogen,
Zu denen die Stürme des Lebens nicht kom-
    men.

You marvel, O man, at our sacred
    radiance,
If only you followed the heavenly signs,
You would understand better our friendly
    glimmer,
And mortal suffering would vanish!
Then love would flow from eternal vessels,
All would breathe deep the pure blue sky,
The light-blue sea would lap the fields,
And stars would glitter in our native
    valleys.

    We all spring from a divine source,
Is not all creation united in a single choir?
Now all the gates of heaven stand open,
What can dread despair avail?
If you had already conquered the depths,
You would see stars circling your head,
And child-like waves, untouched by life's
    tempests,
Playing about your heart.

?1820 Abendröte / Sunset D690

Tiefer sinket schon die Sonne,	The sun sinks lower,
Und es atmet alles Ruhe,	All things breathe peace,
Tages Arbeit ist vollendet,	The day's work is ended,
Und die Kinder scherzen munter.	And the children laugh and play.
Grüner glänzt die grüne Erde,	The green earth glows greener
Eh' die Sonne ganz versunken;	Before the sun has finally set;
Milden Balsam hauchen leise	The flowers now breathe sweet balm
In die Lüfte nun die Blumen,	Softly into the air,
Der die Seele zart berühret,	Tenderly caressing the soul,
Wenn die Sinne selig trunken.	While the senses are drunk with rapture.
Kleine Vögel, ferne Menschen,	Small birds, distant figures,
Berge himmelan geschwungen,	Mountains soaring heavenward,
Und der große Silberstrom,	And the great silver river
Der im Tale schlank gewunden,	Winding its slender course through the valley,
Alles scheint dem Dichter redend,	All things seem to speak to the poet,
Denn er hat den Sinn gefunden;	For he has discovered their meaning;
Und das All ein einzig Chor,	And the universe becomes a single choir,
Manches Lied aus einem Munde.	Many a song from one mouth.

March 1820 Der Schiffer / The boatman D694

Friedlich lieg' ich hingegossen,	Peacefully I lie stretched out,
Lenke hin und her das Ruder,	Move the rudder to and fro,
Atme kühl im Licht des Mondes,	Breathe the cool moonlit air,
Träume süß im stillen Mute;	Dream in sweet tranquillity;
Gleiten lass' ich auch den Kahn,	And I let the boat drift,
Schaue in die blanken Fluten,	Gaze into the shining waters,
Wo die Sterne lieblich schimmern,	Where the lovely stars glimmer,
Spiele wieder mit dem Ruder.	Play once more with the rudder.
Säße doch das blonde Mägdlein	If only that fair-haired girl
Vor mir auf dem Bänkchen ruhend,	Were resting on the bench beside me,
Sänge schmachtend zarte Lieder,	Longingly singing tender songs,
Himmlisch wär' mir dann zu Mute.	I should feel I were in heaven,
Ließ mich necken von dem Kinde,	Would submit to the child's banter,
Wieder tändelnd mit der Guten. –	Flirt again with the dear creature. –
Friedlich lieg' ich hingegossen,	Peacefully I lie stretched out,
Träume süß im stillen Mute,	Dream in sweet tranquillity,
Atme kühl im Licht des Mondes,	Breathe the cool moonlit air,
Führe hin und her das Ruder.	Move the rudder to and fro.

December 1820 Im Walde / In the forest (D708)
THE SONG WAS ORIGINALLY PUBLISHED AS 'WALDESNACHT'.

Windes Rauschen, Gottes Flügel,	The roar of the wind, God's own wings,
Tief in kühler Waldesnacht,	Deep in the cool forest night,

Wie der Held in Rosses Bügel,	As the hero leaps into his horse's stirrups,
Schwingt sich des Gedankens Macht.	So does the power of thought leap up.
Wie die alten Tannen sausen,	As the old pine-trees sough,
Hört man Geistes Wogen brausen.	So we hear the spirit's surging waves.
Herrlich ist der Flamme Leuchten	Glorious is the fiery glow
In des Morgenglanzes Rot,	In the red dawn,
Oder die das Feld beleuchten,	Or the flashes that light up the fields,
Blitze, schwanger oft von Tod.	Often pregnant with death.
Rasch die Flamme zuckt und lodert,	Swiftly the flame flickers and flares,
Wie zu Gott hinaufgefodert.	As though summoned to God.
Ewig's Rauschen sanfter Quellen,	The eternal murmuring of gentle springs
Zaubert Blumen aus dem Schmerz;	Entices flowers from sorrow;
Trauer doch in linden Wellen	Yet sadness breaks alluringly
Schlägt uns lockend an das Herz;	Against our hearts in gentle waves;
Fernab hin der Geist gezogen,	The Spirit is borne far away
Die uns locken, durch die Wogen.	By those alluring waves.
Drang des Lebens aus der Hülle,	The urge to escape life's fetters,
Kampf der starken Triebe wild;	The struggle of strong, untamed impulses,
Wird zur schönsten Liebesfülle,	Become love's fairest fulfilment,
Durch des Geistes Hauch gestillt.	Stilled by the Spirit's breath.
Schöpferischer Lüfte Wehen	We feel the winds of creation
Fühlt man durch die Seele gehen.	Permeate our souls.
Windes Rauschen, Gottes Flügel,	The roar of the wind, God's own wings,
Tief in dunkler Waldesnacht,	Deep in the dark forest night,
Frei gegeben alle Zügel,	Freed from all fetters,
Schwingt sich des Gedankens Macht,	The power of thought leaps up,
Hört in Lüften ohne Grausen	Listen without dread to the Spirit's song
Den Gesang der Geister brausen.	Soughing in the wind.

Georg Philipp Schmidt (1766–1849)

Usually known as Schmidt von Lübeck, he studied law, before turning to medicine. He practised as a physician in Lübeck and then became Danish Justizrat in 1816. His fame rests on a single poem, 'Des Fremdlings Abschied', the title of which was altered by Schubert to 'Der Wanderer', when he set the poem in October 1816. He also changed the famous final line from 'Da, wo du nicht bist, ist das Glück!' to 'Dort, wo du nicht bist, dort ist das Glück!' Next to 'Erlkönig', 'Der Wanderer' was Schubert's most popular song during his lifetime and for many years after his death. Bars 23–30 are used by Schubert in the Adagio section of his *Wandererfantasie* for piano, D760.

Ich komme vom Gebirge her;	From the mountains I have come,
Es dampft das Tal, es braust das Meer,	The valley steams, the ocean roars,
Ich wandle still, bin wenig froh,	I walk in silence, with little joy,
Und immer fragt der Seufzer – wo?	And my sighs keep asking – Where?
Die Sonne dünkt mich hier so kalt,	Here the sun seems so cold,
Die Blüte welk, das Leben alt;	Blossom faded, life old;
Und, was sie reden, leerer Schall –	What men say – just empty sound:
Ich bin ein Fremdling überall.	I am a stranger everywhere.
Wo bist du, mein geliebtes Land!	Where are you, my beloved land?
Gesucht, geahnt, und nie gekannt,	Sought for, sensed, and never known,
Das Land, das Land, so hoffnungsgrün,	The land, the land, so green with hope,
Das Land, wo meine Rosen blüh'n;	The land where my roses bloom;
Wo meine Freunde wandelnd geh'n,	Where my friends roam,
Wo meine Toten aufersteh'n,	Where my dead friends rise again,
Das Land, das meine Sprache spricht,	The land that speaks my tongue,
O Land, wo bist du?	O land, where are you?
Ich wandle still, bin wenig froh,	I walk in silence, with little joy,
Und immer fragt der Seufzer – wo? –	And my sighs keep asking – Where? –
Im Geisterhauch tönt's mir zurück,	A ghostly whisper makes reply,
„D o r t , wo du n i c h t b i s t, dort ist das G l ü c k!"	'*There*, where you *are not*, there *fortune* lies!'

Franz von Schober (1796–1882)

Franz von Schober, born a year before Schubert, became one of his closest friends. It was he who offered the composer accommodation, when Schubert left home in 1816, and again on several occasions later in his life; and it was at Schober's Viennese apartment that many of the reading parties and Schubertiads took place. Schober was something of a dilettante, and with his restless temperament never settled. He tried his hand at acting and writing and provided the libretto for Schubert's most successful opera *Alfonso und Estrella* and the text to possibly his best-loved song ('An die Musik'). He went to Hungary as a companion to several noble families and was asked by Liszt to accompany him on his concert tours as secretary. Schober was the most worldly of Schubert's circle, and was blamed by some for corrupting him morally. His poems were not published until 1842, which means that all of Schubert's twelve solo songs were set from manuscript.

?1816 Am Bach im Frühling / By the stream in spring D361

Du brachst sie nun die kalte Rinde,	Now you have broken the cold crust,
Und rieselst froh und frei dahin;	And ripple along, free and happy;

Die Lüfte wehen wieder linde,
Und Moos und Gras wird neu und grün.

The breezes blow gently again,
Moss and grass grow fresh and green.

Allein mit traurigem Gemüte
Tret' ich wie sonst zu deiner Flut,
Der Erde allgemeine Blüte
Kommt meinem Herzen nicht zu gut.

Alone and heavy-hearted,
I come to your banks, as of old,
The flowering of the entire earth
Cannot gladden my heart.

Hier treiben immer gleiche Winde,
Kein Hoffen kommt in meinen Sinn –
Als daß ich hier ein Blümchen finde,
Blau, wie sie der Erinn'rung blühn.

Here the same winds still are blowing,
No hope enters my heart –
Unless I find a flower here,
Blue, like the flowers of remembrance.

March 1817 An die Musik / To music D547

Du holde Kunst, in wieviel grauen Stunden,
Wo mich des Lebens wilder Kreis umstrickt,
Hast du mein Herz zu warmer Lieb entzun-
den,
Hast mich in eine beßre Welt entrückt.

O sweet art, in how many a grey hour,
When I am caught in life's tempestuous
round,
Have you kindled my heart to loving warmth,
And borne me away to a better world.

Oft hat ein Seufzer, deiner Harf entflossen,
Ein süßer, heiliger Akkord von dir
Den Himmel beßrer Zeiten mir erschlossen,
Du holde Kunst, ich danke dir dafür!

Often a sigh, escaping your harp,
A chord of sweet celestial harmony,
Has opened a heaven of better times,
O sweet art, for this I thank you!

March 1817 Trost im Liede / Consolation in song D546

Braust des Unglücks Sturm empor:
Halt' ich meine Harfe vor.
Schützen können Saiten nicht,
Die er leicht und schnell durchbricht;
Aber durch des Sanges Tor
Schlägt er milder an mein Ohr.
Sanfte Laute hör' ich klingen,
Die mir in die Seele dringen,
Die mir auf des Wohllauts Schwingen
Wunderbare Tröstung bringen;
Und ob Klagen mir entschweben,
Ob ich still und schmerzlich weine,
Fühl ich mich doch so ergeben,
Daß ich fest und gläubig meine:
Es gehört zu meinem Leben,
Daß sich Schmerz und Freude eine.

When misfortune's tempest rages,
I hold my harp aloft.
Strings can give no protection,
The storm snaps them with swift ease;
But it strikes the ear more gently
Through the gates of song.
I hear sweet sounds
That pierce my soul,
Bringing wondrous comfort
On the wings of harmony;
And though my lips lament,
And though I weep in silent sorrow,
I feel such humility
That I firmly and devoutly believe
That this mingled joy and pain
Is part of my very life.

Christian Friedrich Daniel Schubart (1739–1791)

Poet, composer and pianist, who wrote over eighty songs, many of them, including 'Die Forelle', to his own texts. Much of his work was written in prison, where he languished for ten years – a punishment for his outspoken criticism of the tyrannical duke Karl Eugen and his mistress.

1817 Die Forelle / The trout D550

In einem Bächlein helle,
    Da schoß in froher Eil'
Die launische Forelle
    Vorüber wie ein Pfeil.
Ich stand an dem Gestade,
    Und sah in süßer Ruh'
Des muntern Fischleins Bade
    Im klaren Bächlein zu.

Ein Fischer mit der Rute
    Wohl an dem Ufer stand,
Und sah's mit kaltem Blute,
    Wie sich das Fischlein wand.
So lang dem Wasser Helle,
    So dacht' ich, nicht gebricht,
So fängt er die Forelle
    Mit seiner Angel nicht.

Doch endlich ward dem Diebe
    Die Zeit zu lang. Er macht
Das Bächlein tückisch trübe,
    Und eh' ich es gedacht,
So zuckte seine Rute,
    Das Fischlein zappelt dran,
Und ich mit regem Blute
    Sah die Betrogne an.

In a clear stream,
    In lively haste,
The capricious trout
    Darted by like an arrow.
I stood on the bank,
    Contentedly watching
The frisky fish
    In the clear stream.

An angler with his rod
    Stood on the bank,
And cold-bloodedly watched
    The fish twist and turn.
As long as the water,
    I thought, stays clear,
He'll never catch
    The trout with his hook.

But finally the thief
    Lost patience. Cunningly
He muddied the stream,
    And before I realized,
There was a flick of his rod,
    Where the little fish writhed,
And I, my blood boiling,
    Looked at the cheated creature.

Franz Schubert (1797–1828)

'Abschied von einem Freunde' was occasioned by the departure from Vienna of Franz von Schober, the 'lieber Freund' of the first line, whose brother, an officer in the French army, was ill in France. Schubert, who had been living as a guest in Schober's home, presumably wrote the poem to express his gratitude.

24 August 1817 Abschied von einem Freunde / Farewell to a friend D578

Lebe wohl! Du lieber Freund!
Ziehe hin in fernes Land,

Farewell, dear friend!
Depart to a distant land,

Nimm der Freundschaft trautes Band –	Take this cherished bond of friendship –
Und bewahr's in treuer Hand!	And preserve it faithfully!
Lebe wohl! Du lieber Freund!	Farewell, dear friend!
Lebe wohl! Du lieber Freund!	Farewell, dear friend!
Hör' in diesem Trauersang	Hear in this sad song
Meines Herzens innern Drang,	My heart's deep yearning,
Tönt er doch so dumpf und bang.	So heavy and so anxious.
Lebe wohl! Du lieber Freund!	Farewell, dear friend!
Lebe wohl! Du lieber Freund!	Farewell, dear friend!
Scheiden heißt das bitt're Wort,	Parting is a bitter word,
Weh, es ruft Dich von uns fort	Alas, it calls you from us
Hin an den Bestimmungsort.	To the place where you must go.
Lebe wohl! Du lieber Freund!	Farewell, dear friend!
Lebe wohl! Du lieber Freund!	Farewell, dear friend!
Wenn dies Lied Dein Herz ergreift,	Should this song move your heart,
Freundes Schatten näher schweift,	A friend's spirit shall draw near,
Meiner Seele Saiten streift.	Touching the strings of my soul.
Lebe wohl! Du lieber Freund!	Farewell, dear friend!

Ernst Schulze (1789–1817)

Ernst Konrad Friedrich Schulze was born on 22 March 1789 in Celle. His mother died when Ernst was two, and he seems to have inherited her sickly constitution; he considered himself inferior to his older brother August, and would often seek refuge in imagination and dreams. He vented his frustration in poetry, which eventually led to the hundred poems of his *Poetisches Tagebuch* (*Verse diary*), which were almost entirely inspired by his love for Adelheid and Cäcilie Tychsen, the daughters of a celebrated orientalist and archaeologist. Neither sister returned his affection, and Schulze poured out his obsession in verse that often deludedly depicts his love as requited. There are ten Schulze songs and one male quartet, 'Ewige Liebe'.

?March 1825 Im Walde / In the forest D834

Ich wandre über Berg und Tal	I wander over hill and dale
Und über grüne Heiden,	And over green moors,
Und mit mir wandert meine Qual,	And with me wanders all my woe,
Will nimmer von mir scheiden.	That never leaves my side.
Und schifft' ich auch durch's weite Meer,	And were I to sail across the wide sea,
Sie käm' auch dort wohl hinterher.	It would follow in my wake.
Wohl blühn viel Blumen auf der Flur,	Though many flowers bloom in the field,
Die hab' ich nicht gesehen.	I have not noticed them,
Denn e i n e Blume seh' ich nur	For I see but a *single* flower,

Auf allen Wegen stehen.
Nach ihr hab' ich mich oft gebückt
Und doch sie nimmer abgepflückt.

Die Bienen summen durch das Gras
Und hängen an den Blüten;
Das macht mein Auge trüb' und naß,
Ich kann mir's nicht verbieten.
Ihr süßen Lippen, rot und weich,
Wohl hing ich nimmer so an euch!

Gar lieblich singen nah und fern
Die Vögel auf den Zweigen;
Wohl säng' ich mit den Vögeln gern,
Doch muß ich traurig schweigen.
Denn Liebeslust und Liebespein,
Die bleiben jedes gern allein.

Am Himmel seh' ich flügelschnell
Die Wolken weiter ziehen,
Die Welle rieselt leicht und hell,
Muß immer nahn und fliehen.
Doch haschen, wenn's vom Winde ruht,
Sich Wolk' und Wolke, Flut und Flut.

Ich wandre hin, ich wandre her,
Bei Sturm und heitern Tagen,
Und doch erschau' ich's nimmermehr
Und kann es nicht erjagen.
O Liebessehnen, Liebesqual,
Wann ruht der Wanderer einmal?

Whatever path I tread.
I've often stooped before it,
But never yet plucked it.

The bees are humming through the grass,
Hanging from the blossoms;
My eyes grow dim and fill with tears,
I cannot prevent myself.
I never drew so close to you,
Sweet lips so red and soft!

Far and near the birds are singing
Sweetly on the branches;
I'd gladly join them in their song,
But must remain sad and silent.
For love's joy and love's sorrow –
Both prefer to be alone.

I watch the clouds wing their way
Swiftly across the sky,
The brightly rippling waves
Must ever ebb and flow.
Yet when the winds abate,
Clouds and waves still chase each other.

I wander to and fro
Through storms and cloudless days,
Yet I shall never behold it again,
Shall never track it down.
O love's desire, O love's torment,
When shall the wanderer finally rest?

?March 1825 Auf der Brücke* / On the bridge D853

Frisch trabe sonder Ruh und Rast,
Mein gutes Roß, durch Nacht und Regen!
Was scheust du dich vor Busch und Ast
Und strauchelst auf den wilden Wegen?
Dehnt auch der Wald sich tief und dicht,
Doch muß er endlich sich erschließen,
Und freundlich wird ein fernes Licht
Uns aus dem dunkeln Tale grüßen.

Wohl könnt' ich über Berg und Feld
Auf deinem schlanken Rücken fliegen
Und mich am bunten Spiel der Welt,
An holden Bildern mich vergnügen.
Manch Auge lacht mir traulich zu
Und beut mir Frieden, Lieb' und Freude.

Gallop briskly on without respite,
Good horse, through night and rain!
Why do you shy at bushes and boughs
And stumble on wild paths?
Though the forest stretch deep and dense,
It must finally come to an end,
And a distant light will greet us warmly
From the dark valley.

I could happily speed on your slender back
Over mountain and field,
Enjoy the world's varied pleasures
And all its wondrous sights.
Many an eye smiles with affection,
Offering me peace, love and joy.

* Schulze's title 'Auf der Bruck' refers to a lookout point on a hill near Göttingen.

Und dennoch eil' ich ohne Ruh
Zurück, zurück zu meinem Leide.

   Denn schon drei Tage war ich fern
Von ihr, die ewig mich gebunden,
Drei Tage waren Sonn' und Stern
Und Erd' und Himmel mir verschwunden.
Von Lust und Leiden, die mein Herz
Bei ihr bald heilten, bald zerrissen,
Fühlt' ich drei Tage nur den Schmerz,
Und ach, die Freude mußt' ich missen!

   Weit sehn wir über Land und See
Zur wärmern Flur den Vogel fliegen;
Wie sollte denn die Liebe je
In ihrem Pfade sich betrügen?
Drum trabe mutig durch die Nacht!
Und schwinden auch die dunkeln Bahnen,
Der Sehnsucht helles Auge wacht,
Und sicher führt mich süßes Ahnen.

And yet I hurry without rest
Back, back to my sorrow.

   For three whole days I've been away
From her, to whom I'm ever bound,
For three whole days sun and stars,
Earth and sky have vanished from view.
Of the joy and pain which, with her,
Now healed, now broke my heart,
I've for three days felt only the pain,
And have had, alas, to forgo the joy!

   We watch the bird fly far away
Over land and sea to warmer climes;
Why, then, should love ever be
Deceived in its own course?
So gallop bravely through the night!
And though the dark tracks disappear,
The bright eye of longing is awake,
Sweet expectation will guide me safely.

?March 1826 Tiefes Leid / Deep sorrow D876

Ich bin von aller Ruh geschieden,
Ich treib' umher auf wilder Flut;
An e i n e m Ort nur find' ich Frieden,
Das ist der Ort, wo Alles ruht.
Und wenn die Wind' auch schaurig sausen,
Und kalt der Regen niederfällt,
Doch will ich dort viel lieber hausen,
Als in der unbeständ'gen Welt.

   Denn wie die Träume spurlos schweben,
Und einer schnell den andern treibt,
Spielt mit sich selbst das irre Leben,
Und jedes naht und keines bleibt.
Nie will die falsche Hoffnung weichen,
Nie mit der Hoffnung Furcht und Müh;
Die Ewigstummen, Ewigbleichen
Verheißen und versagen nie.

   Nicht weck' ich sie mit meinen Schritten
In ihrer dunklen Einsamkeit.
Sie wissen nicht, was ich gelitten,
Und Keinen stört mein tiefes Leid.
Dort kann die Seele freier klagen
Bei Jener, die ich treu geliebt,
Nicht wird der kalte Stein mir sagen,
Ach, daß auch sie mein Schmerz betrübt!

I have lost all peace of mind
And drift on wild waters;
In *one* place alone shall I find peace,
The place where all things rest.
And though the wind roar fearfully,
And though the falling rain be cold,
I'd prefer by far to dwell there
Than in this inconstant world.

   For as dreams vanish without trace,
Swiftly succeeding each other,
So is life one mad whirl,
All things draw near and nothing stays.
False hopes will never fade,
Nor with those hopes our fear and toil;
The ever-silent, the ever-pale
Promise and deny us nothing.

   I shall not wake them with my footsteps
In their dark solitude.
They do not know what I have suffered,
My deep sorrow disturbs none of them.
There my soul can lament more freely
With her whom I have truly loved,
The cold stone will not tell me, alas,
That my suffering grieves her too!

March 1826 Im Frühling / In Spring D882

Still sitz' ich an des Hügels Hang,
Der Himmel ist so klar,
Das Lüftchen spielt im grünen Tal,
Wo ich bei'm ersten Frühlingsstrahl
Einst, ach, so glücklich war;

 Wo ich an ihrer Seite ging
So traulich und so nah,
Und tief im dunkeln Felsenquell
Den schönen Himmel blau und hell,
Und sie im Himmel sah.

 Sieh, wie der bunte Frühling schon
Aus Knosp' und Blüte blickt!
Nicht alle Blüten sind mir gleich,
Am liebsten pflückt' ich von dem Zweig,
Von welchem sie gepflückt.

 Denn Alles ist wie damals noch,
Die Blumen, das Gefild,
Die Sonne scheint nicht minder hell,
Nicht minder freundlich schwimmt im Quell
Das blaue Himmelsbild.

 Es wandeln nur sich Will' und Wahn,
Es wechseln Lust und Streit,
Vorüber flieht der Liebe Glück,
Und nur die Liebe bleibt zurück,
Die Lieb' und ach, das Leid!

 O wär' ich doch ein Vöglein nur
Dort an dem Wiesenhang!
Dann blieb' ich auf den Zweigen hier
Und säng' ein süßes Lied von ihr
Den ganzen Sommer lang.

I sit silently on the hillside,
The sky is so clear,
The breeze plays in the green valley
Where once, at the first gleam of spring,
I was, ah, so happy;

 Where I walked by her side
So fondly and so close,
And saw deep in the dark rocky stream
The lovely sky blue and bright,
And her reflected in the sky.

 See how colourful spring
Already peers from bud and flower!
Not all flowers are the same to me,
I'd like best to pluck them from the branch
From which she has plucked.

 For all is as it used to be,
The flowers and the fields,
The sun shines no less brightly,
And the blue sky ripples
No less cheerfully in the stream.

 It's only will and whim that change,
Joy alternates with strife,
The happiness of love slips by,
And love alone remains,
Love and, alas, sorrow!

 Ah, if only I were a little bird
There on the hillside meadow!
Then I'd stay on these branches here
And sing a sweet song about her
All summer long.

March 1826 Über Wildemann* / Above Wildemann D884

Die Winde sausen
Am Tannenhang,
Die Quellen brausen
Das Tal entlang;
Ich wand're in Eile
Durch Wald und Schnee,
Wohl manche Meile
Von Höh zu Höh.

The winds roar
Across the pine slopes,
The rivers rush
Along the valley;
I hurry
Through forest and snow
For many a mile
From peak to peak.

*A small town in the Harz mountains

Und will das Leben	And though life
Im freien Tal	In the open valley
Sich auch schon heben	Already stirs
Zum Sonnenstrahl;	To greet the sun,
Ich muß vorüber	I must go on my way
Mit wildem Sinn	In a wild mood,
Und blicke lieber	Preferring to look
Zum Winter hin.	Towards winter.
Auf grünen Heiden,	On green moors
Auf bunten Aun,	And colourful meadows,
Müßt' ich mein Leiden	I'd only suffer
Nur immer schaun,	Constantly,
Daß selbst am Steine	Seeing life burgeon
Das Leben sprießt,	From the very stones,
Und ach! nur Eine	Knowing, alas! that she alone
Ihr Herz verschließt.	Closes up her heart.
O Liebe, Liebe,	O love, O love,
O Maienhauch!	O breath of May!
Du drängst die Triebe	You force the buds
Aus Baum und Strauch!	From tree and bush!
Die Vögel singen	The birds sing
Auf grünen Höhn,	On the green hills,
Die Quellen springen	Springs gush forth,
Bei deinem Wehn!	When your breezes blow!
Mich läßt du schweifen	You leave me to roam
Im dunklen Wahn	In my dark delusion
Durch Windespfeifen	Through roaring winds
Auf rauher Bahn.	On rough paths.
O Frühlingsschimmer,	O shimmering spring,
O Blütenschein,	O gleaming blossom,
Soll ich denn nimmer	Shall I nevermore
Mich dein erfreun?	Delight in you?

Sir Walter Scott (1771–1832)

Scott's historical romances enjoyed enormous popularity across Europe in the early years of the nineteenth century and were frequently adapted as plays and operas. Schubert's interest in the Scottish poet dates from the summer of 1823. However much Schubert struggled in his lifetime to win public acceptance for his Lieder, the recital tour he made of Upper Austria in 1825 with Johann Michael Vogl was ecstatically received. They often performed 'Ave Maria', composed that spring, but though the song represented a great triumph, the success was only parochial, and in a letter to his parents of late July 1825 Schubert writes that he intended to have the songs printed with Scott's original words, so that he might 'become better known in England'. Schubert composed eight solo songs from Scott's novels: 'Gesang der Norna' (*The Pirate*); 'Lied der Anna Lyle' (*A Legend of Montrose*); 'Raste Krieger, Krieg ist aus', 'Jäger, ruhe von der Jagd', 'Ave Maria', 'Lied des gefangenen Jägers', 'Normans Gesang' (*The Lady of the Lake*); and 'Romanze des Richard Löwenherz' (*Ivanhoe*).

1825 Ellens erster Gesang / Ellen's song I D837
FROM *The Lady of the Lake*, TRANSLATED BY ADAM STORCK (1780–1822)

Raste Krieger! Krieg ist aus,	Warrior, rest! Your war is over,
Schlaf den Schlaf, nichts wird dich wecken,	Sleep the sleep, nothing shall wake you,
Träume nicht von wildem Strauß,	Do not dream of fierce battles,
Nicht von Tag und Nacht voll Schrecken.	Of days and nights filled with terror.
In der Insel Zauberhallen	In the isle's enchanted halls,
Wird ein weicher Schlafgesang	A gentle lullaby
Um das müde Haupt dir wallen	Shall caress your weary head
Zu der Zauberharfe Klang.	To the harp's magic strains.
Feen mit unsichtbaren Händen	Fairies with invisible hands
Werden auf dein Lager hin	Shall strew on your bed
Holde Schlummerblumen senden,	Sweet flowers of slumber
Die im Zauberlande blühn.	That bloom in the magic land.
Raste Krieger! Krieg ist aus,	Warrior, rest! Your war is over,
Schlaf den Schlaf, nichts wird dich wecken.	Sleep the sleep, nothing shall wake you,
Träume nicht von wildem Strauß,	Do not dream of fierce battles,
Nicht von Tag und Nacht voll Schrecken.	Of days and nights filled with terror.
Nicht der Trommel wildes Rasen,	Neither the wild crash of drums,
Nicht des Kriegs gebietend Wort,	Nor the summons to enter battle,
Nicht der Todeshörner Blasen	Nor the blaring horns of Death
Scheuchen deinen Schlummer fort.	Shall banish your sleep.
Nicht das Stampfen wilder Pferde,	Neither the stamping of wild horses,
Nicht der Schreckensruf der Wacht,	Nor the sentry's fearful cry,
Nicht das Bild von Tagsbeschwerde	Nor the image of daily cares
Stören deine stille Nacht.	Shall disturb your tranquil night.
Doch der Lerche Morgensänge	Yet the lark's morning songs
Wecken sanft dein schlummernd Ohr,	Shall softly wake your slumbering ear,
Und des Sumpfgefieders Klänge	And the sounds of marshland birds,
Steigend aus Geschilf und Rohr.	Rising from the reeds and rushes.
Raste Krieger! Krieg ist aus,	Warrior, rest! Your war is over,
Schlaf den Schlaf, nichts wird dich wecken.	Sleep the sleep, nothing shall wake you,
Träume nicht von wildem Strauß,	Do not dream of fierce battles,
Nicht von Tag und Nacht voll Schrecken.	Of days and nights filled with terror.

1825 Ellens zweiter Gesang / Ellen's song II D838
FROM *The Lady of the Lake*, TRANSLATED BY ADAM STORCK (1780–1822)

Jäger, ruhe von der Jagd!
Weicher Schlummer soll dich decken,
Träume nicht, wenn Sonn' erwacht
Daß Jagdhörner dich erwecken.

Schlaf! der Hirsch ruht in der Höhle,
Bei dir sind die Hunde wach,
Schlaf, nicht quäl' es deine Seele,
Daß dein edles Roß erlag.

Jäger, ruhe von der Jagd!
Weicher Schlummer soll dich decken;
Wenn der junge Tag erwacht,
Wird kein Jägerhorn dich wecken.

Huntsman, rest from the chase!
Gentle slumber shall enshroud you,
Do not dream, when the sun rises,
That hunting horns will wake you.

Sleep! The stag is resting in its cave,
Your hounds beside you are awake,
Sleep! Let it not torment your soul
That your noble horse has died.

Huntsman, rest from the chase!
Gentle slumber shall enshroud you;
When the young day rises,
No hunting horns shall wake you.

1825 Ellens dritter Gesang / Ellen's song III D839
FROM *The Lady of the Lake*, TRANSLATED BY ADAM STORCK (1780–1822)

Ave Maria! Jungfrau mild,
Erhöre einer Jungfrau Flehen,
Aus diesem Felsen starr und wild
Soll mein Gebet zu dir hinwehen.
Wir schlafen sicher bis zum Morgen,
Ob Menschen noch so grausam sind.
O Jungfrau, sieh der Jungfrau Sorgen,
O Mutter, hör ein bittend Kind!
Ave Maria!

Ave Maria! Unbefleckt!
Wenn wir auf diesen Fels hinsinken
Zum Schlaf, und uns dein Schutz bedeckt,
Wird weich der harte Fels uns dünken.
Du lächelst, Rosendüfte wehen
In dieser dumpfen Felsenkluft,
O Mutter, höre Kindes Flehen,
O Jungfrau, eine Jungfrau ruft!
Ave Maria!

Ave Maria! Reine Magd!
Der Erde und der Luft Dämonen,
Von deines Auges Huld verjagt,
Sie können hier nicht bei uns wohnen.
Wir woll'n uns still dem Schicksal beugen,
Da uns dein heil'ger Trost anweht;
Der Jungfrau wolle hold dich neigen,

Ave Maria! Virgin mild,
Listen to a virgin's pleading,
From this wild, unyielding rock
My prayer shall be wafted to you.
We shall sleep safely till morning dawns,
However cruel men may be.
O Virgin, behold a virgin's cares,
O Mother, hear a pleading child!
Ave Maria!

Ave Maria! Undefiled!
When, beneath your protection,
We sink down on this rock to sleep,
The hard rock shall seem soft to us.
You smile, and the fragrance of roses
Wafts through this gloomy cavern,
O Mother, hear a child's entreaty,
O Virgin, a virgin cries out to you!
Ave Maria!

Ave Maria! Pure Maiden!
Demons of the earth and air,
Banished by the grace of your gaze,
Cannot dwell with us here.
We shall silently submit to fate,
Since your holy comfort breathes on us;
Bow down, I pray, to this virgin,

Dem Kind, das für den Vater fleht.
Ave Maria!
(*Hensel*)

This child who prays for her father.
Ave Maria!

Johann Gabriel Seidl (1804–75)

Seidl was a close friend of Schubert, and spent much of his life in Vienna as curator, schoolmaster, book-censor, poet and civil servant. He was responsible for modernizing the text of the Austrian national anthem, and published poems both in dialect and High German, including a long and touching poem written the day before Schubert's funeral, entitled 'Meinem Freunde Franz Schubert!'

?1828 Bei dir allein! / With you alone! D866

Bei dir allein
Empfind ich, daß ich lebe,
Daß Jugendmut mich schwellt,
Daß eine heit're Welt
Der Liebe mich durchbebe;
  Mich freut mein Sein
  Bei dir allein!

With you alone
I feel I am alive,
That I am fired by youthful vigour,
That a serene world
Of love quivers through me;
  I rejoice in being
  With you alone!

Bei dir allein
Weht mir die Luft so labend,
Dünkt mich die Flur so grün,
So mild des Lenzes Blüh'n,
So balsamreich der Abend,
  So kühl der Hain,
  Bei dir allein!

With you alone
The breeze blows so bracingly,
The fields seem so green,
The flowering spring so gentle,
The evening so fragrant,
  The grove so cool,
  With you alone!

Bei dir allein
Verliert der Schmerz sein Herbes,
Gewinnt die Freud' an Lust!
Du sicherst meine Brust
Des angestammten Erbes;
  Ich fühl' mich mein
  Bei dir allein!

With you alone
Pain's bitterness is lost,
Joy gains in sweetness!
You assure my heart
Of its natural heritage;
  I feel I am myself
  With you alone!

?1828 Die Männer sind mechant! / Men are rogues! D866

Du sagtest mir es, Mutter:
Er ist ein Springinsfeld!
Ich würd' es dir nicht glauben,
Bis ich mich krank gequält!
Ja, ja, nun ist er's wirklich;
Ich hatt' ihn nur verkannt!

You told me, mother:
He's a young rogue!
I would not believe you,
Till I was sick with torment!
Yes, yes, he really is;
I was quite mistaken!

Du sagtest mir's, o Mutter:
  „Die Männer sind mechant!"

Vor'm Dorf im Busch, als gestern
Die stille Dämm'rung sank,
Da rauscht' es: „Guten Abend!"
Da rauscht' es: „Schönen Dank!"
Ich schlich hinzu, ich horchte;
Ich stand wie festgebannt:
Er war's mit einer Andern. –
  „Die Männer sind mechant!"

O Mutter, welche Qualen!
Es muß heraus, es muß! –
Es blieb nicht bloß beim Rauschen,
Es blieb nicht bloß bei'm Gruß!
Von Gruße kam's zum Kusse,
Vom Kuß zum Druck der Hand,
Vom Druck, ach liebe Mutter! –
  „Die Männer sind mechant!"

You told me so, mother:
  'Men are rogues!'

In the bushes near the village
Last night as dusk fell silently,
I heard a whispered 'Good evening!'
I heard a whispered 'Thank you so much!'
I crept up, I listened;
I stood as if transfixed:
There he was with another girl –
  'Men are rogues!'

O mother, what torture!
I must speak out, I must! –
It did not stop at whisperings,
It did not stop at greetings!
It went from greetings to kissing,
From kissing to holding hands,
From holding hands – ah, dear mother! –
  'Men are rogues!'

?1826 Wiegenlied / Cradle song D867

Wie sich der Äuglein
Kindlicher Himmel,
Schlummerbelastet,
Lässig verschließt! –
  Schließe sie einst so,
  Lockt dich die Erde:
  D r i n n e n   i s t   H i m m e l,
  A u ß e n   i s t   L u s t!

Wie dir so schlafrot
Glühet die Wange!
Rosen aus Eden
Hauchten sie an;
  Rosen die Wangen,
  Himmel die Augen,
  H e i t e r e r   M o r g e n,
  H i m m l i s c h e r   T a g!

Wie des Gelockes
Goldige Wallung
Kühlet der Schläfe
Glühenden Saum.
  Schön ist das Goldhaar,
  Schöner der Kranz drauf:
  T r ä u m'   d u   v o m   L o r b e e r,
  B i s   e r   d i r   b l ü h t.

How free of care those little eyes
With their childlike heaven
Close,
Laden with slumber!
  Close them thus,
  When the earth one day calls you,
  Heaven lies within,
  Joy lies without!

How your cheeks are glowing
Red with sleep!
Roses from Eden
Breathed on them;
  Your cheeks are roses,
  Your eyes are heaven,
  Cloudless morning,
  Heavenly day!

How the golden waves
Of your curly hair
Cool your burning
Temples.
  Lovely golden hair,
  Lovelier still the garland on it:
  Dream of the laurel
  Until it blooms for you.

Liebliches Mündchen,	Dear little mouth,
Engel umwehn dich:	Angels hover round you:
Drinnen die Unschuld,	Within is innocence,
Drinnen die Lieb';	Within is love;
Wahre sie, Kindchen,	Guard them, my child,
Wahre sie treulich;	Faithfully guard them:
L i p p e n s i n d R o s e n,	*Lips are roses,*
L i p p e n s i n d G l u t.	*Lips are warmth.*

Wie dir ein Engel	Just as an angel
Faltet die Händchen;	Folds your little hands,
Falte sie einst so,	Fold them thus one day
Gehst du zur Ruh;	When you go to rest;
Schön sind die Träume,	Dreams are beautiful,
Wenn man gebetet:	When you've said your prayers:
U n d d a s E r w a c h e n	*And waking rewards you*
L o h n t m i t d e m T r a u m.	*Along with the dream.*

?March 1826 Der Wanderer an den Mond / The wanderer addresses the moon D870

Ich auf der Erd', am Himmel du,	I on earth, you in the heavens,
Wir wandern Beide rüstig zu: –	Both of us journey briskly on:
Ich ernst und trüb, du mild und rein,	I sad and cheerless, you pure and gentle,
Was mag der Unterschied wohl sein?	I wonder what the difference can be?

Ich wandre fremd von Land zu Land,	I journey, a stranger, from land to land,
So heimatlos, so unbekannt;	So homeless, so unknown;
Bergauf, bergab, waldein, waldaus,	Up and down mountains, into forests and out,
Doch bin ich nirgend, ach! zu Haus.	But nowhere, alas! am I at home.

Du aber wanderst auf und ab	But you journey up and down
Aus Ostens Wieg' in Westens Grab, –	From eastern cradle to western grave,
Wallst Länder ein und Länder aus,	Wander, a pilgrim, from land to land,
Und bist doch, wo du bist, zu Haus.	Yet are, wherever you be, at home.

Der Himmel, endlos ausgespannt,	The infinite expanse of sky
Ist dein geliebtes Heimatland:	Is your beloved native land:
O glücklich, wer wohin er geht,	O happy is he who, wherever he goes,
Doch auf der Heimat Boden steht!	Still stands upon his native soil!

?March 1826 Das Zügenglöcklein* / The passing bell D871

Kling' die Nacht durch, klinge,	Ring the night through, ring,
Süßen Frieden bringe	Bring sweet peace
Dem, für den du tönst!	To him you toll for!
Kling' in weite Ferne,	Ring out afar,
So du Pilger gerne	You who love to reconcile
Mit der Welt versöhnst!	Pilgrims with the world!

* Passing bells used to be found in most Austrian Catholic churches and were rung only when one of the parishioners was known to be dying.

Aber wer will wandern	But who would wish to join
Zu den lieben Andern,	Their dear loved ones,
Die voraus gewallt?	Who have gone on before?
Zog er gern die Schelle?	Did he ring the bell gladly?
Bebt er an der Schwelle,	Did he tremble on the threshold,
Wann „Herein" erschallt?	At the cry of 'Enter'?
Gilt's dem bösen Sohne,	Does it ring for the wicked son,
Der noch flucht dem Tone,	Who still curses its sound,
Weil er heilig ist?!	Because it is holy?!
Nein, es klingt so lauter,	No, it rings as purely
Wie ein Gottvertrauter	As when one who trusts in God
Seine Laufbahn schließt!	Ends his life on earth!
Aber ist's ein Müder,	But if it is a weary man,
Den verwaist die Brüder, –	Whose brothers have died –
Dem ein treues Tier	Whose faith in the world
Einzig ließ den Glauben	Has only been kept alive
An die Welt nicht rauben: –	By some loyal animal –
Ruft ihn Gott zu Dir!	Call him, O God, to Thee!
Ist's der Frohen Einer,	If it be one of that happy band
Der die Freuden reiner	Who shares in the joys
Lieb' und Freundschaft teilt,	Of pure love and friendship,
Gönn' ihm noch die Wonnen	Allow him still to live blissfully
Unter dieser Sonnen,	Beneath this sun,
Wo er gerne weilt!	Where he loves to dwell!

March 1826 Am Fenster / At the window D878

Ihr lieben Mauern, hold und traut,	Dear, friendly, familiar walls
Die ihr mich kühl umschließt,	That enclose me with your coolness,
Und silberglänzend niederschaut,	And gaze down with silvery sheen
Wenn droben Vollmond ist:	When the full moon shines above:
Ihr saht mich einst so traurig da,	Once you saw me here so sad,
Mein Haupt auf schlaffer Hand, –	Head sunk in weary hands –
Als ich in mir allein mich sah,	When my thoughts turned in on myself,
Und keiner mich verstand.	And no one understood me.
Jetzt brach ein ander Licht heran:	But now another light has dawned:
Die Trauerzeit ist um:	The time for mourning is past:
Und manche ziehn mit mir die Bahn	Now many keep me company
Durch's Lebensheiligtum.	Along life's blessed way.
Sie raubt der Zufall ewig nie	Chance shall never banish them
Aus meinem treuen Sinn:	From my loyal thoughts:
In tiefster Seele trag' ich sie, –	They are ever there in my inmost soul –
Da reicht kein Zufall hin.	Where chance can never reach.
Du Mauer wähnst mich trüb' wie einst,	You walls think I'm sad as once I was,
Das ist die stille Freud';	That is my silent joy;

Wenn du vom Mondlicht wiederscheinst,	When you shimmer in the moonlight,
Wird mir die Brust so weit.	My heart swells.
An jedem Fenster wähnt' ich dann	Then I imagine I see at every window
Ein Freundeshaupt, gesenkt,	A friendly face with lowered gaze,
Das auch so schaut zum Himmel an,	That also gazes up to heaven
Das auch so meiner denkt!	And thinks of me as well!

March 1826 Sehnsucht / Longing D879

Die Scheibe friert, der Wind ist rauh,	The window pane freezes, the wind is raw,
Der nächt'ge Himmel rein und blau:	The night sky blue and clear:
Ich sitz' in meinem Kämmerlein	I sit inside my little room
Und schau in's reine Blau hinein!	And gaze into the clear blue!
Mir fehlt etwas, das fühl' ich gut,	Something is missing, that I know,
Mir fehlt mein Lieb, das treue Blut:	My love is missing, my faithful love:
Und will ich in die Sterne sehn,	And when I look up at the stars,
Muß stets das Aug mir übergehn!	My eyes always fill with tears!
Mein Lieb, wo weilst du nur so fern,	My love, where are you so far away,
Mein schöner Stern, mein Augenstern?!	My lovely star, my treasure?!
Du weißt, dich lieb' und brauch' ich ja, –	You know I love you, know I need you –
Die Träne tritt mir wieder nah.	Again I am close to tears.
Da quält' ich mich so manchen Tag,	For many a day I've been in torment,
Weil mir kein Lied gelingen mag, –	Since no song has turned out well –
Weil's nimmer sich erzwingen läßt	Because a song can never be forced
Und frei hinsäuselt, wie der West!	To blow as freely as the West Wind!
Wie mild mich's wieder grad durchglüht! –	How gentle the glow that warms me again!
Sieh nur – das ist ja schon ein Lied!	Lo and behold – a song appears!
Wenn mich mein Los vom Liebchen warf,	When fate has severed me from my love,
Dann fühl' ich, daß ich singen darf.	I feel in my heart that I can sing.

March 1826 Im Freien / In the open D880

Draussen in der weiten Nacht	Once more I stand outside
Steh' ich wieder nun:	In the vastness of the night:
Ihre helle Sternenpracht	Its bright starry splendour
Läßt mein Herz nicht ruhn!	'Greetings, dear friend!'
Tausend Arme winken mir	A thousand arms beckon me
Süßbegehrend zu,	With sweet longing,
Tausend Stimmen rufen hier:	A thousand voices call:
„Grüß' dich, Trauter, du!"	'Greetings, dear friend!'
O ich weiß auch, was mich zieht,	Oh I am well aware
Weiß auch, was mich ruft,	What draws me and what calls me,
Was wie Freundesgruß und Lied	Like a friendly word and song
Locket durch die Luft.	Floating enticingly through the air.

Siehst du dort das Hüttchen stehn,	Can you see that cottage there,
Drauf der Mondschein ruht?	Where the moon sheds its light?
Durch die blanken Scheiben sehn	From its shining windows
Augen, die mir gut!	A pair of loving eyes look out!

Siehst du dort das Haus am Bach,	Can you see the house by the stream,
Das der Mond bescheint?	Lit up by the moon?
Unter seinem trauten Dach	Underneath its cosy roof
Schläft mein liebster Freund.	My dearest friend is sleeping.

Siehst du jenen Baum, der voll	Can you see that tree over there,
Silberflocken flimmt?	Laden with silver flakes?
O wie oft mein Busen schwoll,	Oh! how often my heart
Froher dort gestimmt!	Used to swell there with joy!

Jedes Plätzchen, das mir winkt,	Every little place that beckons me
Ist ein lieber Platz;	Is dear to my heart,
Und wohin ein Strahl nur sinkt,	And wherever a moonbeam shines,
Lockt ein teurer Schatz.	A dear loved one entices.

Drum auch winkt mir's überall	So everything here
So begehrend hier,	Beckons me with longing,
Drum auch ruft es, wie der Schall	Calling to me with the sounds
Trauter Liebe mir.	Of true love.

October 1828 Die Taubenpost / Pigeon post D957/14
FROM *Schwanengesang*

Ich hab' eine Brieftaub in meinem Sold,	I've a carrier-pigeon in my pay,
Die ist gar ergeben und treu,	She's so devoted and true,
Sie nimmt mir nie das Ziel zu kurz,	She never stops short of her goal,
Und fliegt auch nie vorbei.	And never flies too far.

Ich sende sie vieltausendmal	I send her many thousands of times
Auf Kundschaft täglich hinaus,	Each day to spy out the land,
Vorbei an manchem lieben Ort,	Past many a beloved spot,
Bis zu der Liebsten Haus.	Till she reaches my sweetheart's house.

Dort schaut sie zum Fenster heimlich hinein,	There she peeps in at the window,
Belauscht ihren Blick und Schritt,	Observing every look and step,
Gibt meine Grüße scherzend ab	Delivers my greeting cheerfully
Und nimmt die ihren mit.	And brings hers back to me.

Kein Briefchen brauch' ich zu schreiben mehr,	I no longer need to write a letter,
Die Träne selbst geb' ich ihr;	I can entrust to her my very tears;
O, sie verträgt sie sicher nicht,	She'll certainly not mistake the address,
Gar eifrig dient sie mir.	For she serves me so fervently.

| Bei Tag, bei Nacht, im Wachen, im Traum, | Day or night, awake or dreaming, |
| Ihr gilt das alles gleich: | It's all the same to her: |

Wenn sie nur wandern, wandern kann,	As long as she can range and roam,
Dann ist sie überreich!	She's richly satisfied!

Sie wird nicht müd', sie wird nicht matt,	She does not tire, she does not flag,
Der Weg ist stets ihr neu;	To her the route seems always new;
Sie braucht nicht Lockung, braucht nicht Lohn,	She needs no enticement, no reward,
D i e Taub' ist so mir treu!	*That* pigeon is so loyal!

Drum heg' ich sie auch so treu an der Brust,	That's why I cherish her in my heart,
Versichert des schönsten Gewinns;	Certain of the fairest prize;
Sie heißt – die Sehnsucht! Kennt ihr sie? –	Her name is – Longing! Do you know her?
Die Botin treuen Sinns.	The messenger of faithfulness.

Johann Chrysostomus Senn (1792–1857)

Senn, a schoolfriend of the composer, was greatly influenced in his political views by his father, Franz Michael Senn, a judge who supported the Tyrolean movement for independence. Johann Senn was described by Josef Kenner in his *Memoirs* as a 'Hasser äußerlichen Zwanges' – a man who hated all constraint. In Metternich's Austria, where suppression of liberty and the arts was rife, the arrest of any opponent of state or church was a commonplace – and so it was that the police detained Senn one evening in March 1820; he was imprisoned for some fourteen months and then deported to Tyrol. Schubert, who had been with him on the evening of his arrest, was let off with a caution. The two friends never met again.

1822 Schwanengesang / Swan song D744

„Wie klag' ich's aus	'How shall I express
„Das Sterbegefühl,	This sense of death,
„Das auflösend	The dissolution
„Durch die Glieder rinnt?	That flows through my limbs?

„Wie sing' ich's aus	How shall I sing
„Das Werdegefühl,	This sense of life
„Das erlösend	That redeems you, O spirit,
„Dich, o Geist, anweht?"	With its breath?'

Er klagt', er sang	It lamented, it sang,
Vernichtungsbang,	Fearful of extinction,
Verklärungsfroh,	Rapturously transfigured,
Bis das Leben floh.	Until life ebbed away.

Das bedeutet des Schwanen Gesang!	That is the swan's song!

William Shakespeare (1564–1616)

Schubert set three songs from Shakespeare's plays: 'Was ist Silvia' from *The Two Gentlemen of Verona*, 'Ständchen: Horch, horch! die Lerch im Ätherblau' from *Cymbeline*, and 'Trinklied: Bacchus, feister Fürst des Weins' from *Antony and Cleopatra*.

July 1826 Ständchen / Serenade D889
FROM *Cymbeline*
[VERSE ONE TRANSLATED BY SCHLEGEL, BAUERNFELD, MAYERHOFER; VERSES TWO AND THREE ADDED BY FRIEDRICH REIL AFTER SCHUBERT'S DEATH]

Horch! horch! die Lerch' im Ätherblau;
　Und Phöbus, neu erweckt,
Tränkt seine Rosse mit dem Tau,
　Der Blumenkelche deckt;
Der Ringelblume Knospe schleußt
　Die goldnen Äuglein auf;
Mit allem, was da reizend ist,
　Du süße Maid, steh auf!
　Steh auf, steh auf!

Wenn schon die liebe ganze Nacht
　Der Sterne lichtes Heer
Hoch über dir im Wechsel wacht,
　So hoffen sie noch mehr,
Daß auch dein Augenstern sie grüßt.
　Erwach! Sie warten drauf,
Weil du doch gar so reizend bist,
　Du süße Maid, steh auf,
　Steh auf, steh auf!

Und wenn dich alles das nicht weckt,
　So werde durch den Ton
Der Minne zärtlich aufgeneckt!
　O dann erwachst du schon,
Wie oft sie dich an's Fenster trieb,
　Das weiß sie, drum steh auf,
Und habe deinen Sänger lieb,
　Du süße Maid, steh auf,
　Steh auf, steh auf!

Hark, hark! the lark in heaven's blue;
　And Phoebus, newly awakened,
Waters his steeds with the dew,
　That lies on chaliced flowers;
The marigold bud unfolds
　Its little golden eyes;
With every pretty thing,
　Sweet maid, arise!
　Arise, arise!

When throughout the livelong night
　The radiant host of stars
Keep watch in turn high over you,
　They hope for even more,
To be greeted by your star-like eyes.
　Awake! They are waiting;
Because you are so pretty,
　Sweet maid, arise!
　Arise, arise!

And should all this fail to wake you,
　Then be teased awake tenderly
By sounds of love!
　O then, for sure, you will awake,
Love knows how often she's drawn you
　To the window, so arise
And love your minstrel,
　Sweet maid, arise!
　Arise, arise!

July 1826 An Silvia / To Sylvia D891
FROM *The Two Gentlemen of Verona*, TRANSLATED BY EDWARD VON BAUERNFELD (1802–90)

Was ist Silvia, saget an,
　Daß sie die weite Flur preist?
Schön und zart seh' ich sie nah'n,

What is Sylvia, tell me,
　That the wide fields praise her?
I see her draw near, delicate and fair,

Auf Himmels Gunst und Spur weist,	It is a mark of heaven's favour
Daß ihr Alles untertan.	That all are subject to her.

Ist sie schön und gut dazu?	Is she fair and kind as well?
Reiz labt wie milde Kindheit;	Her gentle child-like charm refreshes;
Ihrem Aug' eilt Amor zu,	Cupid hastens to her eyes,
Dort heilt er seine Blindheit,	Is cured of his blindness there,
Und verweilt in süßer Ruh.	And lingers in sweet peace.

Darum Silvia, tön', o Sang,	To Sylvia, then, let our song resound,
Der holden Silvia Ehren;	In sweetest Sylvia's honour;
Jeden Reiz besiegt sie lang,	She's long excelled every grace
Den Erde kann gewähren:	That this earth can bestow:
Kränze ihr und Saitenklang!	Bring her garlands and the sound of strings!

Josef Freiherr von Spaun (1788–1865)

Josef von Spaun entered the Imperial College two years before Schubert, and was responsible for running the school orchestra. He quickly showed a protective interest in the withdrawn new boy, supplied him with manuscript paper and often took him to the opera. He was the first of Schubert's friends to recognize his genius, and it was through Spaun that Schubert was introduced to Mayrhofer, Schober, Vogl and many others who were to play a crucial part in his life. They lived together for a short time in 1816, and a year later Schubert composed 'Der Jüngling und der Tod', the only setting of his friend's verse. Spaun left Vienna in 1821 to become a distinguished civil servant in Linz, and though the friends kept in touch, he did not return to the capital until 1826. His *Memoirs* are extremely reliable (Spaun was a noted lawyer) and required reading for anyone interested in a factual account of Schubert's life.

March 1817 Der Jüngling und der Tod / The youth and death D545

DER JÜNGLING

Die Sonne sinkt, o könnt' ich mit ihr scheiden,	THE YOUTH
Mit ihrem letzten Strahl entfliehen,	The sun sinks, O that I could part with it,
Ach diese namenlosen Qualen meiden	And vanish with its dying rays,
Und weit in schön're Welten zieh'n!	Escape, ah! these nameless torments,
	And move far away to fairer worlds!

O komme, Tod, und löse diese Bande!	Come, O Death, and loose these bonds!
Ich lächle dir, o Knochenmann,	I smile on you, O bony death,
Entführe mich leicht in geträumte Lande,	Lead me gently to dreamed-of lands,
O komm' und rühre mich doch an!	O come, and lay your hand on me!

DER TOD

Es ruht sich kühl und sanft in meinen Armen,	DEATH
Du rufst, ich will mich deiner Qual erbarmen!	My calm embrace is cool and gentle,
	You call, I shall take pity on your torment!

Friedrich Leopold Graf zu Stolberg-Stolberg (1750–1819)

Friedrich Leopold Graf zu Stolberg-Stolberg, was an aristocratic friend of Goethe's who accompanied him on a tour of Switzerland in 1775. He translated Homer and Plato, but it is as the poet of this one Schubert song that he is remembered today. It was composed in 1823, when Schubert's syphilis was diagnosed and he became acutely aware of his own mortality. Stolberg dedicated the poem to the memory of his first wife Agnes von Witzleben, who had died in 1788, aged twenty-seven, almost exactly Schubert's age when he composed this bitter-sweet hymn to ephemerality. With Voss, he was responsible for 'improving' Hölty's poetry – see p. 325.

1823 Auf dem Wasser zu singen / To be sung on the water D774

Mitten im Schimmer der spiegelnden Wellen	Amid the shimmer of mirroring waves
Gleitet, wie Schwäne, der wankende Kahn;	The swaying boat glides like a swan;
Ach, auf der Freude sanftschimmernden	Ah, on joy's gently gleaming
Wellen	waves
Gleitet die Seele dahin wie der Kahn;	The soul glides onward like the boat;
Denn von dem Himmel herab auf die Wellen	For the sunset glow from heaven
Tanzet das Abendrot rund um den Kahn.	Dances on the waves around the boat.
Über den Wipfeln des westlichen Haines,	Above the tree-tops of the western grove,
Winket uns freundlich der rötliche Schein;	The reddish light beckons us;
Unter den Zweigen des östlichen Haines	Beneath the branches of the easterly grove,
Säuselt der Calmus im rötlichen Schein;	The sweet-flag rustles in the reddish light;
Freude des Himmels und Ruhe des Haines	The soul breathes in the joy of heaven,
Atmet die Seel' im errötenden Schein.	The peace of the grove in the reddening glow.
Ach es entschwindet mit tauigem Flügel	For me, alas, time vanishes
Mir auf den wiegenden Wellen die Zeit.	With dewy wings on the rocking waves.
Morgen entschwindet mit schimmerndem	Time vanishes tomorrow with shimmering
Flügel	wings,
Wieder wie gestern und heute die Zeit,	As it did yesterday and today,
Bis ich auf höherem strahlenden Flügel	Till I on loftier, radiant wings,
Selber entschwinde der wechselnden Zeit.	Myself escape the flux of time.

Johann Ludwig Uhland (1787–1862)

See Kreutzer

September 1820 Frühlingsglaube / Faith in Spring D686

Die linden Lüfte sind erwacht,	The gentle breezes are awakened,
Sie säuseln und weben Tag und Nacht,	They stir and whisper night and day,
Sie schaffen an allen Enden.	Everywhere active, creative.
O frischer Duft, o neuer Klang!	O fresh fragrance, O new sounds!

| Nun, armes Herze, sei nicht bang! | Now, poor heart, be not afraid! |
| Nun muß sich alles, alles wenden. | Now must all things, all things change. |

Die Welt wird schöner mit jedem Tag,	The world grows fairer with every day,
Man weiß nicht, was noch werden mag,	We do not know what might yet be,
Das Blühen will nicht enden.	The blooming will not end.
Es blüht das fernste, tiefste Tal;	The deepest, most distant valley blooms;
Nun, armes Herz, vergiß der Qual!	Now, poor heart, forget your torment!
Nun muß sich alles, alles wenden.	Now must all things, all things change.
(*Curschmann, Kreutzer, Lachner,*	
Mendelssohn, Ries, Silcher, Spohr)	

Marianne von Willemer (1784–1860)

See Wolf

Marianne Jung, the illegitimate daughter of an Austrian travelling actress, was brought up by the Frankfurt banker Johann Jakob von Willemer, who later married her. Willemer was a great admirer of Goethe who, during an extended stay at the banker's country seat in the autumn of 1815, fell passionately in love with the thirty-year-old Marianne. Schubert, like Mendelssohn, set two of her poems: 'Was bedeutet die Bewegung', which was written on her way eastward from Frankfurt to Heidelberg on 23 September 1815 to meet Goethe; and 'Ach, um deine feuchten Schwingen' a few days later, as she left Goethe for what turned out to be the last time. He continued to correspond with her for the rest of his life, and in his last letter, dated 10 February 1832, he enclosed all her correspondence, with the request that it should be left unopened 'bis zu unbestimmter Stunde' ('until an unspecified time'). Both 'Suleika' poems were revised by Goethe and included in Book 8 of the *West-östlicher Divan* (1819). Goethe never acknowledged Marianne's participation (probably to protect her reputation as a married woman), which means that when Schubert, Schumann and Mendelssohn set her poems, they had no idea that Marianne was the author. It was only in 1873, when Theodor Creizenach published the complete correspondence, that her talent as a poet was fully recognized.

March 1821 Suleika I / Suleika I D720
IN COLLABORATION WITH JOHANN WOLFGANG VON GOETHE; ALSO 'SULEIKA II'

Was bedeutet die Bewegung?	What does this stirring mean?
Bringt der Ost mir frohe Kunde?	Does the East Wind bring good tidings?
Seiner Schwingen frische Regung	The fresh motion of its wings
Kühlt des Herzens tiefe Wunde.	Cools the deep wound in my heart.

| Kosend spielt er mit dem Staube, | It plays caressingly with the dust, |
| Jagt ihn auf in leichten Wölkchen, | Whipping it into puffs of cloud, |

Treibt zur sichern Rebenlaube
Der Insekten frohes Völkchen.

Lindert sanft der Sonne Glühen,
Kühlt auch mir die heißen Wangen,
Küßt die Reben noch im Fliehen,
Die auf Feld und Hügel prangen.

Und mir bringt sein leises Flüstern
Von dem Freunde tausend Grüße;
Eh' noch diese Hügel düstern,
Grüßen mich wohl tausend Küsse.

Und so kannst du weiter ziehen!
Diene Freunden und Betrübten.
Dort wo hohe Mauern glühen,
Dort find ich bald den Vielgeliebten.

Ach, die wahre Herzenskunde,
Liebeshauch, erfrischtes Leben
Wird mir nur aus seinem Munde,
Kann mir nur sein Atem geben.
(*Hensel, Mendelssohn*)

Driving the happy insects
To the vine-leaves' safe retreat.

It gently soothes the heat of the sun,
And also cools my burning cheeks,
Flitting by, it kisses the grapes
That deck the hillsides and the fields.

And its soft murmur brings me
A thousand greetings from my friend;
Even before these hills darken,
I'll be greeted by a thousand kisses.

You may then go on your way!
Serving friends and those afflicted.
There, where lofty walls are glowing,
I'll soon find my dear beloved.

Ah, the heart's true message,
The breath of love and life's renewal,
Will come to me only from his lips,
Can be given me only by his breath.

?December 1824 Suleika II / Suleika II D717

Ach, um deine feuchten Schwingen,
West, wie sehr ich dich beneide:
Denn du kannst ihm Kunde bringen
Was ich in der Trennung leide!

Die Bewegung deiner Flügel
Weckt im Busen stilles Sehnen;
Blumen, Auen, Wald und Hügel
Stehn bei deinem Hauch in Tränen.

Doch dein mildes sanftes Wehen
Kühlt die wunden Augenlider;
Ach, für Leid müßt' ich vergehen,
Hofft' ich nicht zu sehn ihn wieder.

Eile denn zu meinem Lieben,
Spreche sanft zu seinem Herzen;
Doch vermeid' ihn zu betrüben
Und verbirg ihm meine Schmerzen.

Sag ihm, aber sag's bescheiden:
Seine Liebe sei mein Leben,
Freudiges Gefühl von beiden
Wird mir seine Nähe geben.
(*Hensel, Mendelssohn, Zelter*)

Ah, West Wind, how I envy you
Your moist pinions:
For you can bring him word
Of what I suffer away from him!

The movement of your wings
Wakes silent longing in my heart;
Flowers, meadows, woods and hills,
Dissolve in tears where you blow.

Yet your mild, gentle breeze
Cools my sore eyelids;
Ah, I'd surely die of grief,
Did I not hope to see him again.

Hurry, then, to my beloved,
Whisper softly to his heart;
Take care, though, not to sadden him,
And hide from him my anguish.

Tell him, but tell him humbly:
That his love is my life,
His presence here will fill me
With happiness in both.

Johann Abraham Peter Schulz (1747–1800)

Although he composed a dozen operas in French and German, a number of cantatas and oratorios, six pieces for harpsichord or piano and a harpsichord sonata, it is as a Lieder composer that Schulz is remembered. His version of Claudius's 'Abendlied' ('Der Mond ist aufgegangen') is better known in German-speaking countries than Schubert's setting, and there are many other fine songs in his prolific output. The importance Schulz attached to literary quality guarantees him a special place in the history of German song – two of his collections, published in 1784 and 1786, were called, significantly, *Religiöse Lieder und Oden aus den besten deutschen Dichtern*. He had a predilection for the poetry of Bürger, Claudius, Hölty and Klopstock and, according to his own testimony, always strove to write folk-like Lieder with a melodic line that enhanced the meaning of the words. His most influential collection was *Lieder im Volkston* that appeared in three volumes in 1782, 1785 and 1790. The Preface to the second volume contains his aesthetic of Lieder composition:

> Zu dem Ende habe ich nur solche Texte aus unseren besten Liederdichtern gewählt, die mir zu diesem Volksgesange gemacht zu sein schienen, und mich in den Melodien selbst der höchsten Simplizität und Faßlichkeit beflissen, ja auf alle Weise den Schein des Bekannten darzubringen versucht. In diesem Schein des Bekannten liegt das ganze Geheimnis des Volkstons.

> To this end I have chosen only those texts by our best poets which seemed to me tailor-made for folksong, and I have been at pains to write melodies of the greatest simplicity and comprehensibility and have always tried to create the appearance of familiarity. The whole secret of this folk style depends on this appearance of familiarity.

Schulz is the forerunner of Reichardt and Zelter and deserves to be better known.

Matthias Claudius (1740–1815)

See Schubert

1790 Abendlied / Evening song

Der Mond ist aufgegangen,	The moon has risen,
Die goldnen Sternlein prangen	The golden stars are gleaming
Am Himmel hell und klar;	Bright and clear in heaven;
Der Wald steht schwarz und schweiget,	The woods are dark and silent,
Und aus den Wiesen steiget	And wondrously the white mist
Der weiße Nebel wunderbar.	Rises from the meadows.

Wie ist die Welt so stille,
Und in der Dämmrung Hülle
  So traulich und so hold!
Als eine stille Kammer,
Wo ihr des Tages Jammer
  Verschlafen und vergessen sollt.

Seht ihr den Mond dort stehen? –
Er ist nur halb zu sehen,
  Und ist doch rund und schön!
So sind wohl manche Sachen,
Die wir getrost belachen,
  Weil unsre Augen sie nicht sehn.

Wir stolze Menschenkinder
Sind eitel arme Sünder,
  Und wissen gar nicht viel;
Wir spinnen Luftgespinste,
Und suchen viele Künste,
  Und kommen weiter von dem Ziel.

Gott, laß d e i n Heil uns schauen,
Auf nichts Vergänglichs trauen,
  Nicht Eitelkeit uns freun!
Laß uns einfältig werden,
Und vor dir hier auf Erden
  Wie Kinder fromm und fröhlich sein!
(*C. P. E. Bach, Reichardt, Schoeck, Schubert,
Tomášek*)

How silent the world is,
And, beneath twilight's mantle,
  How lovely and how close!
Like a peaceful room
Where you may forget in sleep
  The anguish of the day.

Do you see the moon up there?
Though only half is visible,
  It is so round and fair!
So are many things
Which we are quick to mock,
  Because we do not see them.

We proud sons of men
Are but wretched sinners,
  And know so very little;
We weave our airy fantasies,
And seek out many skills
  And wander further from our goal.

God, may we behold *Thy* grace,
Mistrust all that is transitory
  And delight not in vanity!
Let us all attain simplicity,
And before Thee on earth
  Be devout and glad as children!

Clara Schumann (1819–96)

Before her marriage to Robert Schumann on 12 September 1840, Clara Wieck composed almost exclusively for her own instrument, the piano. Although it was the custom of the time to include songs – as a sort of leavening device – into piano recitals, and though Ferdinand Wieck had made sure that Clara received a solid education in song, vocal compositions played a secondary role in her output. She eventually composed some thirty Lieder, the best of which are well crafted and extremely expressive. On 13 March 1840, Schumann, busy composing his *Liederfrühling*, wrote a revealing letter to his betrothed:

> Clärchen, hast du nichts für meine Beilagen? Mir fehlt Manuskript ... Denkst du denn etwa, weil ich so componire, kannst du müßig sein. Mach' doch ein Lied einmal! Hast Du angefangen, so kannst Du nicht wieder los. Es ist gar zu verführerisch.

> Clara dear, don't you have anything for my supplements [music supplements to the 'Neue Zeitschrift für Musik']? I need some more pages ... Perhaps you think that, since I compose so much, you can be idle. Come on, write a song! Once you've begun, you won't be able to drag yourself away. It's far too enticing.

From now on, despite Clara's doubts, Schumann became obsessed with the idea of a joint publication with his wife. When he approached Friedrich Kistner, his Leipzig publisher, on 22 April 1841 with his proposal of publishing a joint collection of songs with Clara [see ROBERT SCHUMANN], Clara had not completed her contributions; in fact she had not even begun them. It was not until the beginning of June 1841 that she wrote in the marriage journal:

> Mit dem Componiren will's nun gar nicht gehen – ich möchte mich manchmal an meinen dummen Kopf schlagen! ... Ich habe diese Woche viel am Componiren gesessen, und denn auch vier Gedichte von Rückert für meinen lieben Robert zu Stande gebracht. Möchten sie ihm nur einigermassen genügen, dann ist mein Wunsch erfüllt.

> I'm not making any progress with composition; sometimes I'd like to give my thick skull a good whack! ... I've spent a lot of time on composition this week and did in fact succeed in setting four poems by Rückert for my dear Robert. Now, if they satisfy him in some small measure, then my wish shall have been fulfilled.

Three of these four songs, 'Er ist gekommen', 'Liebst du um Schönheit' and 'Warum willst du and're fragen' appeared as nos. 2, 4 and 11 in Schumann's *Liebesfrühling*, Op. 37, while the fourth, 'Die gute Nacht', though of equal quality, was not included.

Friedrich Rückert (1788–1866)

See Robert Schumann

June 1841 Er ist gekommen / He came in storm and rain Op. 12 , no. 2

Er ist gekommen	He came
In Sturm und Regen,	In storm and rain,
Ihm schlug beklommen	My anxious heart
Mein Herz entgegen.	Beat against his.
Wie konnt ich ahnen,	How could I have known
Daß seine Bahnen	That his path
Sich einen sollten meinen Wegen?	Should unite itself with mine?
Er ist gekommen	He came
In Sturm und Regen,	In storm and rain,
Er hat genommen	Audaciously
Mein Herz verwegen.	He took my heart.
Nahm er das meine?	Did he take mine?
Nahm ich das seine?	Did I take his?
Die beiden kamen sich entgegen.	Both drew near to each other.
Er ist gekommen	He came
In Sturm und Regen.	In storm and rain.
Nun ist gekommen	Now spring's blessing
Des Frühlings Segen.	Has come.
Der Freund zieht weiter,	My friend journeys on,
Ich seh es heiter,	I watch with good cheer,
Denn er bleibt mein auf allen Wegen.	For he shall be mine wherever he goes.
(*Franz*)	

June 1841 Liebst du um Schönheit / If you love for beauty Op. 12, no. 4
See Gustav Mahler, p. 208

June 1841 Warum willst du andre fragen / Why enquire of others Op. 12, no. 11

Warum willst du andre fragen,	Why enquire of others,
Die's nicht meinen treu mit dir?	Who are not loyal to you?
Glaube nichts, als was dir sagen	Only believe what these two eyes
Diese beiden Augen hier.	Here tell you.
Glaube nicht den fremden Leuten,	Do not believe what strangers say,
Glaube nicht dem eignen Wahn;	Do not believe your own delusions;
Nicht mein Tun auch sollst du deuten,	Nor should you interpret my deeds,
Sondern sieh die Augen an!	But instead look at these eyes!
Schweigt die Lippe deinen Fragen,	Are my lips silent to your questions
Oder zeugt sie gegen mich?	Or do they testify against me?
Was auch meine Lippen sagen,	Whatever my lips might say;
Sieh mein Aug' – ich liebe dich.	Look at my eyes – I love you.

Die gute Nacht, die ich dir sage,
  Freund, hörest du;
  Ein Engel, der die Botschaft trage,
  Geht ab und zu.
Er bringt sie dir, und hat mir wieder
  Den Gruß gebracht:
  Dir sagen auch des Freundes Lieder
  Jetzt gute Nacht.
(*Robert Schumann*)

Listen, my friend,
  To the good night I bid you;
  An angel, bearing the message,
  Flits to and fro.
He brings you it and has brought the greeting
  Back to me:
  A friend's songs too
  Now wish you good night.

Robert Schumann (1810–56)

Schumann was one of the most literary composers in the entire history of the Lied. His father owned a small book-publishing business in Zwickau, wrote long historical and Gothic novels and was famous throughout Germany as a translator of English literature, especially Byron and Scott. Schumann himself toyed with the idea of becoming a writer, and wrote a number of unfinished novels, plays and poetry. He keeps insisting in his letters and music criticism on the importance of literary quality in the composition of Lieder. In an article on the songs of W. H. Veit, he wrote:

> Weshalb also nach mittelmäßigen Gedichten greifen, was sich immer an der Musik rächen muß? Einen Kranz von Musik um ein wahres Dichterhaupt schlingen – nichts Schöneres; aber ihn an ein Alltagsgesicht verschwenden, wozu die Mühe?

> Why choose mediocre poems, when this will always take revenge on the music? To braid a wreath of music around a true poet's brow – nothing more beautiful; but to waste it on an everyday face, why bother?

It is therefore not surprising that the majority of his finest Lieder are settings of Eichendorff, Goethe, Heine, Kerner, Mörike and Lenau, or that he had a predilection for Friedrich Rückert, a poet who, though he produced too much, also wrote a number of undisputed gems. Less easy to explain is his devotion to the feeble verse of Elisabeth Kulmann, Wilfried von der Neun and Gustav Pfarrius. Some critics have attributed this decline in literary perception to a decline in musical creativity (all these third-rate poets were set some ten years after the annus mirabilis of 1840) – a charge that is refuted by such wonderful late songs as the *Wilhelm Meister* settings and 'Nachtlied' (Goethe), 'Der Einsiedler' (Eichendorff), 'Aufträge' (L'Egru), 'Mein schöner Stern' (Rückert), 'Requiem' (Dreves) and the Lenau settings of Op. 90 – all of which are, in their own way, as fine as anything he wrote in 1840.

Schumann's first songs date from 1827–28, including the charming 'Sehnsucht', composed to his own text, Goethe's 'Der Fischer' and five songs to texts by Justinus Kerner. Schumann's first twenty-three opus numbers, composed between 1830 and 1839, were all devoted to the piano; small wonder, therefore, that his Op. 24, the Heine *Liederkreis*, written in February 1840, should contain echoes of these piano works: the first Novellette of Op. 21 in 'Mit Myrten und Rosen', for example, and *Kreisleriana* at the end of 'Morgens steh' ich auf und frage'. Schumann now turned his back on piano composition, and became wholly absorbed by song. During 1840 he composed some 140 Lieder, and only one new piano piece, the *Sonatina* in B flat. He quite clearly saw himself as the pioneer of a new type of song in which the piano assumes unprecedented importance, particularly in the extensive preludes and postludes of such works as *Dichterliebe* and *Frauenliebe und -leben*. The piano was now to be an equal partner, instead of just contributing 'schlotternde Begleitungsformeln'('formulaic accompaniments that merely move along with the poem'), as he wrote in a glowing essay on the songs of Robert Franz. Or as Grieg put it, more fairly:

> It cannot be maintained that Schumann was the first to accord a conspicuous role to the accompaniment of his songs. Schubert had anticipated him as no other of his predecessors had done, in making the piano depict the mood. But what Schubert began, Schumann further developed; and woe to the singer who tries to render Schumann without keeping a close watch on what the piano is doing, even to the finest shades of sound. I have no faith in a performer of Schumann's songs who does not appreciate that the piano has just as great a claim on interest and study as the voice of the singer; I would even go so far as to say that, up to a certain point, he who cannot play Schumann cannot sing him either.

Like Wolf (see p. 579), Schumann expressed dissatisfaction with composing music for modest forces. Having completed the Eichendorff cycle he wrote to Clara, on 22 May 1840: „Aber ich will auch nicht so viel Kleines machen und nun bald ernstlich an die Oper gehen." ('But I do not want to compose so many small things and plan to begin serious work on the opera.')

Hans Christian Andersen (1805–75)

Born of humble stock – his father was a cobbler, his mother a domestic servant – Andersen attended a school for the poor, and in the wake of Denmark's economic collapse eked out a living as a labourer in a textile mill and a tobacco factory. With the financial backing of the composer Weyse, he took singing and ballet lessons, and was briefly engaged by the Royal Theatre in Copenhagen. Having left school, he served in the army until 1834. His first books were published under a pseudonym, but gradually he became celebrated as a writer of plays, novels, poems and fairy tales. After his death in 1875 he was given a state funeral. Schumann presented Andersen with a copy of his Op. 40 and wrote in the accompanying letter:

> Sie wird Ihnen vielleicht im ersten Augenblick sonderbar vorkommen. Ging es mir doch selbst erst mit Ihren Gedichten so! Wie ich mich aber hineinlebte, nahm auch meine Musik einen immer fremdartigeren Charakter an.

> Perhaps the settings will seem strange to you. So at first did your poems to me! But as I grew to understand them better, my music took on a more and more unusual style.

July 1840 aus: *Fünf Lieder* / from: *Five songs* Op. 40

TRANSLATED BY ADELBERT VON CHAMISSO (1781–1838)

Märzveilchen / March violets

Der Himmel wölbt sich rein und blau,
Der Reif stellt Blumen aus zur Schau.

The sky arches clear and blue;
The hoar-frost fashions flowers.

Am Fenster prangt ein flimmernder Flor.
Ein Jüngling steht, ihn betrachtend, davor.

Shimmering blossom gleams on the window,
A young man stands there, looking on.

Und hinter den Blumen blühet noch gar
Ein blaues, ein lächelndes Augenpaar.

And blossoming behind those flowers
A pair of blue eyes smile.

Märzveilchen, wie jener noch keine gesehn.
Der Reif wird, angehaucht, zergehn.

March violets, sweeter than he'd ever seen.
A single breath will melt the frost.

Eisblumen fangen zu schmelzen an,
Und Gott sei gnädig dem jungen Mann.
(*Nils Gade*)

Jack Frost's flowers begin to thaw –
May the Lord have mercy on that young man.

Muttertraum / A mother's dream

Die Mutter betet herzig und schaut
Entzückt auf den schlummernden Kleinen.
Er ruht in der Wiege so sanft und traut.
Ein Engel muß er ihr scheinen.

A mother prays fervently and looks
Enraptured at her slumbering child;
He sleeps in the cradle all soft and snug,
To her he must seem like an angel.

Sie küßt ihn und herzt ihn; sie hält sich kaum.
Vergessen der irdischen Schmerzen,
Es schweift in der Zukunft ihr Hoff-
    nungstraum;
So träumen Mütter im Herzen.

She kisses and hugs him; can hardly hold
    back,
And forgets her earthly sorrows;
Her hopes and dreams fly to the future –
The way all mothers dream in their hearts.

Der Rab' indes mit der Sippschaft sein
Kreischt draußen am Fenster die Weise:
Dein Engel, dein Engel wird unser sein!
Der Räuber dient uns zur Speise!

The raven meanwhile with its brood
Croaks this tune outside the window:
Your angel, your angel shall be our prey!
The thief will provide us with food!

Der Soldat / The soldier

Es geht bei gedämpfter Trommel Klang.
Wie weit noch die Stätte! der Weg wie lang!
O wär' er zur Ruh und alles vorbei!
Ich glaub', es bricht mir das Herz entzwei.

He walks to the sound of the muffled drum.
How far the place! the way how long!
Ah, were he at rest and all this done!
My heart, I think, will break in two.

Ich hab' in der Welt nur ihn geliebt,
Nur ihn, dem jetzt man den Tod doch gibt.
Bei klingendem Spiele wird paradiert,
Dazu bin auch ich kommandiert.

None but him in the world have I loved,
Him, who now they're putting to death.
The firing squad parades with full band,
I too am detailed for the task.

Nun schaut er auf zum letztenmal	Now he looks up for one last time
In Gottes Sonne freudigen Strahl, –	At the joyous rays of God's sun, –
Nun binden sie ihm die Augen zu, –	Now they put his blindfold on, –
Dir schenke Gott die ewige Ruh'!	May God grant you eternal peace!
Es haben dann Neun wohl angelegt,	The nine of us took good aim,
Acht Kugeln haben vorbeigefegt;	Eight bullets whistled wide of the mark;
Sie zitterten alle vor Jammer und Schmerz –	Every man shook with pity and grief –
Ich aber, ich traf ihn mitten in das Herz.	But I, I shot him clean through the heart.
(*Franz, Marschner, Silcher*)	

Der Spielmann / The fiddler

Im Städtchen gibt es des Jubels viel,	In the little town there's much rejoicing,
Da halten sie Hochzeit mit Tanz und mit Spiel,	They're holding a wedding with music and dance,
Dem Fröhlichen blinket der Wein so rot,	The happy man quaffs the glinting red wine,
Die Braut nur gleicht dem getünchten Tod.	But the bride's as pale as death.
Ja tot für den, den nicht sie vergißt,	She's dead for the one she cannot forget,
Der doch beim Fest nicht Bräutigam ist;	Who's at the feast but not as groom;
Da steht er inmitten der Gäste im Krug,	He stands among the guests at the inn,
Und streichet die Geige lustig genug!	And plays his fiddle gaily enough!
Er streichet die Geige, sein Haar ergraut,	He plays his fiddle, his hair turns grey,
Es schwingen die Saiten gellend und laut,	The strings resound shrill and loud,
Er drückt sie ans Herz und achtet es nicht,	He presses the fiddle close to his heart,
Ob auch sie in tausend Stücken zerbricht.	Though it breaks into a thousand pieces.
Es ist gar grausig, wenn einer so stirbt,	It's hideous for a man to die this way,
Wenn jung sein Herz um Freude noch wirbt;	When his heart's still young and striving for joy;
Ich mag und will nicht länger es sehn!	I cannot and will not watch any more!
Das möchte den Kopf mir schwindelnd ver-	My head might reel in a fatal whirl. –
drehn. –	
Wer heißt euch mit Fingern zeigen auf mich?	Who said to point a finger at me?
O Gott! bewahr' uns gnädiglich,	O God! have mercy,
Daß Keinen der Wahnsinn übermannt;	Let none of us go mad;
Bin selber ein armer Musikant.	I too am just a poor musician.
(*Fibich*)	

Adelbert von Chamisso (1781–1838)

See Loewe

Chamisso, a Frenchman who at the age of nine fled the Revolution to live in Prussia, was committed throughout his life to the ideals of liberty, equality and women's rights. Many of his poems show his concern for soldiers, servants, invalids, barbers, madmen, millers, orphans, beggars, the blind and the dispossessed. Chamisso, when he wrote the *Frauenliebe und -leben* poems, to which he gave pride of place in his Collected Works, had just married a girl many years his junior. Perhaps the autobiographical similarity attracted Schumann – he too was about to marry a much younger woman. Carl Loewe's setting of the cycle, more 'complete' than Schumann's, since Loewe set the final poem that Schumann omitted, had appeared the previous year. Chamisso was also a most skilled translator: Schumann opened his Op. 40 with four translations of Hans Andersen poems, and ended Op. 31 with two ballads ('Die Kartenlegerin' and 'Die rote Hanne') which Chamisso based on poems by Jean-Pierre Béranger (1780–1857), the idolized poet and song-writer of the Parisian working class, whose satirical songs at the expense of Napoleon's regime earned him two bouts of imprisonment.

c.July 1840 Die Löwenbraut / The lion's bride Op. 31, no. 1

Mit der Myrte geschmückt und dem Braut- geschmeid,	Adorned with myrtle and bridal jewels,
Des Wärters Tochter, die rosige Maid,	The keeper's daughter, the rosy maid,
Tritt ein in den Zwinger des Löwen; er liegt	Steps into the lion's cage;
Der Herrin zu Füßen, vor der er sich schmiegt.	The lion lies fawning at his mistress's feet.
Der Gewaltige, wild und unbändig zuvor,	The powerful beast, once wild and untamed,
Schaut fromm und verständig zur Herrin empor;	Looks up at his mistress, understanding and meek;
Die Jungfrau, zart und wonnereich,	The gentle and radiant girl
Liebstreichelt ihn sanft und weinet zugleich:	Caresses him tenderly, weeping the while:
„Wir waren in Tagen, die nicht mehr sind,	'We were in days that now are past
Gar treue Gespielen wie Kind und Kind,	True playmates, like two children,
Und hatten uns lieb und hatten uns gern;	And loved and liked each other;
Die Tage der Kindheit, sie liegen uns fern.	Those days of childhood are long since gone.
Du schütteltest machtvoll, eh wir's geglaubt,	Before we knew it, you were shaking
Dein mähnenumwogtes königlich Haupt;	Your mighty, mane-rippling regal head;
Ich wuchs heran, du siehst es: ich bin	I grew up too, as you can see: I am
Das Kind nicht mehr mit kindischem Sinn.	No longer a child with a childish mind.
O wär' ich das Kind noch und bliebe bei dir,	Were I still that child, and could stay with you,
Mein starkes, getreues, mein redliches Tier;	My strong, faithful, my honest beast!
Ich aber muß folgen, sie taten mir's an,	But I must follow – they have forced me –
Hinaus in die Fremde dem fremden Mann.	A stranger, far off into foreign lands.
Es fiel ihm ein, daß schön ich sei,	He thought me beautiful,
Ich wurde gefreit, es ist nun vorbei:	I was wooed, and now it is done:
Der Kranz im Haar, mein guter Gesell,	The wreath, trusty friend, garlands my hair,
Und vor Tränen nicht die Blicke mehr hell.	And my eyes are now dim with tears.
Verstehst du mich ganz? schaust grimmig dazu,	Do you really understand? You look at me wildly,
Ich bin ja gefaßt, sei ruhig auch du;	But I am resigned, and you must be too;

Dort seh' ich ihn kommen, dem folgen ich muß,	There he comes whom I must follow,
So geb ich denn, Freund, dir den letzten Kuß!"	So I'll give you, my friend, a final kiss.'
Und wie ihn die Lippe des Mädchens berührt,	And as the girl's lips touched his own,
Da hat man den Zwinger erzittern gespürt,	The cage was seen to shake,
Und wie er am Zwinger den Jüngling erschaut,	And as he glimpsed the youth outside the cage,
Erfaßt Entsetzen die bangende Braut.	The anxious bride was seized with terror.
Er stellt an die Tür sich des Zwingers zur Wacht,	He stands on guard by the door of the cage,
Er schwinget den Schweif, er brüllet mit Macht;	He lashes his tail and roars with might,
Sie flehend, gebietend und drohend begehrt	She pleads with him, issuing orders and threats,
Hinaus; er im Zorn den Ausgang wehrt.	To let her out; angrily, he won't let her pass.
Und draußen erhebt sich verworren Geschrei.	Confusing shouts are heard outside.
Der Jüngling ruft: „Bringt Waffen herbei,	The young man cries: 'bring me arms,
Ich schieß' ihn nieder, ich treff' ihn gut."	I'll fire at him, I'll shoot him down.'
Aufbrüllt der Gereizte, schäumend vor Wut.	Provoked, the growling lion foams with rage.
Die Unselige wagt', sich der Türe zu nahn,	The luckless girl ventured to the door,
Da fällt er verwandelt die Herrin an;	The transformed beast falls on his mistress:
Die schöne Gestalt, ein gräßlicher Raub,	Her fair form, now a fearful prey,
Liegt blutig zerrissen entstellt in dem Staub.	Lies bleeding and mangled in the dust.
Und wie er vergossen das teure Blut,	And having shed that dear blood,
Er legt sich zur Leiche mit finsterem Mut,	The lion lies brooding down by the corpse,
Er liegt so versunken in Trauer und Schmerz,	Sunk in grief and sunk in sorrow,
Bis tödlich die Kugel ihn trifft in das Herz.	Till the fatal bullet strikes his heart.

July 1840 Die Kartenlegerin / The fortune-teller Op. 31, no. 2
AFTER PIERRE JEAN DE BÉRANGER (1780–1857)

Schlief die Mutter endlich ein	Has mother finally fallen asleep
Über ihrer Hauspostille?	Over her book of sermons?
Nadel, liege du nun stille,	You, my needle, now be still,
Nähen, immer nähen, –nein!	Stop this constant sewing!
Ei, was hab' ich zu erwarten?	Oh, what things can I expect?
Ei, was wird das Ende sein?	Oh, how will it all end?
Trüget mich die Ahnung nicht,	If I'm not deceived,
Zeigt sich Einer, den ich meine, –	One, I think of, will appear,
Schön, da kommt er ja, der Eine,	Excellent, here he comes,
Cœurbub kannte seine Pflicht. –	The knave of hearts has done his duty.
Eine reiche Witwe? – wehe!	A rich widow? Dear, oh dear.
Ja, er freit sie, ich vergehe!	Yes, he woos her, I'm undone,
O verruchter Bösewicht!	Oh! the wicked scoundrel!
Herzeleid und viel Verdruß, –	Heartache and much vexation,
Eine Schul' und enge Mauern, –	A school with restricting walls,

Carreaukönig, der bedauern,	But the king of diamonds will take pity
Und zuletzt mich trösten muß. –	And eventually comfort me.
Ein Geschenk auf artge Weise –	A nicely delivered present,
Er entführt mich – Eine Reise –	He elopes with me, a journey,
Geld und Lust in Überfluß!	Money and happiness in abundance!
Dieser Carreaukönig da	This king of diamonds
Muß ein Fürst sein oder König,	Must be a prince or king,
Und es fehlt daran nur wenig,	Which means it won't take much
Bin ich selber Fürstin ja. –	For me to be a princess.
Hier ein Feind, der mir zu schaden	Here's a foe, who strives to soil
Sich bemüht bei seiner Gnaden,	My name before His Majesty,
Und ein Blonder steht mir nah.	And a fair-haired man stands close by too.
Ein Geheimnis kommt zu Tage,	A secret comes to light,
Und ich flüchte noch bei Zeiten, –	And I escape just in time,
Fahret wohl, ihr Herrlichkeiten,	Farewell, O life of splendour,
O das war ein harter Schlag! –	Ah, that was a cruel blow!
Hin ist Einer, eine Menge	The one is gone, such a crowd
Bilden um mich ein Gedränge,	Surges around me
Daß ich sie kaum zählen mag.	That I can scarcely count them all.
Kommt das dumme Frau'ngesicht,	What's this? A dumb female apparition,
Kommt die Alte da mit Keuchen,	A wheezing old woman coming my way,
Lieb' und Lust mir zu verscheuchen,	To banish love and happiness
Eh' die Jugend mir gebricht?–	Before my youth has gone?
Ach, die Mutter ist's, die aufwacht,	Ah, it's mother who's woken up,
Und den Mund zu schelten aufmacht. –	Opening wide her mouth to scold. –
Nein, die Karten lügen nicht!	No, the cards do not lie!

July 1840 Die rote Hanne / Red Hannah Op. 31, no. 3
AFTER PIERRE JEAN DE BÉRANGER (1780–1857)

Den Säugling an der Brust, den zweiten	With her baby at her breast
Der Knaben auf dem Rücken, führt	And her second boy astride her back,
Sie an der Hand den Erstgeborenen,	She leads by the hand her oldest boy
Der fast entkleidet, barfuß friert.	Who's half-naked, barefoot and freezing.
Den Vater haben sie gefangen,	The father has been arrested,
Er kühlt im Kerker seinen Mut.	He's cooling off in jail.
Sei Gott du mit der roten Hanne!	God be with you, red-haired Hannah!
Der Wilddieb sitzt in sich'rer Hut.	The poacher's under lock and key.
Ich sah sie oft in bessern Tagen,	I often saw her in happier days,
Schulmeisters liebes Töchterlein;	The schoolmaster's gentle daughter;
Sie spann und sang und las und nähte,	She would sing and spin and read and sew,
Ein herzig Kind und schmuck und fein;	A charming child, so spruce and clean;
Bei'm Sonntagstanz im Kreis der Linden,	Each Sunday she danced beneath the limes,
Wie war sie froh und wohlgemut!	So happily and joyfully!
Sei Gott du mit der roten Hanne!	God be with you, red-haired Hannah!
Der Wilddieb sitzt in sich'rer Hut.	The poacher's under lock and key.

Ein junger reicher hübscher Pächter
   Versprach ihr einst ein beß'res Glück;
Ihr rotes Haar, das ward verspottet,
   Der reiche Freier trat zurück;
Es kamen andre, gingen wieder,
   Sie hatte ja kein Heiratsgut.
Sei Gott du mit der roten Hanne!
   Der Wilddieb sitzt in sich'rer Hut.

Ein Taugenichts war schnell entschlossen:
   Ich nehm' dich zum Weibe, blond oder rot;
Drei Büchsen hab ich, weiß die Schliche,
   Der Förster macht mir keine Not;
Den Schwarzrock will ich auch bezahlen,
   Des Sprüchlein uns zusammentut.
Sei Gott du mit der roten Hanne!
   Der Wilddieb sitzt in sich'rer Hut.

Sie sprach nicht nein, mit sanfter Lockung
   Gebot Natur in ihrer Brust,
Und dreimal ward allein im Walde
   Sie Mutter unter bittrer Lust.
Die Kinder treiben und gedeihen,
   Ein blühend frisch gesundes Blut;
Sei Gott du mit der roten Hanne!
   Der Wilddieb sitzt in sich'rer Hut.

Des treuen Weibes näcbt'gen Jammer
   Erhellet noch ein milder Schein.
Sie lächelt: ihre Kleinen werden
   Schwarzlockig wie der Vater sein;
Sie lächelt, ach! aus ihrem Lächeln
   Schöpft der Gefang'ne frischen Mut.
Sei Gott du mit der roten Hanne!
   Der Wilddieb sitzt in sich'rer Hut.

A young, rich and handsome farmer
   Once promised her a better fate;
People laughed at her red hair,
   The wealthy suitor jilted her;
Others came and likewise went,
   Because she had no dowry.
God be with you, red-haired Hannah!
   The poacher's under lock and key.

A lay-about quickly made up his mind:
   Blonde or red, I'll marry you;
I have three guns and know all the tricks –
   The gamekeeper doesn't bother me;
I'll even pay the parson
   Who will marry us.
God be with you, red-haired Hannah!
   The poacher's under lock and key.

She did not refuse him, her heart quickened
   With nature's gentle promptings,
And three times alone in the forest
   She knew the bitter joys of giving birth.
The children grew up and flourished,
   And all enjoyed rude health;
God be with you, red-haired Hannah!
   The poacher's under lock and key.

The faithful wife's nightly distress
   Is brightened by a gentle glow.
She smiles: her children will have
   Their father's curly black hair;
She smiles, ah! and her smile
   Gives the prisoner fresh courage.
God be with you, red-haired Hannah!
   The poacher's under lock and key.

July 1840 *Frauenliebe und -leben / A woman's love and life* Op. 42

1

Seit ich ihn gesehen,
   Glaub' ich blind zu sein;
Wo ich hin nur blicke,
   Seh' ich ihn allein;
Wie im wachen Traume
   Schwebt sein Bild mir vor,
Taucht aus tiefstem Dunkel
   Heller nur empor.

Sonst ist licht- und farblos
   Alles um mich her,

Since first seeing him,
   I think I am blind;
Wherever I look,
   I see only him;
As in a waking dream
   His image hovers before me,
Rising out of deepest darkness
   Ever more brightly.

All else is dark and pale
   Around me,

Nach der Schwestern Spiele
    Nicht begehr ich mehr,
Möchte lieber weinen
    Still im Kämmerlein;
Seit ich ihn gesehen,
    Glaub' ich blind zu sein.
(*Kugler, Lachner, Loewe, Marscher, Reissiger*)

My sisters's games
    I no more long to share,
I would rather weep
    Quietly in my room;
Since first seeing him,
    I think I am blind.

2

Er, der Herrlichste von allen,
    Wie so milde, wie so gut!
Holde Lippen, klares Auge,
    Heller Sinn und fester Mut.

He, the most wonderful of all,
    How gentle and loving he is!
Sweet lips, bright eyes,
    A clear mind and firm resolve.

So wie dort in blauer Tiefe,
    Hell und herrlich, jener Stern,
Also er an meinem Himmel,
    Hell und herrlich, hehr und fern.

Just as there in the deep-blue distance
    That star gleams bright and brilliant,
So does he shine in my sky,
    Bright and brilliant, distant and sublime.

Wandle, wandle deine Bahnen;
    Nur betrachten deinen Schein,
Nur in Demut ihn betrachten,
    Selig nur und traurig sein!

Wander, wander on your way;
    Just to gaze on your radiance,
Just to gaze on in humility,
    To be but blissful and sad!

Höre nicht mein stilles Beten,
    Deinem Glücke nur geweiht;
Darfst mich niedre Magd nicht kennen,
    Hoher Stern der Herrlichkeit!

Do not heed my silent prayer,
    Uttered for your happiness alone;
You shall never know my lowly self,
    You noble star of splendour!

Nur die Würdigste von allen
    Darf beglücken deine Wahl,
Und ich will die Hohe segnen,
    Viele tausendmal.

Only the worthiest woman of all
    May your choice bless,
And I shall bless that exalted one
    Many thousands of times.

Will mich freuen dann und weinen,
    Selig, selig bin ich dann;
Sollte mir das Herz auch brechen,
    Brich, o Herz, was liegt daran?
(*Kugler, Loewe*)

I shall then rejoice and weep,
    Blissful, blissful I shall be;
Even if my heart should break,
    Break, O heart, what does it matter?

3

Ich kann's nicht fassen, nicht glauben,
    Es hat ein Traum mich berückt;
Wie hätt' er doch unter allen
    Mich Arme erhöht und beglückt?

I cannot grasp it, believe it,
    A dream has beguiled me;
How, from all women, could he
    Have exalted and favoured poor me?

Mir war's, er habe gesprochen:
    „Ich bin auf ewig dein" –
Mir war's – ich träume noch immer,
    Es kann ja nimmer so sein.

He said, I thought,
    'I am yours forever,'
I was, I thought, still dreaming,
    After all, it can never be.

O laß im Traume mich sterben,
    Gewieget an seiner Brust,
Den seligsten Tod mich schlürfen
    In Tränen unendlicher Lust.
(*Kugler, Lachner, Loewe, Marschner, Reissiger*)

O let me, dreaming, die,
    Cradled on his breast;
Let me savour blissful death
    In tears of endless joy.

4

Du Ring an meinem Finger,
    Mein goldenes Ringelein,
Ich drücke dich fromm an die Lippen,
    Dich fromm an das Herze mein.

You ring on my finger,
    My golden little ring,
I press you devoutly to my lips,
    To my heart.

Ich hatt' ihn ausgeträumet,
    Der Kindheit friedlich schönen Traum,
Ich fand allein mich, verloren
    Im öden unendlichen Raum.

I had finished dreaming
    Childhood's peaceful dream,
I found myself alone, forlorn
    In boundless desolation.

Du Ring an meinem Finger
    Da hast du mich erst belehrt,
Hast meinem Blick erschlossen
    Des Lebens unendlichen, tiefen Wert.

You ring on my finger,
    You first taught me,
Opened my eyes
    To life's deep eternal worth.

Ich will ihm dienen, ihm leben,
    Ihm angehören ganz,
Hin selber mich geben und finden
    Verklärt mich in seinem Glanz.

I shall serve him, live for him,
    Belong to him wholly,
Yield to him and find
    Myself transfigured in his light.

Du Ring an meinem Finger,
    Mein goldenes Ringelein,
Ich drücke dich fromm an die Lippen
    Dich fromm an das Herze mein.
(*Kugler, Loewe*)

You ring on my finger,
    My golden little ring,
I press you devoutly to my lips,
    To my heart.

5

Helft mir, ihr Schwestern
Freundlich mich schmücken,
Dient der Glücklichen heute mir,
Windet geschäftig
Mir um die Stirne
Noch der blühenden Myrte Zier.

Help me, O sisters,
With my bridal attire,
Serve me today in my joy,
Busily braid
About my brow
The wreath of blossoming myrtle.

Als ich befriedigt,
Freudigen Herzens,
Sonst dem Geliebten im Arme lag,
Immer noch rief er,
Sehnsucht im Herzen,
Ungeduldig den heutigen Tag.

When with contentment
And joy in my heart
I lay in my beloved's arms,
He still called,
With longing heart,
Impatiently for this day.

Helft mir, ihr Schwestern,
Helft mir verscheuchen

Help me, my sisters,
Help me banish

Eine törichte Bangigkeit;
Daß ich mit klarem
Aug' ihn empfange,
Ihn, die Quelle der Freudigkeit.

A foolish fearfulness;
So that I with bright eyes
May receive him,
The source of my joy.

Bist, mein Geliebter,
Du mir erschienen,
Gibst du mir, Sonne, deinen Schein?
Laß mich in Andacht,
Laß mich in Demut,
Laß mich verneigen dem Herren mein.

Have you, my love,
Really entered my life,
Do you, O sun, give me your glow?
Let me in reverence,
Let me in humility
Bow before my lord.

Streuet ihm, Schwestern,
Streuet ihm Blumen,
Bringet ihm knospende Rosen dar,
Aber euch, Schwestern,
Grüß' ich mit Wehmut,
Freudig scheidend aus eurer Schar.
(*Kugler, Loewe*)

Scatter flowers, O sisters,
Scatter flowers before him,
Bring him budding roses.
But you, sisters,
I greet with sadness,
As I joyfully take leave of you.

6

Süßer Freund, du blickest
    Mich verwundert an,
Kannst es nicht begreifen,
    Wie ich weinen kann;
Laß der feuchten Perlen
    Ungewohnte Zier
Freudig hell erzittern
    In dem Auge mir!

Sweet friend, you look
    At me in wonder,
You cannot understand
    How I can weep;
Let the unfamiliar beauty
    Of these moist pearls
Tremble joyfully bright
    In my eyes!

Wie so bang mein Busen,
    Wie so wonnevoll!
Wüßt' ich nur mit Worten,
    Wie ich's sagen soll;
Komm und birg dein Antlitz
    Hier an meiner Brust,
Will ins Ohr dir flüstern
    Alle meine Lust.

How anxious my heart is,
    How full of bliss!
If only I knew
    How to say it in words;
Come and hide your face
    Here against my breast,
For me to whisper you
    All my joy.

Weißt du nun die Tränen,
    Die ich weinen kann,
Sollst du nicht sie sehen,
    Du geliebter Mann?
Bleib' an meinem Herzen,
    Fühle dessen Schlag,
Daß ich fest und fester
    Nur dich drücken mag.

Do you now understand the tears
    That I can weep,
Should you not see them,
    Beloved husband?
Stay by my heart,
    Feel how it beats,
That I may press you
    Closer and closer.

Hier an meinem Bette
    Hat die Wiege Raum,
Wo sie still verberge
    Meinen holden Traum;
Kommen wird der Morgen,
    Wo der Traum erwacht,
Und daraus dein Bildnis
    Mir entgegen lacht.
(*Kugler, Loewe*)

Here by my bed
    There is room for the cradle,
Silently hiding
    My blissful dream;
The morning shall come
    When the dream awakens,
And your likeness
    Laughs up at me.

7

An meinem Herzen, an meiner Brust,
Du meine Wonne, du meine Lust!

On my heart, at my breast,
You my delight, my joy!

Das Glück ist die Liebe, die Lieb' ist das Glück,
Ich hab's gesagt und nehm's nicht zurück.

Happiness is love, love is happiness,
I've always said and say so still.

Hab' überschwenglich mich geschätzt,
Bin überglücklich aber jetzt.

I thought myself rapturous,
But now am delirious with joy.

Nur die da säugt, nur die da liebt
Das Kind, dem sie die Nahrung gibt;

Only she who suckles, only she who loves
The child that she nourishes;

Nur eine Mutter weiß allein,
Was lieben heißt und glücklich sein.

Only a mother knows
What it means to love and be happy.

O, wie bedaur' ich doch den Mann,
Der Mutterglück nicht fühlen kann!

Ah, how I pity the man
Who cannot feel a mother's bliss!

Du lieber, lieber Engel, Du,
Du schauest mich an und lächelst dazu!

You dear, dear angel, you,
You look at me and you smile!

An meinem Herzen, an meiner Brust,
Du meine Wonne, du meine Lust!
(*Kugler, Lachner, Loewe*)

On my heart, at my breast,
You my delight, my joy!

8

Nun hast du mir den ersten Schmerz getan,
    Der aber traf.
Du schläfst, du harter, unbarmherz'ger Mann,
    Den Todesschlaf.

Now you have caused me my first pain,
    But it struck hard.
You sleep, you harsh and pitiless man,
    The sleep of death.

Es blicket die Verlaßne vor sich hin,
    Die Welt ist leer.
Geliebet hab' ich und gelebt, ich bin
    Nicht lebend mehr.

The deserted one stares ahead,
    The world is void.
I have loved and I have lived,
    And now my life is done.

Ich zieh' mich in mein Innres still zurück,
    Der Schleier fällt,
Da hab' ich dich und mein verlornes Glück,
    Du meine Welt!
(*Kugler, Loewe*)

Silently I withdraw into myself,
    The veil falls,
There I have you and my lost happiness,
    You, my world!

Leberecht Blücher Dreves (1816–70)

A lawyer who edited the *Neue Hamburger Blätter*, Dreves also published several volumes of poetry, including *Lieder der Kirche – deutsche Nachbildungen alt-lateinischer Originale* (1846). 'Requiem' is a translation of the Latin poem in which Héloïse, now an abbess, looks back on her love for Peter Abelard (1079–1142), which resulted in an illegitimate child, their secret marriage and Abelard's castration. Eichendorff wrote an enthusiastic foreword to Dreve's *Gedichte* (1849).

August 1850 Requiem / Requiem Op. 90, no. 7
OLD CATHOLIC POEM

Ruh' von schmerzensreichen Mühen	Rest from pain-wracked toil
Aus und heißem Liebesglühen;	And love's passionate ardour;
Der nach seligem Verein	He who desired
Trug Verlangen,	Blessed reunion in Heaven
Ist gegangen	Has entered
Zu des Heilands Wohnung ein.	The Saviour's dwelling.
Dem Gerechten leuchten helle	For the righteous, bright stars
Sterne in des Grabes Zelle,	Shine within the tomb,
Ihm, der selbst als Stern der Nacht	For him, who will himself
Wird erscheinen,	Appear as a night star,
Wenn er seinen	When he beholds his Lord
Herrn erschaut in Himmelspracht.	In Heavenly glory.
Seid Fürsprecher, heil'ge Seelen,	Intercede for him, holy souls,
Heil'ger Geist, laß Trost nicht fehlen;	Holy spirit, let comfort not be lacking.
Hörst du? Jubelsang erklingt,	Do you hear? Songs of joy resound,
Feiertöne,	Solemn tones,
Darein die schöne	Among them the lovely song
Engelsharfe singt:	Of the angels' harp:
Ruh' von schmerzensreichen Mühen	Rest from pain-wracked toil
Aus und heißem Liebesglühen;	And love's passionate ardour;
Der nach seligem Verein	He who desired
Trug Verlangen,	Blessed reunion in Heaven
Ist gegangen	Has entered
Zu des Heilands Wohnung ein.	The Saviour's dwelling.

Joseph von Eichendorff (1788–1857)

See Pfitzner, Schoeck, Wolf

Although the Eichendorff *Liederkreis* is Schumann's only cycle to bear no dedication on the title-page, it is clear that Clara was the inspiration behind this outpouring. On May 15 he writes:

Ich habe wieder so viel komponiert, daß mirs manchmal ganz unheimlich vorkommt. Ach, ich kann nicht anders, ich möchte mich tot singen wie eine Nachtigall. Eichendorffsche sind es zwölf.

I have been composing so much again, that sometimes it seems quite uncanny. Ah, I can't help it, I want to sing myself to death like a nightingale. There are twelve Eichendorff songs.

And on 22 May, he writes a letter that lurches between despair, outrage, pride and rapture, and gives us a glimpse of those mood-swings that were an integral part of his psychological make-up and eventually led to his mental decline:

Der Eichendorffsche Zyklus ist wohl mein Allerromantischstes und es steht viel von Dir darin [. . .] Heute war ich schon recht froh und trübe . . . sonst ist alles still und schlicht in diesen Tagen hingeschlichen – das Wetter abscheulich und ich sitze den ganzen Tag in meiner Klause . . . Gibt es denn noch Worte für die bestialische Frechheit: In meinen Eichendorffschen Zyklus paßt das schlecht. Ich hatte den Skandal auch eine Weile vergessen, manchmal packt es mich aber auch zum Niederwerfen.
Und sieh, es ist doch auch nicht unbedeutend, was ich mir verdiene durch Komposition, und es wird auch immer besser, weißt Du wohl, daß ich in diesem halben Jahr beinahe gegen 400 Taler einnahm durch Komposition – ja staune nur, ich gebe kein Heft Lieder von fünf Bogen unter sechs Louisdor. Das fällt ins Gewicht, denn bei guter Stimmung schreibe ich an einem Tag zwei Bogen Gesang, auch mehr, wenn Du es z.B. verlangtest . . . Übrigens macht der Heinesche Zyklus, wie ich höre, viel Sprechens, und das ist mir ganz lieb. Die andern Eichendorffschen, kann ich Dir versprechen, sind noch viel melancholischer und glücklicher, als das kleine, das Du kennst. Geschwärmt habe ich in diesen Gedichten – und nun auch Deine Schrift machts.

The Eichendorff cycle must be my most romantic and it contains much of you. Today I was so happy and so sad . . . The days all slip past quietly and simply. The weather is foul, and I sit all day long in my retreat . . . Do words exist that can describe his [Wieck's] inhuman cheek: it suits ill my Eichendorff cycle. I had forgotten the scandal for a while, but sometimes it overwhelms me so. And listen – it's not insubstantial, the amount I earn through composing, and things are improving too. Do you know that in the last six months I've received about 400 Taler for my works – you'd be amazed, but it's true. I don't accept less than 6 Louisdor for five sheets of song. And that's important, for when the mood's on me, I can write two sheets of song a day, even more if you, for example, insist on it . . . I know that my Heine cycle is being much talked about, and that pleases me. But the Eichendorff songs, I can promise you, are much more melancholy and happy than the few things you have heard. I've revelled in these poems – and your handwriting too plays a part.

May 1840 *Liederkreis* / Song cycle* Op. 39

1

In der Fremde / In a foreign land
FROM *Viel Lärmen um nichts*

Aus der Heimat hinter den Blitzen rot
Da kommen die Wolken her,
Aber Vater und Mutter sind lange tot,
Es kennt mich dort keiner mehr.

Wie bald, ach wie bald kommt die stille
Zeit,
Da ruhe ich auch, und über mir
Rauscht die schöne Waldeinsamkeit,
Und keiner kennt mich mehr hier.
(*Brahms, Eisler*)

From my homeland, beyond the red lightning,
The clouds come drifting in,
But father and mother have long been dead,
Now no one knows me there.

How soon, ah! how soon till that quiet
time
When I too shall rest
Beneath the sweet murmur of lonely woods,
Forgotten here as well.

2

Intermezzo / Intermezzo

Dein Bildnis wunderselig
Hab' ich im Herzensgrund,
Das sieht so frisch und fröhlich
Mich an zu jeder Stund'.

Mein Herz still in sich singet
Ein altes, schönes Lied,
Das in die Luft sich schwinget
Und zu dir eilig zieht.
(*Willy Burkhard*)

I bear your beautiful likeness
Deep within my heart,
It gazes at me every hour
So freshly and happily.

My heart sings softly to itself
An old and beautiful song
That soars into the sky
And swiftly wings its way to you.

3

Waldesgespräch / A forest dialogue
FROM *Ahnung und Gegenwart*

Es ist schon spät, es ist schon kalt,
Was reit'st du einsam durch den Wald?
Der Wald ist lang, du bist allein,
Du schöne Braut! Ich führ dich heim!

„Groß ist der Männer Trug und List,
Vor Schmerz mein Herz gebrochen ist,
Wohl irrt das Waldhorn her und hin,
O flieh! Du weißt nicht, wer ich bin."

It is already late, already cold,
Why ride lonely through the forest?
The forest is long, you are alone,
You lovely bride! I'll lead you home!

'Great is the deceit and cunning of men,
My heart is broken with grief,
The hunting horn echoes here and there,
O flee! You do not know who I am.'

---

* The original thirteen-song version of *Liederkreis* (1842) opened with 'Der frohe Wandersmann' (p. 450);
The twelve-song version appeared only in 1850.

So reich geschmückt ist Roß und Weib,
So wunderschön der junge Leib,
Jetzt kenn ich dich – Gott steh mir bei!
Du bist die Hexe Loreley.

„Du kennst mich wohl – von hohem Stein
Schaut still mein Schloß tief in den Rhein.
Es ist schon spät, es ist schon kalt,
Kommst nimmermehr aus diesem Wald!"
(*Jensen, Pfitzner [fragment], Zemlinsky*)

So richly adorned are steed and lady,
So wondrous fair her youthful form,
Now I know you – may God protect me!
You are the enchantress Lorelei.

'You know me well – from its towering rock
My castle looks deep and silent down into the Rhine.
It is already late, already cold,
You shall never leave this forest again!'

4
Die Stille / Silence
FROM *Ahnung und Gegenwart*

Es weiß und rät es doch Keiner,
Wie mir so wohl ist, so wohl!
Ach, wüßt' es nur Einer, nur Einer,
Kein Mensch es sonst wissen soll!

So still ist's nicht draußen im Schnee,
So stumm und verschwiegen sind
Die Sterne nicht in der Höh',
Als meine Gedanken sind.

Ich wünscht', ich wär' ein Vöglein
Und zöge über das Meer,
Wohl über das Meer und weiter,
Bis daß ich im Himmel wär'!
(*Hensel, Hiller, Mendelssohn*)

No one knows and no one can guess
How happy I am, how happy!
If only one, just one man knew,
No one else ever should!

The snow outside is not so silent,
Nor are the stars on high
So still and silent
As my own thoughts.

I wish I were a little bird,
And could fly across the sea,
Across the sea and further,
Until I were in heaven!

5
Mondnacht / Moonlit night

Es war, als hätt' der Himmel
Die Erde still geküßt,
Daß sie im Blütenschimmer
Von ihm nur träumen müßt'.

Die Luft ging durch die Felder,
Die Ähren wogten sacht,
Es rauschten leis die Wälder,
So sternklar war die Nacht.

Und meine Seele spannte
Weit ihre Flügel aus,
Flog durch die stillen Lande,
Als flöge sie nach Haus.
(*Brahms, Marschner*)

It was as though Heaven
Had softly kissed the Earth,
So that she in a gleam of blossom
Had now to dream of him.

The breeze passed through the fields,
The corn swayed gently to and fro,
The forests murmured softly,
The night was so clear with stars.

And my soul spread
Its wings out wide,
Flew across the silent land,
As though flying home.

6

Schöne Fremde / A beautiful foreign land
FROM *Dichter und ihre Gesellen*

Es rauschen die Wipfel und schauern,
Als machten zu dieser Stund'
Um die halb versunkenen Mauern
Die alten Götter die Rund'.

Hier hinter den Myrtenbäumen
In heimlich dämmernder Pracht,
Was sprichst du wirr, wie in Träumen,
Zu mir, phantastische Nacht?

Es funkeln auf mich alle Sterne
Mit glühendem Liebesblick,
Es redet trunken die Ferne
Wie von künftigem großen Glück!
(*Hensel*)

The tree-tops rustle and shudder
As if at this very hour
The ancient gods
Were pacing these half-sunken walls.

Here beyond the myrtle trees
In secret twilit splendour,
What are you telling me, fantastic night,
Obscurely, as in a dream?

The glittering stars gaze down on me,
Fierily and full of love,
The distant horizon speaks with rapture
Of some great happiness to come!

7

Auf einer Burg / In a castle

Eingeschlafen auf der Lauer
Oben ist der alte Ritter;
Drüben gehen Regenschauer,
Und der Wald rauscht durch das Gitter.

Eingewachsen Bart und Haare,
Und versteinert Brust und Krause,
Sitzt er viele hundert Jahre
Oben in der stillen Klause.

Draußen ist es still und friedlich,
Alle sind in's Tal gezogen,
Waldesvögel einsam singen
In den leeren Fensterbogen.

Eine Hochzeit fährt da unten
Auf dem Rhein im Sonnenscheine,
Musikanten spielen munter,
Und die schöne Braut, die weinet.
(*Schoeck*)

Up there at his look-out
The old knight has fallen asleep;
Rain-storms pass overhead,
And the wood stirs through the portcullis.

Beard and hair matted together,
Ruff and breast turned to stone,
For centuries he's sat up there
In his silent cell.

Outside it's quiet and peaceful,
All have gone down to the valley,
Forest birds sing lonely songs
In the empty window-arches.

Down there on the sunlit Rhine
A wedding-party's sailing by,
Musicians strike up merrily,
And the lovely bride – weeps.

8

In der Fremde / In a foreign land

Ich hör' die Bächlein rauschen
Im Walde her und hin,

I hear the brooklets murmuring
Through the forest, here and there,

Im Walde, in dem Rauschen
Ich weiß nicht, wo ich bin.

Die Nachtigallen schlagen
Hier in der Einsamkeit,
Als wollten sie was sagen
Von der alten, schönen Zeit.

Die Mondesschimmer fliegen,
Als säh' ich unter mir
Das Schloß im Tale liegen,
Und ist doch so weit von hier!

Als müßte in dem Garten
Voll Rosen weiß und rot,
Meine Liebste auf mich warten,
Und ist doch so lange tot.
(*Marx, Schoeck*)

In the forest, in the murmuring
I do not know where I am.

Nightingales are singing
Here in the solitude,
As though they wished to tell
Of lovely days now past.

The moonlight flickers,
As though I saw below me
The castle in the valley,
Yet it lies so far from here!

As though in the garden,
Full of roses, white and red,
My love were waiting for me,
Yet she died so long ago.

9

Wehmut / Sadness
FROM *Ahnung und Gegenwart*

Ich kann wohl manchmal singen,
Als ob ich fröhlich sei,
Doch heimlich Tränen dringen,
Da wird das Herz mir frei.

Es lassen Nachtigallen,
Spielt draußen Frühlingsluft,
Der Sehnsucht Lied erschallen
Aus ihres Kerkers Gruft.

Da lauschen alle Herzen,
Und alles ist erfreut,
Doch keiner fühlt die Schmerzen,
Im Lied das tiefe Leid.
(*Hensel, Schoeck*)

True, I can sometimes sing
As though I were content;
But secretly tears well up,
And my heart is set free.

Nightingales, when spring breezes
Play outside, sing
Their song of longing
From their dungeon cell.

Then all hearts listen
And everyone rejoices,
Yet no one feels the pain,
The deep sorrow in the song.

10

Zwielicht / Twilight
FROM *Ahnung und Gegenwart*

Dämmrung will die Flügel spreiten,
Schaurig rühren sich die Bäume,
Wolken ziehn wie schwere Träume –
Was will dieses Graun bedeuten?

Hast ein Reh du lieb vor andern,
Laß es nicht alleine grasen,

Dusk is about to spread its wings,
The trees now shudder and stir,
Clouds drift by like oppressive dreams –
What can this dusk and dread imply?

If you have a fawn you favour,
Do not let her graze alone,

Jäger ziehn im Wald und blasen,
Stimmen hin und wieder wandern.

   Hast du einen Freund hienieden,
Trau ihm nicht zu dieser Stunde,
Freundlich wohl mit Aug' und Munde,
Sinnt er Krieg im tück'schen Frieden.

   Was heut gehet müde unter,
Hebt sich morgen neugeboren.
Manches geht in Nacht verloren –
Hüte dich, sei wach und munter!

Hunters sound their horns through the forest,
Voices wander to and fro.

   If here on earth you have a friend,
Do not trust him at this hour,
Though his eyes and lips be smiling,
In treacherous peace he's scheming war.

   That which wearily sets today,
Will rise tomorrow, newly born.
Much can go lost in the night –
Be wary, watchful, on your guard!

11
Im Walde / In the forest

   Es zog eine Hochzeit den Berg entlang,
Ich hörte die Vögel schlagen,
Da blitzten viel Reiter, das Waldhorn klang,
Das war ein lustiges Jagen!

   Und eh' ich's gedacht, war alles verhallt,
Die Nacht bedecket die Runde;
Nur von den Bergen noch rauschet der Wald
Und mich schauert's im Herzensgrunde.
(*Medtner*)

   A wedding procession wound across the
     mountain,
I heard the warbling of birds,
Riders flashed by, hunting horns blared,
That was a merry chase!

   And before I knew, all had faded,
Darkness covers the land;
Only the forest still sighs from the mountain,
And deep in my heart I quiver with fear.

12
Frühlingsnacht / Spring night

   Überm Garten durch die Lüfte
Hört' ich Wandervögel zieh'n,
Das bedeutet Frühlingsdüfte,
Unten fängt's schon an zu blühn.

   Jauchzen möcht' ich, möchte weinen,
Ist mir's doch, als könnt's nicht sein!
Alte Wunder wieder scheinen
Mit dem Mondesglanz herein.

   Und der Mond, die Sterne sagen's,
Und im Traume rauscht's der Hain
Und die Nachtigallen schlagen's:
Sie ist Deine, sie ist Dein!
(*Curschmann, Hensel, Jensen, Marschner*)

   Over the garden, through the air
I heard birds of passage fly,
A sign that spring is in the air,
Flowers already bloom below.

   I could shout for joy, could weep,
For it seems to me it cannot be!
All the old wonders come flooding back,
Gleaming in the moonlight.

   And the moon and stars say it,
And the dreaming forest whispers it,
And the nightingales sing it:
She is yours, is yours!

May 1840 Der frohe Wandersmann / The happy wanderer Op. 77, no. 1

   Wem Gott will rechte Gunst erweisen,
Den schickt er in die weite Welt;

   He whom God means to favour
Is sent out into the wide world;

Dem will er seine Wunder weisen	And is shown His many wonders
In Berg und Wald und Strom und Feld.	In mountain and forest and river and field.
Die Trägen, die zu Hause liegen,	The idlers who remain at home
Erquicket nicht das Morgenrot,	Are not refreshed when dawn turns red,
Sie wissen nur vom Kinderwiegen,	They only know of children's cradles,
Von Sorgen, Last und Not um Brot.	Of sorrow, trouble and hunger.
Die Bächlein von den Bergen springen,	The streams go rushing down the moun-
Die Lerchen schwirren hoch vor Lust,	tains,
Was sollt' ich nicht mit ihnen singen	Larks soar heavenwards with joy,
Aus voller Kehl' und frischer Brust?	Why should I not join their singing
	Full-throatedly and with fresh heart?
Den lieben Gott nur laß ich walten;	Let the good Lord bring what He will;
Der Bächlein, Lerchen, Wind und Feld,	Brooklets, larks, wind and field,
Und Erd und Himmel will erhalten,	Earth and Heaven are in His keeping –
Hat auch mein' Sach' auf's Best' bestellt!	He has ordered my life for the best!
(*Mendelssohn, Schoeck*)	

November 1840 Der Schatzgräber / The treasure-seeker Op. 45, no. 1

Wenn alle Wälder schliefen,	When all forests were sleeping,
Er an zu graben hub.	He began to dig.
Rastlos in Berges Tiefen	Ceaselessly in the mountain gorge
Nach einem Schatz er grub.	He dug for treasure.
Die Engel Gottes sangen	The angels of God were singing
Dieweil in stiller Nacht,	In the silent night,
Wie rote Augen drangen	Metals, like red eyes,
Metalle aus dem Schacht.	Were emerging from the shaft.
„Und wirst doch mein!" und grimmer	'You shall be mine!' More grimly
Wühlt er und wühlt hinab!	He burrows and burrows down!
Da stürzen Steine und Trümmer	Stones and rubbles
Über den Narren herab.	Fall in on the fool.
Hohnlachen wild erschallte	Wild mocking laughter echoed
Aus der verfall'nen Gruft,	From the crumbled vault,
Der Engelsang verhallte	The song of angels died away
Wehmütig in der Luft.	Sadly in the air.

November 1840 Frühlingsfahrt / A spring journey Op. 45, no. 2

Es zogen zwei rüst'ge Gesellen	Two sturdy lads set out
Zum erstenmal von Haus,	From home for the first time,
So jubelnd recht in die hellen,	Exultantly into the bright,
In die klingenden, singenden Wellen	Sounding and singing waves
Des vollen Frühlings hinaus.	Of springtime at its height.
Die strebten nach hohen Dingen,	They strove for lofty things,
Die wollten, trotz Lust und Schmerz,	Desired, despite joy and pain,

Was Rechts in der Welt vollbringen,	To achieve something in the world,
Und wem sie vorüber gingen,	And those they passed on their way
Dem lachten Sinnen und Herz.	Were happy in heart and mind.
Der Erste, der fand ein Liebchen,	The first, he found a loved-one,
Die Schwieger kauft' Hof und Haus;	Her family bought them house and home;
Der wiegte gar bald ein Bübchen,	Soon he was rocking a baby boy,
Und sah aus heimlichem Stübchen	And gazing from a homely room
Behaglich in's Feld hinaus.	At ease into his field.
Dem Zweiten sangen und logen	The second was sung and lied to
Die tausend Stimmen im Grund,	By a thousand voices from the deep –
Verlockend Sirenen, und zogen	Enticing sirens, who drew him
Ihn in die buhlenden Wogen,	Into the amorous waves,
In der Wogen farbigen Schlund.	The oceans' colourful depths.
Und wie er auftaucht' vom Schlunde,	And when he surfaced from the depths,
Da war er müde und alt,	He was weary and old,
Sein Schifflein das lag im Grunde,	His vessel lay on the sea-bed,
So still war's rings in der Runde,	Such silence reigned around him,
Und über den Wassern weht's kalt.	And the wind blew cold above the waves.
Es klingen und singen die Wellen	The waves of spring are singing
Des Frühlings wohl über mir;	And sounding over me;
Und seh' ich so kecke Gesellen,	And when I see such bold lads,
Die Tränen im Auge mir schwellen	Tears come welling to my eyes –
Ach Gott, führ' uns liebreich zu Dir!	Ah, guide us, God, lovingly to Thee!
(*Vesque von Püttlingen*)	

April 1850 Der Einsiedler / The hermit Op. 83, no. 3

Komm, Trost der Welt, du stille Nacht!	Come, comfort of the world, quiet night!
Wie steigst du von den Bergen sacht,	How softly you climb from the hills,
Die Lüfte alle schlafen.	The breezes all are sleeping,
Ein Schiffer nur noch, wandermüd,	One sailor still, travel-wearied,
Singt über's Meer sein Abendlied	Sings over the water his evening song
Zu Gottes Lob im Hafen.	In praise of God in the harbour.
Die Jahre wie die Wolken gehn,	The years, like the clouds, go by
Und lassen mich hier einsam stehn,	And leave me here in solitude,
Die Welt hat mich vergessen,	Forgotten by the world,
Da tratst du wunderbar zu mir,	Then wondrously you came to me,
Wenn ich beim Waldesrauschen hier	As I sat here lost in thought
Gedankenvoll gesessen.	Beside the murmuring wood.
O Trost der Welt, du stille Nacht!	O comfort of the world, quiet night!
Der Tag hat mich so müd gemacht,	The day has tired me so,
Das weite Meer schon dunkelt,	The wide sea darkens now,
Laß ausruhn mich von Lust und Not,	Let me rest from joy and pain,

| Bis daß das ew'ge Morgenrot | Until eternal dawn |
| Den stillen Wald durchfunkelt. | Flashes through the silent wood. |

(*Dessauer, Schoeck, Wolf*)

Emanuel Geibel (1815–84)

See Wolf

March 1849 Der Knabe mit dem Wunderhorn / The boy with the magic horn Op. 30, no. 1

Ich bin ein lust'ger Geselle,	I am a merry fellow,
Wer könnt auf Erden fröhlicher sein!	Who on earth could be happier?
Mein Rößlein so helle, so helle,	My steed is so swift,
Das trägt mich mit Windesschnelle	It bears me like the wind
Ins blühende Leben hinein –	Into a world in flower –
Trarah!	Trara!
Ins Leben hinein.	Into the world.
Es tönt an meinem Munde	I blow my silver horn
Ein silbernes Horn von süßem Schall,	With its sweet sound
Es tönt wohl manche Stunde,	It sounds for hours on end,
Von Fels und Wald in der Runde	From rocks and forest all around
Antwortet der Widerhall –	The echo answers –
Trarah!	Trara!
Der Widerhall.	The echo.
Und komm' ich zu festlichen Tänzen,	And when I come upon dancing,
Zu Scherz und Spiel im sonnigen Wald,	Laughing and playing in the sunlit wood,
Wo schmachtende Augen mir glänzen	Where languishing eyes gaze on me,
Und Blumen den Becher bekränzen,	And flowers garland the goblets,
Da schwing ich vom Roß mich alsbald –	I swiftly leap down from my steed –
Trarah!	Trara!
Da schwing ich vom Roß mich alsbald.	I swiftly leap down from my steed.
Süß lockt die Gitarre zum Reigen,	Guitars summon me sweetly to the dance,
Ich küsse die Mädchen, ich trinke den Wein;	I kiss the girls and drink the wine;
Doch will hinter blühenden Zweigen	But when behind blossoming branches
Die purpurne Sonne sich neigen,	The crimson sun begins to sink,
Da muß geschieden sein –	Then I must take my leave –
Trarah!	Trara!
Da muß geschieden sein.	Then I must take my leave.
Es zieht mich hinaus in die Ferne,	Faraway lands now beckon me,
Ich gebe dem flüchtigen Rosse den Sporn –	I spur my swift steed –
Ade! Wohl blieb' ich noch gerne,	Farewell! I'd willingly stay,
Doch winken schon andre Sterne,	But other stars already beckon,
Und grüßend vertönet das Horn –	And my horn sounds in greeting –
Trarah!	Trara!

Und grüßend vertönet das Horn.
Ade!
(*Raff*)

And my horn sounds in greeting.
Farewell!

August 1840 Der Page / The page Op. 30, no. 2

Da ich nun entsagen müssen
Allem, was mein Herz erbeten,
Laß mich diese Stelle küssen,
Die dein schöner Fuß betreten.

Since I must now renounce
All my heart's desire,
Let me kiss this spot,
Where your sweet foot has trod.

Darf ich auch als Ritter nimmer
Dir beglückt zur Seite schreiten,
Laß mich doch als Pagen immer
In die Messe dich begleiten.

And if I may never as a knight
Walk joyously by your side,
Let me always as a page
Escort you into mass.

Will ja treu sein und verschwiegen,
Tags dem kleinsten Winke lauschen,
Nachts auf deiner Schwelle liegen,
Mag auch Sturm und Hagel rauschen.

For I will be faithful and discreet,
Be alert by day for your slightest sign,
Lie by night outside your home,
Even in hail or storm.

Will dir stets mit sittgem Grüßen
Morgens frische Rosen bringen,
Will des Abends, dir zu Füßen,
Lieder zur Gitarre singen.

Always with a modest greeting
I'll bring fresh flowers each morning,
And every evening at your feet
Sing you songs to my guitar.

Will den weißen Renner zäumen,
Wenn's dich lüstet frisch zu jagen,
Will dir in des Waldes Räumen
Dienend Speer und Falken tragen;

And I shall bridle the white courser,
When it pleases you to hunt,
And in the forest's wide spaces
I shall carry your spear and falcon;

Will auf deinen Liebes Wegen
Selbst den Fackelträger machen,
Und am Tor mit blankem Degen,
Wenn du andre küssest, wachen;

And I shall be your torchbearer,
When you go to meet your lover,
And at the gate with naked dagger
I'll keep watch, when you kiss another;

Und das Alles ohne Klage,
Ohne Flehn, nicht laut noch leise,
Wenn mir nach vollbrachtem Tage
Nur ein Lächeln wird zum Preise,

And do all this without complaining,
Without a sigh loud or soft,
If when every day is ended,
A single smile be my reward,

Wenn gleich einem Segensterne,
Der mein ganzes Wesen lenket,
Nur dein Aug aus weiter Ferne
Einen einz'gen Strahl mir schenket.

If, like blessed starlight,
Guiding all my being,
You bestow on me from afar
Just a single glance.

August 1840 Der Hidalgo / The Hidalgo Op. 30, no. 3

Es ist so süß, zu scherzen
Mit Liedern und mit Herzen
Und mit dem ernsten Streit!

So sweet it is to sport
With songs and hearts
And serious quarrel!

Erglänzt des Mondes Schimmer,	When the moon gleams,
Da treibt's mich fort vom Zimmer,	I'm drawn from my room
Durch Platz und Gassen weit;	Through squares and streets;
Da bin zur Lieb ich immer	As ready for love
Wie zum Gefecht bereit.	As for a fight.
Die Schönen von Sevilla	The beauties of Seville
Mit Fächer und Mantilla	With fan and mantilla
Blicken den Strom entlang,	Gaze up the river;
Sie lauschen mit Gefallen,	They listen with favour
Wenn meine Lieder schallen	When my songs sound
Zum Mandolinenklang,	To the mandolin,
Und dunkle Rosen fallen	And dark roses drop
Mir vom Balkon zum Dank.	From the balcony as thanks.
Ich trage, wenn ich singe,	Singing, I carry
Die Zither und die Klinge,	My zither and blade
Vom Toledan'schen Stahl.	Of Toledo steel.
Ich sing' an manchem Gitter	I sing at many a lattice
Und höhne manchen Ritter	And mock many a knight
Mit keckem Lied zumal,	With insolent songs,
Den Damen gilt die Zither,	The zither's for the ladies,
Die Klinge dem Rival.	The blade for my rival.
Auf denn zum Abenteuer!	Off, then, for adventure!
Schon losch der Sonne Feuer	The sun's now extinguished
Jenseits der Berge aus;	Beyond the mountain range;
Der Mondnacht Dämmrungstunden,	The moonlit hours of night
Sie bringen Liebeskunden,	Will bring tidings of love,
Sie bringen blut'gen Strauß,	Bring bloody combat,
Und Blumen oder Wunden	And flowers or wounds
Trag' morgen ich nach Haus.	I'll bring home tomorrow.

March 1849 Melancholie / Melancholy Op. 74, no. 6
AFTER FRANCISCO SÁO DE MIRANDA

Wann, wann erscheint der Morgen,	When, when will the morning come,
Wann denn, wann denn!	When, O when!
Der mein Leben löst	That will free my life
Aus diesen Banden?	From these bonds?
Ihr Augen, vom Leide	You my eyes,
So trübe, so trübe!	So clouded by sorrow!
Saht nur Qual für Liebe,	Saw only torment instead of love,
Saht nicht eine Freude;	Saw no joy at all;
Saht nur Wunde auf Wunde,	Saw only wound on wound,
Schmerz auf Schmerz mir geben,	Agony on agony inflicted on me,
Und im langen Leben	And in my long life
Keine frohe Stunde.	Not a single cheerful hour.

Wenn es endlich doch	If only the hour
Endlich doch geschähe,	Would finally,
Daß ich säh' die Stunde,	Finally arrive,
Wo ich nimmer sähe!	When I could no longer see!

March 1849 Gestädnis / Confession Op. 74, no. 7
AFTER CONDE DI VIMIOSO

Also lieb' ich euch, Geliebte,	This is how I love you, beloved,
Daß mein Herz es nicht mag wagen,	My heart does not dare
Irgend einen Wunsch zu tragen.	To express a single wish.

Denn wenn ich zu wünschen wagte,	For if I dared to wish,
Hoffen würd' ich auch zugleich;	I would immediately hope;
Wenn ich nicht zu hoffen zagte,	And if I were bold in my hopes,
Weiß ich wohl, erzürnt' ich euch.	I know I should anger you.
Darum ruf ich ganz alleine	So I summon
Nur dem Tod, daß er erscheine,	Death alone to appear,
Weil mein Herz es nicht mag wagen,	For my heart does not dare
Einen andern Wunsch zu tragen.	To express another wish.

March 1849 Der Contrabandiste / The smuggler Op. 74, Annex
FROM *El Contrabandista* BY MANUEL GARCIA (1775–1832)

Ich bin der Contrabandiste,	I am the smuggler,
Weiß wohl Respekt mir zu schaffen.	I know how to get respect.
Allen zu trotzen, ich weiß es,	I know how to defy the world,
Furcht nur, die hab' ich vor Keinem.	I fear no one.
Drum nur lustig, nur lustig!	So let's be merry!

Wer kauft Seide, Tabak!	Who'll buy silk, tobacco?
Ja wahrlich, mein Rößlein ist müde,	But truly, my pony's tired,
Ich eil', ich eile, ja eile,	I must make haste, make haste,
Sonst faßt mich noch gar die Runde,	Or the patrol will catch me,
Los geht der Spektakel dann.	Then sparks will fly.
Lauf zu, mein lustiges Pferdchen,	So, off at a gallop, my merry horse,
Ach, mein liebes, gutes Pferdchen!	Ah, my dear good little horse!
Weißt ja davon mich zu tragen!	You know how to bear me away!

November 1849 O wie lieblich ist das Mädchen / Oh, how lovely is the girl Op. 138, no. 3
AFTER GIL VICENTE (?1465–?1536)

| O wie lieblich ist das Mädchen, | Oh, how lovely is the girl, |
| Wie so schön und voll Anmut! | How beautiful and full of grace! |

Sag mir an, du wackrer Seemann,	Tell me, brave sailor,
Der du lebst auf deinem Schiffe,	You who live on board your ship,
Ob das Schiff und seine Segel,	If the ship and its sails,
Ob die Sterne wohl so schön sind?	If the stars are as beautiful?

Sag mir an, du stolzer Ritter,	Tell me, proud knight,
Der du gehst im blanken Harnisch,	Clad in shining armour,
Ob das Roß und ob die Rüstung,	If your horse and your arms,
Ob die Schlachten wohl so schön sind?	If your battles are as beautiful?
Sag mir an, du Hirtenknabe,	Tell me, shepherd boy,
Der du deine Herde weidest,	You who tend your flock,
Ob die Lämmer, ob die Matten,	If lambs and pastures,
Ob die Berge wohl so schön sind?	If mountains are as beautiful?

April 1849 Romanze / Romance Op. 138, no. 5
AFTER AN ANONYMOUS SPANISH POEM

Flutenreicher Ebro,*	Surging River Ebro,
Blühendes Ufer,	Blossoming banks,
All ihr grünen Matten,	All you green pastures,
Schatten des Waldes,	And forest shadows,
Fraget die Geliebte,	Ask my beloved,
Die unter euch ruhet,	Who dwells among you,
Ob in ihrem Glücke	If in her happiness
Sie meiner gedenket!	She thinks of me!
Und ihr tauigen Perlen,	And you dewy pearls,
Die ihr im Frührot	Who in the rosy dawn
Den grünenden Rasen	Beautify the green grass
Bunt mit Farben schmückt,	With many bright colours,
Fraget die Geliebte	Ask my beloved,
Wenn sie Kühlung atmet,	When she breathes the cool air,
Ob in ihrem Glücke	If in her happiness
Sie meiner gedenket!	She thinks of me!
Ihr laubigen Pappeln,	You leafy poplars,
Schimmernde Pfade,	Shimmering paths,
Wo leichten Fußes	Where with light tread
Mein Mädchen wandelt,	My girl roams,
Wenn sie euch begegnet,	When she encounters you,
Fragt sie, fragt sie,	Ask her, ask her
Ob in ihrem Glücke	If in her happiness
Sie meiner gedenket!	She thinks of me!
Ihr schwärmenden Vögel,	You swarming birds,
Die den Sonnenaufgang	Who greet the sunrise
Singend ihr begrüßet	With flute-like
Mit Flötenstimmen,	Songs,
Fraget die Geliebte,	Ask my beloved,
Dieses Ufers Blume,	The flower of this shore,
Ob in ihrem Glücke	If in her happiness
Sie meiner gedenket!	She thinks of me!

* Spanish river that rises at Fuentibre in Santandes and flows into the Mediterranean.

November 1849 Weh, wie zornig ist das Mädchen / Alas, how angry the girl is Op. 138, no. 7
AFTER GIL VICENTE (1465?–1536?)

Weh, wie zornig ist das Mädchen,	Alas, how angry the girl is,
Weh, wie zornig, weh, weh!	Alas, how angry, alas!
Im Gebirge geht das Mädchen	In the mountains
Ihrer Herde hinterher,	The girl follows her herd –
Ist so schön wie die Blumen,	She's as fair as the flowers,
Ist so zornig wie das Meer.	As angry as the sea.

April 1849 Hoch, hoch sind die Berge / The mountains are high Op. 138, no. 8
AFTER PEDRO DE PADILLA (*fl.* 1585–99)

Hoch, hoch sind die Berge,	The mountains are high,
Und steil ist ihr Pfad;	Their paths are sheer;
Die Brunnen sprühn Wasser,	The fountains spray water
Und rieseln ins Kraut.	Which flows into the heather.
O Mutter, o Mutter,	O mother, O mother,
Lieb Mütterlein du;	O dearest mother;
Dort, dort in die Berge,	Up into those mountains
Mit den Gipfeln so stolz,	With their proud peaks
Da ging eines Morgens	My sweetest friend
Mein süßester Freund.	Went one morning.
Wohl rief ich zurück ihn	I called him back
Mit Zeichen und Wort,	With gesture and words,
Wohl winkt' ich mit allen	I waved him back
Fünf Fingern zurück –	With every finger of my hand –
Die Brunnen sprühn Wasser	The fountains spray water
Und rieseln ins Kraut.	Which flows into the heather.

Heinrich Heine (1797–1856)

See Brahms, Mendelssohn, Wolf

Heinrich Heine, whose name alongside Goethe's is almost synonymous with German art song, has been prodigiously set by Lieder composers. Vesque von Püttlingen leads with one hundred and nineteen – mostly ironic settings – followed by Robert Franz (sixty-eight), Schumann (forty-one), Wolf (eighteen), Liszt and Mendelssohn (seven), Schubert, Brahms, Pfitzner (six) and Richard Strauss (five). He has also attracted composers from an astonishing array of non German-speaking countries, such as Norway (Grieg), Russia (Balakirev, Borodin, Mussorgsky, Tchaikovsky), France (Meyerbeer), America (Ives, Macdowell, Griffes) and England (Maude Valérie White) among many others. Almost all these songs were based on poems taken from Heine's *Buch der Lieder* (1827).

The identity of the woman behind these unrequited love poems remains shrouded in mystery. Some scholars have cited cousin Amalie, daughter of his rich Uncle Salomon, others have suggested her sister Therese. That Heine suffered some sort of traumatic experience is proved by a letter to his schoolfriend Christian Sethe of 27 October 1816. Something shattering must have occurred, for the letter scorns all preliminary niceties and plunges straight into his grief:

Sie liebt mich *nicht* – Mußt, lieber Christian, dieses letzte Wörtchen ganz leise, leise aussprechen. In dem ersten Wörtchen liegt der ewig lebendige Himmel, aber auch in dem letzten liegt die ewig lebende Hölle.

She loves me *not* – Dear Christian, you must utter this last little word quietly, very quietly. Eternal Heaven dwells in the first word, just as eternal damnation dwells in the last.

The letter, which goes on to describe how the woman had scoffed at the 'schöne Lieder' he had written especially for her, also criticizes the philistine atmosphere of Hamburg, and states bitterly that the poems of a Jew would not be received kindly by the Christian community.

Heine's increasing fears of isolation and anti-semitism were only too well founded. In December 1820 he was expelled from the Göttingen Burschenschaft (student fraternity): at a secret meeting on 28 September 1820 in Dresden, the Burschenschaft decided not to accept any more Jews, since they had 'kein Vaterland und für unseres kein Interesse haben können' ('no fatherland, and could not be interested in ours'). That the rampant anti-semitism was threatening not only his confidence but his very sense of identity, is clear from an extraordinary letter to Sethe, dated 14 April 1822:

Alles, was deutsch ist, ist mir zuwider; und Du bist leider ein Deutscher. Alles Deutsche wirkt auf mich wie ein Brechpulver. Die deutsche Sprache zerreißt meine Ohren. Die eigenen Gedichte ekeln mich zuweilen an, wenn ich sehe, daß sie auf deutsch geschrieben sind. [...] Des Tags verfolgt mich ein ewiges Mißtrauen. Überall höre ich meinen Namen und hintendrein ein höhnisches Gelächter.

All that is German repulses me; and you, unfortunately, are German. Everything German acts on me like an emetic. The German language shrills in my ears. There are times when my own poems disgust me, when I see that they are written in German. [...] An eternal mistrust pursues me each day, I hear my name uttered everywhere, followed by mocking laughter.

The theme of unrequited love that runs through the early poetry is also a metaphor for Heine's rejection by society and his increasing fear of isolation.

February 1840 *Liederkreis / Song cycle* Op. 24

1

Morgens steh' ich auf und frage:
Kommt feins Liebchen heut?
Abends sink' ich hin und klage:
Ausblieb sie auch heut.

In der Nacht mit meinem Kummer
Lieg' ich schlaflos, lieg' ich wach;
Träumend, wie im halben Schlummer,
Wandle ich bei Tag.
(*Franz, Liszt*)

Every morning I wake and ask:
Will my sweetheart come today?
Every evening I lie down,
Complaining she stayed away.

All night long with my grief
I lie sleepless, lie awake;
Dreaming, as if half asleep,
I wander through the day.

2

Es treibt mich hin, es treibt mich her!
Noch wenige Stunden, dann soll ich sie
    schauen,
Sie selber, die schönste der schönen
    Jungfrauen;–
Du armes Herz, was pochst du schwer?

Die Stunden sind aber ein faules Volk!
Schleppen sich behaglich träge,
Schleichen gähnend ihre Wege;–
Tummle dich, du faules Volk!

Tobende Eile mich treibend erfaßt!
Aber wohl niemals liebten die Horen;–*
Heimlich im grausamen Bunde verschworen,
Spotten sie tückisch der Liebenden Hast.
(*Franz*)

I'm driven this way, driven that!
A few more hours, and I shall see
    her,
She, the fairest of the fair –
Faithful heart, why pound so
    hard?

But the Hours are a lazy breed!
They dawdle along and take their time,
Crawl yawningly on their way –
Get a move on, you lazy breed!

Raging haste drives me onward!
But the Horae can never have loved –
Cruelly and secretly in league,
They spitefully mock a lover's haste.

3

Ich wandelte unter den Bäumen
Mit meinem Gram allein;
Da kam das alte Träumen,
Und schlich mir ins Herz hinein.

Wer hat euch dies Wörtlein gelehret,
Ihr Vöglein in luftiger Höh'?
Schweigt still! wenn mein Herz es höret,
Dann tut es noch einmal so weh.

„Es kam ein Jungfräulein gegangen,
Die sang es immerfort,

I wandered among the trees,
Alone with my own grief,
But then the old dreams returned
And stole into my heart.

Who taught you this little word,
You birds up there in the breeze?
Be silent! If my heart hears it,
My pain will return once more.

'A young woman once passed by,
She sang it again and again,

* The Horae were three sisters, daughters of Jupiter and Themis, who presided over spring, summer and winter. Poets often represented them as opening the gates of heaven and Olympus.

Da haben wir Vöglein gefangen
Das hübsche, goldne Wort."

Das sollt ihr mir nicht erzählen,
Ihr Vöglein wunderschlau;
Ihr wollt meinen Kummer mir stehlen,
Ich aber niemandem trau'.
(*Hensel, Lachner*)

4

Lieb Liebchen, leg's Händchen aufs Herze
    mein;–
Ach, hörst du, wie's pochet im Kämmerlein?
Da hauset ein Zimmermann schlimm und arg,
Der zimmert mir einen Totensarg.

Es hämmert und klopfet bei Tag und bei
    Nacht;
Es hat mich schon längst um den Schlaf
    gebracht.
Ach! sputet Euch, Meister Zimmermann,
Damit ich balde schlafen kann.
(*Franz, Lachner, Medtner, Ries*)

5

Schöne Wiege meiner Leiden,
Schönes Grabmal meiner Ruh,
Schöne Stadt, wir müssen scheiden,–
Lebe wohl! ruf' ich dir zu.

Lebe wohl, du heil'ge Schwelle,
Wo da wandelt Liebchen traut;
Lebe wohl! du heil'ge Stelle,
Wo ich sie zuerst geschaut.

Hätt' ich dich doch nie gesehn,
Schöne Herzenskönigin!
Nimmer wär es dann geschehen,
Daß ich jetzt so elend bin.

Nie wollt' ich dein Herze rühren,
Liebe hab' ich nie erfleht;
Nur ein stilles Leben führen
Wollt' ich, wo dein Odem weht.

Doch du drängst mich selbst von hinnen,
Bittre Worte spricht dein Mund;
Wahnsinn wühlt in meinen Sinnen,
Und mein Herz ist krank und wund.

And we birds snatched it up,
That lovely golden word.'

You shouldn't tell me such things,
You wondrously cunning birds;
You thought to steal my grief from me,
But I trust no one.

Lay your hand on my heart, my
    love;–
Ah, can you not hear it throbbing?
A wicked, evil carpenter's there,
Fashioning me my coffin.

He bangs and hammers day and
    night;
The noise has long since robbed me of
    sleep.
Ah! master carpenter, make haste,
So that I soon might sleep.

Lovely cradle of my sorrows,
Lovely tombstone of my peace,
Lovely city, we must part –
Farewell! I call to you.

Farewell, O sacred threshold,
Where my dear beloved treads;
Farewell! O sacred spot,
Where I first beheld her.

Had I never seen you though,
Fair queen of my heart!
It would never then have happened
That I'm now so wretched.

I never wished to touch your heart,
I never begged for love;
To live in peace was all I wished,
And to breathe the air you breathe.

But you yourself drive me away,
Your lips speak bitter words;
Madness rages in my mind,
And my heart is sick and wounded.

Und die Glieder matt und träge
Schlepp' ich fort am Wanderstab,
Bis mein müdes Haupt ich lege
Ferne in ein kühles Grab.

And my limbs, weary and feeble,
I drag along, staff in hand,
Until I lay my tired head down
In a cool and distant grave.

6

Warte, warte, wilder Schiffmann,
Gleich folg' ich zum Hafen dir;
Von zwei Jungfraun nehm' ich Abschied,
Von Europa und von Ihr.

Wait, O wait, wild sailor,
Soon I'll follow to the harbour;
I'm taking leave of two maidens,
Of Europe and of her.

Blutquell, rinn' aus meinen Augen,
Blutquell, brich aus meinem Leib,
Daß ich mit dem heißen Blute
Meine Schmerzen niederschreib'.

Stream from my eyes, O blood,
Gush from my body, O blood,
That with my hot blood
I may write down my agonies.

Ei, mein Lieb, warum just heute
Schaudert dich, mein Blut zu sehn?
Sahst mich bleich und herzeblutend
Lange Jahre vor dir stehn!

Why today of all days, my love,
Do you shudder to see my blood?
You've seen me pale with bleeding heart
Before you for years on end!

Kennst du noch das alte Liedchen
Von der Schlang' im Paradies,
Die durch schlimme Apfelgabe
Unsern Ahn ins Elend stieß?

Do you remember the old story
Of the serpent in Paradise,
Who, through the evil gift of an apple,
Plunged our forbears into woe?

Alles Unheil brachten Äpfel!
Eva bracht' damit den Tod,
Eris* brachte Trojas Flammen,
Du bracht'st beides, Flamm' und Tod.

The apple's the cause of all our ills!
Eve brought death with it,
Eris brought flames to Troy,
And you – both flames and death.

7

Berg' und Burgen schau'n herunter
In den spiegelhellen Rhein,
Und mein Schiffchen segelt munter,
Rings umglänzt von Sonnenschein.

Mountains and castles look down
Into the mirror-bright Rhine,
And my boat sails merrily on,
With sunshine glistening all around.

Ruhig seh' ich zu dem Spiele
Goldner Wellen, kraus bewegt;
Still erwachen die Gefühle,
Die ich tief im Busen hegt'.

Calmly I watch the play
Of golden, ruffled waves;
Quietly the feelings awaken
I'd nursed deep in my heart.

Freundlich grüßend und verheißend
Lockt hinab des Stromes Pracht;
Doch ich kenn' ihn, oben gleißend,
Birgt sein Innres Tod und Nacht.

With friendly greetings and promises
The river's splendour beckons me;
But I know how, gleaming above,
It hides death and night within.

Oben Lust, im Busen Tücken,
Strom, du bist der Liebsten Bild!

On the surface – pleasure, at heart – malice,
River, how you resemble my love!

* The goddess of discord.

Die kann auch so freundlich nicken,
Lächelt auch so fromm und mild.

8

Anfangs wollt' ich fast verzagen,
Und ich glaubt', ich trüg' es nie;
Und ich hab' es doch getragen –
Aber fragt mich nur nicht, wie?
(*Liszt*)

9

Mit Myrten und Rosen, lieblich und hold,
Mit duft'gen Zypressen und Flittergold,
Möcht' ich zieren dies Buch wie 'nen Toten-
schrein,
Und sargen meine Lieder hinein.

O könnt' ich die Liebe sargen hinzu!
Auf dem Grabe der Liebe wächst Blümlein
der Ruh',
Da blüht es hervor, da pflückt man es ab, –
Doch mir blüht's nur, wenn ich selber im
Grab.

Hier sind nun die Lieder, die einst so wild,
Wie ein Lavastrom, der dem Ätna entquillt,
Hervorgestürzt aus dem tiefsten Gemüt,
Und rings viel blitzende Funken versprüht!

Nun liegen sie stumm und totengleich,
Nun starren sie kalt und nebelbleich,
Doch aufs neu' die alte Glut sie belebt,
Wenn der Liebe Geist einst über sie schwebt.

Und es wird mir im Herzen viel Ahnung
laut:
Der Liebe Geist einst über sie taut;
Einst kommt dies Buch in deine Hand,
Du süßes Lieb im fernen Land.

Dann löst sich des Liedes Zauberbann,
Die blassen Buchstaben schaun dich an,
Sie schauen dir flehend ins schöne Aug',
Und flüstern mit Wehmut und Liebeshauch.

February 1840 Belsazar / Belshazzar Op. 57

Die Mitternacht zog näher schon;
In stummer Ruh' lag Babylon.

She too can be kind and friendly,
Smiles her gentle, innocent smile.

At first I almost lost heart,
And thought I could never bear it;
And yet I have borne it –
Only do not ask me how.

With myrtles and roses, sweet and fair,
With fragrant cypress and golden tinsel,
I should like to adorn this book like a
coffin
And bury my songs within.

Could I but bury my love here too!
On Love's grave grows the flower of
peace,
There it blossoms, there is plucked,
But only when I'm buried will it bloom for
me.

Here now are the songs, which once
Streamed like lava from Etna,
Wildly from the depths of my soul,
Scattering sparks all around!

Now they lie mute, as though dead,
Now they stare coldly, as pale as mist,
But the old glow shall revive them again,
When one day Love's spirit floats over them.

And a thought speaks loudly in my
heart:
That Love's spirit will one day thaw them;
One day this book will fall into your hands,
My sweetest love, in a distant land.

And on that day the spell will break,
The pale letters will gaze at you,
Gaze imploringly into your beautiful eyes,
And whisper with sadness and the breath of love.

The midnight hour was drawing on;
In hushed repose lay Babylon.

Nur oben in des Königs Schloß,	But high in the castle of the king
Da flackert's, da lärmt des Königs Troß.	Torches flare, the king's men clamour.
Dort oben in dem Königssaal	Up there in the royal hall
Belsazar hielt sein Königsmahl.	Belshazzar was holding his royal feast.
Die Knechte saßen in schimmernden Reihn,	The vassals sat in shimmering rows,
Und leerten die Becher mit funkelndem Wein.	And emptied the beakers of glistening wine.
Es klirrten die Becher, es jauchzten die Knecht';	The vassals made merry, the goblets rang;
So klang es dem störrigen Könige recht.	Noise pleasing to that obdurate king.
Des Königs Wangen leuchten Glut;	The king's cheeks glow like coals;
Im Wein erwuchs ihm kecker Mut.	His impudence grew as he quaffed the wine.
Und blindlings reißt der Mut ihn fort;	And arrogance carries him blindly away;
Und er lästert die Gottheit mit sündigem	And he blasphemes God with sinful
Wort.	words.
Und er brüstet sich frech, und lästert wild;	And he brags insolently, blasphemes wildly;
Die Knechtschar ihm Beifall brüllt.	The crowd of vassals roar him on.
Der König rief mit stolzem Blick;	The king called out with pride in his eyes;
Der Diener eilt und kehrt zurück.	The servant hurries out and then returns.
Er trug viel gülden Gerät auf dem Haupt;	He bore many vessels of gold on his head;
Das war aus dem Tempel Jehovas geraubt.	Plundered from Jehovah's temple.
Und der König ergriff mit frevler Hand	With impious hand the king
Einen heiligen Becher, gefüllt bis am Rand.	Grabs a sacred beaker filled to the brim.
Und er leert' ihn hastig bis auf den Grund	And he drains it hastily down to the dregs,
Und rufet laut mit schäumendem Mund:	And shouts aloud through foaming lips:
Jehova! dir künd' ich auf ewig Hohn, –	Jehovah! I offer you eternal scorn –
Ich bin der König von Babylon!	I am the king of Babylon!
Doch kaum das grause Wort verklang,	Those terrible words had hardly faded,
Dem König ward's heimlich im Busen bang.	Than the king was filled with secret fear.
Das gellende Lachen verstummte zumal;	The shrill laughter was suddenly silent;
Es wurde leichenstill im Saal.	It became deathly still in the hall.
Und sieh! und sieh! an weißer Wand	And see! and see! on the white wall
Da kam's hervor wie Menschenhand;	A shape appeared like a human hand;
Und schrieb und schrieb an weißer Wand	And wrote and wrote on the white
Buchstaben von Feuer, und schrieb und	wall
schwand.	Letters of fire, and wrote and went.
Der König stieren Blicks da saß,	The king sat there with staring eyes,
Mit schlotternden Knien und totenblaß.	With trembling knees and pale as death.
Die Knechteschar saß kalt durchgraut,	The host of vassals sat stricken with horror,
Und saß gar still, gab keinen Laut.	And sat quite still, and made no sound.

| Die Magier kamen, doch keiner verstand | The soothsayers came, not one of them all |
| Zu deuten die Flammenschrift an der Wand. | Could interpret the letters of fire on the wall. |

| Belsazar ward aber in selbiger Nacht | Belshazzar however in that same night |
| Von seinen Knechten umgebracht. | Was done to death by his own vassals. |

*c.*April 1840 *Der arme Peter / Poor Peter* Op. 53, no. 3

I

Der Hans und die Grete tanzen herum,	Hans and Grete are dancing about,
Und jauchzen vor lauter Freude.	And crying aloud for sheer joy.
Der Peter steht so still und stumm,	Peter stands there speechless and still,
Und ist so blaß wie Kreide.	Looking as white as chalk.

Der Hans und die Grete sind Bräut'gam und Braut,	Hans and Grete are groom and bride,
Und blitzen im Hochzeitgeschmeide.	And gleam in wedding finery.
Der arme Peter die Nägel kaut	Poor Peter is biting his nails
Und geht im Werkeltagkleide.	And wears his working clothes.

Der Peter spricht leise vor sich her,	Peter mumbles to himself
Und schauet betrübet auf beide:	And looks sadly at the pair:
Ach! wenn ich nicht gar zu vernünftig wär',	If I weren't such a sensible lad,
Ich täte mir was zu leide.	I'd do myself some harm.

II

„In meiner Brust, da sitzt ein Weh,	'The pain in my breast
Das will die Brust zersprengen;	Will break my heart;
Und wo ich steh' und wo ich geh',	Wherever I am, wherever I go,
Will's mich von hinnen drängen.	It drives me somewhere else.

„Es treibt mich nach der Liebsten Näh',	'It drives me to be near my love,
Als könnt's die Grete heilen;	As if Grete could ease the pain;
Doch wenn ich der ins Auge seh',	But when I look into her eyes,
Muß ich von hinnen eilen.	I must hurry away again.

„Ich steig' hinauf des Berges Höh',	'I climb the high mountain,
Dort ist man doch alleine;	For there one is alone;
Und wenn ich still dort oben steh',	And when I'm standing still up there,
Dann steh' ich still und weine."	I stand still and weep.'

III

Der arme Peter wankt vorbei,	Poor Peter staggers past,
Gar langsam, leichenblaß und scheu.	So slowly, timid and pale as death.
Es bleiben fast, wie sie ihn sehn,	Folk in the streets almost stop,
Die Leute auf den Straßen stehn.	When they see him passing by.

| Die Mädchen flüstern sich ins Ohr: | The girls whisper to each other: |
| „Der stieg wohl aus dem Grab hervor." | 'He must have risen from his grave.' |

Ach nein, ihr lieben Jungfräulein,	Ah no, you dear young maidens,
Der steigt erst in das Grab hinein.	He's about to lie down in it.

Er hat verloren seinen Schatz,	He's lost his own true love,
Drum ist das Grab der beste Platz,	And so the grave's the best place
Wo er am besten liegen mag,	For him to lie and sleep
Und schlafen bis zum Jüngsten Tag.	Till Judgement Day arrives.

*c.*April 1840 Abends am Strand / Evening by the sea Op. 45, no. 3

Wir saßen am Fischerhause,	We sat by the fisherman's house,
Und schauten nach der See;	And gazed out at the sea;
Die Abendnebel kamen,	The evening mists gathered
Und stiegen in die Höh'.	And rose into the sky.

Im Leuchtturm wurden die Lichter	The lamps in the lighthouse
Allmählich angesteckt,	Were gradually lit,
Und in der weiten Ferne	And in the far distance
Ward noch ein Schiff entdeckt.	Another ship was sighted.

Wir sprachen von Sturm und Schiffbruch,	We talked of storm and shipwreck,
Vom Seemann, und wie er lebt,	Of the sailor and how he lives,
Und zwischen Himmel und Wasser,	Afloat between ocean and heaven,
Und Angst und Freude schwebt.	Afloat between joy and fear.

Wir sprachen von fernen Küsten,	We talked of distant shores,
Vom Süden und vom Nord,	Of South and of North,
Und von den seltsamen Menschen	And of the strange people
Und seltsamen Sitten dort.	And strange customs there.

Am Ganges duftet's und leuchtet's,	By the Ganges it's fragrant and sunny,
Und Riesenbäume blühn,	And huge trees blossom there,
Und schöne, stille Menschen	And beautiful, silent people
Vor Lotosblumen knien.	Kneel down before lotus flowers.

In Lappland sind schmutzige Leute,	In Lapland the people are dirty,
Plattköpfig, breitmäulig, klein;	Flat-headed, wide-mouthed, small;
Sie kauern ums Feuer, und backen	They squat around fires, and bake
Sich Fische, und quäken und schrei'n.	Fish, and squeal and scream.

Die Mädchen horchten ernsthaft,	Earnestly the girls listened,
Und endlich sprach niemand mehr;	At last no one spoke any more;
Das Schiff war nicht mehr sichtbar,	The ship was no more to be sighted,
Es dunkelte gar zu sehr.	It was growing far too dark.
(*Vesque von Püttlingen*)	

April 1840 Die feindlichen Brüder / The warring brothers Op. 49, no. 2

Oben auf des Berges Spitze	High on the mountain summit
Liegt das Schloß in Nacht gehüllt;	Stands the castle, veiled in night;

| Doch im Tale leuchten Blitze, | But in the valley lightning flashes, |
| Helle Schwerter klirren wild. | Bright swords fiercely clash. |

Das sind Brüder, die dort fechten	Those are brothers fighting there,
Grimmen Zweikampf, wutentbrannt.	Rage-inflamed, a dreadful duel.
Sprich, warum die Brüder rechten	Pray, why are those brothers fighting,
Mit dem Schwerte in der Hand?	Each of them with sword in hand?

Gräfin Lauras Augenfunken	Countess Laura's sparkling eyes
Zündeten den Brüderstreit;	Kindled the brothers' quarrel;
Beide glühen liebestrunken	Both burn with love and passion
Für die adlig holde Maid.	For that sweet and noble maid.

Welchem aber von den beiden	But to which of them
Wendet sich ihr Herze zu?	Does her heart incline?
Kein Ergrübeln kann's entscheiden, –	No pondering can resolve it –
Schwert heraus, entscheide du!	Out, then, sword, let you decide!

Und sie fechten kühn verwegen,	And bold and rash they do battle,
Hieb auf Hiebe niederkracht's.	Blow on blow crashes down.
Hütet euch, ihr wilden Degen,	Beware, O savage warriors,
Grausig Blendwerk schleichet nachts.	Night brings cruel deception.

Wehe! Wehe! blut'ge Brüder!	Alack, alack now, bloody brothers!
Wehe! Wehe! blut'ges Tal!	Alack, alack now, bloody vale!
Beide Kämpfer stürzen nieder,	Both fighters are felled,
Einer in des andern Stahl. –	Each by the other's sword.

Viel Jahrhunderte verwehen,	Many centuries pass by,
Viel Geschlechter deckt das Grab;	Many generations die away;
Traurig von des Berges Höhen	Sadly from the mountain heights
Schaut das öde Schloß herab.	The desolate castle looks down.

Aber nachts, im Talesgrunde,	But at night, deep in the valley,
Wandelt's heimlich, wunderbar;	The scene changes mysteriously;
Wenn da kommt die zwölfte Stunde,	At the first stroke of midnight,
Kämpfet dort das Brüderpaar.	Still the brothers fight it out.

May 1840 Die beiden Grenadiere / The two grenadiers Op. 49, no. 1

Nach Frankreich zogen zwei Grenadier',	Two grenadiers, held captive in Russia,
Die waren in Rußland gefangen.	Were marching back to France.
Und als sie kamen ins deutsche Quartier,	And when they set foot on German soil,
Sie ließen die Köpfe hangen.	They hung their heads.

Da hörten sie beide die traurige Mär:	For here they learnt the sorry tale
Daß Frankreich verloren gegangen,	That France was lost forever,
Besiegt und geschlagen das tapfere Heer –	Her valiant army beaten and shattered –
Und der Kaiser, der Kaiser gefangen.	And the Emperor, the Emperor captured.

| Da weinten zusammen die Grenadier' | The grenadiers then wept together, |
| Wohl ob der kläglichen Kunde. | As they heard of these sad tidings. |

Der eine sprach: Wie weh wird mir,	The first said: Ah, the agony,
Wie brennt meine alte Wunde!	How my old wound is burning!
Der andre sprach: Das Lied ist aus,	The second said: This is the end,
Auch ich möcht mit dir sterben,	If only we could die together,
Doch hab ich Weib und Kind zu Haus,	But I've a wife and child at home,
Die ohne mich verderben.	Who without me would perish.
Was schert mich Weib, was schert mich Kind,	To hell with wife, to hell with child,
Ich trage weit beß'res Verlangen;	I strive for far higher things;
Laß sie betteln gehn, wenn sie hungrig sind, –	Let them beg, if they are hungry –
Mein Kaiser, mein Kaiser gefangen!	My Emperor, my Emperor captured!
Gewähr mir, Bruder, eine Bitt':	Grant me brother one request:
Wenn ich jetzt sterben werde,	If I am now to die,
So nimm meine Leiche nach Frankreich mit,	Take my corpse with you to France,
Begrab' mich in Frankreichs Erde.	Bury me in French soil.
Das Ehrenkreuz am roten Band	You shall lay on my heart
Sollst du aufs Herz mir legen;	The Cross of Valour with its red ribbon;
Die Flinte gib mir in die Hand,	And place my musket in my hand
Und gürt' mir um den Degen.	And gird my sword about me.
So will ich liegen und horchen still,	So shall I lie and listen
Wie eine Schildwach', im Grabe,	Like a silent sentry in my grave,
Bis einst ich höre Kanonengebrüll	Until I hear the cannons' roar
Und wiehernder Rosse Getrabe.	And the horses gallop and neigh.
Dann reitet mein Kaiser wohl über mein Grab,	My Emperor will then ride over my grave,
Viel Schwerter klirren und blitzen;	Swords will be clashing and flashing;
Dann steig' ich gewaffnet hervor aus dem Grab, –	I shall then rise armed from the grave –
Den Kaiser, den Kaiser zu schützen.	To defend the Emperor, my Emperor.
(*Reissiger, Wagner*)	

May 1840 *Dichterliebe* / A poet's love* Op. 48

1

Im wunderschönen Monat Mai,	In the wondrous month of May,
Als alle Knospen sprangen,	When all buds were bursting into bloom,
Da ist in meinem Herzen	Then it was that in my heart
Die Liebe aufgegangen.	Love began to blossom.
Im wunderschönen Monat Mai,	In the wondrous month of May,
Als alle Vögel sangen,	When all the birds were singing,

---

* *Dichterliebe* originally contained twenty songs, but Schumann, having had the cycle refused by Bote & Bock and Breitkopf & Härtel, decided to leave out 'Dein Angesicht', 'Es leuchtet meine Liebe', 'Lehn' deine Wang" and 'Mein Wagen rollet langsam'.

Da hab' ich ihr gestanden
Mein Sehnen und Verlangen.
(*Franz, Hensel, Lachner*)

Then it was I confessed to her
My longing and desire.

2

Aus meinen Tränen sprießen
Viel blühende Blumen hervor,
Und meine Seufzer werden
Ein Nachtigallenchor.

From my tears will spring
Many blossoming flowers,
And my sighs will become
A choir of nightingales.

Und wenn du mich lieb hast, Kindchen,
Schenk' ich dir die Blumen all',
Und vor deinem Fenster soll klingen
Das Lied der Nachtigall.
(*Borodin, Hensel, Mussorgsky, Rimsky-Korsakov*)

And if you love me, child,
I'll give you all the flowers,
And at your window shall sound
The nightingale's song.

3

Die Rose, die Lilie, die Taube, die Sonne,
Die liebt' ich einst alle in Liebeswonne.
Ich lieb' sie nicht mehr, ich liebe alleine
Die Kleine, die Feine, die Reine, die Eine;
Sie selber, aller Liebe Wonne,
Ist Rose und Lilie und Taube und Sonne.
(*Franz, Lachner, Meyerbeer*)

Rose, lily, dove, sun,
I loved them all once in the bliss of love.
I love them no more, I only love
She who is small, fine, pure, rare;
She, most blissful of all loves,
Is rose and lily and dove and sun.

4

Wenn ich in deine Augen seh',
So schwindet all mein Leid und Weh;
Doch wenn ich küsse deinen Mund,
So werd ich ganz und gar gesund.

When I look into your eyes,
All my pain and sorrow vanish;
But when I kiss your lips,
Then I am wholly healed.

Wenn ich mich lehn' an deine Brust,
Kommt's über mich wie Himmelslust;
Doch wenn du sprichst: Ich liebe dich!
So muß ich weinen bitterlich.
(*Franz, Glazunov, Hensel, Lachner, Rimsky-Korsakov, Wolf*)

When I lay my head against your breast,
Heavenly bliss steals over me;
But when you say: I love you!
I must weep bitter tears.

5

Ich will meine Seele tauchen
In den Kelch der Lilie hinein;
Die Lilie soll klingend hauchen
Ein Lied von der Liebsten mein.

Let me bathe my soul
In the lily's chalice;
The lily shall resound
With a song of my love.

Das Lied soll schauern und beben,
Wie der Kuß von ihrem Mund,
Den sie mir einst gegeben
In wunderbar süßer Stund'.
(*Franz*)

The song shall tremble and quiver
Like the kiss her lips
Once gave me
In a sweet and wondrous hour.

469

6

Im Rhein, im heiligen Strome,
Da spiegelt sich in den Well'n,
Mit seinem großen Dome,
Das große, heilige Köln.

Im Dom da steht ein Bildnis,*
Auf goldenem Leder gemalt;
In meines Lebens Wildnis
Hat's freundlich hineingestrahlt.

Es schweben Blumen und Englein
Um unsre liebe Frau;
Die Augen, die Lippen, die Wänglein,
Die gleichen der Liebsten genau.
(*Franz, Liszt*)

In the Rhine, the holy river,
There is reflected in the waves,
With its great cathedral,
Great and holy Cologne.

In the cathedral hangs a picture,
Painted on gilded leather;
Into my life's wilderness
It has cast its friendly rays.

Flowers and cherubs hover
Around Our beloved Lady;
Her eyes, her lips, her cheeks
Are the image of my love's.

7

Ich grolle nicht, und wenn das Herz auch
bricht,
Ewig verlornes Lieb! ich grolle nicht.
Wie du auch strahlst in Diamantenpracht,
Es fällt kein Strahl in deines Herzens Nacht.

Das weiß ich längst. Ich sah dich ja im
Traume,
Und sah die Nacht in deines Herzens Raume,
Und sah die Schlang', die dir am Herzen frißt,
Ich sah, mein Lieb, wie sehr du elend bist.
(*Ives*)

I bear no grudge, though my heart is
breaking,
O love forever lost! I bear no grudge.
However you gleam in diamond splendour,
No ray falls in the night of your heart.

I've known that long. For I saw you in my
dreams,
And saw the night within your heart,
And saw the serpent gnawing your heart –
I saw, my love, how pitiful you are.

8

Und wüßten's die Blumen, die kleinen,
Wie tief verwundet mein Herz,
Sie würden mit mir weinen,
Zu heilen meinen Schmerz.

Und wüßten's die Nachtigallen,
Wie ich so traurig und krank,
Sie ließen fröhlich erschallen
Erquickenden Gesang.

Und wüßten sie mein Wehe,
Die goldenen Sternelein,
Sie kämen aus ihrer Höhe,
Und sprächen Trost mir ein.

Sie alle können's nicht wissen,
Nur Eine kennt meinen Schmerz;

If the little flowers knew
How deeply my heart is hurt,
They would weep with me
To heal my pain.

If the nightingales knew
How sad I am and sick,
They would joyfully make the air resound
With refreshing song.

And if they knew of my grief,
Those little golden stars,
They would come down from the sky
And console me with their words.

But none of them can know,
My pain is known to one alone;

* Stephan Lochner's 'Muttergottes in der Rosenlaube' (1448)

Sie hat ja selbst zerrissen,
Zerrissen mir das Herz.
(*Franz, Hensel, Josefine Lang, Mendelssohn,
Reissiger*)

For she it was who broke,
Broke my heart in two.

9

Das ist ein Flöten und Geigen,
Trompeten schmettern darein;
Da tanzt wohl den Hochzeitreigen
Die Herzallerliebste mein.

What a fluting and fiddling,
What a blaring of trumpets;
That must be my dearest love
Dancing at her wedding feast.

Das ist ein Klingen und Dröhnen,
Ein Pauken und ein Schalmei'n;
Dazwischen schluchzen und stöhnen
Die lieblichen Engelein.

What a booming and ringing,
What a drumming and piping;
With lovely little angels
Sobbing and groaning between.

10

Hör' ich das Liedchen klingen,
Das einst die Liebste sang,
So will mir die Brust zerspringen
Von wildem Schmerzendrang.

When I hear the little song
My beloved once sang,
My heart almost bursts
With the wild rush of pain.

Es treibt mich ein dunkles Sehnen
Hinauf zur Waldeshöh',
Dort löst sich auf in Tränen
Mein übergroßes Weh.
(*Franz, Meyerbeer*)

A dark longing drives me
Up to the wooded heights,
Where my overwhelming grief
Dissolves into tears.

11

Ein Jüngling liebt ein Mädchen,
Die hat einen andern erwählt;
Der andre liebt eine andre,
Und hat sich mit dieser vermählt.

A boy loves a girl
Who chooses another;
He in turn loves another
And marries her.

Das Mädchen nimmt aus Ärger
Den ersten besten Mann,
Der ihr in den Weg gelaufen;
Der Jüngling ist übel dran.

The girl, out of pique,
Takes the very first man
To come her way;
The boy is badly hurt.

Es ist eine alte Geschichte,
Doch bleibt sie immer neu;
Und wem sie just passieret,
Dem bricht das Herz entzwei.
(*Lachner, Vesque von Püttlingen*)

It's an old story,
Yet remains ever new;
And he to whom it happens,
It breaks his heart in half.

12

Am leuchtenden Sommermorgen
Geh' ich im Garten herum.

One bright summer morning
I walk round the garden.

Es flüstern und sprechen die Blumen,
Ich aber wandle stumm.

Es flüstern und sprechen die Blumen,
Und schaun mitleidig mich an:
Sei unsrer Schwester nicht böse,
Du trauriger, blasser Mann.
(*Franz, Glazunov, Hensel*)

13
Ich hab' im Traum geweinet,
Mir träumte, du lägest im Grab.
Ich wachte auf, und die Träne
Floß noch von der Wange herab.

Ich hab' im Traum geweinet,
Mir träumt', du verließest mich.
Ich wachte auf, und ich weinte
Noch lange bitterlich.

Ich hab' im Traum geweinet,
Mir träumte, du wärst mir noch gut.
Ich wachte auf, und noch immer
Strömt meine Tränenflut.
(*Cui, Franz, Lachner, Lassen, Loewe,
Reissiger, Ries*)

14
Allnächtlich im Traume seh' ich dich,
Und sehe dich freundlich grüßen,
Und laut aufweinend stürz' ich mich
Zu deinen süßen Füßen.

Du siehest mich an wehmütiglich
Und schüttelst das blonde Köpfchen;
Aus deinen Augen schleichen sich
Die Perlentränentröpfchen.

Du sagst mir heimlich ein leises Wort,
Und gibst mir den Strauß von Zypressen.
Ich wache auf, und der Strauß ist fort,
Und's Wort hab' ich vergessen.
(*Franz, Hensel, Mendelssohn*)

15
Aus alten Märchen winkt es
Hervor mit weißer Hand,
Da singt es und da klingt es
Von einem Zauberland;

The flowers whisper and talk,
But I move silently.

The flowers whisper and talk,
And look at me in pity:
Be not angry with our sister,
You sad, pale man.

I wept in my dream,
I dreamt you lay in your grave.
I woke, and tears
Still flowed down my cheeks.

I wept in my dream,
I dreamt you were leaving me.
I woke, and wept on
Long and bitterly.

I wept in my dream,
I dreamt you loved me still.
I woke, and still
My tears stream.

Nightly in my dreams I see you,
And see your friendly greeting,
And weeping loud, I hurl myself
Down at your sweet feet.

Wistfully you look at me,
Shaking your fair little head;
Tiny little pearl-like tears
Trickle from your eyes.

You whisper me a soft word
And hand me a wreath of cypress.
I wake up and the wreath is gone,
And I cannot remember the word.

A white hand beckons
From fairy tales of old,
Where there are sounds and songs
Of a magic land;

Wo bunte Blumen blühen	Where brightly coloured flowers
Im goldnen Abendlicht,	Bloom in golden twilight,
Und lieblich duftend glühen,	And glow sweet and fragrant
Mit bräutlichem Gesicht;	With a bride-like face;
Und grüne Bäume singen	And green trees
Uralte Melodein,	Sing primeval melodies,
Die Lüfte heimlich klingen,	Mysterious breezes murmur,
Und Vögel schmettern drein;	And birds warble;
Und Nebelbilder steigen	And misty shapes rise up
Wohl aus der Erd' hervor,	From the very ground,
Und tanzen luft'gen Reigen	And dance airy dances
Im wunderlichen Chor;	In a strange throng;
Und blaue Funken brennen	And blue sparks blaze
An jedem Blatt und Reis,	On every leaf and twig,
Und rote Lichter rennen	And red fires race
Im irren, wirren Kreis;	Madly round and round;
Und laute Quellen brechen	And loud springs gush
Aus wildem Marmorstein,	From wild marble cliffs.
Und seltsam in den Bächen	And strangely in the streams
Strahlt fort der Widerschein.	The reflection shines on.
Ach, könnt ich dorthin kommen,	Ah, could I but reach that land,
Und dort mein Herz erfreu'n,	And there make glad my heart,
Und aller Qual entnommen,	And be relieved of all pain,
Und frei und selig sein!	And be blissful and free!
Ach! jenes Land der Wonne,	Ah! that land of delight,
Das seh' ich oft im Traum,	I see it often in my dreams,
Doch kommt die Morgensonne,	But with the morning sun
Zerfließt's wie eitel Schaum.	It melts like mere foam.

16

Die alten, bösen Lieder,	The bad old songs,
Die Träume bös und arg,	The bad and bitter dreams,
Die laßt uns jetzt begraben,	Let us now bury them,
Holt einen großen Sarg.	Fetch me a large coffin.
Hinein leg' ich gar manches,	I have much to put in it,
Doch sag' ich noch nicht was;	Though what I won't yet say;
Der Sarg muß sein noch größer	The coffin must be even larger
Wie's Heidelberger Faß.*	Than the Vat at Heidelberg.
Und holt eine Totenbahre,	And fetch a bier
Und Bretter fest und dick;	Made of firm thick timber;
Auch muß sie sein noch länger,	And it must be even longer
Als wie zu Mainz die Brück'.	Than the bridge at Mainz.

* With a capacity of 48,780 gallons, the Heidelberg Vat was installed during the reign of Charles Theodore.

Und holt mir auch zwölf Riesen,	And fetch for me twelve giants,
Die müssen noch stärker sein,	They must be even stronger
Als wie der starke Christoph,*	Than Saint Christopher the Strong
Im Dom zu Köln am Rhein.	In Cologne cathedral on the Rhine.

Die sollen den Sarg forttragen,	They shall bear the coffin away,
Und senken in's Meer hinab;	And sink it deep into the sea;
Denn solchem großen Sarge	For such a large coffin
Gebührt ein großes Grab.	Deserves a large grave.

Wißt ihr, warum der Sarg wohl	Do you know why the coffin
So groß und schwer mag sein?	Must be so large and heavy?
Ich senkt' auch meine Liebe	I'd like to bury there my love
Und meinen Schmerz hinein.	And my sorrow too.

May 1840 Dein Angesicht / Your face Op. 127, no. 2

Dein Angesicht, so lieb und schön,	Your face so lovely and fair
Das hab' ich jüngst im Traum gesehn,	Appeared to me in a recent dream,
Es ist so mild und engelgleich,	So mild, it looks, and angel-like,
Und doch so bleich, so schmerzenreich.	And yet so pale, so full of pain.

Und nur die Lippen, die sind rot;	And your lips alone are red;
Bald aber küßt sie bleich der Tod.	But death shall soon kiss them pale.
Erlöschen wird das Himmelslicht,	The heavenly light will be extinguished
Das aus den frommen Augen bricht.	That gleams from your innocent eyes.

May 1840 Es leuchtet meine Liebe / The gleam of my love Op. 127, no. 3

Es leuchtet meine Liebe	The gleam of my love
In ihrer dunkeln Pracht,	In its dark splendour
Wie'n Märchen, traurig und trübe,	Is like a tale, sad and gloomy,
Erzählt in der Sommernacht.	Told on a summer night.

Im Zaubergarten wallen	In the magic garden wander
Zwei Buhlen, stumm und allein;	Two lovers, silent and alone;
Es singen die Nachtigallen,	The nightingales are singing,
Es flimmert der Mondenschein.	The moon is shimmering.

Die Jungfrau steht still wie ein Bildnis,	The maiden stands as silent as a picture,
Der Ritter vor ihr kniet.	The knight kneels down before her.
Da kommt der Riese der Wildnis,	Suddenly the wild giant appears,
Die bange Jungfrau flieht.	The frightened maiden flees.

Der Ritter sinkt blutend zur Erde,	The knight sinks bleeding to the ground,
Es stolpert der Riese nach Haus;	The giant stumbles home;
Wenn ich begraben werde,	And when I'm dead and buried;
Dann ist das Märchen aus.	This story shall be done.

* The giant who carried travellers across the water on his back; legend has it that in carrying the Christ-child he almost buckled under his weight, since he was bearing the weight of all the world's sorrows.

May 1840 Lehn' deine Wang' / Rest your cheek against my cheek Op. 142, no. 2

Lehn' deine Wang' an meine Wang',
Dann fließen die Tränen zusammen;
Und an mein Herz drück' fest dein Herz,
Dann schlagen zusammen die Flammen!

Und wenn in die große Flamme fließt
Der Strom von unsern Tränen,
Und wenn dich mein Arm gewaltig
      umschließt –
Sterb' ich vor Liebessehnen!
(*Jensen, Rimsky-Korsakov*)

Rest your cheek against my cheek,
Together our tears shall flow;
And against my heart press firm your heart,
Together the flames shall leap!

And when into that great flame
Our river of tears shall flow,
And when I clasp you wildly in my
      arms –
I shall die of love's desire!

May 1840 Mein Wagen rollet langsam / My carriage rolls slowly Op. 142, no. 4

Mein Wagen rollet langsam
Durch lustiges Waldesgrün,
Durch blumige Täler, die zaubrisch
Im Sonnenglanze blühn.

Ich sitze und sinne und träume,
Und denk' an die Liebste mein;
Da huschen drei Schattengestalten
Kopfnickend zum Wagen herein.

Sie hüpfen und schneiden Gesichter,
So spöttisch und doch so scheu,
Und quirlen wie Nebel zusammen,
Und kichern und huschen vorbei.
(*Strauss*)

My carriage rolls slowly
Through cheerful green woodlands,
Through flowery valleys
Magically blooming in sun.

I sit and muse and dream,
And think of my dear love;
Three shadowy forms nod at me
Through the carriage window.

They hop and pull faces,
So mocking yet so shy,
And whirl together like mist
And flit chuckling by.

?1841 Tragödie / Tragedy Op. 64, no. 3
THE SECOND POEM IS A FOLKSONG HEARD BY HEINE ON THE RHINE.

I
Entflieh' mit mir und sei mein Weib,
Und ruh an meinem Herzen aus!
In weiter Ferne sei mein Herz
Dein Vaterland und Vaterhaus!

Entflieh'n wir nicht, so sterb' ich hier
Und du bist einsam und allein;
Und bleibst du auch im Vaterhaus,
Wirst doch wie in der Fremde sein.
(*Griffes*)

Elope with me and be my wife,
And rest against my heart!
In distant lands let my heart be
Your fatherland and your home!

If we don't flee, then I'll die here,
And you shall be lonely and alone;
And though you stay in your father's home,
It shall be like a foreign land!

II

Es fiel ein Reif in der Frühlingsnacht,
Er fiel auf die zarten Blaublümelein.
Sie sind verwelket, verdorret.

There fell a frost one night in spring,
It fell on the tender forget-me-nots.
They are now blighted, withered.

Ein Jüngling hatte ein Mädchen lieb,
Sie flohen heimlich vom Hause fort,
Es wußt' weder Vater noch Mutter.

A young man loved a maiden,
In secret they eloped together,
Neither father nor mother knew.

Sie sind gewandert hin und her,
Sie haben gehabt weder Glück noch Stern,
Sie sind gestorben, verdorben.
(*Griffes, Hiller, Knab, Clara Schumann,
Tomášek*)

They wandered to and fro,
They had neither luck nor guiding star,
They perished, died.

III

Auf ihrem Grab, da steht eine Linde,
Drin pfeifen die Vögel und Abendwinde,
Und drunter sitzt, auf dem grünen Platz,
Der Müllersknecht mit seinem Schatz.

On their grave a lime-tree grows,
Where birds and evening breezes sing,
And on the turf beneath it sit
The miller-lad and his love.

Die Winde, die wehen so lind und so schaurig,
Die Vögel, die singen so süß und so traurig,
Die schwatzenden Buhlen, sie werden stumm,
Sie weinen und wissen selbst nicht warum.
(*Griffes, Hiller*)

The breezes are so faint and fearful,
The birdsong sounds so sweet and sad,
The chattering lovers fall silent,
They weep without knowing why.

Justinus Kerner (1786–1862)

While studying medicine at Tübingen, where he supervised the mentally deranged poet Hölderlin, Kerner formed a life-long friendship with Uhland, and together with Gustav Schwab formed a Swabian group of poets that included Mörike. In true Romantic spirit he restored Weibertreu castle and lived nearby in a house that became a centre of pilgrimage. He was fascinated by occult and psychic phenomena and wrote medical histories of hysterical or mesmerized patients (*Geschichte zweier Somnambulen* (1824) and *Die Seherin von Prevorst* (1829). *Die somnambulistischen Tische* probably influenced Schumann's own spiritualistic interests, especially table-turning, which preoccupied him towards the end of his life. His poems, which Schumann set as early as 1827, were greatly influenced by folk-song.

Zwölf Gedichte von Justinus Kerner / Twelve poems by Justinus Kerner Op. 35

1

Lust der Sturmnacht / Joy in a stormy night
NOVEMBER 1840

Wenn durch Berg' und Tale draußen

When rainstorms gust and rage outside

Regen schauert, Stürme brausen,
Schild und Fenster hell erklirren,
Und in Nacht die Wandrer irren,

Ruht es sich so süß hier innen,
Aufgelöst in sel'ges Minnen;
All der goldne Himmelsschimmer
Flieht herein in's stille Zimmer:

Reiches Leben! hab' Erbarmen!
Halt mich fest in linden Armen!
Lenzesblumen aufwärts dringen,
Wölklein ziehn und Vöglein singen.

Ende nie, du Sturmnacht wilde!
Klirrt, ihr Fenster! schwankt, ihr Schilde!
Bäumt euch, Wälder! braus', o Welle!
Mich umfängt des Himmels Helle!

Over mountains and valleys,
When inn-signs and windows rattle loud
And travellers are lost in the night,

How sweet to be at peace indoors,
To surrender to blissful love;
All the golden glow of heaven
Takes refuge in this quiet room.

Abundant life, have mercy on me!
Let gentle arms hold me tight!
Spring flowers will shoot up,
Clouds disperse and birds sing.

Never end, O wild night of storm!
Let windows rattle, let inn-signs sway!
Rear up, O forests; roar, O waves!
I'm locked in heaven's bright embrace!

2

Stirb, Lieb' und Freud'! / Die, love and joy!
NOVEMBER 1840

Zu Augsburg steht ein hohes Haus,
Nah' bei dem alten Dom,
Da tritt am hellen Morgen aus
Ein Mägdelein gar fromm;
  Gesang erschallt,
  Zum Dome wallt
  Die liebe Gestalt.

Dort vor Marias heilig Bild
Sie betend niederkniet,
Der Himmel hat ihr Herz erfüllt,
Und alle Weltlust flieht:
  „O Jungfrau rein!
  Laß mich allein
  Dein eigen sein!"

Alsbald der Glocken dumpfer Klang
Die Betenden erweckt,
Das Mägdlein wallt die Hall' entlang,
Es weiß nicht, was es trägt;
  Am Haupte, ganz
  Von Himmelsglanz,
  Einen Lilienkranz.

Mit Staunen schauen all die Leut'
Dies Kränzlein licht im Haar,
Das Mägdlein aber wallt nicht weit,

In Augsburg stands a lofty house
Nearby the old cathedral,
From where, one bright morning,
A devout young girl steps out;
  Hymns resound,
  The lovely figure
  Walks to the cathedral.

There before the Virgin Mary
She kneels down in prayer,
Heaven has pervaded her heart
And all worldly pleasures flee:
  'O Virgin pure!
  Let me be
  Yours alone!'

As soon as the sound of muffled bells
Summons the worshippers,
The young girl walks down the nave,
Not knowing what she wears;
  Upon her head
  A heavenly bright
  Lily crown.

All the people gaze in wonder
At her halo of bright flowers,
The young girl though only moves

Tritt vor den Hochaltar:
  „Zur Nonne weiht
  Mich arme Maid!
  Stirb, Lieb' und Freud'!"

Gott gib, daß dieses Mägdlein
Ihr Kränzlein friedlich trag'!
Es ist die Herzallerliebste mein,
Bleibt's bis zum jüngsten Tag.
  Sie weiß es nicht. –
  Mein Herz zerbricht –
  Stirb, Lieb' und Licht!
(*Spohr*)

As far as the high altar:
  'Take me, poor maid,
  To be a nun!
  Die, love and joy!'

God grant that this young girl
Might wear her crown in peace!
She is my own true love
And shall be till Judgment Day.
  She does not know. –
  My heart is breaking –
  Die, love and light!

3
Wanderlied / Song of travel
DECEMBER 1840

Wohlauf! noch getrunken
Den funkelnden Wein!
Ade nun, ihr Lieben!
Geschieden muß sein.
Ade nun, ihr Berge,
Du väterlich Haus!
Es treibt in die Ferne
Mich mächtig hinaus.

Come! One more draught
Of sparkling wine!
Farewell now, loved ones!
It's time to part.
Farewell now, you mountains,
You my father's house!
I've a great urge
To journey afar.

Die Sonne, sie bleibet
Am Himmel nicht stehn,
Es treibt sie, durch Länder
Und Meere zu gehn.
Die Woge nicht haftet
Am einsamen Strand,
Die Stürme, sie brausen
Mit Macht durch das Land.

The sun does not
Stand still in the sky,
But is urged to go
Over land and sea.
The waves don't cling
To the lonely shore,
And tempests roar
Mightily over the land.

Mit eilenden Wolken
Der Vogel dort zieht,
Und singt in der Ferne
Ein heimatlich Lied.
So treibt es den Burschen
Durch Wälder und Feld,
Zu gleichen der Mutter,
Der wandernden Welt.

The bird joins in flight
The scudding clouds,
And in a far-off land
Sings a homely song.
The young man too is urged,
Through forests and fields,
To match his mother,
The journeying earth.

Da grüßen ihn Vögel
Bekannt über'm Meer,
Sie flogen von Fluren
Der Heimat hieher;

Birds greet him as friends
Over the sea,
They flew from the fields
Of his native land;

Da duften die Blumen
Vertraulich um ihn,
Sie trieben vom Lande
Die Lüfte dahin.

Die Vögel die kennen
Sein väterlich Haus,
Die Blumen, die pflanzt' er
Der Liebe zum Strauß,
Und Liebe die folgt ihm,
Sie geht ihm zur Hand:
So wird ihm zur Heimat
Das ferneste Land.

He knows the scent
Of the flowers around him,
They were borne on the winds
Of his own country.

Those birds know well
His father's house,
He once planted those flowers
For his sweetheart's bouquet,
And love now follows,
And succours him:
Thus he feels at home
In the most distant of lands.

4
Erstes Grün / First green
DECEMBER 1840

Du junges Grün, du frisches Gras!
Wie manches Herz durch dich genas,
Das von des Winters Schnee erkrankt,
O wie mein Herz nach dir verlangt!

Schon wächst du aus der Erde Nacht,
Wie dir mein Aug' entgegen lacht!
Hier in des Waldes stillem Grund
Drück' ich dich, Grün, an Herz und Mund.

Wie treibt's mich von den Menschen fort!
Mein Leid das hebt kein Menschenwort;
Nur junges Grün, an's Herz gelegt,
Macht, daß mein Herze stiller schlägt.

You young green, you fresh grass!
How many hearts have you healed
That fell ill from the winter's snow,
O how my heart longs for you!

Already you wake from the earth's night,
How my eyes laugh to behold you!
Here in the forest's silent depths
I press you, O green, to my heart and lips.

How I'm driven to shun mankind!
No human word can ease my sorrow;
Only young grass laid on my heart
Can make it beat more calmly.

5
Sehnsucht nach der Waldgegend / Longing for woodland
c.NOVEMBER 1840

Wär' ich nie aus euch gegangen,
Wälder, hehr und wunderbar!
Hieltet liebend mich umfangen
Doch so lange, lange Jahr! –

Wo in euren Dämmerungen
Vogelsang und Silberquell,
Ist auch manches Lied entsprungen
Meinem Busen, frisch und hell;

Eure Wogen, euer Hallen,
Euer Säuseln nimmer müd,

Would that I had never left you,
Majestic, wondrous woods!
You surrounded me lovingly
For many a long year! –

Where in your twilit places
Birds and silvery streams were heard,
Many a song also flowed,
Fresh and bright, from my heart;

Your waving, your echoing,
Your untiring murmur,

| Eure Melodien alle | All your melodies |
| Weckten in der Brust das Lied. | Awoke in my breast the songs. |

Hier in diesen weiten Triften	Here in these wide pastures
Ist mir alles öd' und stumm,	All is desolate and silent,
Und ich schau' in blauen Lüften	And I search the blue skies
Mich nach Wolkenbildern um.	For any sign of cloud.

Wenn ihr's in den Busen zwinget,	If you try to force a song,
Regt sich selten nur das Lied;	It will seldom succeed;
Wie der Vogel halb nur singet,	Just as caged birds only half sing,
Den von Baum und Blatt man schied.	When severed from leafy trees.

6

Auf das Trinkglas eines verstorbenen Freundes* / To the wine glass of a departed friend
NOVEMBER 1840

Du herrlich Glas, nun stehst du leer,	Glorious glass, now you stand empty,
Glas, das er oft mit Lust gehoben;	Glass he raised often with delight;
Die Spinne hat rings um dich her	The spider meanwhile has spun
Indes den düstern Flor gewoben.	His sombre web around you.

Jetzt sollst du mir gefüllet sein	Now shall you be filled for me
Mondhell mit Gold der deutschen Reben!	Moonbright with the gold of German vines!
In deiner Tiefe heil'gen Schein	I tremble devoutly as I gaze
Schau' ich hinab mit frommem Beben.	Into the sacred lustre of your depths.

Was ich erschau' in deinem Grund	What I behold deep within you
Ist nicht Gewöhnlichen zu nennen,	Should not be told to ordinary mortals,
Doch wird mir klar zu dieser Stund',	Yet at this hour I realize
Wie nichts den Freund vom Freund kann	How nothing can part friend from
trennen.	friend.

Auf diesen Glauben, Glas so hold!	To that belief, then, sweetest glass!
Trink' ich dich aus mit hohem Mute.	I drain you in exalted mood.
Klar spiegelt sich der Sterne Gold,	Clear in your precious blood, O chalice,
Pokal, in deinem teuren Blute.	The golden stars are mirrored.

Still geht der Mond das Tal entlang,	The moon slips silently down the valley,
Ernst tönt die mitternächt'ge Stunde,	Gravely sounds the midnight hour,
Leer steht das Glas, der heil'ge Klang	The glass stands empty, the sacred sound
Tönt nach in dem kristall'nen Grunde.	Still echoes in its crystal depths.

7

Wanderung / Wandering
NOVEMBER 1840

| Wohlauf und frisch gewandert | Arise and travel briskly |
| Ins unbekannte Land! | Into unknown lands! |

* Kerner's poem is dedicated to his friend and patron Stierlein von Lorch.

Zerrissen, ach! zerrissen,
Ist manches teure Band.

Ihr heimatlichen Kreuze,
Wo ich oft betend lag,
Ihr Bäume, ach! ihr Hügel,
O blickt mir segnend nach!

Noch schläft die weite Erde,
Kein Vogel weckt den Hain,
Doch bin ich nicht verlassen,
Doch bin ich nicht allein:

Denn, ach! auf meinem Herzen
Trag' ich ihr teures Pfand,
Ich fühl's, und Erd' und Himmel
Sind innig mir verwandt.

Severed, ah! severed
Is many a true bond.

You crosses of my homeland,
Where often I prayed,
You trees, ah! you hills,
Give me your blessing as I go!

The wide world is still asleep,
No bird yet wakes the wood,
Yet I am not forsaken,
Yet I am not alone:

For ah! on my heart
I wear her precious pledge,
I press it, and earth and heaven
Are near and dear to me.

8
Stille Liebe / Silent love
NOVEMBER 1840

Könnt' ich dich in Liedern preisen,
Säng'ich dir das längste Lied,
Ja, ich würd' in allen Weisen
Dich zu singen, nimmer müd'.

Doch was immer mich betrübte,
Ist, daß ich nur immer stumm,
Tragen kann dich, Herzgeliebte!
In des Busens Heiligtum.

Dieser Schmerz hat mich bezwungen,
Daß ich sang dies kleine Lied,
Doch von bitterm Leid durchdrungen,
Daß noch keins auf dich geriet.

If I could praise you in songs,
I'd sing you the longest song,
Yes, I'd never tire of singing
Every tune in praise of you.

But to my eternal sadness
I can only carry you silently,
My dearest love,
In the shrine of my heart!

This anguish has compelled me
To sing you this little song,
Most bitterly regretting
That none has done you justice yet.

9
Frage / Question
c.NOVEMBER 1840

Wärst du nicht, heil'ger Abendschein!
Wärst du nicht, sternerhellte Nacht!
Du Blütenschmuck! du üpp'ger Hain!
Und du, Gebirg' voll ernster Pracht!
Du Vogelsang aus Himmeln hoch!
Du Lied aus voller Menschenbrust!
Wärst du nicht – ach! was füllte noch
In arger Zeit ein Herz mit Lust? –

If you did not exist, holy light of evening!
If you did not exist, starlit night!
You, flowery bouquets! You, lush groves!
And you, mountain ranges of grave splendour!
You, birdsong from heaven on high!
You, full-throated human song!
If you did not exist – ah! what could delight
The heart in adversity?

Stille Tränen / Silent tears
NOVEMBER 1840

Du bist vom Schlaf erstanden
Und wandelst durch die Au,
Da liegt ob allen Landen
Der Himmel wunderblau.

So lang du ohne Sorgen
Geschlummert schmerzenlos,
Der Himmel bis zum Morgen
Viel Tränen niedergoß.

In stillen Nächten weinet
Oft mancher aus den Schmerz,
Und Morgens dann ihr meinet,
Stets fröhlich sei sein Herz.

You have arisen from sleep
And wander through the meadow,
Over all the countryside
The sky lies wondrously blue.

While you slumbered free of care
And free of sorrow,
The sky shed many tears
Until morning dawned.

Many a man in silent nights
Will often weep out his sorrow,
And then in the morning you imagine
His heart is always happy.

Wer machte dich so krank? / Who made you so ill?
DECEMBER 1840

Daß du so krank geworden,
Wer hat es denn gemacht? –
Kein kühler Hauch aus Norden,
Und keine Sternennacht.

Kein Schatten unter Bäumen,
Nicht Glut des Sonnenstrahls,
Kein Schlummern und kein Träumen
Im Blütenbett' des Tals.

Daß ich trag' Todeswunden,
Das ist der Menschen Tun;
Natur ließ mich gesunden,
Sie lassen mich nicht ruhn.

Who has caused you
To become so ill?
No cool north wind,
No starlit night.

No shade-giving tree,
Nor heat of the sun,
Neither sleep nor dreams
Among the valley's flowers.

That I bear mortal wounds,
That is the work of men;
Nature healed me,
Mankind gives me no peace.

Alte Laute / Sounds from the past
DECEMBER 1840

Hörst du den Vogel singen?
Siehst du den Blütenbaum?
Herz! kann dich das nicht bringen
Aus deinem bangen Traum?

Was hör' ich? alte Laute
Wehmüt'ger Jünglingsbrust

Can you hear the bird singing?
Can you see the blossoming tree?
Can that not deliver you, O heart!
From your anxious dream?

What do I hear? Sounds from the past
From the breast of a melancholy young man,

| Der Zeit als ich vertraute | From the time when I trusted |
| Der Welt und ihrer Lust. | The world and its pleasures. |

D i e Tage sind vergangen,	*Those* days have now passed,
Mich heilt kein Kraut der Flur;	No meadow herb will heal me;
Und aus dem Traum, dem bangen,	And from my anxious dream
Weckt mich ein Engel nur.	Only an angel shall wake me.

Christian L'Egru (*fl.* 1850)

Little is known about the poet Christian L'Egru. He published a volume of verse entitled *Das Gewächshaus. Eine Sammlung selbstgezogener Blumen* in 1851, which contains neither 'Aufträge' nor 'Triolett', the two L'Egru poems set by Schumann. We know that on 6 April 1850 he sent Schumann some poems accompanied by this letter:

> Hochgeehrtester Herr!
> Ew. Wohlgeboren bin ich so frei, vorstehende Liedertexte zu übersenden. Es würde mich sehr glücklich machen, wenn Sie dieselben für werth hielten, durch Ihre Composition verherrlicht zu werden.
> Mit besondrer Hochachtung
> Ew. Wohlgeboren
> Ergebenster Diener
> Ch. L'Egru

> I take the liberty of sending you, sir, the enclosed song texts. It would make me very happy if you were to consider them worthy of the honour of being set to music by yourself.

Whether 'Aufträge' was among the poems sent the composer is unclear, but there is some evidence to show that it was. Six days after this letter, Schumann noted in the *Haushaltbuch* that he had composed 'Aufträge' – a song by L'egru [*sic*].

April 1850 Aufträge / Messages Op. 77, no. 5

Nicht so schnelle, nicht so schnelle!	Not so fast, not so fast!
Wart' ein wenig, kleine Welle!	Wait a moment, little wave!
Will dir einen Auftrag geben	I've a message to give you
An die Liebste mein.	For my sweetheart.
Wirst du ihr vorüberschweben,	If you glide past her,
Grüße sie mir fein!	Greet her fondly!

Sag, ich wäre mitgekommen,	Say I'd have come too,
Auf dir selbst herab geschwommen:	Sailing on your back:
Für den Gruß einen Kuß	And would have boldly
Kühn mir zu erbitten,	Begged a kiss for my greeting,

Doch der Zeit Dringlichkeit	But pressing time
Hätt' es nicht gelitten.	Did not allow it.

Nicht so eilig! halt! erlaube,	Not so fast! Stop! Allow me,
Kleine, leichtbeschwingte Taube!	Little light-winged dove,
Habe dir was aufzutragen	To entrust you with something
An die Liebste mein!	For my sweetheart!
Sollst ihr tausend Grüße sagen,	Give her a thousand greetings,
Hundert obendrein.	And a hundred more.

Sag, ich wär' mit dir geflogen,	Say, I'd have flown with you
Über Berg und Strom gezogen:	Over mountain and river:
Für den Gruß einen Kuß	And would have boldly
Kühn mir zu erbitten;	Begged a kiss for my greeting,
Doch der Zeit Dringlichkeit	But pressing time
Hätt' es nicht gelitten.	Did not allow it.

Warte nicht, daß ich dich treibe,	Don't wait for me to drive you on,
O du träge Mondesscheibe!	You lazy old moon!
Weißt's ja, was ich dir befohlen	You know what I ordered you to do
Für die Liebste mein:	For my sweetheart:
Durch das Fensterchen verstohlen	Peep secretly through the window-pane
Grüße sie mir fein!	And give her my love!

Sag, ich wär' auf dich gestiegen,	Say I'd have climbed on you
Selber zu ihr hinzufliegen:	And flown to her in person:
Für den Gruß einen Kuß	And would have boldly
Kühn mir zu erbitten,	Begged a kiss for my greeting,
Du seist schuld, Ungeduld	That it's my fault
Hätt' mich nicht gelitten.	Impatience did not allow it.

Nikolaus Lenau (1802–50)

Perhaps the most melancholy of all German poets, Nikolaus Franz Niembsch, Edler von Strehlenau (the pseudonym Lenau is derived from the final two syllables) was the son of a dissipated Austrian cavalry officer and a middle-class Hungarian girl from a good family. He lost his father when he was five and suffered in his youth from deep depressions. He studied numerous subjects at several different universities and qualified in none. On receiving a substantial inheritance in 1830, he moved to Stuttgart, where he was in regular contact with Uhland, Schwab and, above all, Kerner.

Disappointed by the social and political conditions in Austria, he emigrated in 1832 to America where he tried unsuccessfully to become a farmer. On his return to Stuttgart, he fell in love with Sophie von Löwenthal, and though he remained devoted to her for the rest of his life, he soon became engaged to the singer Caroline Unger. When that relationship failed, he became engaged once more, this time to Marie Behrends, after which he suffered a mental breakdown in 1844 and entered the asylum at Winnental. Though Lenau published several epics such as *Faust. Ein Gedicht* (1836), *Savonarola* (1837), *Die Albingenser* (1842) and *Don Juan*, which was published posthumously in 1851, he is best remembered by his lyric poetry that has attracted numerous composers, most notably Berg, Franz, Liszt, Mendelssohn, Pfitzner, Schoeck, Strauss and Wolf. Schumann was convinced, when composing his Lenau songs, that the poet had already died, and 'Requiem' (see p. 444) was appended to the group as a tribute to the 'dead' poet. News of his actual death reached Schumann during the first performance of Op. 90 at the house of Eduard Bendemann in Dresden, where Robert and Clara were being fêted before their departure to Düsseldorf. Schumann now wrote urgently to Kistner, requesting him to publish Op. 90 as quickly as possible to mark the poet's death:

> Es soll mich freuen, wenn Sie mir die Hand reichten, dem unglücklichen, aber so herrlichen Dichter mit diesem Werk ein kleines Denkmal zu setzen.

> I should be pleased if you could help me furnish with this work a small monument to the unhappy but marvellous poet.

August 1850 *Sechs Gedichte von N. Lenau / Six poems of N. Lenau* Op. 90

1
Lied eines Schmiedes / Blacksmith's song
FROM *Faust*

Fein Rößlein, ich	Fine little steed,
Beschlage dich,	You'll soon be shod,
Sei frisch und fromm,	Be frisky and good,
Und wieder komm!	And come back again!
Trag deinen Herrn	Carry your master
Stets treu dem Stern,	Ever true to the star
Der seiner Bahn	That shines brightly
Hell glänzt voran!	On his path!
Trag auf dem Ritt	With each step
Mit jedem Tritt	As you go,
Den Reiter du	Carry your rider
Dem Himmel zu!	Nearer heaven!
Nun, Rößlein, ich	There, little steed,
Beschlagen dich,	Now you're shod,
Sei frisch und fromm,	Be frisky and good,
Und wieder komm!	And come back again!

2
Meine Rose / My rose

Dem holden Lenzgeschmeide,	To spring's fair jewel,

Der Rose, meiner Freude,
Die schon gebeugt und blasser
Vom heißen Strahl der Sonnen,
Reich' ich den Becher Wasser
Aus dunklem, tiefen Bronnen.

Du Rose meines Herzens!
Vom stillen Strahl des Schmerzens
Bist du gebeugt und blasser;
Ich möchte dir zu Füßen,
Wie dieser Blume Wasser,
Still meine Seele gießen!
Könnt' ich dann auch nicht sehen
Dich freudig auferstehen.

To the rose, my delight,
Already drooping and pale
From the heat of the sun,
I bring a beaker of water
From the deep, dark well.

Rose of my heart!
You droop and pale
From the silent shaft of pain;
I would silently pour out
My soul at your feet,
As I pour water for this flower!
Even though I might not then
See you happily revive.

3
Kommen und Scheiden / Meeting and parting

So oft sie kam, erschien mir die Gestalt
So lieblich wie das erste Grün im Wald.

Each time we met, the sight of her
Seemed as dear as the first green in the wood.

Und was sie sprach, drang mir zum Herzen ein
Süß wie des Frühlings erstes Lied.

And what she said, pierced my heart
As sweetly as the spring's first song.

Und als Lebwohl sie winkte mit der Hand,
War's, ob der letzte Jugendtraum mir schwand.
(*Hensel, Schoeck*)

And when she waved to me in parting,
Youth's last dream seemed to vanish.

4
Die Sennin / The cowgirl

Schöne Sennin, noch einmal
Singe deinen Ruf ins Tal,
Daß die frohe Felsensprache
Deinem hellen Ruf erwache.

Lovely cowgirl, sing once more
Your song into the valley,
That the cliffs wake with joyful speech
At your clear summons.

Horch, o Sennin, wie dein Sang
In die Brust den Bergen drang,
Wie dein Wort die Felsenseelen
Freudig fort und fort erzählen!

Listen, girl, how your song
Has pierced the heart of the mountains,
How the souls of the crags joyfully
Keep echoing your words!

Aber einst, wie Alles flieht,
Scheidest du mit deinem Lied,
Wenn dich Liebe fortbewogen,
Oder dich der Tod entzogen.

But all things pass, and one day
You will depart with your song,
When love has drawn you away
Or death has claimed you.

Und verlassen werden stehn,
Traurig stumm herübersehn
Dort die grauen Felsenzinnen
Und auf deine Lieder sinnen.

And the towering grey crags
Will then stand deserted,
Sadly looking down in silence,
Remembering your songs.

5

Einsamkeit / Solitude

Wild verwachs'ne dunkle Fichten,	A wild tangle of dark spruce,
Leise klagt die Quelle fort;	The fountain's soft and ceaseless lament;
Herz, das ist der rechte Ort	Heart, this is a fitting place
Für dein schmerzliches Verzichten!	For your painful renunciation!
Grauer Vogel in den Zweigen,	A grey bird alone in the branches
Einsam deine Klage singt,	Sings of your sorrow,
Und auf deine Frage bringt	And to your questioning
Antwort nicht des Waldes Schweigen.	The silent forest brings no reply.
Wenn's auch immer Schweigen bliebe,	Even if silence reigned forever,
Klage, klage fort; es weht,	Continue, continue your lament;
Der dich höret und versteht,	The spirit of love blows silently here,
Stille hier der Geist der Liebe.	It hears and understands you.
Nicht verloren hier im Moose,	Heart, your secret weeping
Herz, dein heimlich Weinen geht,	Is not lost here amongst the moss,
Deine Liebe Gott versteht,	God understands your love,
Deine tiefe, hoffnungslose!	Your deep and hopeless love!

6

Der schwere Abend / The oppressive evening

Die dunklen Wolken hingen	The dark clouds hung
Herab so bang und schwer,	So anxiously and heavy,
Wir beide traurig gingen	We both walked up and down
Im Garten hin und her.	Sadly in the garden.
So heiß und stumm, so trübe	The night was so sultry and silent,
Und sternlos war die Nacht,	So gloomy and starless,
So ganz wie unsre Liebe	Just like our love,
Zu Tränen nur gemacht.	Fit only for tears.
Und als ich mußte scheiden,	And when I had to leave
Und gute Nacht dir bot,	And bade you good night,
Wünscht' ich bekümmert beiden	I wished us both dead
Im Herzen uns den Tod.	In the anguish of my heart.
(Franz, Schoeck)	

Mary, Queen of Scots (1542–87)

These five poems, attributed to Mary, Queen of Scots, cover over twenty-five years of her life. At the age of five she was sent to France where, on the accession of François II in 1559, she became Queen of France, Scotland and, due to the technical illegitimacy of Elizabeth Tudor, England. When François died in 1560, she was sent back to Scotland, although she wished to remain in France ('Abschied von

Frankreich'). She was permitted to practise her own Catholic religion in Scotland, but life there became increasingly difficult when, having married the dissolute Henry, Lord Darnley, in July 1565, she turned for emotional support to the Italian musician David Rizzio, who was murdered by Darnley's men in her presence, when she was six months pregnant. 'Nach der Geburt ihres Sohnes' describes the birth of her son (Darnley suspected that Rizzio was the father) who was almost immediately taken away from her. Three months after Darnley was murdered on 9 February 1567 (probably by the Scottish nobles who detested him), Mary married James Hepburn, Earl of Bothwell – a decision which her enemies interpreted as complicity in Darnley's murder. Mary and Bothwell were captured in June 1567, Bothwell was imprisoned in Denmark, Mary on the island of Loch Leven, from where she escaped. Her supporters rallied to her cause but were defeated at the battle of Langside in May 1568. Mary now decided to plead with Elizabeth I for mercy. On 16 May 1568 she crossed the Solway Firth, but was detained in Carlisle Castle, from where she wrote some twenty letters to her 'Chère sœur' and a poem, 'An die Königin Elisabeth' (in Baron Gisbert Vincke's translation). Her request for an audience was not granted. The so-called 'casket letters' were produced to 'prove' her complicity in Darnley's murder, and for the next eighteen years of her life Mary languished in a number of English prisons. 'Abschied von der Welt' is an expression of her helplessness, despair and realisation that only death will release her from suffering. Death was not long in coming. Realizing that Mary's continued presence in England was an encouragement to those who wished to restore Catholic rule in England, Walsingham tricked her into becoming involved in the Babington Plot of 1586. She was put on trial for treason. Queen Elizabeth, after months of temporizing, finally signed the death warrant, and Mary was given less than twelve hours to prepare for the end. According to legend, the poem 'Gebet' was written in Latin a few hours before her execution on the morning of 8 February 1587. She was forty-four years old.

December 1852 *Gedichte der Königin Maria Stuart / Poems of Mary, Queen of Scots* Op. 135
TRANSLATED BY GISBERT FREIHERR VON VINCKE (1813–92)

1

Abschied von Frankreich / Farewell to France

Ich zieh dahin!	I am going away!
Ade, mein fröhlich Frankenland,	Farewell, my happy France,
Wo ich die liebste Heimat fand,	Where I found the dearest homeland,
Du meiner Kindheit Pflegerin!	You the guardian of my childhood!
Ade, du Land, du schöne Zeit –	Farewell, O land, O happy time –
Mich trennt das Boot vom Glück so weit!	The ship bears me far away from joy!
Doch trägt's die Hälfte nur von mir:	Yet it takes but half of me:
Ein Teil für immer bleibet dein,	One part will be forever yours,

Mein fröhlich Land, der sage dir,
Des andern eingedenk zu sein!
Ade!

My happy land, and it asks you
Always to remember me!
Farewell!

2
Nach der Geburt ihres Sohnes / After the birth of her son

Herr Jesu Christ, den sie gekrönt mit Dornen,
Beschütze die Geburt des hier Gebornen.
Und sei's dein Will', laß sein Geschlecht
    zugleich
Lang herrschen noch in diesem Königreich,
Und Alles, was geschieht in seinem Namen,
Sei dir zu Ruhm und Preis und Ehre, Amen.

Lord Jesus Christ, whom they crowned with
    thorns,
Protect this new-born boy.
And, if it be Thy will, let his race
Long rule in this realm.
And let all that is done in his name
Be to Thy glory, praise and honour, Amen.

3
An die Königin Elisabeth / To Queen Elizabeth

Nur ein Gedanke, der mich freut und quält,
Hält ewig mir den Sinn gefangen,
So daß der Furcht und Hoffnung Stimmen
    klangen,
Als ich die Stunden ruhelos gezählt.

One thought alone gladdens and grieves me
And always dominates my mind,
So that the voices of fear and hope
    resounded,
When sleepless I counted the hours.

Und wenn mein Herz dies Blatt zum Boten
    wählt,
Und kündet, Euch zu sehen, mein Verlangen,
Dann, teure Schwester, faßt mich neues Bangen,
Weil ihm die Macht, es zu beweisen, fehlt.

And when my heart chooses this letter as
    messenger,
Revealing how I long to see you,
Then, dear sister, a new anguish seizes me,
Because the letter lacks the power to prove it.

Ich seh' den Kahn, im Hafen fast geborgen,
Vom Sturm und Kampf der Wogen festge-
    halten,
Des Himmels heit'res Antlitz nachtumgraut.
So bin auch ich bewegt von Furcht und Sorgen,
Vor Euch nicht, Schwester! Doch des Schick-
    sals Walten
Zerreißt das Segel oft, dem wir vertraut.

I see the boat half hidden in the harbour,
Held back by the storm and warring waves,
And heaven's serene face blackened by
    night.
So am I likewise beset by cares and fear,
Not of you, my sister! But the force of
    fate
Often lacerates the sail in which we trust.

4
Abschied von der Welt / Farewell to the world

Was nützt die mir noch zugemess'ne Zeit?
Mein Herz erstarb für irdisches Begehren,
Nur Leiden soll mein Schatten nicht ent-
    behren,
Mir blieb allein die Todesfreudigkeit.

What use is the time still allotted me?
My heart is dead to earthly desires,
My shadow is severed from all but
    sorrow,
The joy of death alone remains.

Ihr Feinde, laßt von eurem Neid:	Cease envying me, O enemies:
Mein Herz ist abgewandt der Hoheit Ehren,	My heart abjures all honour and nobility,
Des Schmerzes Übermaß wird mich verzehren,	Excess of anguish will devour me,
Bald geht mit mir zu Grabe Haß und Streit.	Hatred and schism will soon be buried with me.
Ihr Freunde, die ihr mein gedenkt in Liebe,	O friends, who will remember me with love,
Erwägt und glaubt, daß ohne Kraft und Glück	Consider and believe that without power or fortune
Kein gutes Werk mir zu vollenden bliebe.	There is nothing good I can achieve.
So wünscht mir bess're Tage nicht zurück,	So do not wish for the return of happier days,
Und weil ich schwer gestrafet werd' hienieden,	And because I've been sorely punished here on earth,
Erfleht mir meinen Teil am ew'gen Frieden!	Pray that a share of eternal peace might be mine!

5
Gebet / Prayer

O Gott, mein Gebieter,	O Lord God,
Ich hoffe auf Dich!	I put my trust in Thee!
O Jesu, Geliebter,	O beloved Jesus,
Nun rette Du mich!	Rescue me!
Im harten Gefängnis,	In my harsh prison,
In schlimmer Bedrängnis	In dire affliction
Ersehne ich Dich;	I long for Thee;
In Klagen dir klagend,	Lamenting I cry to Thee,
Im Staube verzagend,	Despairing in the dust,
Erhör, ich beschwöre,	Hearken, I implore Thee,
Und rette Du mich!	And rescue me!

Robert Reinick (1805–52)

See Brahms, Wolf

Schumann and Reinick first met in 1845 and soon became close friends: there were many reciprocal visits and in 1848 Reinick became godfather to Ludwig Schumann. Reinick spent some time writing an opera libretto (*Genoveva*) for Schumann, but his contribution eventually came to nothing.

July–August 1840 *Sechs Lieder nach R. Reinick / Six songs to poems by R. Reinick* **Op. 36**

1

Sonntags am Rhein / Sunday on the Rhine

Des Sonntags in der Morgenstund'	How good to walk beside the Rhine

Wie wandert's sich so schön
Am Rhein, wenn rings in weiter Rund'
Die Morgenglocken gehn!

   Ein Schifflein zieht auf blauer Flut,
Da singt's und jubelt's drein;
Du Schifflein, gelt, das fährt sich gut
In all die Lust hinein?

   Vom Dorfe hallet Orgelton,
Es tönt ein frommes Lied,
Andächtig dort die Prozession
Aus der Kapelle zieht.

   Und ernst in all die Herrlichkeit
Die Burg hernieder schaut
Und spricht von alter, guter Zeit,
Die auf den Fels gebaut.

   Das alles beut der prächt'ge Rhein
An seinem Rebenstrand,
Und spiegelt recht im hellsten Schein
Das ganze Vaterland,

   Das fromme, treue Vaterland
In seiner vollen Pracht,
Mit Lust und Liedern allerhand
Vom lieben Gott bedacht.

On Sunday at the break of day,
When ringing out for miles around
The morning bells resound!

   A skiff floats by on blue waves,
Amid singing and rejoicing;
Is it not good, O little ship,
To sail into such happiness?

   The village organ rings out
With its solemn hymn,
The procession, reverently,
Sets out from the church.

   And grave in the midst of such splendour
The castle gazes down
And tells of the good old days
When men built on firm rock.

   The mighty Rhine offers all this
On its vine-clad shore,
And mirrors in brightest reflection
All the fatherland,

   That fatherland, devout and true,
In its splendid glory,
With all kinds of joy and song,
Protected by God's dear hand.

2
Ständchen / Serenade

Komm' in die stille Nacht! –
   Liebchen! was zögerst du?
   Sonne ging längst zur Ruh',
   Welt schloß die Augen zu,
Rings nur einzig die Liebe wacht!

Liebchen, was zögerst du?
   Schon sind die Sterne hell,
   Schon ist der Mond zur Stell',
   Eilen so schnell, so schnell!
Liebchen, mein Liebchen, drum eil' auch du!

Einzig die Liebe wacht,
   Ruft dich allüberall;
   Höre die Nachtigall,
   Hör' meiner Stimme Schall,
Liebchen, o komm in die stille Nacht!
(*Lassen, Wolf*)

Come into the silent night! –
   Why delay, my dearest?
   The sun has set long ago,
   The world has closed its eyes.
Love alone keeps watch around us!

Why delay, my dearest?
   Already the stars are bright,
   Already the moon's at her post,
   They make such haste, such haste!
Dearest, my dearest, so make haste too!

Love alone keeps watch,
   Calling for you everywhere;
   Listen to the nightingale,
   Listen to my voice ring out,
Dearest, O come into the silent night!

3
Nichts Schöneres / Nothing more beautiful

Als ich zuerst dich hab' gesehn,
Wie du so lieblich warst, so schön,
Da fiel's mein Lebtag mir nicht ein,
Daß noch was Schön'res sollte sein,
Als in dein liebes Augenpaar
Hinein zu schauen immerdar.

Da hab' ich denn so lang' geschaut,
Bis du geworden meine Braut;
Und wieder fiel es mir nicht ein,
Daß noch was Schön'res könnte sein,
Als so an deinem roten Mund
Sich satt zu küssen alle Stund.

Da hab' ich denn so lang' geküßt,
Bis du mein Weibchen worden bist,
Und kann nun wohl versichert sein,
Daß noch was Schön'res nicht kann sein,
Als wie mit seinem lieben Weib
Zu sein so ganz ein' Seel' und Leib!
(*Spohr*)

When first I saw you,
Saw how sweet and beautiful you were,
I did not think in all my days
That anything could be more beautiful
Than to gaze for evermore
Into your lovely eyes.

But then I gazed on you so long
Till you became my bride;
And again I did not think in all my days
That any thing could be more beautiful
Than to kiss your red lips endlessly
Till I was surfeited.

But then I kissed you so long
Till you became my wife,
And now I may rest assured
That nothing could be more beautiful
Than to be entirely at one with a dear wife
In body and in soul!

4
An den Sonnenschein / To the sunshine

O Sonnenschein! o Sonnenschein!
Wie scheinst du mir ins Herz hinein,
Weckst drinnen lauter Liebeslust,
Daß mir so enge wird die Brust!

Und enge wird mir Stub' und Haus,
Und wenn ich lauf' zum Tor hinaus,
Da lockst du gar ins frische Grün
Die allerschönsten Mädchen hin!

O Sonnenschein! Du glaubest wohl,
Daß ich wie du es machen soll,
Der jede schmucke Blume küßt,
Die eben nur sich dir erschließt?

Hast doch so lang' die Welt erblickt,
Und weißt, daß sich's für mich nicht schickt;
Was machst du mir denn solche Pein?
O Sonnenschein! o Sonnenschein!

O sunshine! O sunshine!
How you shine into my heart,
Waking there such sheer love
That my breast becomes constricted!

House and room become constricted too,
And when I run out through the gate,
I see you've tempted the loveliest girls
Out into the fresh green countryside!

O sunshine! Do you really think
I should follow your example,
You that kiss all the lovely flowers
That only open to your caress?

But you have observed the world so long
And know that this does not become me;
So why do you torment me so?
O sunshine! O sunshine!

5

Dichters Genesung / The poet's recovery

Und wieder hatt' ich der Schönsten gedacht,
Die nur in Träumen bisher ich gesehen;
Es trieb mich hinaus in die lichte Nacht,
Durch stille Gründe mußt' ich gehen:
  Da auf einmal
  Glänzte das Tal,
  Schaurig, als wär es ein Geistersaal.

Da rauschten zusammen zur Tanzmelodei
Der Strom und die Winde mit Klingen und
  Zischen,
Da weht' es im flüchtigen Zuge herbei
Aus Felsen und Tale, aus Wellen und Büschen,
  Und im Mondesglanz
  Ein weißer Kranz
  Tanzten die Elfen den Reigentanz.

Und mitten im Kreis' ein luftiges Weib,
Die Königin war es, ich hörte sie singen:
„Laß ab von dem schweren irdischen Leib!
Laß ab von den törichten irdischen Dingen!
  Nur im Mondenschein
  Ist Leben allein!
  Nur im Träumen zu schweben ein ewiges
Sein!

Ich bin's, die in Träumen du oft gesehn,
Ich bin's, die als Liebchen du oft besungen,
Ich bin es, die Elfenkönigin,
Du wolltest mich schauen, es ist dir gelungen!
  Nun sollst du mein
  Auf ewig sein.
  Komm' mit, komm' mit in den Elfen-
reihn!"

Schon zogen, schon flogen sie all um mich
  her,
Da wehte der Morgen, da bin ich genesen.
Fahr' wohl nun, du Elfenkönigin,
Jetzt will ein andres Lieb ich mir erlesen;
  Ohn Trug und Schein
  Und von Herzen rein
  Wird wohl auch für mich eins zu finden
sein!

And once again I thought of my beloved,
Whom till then I had seen but in dreams;
I was drawn out into the bright night,
I had to wander through silent valleys:
  Then suddenly
  The valley began to gleam
  Eerily, like a hall full of ghosts.

The river and winds whistled together a
  dance melody
With a hissing and a roar.
A fleeting throng came rushing by
From rocks and valleys, bushes and waves,
  And in the moonlight,
  Like a white wreath,
  The elves began to dance their rounds.

And I heard in their midst an airy
  maiden,
The Queen of the Elves, begin to sing:
'Leave your heavy earthly body!
Leave all foolish earthly things!
  Only in moonlight
  Can true life be found!
  Eternity only in floating dreams!

I am she you've often seen in dreams,
I am she you've often hymned as your love,
I am the Queen of the Elves,
You wanted to see me – your wish is fulfilled!
  You shall now be mine
  For evermore,
  Come, come dance with me in our fairy
ring!'

They were fluttering and flying all around
  me now,
Then the dawn wind blew, and I recovered.
Farewell now, O Queen of the Elves,
For now I shall choose another love;
  Without deceit and wiles,
  And pure of heart,
  There must be one out there for me!

Liebesbotschaft / A message of love

Wolken, die ihr nach Osten eilt,
Wo die Eine, die Meine, die Eine weilt,
All meine Wünsche, mein Hoffen und Singen
Sollen auf eure Flügel sich schwingen,
    Sollen euch, Flüchtige,
    Zu ihr lenken,
    Daß die Züchtige
Meiner in Treuen mag gedenken!

Singen noch Morgenträume sie ein,
Schwebet leise zum Garten hinein,
Senket als Tau euch in schattige Räume,
Streuet Perlen auf Blumen und Bäume,
    Daß der Holdseligen,
    Kommt sie gegangen,
    All die fröhlichen
Blüten sich öffnen mit lichterem Prangen!

Und am Abend in stiller Ruh'
Breitet der sinkenden Sonne euch zu!
Mögt mit Purpur und Gold euch malen,
Mögt in dem Meere von Gluten und Strahlen
    Leicht sich schwingende
    Schifflein fahren,
    Daß sie singende
Engel glaubt auf euch zu gewahren.

Ja, wohl möchten es Engel sein,
Wär mein Herz gleich ihrem rein;
All meine Wünsche, mein Hoffen und Singen
Zieht ja dahin auf euren Schwingen,
    Euch, ihr Flüchtigen,
    Hinzulenken,
    Zu der Züchtigen,
Der ich einzig nur mag gedenken!
(*Wolf*)

You clouds that hasten eastwards
To where my own love lives,
All my wishes, hopes and songs
Shall go flying on your wings,
    Shall lead you,
    Fleeting messengers, to her,
    That the chaste child
Shall faithfully think of me!

If morning dreams still lull her asleep,
Drift gently down into her garden,
Alight as dew in the shadows,
Strew pearls on flowers and trees,
    So that if my sweetheart
    Passes by,
    She shall see all the joyous flowers
Bud in even brighter splendour!

And at evening, in calm and silence,
Sail away to the setting sun!
Paint yourselves in purple and gold,
Immersed in the sea of bright fire,
    Lightly swinging
    Like little ships,
    That she might think
You are singing angels.

And well might my thoughts be angels,
If my heart were as pure as hers;
All my wishes, hopes and songs
Shall go flying on your wings,
    Shall lead you,
    Fleeting messengers, to her,
    The chaste child,
I think of all the time!

Friedrich Rückert (1788–1866)

See Brahms, Mahler

Greatly influenced by Joseph Hammer-Purgstall, Rückert studied Arabic, Turk-ish and Persian and in 1826 was appointed Professor of Oriental Languages and Literature at the University of Erlangen. Rückert's huge output includes a versi-fied 'Life of Jesus', translations and adaptations of oriental literature and more than ten thousand poems. *Östliche Rosen*, written in 1822, was dedicated to Goethe, whose *West-östlicher Divan* had appeared in 1819. Schumann selected several songs from this collection, including 'Aus den Östlichen Rosen' in *Myrten*, but it was the four hundred or so poems from Rückert's *Liebesfrühling* (1823) that especially appealed to Schumann. These poems, which celebrate Rückert's love for Luise Wiethaus-Fischer (whom he married in 1821) were an ideal choice for Schumann who had just married Clara. In 1841 he wrote to his publishers, Breitkopf und Härtel:

> Ich möchte meiner Frau an ihrem Geburtstag, der Mitte September fällt, eine kleine Freude bereiten mit Folgendem: Wir haben zusammen eine Anzahl Rückertscher Lieder componiert, die sich wie Fragen aufeinander beziehen. Diese Sammlung hätte ich nun gern an jenem Tag gedruckt beschert. Ist es Ihnen nun möglich, das Heft bis zu jener Zeit fertig zu bringen? Ich denke mir, die Lieder müssen Interesse erregen; auch sind sie fast durchgängig leicht und einfach gehalten, und recht mit Lust und Liebe geschrieben.

> I should like to surprise my wife on her birthday – in mid-September – in the following manner. We have composed a number of Rückert songs together in the form of questions and answers. I should like to see this collection in print by her birthday. Would it be possible to have the volume ready by that time? These songs should arouse interest; they are kept light and simple throughout, and were written with much joy and love.

March 1840 Jasminenstrauch / The jasmine bush Op. 27, no. 4

Grün ist der Jasminenstrauch	The jasmine bush was green
Abends eingeschlafen.	As it fell asleep last night.
Als ihn mit des Morgens Hauch	When woken by the morning breeze
Sonnenlichter trafen,	And sunlight,
Ist er schneeweiß aufgewacht:	It was snowy white:
„Wie geschah mir in der Nacht?"	'What happened to me overnight?'
Seht, so geht es Bäumen,	That, you see, is the fate of trees
Die im Frühling träumen!	Which dream in Spring!

c.March 1840 Volksliedchen / Folksong Op. 51, no. 2

Wenn ich früh in den Garten geh'	When at dawn I enter the garden,
In meinem grünen Hut,	Wearing my green hat,
Ist mein erster Gedanke,	My thoughts first turn
Was nun mein Liebster tut?	To what my love is doing.
Am Himmel steht kein Stern,	Every star in the sky
Den ich dem Freund nicht gönnte.	I'd give to my friend.
Mein Herz gäb' ich ihm gern,	I'd willingly give him my very heart,
Wenn ich's heraustun könnte.	If I could tear it out.

January 1841 *Zwölf Gedichte aus Rückerts* Liebesfrühling / *Twelve poems from Rückert's* Love's springtime Op. 37

1

Der Himmel hat eine Träne geweint / Heaven shed a tear

Der Himmel hat eine Träne geweint,
Die hat sich ins Meer verlieren gemeint.
Die Muschel kam und schloß sie ein;
Du sollst nun meine Perle sein.
Du sollst nicht vor den Wogen zagen,
Ich will hindurch dich ruhig tragen.
O du mein Schmerz, du meine Lust,
Du Himmelstärn' in meiner Brust!
Gib, Himmel, daß ich in reinem Gemüte
Den reinsten deiner Tropfen hüte!
(*Franz, Reger*)

Heaven shed a tear
That thought to lose itself in the sea.
The seashell came and locked it in;
My pearl shall you now be.
You shall not fear the waves,
I shall bear you calmly through them.
O you, my pain, O you, my joy,
You tear of heaven in my breast!
Grant, heaven, that with pure soul
I might guard the purest of your drops!

2

Er ist gekommen in Sturm und Regen / He came in storm and rain

See Clara Schumann, p. 430

3

O ihr Herren / O you lords

O ihr Herren, o ihr werten
  Großen, reichen Herren all!
  Braucht in euren schönen Gärten
  Ihr denn keine Nachtigall?
Hier ist eine, die ein stilles
  Plätzchen sucht die Welt entlang!
  Räumt mir eines ein, ich will es
  Euch bezahlen mit Gesang.

O you lords, O all you worthy,
  Great and wealthy lords!
  Have you no need in your beautiful gardens
  Of a single nightingale?
Here is one who searches
  For a quiet corner throughout the world!
  Grant me but this, and I shall
  Repay you with song.

4

Liebst du um Schönheit / If you love for beauty

See Gustav Mahler, p. 208

5

Ich hab' in mich gesogen / I have drawn into myself

Ich hab' in mich gesogen
  Den Frühling treu und lieb,
  Daß er, der Welt entflogen,
  Hier in der Brust mir blieb.
Hier sind die blauen Lüfte,
  Hier sind die grünen Aun,

I have drawn into myself
  The sweet and loyal spring,
  That, having fled the world,
  It might dwell here in my heart.
Here are blue skies,
  Here are green meadows,

Die Blumen hier, die Düfte,
Der blüh'nde Rosenzaun.
Und hier am Busen lehnet
Mit süßem Liebesach
Die Liebste, die sich sehnet
Den Frühlingswonnen nach.
Sie lehnt sich an, zu lauschen
Und hört in stiller Lust
Die Frühlingsströme rauschen
In ihres Dichters Brust.
Da quellen auf die Lieder
Und strömen über sie
Den vollsten Frühling nieder,
Den mir der Gott verlieh.
Und wie sie, davon trunken,
Umblicket rings im Raum,
Blüht auch von ihren Funken
Die Welt, ein Frühlingstraum.
(*Franz*)

Here the flowers, here the scents,
The flowering hedge of roses.
And here, leaning on my breast
With sighs of sweetest love,
Is my sweetheart, longing
For springtime rapture.
She leans against me, listens
And hears with quiet joy
The streams of spring
Flow into my, her poet's, heart.
And then my songs arise,
Pouring over her
The full spate
Of God-given spring.
And as she, intoxicated,
Gazes all around her,
The world blossoms too –
A spring dream lit by her joy.

6
Liebste, was kann denn uns scheiden? / Dearest, what can part us?

Liebste, was kann denn uns scheiden?
  Kann's das Meiden?
  Kann uns Meiden scheiden? Nein.
Ob wir uns zu sehn vermieden,
Ungeschieden
Wollen wir im Herzen sein.
  Mein und dein,
  Dein und mein,
  Wollen wir, o Liebste, sein.
Liebste, was kann denn uns scheiden?
  Wald und Haiden?
  Kann die Fern' uns scheiden? Nein.
Unsre Lieb' ist nicht hienieden;
Ungeschieden
Wollen wir im Himmel sein.
  Mein und dein,
  Dein und mein,
  Wollen wir, o Liebste, sein.
Liebste, was kann denn uns scheiden?
  Glück und Leiden?
  Kann uns beides scheiden? Nein.
Sei mir Glück, sei Weh beschieden,
Ungeschieden
Soll mein Los von deinem sein.
  Mein und dein,

Dearest, what can part us?
  Can separation?
  Can separation part us? No.
Though we decline to see each other,
We wish to be
United in our hearts.
  Mine and thine,
  Thine and mine,
  Is what, my love, we wish to be.
Dearest, what can part us?
  Forest and heath?
  Can distance part us? No.
Our love is not of this earth;
We wish to be
United in heaven.
  Mine and thine,
  Thine and mine
  Is what, my love, we wish to be.
Dearest, what can part us?
  Happiness and sorrow?
  Can both part us? No.
Whether happiness or grief be granted me,
My fate shall be
United with yours.
  Mine and thine,

Dein und mein,
Wollen wir, o Liebste, sein.
Liebste, was kann denn uns scheiden?
Haß und Neiden?
Kann die Welt uns scheiden? Nein.
Niemand störe deinen Frieden,
Ungeschieden
Wollen wir auf ewig sein.
Mein und dein,
Dein und mein,
Wollen wir, o Liebste, sein.

Thine and mine
Is what, my love, we wish to be.
Dearest, what can part us?
Hatred and envy?
Can the world part us? No.
Let no one disturb your peace!
We shall be
United forever.
Mine and thine,
Thine and mine
Is what, my love, we wish to be.

7
Schön ist das Fest des Lenzes / Fair is the festival of spring [Duet]

Schön ist das Fest des Lenzes.
Doch währt es nur der Tage drei!
Hast du ein Lieb, bekränz es
Mit Rosen, eh' sie gehn vorbei!
Hast du ein Glas, kredenz es,
O Schenk, und singe mir dabei:
Schön ist das Fest des Lenzes,
Doch währt es nur der Tage drei!

Fair is the festival of spring.
Yet it only lasts three days!
If you have a love, garland her
With roses, before they fade!
If you have a goblet, offer it,
Mine host, and in doing so, sing to me:
Fair is the festival of spring.
Yet it only lasts three days!

8
Flügel! Flügel! um zu fliegen / Wings! Wings!

Flügel! Flügel! um zu fliegen
 Über Berg und Tal,
 Flügel, um mein Herz zu wiegen
 Auf des Morgens Strahl.
Flügel, übers Meer zu schweben
 Mit dem Morgenrot,
 Flügel, Flügel übers Leben,
 Über Grab und Tod.
Flügel, wie sie Jugend hatte,
 Da sie mir entflog,
 Flügel, wie des Glückes Schatten,
 Der mein Herz betrog!
Flügel, nachzufliehn den Tagen,
 Die vorüber sind!
 Flügel, Freuden einzujagen,
 Die entflohn im Wind!
Flügel, gleich den Nachtigallen,
 Wann die Rosen blühn,
 Aus dem Land, wo Nebel wallen,
 Ihnen nachzuziehn!

Wings! Wings! To fly
 Over hill and dale,
 Wings, that my heart might float
 On shafts of morning light.
Wings, to soar over the sea
 With the dawn,
 Wings, wings to soar above life,
 Above the grave and death.
Wings, such as youth had,
 That now has flown away,
 Wings, like rapture's shadow
 That deceived my heart!
Wings, to fly after days
 Now fled!
 Wings, to hunt down joys
 Now blown away on the wind!
Wings, like nightingales,
 When roses bloom,
 To escape this land of mists
 And fly in search of them!

Ach! von dem Verbannungsstrande,
　Wo kein Nachen winkt,
Flügel nach dem Heimatlande,
　Wo die Krone blinkt!
Freiheit, wie zum Schmetterlinge
　Raupenleben reift,
Wenn sich dehnt des Geistes Schwinge
　Und die Hüll' entstreift!
Oft in stillen Mitternächten
　Fühl' ich mich empor
Flügeln von des Traumes Mächten
　Zu dem Sternentor.
Doch gewachsenes Gefieder
　In der Nächte Duft,
Mir entträufeln seh' ichs wieder
　An des Morgens Luft.
Sonnenbrand den Fittig schmelzet,
　Ikar stürzt ins Meer,
Und der Sinne Brausen wälzet
　Überm Geist sich her.

Ah! from exile's shore,
　Where no ship can be seen,
To wing to the homeland
　Where my crown is gleaming!
O for freedom, as when butterflies
　Slip from the chrysalis,
　When it splits
And nature's spirit spreads its wings!
Often during silent midnights
　I feel myself winged aloft
By the power of dreams
　To the gateway of the stars.
Yet the wings I grew
　In the fragrant night
I now see vanish
　In the morning breeze.
The scorching sun melts my pinions,
　Icarus plunges into the sea,
　And the pulse of the senses
Spills over the spirit.

9
Rose, Meer und Sonne / Rose, sea and sun

Rose, Meer und Sonne
　Sind ein Bild der Liebsten mein,
　Die mit ihrer Wonne
　Faßt mein ganzes Leben ein.
Aller Glanz, ergossen,
　Aller Tau der Frühlingsflur
　Liegt vereint beschlossen
　In dem Kelch der Rose nur.
Alle Farben ringen,
　Aller Duft im Lenzgefild,
　Um hervorzubringen
　Im Verein der Rose Bild.
Rose, Meer und Sonne
　Sind ein Bild der Liebsten mein,
　Die mit ihrer Wonne
　Faßt mein ganzes Leben ein.
Alle Ströme haben
　Ihren Lauf auf Erden bloß,
　Um sich zu begraben
　Sehnend in des Meeres Schoß.
Alle Quellen fließen
　In den unerschöpften Grund,
　Einen Kreis zu schließen
　Um der Erde blüh'ndes Rund.

Rose, sea and sun
　Are an image of my beloved,
　Who with her radiance
　Frames my whole life.
All the beams of the sun,
　All the dew of the spring meadow
　Are mingled
　Only in the heart of the rose.
All colours,
　All the scents of spring fields
　Vie with each other
　To produce the rose's likeness.
Rose, sea and sun
　Are an image of my beloved,
　Who with her radiance
　Frames my whole life.
All rivers flow
　Through the land,
　Merely to bury themselves
　Longingly into the lap of the sea.
All springs flow
　Into the inexhaustible abyss,
　In order to describe a circle
　Around the blossoming world.

Rose, Meer und Sonne	Rose, sea and sun
Sind ein Bild der Liebsten mein,	Are an image of my beloved,
Die mit ihrer Wonne	Who with her radiance
Faßt mein ganzes Leben ein.	Frames my whole life.
Alle Stern' in Lüften	All the stars in the sky
Sind ein Liebesblick der Nacht,	Are the eyes of night looking down in love,
In des Morgens Düften	Dying in the morning's mist,
Sterbend, wann der Tag erwacht.	When the day awakes.
Alle Weltenflammen,	All the world's flames,
Der zerstreute Himmelsglanz,	All the scattered radiance of heaven,
Fließen hell zusammen	Mingle brightly together
In der Sonne Strahlenkranz.	In the sun's shining crown.
Rose, Meer und Sonne	Rose, sea and sun
Sind ein Bild der Liebsten mein,	Are an image of my beloved,
Die mit ihrer Wonne	Who with her radiance
Faßt mein ganzes Leben ein.	Frames my whole life.

10

O Sonn', O Meer, O Rose! / O sun, O sea, O rose!

O Sonn', o Meer, o Rose!	O sun, O sea, O rose!
Wie wenn die Sonne triumphierend sich	Just as the sun triumphantly rises
Hebt über Sterne, die am Himmel stunden,	Above stars that stood in the sky,
Ein Schimmer nach dem andern leis' erblich,	Which gradually faded
Bis alle sind in einen Glanz geschwunden,	Till all had vanished in a glow,
So hab' ich, Liebste, dich	Thus it was, my love, when I
Gefunden:	Found you:
Du kamst, da war, was je mein Herz emp-	You came, and what my heart
funden,	Ever loved,
Geschwunden	Vanished
In dich.	In you.
O Sonn', o Meer, o Rose!	O sun, O sea, O rose!
Wie wenn des Meeres Arme auftun sich	Just as the sea opens its arms
Den Strömen, die nach ihnen sich gewunden,	To the rivers that have meandered
Hinein sich diese stürzen brünstiglich,	And ardently pour themselves
	into it,
Bis sie die Ruh im tiefen Schoß gefunden;	Until they have found peace in its depths,
So, Liebste, hab' ich dich	Thus, I felt, my love, when I
Empfunden:	Found you:
Sich hat mein Herz mit allen Sehn-	My wounded heart's longing
suchtswunden	Was set free
Entbunden	In you.
In dich.	
O Sonn', o Meer, o Rose!	O sun, O sea, O rose!
Wie wenn im Frühling tausendfältig sich	Just as in a thousand ways spring's fresh green
Ein buntes Grün hat ringend losgewunden,	Breaks out all around,
Ein haderd Volk, bis Rose, königlich	And all argue, till regally the rose appears
Eintretend, es zum Kranz um sich verbunden,	And wraps it in a garland about itself –
So, Liebste, hab' ich dich	Thus, my love, did I entwine myself

Umwunden:	About you:
Der Kranz des Daseins muß sich blühend	The garland of my life flourishes
runden,	and finds its fulfilment,
Gebunden	When bound up
In dich.	In you.

11

Warum willst du andre fragen / Why enquire of others [Duet]

See Clara Schumann, p. 430

12

So wahr die Sonne scheinet / Truly as the sun shines

So wahr die Sonne scheinet,	Truly as the sun shines,
So wahr die Wolke weinet,	Truly as the cloud weeps,
So wahr die Flamme sprüht,	Truly as the flame flashes,
So wahr der Frühling blüht;	Truly as spring blossoms;
So wahr hab ich empfunden,	As truly did I feel
Wie ich dich halt umwunden:	Holding you in my embrace:
Du liebst mich, wie ich dich,	You love me, as I love you,
Dich lieb' ich wie du mich.	I love you, as you love me.
Die Sonne mag verscheinen,	The sun may cease to shine,
Die Wolke nicht mehr weinen,	The cloud may weep no more,
Die Flamme mag versprühn,	The flame may flash and fade,
Der Frühling nicht mehr blühn!	The spring may blossom no more!
Wir wollen uns umwinden	We shall both embrace
Und immer so empfinden:	And always feel:
Du liebst mich, wie ich dich,	You love me, as I love you,
Dich lieb' ich wie du mich.	I love you, as you love me.
(*Wolf*)	

June 1849 Mein schöner Stern! / My lovely star! Op 101, no. 4

Mein schöner Stern!	My lovely star!
Ich bitte dich,	I beg of you,
O lasse du	O do not let
Dein heitres Licht	Your serene radiance
Nicht trüben durch	Be dimmed by
Den Dampf in mir,	Dark clouds in me,
Vielmehr den Dampf	Rather help,
In mir zu Licht,	My lovely star,
Mein schöner Stern,	To transfigure the dark
Verklären hilf!	Into light!
Mein schöner Stern!	My lovely star!
Ich bitte dich,	I beg of you
Nicht senk' herab	Not to descend
Zur Erde dich,	To earth,

Weil du mich noch	Because you still
Hier unten siehst,	See me down here,
Heb' auf vielmehr	Rather lift me
Zum Himmel mich,	Up to heaven,
Mein schöner Stern,	My lovely star,
Wo du schon bist!	Where you already are!

Friedrich Schiller (1759–1805)

See Schubert

*c.*April 1850 Der Handschuh / The glove Op. 87

Vor seinem Löwengarten,	Before his lion arena,
Das Kampfspiel zu erwarten,	Awaiting the contest,
Saß König Franz,	Sat King Francis,
Und um ihn die Großen der Krone,	Surrounded by the lords of the realm,
Und rings auf hohem Balkone	And on the high balcony,
Die Damen in schönem Kranz.	By a fair circle of ladies.

Und, wie er winkt mit dem Finger,	And as he raises his finger,
Auf tut sich der Zwinger	The cage opens,
Und hinein mit bedächtigem Schritt	And with measured tread
Ein Löwe tritt,	A lion pads in,
Und sieht sich stumm	Silently looking
Rings um,	Around
Mit langem Gähnen,	With a long yawn,
Und schüttelt die Mähnen,	He shakes his mane,
Und streckt die Glieder	Stretches his limbs
Und legt sich nieder.	And then lies down.

Und der König winkt wieder,	And again the king gives a sign,
Da öffnet sich behend	A second gate
Ein zweites Tor,	Swiftly opens,
Daraus rennt	And from it,
Mit wildem Sprunge	With savage leap,
Ein Tiger hervor.	A tiger springs.
Wie der den Löwen erschaut,	On seeing the lion,
Brüllt er laut,	He roars mightily,
Schlägt mit dem Schweif	Lashing his tail
Einen furchtbaren Reif	In a fearful arc
Und recket die Zunge,	And lolls out its tongue,
Und im Kreise scheu	And stealthily
Umgeht er den Leu,	Circles the lion,
Grimmig schnurrend;	And then, with a growl,
Drauf streckt er sich murrend	Lies down
Zur Seite nieder.	By its side.

Und der König winkt wieder,	And again the king gives a sign,
Da speit das doppelt geöffnete Haus	The gates open a second time,
Zwei Leoparden auf einmal aus;	Spewing out two leopards at once.
Die stürzen mit mutiger Kampfbegier	They pounce with murderous might
Auf das Tigertier;	On the tiger,
Das packt sie mit seinen grimmigen Tatzen,	Which seizes them in his cruel claws,
Und der Leu mit Gebrüll	And the lion, with a roar,
Richtet sich auf, da wird's still;	Rises – all fall silent;
Und herum im Kreis	And in a circle,
Von Mordsucht heiß	Hot with bloodlust,
Lagern sich die gräulichen Katzen.	The savage cats crouch down.
Da fällt von des Altans Rand	Then, from the balcony's edge,
Ein Handschuh von schöner Hand,	A glove falls from a fair hand,
Zwischen den Tiger und den Leun	Right between
Mitten hinein.	The tiger and lion.
Und zu Ritter Delorges spottender Weis'	And to Sir Delorges, tauntingly
Wendet sich Fräulein Kunigund:	Lady Kunigunde turns:
„Herr Ritter, ist Eure Lieb so heiß,	'Knight, if you love me as ardently
Wie Ihr mir schwört zu jeder Stund,	As you constantly avow –
Ei, so hebt mir den Handschuh auf!"	Why then, bring me up my glove!'
Und der Ritter, in schnellem Lauf	And the knight swiftly
Steigt hinab in den furchtbaren Zwinger	Descends into the terrible den,
Mit festem Schritte,	Unflinchingly,
Und aus der Ungeheuer Mitte	And from between the monstrous beasts
Nimmt er den Handschuh mit keckem Finger.	Audaciously recovers the glove.
Und mit Erstaunen und mit Grauen	And with amazement and terror
Sehen's die Ritter und Edelfrauen,	The knights and noble ladies watch,
Und gelassen bringt er den Handschuh zurück.	As calmly he returns with the glove.
Da schallt ihm sein Lob aus jedem Munde,	All then praise him;
Aber mit zärtlichem Liebesblick,	But with tender loving glances –
Er verheißt ihm sein nahes Glück,	A promise of the bliss in store –
Empfängt ihn Fräulein Kunigunde.	Lady Kunigunde receives him.
Und er wirft ihr den Handschuh in's Gesicht!	And he flings the glove in her face:
„Den Dank, Dame, begehr' ich nicht!"	'I desire no thanks from you, my Lady!'
Und verläßt sie zur selben Stunde.	And forthwith takes his leave.
(*Zelter*)	

Robert Schumann (1810–56)

Schumann wrote the poems to four of his own songs. 'Lied für Lxxxx' (Liddy Hempel, the sweetheart of his youth) and 'Sehnsucht' date from 1827, 'Hirtenknabe' (for which, as with 'Sehnsucht', he gives his own pseudonym Ekert as author) from 1828. The poem 'Bei Schenkung eines Flügels', written in 1840 to mark the occasion on 5 July when he made a gift to Clara Wieck of a grand piano adorned with orange and myrtle twigs, was not set by Schumann until August 1853.

1827 Sehnsucht / Longing WoO 121

Sterne der blauen	O stars up on high
Himmlischen Auen,	In the fields of heaven,
Grüßt mir das Mädchen,	Greet for me the girl
Das ich geliebt!	I have loved!
Weit in die Ferne	Far away I should
Möcht' ich so gerne	Love to journey
Wo das geliebte	To where my dear
Mädchen mir weilt.	Girl dwells.
Schweigende Sterne,	O silent stars,
Grüßt mir die Ferne,	Greet for me the distance,
Grüßt mir das Mädchen,	Greet for me the girl
Das ich geliebt!	I have loved!
Sterne der blauen	O stars up on high
Himmlischen Auen,	In the fields of heaven,
Treuliche Winde,	O faithful winds,
Küßt sie von mir!	Kiss her for me!
Stumme Vertraute	O you silent accomplices,
Küßt mir die Braut,	Kiss for me the bride,
Bringt ihr auch Tränen,	Bring tears too,
Tränen von mir.	Tears from me.
Ach, ich muß weinen,	Ah! I must weep tears
Tränen der Einen,	For my own darling,
Tränen der Sehnsucht,	Tears of longing,
Teuere, dir!	Tears for you, my love!

February–April 1840 *Myrten / Myrtles* Op. 25

As the year 1840 approached, when Clara would be twenty-one and free to marry, despite her father's opposition to their union, Schumann set about composing his wedding gift, though he found it difficult to keep the secret. Clara guessed what he was up to, either through the broad hint of Op. 24, no. 9 ('Mit Myrten und Rosen') or through feminine intuition. In February 1840 she writes from Hamburg:

> [. . .] Sag mir, was das ist, was Du komponierst? Ich wüßte es doch gar zu gern! O bitte, bitte. Ist es ein Quartett? Eine Ouvertüre, oder wohl gar eine Symphonie? Soll es vielleicht ein Hochzeitsgeschenk für mich sein? Sag mir nur den ersten Buchstaben!

[. . .] Tell me what you are composing, I'd so love to know; oh please, please. A quartet, an overture, or a symphony even? Could it by any chance be . . . a wedding present? Just give me the first letter.

1

Widmung / Dedication
FRIEDRICH RÜCKERT (1788–1866)

Du meine Seele, du mein Herz,	You my soul, you my heart,
Du meine Wonn', o du mein Schmerz,	You my rapture, O you my pain,
Du meine Welt, in der ich lebe,	You my world in which I live,
Mein Himmel du, darein ich schwebe,	My heaven you, in which I float,
O du mein Grab, in das hinab	O you my grave, into which
Ich ewig meinen Kummer gab!	My grief forever I've consigned!
Du bist die Ruh, du bist der Frieden,	You are repose, you are peace,
Du bist vom Himmel mir beschieden.	You are bestowed on me from heaven.
Daß du mich liebst, macht mich mir wert,	Your love for me gives me my worth,
Dein Blick hat mich vor mir verklärt,	Your eyes transfigure me in mine,
Du hebst mich liebend über mich,	You raise me lovingly above myself,
Mein guter Geist, mein beß'res Ich!	My guardian angel, my better self!

2

Freisinn / Free spirit
JOHANN WOLFGANG VON GOETHE (1749–1832)

Laßt mich nur auf meinem Sattel gelten!	Let me hold sway in the saddle!
Bleibt in euren Hütten, euren Zelten!	Stay in your huts and your tents!
Und ich reite froh in alle Ferne,	And I'll ride happily far away,
Über meiner Mütze nur die Sterne.	With only the stars above me.
Er hat euch die Gestirne gesetzt	He has set the constellations
Als Leiter zu Land und See;	To guide you over land and sea,
Damit ihr euch daran ergötzt,	That you may delight in them,
Stets blickend in die Höh'.	As you gaze forever aloft.
(*Rubinstein*)	

3

Der Nußbaum / The walnut tree
JULIUS MOSEN (1803–67)

Es grünet ein Nußbaum vor dem Haus,	A walnut tree blossoms outside the house,
Duftig,	Fragrantly,
Luftig	Airily,
Breitet er blättrig die Blätter aus.	It spreads its leafy boughs.
Viel liebliche Blüten stehen d'ran;	Many lovely blossoms it bears;
Linde	Gentle
Winde	Winds
Kommen, sie herzlich zu umfahn.	Come to caress them tenderly.

Es flüstern je zwei zu zwei gepaart,	Paired together, they whisper,
Neigend,	Inclining,
Beugend	Bending
Zierlich zum Kusse die Häuptchen zart.	Gracefully their delicate heads to kiss.
Sie flüstern von einem Mägdlein, das	They whisper of a maiden who
Dächte	Dreamed
Die Nächte	For nights
Und Tage lang, wußte, ach! selber nicht was.	And days, of, alas! she knew not what.
Sie flüstern, – wer mag verstehn so gar	They whisper – who can understand
Leise	So soft
Weis'?	A song?
Flüstern von Bräut'gam und nächstem Jahr.	Whisper of a bridegroom and next year.
Das Mägdlein horchet, es rauscht im Baum;	The maiden listens, the tree rustles;
Sehnend,	Yearning,
Wähnend	Musing
Sinkt es lächelnd in Schlaf und Traum.	She drifts smiling into sleep and dreams.

4

Jemand / Somebody

ROBERT BURNS (1759–96), TRANSLATED BY WILHELM GERHARD (1780–1858)

Mein Herz ist betrübt – ich sag' es nicht –	My heart is sad, I cannot reveal it,
Mein Herz ist betrübt um Jemand;	My heart is sad for somebody;
Ich könnte wachen die längste Nacht,	I could lie awake during the longest night
Und immer träumen von Jemand.	And always dream of somebody.
O Wonne! von Jemand;	Oh bliss! Of somebody;
O Himmel! von Jemand;	Oh heavens! Of somebody!
Durchstreifen könnt' ich die ganze Welt,	I could roam through the whole world,
Aus Liebe zu Jemand.	For the love of somebody.
Ihr Mächte, die ihr der Liebe hold,	Ye powers that smile on love,
O lächelt freundlich auf Jemand!	Oh! smile sweetly on somebody!
Beschirmet ihn, wo Gefahren drohn;	Protect him from perils;
Gebt sicher Geleite dem Jemand!	And guide my somebody safely!
O Wonne! dem Jemand;	Oh bliss! My somebody;
O Himmel! dem Jemand;	Oh heavens! My somebody;
Ich wollt' – ich wollte – was wollt' ich nicht	I'd love, I'd love, what wouldn't I love to do
Für meinen Jemand!	For my somebody!

5 AND 6

Lieder aus dem Schenkenbuch im Divan / Songs from the 'Book of the Cupbearer' from
West-östlicher Divan

JOHANN WOLFGANG VON GOETHE (1749–1832)

5

Sitz ich allein,	If I sit alone,
Wo kann ich besser sein?	Where could I be better off?

Meinen Wein
Trink' ich allein;
Niemand setzt mir Schranken,
Ich hab' so meine eignen Gedanken.

I drink my wine
All by myself;
Nobody hampers me,
And I can think my own thoughts.

6

DEM KELLNER
Setze mir nicht, du Grobian,
Mir den Krug so derb vor die Nase!
Wer mir Wein bringt sehe mich freundlich an.
Sonst trübt sich der Eilfer* im Glase.

TO THE WAITER
You oaf, don't bang down the jug like that
Beneath my nose!
Whoever serves me wine, must smile at me,
Or the 1811 will cloud in the glass.

DEM SCHENKE
Du lieblicher Knabe, du komm herein,
Was stehst du denn da auf der Schwelle?
Du sollst mir künftig der Schenke sein,
Jeder Wein ist schmackhaft und helle.

TO THE CUP-BEARER
You lovely boy, come on in,
Why stand there on the threshold?
You shall in future bring my wine,
Each wine shall taste delicious and bright.

7

Die Lotosblume / The lotus-flower
HEINRICH HEINE (1797–1856)

Die Lotosblume ängstigt
Sich vor der Sonne Pracht,
Und mit gesenktem Haupte
Erwartet sie träumend die Nacht.

The lotus-flower fears
The sun's splendour,
And with bowed head,
Dreaming, awaits the night.

Der Mond, der ist ihr Buhle,
Er weckt sie mit seinem Licht,
Und ihm entschleiert sie freundlich
Ihr frommes Blumengesicht.

The moon is her lover,
He wakes her with his light,
And to him she tenderly unveils
Her innocent flower-like face.

Sie blüht und glüht und leuchtet
Und starret stumm in die Höh';
Sie duftet und weinet und zittert
Vor Liebe und Liebesweh.
(*Franz, Loewe*)

She blooms and glows and gleams,
And gazes silently aloft –
Fragrant and weeping and trembling
With love and the pain of love.

8

Talismane / Talismans
JOHANN WOLFGANG VON GOETHE (1749–1832)

Gottes ist der Orient!
Gottes ist der Occident!
Nord- und südliches Gelände
Ruht im Frieden seiner Hände.

God's is the East!
God's is the West!
Northern and southern lands
Repose in the peace of his hands.

Er, der einzige Gerechte,

He, who alone is just,

* 1811 was an outstanding year for German wines.

Will für jedermann das Rechte.
Sei, von seinen hundert Namen,
Dieser hochgelobet! Amen.

Wills what is right for each.
Of His hundred names,
Let this one be highly praised! Amen.

Mich verwirren will das Irren;
Doch du weißt mich zu entwirren.
Wenn ich handle, wenn ich dichte,
Gib du meinem Weg die Richte!
(*Loewe*)

Error may lead me astray;
But You can disentangle me.
When I act, when I write,
May You guide me on my way!

9

Lied der Suleika / Suleika's song

MARIANNE VON WILLEMER (1784–1869) IN COLLABORATION WITH JOHANN WOLFGANG VON GOETHE (1749–1832)

Wie mit innigstem Behagen,
Lied, empfind' ich deinen Sinn!
Liebevoll du scheinst zu sagen:
Daß ich ihm zur Seite bin.

With what heartfelt contentment,
O song, do I sense your meaning!
Lovingly you seem to say:
That I am at his side;

Daß er ewig mein gedenket,
Seiner Liebe Seligkeit
Immerdar der Fernen schenket,
Die ein Leben ihm geweiht.

That he ever thinks of me,
And ever bestows his love's rapture
On her who, far away,
Dedicates her life to him.

Ja, mein Herz, es ist der Spiegel,
Freund, worin du dich erblickt,
Diese Brust, wo deine Siegel
Kuß auf Kuß hereingedrückt.

For my heart, dear friend, is the mirror,
Wherein you have seen yourself;
And this the breast where your seal is imprinted
Kiss upon kiss.

Süßes Dichten, lautre Wahrheit,
Fesselt mich in Sympathie!
Rein verkörpert Liebesklarheit
Im Gewand der Poesie.
(*Meyerbeer*)

Sweet verses, unsullied truth
Chain me in sympathy;
Love's pure embodied radiance
In the garb of poetry!

10

Die Hochländer-Witwe / The Highland widow

ROBERT BURNS (1759–96), TRANSLATED BY WILHELM GERHARD (1780–1858)

Ich bin gekommen in's Niederland,
O weh! o weh! o weh!
So ausgeplündert haben sie mich,
Daß ich vor Hunger vergeh!

I am come to the Lowlands,
Alas! Alas! Alas!
They have taken all I had,
So that now I've nothing to eat.

So war's in meinem Hochland nicht;
O weh! o weh! o weh!
Ein hochbeglückter Weib, als ich,
War nicht auf Tal und Höh!

It was not like this in the Highlands,
Alas! Alas! Alas!
No woman was happier than I
In the valleys or on the hills!

Denn damals hatt' ich zwanzig Küh';
O weh! o weh! o weh!
Die gaben Milch und Butter mir,
Und weideten im Klee.

Und sechzig Schafe hatt' ich dort;
O weh! o weh! o weh!
Die wärmten mich mit weichem Vließ
Bei Frost und Winterschnee.

Es konnte Kein' im ganzen Clan
Sich größern Glückes freu'n;
Denn Donald war der schönste Mann,
Und Donald, der war mein!

So blieb's, bis Charlie Stuart kam,
Alt-Schottland zu befrein;
Da mußte Donald seinen Arm
Ihm und dem Lande leihn.

Was sie befiel, wer weiß es nicht?
Dem Unrecht wich das Recht,
Und auf Culloden's blut'gem Feld
Erlagen Herr und Knecht.

O! daß ich kam in's Niederland!
O weh! o weh! o weh!
Nun gibt's kein unglücksel'ger Weib
Vom Hochland bis zur See!

For then I'd a herd of twenty cows;
Alas! Alas! Alas!
Who used to give me milk and butter
And used to graze in clover.

And there I had threescore sheep;
Alas! Alas! Alas!
Who warmed me with their soft fleece
In the frost and winter snow.

No one in all the clan
Enjoyed greater fortune than I;
For Donald was the most handsome of men,
And Donald, he was mine!

And so it remained till Charlie Stuart came
To set Old Scotland free:
Donald's arm was wanted then
For Scotland and for him.

What befell – who does not know it?
Right did yield to wrong,
And on Culloden's bloody field
Master and servant perished.

Ah! Had I never come to the Lowlands!
Alas! Alas! Alas!
No one can now be unhappier than I
From the Highlands down to the sea!

11
Lied der Braut (1) / Song of the bride (1)
FRIEDRICH RÜCKERT (1788–1866)

Mutter, Mutter! glaube nicht,
  Weil ich ihn lieb' also sehr,
  Daß nun Liebe mir gebricht,
  Dich zu lieben, wie vorher.
Mutter, Mutter! seit ich ihn
  Liebe, lieb' ich erst dich sehr.
  Laß mich an mein Herz dich ziehn,
  Und dich küssen, wie mich er.
Mutter, Mutter! seit ich ihn
  Liebe, lieb' ich erst dich ganz,
  Daß du mir das Sein verliehn,
  Das mir ward zu solchem Glanz.

Mother, mother! never believe,
  Because I love him too much,
  That I now lack the love
  To love you as before.
Mother, mother! since loving him
  I love you all the more.
  Let me press you to my heart
  And kiss you, as he kisses me.
Mother, mother! Only since loving him
  Do I truly love you now,
  For giving me my life
  That has become so radiant.

12

Lied der Braut (2) / Song of the bride (2)
FRIEDRICH RÜCKERT (1788–1866)

Laß mich ihm am Busen hangen,
Mutter, Mutter! laß das Bangen.
Frage nicht: wie soll sich's wenden?
Frage nicht: wie soll das enden?
Enden? enden soll sichs nie,
Wenden, noch nicht weiß ich, wie!

Let me lay my head on his heart,
Mother, mother! be not afraid.
Do not ask: how will things change?
Do not ask: how will it end?
End? Never shall it end,
Change? I don't know how it could!

13

Hochländers Abschied / The highlander's farewell
ROBERT BURNS (1759–1796), TRANSLATED BY WILHELM GERHARD (1780–1858)

Mein Herz ist im Hochland, mein Herz ist nicht hier;
Mein Herz ist im Hochland, im Waldes Revier;
Dort jagt es den Hirsch und verfolget das Reh;
Mein Herz ist im Hochland, wohin ich auch geh!

My heart's in the Highlands, my heart is not here;
My heart's in the Highlands, in the forests up there;
Chasing the wild deer, and following the roe;
My heart's in the Highlands wherever I go!

Leb wohl, mein Hochland, mein heimischer Ort!
Die Wiege der Freiheit, des Mutes ist dort.
Wohin ich auch wandre, wo immer ich bin:
Auf die Berg', auf die Berge zieht es mich hin.

Farewell to the Highlands, farewell to my home!
The birthplace of freedom, of valour is there.
Wherever I wander, wherever I am:
It's the hills of the Highlands that draw me on.

Lebt wohl, ihr Berge, bedecket mit Schnee,
Lebt wohl, ihr Täler voll Blumen und Klee!
Lebt wohl, ihr Wälder, bemoostes Gestein,
Ihr stürzenden Bächlein im farbigen Schein!

Farewell, you mountains, covered with snow,
Farewell, you valleys, full of clover and flowers!
Farewell, you forests and moss-covered rocks,
Farewell, you torrents, with your colourful glow!

Mein Herz ist im Hochland, mein Herz ist nicht hier;
Mein Herz ist im Hochland, im Waldes Revier;
Dort jagt es den Hirsch und verfolget das Reh;
Mein Herz ist im Hochland, wohin ich auch geh!
(*Franz, Jensen*)

My heart's in the Highlands, my heart is not here;
My heart's in the Highlands, in the forests up there;
Chasing the wild deer, and following the roe;
My heart's in the Highlands wherever I go!

14

Hochländisches Wiegenlied / Highland lullaby
ROBERT BURNS (1759–1796), TRANSLATED BY WILHELM GERHARD (1780–1858)

Schlafe, süßer, kleiner Donald,
Ebenbild des großen Ronald!
Wer ihm kleinen Dieb gebar,
Weiß der edle Clan aufs Haar.

Sleep, sweet little Donald,
The very image of great Ronald!
Our noble clan knows all too well
Who conceived with him the little thief.

Schelm, hast Äuglein schwarz wie Kohlen!	You little rogue, you've coal-black eyes!
Wenn du groß bist, stiehl ein Fohlen;	When you grow up, you'll steal a foal;
Geh die Ebne ab und zu,	You'll travel the plains up and down,
Bringe heim 'ne Carlisle-Kuh!	And bring home a Carlisle cow!
Darfst in Niederland nicht fehlen;	Make sure you go to the Lowlands;
Dort, mein Bübchen, magst du stehlen;	There, my boy, you may steal;
Stiehl dir Geld und stiehl dir Glück,	Steal money and steal happiness
Und in's Hochland komm zurück!	And come back to the Highlands!

15

Aus den hebräischen Gesängen / From 'Hebrew melodies'

GEORGE GORDON, LORD BYRON (1788–1824), TRANSLATED BY KARL JULIUS KÖRNER
(1783–1873)

Mein Herz ist schwer! auf! von der Wand	My heart is heavy! Take the lute
Die Laute, nur s i e allein mag ich noch hören;	From the wall, *it* alone can I still bear to hear,
Entlocke mit geschickter Hand	Draw from it with your skilled hands
Ihr Töne, die das Herz betören!	Sounds that will beguile my heart!
Kann noch mein Herz ein Hoffen nähren,	If hope can still nourish my heart,
Es zaubern diese Töne her;	These sounds will charm it forth;
Und birgt mein trocknes Auge Zähren,	And if tears lurk in my dry eyes,
Sie fließen, und mich brennt's nicht mehr!	They will flow, and burn me no more!
Nur tief sei, wild der Töne Fluß,	But let the strain be wild and deep
Und von der Freude weggekehret!	And devoid of every joy!
Ja, Sänger, daß ich weinen muß,	I tell thee, minstrel, I must weep,
Sonst wird das schwere Herz verzehret!	Or this heavy heart will be consumed!
Denn sieh! vom Kummer ward's genähret;	For see! It has been been nursed by sorrow;
Mit stummem Wachen trug es lang;	And ached for long in sleepless silence;
Und jetzt vom Äußersten belehret –	And now it is doomed to know the worst –
Da brech' es, oder heil im Sang.	Let it break or be healed in song.

16

Räthsel* / Riddle

CATHERINE MARIA FANSHAWE (1765–1834), ATTRIBUTED TO LORD BYRON (1788–1824),
TRANSLATED BY KARL KANNEGIESSER (1781–1861)

Es flüstert's der Himmel, es murrt es die Hölle,	Heaven whispers it, Hell mutters it,
Nur schwach klingt's nach in des Echos Welle,	It resounds but faintly in the echo's waves;
Und kommt es zur Fluth, so wird es stumm,	And when it comes to the sea, it falls silent,
Auf den Höhn, da hörst du sein zwiefach Gesumm.	On the heights you can hear its twofold hum.
Das Schlachtengewühl liebt's, fliehet den Frieden,	It loves the thick of the battle, it flees peace,
Es ist nicht Männern noch Frauen beschieden,	It's granted to neither men nor women,
Doch jeglichem Thier, nur mußt du's seciren.	But to every animal, only you must dissect it.

* The solution to the riddle is the letter H (in German notation B) and the final suppressed answer is 'Hauch'.

Nicht ist's in der Poesie zu erspüren,	It's not to be found in poetry,
Die Wissenschaft hat es, vor allem sie,	Science has it, science above all,
Die Gottesgelahrtheit und Philosophie.	And theology and philosophy.
Bei den Helden führt es den Vorsitz immer,	It always presides amongst heroes,
Doch mangelt's den Schwachen auch inner-	Yet the weak never lack it in their
lich nimmer,	souls,
Es findet sich richtig in jedem Haus,	It can be found in any house,
Denn ließe man's fehlen, so wär es aus.	For were it missing, all would be over.
In Griechenland klein, an den Tiber Borden	Small in Greece, on the banks of the Tiber
Ist's größer, am größten in Deutschland	It grew bigger, but biggest of all in Germany.
geworden.	
Im Schatten birgt sich's, im Blümchen auch;	It's concealed in the shade, and the tiny
Du hauchst es täglich, es ist nur ein (was ist's?)	flower;
Es ist nur ein	You breathe it daily, it's merely a . . . (what is it?)
	It's only a

17 AND 18
Zwei Venetianische Lieder / Two Venetian airs
THOMAS MOORE (1779–1852), TRANSLATED BY FERDINAND FREILIGRATH (1810–76)

17

Leis' rudern hier, mein Gondolier! die Flut	Row gently here, my gondolier, ply the water
vom Ruder sprühn	gently,
So leise laß, daß sie uns nur vernimmt, zu	So that only she, to whom we glide, shall hear
der wir zieh'n!	us coming!
O könnte, wie er schauen kann, der Himmel	Oh, if only heaven could speak as it can
reden – traun,	see,
Er spräche Vieles wohl von dem, was Nachts	It would tell much about what the stars dis-
die Sterne schau'n!	cern at night!
Nun rasten hier, mein Gondolier! Ins Boot	Now stay here, my gondolier, gently into the
die Ruder! sacht!	boat with your oar!
Auf zum Balkone schwing' ich mich, doch du	While I climb the balcony, you keep watch
hältst unten Wacht.	beneath.
O, wollten halb so eifrig nur dem Himmel	Oh, if we devoted ourselves to heaven half as
wir uns weih'n,	eagerly
Als schöner Weiber Diensten – traun, wir	As we seek favours of fair women, we could
könnten Engel sein!	be angels!
(*Mendelssohn*)	

18

Wenn durch die Piazzetta	When through the Piazzetta
Die Abendluft weht,	The night air drifts,
Dann weißt du, Ninetta,	Then you know, Ninetta,
Wer wartend hier steht.	Who's waiting here.
Du weißt, wer trotz Schleier	You know who, despite your veil
Und Maske dich kennt,	And mask, recognizes you,
Wie Amor die Venus	As Amor knows Venus
Am Nachtfirmament.	In the night sky.

Ein Schifferkleid trag' ich
Zur selbigen Zeit,
Und zitternd dir sag' ich:
Das Boot liegt bereit!
O, komm' jetzt, wo Lunen
Noch Wolken umzieh'n,
Laß durch die Lagunen,
Mein Leben, uns flieh'n!

At that very hour
I'll come dressed as a gondolier,
And trembling, tell you:
The boat lies ready!
O come now, while the moon
Is still covered in clouds,
Let us flee, my love,
Across the lagoons!

19

Hauptmanns Weib / The captain's lady

ROBERT BURNS (1759–96), TRANSLATED BY WILHELM GERHARD (1780–1858)

Hoch zu Pferd!
Stahl auf zartem Leibe,
Helm und Schwert
Ziemen Hauptmanns Weibe.
Tönet Trommelschlag
Unter Pulverdampf,
Siehst du blut'gen Tag
Und dein Lieb' im Kampf. –

Mount your horse!
Steel across your tender body,
Helmet and sword
Become a captain's lady.
When the drums beat
And the powder smokes,
You'll behold a bloody day
And your love in battle. –

Schlagen wir den Feind,
Küssest du den Gatten,
Wohnst mit ihm vereint
In des Friedens Schatten.

When the foe is vanquished,
You'll kiss your husband,
You'll live united with him
In the shadow of peace.

20

Weit, weit! / Far far!

ROBERT BURNS (1759–96), TRANSLATED BY WILHELM GERHARD (1780–1858)

Wie kann ich froh und munter sein,
Und flink mich drehn bei meinem Leid?
Der schmucke Junge, der mich liebt,
Ist über die Berge weit, weit!

How can I be cheerful and merry
And brisk with all my sorrow?
The handsome boy who loves me
Is far far across the mountains!

Was kümmert mich des Winters Frost,
Und ob es draußen stürmt und schneit?
Im Auge blinkt die Träne mir,
Denk' ich an ihn, der weit, weit!

What do I care about winter frost
And whether it storms and snows outside?
Tears glisten in my eyes
When I think of him, who's far far away!

Er hat die Handschuh' mir geschenkt,
Das bunte Tuch, das seidne Kleid:
Doch er, dem ich's zur Ehre trag',
Ist über die Berge weit, weit!

He gave these gloves as a gift to me,
The colourful cloth, the silken dress:
But he, in whose honour I wear it,
Is far far across the mountains!

21

Was will die einsame Träne? / Why this solitary tear?

HEINRICH HEINE (1797–1856)

Was will die einsame Träne?
Sie trübt mir ja den Blick.
Sie blieb aus alten Zeiten
In meinem Auge zurück.

Sie hatte viel leuchtende Schwestern,
Die alle zerflossen sind,
Mit meinen Qualen und Freuden,
Zerflossen in Nacht und Wind.

Wie Nebel sind auch zerflossen
Die blauen Sternelein,
Die mir jene Freuden und Qualen
Gelächelt ins Herz hinein.

Ach, meine Liebe selber
Zerfloß wie eitel Hauch!
Du alte, einsame Träne,
Zerfließe jetzunder auch!
(*Cornelius, Franz, Hensel, Lachner*)

Why this solitary tear?
It troubles my gaze.
It has remained in my eye
From days long past.

It had many shining sisters
Who have all vanished,
Vanished with my joys and sorrows
In night and wind.

Like mist, those tiny blue stars
Have also vanished
That smiled those joys and sorrows
Into my heart.

Ah, my love itself
Vanished like a mere breath of air!
Old, solitary tear,
Vanish now as well!

22

Niemand / Nobody

ROBERT BURNS (1759–96), TRANSLATED BY WILHELM GERHARD (1780–1858)

Ich hab mein Weib allein,
Und teil' es, traun! mit Niemand;
Nicht Hahnrei will ich sein,
Zum Hahnrei mach' ich Niemand.
Ein Säckchen Gold ist mein,
Doch – dafür dank' ich Niemand;
Nichts hab' ich zu verleihn,
Und borgen soll mir Niemand.

Ich bin nicht Andrer Herr,
Und untertänig Niemand;
Doch meine Klinge sticht,
Ich fürchte mich vor Niemand.
Ein lustger Kauz bin ich,
Kopfhängerisch mit Niemand;
Schiert Niemand sich um mich,
So scher' ich mich um Niemand.

I've a wife of my own,
And share her, forsooth, with nobody;
I'll not be a cuckold
Or cuckold anyone either.
I've a purse of gold,
Thanks to nobody;
I have nothing to lend,
And I'll borrow from nobody.

I'm nobody's lord,
And I'll be nobody's slave;
But my sword is sharp,
I fear nobody.
I'm a merry fellow,
Nobody gets me down;
If nobody cares about me,
I'll care about nobody.

23

Im Westen / In the West

ROBERT BURNS (1759–96), TRANSLATED BY WILHELM GERHARD (1780–1858)

Ich schau' über Forth hinüber nach Nord:
Was helfen mir Nord und Hochlands Schnee?
Was Osten und Süd, wo die Sonne glüht,
Das ferne Land und die wilde See?

Aus Westen winkt, wo die Sonne sinkt,
Was mich im Schlummer und Traume
    beglückt;
Im Westen wohnt, der mir Liebe lohnt,
Mich und mein Kindlein an's Herz gedrückt!

I gaze over the Forth across to the north:
What good's the north and Highland snow to me?
What good's the east and the sun-burning south,
The distant land and the wild sea?

From the west, where the sun sets,
Beckons all that delights me in slumber and dream:
In the west lives the man who rewards me
    with love,
Who pressed me and my little child to his heart!

24

Du bist wie eine Blume / You are like a flower

HEINRICH HEINE (1797–1856)

Du bist wie eine Blume,
So hold und schön und rein;
Ich schau' dich an, und Wehmut
Schleicht mir in's Herz hinein.

Mir ist, als ob ich die Hände
Auf's Haupt dir legen sollt',
Betend, daß Gott dich erhalte
So rein und schön und hold.
(*Lord Berners, Burgmüller, Ives, Liszt, Rach-maninov, Rubinstein, Wolf*)

You are like a flower,
So sweet and fair and pure;
I look at you, and sadness
Steals into my heart.

I feel as if I should lay
My hands upon your head,
Praying that God preserve you
So pure and fair and sweet.

25

Aus den 'Östlichen Rosen' / From 'Eastern roses'

FRIEDRICH RÜCKERT (1788–1866)

Ich sende einen Gruß wie Duft der Rosen,
Ich send' ihn an ein Rosenangesicht.
Ich sende einen Gruß wie Frühlingskosen,
Ich send' ihn an ein Aug' voll Frühlingslicht.
Aus Schmerzensstürmen, die mein Herz
    durchtosen,
Send' ich den Hauch, dich unsanft rühr' er
    nicht!
Wenn du gedenkest an den Freudelosen,
So wird der Himmel meiner Nächte licht.

I send a greeting like the scent of roses,
I send it to a rose-like face.
I send a greeting like Spring's caressing,
I send it to eyes brimming with Spring's light.
From anguished storms that rage through
    my heart
I send a breath – may it cause you no harm!
When you think of me in my sadness,
The sky of my nights will then be made
    bright.

26

Zum Schluß / At the last
FRIEDRICH RÜCKERT (1788–1866)

Hier in diesen erdbeklomm'nen
 Lüften, wo die Wehmut taut,
Hab ich dir den unvollkomm'nen
 Kranz geflochten, Schwester, Braut!
Wenn uns droben aufgenommen
Gottes Sonn' entgegenschaut,
Wird die Liebe den vollkomm'nen
 Kranz uns flechten, Schwester, Braut!

Here in these earth-stifled
 Breezes, where sadness dissolves like dew,
I've fashioned you that imperfect
 Garland, sister, bride!
When we are received above
And God's sun looks on us,
Love shall fashion for us the perfect
 Garland, sister, bride!

April–June 1849 *Liederalbum für die Jugend / Lieder album for the young* Op. 79

By 1849, Clara Schumann had already given birth to five children (her first son died) and was expecting a sixth. In the previous year her husband had composed his *Album für die Jugend* and now, with the imminent birth of another baby and his own thoughts turning to music connected with childhood, Schumann set about writing his *Liederalbum für die Jugend*. Schumann's own view of these delightful Lieder – there are twenty-five solo songs and four duets – is expressed in a letter to his publisher Emanuel Klitzsch:

> Sie werden es am besten aussprechen, was ich damit gemeint habe, wie ich namentlich dem Jugendalter angemessene Gedichte, und zwar nur von den besten Dichtern gewählt, und wie ich vom Leichten und Einfachen zum Schwierigen überzugehen mich bemühe. Mignon schließt ahnungsvoll, den Blick in ein bewegteres Seelenleben richtend.

> They will best express what I had in mind. I have selected poems appropriate to childhood, exclusively from the best poets, and have tried to arrange them in order of difficulty, progressing from the easy and simple to the difficult and complex. At the end comes Mignon, gazing into a more troubled emotional life.

1

Der Abendstern / The evening star
HOFFMANN VON FALLERSLEBEN (1798–1874)

Du lieblicher Stern,
Du leuchtest so fern.
Doch hab' ich dich dennoch
Von Herzen so gern.

You lovely star,
You shine from afar.
Yet I love you dearly
With all my heart.

Wie lieb' ich doch dich
So herzinniglich!

How fervently
I love you!

| Dein funkelndes Äuglein | Your twinkling eye |
| Blickt immer auf mich. | Watches over me always. |

So blick' ich nach dir,	So I look at you,
Sei's dort oder hier:	Be you here or there:
Dein freundliches Äuglein	Your friendly eye
Steht immer vor mir.	Is always before me.

Wie nickst du mir zu	How you beckon to me,
In fröhlicher Ruh!	Happy and at peace!
O liebliches Sternlein,	O lovely little star,
O wär' ich wie du!	I wish I were like you!
(*Reinecke*)	

2
Schmetterling / Butterfly
HOFFMANN VON FALLERSLEBEN (1798–1874)

O Schmetterling, sprich,	O butterfly, say,
Was fliehest du mich?	Why fly from me?
Warum doch so eilig,	Why hurry so,
Jetzt fern und dann nah?	First far and then near?

Jetzt fern und dann nah,	First far and then near,
Jetzt hier und dann da –	First here and then there,
Ich will dich nicht haschen,	I don't want to catch you,
Ich tu' dir kein Leid.	I'll do you no harm.

Ich tu' dir kein Leid:	I'll do you no harm,
O bleib allezeit!	Oh stay forever!
Und wär' ich ein Blümchen,	And if I were a flower,
So spräch' ich zu dir,	I'd say to you,

So spräch' ich zu dir:	I'd say to you:
Komm, komm doch zu mir!	Come, come here to me!
Ich schenk' dir mein Herzchen,	I'll give you my heart,
Wie gut bin ich dir!	I love you so!

3
Frühlingsbotschaft / Spring tidings
HOFFMANN VON FALLERSLEBEN (1798–1874)

Kuckuck, Kuckuck ruft aus dem Wald:	Cuckoo, cuckoo calls from the wood:
Lasset uns singen,	Let us sing,
Lasset uns springen!	Let us dance!
Frühling wird es nun bald!	Spring will soon be here!

| Kuckuck, Kuckuck läßt nicht sein Schrein: | Cuckoo, cuckoo does not cease calling: |
| Komm in die Felder, | Come to the fields, |

Wiesen und Wälder!
Frühling, stelle dich ein!

Kuckuck, Kuckuck, trefflicher Held!
Was du gesungen,
Ist dir gelungen:
Winter räumet das Feld.

4
Frühlingsgruß / Spring greeting
HOFFMANN VON FALLERSLEBEN (1798–1874)

So sei gegrüßt viel tausendmal,
   Holder Frühling!
Willkommen hier in unserm Tal,
   Holder Frühling!
Holder Frühling, überall
Grüßen wir dich froh mit Sang und Schall,
   Mit Sang und Schall.

Du kommst, und froh ist alle Welt,
   Holder Frühling!
Es freut sich Wiese, Wald und Feld,
   Holder Frühling!
Jubel tönt dir überall,
Dich begrüßet Lerch' und Nachtigall,
   Und Nachtigall.

So sei gegrüßt viel tausendmal,
   Holder Frühling!
O bleib' recht lang' in unserm Tal,
   Holder Frühling!
Kehr' in alle Herzen ein,
Laß doch alle mit uns fröhlich sein,
   Fröhlich sein!

5
Vom Schlaraffenland / Cockaigne
HOFFMANN VON FALLERSLEBEN (1798–1874)

Kommt, wir wollen uns begeben
Jetzo ins Schlaraffenland!
Seht, da ist ein lustig Leben,
Und das Trauern unbekannt.
Seht, da läßt sich billig leben
Und umsonst recht lustig sein:
Milch und Honig fließt in Bächen,
Aus den Felsen quillt der Wein.

The meadows and woods!
Spring, don't be long in coming!

Cuckoo, cuckoo, gallant hero!
Your singing
Was successful:
Winter's on the run.

A thousand greetings to you,
   Sweetest Spring!
Welcome to our valley here,
   Sweetest Spring!
Sweetest Spring, wherever you be,
We salute you joyously
   With singing and rejoicing.

You come, and all the world's happy,
   Sweetest Spring!
Meadow, forest and field rejoice,
   Sweetest Spring!
Jubilation everywhere:
Lark and nightingale greet you,
   And nightingale.

A thousand greetings to you,
   Sweetest Spring!
O stay a long time in our valley,
   Rejoice with us!
Sweetest Spring!
Enter into every heart,
   Let everyone rejoice with us!

Come, let's now set out
For Cockaigne!
Look, life's merry there
And sorrow's unknown.
Look, you can live cheaply there,
And be happy for nothing at all:
Milk and honey flow in streams,
The waterfalls are wine.

Und von Kuchen, Butterwecken
Sind die Zweige voll und schwer;
Feigen wachsen in den Hecken,
Ananas im Busch umher.
Keiner darf sich müh'n und bücken,
Alles stellt von selbst sich ein.
O, wie ist es zum Entzücken!
Ei, wer möchte dort nicht sein!

Und die Straßen aller Orten,
Jeder Weg und jede Bahn
Sind gebaut aus Zuckertorten,
Und Bonbons und Marzipan.
Und von Brezeln sind die Brücken
Aufgeführt gar hübsch und fein.
O wie ist es zum Entzücken!
Ei, wer möchte dort nicht sein!

Ja, das mag ein schönes Leben
Und ein herrlich Ländchen sein!
Mancher hat sich hinbegeben,
Aber keiner kam hinein.
Ja, und habt ihr keine Flügel,
Nie gelangt ihr bis ans Tor,
Denn es liegt ein breiter Hügel
Ganz von Pflaumenmus davor.

And the boughs are weighed down
With cakes and buttered buns;
Figs grow in the hedgerows,
Pineapples in every copse.
No one there must work or slave,
Everything happens of its own accord.
O how delightful it is!
Who wouldn't wish to live there!

And every single street,
Every road and every path
Are made of sugar-plums
And sweets and marzipan.
And all the bridges are built
Of crisp, delicate pretzels.
O how delightful it is!
Who wouldn't wish to live there!

Yes, it must be a wonderful life
And a splendid little country!
Many have set out for it,
But no one's ever entered.
And unless you have wings,
You'll never reach the gate,
For outside stands a large hill,
Made entirely of plum jam.

6

Sonntag / Sunday
HOFFMANN VON FALLERSLEBEN (1798–1874)

Der Sonntag ist gekommen,
Ein Sträußchen auf dem Hut;
Sein Aug' ist mild und heiter,
Er meint's mit Allen gut.

Er steiget auf die Berge,
Er wandelt durch das Tal,
Und ladet zum Gebete
Die Menschen allzumal.

Und wie in schönen Kleidern
Nun pranget Jung und Alt,
Hat er für sie geschmücket
Die Flur und auch den Wald.

Und wie er Allen Freude
Und Frieden bringt und Ruh,
So ruf' auch du nun Jedem
„Gott grüß dich!" freundlich zu.

Sunday has come,
A posy in his hat,
His eyes are smiling and gentle,
He's friendly to everyone.

He climbs the mountains,
He walks through the valley,
Inviting everyone
To say their prayers.

And just as young and old are dressed
In their Sunday best,
He's beautified for them
The fields and the woods.

And just as he brings joy
And peace and rest to everyone,
So you should say a friendly 'God bless!'
To everyone you meet.

7
Zigeunerliedchen (1) / Gypsy song (1)

TRANSLATED FROM THE SPANISH BY EMANUEL GEIBEL (1815–84)

Unter die Soldaten ist
Ein Zigeunerbub' gegangen,
Mit dem Handgeld ging er durch,
Und morgen muß er hangen.

A gypsy lad
Joined the soldiers,
He ran off with the bounty
And tomorrow must hang.

Holten mich aus meinem Kerker,
Setzten auf den Esel mich,
Geißelten mir meine Schultern,
Daß das Blut floß auf den Weg.

They took me from my cell,
They set me on a donkey,
They scourged my shoulders
Till blood ran on the road.

Holten mich aus meinem Kerker,
Stießen mich ins Weite fort,
Griff ich rasch nach meiner Büchse,
Tat auf sie den ersten Schuß.

They took me from my cell,
They made me run for my life,
I swiftly drew my gun,
Fired at them the first shot.

8
Zigeunerliedchen (2) / Gypsy song (2)

TRANSLATED FROM THE SPANISH BY EMANUEL GEIBEL (1815–84) VERSE 2 ANON.

Jeden Morgen, in der Frühe,
Wenn mich weckt das Tageslicht,
Mit dem Wasser meiner Augen
Wasch' ich dann mein Angesicht.

Early every morning,
When daylight wakes me,
I wash my face
With water from my eyes.

Wo die Berge hoch sich türmen
An dem Saum des Himmels dort,
Aus dem Haus, dem schönen Garten
Trugen sie bei Nacht mich fort.

Where the mountains tower up high
On the horizon over there,
From my house and lovely garden
They dragged me away by night.

Jeden Morgen, in der Frühe,
Wenn mich weckt das Tageslicht,
Mit dem Wasser meiner Augen
Wasch' ich dann mein Angesicht.

Early every morning,
When daylight wakes me,
I wash my face
With water from my eyes.

9
Des Knaben Berglied / Song of the mountain lad

LUDWIG UHLAND (1787–1862)

Ich bin vom Berg der Hirtenknab',
Seh' auf die Schlösser all herab.
Die Sonne strahlt am ersten hier,
Am längsten weilet sie bei mir.
Ich bin der Knab' vom Berge,
Vom Berg der Hirtenknab'!

I'm the mountain shepherd lad,
I look down on all the castles.
This is where the sun shines first,
With me it lingers longest.
I'm the lad from the mountain,
The shepherd of the hills!

Der Berg, der ist mein Eigentum,
Da ziehn die Stürme rings herum,
Und heulen sie von Nord und Süd,
So überschallt sie doch mein Lied:
Ich bin der Knab' vom Berge,
Vom Berg der Hirtenknab'!

Sind Blitz und Donner unter mir,
So steh' ich hoch im Blauen hier;
Ich kenne sie und rufe zu:
Laßt meines Vaters Haus in Ruh!
Ich bin der Knab' vom Berge,
Vom Berg der Hirtenknab'!

Und wann die Sturmglock' einst erschallt,
Manch Feuer auf den Bergen wallt,
Dann steig' ich nieder, tret' ins Glied,
Und schwing' mein Schwert und sing' mein
    Lied:
Ich bin der Knab' vom Berge,
Vom Berg der Hirtenknab'!
(*Loewe*)

The mountain belongs to me,
The storms rage right round it,
And though they howl from north and south,
My song's louder than theirs:
I'm the lad from the mountain,
The shepherd of the hills!

Though thunder and lightning flash below me,
I stand up here in the blue sky;
I know them well and cry:
Leave my father's house alone!
I'm the lad from the mountain,
The shepherd of the hills!

And if the alarum should ever sound,
And fires should blaze on the mountain,
Then down I'll come and join the ranks
And brandish my sword and sing my
    song:
I'm the lad from the mountain,
The shepherd of the hills!

10

Mailied / May song [Duet]
CHRISTIAN ADOLF OVERBECK (1755–1821)

Komm' lieber Mai und mache
Die Bäume wieder grün,
Und laß uns an dem Bache
Die kleinen Veilchen blühn!
Wie möchten wir so gerne
Ein Blümchen wieder sehn,
Und in die frische Ferne,
In's grüne Freie gehn!

Komm, mach es bald gelinder,
Daß alles wieder blüht!
Dann wird das Flehn der Kinder
Ein lautes Jubellied.
O komm und bring vor allen
Uns viele Rosen mit!
Bring auch viel Nachtigallen
Und schöne Kuckucks mit.
(*Mozart*)

Come, sweet May, and turn
The trees green again,
And make the little violets
Bloom for us by the brook!
How we should love to see
A little flower again,
And journey into fresh open spaces
And go into the green outdoors!

Come, make the weather milder soon
That all things may bloom again!
Then the children's pleading
Will turn to loud rejoicing.
O come, and above all bring us
Many roses with you,
Bring many nightingales as well
And lovely cuckoos too.

Käuzlein / Owlet
FROM *Des Knaben Wunderhorn*

Ich armes Käuzlein kleine,	Poor owlet that I am,
Wo soll ich fliegen aus,	Where shall I fly,
Bei Nacht so gar alleine	Being so alone at night
Bringt mir so manchen Graus;	Makes me so afraid:
Das macht der Eulen Ungestalt,	That's because of that monster owl,
Ihr Trauern mannigfalt,	Who's always grieving one way or the other,
Ich armes Käuzlein!	Poor owlet that I am!

Ich will's Gefieder schwingen
Gen Holz im grünen Wald,
Die Vöglein hören singen
In mancherlei Gestalt.
Vor allen lieb ich Nachtigall,
Vor allen liebt mich Nachtigall,
Ich armes Käuzlein!

I'll fly off
To the green wood,
To hear all kinds
Of little birds sing.
I love the nightingale best of all,
The nightingale loves me best of all,
Poor owlet that I am!

Die Kinder unten glauben,
Ich deute Böses an,
Sie wollen mich vertreiben,
Daß ich nicht schreien kann:
Wenn ich was deute, tut mir's leid,
Und was ich schrei, ist keine Freud,
Ich armes Käuzlein!

The children down there
Believe I bring bad luck,
They want to drive me away,
So as not to hear me hoot:
I'm sorry if I'm an ill-omen,
And if my hooting brings no joy,
Poor owlet that I am!

Mein Ast ist mir entwichen,
Darauf ich ruhen sollt,
Sein Blättlein all verblichen,
Frau Nachtigall geholt:
Das schafft der Eulen falsche Tück,
Die störet all mein Glück,
Ich armes Käuzlein!
(*Louise Reichardt*)

The branch has withered
Where I'd planned to rest,
All its little leaves have faded,
And Mistress Nightingale has gone:
That's because of that treacherous owl,
It ruins all my happiness,
Poor owlet that I am!

Hinaus ins Freie! / Out into the open air!
HOFFMANN VON FALLERSLEBEN (1798–1874)

Wie blüht es im Tale,
Wie grünt's auf den Höh'n!
Und wie ist es doch im Freien,
Im Freien so schön!

How the valley's blooming,
How the hills are turning green!
How lovely it is
Out in the open air!

Es ladet der Frühling,
Der Frühling uns ein:

Spring invites us,
Spring bids us:

Nach der Weidenflöte sollen	To dance to the sound
Wir springen zum Reih'n.	Of the willow flute.
Es ladet der Frühling,	Spring invites us,
Der Frühling uns ein:	Spring bids us
Nach der Weidenflöte sollen	To dance to the sound
Wir springen zum Reih'n.	Of the willow flute.
Wer wollte nicht tanzen	Who wouldn't dance
Dem Frühling zu lieb?	In honour of spring?
Der den schlimmen langen Winter	Who finally banished
Uns endlich vertrieb?	The long wicked winter?
Wer wollte nicht tanzen	Who wouldn't dance
Dem Frühling zu lieb,	In honour of spring,
Der den schlimmen langen	Who finally banished
Winter uns endlich vertrieb?	The long wicked winter?
So kommet, so kommet	So come out, come out
Ins Freie hinaus!	Into the open air!
Wann die Abendglocke läutet,	When the evening bell rings,
Geht's wieder nach Haus.	We'll go back home.

13
Der Sandmann / The sandman
HERMANN KLETKE (1813–86)

Zwei feine Stieflein hab' ich an,	I wear two little soft boots
Mit wunderweichen Söhlchen d'ran,	With marvellously soft little soles,
Ein Säcklein hab' ich hinten auf,	I carry a little sack on my back,
Husch! trippl' ich rasch die Trepp' hinauf;	In a flash I slip upstairs;
Und wenn ich in die Stube tret',	And when I step into their room
Die Kinder beten ihr Gebet,	The children are saying their prayers,
Von meinem Sand zwei Körnelein	I sprinkle on their little eyes
Streu' ich auf ihre Äugelein,	Two little grains of my sand,
Da schlafen sie die ganze Nacht	Then they sleep all night long,
In Gottes und der Englein Wacht.	In the care of God and angels.
Von meinem Sand zwei Körnelein	I've sprinkled on their little eyes
Streut' ich auf ihre Äugelein,	Two little grains of my sand,
Den frommen Kindern soll gar schön	For all good children
Ein froher Traum vorübergehn.	Ought to have happy dreams.
Nun risch und rasch mit Sack und Stab	Quick as a flash with sack and wand
Nur wieder jetzt die Trepp' hinab,	I steal downstairs again,
Ich kann nicht länger müßig stehn,	I can't afford to linger longer,
Muß heut noch zu gar Vielen gehn, –	There are many more to visit tonight, –
Da nickt ihr schon und lacht im Traum,	You're nodding and smiling in your dreams,
Und öffnete doch mein Säcklein kaum!	Yet I hardly opened my sack at all!

14

Marienwürmchen / Ladybird

CAROLINE RUDOLPHI (1754–1811), INCLUDED IN *Des Knaben Wunderhorn*

Marienwürmchen, setze dich	Ladybird, come and settle
Auf meine Hand, auf meine Hand,	On my hand, on my hand,
Ich tu dir nichts zu Leide,	I shall do you no harm,
Es soll dir nichts zu Leid geschehn,	You shall suffer no harm,
Will nur deine bunten Flügel sehn,	I just want to see your bright wings,
Bunte Flügel, meine Freude!	Bright wings are my joy!
Marienwürmchen, fliege weg,	Ladybird, fly away home,
Dein Häuschen brennt, die Kinder schrein	Your house is on fire, the children are crying
So sehre, wie so sehre,	So much, so very much,
Die böse Spinne spinnt sie ein,	The wicked spider's spinning them in,
Marienwürmchen flieg hinein,	Ladybird, fly away home,
Deine Kinder schreien sehre.	Your children are crying so much.
Marienwürmchen, fliege hin	Ladybird, fly off
Zu Nachbars Kind, zu Nachbars Kind,	To the children next door, next door,
Sie tun dir nichts zu Leide,	They will do you no harm,
Es soll dir da kein Leid geschehn,	You shall suffer no harm,
Sie wollen deine bunten Flügel sehn,	They want to see your bright wings,
Und grüß sie alle beide.	And say hallo to them from me.

15

Die Waise / The orphan girl

HOFFMANN VON FALLERSLEBEN (1798–1874)

Der Frühling kehret wieder	Spring comes again
Und Alles freuet sich.	And everyone rejoices.
Ich blicke traurig nieder,	I look downcast,
Er kam ja nicht für mich.	It has not come for me.
Was soll mir armen Kinde	What am I, poor child, to make
Des Frühlings Pracht und Glanz?	Of spring's splendour and radiance?
Denn wenn ich Blumen winde,	For if I twine flowers,
Ist es zum Totenkranz.	It's for a funeral wreath.
Ach! keine Hand geleitet	Ah! there's no hand to guide me
Mich heim ins Vaterhaus,	Back to a father's house,
Und keine Mutter breitet	And no mother to hold out
Die Arme nach mir aus.	Her arms towards me.
O Himmel, gib mir wieder,	O Heaven, give me back
Was deine Liebe gab –	What your love once gave –
Blick' ich zur Erde nieder,	If I look down at the earth,
So seh' ich nur ihr Grab.	Their grave is all I see.

16

Das Glück / Fortune [Duet]
FRIEDRICH HEBBEL (1813–63)

Vöglein vom Zweig,
  Gaukelt hernieder;
Lustig sogleich
  Schwingt es sich wieder.

The bird on the bough
  Flits down;
He's back in a trice,
  Fluttering his wings.

Jetzt dir so nah,
  Jetzt sich versteckend,
Abermals da,
  Scherzend und neckend.

Now he's so near,
  Now's he's in hiding,
Then back once again,
  Joking and teasing.

Tastest du zu,
  Bist du betrogen,
Spottend im Nu
  Ist es entflogen.

Try to catch him
  And you're deceived,
Mocking, he's
  Gone in a flash.

Still! Bis zur Hand
  Wird's dir noch hüpfen,
Bist du gewandt,
  Kann's nicht entschlüpfen.

Shh! There he hops
  Onto your hand,
Now if you're quick,
  He won't get away.

Ist's denn so schwer,
  Das zu erwarten?
Schau' um dich her;
  Blühender Garten!

Is it so hard
  To exercise patience?
Just look around you;
  A garden in bloom!

Ei du verzagst?
  Laß es gewähren,
Bis du's erjagst,
  Kannst du's entbehren.

What, are you timid?
  Just let things be,
Until you catch him,
  You can do without him.

Wird's doch auch dann
  Wenig nur bringen,
Aber es kann
  Süßestes bringen.
(*Wolf*)

He'll not bring much
  Even then,
But he can
  Bring great sweetness.

17

Weihnachtslied / Christmas carol
HANS CHRISTIAN ANDERSEN (1805–75)

  Als das Christkind ward zur Welt gebracht,
Das uns von der Hölle gerettet,
Da lag's auf der Krippe bei finstrer Nacht,
Auf Stroh und Heu gebettet;
Doch über der Hütte glänzte der Stern,

  When the Christ-child was born,
Who saved us from Hell,
He lay in his crib when the night was dark,
With straw and hay for bedding;
Yet over the stable there shone the star,

Und der Ochse küßte den Fuß des Herrn;	And the ox kissed the feet of the Lord.
Halleluja, Kind Jesus!	Hallelujah, Child Jesus!
Ermanne dich, Seele, die krank und matt,	Take courage, sick and weary soul,
Vergiß die nagenden Schmerzen.	Forget your nagging sorrows.
Ein Kind ward geboren in Davids Stadt	A child was born in David's town
Zum Trost für alle Herzen.	To comfort every heart.
O, laßt uns wallen zum Kindlein hin,	O let us pilgrimage to the little child,
Und Kinder werden in Geist und Sinn;	And ourselves become children in mind and spirit;
Halleluja, Kind Jesus!	Hallelujah, Child Jesus!

18

Die wandelnde Glocke / The walking bell
JOHANN WOLFGANG VON GOETHE (1749–1832)
See Loewe, p. 172

19

Frühlingslied / Spring song [Duet]
HOFFMANN VON FALLERSLEBEN (1798–1874)

Schneeglöckchen klingen wieder,	Snowdrops sound their bells again,
Schneeglöckchen bringen wieder	Snowdrops bring back again
Uns heit're Tag' und Lieder.	Our happy days and songs.
Wie läuten sie so schön	How beautifully they peal
Im Tal und auf den Höh'n:	In the valley and on the hills:
Der König ziehet ein!	The king's marching in!
Der König ist erschienen,	The king's here again,
Ihr sollt ihm treulich dienen	You should serve him faithfully
Mit heit'rem Blick und Mienen!	With cheerful gaze and countenance!
O, laßt den König ein!	O let the king enter in!
Er kommt vom Sterngefilde	He comes from the starry spheres,
Und führt in seinem Schilde	And the only things he has in mind
Die Güte nur und Milde;	Are gentleness and kindness;
Er trägt die Freud' und Lust	The star on his breast
Als Stern an seiner Brust:	Is the star of happiness and joy:
Ist gnädig Jedermann,	He's gracious to everyone,
Den Herren und den Knechten,	To gentlemen and servants,
Den Guten und den Schlechten,	To the good and the bad,
Den Bösen und Gerechten,	To the wicked and the just –
Sieht alle liebreich an.	On all he turns a loving eye.
Ihr aber fragt und wißt es,	But you ask and you know,
Und wer's auch weiß, vergißt es,	And whoever knows forgets,
Der König Frühling ist es.	This monarch is the spring.
Entgegen ihm mit Sang,	Go to him with song
Mit Saitenspiel und Klang!	And the playing of strings!
Der König ziehet ein!	The king's marching in!
Der König ist erschienen,	The king's here again,

Ihr sollt ihm treulich dienen
Mit heit'rem Blick und Mienen!
O, laßt den König ein!

You should serve him faithfully
With cheerful gaze and countenance!
O let the king enter in!

20

Frühlingsankunft / Spring's arrival
HOFFMANN VON FALLERSLEBEN (1798–1874)

Nach diesen trüben Tagen,
Wie ist so hell das Feld!
Zerrißne Wolken tragen
Die Trauer aus der Welt.

After these dull days
How bright the fields are!
Tattered clouds bear
The world's sorrows away.

Und Keim und Knospe mühet
Sich an das Licht hervor,
Und manche Blume blühet
Zum Himmel still empor.

And seeds and buds
Struggle towards the light;
And many a flower blossoms
In silence up to heaven.

Ja, auch sogar die Eichen
Und Reben werden grün!
O Herz, das sei dein Zeichen!
Werde froh und kühn!

Yes, even the oaks
And vines turn green!
O heart, let this be your sign!
Be joyous and bold!

21

Die Schwalben / The swallows [Duet]
AUGUSTE VON PATTBERG (1769–1850), INCLUDED IN *Des Knaben Wunderhorn*

Es fliegen zwei Schwalben in's Nachbar sein
    Haus,
Sie fliegen bald hoch, bald nieder,
Auf's Jahr da kommen sie wieder
Und suchen ihr voriges Haus.

Up and down two swallows
    fly
Into the house next door,
In a year they'll be back again
In search of their former home.

Sie gehen jetzt fort in's neue Land,
Und ziehen jetzt eilig hinüber;
Doch kommen sie wieder herüber,
Das ist einem jeden bekannt.

Now they set out for pastures new,
And hasten across the sky;
But they'll be back here again,
As everybody knows.

Und kommen sie wieder zu uns zurück,
Der Bauer geht ihnen entgegen,
Sie bringen ihm vielmal den Segen,
Sie bringen ihm Wohlstand und Glück!

And when they return to us again,
The farmer will go to meet them,
They bring him blessings in abundance,
Good fortune and prosperity!

22

Kinderwacht / Watching over children
MELCHIOR VON DIEPENBROCK (1798–1853)

Wenn fromme Kindlein schlafen gehn,
An ihrem Bett zwei Englein stehn,

When good children go to sleep,
Two little angels stand by their beds,

| Decken sie zu, decken sie auf, | They tuck them in and pull back the covers, |
| Haben ein liebendes Auge d'rauf. | And keep a loving eye on them. |

Wenn aber auf die Kindlein stehn,	But when the children get up,
Die beiden Engel schlafen gehn,	Both the angels go to sleep,
Reicht nun nicht mehr der Englein Macht,	If the angels' strength is no longer enough,
Der liebe Gott hält selbst die Wacht.	The good Lord himself keeps watch.

23
Des Sennen Abschied / The alpine herdsman's farewell
FRIEDRICH VON SCHILLER (1759–1805), FROM *Wilhelm Tell*

Ihr Matten, lebt wohl!	Farewell, you meadows!
Ihr sonnigen Weiden!	You sunny pastures!
Der Senne muß scheiden,	The herdsman must leave you,
Der Sommer ist hin.	Summer is over.

Wir fahren zu Berg, wir kommen wieder,	We'll return to the mountains, we'll come again,
Wenn der Kuckuck ruft, wenn erwachen die Lieder,	When the cuckoo calls, when songs awaken,
Wenn mit Blumen die Erde sich kleidet neu,	When the earth is freshly clothed with flowers,
Wenn die Brünnelein fließen im lieblichen Mai.	When the brooklets are flowing in lovely May.

Ihr Matten, lebt wohl!	Farewell, you meadows!
Ihr sonnigen Weiden!	You sunny pastures!
Der Senne muß scheiden,	The herdsman must leave you,
Der Sommer ist hin.	Summer is over.
(*Liszt*)	

24
Er ists / Spring is here
EDUARD MÖRIKE (1804–75)
See Wolf, p. 639

25
Spinnelied / Spinning song [Duet]
ANON.

Spinn', Mägdlein, spinn'!	Spin, maiden, spin!
So wachsen dir die Sinn',	Then your wits will grow,
Wachsen dir die gelben Haar',	And when your blond hair grows,
Kommen dir die klugen Jahr'.	Your years of wisdom will come.
Spinn', Mägdlein, spinn'!	Spin, maiden, spin!

Sing', Mägdlein, sing',	Sing, maiden, sing,
Und sei fein guter Ding',	And be of good cheer,
Fang' dein Spinnen lustig an,	Start your spinning cheerily,

Mach' ein frommes End' daran.
Sing', Mägdlein, sing'!

Lern', Mägdlein, lern',
So hast du Glück und Stern;
Lerne bei dem Spinnen fort
Gottesfurcht und Gotteswort.
Lern', Mägdlein, lern'!

Lob', Mägdlein, lob',
Dem Schöpfer halte Prob';
Daß dir Glaub und Hoffnung wachs'
Wie dein Garn und wie dein Flachs.
Lob', Mägdlein, lob'!

Dank', Mägdlein, dank'
Dem Herrn, daß du nicht krank,
Daß du kannst fein oft und viel
Treiben dieses Rockenspiel.
Dank', Mägdlein, dank'!
(*Reinecke*)

Conclude it dutifully,
Sing, maiden, sing!

Learn, maiden, learn,
Then fortune will smile on you;
Learn, as you spin,
The fear of God and God's word.
Learn, maiden, learn!

Praise, maiden, praise,
Rehearse for your Creator,
So your faith and hope might grow
Like your yarn and like your flax.
Praise, maiden, praise!

Thank, maiden, thank
The Lord you are not sick,
That you can work this distaff
Many a time and oft.
Thank, maiden, thank!

26

Des Buben Schützenlied / The boy's hunting song
FRIEDRICH VON SCHILLER (1759–1805), FROM *Wilhelm Tell*

Mit dem Pfeil, dem Bogen
Durch Gebirg und Tal,
Kommt der Schütz gezogen
Früh im Morgenstrahl.

Wie im Reich der Lüfte
König ist der Weih',
Durch Gebirg und Klüfte
Herrscht der Schütze frei.

Ihm gehört das Weite;
Was sein Pfeil erreicht,
Das ist seine Beute,
Was da kreucht und fleugt.

With the arrow, with the bow,
Through mountains and valleys
The archer goes his way
In the early light of dawn.

As in the breezes' realm,
The kite is king,
So, over peak and gorge,
The archer holds sway.

The wide spaces belong to him;
Whatever his arrow hits,
That is his prey,
Be it bird or beast.

27

Schneeglöckchen / Snowdrop
FRIEDRICH RÜCKERT (1788–1866)

Der Schnee, der gestern noch in Flöckchen
Vom Himmel fiel,
Hängt nun geronnen heut als Glöckchen
Am zarten Stiel.

The snow that only yesterday fell in flakes
From the sky,
Hangs now, frozen, as a little bell
From a delicate stem.

Schneeglöckchen läutet; was bedeutet's	A snowdrop rings; what can it mean
Im stillen Hain?	In the silent grove?
O komm geschwind! im Haine läutet's	O come quickly! In the grove it's ringing
Den Frühling ein.	Springtime in.

O kommt, ihr Blätter, Blüt und Blume,	Come quickly, leaves, blossom and flowers,
Die ihr noch träumt,	You who still dream,
All' zu des Frühlings Heiligtume!	Into spring's sanctuary!
Kommt ungesäumt!	Come without delay!

28
Lied Lynceus' des Türmers / Song of Lynceus the watchman
JOHANN WOLFGANG VON GOETHE (1749–1832)
See Loewe, p. 175

See Loewe, p. 175

29
Mignon / Mignon
JOHANN WOLFGANG VON GOETHE (1749–1832)
See Wolf, p. 594

See Wolf, p. 594

Friedrich Silcher (1789–1860)

Having studied piano and composition with Kreutzer and Hummel, Silcher became Director of Tübingen University, where he founded the Akademische Liedertafel in 1820 and the Oratorienchor in 1839. In 1816 he met Pestalozzi, with whom he shared the view that music and singing were the most important means to the improvement and education of man – a conviction which led him to compose some 250 strophic songs with piano accompaniment and countless pieces for men's choir. His *Melodies from Beethoven's Sonatas and Symphonies, arranged as Songs* were published by Zumsteeg in 1840 – with the aim of popularizing Beethoven's melodies in domestic music circles. Though Silcher collected and arranged a great number of folksongs from Germany and other countries, many of his own songs, such as 'Lore-Ley', 'Ännchen von Tharau' and 'Morgen muß ich weg von hier', have acquired folksong status in Germany.

Simon Dach (1605–59)

The poem was written in 1637 to celebrate the wedding of Dach's schoolfriend Johannes Portatius to Anna, the daughter of Pastor Andreas Neander of Tharau near Königsberg. The original, written in East-Prussian dialect, was rendered by Herder in his *Stimmen der Völker in Liedern* (1778) into High German. Dach worked as a schoolmaster in Königsberg, where he was appointed professor of poetry in 1639. He wrote a great deal of occasional verse for weddings, funerals, christenings and graduations. 'Ännchen von Tharau' is now thought by some scholars to be the work of Heinrich Albert.

Ännchen von Tharau / Annie of Tharau

Ännchen von Tharau ist, die mir gefällt;	Annie of Tharau is the one whom I love,
Sie ist mein Leben, mein Gut und mein Geld.	She is my life, my riches, my wealth.
Ännchen von Tharau hat wieder ihr Herz	Annie of Tharau has once again
Auf mich gerichtet in Lieb' und in Schmerz.	Pledged me her heart in love and pain.
Ännchen von Tharau, mein Reichtum, mein Gut,	Annie of Tharau, my wealth, my riches,
Du meine Seele, mein Fleisch und mein Blut!	O you my soul, my flesh and my blood!
Käm' alles Wetter gleich auf uns zu schlahn,	Though wild weather were to smite us,
Wir sind gesinnt bei einander zu stahn.	We are resolved to stand by each other.
Krankheit, Verfolgung, Betrübnis und Pein	Persecution, sickness, sorrow and pain
Soll unsrer Liebe Verknotigung sein.	Shall only serve to strengthen our love.

Recht als ein Palmenbaum über sich steigt,	Just as a palm tree stands straight and tall,
Je mehr ihn Hagel und Regen anficht;	The more it's lashed by hail and rain;
So wird die Lieb' in uns mächtig und groß	So shall our love grow mighty and strong
Durch Kreuz, durch Leiden, durch allerlei Not.	Through hardship, suffering and distress.
Würdest du gleich einmal von mir getrennt,	Were you even to be parted from me,
Lebtest da, wo man die Sonne kaum kennt:	Were to live where the sun scarcely shines:
Ich will dir folgen durch Wälder, durch Meer,	I shall follow you across forest and ocean,
Durch Eis, durch Eisen, durch feindliches Heer.	Through ice, through swords and enemy ranks.
Ännchen von Tharau, mein Licht, meine Sonn',	Annie of Tharau, my light, my sun,
Mein Leben schließ' ich um deines herum.	I'll weave our two lives into one.

Heinrich Heine (1797–1856)

See Mendelssohn, Robert Schumann, Wolf

Lore-Ley / Loreley

Ich weiß nicht, was soll es bedeuten,	I do not know what it means
Daß ich so traurig bin;	That I should feel so sad;
Ein Märchen aus alten Zeiten,	There is a tale from olden times
Das kommt mir nicht aus dem Sinn.	I cannot get out of my mind.
Die Luft ist kühl und es dunkelt,	The air is cool, and twilight falls,
Und ruhig fließt der Rhein;	And the Rhine flows quietly by;
Der Gipfel des Berges funkelt	The summit of the mountain glitters
Im Abendsonnenschein.	In the evening sun.
Die schönste Jungfrau sitzet	The fairest maiden is sitting
Dort oben wunderbar,	In wondrous beauty up there,
Ihr goldnes Geschmeide blitzet,	Her golden jewels are sparkling,
Sie kämmt ihr goldenes Haar.	She combs her golden hair.
Sie kämmt es mit goldenem Kamme	She combs it with a golden comb
Und singt ein Lied dabei;	And sings a song the while;
Das hat eine wundersame,	It has an awe-inspiring,
Gewaltige Melodei.	Powerful melody.
Den Schiffer im kleinen Schiffe	It seizes the boatman in his skiff
Ergreift es mit wildem Weh;	With wildly aching pain;
Er schaut nicht die Felsenriffe,	He does not see the rocky reefs,
Er schaut nur hinauf in die Höh'.	He only looks up to the heights.
Ich glaube, die Wellen verschlingen	I think at last the waves swallow
Am Ende Schiffer und Kahn;	The boatman and his boat;
Und das hat mit ihrem Singen	And that, with her singing,
Die Lorelei getan.	The Loreley has done.
(*Gade, Lachner, Liszt, Raff*)	

Louis Spohr (1784–1859)

Due to his long life, Spohr was a contemporary of Beethoven, Schubert, Schumann and the young Wagner, whose *Der fliegende Holländer* and *Tannhäuser* he championed. He was a well-known conductor and celebrated virtuoso violinist. A friend of both Beethoven and Weber, he wrote some ten operas, fifteen violin concertos, over thirty string quartets, a great deal of chamber and choral music and about a hundred Lieder. He was one of the first opera composers to use the leitmotif (*Faust*, 1813), and the first to compose a German grand opera (*Jessonda*, 1823); he also used the *Tristan* chord as early as 1830, in his opera *Der Alchymist*. Yet despite such originality, much of his music fell into oblivion, including his songs. Six of these were composed to Goethe texts: 'Gretchen am Spinnrade' five years before Schubert's version, 'Ziegeunerlied' (1809), 'Vanitas! Vanitatum vanitas', 'Kennst du das Land', 'An Mignon' (1815) and an 'Erlkönig' (1856) for baritone, violin and piano. His most successful songs are the *Sechs Lieder für Sopran, Klarinette und Klavier* (1837), which were written expressly for his friend Johann Simon Hermstedt, who premiered all of Spohr's works for the clarinet.

1837 *Sechs Lieder für Sopran mit Begleitung von Klarinette und Klavier / Six songs for soprano with clarinet and piano accompaniment* Op. 103

1

Sei still, mein Herz / Be still, my heart
KARL VON SCHWEIZER (1797–1847)

Ich wahrte die Hoffnung tief in der Brust,	I harboured a hope deep in my heart
Die sich ihr vertrauend erschlossen,	I had trustingly surrendered to her,
Mir strahlten die Augen voll Lebenslust,	My eyes sparkled with zest for life,
Wenn mich ihre Zauber umflossen,	When her charms streamed round me,
Wenn ich ihrer schmeichelnden Stimme	When I heard her cajoling
gelauscht –	voice –
Im Wettersturm ist ihr Echo verrauscht,	Now its echo is lost in the storm,
Sei still, mein Herz, und denke nicht d'ran,	Be still, my heart, think no more of it,
Das ist nun die Wahrheit, das And're war	This is the truth, the rest was
Wahn.	delusion.
Die Erde lag vor mir im Frühlingstraum,	The earth lay before me in a Spring dream
Den Licht und Wärme durchglühte,	That glowed with light and warmth,
Und wonnetrunken durchwallt' ich den Raum,	Drunk with joy I wandered up and down,
Der Brust entsproßte die Blüte,	Blossoms burgeoned in my heart,
Der Liebe Lenz war in mir erwacht –	Love's Spring had woken in me –
Mich durchrieselt Frost, in der Seele ist Nacht.	Frost now chills me, my soul is benighted,
Sei still, mein Herz, und denke nicht d'ran,	Be still, my heart, think no more of it,
Das ist nun die Wahrheit, das And're war	This is the truth, the rest was
Wahn.	delusion.

Ich baute von Blumen und Sonnenglanz
Eine Brücke mir durch das Leben,
Auf der ich wandelnd im Lorbeerkranz
Mich geweiht dem hochedelsten Streben;
Der Menschen Dank war mein schönster
Lohn –
Laut auflacht' die Menge mit frechem Hohn,
Sei still, mein Herz und denke nicht d'ran,
Das ist nun die Wahrheit, das And're war
Wahn.

Throughout my life I built a bridge
Of flowers and sunny radiance,
On which, wreathed in laurel, I devoted
myself
To the noblest of aspirations;
Human gratitude was my richest reward –
The mob laughed in derisive scorn
Be still, my heart, think no more of it,
This is the truth, the rest was delusion.

2
Zwiegesang / Duet
ROBERT REINICK (1805–52)

Im Fliederbusch ein Vöglein saß
In der stillen, schönen Maiennacht,
Darunter ein Mägdlein im hohen Gras
In der stillen, schönen Maiennacht.
Sang Mägdlein, hielt das Vöglein Ruh,
Sang Vöglein, hört' das Mägdlein zu,
    Und weithin klang
    Der Zwiegesang
Das mondbeglänzte Tal entlang.

A bird sat perched in the lilac-bush
One silent, lovely May night,
A girl sat in the tall grass below,
One silent, lovely May night.
When the girl sang, the bird fell silent,
When the bird sang, the girl listened,
    And their dialogue echoed
    Far and wide
Along the moonlit valley.

Was sang das Vöglein im Gezweig
Durch die stille, schöne Maiennacht?
Was sang doch wohl das Mägdlein gleich
Durch die stille, schöne Maiennacht?
Von Frühlingssonne das Vögelein,
Von Liebeswonne das Mägdelein;
    Wie der Gesang
    Zum Herzen drang,
Vergeß' ich nimmer mein Leben lang!
(*Schoenberg*)

What did the bird sing in the branches
Through the silent, lovely May night?
And what did the girl sing too
Through the silent, lovely May night?
The bird sang of springtime sun,
The girl of love's rapture;
    How that song
    Pierced my heart,
I shall remember all my life!

3
Sehnsucht / Longing
EMANUEL GEIBEL (1815–84)

Ich blick' in mein Herz und ich blick' in die
Welt,
Bis vom schwimmenden Auge die Träne mir
fällt;
Wohl leuchtet die Ferne mit goldenem Licht,
Doch hält mich der Nord, ich erreiche sie
nicht.
O die Schranken so eng und die Welt so weit,
Und so flüchtig die Zeit!

I look in my heart and I look out into the
world,
Till tears fall from my brimming eyes;
Though the distant horizon gleams
golden,
The North holds me back, I cannot reach it.
Oh, the bounds are so narrow and the world
is so wide,
And time so fleeting!

Ich weiß ein Land, wo aus sonnigem Grün
Um versunkene Tempel die Trauben glüh'n,
Wo die purpurne Woge das Ufer beschäumt
Und von kommenden Sängern der Lorbeer
    träumt.
Fern lockt es und winkt dem verlangenden
    Sinn,
Und ich kann nicht hin!

O hätt' ich Flügel, durch Blau der Luft
Wie wollt' ich baden im Sonnenduft!
Doch umsonst! Und Stunde auf Stunde ent-
    flieht –
Vertraure die Jugend, begrabe das Lied! –
O die Schranken so eng und die Welt so weit,
Und so flüchtig die Zeit!
(*Robert Schumann*)

I know a land where grapes glow
Among sunny foliage round sunken
    temples,
Where purple waves foam on the shore
And the laurel dreams of poets to come.
It lures from afar, beckons my yearning
    mind,
And I cannot go there!

Oh! if I had wings, in the blue sky
I'd bathe in the sun's vapour!
But in vain! Hour after hour goes by –
Mourn for lost youth, bury the song! –
Oh, the bounds are so narrow and the world
    is so wide,
And time so fleeting!

4
Wiegenlied (in drei Tönen) / Cradle song (on three notes)
HOFFMANN VON FALLERSLEBEN (1798–1874)

Alles still in süßer Ruh,
Drum, mein Kind, so schlaf auch du!
Draußen säuselt nur der Wind,
Su susu, schlaf ein, mein Kind!

Schließ du deine Äugelein,
Laß sie wie zwei Knospen sein!
Morgen, wenn die Sonn' erglüht,
Sind sie wie die Blum' erblüht.

Und die Blümlein schau' ich an,
Und die Äuglein küß' ich dann,
Und der Mutter Herz vergißt,
Daß es draußen Frühling ist.

All is silent in sweet peace,
So go to sleep too, my child!
The wind is rustling outside:
Lullaby! go to sleep, my child!

Shut tight your little eyes,
Let them be like two buds!
Tomorrow, when the sun shines,
They will have opened like the flowers.

And I'll gaze at the little flowers,
And kiss those little eyes,
And your mother's heart shall forget
That it's Spring outside.

5
Das heimliche Leid / Secret grief
ERNST KOCH (1808–58)

Es gibt geheime Schmerzen,
Sie klaget nie der Mund,
Getragen tief im Herzen
Sind sie der Welt nicht kund.
Es gibt ein heimlich Sehnen,
Das scheuet stets das Licht,
Es gibt verborgne Tränen,
Der Fremde sieht sie nicht.

There is a secret ache
That lips never utter,
Borne deep in the heart,
Unknown to the world.
There is a secret longing
That always shuns the light,
There are hidden tears
The stranger does not see.

Es gibt ein still Versinken
In eine inn're Welt,
Wo Friedensauen winken
Von Sternenglanz erhellt,
Wo auf gefall'nen Schranken
Die Seele Himmel baut,
Und jubelnd den Gedanken
Den Lippen anvertraut.

Es gibt ein still' Vergehen
In stummen, öden Schmerz,
Und niemand darf es sehen,
Das schwergepreßte Herz.
Es sagt nicht was ihm fehlet,
Und wenn's im Grame bricht,
Verblutet und zerquälet,
Der Fremde sieht es nicht.

Es gibt einen sanften Schlummer,
Wo süßer Frieden weilt,
Wo stille Ruh' den Kummer
Der müden Seele heilt.
Doch gibt's ein schöner Hoffen,
Das Welten überfliegt,
Da wo am Herzen offen
Das Herz voll Liebe liegt.

There is a quiet sinking
Into an inner world,
Where peaceful meadows beckon,
Lit by gleaming stars,
Where on fallen barriers
The soul erects a heaven
And joyfully entrusts
Thoughts to its lips.

There is a quiet dying
In desolate, mute grief,
And not a soul may see
The heaviness of heart.
It does not say what ails it,
And when it breaks in anguish,
Bleeding and tormented,
The stranger does not see.

There is a gentle sleep
Where sweet peace dwells,
Where quiet rest heals
The weary soul's sorrow.
Yet there is a sweeter hope
That flies above the earth,
Where a heart brimming with love
Rests against an open heart.

6

Wach auf! / Awaken!
ANON.

Was stehst du lange und sinnest nach?
Ach, schon so lange ist Liebe wach!
Hörst du das Klingen allüberall?
Die Vöglein singen mit süßem Schall;
Aus Starrem sprießet Baumblättlein weich,
Das Leben fließet um Ast und Zweig.
Das Tröpflein schlüpfet aus Waldesschacht,
Das Bächlein hüpfet mit Wallungsmacht;
Der Himmel neiget in's Wellenklar,
Die Bläue zeiget sich wunderbar.
Ein heit'res Schwingen zu Form und Klang,
Ein ew'ges Fügen im ew'gen Drang!
Was stehest du bange und sinnest nach?
Ach, schon so lange ist Liebe wach!

Why stand there so long, lost in thought?
Ah, love has been awake so long!
Can you not hear the ringing all about you?
The birds are singing sweet songs;
Leaves shoot gently from frozen trees,
Life flows around branches and twigs.
Drops slip down woodland ravines,
The little stream foams along;
The sky leans down to the limpid waves,
Its blueness shows wondrously clear.
Joy vibrates in shapes and sounds,
Eternally part of eternal creation!
Why stand there fearfully, lost in thought?
Ah, love has been awake so long!

Richard Strauss (1864–1949)

Strauss's first song, 'Weihnachtslied' (wonderfully set by Schubart), was written when he was six years old, and 41 more juvenilia followed before he composed the eight songs of Op. 10 in 1882–3. Most of his two hundred or so Lieder were composed between 1882 and 1905, the year of his Op. 56, published by Bote & Bock, with a clause in Strauss's contract which stipulated that the Berlin publishing house would hold the rights to his next group of songs. Such a clause was now anathema to Strauss, whose ambitions to protect the rights of German composers in matters of fees and royalties had led to the founding of a Society of German Composers and – subsequently – the founding of a rival Society by Bote & Bock to protect their own interests. Strauss's refusal to write a group of songs for them meant that for twelve years after the publication of Op. 56 he composed no further Lieder – until in 1918 the Berlin publishers threatened him with legal action. Strauss's response was to compose the scurrilous *Krämerspiegel*, a virulent attack on music publishers, which Bote & Bock refused to accept. To break the deadlock, Strauss dashed off his Op. 67, comprising three mad Ophelia songs (paradoxically among his best) and three bad-tempered songs from the 'Book of Ill-humour' from Goethe's *West-östlicher Divan*. Strauss now continued to write songs again, but less prolifically than before. His last songs, the *Vier letzte Lieder*, date from 1948, a year before his death.

Strauss's songs divide music-lovers more than those of any other Lieder composer. His detractors criticize him for his choice of banal or saccharine texts, and it is true that the Lieder of Opp. 10, 15, 17, 19, 21, and 22 set second-rate poems by Gilm, Schack and Dahn – contemporaries who were known to his father. But the important thing for Strauss was melodic inspiration. As he wrote to Joseph Gregor on 12 May 1939:

> Viele Lieder verdanken ihre Entstehung dem Umstand, daß der Componist zu einem schönen melodischen Einfall und einer poetischen musikalischen Stimmung ein Gedicht sucht: Brahmssche Lieder!

> Many songs owe their origin to the circumstance that the composer looks for a poem that will match a fine melodic idea and the poetically musical atmosphere: Brahmsian songs!

And the same letter contains the much-quoted statement: 'ein vollendetes Göthesches Gedicht braucht keine Musik, gerade bei Göthe schwächt die Musik und verflacht das Wort' ('a perfect Goethe poem does not need any music, because precisely in the case of Goethe, music weakens and flattens out every word'). Unlike many other great Lieder composers, Strauss seldom devoted an entire opus

to a single poet, the exceptions being the four Dahn Lieder of Op. 22, the five
Uhland Lieder of Op. 47, the twelve Kerr Lieder of Op. 66, the Brentano-Lieder of
Op. 68 and Shakespeare's *Ophelia-Lieder* of Op. 67. Yet Strauss was widely read,
and as he grew more famous through the success of his operas and tone-poems,
his choice of poets became more sophisticated. He turns his attention to the more
contemporary verse of Liliencron, Bierbaum, Dehmel and Hesse, and also
explores the nineteenth century poetic world of Goethe, Eichendorff, Heine,
Uhland, Klopstock, Lenau, Rückert, Arnim, Brentano and Meyer. Even the detrac-
tors of pieces such as 'Zueignung', 'Morgen! . . .', 'Ständchen', 'Traum durch die
Dämmerung', 'Allerseelen', 'Die Nacht' and 'Waldseligkeit' would have to concede
that in songs like 'Befreit', 'Gefunden' and 'Im Spätboot' Strauss created songs that
are a match for any of the most serious songs of his predecessors.

Anonymous

31 March 1898 **Hat gesagt – bleibt's nicht dabei / It won't stop there Op. 36, no. 3**
FROM *Des Knaben Wunderhorn*, EDITED BY ACHIM VON ARNIM AND CLEMENS BRENTANO

Mein Vater hat gesagt,	My father told me
Ich soll das Kindlein wiegen,	To rock the baby,
Er will mir auf den Abend	In the evening, he said,
Drei Gaggeleier sieden;	He'd boil me three eggs;
Siedt er mir drei,	If he boils me three,
Ißt er mir zwei,	He'll eat two,
Und ich mag nicht wiegen	And I don't want to rock
Um ein einziges Ei.	For a single egg.
Mein Mutter hat gesagt,	My mother told me
Ich soll die Mägdlein verraten,	To tell on the maids,
Sie wollt mir auf den Abend	In the evening, she said,
Drei Vögelein braten, ja braten;	She'd roast me three birds;
Brat sie mir drei,	If she roasts me three,
Ißt sie mir zwei,	She'll eat two,
Um ein einzig Vöglein,	For a single bird
Treib ich kein Verräterei.	I'll not turn traitor.
Mein Schätzlein hat gesagt,	My sweetheart told me
Ich soll sein gedenken,	I should think of him,
Er wollt mir auf den Abend	In the evening, he said,
Drei Küßlein auch schenken;	He'd give me three kisses;
Schenkt er mir drei,	If he gives me three,
Bleibt's nicht dabei,	It won't stop there,
Was kümmert mich's Vöglein,	What do I care for the bird,
Was schiert mich das Ei.	What do I care for the egg.
(*Reger*)	

Ludwig Achim von Arnim (1781–1831)

Poet, novelist and dramatist. After a three-year tour of Europe he settled with Clemens Brentano in Heidelberg where the two friends devoted themselves to collecting German folk-poems, which they frequently reworked or rewrote before publishing them in the three volumes of *Des Knaben Wunderhorn* between 1805–8. The success of these volumes made Arnim and Brentano the undisputed leaders of the Heidelberg Romantic school. Arnim's poem, which he simply called 'Stern', refers to the appearance in 1811 of the comet which the people of Prussia hailed as an encouraging omen after the disastrous campaign against Russia. Arnim, with his aristocratic connexions, was an ardent patriot and volunteered for service when Prussia mobilized against Napoleon.

21 June 1918 Der Stern / The star Op. 69, no. 1
FROM *Raphael und seine Nachbarinnen*

Ich sehe ihn wieder	I see it again
Den lieblichen Stern;	The beautiful star;
Er winket hernieder,	It beckons to me,
Er nahte mir gern;	And would like to draw near;
Er wärmet und funkelt,	It warms and it glitters,
Je näher er kömmt,	The closer it comes,
Die andern verdunkelt,	It dims the others,
Die Herzen beklemmt.	Oppresses hearts.
Die Haare im Fliegen	With flowing mane
Er eilet mir zu,	It hurries towards me,
Das Volk träumt von Siegen,	The people dream of victory,
Ich träume von Ruh',	I dream of peace,
Die andern sich deuten	From it the others
Die Zukunft daraus,	Predict the future,
Vergangene Zeiten	For me it merely
Mir leuchten ins Haus.	Illumines the past.

25 June 1918 Einerlei / Sameness Op. 69, no. 3

Ihr Mund ist stets derselbe,	Her mouth is always the same,
Sein Kuß mir immer neu,	Its kiss is ever new,
Ihr Auge noch dasselbe,	Her eyes remain the same,
Sein freier Blick mir treu;	Their frank gaze true to me;
O du liebes Einerlei,	O you dear sameness,
Wie wird aus dir so mancherlei!	The diversity that comes of you!

Otto Julius Bierbaum (1865–1910)

Although Bierbaum wrote novels, Novellen and plays, it was as a poet that this successful journalist made his mark, especially the satirical verse he wrote for Ernst von Wolzogen's 'Überbrettl' cabaret, which influenced both Wedekind, Brecht and Schoenberg, who set Bierbaum's 'Gigerlette' as one of his *Brettl-Lieder* (1901).

4 May 1895 Traum durch die Dämmerung / Dream into dusk Op. 29, no. 1

Weite Wiesen im Dämmergrau;	Broad meadows in grey dusk;
Die Sonne verglomm, die Sterne ziehn;	The sun has set, the stars come out;
Nun geh' ich hin zu der schönsten Frau,	I go now to the loveliest woman,
Weit über Wiesen im Dämmergrau,	Far across meadows in grey dusk,
Tief in den Busch von Jasmin.	Deep into the jasmine grove.
Durch Dämmergrau in der Liebe Land;	Through grey dusk into the land of love;
Ich gehe nicht schnell, ich eile nicht;	I do not go fast, I do not hurry;
Mich zieht ein weiches, sammtenes Band	I am drawn by a soft velvet ribbon
Durch Dämmergrau in der Liebe Land,	Through grey dusk into the land of love,
In ein blaues, mildes Licht.	Into a gentle blue light.
(*Reger*)	

5 June 1895 Schlagende Herzen / Beating hearts Op. 29, no. 2

Über Wiesen und Felder ein Knabe ging,	A boy was walking across meadows and fields,
Kling-klang schlug ihm das Herz,	Pit-a-pat went his heart,
Es glänzt ihm am Finger von Golde ein Ring,	A golden ring gleamed on his finger,
Kling-klang schlug ihm das Herz.	Pit-a-pat went his heart.
„Oh Wiesen, oh Felder,	'O meadows, O fields,
Wie seid ihr schön!	How fair you are!'
Oh Berge, oh Täler	O mountains, O valleys,
Wie seid ihr schön!	How fair you are!
Wie bist du gut, wie bist du schön,	How good you are, how fair you are,
Du gold'ne Sonne in Himmeshöh'n!"	You golden sun in heaven above!'
Kling-klang schlug ihm das Herz.	Pit-a-pat went his heart.
Schnell eilte der Knabe mit fröhlichem Schritt,	The boy hurried on with happy steps,
Kling-klang schlug ihm das Herz,	Pit-a-pat went his heart,
Nahm manche lachende Blume mit,	Took with him many a laughing flower,
Kling-klang schlug ihm das Herz.	Pit-a-pat went his heart.
„Über Wiesen und Felder	'Over meadows and fields
Weht Frühlingswind,	A spring wind blows,
Über Berge und Wälder	Over mountains and woods
Weht Frühlingswind.	A spring wind blows.
Im Herzen mir innen weht Frühlingswind,	A spring wind is blowing in my heart,
Der treibt zu Dir mich leise, lind!"	Driving me to you, softly and gently!'
Kling-klang schlug ihm das Herz.	Pit-a-pat went his heart.

Zwischen Wiesen und Feldern ein Mädel stand,	Between meadows and fields a young girl stood,
Kling-klang schlug ihr das Herz,	Pit-a-pat went her heart,
Hielt über die Augen zum Schauen die Hand,	She shaded her eyes with her hand as she gazed,
Kling-klang schlug ihr das Herz.	Pit-a-pat went her heart.
„Über Wiesen und Felder,	'Over meadows and fields,
Über Berge und Wälder	Over mountains and woods,
Zu mir, zu mir schnell kommt er her!	To me, to me he's hurrying!
Oh wenn er bei mir nur, bei mir schon wär!"	Ah! would he were with me, with me already!'
Kling-klang schlug ihr das Herz.	Pit-a-pat went her heart.

7 June 1895 Nachtgang / A Walk at Night Op. 29, no. 3

Wir gingen durch die dunkle, milde Nacht, dein Arm in meinem, dein Auge in meinem; der Mond goss silbernes Licht über dein Angesicht; wie auf Goldgrund ruhte dein schönes Haupt, und du erschienst mir wie eine Heilige: mild, mild und gross, und seelenübervoll, heilig und rein wie die liebe Sonne. Und in die Augen schwoll mir ein warmer Drang, wie Tränenahnung. Fester fasst' ich dich und küsste – küsste dich ganz leise, – meine Seele weinte.

(*Berg, Reger*)

We walked through the gentle silent night, your arm in mine, your eyes gazing into mine; the moon shed silver light over your face; as though on gold your fair head lay, and you seemed to me like a saint: gentle, gentle and great, with a brimming soul, holy and pure like the dear sun. And a pressing warmth welled into my eyes, like impending tears. I held you closer and kissed you – kissed you so gently, – my soul wept.

5 October 1900 Freundliche Vision / A pleasant vision Op. 48, no. 1
ORCHESTRATED 1 JULY 1918

Nicht im Schlafe hab ich das geträumt,	I did not dream it in my sleep,
Hell am Tage sah ich's schön vor mir:	In broad daylight I saw it fair before me:
Eine Wiese voller Margeritten;	A meadow full of daisies;
Tief ein weißes Haus in grünen Büschen;	A white house deep in green bushes;
Götterbilder leuchten aus dem Laube.	Statues of gods gleaming from the foliage.
Und ich geh' mit Einer, die mich lieb hat	And I walk with one who loves me,
Ruhigen Gemütes in die Kühle	My heart at peace, into the coolness
Dieses weißen Hauses, in den Frieden,	Of this white house, into the peace,
Der voll Schönheit wartet, daß wir kommen.	Brimming with beauty, that awaits our coming.
(*Reger*)	

Clemens Brentano (1778–1842)

See Brahms

4 February 1918 Als mir dein Lied erklang! / As your song rang out! Op. 68, no. 4
FROM *Aloys und Imelde*; ORCHESTRATED 22 JULY 1940

Dein Lied erklang, ich habe es gehört
Wie durch die Rosen es zum Monde zog,
Den Schmetterling, der bunt im Frühling flog
Hast du zur frommen Biene dir bekehrt;
Zur Rose ist mein Drang
Seit mir dein Lied erklang!

Dein Lied erklang, die Nachtigallen klagen,
Ach, meiner Ruhe süßes Schwanenlied
Dem Mond, der lauschend von dem Himmel
    sieht,
Den Sternen und den Rosen muß ich's klagen,
Wohin sie sich nun schwang,
Der dieses Lied erklang!

Dein Lied erklang, es war kein Ton
    vergebens,
Der ganze Frühling, der von Liebe haucht,
Hat als du sangest nieder sich getaucht
Im sehnsuchtsvollen Strome meines Lebens,
Im Sonnenuntergang,
Als mir dein Lied erklang!
(*Hermann Reutter*)

Your song rang out, I heard it
Soaring through roses to the moon,
The butterfly, flying brightly in spring,
You have turned into a virtuous bee;
I yearn for the rose
Since your song rang out!

Your song rang out! The nightingales com-
    plain –
Ah! sweet swansong of my peace –
To the moon, who listens and looks down
    from heaven,
And I must complain to the stars and the roses,
To where she flew,
She for whom this song was sung!

Your song rang out, no note was in vain,
The entire spring, breathing love,
Has, while you sang, immersed itself
In the passionate stream of my life,
At sunset,
As your song rang out!

6 February 1918 Ich wollt ein Sträußlein binden / I meant to make you a posy Op. 68, no. 2
FROM *Ponce de Leon*; ORCHESTRATED 6 JULY 1940

Ich wollt ein Sträußlein binden,
Da kam die dunkle Nacht,
Kein Blümlein war zu finden,
Sonst hätt' ich dir's gebracht.

Da flossen von den Wangen
Mir Tränen in den Klee,
Ein Blümlein aufgegangen
Ich nun im Garten seh.

Das wollte ich dir brechen
Wohl in dem dunklen Klee,
Da fing es an zu sprechen:
„Ach, tue mir nicht weh!

I meant to make you a posy,
But dark night then came,
There were no flowers to be found,
Or I'd have brought you some.

Tears then flowed from my cheeks
Into the clover,
And now I saw a flower
That had sprung up in the garden.

I meant to pick it for you
There in the dark clover,
When it started to speak:
'Ah, do not hurt me!

"Sei freundlich in dem Herzen,
Betracht dein eigen Leid,
Und lasse mich in Schmerzen
Nicht sterben vor der Zeit!"

Und hätt's nicht so gesprochen,
Im Garten ganz allein,
So hätt' ich dir's gebrochen,
Nun aber darf's nicht sein.

Mein Schatz ist ausgeblieben,
Ich bin so ganz allein.
Im Lieben wohnt Betrüben,
Und kann nicht anders sein.
(*Louise Reichardt, Ludwig Thuille*)

Be kind in your heart,
Consider your own suffering,
And do not make me die
In torment before my time!'

And had it not spoken these words,
All alone in the garden,
I'd have picked it for you,
But now that cannot be.

My sweetheart stayed away,
I am utterly alone.
Sadness dwells in loving,
And cannot be otherwise.

9 February 1918 Säus'le, liebe Myrte! / Rustle, dear myrtle! Op. 68, no. 3
FROM *Mirtenfräulein*; ORCHESTRATED 2 AUGUST 1940

"Säus'le, liebe Myrte!
Wie still ist's in der Welt,
Der Mond, der Sternenhirte
Auf klarem Himmelsfeld,
Treibt schon die Wolkenschafe
Zum Born des Lichtes hin,
Schlaf, mein Freund, o schlafe,
Bis ich wieder bei dir bin!

"Säus'le, liebe Myrte!
Und träum im Sternenschein,
Die Turteltaube girrte
Auch ihre Brut schon ein.
Still ziehn die Wolkenschafe
Zum Born des Lichtes hin,
Schlaf, mein Freund, o schlafe,
Bis ich wieder bei dir bin!

"Hörst du, wie die Brunnen rauschen?
Hörst du, wie die Grille zirpt?
Stille, stille, laß uns lauschen,
Selig, wer in Träumen stirbt;
Selig, wen die Wolken wiegen,
Wenn der Mond ein Schlaflied singt;
O! wie selig kann der fliegen,
Den der Traum den Flügel schwingt,
Daß an blauer Himmelsdecke
Sterne er wie Blumen pflückt;
Schlafe, träume, flieg', ich wecke
Bald dich auf und bin beglückt!"
(*Knab*)

'Rustle, dear myrtle!
How silent the world is,
The moon, that shepherd of the stars,
In the bright Elysian fields,
Already drives the herd of clouds
To the spring of light,
Sleep, my friend, ah sleep,
Till I am with you again!

'Rustle, dear myrtle!
And dream in the starlight,
The turtledove has already cooed
Her brood to sleep.
Quietly the herd of clouds
Travel to the spring of light,
Sleep, my friend, ah sleep,
Till I am with you again!

'Do you hear the fountains murmur?
Do you hear the cricket chirping?
Hush, hush, let us listen,
Happy is he who dies while dreaming;
Happy he who is cradled by clouds,
While the moon sings a lullaby;
Ah, how happily he can fly
Who takes flight in dreams,
So that from heavens' blue vault
He gathers stars as though they were flowers;
Sleep, dream, fly, I shall wake
You soon and be made happy!'

18 February 1918 An die Nacht / To night Op. 68, no. 1
FROM *Die Gründung Prags*; ORCHESTRATED 27 JULY 1940

Heilige Nacht, heilige Nacht!	Holy night, holy night!
Sterngeschloss'ner Himmelsfrieden!	Heavenly peace, encircled in stars!
Alles, was das Licht geschieden,	All things divided by light
Ist verbunden,	Are united,
Aller Wunden	All our wounds
Bluten süß im Abendrot!	Bleed sweetly in the sunset!
Bjelbog's* Speer, Bjelbog's Speer	Bielbog's spear, Bielbog's spear
Sinkt in's Herz der trunknen Erde,	Plunges into the heart of the drunken earth,
Die mit seliger Geberde	Which with a gesture of bliss
Eine Rose	Immerses a rose
In dem Schoße	In the womb
Dunkler Lüste niedertaucht!	Of darkened desire!
Heilige Nacht! züchtige Braut, züchtige Braut!	Holy night! chaste bride, chaste bride!
Deine süße Schmach verhülle,	Veil your sweet shame,
Wenn des Hochzeitbechers Fülle	When the wedding-cup
Sich ergießet.	Overflows.
Also fließet	Thus does day
In die brünstige Nacht der Tag!	Stream into fervent night!

Gottfried August Bürger (1747–94)

A colourful character whose poems were set by Beethoven, Cornelius, Haydn and Pfitzner. He was appointed magistrate in 1772 but neglected his official duties and got into financial difficulties; he later became a lecturer in Göttingen. His collected poems, including the celebrated ballad 'Lenore', were published in 1789 and savaged by Schiller in 1791 ('Über Bürgers Gedichte'). It is said that this criticism and a disastrous third marriage hastened his early death. 'Muttertändelei' was probably written by his first wife, Dorette Leonhard, who bore him a son, the subject of this poem, in 1782.

15 August 1899 Muttertändelei / Mother-talk Op. 43, no. 2

Seht mir doch mein schönes Kind!	Just look at my pretty child!
Mit den goldnen Zottellöckchen,	With his golden tassels of hair,
Blauen Augen, roten Bäckchen!	Blue eyes, red cheeks!
Leutchen, habt ihr auch so eins? –	Well folks, do you have such a child? –
Leutchen, nein, ihr habet keins!	No, folks, you don't!
Seht mir doch mein süßes Kind!	Just look at my sweet child!
Fetter als ein fettes Schneckchen,	Fatter than a fat snail,

---

* The God of Light, according to Bohemian mythology.

Süßer als ein Zuckerweckchen!	Sweeter than a sugar roll!
Leutchen, habt ihr auch so eins? –	Well folks, do you have such a child? –
Leutchen, nein, ihr habt keins!	No, folks, you don't!
Seht mir doch mein holdes Kind!	Just look at my lovely child!
Nicht zu mürrisch, nicht zu wählig,	Not too moody, not too choosy,
Immer freundlich, immer fröhlich!	Always friendly, always happy!
Leutchen, habt ihr auch so eins? –	Well folks, do you have such a child? –
Leutchen, nein, ihr habet keins!	No, folks, you don't!
Seht mir doch mein frommes Kind!	Just look at my gentle child!
Keine bitterböse Sieben	No wicked shrew
Würd' ihr Mütterchen so lieben.	Would love her mother so.
Leutchen, möchtet ihr so eins? –	Well folks, do you want such a child? –
O, ihr kriegt gewiß nicht meins!	Oh! you'll certainly not get mine!
Komm' einmal ein Kaufmann her!	Let a merchant come along!
Hunderttausend blanke Taler,	One hundred thousand thalers
Alles Gold der Erde zahl' er!	Let him pay, all the gold on earth!
O, er kriegt gewiß nicht meins!	Oh! he certainly won't get mine!
Kauf' er sich wo anders eins!	Let him buy one somewhere else!

Felix Dahn (1834–1912)

A once celebrated writer of *Professorenromane* – a somewhat derogatory term for meticulously researched historical novels that lack imagination. The four volumes of *Ein Kampf um Rom* (1876) spawned a series of novels on early German history which, like Dahn's epic poetry and tragedies, have been forgotten. The poems of *Schlichte Weisen*, which attracted both Strauss and Reger, were inspired by an index of first words of ancient folksongs he found in a museum: the catalogue merely mentioned the opening of each poem, on to which Dahn grafted the continuation.

12 February 1889 All' mein Gedanken / All my thoughts Op. 21, no. 1

All' mein Gedanken, mein Herz und mein Sinn,	*All my thoughts*, my heart and my mind,
Da wo die Liebste ist, wandern sie hin.	Wander to where my beloved is.
Geh'n ihres Weges trotz Mauer und Tor,	They go on their way despite wall and gate,
Da hält kein Riegel, kein Graben nicht vor,	No bolt, no ditch can stop them,
Gehn wie die Vögelein hoch durch die Luft,	Go high in the air like little birds,
Brauchen kein' Brücken über Wasser und Kluft,	Needing no bridge over water or chasm,
Finden das Städtlein und finden das Haus,	They find the town and find the house,
Finden ihr Fenster aus allen heraus,	Find her window among all the others,
Und klopfen und rufen: „mach' auf, laß uns ein,	And knock and call: 'Open up, let us in,

Wir kommen vom Liebsten und grüßen Dich
fein."
(Reger)

We come from your sweetheart who sends
his love.'

7 April 1889 Du meines Herzens Krönelein / You, my heart's coronet Op. 21, no. 2

Du meines Herzens Krönelein, du
bist von lautrem Golde,
Wenn Andere daneben sein, dann bist du
noch viel holde.
Die Andern tun so gern gescheut, du bist gar
sanft und stille;
Daß jedes Herz sich dein erfreut, dein Glück
ist's, nicht dein Wille.

Die Andern suchen Lieb' und Gunst mit
tausend falschen Worten,
Du ohne Mund- und Augenkunst bist wert
an allen Orten,
Du bist als wie die Ros' im Wald, sie weiß
nichts von ihrer Blüte,
Doch Jedem, der vorüberwallt, erfreut sie das
Gemüte.
(Reger)

You, my heart's coronet, you are of pure
gold,
When others stand beside you, you are more
lovely still.
Others love to appear clever, you are so gen-
tle and quiet;
That every heart delights in you, is your for-
tune not your will.

Others seek love and favours with a thousand
false words,
You, without artifice of mind or eye, are
esteemed in every place,
You are like the rose in the forest, knowing
nothing of its flowers,
Yet rejoicing the heart of every passer-by.

17 April 1889 Ach weh mir unglückhaftem Mann / Ah, unhappy man that I am Op. 21, no. 4

Ach weh mir unglückhaftem Mann,
daß ich Geld und Gut nicht habe,
Sonst spannt' ich gleich vier Schimmel an
und führ' zu Dir im Trabe.
Ich putzte sie mit Schellen aus, daß Du mich
hört'st von Weitem,
Ich steckt' ein'n großen Rosenstrauß an
meine linke Seiten,
Und käm' ich an Dein kleines Haus, tät ich
mit der Peitsche schlagen,
Da gucktest Du zum Fenster 'naus: „Was
willst Du? tätst Du fragen.
Was soll der große Rosenstrauß, die Schim-
mel an dem Wagen?"
„Dich will ich, rief ich, komm heraus!" Da
tätst du nimmer fragen.
„Nun Vater, Mutter, seht sie an und küßt sie
rasch zum Scheiden,
Weil ich nicht lange warten kann, meine
Schimmel woll'ns nicht leiden."

Ah, unhappy man that I am to have neither
property nor money,
Else I'd harness four white horses and drive
to you at a canter.
I'd deck them out with little bells for you to
hear from afar,
I'd place a huge bouquet of roses on my left
side,
And when I reached your little house, I'd
crack my whip,
You'd lean out of the window and ask: 'What
do you want?
Why the huge bouquet of roses, why the car-
riage and the horses?'
'It's you I want,' I'd cry, 'come down!' And
there would be no more questions.
'Take one last look at her, mother, father, and
kiss her quickly goodbye,
For I can't wait long, my horses wouldn't
allow it.'

Richard Dehmel (1863–1920)

See Schoenberg

30 December 1895 Stiller Gang / Silent walk Op. 31, no. 4

Der Abend graut; Herbstfeuer brennen.
Über den Stoppeln geht der Rauch entzwei.
Kaum ist mein Weg noch zu erkennen.
Bald kommt die Nacht; ich muß mich trennen.
Ein Käfer surrt an meinem Ohr vorbei.
Vorbei.
(*Conrad Ansorge, Willy Burkhard*)

Dusk falls; autumn fires are burning.
Smoke breaks up above the stubble.
My way can barely be seen.
Night will soon be here; I must depart.
A beetle whirrs away past my ear.
Away.

2 June 1898 Befreit / Released Op. 39, no. 4

Du wirst nicht weinen. Leise, leise
wirst du lächeln; und wie zur Reise
geb ich dir Blick und Kuß zurück.
Unsre lieben vier Wände! Du hast sie bereitet,
ich habe sie dir zur Welt geweitet –
o Glück!

You will not weep. Gently, gently
you will smile; and as before a journey
I shall return your gaze and kiss.
Our dear four walls! You prepared them,
I have widened them into a world for you –
O happiness!

Dann wirst du heiß meine Hände fassen
und wirst mir deine Seele lassen,
läßt unsern Kindern mich zurück.
Du schenktest mir dein ganzes Leben,
ich will es ihnen wiedergeben –
o Glück!

Then ardently you will seize my hands
and you will leave me your soul,
leave me to care for our children.
You gave your whole life to me,
I shall give it back to them –
O happiness!

Es wird sehr bald sein, wir wissen's Beide,
wir haben einander befreit vom Leide,
so gab ich dich der Welt zurück.
Dann wirst du mir nur noch im Traum
    erscheinen
und mich segnen und mit mir weinen –
o Glück!

It will be very soon, we both know it,
we have released each other from suffering,
so I returned you to the world.
Then you'll appear to me only in
    dreams,
and you will bless me and weep with me –
O happiness!

22 August 1899 Wiegenlied / Cradle song Op. 41, no. 1

Träume, träume, du mein süßes Leben,
von dem Himmel, der die Blumen bringt;
    Blüten schimmern da, die beben
von dem Lied, das deine Mutter singt.

Dream, dream, my sweet, my life,
of heaven that brings the flowers;
    blossoms shimmer there, they quiver
from the song your mother sings.

Träume, träume, Knospe meiner Sorgen,
von dem Tage, da die Blume sproß;
    von dem hellen Blütenmorgen,
da dein Seelchen sich der Welt erschloß.

Dream, dream, bud born of my anxiety,
of the day the flower unfolded;
    of that morning bright with blossom,
when your little soul opened to the world.

Träume, träume, Blüte meiner Liebe,
  von der stillen, von der heiligen Nacht,
    da die Blume Seiner Liebe
diese Welt zum Himmel mir gemacht.
(*Pfitzner, Reger, Salmhofer*)

Dream, dream, blossom of my love,
  of the silent, of the sacred night,
    when the flower of His love
made this world my heaven.

21 September 1901 Waldseligkeit / Woodland rapture Op. 49, no. 1
ORCHESTRATED 24 JUNE 1918

Der Wald beginnt zu rauschen,
  den Bäumen naht die Nacht;
    als ob sie selig lauschen,
    berühren sie sich sacht.

The wood begins to stir,
  night draws near the trees;
    as if blissfully listening,
    they gently touch each other.

Und unter ihren Zweigen,
  da bin ich ganz allein,
da bin ich ganz mein eigen:
    ganz nur Dein.
(*Conrad Ansorge, Alma Mahler, Marx, Reger*)

And beneath their branches
  I am utterly alone,
utterly my own:
    utterly and only yours.

Joseph von Eichendorff (1788–1857)

*See **Vier letzte Lieder**, p. 562*

Gustav Falke (1853–1916)

A bookseller and music teacher whose literary gifts were admired and promoted by Liliencron. He wrote novels and stories, but it is through the settings of his poems, published in *Gesammelte Dichtungen* (1912), by Marx, Reger and Strauss that his name is still known.

7 February 1897 Meinem Kinde / To my child Op. 37, no. 3
ORCHESTRATED ?1897

Du schläfst und sachte neig' ich mich
Über dein Bettchen und segne dich.
Jeder behutsame Atemzug
Ist ein schweifender Himmelsflug,
Ist ein Suchen weit umher,
Ob nicht doch ein Sternlein wär',
Wo aus eitel Glanz und Licht
Liebe sich ein Glückskraut bricht,
Das sie geflügelt herniederträgt
Und dir aufs weiße Deckchen legt.
(*Reger*)

You sleep and softly I bend down
Over your cot and bless you.
Every cautious breath you take
Soars up towards heaven,
Searches far and wide to see
If there might not be some star,
From whose pure radiance and light
Love may pluck a herb of grace,
To descend with it on her wings
And lay it on your white coverlet.

Hermann von Gilm (1812–64)

Aristocratic, Austrian civil servant from the Tyrol, whose anti-Jesuitical verse met with widespread condemnation. His poems, published in *Tiroler Schützenleben* (1863) and *Gedichte* (1864–65) were set by both Reger and Strauss.

11 August 1885 Die Nacht / The night Op. 10, no. 3

Aus dem Walde tritt die Nacht,
Aus den Bäumen schleicht sie leise,
Schaut sich um in weitem Kreise,
    Nun gib Acht!

Alle Lichter dieser Welt,
Alle Blumen, alle Farben
Löscht sie aus und stiehlt die Garben
    Weg vom Feld.

Alles nimmt sie, was nur hold,
Nimmt das Silber weg des Stroms
Nimmt vom Kupferdach des Doms
    Weg das Gold.

Ausgeplündert steht der Strauch:
Rücke näher, Seel' an Seele,
O die Nacht, mir bangt, sie stehle
    Dich mir auch.
(*Ernest Vietor*)

Night steps from the woods,
Slips softly from the trees,
Gazes about her in a wide arc,
    Now beware!

All the lights of this world,
All the flowers, all the colours
She extinguishes and steals the sheaves
    From the field.

She takes all that is fair,
Takes the silver from the river,
Takes from the cathedral's copper roof
    The gold.

The bush stands plundered:
Draw closer, soul to soul,
Ah the night, I fear, will steal
    You too from me.

13 August 1885 Zueignung / Dedication Op. 10, no. 1
ORCHESTRATED 14 APRIL 1940

Ja du weißt es, teure Seele,
Daß ich fern von dir mich quäle,
Liebe macht die Herzen krank,
    Habe Dank.

Einst hielt ich, der Freiheit Zecher,
Hoch den Amethisten-Becher
Und du segnetest den Trank,
    Habe Dank.

Und beschworst darin die Bösen,
Bis ich, was ich nie gewesen,
Heilig, heilig an's Herz dir sank,
    Habe Dank.

Yes, dear soul, you know
That I'm in torment far from you,
Love makes hearts sick,
    Be thanked.

Once, revelling in freedom, I held
The amethyst cup aloft
And you blessed that draught,
    Be thanked.

And you banished the evil spirits,
Till I, as never before,
Holy, sank holy upon your heart,
    Be thanked.

15 August 1885 Nichts / Nothing Op. 10, no. 2

Nennen soll ich, sagt ihr, meine	You say I should name
Königin im Liederreich!	My queen in the realm of song!
Toren, die ihr seid, ich kenne	Fools that you are, I know
Sie am wenigsten von euch.	Her least of all of you.
Fragt mich nach der Augen Farbe,	Ask me the colour of her eyes,
Fragt mich nach der Stimme Ton,	Ask me about the sound of her voice,
Fragt nach Gang und Tanz und Haltung,	Ask me about her walk, her dancing, her bearing,
Ach, und was weiß ich davon.	Ah! what do I know of all that.
Ist die Sonne nicht die Quelle	Is not the sun the source
Alles Lebens, alles Licht's	Of all life, of all light,
Und was wissen von derselben	And what do we know about it,
Ich, und ihr, und alle? – nichts.	I and you and everyone? – nothing.

18 August 1885 Die Georgine / The dahlia Op. 10, no. 4

Warum so spät erst Georgine?	Why, dahlia, appear so late?
Das Rosenmärchen ist erzählt	The roses have told their tale
Und honigsatt hat sich die Biene	And the honey-sated bee
Ihr Bett zum Schlummer ausgewählt.	Has chosen where to lay its head.
Sind nicht zu kalt dir diese Nächte?	Are these nights not too cold for you?
Wie lebst du diese Tage hin?	How do you survive these days?
Wenn ich dir jetzt den Frühling brächte,	What if I brought you springtime now,
Du feuergelbe Träumerin.	You fiery yellow dreamer?
Wenn ich mit Maitau dich benetzte,	What if I watered you with May dew,
Begösse dich mit Juni-Licht,	Drenched you in the light of June,
Doch ach, dann wärst du nicht die Letzte,	But ah! you would not be then the last,
Die stolze Einzige auch nicht.	Nor proud to be unique.
Wie, Träum'rin, lock' ich vergebens?	What, O dreamer, do I tempt you in vain?
So reich' mir schwesterlich die Hand,	Then give me your sisterly hand,
Ich hab' den Maitag dieses Lebens	I've not known May-time in this life,
Wie du den Frühling nicht gekannt.	Just as you've not known the spring.
Und spät wie dir, du feuergelbe,	And as with you, fiery yellow flower,
Stahl sich die Liebe mir in's Herz,	Love stole late into my heart,
Ob spät, ob früh, es ist dasselbe	Late or early, it is the same
Entzücken und derselbe Schmerz.	Enchantment and the same pain.

3 October 1885 Allerseelen / All Souls' Day Op. 10, no. 8

Stell' auf den Tisch die duftenden Reseden,	Set on the table the fragrant mignonettes,
Die letzten roten Astern trag' herbei	Bring in the last red asters,
Und laß uns wieder von der Liebe reden	And let us talk of love again
Wie einst im Mai.	As once in May.

Gib mir die Hand, daß ich sie heimlich drücke,
Und wenn man's sieht, mir ist es einerlei,
Gib mir nur einen deiner süßen Blicke
       Wie einst im Mai.

Es blüht und duftet heut' auf jedem Grabe,
Ein Tag im Jahr ist ja den Toten frei;
Komm' an mein Herz, daß ich dich wieder
   habe,
       Wie einst im Mai.
(*Eduard Lassen, Ludwig Thuille*)

Give me your hand to press in secret,
And if people see, I do not care,
Give me but one of your sweet glances
       As once in May.

Each grave today has flowers and is fragrant,
One day each year is devoted to the dead;
Come to my heart and so be mine
   again,
       As once in May.

Johann Wolfgang von Goethe (1749–1832)

See Beethoven, Brahms, Hensel, Loewe, Mendelssohn, Mozart, Reichardt, Schubert, Zelter, Wolf

Goethe wrote 'Gefunden' on 26 August 1813, and sent it to his wife Christiane, whom he had first met twenty-five years previously in the park at Weimar. This allegory on marriage was aptly dedicated by Strauss to his wife, the soprano Pauline de Ahna, who gave many of his songs their first performance.

31 July 1903 Gefunden / Found Op. 56, no. 1

Ich ging im Walde
So für mich hin,
Und nichts zu suchen,
Das war mein Sinn.

I was walking
In the wood alone,
And intended
To look for nothing.

Im Schatten sah ich
Ein Blümchen stehn,
Wie Sterne leuchtend,
Wie Äuglein schön.

In the shade I saw
A little flower growing
Gleaming like stars,
Lovely as eyes.

Ich wollt es brechen,
Da sagt' es fein:
Soll ich zum Welken
Gebrochen sein?

I was going to pick it,
When gently it said:
Must I be picked
To wilt and die?

Ich grubs mit allen
Den Würzlein aus,
Zum Garten trug ichs
Am hübschen Haus.

I dug it out
With all its roots,
Took it to the garden
Of my pretty home.

Und pflanzt es wieder
Am stillen Ort;
Nun zweigt es immer
Und blüht so fort.
(*Wilhelm Kienzl, Loewe, Medtner, Viana da Mota*)

And planted it again
In a quiet corner;
Where still it grows
And continues to bloom.

Heinrich Hart (1855–1906)

A celebrated literary critic who, with his brother Julius, edited the *Deutscher Literaturkalender* (1879–82) and the *Kritische Waffengänge* (1882–4) which promoted a new realism in literature. Cäcilie was the name of Hart's wife, and Strauss set the poem on the eve of his own wedding.

9 September 1894 Cäcilie / Cecily Op. 27, no. 2

Wenn Du es wüßtest,	If you knew
Was träumen heißt	What it is to dream
Von brennenden Küssen,	Of burning kisses,
Vom Wandern und Ruhen	Of walking and resting
Mit der Geliebten,	With one's love,
Aug' in Auge	Gazing at each other
Und kosend und plaudernd –	And caressing and talking –
Wenn Du es wüßtest,	If you knew,
Du neigtest Dein Herz.	Your heart would turn to me.
Wenn Du es wüßtest,	If you knew
Was bangen heißt	What it is to worry
In einsamen Nächten,	On lonely nights,
Umschauert vom Sturm,	In the frightening storm,
Da Niemand tröstet	With no soft voice
Milden Mundes	To comfort
Die kampfmüde Seele –	The struggle-weary soul –
Wenn Du es wüßtest,	If you knew,
Du kämest zu mir.	You would come to me.
Wenn Du es wüßtest,	If you knew
Was leben heißt	What it is to live
Umhaucht von der Gottheit	Enveloped in God's
Weltschaffendem Atem,	World-creating breath,
Zu schweben empor	To soar upwards,
Lichtgetragen	Borne on light
Zu seligen Höh'en –	To blessed heights –
Wenn Du es wüßtest,	If you knew,
Du lebtest mit mir.	You would live with me.

Heinrich Heine (1797–1856)

See Mendelssohn, Robert Schumann, Wolf

7 October 1906 Die heiligen drei Könige aus Morgenland / The three holy kings Op. 56, no. 6

Die heil'gen drei Kön'ge aus Morgenland,	The three holy kings from Eastern lands,
Sie frugen in jedem Städtchen:	They asked in every town:

„Wo geht der Weg nach Bethlehem,
Ihr lieben Buben und Mädchen?"

    Die Jungen und Alten, sie wußten's nicht,
Die Könige zogen weiter;
Sie folgten einem goldenen Stern,
Der leuchtete lieblich und heiter.

    Der Stern blieb stehn über Josephs Haus,
Da sind sie hineingegangen;
Das Öchslein brüllte, das Kindlein schrie,
Die heil'gen drei Könige sangen.
(*Lord Berners, Vesque von Püttlingen*)

'Where is the way to Bethlehem,
Dear little boys and girls?'

    Young and old, they did not know,
The three kings journeyed on;
They followed a star of golden light
That shone down bright and cheerily.

    The star stood still over Joseph's house,
And there they went inside;
The little ox bellowed, the baby cried,
The three holy kings, they sang.

12 June 1918 Schlechtes Wetter / Dreadful weather Op. 69, no. 5

    Das ist ein schlechtes Wetter,
Es regnet und stürmt und schneit;
Ich sitze am Fenster und schaue
Hinaus in die Dunkelheit.

    Da schimmert ein einsames Lichtchen,
Das wandelt langsam fort;
Ein Mütterchen mit dem Laternchen
Wankt über die Straße dort.

    Ich glaube, Mehl und Eier
Und Butter kaufte sie ein;
Sie will einen Kuchen backen
Fürs große Töchterlein.

    Die liegt zu Haus im Lehnstuhl,
Und blinzelt schläfrig ins Licht;
Die goldnen Locken wallen
Über das süße Gesicht.

    This is dreadful weather,
It's raining and blowing and snowing;
I sit at my window and stare
Out into the darkness.

    One solitary light flickers out there,
Moving slowly along;
A little old woman with a lantern
Totters across the street.

    I fancy it's flour and eggs
And butter she's been buying;
She's going to bake a cake
For her big little daughter.

    She lolls at home in the armchair,
Blinking sleepily into the light;
Her golden curls tumble down
Over her sweet face.

Karl Henckell (1864–1929)

Henckell was one of a number of poets – Mackay, Hart and Dehmel were others –
who reacted against the sentimentality of the mid-nineteenth century and sought
to instil a new spirit into German poetry, while retaining its traditional form.
Some of his proletarian poetry, such as 'Das Lied des Steinklopfers' (set by Strauss)
which describes a stone-breaker 'who has no title, no decorations and also no
money', was so inflammatory that it was banned in Germany. Henckell, who dis-
approved violently of Bismarck and the Prussians, circumvented the ban by emi-
grating to Switzerland. Despite his polemical nature, he also wrote a great number
of delicate love poems.

17 May 1894 Ruhe, meine Seele! / Rest, my soul! Op. 27, no. 1
ORCHESTRATED 9 JUNE 1948

Nicht ein Lüftchen,	Not even
Regt sich leise,	A soft breeze stirs,
Sanft entschlummert	In gentle sleep
Ruht der Hain;	The wood rests;
Durch der Blätter	Through the leaves'
Dunkle Hülle	Dark veil
Stiehlt sich lichter	Bright sunshine
Sonnenschein.	Steals.
Ruhe, ruhe,	Rest, rest,
Meine Seele,	My soul,
Deine Stürme	Your storms
Gingen wild,	Were wild,
Hast getobt und	You raged and
Hast gezittert,	You quivered,
Wie die Brandung,	Like breakers,
Wenn sie schwillt!	When they surge!
Diese Zeiten	These times
Sind gewaltig,	Are violent,
Bringen Herz und	Cause heart and
Hirn in Not –	Mind distress –
Ruhe, ruhe,	Rest, rest,
Meine Seele,	My soul,
Und vergiß,	And forget
Was dich bedroht!	What threatens you!

26 January 1896 Ich trage meine Minne / I bear my love Op. 32, no. 1

Ich trage meine Minne	I bear my love
Vor Wonne stumm	In silent bliss
Im Herzen und im Sinne	About with me
Mit mir herum.	In heart and mind.
Ja, daß ich dich gefunden,	Yes, that I have found you,
Du liebes Kind,	Sweet child,
Das freut mich alle Tage,	Will cheer me all
Die mir beschieden sind.	My allotted days.
Und ob auch der Himmel trübe,	Though the sky be dim,
Kohlschwarz die Nacht,	And the night pitch-black,
Hell leuchtet meiner Liebe	My loves shines brightly
Goldsonnige Pracht.	In golden splendour.
Und lügt auch die Welt in Sünden,	And though the world lies and sins,
So tut mir's weh –	And it hurts to see it so –
Die arge muß erblinden	The bad world must be blinded
Vor deiner Unschuld Schnee.	By your snowy innocence.

Hermann Hesse (1877–1962)

*See **Vier letzte Lieder**, p. 562*

Detlev von Liliencron (1844–1909)

See Brahms

7 February 1898 Ich liebe dich / I love you Op. 37, no. 2

Vier adlige Rosse	Four noble horses
Voran unserm Wagen,	Draw our carriage,
Wir wohnen im Schlosse,	We live in the castle
In stolzem Behagen.	Proud and content.
Die Frühlichterwellen	The rays of dawn
Und nächtens der Blitz,	And the lightning at night,
Was all' sie erhellen,	All that they shine on
Ist unser Besitz.	Belongs to us.
Und irrst du verlassen,	And though you roam the land,
Verbannt durch die Lande:	Abandoned and banished:
Mit dir durch die Gassen	I'll walk through the streets with you
In Armut und Schande!	In poverty and shame!
Es bluten die Hände,	Our hands will bleed,
Die Füße sind wund,	Our feet be sore,
Vier trostlose Wände,	Four desolate walls,
Es kennt uns kein Hund.	Not a dog to know us.
Steht silberbeschlagen	When your silver-edged coffin
Dein Sarg am Altar,	Stands at the altar,
Sie sollen mich tragen	They must lay me
Zu dir auf die Bahr.	Beside you on the bier.
Und fern auf der Heide,	Whether you die on the heath
Und stirbst du in Not:	Or die in distress,
Den Dolch aus der Scheide,	I'll draw my dagger
Dir nach in den Tod!	And join you in death!

8 February 1898 Glückes genug / Abundant happiness Op. 37, no. 1

Wenn sanft du mir im Arme schliefst,	When softly in my arms you slept,
Ich deinen Atem hören konnte,	I could hear you breathing,
Im Traum du meinen Namen riefst,	In your dreams you called out my name,
Um deinen Mund ein Lächeln sonnte –	A smile shone on your mouth –
Glückes genug.	Abundant happiness.
Und wenn nach heißem, ernstem Tag	And when after a hot, exhausting day
Du mir verscheuchtest schwere Sorgen,	You banished my grievous cares,
Wenn ich an deinem Herzen lag	When I lay on your heart

Und nicht mehr dachte an ein Morgen –
   Glückes genug.
(*Reger*)

And thought no more about the morrow –
   Abundant happiness.

John Henry Mackay (1864–1933)

Born in Greenock, Scotland, Mackay was brought up in Germany by a German
mother and a Scottish father. In the 1890s he settled in Berlin where, as a left-wing
thinker with anarchist leanings (one of his novels was called *Die Anarchisten*) he
was constantly at loggerheads with authority. With Arno Holz, Johannes Schlaf,
the Hart brothers and Gerhart Hauptmann he was a member of the 'Durch' group
of writers, whose aim was to do away with convention. Most of Mackay's work has
a homosexual subtext, and 'Morgen! . . .' looks forward to a time when gay people
can live and love without persecution. He wrote his stories of homosexual love
under the pseudonym of Sagitta, and published a novel on male prostitution, *Der
Puppenjunge* (*The Hustler*) in 1926.

21 May 1894 Morgen! . . . / Tomorrow! . . . Op. 27, no. 4

Und morgen wird die Sonne wieder scheinen
Und auf dem Wege, den ich gehen werde,
   Wird uns, die Glücklichen, sie wieder einen,
Inmitten dieser sonnenatmenden Erde . . .

And tomorrow the sun will shine again
And on the path that I shall take,
   It will unite us, happy ones, again,
Amid this same sun-breathing earth . . .

   Und zu dem Strand, dem weiten, wogen-
     blauen,
Werden wir still und langsam niedersteigen,
   Stumm werden wir uns in die Augen
     schauen,
Und auf uns sinkt des Glückes stummes
     Schweigen . . .
(*Reger*)

   And to the shore, broad, blue-
     waved,
We shall quietly and slowly descend,
   Speechless we shall gaze into each other's
     eyes,
And the speechless silence of bliss shall fall
     on us . . .

22 May 1894 Heimliche Aufforderung / Secret invitation Op. 27, no. 3

Auf, hebe die funkelnde Schale
   empor zum Mund,
Und trinke beim Freudenmahle
   dein Herz gesund.

Come, raise to your lips
   the sparkling goblet,
And drink at this joyful feast
   your heart to health.

Und wenn du sie hebst, so winke
   mir heimlich zu,
Dann lächle ich, und dann trinke
   ich still wie du . . .

And when you raise it, give
   me a secret sign,
Then I shall smile and drink,
   as quietly as you . . .

Und still gleich mir betrachte
   um uns das Heer

And quietly like me, look
   around at the hordes

Der trunkenen Schwätzer – verachte
    sie nicht zu sehr.
	Of drunken gossips – do not
	    despise them too much.

Nein, hebe die blinkende Schaale,
    gefüllt mit Wein,
Und laß beim lärmenden Mahle
    sie glücklich sein.
	No, raise the glittering goblet,
	    filled with wine,
	And let them be happy
	    at the noisy feast.

Doch hast du das Mahl genossen,
    den Durst gestillt,
Dann verlasse der lauten Genossen
    festfreudiges Bild,
	But once you have savoured the meal,
	    quenched your thirst,
	Leave the loud company
	    of happy revellers,

Und wandle hinaus in den Garten
    zum Rosenstrauch, –
Dort will ich dich dann erwarten
    nach altem Brauch,
	And come out into the garden
	    to the rose-bush, –
	There I shall wait for you
	    As I've always done,

Und will an die Brust dir sinken
    eh' du's gehofft,
Und deine Küsse trinken,
    wie ehmals oft,
	And I shall sink on your breast,
	    before you could hope,
	And drink your kisses,
	    As often before,

Und flechten in deine Haare
    der Rose Pracht –
O komm, du wunderbare,
    ersehnte Nacht!
	And twine in your hair
	    the glorious rose –
	Ah! come, o wondrous,
	    longed-for night!

Conrad Ferdinand Meyer (1825–98)

See Pfitzner

?1906 Im Spätboot / On the night boat Op. 56, no. 3

Aus der Schiffsbank mach' ich meinen Pfühl, Endlich wird die heiße Stirne kühl! O wie süß erkaltet mir das Herz! O wie weich verstummen Lust und Schmerz! Über mir des Rohres schwarzer Rauch Wiegt und biegt sich in des Windes Hauch. Hüben hier und drüben wieder dort Hält das Boot an manchem kleinen Port: Bei der Schiffslaterne kargem Schein Steigt ein Schatten aus und niemand ein. Nur der Steurer noch, der wacht und steht! Nur der Wind, der mir im Haare weht! Schmerz und Lust erleiden sanften Tod. Einen Schlumm'rer trägt das dunkle Boot.	I lay my head on the ship's bench, At last my burning brow is chilled! Ah, how sweetly my heart grows cool! How gently joy and pain are stilled! Over my head the funnel's black smoke Curls and sways in the gusting wind. First on this side and then on that The boat puts in at many a port: In the faint light of the ship's lantern A shadow disembarks and no one boards. Only the helmsman's awake, on his feet! Only the wind, which blows through my hair! Pain and pleasure die a gentle death. The dark boat bears a slumbering form.

Michelangelo Buonarroti (1475–1564)

See Wolf

Strauss's song sets a Michelangelo madrigal, 'Porgo umilmente all'aspro giogo il collo'.

?1886 Madrigal / Madrigal Op. 15, no. 1
TRANSLATED BY SOPHIE HASENCLEVER (1824–92)

Ins Joch beug' ich den Nacken demutvoll,	Humbly I submit to the yoke,
Beug' lächelnd vor dem Mißgeschick dies Haupt,	Bow, smiling, this head before misfortune,
Dies Herz, das liebt und glaubt,	And this heart too that loves and has faith,
Vor meiner Feindin. Wider diese Qual	Before my enemy. I do not rise
Bäum' ich mich nicht mit Groll,	Resentfully against this torment,
Mir bangt vielmehr, sie lindre sich einmal.	I'm more afraid it will one day abate.
Wenn deines Auges Strahl	When the radiance of your eyes
Dies Leid verwandelt hat in Lebenssaft,	Has translated this pain into vital sap,
Welch' Leid hat dann zu töten mich die Kraft?	What pain will have the power to kill me?
(*Schoeck*)	

Adolph Friedrich von Schack (1815–94)

A cultured aristocrat, art-collector (the purpose-built Schack Gallerie in Munich houses a rich collection of nineteenth-century German painting including works by Böcklin, Feuerbach, Lenbach, von Schwind and Spitzweg), diplomat and linguist. Although the Naturalists admired his poetry, it lives on only through the songs of Brahms, Marx and Strauss. Schack was a distinguished translator, and his *Epische Dichtungen des Firdusi* (1853) is still admired.

?December 1886 Heimkehr / Homecoming Op. 15, no. 5

Leiser schwanken die Äste,	The boughs are swaying more gently,
Der Kahn fliegt uferwärts,	The small boat races ashore,
Heim kehrt die Taube zum Neste,	The dove's coming home to its nest,
Zu dir kehrt heim mein Herz.	My heart's coming home to you.
Genug am schimmernden Tage,	Often enough by shimmering day,
Wenn rings das Leben lärmt,	Amidst the clamour of life,
Mit irrem Flügelschlage	It has winged its roving way
Ist es ins Weite geschwärmt.	Far into the distance.
Doch nun die Sonne geschieden	But now the sun's departed
Und Stille sich senkt auf den Hain,	And silence descends on the grove,

Fühlt es: bei dir ist der Frieden,
Die Ruh' bei dir allein.

It feels: peace is where you are,
Repose is with you alone.

22 December 1886 Ständchen / Serenade Op. 17, no. 2

Mach auf, mach auf! doch leise, mein Kind,
Um Keinen vom Schlummer zu wecken!
Kaum murmelt der Bach, kaum zittert im Wind
Ein Blatt an den Büschen und Hecken;
Drum leise, mein Mädchen, daß nichts sich
    regt,
Nur leise die Hand auf die Klinke gelegt!

Open up, open up! but softly, my child,
So that no one's roused from slumber!
The brook hardly murmurs, the breeze
    hardly moves
A leaf on the bushes and hedges;
Gently, my love, so nothing shall stir,
Gently with your hand as you lift the latch!

Mit Tritten, wie Tritte der Elfen so sacht,
Um über die Blumen zu hüpfen,
Flieg leicht hinaus in die Mondscheinnacht,
Zu mir in den Garten zu schlüpfen!
Rings schlummern die Blüten am rieselnden
    Bach
Und duften im Schlaf, nur die Liebe ist wach.

With steps as light as the steps of elves,
As they hop their way over flowers,
Flit out into the moonlit night,
Slip out to me in the garden!
The flowers are fragrant in sleep
By the rippling brook, only love is
    awake.

Sitz nieder! Hier dämmerts geheimnisvoll
Unter den Lindenbäumen.
Die Nachtigall uns zu Häupten soll
Von unseren Küssen träumen
Und die Rose, wenn sie am Morgen erwacht,
Hoch glühn von den Wonneschauern der
    Nacht.
(*Robert Kahn, Pfitzner*)

Sit down! Dusk falls mysteriously here
Beneath the linden trees.
The nightingale above us
Shall dream of our kisses
And the rose, when it wakes at dawn,
Shall glow from our night's rapture.

2 January 1888 Wie sollten wir geheim sie halten / How could we keep it secret Op. 19, no. 4

Wie sollten wir geheim sie halten,
Die Seligkeit, die uns erfüllt?
Nein, bis in seine tiefsten Falten
Sei Allen unser Herz enthüllt!

How could we keep it secret,
This bliss with which we're filled?
No, into its deepest recesses
Our hearts must be revealed to all!

Wenn Zwei in Liebe sich gefunden,
Geht Jubel hin durch die Natur,
In längern wonnevollen Stunden
Legt sich der Tag auf Wald und Flur.

When two souls have fallen in love,
Nature's filled with exultation,
And daylight lingers on wood and fields
In longer hours of rapture.

Selbst aus der Eiche morschem Stamm,
Die ein Jahrtausend überlebt,
Steigt neu des Wipfels grüne Flamme
Und rauscht von Jugendlust durchbebt.

Even the oak tree's rotten trunk,
That has survived a thousand years,
Sends fresh flaming green to its crown
And rustles with the thrill of youth.

Zu höherm Glanz und Dufte brechen
Die Knospen auf beim Glück der Zwei,

The buds, seeing the lovers' bliss,
Flower more brightly and fragrantly,

Und süßer rauscht es in den Bächen,	And the brooks babble more sweetly,
Und reicher blüht und reicher glänzt der Mai.	And May gleams and blooms more lavishly.

1 February 1888 Breit' über mein Haupt / Unbind your black hair Op. 19, no. 2

Breit' über mein Haupt dein schwarzes Haar,	Unbind your black hair over my head,
Neig' zu mir dein Angesicht!	Incline to me your face!
Da strömt in die Seele so hell und klar	Then clearly and brightly into my soul
Mir deiner Augen Licht.	The light of your eyes will stream.
Ich will nicht droben der Sonne Pracht,	I want neither the glory of the sun above
Noch der Sterne leuchtenden Kranz,	Nor the gleaming garland of stars,
Ich will nur deiner Locken Nacht	All I want are your black tresses
Und deiner Blicke Glanz.	And the radiance of your eyes.

5 February 1888 Wozu noch, Mädchen / What is the purpose, my sweet Op. 19, no. 1

Wozu noch, Mädchen, soll es frommen,	What is the purpose, my sweet,
Daß du vor mir Verstellung übst?	Of trying to deceive me?
Heiß froh das neue Glück willkommen	Bid your new bliss a joyful welcome
Und sag es offen, daß du liebst!	And say openly that you're in love!
An deines Busens höherm Schwellen,	The quickened stirring of your breast,
Dem Wangenrot, das kommt und geht,	The way your blushes come and go,
Ward dein Geheimnis von den Quellen,	Have long since revealed your secret
Den Blumengeistern längst erspäht.	To fountains and flower-sprites.
Die Wogen murmelns in den Grotten,	The waves murmur it in caverns,
Es flüsterts leis der Abendwind,	The evening breezes whisper it,
Wo du vorbeigehst, hörst dus spotten:	Wherever you go, you hear them mocking:
Wir wissen es seit lange, Kind!	We've known it a long time, child!

William Shakespeare (1564–1616)

Karl Simrock's translations owe a great deal to those by Tieck and Schlegel. All three fragments are chanted by the demented Ophelia in Act 4, scene 5 of *Hamlet*; unlike Brahms's five *Ophelia-Lieder*, which were intended to be sung unaccompanied, Strauss's are set to piano accompaniments that stress Ophelia's insanity: the little wandering motif and dissonances of 'Wie erkenn ich mein Treulieb', the bizarre flapping syncopations of 'Guten Morgen, 's ist Sankt Valentinstag', and in 'Sie trugen ihn auf der Bahre bloß' the abrupt shifts in tempi.

1918 *Drei Lieder der Ophelia aus 'Hamlet' / Three Ophelia songs from 'Hamlet'*
Op. 67

TRANSLATED BY KARL SIMROCK (1802–76)

1

Wie erkenn' ich mein Treulieb
Vor andern nun?
An dem Muschelhut und Stab
Und den Sandalschuh'n.

How shall I know my true love
From others now?
By his cockle hat and staff
And his sandal shoes.

Er ist tot und lange hin,
Tot und hin, Fräulein.
Ihm zu Häupten grünes Gras,
Ihm zu Fuß ein Stein. – O, ho!

He is dead and long gone,
Dead and gone, lady!
At his head green grass,
At his feet a stone. – O, ho!

Auf seinem Bahrtuch, weiß wie Schnee,
Viel liebe Blumen trauern:
Sie gehn zu Grabe naß, o weh,
Vor Liebesschauern.
(*Brahms*)

On his shroud white as snow
Many sweet flowers mourn:
They'll go wet to the grave, alas,
Wet with love's showers.

2

Guten Morgen, 's ist Sankt Valentinstag,
    So früh vor Sonnenschein.
Ich junge Maid am Fensterschlag
    Will euer Valentin sein.

Good morning, it's St Valentine's Day,
    So early before sunrise.
I, young maid at the window,
    Shall be your Valentine.

Der junge Mann tut Hosen an,
    Tät auf die Kammertür,
Ließ ein die Maid, die als Maid
    Ging nimmermehr herfür.

The young man put trousers on,
    Opened up the chamber door,
Let in the maid who as a maid
    Departed nevermore.

Bei Sankt Niklas und Charitas,
    Ein unverschämt Geschlecht!
Ein junger Mann tut's wenn er kann,
    Fürwahr, das ist nicht recht.

By St Nicholas and Charity,
    What a shameless breed!
A young man does it when he can,
    Which is, forsooth, not right.

Sie sprach: Eh' ihr gescherzt mit mir,
    Verspracht ihr mich zu frei'n.
Ich bräch's auch nicht, bei'm Sonnenlicht!
    Wär'st du nicht kommen herein.
(*Brahms*)

She said: before you trifled with me,
    You promised to marry me.
I'd not, by sunlight! have broken my word,
    If you had not come in.

3

Sie trugen ihn auf der Bahre bloß,
    Leider, ach leider den Liebsten!
Manche Träne fiel in des Grabes Schoß:
    Fahr' wohl, meine Taube!

They carried him naked on the bier,
    Alas, alas, the dear one!
Many a tear dropped in the grave:
    Farewell, farewell, my dove!

Mein junger frischer Hansel ist's der mir gefällt,
Und kommt er nimmermehr?
Und kommt er nimmermehr?
   Er ist tot, o weh!
   In dein Todbett geh,
Er kommt dir nimmermehr.

Sein Bart war weiß wie Schnee,
Sein Haupt wie Flachs dazu:
   Er ist hin, er ist hin,
   Kein Trauern bringt Gewinn:
Mit seiner Seele Ruh!

Und mit allen Christenseelen! darum bet' ich! –
Gott sei mit euch.
(*Brahms*)

My young fresh Johnnie it is I love
And will he not come again?
And will he not come again?
   He is dead, ah woe!
   To your deathbed go,
He will never come to you again.

His beard was white as snow,
His head was like flax:
   He is gone, he is gone,
   Nothing comes of mourning:
May his soul rest in peace!

With all Christian souls!
That is my prayer! God be with you!

Vier letzte Lieder / *Four last songs*

1

18 July 1948 Frühling / Spring
HERMANN HESSE (1877–1962)

In dämmrigen Grüften
Träumte ich lang
Von deinen Bäumen und blauen Lüften,
Von deinem Duft und Vogelsang.

Nun liegst du erschlossen
In Gleiß und Zier
Von Licht übergossen
Wie ein Wunder vor mir.

Du kennst mich wieder,
Du lockst mich zart,
Es zittert durch all meine Glieder
Deine selige Gegenwart.

In twilit caverns
I have long dreamt
Of your trees and blue skies,
Your fragrance and birdsong.

Now you lie revealed
In shining graceful splendour,
Bathed in light
Like a miracle before me.

You recognize me once more,
You lure me tenderly,
My whole frame quivers
With your blissful presence.

2

20 September 1948 September / September
HERMANN HESSE (1877–1962)

Der Garten trauert,
Kühl sinkt in die Blumen der Regen.
Der Sommer schauert
Still seinem Ende entgegen.

Golden tropft Blatt um Blatt
Nieder vom hohen Akazienbaum.

The garden mourns,
The cool rain sinks into the flowers.
Summer shudders
Quietly to its close.

Leaf after golden leaf
Falls from the tall acacia.

Sommer lächelt erstaunt und matt   Summer smiles, astonished and drained,
In den sterbenden Gartentraum.   Into the garden's dying dream.

Lange noch bei den Rosen   For a long time it lingers
Bleibt er stehn, sehnt sich nach Ruh.   By the roses, yearning for rest.
Langsam tut er die   Slowly it closes
Müdgewordnen Augen zu.   Its now wearied eyes.

3
4 August 1948 Beim Schlafengehen / Going to sleep
HERMANN HESSE (1877–1962)

Nun der Tag mich müd gemacht,   Now that day has wearied me,
Soll mein sehnliches Verlangen   May my yearning desire
Freundlich die gestirnte Nacht   Be received by the starlit night
Wie ein müdes Kind empfangen.   Like a tired child.

Hände laßt von allem Tun,   Hands, refrain from all work,
Stirn vergiß du alles Denken,   Brow, forget all thought,
Alle meine Sinne nun   All my senses now
Wollen sich in Schlummer senken.   Long to sink in slumber.

Und die Seele unbewacht   And the unwatched soul
Will in freien Flügen schweben,   Longs to soar up freely,
Um im Zauberkreis der Nacht   To live in night's magic circle
Tief und tausendfach zu leben.   Profoundly and a thousandfold.

4
6 May 1948 Im Abendrot / At sunset
JOSEPH VON EICHENDORFF (1788–1857)

  Wir sind durch Not und Freude   We have gone hand in hand
Gegangen Hand in Hand,   Through joys and distress,
Vom Wandern ruhen wir   Now we rest from our wanderings
Nun überm stillen Land.   High above the quiet land.

  Rings sich die Täler neigen,   Around us the valleys slope down,
Es dunkelt schon die Luft,   The skies have begun to darken,
Zwei Lerchen nur noch steigen   Only two larks, recalling a dream,
Nachträumend in den Duft.   Soar up into the haze.

  Tritt her, und laß sie schwirren,   Come, and leave them to fly,
Bald ist es Schlafenszeit,   Soon it will be time to sleep,
Daß wir uns nicht verirren   We must not lose our way
In dieser Einsamkeit.   In this solitude.

  O weiter stiller Friede!   O vast and silent peace!
So tief im Abendrot   So deep in the sunset glow,
Wie sind wir wandermüde –   How weary we are with wandering –
Ist dies etwa der Tod?   Could this perhaps be death?
(*Pepping*)

Václav Tomášek (1774–1850)

Václav Tomášek fared much better than Schubert in his correspondence with Goethe. Not only did the great poet deign to reply to Tomášek's gift of songs, he invited the composer in 1818 to perform them in his presence; Tomášek gives an account of his two meetings with the poet in his memoirs, published between 1845 and 1850 in the Prague periodical *Libussa*. By 1818, he had made a name for himself in Prague as music-teacher, pianist and composer, had already met Haydn and Beethoven in Vienna, and was clearly known to Goethe who, though they had not yet met, was almost certainly attracted to a composer who had spent years studying mathematics, history, aesthetics, philosophy and law, before devoting himself to music. His forty-one Goethe Lieder were composed in 1815, the great Schubert–Goethe year. Though many of them are better known in settings by other composers – 'Der Fischer', 'Wandrers Nachtlied' ('Der du von dem Himmel bist'), 'Erlkönig', 'Auf dem See', 'Mit einem gemalten Band', 'Mailied', 'Am Flusse', 'Der König in Thule', 'Der Rattenfänger', 'Schäfers Klagelied', 'Erster Verlust', 'Jägers Abendlied', 'Rastlose Liebe', 'Trost in Tränen', 'Nähe des Geliebten', 'Philine' – they all repay study.

Johann Wolfgang von Goethe (1749–1832)

See Beethoven, Brahms, Hensel, Loewe, Mendelssohn, Mozart, Reichardt, Schubert, Strauss, Wolf, Zelter

Selbstbetrug / Self-deception

Der Vorhang schwebet hin und her	The curtain moves to and fro
Bei meiner Nachbarin.	At my neighbour's window.
Gewiß, sie lauschet überquer,	I bet she's listening across the way
Ob ich zu Hause bin.	To see if I'm at home
Und ob der eifersücht'ge Groll,	And if the jealous rancour
Den ich am Tag gehegt,	I'd harboured in the day
Sich, wie er nun auf immer soll,	Stirs, as it now always shall,
Im tiefen Herzen regt.	Deep in my heart.
Doch leider hat das schöne Kind	But I'm sorry to say, the lovely child
Dergleichen nicht gefühlt.	Felt nothing of the sort.
Ich seh, es ist der Abendwind,	I see it's the evening breeze
Der mit dem Vorhang spielt.	Playing with the curtain.
(*Reichardt, Medtner*)	

Richard Wagner (1813–83)

Wagner's earliest Lieder, the *Sieben Compositionen zu Goethes Faust*, date from 1832 and include a 'Flohlied' (see BEETHOVEN), and two of Gretchen's songs, more familiar to us from Schubert's settings: 'Ach neige' and 'Meine Ruh' ist hin'. It was not until a quarter of a century later that he composed the *Fünf Gedichte für eine Frauenstimme*, the so-called *Wesendonck-Lieder*, on which his reputation as a Lieder composer rests. Wagner himself had a high opinion of these songs, and in a letter to Mathilde of 9 October 1858 he wrote: „Beßeres, als diese Lieder, habe ich nie gemacht, und nur weniges von meinen Werken wird ihnen zur Seite gestellt werden können." ('I have never done anything better than these songs, and few of my works will bear comparison with them.')

Mathilde Wesendonck (1828–1902)

Apart from poetry, Mathilde Wesendonck wrote a number of plays, including *Gudrun* (1868), *Edith oder die Schlacht bei Hastings* (1872), and the dramatic poem *Odysseus* (1878). The confusion over the correct orthography of her surname was caused by her son, who in the early years of the twentieth century reverted to the original spelling (Wesendonk) of the family name. Wagner first met Mathilde Wesendonck in Zurich, after he had fled Germany in the wake of his revolutionary activities of 1849. She was the wife of Otto Wesendonck, a wealthy Rhenish silk merchant who supported Wagner financially. Wagner's attachment to her developed into a passion, and the relationship yielded rich artistic results: the composer's decision in 1857 to shelve work on the *Ring* and turn to *Tristan und Isolde* must have been partly inspired by his love for Mathilde. The *Fünf Gedichte für eine Frauenstimme*, written during the early stages of his work on the new opera, all inhabit the same harmonic world as *Tristan*, while two of them employ actual material from the opera: the Prelude to Act III can be heard in 'Im Treibhaus', and 'Träume' anticipates that section of the Act II love duet beginning 'O sink hernieder, Nacht der Liebe'. Although they were conceived for piano accompaniment, Wagner made an orchestral transcription of 'Träume' as a birthday present for Mathilde on 23 December, when an ensemble of eighteen players performed it outside her villa near Zurich. The other songs were orchestrated by Friedrich Mottl, the Austrian conductor who was to perform *Tristan* at Bayreuth after Wagner's death.

Fünf Gedichte für eine Frauenstimme und Klavier / Five poems for woman's voice and piano

1

30 November 1857 Der Engel / The angel

In der Kindheit frühen Tagen
Hört' ich oft von Engeln sagen,
Die des Himmels hehre Wonne
Tauschen mit der Erdensonne,

Daß, wo bang ein Herz in Sorgen
Schmachtet vor der Welt verborgen,
Daß, wo still es will verbluten,
Und vergehn in Tränenfluten,

Daß, wo brünstig sein Gebet
Einzig um Erlösung fleht,
Da der Engel niederschwebt,
Und es sanft gen Himmel hebt.

Ja, es stieg auch mir ein Engel nieder,
Und auf leuchtendem Gefieder
Führt er, ferne jedem Schmerz,
Meinen Geist nun himmelwärts!

In the early days of childhood
I often heard tell of angels
Who exchange heaven's pure bliss
For the sun of earth,

So that, when a sorrowful heart
Hides its yearning from the world,
And would silently bleed away
And dissolve in streams of tears,

And when its fervent prayer
Begs only for deliverance,
That angel will fly down
And gently raise the heart to heaven.

And to me too an angel descended,
And now on shining wings
Bears my spirit, free from all pain,
Towards heaven!

2

February 1858 Stehe still! / Stand still!

Sausendes, brausendes Rad der Zeit,
Messer du der Ewigkeit;
Leuchtende Sphären im weiten All,
Die ihr umringt den Weltenball;
Urewige Schöpfung, halte doch ein,
Genug des Werdens, laß mich sein!

Halte an dich, zeugende Kraft,
Urgedanke, der ewig schafft!
Hemmet den Atem, stillet den Drang,
Schweigend nur eine Sekunde lang!
Schwellende Pulse, fesselt den Schlag;
Ende, des Wollens ew'ger Tag!

Daß in selig süßem Vergessen
Ich mög alle Wonne ermessen!
Wenn Auge in Auge wonnig trinken,
Seele ganz in Seele versinken;
Wesen in Wesen sich wiederfindet,
Und alles Hoffens Ende sich kündet,
Die Lippe verstummt in staunendem
    Schweigen,

Rushing, roaring wheel of time,
You that measure eternity;
Gleaming spheres in the vast universe,
You that surround our earthly sphere;
Eternal creation – cease:
Enough of becoming, let me be!

Hold yourselves back, generative powers,
Primal Thought that always creates!
Stop your breath, still your urge,
Be silent for a single moment!
Swelling pulses, restrain your beating;
Eternal day of the Will – end!

That in blessed, sweet oblivion
I might measure all my bliss!
When eye gazes blissfully into eye,
When soul drowns utterly in soul;
When being finds itself in being,
And the goal of every hope is near,
When lips are mute in silent wonder,

Keinen Wunsch mehr will das Innre zeugen:	When the soul wishes for nothing more:
Erkennt der Mensch des Ew'gen Spur,	Then man perceives Eternity's footprint,
Und löst dein Rätsel, heil'ge Natur!	And solves your riddle, holy Nature!

3

1 May 1858 Im Treibhaus / In the greenhouse
(STUDY FOR *Tristan und Isolde*)

Hochgewölbte Blätterkronen,	High-arching leafy crowns,
Baldachine von Smaragd,	Canopies of emerald,
Kinder ihr aus fernen Zonen,	You children who dwell in distant climes,
Saget mir, warum ihr klagt?	Tell me, why do you lament?
Schweigend neiget ihr die Zweige,	Silently you bend your branches,
Malet Zeichen in die Luft,	Inscribe your symbols on the air,
Und der Leiden stummer Zeuge	And a sweet fragrance rises,
Steiget aufwärts, süßer Duft.	As silent witness to your sorrows.
Weit in sehnendem Verlangen	With longing and desire
Breitet ihr die Arme aus,	You open wide your arms,
Und umschlinget wahnbefangen	And embrace in your delusion
Öder Leere nicht'gen Graus.	Desolation's awful void.
Wohl, ich weiß es, arme Pflanze;	I am well aware, poor plant;
Ein Geschicke teilen wir,	We both share a single fate,
Ob umstrahlt von Licht und Glanze,	Though bathed in gleaming light,
Unsre Heimat ist nicht hier!	Our homeland is not here!
Und wie froh die Sonne scheidet	And just as the sun is glad to leave
Von des Tages leerem Schein,	The empty gleam of day,
Hüllet der, der wahrhaft leidet,	The true sufferer veils himself
Sich in Schweigens Dunkel ein.	In the darkness of silence.
Stille wird's, ein säuselnd Weben	It grows quiet, a whirring whisper
Füllet bang den dunklen Raum:	Fills the dark room uneasily:
Schwere Tropfen seh ich schweben	I see heavy droplets hanging
An der Blätter grünem Saum.	From the green edge of the leaves.

4

17 December 1857 Schmerzen / Agonies

Sonne, weinest jeden Abend	Every evening, sun, you redden
Dir die schönen Augen rot,	Your lovely eyes with weeping,
Wenn im Meeresspiegel badend	When, bathing in the sea,
Dich erreicht der frühe Tod;	You die an early death;
Doch erstehst in alter Pracht,	Yet you rise in your old splendour,
Glorie der düstren Welt,	The glory of the dark world,
Du am Morgen neu erwacht,	When you wake in the morning
Wie ein stolzer Siegesheld!	As a proud and conquering hero!

Ach, wie sollte ich da klagen,
Wie, mein Herz, so schwer dich sehn,
Muß die Sonne selbst verzagen,
Muß die Sonne untergehn?

Und gebieret Tod nur Leben,
Geben Schmerzen Wonne nur:
O wie dank ich, daß gegeben
Solche Schmerzen mir Natur!

Ah, why should I complain,
Why should I see you, my heart, so depressed,
If the sun itself must despair,
If the sun itself must set?

If only death gives birth to life,
If only agony brings bliss:
O how I give thanks to Nature
For giving me such agony!

5

4–5 December 1857 **Träume / Dreams**
(STUDY FOR *Tristan und Isolde*)

Sag, welch wunderbare Träume
Halten meinen Sinn umfangen,
Daß sie nicht wie leere Schäume
Sind in ödes Nichts vergangen?

Träume, die in jeder Stunde,
Jedem Tage schöner blühn,
Und mit ihrer Himmelskunde
Selig durchs Gemüte ziehn!

Träume, die wie hehre Strahlen
In die Seele sich versenken,
Dort ein ewig Bild zu malen:
Allvergessen, Eingedenken!

Träume, wie wenn Frühlingssonne
Aus dem Schnee die Blüten küßt,
Daß zu nie geahnter Wonne
Sie der neue Tag begrüßt,

Daß sie wachsen, daß sie blühen,
Träumend spenden ihren Duft,
Sanft an deiner Brust verglühen,
Und dann sinken in die Gruft.

Say, what wondrous dreams are these
Embracing all my senses,
That they have not, like bubbles,
Vanished to a barren void?

Dreams, that with every hour
Bloom more lovely every day,
And with their heavenly tidings
Float blissfully through the mind!

Dreams, that with glorious rays
Penetrate the soul,
There to paint an eternal picture:
Forgetting all, remembering one!

Dreams, as when the Spring sun
Kisses blossoms from the snow,
So the new day might welcome them
In unimagined bliss,

So that they grow and flower,
Bestow their scent as in a dream,
Fade softly away on your breast
And sink into their grave.

Carl Maria von Weber (1786–1826)

When Wilhelm Müller dedicated *Die Winterreise* to 'Carl Maria von Weber, master of German song, in friendship and admiration', he was, above all, expressing his approval of Weber's operas which combined national characteristics in both plot and music. Song had always been important for Weber from the time when, in his youth, he travelled the countryside with his guitar. Max Maria wrote in the biography of his father:

> Weber war Meister auf der Gitarre wie auf dem Flügel. Seine damals noch wenig bekannten Lieder, von ihm selbst mit schwacher aber ungemein wohlklingender Stimme in unnachahmlichem Ausdruck vorgetragen und mit höchster Virtuosität von der Gitarre begleitet, sind das Vollendetste, was vielleicht je in dieser Gattung geleistet worden ist und gewann ihm alle Herzen.

> Weber was a great master of the guitar as he was of the piano. His songs, which were not yet well-known, and which he would sing with incomparable expression in his weak but uncommonly sweet voice and accompany with real virtuosity on the guitar, were perhaps the most perfect of their kind and won all hearts.

Although some of his hundred or so songs were originally written for voice and guitar, including the celebrated 'Wiegenlied', the majority were composed with piano accompaniment. Melody was of paramount importance, as he explains in a letter to Friedrich Wieck, who had sent him some songs for criticism:

> Die Schaffung einer neuen Form muß über das von einem geschriebene Gedicht geschehen. In meinen Liedern bedarf es immer der größten Anstrengung, meinen Dichter treu, wiederzugeben, wahrhaftig und richtig deklamiert, was zu einer Menge von neuen melodischen Formen geführt hat.

> The creation of a new form must be achieved through the poem one sets. In my songs, it is always through taking the greatest pains to reproduce my poet truthfully and correctly declaimed that I have created a number of new melodic forms.

One of these new forms was none other than a mini song-cycle: *Die Temperamente beim Verluste der Geliebten*; composed in 1816, the year of Beethoven's *An die ferne Geliebte*, it explores four contrasting emotions at the poet's loss of his beloved.

Friedrich Wilhelm Gubitz (1786–1870)

A playwright and friend of Weber's, for whose play, *Lieb' und Versöhnen oder die Schlacht bei Leipzig*, produced in Prague on the anniversary of the battle (18 October 1815), the composer wrote two patriotic songs: 'Wer stets hinter'n Ofen kroch' and 'Wie wir voll Glut'.

1816 *Die vier Temperamente beim Verlust der Geliebten / The four humours at the loss of the beloved* Op. 46

1

Der Leichtmütige / The lighthearted lover

Lust entfloh und hin ist hin!	Joy has fled, what's gone is gone!
Blanda will mich nicht mehr lieben!	Blanda loves me no more!
Ich wär ihr (so wahr ich bin!)	I would have stayed faithful
Noch acht Tage treu geblieben,	(Honestly!) for another week,
Kam ihr Hochzeit nicht zu Sinn;	If she hadn't mentioned marriage;
Dafür hat mich Gott bewahrt!	God saved me from that!
Lebe wohl, mein Kind, ich wandre	Farewell, my child, I'm on my way
Schon zu frischer Liebesfahrt!	In search of new love experiences!
Heute die und dann die andre:	One girl today, and another tomorrow:
Das ist so die rechte Art!	That's the way to do it!
Scheiden macht mein Herz nicht schwer,	Parting doesn't pain my heart,
Weinen kann ich nicht noch fluchen.	I can neither weep nor curse.
Doch da kommt ein Mädchen her,	But there comes a girl,
Schnell muß ich mein Glück versuchen;	I must try my luck at once;
Ohne Lieb' ist alles leer!	Without love the world's empty!
Sprödes Kind, wirf ab dein Joch,	Prudish child, away with restraint,
Laß' von Himmelskost mich nippen;	Let me sip the heavenly nectar;
Eh' wir bleichen, lebe noch!	Let us live before we die!
Mädchen, reiche mir die Lippen,	Offer me your lips, my girl,
Denn geküßt wirst du ja doch!	For kiss you I certainly shall!
Sieh, man darf sich in Genuß	Pleasures, you see, can make up
Für versehnte Träume rächen.	For dreams we craved in vain.
Laß der Seelen Genius	Let the spirit of the soul
Aus dem Schlag der Herzen sprechen;	Speak in the beating of the heart;
Doppelsprache ist der Kuß!	A kiss has a double meaning!
Ah, du magst mich nicht? Nun gut!	Ah, you don't like me? Very well, then!
Mag ich's auch nicht gern ertragen,	Even though it's hard to bear,
Halt' ich doch mir frischen Mut;	It doesn't dampen my exuberance;
Morgen will ich wieder fragen,	I'll ask again tomorrow,
Hast vielleicht dann wärmer Blut.	When you might have hotter blood.
Wer wie ich, mein' Lieb', gesinnt,	Whoever thinks as I do, my love,
Kann nur liebend selig werden!	Can only be happy in loving!

Fahr' ich einst zum Himmel, Kind,	If I get to Heaven, my child,
Frag' ich gleich den Herrn der Erden,	I'll ask the Lord immediately
Ob die Engel weiblich sind!	If the angels there are women!
Wenn er etwa „Nein!" nun spricht,	If he happens to answer 'No',
Sag' ich keck und voll Vertrauen:	I'll say boldly and with confidence:
„Herr, dein Reich gefällt mir nicht;	'Lord, your kingdom's not to my taste,
Denn ein Himmel ohne Frauen	For a heaven without women
Ist die Sonne ohne Licht."	Is like the sun without light.'
Hebt die Treue hoch empor,	Raise faithfulness aloft –
Quälend Glück will ich euch schenken.	I can do without agonized joy.
Schwatzt nur mir Moral nicht vor;	But don't talk to me of morals;
Bei der Liebe will ich denken,	I shall be thinking of love
Wenn ich den Verstand verlor.	Even when I've lost my reason.
Alle Wesen huld'gen ihr;	All creatures pay homage to love;
Liebe ist das Herz vom Leben,	Love is the heart of life,
Nur durch Liebe sind wir hier;	It's only through love that we are here;
Liebe will ich wieder geben,	I wish to continue loving,
Mädchen alle, kommt zu mir!	Come to me, all you girls!

2

Der Schwermütige / The melancholy lover

Sel'ge Zeiten sah ich prangen,	I saw the splendour of blissful days
Und den Erdball glaubt' ich mein	And I believed the earth was mine
Als mich Lyddis Blick befangen,	When Lydia bewitched me with her eyes,
Unschuldklar wie Heil'genschein.	Innocent like a halo.
Als der Lippen Siegel sprangen,	When the seal of her lips was broken,
Herrschte Gott nicht mehr allein,	God no longer reigned alone,
Denn der Liebe Klänge schwangen	For the sounds of love made me soar
Siegend mich zum Himmel ein.	Victoriously up to heaven.
Ach, die Wonnen all' verklangen!	Alas! all the rapture has died away!
Ewig kann nicht Frühling sein!	Spring cannot last forever!
Traum und Treue sind vergangen,	Dream and faithfulness have vanished,
Ausgelöscht der Heil'genschein!	The halo has been extinguished!
Fern von ihr muß ich verbangen,	Far from her I must die of anguish,
Von der Welt ist nichts mehr mein;	Nothing more in the world is mine;
Glühend fasset all' Verlangen	All that I passionately desire
Nur der Hoffnung Leichenstein.	Is the tombstone of hope.
Doch zum Todesengel drangen	Yet news of my bleak heart's anguish
Meines Herzens Öd' und Pein,	Has reached the angel of death,
Liebend bald von Erd' umfangen	Soon, lovingly embraced by earth,
Wird der Himmel wieder mein.	Heaven will be mine again.

3
Der Liebewütige / The raging lover

„Verraten! Verschmähet!
Wer drängte mich aus?
Auf, Diener, umspähet
Heut' Abend ihr Haus;
Und wagt zur Megäre
Ein Einz'ger den Blick,
So fragt: wer er wäre?
Und brecht ihm's Genick!"

Don Marco trieb Alle
Recht wachsam zu sein,
Dann stürmt' ihn die Galle
Bergauf und talein.
Er fluchte nun trabend
Hinein in die Luft
Und passte am Abend
Noch selbst auf den Schuft.

Mit Hast spionieret
Das Dienervolk stumm;
Don Marco begieret
Die Türen rings um.
Wie schleichend und sinnig
Im Dämmern er wallt,
Gebieten recht innig
Sechs Fäuste ihm: „Halt!"

„Wer sind Sie?" nach Regel
Klingt dies zum Gezerr.
„Ihr Lümmel, ihr Flegel!
Ich bin euer Herr!"
Und wie ihn am Toben
Die Diener erkannt,
Spricht Clara von oben:
„Das ist ja charmant!

Die Eifersucht hordet
Schon Söldner heran –
Der Argwohn ermordet,
Was Liebe gewann!
Drum hab' ich vernünftig
Den Leichtsinn bereut!
Nun quälen Sie künftig
Sich selber gescheut!"

Nichts halfen Sonette
Von Gram und von Grab.

'Betrayed! Disdained!
Who has usurped me?
Servants, keep watch tonight
Round her house;
And if any man
Dares look at the harpy,
Ask him his name
And break his neck!'

Don Marco urged everyone
To be on their guard,
Bitterness then drove him
Up hill and down dale.
He uttered curses on horseback
Into the air,
And in the evening kept watch
For the villain himself.

The servants swiftly and quietly
Spy out the land;
Zealously Don Marco
Keeps an eye on the doors.
As he pensively, stealthily
Walks at dusk,
Six fists command him
With passion: 'Halt!'

'Who are you?' they scream
To order, as they drag him away.
'You louts, you idiots!
It's me, your master!'
And now as his servants
Recognize his roar,
Clara says from above:
'How very appealing!

Your jealousy's caused you
To call in hirelings –
Suspicion has killed
What was gained through love!
So now I've sensibly
Regretted my folly!
You must try hard in future
To be sensible yourself!'

In vain he wrote sonnets
On grief and the grave,

572   CARL MARIA VON WEBER

Da riß er vom Brette	So he went to the shelf
Die Flinte herab;	And snatched up his gun;
Er jagte mit Rasen	He stormed out raging
Zum Walde hinaus,	Into the forest,
Und schoß einen Hasen	And shot a hare
Zum lärmenden Schmaus.	For a riotous feast.

4

Der Gleichmütige / The apathetic lover

Nun, ich bin befreit!	Now I'm free!
Wie behäglich!	How very pleasant!
Mir ist Zärtlichkeit	I cannot abide
Unerträglich;	Tenderness;
Treibt sie Keine lau,	If women can't be moderate,
Werd' ich ohne Frau	I'll gladly grow old
Ruhig alt und grau.	And grey unwed.
Hätt' sie wohl gemocht	I liked her well enough
So bei Festen;	On festival days.
Plumperpuddings kocht	No one can cook
Sie am besten.	Plum pudding like her.
Doch die Lust ward matt,	But my passion waned,
Denn am Ende hatt'	Because her puddings
Ich die Puddings satt.	Finally palled.
Sie gefiel mir gut	When I was on my travels
So beim Wandern;	She pleased me well enough;
Und weil man gern tut,	And since one likes
Wie die Andern,	To do as others do,
Bot ich mich zum Mann,	I offered my hand in marriage
Und sie nahm es an,	And she accepted
Eh' ich mich besann.	Before I could change my mind.
Doch das gab ein Joch	O what a burden!
Und ein Laufen!	And how I had to run after her!
Was nach Ausland roch,	I had to buy
Mußt' ich kaufen,	Anything foreign,
Und tagaus, tagein,	And day in, day out,
Und bei Mondenschein,	Even in the moonlight,
Auch noch zärtlich sein!	I had to be loving and tender as well!
Ohne Ruh und Rast	I had to kiss her
Mußt' ich küssen.	Incessantly.
Das ist Höllenlast,	How hellish it is
Küssen müssen!	To have to kiss!
Drum recht eisig hart	So I deceived her,
Hab' ich sie genarrt,	Acting very cold,
Bis mein Wunsch mir ward.	Until I had my way.

Aus dem Hause warf	Yesterday she threw me
Sie mich gestern,	Out of the house,
Und beliebte scharf	And even took the liberty
Noch zu lästern;	Of abusing me;
„Hätt' ich nicht viel Geld,	'If I, the great trencherman
Wär ich Schüßelheld	Had no money,
Gar nichts nutz der Welt!"	I'd be totally useless!'
Doch mich macht der Hieb	But that affront
Nimmer grämlich,	No longer upsets me,
Denn die Liebe lieb'	For I like love
Ich bequemlich;	To be easy-going;
Treibt sie Keine lau,	If women can't be moderate,
Werd' ich ohne Frau	I'll gladly grow old
Ruhig alt und grau!	And grey unwed.

Franz Karl Hiemer (1768–1822)

Officer, actor, poet and painter, Hiemer was one of those dilettante friends in whom Weber delighted. Weber asked him to refashion and expand the discarded libretto of *Das Waldmädchen* which Hiemer, after a number of humorously pleading letters from the composer, eventually finished and re-titled *Silvana*.

1810 Wiegenlied / Cradle song Op. 13, no. 2

Schlaf, Herzenssöhnchen, mein Liebling bist du,	Sleep my darling, my dearest boy,
Schließe die blauen Guckäugelein zu.	Close your little blue peeping eyes.
Alles ist ruhig, ist still wie im Grab,	All is quiet, silent as the grave,
Schlaf nur, ich wehre die Fliegen dir ab.	Sleep, and I'll wave the flies away from you.
Jetzt noch, mein Püppchen, ist goldene Zeit,	Now, little lad, is your golden age,
Später, ach später ist's nimmer wie heut.	Later, ah later will not be the same.
Stellen einst Sorgen ums Lager sich her,	When troubles one day surround your bed,
Herzchen, da schläft sich's so ruhig nicht mehr.	You'll not sleep so peacefully, my darling.
Engel vom Himmel, so lieblich wie du,	Angels from heaven, as sweet as you,
Schweben ums Bettchen und lächeln dir zu.	Hover round your bed and smile at you.
Später zwar steigen sie auch noch herab,	They'll come down to you later in life,
Aber sie wischen nur Tränen dir ab.	But only to wipe away your tears.
Schlaf, liebes Söhnchen, und kommt gleich die Nacht,	Sleep, little boy, and as soon as night falls,
Sitzt deine Mutter am Bettchen und wacht.	Mother will sit and watch by your cot.
Sei es so spät auch und sei es so früh,	However late or early it be,
Mutterlieb, Herzchen, entschlummert doch nie.	Your mother's love, my darling, will never die.

Anton Webern (1883–1945)

While still a student at Vienna University, Webern met Schoenberg and became his pupil. At the same time as Schoenberg was composing *Das Buch der hängenden Gärten* (1908–9) to George texts, Webern – presumably influenced by his teacher – wrote the first of his fourteen settings of the same poet: the *Fünf Lieder aus 'Der siebente Ring'* (Op. 3), the *Fünf Lieder nach Stefan George* (Op. 4) and the *Vier Lieder* without opus number. Webern was aware that the public would find it difficult to accept the revolutionary nature of his Op. 3, the suspension of tonality, the lack of regular pulse, the changing bar lengths and the irregular grouping within the beat:

> Of course it was a fierce struggle, inhibitions of the most fearful kind had to be overcome, a panic fear as to whether it was possible [. . .] Never in the history of music has such resistance been shown as there was to these things.

Still largely misunderstood by the Lieder-going public, he has always had his passionate followers, among them Stravinsky who in 1955 acknowledged his influence and paid him this wonderful tribute: 'Doomed to failure in a deaf world of ignorance and indifference, he inexorably went on cutting his diamonds, his dazzling diamonds, of whose mines he had such perfect knowledge.' Webern's œuvre is dominated by vocal music, and from 1924 he developed the 'serial' method he had learned from Schoenberg and first used in his *Drei Lieder*, Op. 17.

Stefan George (1868–1933)

The son of a prosperous wine merchant, George never worked for his living, married or established his own home. His extensive travels through central and western Europe brought him into contact with Mallarmé and Verlaine, both of whom he translated into German, as well as Baudelaire and Swinburne. His early books of verse contain all the characteristic features of his personality and work. *Algabal* (1892), in particular, enshrines his concept of the superman, embodied by the Roman emperor Heliogabalus, whose cruelty, effeminacy and perversity are turned by George into virtues. Whereas Dehmel and Liliencron identified themselves with the vital forces of the age, George did his utmost to avoid all contamination with modern life. His poetry and behaviour is characterized by an aristocratic aloofness; he trained a small band of followers to pursue his goal, which was, in his own words, 'Die Vergottung des Leibes und die Verleibung des Gottes' ('the deification of the body and the incarnation of the deity'). He saw himself as an educator, a leader – and his goal was the renewal of what he regarded to be a debased culture. He even created a new God incarnate in the person of the handsome Maximilian Kronberger, a fifteen-year-old Munich boy, who died soon after George had met him. Maximin became the central figure of *Der Siebente Ring*, a collection of 184 poems which deal with the new elite youth which will bring about a renewal of civilization. The esoteric nature of George's poetry and message was emphasized by the presentation of his books. He invented a special fount for the exclusive printing of his works on the finest quality paper, dispensed with capital letters (even for nouns!) except for titles and the beginning of lines, and employed a minimalist and idiosyncratic punctuation of his own devising – not as an affectation or a means of frightening away the uninitiated, but as a way of pursuing his ideal of beauty. Following the publication of *Das neue Reich* (1933), Hitler offered him the presidency of the new Dichter-Akademie, which he declined. Although he had hailed the Great War as a mere forerunner of another 'German' war, which would usher in the Third Empire under its anointed leader, he was appalled by Hitler and fled to Switzerland, where he died. His last will stipulated that his ashes should be interred in free Switzerland – a directive that was immediately suppressed by Goebbels. Despite the unattractive nature of his philosophy, there is an elegance and highly polished beauty to much of his verse (especially his nature poetry such as 'An baches ranft' and 'Im morgen-taun'), which Webern captures in the dazzling atonal vocabulary of his Op. 3.

Fünf Lieder aus 'Der siebente Ring' / Five songs from 'The Seventh Ring' of Stefan George

1

Dies ist ein lied	This is a song
Für dich allein:	For you alone:
Von kindischem wähnen	Of childish dreams
Von frommen tränen . .	Of pious tears . .
Durch morgengärten klingt es	Through morning gardens
Ein leichtbeschwingtes.	It sounds its light way.
Nur dir allein	Only for you
Möcht es ein lied	Would it be a song
Das rühre sein.	To stir the heart.

2

Im windes-weben	In the murmuring wind
War meine frage	My question
Nur träumerei.	Was but a dream.
Nur lächeln war	A smile was all
Was du gegeben.	You had given.
Aus nasser nacht	From the wet night
Ein glanz entfacht –	A radiance was kindled –
Nun drängt der mai ·	May now wakens desire ·
Nun muss ich gar	I must now
Um dein aug und haar	Live in longing

Alle tage
In sehnen leben.
(*Egon Wellesz*)

All my days
For your eyes and hair.

3

An baches ranft
Die einzigen frühen
Die hasel blühen.
Ein vogel pfeift
In kühler au.
Ein leuchten streift
Erwärmt uns sanft
Und zuckt und bleicht.
Das feld ist brach ·
Der baum noch grau . .
Blumen streut vielleicht
Der lenz uns nach.
(*Wolfgang Rihm*)

Beside the stream
The only early creatures
The hazels are in bloom.
A bird whistles
In the cool meadow.
A gleaming touches us
Warms us gently
And quivers and pales.
The field is fallow ·
The tree still grey . .
Spring perhaps
Will bestrew us with flowers.

4

Im morgen-taun
Trittst du hervor
Den kirschenflor
Mit mir zu schaun ·
Duft einzuziehn
Des rasenbeetes.
Fern fliegt der staub . .
Durch die natur
Noch nichts gediehn
Von frucht und laub –
Rings blüte nur . . .
Von süden weht es.
(*Egon Wellesz*)

In the morning dew
You emerge
To gaze with me
On the flowering cherry ·
To drink in the fragrance
Of the lawn.
Dust swirls afar . .
Nature has not yet
Brought forth
Leaf or fruit –
Only blossom abounds . . .
The South Wind blows.

5

Kahl reckt der baum
Im winterdunst
Sein frierend leben ·
Lass deinen traum
Auf stiller reise
Vor ihm sich heben!
Er dehnt die arme –
Bedenk ihn oft
Mit dieser gunst
Dass er im harme
Dass er im eise
Noch frühling hofft!
(*Egon Wellesz*)

The bare tree stretches
Its freezing life
In winter mist ·
Let your dream
On its quiet journey
Rise before it!
It stretches its arms –
Think of it often
With favour
That in pain
That in ice
It might still hope for spring!

Hugo Wolf (1860–1903)

Hugo Wolf was the only important Lieder composer to select verse written almost exclusively by the great poets of the past. If we exclude the juvenilia, composed before he turned twenty, unpublished during his lifetime and featuring such ephemera as Zshokke, Kind, von Zusner, Roquette, Herloßsohn and Steinebach, we find that from February 1888 – with the exception of three poems by Reinick – he set only German poets of indisputable pedigree: fifty-three poems by Mörike, twenty by Eichendorff, fifty-one by Goethe and six by Keller. Having composed his final Keller song in June 1890, however, he turned his back on German poetry, and for the remaining seven years of his composing life set nothing but German translations of Italian, Spanish, English and Norwegian verse.

Wolf was not the first composer to devote a series of songs to a particular poet – C. P. E. Bach, Reichardt, Schubert and Schumann, for example, had already concentrated in depth on Gellert, Goethe and Heine – but the way in which Wolf immersed himself in his poets and created musical anthologies of Eichendorff, Mörike and Goethe was something new. And his fidelity to the poetic text was extraordinary. Although on occasion he was guilty of repeating ('Wer sein holdes Lieb verloren') or omitting ('Geh, Geliebter, geh jetzt') stanzas; although he sometimes repeated phrases seemingly at random ('Er ist's'); although his prosody was not always faultless ('Leibrößlein' in 'Der Gärtner' should be stressed on the first and not the second syllable); although he occasionally composed a song to a corrupt text ('Das verlassene Mägdlein') – he was normally scrupulous in respecting the integrity of a poem. In the vast majority of the Eichendorff, Mörike and Goethe songs, not a single word or syllable is altered; and Wolf's practice of prefacing a performance of a song with a recitation of the poem was unprecedented. The first page of the Mörike volume gave pride of place to the poet's portrait, inspiring Detlev von Liliencron, who was present at the premiere of the *Mörike-Lieder*, to write in his poem 'An Hugo Wolf':

> Vorn im Mörike-Heft,
> Auf erster Seite,
> Hattest Du, Bescheidener,
> Des Dichters Bild verehrend aufgestellt.
> Welcher Tonsetzer tat je so?

> In the Mörike volume,
> On the first page,
> You, modest man,
> Had set the poet's portrait in admiration.
> What composer ever did that?

Wolf's subtitling of his songbooks also mirrored his special response to word-setting: 'Gedichte von . . . für eine Singstimme und Klavier' ('Poems by . . . for voice and piano) instead of the usual 'Songs by . . . for voice with piano'; and in preferring the conjunction 'and' to the more conventional 'with', he attaches an importance to the piano which renders the term 'accompaniment' obsolete.

Yet Wolf, despite the perfection and emotional range of his songbooks (no other Lieder composer, with the possible exception of Carl Loewe, composed so many comic songs), grew increasingly disillusioned by the small-scale format of his works, and the title of songwriter became anathema to him. In a letter to his friend Grohe, he complains that he cannot continue to write songs for another thirty years; instead of being flattered by the increasing success of his Lieder, he saw in the public's praise an implied reproach that he was master of what was only a minor genre. Wolf harboured great ambitions, at times bordering on megalomania, to master symphonic form, and it was perhaps for this reason that he orchestrated some thirty of his songs, more than any other Lieder composer before him.

Joseph von Eichendorff (1788–1857)

See Pfitzner, Robert Schumann, Schoeck

In a letter to Engelbert Humperdinck, dated 12 March 1891, Wolf made it clear that, following the current trend of realism ('übereinstimmend mit der realistischen Kunstrichtung'), he wished to abandon the romantic element in Eichendorff's poetry, and turn instead to the comparatively unknown, the saucily humorous and robustly sensual side of the poet ('der ziemlich unbekannten, keck humoristischen, derb-sinnlichen Seite des Dichters'). And a glance at Challier's *Grosser Lieder-Katalog* tells us that he was the first Lieder composer to have attended to this side of Eichendorff's poetry. Wolf's original order of the Eichendorff songs is indicated in square brackets.

26 January 1880 Erwartung / Anticipation [18]

Grüß' euch aus Herzensgrund:	I greet you from the depths of my heart:
Zwei Augen hell und rein,	Two eyes bright and clear,
Zwei Röslein auf dem Mund,	Two small roses on your lips,
Kleid blank aus Sonnenschein!	A gleaming dress of sunlight!
Nachtigall klagt und weint,	The nightingale laments and weeps,
Wollüstig rauscht der Hain,	The grove rustles voluptuously,
Alles die Liebste meint:	Everything speaks of my sweetheart:
Wo weilt sie so allein?	Where does she tarry, so alone?
Weil's draußen finster war,	Because it was dark outside,
Sah ich viel hellern Schein,	I saw many a brighter glow,

Jetzt ist es licht und klar,
Ich muß im Dunkeln sein.

  Sonne nicht steigen mag,
Sieht so verschlafen drein,
Wünschet den ganzen Tag,
Daß wieder Nacht möcht' sein.

  Liebe geht durch die Luft,
Holt fern die Liebste ein;
Fort über Berg und Kluft!
Und sie wird doch noch mein!

Now it is light and clear,
I must dwell in darkness.

  The sun, reluctant to rise,
Looks down so sleepy-eyed,
Wishing all day long
Night could come again.

  Love moves through the air,
Catches up my distant love;
Quickly away, over mountain and chasm!
And she will yet be mine!

3 February 1880 Die Nacht / Night [19]

  Nacht ist wie ein stilles Meer,
Lust und Leid und Liebesklagen
Kommen so verworren her
In den linden Wellenschlagen.

  Wünsche wie die Wolken sind,
Schiffen durch die stillen Räume,
Wer erkennt im lauen Wind,
Ob's Gedanken oder Träume? –

  Schließ' ich nun auch Herz und Mund,
Die so gern den Sternen klagen:
Leise doch im Herzensgrund
Bleibt das linde Wellenschlagen.
(*Hensel*)

  Night is like a silent sea,
Joy and pain and lovers' laments
Mingle in such confusion
In the gently lapping waves.

  Wishes are like clouds,
Sailing through silent space,
Who can tell in the warm breeze
If they be thoughts or dreams?

  Though I now close my heart and lips
That love lamenting to the stars:
Still in the depths of my heart,
The waves pulse gently on.

14 December 1886 Der Soldat II / The soldier II [6]

Wagen mußt du und flüchtig erbeuten,
Hinter uns schon durch die Nacht hör' ich's
    schreiten,
Schwing' auf mein Roß dich nur schnell
Und küß' noch im Flug mich, wildschönes
    Kind.
Geschwind,
Denn der Tod ist ein rascher Gesell.
(*Cornelius*)

You must be bold and swift to seize your
    prey,
Already I hear footsteps behind us in the
    night,
Quickly leap up onto my horse
And kiss me as we flee, wild and lovely child.
Make haste,
For Death is fleet of foot.

7 March 1887 Der Soldat I / The soldier I [5]

  Ist auch schmuck nicht mein Rößlein,
So ist's doch recht klug,
Trägt im Finstern zu 'nem Schlößlein
Mich rasch noch genug.

  Though my little horse isn't handsome,
He's really rather clever,
He carries me to a little castle
Quickly enough in the dark.

Ist das Schloß auch nicht prächtig:	Though the castle's not palatial:
Zum Garten aus der Tür	From the gate into the garden
Tritt ein Mädchen doch allnächtig	A girl steps every night
Dort freundlich herfür.	In friendly fashion.
Und ist auch die Kleine	And though the little creature
Nicht die Schönst' auf der Welt,	Isn't the prettiest in the world,
So gibt's doch just keine,	There's simply no one else
Die mir besser gefällt.	I like better.
Und spricht sie vom Freien:	But if she speaks of marriage,
So schwing' ich mich auf mein Roß –	I leap onto my horse –
Ich bleibe im Freien,	I'll stay outside and be free,
Und sie auf dem Schloß.	And she can stay in the castle.
(*Bruno Walter*)	

8 March 1887 Die Kleine / The little girl

Zwischen Bergen, liebe Mutter,	Between mountains, dear mother,
Weit den Wald entlang,	By the woodland ways,
Reiten da drei junge Jäger	Three young hunters come riding by
Auf drei Rößlein blank,	On three young gleaming steeds,
lieb' Mutter,	dear mother,
Auf drei Rößlein blank.	On three young gleaming steeds.
Ihr könnt fröhlich sein, lieb' Mutter:	*You*, dear mother, can be happy:
Wird es draußen still,	When outside all falls quiet,
Kommt der Vater heim vom Walde,	When father comes home from the forest,
Küsst Euch, wie er will,	He'll kiss you to his heart's content,
lieb' Mutter,	dear mother,
Küsst Euch, wie er will.	He'll kiss you to his heart's content.
Und ich werfe mich im Bettchen	And I toss and turn in bed
Nachts ohn' Unterlaß,	All night long without respite,
Kehr' mich links und kehr' mich rechts hin,	Roll to the left and roll to the right,
Nirgends hab' ich was,	Finding nothing anywhere,
lieb' Mutter,	dear mother,
Nirgends hab' ich was.	Finding nothing anywhere.
Bin ich eine Frau erst einmal,	When I've once become a woman,
In der Nacht dann still,	In the night I'll quietly turn
Wend' ich mich nach allen Seiten,	Whichever way I wish,
Küss', so viel ich will,	Kiss to my heart's content,
lieb' Mutter,	dear mother,
Küss', so viel ich will.	Kiss to my heart's content.

19 March 1887 Die Zigeunerin / The gypsy girl [7]

Am Kreuzweg da lausche ich, wenn die Stern'	At the crossroads I listen, when the stars
Und die Feuer im Walde verglommen,	And fires in the wood have faded,

Und wo der erste Hund bellt von fern,
Da wird mein Bräut'gam herkommen.
La, la, la –

"Und als der Tag graut', durch das Gehölz
Sah ich eine Katze sich schlingen,
Ich schoß ihr auf den nußbraunen Pelz,
Wie tat die weitüber springen! –
Ha, ha, ha!"

Schad' nur ums Pelzlein, du kriegst mich nit!
Mein Schatz muß sein wie die andern:
Braun und ein Stutzbart auf ung'rischen
Schnitt
Und ein fröhliches Herze zum Wandern.
La, la, la . . .

And where, afar, the first dog barks,
From there my bridegroom will come.
La, la, la –

'And at dawn, through the copse,
I saw a cat slinking,
I fired a shot at her nut-brown coat,
How that made her jump –
Ha, ha, ha!'

A shame about the coat, you won't catch
me!
My sweetheart must be like the others:
Swarthy, with a beard of Hungarian trim,
And a happy heart for wandering.
La, la, la . . .

20 April 1887 Waldmädchen / Forest-nymph [20]

Bin ein Feuer hell, das lodert
Von dem grünen Felsenkranz,
Seewind ist mein Buhl' und fordert
Mich zum lust'gen Wirbeltanz,
Kommt und wechselt unbeständig.
Steigend wild,
Neigend mild,
Meine schlanken Lohen wend' ich:
Komm nicht nah' mir, ich verbrenn' dich!

Wo die wilden Bäche rauschen
Und die hohen Palmen stehn,
Wenn die Jäger heimlich lauschen,
Viele Rehe einsam gehn.
Bin ein Reh, flieg' durch die Trümmer,
Über die Höh',
Wo im Schnee
Still die letzten Gipfel schimmern,
Folg' mir nicht, erjagst mich nimmer!

Bin ein Vöglein in den Lüften,
Schwing mich übers blaue Meer,
Durch die Wolken von den Klüften
Fliegt kein Pfeil mehr bis hieher,
Und die Aun, die Felsenbogen,
Waldeseinsamkeit
Weit, wie weit,
Sind versunken in die Wogen –
Ach, ich habe mich verflogen!
(*Robert Schumann*)

I'm a bright fire that blazes
From the green-garlanded cliff,
The sea-wind's my lover,
Who, asking me to pirouette,
Comes in his inconstant way.
Madly rising,
Gently falling,
I turn on him my slender fires:
Don't come near me, or I'll burn you!

Where the wild streams roar,
And the palm trees soar up,
When the hidden hunters listen,
Many a lonely deer goes by.
I'm a deer, leaping over rubble,
Over the mountains,
Where in the snow
The last peaks shimmer quietly,
Don't follow, you'll never catch me!

I'm a little bird in the air,
Winging over the blue sea,
Here no arrow, shot from chasms,
Can reach me through the clouds,
And the meadows and rocks,
Lonely woods
Left far, far behind,
Have vanished beneath the waves –
Ah, I've lost my way!

24 May 1887 Nachtzauber / Night magic [8]

Hörst du nicht die Quellen gehen
Zwischen Stein und Blumen weit
Nach den stillen Waldesseen,
Wo die Marmorbilder stehen
In der schönen Einsamkeit?
Von den Bergen sacht hernieder,
Weckend die uralten Lieder,
Steigt die wunderbare Nacht,
Und die Gründe glänzen wieder,
Wie du's oft im Traum gedacht.

Kennst die Blume du, entsprossen
In dem mondbeglänzten Grund?
Aus der Knospe, halb erschlossen,
Junge Glieder blühend sprossen,
Weiße Arme, roter Mund,
Und die Nachtigallen schlagen,
Und rings hebt es an zu klagen,
Ach, vor Liebe todeswund,
Von versunk'nen schönen Tagen –
Komm, o komm zum stillen Grund!
(*Trunk*)

Can you not hear the brooks running
Amongst the stones and flowers
To the silent woodland lakes
Where the marble statues stand
In the lovely solitude?
Softly from the mountains,
Awakening age-old songs,
Wondrous night descends,
And the valleys gleam again,
As you often dreamed.

Do you know the flower that blossomed
In the moonlit valley?
From its half-open bud
Young limbs have flowered forth,
White arms, red lips,
And the nightingales are singing,
And all around a lament is raised,
Ah, wounded to death with love,
For the lovely days now lost –
Come, ah come to the silent valley!

31 August 1888 Verschwiegene Liebe / Silent love [3]
FROM *Robert und Guiscard*

Über Wipfel und Saaten
In den Glanz hinein –
Wer mag sie erraten,
Wer holte sie ein?
Gedanken sich wiegen,
Die Nacht ist verschwiegen,
Gedanken sind frei.

Errät' es nur eine,
Wer an sie gedacht
Beim Rauschen der Haine,
Wenn niemand mehr wacht
Als die Wolken, die fliegen –
Mein Lieb ist verschwiegen
Und schön wie die Nacht.

Over treetops and cornfields
Into the gleaming light –
Who may guess them,
Who catch them up?
Thoughts go floating,
The night is silent,
Thoughts are free.

If only she could guess
Who has thought of her
In the rustling groves,
When no one else is awake
But the scudding clouds –
My love is silent
And lovely as night.

14 September 1888 Der Schreckenberger / The swashbuckler [9]

Aufs Wohlsein meiner Dame,
Eine Windfahn' ist ihr Panier,

Let's drink to my lady!
A weather vane's her banner,

Fortuna ist ihr Name,	Fortune's her name,
Das Lager ihr Quartier!	The camp's her billet!
Und wendet sie sich weiter,	And if she goes on her way,
Ich kümmre mich nicht drum,	It won't bother me,
Da draußen ohne Reiter,	For life in the outside world
Da geht die Welt so dumm.	Is dull without a rider.
Statt Pulverblitz und Knattern	Instead of gunpowder and rattling muskets,
Aus jedem wüsten Haus	Old gossips peer from drab houses
Gevattern sehn und schnattern	And prattle
Alle Lust zum Land hinaus.	All pleasure from life.
Fortuna weint vor Ärger,	Fortune sheds tears of anger,
Es rinnet Perl' auf Perl'.	Trickling pearl on pearl:
„Wo ist der Schreckenberger?	'Where's my swashbuckling fellow?
Das war ein andrer Kerl."	He was a real man.'
Sie tut den Arm mir reichen,	She offers me her arm,
Fama bläst das Geleit,	Fame sounds the advance,
So zu dem Tempel steigen	Thus do we ascend
Wir der Unsterblichkeit.	To the Temple of Immortality.

16 September 1888 Der Glücksritter / The soldier of fortune [10]

Wenn Fortuna spröde tut,	When Fortune acts coyly,
Laß ich sie in Ruh,	I leave her in peace,
Singe recht und trinke gut,	Sing out and drink my fill,
Und Fortuna kriegt auch Mut,	And Fortune too takes heart
Setzt sich mit dazu.	And sits down beside me.
Doch ich geb' mir keine Müh':	But I don't exert myself:
„He, noch eine her!"	'Hey, another beer!'
Kehr' den Rücken gegen sie,	I turn my back on her,
Laß hoch leben die und die –	Drink to the health of other girls –
Das verdrießt sie sehr.	Which makes her very cross.
Und bald rückt sie sacht zu mir:	And soon she nestles beside me:
„Hast du deren mehr?"	'Any more of them?'
„Wie Sie sehn – drei Kannen schier,	'As you see, almost three tankards
Und das lauter Klebebier! –	Of pure malt beer! –
's wird mir gar nicht schwer."	That's not too much for me!'
Drauf sie zu mir lächelt fein:	Then she smiles at me slyly:
„Bist ein ganzer Kerl!"	'You're a real man!'
Ruft den Kellner, schreit nach Wein,	She summons the waiter, shouts for wine,
Trinkt mir zu und schenkt mir ein,	Drinks my health and fills my glass,
Echte Blum' und Perl'.	Real bouquet and sparkle.
Sie bezahlet Wein und Bier,	She pays for both wine and beer,
Und ich, wieder gut,	And I, good-humoured once more,

Führe sie am Arm mit mir
Aus dem Haus wie 'n Kavalier,
Alles zieht den Hut.

Lead her out of the inn
On my arm, like a cavalier,
Everyone doffs his hat.

21 September 1888 Seemanns Abschied / Sailor's farewell [17]

Ade, mein Schatz, du mocht'st mich nicht,
Ich war dir zu geringe.
Einst wandelst du bei Mondenlicht
Und hörst ein süßes Klingen,
Ein Meerweib singt, die Nacht ist lau,
Die stillen Wolken wandern.
Da denk' an mich, 's ist meine Frau,
Nun such' dir einen andern!

Farewell, my sweet, you never loved me,
I was too lowly for you.
One night you'll wander by moonlight
And hear sweet music.
A mermaid's singing, the night is mild,
The silent clouds drift by.
Then think of me, it's my mermaid wife,
Now find yourself another!

Ade, ihr Landsknecht', Musketier'!
Wir zieh'n auf wildem Rosse,
Das bäumt und überschlägt sich schier
Vor manchem Felsenschlosse,
Der Wassermann bei Blitzesschein
Taucht auf in dunklen Nächten,
Der Haifisch schnappt, die Möwen schrein –
Das ist ein lustig Fechten!

Farewell, you troopers, musketeers!
We ride on a wild horse
That rears and almost somersaults
Before many a mountain castle.
The merman, lit by lightning,
Looms up on dark nights,
The shark snaps, the gull shrieks –
What a merry skirmish!

Streckt nur auf eurer Bärenhaut
Daheim die faulen Glieder,
Gott Vater aus dem Fenster schaut,
Schickt seine Sündflut wieder,
Feldwebel, Reiter, Musketier,
Sie müssen all' ersaufen,
Derweil mit frischem Winde wir
Im Paradies einlaufen.

Just stretch out your lazy limbs
On your bearskin rug at home,
God the Father looks out of His window
And sends a second flood,
Sergeants, horsemen, musketeers,
All will have to drown,
While we, before a brisk wind,
Sail into Paradise.

22 September 1888 Der Musikant / The minstrel [2]

Wandern lieb' ich für mein Leben,
Lebe eben wie ich kann,
Wollt' ich mir auch Mühe geben,
Paßt es mir doch gar nicht an.

I simply love to wander,
And live as best I can,
And were I to exert myself,
It wouldn't suit at all.

Schöne alte Lieder weiß ich,
In der Kälte, ohne Schuh'
Draußen in die Saiten reiß' ich,
Weiß nicht, wo ich abends ruh'.

Beautiful old songs I know,
Barefoot out in the cold
I pluck my strings,
Not knowing where I'll rest at night.

Manche Schöne macht wohl Augen,
Meinet, ich gefiel ihr sehr,
Wenn ich nur was wollte taugen,
So ein armer Lump nicht wär'. –

Many a beauty gives me looks,
Says she'd fancy me,
If I'd make something of myself,
Were not such a beggar wretch. –

Mag dir Gott ein'n Mann bescheren,
Wohl mit Haus und Hof versehn!
Wenn wir zwei zusammen wären,
Möcht' mein Singen mir vergehn.
(*Schwarz-Schilling*)

May God give you a husband,
Well provided with house and home!
If we two were together,
My singing might fade away.

22 September 1888 Der Scholar / The scholar [13]

Bei dem angenehmsten Wetter
Singen alle Vögelein,
Klatscht der Regen auf die Blätter,
Sing ich so für mich allein.

In the most pleasant of weathers
All the little birds are singing,
When rain rattles on the leaves,
I sing to myself alone.

Denn mein Aug' kann nichts entdecken,
Wenn der Blitz auch grausam glüht,
Was im Wandern könnt' erschrecken
Ein zufriedenes Gemüt.

For my eyes see nothing,
However cruelly lightning flashes,
That could alarm a contented soul
In its wanderings.

Frei von Mammon will ich schreiten
Auf dem Feld der Wissenschaft,
Sinne ernst und nehm' zuzeiten
Einen Mund voll Rebensaft.

Free from Mammon I'll roam
The field of knowledge,
Think deeply, and at times
Quaff the juice of the grape.

Bin ich müde vom Studieren,
Wann der Mond tritt sanft herfür,
Pfleg' ich dann zu musizieren
Vor der Allerschönsten Tür.

When I'm tired of studying,
When gently the moon climbs the sky,
I'm wont to make music
Before my sweetheart's door.

23 September 1888 Der verzweifelte Liebhaber / The despairing lover [14]

Studieren will nichts bringen,
Mein Rock hält keinen Stich,
Meine Zither will nicht klingen,
Mein Schatz, der mag mich nicht.

Studying's unprofitable,
My coat's all unstitched,
My zither won't sound,
My sweetheart doesn't love me.

Ich wollt', im Grün spazierte
Die allerschönste Frau,
Ich wär' ein Drach' und führte
Sie mit mir fort durchs Blau.

I wish the fairest of women
Were walking in the fields,
And I were a kite to bear
Her off into the blue.

Ich wollt', ich jagt' gerüstet
Und legt' die Lanze aus,
Und jagte alle Philister
Zur schönen Welt hinaus.

I wish I were armed for the hunt
To chase with couched lance
Every Philistine
Out of sight.

Ich wollt', ich läg' jetzunder
Im Himmel still und weit,
Und fragt' nach all' dem Plunder
Nichts vor Zufriedenheit.

I wish I were now lying
In Heaven's silent spaces,
Enquiring nothing of such rubbish,
Filled with content.

25 September 1888 Unfall / Mishap 15]

Ich ging bei Nacht einst über Land,	Once, when travelling by night over land,
Ein Bürschlein traf ich draußen,	I met a little boy
Das hat 'nen Stutzen in der Hand	With a gun in his hand
Und zielt auf mich voll Grausen.	Which he aimed at me most frighteningly.
Ich renne, da ich mich erbos',	Provoked, I rush at him
Auf ihn in vollem Rasen,	In a mighty rage,
Da drückt das kecke Bürschlein los	The impish boy fires,
Und ich stürzt' auf die Nasen.	I fall flat on my nose.
Er aber lacht mir ins Gesicht,	But he laughs in my face
Daß er mich angeschossen,	For having shot at me.
Cupido war der kleine Wicht –	Cupid was the wretch's name –
Das hat mich sehr verdrossen.	I was sorely vexed.

26 September 1888 Der Freund / The friend [1]

Wer auf den Wogen schliefe	Whoever would sleep on the waves,
Ein sanft gewiegtes Kind,	A gently cradled child,
Kennt nicht des Lebens Tiefe,	Knows not the depths of life,
Vor süßem Träumen blind.	Blinded by sweet dreams.
Doch wen die Stürme fassen	But he whom the storms seize
Zu wildem Tanz und Fest,	For wild dances and feasts,
Wen hoch auf dunklen Straßen	Whom, high on dark paths,
Die falsche Welt verläßt:	The false world abandons:
Der lernt sich wacker rühren,	He learns to bear himself bravely,
Durch Nacht und Klippen hin	Through night and past cliffs,
Lernt der das Steuer führen	He learns to steer a course
Mit sichrem, ernstem Sinn.	With sure and serious mind.
Der ist von echtem Kerne,	He is a man of true worth,
Erprobt zu Lust und Pein,	Proven in joy and pain,
Der glaubt an Gott und Sterne,	He believes in God and the stars,
Der soll mein Schiffmann sein!	He shall be my helmsman.

27 September 1888 Liebesglück / Love's happiness [16]

Ich hab' ein Liebchen lieb recht von Herzen,	I've a sweetheart I love with all my heart,
Hellfrische Augen hat's wie zwei Kerzen,	Her bright eyes sparkle like two candles,
Und wo sie spielend streifen das Feld,	And when they playfully gaze on the field,
Ach, wie so lustig glänzet die Welt!	Ah, how joyously the world shines!
Wie in der Waldnacht zwischen den Schlüften	Just as in dark forests between ravines
Plötzlich die Täler sonnig sich klüften,	The valleys suddenly divide into sunlight,
Funkeln die Ströme, rauscht himmelwärts	The streams sparkle, and the blossoming
Blühende Wildnis – so ist mein Herz!	Wilderness rustles heavenward – so does my heart!

Wie vom Gebirge ins Meer zu schauen,	Like gazing from summits into the sea,
Wie wenn der Seefalk, hangend im Blauen,	Like a sea-falcon, hovering in the blue sky,
Zuruft der dämmernden Erd', wo sie blieb –	Asks the twilit earth where she's been –
So unermeßlich ist rechte Lieb'!	So immeasurable is true love!

28 September 1888 Das Ständchen / The serenade [4]

Auf die Dächer zwischen blassen	The moon from pallid clouds
Wolken schaut der Mond herfür,	Gazes out across the roofs,
Ein Student dort auf der Gassen	There in the street a student sings
Singt vor seiner Liebsten Tür.	Before his sweetheart's door.
Und die Brunnen rauschen wieder	And again the fountains murmur
Durch die stille Einsamkeit,	In the silent loneliness,
Und der Wald vom Berge nieder,	And the woods on the mountain
Wie in alter, schöner Zeit.	Murmur, as in the good old days.
So in meinen jungen Tagen	Likewise in my young days,
Hab' ich manche Sommernacht	Often on a summer's night
Auch die Laute hier geschlagen	I too plucked my lute here,
Und manch lust'ges Lied erdacht.	And composed some merry songs.
Aber von der stillen Schwelle	But from that silent threshold
Trugen sie mein Lieb zur Ruh' –	My love's been taken to rest –
Und du, fröhlicher Geselle,	And you, my blithe friend,
Singe, sing' nur immer zu!	Sing on, just sing on!
(*Korngold, Trunk*)	

29 September 1888 Lieber alles / Sooner all three [11]

Soldat sein ist gefährlich,	Soldiering's dangerous,
Studieren sehr beschwerlich,	Studying's most arduous,
Das Dichten süß und zierlich,	Poetry's sweet and graceful,
Der Dichter gar possierlich	The poet's a figure of fun
In diesen wilden Zeiten.	In these barbarous times.
Ich möcht' am liebsten reiten,	Most of all I'd like to ride,
Ein gutes Schwert zur Seiten,	A good sword at my side,
Die Laute in der Rechten,	A lute in my right hand,
Studentenherz zum Fechten.	With a student's heart for the fight.
Ein wildes Roß ist's Leben,	Life's an untamed steed,
Die Hufe Funken geben,	Its hooves strike sparks,
Wer's ehrlich wagt, bezwingt es,	The truly bold man will tame it,
Und wo es tritt, da klingt es!	And where it treads it resounds!

29 September 1888 Heimweh / Homesickness [12]

Wer in die Fremde will wandern,	He who would journey abroad
Der muß mit der Liebsten gehn,	Must go with his beloved,

Es jubeln und lassen die andern	Others, in their joy, leave
Den Fremden alleine stehn.	The stranger all alone.
Was wisset ihr, dunkle Wipfel,	What do you know, dark summits,
Von der alten, schönen Zeit?	Of the happy days now past?
Ach, die Heimat hinter den Gipfeln,	Ah, my homeland beyond the mountains,
Wie liegt sie von hier so weit.	How far it lies from here.
Am liebsten betracht' ich die Sterne,	I love best to watch the stars
Die schienen, wie ich ging zu ihr,	That shone as I went to her,
Die Nachtigall hör' ich so gerne,	I love to hear the nightingale
Sie sang vor der Liebsten Tür.	That sang at my loved one's door.
Der Morgen, das ist meine Freude!	The morning is my delight!
Da steig' ich in stiller Stund'	At that peaceful hour I climb
Auf den höchsten Berg in die Weite,	The highest mountain far and wide,
Grüß dich, Deutschland, aus Herzensgrund!	And greet you, Germany, from the depth of my heart!

Johann Wolfgang von Goethe (1749–1832)

See Beethoven, Brahms, Hensel, Loewe, Mendelssohn, Mozart, Reichardt, Schubert, Strauss, Zelter

Wolf, when he embarked on his *Goethe-Lieder* in October 1888, was well aware of the gargantuan task confronting him. How could he do justice to the depth and range of Germany's greatest poet? And how dare he invite comparisons with the finest Goethe Lieder by Reichardt, Zelter, Beethoven, Schubert, Schumann, Loewe and others? It was Wolf's policy never to choose a poem that had in his view already been successfully set by previous composers; his decision, therefore, to compose thirteen Goethe poems that had inspired Schubert implied a criticism of his predecessor. In the Harper and Mignon songs from *Wilhelm Meister*, which he proudly placed at the head of his Goethe volume, Wolf manages through intense chromaticism, dissonance, tortuous melody and even on occasion a veiling of tonality to stress the pathological nature of his characters, to probe into the half-crazed minds of the Harper and Mignon more deeply than any other composer before him. The background to many of these poems is one of incest, madness and suicide, and however much Wolf admired Schubert, he felt that the older composer had not fully explored these poems. Or as he put it to Paul Müller: 'Da hat Schubert den Goethe halt nicht verstanden' ('In these songs Schubert simply didn't understand Goethe'). Wolf also selected many Goethe poems that had seldom been set, especially the seventeen poems from the *West-östlicher Divan*. The songs are printed in chronological order of composition, except for 'Gutmann und Gutweib', listed under Loewe, and 'Prometheus', 'Ganymed' and 'Grenzen der Menschheit', listed under Schubert. Wolf's order is indicated in square brackets.

Aus *Wilhelm Meister*/ Songs from *Wilhelm Meister*

The eight books of Goethe's *Wilhelm Meisters Lehrjahre* were published in 1795–6 and immediately found favour with the new generation of Romantics. Thomas Carlyle translated the novel into English in 1824 and it was for a while one of the most popular of all Goethe's works. Although it is rarely read today, the lyrics that punctuate the novel have become known to millions of music lovers across the globe, thanks to Beethoven, Spohr, Schubert, Loewe, Schumann, Liszt, Wolf and countless other Lieder composers.

Wilhelm, the son of prosperous middle-class parents, has a passion for the theatre. Believing he has been jilted by Mariane, he destroys his poems and devotes himself to business. Later in the novel he sets out on a journey and meets Philine, one of a strolling company of actors, a lighthearted soubrette, who impatiently interrupts the company's discussion of their production of *Hamlet*: not for her their restrained and calculated performances, she wants something more extrovert and impulsive. To make her point she sings a ditty to a very 'zierliche und gefällige Melodie' (delicate and pleasing melody) – which is what Wolf provides. Wilhelm meets the mysterious Harper and the enigmatic Mignon among a group of itinerant actors. The Harper, of noble Italian birth, had been destined by his father for the Church; having spent some time in a monastery, he returned home after his father's death and struck up a friendship with Sperata. The friendship developed into an illicit affair: she turned out to be his sister, and the child of their incestuous union was Mignon. He fled to Germany where, devoured by guilt and despair (he refers to his incest in the final line of 'Wer nie sein Brot mit Tränen aß'), he kills himself at the end of the novel. Mignon, having been abducted from Italy, joined the group of actors and gradually fell in love with Wilhelm, while hiding her affection from him. Wolf's Mignon songs describe her sadness and longing to return to her Italian homeland: 'Kennst du das Land' is addressed to Wilhelm, and 'Nur wer die Sehnsucht kennt' is sung with him as a duet. Wilhelm had bought the freedom of the twelve-year-old girl, but she dies of grief when she sees him in the arms of another woman. The only other character from the novel to be mentioned in Wolf's songs is the Baron ('Spottlied aus *Wilhelm Meister*'). This pretentious aristocrat has mocked the troupe of actors, who gain their revenge when the poem that satirizes him (the 'Spottlied') is circulated anonymously at the castle.

27 October 1888 Harfenspieler I / The Harper I [1]
ORCHESTRATED 2 DECEMBER 1890

Wer sich der Einsamkeit ergibt,	Who gives himself to loneliness,
Ach, der ist bald allein;	Ah, he is soon alone;
Ein jeder lebt, ein jeder liebt,	Others live, others love,
Und läßt ihn seiner Pein.	And leave him to his pain.

Ja! laßt mich meiner Qual!	Yes! leave me to my torment!
Und kann ich nur einmal	And if I can but once
Recht einsam sein,	Be truly lonely,
Dann bin ich nicht allein.	Then I'll not be alone.
Es schleicht ein Liebender lauschend sacht,	A lover steals up listening
Ob seine Freundin allein?	To learn if his love's alone.
So überschleicht bei Tag und Nacht	So in my solitude
Mich Einsamen die Pein,	Do pain and torment
Mich Einsamen die Qual.	Steal over me by day and night.
Ach, werd ich erst einmal	Ah, when once I lie
Einsam im Grabe sein,	Lonely in my grave,
Da läßt sie mich allein!	Loneliness will leave me alone!

(*Hensel, Reichardt, Schubert, Robert Schumann, Zelter*)

29 October 1888 Harfenspieler II / The Harper II [2]
ORCHESTRATED 4 DECEMBER 1890

An die Türen will ich schleichen,	I'll steal from door to door,
Still und sittsam will ich stehn;	Quietly and humbly I'll stand;
Fromme Hand wird Nahrung reichen,	A kindly hand will offer food,
Und ich werde weitergehn.	And I'll go on my way.
Jeder wird sich glücklich scheinen,	Men will think themselves happy,
Wenn mein Bild vor ihm erscheint;	When they see me standing there;
Eine Träne wird er weinen,	They will shed a tear,
Und ich weiß nicht, was er weint.	And I'll not know why they weep.

(*Burgmüller, Medtner, Mussorgsky, Reichardt, Robert Schumann, Schubert, Zelter*)

30 October 1888 Harfenspieler III / The Harper III [3]
ORCHESTRATED 4 DECEMBER 1890

Wer nie sein Brot mit Tränen aß,	Who never ate his bread with tears,
Wer nie die kummervollen Nächte	Who never through the anxious nights
Auf seinem Bette weinend saß,	Sat weeping on his bed,
Der kennt euch nicht, ihr himmlischen Mächte!	He knows you not, you heavenly powers!
Ihr führt ins Leben uns hinein,	You bring us into life,
Ihr laßt den Armen schuldig werden,	You let the poor incur guilt,
Dann überlaßt ihr ihn der Pein:	Then abandon him to pain:
Denn alle Schuld rächt sich auf Erden.	For all guilt is avenged on earth.

(*Burgmüller, Liszt, Marschner, Reichardt, Schubert, Robert Schumann, Zelter*)

30 October 1888 Philine / Philine [8]

Singet nicht in Trauertönen	Do not sing in mournful tones
Von der Einsamkeit der Nacht;	Of the solitude of night;

Nein, sie ist, o holde Schönen,
Zur Geselligkeit gemacht.

Wie das Weib dem Mann gegeben
Als die schönste Hälfte war,
Ist die Nacht das halbe Leben,
Und die schönste Hälfte zwar.

Könnt ihr euch des Tages freuen,
Der nur Freuden unterbricht?
Er ist gut, sich zu zerstreuen;
Zu was anderm taugt er nicht.

Aber wenn in nächt'ger Stunde
Süßer Lampe Dämmrung fließt
Und vom Mund zum nahen Munde
Scherz und Liebe sich ergießt,

Wenn der rasche lose Knabe,
Der sonst wild und feurig eilt,
Oft bei einer kleinen Gabe
Unter leichten Spielen weilt,

Wenn die Nachtigall Verliebten
Liebevoll ein Liedchen singt,
Das Gefangnen und Betrübten
Nur wie Ach und Wehe klingt:

Mit wie leichtem Herzensregen
Horchet ihr der Glocke nicht,
Die mit zwölf bedächt'gen Schlägen
Ruh und Sicherheit verspricht!

Darum an dem langen Tage
Merke dir es, liebe Brust:
Jeder Tag hat seine Plage,
Und die Nacht hat ihre Lust.
(*Reichardt, Rubinstein, Robert Schumann,*
Tomášek)

No, fair ladies, night is made
For conviviality.

Woman was given to man
As his better half,
Night is likewise half of life,
And the better half by far.

Can you take delight in day,
Which only curtails pleasure?
It may serve as a distraction;
But is good for nothing else.

But when in hours of darkness
The sweet lamp's twilight flows,
And love as well as laughter
Streams from almost touching lips,

When impulsive, roguish Cupid,
Used to wild and fiery haste,
In return for some small gift,
Often lingers, dallying,

When, full of love, the nightingale
Sings a little song for lovers,
Which to the imprisoned and sad
Seems only to tell of grief and pain:

With what lightly pounding heart
Do you then listen to the bell,
That with twelve solemn strokes
Pledges security and rest!

And so remember this, dear heart,
Throughout the livelong day:
Every day has its troubles,
And every night its joys.

2 November 1888 Spottlied / Lampoon [4]

Ich armer Teufel, Herr Baron,
Beneide Sie um Ihren Stand,
Um Ihren Platz so nah dem Thron,
Und um manch schön Stück Ackerland,
Um Ihres Vaters festes Schloß,
Um seine Wildbahn und Geschoß.

Mich armen Teufel, Herr Baron,
Beneiden Sie, so wie es scheint,

Poor devil that I am,
I envy you, my Lord Baron, your rank,
Your position so near the throne,
Your many stretches of fine fertile land,
Your father's fortified castle,
His hunting grounds and firearms.

Poor devil that I am, it seems to me,
My Lord Baron, that you envy me

Weil die Natur vom Knaben schon	Because Nature, from boyhood on,
Mit mir es mütterlich gemeint.	Treated me like a mother.
Ich ward mit leichtem Mut und Kopf,	With a light heart and free of care,
Zwar arm, doch nicht ein armer Tropf.	I grew up to be poor but not a poor wretch.
Nun dächt' ich, lieber Herr Baron,	Well now, my dear Lord Baron, I rather think
Wir ließen's bleiben wie wir sind:	We should remain as we are:
Sie blieben des Herrn Vaters Sohn,	You your noble father's son,
Und ich blieb' meiner Mutter Kind.	And I my mother's child.
Wir leben ohne Neid und Haß,	Let us live without hate or envy,
Begehren nicht des andern Titel,	Let us not covet each other's title,
Sie keinen Platz auf dem Parnaß,	No place on Parnassus for you,
Und keinen ich in dem Kapitel.	And none in the Peerage for me.
(*Rubinstein*)	

14 December 1888 Der Sänger / The minstrel [10]

„Was hör ich draußen vor dem Tor,	'What do I hear outside the gate,
Was auf der Brücke schallen?	What sounds from the bridge?
Laß den Gesang vor unserm Ohr	Let that song resound for us
Im Saale widerhallen!	Here inside this hall!
Der König sprach's, der Page lief;	So spake the king, the page ran,
Der Knabe kam, der König rief:	The boy returned, the king exclaimed:
Laßt mir herein den Alten!"	Let the old man enter!'
„Gegrüßet seid mir, edle Herrn,	'Hail to you, O noble lords,
Gegrüßt ihr, schöne Damen!	Hail to you, fair ladies!
Welch reicher Himmel! Stern bei Stern!	How rich a heaven! Star on star!
Wer kennet ihre Namen?	Who can tell their names?
Im Saal voll Pracht und Herrlichkeit	In this hall of pomp and splendour,
Schließt, Augen, euch; hier ist nicht Zeit,	Close, O eyes; here is no time
Sich staunend zu ergötzen."	For amazement and delight.'
Der Sänger drückt' die Augen ein,	The minstrel shut tight his eyes
Und schlug in vollen Tönen;	And struck up with full voice;
Die Ritter schauten mutig drein	The knights looked on gallantly,
Und in den Schoß die Schönen.	The ladies gazed into their laps.
Der König, dem das Lied gefiel,	The king, enchanted with the song,
Ließ, ihn zu ehren für sein Spiel,	Sent for a golden chain
Eine goldne Kette reichen.	To reward him for his playing.
„Die goldne Kette gib mir nicht,	'Give not the golden chain to me,
Die Kette gib den Rittern,	Give it to your knights,
Vor deren kühnem Angesicht	Before whose bold countenance
Der Feinde Lanzen splittern;	The enemy lances shatter;
Gib sie dem Kanzler, den du hast,	Give it to your chancellor
Und laß ihn noch die goldne Last	And let him add its golden weight
Zu andern Lasten tragen.	To his other burdens.

Ich singe, wie der Vogel singt,
Der in den Zweigen wohnet;
Das Lied, das aus der Kehle dringt,
Ist Lohn, der reichlich lohnet.
Doch darf ich bitten, bitt ich eins:
Laß mir den besten Becher Weins
In purem Golde reichen."

I sing as the bird sings
In the branches;
The song that bursts from the throat
Is its own abundant reward.
But if I may, I'll beg one boon:
Let the best wine be brought me
In a beaker of pure gold.'

Er setzt' ihn an, er trank ihn aus:
"O Trank voll süßer Labe!
O wohl dem hochbeglückten Haus,
Wo das ist kleine Gabe!
Ergeht's euch wohl, so denkt an mich,
Und danket Gott so warm, als ich
Für diesen Trunk euch danke."
(*Loewe, Reichardt, Schubert, Robert Schumann, Zelter*)

He put it to his lips, he drank it dry:
'O draught full of sweet refreshment!
O happy that highly-favoured house,
Where that is a trifling gift!
If you prosper, then think of me,
And thank God as warmly,
As I thank you for this draught.'

17 December 1888 Mignon / Mignon [9]
ORCHESTRATED 1890 AND 31 OCTOBER 1893

Kennst du das Land, wo die Zitronen blühn,
Im dunkeln Laub die Goldorangen glühn,
Ein sanfter Wind vom blauen Himmel weht,
Die Myrte still und hoch der Lorbeer steht,
Kennst du es wohl?
        Dahin! Dahin
Möcht ich mit dir, o mein Geliebter, ziehn.

Do you know the land where lemons blossom,
Where oranges grow golden among dark leaves,
A gentle wind drifts across blue skies,
The myrtle stands silent, the laurel tall,
Do you know it?
        It's there, it's there
I long to go with you, my love.

Kennst du das Haus? Auf Säulen ruht sein
   Dach,
Es glänzt der Saal, es schimmert das Gemach,
Und Marmorbilder stehn und sehn mich an:
Was hat man dir, du armes Kind, getan?
Kennst du es wohl?
        Dahin! Dahin
Möcht ich mit dir, o mein Beschützer, ziehn.

Do you know the house? Columns support
   its roof,
Its hall gleams, its apartment shimmers,
And marble statues stand and stare at me:
What have they done to you, poor child?
Do you know it?
        It's there, it's there
I long to go with you, my protector.

Kennst du den Berg und seinen Wolkensteg?
Das Maultier sucht im Nebel seinen Weg;
In Höhlen wohnt der Drachen alte Brut;
Es stürzt der Fels und über ihn die Flut,
Kennst du ihn wohl?
        Dahin! Dahin
Geht unser Weg! o Vater, laß uns ziehn!
(*Beethoven, Hensel, Liszt, Moniuszko, Reichardt, Rubinstein, Schubert, Robert Schumann, Spohr, Tomášek, Zelter*)

Do you know the mountain and its cloudy path?
The mule seeks its way through the mist,
In caverns dwell the dragons' ancient brood;
The cliff falls sheer, the torrent over it,
Do you know it?
        It's there, it's there
Our pathway lies! O father, let us go!

18 December 1888 Mignon II / Mignon II [6]

Nur wer die Sehnsucht kennt,	Only those who know longing
Weiß, was ich leide!	Know what I suffer!
Allein und abgetrennt	Alone and cut off
Von aller Freude,	From every joy,
Seh' ich ans Firmament	I search the sky
Nach jener Seite.	In that direction.
Ach! der mich liebt und kennt,	Ah! he who loves and knows me
Ist in der Weite.	Is far away.
Es schwindelt mir, es brennt	My head reels,
Mein Eingeweide.	My body blazes.
Nur wer die Sehnsucht kennt,	Only those who know longing
Weiß, was ich leide!	Know what I suffer!

(*Beethoven, Hensel, Kreutzer, Loewe, Medtner, Reichardt, Schubert, Robert Schumann, Tomášek, Tchaikovsky, Zelter*)

19 December 1888 Mignon I / Mignon I [5]

Heiß mich nicht reden, heiß mich schweigen,	Bid me not speak, bid me be silent,
Denn mein Geheimnis ist mir Pflicht;	For I am bound to secrecy;
Ich möchte dir mein ganzes Innre zeigen,	I should love to bare you my soul,
Allein das Schicksal will es nicht.	But Fate has willed it otherwise.
Zur rechten Zeit vertreibt der Sonne Lauf	At the appointed time the sun dispels
Die finstre Nacht, und sie muß sich erhellen;	The dark, and night must turn to day;
Der harte Fels schließt seinen Busen auf,	The hard rock opens up its bosom,
Mißgönnt der Erde nicht die tiefverborgnen	Does not begrudge earth its deeply hidden
Quellen.	springs.
Ein jeder sucht im Arm des Freundes Ruh,	All humans seek peace in the arms of a friend,
Dort kann die Brust in Klagen sich ergießen;	There the heart can pour out its sorrow;
Allein ein Schwur drückt mir die Lippen zu,	But my lips, alas, are sealed by a vow,
Und nur ein Gott vermag sie aufzuschließen.	And only a god can open them.

(*Reichardt, Rubinstein, Schubert, Robert Schumann, Tomášek, Zelter*)

22 December 1888 Mignon III / Mignon III [7]

So laßt mich scheinen, bis ich werde;	Let me appear an angel till I become one;
Zieht mir das weiße Kleid nicht aus!	Do not take my white dress from me!
Ich eile von der schönen Erde	I hasten from the beautiful earth
Hinab in jenes feste Haus.	Down to that impregnable house.
Dort ruh ich eine kleine Stille,	There in brief repose I'll rest,
Dann öffnet sich der frische Blick,	Then my eyes will open, renewed;

Ich lasse dann die reine Hülle,
Den Gürtel und den Kranz zurück.

My pure raiment then I'll leave,
With girdle and rosary, behind.

Und jene himmlischen Gestalten,
Sie fragen nicht nach Mann und Weib,
Und keine Kleider, keine Falten
Umgeben den verklärten Leib.

And those heavenly beings,
They do not ask who is man or woman,
And no garments, no folds
Cover the transfigured body.

Zwar lebt ich ohne Sorg und Mühe,
Doch fühlt ich tiefen Schmerz genung.
Vor Kummer altert ich zu frühe;
Macht mich auf ewig wieder jung!
(*Reichardt, Rubinstein, Schubert, Robert Schumann*)

Though I lived without trouble and toil,
I have felt deep pain enough.
I grew old with grief before my time;
O make me forever young again!

* * *

4 November 1888 Anakreons Grab / Anacreon's grave [29]

Wo die Rose hier blüht, wo Reben um Lorbeer sich schlingen,
    Wo das Turtelchen lockt, wo sich das Grillchen ergötzt,
Welch ein Grab ist hier, das alle Götter mit Leben
    Schön bepflanzt und geziert? Es ist Anakreons Ruh.
Frühling, Sommer und Herbst genoß der glückliche Dichter;
    Vor dem Winter hat ihn endlich der Hügel geschützt.

Where the rose is in flower, where vine interlaces with laurel,
    Where the turtle-dove calls, where the cricket rejoices,
Whose grave is this that all the gods have decked with life
    And beautiful plants? It is Anacreon's resting place.
The happy poet savoured spring, summer and autumn;
    This mound has at the last protected him from winter.

4 November 1888 Der Schäfer / The shepherd [22]
FROM *Jery und Bätely*

Es war ein fauler Schäfer,
Ein rechter Siebenschläfer,
Ihn kümmerte kein Schaf.

There was once a lazy shepherd,
A veritable lay-abed,
He never bothered about his sheep.

Ein Mädchen konnt' ihn fassen,
Da war der Tropf verlassen,
Fort Appetit und Schlaf!

A girl took his fancy,
The fool was then forlorn,
Gone all appetite and sleep!

Es trieb ihn in die Ferne,
Des Nachts zählt' er die Sterne,
Er klagt' und härmt' sich brav.

He was driven to distant parts,
Counting the stars at night,
Moaning and complaining mightily.

Nun da sie ihn genommen,
Ist alles wieder kommen,
Durst, Appetit und Schlaf.
(*Knab, Reichardt*)

Now she's accepted him,
He's got them all back again,
Thirst, appetite and sleep.

6 November 1888 Der Rattenfänger / The ratcatcher [11]
ORCHESTRATED 5 FEBRUARY 1890

Ich bin der wohlbekannte Sänger,
Der vielgereiste Rattenfänger,
Den diese altberühmte Stadt
Gewiß besonders nötig hat.
Und wären's Ratten noch so viele,
Und wären Wiesel mit im Spiele;
Von allen säubr' ich diesen Ort,
Sie müssen miteinander fort.

I am that celebrated singer,
The much-travelled ratcatcher,
Of whom this famous old city
Assuredly has special need.
And however many rats there are,
And even if there were weasels too;
I'll rid the place of every one,
One and all, they must away.

Dann ist der gutgelaunte Sänger
Mitunter auch ein Kinderfänger,
Der selbst die wildesten bezwingt,
Wenn er die goldnen Märchen singt.
Und wären Knaben noch so trutzig,
Und wären Mädchen noch so stutzig,
In meine Saiten greif ich ein,
Sie müssen alle hinterdrein.

Then this good-humoured singer
Is a child-catcher too from time to time,
Who can tame even the wildest,
When he sings his golden tales.
And however defiant the boys might be,
And however rebellious the girls,
I only have to pluck my strings,
For them all to follow me.

Dann ist der vielgewandte Sänger
Gelegentlich ein Mädchenfänger;
In keinem Städtchen langt er an,
Wo er's nicht mancher angetan.
Und wären Mädchen noch so blöde,
Und wären Weiber noch so spröde:
Doch allen wird so liebebang
Bei Zaubersaiten und Gesang.
(*Schubert, Tomášek*)

And then this many-sided singer
Is occasionally a girl-catcher;
He's never arrived in any town,
Without captivating many.
And however bashful the girls might be,
And however prudish the women,
All of them grow weak with love
At the sound of magic lute and song.

6 November 1888 Gleich und gleich / Like to like [25]

Ein Blumenglöckchen
Vom Boden hervor
War früh gesprosset
In lieblichem Flor;
Da kam ein Bienchen
Und naschte fein: –
Die müssen wohl beide
Füreinander sein.
(*Franz, Medtner, Webern, Zelter*)

A little flower-bell
Had sprung up early
From the ground
In lovely blossom;
Along came a little bee
And sipped most daintily: –
They must have been
Made for each other.

14 November 1888 Frech und froh I / Cheerful impudence I [16]
FROM *Claudine von Villa Bella*

Mit Mädchen sich vertragen,
Mit Männern 'rumgeschlagen,

Getting on well with girls,
Knocking about with men,

Und mehr Kredit als Geld:	And with more credit than cash;
So kommt man durch die Welt.	That's how to get through life.
Mit vielem läßt sich schmausen,	You can feast with a lot;
Mit wenig läßt sich hausen;	Find a roof with a little;
Daß wenig vieles sei,	Only pleasure can succeed
Schafft nur die Lust herbei.	In making a lot out of little.
Will sie sich nicht bequemen,	If she won't consent,
So müßt ihr's eben nehmen.	Simply take what you want.
Will einer nicht vom Ort,	If someone won't leave,
So jagt ihn grade fort.	Then chase him away.
Laßt alle nur mißgönnen,	Let them all begrudge
Was sie nicht nehmen können,	What they're unable to have,
Und seid von Herzen froh;	And be heartily happy;
Das ist das A und O.	That's the alpha and omega.
So fahret fort zu dichten,	Continue writing,
Euch nach der Welt zu richten.	Continue conforming.
Bedenkt in Wohl und Weh –	Always remember in good times and bad
Dies goldne ABC.	This golden ABC.
(*Beethoven, Reichardt*)	

15 November 1888 Sankt Nepomuks* Vorabend / St Nepomuk's eve [20]

Lichtlein schwimmen auf dem Strome,	Little lights are gleaming on the river,
Kinder singen auf der Brücken,	Children are singing on the bridge,
Glocke, Glöckchen fügt vom Dome	Small and large bells from the cathedral
Sich der Andacht, dem Entzücken.	Match the enchantment and devotion.
Lichtlein schwinden, Sterne schwinden;	The little lights fade, the stars fade;
Also löste sich die Seele	Thus our Saint gave up his soul,
Unsres Heil'gen, nicht verkünden	Rather than betray
Durft er anvertraute Fehle.	A man's confession of his guilt.
Lichtlein, schwimmet! Spielt, ihr Kinder!	Float, little lights! Play, you children!
Kinderchor, o singe, singe!	Children's voices, sing, O sing!
Und verkündiget nicht minder,	And do not cease proclaiming
Was den Stern zu Sternen bringe.	What brings this star to other stars.
(*Zelter*)	

21 December 1888 Frühling übers Jahr / Perennial spring [28]

Das Beet, schon lockert	The flower-bed's
Sich's in die Höh,	Already pushing upwards,
Da wanken Glöckchen	Little bells wave there

* John of Nepomuk (*c*.1350–93) was thrown into the Vltava (Moldau) by King Wenceslas IV for refusing to divulge the sins confessed to him by Queen Johanna of Bohemia.

So weiß wie Schnee;	As white as snow;
Safran entfaltet	Crocuses blaze
Gewalt'ge Glut,	With intense colour,
Smaragden keimt es	Shoots of emerald
Und keimt wie Blut.	And shoots like blood.
Primeln stolzieren	Primroses strut
So naseweis,	So saucily,
Schalkhafte Veilchen,	Mischievous violets
Versteckt mit Fleiß;	Carefully hidden;
Was auch noch alles	And a great deal else
Da regt und webt,	Is stirring and moving,
Genug, der Frühling,	Enough – it's spring,
Er wirkt und lebt.	Active and alive.
Doch was im Garten	But in all the garden
Am reichsten blüht,	The richest flower
Das ist des Liebchens	Is my sweetheart's
Lieblich Gemüt.	Lovely soul.
Da glühen Blicke	She looks at me ardently
Mir immerfort,	All the time,
Erregend Liedchen,	Inspiring songs,
Erheiternd Wort,	Provoking words,
Ein immer offen,	An ever-open
Ein Blütenherz,	Blossoming heart,
Im Ernste freundlich	Friendly in grave matters,
Und rein im Scherz.	And pure in jesting.
Wenn Ros und Lilie	Summer may bring
Der Sommer bringt,	The rose and lily,
Er doch vergebens	But it vies in vain
Mit Liebchen ringt.	With my darling.
(*Loewe*)	

27 December 1888 Epiphanias / Epiphany [19]

Die Heiligen Drei König' mit ihrem Stern,	The Three Kings of Orient with their star,
Sie essen, sie trinken, und bezahlen nicht gern;	They eat, they drink, and don't like to pay;
Sie essen gern, sie trinken gern,	They like eating, they like drinking,
Sie essen, trinken, und bezahlen nicht gern.	They eat, drink and don't like to pay.
Die Heil'gen Drei König' sind kommen allhier,	The Three Kings of Orient have come to this place,
Es sind ihrer drei und sind nicht ihrer vier;	They are three in number and not four;
Und wenn zu dreien der vierte wär,	And if to the three a fourth were added,
So wär ein Heil'ger-Drei-König mehr.	There'd be one Three Kings of Orient more.
Ich erster bin der weiß' und auch der schön',	I, the first, am the handsome white one,
Bei Tage solltet ihr erst mich sehn!	Just wait till you see me by day!
Doch ach, mit allen Spezerein	But ah! despite all my spices,
Werd ich sein Tag kein Mädchen mir erfrein.	I'll never win a girl again.

Ich aber bin der braun' und bin der lang',
Bekannt bei Weibern wohl und bei Gesang.
Ich bringe Gold statt Spezerein,
Da werd ich überall willkommen sein.

But I'm the brown one, I'm the tall one,
Well known to women and to song.
I bring gold instead of spices,
So I'll be welcome everywhere.

Ich endlich bin der schwarz' und bin der
    klein'
Und mag auch wohl einmal recht lustig sein.
Ich esse gern, ich trinke gern,
Ich esse, trinke und bedanke mich gern.

I, lastly, am the little black one,
And would like a good time too for
    once.
I like eating, I like drinking,
I like eating, drinking and saying thank you.

Die Heiligen Drei König' sind wohlgesinnt,
Sie suchen die Mutter und das Kind;
Der Joseph fromm sitzt auch dabei,
Der Ochs und Esel liegen auf der Streu.

The Three Kings of Orient are well-disposed,
They seek the Mother and the Child;
Pious Joseph is sitting there too,
The ox and ass lie in the straw.

Wir bringen Myrrhen, wir bringen Gold,
Dem Weihrauch sind die Damen hold;
Und haben wir Wein von gutem Gewächs,
So trinken wir drei so gut als ihrer sechs.

We're bringing myrrh, we're bringing gold,
The ladies will like our frankincense;
And if we've wine from a fine year,
We drink enough, we three, for six.

Da wir nun hier schöne Herrn und Fraun,
Aber keine Ochsen und Esel schaun,
So sind wir nicht am rechten Ort
Und ziehen unseres Weges weiter fort.
(*Pepping, Zelter*)

But since we see fine squires and ladies,
But no oxen or asses here,
We cannot be in the right place,
And so must proceed on our way.

28 December 1888 Cophtisches* Lied I / Cophtic song I [14]
FROM *Der Großkophta*

Lasset Gelehrte sich zanken und streiten,
Streng und bedächtig die Lehrer auch sein!
Alle die Weisesten aller der Zeiten
Lächeln und winken und stimmen mit ein:
„Töricht, auf Beßrung der Toren zu harren!
Kinder der Klugheit, o habet die Narren
Eben zum Narren auch, wie sich's gehört!"

Let scholars quarrel and squabble,
Let teachers too be prudent and strict!
All the wisest men in all the ages
Nod and smile in agreement with me:
'Foolish to wait till fools grow wiser!
Children of wisdom, simply make fools
Of the fools, as is fit!'

Merlin der Alte, im leuchtenden Grabe,
Wo ich als Jüngling gesprochen ihn habe,
Hat mich mit ähnlicher Antwort belehrt:
„Töricht, auf Beßrung der Toren zu harren!
Kinder der Klugheit, o habet die Narren
Eben zum Narren auch, wie sich's gehört!"

Old Merlin from his shining grave,
Where I consulted him in my youth,
Gave me a similar answer too:
'Foolish to wait till fools grow wiser!
Children of wisdom, simply make fools
Of the fools, as is fit!'

Und auf den Höhen der indischen Lüfte
Und in den Tiefen ägyptischer Grüfte
Hab ich das heilige Wort nur gehört:

And on India's airy heights,
And in the depths of Egyptian tombs,
I have only heard those sacred words:

---

* Coptic is the language of the Christian descendants of the ancient Egyptians.

„Töricht, auf Beßrung der Toren zu harren!
Kinder der Klugheit, o habet die Narren
Eben zum Narren auch, wie sich's gehört!"
(*Bruch*)

'Foolish to wait till fools grow wiser!
Children of wisdom, simply make fools
Of the fools, as is fit!'

28 December 1888 Cophtisches Lied II / Cophtic song II [15]
FROM *Der Großkophta*

Geh! gehorche meinen Winken,
Nutze deine jungen Tage,
Lerne zeitig klüger sein:
Auf des Glückes großer Waage
Steht die Zunge selten ein;
Du mußt steigen oder sinken,
Du mußt herrschen und gewinnen
Oder dienen und verlieren,
Leiden oder triumphieren,
Amboß oder Hammer sein.
(*Bruch, Reichardt*)

Go! do what I suggest,
Make use of your young days,
Learn in good time to be wiser:
On the mighty scales of Fortune
The pointer is seldom at rest:
You must rise or you must fall,
You must win and be a master
Or you must lose and be a slave,
You must suffer or triumph,
Be the anvil or the hammer.

30 December 1888 Beherzigung / Take this to heart [18]

Ach, was soll der Mensch verlangen?
Ist es besser, ruhig bleiben?
Klammernd fest sich anzuhangen?
Ist es besser, sich zu treiben?
Soll er sich ein Häuschen bauen?
Soll er unter Zelten leben?
Soll er auf die Felsen trauen?
Selbst die festen Felsen beben.

Ah, what should a man desire?
Is it better to remain quiet?
Or hang on, holding tight?
Is it better to press on?
Should he build himself a house?
Should he live in tents?
Should he trust the rocks?
Even solid rocks can quake.

Eines schickt sich nicht für alle!
Sehe jeder, wie er's treibe,
Sehe jeder, wo er bleibe,
Und wer steht, daß er nicht falle!
(*Zelter, Zillig*)

There is no answer fit for all!
Let each man look to himself,
Let each man decide where to dwell,
And he who stands, let him not fall!

31 December 1888 Blumengruß / Flower greeting [24]

Der Strauß, den ich gepflücket,
Grüße dich vieltausendmal!
Ich habe mich oft gebücket,
Ach, wohl eintausendmal,
Und ihn ans Herz gedrücket
Wie hunderttausendmal!
(*Graener, Knab, Reichardt, Webern, Zelter*)

May this garland I have gathered
Greet you many thousand times!
I have often stooped down,
Ah, at least a thousand times,
And pressed it to my heart
Something like a hundred thousand!

Ha, ich bin Herr der Welt! mich lieben	Ha, I am master of the world! I am loved
Die Edlen, die mir dienen.	By the nobles, who are my servants.
Ha, ich bin Herr der Welt! ich liebe	Ha, I am master of the world! I love
Die Edlen, denen ich gebiete.	The nobles, whom I command.
O gib mir, Gott im Himmel! daß ich mich	O grant me, God in Heaven! that I never
Der Höh und Lieb nicht überhebe.	Take this power and this love for granted.

Aus *West-östlicher Divan* / Songs from the *West-Eastern Divan*

Goethe's *West-östlicher Divan*, published in 1819, owes its inspiration to the Persian poet Hafiz (1320–89) whose verse he had first read in a translation by Joseph, Freiherr von Hammer-Purgstall. Goethe prepared the poems for publication in a cycle of twelve books; and to accentuate the close collaboration of two kindred spirits and the mingling of two cultures ('west-östlich'), he gave each book a transliterated title and its German equivalent. He did not attempt to imitate the metrical form of the originals, which were Ghasels, but wrote instead rhyming verse, mostly arranged in four-line stanzas, that is characterized by a sort of mellifluous wiriness. Wolf chose seventeen poems from the *West-östlicher Divan*: three from 'The Book of the Minstrel', five from the '*Book of the Cup-bearer*' and ten from the '*Book of Suleika*', none of which, according to Ernst Challier's *Großer Lieder-Katalog*, had ever been set to music before, apart from 'Phänomen' (Brahms), 'Erschaffen und Beleben' (Zelter) and 'Als ich auf dem Euphrat schiffte' which already existed in long-since forgotten settings by K. Heubner and J. Mathieux. The *Buch der Suleika* poems were inspired by Goethe's infatuation with Marianne von Willemer (see SCHUBERT, p. 425). In these poems Goethe appears as Hatem and Marianne as Suleika; she also contributed to the volume, writing two Suleika poems (see SCHUBERT) and 'Hochbeglückt in deiner Liebe'.

16 January 1889 Solang man nüchtern ist / As long as a man's sober [36]

Solang man nüchtern ist,	As long as a man's sober,
Gefällt das Schlechte;	Badness pleases;
Wie man getrunken hat,	When he's imbibed,
Weiß man das Rechte;	He knows what's right;
Nur ist das Übermaß	Yet excess too
Auch gleich zuhanden;	Is imminent;
Hafis, o lehre mich,	Teach me, O Hafiz,
Wie du's verstanden!	The fruits of your wisdom!
Denn meine Meinung ist	Because what I think
Nicht übertrieben:	Is no exaggeration:
Wenn man nicht trinken kann,	If one can't drink,
Soll man nicht lieben;	One shouldn't love;

Doch sollt ihr Trinker euch
Nicht besser dünken,
Wenn man nicht lieben kann,
Soll man nicht trinken.
(*Mendelssohn, Zelter*)

But you drinkers
Shouldn't think yourselves better,
If one can't love,
One shouldn't drink.

16 January 1889 Was in der Schenke waren heute / What a commotion at the inn [38]

Was in der Schenke waren heute
Am frühsten Morgen für Tumulte!
Der Wirt und Mädchen! Fackeln, Leute!
Was gab's für Händel, für Insulte!

What a commotion at the inn
In the early morning today!
Landlord and girls! Torches, crowds!
Such haggling and such insults!

Die Flöte klang, die Trommel scholl!
Das war ein wüstes Wesen –
Doch bin ich, Lust und Liebe voll,
Auch selbst dabeigewesen.

Flutes and drums rang out!
It was Bedlam –
But full of love and joy,
I was there as well.

Daß ich von Sitte nichts gelernt,
Darüber tadelt mich ein jeder;
Doch bleib ich weislich weit entfernt
Vom Streit der Schulen und Katheder.

I'm rebuked by all and sundry
For not knowing how to behave;
But I wisely keep far away
From the bickering of pedants.

17 January 1889 Ob der Koran von Ewigkeit sei? / Has the Koran existed since time began? [34]

Ob der Koran von Ewigkeit sei?
Darnach frag ich nicht!
Ob der Koran geschaffen sei?
Das weiß ich nicht!
Daß er das Buch der Bücher sei,
Glaub ich aus Mosleminenpflicht.
Daß aber der Wein von Ewigkeit sei,
Daran zweifl' ich nicht;
Oder daß er vor den Engeln geschaffen sei,
Ist vielleicht auch kein Gedicht.
Der Trinkende, wie es auch immer sei,
Blickt Gott frischer ins Angesicht.

Has the Koran existed since time began?
I do not enquire!
Was the Koran created?
I do not know!
That it is the Book of Books,
I, as a dutiful Muslim, believe.
That wine has existed since time began,
I do not doubt;
And that it was created before the angels,
May also well be true.
Be that as it may, he who imbibes
Sees God's countenance more clearly.

18 January 1889 Sie haben wegen der Trunkenheit / They accuse me of drunkenness [37]

Sie haben wegen der Trunkenheit
Vielfältig uns verklagt
Und haben von unsrer Trunkenheit
Lange nicht genug gesagt.
Gewöhnlich der Betrunkenheit
Erliegt man, bis es tagt;
Doch hat mich meine Betrunkenheit
In der Nacht umhergejagt.

They accuse me of drunkenness
In a variety of guises
And still have not fully
Exhausted the topic.
The norm is to lie in a stupor
Until day breaks;
But my drunkenness harries me
All through the night.

Es ist die Liebestrunkenheit,
Die mich erbärmlich plagt,
Von Tag zu Nacht, von Nacht zu Tag
In meinem Herzen zagt.
Dem Herzen, das in Trunkenheit
Der Lieder schwillt und ragt,
Daß keine nüchterne Trunkenheit
Sich gleich zu heben wagt.
Lieb-, Lied- und Weinestrunkenheit,
Ob's nachtet oder tagt,
Die göttlichste Betrunkenheit,
Die mich entzückt und plagt.

For I am drunk with love,
That is what plagues me so,
Day and night, night and day,
It quakes in my heart.
My heart so swells
With the drunkenness of song,
That sober drunkenness
Dares not raise its head.
I am drunk with love, poetry and wine,
Whether by day or by night,
This divinest drunkenness
Torments and delights me.

18 January 1889 Trunken müssen wir alle sein! / We must all be drunk! [35]

Trunken müssen wir alle sein!
Jugend ist Trunkenheit ohne Wein;
Trinkt sich das Alter wieder zu Jugend,
So ist es wundervolle Tugend.
Für Sorgen sorgt das liebe Leben,
Und Sorgenbrecher sind die Reben.

We must all be drunk!
Young men get drunk without wine;
If old men drink themselves young again,
That is a wondrous virtue.
Dear life ensures we're full of care,
The grape makes us all carefree.

Da wird nicht mehr nachgefragt!
Wein ist ernstlich untersagt.
Soll denn doch getrunken sein,
Trinke nur vom besten Wein:
Doppelt wärest du ein Ketzer
In Verdammnis um den Krätzer.

No more questions, then!
Wine is strictly forbidden.
But if you are to get drunk,
Drink only the best:
You'd be a heretic twice over,
If damned for bad wine.

19 January 1889 Phänomen / Phenomenon [32]

Wenn zu der Regenwand
Phöbus sich gattet,
Gleich steht ein Bogenrand
Farbig beschattet.

When the Sun-god mates
With a curtain of rain,
A rainbow springs up,
Shaded with colours.

Im Nebel gleichen Kreis
Seh ich gezogen,
Zwar ist der Bogen weiß,
Doch Himmelsbogen.

I see this same circle
Drawn in the mist;
Though the bow is white,
It is there in the heavens.

So sollst du, muntrer Greis,
Dich nicht betrüben,
Sind gleich die Haare weiß,
Doch wirst du lieben.
(*Brahms*)

So be of good cheer, old fellow,
Do not lose heart;
Though your hair be white,
You shall still find love.

21 January 1889 Erschaffen und Beleben / Creation and animation [33]

Hans Adam war ein Erdenkloß,
Den Gott zum Menschen machte,
Doch bracht er aus der Mutter Schoß
Noch vieles Ungeschlachte.

Hans Adam was a lump of clay
That God made into man,
But he produced from Mother Earth
Much else that was uncouth.

Die Elohim zur Nas' hinein
Den besten Geist ihm bliesen,
Nun schien er schon was mehr zu sein,
Denn er fing an zu niesen.

Jehovah, via his nose,
Blew the best spirit in,
Now he seemed to make progress,
He began to sneeze.

Doch mit Gebein und Glied und Kopf
Blieb er ein halber Klumpen,
Bis endlich Noah für den Tropf
Das Wahre fand, den Humpen.

Despite his head and bones and limbs,
He still remained half a lump,
Till Noah for the clot at last
Found the very thing – a tankard.

Der Klumpe fühlt sogleich den Schwung,
Sobald er sich benetzet,
So wie der Teig durch Säuerung
Sich in Bewegung setzet.

That brought life into the lump
As soon as he partook,
Just as dough, through leavening,
Is quickened into life.

So, Hafis, mag dein holder Sang,
Dein heiliges Exempel,
Uns führen, bei der Gläser Klang,
Zu unsres Schöpfers Tempel.
(*Von Schillings, Strauss, Zelter*)

So, Hafiz, may your sweet song
And your sacred example
Conduct us, as the glasses clink,
To our Creator's temple.

21 January 1889 Nicht Gelegenheit macht Diebe / It is not opportunity that makes thieves [39]

HATEM
Nicht Gelegenheit macht Diebe,
Sie ist selbst der größte Dieb;
Denn sie stahl den Rest der Liebe,
Die mir noch im Herzen blieb.

HATEM
It is not opportunity that makes thieves,
It is itself the greatest thief;
For it stole the rest of the love
That still remained in my heart.

Dir hat sie ihn übergeben,
Meines Lebens Vollgewinn,
Daß ich nun, verarmt, mein Leben
Nur von dir gewärtig bin.

It stole and gave away to you
All that I had gained in life,
So that now, impoverished,
I am dependent on you.

Doch ich fühle schon Erbarmen
Im Karfunkel deines Blicks
Und erfreu in deinen Armen
Mich erneuerten Geschicks.

But I sense compassion
In your sapphire glances,
And in your embrace
Rejoice in fate once more.

23 January 1889 Hochbeglückt in deiner Liebe / Sublimely happy in your love [40]

SULEIKA
Hochbeglückt in deiner Liebe
Schelt ich nicht Gelegenheit;

SULEIKA
Sublimely happy in your love,
I do not chide opportunity;

Ward sie auch an dir zum Diebe,
Wie mich solch ein Raub erfreut!

Und wozu denn auch berauben?
Gib dich mir aus freier Wahl;
Gar zu gerne möcht ich glauben –
Ja, ich bin's, die dich bestahl.

Was so willig du gegeben,
Bringt dir herrlichen Gewinn,
Meine Ruh, mein reiches Leben
Geb ich freudig, nimm es hin!

Scherze nicht! Nichts von Verarmen!
Macht uns nicht die Liebe reich?
Halt ich dich in meinen Armen,
Jedem Glück ist meines gleich.

Though it played the thief on you,
How such a theft delights me!

But why speak of stealing?
Surrender to me of your own free will;
All too gladly I would believe –
Yes, I'm the one who robbed you.

What you gave so willingly
Brings you glorious gain,
My peace, my rich life
I gladly give, take it from me!

Do not jest! Say nothing of impoverishment!
Does not love make us rich?
When I hold you in my arms,
My fortune's the match of anyone's.

24 January 1889 Als ich auf dem Euphrat schiffte / As I sailed on the Euphrates [41]

SULEIKA

Als ich auf dem Euphrat schiffte,
Streifte sich der goldne Ring
Fingerab in Wasserklüfte,
Den ich jüngst von dir empfing.

Also träumt ich. Morgenröte
Blitzt ins Auge durch den Baum,
Sag, Poete, sag, Prophete!
Was bedeutet dieser Traum?

SULEIKA

As I sailed on the Euphrates,
The golden ring you recently gave me
Slipped from my fingers
Down into the watery depths.

So I dreamed. Red dawn
Flashed into my eyes through the trees,
Tell me, poet, tell me, prophet!
What is the meaning of this dream?

24 January 1889 Dies zu deuten, bin erbötig! / I am disposed to interpret this dream! [42]

HATEM

Dies zu deuten, bin erbötig!
Hab ich dir nicht oft erzählt,
Wie der Doge von Venedig
Mit dem Meere sich vermählt?

So von deinen Fingergliedern
Fiel der Ring dem Euphrat zu.
Ach, zu tausend Himmelsliedern,
Süßer Traum, begeisterst du!

Mich, der von den Indostanen
Streifte bis Damaskus hin,
Um mit neuen Karawanen
Bis ans Rote Meer zu ziehn,

HATEM

I am disposed to interpret this dream!
Have I not often told you
How the Doge of Venice
Was wedded to the sea?

Thus from your fingers
The ring fell into the Euphrates.
Ah, sweet dream, you inspire me
To a thousand heavenly songs!

You wed me, who wandered
from Hindustan to Damascus
To reach the Red Sea
With new caravans,

* The Doge on Ascension Day casts a golden ring from the state gondola, the 'Bucintoro', to symbolize the marriage of Venice with the sea.

Mich vermählst du deinem Flusse,	To your river,
Der Terrasse, diesem Hain,	To the terraces, to this grove,
Hier soll bis zum letzten Kusse	Here, until our final kiss,
Dir mein Geist gewidmet sein.	Shall my soul be dedicated to you.

23 January 1889 Wie sollt ich heiter bleiben / How could I remain cheerful [45]

HATEM	HATEM
Wie sollt ich heiter bleiben,	How could I remain cheerful,
Entfernt von Tag und Licht?	When parted from day and light?
Nun aber will ich schreiben,	But now I shall write,
Und trinken mag ich nicht.	And do not wish to drink.
Wenn sie mich an sich lockte,	When she enticed me to her,
War Rede nicht im Brauch,	There was no need of words;
Und wie die Zunge stockte,	And as my tongue faltered,
So stockt die Feder auch.	So my quill did too.
Nur zu! geliebter Schenke,	But come, dear Saki,
Den Becher fülle still!	Fill my cup in silence!
Ich sage nur: Gedenke!	I've only to say: 'Remember!'
Schon weiß man, was ich will.	And my meaning is clear.

25 January 1889 Wenn ich dein gedenke / When I think of you [46]

HATEM	HATEM
Wenn ich dein gedenke,	When I think of you,
Fragt mich gleich der Schenke:	Saki at once enquires:
„Herr, warum so still?	'Why are you so silent, sir?
Da von deinen Lehren	For Saki would always
Immer weiter hören	Gladly hear more
Saki* gerne will."	Of your teaching.'
Wenn ich mich vergesse	When I forget myself
Unter der Zypresse,	Under the cypresses,
Hält er nichts davon,	He's not impressed at all,
Und im stillen Kreise	And yet in quiet surroundings
Bin ich doch so weise,	I am as wise
Klug wie Salomon.	And clever as Solomon.

25 January 1889 Komm, Liebchen, komm! / Come, my love, come! [44]

HATEM	HATEM
Komm, Liebchen, komm! umwinde mir die Mütze!	Come, my love, come! Wind my head-dress on!
Aus deiner Hand nur ist der Tulbend schön.	Only when wound by you is the turban beautiful.

* Persian for 'publican', here used as a proper noun.

Hat Abbas* doch, auf Irans höchstem Sitze,
Sein Haupt nicht zierlicher umwinden sehn!

Ein Tulbend war das Band, das Alexandern
In Schleifen schön vom Haupte fiel
Und allen Folgeherrschern, jenen andern,
Als Königszierde wohlgefiel.

Ein Tulbend ist's, der unsern Kaiser
   schmücket,
Sie nennen's Krone. Name geht wohl hin!
Juwel und Perle! sei das Aug entzücket!
Der schönste Schmuck ist stets der Musselin.

Und diesen hier, ganz rein und silberstreifig,
Umwinde, Liebchen, um die Stirn umher.
Was ist denn Hoheit? Mir ist sie geläufig!
Du schaust mich an, ich bin so groß als er.

Even Abbas, on Iran's loftiest throne,
Did not see his head more gracefully bound!

It was a turban that cascaded
In fine folds from Alexander's head,
And with all rulers that succeeded him
Found favour as a royal embellishment.

It is a turban that adorns our emperor,
A crown they call it. What's in a name?
Jewels and pearls! Let the eyes be delighted:
The most beautiful ornament remains muslin.

So wind this muslin here, so pure and silver-
   threaded,
Wind it, my love, about my brow.
What, then, is majesty? A familiar thing to me!
You gaze at me, I am as great as He.

26 January 1889 Hätt ich irgend wohl Bedenken / Could I ever hesitate [43]

HATEM

Hätt ich irgend wohl Bedenken,
Balch,† Bochâra,‡ Samarkand,
Süßes Liebchen, dir zu schenken,
Dieser Städte Rausch und Tand?

Aber frag einmal den Kaiser,
Ob er dir die Städte gibt?
Er ist herrlicher und weiser;
Doch er weiß nicht, wie man liebt.

Herrscher, zu dergleichen Gaben
Nimmermehr bestimmst du dich!
Solch ein Mädchen muß man haben
Und ein Bettler sein wie ich.

HATEM

Could I ever hesitate to offer you
Balkh, Bokhara, Samarkand,
O my sweetest love,
With all their gaudy heady delights?

But try asking the emperor
Whether he would give you these cities?
He may be grander and wiser;
But he does not know what Love is.

Sovereign, you will never resolve
To give such gifts!
Better by far to have such a girl
And be a beggar like me.

29 January 1889 Locken, haltet mich gefangen / O curls, hold me captive [47]

HATEM

Locken, haltet mich gefangen
In dem Kreise des Gesichts!
Euch geliebten braunen Schlangen
Zu erwidern hab ich nichts.

HATEM

O curls, hold me captive
In the circle of her face!
I have nothing, sweet dark serpents,
That can requite you.

---

*Abbas II, shah of Persia, 1642–66. Promoted the prosperity of his people and tolerated the Christians.
† Capital of a principality of that name in N. Afghanistan, once known by its Persian name Bakhtri as the capital of Bactria.
‡ An ancient town, formerly the capital of the Khanate, renowned as the centre of Islamic culture.

Nur dies Herz, es ist von Dauer,
Schwillt in jugendlichstem Flor;
Unter Schnee und Nebelschauer
Rast ein Ätna dir hervor.

Du beschämst wie Morgenröte
Jener Gipfel ernste Wand,
Und noch einmal fühlet Hatem
Frühlingshauch und Sommerbrand.

Schenke, her! Noch eine Flasche!
Diesen Becher bring ich ihr!
Findet sie ein Häufchen Asche,
Sagt sie: der verbrannte mir.

This heart alone is constant
And swells in youthful blossom;
From beneath the snow and veils of mist
An Etna gushes out towards you.

Like the dawn, you put to shame
The earnest brow of those peaks,
And once again Hatem feels
The breath of Spring and Summer's fire.

Cup-bearer, here! Another bottle!
I raise this glass to her!
If she finds a small heap of ashes,
She'll say: 'He burned away for me.'

30 January 1889 Nimmer will ich dich verlieren! / May I never lose you! [48]

SULEIKA
Nimmer will ich dich verlieren!
Liebe gibt der Liebe Kraft.
Magst du meine Jugend zieren
Mit gewaltiger Leidenschaft.
Ach! wie schmeichelt's meinem Triebe,
Wenn man meinen Dichter preist.
Denn das Leben ist die Liebe,
Und des Lebens Leben Geist.

SULEIKA
May I never lose you!
Love gives strength to love.
May you adorn my youth
With your powerful passion.
Ah! how flattered my own impulses feel
When I hear my poet praised.
For life is love,
And the mind is the life of life itself.

* * *

2 February 1889 Frech und froh II / Cheerful impudence II [17]

Liebesqual verschmäht mein Herz,
Sanften Jammer, süßen Schmerz;
Nur vom Tücht'gen will ich wissen,
Heißem Äugeln, derben Küssen.
Sei ein armer Hund erfrischt,
Von der Lust, mit Pein gemischt!
Mädchen, gib der frischen Brust
Nichts von Pein und alle Lust.

My heart scorns the torment of love,
The gentle moan, the sweet distress;
I'm only interested in someone proficient,
Passionate ogling, rough kisses.
Only poor devils could be refreshed
By pleasure mingled with pain!
Give this lively heart, my girl,
No pain at all and lots of pleasure.

5 February 1889 Der neue Amadis* / A latter-day Amadis [23]

Als ich noch ein Knabe war,
Sperrte man mich ein;
Und so saß ich manches Jahr
Über mir allein,
Wie in Mutterleib.

When I was still a little boy,
They used to lock me in;
So for many a year I had
To sit there all alone,
As in my mother's womb.

*Amadis de Gaul was a pseudo-historical hero of fourteenth century Spanish romance.

Doch du warst mein Zeitvertreib,	But you passed the time for me,
Goldne Phantasie,	Golden Fantasy,
Und ich ward ein warmer Held,	And I became an ardent hero,
Wie der Prinz Pipi,	Like young prince Pipi,
Und durchzog die Welt.	And I roamed the world.

Baute manch kristallen Schloß	I built and shattered
Und zerstört es auch,	Many a castle of glass,
Warf mein blinkendes Geschoß	I hurled my shining spear
Drachen durch den Bauch,	Into dragons' bellies,
Ja, ich war ein Mann!	Yes, I was a man!

Ritterlich befreit ich dann	Chivalrously I then freed
Die Prinzessin Fisch;	Princess Fish;
Sie war gar zu obligeant,	She was most obliging,
Führte mich zu Tisch,	Conducted me to table,
Und ich war galant.	And I was gallant.

Und ihr Kuß war Götterbrot,	And her kiss was ambrosia,
Glühend wie der Wein.	Glowing like the wine.
Ach! ich liebte fast mich tot!	Ah! I almost died of love!
Rings mit Sonnenschein	She glittered, enamel-like,
War sie emailliert.	In sunshine.

Ach! wer hat sie mir entführt?	Ah, who has abducted her?
Hielt kein Zauberband	Did no magic wand
Sie zurück vom schnellen Fliehn?	Hold her back from hasty flight?
Sagt, wo ist ihr Land?	Say, where is her country?
Wo der Weg dahin?	Where the way to it?

(*Corona Schröter, Knab, Krenek, Reichardt*)

10 February 1889 Genialisch Treiben / Genius at work [21]

So wälz ich ohne Unterlaß	So I trundle my tub relentlessly,
Wie Sankt Diogenes* mein Faß.	Like Saint Diogenes.
Bald ist es Ernst, bald ist es Spaß;	Sometimes in earnest, sometimes in jest;
Bald ist es Lieb, bald ist es Haß;	Sometimes it's love, sometimes it's hate;
Bald ist es dies, bald ist es das;	Sometimes it's this, sometimes it's that;
Es ist ein Nichts und ist ein Was.	Achieving nothing, achieving something.
So wälz ich ohne Unterlaß	So I trundle my tub relentlessly,
Wie Sankt Diogenes mein Faß.	Like Saint Diogenes.

(*Zelter*)

12 February 1889 Die Bekehrte† / Converted [27]

Bei dem Glanz der Abendröte	In the red glow of sunset
Ging ich still den Wald entlang,	I wandered quietly through the wood,

---

* Diogenes, the Cynic philosopher, was said to live in a tub.
† Both 'Die Bekehrte' and 'Die Spröde' were written by Goethe for inclusion in *L'Impresario in angustie*.

Damon saß und blies die Flöte,
Daß es von den Felsen klang,
So la la!

Und er zog mich zu sich nieder,
Küßte mich so hold, so süß.
Und ich sagte: „Blase wieder!"
Und der gute Junge blies,
So la la!

Meine Ruh' ist nun verloren,
Meine Freude floh davon,
Und ich hör' vor meinen Ohren
Immer nur den alten Ton,
So la la! le ralla!
(*Busoni, Cimarosa, Knab, Medtner, Tomášek,
Zelter*)

Damon sat and played his flute,
Making the rocks resound,
So la la!

And he drew me down to him,
Kissed me so gently, so sweetly.
And I said: 'Play once more!'
And the good lad played,
So la la!

Now my peace is lost,
My joy has flown away,
And ringing in my ears I hear
Nothing but the old refrain,
So la la, le ralla!

21 October 1889 Die Spröde / Coy [26]

An dem reinsten Frühlingsmorgen
Ging die Schäferin und sang,
Jung und schön und ohne Sorgen,
Daß es durch die Felder klang,
So la la! le ralla!

Thyrsis bot ihr für ein Mäulchen
Zwei, drei Schäfchen gleich am Ort,
Schalkhaft blickte sie ein Weilchen;
Doch sie sang und lachte fort,
So la la! le ralla!

Und ein andrer bot ihr Bänder,
Und der dritte bot sein Herz;
Doch sie trieb mit Herz und Bändern
So wie mit den Lämmern Scherz,
Nur la la! le ralla!
(*Cimarosa, Knab, Medtner, Tomášek, Zelter*)

On the clearest of spring mornings
The shepherdess went out and sang,
Carefree, young and beautiful,
Till it echoed through the fields,
So la la! le ralla!

Thyrsis offered her for a kiss
Two, three lambs without delay,
She looked on archly for a while;
But went laughing and singing on her way,
So la la! le ralla!

And another offered ribbons,
And a third bid his heart;
But she made fun of heart and ribbons,
As she had done with the lambs,
Only la la, le ralla!

Heinrich Heine (1797–1856)

See Mendelssohn, Robert Schumann

Wolf published only one Heine song in his lifetime, 'Wo wird einst' (1888), a setting of a poem ('Wo') Heine had written in Paris on his 'Matratzengruft', the 'mattress grave' on which he languished for the last eight years of his life, suffering from a spinal tuberculosis of syphilitic origin which gradually paralysed him. Heine's wonderful late poetry – 'Wo' is inscribed on his grave in Paris – has inspired very few Lieder composers, almost all of whom, apart from David Blake in *From the Mattress Grave* (1978), concentrated instead on the earlier verse of unrequited love. Wolf also set seventeen of these *Buch der Lieder* poems, seven of which were composed in quick succession in the spring of 1878 to form a *Liederstrauß*, the title-page of which reads: 'Seven poems from the *Buch der Lieder* of Heinrich Heine, for voice and pianoforte, composed by Hugo Wolf, Volume I. Summer 1878' – an early example of Wolf's method of concentrating in depth on a single poet. Though the Mörike songs of his maturity are a decade away, these Heine Lieder are far from negligible. Or as Wolf put it in a letter to his friend Edmund Lang, dated February 1888: 'Mein Lodi im Lied ist bekanntlich das Jahr 1878 gewesen; damals komponierte ich fast jeden Tag e i n gutes Lied, mitunter auch z w e i. ('My Lodi in song [a reference to Napoleon's victory at Lodi in Northern Italy that brought him recognition and a boost in self-confidence] is known to have been the year 1878; in those days I composed almost every day *one* good song, and sometimes *two*.' Hyperbole, perhaps, but a song like 'Sie haben heut' abend Gesellschaft', with its Schumann-like postlude that takes up a quarter of the entire piece, compares well with the setting by Pfitzner.

18–25 May 1878 Sie haben heut abend Gesellschaft / They have company tonight

Sie haben heut abend Gesellschaft,	They have company tonight
Und das Haus ist lichterfüllt.	And the house is full of light.
Dort oben am hellen Fenster	Up there at the bright window
Bewegt sich ein Schattenbild.	A shadowy figure moves.
Du schaust mich nicht, im Dunkeln	You do not see me, in the dark
Steh' ich hier unten allein;	I stand alone down here below,
Noch wen'ger kannst du schauen	Even less can you see
In mein dunkles Herz hinein.	Into my dark heart.
Mein dunkles Herze liebt dich,	My dark heart loves you,
Es liebt dich und es bricht,	It loves you and it breaks,
Und bricht und zuckt und verblutet,	It breaks and quivers and bleeds to death,
Du aber siehst es nicht.	But you see none of this.
(*Pfitzner*)	

24 January 1888 Wo wird einst / Where shall the weary traveller

Wo wird einst des Wandermüden	Where shall the weary traveller
Letzte Ruhestätte sein?	Find his final resting-place?
Unter Palmen in dem Süden?	Under palm trees in the south?
Unter Linden an dem Rhein?	Under lime trees by the Rhine?
Werd' ich wo in einer Wüste	Will I, somewhere in a desert,
Eingescharrt von fremder Hand?	Be buried by a stranger's hand?

Oder ruh' ich an der Küste	Or shall I find rest on the shore
Eines Meeres in dem Sand?	Of some ocean in the sand?
Immerhin! Mich wird umgeben	No matter! I shall be surrounded
Gotteshimmel, dort wie hier,	By God's Heaven, there as here,
Und als Totenlampen schweben	And, as funeral lamps, the stars
Nachts die Sterne über mir.	Shall float above me every night.
(*Schoeck, Tchaikovsky*)	

Gottfried Keller (1819–90)

See Schoeck

The six *Alte Weisen* were composed by Wolf in May–June 1890 as a tribute to the Swiss novelist, short story writer and poet Gottfried Keller on his seventieth birthday. Keller was of even smaller stature than Wolf (1.50 m. to Wolf's 1.54 m.) and throughout his life had difficulties sustaining relationships with women – he was pathologically shy and often unable to confess his love. In 1846, he wrote a set of poems to which he gave the title: *Von Weibern – alte Lieder* (*Ancient songs about wenches*). Wolf chose six* of Keller's eighteen poems, mostly about dominant women.

Alte Weisen / Old saws

1

25 May 1890 Tretet ein, hoher Krieger / Enter, lofty warrior

Tretet ein, hoher Krieger,	Enter, lofty warrior,
Der sein Herz mir ergab!	You who gave your heart to me!
Legt den purpurnen Mantel	Lay that crimson cloak aside
Und die Goldsporen ab.	And those golden spurs.
Spannt das Roß in den Pflug,	Yoke your charger to the plough,
Meinem Vater zum Gruß!	As a greeting for my father!
Die Schabrack' mit dem Wappen	The crested saddle-cloth
Gibt 'nen Teppich meinem Fuß.	Provides a carpet for my feet.
Euer Schwertgriff muß lassen	Your sword-hilt must yield to me
Für mich Gold und Stein,	Its jewels and its gold,
Und die blitzende Klinge	And its flashing blade
Wird ein Schüreisen sein.	Shall serve as a poker.
Und die schneeweiße Feder	And the snow-white feather
Auf dem blutroten Hut	On your blood-red hat
Ist zu 'nem kühlenden Wedel	Shall make a useful cooling fan
In der Sommerszeit gut.	In summertime.

* Brahms's settings of 'Salome' and 'Therese' have a slightly different wording, explained by the two different editions: Brahms owned the *Neuere Gedichte* (1851), Wolf the revised *Gedichte* of 1883.

Und der Marschalk muß lernen
Wie man Weizenbrot backt,
Wie man Wurst und Gefüllsel
Um die Weihnachtszeit hackt!

Nun befehlt Eure Seele
Dem heiligen Christ!
Euer Leib ist verkauft,
Wo kein Erlösen mehr ist!
(*Pfitzner*)

And the Marshall must learn
How to bake wheaten bread,
How sausages and stuffing
Are chopped at Christmastide!

Commend now your soul
To Christ our Lord!
Your body is sold
When redemption no longer exists!

2

2 June 1890 Singt mein Schatz wie ein Fink / If my love sings like a finch

Singt mein Schatz wie ein Fink,
Sing' ich Nachtigallensang;
Ist mein Liebster ein Luchs,
O so bin ich eine Schlang'!

O ihr Jungfraun im Land,
Vom Gebirg und über See,
Überlaßt mir den Schönsten,
Sonst tut ihr mir weh!

Er soll sich unterwerfen
Zum Ruhm uns und Preis!
Und er soll sich nicht rühren
Nicht laut und nicht leis!

O ihr teuern Gespielen,
Überlaßt mir den stolzen Mann,
Er soll sehn, wie die Liebe
Ein feurig Schwert werden kann!
(*Brahms* ['Salome'], *Pfitzner*)

If my love sings like a finch,
I'll sing like a nightingale;
If my sweetheart is a lynx,
Then I shall be a snake!

O you maidens on land,
From the mountains and across the sea,
Leave the most handsome one to me,
Or else you'll do me harm!

He shall have to submit
To our glory and our praise!
And he shall not move an inch
Either noisily or softly!

O my dear playmates,
Leave the proud fellow to me,
He shall see how Love
Can become a fiery sword!

3

16 June 1890 Du milchjunger Knabe / You beardless boy

Du milchjunger Knabe,
Wie siehst du mich an?
Was haben deine Augen
Für eine Frage getan!

Alle Ratsherrn in der Stadt
Und alle Weisen der Welt
Bleiben stumm auf die Frage,
Die deine Augen gestellt!

Ein leeres Schneckhäusel,
Schau, liegt dort im Gras;

You beardless boy,
Why do you look at me so?
What kind of question
Have your eyes been asking!

All the councillors in the city
And all the wise men in the world
Are dumbfounded by the question
Your eyes have put!

Look, there's an empty snail-shell,
Lying there in the grass;

Da halte dein Ohr dran,
Drin brümmelt dir was!
(*Brahms* ['Therese'], *Pfitzner*)

Just put it to your ear,
And you'll hear something hum inside!

4

8–23 June 1890 Wandl' ich in dem Morgentau / When I walk in the morning dew

Wandl' ich in dem Morgentau
Durch die dufterfüllte Au',
Muß ich schämen mich so sehr
Vor den Blümlein ringsumher!

When I walk in the morning dew
Through the scent-filled meadow,
I'm forced to feel so ashamed
In front of all the flowers!

Täublein auf dem Kirchendach,
Fischlein in dem Mühlenbach
Und das Schlänglein still im Kraut,
Alles fühlt und nennt sich Braut.

The doves on the church roof,
The little fish in the millstream,
And the still snake in the heather,
All know what it is to wed.

Apfelblüt' im lichten Schein
Dünkt sich stolz ein Mütterlein;
Freudig stirbt so früh im Jahr
Schon das Papilionenpaar.

Apple-blossom in the sunlight
Proudly deems itself a mother;
Butterfly and mate are glad
To die so early in the year.

Gott, was hab' ich denn getan,
Daß ich ohne Lenzgespan,
Ohne einen süßen Kuß
Ungeliebet sterben muß?
(*Pfitzner*)

God, what then have I done
That, with no springtime mate,
And not a single sweet kiss,
I must die unloved?

5

7–23 June 1890 Das Köhlerweib ist trunken / The charcoal-burner's wife is drunk

Das Köhlerweib ist trunken
Und singt im Wald,
Hört, wie die Stimme gellend
Im Grünen hallt!

The charcoal-burner's wife is drunk
And singing in the wood,
Listen how her screeching voice
Echoes through the green countryside!

Sie war die schönste Blume,
Berühmt im Land;
Es warben Reich' und Arme
Um ihre Hand.

She was once the fairest flower,
Celebrated far and wide,
Rich and poor came wooing
To win her hand.

Sie trat in Gürtelketten
So stolz einher;
Den Bräutigam zu wählen
Fiel ihr zu schwer.

She wore a chatelaine
And walked with haughty pride;
To choose a bridegroom
Proved too hard a task.

Da hat sie überlistet
Der rote Wein –
Wie müssen alle Dinge
Vergänglich sein!

Then red wine
Outwitted her –
How transitory
Must all things be!

Das Köhlerweib ist trunken
Und singt im Wald;
Wie durch die Dämmerung gellend
Ihr Lied erschallt!

The charcoal-burner's wife is drunk
And singing in the wood;
How her screeching song resounds
In the gathering dusk!

6

5–23 June 1890 Wie glänzt der helle Mond so kalt und fern / How cold and distant the bright moon shines

Wie glänzt der helle Mond so kalt und fern,
Doch ferner schimmert meiner Schönheit
　　Stern!

How cold and distant the bright moon
　　shines,
But my beauty's star gleams more distant still!

Wohl rauschet weit von mir des Meeres
　　Strand,
Doch weiterhin liegt meiner Jugend Land!

The sea pounds the shore far away from me,
Farther still lies the land of my youth!

Ohn' Rad und Deichsel gibt's ein Wägelein,
Drin fahr' ich bald zum Paradies hinein.

There is a wagon without wheels or shafts,
I'll soon drive in it to Paradise.

Dort sitzt die Mutter Gottes auf dem Thron,
Auf ihren Knieen schläft ihr sel'ger Sohn.

The Mother of God sits there on her throne,
With her blessed Son asleep on her lap.

Dort sitzt Gott Vater, der den heil'gen Geist
Aus seiner Hand mit Himmelskörnern speist.

There sits God the Father, with the Holy
　　Ghost
Whom He feeds from His hand with manna.

In einem Silberschleier sitz' ich dann
Und schaue meine weißen Finger an.

Then I'll sit in a silver veil
And gaze at my white fingers.

Sankt Petrus aber gönnt sich keine Ruh,
Hockt vor der Tür und flickt die alten Schuh.
(*Pfitzner*)

But Saint Peter will not take a rest,
He squats at the Gate and cobbles old shoes.

Justinus Kerner (1786–1862)

See Robert Schumann

The opening of this song was quoted at Wolf's funeral at the end of Dr Michael Haberlandt's oration. 'Take the late, all too late thanks of the world with you into your final resting-place. And now as you sang in one of your loveliest songs . . .'

16 June 1883 Zur Ruh, zur Ruh! / To rest, to rest!

Zur Ruh, zur Ruh
Ihr müden Glieder!
Schließt fest euch zu,
Ihr Augenlider!
Ich bin allein,

To rest, to rest,
You weary limbs!
Close tight,
You eyelids!
I am alone,

Fort ist die Erde;	The world is left behind;
Nacht muß es sein,	Night must come
Daß Licht mir werde.	That I may find light.
O führt mich ganz,	O lead me on,
Ihr innern Mächte!	You inner powers!
Hin zu dem Glanz	To the radiance
Der tiefsten Nächte.	Of the darkest nights.
Fort aus dem Raum	Far away from earth
Der Erdenschmerzen	And its anguish
Durch Nacht und Traum	Through night and dream
Zum Mutterherzen!	To a mother's heart!

Michelangelo Buonarroti (1475–1564)

See Strauss

Though Michelangelo wrote poetry from an early age, it was not until the sonnets to Tornasso Cavaliere and the poems to Vittoria Colonna that he found his characteristic voice. Wolf's Michelangelo settings were the last he composed before he was taken to the asylum where he died. 'Wohl denk ich oft' translates an eight-line stanza by Michelangelo, 'I' vo pensando al mio viver di prima'; 'Alles endet, was entstehet' comes from one of the *Canti de' Morti* ('Chiunche nascie a morte arriva'); and 'Fühlt meine Seele' is a translation of Sonnet 50, 'Non so se s'è la desiata luce', addressed to Vittoria Colonna, the object of Michelangelo's mystical love. Wolf had received a copy of the original Italian poems with German translations by Walter Robert-tornow during Christmas 1896, and intended to set at least six of them. Four were eventually composed, but he was dissatisfied with 'Irdische und himmlische Liebe' and later destroyed it. When asked by Edmund Hellmer why he had composed the songs for bass, he replied: 'Selbstverständlich muß ein Bildhauer Baß singen' ('Of course a sculptor has to sing bass.')

Drei Gedichte von Michelangelo / Three Michelangelo poems
TRANSLATED BY WALTER ROBERT-TORNOW (1852–95)

18 March 1897 Wohl denk' ich oft / I often recall

Wohl denk' ich oft an mein vergang'nes Leben,	I often recall my past life,
Wie es, vor meiner Liebe für Dich, war;	As it was before I loved you;
Kein Mensch hat damals Acht auf mich gegeben,	No one then paid heed to me,
Ein jeder Tag verloren für mich war.	Each day for me was a loss.
Ich dachte wohl, ganz dem Gesang zu leben,	I thought to live for song alone,
Auch mich zu flüchten aus der Menschen Schar	And flee the thronging crowd . . . . .

Genannt in Lob und Tadel bin ich heute,
Und, daß ich da bin, wissen alle Leute!

Today my name is praised and censured,
And the entire world knows that I exist!

20 March 1897 Alles endet, was entstehet / All must end that has beginning

Alles endet, was entstehet,
    Alles, alles rings vergehet,
    Denn die Zeit flieht, und die Sonne sieht,
    Sieht, daß Alles rings vergehet,
    Denken, Reden, Schmerz und Wonne;
    Und die wir zu Enkeln hatten
Schwanden wie bei Tag die Schatten,
Wie ein Dunst im Windeshauch.
Menschen waren wir ja auch,
Froh und traurig, so wie ihr;
Und nun sind wir leblos hier,
Sind nur Erde, wie ihr sehet;
Alles endet, was entstehet,
Alles, alles rings vergehet!

All must end that has beginning,
    All things round us perish,
    For time is fleeting, and the sun
    Sees that all things round us perish,
    Thought, speech, pain and rapture;
    And our children's children
Vanished as shadows by day,
As mists in a breeze.
We were also human beings,
With joys and sorrows like your own;
And now there is no life in us here,
We are but earth, as you can see;
All must end that has beginning,
All things round us perish!

25 March 1897 Fühlt meine Seele / Is it the longed-for light of God

Fühlt meine Seele das ersehnte Licht
    Von Gott, der sie erschuf? Ist es der Strahl
    Von and'rer Schönheit aus dem Jammertal,
    Der in mein Herz erinnrungweckend
bricht?
Ist es ein Klang, ein Traumgesicht,
    Das Aug' und Herz mir füllt mit einem Mal
    In unbegreiflich glühn'der Qual,
    Die mich zu Tränen bringt? Ich weiß es
nicht.
Was ich ersehne, fühle, Was mich lenkt,
    Ist nicht in mir: Sag' mir, wie ich's erwerbe?
    Mir zeigt es wohl nur eines And'ren Huld.
Darein bin ich, seit ich Dich sah, versenkt;
    Mich treibt ein Ja und Nein, ein Süß und
Herbe...
    Daran sind, Herrin, Deine Augen Schuld!

Does my soul feel the longed-for light
    Of God who created it? Is it the ray
    Of some other beauty from this vale of tears
    That storms my heart, awakening
memories?
Is it a sound, a vision in a dream
    That suddenly fills my eyes and heart
    With inconceivable, searing pain,
    Reducing me to tears? I do not
know.
What I long for, what I feel, what guides me
    Is not in me: tell me how to achieve it!
    Only another's favour is likely to reveal it.
This has absorbed me, since seeing you;
    I am torn between yes and no, bitterness
and sweetness...
    Your eyes, my lady, are the cause!

Eduard Mörike (1804–75)

Eduard Mörike used to be regarded as a naive romantic, untouched by the events of his time, the epitome of Biedermeier, the author of poetic idylls and delightful fairy tales, a bucolic, charmingly inadequate, ineffectual clergyman at one with his surroundings in Cleversulzbach, a nature poet par excellence with an engaging sense of humour. Gottfried Keller unwittingly encouraged this assessment when, on Mörike's death in 1875, he said: „es ist als ob ein schöner Junitag dahin wäre mit Mörike" ('it was as if a fine June day had passed away with Mörike'); and the sweet, bespectacled face that stares at us from many portraits has also been partially responsible for this distorted picture of one of Germany's greatest lyric poets. The naivety, the idylls and the humour of many Mörike poems are, in fact, a bastion erected by the poet against those extreme emotions which threatened to overwhelm him throughout his life. The idyll protects him from the demonic, humour helps him cope with emotional turmoil, and the quest for moderation banishes or at least controls erotic undercurrents.

Much of Mörike's love poetry was written in the wake of his failed relationship with Maria Meyer, an experience he tried to exorcise in the five Peregrina poems, of which Wolf set two and Schoeck three. She was born on 27 February 1802 as the illegitimate child of a certain Helena Meyer in Schaffhausen and an apprentice tawer. We actually know little about her and even less about the details of her relationship with Mörike. She was a Swiss girl of obscure origin, extremely well read, a member of the wandering sect of Julia von Krüdener, and affected at times by a sort of religious fervour. The first Mörike heard of her was when Herr Mergenthaler, the owner of a Ludwigsburg brewery, found her unconscious on the Stuttgart–Ludwigsburg road – it later turned out that she was prone to epileptic fits and bouts of sleepwalking. She was now taken in by the mother of one of Mörike's seminary friends, Rudolf Lohbauer. Overnight, Maria Meyer had become something of a celebrity in the little town, and Mörike, living in Tübingen, exchanged passionate letters with her, despite the warnings of his sister Luise. Rumours soon reached him, however, that led him to call her moral integrity into question. He was thrown into utter confusion – all the more so, when he heard that she had suddenly left Ludwigsburg. Soon afterwards, she was found in Heidelberg in exactly the same circumstances in which she had first appeared on the Ludwigsburg road. This time she was arrested, but later bailed by influential friends and admirers and left to go her way. In the early summer of 1824 she turned up in Tübingen and wrote Mörike a letter, requesting a meeting and a short dedicatory poem. He refused and fled in turmoil to his mother in Stuttgart.

Mörike was one of Wolf's favourite poets, and it was with a volume of his poems that he withdrew to Perchtoldsdorf after his father's death on 9 May 1887. He had already set 4 Mörike poems – 'Suschens Vogel' in 1880, 'Die Tochter der Heide' in 1884, 'Mausfallensprüchlein' in 1882 and 'Der König bei der Krönung' in 1886 – but bereavement now paralysed his creative urge, and for the rest of 1887 he composed nothing and was inconsolable. At Perchtoldsdorf, however, the Mörike poems unleashed within him a period of creativity, comparable to Schubert's in 1815 and Schumann's in 1840. Between 10 February and 26 November 1888 he composed the fifty-three songs of the *Mörike-Liederbuch,* and symbolically placed 'Der Genesene an die Hoffnung' ('He who has recovered addresses hope') at the head of the published volume. Although the seasons partially dictated his choice of poem – 'Er ist's', 'Fußreise', 'Im Frühling' and 'Zitronenfalter im April', all Spring poems, were composed in March and May, while the approach of Christmas inspired 'Auf eine Christblume 1', 'Schlafendes Jesuskind' and 'Zum neuen Jahr' – he was composing maniacally, almost somnambulistically, in much the same way as Mörike wrote many of his poems ('Im Frühling', for example, was written at one sitting in the early morning of 13 May 1828).

The Mörike songs are printed in chronological order of composition; Wolf's published order is indicated in square brackets.

18 June 1882 Mausfallen-Sprüchlein / Mousetrap incantation

DAS KIND GEHT DREIMAL UM DIE FALLE UND SPRICHT:	THE CHILD WALKS THREE TIMES ROUND THE TRAP AND SAYS:
Kleine Gäste, kleines Haus.	Little guests, little house,
Liebe Mäusin oder Maus,	Dear Mrs or Mr Mouse,
Stell dich nur kecklich ein	Just drop boldly by
Heut nacht bei Mondenschein!	Tonight in the moonlight!
Mach aber die Tür fein hinter dir zu,	But be sure to close the door behind you,
Hörst du?	Do you hear?
Dabei hüte dein Schwänzchen!	And watch out for your tail!
Nach Tische singen wir,	After supper we'll sing,
Nach Tische springen wir	After supper we'll leap
Und machen ein Tänzchen:	And dance a little dance:
Witt witt:	Witt, witt!
Meine alte Katze tanzt wahrscheinlich mit.	My old cat might well dance with us too.
(*Distler*)	

Mörike-Lieder / The Mörike songs

16 February 1888 Der Tambour / The drummer-boy [5]

Wenn meine Mutter hexen könnt,	If my mother could work magic,
Da müßt sie mit dem Regiment	She'd have to go with the regiment
Nach Frankreich, überall mit hin,	To France and everywhere,
Und wär die Marketenderin.	And be the vivandière.
Im Lager, wohl um Mitternacht	In camp, at midnight,
Wenn niemand auf ist als die Wacht,	When no one's up save the guard,
Und alles schnarchet, Roß und Mann,	And everyone – man and horse – is snoring,
Vor meiner Trommel säß ich dann:	Then I'd sit by my drum:
Die Trommel müßt eine Schüssel sein,	My drum would be a bowl,
Ein warmes Sauerkraut darein,	With warm sauerkraut in it,
Die Schlegel Messer und Gabel,	The sticks would be a knife and fork,
Eine lange Wurst mein Sabel;	My sabre – a long sausage;

Mein Tschako wär ein Humpen gut,	My shako would be a tankard
Den füll ich mit Burgunderblut.	Filled with red Burgundy.
Und weil es mir an Lichte fehlt,	And because I lack light,
Da scheint der Mond in mein Gezelt;	The moon shines into my tent;
Scheint er auch auf franzö'sch herein,	And though it shines in French,
Mir fällt doch meine Liebste ein:	It still reminds me of my beloved:
Ach weh! Jetzt hat der Spaß ein End!	Oh dear! There's an end to my fun!
– Wenn nur meine Mutter hexen könnt!	– If only my mother could work magic!
(*Distler*)	

22 February 1888 Der Knabe und das Immlein / The boy and the bee [2]

Im Weinberg auf der Höhe	On the hill-top vineyard
Ein Häuslein steht so windebang,	There stands a hut so timidly,
Hat weder Tür noch Fenster,	It has neither door nor window
Die Weile wird ihm lang.	And feels time dragging by.
Und ist der Tag so schwüle,	And when the day's so sultry
Sind all verstummt die Vögelein,	And every little bird is silent,
Summt an der Sonnenblume	A solitary bee
Ein Immlein ganz allein.	Buzzes round the sunflower.
Mein Lieb hat einen Garten,	My sweetheart has a garden
Da steht ein hübsches Immenhaus:	With a pretty beehive in it:
Kommst du daher geflogen?	Is that where you've flown from?
Schickt sie dich nach mir aus?	Did she send you to me?
„O nein, du feiner Knabe,	'Oh no, you handsome boy,
Es hieß mich niemand Boten gehn;	No one bade me bear messages;
Dies Kind weiß nichts von Lieben,	This child knows nothing of love,
Hat dich noch kaum gesehn.	Has scarcely even noticed you.
Was wüßten auch die Mädchen,	What can girls know
Wenn sie kaum aus der Schule sind!	When hardly out of school!
Dein herzallerliebstes Schätzchen	Your beloved sweetheart
Ist noch ein Mutterkind.	Is still her mother's child.
Ich bring ihm Wachs und Honig;	I bring her wax and honey;
Ade! – ich hab ein ganzes Pfund;	Farewell! – I've gathered a whole pound;
Wie wird das Schätzchen lachen,	How your beloved will laugh!
Ihm wässert schon der Mund."	Her mouth's already watering.'
Ach, wolltest du ihr sagen,	Ah, if only you would tell her,
Ich wüßte, was viel süßer ist:	I know of something much sweeter:
Nichts Lieblichers auf Erden	There's nothing lovelier on earth
Als wenn man herzt und küßt!	Than when one hugs and kisses!
(*Distler*)	

22 February 1888 Ein Stündlein wohl vor Tag / An hour before day [3]

Derweil ich schlafend lag,
Ein Stündlein wohl vor Tag,
Sang vor dem Fenster auf dem Baum
Ein Schwälblein mir, ich hört es kaum,
Ein Stündlein wohl vor Tag:

As I lay sleeping,
An hour before day,
A swallow sang to me – I could hardly hear it –
From a tree by my window,
An hour before day:

„Hör an, was ich dir sag,
Dein Schätzlein ich verklag:
Derweil ich dieses singen tu,
Herzt er ein Lieb in guter Ruh,
Ein Stündlein wohl vor Tag.“

'Listen well to what I say,
It's your lover I accuse:
While I'm singing this,
He's cuddling a girl in sweet repose,
An hour before day.'

O weh! nicht weiter sag!
O still! nichts hören mag!
Flieg ab! flieg ab von meinem Baum!
– Ach, Lieb und Treu ist wie ein Traum
Ein Stündlein wohl vor Tag.
(*Franz, Distler*)

Oh! don't say another word!
Oh quiet! I don't wish to hear!
Fly away! fly away from off my tree!
– Ah, love and loyalty are like a dream
An hour before day.

23 February 1888 Der Jäger / The huntsman [40]
FROM *Maler Nolten*

Drei Tage Regen fort und fort,
Kein Sonnenschein zur Stunde;
Drei Tage lang kein gutes Wort
Aus meiner Liebsten Munde!

Three days of endless rain,
No sunshine even now;
Not one kind word for three whole days
From my beloved's lips!

Sie trutzt mit mir und ich mit ihr,
So hat sie's haben wollen;
Mir aber nagts am Herzen hier,
Das Schmollen und das Grollen.

She sulks and so do I,
That's how she wanted it;
But it gnaws at my heart,
This sulkiness and sullenness.

Willkommen denn, des Jägers Lust,
Gewittersturm und Regen!
Fest zugeknöpft die heiße Brust
Und jauchzend euch entgegen!

Welcome, then, to the hunter's joy,
To thunderstorm and rain!
I'll button tight the ardent breast,
And fly to you rejoicing!

Nun sitzt sie wohl daheim und lacht
Und scherzt mit den Geschwistern;
Ich höre in des Waldes Nacht
Die alten Blätter flüstern.

She'll be sitting at home and laughing now,
And joking with her siblings;
I can hear the old leaves whispering
In the forest night.

Nun sitzt sie wohl und weinet laut
Im Kämmerlein, in Sorgen;
Mir ist es wie dem Wilde traut,
In Finsternis geborgen.

Now she'll be sitting and weeping aloud
For sorrow in her little room;
I feel as cosy as any deer,
Hidden in the darkness.

Kein Hirsch und Rehlein überall!
Ein Schuß zum Zeitvertreibe!

No stag or roe anywhere!
A shot will pass the time!

Gesunder Knall und Widerhall
Erfrischt das Mark im Leibe. –

The healthy crack and echo
Refresh the marrow in my bones. –

Doch wie der Donner nun verhallt
In Tälern, durch die Runde,
Ein plötzlich Weh mich überwallt,
Mir sinkt das Herz zu Grunde.

But as the thunder dies away
In the valleys all around,
I'm assailed by sudden pain,
My heart sinks like a stone.

Sie trutzt mit mir und ich mit ihr,
So hat sie's haben wollen;
Mir aber frißts am Herzen hier,
Das Schmollen und das Grollen.

She sulks with me and I with her,
That's how she wanted it;
But it gnaws at my heart,
This sulkiness and sullenness.

Und auf! und nach der Liebsten Haus!
Und sie gefaßt ums Mieder!
„Drück mir die nassen Locken aus,
Und küß und hab mich wieder!"

So let's away to my love's house!
And clasp her round the waist!
'Wring out these soaking locks of mine
And kiss and take me back again!'

23 February 1888 Jägerlied / Huntsman's song [4]

Zierlich ist des Vogels Tritt im Schnee,
Wenn er wandelt auf des Berges Höh:
Zierlicher schreibt Liebchens liebe Hand,
Schreibt ein Brieflein mir in ferne Land'.

A bird steps daintily in the snow
On the mountain heights:
Daintier still is my sweetheart's hand,
When she writes to me in far-off lands.

In die Lüfte hoch ein Reiher steigt,
Dahin weder Pfeil noch Kugel fleugt:
Tausendmal so hoch und so geschwind
Die Gedanken treuer Liebe sind.
(*Distler, Robert Kahn, Marx, Robert Schumann*)

A heron soars high into the air,
Beyond the reach of shot or shaft:
The thoughts of faithful love
Are a thousand times as swift and high.

24 February 1888 Nimmersatte Liebe / Insatiable love [9]

So ist die Lieb! So ist die Lieb!
Mit Küssen nicht zu stillen:
Wer ist der Tor und will ein Sieb
Mit eitel Wasser füllen?
Und schöpfst du an die tausend Jahr,
Und küssest ewig, ewig gar,
Du tust ihr nie zu Willen.

Such is love! Such is love!
Not to be quieted with kisses:
What fool would wish to fill a sieve
With nothing else but water?
And were you to draw water for some thousand years,
And were you to kiss for ever and ever,
You'd never satisfy love.

Die Lieb, die Lieb hat alle Stund
Neu wunderlich Gelüsten;
Wir bissen uns die Lippen wund,
Da wir uns heute küßten.
Das Mädchen hielt in guter Ruh,
Wie's Lämmlein unterm Messer;
Ihr Auge bat: „Nur immer zu!
Je weher, desto besser!"

Love, love, has every hour
New and strange desires;
We bit until our lips were sore,
When we kissed today.
The girl kept nicely quiet and still,
Like a lamb beneath the knife;
Her eyes pleaded: 'Go on, go on!
The more it hurts the better!'

So ist die Lieb! und war auch so,
Wie lang es Liebe gibt,
Und anders war Herr Salomo,
Der Weise, nicht verliebt.
(*Distler*)

Such is love, and has been so
As long as love's existed,
And wise old Solomon himself
Was no differently in love.

25 February 1888 Auftrag / A commission [50]

In poetischer Epistel
Ruft ein desperater Wicht:
Lieber Vetter! Vetter Christel!
Warum schreibt Er aber nicht?

A desperate fellow cries for help
In this poetic letter:
My dear cousin, cousin Christel!
Why do you not write?

Weiß Er doch, es lassen Herzen,
Die die Liebe angeweht,
Ganz und gar nicht mit sich scherzen,
Und nun vollends ein Poet!

You know that people
Smitten with love
Cannot be trifled with,
Especially a poet!

Denn ich bin von dem Gelichter,
Dem der Kopf beständig voll;
Bin ich auch nur halb ein Dichter,
Bin ich doch zur Hälfte toll.

For I am one of those creatures
Whose head is always full;
And though I'm only half a poet,
I am half-demented.

Amor hat Ihn mir verpflichtet,
Seinen Lohn weiß Er voraus.
Und der Mund, der Ihm berichtet,
Geht dabei auch leer nicht aus.

Cupid has pledged you to me,
You know what your reward will be.
And the mouth that tells you all
Shall not go away empty.

Pass Er denn zur guten Stunde,
Wenn Sein Schatz durchs Lädchen schaut,
Lock ihr jedes Wort vom Munde,
Das mein Schätzchen ihr vertraut.

So wait for the right moment
When your love looks from her window,
Go and find out every word
My sweetheart's said to her.

Schreib Er mir dann von dem Mädchen
Ein halb Dutzend Bogen voll
Und daneben ein Traktätchen,
Wie ich mich verhalten soll!

Write me a letter six pages long
All about the girl,
And enclose a treatise of advice
On how I should respond!

25 February 1888 Zur Warnung / By way of warning [49]

Einmal nach einer lustigen Nacht
War ich am Morgen seltsam aufgewacht:
Durst, Wasserscheu, ungleich Geblüt,
Dabei gerührt und weichlich im Gemüt,
Beinah poetisch, ja, ich bat die Muse um ein
    Lied.

Once, after a convivial night,
I woke in the morning, feeling odd:
Thirst – but not for water – unsteady pulse,
Emotional and sentimental,
Almost poetic, yes, I asked my Muse for a
    song.

Sie, mit verstelltem Pathos, spottet' mein,
Gab mir den schnöden Bafel ein:

With feigned pathos she mocked me,
Served up this vile doggerel:

„Es schlagt eine Nachtigall	'Nightingale doth call
Am Wasserfall;	By waterfall;
Und ein Vogel ebenfalls,	Another bird does the same –
Der schreibt sich Wendehals,*	Wryneck is his name,
Johann Jakob Wendehals;	Johann Jakob Wryneck;
Der tut tanzen	Who doth dance
Bei den Pflanzen	By the plants
Obbemeld'ten Wasserfalls –"	Of said waterfall –'

So ging es fort; mir wurde immer bänger.	And so it went on; I grew ever uneasier.
Jetzt sprang ich auf: zum Wein! Der war	Now I leapt up: Wine! That was my
denn auch mein Retter.	salvation.
– Merkts euch, ihr tränenreichen Sänger,	– Mark well, you weepy bards,
Im Katzenjammer ruft man keine Götter!	Call not on the gods, when you're hung-over!

29 February 1888 Lied vom Winde / Song of the wind [38]
FROM *Maler Nolten*

Sausewind, Brausewind,	Storming wind, roaring wind,
Dort und hier!	Now here, now there!
Deine Heimat sage mir!	Tell me where your homeland is!
„Kindlein, wir fahren	'Child, we've travelled
Seit viel vielen Jahren	For many many years
Durch die weit weite Welt,	Through the wide wide world,
Und möchtens erfragen,	We too want to know,
Die Antwort erjagen	Seek out the answer
Bei den Bergen, den Meeren,	From the mountains, the seas,
Bei des Himmels klingenden Heeren:	The resounding hosts of heaven:
Die wissen es nie.	They never know.
Bist du klüger als sie,	If you're smarter than they,
Magst du es sagen.	You can tell us.
– Fort, wohlauf!	– Off, away!
Halt uns nicht auf!	Don't delay us!
Kommen andre nach, unsre Brüder,	Others follow, our brothers,
Da frag wieder!"	Ask them!'
Halt an! Gemach,	Stop! Stay
Eine kleine Frist!	A little while!
Sagt, wo der Liebe Heimat ist,	Say where love's home is,
Ihr Anfang, ihr Ende?	Where does it begin and end?
„Wers nennen könnte!	'Who could say!
Schelmisches Kind,	Impish child,
Lieb ist wie Wind,	Love's like the wind,
Rasch und lebendig,	Swift and brisk,

* Possibly a veiled reference to the poet Reinick (Wendehals = wryneck)

Ruhet nie,	Never resting,
Ewig ist sie,	Everlasting,
Aber nicht immer beständig.	But not always constant.
– Fort, wohlauf!	– Off, away!
Halt uns nicht auf!	Don't delay us!
Fort über Stoppel und Wälder und Wiesen!	Away over stubble and woods and fields!
Wenn ich dein Schätzchen seh,	If I see your sweetheart,
Will ich es grüßen.	I'll blow her a kiss.
Kindlein, ade!"	Child, farewell!'
(*Distler*)	

1 March 1888 Bei einer Trauung / At a wedding [51]

Vor lauter hochadligen Zeugen	Before exclusively highborn witnesses,
Kopuliert man ihrer zwei;	Two exclusive people are being wed;
Die Orgel hängt voll Geigen,	The organ pours forth joyful music,
Der Himmel nicht, mein Treu!	But there'll be no joy in heaven, I vow!
Seht doch! *sie* weint ja greulich,	Just look, *she's* crying her eyes out,
Er macht ein Gesicht abscheulich!	*He's* making a dreadful face!
Denn leider freilich, freilich,	For I'm very very sorry to say,
Keine Lieb ist nicht dabei.	That love is wholly absent.

6 March 1888 Der Genesene an die Hoffnung / He who has recovered addresses hope [1]

Tödlich graute mir der Morgen:	Day dawned deathly grey:
Doch schon lag mein Haupt, wie süß!	Yet my head lay, how sweetly!
Hoffnung, dir im Schoß verborgen,	O Hope, hidden in your lap,
Bis der Sieg gewonnen hieß.	Till victory was reckoned won.
Opfer bracht ich allen Göttern,	I had made sacrifices to all the gods,
Doch vergessen warest du;	But you I had forgotten;
Seitwärts von den ewgen Rettern	Aside from the eternal saviours
Sahest du dem Feste zu.	You gazed on at the feast.
O vergib, du Vielgetreue!	Oh forgive, most true one!
Tritt aus deinem Dämmerlicht,	Step forth from your twilight
Daß ich dir ins ewig neue,	That I, just *once*, might gaze
Mondenhelle Angesicht	From my very heart
Einmal schaue, recht von Herzen,	At your eternally new and moonbright face,
Wie ein Kind und sonder Harm;	Like a child and without sorrow;
Ach, nur *einmal* ohne Schmerzen	Ah, just *once*, without pain,
Schließe mich in deinen Arm!	Enfold me in your arms!

3 March 1888 Zitronenfalter im April / Brimstone butterfly in April [18]

Grausame Frühlingssonne,	Merciless spring sun,
Du weckst mich vor der Zeit,	You wake me before my time,
Dem nur im Maienwonne	For only in blissful May
Die zarte Kost gedeiht!	Can my delicate food grow!

Ist nicht ein liebes Mädchen hier,	If there's no dear girl here
Das auf der Rosenlippe mir	To offer me a drop of honey
Ein Tröpfchen Honig beut,	From her rosy lips,
So muß ich jämmerlich vergehn	Then I must perish miserably
Und wird der Mai mich nimmer sehn	And May shall never see me
In meinem gelben Kleid.	In my yellow dress.
(*Felix Weingartner*)	

7 March 1888 Der Gärtner / The gardener [17]

Auf ihrem Leibrößlein,	On her favourite mount,
So weiß wie der Schnee,	As white as snow,
Die schönste Prinzessin	The loveliest princess
Reit't durch die Allee.	Rides down the avenue.
Der Weg, den das Rößlein	On the path her horse
Hintanzet so hold,	Prances so sweetly along,
Der Sand, den ich streute,	The sand I scattered
Er blinket wie Gold.	Glitters like gold.
Du rosenfarbs Hütlein,	You rose-coloured bonnet
Wohl auf und wohl ab,	Bobbing up and down,
O wirf eine Feder	O throw me a feather
Verstohlen herab!	Discreetly down!
Und willst du dagegen	And if you in exchange
Eine Blüte von mir,	Want a flower from me,
Nimm tausend für *eine*,	Take a thousand for *one*,
Nimm alle dafür!	Take all in return!
(*Distler, Robert Kahn, Robert Schumann*)	

7 March 1888 Elfenlied / Elf-song [16]
FROM *Maler Nolten*

Bei Nacht im Dorf der Wächter rief:	The village watch cried out at night:
„Elfe!"*	'Eleven!'
Ein ganz kleines Elfchen im Walde schlief –	An elfin elf was asleep in the wood –
Wohl um die Elfe –	Just at eleven –
Und meint, es rief ihm aus dem Tal	And thinks the nightingale was calling
Bei seinem Namen die Nachtigall,	Him by name from the valley,
Oder Silpelit† hätt ihm gerufen.	Or Silpelit had sent for him.
Reibt sich der Elf die Augen aus,	The elf rubs his eyes,
Begibt sich vor sein Schneckenhaus,	Steps from his snail-shell home,
Und ist als wie ein trunken Mann,	Looking like a drunken man,
Sein Schläflein war nicht voll getan,	Not having slept his fill,
Und humpelt also tippe tapp	And hobbles down, tippety tap,

* Elfe = elf and eleven
† A lady elf in Mörike's novel *Maler Nolten*

Durchs Haselholz ins Tal hinab,	Through the hazels to the valley,
Schlupft an der Mauer hin so dicht,	Slips right up against the wall,
Da sitzt der Glühwurm, Licht an Licht.	Where the glow-worm sits, shining bright.
„Was sind das helle Fensterlein?	'What bright windows are these?
Da drin wird eine Hochzeit sein:	There must be a wedding inside:
Die Kleinen sitzen beim Mahle	The little folk are sitting at the feast
Und treibens in dem Saale;	And skipping round the ballroom;
Da guck ich wohl ein wenig 'nein!"	I'll take a little peek inside!'
– Pfui, stößt den Kopf an harten Stein!	Shame! he hits his head on hard stone!
Elfe, gelt, du hast genug?	Elf, don't you think you've had enough?
Gukuk! Gukuk!	Cuckoo! Cuckoo!

8 March 1888 Abschied / Goodbye [53]

Unangeklopft ein Herr tritt abends bei mir ein:	Without knocking a man one evening enters my room:
„Ich habe die Ehr, Ihr Rezensent zu sein."	'I have the honour, sir, to be your critic.'
Sofort nimmt er das Licht in die Hand,	He instantly takes my lamp in his hand,
Besieht lang meinen Schatten an der Wand,	Inspects at length my shadow on the wall,
Rückt nah und fern: „Nun, lieber junger Mann,	Moves back and forth: 'Now, young man,
Sehn Sie doch gefälligst mal Ihre Nas so von der Seite an!	Be so good as to view your nose from the side!
Sie geben zu, daß das ein Auswuchs is." –	You'll admit that it's a monstrosity.' –
– Das? Alle Wetter – gewiß!	– What? Good god – you're right!
Ei Hasen! ich dachte nicht,	Bless my soul! I never thought,
All mein Lebtage nicht,	In all my life,
Daß ich so eine Weltsnase führt im Gesicht!!	I had a nose of such cosmic size!!

Der Mann sprach noch Verschiednes hin und her,	The man said various other things,
Ich weiß, auf meine Ehre, nicht mehr;	What – I truly no longer recall;
Meinte vielleicht, ich sollt ihm beichten.	Maybe he thought I should confess to him.
Zuletzt stand er auf; ich tat ihm leuchten.	At last he got up; I lit his way.
Wie wir nun an der Treppe sind,	As we stood at the top of the stairs,
Da geb ich ihm, ganz froh gesinnt,	I give him, in the best of spirits,
Einen kleinen Tritt	A wee little kick
Nur so von hinten aufs Gesäße mit –	On his derrière –
Alle Hagel! ward das ein Gerumpel,	Goodness me! What a rumbling,
Ein Gepurzel, ein Gehumpel!	A tumbling, a stumbling!
Dergleichen hab ich nie gesehn,	I've never before seen the like,
All mein Lebtage nicht gesehn,	Never in all my born days have I seen
Einen Menschen so rasch die Trepp hinabgehn!	A man go downstairs so fast!

10 March 1888 Denk es, o Seele! / O soul, remember! [39]
FROM *Mozart auf der Reise nach Prag*

Ein Tännlein grünet wo,	A young fir is growing, where,
Wer weiß, im Walde,	Who knows, in the wood?

Ein Rosenstrauch, wer sagt,	A rosebush, who can say,
In welchem Garten?	In what garden?
Sie sind erlesen schon,	Already they are pre-ordained,
Denk es, o Seele,	O soul, remember,
Auf deinem Grab zu wurzeln	To root and grow
Und zu wachsen.	On your grave.
Zwei schwarze Rößlein weiden	Two black colts are grazing
Auf der Wiese,	On the field,
Sie kehren heim zur Stadt	Homewards at a merry pace
In muntern Sprüngen.	They return to the town.
Sie werden schrittweis gehn	At a walking pace they'll go
Mit deiner Leiche;	With your corpse;
Vielleicht, vielleicht noch eh	Perhaps, perhaps even before
An ihren Hufen	Their hooves
Das Eisen los wird,	Will lose the shoes
Das ich blitzen sehe.	That I see flashing.
(*Distler, Franz, Pfitzner*)	

11–25 March 1888 Auf einer Wanderung / On a walk [15]

In ein freundliches Städtchen tret ich ein,	I arrive in a friendly little town,
In den Straßen liegt roter Abendschein.	The streets glow in red evening light.
Aus einem offnen Fenster eben,	From an open window,
Über den reichsten Blumenflor	Across the richest array of flowers
Hinweg, hört man Goldglockentöne	And beyond, golden bell-chimes come
schweben,	floating,
Und *eine* Stimme scheint ein Nachtigallen-	And *one* voice seems a choir of nightin-
chor,	gales,
Daß die Blüten beben,	Causing blossoms to quiver,
Daß die Lüfte leben,	Bringing breezes to life,
Daß in höherem Rot die Rosen leuchten vor.	Making roses glow a brighter red.
Lang hielt ich staunend, lustbeklommen.	Long I halted marvelling, oppressed by joy.
Wie ich hinaus vors Tor gekommen,	How I came out through the gate,
Ich weiß es wahrlich selber nicht.	I cannot in truth remember.
Ach hier, wie liegt die Welt so licht!	Ah, how bright the world is here!
Der Himmel wogt in purpurnem Gewühle,	The sky billows in a crimson whirl,
Rückwärts die Stadt in goldnem Rauch;	The town lies behind in a golden haze;
Wie rauscht der Erlenbach, wie rauscht im	How the alder brook chatters, and the mill
Grund die Mühle!	below!
Ich bin wie trunken, irrgeführt –	I am as if drunk, led astray –
O Muse, du hast mein Herz berührt	O Muse, you have touched my heart
Mit einem Liebeshauch!	With a breath of love!

13 March 1888 Verborgenheit / Seclusion [12]

Laß, o Welt, o laß mich sein!	Let, O world, O let me be!
Locket nicht mit Liebesgaben,	Do not tempt with gifts of love,

Laßt dies Herz alleine haben
Seine Wonne, seine Pein!

Was ich traure, weiß ich nicht,
Es ist unbekanntes Wehe;
Immerdar durch Tränen sehe
Ich der Sonne liebes Licht.

Oft bin ich mir kaum bewußt,
Und die helle Freude zücket
Durch die Schwere, so mich drücket
Wonniglich in meiner Brust.

Laß, o Welt, o laß mich sein!
Locket nicht mit Liebesgaben,
Laßt dies Herz alleine haben
Seine Wonne, seine Pein!
(*Burkhard, Distler, Franz, Robert Fuchs*)

Let this heart keep to itself
Its rapture, its pain!

I do not know why I grieve,
It is unknown sorrow;
Always through a veil of tears
I see the sun's beloved light.

Often, I am lost in thought,
And bright joy flashes
Through the oppressive gloom,
Bringing rapture to my breast.

Let, O world, O let me be!
Do not tempt with gifts of love,
Let this heart keep to itself
Its rapture, its pain!

14 March 1888 Lied eines Verliebten / A lover's song [43]

In aller Früh, ach, lang vor Tag,
Weckt mich mein Herz, an dich zu denken,
Da doch gesunde Jugend schlafen mag.

Hell ist mein Aug um Mitternacht,
Heller als frühe Morgenglocken:
Wann hättst du je am Tage mein gedacht?

Wär ich ein Fischer, stünd ich auf,
Trüge mein Netz hinab zum Flusse,
Trüg herzlich froh die Fische zum Verkauf.

In der Mühle, bei Licht, der Müllerknecht
Tummelt sich, alle Gänge klappern;
So rüstig Treiben wär mir eben recht!

Weh, aber ich! o armer Tropf!
Muß auf dem Lager mich müßig grämen,
Ein ungebärdig Mutterkind im Kopf.
(*Distler*)

At first dawn, ah! long before day,
My heart wakes me to think of you,
When healthy lads would love to sleep.

My eyes are bright at midnight,
Brighter than early morning bells:
Did you ever think of me by day?

If I were a fisherman, I'd get up,
Carry my net down to the river,
Gladly carry the fish to market.

The miller's lad, at first light,
Is hard at work, the machinery clatters;
Such hearty work would suit me well!

But I, alas, poor wretch,
Must lie idly grieving on my bed,
Obsessed with that unruly girl!

17 March 1888 Selbstgeständnis / Self-confession [52]

Ich bin meiner Mutter einzig Kind,
Und weil die andern ausblieben sind
– Was weiß ich wieviel, die sechs oder sieben, –
Ist eben alles an mir hängen blieben;
Ich hab müssen die Liebe, die Treue, die Güte
Für ein ganz halb Dutzend allein aufessen,
Ich wills mein Lebtag nicht vergessen.

I am my mother's only child,
And since the others failed to appear
– Who knows how many, six or seven, –
Everything had to centre on me;
I've had to devour all by myself
The love, loyalty and kindness for a full half-dozen,
I'll never forget it, as long as I live.

Es hätte mir aber noch wohl mögen frommen,
Hätt ich nur auch Schläg für Sechse bekom-
men!

I dare say it would have done me no harm,
If I'd been whipped for six as well!

20 March 1888 Erstes Liebeslied eines Mädchens / A girl's first love song [42]

Was im Netze? Schau einmal!
Aber ich bin bange;
Greif ich einen süßen Aal?
Greif ich eine Schlange?

What's in the net? Take a look!
But I'm afraid;
Is a sweet eel?
Is it a snake?

Lieb ist blinde
Fischerin;
Sagt dem Kinde,
Wo greifts hin?

Love's a blind
Fisher-girl;
Tell the child
What she's caught.

Schon schnellt mirs in Händen!
Ach Jammer! o Lust!
Mit Schmiegen und Wenden
Mir schlüpfts an die Brust.

It's rearing up in my hands!
Ah misery, oh joy!
Nestling and wriggling
It slithers to my bosom.

Es beißt sich, o Wunder!
Mir keck durch die Haut,
Schießt's Herze hinunter!
O Liebe, mir graut!

Incredible! It bites its way
Boldly through my skin,
Plunges down to my heart!
O Love, I shudder!

Was tun, was beginnen?
Das schaurige Ding,
Es schnalzet da drinnen,
Es legt sich im Ring.

What can I do?
The ghastly thing's
Snapping in there,
Coiling into a ring.

Gift muß ich haben!
Hier schleicht es herum,
Tut wonniglich graben
Und bringt mich noch um.
(*Distler*)

I must have poison!
It's creeping about,
It burrows deliciously
And will be the death of me yet.

21 March 1888 Fußreise / A journey on foot [10]

Am frischgeschnittnen Wanderstab,
Wenn ich in der Frühe
So durch Wälder ziehe,
Hügel auf und ab:
Dann, wie's Vög'lein im Laube
Singet und sich rührt,
Oder wie die goldne Traube
Wonnegeister spürt
In der ersten Morgensonne:
So fühlt auch mein alter, lieber
Adam Herbst- und Frühlingsfieber,

When, with a freshly cut stick,
I set off early like this
Through the woods
And over the hills:
Then, as the bird in the branches
Sings and stirs,
Or as the golden cluster of grapes
Feels the rapture
Of the early morning sun:
So too my dear old Adam
Feels autumn and spring fever,

Gottbeherzte,	The God-inspired,
Nie verscherzte	Never forfeited
Erstlings-Paradieseswonne.	Primal bliss of Paradise.
Also bist du nicht so schlimm, o alter	So you are not as bad, old
Adam, wie die strengen Lehrer sagen;	Adam, as strict teachers say;
Liebst und lobst du immer doch,	You still love and extol,
Singst und preisest immer noch,	Still sing and praise,
Wie an ewig neuen Schöpfungstagen,	As if Creation were forever new,
Deinen lieben Schöpfer und Erhalter.	Your dear Maker and Preserver.
Möcht es dieser geben,	If only He would grant it,
Und mein ganzes Leben	My whole life
Wär im leichten Wanderschweiße	Would be, gently perspiring,
Eine solche Morgenreise!	Just such a morning journey!

21 March 1888 Rat einer Alten / Old woman's advice [41]

Bin jung gewesen,	I was young once,
Kann auch mitreden,	So I can talk,
Und alt geworden,	And now I've grown old,
Drum gilt mein Wort.	My word carries weight.
Schön reife Beeren	Lovely ripe berries
Am Bäumchen hangen:	Hang from the tree:
Nachbar, da hilft kein	Neighbour, it's no use
Zaun um den Garten;	Fencing the garden;
Lustige Vögel	Cheerful birds
Wissen den Weg.	Know the way in.
Aber, mein Dirnchen,	But young lady –
Du laß dir raten:	A piece of advice:
Halte dein Schätzchen	Make sure your sweetheart
Wohl in der Liebe,	Loves
Wohl im Respekt!	And respects you!
Mit den zwei Fädlein	With those two threads
In eins gedrehet,	Twined into one,
Ziehst du am kleinen	You'll lead him
Finger ihn nach.	By the little finger.
Aufrichtig Herze,	Be open of heart,
Doch schweigen können,	Yet know how to keep quiet,
Früh mit der Sonne	Be up with the sun
Mutig zur Arbeit,	And go to work with a will,
Gesunde Glieder,	A healthy body
Saubere Linnen,	And clean linen –
Das machet Mädchen	These things become a girl
Und Weibchen wert.	And a wife.

Bin jung gewesen,	I was young once,
Kann auch mitreden,	So I can talk,
Und alt geworden,	And now I've grown old,
Drum gilt mein Wort.	My word carries weight.

22 March 1888 Begegnung / Encounter [8]

Was doch heut nacht ein Sturm gewesen,	What a storm there was last night,
Bis erst der Morgen sich geregt!	It raged until this morning dawned!
Wie hat der ungebetne Besen	How that uninvited broom
Kamin und Gassen ausgefegt!	Swept the streets and chimneys clean!
Da kommt ein Mädchen schon die Straßen,	Here comes a girl along the street,
Das halb verschüchtert um sich sieht;	Glancing half bashfully about her;
Wie Rosen, die der Wind zerblasen,	Like roses the wind has scattered,
So unstet ihr Gesichtchen glüht.	Her pretty face keep changing colour.
Ein schöner Bursch tritt ihr entgegen,	A handsome lad steps up to meet her,
Er will ihr voll Entzücken nahn:	Approaches her full of bliss,
Wie sehn sich freudig und verlegen	How joyfully and awkwardly
Die ungewohnten Schelme an!	Those novice rascals exchange looks!
Er scheint zu fragen, ob das Liebchen	He seems to ask if his sweetheart
Die Zöpfe schon zurecht gemacht,	Has tidied up her plaited locks,
Die heute nacht im offnen Stübchen	That last night a storm dishevelled
Ein Sturm in Unordnung gebracht.	In her gaping wide room.
Der Bursche träumt noch von den Küssen,	The lad's still dreaming of the kisses
Die ihm das süße Kind getauscht,	The sweet child exchanged with him,
Er steht, von Anmut hingerissen,	He stands enraptured by her charm,
Derweil sie um die Ecke rauscht.	As she whisks round the corner.
(*Reger*)	

24 March 1888 Das verlassene Mägdlein / The forsaken servant-girl [7]
FROM *Maler Nolten*

Früh, wann die Hähne krähn,	Early, when the cocks crow,
Eh die Sternlein schwinden,	Before the tiny stars recede,
Muß ich am Herde stehn,	I must be at the hearth,
Muß Feuer zünden.	I must light the fire.
Schön ist der Flammen Schein,	The flames are beautiful,
Es springen die Funken;	The sparks fly;
Ich schaue so darein,	I gaze at them,
In Leid versunken.	Sunk in sorrow.
Plötzlich, da kommt es mir,	Suddenly I realize,
Treuloser Knabe,	Faithless boy,
Daß ich die Nacht von dir	That in the night
Geträumet habe.	I dreamt of you.

Träne auf Träne dann	Tear after tear
Stürzet hernieder;	Then tumbles down;
So kommt der Tag heran –	So the day dawns –
O ging er wieder!	O would it were gone again!
(*Distler, Franz, Lachner, Pfitzner, Robert Schumann*)	

27 March 1888 Storchenbotschaft / Stork-tidings [48]

Des Schäfers sein Haus und das steht auf zwei Rad,	The shepherd's house stands on two wheels,
Steht hoch auf der Heiden, so frühe wie spat;	High on the moor, morning and night,
Und wenn nur ein mancher so'n Nachtquartier hätt!	A lodging most would be glad of!
Ein Schäfer tauscht nicht mit dem König sein Bett.	No shepherd would change his bed with a king.
Und käm ihm zu Nacht auch was Seltsames vor,	And should by night any strange thing occur,
Er betet sein Sprüchel und legt sich aufs Ohr;	He prays a brief prayer and lies down to sleep;
Ein Geistlein, ein Hexlein, so lustige Wicht,	A ghost, a witch, some airy creature –
Sie klopfen ihm wohl, doch er antwortet nicht.	They might come knocking, but he'll not answer.
Einmal doch, da ward es ihm wirklich zu bunt:	But one night it really became too much:
Es knopert am Laden, es winselt der Hund;	A tap on the shutters, a whine from the dog;
Nun ziehet mein Schäfer den Riegel – ei schau!	So my shepherd unbolts – lo and behold!
Da stehen zwei Störche, der Mann und die Frau.	Two storks stand there, a husband and wife.
Das Pärchen, es machet ein schön Kompliment,	The couple, they make a beautiful bow,
Es möchte gern reden, ach, wenn es nur könnt!	They'd like to speak, if only they could!
Was will mir das Ziefer! – ist so was erhört?	What can these feathered friends want of me! Whoever heard the like?
Doch ist mir wohl fröhliche Botschaft beschert.	They must have joyful tidings for me.
Ihr seid wohl dahinten zu Hause am Rhein?	You live over there, down by the Rhine?
Ihr habt wohl mein Mädel gebissen ins Bein?	I guess you've paid my girl a visit?
Nun weinet das Kind und die Mutter noch mehr,	The child's now crying, the mother even louder,
Sie wünschet den Herzallerliebsten sich her?	She wants her sweetheart by her side?
Und wünschet daneben die Taufe bestellt:	And wants the christening feast arranged:
Ein Lämmlein, ein Würstlein, ein Beutelein Geld?	A lambkin, a sausage, a purse of money?
So sagt nur, ich käm in zwei Tag' oder drei,	Well, tell her I'm coming in two days or three,
Und grüßt mir mein Bübel und rührt ihm den Brei!	Say hello to my boy, give his pap a stir!
Doch halt! warum stellt ihr zu zweien euch ein?	But wait! Why have two of you come?

Es werden doch, hoff ich, nicht Zwillinge
    sein? –
	It can't, I hope, be a case of
	    twins? –

Da klappern die Störche im lustigsten Ton,	At that the storks clatter most merrily,
Sie nicken und knixen und fliegen davon.	They nod and curtsey and fly away.
(*Distler*)	

29 March 1888 Frage und Antwort / Question and answer [35]

Fragst du mich, woher die bange	You ask me where it came from,
Liebe mir zum Herzen kam,	This timid love that entered my heart,
Und warum ich ihr nicht lange	And why I did not long ago
Schon den bittern Stachel nahm?	Draw its bitter sting?
Sprich, warum mit Geisterschnelle	Tell me, why with ghostly speed
Wohl der Wind die Flügel rührt,	The wind whirrs its wings,
Und woher die süße Quelle	And from where the sweet spring
Die verborgnen Wasser führt?	Draws its hidden waters?
Banne du auf seiner Fährte	You might as well try to halt
Mir den Wind in vollem Lauf!	The wind in full career!
Halte mit der Zaubergerte	Or conjure with a magic wand
Du die süßen Quellen auf!	The sweet springs to be still!
(*Distler*)	

31 March 1888 Lebe wohl / Farewell [36]

„Lebewohl!" – Du fühlest nicht,	'Farewell!' – You do not feel
Was es heißt, dies Wort der Schmerzen;	What it means, this word of pain;
Mit getrostem Angesicht	With hopeful countenance
Sagtest du's und leichtem Herzen.	You said it, and a light heart.
Lebe wohl! – Ach, tausendmal	Farewell! – Ah, a thousand times
Hab ich mir es vorgesprochen,	I have uttered it aloud,
Und in nimmersatter Qual	And with never-ending anguish
Mir das Herz damit gebrochen.	Have broken my heart in doing so.
(*Distler*)	

1 April 1888 Heimweh / Longing for home [37]

Anders wird die Welt mit jedem Schritt,	The world changes with every step
Den ich weiter von der Liebsten mache;	That takes me further from my love;
Mein Herz, das will nicht weiter mit.	My heart's reluctant to follow me.
Hier scheint die Sonne kalt ins Land,	Here the sun shines coldly on the land,
Hier deucht mir alles unbekannt,	Here all seems unfamiliar,
Sogar die Blumen am Bache!	Even the flowers by the brook!
Hat jede Sache	Each thing
So fremd eine Miene, so falsch ein Gesicht.	Has so foreign a look, so false a face.
Das Bächlein murmelt wohl und spricht:	The stream, it's true, murmurs and says:
„Armer Knabe, komm bei mir vorüber,	'Poor boy, come to me,

Siehst auch hier Vergißmeinnicht!"
– Ja, die sind schön an jedem Ort,
Aber nicht wie dort.
Fort, nur fort!
Die Augen gehn mir über!

You'll see forget-me-nots here too!'
– Yes, they are lovely everywhere,
But not so lovely as those I left.
Onwards, onwards!
My eyes fill with tears!

12 April 1888 Seufzer / Sighs [22]
FROM *Maler Nolten*

Dein Liebesfeuer,
Ach Herr! wie teuer
Wollt ich es hegen,
Wollt ich es pflegen!
Habs nicht geheget
Und nicht gepfleget,
Bin tot im Herzen –
O Höllenschmerzen!

The fire of your love,
O Lord!
How I longed to tend it,
How I longed to cherish it,
Have failed to tend it
And failed to cherish it,
Am dead at heart –
O hellish pain!

14 April 1888 Auf ein altes Bild / On an old painting [23]

In grüner Landschaft Sommerflor,
Bei kühlem Wasser, Schilf und Rohr,
Schau, wie das Knäblein Sündelos
Frei spielet auf der Jungfrau Schoß!
Und dort im Walde wonnesam,
Ach, grünet schon des Kreuzes Stamm!

In the summer haze of a green landscape,
By cool water, rushes and reeds,
See how the Child, born without sin,
Plays freely on the Virgin's lap!
And ah! growing blissfully there in the wood,
Already the tree of the cross is turning green!

15 April 1888 An eine Äolsharfe / To an Aeolian harp [11]

Angelehnt an die Efeuwand
Dieser alten Terrasse,
Du, einer luftgebornen Muse
Geheimnisvolles Saitenspiel,
Fang an,
Fange wieder an
Deine melodische Klage!

Leaning against the ivy-clad wall
Of this old terrace,
O mysterious lyre
Of a zephyr-born Muse,
Begin,
Begin again
Your melodious lament!

Ihr kommet, Winde, fern herüber
Ach! von des Knaben,*
Der mir so lieb war,
Frisch grünendem Hügel.
Und Frühlingsblüten unterweges streifend,
Übersättigt mit Wohlgerüchen,
Wie süß bedrängt ihr dies Herz!
Und säuselt her in die Saiten,
Angezogen von wohllautender Wehmut,

Winds, you come from afar,
Ah! from the fresh green mound
Of the boy
Who was so dear to me.
And brushing spring flowers along the way,
Saturated with fragrance,
How sweetly you afflict this heart!
And you murmur into these strings,
Drawn by their sweet-sounding sorrow,

*Mörike's younger brother August who died in 1824, aged seventeen.

Wachsend im Zug meiner Sehnsucht,
Und hinsterbend wieder.

Aber auf einmal,
Wie der Wind heftiger herstößt,
Ein holder Schrei der Harfe
Wiederholt, mir zu süßem Erschrecken,
Meiner Seele plötzliche Regung;
Und hier – die volle Rose streut, geschüttelt,
All ihre Blätter vor meine Füße!
(*Brahms*)

Waxing with my heart's desire,
Then dying away once more.

But all at once,
As the wind gusts more strongly,
The harp's gentle cry
Echoes, to my sweet alarm,
The sudden commotion of my soul;
And here – the full-blown rose, shaken,
Strews all its petals at my feet!

20 April 1888 Um Mitternacht / At midnight [19]

Gelassen stieg die Nacht ans Land,
Lehnt träumend an der Berge Wand,
Ihr Auge sieht die goldne Waage nun
Der Zeit in gleichen Schalen stille ruhn;
    Und kecker rauschen die Quellen hervor,
    Sie singen der Mutter, der Nacht, ins Ohr
    Vom Tage,
    Vom heute gewesenen Tage.

Das uralt alte Schlummerlied,
Sie achtets nicht, sie ist es müd;
Ihr klingt des Himmels Bläue süßer noch,
Der flüchtgen Stunden gleichgeschwungnes
    Joch.
    Doch immer behalten die Quellen das Wort,
    Es singen die Wasser im Schlafe noch fort
    Vom Tage,
    Vom heute gewesenen Tage.
(*Bruch, Distler, Erbse, Franz*)

Night has serenely stepped ashore,
Leans dreaming against the mountain wall,
Watches now the golden scales of time
Quietly at rest in equipoise;
    And the springs babble more boldly,
    They sing in the ear of their mother, the night,
    Of the day,
    Of the day that has been today.

That old, that age-old lullaby,
She disregards, she is tired of it;
The blue of the sky sounds sweeter to her,
The evenly curved yoke of the fleeting
    hours.
    But still the streams murmur on,
    They babble in sleep as their waters run
    Of the day,
    Of the day that has been today.

21 April 1888 Auf eine Christblume II / On a Christmas rose II [21]

Im Winterboden schläft, ein Blumenkeim,
Der Schmetterling, der einst um Busch und
    Hügel
In Frühlingsnächten wiegt den samtnen Flügel;
Nie soll er kosten deinen Honigseim.

Wer aber weiß, ob nicht sein zarter Geist,
Wenn jede Zier des Sommers hingesunken,
Dereinst, von deinem leisen Dufte trunken,
Mir unsichtbar, dich blühende umkreist?

There sleeps within the wintry ground, itself
    a flower-seed,
The butterfly that one day over hill and dale
Will flutter its velvet wings in spring nights.
Never shall it taste your liquid honey.

But who knows if perhaps its gentle ghost,
When summer's loveliness has faded,
Might some day, dizzy with your faint fragrance,
Unseen by me, circle you as you flower?

28 April 1888 Peregrina I / Peregrina I [33]
FROM *Maler Nolten*

Der Spiegel dieser treuen, braunen Augen
Ist wie von innerm Gold ein Widerschein;
Tief aus dem Busen scheint ers anzusaugen,
Dort mag solch Gold in heilgem Gram ge-
deihn.
In diese Nacht des Blickes mich zu tauchen,
Unwissend Kind, du selber lädst mich ein –
Willst, ich soll kecklich mich und dich
entzünden,
Reichst lächelnd mir den Tod im Kelch der
Sünden!

The surface of these faithful brown eyes
Seems to mirror the gleam of inner gold;
Seems to draw it from deep within your
breast –
There, in hallowed grief such gold may
thrive.
To plunge into this dark night of your gaze,
Innocent child, you yourself invite me –
Wish me boldly to consume us both in fire,
Smile as you offer me death in the chalice of
sin!

30 April 1888 Peregrina II / Peregrina II [34]
FROM *Maler Nolten*

Warum, Geliebte, denk ich dein
Auf einmal nun mit tausend Tränen,
Und kann gar nicht zufrieden sein,
Und will die Brust in alle Weite dehnen?

Ach, gestern in den hellen Kindersaal,
Beim Flimmer zierlich aufgesteckter Kerzen,
Wo ich mein selbst vergaß in Lärm und
Scherzen,
Tratst du, o Bildnis mitleid-schöner Qual;
Es war dein Geist, er setzte sich ans Mahl,
Fremd saßen wir mit stumm verhaltnen
Schmerzen;
Zuletzt brach ich in lautes Schluchzen aus,
Und Hand in Hand verließen wir das Haus.

Why, beloved, do I now think of you
Suddenly and with a thousand tears,
And cannot be satisfied at all,
And long to extend my heart into infinity?

Ah, you came yesterday to the bright nursery,
In the gleam of decorative candles,
As I forgot myself in noise and mirth,
You came, agony's image, lovely in compas-
sion;
It was your ghost, it joined us at the feast,
Strangers we sat, our sorrows mutely
hidden;
At last I broke out into loud sobs,
And hand in hand we left the house.

3 May 1888 Agnes / Agnes [14]
FROM *Maler Nolten*

Rosenzeit! Wie schnell vorbei,
    Schnell vorbei
Bist du doch gegangen!
Wär mein Lieb nur blieben treu,
    Blieben treu,
Sollte mir nicht bangen.

Um die Ernte wohlgemut,
    Wohlgemut,
Schnitterinnen singen.
Aber ach! mir kranken Blut,

Time of roses! How swiftly by,
    Swiftly by
You have sped!
Had my love but stayed true,
    Stayed true,
I should feel no fear.

Joyously at harvest-time,
    Joyously,
Reaping women sing.
But ah! I'm sick,

Mir kranken Blut
Will nichts mehr gelingen.

Schleiche so durchs Wiesental,
  So durchs Tal,
Als im Traum verloren,
Nach dem Berg, da tausendmal,
  Tausendmal
Er mir Treu geschworen.

Oben auf des Hügels Rand,
  Abgewandt,
Wein ich bei der Linde;
An dem Hut mein Rosenband,
  Von seiner Hand,
Spielet in dem Winde.
(*Brahms, Distler, Franz, Hiller, Schoeck*)

Sick at heart
I fail at everything.

So I steal through the meadow vale,
  Meadow vale,
As if lost in dreams,
Up to the hill where a thousand times,
  Thousand times,
He promised to be true.

Up there on the hillside,
  Turning away,
I weep by the lime-tree;
On my hat the rosy ribbon,
  A gift from him,
Flutters in the wind.

5 May 1888 In der Frühe / Early morning [24]

Kein Schlaf noch kühlt das Auge mir,
Dort gehet schon der Tag herfür
An meinem Kammerfenster.
Es wühlet mein verstörter Sinn
Noch zwischen Zweifeln her und hin
Und schaffet Nachtgespenster.
– Ängste,* quäle
Dich nicht länger, meine Seele!
Freu dich! schon sind da und dorten
Morgenglocken wach geworden.
(*Reger*)

Still no sleep cools my eyes,
The day's already dawning there
At my bedroom window.
My troubled mind still races on,
Torn by doubts, to and fro,
Creating night phantoms.
– Frighten, torment
Yourself no more, my soul!
Rejoice! Already here and there
Morning bells have woken.

5 May 1888 Er ists / Spring is here [6]
FROM *Maler Nolten*

Frühling läßt sein blaues Band
Wieder flattern durch die Lüfte;
Süße, wohlbekannte Düfte
Streifen ahnungsvoll das Land.
Veilchen träumen schon,
Wollen balde kommen.
– Horch, von fern ein leiser Harfenton!
Frühling, ja du bists!
Dich hab ich vernommen!
(*Distler, Franz, Lachner, Lassen, Reger,
Schoeck, Robert Schumann*)

Spring sends its blue banner
Fluttering on the breeze again;
Sweet, well-remembered scents
Drift propitiously across the land.
Violets dream already,
Will soon begin to bloom.
– Listen, the soft sound of a distant harp!
Spring, that must be you!
It's you I've heard!

---

* The first edition has 'Ängst'ge', surely a mistake; Mörike's deliberately archaic 'Ängste' should be restored.

8 May 1888 Im Frühling / In spring [13]

FROM *Maler Nolten*

Hier lieg ich auf dem Frühlingshügel:
Die Wolke wird mein Flügel,
Ein Vogel fliegt mir voraus.
Ach, sag mir, alleinzige Liebe,
Wo du bleibst, daß ich bei dir bliebe!
Doch du und die Lüfte, ihr habt kein Haus.

Der Sonnenblume gleich steht mein Gemüte
   offen,
Sehnend,
Sich dehnend
In Lieben und Hoffen.
Frühling, was bist du gewillt?
Wann werd ich gestillt?

Die Wolke seh ich wandeln und den Fluß,
Es dringt der Sonne goldner Kuß
Mir tief bis ins Geblüt hinein;
Die Augen, wunderbar berauschet,
Tun, als schliefen sie ein,
Nur noch das Ohr dem Ton der Biene lauschet.
Ich denke dies und denke das,
Ich sehne mich und weiß nicht recht nach was:
Halb ist es Lust, halb ist es Klage;
Mein Herz, o sage,
Was webst du für Erinnerung
In golden grüner Zweige Dämmerung?
– Alte unnennbare Tage!

Here I lie on the springtime hill:
The clouds become my wings,
A bird flies on ahead of me.
Ah tell me, one-and-only love,
Where you are, that I might be with you!
But you and the breezes, you have no home.

Like a sunflower my soul has
   opened,
Yearning,
Expanding
In love and hope.
Spring, what is it you want?
When shall I be stilled?

I see the clouds drift by, the river too,
The sun kisses its golden glow
Deep into my veins;
My eyes, wondrously enchanted,
Close, as if in sleep,
Only my ears still harken to the humming bee.
I muse on this, I muse on that,
I yearn, and yet for what I cannot say:
It is half joy, half lament;
Tell me, O heart,
What memories you weave
Into the twilit green and golden leaves?
– Past, unmentionable days!

13 May 1888 Nixe Binsefuß / The water-sprite Reedfoot [45]

Des Wassermanns sein Töchterlein
Tanzt auf dem Eis im Vollmondschein,
Sie singt und lachet sonder Scheu
Wohl an des Fischers Haus vorbei.

„Ich bin die Jungfer Binsefuß,
Und meine Fisch wohl hüten muß;
Meine Fisch, die sind im Kasten,
Sie haben kalte Fasten;
Von Böhmerglas mein Kasten ist,
Da zähl ich sie zu jeder Frist.

Gelt, Fischer-Matz? gelt, alter Tropf,
Dir will der Winter nicht in Kopf?
Komm mir mit deinen Netzen!

The water spirit's little daughter
Dances on the ice in the full moon,
Singing and laughing without fear
Past the fisherman's house.

'I am the maiden Reedfoot,
And I must look after my fish;
My fish are in this casket,
Having a cold Lent;
My casket's made of Bohemian glass,
And I count them whenever I can.

Not so, Matt? Not so, foolish old fisherman,
You cannot understand it's winter?
If you come near me with your nets,

Die will ich schön zerfetzen!	I'll tear them all to shreds!
Dein Mägdlein zwar ist fromm und gut,	But your little girl is good and devout,
Ihr Schatz ein braves Jägerblut.	And her sweetheart's an honest huntsman.
Drum häng ich ihr, zum Hochzeitsstrauß,	That's why I'll hang a wedding bouquet,
Ein schilfen Kränzlein vor das Haus,	A wreath of rushes outside her house,
Und einen Hecht, von Silber schwer,	And a pike of solid silver,
Er stammt von König Artus her,	From King Arthur's time,
Ein Zwergen-Goldschmieds-Meisterstück,	The masterwork of a dwarf goldsmith,
Wers hat, dem bringt es eitel Glück:	Which brings its owner the best of luck:
Er läßt sich schuppen Jahr für Jahr,	Each year it sheds its scales,
Da sinds fünfhundert Gröschlein bar.	Worth five hundred groschen in cash.
Ade, mein Kind! Ade für heut!	Farewell, child! Farewell for today!
Der Morgenhahn im Dorfe schreit."	The cock in the village cries morning.'

18 May 1888 Die Geister am Mummelsee* / Ghosts on Mummelsee [47]
FROM *Maler Nolten*

Vom Berge was kommt dort um Mitternacht spät	What's this winding down the mountain at midnight
Mit Fackeln so prächtig herunter?	With torches and such splendour?
Ob das wohl zum Tanze, zum Feste noch geht?	Can they be going to a ball or banquet?
Mir klingen die Lieder so munter.	Their singing sounds so joyful.
O nein!	Oh no!
So sage, was mag es wohl sein?	Then tell me what it can be?
Das, was du da siehest, ist Totengeleit,	What you see is a funeral procession,
Und was du da hörest, sind Klagen.	And what you hear are laments.
Dem König, dem Zauberer, gilt es zu Leid,	They are mourning the king, the sorcerer,
Sie bringen ihn wieder getragen.	They are bearing him back down again.
O weh!	Oh mercy!
So sind es die Geister vom See!	They must be the ghosts of the lake!
Sie schweben herunter ins Mummelseetal –	They're gliding down to the Mummel valley –
Sie haben den See schon betreten –	Already they've alighted on the lake –
Sie rühren und netzen den Fuß nicht einmal –	They neither move nor even wet their feet –
Sie schwirren in leisen Gebeten –	They whirr their wings while murmuring prayers –
O schau,	Oh look,
Am Sarge die glänzende Frau!	There by the coffin the glistening woman!
Jetzt öffnet der See das grünspiegelnde Tor;	The lake now opens its mirror-green doors;
Gib acht, nun tauchen sie nieder!	Look out, already they're diving down!
Es schwankt eine lebende Treppe hervor,	A living, wavering staircase rises,
Und – drunten schon summen die Lieder.	And down in the depths they're droning songs.
Hörst du?	Can you hear?
Sie singen ihn unten zur Ruh.	They're singing him to rest below.

* The name of a tarn in the Black Forest.

Die Wasser, wie lieblich sie brennen und
     glühn!
Sie spielen in grünendem Feuer;
Es geisten die Nebel am Ufer dahin,
Zum Meere verzieht sich der Weiher –
          Nur still!
Ob dort sich nichts rühren will?

Es zuckt in der Mitten – o Himmel! ach hilf!
Nun kommen sie wieder, sie kommen!
Es orgelt im Rohr und es klirret im Schilf;
Nur hurtig, die Flucht nur genommen!
          Davon!
Sie wittern, sie haschen mich schon!

How sweetly the waters burn and
     glow!
Their fire flickers green as they dance;
The mists are swirling around the shore,
The lake vanishes into the sea –
          Hush now!
Will nothing ever move there again?

A swirl in the middle – O heavens! ah help!
The ghosts – they're coming again!
There's a roar in the reeds and a wind in the rushes
Quick now, run, take flight!
          Away!
They've caught my scent, they're catching me!

4 October 1888 Neue Liebe / New love [30]
ORCHESTRATED 5 SEPTEMBER 1890

Kann auch ein Mensch des andern auf der
     Erde
Ganz, wie er möchte, sein?
– In langer Nacht bedacht ich mirs und
     mußte sagen, nein!

So kann ich niemands heißen auf der Erde,
Und niemand wäre mein?
– Aus Finsternissen hell in mir aufzückt ein
     Freudenschein:

Sollt ich mit Gott nicht können sein,
So wie ich möchte, mein und dein?
Was hielte mich, daß ichs nicht heute werde?

Ein süßes Schrecken geht durch mein Gebein!
Mich wundert, daß es mir ein Wunder wollte
     sein,
Gott selbst zu eigen haben auf der Erde!

Can one ever belong to another here on
     earth
Wholly, as one would wish to be?
Long I pondered this at night and had to
     answer, no!

So can I belong to no one here on earth,
And can no one be mine ?
– From dark recesses in me a bright flame of
     joy flashes:

Could I not be with God,
Just as I would wish, mine and Thine?
What could keep me from being so today?

A sweet tremor pervades my very frame!
I marvel that it should have ever seemed a
     marvel
To have God for one's own on earth!

4 October 1888 An den Schlaf / To sleep [29]

Schlaf! süßer Schlaf! obwohl dem Tod wie du
     nichts gleicht,
Auf diesem Lager doch willkommen heiß ich
     dich!
Denn ohne Leben so, wie lieblich lebt es sich!
So weit vom Sterben, ach, wie stirbt es sich so
     leicht!
(*Eisler*)

Sleep! sweet sleep! though nothing so resem-
     bles death as you,
I bid you welcome to this couch!
For thus without life, how sweet it is to
     live!
So far from dying, ah, how easy it is to die!

5 October 1888 Zum neuen Jahr / A poem for the New Year [27]

Wie heimlicher Weise	Just as a cherub,
Ein Engelein leise	Secretly and softly
Mit rosigen Füßen	Alights on earth
Die Erde betritt,	With rosy feet,
So nahte der Morgen.	So the morning dawned.
Jauchzt ihm, ihr Frommen,	Rejoice, you gentle souls, with
Ein heilig Willkommen!	A holy welcome!
Ein heilig Willkommen,	A holy welcome,
Herz, jauchze du mit!	O heart, rejoice as well!
In ihm sei's begonnen,	May the New Year begin in Him,
Der Monde und Sonnen	Who moves
An blauen Gezelten	Moons and suns
Des Himmels bewegt.	In the blue firmament.
Du, Vater, du rate!	O Father, counsel us!
Lenke du und wende!	Lead us and guide us!
Herr, dir in die Hände	Lord, let all things,
Sei Anfang und Ende,	Beginning and End,
Sei alles gelegt!	Be entrusted into Thy keeping!

6 October 1888 Schlafendes Jesuskind / The sleeping Christ-child [25]

Sohn der Jungfrau, Himmelskind! am Boden	Son of the Virgin, Heavenly Child!
Auf dem Holz der Schmerzen eingeschlafen,	Asleep on the ground, on the wood of suffering,
Das der fromme Meister, sinnvoll spielend,	Which the pious painter, in meaningful play,
Deinen leichten Träumen unterlegte;	Has laid beneath Thy gentle dreams;
Blume du, noch in der Knospe dämmernd	O flower, still the Glory of God the Father,
Eingehüllt die Herrlichkeit des Vaters!	Though still hidden in the dark bud!
O wer sehen könnte, welche Bilder	Ah, if one could see what pictures, behind
Hinter dieser Stirne, diesen schwarzen	this brow and these dark
Wimpern sich in sanftem Wechsel malen!	Lashes, are reflected in gentle succession!

6 October 1888 Wo find ich Trost? / Where shall I find comfort? [31]
FROM *Maler Nolten*; ORCHESTRATED 6 SEPTEMBER 1890

Eine Liebe kenn ich, die ist treu,	I know a love that is true,
War getreu, solang ich sie gefunden,	And has been since I first found it,
Hat mit tiefem Seufzen immer neu,	It has, deeply sighing, always forgivingly renewed,
Stets versöhnlich, sich mit mir verbunden.	Bonds between us.
Welcher einst mit himmlischem Gedulden	He it was who once, with heavenly forbearance,
Bitter bittern Todestropfen trank,	Drank death's bitter, bitter drops,
Hing am Kreuz und büßte mein Verschulden,	Hung on the cross and atoned for my sins,
Bis es in ein Meer von Gnade sank.	Until they sank in a sea of mercy.
Und was ists nun, daß ich traurig bin,	And why is it that I am now sad,
Daß ich angstvoll mich am Boden winde?	That I writhe in terror on the ground?

Frage: „Hüter*, ist die Nacht bald hin?"	That I ask: 'Watchman, is the night soon done?'
Und: „was rettet mich von Tod und Sünde?"	And 'What shall save me from death and sin?'
Arges Herze! ja gesteh es nur,	Evil heart! why not confess it,
Du hast wieder böse Lust empfangen;	Once more you have felt wicked desires;
Frommer Liebe, frommer Treue Spur,	All trace of pious love, of pious faith,
Ach, das ist auf lange nun vergangen.	Has vanished, alas, for a long time.
Ja, das ists auch, daß ich traurig bin,	Yes, that is why I am sad,
Daß ich angstvoll mich am Boden winde!	Why I writhe in terror on the ground!
Hüter, Hüter, ist die Nacht bald hin?	Watchman, watchman, is the night soon done?
Und was rettet mich von Tod und Sünde?	What shall save me from death and sin?

8 October 1888 Karwoche / Holy week [26]

FROM *Maler Nolten*; ORCHESTRATED 29 MAY 1889

O Woche, Zeugin heiliger Beschwerde!	O week, witness of sacred sorrow!
Du stimmst so ernst zu dieser Früh-	Your gravity does not become this spring-
lingswonne,	time rapture,
Du breitest im verjüngten Strahl der Sonne	In the fresh sunlight you spread
Des Kreuzes Schatten auf die lichte Erde	The cross's shadow on the bright earth
Und senkest schweigend deine Flöre nieder;	And silently lower your veils;
Der Frühling darf indessen immer keimen,	Spring meanwhile continues to bloom,
Das Veilchen duftet unter Blütenbäumen,	Violets smell sweet beneath blossoming trees,
Und alle Vöglein singen Jubellieder.	And all the birds sing songs of praise.
O schweigt, ihr Vöglein auf den grünen Auen!	Oh hush, you birds on the green meadows!
Es hallen rings die dumpfen Glockenklänge,	Muffled bells are tolling all around,
Die Engel singen leise Grabgesänge;	Angels are singing their soft dirges;
O still, ihr Vöglein hoch im Himmelblauen!	Oh hush, you birds in the blue skies above!
Ihr Veilchen, kränzt heut keine Lockenhaare!	You violets, adorn no maiden's hair today!
Euch pflückt mein frommes Kind zum	My pious child has picked you for the dark
dunkeln Sträuße,	bouquet,
Ihr wandert mit zum Muttergotteshause,	You shall go with her to the church of the Virgin,
Da sollt ihr welken auf des Herrn Altare.	There you shall wither on the altar of our Lord.
Ach dort, von Trauermelodien trunken,	Ah, there, drunk with mourning melodies
Und süß betäubt von schweren	And dazed by sweet and heavy
Weihrauchdüften,	incense,
Sucht sie den Bräutigam in Todesgrüften,	She seeks the Bridegroom in the tomb,
Und Lieb und Frühling, alles ist versunken.	And love and spring – all is lost forever.

9 October 1888 Gesang Weylas / Weyla's song [46]

Du bist Orplid†, mein Land!	You are Orplid, my land!

* The watchman from Isaiah XXI, 11, who heralds the Day of Judgement.
† The magical island in Mörike's *Der letzte König von Orplid*, the shadow-play he included in his novel *Maler Nolten*. Weyla is the tutelary goddess of the island, from which she derives her magic power.

Das ferne leuchtet;	That shines afar;
Vom Meere dampfet dein besonnter Strand	Your sunlit shore sends up sea-
Den Nebel, so der Götter Wange feuchtet.	Mists, that moisten the cheeks of the gods.
Uralte Wasser steigen	Ancient waters climb,
Verjüngt um deine Hüften, Kind!	Rejuvenated, child, about your waist!
Vor deiner Gottheit beugen	Kings, who attend you,
Sich Könige, die deine Wärter sind.	Bow down before your divinity.

10 October 1888 Der Feuerreiter / Fire-rider [44]
FROM *Maler Nolten*; VERSION FOR CHORUS AND ORCHESTRA OCTOBER–NOVEMBER 1892

Sehet ihr am Fensterlein	See, at the window
Dort die rote Mütze wieder?	There, his red cap again?
Nicht geheuer muß es sein,	Something must be wrong,
Denn er geht schon auf und nieder.	For he's pacing to and fro.
Und auf einmal welch Gewühle	And all of a sudden, what a throng
Bei der Brücke, nach dem Feld!	At the bridge, heading for the fields!
Horch! das Feuerglöcklein gellt:	Listen to the fire-bell shrilling:
Hinterm Berg,	Behind the hill,
Hinterm Berg	Behind the hill,
Brennt es in der Mühle!	The mill's on fire!
Schaut! da sprengt er wütend schier	Look, there he gallops frenziedly
Durch das Tor, der Feuerreiter,	Through the gate, the fire-rider,
Auf dem rippendürren Tier,	Straddling his skinny mount
Als auf einer Feuerleiter!	Like a fireman's ladder!
Querfeldein! Durch Qualm und Schwüle	Across the fields! Through thick smoke and heat
Rennt er schon und ist am Ort!	He rides and has reached his goal!
Drüben schallt es fort und fort:	The distant bell peals on and on:
Hinterm Berg,	Behind the hill,
Hinterm Berg	Behind the hill
Brennt es in der Mühle!	The mill's on fire!
Der so oft den roten Hahn	You who have often smelt a fire
Meilenweit von fern gerochen,	From many miles away,
Mit des heilgen Kreuzes Span	And blasphemously conjured the blaze
Freventlich die Glut besprochen –	With a fragment of the True Cross –
Weh! dir grinst vom Dachgestühle	Look out! there, grinning at you from the rafters,
Dort der Feind im Höllenschein.	Is the Devil amid the flames of hell.
Gnade Gott der Seele dein!	God have mercy on your soul!
Hinterm Berg,	Behind the hill,
Hinterm Berg	Behind the hill
Rast er in der Mühle!	He's raging in the mill!
Keine Stunde hielt es an,	In less than an hour
Bis die Mühle barst in Trümmer;	The mill collapsed in rubble;
Doch den kecken Reitersmann	But from that hour the bold rider
Sah man von der Stunde nimmer.	Was never seen again.

Volk und Wagen im Gewühle	Thronging crowds and carriages
Kehren heim von all dem Graus;	Turn back home from all the horror;
Auch das Glöcklein klinget aus:	And the bell stops ringing too:
Hinterm Berg,	Behind the hill,
Hinterm Berg	Behind the hill
Brennts ! –	A fire! –
Nach der Zeit ein Müller fand	Some time after a miller found
Ein Geripppe samt der Mützen	A skeleton, complete with cap,
Aufrecht an der Kellerwand	Upright against the cellar wall,
Auf der beinern Mähre sitzen:	Mounted on the fleshless mare:
Feuerreiter, wie so kühle	Fire-rider, how coldly
Reitest du in deinem Grab!	You ride in your grave!
Husch! da fällts in Asche ab.	Hush! now it flakes into ash.
Ruhe wohl,	Rest in peace,
Ruhe wohl	Rest in peace
Drunten in der Mühle!	Down there in the mill!
(*Distler*)	

11 October 1888 An die Geliebte / To the beloved [32]
FROM *Maler Nolten*

Wenn ich, von deinem Anschaun tief gestillt,	When I, deeply calmed at beholding you,
Mich stumm an deinem heilgen Wert	
vergnüge,	Take silent delight in your sacred worth,
Dann hör ich recht die leisen Atemzüge	Then I truly hear the gentle breathing
Des Engels, welcher sich in dir verhüllt,	Of that angel concealed within you.
Und ein erstaunt, ein fragend Lächeln quillt	And an amazed, a questioning smile
Auf meinem Mund, ob mich kein Traum	Rises to my lips: does not a dream deceive
betrüge,	me,
Daß nun in dir, zu ewiger Genüge,	Now that in you, to my eternal joy,
Mein kühnster Wunsch, mein ein'zger, sich	My boldest, my only wish is being
erfüllt?	fulfilled?
Von Tiefe dann zu Tiefen stürzt mein Sinn,	My soul then plunges from depth to depth,
Ich höre aus der Gottheit nächtger Ferne	From the dark distances of Godhead I
Die Quellen des Geschicks melodisch	hear
rauschen.	The springs of fate ripple in melody.
Betäubt kehr ich den Blick nach oben hin,	Dazed I raise my eyes
Zum Himmel auf – da lächeln alle Sterne;	To heaven – where all the stars are smiling;
Ich kniee, ihrem Lichtgesang zu lauschen.	I kneel to listen to their song of light.

13 October 1888 Gebet / Prayer [28]
FROM *Maler Nolten*

Herr! schicke, was du willt,	Lord! send what Thou wilt,
Ein Liebes oder Leides;	Pleasure or pain;

Ich bin vergnügt, daß beides
Aus deinen Händen quillt.

Wollest mit Freuden
Und wollest mit Leiden
Mich nicht überschütten!
Doch in der Mitten
Liegt holdes Bescheiden.
(*Bruch, Distler, Schoeck*)

I am content that both
Flow from Thy hands.

Do not, I beseech Thee,
Overwhelm me
With joy or suffering!
But midway between
Lies blessed moderation.

26 November 1888 Auf eine Christblume I / On a Christmas rose I [20]
ORCHESTRATED 25 SEPTEMBER 1890

Tochter des Walds, du Lilienverwandte,
So lang von mir gesuchte, unbekannte,
Im fremden Kirchhof, öd und winterlich,
Zum erstenmal, o schöne, find ich dich!

Daughter of the forest, close kin to the lily,
You whom I sought so long and never knew,
Now in a strange churchyard, desolate and wintry,
For the first time, O lovely one, I find you!

Von welcher Hand gepflegt du hier erblühtest,
Ich weiß es nicht, noch wessen Grab du hütest;
Ist es ein Jüngling, so geschah ihm Heil,
Ists eine Jungfrau, lieblich fiel ihr Teil.

Whose hand helped you to blossom here,
I do not know, nor whose grave you guard;
If a young man lies here, he has found salvation,
If a maiden, a fair lot befell her.

Im nächtgen Hain, von Schneelicht überbreitet,
Wo fromm das Reh an dir vorüberweidet,
Bei der Kapelle, am kristallnen Teich,
Dort sucht ich deiner Heimat Zauberreich.

In the darkling grove, overspread with snowy light,
Where the gentle deer moves past you grazing,
By the chapel, beside the crystal pond,
There I sought your enchanted realm.

Schön bist du, Kind des Mondes, nicht der
    Sonne;
Dir wäre tödlich andrer Blumen Wonne,
Dich nährt, den keuschen Leib voll Reif und
    Duft,
Himmlischer Kälte balsamsüße Luft.

How fair you are, child of the moon, not of the
    sun;
Fatal to you would be the bliss of other flowers,
Your pure body, all rime and scent, feeds
On heavenly cold and balsam-scented air.

In deines Busens goldner Fülle gründet
Ein Wohlgeruch, der sich nur kaum verkündet;
So duftete, berührt von Engelshand,
Der benedeiten Mutter Brautgewand.

There dwells within the golden fullness of your
    heart
A perfume so faint it can scarcely be perceived;
Such was the scent, touched by angelic hands,
Of the Blessed Mother's bridal robe.

Dich würden, mahnend an das heilge Leiden,
Fünf Purpurtropfen schön und einzig kleiden:
Doch kindlich zierst du, um die Weih-
    nachtzeit,
Lichtgrün mit einem Hauch dein weißes Kleid.

Five crimson drops, a reminder of the sacred Pas-
    sion,
Would suffice as your sole and lovely ornament:
Yet child-like at Christmas-time you adorn
Your white dress with a hint of palest green.

Der Elfe, der in mitternächtger Stunde
Zum Tanze geht im lichterhellen Grunde,
Vor deiner mystischen Glorie steht er scheu
Neugierig still von fern und huscht vorbei.

The elf, who at the midnight hour
Goes to dance in the glistening glade,
Stands awestruck from afar by your mystic halo,
Looks on in inquiring silence and scurries by.

Robert Reinick (1805–52)

See Brahms, Robert Schumann

Reinick was a poet and painter who, like William Blake, illustrated many of his own poems; but whereas Blake was a genius, Reinick painted unremarkable pictures of historical and romantic scenes (his woodcuts are more skilled) and wrote unremarkable poetry. It is strange that Wolf, normally so fastidious in his choice of texts, should have set Reinick so many times: twice in 1882, six times in 1883, once each in 1888 and 1889, twice in 1890 and once in 1896. Only those songs published during Wolf's lifetime are included here.

17 December 1882 Wiegenlied im Sommer / A lullaby in summer

Vom Berg hinabgestiegen	What remains of day
Ist nun des Tages Rest,	Has now descended from the mountain,
Mein Kind liegt in der Wiegen,	My child lies in its cradle,
Die Vögel all im Nest,	The birds are all in their nests,
Nur ein ganz klein Singvögelein	Just one tiny little song-bird
Ruft weit daher im Dämmerschein:	Calls from afar in the twilight:
„Gut' Nacht! gut' Nacht!	'Good night! good night!
Lieb Kindlein, gute Nacht!"	Dearest child, good night!'
Die Wiege geht im Gleise,	The cradle goes on rocking,
Die Uhr tickt hin und her,	The clock ticks to and fro,
Die Fliegen nur ganz leise	The flies very quietly still
Sie summen noch daher.	Come buzzing through the air.
Ihr Fliegen, laßt mein Kind in Ruh!	Leave my child in peace, you flies!
Was summt ihr ihm so heimlich zu?	Why buzz at him so secretly?
„Gut' Nacht! gut' Nacht!	'Good night! good night!
Lieb Kindlein, gute Nacht!"	Dearest child, good night!'
Der Vogel und die Sterne	The bird and the stars,
Und Alle rings umher,	And all things round about,
Sie haben mein Kind so gerne,	Are so very fond of my child,
Die Engel noch viel mehr.	The angels even fonder.
Sie decken's mit den Flügeln zu	They cover him with their wings
Und singen leise: „Schlaf in Ruh!	And softly sing: 'Sleep in peace!
„Gut' Nacht! gut' Nacht!	'Good night! good night!
Lieb Kindlein, gute Nacht!"	Dearest child, good night!'

(*Leo Blech*)

20 December 1882 Wiegenlied im Winter / A lullaby in winter

Schlaf ein, mein süßes Kind,	Go to sleep, my sweet child,
Da draußen geht der Wind,	Outside the wind is blowing,
Er pocht ans Fenster und schaut hinein,	He knocks at the window and looks inside,

Und hört er wo ein Kindlein schrein,
  Da schilt und summt und brummt er sehr,
Holt gleich ein Bett voll Schnee daher,
Und deckt es auf die Wiegen,
Wenn's Kind nicht still will liegen.

Schlaf ein, mein süßes Kind,
Da draußen geht der Wind,
Er rüttelt an dem Tannenbaum,
Da fliegt heraus ein schöner Traum,
Der fliegt durch Schnee und Nacht und Wind
Geschwind, geschwind zum lieben Kind,
Und singt von Licht und Kränzen,
Die bald am Christbaum glänzen.

  Schlaf ein, mein süßes Kind,
  Da draußen bläst der Wind,
Doch ruft die Sonne: „Grüß euch Gott!"
Bläst er dem Kind die Backen rot,
Und sagt der Frühling: „Guten Tag!"
Bläst er die ganze Erde wach,
Und was erst still gelegen,
Springt lustig allerwegen.
  Jetzt schlaf, mein süßes Kind,
  Da draußen bläst der Wind.

And if he hears a baby cry,
  He scolds and hums and mutters aloud,
Fetches at once a bedful of snow
And lays it on the cradle,
If the child will not lie still.

Go to sleep, my sweet child,
  Outside the wind is blowing,
He rattles on the fir tree,
And out flies a lovely dream,
Flies through snow and night and wind,
Quickly, quickly to the darling child,
And sings of lights and wreaths
That soon will shine on the Christmas tree.

  Go to sleep, my sweet child,
  Outside the wind is blowing,
But when the sun cries: 'Good morning!',
He blows till my child's cheeks are red,
And if the Spring should cry: 'Good day!',
It blows till all the world's awake,
And all that was lying still
Leaps merrily around.
  Go to sleep now, sweet child,
  Outside the wind is blowing.

24 January 1888 Gesellenlied / The journeyman's song

  „Kein Meister fällt vom Himmel!"
Und das ist auch ein großes Glück!
    Der Meister sind schon viel zuviel;
    Wenn noch ein Schock vom Himmel fiel',
Wie würden uns Gesellen
Die vielen Meister prellen
Trotz unserm Meisterstück!

  „Kein Meister fällt vom Himmel!"
Gottlob, auch keine Meisterin!
    Ach, lieber Himmel, sei so gut,
    Wenn droben eine brummen tut,
Behalte sie in Gnaden,
Daß sie zu unserm Schaden
Nicht fall' zur Erden hin!

  „Kein Meister fällt vom Himmel!"
Auch keines Meisters Töchterlein!
    Zwar hab' ich das schon lang' gewußt,
    Und doch, was wär' das eine Lust,
Wenn jung und hübsch und munter
Solch Mädel fiel' herunter
Und wollt' mein Herzlieb sein!

  'Masters don't fall from Heaven!'
And it's a very good thing they don't!
    There are far too many masters already;
    If another batch were to fall from Heaven,
How all those masters
Would cheat us journeymen,
Despite our masterpieces!

  'Masters don't fall from Heaven!'
Nor masters' wives either, thank God!
    Ah, dear Lord above, be so kind,
    And if one's bleating away up there,
Keep her, I beg you, where she is,
That she won't, to our detriment,
Fall to earth as well!

  'Masters don't fall from Heaven!'
Nor masters' daughters either!
    I've long been well aware of that.
    And yet what a pleasure that would be,
If such a maid, young and pretty
And lively, were to fall from Heaven
And fall for me as well!

„Kein Meister fällt vom Himmel!"	'Masters don't fall from Heaven!'
Das ist mein Trost auf dieser Welt;	That's my comfort here on earth;
Drum mach' ich , daß ich Meister werd',	So I'm set on becoming one,
Und wird mir dann ein Weib beschert,	And if I'm also granted a wife,
Dann soll aus dieser Erden	Then my life on earth
Mir schon ein Himmel werden,	Shall become a Heaven
Aus dem kein Meister fällt.	From which no master falls.

1 August 1889 Skolie / Banqueting song

Reich den Pokal mir schäumenden Weines voll,	Give me the goblet brimming with sparkling wine,
Reich mir die Lippen zum Kusse, die blühenden,	Give me your rosy lips to kiss,
Rühre die Saiten, die seelenberauschenden! –	Play the lyre that can ravish the soul! –
Feuer des Mutes brennt im Pokale mir,	The goblet's wine inflames me,
Gluten der Liebe glühn auf der Lippe dir,	The ardour of love glows on your lips,
Flammen des Lebens rauschen die Saiten mir. –	The lyre kindles in me the flame of life. –
Woge des Kampfes, reiß in die Brandung mich!	Wave of battle, bear me into the breakers!
Wogen der Liebe, hebt zu den Wolken mich!	Waves of love, raise me to the clouds!
Schäumendes Leben, jubelnd begrüß ich dich!	Surging life, I greet you with exultation!

8 September–23 October 1896 Morgenstimmung / Morning mood

Bald ist der Nacht	Night will soon
Ein End' gemacht,	Be over,
Schon fühl' ich Morgenlüfte wehen.	Already I feel morning breezes stir.
Der Herr, der spricht:	The Lord says:
„Es werde Licht!"	'Let there be light!'
Da muß, was dunkel ist, vergehen. –	Then all that's dark must vanish. –
Vom Himmelszelt	Angels flying across
Durch alle Welt	The world
Die Engel freudejauchzend fliegen;	Come down from the skies, singing with joy;
Der Sonne Strahl	Sunlight blazes
Durchflammt das All. –	Across the universe. –
Herr, laß uns kämpfen, laß uns siegen!	Lord, let us fight, let us conquer!

Spanisches Liederbuch / The Spanish Songbook
TRANSLATED BY EMANUEL GEIBEL° AND PAUL HEYSE°°

The main source of the translations by Paul Heyse and Emanuel Geibel (1852) was the *Floresta de Rimas Antiguas Castellanas*, edited by J. N. Böhl de Faber, a three-volume anthology that had been published between 1821 and 1825. Wolf follows his poets by separating the *Geistliche Lieder* (*Sacred songs*) from the *Weltliche Lieder* (*Secular songs*), which depict lovers at peace and war. Over half the poems are by anonymous authors, two by Geibel and Heyse themselves (masquerading as Don

Manuel del Rio and Don Luis el Chico), the rest by such poets as Cervantes, Lope de Vega and Camoens.

The poetry of Emanuel Geibel (1815–84) and Paul Heyse (1830–1914) enjoyed enormous popularity in the early 1850s (Heyse also wrote over 100 Novellen), and they were invited to Munich by Maximilian II of Bavaria where they became prominent members of the Münchner Dichterkreis; Heyse was awarded the Nobel Prize for literature in 1910.

The songs are printed in chronological order of composition; the numbers at the start of each song indicate Wolf's published order.

Geistliche Lieder / Spiritual songs

3 °°

4 November 1889
Caminad, esposa BY OCAÑA (*fl. c.*1600)

DER HEILIGE JOSEPH SINGT	SAINT JOSEPH SINGS
Nun wandre, Maria,	Journey on, now, Mary,
Nun wandre nur fort.	Keep journeying.
Schon krähen die Hähne,	The cocks are crowing,
Und nah ist der Ort.	And the place is near.
Nun wandre, Geliebte,	Journey on, beloved,
Du Kleinod mein,	My jewel,
Und balde wir werden	And soon we shall
In Bethlehem sein.	Be in Bethlehem.
Dann ruhest du fein	Then shall you rest well
Und schlummerst dort.	And slumber there.
Schon krähen die Hähne	The cocks are crowing,
Und nah ist der Ort.	And the place is near.
Wohl seh ich, Herrin,	I well see, my lady,
Die Kraft dir schwinden;	That your strength is failing;
Kann deine Schmerzen	I can hardly, alas,
Ach, kaum verwinden.	Bear your agony.
Getrost! Wohl finden	Courage! We shall find
Wir Herberg dort.	Some shelter there.
Schon kräh'n die Hähne,	The cocks are crowing,
Und nah ist der Ort.	And the place is near.
Wär' erst bestanden	If only your hour of pain
Dein Stündlein, Marie,	Were over, O Mary,
Die gute Botschaft	I should handsomely reward
Gut lohnt' ich sie.	The happy tidings.
Das Eselein hie	This little ass here
Gäb ich drum fort!	I'd gladly give away!
Schon Krähen die Hähne,	The cocks are crowing,
Komm! Nah ist der Ort.	Come! The place is near.

$2°°$

5 November 1889

O Virgen que á Dios pariste BY NICOLÁS NUÑEZ (15TH CENTURY)

Die du Gott gebarst, du Reine,	Thou who didst bear God, O pure one,
Und alleine	And who alone
Uns gelös't aus unsern Ketten,	Delivered us from our chains,
Mach mich fröhlich, der ich weine,	Make me glad, I who weep,
Denn nur deine	For only thy
Huld und Gnade mag uns retten.	Grace and mercy can save us.
Herrin, ganz zu dir mich wende,	Lady, turn me to thee entirely,
Daß sich ende	That they might end,
Diese Qual und dieses Grauen,	This torment and this dread,
Daß der Tod mich furchtlos fände,	That death might find me unafraid,
Und nicht blende	And I be not blinded
Mich das Licht der Himmelsauen.	By the light of the heavenly pastures.
Weil du unbefleckt geboren,	Because thou wert born immaculate,
Auserkoren	Chosen
Zu des ew'gen Ruhmes Stätten –	To dwell in eternal glory –
Wie mich Leiden auch umfloren,	However much sorrow dims my eyes,
Unverloren	I am not lost,
Bin ich doch, willst du mich retten.	If thou wilt save me.

$4°$

5 November 1889

Pues andais en las palmas BY LOPE DA VEGA (1562–1613)

Die ihr schwebet	You who hover
Um diese Palmen	About these palms
In Nacht und Wind,	In night and wind,
Ihr heil'gen Engel,	You holy angels,
Stillet die Wipfel!	Silence the tree-tops!
Es schlummert mein Kind.	My child is sleeping.
Ihr Palmen von Bethlehem	You palms of Bethlehem
Im Windesbrausen,	In the raging wind,
Wie mögt ihr heute	Why do you bluster
So zornig sausen!	So angrily today!
O rauscht nicht also!	Oh roar not so!
Schweiget, neiget	Be still, lean
Euch leis' und lind;	Calmly and gently over us;
Stillet die Wipfel!	Silence the tree-tops!
Es schlummert mein Kind.	My child is sleeping.
Der Himmelsknabe	The heavenly babe
Duldet Beschwerde,	Suffers distress,
Ach, wie so müd' er ward	Ah, how weary He has grown

Vom Leid der Erde.
Ach nun im Schlaf ihm
Leise gesänftigt
Die Qual zerrinnt,
Stillet die Wipfel!
Es schlummert mein Kind.

Grimmige Kälte
Sauset hernieder,
Womit nur deck' ich
Des Kindleins Glieder!
O all ihr Engel,
Die ihr geflügelt
Wandelt im Wind,
Stillet die Wipfel!
Es schlummert mein Kind.
(*Brahms*)

With the sorrows of this world.
Ah, now that in sleep
His pains
Are gently eased,
Silence the tree-tops!
My child is sleeping.

Fierce cold
Blows down on us,
With what shall I cover
My little child's limbs?
O all you angels
Who wing your way
On the winds,
Silence the tree-tops!
My child is sleeping.

9 °°

24 November 1889
Qué producirá mi Dios (ANON.)

Herr, was trägt der Boden hier,
Den du tränkst so bitterlich?
„Dornen, liebes Herz, für mich,
Und für dich der Blumen Zier."

Ach, wo solche Bäche rinnen,
Wird ein Garten da gedeihn?
„Ja, und wisse! Kränzelein,
Gar verschiedne, flicht man drinnen."
O mein Herr, zu wessen Zier
Windet man die Kränze? sprich!
„Die von Dornen sind für mich,
Die von Blumen reich' ich dir."

Lord, what will grow in this soil
That Thou dost water with Thy bitter tears?
'Thorns, dear heart, for me,
And for you a wreath of flowers.'

Ah, where such streams flow,
Can a garden flourish there?
'Yes, and know this: many varied
Wreaths are woven there.'
O my Lord, for whose head
Are these wreaths woven, say?
'Those of thorns are for me,
Those of flowers I hand to you.'

5 °°

15 December 1889
Llevadme, niño, á Belen (ANON.)

Führ mich, Kind, nach Bethlehem!
Dich, mein Gott, dich will ich sehn.
Wem geläng' es, wem,
Ohne dich zu dir zu gehn!

Rüttle mich, daß ich erwache,
Rufe mich, so will ich schreiten;

Lead me, child, to Bethlehem!
Thee, my God, Thee will I see.
Whoever managed to come to Thee,
Without Thy help!

Shake me awake,
Call me, and I shall come;

Gib die Hand mir, mich zu leiten,
Daß ich auf den Weg mich mache,
Daß ich schaue Bethlehem,
Dorten meinen Gott zu sehn.
Wem geläng es, wem,
Ohne dich zu dir zu gehn!

Von der Sünde schwerem Kranken
Bin ich träg' und dumpf beklommen.
Willst du nicht zu Hülfe kommen,
Muß ich straucheln, muß ich schwanken.
Leite mich nach Bethlehem,
Dich, mein Gott, dich will ich sehn.
Wem geläng' es, wem,
Ohne dich zu dir zu gehn!

Stretch forth Thy hand to guide me,
That I might set out.
That I might gaze on Bethlehem,
There to see my God.
Whoever managed to come to Thee,
Without Thy help!

I am sorely oppressed and weighed down
With the grievous sickness of sin.
If Thou wilt not come to my aid,
I must stumble and falter.
Lead me to Bethlehem,
Thee, my God, Thee will I see.
Whoever managed to come to Thee,
Without Thy help!

10 °

16 December 1889

Feridas teneis mi vida BY JOSÉ DE VALDIVIELSO (1560–1638)

Wunden trägst du, mein Geliebter,
Und sie schmerzen dich;
Trüg' ich sie statt deiner, ich!

Herr, wer wagt' es, so zu färben
Deine Stirn mit Blut und Schweiß?
„Diese Male sind der Preis,
Dich, o Seele, zu erwerben.
An den Wunden muß ich sterben,
Weil ich dich geliebt so heiß."

Könnt' ich, Herr, für dich sie tragen,
Da es Todeswunden sind.
„Wenn dies Leid dich rührt, mein Kind,
Magst du Lebenswunden sagen:
Ihrer keine ward geschlagen,
Draus für dich nicht Leben rinnt."

Ach, wie mir in Herz und Sinnen
Deine Qual so wehe tut!
„Härtres noch mit treuem Mut
Trüg' ich froh, dich zu gewinnen;
Denn nur der weiß recht zu minnen,
Der da stirbt vor Liebesglut."

Wunden trägst du, mein Geliebter,
Und sie schmerzen dich;
Trüg' ich sie statt deiner, ich!

Thou art wounded, my belovèd Lord,
And dost suffer pain;
Would I could bear it for Thee!

Lord, who dared so to stain
Thy brow with blood and sweat?
'These wounds are the price
Of redeeming you, O soul.
From these wounds I must die
For my great love of you.'

O could I bear them, Lord, for Thee,
Since they are mortal wounds.
'If this suffering moves you, child,
You may call them living wounds:
Not one of them was made, from which
Life does not flow for you.'

Ah, how my heart and mind
Ache with Thy anguish!
'Harsher yet with true courage,
I'd gladly endure to redeem you;
For he alone knows how to love
Who has died for ardent love.'

Thou art wounded, my belovèd Lord,
And dost suffer pain;
Would I could bear it for Thee!

19 December 1889

Mucho ha que el alma duerme (ANON.)

Ach, wie lang die Seele schlummert!	Ah, how long the soul has slumbered!
Zeit ist's, daß sie sich ermuntre.	It is time it roused itself.
Daß man tot sie wähnen dürfte,	My soul might be considered dead,
Also schläft sie schwer und bang,	It sleeps so heavily and fearfully,
Seit sie jener Rausch bezwang,	Since overcome by that intoxication
Den in Sündengift sie schlürfte.	It quaffed from the cup of sin.
Doch nun ihrer Sehnsucht Licht	But now the longed-for light
Blendend ihr ins Auge bricht:	Breaks through and dazzles its eyes:
Zeit ist's, daß sie sich ermuntre.	It is time it roused itself.
Mochte sie gleich taub erscheinen	Though the soul seemed deaf
Bei der Engel süßem Chor:	To the sweet angelic choirs:
Lauscht sie doch wohl zag empor,	It timidly pricks up its ears
Hört sie Gott als Kindlein weinen.	On hearing God weep as a little child.
Da nach langer Schlummernacht	Since after a long night of sleep,
Solch ein Tag der Gnad' ihr lacht,	Such a day of grace now smiles on it,
Zeit ist's, daß sie sich ermuntre.	It is time it roused itself.

6

21 December 1889

Los ojos del niño son BY LOPEZ DE UBEDA (14TH CENTURY)

Ach, des Knaben Augen sind	Ah, the Infant's eyes seemed
Mir so schön und klar erschienen,	So beautiful and clear to me,
Und ein Etwas strahlt aus ihnen,	And a radiance streams from them
Das mein ganzes Herz gewinnt.	That captures my whole heart.
Blickt' er doch mit diesen süßen	If only He would turn
Augen nach den meinen hin!	Those sweet eyes on mine!
Säh' er dann sein Bild darin,	If He saw His image reflected there,
Würd' er wohl mich liebend grüßen.	He would surely greet me lovingly.
Und so geb' ich ganz mich hin,	So I surrender myself
Seinen Augen nur zu dienen,	To the sole service of His eyes,
Denn ein Etwas strahlt aus ihnen,	For a radiance shines from them
Das mein ganzes Herz gewinnt.	That captures my whole heart.

7

10 January 1890

Vengo triste y lastimado BY DON MANUEL DEL RIO = EMANUEL GEIBEL

Mühvoll komm' ich und beladen,	In toil I come and heavy-laden,
Nimm mich an, du Hort der Gnaden!	Receive me, O haven of mercy!
Sieh, ich komm' in Tränen heiß	See, I come with burning tears

Mit demütiger Gebärde,
Dunkel ganz vom Staub der Erde.
Du nur schaffest, daß ich weiß
Wie das Vließ der Lämmer werde.
Tilgen willst du ja den Schaden
Dem, der reuig dich umfaßt;
Nimm denn, Herr, von mir die Last,
Mühvoll komm' ich und beladen.

Laß mich flehend vor dir knie'n,
Daß ich über deine Füße
Nardenduft und Tränen gieße,
Gleich dem Weib, dem du verziehn,
Bis die Schuld wie Rauch zerfließe.
Der den Schächer du geladen:
„Heute noch in Edens Bann
Wirst du sein!" o nimm mich an,
Nimm mich an, du Hort der Gnaden!

And humble mien,
All blackened with the dust of earth.
Thou alone canst make we white
As the fleece of lambs.
Thou shalt eradicate the wrongs
Of the penitent who embraces Thee;
Take, then, Lord, the burden from me,
In toil I come and heavy-laden.

Let me kneel before Thee, pleading,
That I might anoint Thy feet
With scented spikenard and tears,
Like that woman Thou didst forgive,
Until my guilt disperses like smoke.
Thou who didst once tell the thief:
'Today shalt thou be with me
In Paradise!' – O take me,
Receive me, O haven of mercy!

1 °°

15 January 1890
Quiero seguir BY JUAN RUIZ (14TH CENTURY)

Nun bin ich dein,
Du aller Blumen Blume,
Und sing' allein
Allstund zu deinem Ruhme;
Will eifrig sein,
Mich dir zu weihn
Und deinem Duldertume.

Frau auserlesen,
Zu dir steht all mein Hoffen,
Mein innerst Wesen
Ist allezeit dir offen.
Komm, mich zu lösen
Vom Fluch des Bösen,
Der mich so hart betroffen!

Du Stern der See,
Du Port der Wonnen,
Von der im Weh
Die Wunden Heil gewonnen,
Eh' ich vergeh,
Blick' aus der Höh,
Du Königin der Sonnen!

Nie kann versiegen
Die Fülle deiner Gnaden;

Now I am thine,
Thou flower of all flowers,
And I shall sing solely
In Thy praise always;
I shall zealously
Devote myself to Thee
And Thy suffering.

O chosen lady,
In thee is all my hope,
My innermost being
Is forever open to thee.
Come, deliver me
From the curse of the Evil One
Which has so sorely afflicted me!

Thou star of the sea,
Thou haven of delights,
Through whom the afflicted
Can find healing for their wounds,
Before I perish,
Look down on me,
Thou queen of suns!

Never can the abundance
Of thy grace run dry;

Du hilfst zum Siegen
Dem, der mit Schmach beladen.
An dich sich schmiegen,
Zu deinen Füßen liegen
Heilt allen Harm und Schaden.

Thou dost help him to victory
Who is laden with shame.
To cling to thee,
To lie at thy feet
Heals all grief and pain.

Ich leide schwer
Und wohlverdiente Strafen.
Mir bangt so sehr,
Bald Todesschlaf zu schlafen.
Tritt du einher,
Und durch das Meer
O führe mich zum Hafen!

I suffer grievously
Richly deserved punishments.
I am in such dread,
Soon to sleep the sleep of death.
O draw near to me,
And through the ocean
Bring me, ah, to harbour!

Weltliche Lieder / Secular songs

7 °

28 October 1889
Quien gentil señora perde (ANON.)

Wer sein holdes Lieb verloren,
Weil er Liebe nicht versteht,
Besser wär' er nie geboren.

Whoever has lost his loved one
Through not understanding love,
Would have done better not to be born.

Ich verlor sie dort im Garten,
Da sie Rosen brach und Blüten.
Hell auf ihren Wangen glühten
Scham und Lust in holder Zier.
Und von Liebe sprach sie mir;
Doch ich größter aller Toren
Wußte keine Antwort ihr –
Wär' ich nimmermehr geboren.

I lost her in the garden there,
As she was picking roses and blossoms.
Her cheeks were glowing brightly,
Graced by modesty and joy.
And she spoke to me of love;
But I, the greatest of fools,
Knew not how to answer her –
Had I never been born.

Ich verlor sie dort im Garten,
Da sie sprach von Liebesplagen,
Denn ich wagte nicht zu sagen,
Wie ich ganz ihr eigen bin.
In die Blumen sank sie hin,
Doch ich größter aller Toren
Zog auch davon nicht Gewinn –
Wär' ich nimmermehr geboren!

I lost her in the garden there,
As she spoke of the pangs of love,
For I dared not tell her
How utterly I was hers.
She sank down among the flowers,
But I, the greatest of fools,
Gained nothing from that either –
Had I never been born!

8 ° °

31 October 1889
Las tierras corrí (ANON.)

Ich fuhr über Meer,
Ich zog über Land,
Das Glück das fand

I sailed across seas,
I marched across land,
Without ever

Ich nimmermehr.
Die Andern umher
Wie jubelten sie! –
Ich jubelte nie!

Nach Glück ich jagte,
An Leiden krankt' ich;
Als Recht verlangt' ich
Was Liebe versagte.
Ich hofft' und wagte –
Kein Glück mir gedieh,
Und so schaut' ich es nie!

Trug ohne Klage
Die Leiden, die bösen,
Und dacht', es lösen
Sich ab die Tage.
Die fröhlichen Tage
Wie eilen sie! –
Ich ereilte sie nie!

Finding happiness.
How the others
Rejoiced all around! –
I never rejoiced!

I hunted fortune,
I fell ill with grief;
I demanded as a right
What love denied.
I hoped and dared –
No fortune favoured me,
And I never glimpsed it!

I bore uncomplaining
The terrible pain,
And thought these
Days would pass.
How happy days
Speed past! –
I never caught them up!

14°°

31 October 1889
Cabecita, cabecita BY MIGUEL DE CERVANTES (1546–1616)

PRECIOSAS* SPRÜCHLEIN GEGEN KOPFWEH
Köpfchen, Köpfchen, nicht gewimmert,
Halt dich wacker, halt dich munter,
Stütz' zwei gute Säulchen unter,
Heilsam aus Geduld gezimmert!
Hoffnung schimmert,
Wie sich's auch verschlimmert
Und dich kümmert.
Mußt mit Grämen
Dir nichts zu Herzen nehmen,
Ja kein Märchen,
Daß zu Berg dir stehn die Härchen;
Da sei Gott davor
Und der Riese Christophor!
(*Cornelius*)

PRECIOSA'S PRESCRIPTION FOR HEADACHE
Don't whimper, hold your little head up high,
Be brave, be of good cheer,
Prop yourself up on two pillars,
Fashioned wholesomely of patience!
Hope now glimmers,
However bad things get,
However you are vexed.
You must take nothing
Grievously to heart,
Especially stories
That make your hair stand on end;
To avoid that, pray to God
And the giant Christopher!

6°°

1 November 1889
Niña si a la huerta vas (ANON.)

Wenn du zu den Blumen gehst,
Pflücke die schönsten, dich zu schmücken.

When you go to the flowers,
Pick the loveliest to adorn yourself.

* The heroine in Cervantes's short story *La Gitanilla* from which this poem is taken.

Ach, wenn du in dem Gärtlein stehst,
Müßtest du dich selber pflücken.

Alle Blumen wissen ja,
Daß du hold bist ohne gleichen.
Und die Blume, die dich sah –
Farb' und Schmuck muß ihr erbleichen.
Wenn du zu den Blumen gehst,
Pflücke die schönsten, dich zu schmücken.
Ach, wenn du in dem Gärtlein stehst,
Müßtest du dich selber pflücken.

Lieblicher als Rosen sind
Die Küsse, die dein Mund verschwendet,
Weil der Reiz der Blumen endet,
Wo dein Liebreiz erst beginnt.
Wenn du zu den Blumen gehst,
Pflücke die schönsten, dich zu schmücken.
Ach, wenn du in dem Gärtlein stehst,
Müßtest du dich selber pflücken.

Ah, if you were in the garden,
You would have to pick yourself.

All the flowers know well
That you are lovely beyond compare.
And the flower that saw you
Would fade in colour and splendour.
When you go to the flowers,
Pick the loveliest to adorn yourself.
Ah, if you were in the garden,
You would have to pick yourself.

Lovelier than roses are
The kisses your lips lavishly bestow,
For the charm of flowers ceases
Where your fair charms begin.
When you go to the flowers,
Pick the loveliest to adorn yourself.
Ah, if you were in the garden,
You would have to pick yourself.

21 °
2 November 1889
Todos duermen corazon (ANON.)

Alle gingen, Herz, zur Ruh,
Alle schlafen, nur nicht du.

Denn der hoffnungslose Kummer
Scheucht von deinem Bett den Schlummer,
Und dein Sinnen schweift in stummer
Sorge seiner Liebe zu.
(*Robert Schumann*)

All have gone to rest, O heart,
All are sleeping, all but you.

For hopeless grief
Banishes slumber from your bed,
And your thoughts fly in speechless
Sorrow to their love.

26 °
10 November 1889
Cubridme de flores BY ?MARIA DOCEO

Bedeckt mich mit Blumen,
Ich sterbe vor Liebe.

Daß die Luft mit leisem Wehen
Nicht den süßen Duft mir entführe,
                    Bedeckt mich!

Ist ja alles doch dasselbe,
Liebesodem oder Düfte
                    Von Blumen.

Cover me with flowers,
I am dying of love.

Lest the soft breezes
Rob me of their sweet scent,
                    Cover me!

For the breath of love
And the scent of flowers
                    Is all one.

Von Jasmin und weißen Lilien
Sollt ihr hier mein Grab bereiten,
      Ich sterbe.

Und befragt ihr mich: Woran?
Sag' ich: Unter süßen Qualen
      Vor Liebe.
(*Robert Schumann*)

3 °
14 November 1889
Estraño humor tiene Juana (ANON.)

Seltsam ist Juanas Weise.
Wenn ich steh' in Traurigkeit,
Wenn ich seufz' und sage: heut,
„Morgen" spricht sie leise.

Trüb' ist sie, wenn ich mich freue;
Lustig singt sie, wenn ich weine;
Sag' ich, daß sie hold mir scheine,
Spricht sie, daß sie stets mich scheue.
Solcher Grausamkeit Beweise
Brechen mir das Herz in Leid –
Wenn ich seufz' und sage: heut,
„Morgen" spricht sie leise.

Heb' ich meine Augenlider,
Weiß sie stets den Blick zu senken;
Um ihn gleich emporzulenken,
Schlag' ich auch den meinen nieder.
Wenn ich sie als Heil'ge preise,
Nennt sie Dämon mich im Streit –
Wenn ich seufz' und sage: heut,
„Morgen" spricht sie leise.

Sieglos heiß' ich auf der Stelle,
Rühm' ich meinen Sieg bescheiden;
Hoff' ich auf des Himmels Freuden,
Prophezeit sie mir die Hölle.
Ja, so ist ihr Herz von Eise,
Säh' sie sterben mich vor Leid,
Hörte mich noch seufzen: heut,
„Morgen" spräch' sie leise.

4 °°
15 November 1889
Burla bien con desamor (ANON.)

Treibe nur mit Lieben Spott,

With jasmine and white lilies
You shall here prepare my grave,
      I am dying.

And if you ask me: Of what?
I'll say: in sweet torment
      Of love.

Juana's ways are strange.
When I am sad,
When I sigh and say 'today',
She murmurs 'tomorrow'.

She is gloomy when I am glad;
She sings merrily when I weep;
When I say I find her beautiful,
She says I always fill her with dread.
Such tokens of cruelty
Crush my heart in grief –
When I sigh and say 'today',
She murmurs 'tomorrow'.

Whenever I raise my gaze,
She always contrives to lower hers;
Only to look up at me
As soon as I look down.
When I call her a saint,
She, to be contrary, calls me a devil –
When I sigh and say 'today',
She murmurs 'tomorrow'.

She calls me a failure on the spot,
If modestly I claim a victory;
If I hope for heaven's joy,
She prophesies me hell.
Yes, so icy is her heart,
That if she saw me dying of grief
And heard me sigh 'today',
She would murmur tomorrow.

Just keep on mocking love,

Geliebte mein;
Spottet doch der Liebesgott
Dereinst auch dein!

Magst an Spotten nach Gefallen
Du dich weiden;
Von dem Weibe kommt uns Allen
Lust und Leiden.
Treibe nur mit Lieben Spott,
Geliebte mein;
Spottet doch der Liebesgott
Dereinst auch dein!

Bist auch jetzt zu stolz zum
    Minnen,
Glaub', o glaube:
Liebe wird dich doch gewinnen
Sich zum Raube,
Wenn du spottest meiner Not,
Geliebte mein;
Spottet doch der Liebesgott
Dereinst auch dein!

Wer da lebt im Fleisch, erwäge
Alle Stunden:
Amor schläft und plötzlich rege
Schlägt er Wunden.
Treibe nur mit Lieben Spott,
Geliebte mein;
Spottet doch der Liebesgott
Dereinst auch dein!

2 °°
17 November 1889*
A la sombra de mis cabellos (ANON.)

In dem Schatten meiner Locken
Schlief mir mein Geliebter ein.
Weck' ich ihn nun auf? – Ach nein!

Sorglich strählt' ich meine krausen
Locken täglich in der Frühe,
Doch umsonst ist meine Mühe,
Weil die Winde sie zersausen.
Lockenschatten, Windessausen
Schläferten den Liebsten ein.
Weck' ich ihn nun auf? – Ach nein!

My beloved;
But the god of love will mock
You some day too!

You can mock away
To your heart's content;
From women we all derive
Pleasure and pain.
Just keep on mocking love,
My beloved;
But the god of love will mock
You some day too!

Though you are now too proud to
    love,
You may rest assured:
Love will yet seize you
As its prey,
If you mock at my distress,
My beloved;
The god of love will mock
You some day too!

Let him who lives in flesh
Always ponder this:
Cupid sleeps and will suddenly wake
And wound you.
Just keep on mocking love,
My beloved;
But the god of love will mock
You some day too!

In the shadow of my tresses
My lover has fallen asleep.
Shall I wake him now? – Ah no!

Carefully, I combed my curly
Tresses early each morning,
But my efforts are in vain,
For the winds tousle them.
Shade-giving tresses, sighing breezes
Have lulled my lover to sleep.
Shall I wake him now? – Ah no!

---

* Included by Wolf in his opera *Der Corregidor* (1895), where it is sung by Frasquita in Act I.

Hören muß ich, wie ihn gräme,
Daß er schmachtet schon so lange,
Daß ihm Leben geb' und nehme
Diese meine braune Wange.
Und er nennt mich seine Schlange,
Und doch schlief er bei mir ein.
Weck' ich ihn nun auf? – Ach nein!
(*Brahms, Jensen*)

I shall have to hear how he grieves,
How he has languished so long,
How his whole life depends
On these my dusky cheeks.
And he calls me his serpent,
And yet he fell asleep at my side.
Shall I wake him now? – Ah no!

27 °

17 November 1889
Si dormis doncella BY GIL VICENTE (?1465–1537)

Und schläfst du, mein Mädchen,
Auf, öffne du mir;
Denn die Stund' ist gekommen,
Da wir wandern von hier.

And if you're sleeping, my girl,
Get up, and let me in;
Because the time has come
For us to leave.

Und bist ohne Sohlen,
Leg' keine dir an;
Durch reißende Wasser
Geht unsere Bahn.

And if you have no shoes,
Put none on;
For our way lies
Through raging waters.

Durch die tief tiefen Wasser
Des Guadalquivir*;
Denn die Stund' ist gekommen,
Da wir wandern von hier.
(*Robert Schumann*)

Through the deep deep waters
Of the Guadalquivir;
Because the time has come
For us to leave.

11 °°

19 November 1889 †
Corazon no desesperes (ANON.)

Herz, verzage nicht geschwind,
Weil die Weiber Weiber sind.

Heart, do not despair too soon,
Because women are women.

Argwohn lehre sie dich kennen,
Die sich lichte Sterne nennen
Und wie Feuerfunken brennen.
Drum verzage nicht geschwind,
Weil die Weiber Weiber sind.

Teach them to know mistrust,
They who call themselves bright stars
And burn like sparks of fire.
Do not, therefore, despair too soon,
Because women are women.

Laß dir nicht den Sinn verwirren,
Wenn sie süße Weisen girren;

Do not let your wits be confused
When they coo their wheedling words;

---

* Spanish river, some 350 miles long, that rises in the Sierra del Pozo Morena, flows through Andalusia and enters the Atlantic about twenty miles north of Cadiz.
† Included by Wolf in his opera *Der Corregidor* (1895) where it is sung to the sleeping Frasquita by the philandering Corregidor in Act II.

Möchten dich mit Listen kirren,
Machen dich mit Ränken blind;
Weil die Weiber Weiber sind.

Sind einander stets im Bunde,
Fechten tapfer mit dem Munde,
Wünschen, was versagt die Stunde,
Bauen Schlösser in den Wind;
Weil die Weiber Weiber sind.

Und so ist ihr Sinn verschroben,
Daß sie, lobst du, was zu loben,
Mit dem Mund dagegen toben,
Ob ihr Herz auch Gleiches sinnt;
Weil die Weiber Weiber sind.

They would tame you with their cunning,
Blind you with their wiles;
Because women are women.

They are always in league with each other,
Fighting boldly with their tongues,
Wanting what time does not allow,
Building castles in the air;
Because women are women.

And their minds are so perverse
That if you praise what merits praise,
They will rant against it,
Though in their hearts they think the same;
Because women are women.

12 °°
19 November 1889
Dezi si soys vos galan (ANON.)

Sagt, seid Ihr es, feiner Herr,
Der da jüngst so hübsch gesprungen
Und gesprungen und gesungen?

Seid Ihr der, vor dessen Kehle
Keiner mehr zu Wort gekommen?
Habt die Backen voll genommen,
Sangt gar artig, ohne Fehle?
Ja, Ihr seid's, bei meiner Seele,
Der so mit uns umgesprungen
Und gesprungen und gesungen.

Seid Ihr's, der auf Castagnetten
Und Gesang sich nicht verstand,
Der die Liebe nie gekannt,
Der da floh vor Weiberketten?
Ja Ihr seid's; doch möcht' ich wetten,
Manch ein Lieb habt Ihr umschlungen
Und gesprungen und gesungen.

Seid Ihr der, der Tanz und Lieder
So herausstrich ohne Maß?
Seid Ihr's, der im Winkel saß
Und nicht regte seine Glieder?
Ja Ihr seid's, ich kenn' Euch wieder,
Der zum Gähnen uns gezwungen
Und gesprungen und gesungen!

Say, was it you, dear sir,
Who recently danced so nicely,
And danced and sang?

Was it you, whose voice
Stopped all from getting a word in?
Who talked so big,
Who sang so well, without a slip?
Yes, upon my soul, it was you
Who capered with us like this,
And danced and sang.

Was it you who knew nothing
Of castanets and song,
Who had never known love
And fled from female fetters?
Yes, it was you; but I'll wager
That you've embraced many a sweetheart
And danced and sung.

Was it you who praised
Dancing and singing to the skies?
Was it you who sat in the corner
And wouldn't stir a limb?
Yes, it was you, I recognize you now,
Who made us yawn
And danced and sang!

20 November 1889

Tango vos, el mi pandero BY ALVARO FERNANDEZ DE AMEIDA (16TH CENTURY)

Klinge, klinge, mein Pandero,
Doch an andres denkt mein Herz.

Ring out, ring out, my tambourine,
Though my heart thinks of other things.

Wenn du, muntres Ding, verständest
Meine Qual und sie empfändest,
Jeder Ton, den du entsendest,
Würde klagen meinen Schmerz.

If you, blithe instrument, could understand
And feel my torment,
Each one of your sounds
Would bewail my grief.

Bei des Tanzes Drehn und Neigen
Schlag' ich wild den Takt zum Reigen,
Daß nur die Gedanken schweigen,
Die mich mahnen an den Schmerz.

As the dance whirls and turns,
I beat out wildly the dance's rhythm,
Simply in order to silence the thoughts
That remind me of my grief.

Ach, ihr Herrn, dann will im Schwingen
Oftmals mir die Brust zerspringen,
Und zum Angstschrei wird mein Singen,
Denn an andres denkt mein Herz.
(*Rubinstein, Jensen*)

Ah, good sirs, while I whirl around,
My heart often feels like breaking,
And my song becomes a cry of anguish,
For my heart thinks of other things.

9

26 November 1889

Vista ciega, luz oscura BY RODRIGO DE COTA (*fl.* 1510)

Blindes Schauen, dunkle Leuchte,
Ruhm voll Weh, erstorbnes Leben,
Unheil, das ein Heil mir däuchte,
Freud'ges Weinen, Lust voll Beben,
Süße Galle, durst'ge Feuchte,
Krieg in Frieden allerwegen,
Liebe, falsch versprachst du Segen,
Da dein Fluch den Schlaf mir scheuchte.

Seeing yet blind, shining yet dark,
Glory full of sorrow, life that has died,
Disaster that seemed salvation,
Joyful yet weeping, pleasure full of trembling,
Sweet yet bitter, parched yet moist,
War in peace, everywhere, always,
False, O Love, was your promise of bliss,
Since your curse has deprived me of sleep.

26 November 1889

Rogáselo madre (ANON.)

Bitt' ihn, o Mutter,
Bitte den Knaben,
Nicht mehr zu zielen,
Weil er mich tötet.

Tell him, O mother,
Tell Cupid
Not to aim at me any more,
For he's killing me.

Mutter, o Mutter,
Die launische Liebe
Höhnt und versöhnt mich,
Flieht mich und zieht mich.

Mother, O mother,
Capricious love
Mocks and soothes me,
Shuns me and entices me.

Ich sah zwei Augen	I saw two eyes
Am letzten Sonntag,	Last Sunday,
Wunder des Himmels,	The wonder of Heaven,
Unheil der Erde.	The bane of the world.
Was man sagt, o Mutter,	What is said, O mother,
Von Basilisken,	Of basilisks,
Erfuhr mein Herze,	My heart discovered
Da ich sie sah.	When I saw them.
Bitt' ihn, o Mutter,	Tell him, O mother,
Bitte den Knaben,	Tell Cupid
Nicht mehr zu zielen,	Not to aim at me any more,
Weil er mich tötet.	For he's killing me.

30 °

5 December 1889

Qui t'a fet lo mal de peu (ANON.) LIMUSINISCH*

„Wer tat deinem Füßlein weh?	'Who hurt your little foot?
La Marioneta,	La Marioneta,
Deiner Ferse weiß wie Schnee?	Your heel as white as snow?
La Marion."	La Marion.'
Sag' Euch an, was krank mich macht,	I'll tell you what afflicts me,
Will kein Wörtlein Euch verschweigen:	I'll not withhold a single word:
Ging zum Rosenbusch zur Nacht,	Last night I went to the rose-bush,
Brach ein Röslein von den Zweigen;	And plucked a rose;
Trat auf einen Dorn im Gang,	I trod on a thorn as I went,
La Marioneta,	La Marioneta,
Der mir bis ins Herze drang,	Which pierced me to the heart,
La Marion.	La Marion.
Sag' Euch alle meine Pein,	I'll tell you all my woes,
Freund, und will Euch nicht berücken:	My friend, and not deceive you:
Ging in einen Wald allein,	I went into a wood alone
Eine Lilie mir zu pflücken;	To pick myself a lily;
Traf ein Stachel scharf mich dort	A sharp thorn pricked me there,
La Marioneta,	La Marioneta,
War ein süßes Liebeswort,	It was a sweet word of love,
La Marion.	La Marion.
Sag' Euch mit Aufrichtigkeit	I'll tell you frankly
Meine Krankheit, meine Wunde:	Of my sickness, my wounds:
In den Garten ging ich heut,	I went into the garden today,
Wo die schönste Nelke stunde;	Where the loveliest carnation grew;
Hat ein Span mich dort verletzt,	A splinter hurt me there,
La Marioneta,	La Marioneta,

* From Limousin, the département of Corrèze and Haute-Vienne.

Blutet fort und fort bis jetzt,
La Marion.

It bled and still bleeds now,
La Marion.

„Schöne Dame, wenn Ihr wollt,
Bin ein Wundarzt guter Weise,
Will die Wund' Euch stillen leise,
Daß Ihr's kaum gewahren sollt.
Bald sollt Ihr genesen sein,
La Marioneta,
Bald geheilt von aller Pein,
La Marion."

'Beauteous lady, if you will,
I'm a surgeon of good repute,
I'll heal your wound so gently
That you'll scarcely notice it.
You'll soon be well again,
La Marioneta,
Soon be free of all your pain,
La Marion.'

5 °°
12 December
Mirandome está mi niña (ANON.)

Auf dem grünen Balkon mein Mädchen
Schaut nach mir durchs Gitterlein.
Mit den Augen blinzelt sie freundlich,
Mit dem Finger sagt sie mir: Nein!

From her green balcony my love
Peeps at me through the trellis.
With her eyes she leads me on,
But her finger tells me: No!

Glück, das nimmer ohne Wanken
Junger Liebe folgt hienieden,
Hat mir Eine Lust beschieden,
Und auch da noch muß ich schwanken.
Schmeicheln hör' ich oder Zanken,
Komm' ich an ihr Fensterlädchen.
Immer nach dem Brauch der Mädchen
Träuft ins Glück ein bißchen Pein:
Mit den Augen blinzelt sie freundlich,
Mit dem Finger sagt sie mir: Nein!

Fortune, that never here on earth
Lets the course of young love run smooth,
Has granted me joy,
But even so I am still in doubt.
Sometimes I hear flattery, sometimes petulance
When I come to her shuttered window.
That is always the way with women,
Mixing a drop of sadness into pleasure:
With her eyes she leads me on,
But her finger tells me: No!

Wie sich nur in ihr vertragen
Ihre Kälte, meine Glut?
Weil in ihr mein Himmel ruht,
Seh' ich Trüb und Hell sich jagen.
In den Wind gehn meine Klagen,
Daß noch nie die süße Kleine
Ihre Arme schlang um meine;
Doch sie hält mich hin so fein –
Mit den Augen blinzelt sie freundlich,
Mit dem Finger sagt sie mir: Nein!

How can both endure in her,
Her coldness, my fire?
Since she is my heaven,
I see darkness vie with light.
The wind bears away my lament
That my little sweet
Has never yet embraced me.
Yet she puts me off so gently –
With her eyes she leads me on,
But her finger tells me: No!

28 °°
13 December 1889
EN CAMPAÑA, MADRE (ANON.)

Sie blasen zum Abmarsch,
Lieb Mütterlein.

Bugles sound for the march-off,
Dear mother.

Mein Liebster muß scheiden
Und läßt mich allein!

Am Himmel die Sterne
Sind kaum noch geflohn,
Da feuert von ferne
Das Fußvolk schon.
Kaum hört er den Ton,
Sein Ränzelein schnürt er,
Von hinnen marschiert er,
Mein Herz hinterdrein.
Mein Liebster muß scheiden
Und läßt mich allein!

Mir ist wie dem Tag,
Dem die Sonne geschwunden.
Mein Trauern nicht mag
So balde gesunden.
Nach nichts ich frag',
Keine Lust mehr heg' ich,
Nur Zwiesprach pfleg' ich
Mit meiner Pein –
Mein Liebster muß scheiden
Und läßt mich allein!

My beloved must part
And leaves me alone!

The stars in the sky
Have hardly yet faded,
And the infantry already
Fire from afar.
As soon as he heard the sound,
He fastened his pack,
And marched away from here,
Taking my heart with him.
My beloved must part
And leaves me alone!

It is like the day
With no sun.
My sorrow cannot
Be so quickly healed.
I ask for nothing,
I have no more joy,
I commune only
With my agony –
My beloved must part
And leaves me alone!

19 °°
28 March 1890
En los tus amores (ANON.)

Trau nicht der Liebe,
Mein Liebster, gib Acht!
Sie macht dich noch weinen,
Wo heut du gelacht.

Und siehst du nicht schwinden
Des Mondes Gestalt?
Das Glück hat nicht minder
Nur wankenden Halt.
Dann rächt es sich bald;
Und Liebe, gib Acht!
Sie macht dich noch weinen,
Wo heut du gelacht.

Drum hüte dich fein
Vor törigem Stolze!
Wohl singen im Mai'n
Die Grillchen im Holze;
Dann schlafen sie ein,
Und Liebe, gib Acht!

Put no trust in love,
My beloved, take care!
It will make you weep,
Though you laughed today.

Do you not see the moon
Waning?
Happiness is no less
Inconstant.
It soon avenges itself;
And love, beware!
It will make you weep,
Though you laughed today.

So be on your guard
Against foolish pride!
Though crickets in May
Chirp in the trees;
They then fall asleep,
And love, beware!

Sie macht dich noch weinen,
Wo heut du gelacht.

Wo schweifst du nur hin?
Laß Rat dir erteilen:
Das Kind mit den Pfeilen
Hat Possen im Sinn.
Die Tage, die eilen,
Und Liebe, gib Acht!
Sie macht dich noch weinen,
Wo heut du gelacht.

Nicht immer ist's helle,
Nicht immer ist's dunkel;
Der Freude Gefunkel
Erbleichet so schnelle.
Ein falscher Geselle
Ist Amor, gib Acht!
Er macht dich noch weinen,
Wo heut du gelacht.

It will make you weep,
Though you laughed today.

Where are you roaming?
Be well advised:
Cupid with his arrows
Has tricks up his sleeve.
The days hasten by,
And love, beware!
It will make you weep,
Though you laughed today.

It is not always light,
It is not always dark;
The spark of joy
Quickly fades.
A false companion
Is Love, beware!
It will make you weep,
Though you laughed today.

18 °
29 March 1890
Triste placer BY ?EMANUEL GEIBEL

Schmerzliche Wonnen und wonnige
   Schmerzen,
Wasser im Auge und Feuer im Herzen,
Stolz auf den Lippen und Seufzer im Sinne,
Honig und Galle zugleich ist die Minne.

Oft, wenn ein Seelchen vom Leibe
   geschieden,
Möcht' es Sankt Michael tragen zum Frieden;
Aber der Dämon auch möcht' es verschlingen;
Keiner will weichen, da geht es ans Ringen.

Seelchen, gequältes, in ängstlichem Wogen
Fühlst du dich hierhin und dorthin gezogen,
Aufwärts und abwärts. In solches Getriebe
Stürzt zwischen Himmel und Höll' uns die
   Liebe.

Mütterchen, ach, und mit siebenzehn Jahren
Hab' ich dies Hangen und Bangen erfahren,
Hab's dann verschworen mit Tränen der Reue;
Ach, und schon lieb' ich, schon lieb' ich aufs
   neue!

Painful bliss and blissful pain,
Tears in the eyes, and fire in the
   heart,
Pride on the lips and sighs in the mind,
Love is a mixture of honey and gall.

Often, when a soul has departed the
   body,
St Michael would like to bear it to rest;
But the devil too would like to devour it;
Neither will yield, so a tussle ensues.

Tormented soul, you feel yourself
Tugged back and forth, up and down
In anguished distress. Such is the
   commotion
Love hurls us into between heaven and hell.

Ah, mother, I at seventeen
Have already felt this great anxiety,
And then forswore it with tears of
   remorse;
And ah, already I'm in love, in love again!

29 °°

29 March 1890
No lloreis, ojuelos BY LOPE DE VEGA (1562–1613)

Weint nicht, ihr Äuglein!
Wie kann so trübe
Weinen vor Eifersucht,
Wer tötet durch Liebe?

Wer selbst Tod bringt
Der sollt' ihn ersehnen?
Sein Lächeln bezwingt
Was trotzt seinen Tränen.
Weint nicht, ihr Äuglein!
Wie kann so trübe
Weinen vor Eifersucht,
Wer tötet durch Liebe?

Weep not, dear eyes;
How can one who kills through love
Weep so bitterly
From jealousy?

Should he who deals death himself,
Crave it?
Whoever resists his tears
Will be won over by his smiles.
Weep not, dear eyes;
How can one who kills through love
Weep so bitterly
From jealousy?

20 °°

30 March 1890
Que por mayo era por mayo (ANON.)

Ach im Maien war's, im Maien,
Wo die warmen Lüfte wehen,
Wo verliebte Leute pflegen
Ihren Liebchen nachzugehen.

Ich allein, ich armer Trauriger,
Lieg' im Kerker so verschmachtet,
Und ich seh nicht, wann es taget,
Und ich weiß nicht, wann es nachtet.

Nur an einem Vöglein merkt' ich's,
Das dadrauß im Maien sang;
Das hat mir ein Schütz getötet –
Geb' ihm Gott den schlimmsten Dank!

Ah, in May it was, in Maytime,
When warm breezes blow,
When those in love are wont
To seek their loves.

I alone, sad wretch,
Languish in a dungeon cell,
And cannot tell when day dawns,
And cannot tell when night falls.

Only one little bird could tell me,
That sang out there in May;
A hunter killed it –
May God give him the worst of rewards!

10 °°

31 March 1890
Juramentos por amores (ANON.)

Eide, so die Liebe schwur,
Schwache Bürgen sind sie nur.

Sitzt die Liebe zu Gericht,
Dann, Señor, vergesset nicht,
Daß sie nie nach Recht und Pflicht,
Immer nur nach Gunst verfuhr.

Oaths which love has sworn
Are but feeble sureties.

When Love sits in judgement,
Then, senor, do not forget,
That she proceeds not by right or duty,
But always by favour.

Eide, so die Liebe schwur,
Schwache Bürgen sind sie nur.

Werdet dort Betrübte finden,
Die mit Schwüren sich verbinden,
Die verschwinden mit den Winden,
Wie die Blumen auf der Flur.
Eide, so die Liebe schwur,
Schwache Bürgen sind sie nur.

Und als Schreiber an den Schranken
Seht ihr nichtige Gedanken.
Weil die leichten Händlein schwanken,
Schreibt euch keiner nach der Schnur.
Eide, so die Liebe schwur,
Schwache Bürgen sind sie nur.

Sind die Bürgen gegenwärtig,
Allesamt des Spruchs gewärtig,
Machen sie das Urteil fertig; –
Von Vollziehen keine Spur!
Eide, so die Liebe schwur,
Schwache Bürgen sind sie nur.

Oaths which love has sworn
Are but feeble sureties.

There you will find the distressed,
Binding themselves with vows,
Which vanish with the wind
Like flowers in the field.
Oaths which love has sworn
Are but feeble sureties.

And as clerks of the court
You'll find vain thoughts.
Because their feeble hands tremble,
They will not record you accurately.
Oaths which love has sworn
Are but feeble sureties.

And when the sureties are assembled
And all await a verdict,
They will prepare the judgment; –
But never execute it!
Oaths which love has sworn
Are but feeble sureties.

34 °
1 April 1890
Vete amor, y vete (ANON.)

Geh, Geliebter, geh jetzt!
Sieh, der Morgen dämmert.

Leute gehn schon durch die Gasse,
Und der Markt wird so belebt,
Daß der Morgen wohl, der blasse,
Schon die weißen Flügel hebt.
Und vor unsern Nachbarn bin ich
Bange, daß du Anstoß gibst;
Denn sie wissen nicht, wie innig
Ich dich lieb' und du mich liebst.

Drum, Geliebter, geh jetzt!
Sieh, der Morgen dämmert.

Wenn die Sonn' am Himmel scheinend
Scheucht vom Feld die Perlen klar,
Muß auch ich die Perle weinend
Lassen, die mein Reichtum war.
Was als Tag den Andern funkelt,
Meinen Augen dünkt es Nacht,

Go, beloved, go now!
Look, the day is dawning.

Already people are in the streets,
And the market's so busy
That pale morning
Must be spreading its white wings.
And I'm fearful of our neighbours,
That you will offend them;
For they do not know how fervently
I love you and you love me.

Therefore, beloved, go now!
Look, the day is dawning.

When the sun, shining in the sky,
Chases the bright pearls of dew from the fields,
I must also weep and leave the pearl
That was once my treasure.
What to others shines as day,
My eyes see as night,

Da die Trennung bang mir dunkelt,
Wenn das Morgenrot erwacht.

    Geh, Geliebter, geh jetzt!
    Sieh, der Morgen dämmert.

Fliehe denn aus meinen Armen!
Denn versäumest du die Zeit,
Möchten für ein kurz Erwarmen
Wir ertauschen langes Leid.
Ist in Fegefeuersqualen
Doch ein Tag schon auszustehn,
Wenn die Hoffnung fern in Strahlen
Läßt des Himmels Glorie sehn.

    Drum, Geliebter, geh jetzt!
    Sieh, der Morgen dämmert.

For parting darkens my mind,
When the red of morning dawns.

    Go, beloved, go now!
    Look, the day is dawning.

Fly then from my arms!
For if you let time slip by,
We shall pay with long sorrow
For our brief embrace.
One day in Purgatory
Can after all be borne,
When Hope, radiant from afar,
Reveals the glory of heaven.

    Therefore, beloved, go now!
    Look, the day is dawning.

17°°
2 April 1890
En mi helado pecho (ANON.)

Liebe mir im Busen
Zündet' einen Brand.
Wasser, liebe Mutter,
Eh das Herz verbrannt!

Nicht das blinde Kind
Straft für meine Fehle;
Hat zuerst die Seele
Mir gekühlt so lind.
Dann entflammt's geschwind
Ach, mein Unverstand;
Wasser, liebe Mutter,
Eh das Herz verbrannt!

Ach, wo ist die Flut,
Die dem Feuer wehre?
Für so große Glut
Sind zu arm die Meere.
Weil es wohl mir tut
Wein' ich unverwandt;
Wasser, liebe Mutter,
Eh das Herz verbrannt!

Love in my breast
Has kindled a fire.
Water, dear mother,
Before my heart's consumed!

Do not blame blind Cupid
For my faults;
He cooled my soul
So gently at first.
Then, alas, he swiftly
Inflamed my folly.
Water, dear mother,
Before my heart's consumed!

Ah, where is the flood
That might quench this fire?
For so great a flame
The seas are too small.
Since it does me good,
I weep without restraint;
Water, dear mother,
Before my heart's consumed!

31 °°

2 April 1890

La tu madre, o mis amores BY DON LUIS EL CHICO = PAUL HEYSE

Deine Mutter, süßes Kind,
Da sie in den Weh'n gelegen,
Brausen hörte sie den Wind.

Und so hat sie dich geboren
Mit dem falschen wind'gen Sinn.
Hast du heut ein Herz erkoren,
Wirfst es morgen treulos hin.
Doch den zähl' ich zu den Toren,
Der dich schmäht der Untreu wegen:
Dein Geschick war dir entgegen;
Denn die Mutter, süßes Kind,
Da sie in den Weh'n gelegen,
Brausen hörte sie den Wind.

Your mother, sweet child,
When she lay in labour,
Could hear the roaring wind.

And so you were born
As false and fickle as the wind.
If you choose a lover today,
You'll discard him faithlessly tomorrow.
Yet I count him a fool
Who chides you for your infidelity:
Your destiny was against you;
For your mother, sweet child,
When she lay in labour,
Could hear the roaring wind.

13 °

3 April 1890

Dirá cuanto dijere (ANON.)

Mögen alle bösen Zungen
Immer sprechen, was beliebt;
Wer mich liebt, den lieb' ich wieder,
Und ich lieb' und bin geliebt.

Schlimme, schlimme Reden flüstern
Eure Zungen schonungslos;
Doch ich weiß es, sie sind lüstern
Nach unschuld'gem Blute bloß.
Nimmer soll es mich bekümmern,
Schwatzt so viel es euch beliebt;
Wer mich liebt, den lieb' ich wieder
Und ich lieb'und bin geliebt.

Zur Verleumdung sich verstehet
Nur, wem Lieb' und Gunst gebrach,
Weil's ihm selber elend gehet,
Und ihn niemand minnt und mag.
Darum denk' ich, daß die Liebe
Drum sie schmähn, mir Ehre gibt;
Wer mich liebt, den lieb' ich wieder,
Und ich lieb' und bin geliebt.

Wenn ich wär' aus Stein und Eisen,
Möchtet ihr darauf bestehn,
Daß ich sollte von mir weisen

Let all the spiteful tongues
Keep on saying what they please;
He who loves me, I love in return,
And I love and am loved.

Your tongues whisper relentlessly
Wicked, wicked slanders;
But I know, they merely thirst
For innocent blood.
It will never bother me,
You may gossip to your heart's content;
He who loves me, I love in return,
And I love and am loved.

Only those enjoy slander
Who lack affection and kindness,
Because they fare so wretchedly
And no one loves or wants them.
Therefore I think that the love
They revile is to my honour;
He who loves me, I love in return,
And I love and am loved.

If I were made of stone and iron,
You might well insist
That I should reject

Liebesgruß und Liebesflehn.
Doch mein Herzlein ist nun leider
Weich, wie's Gott uns Mädchen gibt;
Wer mich liebt, den lieb' ich wieder,
Und ich lieb' und bin geliebt.
(*Robert Schumann*)

Love's greetings, love's entreaties.
But my little heart is, I fear, soft,
As God fashions it for us girls;
He who loves me, I love in return,
And I love and am loved.

15 °°
4 April 1890
Decidle que me venga á ver (ANON.)

Sagt ihm, daß er zu mir komme,
Denn je mehr sie mich drum schelten,
Ach, je mehr wächst meine Glut!

Tell him to come to me,
For the more they scold me for it,
Ah, the greater my passion grows!

O zum Wanken
Bringt die Liebe nichts auf Erden;
Durch ihr Zanken
Wird sie nur gedoppelt werden.
Sie gefährden
Mag nicht ihrer Neider Wut;
Denn je mehr sie mich drum schelten,
Ach, je mehr wächst meine Glut!

Oh, Love can be shaken
By nothing on earth;
Their chiding
Will only double its power.
Not all the fury of the envious
Can imperil it;
For the more they scold me for it,
Ah, the greater my passion grows!

Eingeschlossen
Haben sie mich lange Tage,
Unverdrossen
Mich gestraft mit schlimmer Plage.
Doch ich trage
Jede Pein mit Liebesmut,
Denn je mehr sie mich drum schelten,
Ach, je mehr wächst meine Glut!

They've locked me in
For days on end,
Have persistently
Punished me severely.
But I bear every pain
With the fortitude of love,
For the more they scold me for it,
Ah, the greater my passion grows!

Meine Peiniger
Sagen oft, ich soll dich lassen,
Doch nur einiger
Wolln wir uns ins Herze fassen.
Muß ich drum erblassen,
Tod um Liebe lieblich tut,
Und je mehr sie mich drum schelten,
Ach, je mehr wächst meine Glut!

My tormentors
Often say I should leave you,
But this only makes us
Cleave to each other more.
And if I must fade away and die,
To die for love will be sweet,
And the more they scold me for it,
Ah, the greater my passion grows!

22 °
11 April 1890
Alguna vez BY CRISTOBAL DE CASTILLEJO (?1492–1550)

Dereinst, dereinst
Gedanke mein
Wirst ruhig sein.

One day, one day,
My thoughts,
You shall be at rest.

Läßt Liebesglut	Though love's ardour
Dich still nicht werden:	Gives you no peace,
In kühler Erden	You shall sleep well
Da schläfst du gut;	In cool earth;
Dort ohne Liebe	There without love
Und ohne Pein	And without pain
Wirst ruhig sein.	You shall be at rest.
Was du im Leben	What you did not
Nicht hast gefunden,	Find in life
Wenn es entschwunden	Will be granted you
Wird dir's gegeben.	When life is ended.
Dann ohne Wunden	Then, free from torment
Und ohne Pein	And free from pain,
Wirst ruhig sein.	You shall be at rest.
(*Grieg, Jensen, Robert Schumann*)	

23 °

12 April 1890

De dentro tengo mi mal BY LUIS DE CAMOENS (1525–80)

Tief im Herzen trag' ich Pein,	Deep in my heart I bear my grief,
Muß nach außen stille sein.	Outwardly I must be calm.
Den geliebten Schmerz verhehle	I conceal this sweet agony
Tief ich vor der Welt Gesicht;	Far from the world's gaze;
Und es fühlt ihn nur die Seele,	It is felt only by my soul,
Denn der Leib verdient ihn nicht.	For the body does not deserve it.
Wie der Funke frei und licht	As sparks, free and bright,
Sich verbirgt im Kieselstein,	Lie hidden in flint,
Trag' ich innen tief die Pein.	So I bear my grief deep within.
(*Robert Schumann*)	

24 °

14 April 1890

Ven muerte tan escondida BY COMENDADOR ESCRIVA (c.1450–c.1520)

Komm, o Tod, von Nacht umgeben,	Come, O Death, shrouded in night,
Leise komm zu mir gegangen,	Come quietly to me,
Daß die Lust, dich zu umfangen,	So that my joy in embracing you
Nicht zurück mich ruf' ins Leben.	Does not recall me to life.
Komm, so wie der Blitz uns rühret,	Come, as the lightning strikes
Den der Donner nicht verkündet,	Unheralded by thunder,
Bis er plötzlich sich entzündet	Until it suddenly flashes,
Und den Schlag gedoppelt führet.	Striking a double blow.
Also seist du mir gegeben,	Thus may you be granted me,
Plötzlich stillend mein Verlangen,	Suddenly stilling my longing,

Daß die Lust, dich zu umfangen,	So that my joy in embracing you
Nicht zurück mich ruf' ins Leben.	Does not recall me to life.

25 °°
16 April 1890
Aunque con semblante airado (ANON.)

Ob auch finstre Blicke glitten,	Even though black looks
Schöner Augenstern, aus dir,	Flashed from your beautiful eyes,
Wird mir doch nicht abgestritten,	It cannot be denied
Daß du hast geblickt nach mir.	That you looked at me.
Wie sich auch der Strahl bemühte,	Even though their rays
Zu verwunden meine Brust,	Sought to wound my breast,
Gibt's ein Leiden, das die Lust,	Is there any suffering which is not requited
Dich zu schaun, nicht reich vergüte?	By the joy of seeing you?
Und so tödlich mein Gemüte	However mortally my feelings
Unter deinem Zorn gelitten,	Have suffered from your anger,
Wird mir doch nicht abgestritten,	It cannot be denied
Daß du hast geblickt nach mir.	That you looked at me.

32 °°
20 April 1890
Pues que no me sabeis dar (ANON.)

Da nur Leid und Leidenschaft	Since only pain and passion
Mich bestürmt in deiner Haft,	Have assailed me in your custody,
Biet' ich nun mein Herz zu Kauf.	I now offer my heart for sale.
Sagt, hat einer Lust darauf?	Speak, does no one want it?
Soll ich sagen, wie ich's schätze,	If I'm to value it,
Sind drei Batzen nicht zuviel.	Then three farthings isn't too much.
Nimmer war's des Windes Spiel,	It was never the wind's plaything,
Eigensinnig blieb's im Netze.	It stayed obstinately in your toils.
Aber weil mich drängt die Not	But because I'm hard pressed,
Biet' ich nun mein Herz zu Kauf,	I now offer my heart for sale,
Schlag' es los zum Meistgebot –	Shall knock it down to the highest bidder –
Sagt, hat einer Lust darauf?	Speak, does no one want it?
Täglich kränkt es mich im Stillen	Each day it silently grieves me
Und erfreut mich nimmermehr.	And delights me no more.
Nun wer bietet? – wer gibt mehr?	So, who'll bid? – who'll give more?
Fort mit ihm und seinen Grillen!	Away with it and all its whims!
Daß sie schlimm sind, leuchtet ein,	It's obvious they are bad,
Biet' ich doch mein Herz zu Kauf.	That's why I offer my heart for sale.
Wär' es froh, behielt's ich's fein –	If it were happy, I'd gladly keep it –
Sagt, hat einer Lust darauf?	Speak, does no one want it?

Kauft ihr's, leb' ich ohne Grämen.	Buy it, and I'll live free of grief.
Mag es haben, wem's beliebt!	Let it go to him who wants it!
Nun wer kauft? Wer will es nehmen?	So, who'll buy? Who'll take it?
Sag' ein Jeder, was er gibt.	Let everyone say what they'll give.
Noch einmal vorm Hammerschlag	Once again, under the hammer,
Biet' ich jetzt mein Herz zu Kauf,	I offer my heart for sale,
Daß man sich entscheiden mag –	So make up your minds –
Sagt, hat einer Lust darauf?	Speak, does no one want it?

Nun zum ersten – und zum zweiten –	Going for the first time – and the second –
Und beim dritten schlag' ich's zu!	Going, going, gone!
Gut denn! Mag dir's Glück bereiten;	Well done! May you have joy of it;
Nimm es, meine Liebste du!	Take it, my sweetheart!
Brenn' ihm mit dem glüh'nden Erz	Brand the slave mark into it
Gleich das Sklavenzeichen auf;	Swiftly with a red-hot iron;
Denn ich schenke dir mein Herz,	For I'll make you a gift of my heart,
Hast du auch nicht Lust zum Kauf.	Though you do not wish to buy it.

33 °°

27 April 1890
Mal haya, quien los envuelve BY GIL VICENTE (?1465–1537)

Wehe der, die mir verstrickte	Woe to the woman
Meinen Geliebten!	Who ensnared my beloved!
Wehe der, die ihn verstrickte!	Woe to the woman who ensnared him!

Ach, der Erste, den ich liebte,	Ah, the first man I loved
Ward gefangen in Sevilla.	Was caught in Seville.
Mein Vielgeliebter,	My best-beloved,
Wehe der, die ihn verstrickte!	Woe to the woman who ensnared him!

Ward gefangen in Sevilla	He was caught in Seville
Mit der Fessel meiner Locken.	By the fetters of my tresses.
Mein Vielgeliebter,	My best-beloved,
Wehe der, die ihn verstrickte!	Woe to the woman who ensnared him!

Italienisches Liederbuch / The Italian Songbook

Hugo Wolf's *Italienisches Liederbuch* comprises forty-six songs to translations by Paul Heyse of anonymous Italian poems, which had been published in 1860. Heyse's source was for the most part four collections of folk and traditional poetry that had been published earlier in the nineteenth century: Tommaseo's *Canti popolari* (1841), Tigri's *Canti popolari Toscani* (1856), Marcoaldi's *Canti popolari inediti* (1855) and Dalmedico's *Canti del popolo Veneziano* (1848). Wolf ignored the ballads and death laments, and concentrated almost exclusively on the *rispetti* – short love poems that depict a wide variety of emotions. Like much demotic verse (*Des Knaben Wunderhorn*, for example), the language is simple and the lines frequently end-stopped. Almost all the poems set by Wolf concern the lover and his sweetheart, and they chart against a Tuscan landscape of Orvieto, Siena and the Arno, the everyday squabbles, tiffs, jealousies, flirtations, machinations, frivolities, joys and despair of men and women in love. Heyse's translations often intensify the simple, unemotional Italian of the original verse, and Wolf's settings, particularly of the more serious poems, represent a further heightening of emotion. The first song of the collection, 'Auch kleine Dinge', states that 'even small things can delight us', and Wolf presumably opened his final songbook with it to indicate the miniature form of these songs. Of forty-six, only six are three pages long, the majority occupy a mere two pages, while two are no longer than a single page. The volume contains no grand-scale songs like Goethe's 'Prometheus' and 'Ganymed' or Mörike's 'Der Feuerreiter'; no religious fervour as in the *Spanisches Liederbuch;* yet there is an *Innigkeit,* an emotional immediacy about these songs and an understanding of the human heart that is in no way diminished by the miniature form.

As Wolf himself described in a letter to Emil Kauffmann, dated 15 December 1891: „Ich halte die Italienischen für das originellste und künstlerisch vollendetste unter allen meinen Sachen." ('I consider the Italian songs the most original and artistically the most perfect of all my things.')

The songs are printed in chronological order of composition; the numbers at the top of each indicate Wolf's published order.

2

25 September 1890
M'è stato detto che voli partire FROM MARCOALDI

Mir ward gesagt, du reisest in die Ferne.	They told me you were going far away.
Ach, wohin gehst du, mein geliebtes Leben?	Ah, where are you going, love of my life?
Den Tag, an dem du scheidest, wüßt ich gerne;	The day you leave, I would gladly know;
Mit Tränen will ich das Geleit dir geben.	I shall accompany you with tears.
Mit Tränen will ich deinen Weg befeuchten –	I shall bedew your path with tears –
Gedenk an mich, und Hoffnung wird mir leuchten!	Think of me, and hope will give me light!
Mit Tränen bin ich bei dir allerwärts –	With tears I'm with you, wherever you are –
Gedenk an mich, vergiß es nicht, mein Herz!	Think of me, do not forget, my heart!

3

2 October 1890
E sete la più bella mentovata FROM TIGRI

Ihr seid die Allerschönste weit und breit,	You are the loveliest for miles around,
Viel schöner als im Mai der Blumenflor.	More lovely by far than flowers in May.
Orvietos Dom steigt so voll Herrlichkeit,	Not even the Cathedral of Orvieto

Viterbos größter Brunnen nicht empor.
So hoher Reiz und Zauber ist dein eigen,
Der Dom von Siena muß sich vor dir neigen.
Ach, du bist so an Reiz und Anmut reich,
Der Dom von Siena selbst ist dir nicht gleich.

Or Viterbo's largest fountain rise with such majesty
Your charms and your magic are such
That Siena Cathedral must bow before you.
Ah, you are so rich in charm and grace,
Even Siena Cathedral cannot compare.

4

3 October 1890
Sia benedetto chi fece lo mondo FROM TIGRI

Gesegnet sei, durch den die Welt entstund;
Wie trefflich schuf er sie nach allen Seiten!
Er schuf das Meer mit endlos tiefem Grund,
Er schuf die Schiffe, die hinübergleiten,
Er schuf das Paradies mit ewgem Licht,
Er schuf die Schönheit und dein Angesicht.

Blessed be he, who created the world;
How excellent on every side he made it!
He made the sea of unfathomable depths,
He made the ships that glide across,
He made Paradise with its eternal light,
He made beauty and your face.

5

4 October 1890
Beati ciechi voi che non vedete FROM MERCOLADI

Selig ihr Blinden, die ihr nicht zu schauen
Vermögt die Reize, die uns Glut entfachen;
Selig ihr Tauben, die ihr ohne Grauen
Die Klagen der Verliebten könnt verlachen;
Selig ihr Stummen, die ihr nicht den Frauen
Könnt eure Herzensnot verständlich machen;
Selig ihr Toten, die man hat begraben!
Ihr sollt vor Liebesqualen Ruhe haben.

Blessed are the blind, who cannot see
The charms that kindle a blaze in us;
Blessed are the deaf, who without fear
Can laugh at the laments of lovers;
Blessed are the dumb, who cannot tell women
Of their heart's anguish;
Blessed are the dead lying in their graves!
You shall have respite from love's torment.

6

13 November 1890
Chi ti ci fa venir, chi ti ci chiama? FROM TOMMASEO

Wer rief dich denn? Wer hat dich herbestellt?
Wer hieß dich kommen, wenn es dir zur Last?
Geh zu dem Liebchen, das dir mehr gefällt,
Geh dahin, wo du die Gedanken hast.
Geh nur, wohin dein Sinnen steht und Denken!
Daß du zu mir kommst, will ich gern dir
    schenken.
Geh zu dem Liebchen, das dir mehr gefällt!
Wer rief dich denn? Wer hat dich herbestellt?

Who called you, then? Who sent for you?
Who asked you to come, if it's a burden?
Go to the sweetheart you like better,
Go there – where your thoughts are.
Just go to her you dream and think of!
I'll gladly spare you from seeing me.
Go to the sweetheart you like better!
Who called you, then? Who sent for
    you?

7

13 November 1890
La luna s'è venuta a lamentare FROM TIGRI

Der Mond hat eine schwere Klag' erhoben
Und vor dem Herrn die Sache kund gemacht;
Er wolle nicht mehr stehn am Himmel droben,
Du habest ihn um seinen Glanz gebracht.
Als er zuletzt das Sternenheer gezählt,
Da hab es an der vollen Zahl gefehlt;
Zwei von den schönsten habest du entwendet,
Die beiden Augen dort, die mich verblendet.

The moon has raised a grave complaint
And made the matter known unto the Lord:
It no longer wants to stay up there in the sky,
For you have robbed it of its radiance.
When last he counted all the stars,
The full number was not complete;
You have purloined two of the loveliest:
Those two eyes that have blinded me.

8

14 November 1890
Facciam la pace, caro bene mio FROM TOMMASEO

Nun laß uns Frieden schließen, liebstes Leben,
Zu lang ist's schon, daß wir in Fehde liegen.
Wenn du nicht willst, will ich mich dir ergeben;
Wie könnten wir uns auf den Tod bekriegen?
Es schließen Frieden Könige und Fürsten,
Und sollten Liebende nicht darnach dürsten?
Es schließen Frieden Fürsten und Soldaten,
Und sollt es zwei Verliebten wohl mißraten?
Meinst du, daß, was so großen Herrn gelingt,
Ein Paar zufriedner Herzen nicht vollbringt?

Let us now make peace, love of my life,
We have been feuding far too long.
If you're not willing, I'll give in to you;
How could we wage war to the death?
Peace is made by kings and princes,
Why should not lovers crave the same?
Peace is made by soldiers and princes,
So why should two lovers not succeed?
Do you think what such great lords can manage
Cannot be done by two contented hearts?

9

29 November 1891
Le tue bellezze fossero dipinti FROM TOMMASEO AND TIGRI

Daß doch gemalt all deine Reize wären,
Und dann der Heidenfürst das Bildnis fände.
Er würde dir ein groß Geschenk verehren,
Und legte seine Kron' in deine Hände.
Zum rechten Glauben müßt' sich bekehren
Sein ganzes Reich, bis an sein fernstes Ende.
Im ganzen Lande würd' es ausgeschrieben,
Christ soll ein jeder werden und dich lieben.
Ein jeder Heide flugs bekehrte sich
Und würd' ein guter Christ und liebte dich.

If only all your charms had been painted,
And the prince of heathens then found the picture!
He would honour you with a great gift
And place his crown into your hands.
His entire kingdom, to its farthest corner,
Would be converted to the true faith.
An edict would be published throughout the land
That everyone must turn Christian and love you.
Every heathen would be converted at once
And become a good Christian and love you.

10

2 November 1891
Ti pensi di legarmi con un filo FROM TOMMASEO

Du denkst mit einem Fädchen mich zu fangen,	You think you can catch me with a thread,
Mit einem Blick schon mich verliebt zu machen?	Make me fall in love with a mere glance?
Ich fing schon andre, die sich höher schwangen;	I've caught others who flew higher;
Du darfst mir ja nicht traun, siehst du mich lachen.	You can't trust me if you see me laugh.
Schon andre fing ich, glaub es sicherlich.	I've caught others, believe you me.
Ich bin verliebt, doch eben nicht in dich.	I am in love – but not with you.

3 December 1891
E lo mio damo è tanto piccolino FROM TIGRI

Mein Liebster ist so klein, daß ohne Bücken	My sweetheart's so small, that without bending down
Er mir das Zimmer fegt mit seinen Locken.	He can sweep my room with his hair.
Als er ins Gärtlein ging, Jasmin zu pflücken,	When he entered the garden to pick jasmine
Ist er vor einer Schnecke sehr erschrocken.	He was terrified by a snail.
Dann setzt er sich ins Haus um zu verschnaufen,	Then when he came indoors to recover,
Da warf ihn eine Fliege übern Haufen;	A fly knocked him head over heels;
Und als er hintrat an mein Fensterlein,	And when he stepped over to my window,
Stieß eine Bremse ihm den Schädel ein.	A horse-fly caved his head in.
Verwünscht sei'n alle Fliegen, Schnaken, Bremsen,	A curse on all flies – crane- and horse-
Und wer ein Schätzchen hat aus den Maremmen!	And anyone with a sweetheart from Maremma!
Verwünscht sei'n alle Fliegen, Schnaken, Mücken	A curse on all flies, craneflies and midges
Und wer sich, wenn er küßt, so tief muß bücken!	And on all who have to stoop for a kiss!

4 December 1891
Se vuoi vedere il tuo servo morire FROM TOMMASEO

Und willst du deinen Liebsten sterben sehen,	And if you would see your lover die,
So trage nicht dein Haar gelockt, du Holde.	Do not wear your hair in tresses, my love.
Laß von den Schultern frei sie niederwehen;	Let it cascade from your shoulders;
Wie Fäden sehn sie aus von purem Golde.	It looks like threads of pure gold.
Wie goldne Fäden, die der Wind bewegt –	Like golden threads blown by the wind –
Schön sind die Haare, schön ist, die sie trägt!	The hair is beautiful, beautiful she that wears it!
Goldfäden, Seidenfäden ungezählt,	Golden threads, silken threads without number –

Schön sind die Haare, schön ist, die sie strählt!	The hair is beautiful, beautiful she who combs it!

11

4 December 1891

Oh quanto tempo l'ho desiderato FROM TIGRI

Wie lange schon war immer mein Verlangen:	How long have I yearned
Ach, wäre doch ein Musikus mir gut!	To have a musician as lover!
Nun ließ der Herr mich meinen Wunsch erlangen	Now the Lord has granted me my wish,
Und schickt mir einen, ganz wie Milch und Blut.	And sends me one, all pink and white.
Da kommt er eben her mit sanfter Miene,	And here he comes with gentle mien,
Und senkt den Kopf und spielt die Violine.	And bows his head and plays the violin.

14

5 December 1891

Campagno mio, vustu che andèmo frate FROM DALMEDICO

Geselle, wolln wir uns in Kutten hüllen,	Comrade, shall we disguise ourselves in cowls
Die Welt dem lassen, den sie mag ergötzen?	And leave the world to those who enjoy it?
Dann pochen wir an Tür um Tür im Stillen:	We'll secretly knock at door after door:
„Gebt einem armen Mönch um Jesu willen."	'Give to a poor monk, for Jesus' sake!'
– O lieber Pater, du mußt später kommen,	– 'O dear Father, you must come later,
Wenn aus dem Ofen wir das Brot genommen.	When we've taken the bread from the oven.
O lieber Pater, komm nur später wieder,	O dear Father, come back later,
Ein Töchterlein von mir liegt krank darnieder.	One of my daughters lies ill in bed.'
– Und ist sie krank, so laßt mich zu ihr gehen,	– 'If she's ill, let me go to her,
Daß sie nicht etwa sterbe unversehen.	So she might not die unshriven.
Und ist sie krank, so laßt mich nach ihr schauen,	And if she's ill, then let me see her,
Daß sie mir ihre Beichte mag vertrauen.	That she may confess her sins to me.
Schließt Tür und Fenster, daß uns keiner störe,	Close doors and windows, let no one disturb us,
Wenn ich des armen Kindes Beichte höre!	When I hear the poor child's confession!'

12

7 December 1891

Giovinottino, non si fa così FROM TOMMASEO

Nein, junger Herr, so treibt man's nicht, für- wahr;	No, young man, that's no way to carry on;
Man sorgt dafür, sich schicklich zu betragen.	People should try to behave properly.
Für alltags bin ich gut genug, nicht wahr?	I'm good enough for weekdays, am I?
Doch beßre suchst du dir an Feiertagen.	But on holidays you look for better.
Nein, junger Herr, wirst du so weiter sünd'gen,	No, young man, if you keep on mis- behaving so,
Wird dir den Dienst dein Alltagsliebchen künd'gen.	Your weekday love will hand in her notice.

13

7/8 December 1891

Bella che troppo in alto vi tenete FROM TOMMASEO

Hoffärtig seid Ihr, schönes Kind, und geht
Mit Euren Freiern um auf stolzem Fuß.
Spricht man Euch an, kaum daß Ihr Rede steht,
Als kostet' Euch zuviel ein holder Gruß.
Bist keines Alexanders Töchterlein,
Kein Königreich wird deine Mitgift sein,
Und willst du nicht das Gold, so nimm das
    Zinn;
Willst du nicht Liebe, nimm Verachtung hin.

You are haughty, beautiful child,
And high and mighty with your suitors.
If you're spoke to, you hardly deign reply,
As if a friendly greeting cost too much.
You are no Alexander's daughter,
No kingdom will be your dowry,
So if you don't want gold, take tin,
If you don't want love, take contempt.

1

9 December 1891

Le cose piccoline son pur belle FROM TOMMASEO AND TIGRI

Auch kleine Dinge können uns entzücken,
Auch kleine Dinge können teuer sein.
Bedenkt, wie gern wir uns mit Perlen
    schmücken;
Sie werden schwer bezahlt und sind nur klein.
Bedenkt, wie klein ist die Olivenfrucht,
Und wird um ihre Güte doch gesucht.
Denkt an die Rose nur, wie klein sie ist
Und duftet doch so lieblich, wie ihr wißt.

Even small things can delight us,
Even small things can be precious.
Think how gladly we deck ourselves with
    pearls;
They fetch a great price but are only small.
Think how small the olive is,
And yet it is prized for its goodness.
Think only of the rose, how small it is,
And yet smells so lovely, as you know.

22

10 December 1891

Io son venuto a farvi serenata FROM TOMMASEO

Ein Ständchen Euch zu bringen kam ich her,
Wenn es dem Herrn vom Haus nicht ungele-
    gen.
Iht habt ein schönes Töchterlein. Es wär
Wohl gut, sie nicht zu streng im Haus zu hegen.
Und liegt sie schon im Bett, so bitt ich sehr,
Tut es zu wissen ihr von meinetwegen,
Daß ihr Getreuer hier vorbeigekommen,
Der Tag und Nacht sie in den Sinn genommen,
Und daß am Tag, der vierundzwanzig zählt,
Sie fünfundzwanzig Stunden lang mir fehlt.

I have come here to sing a serenade,
If the master of the house does not mind.
You have a beautiful daughter. It were
Better not to keep her too strictly indoors.
And should she have gone to bed,
Then kindly tell her on my behalf
That her sweetheart passed this way,
Who thinks of her by day and night,
And that in a day of four and twenty
    hours
I miss her twenty-five.

16

11 December 1891

Giovanettini che andate alla guerra FROM TOMMASEO

Ihr jungen Leute, die ihr zieht ins Feld,	You young men going off to war,
Auf meinen Liebsten sollt ihr Achtung geben.	You must take care of my sweetheart.
Sorgt, daß er tapfer sich im Feuer hält;	Make sure that he's brave under fire;
Er war noch nie im Kriege all sein Leben.	He's never been to war in all his life.
Laßt nie ihn unter freiem Himmel schlafen;	Never let him sleep in the open;
Er ist so zart, es möchte sich bestrafen.	He's so delicate, it might harm him.
Laßt mir ihn ja nicht schlafen unterm Mond;	Don't let him sleep in the moonlight;
Er ginge drauf, er ist's ja nicht gewohnt.	He'd die – he's not used to it, you see.

18

12 December 1891

Alza la bionda testa, e non dormire FROM TIGRI

Heb auf dein blondes Haupt und schlafe nicht,	Raise your fair head and do not sleep,
Und laß dich ja vom Schlummer nicht betören.	And do not be lulled by slumber.
Ich sage dir vier Worte von Gewicht,	Four things of moment I have to tell you,
Von denen darfst du keines überhören.	None of which you must ignore.
Das erste: daß um dich mein Herze bricht,	The first: my heart is breaking for you,
Das zweite: dir nur will ich angehören,	The second: I want to belong to you alone,
Das dritte: daß ich dir mein Heil befehle,	The third: you are my one salvation,
Das letzte: dich allein liebt meine Seele.	The last: my soul loves only you.

20

12 December 1891

Amor, che passi la notte cantando FROM TIGRI

Mein Liebster singt am Haus im Monden- scheine,	My sweetheart's singing outside the moonlit house,
Und ich muß lauschend hier im Bette liegen.	And I must lie in bed and listen.
Weg von der Mutter wend' ich mich und weine,	I turn away from my mother and weep,
Blut sind die Tränen, die mir nicht versiegen.	My tears are blood, which will not dry.
Den breiten Strom am Bett hab' ich geweint,	I have wept that broad stream by the bed,
Weiß nicht vor Tränen, ob der Morgen scheint.	I do not know for tears if day has dawned.
Den breiten Strom am Bett weint' ich vor Sehnen;	I've wept that broad stream out of longing;
Blind haben mich gemacht die blut'gen Tränen.	The tears of blood have blinded me.

19

16 December 1891

Ha tanto tempo ch'eravamo muti FROM TOMMASEO

Wir haben beide lange Zeit geschwiegen,	For a long time we had both been silent,
Auf einmal kam uns nun die Sprache wieder.	Now all at once speech has returned.
Die Engel Gottes sind herabgeflogen,	The angels of God have descended,

Sie brachten nach dem Krieg den Frieden
    wieder.
Die Engel Gottes sind herabgeflogen,
Mit ihnen ist der Frieden eingezogen.
Die Liebesengel kamen über Nacht
Und haben Frieden meiner Brust gebracht.

They brought back peace after
    war.
The angels of God have descended
And with them peace has returned.
The angels of love came in the night
And have brought peace to my breast.

21

23 December 1891
M'è stato detto che tua madre 'n vuole FROM TIGRI

Man sagt mir, deine Mutter wolle es nicht;
So bleibe weg, mein Schatz, tu ihr den Willen.
Ach Liebster, nein! Tu ihr den Willen nicht,
Besuch mich doch, tu's ihr zum Trotz, im
    Stillen!
Nein, mein Geliebter, folg' ihr nimmermehr,
Tu's ihr zum Trotz, komm öfter als bisher!
Nein, höre nicht auf sie, was sie auch sage;
Tu's ihr zum Trotz, mein Lieb, komm all Tage!

They tell me your mother disapproves;
Then stay away, beloved, do as she bids.
Ah no! my love, do not do as she bids,
Defy her, visit me in secret!
No, my love, do not obey her ever again,
Defy her, come more often than before!
No, don't listen to her, whatever she
    says;
Defy her, my love, come every day!

24

25 March 1896
Non posso più mangiarlo il pane asciutto FROM TOMMASEO

Ich esse nun mein Brot nicht trocken mehr,
Ein Dorn ist mir im Fuße stecken blieben.
Umsonst nach rechts und links blick' ich
    umher,
Und keinen find ich, der mich möchte lieben.
Wenn's doch auch nur ein altes Männlein wäre,
Das mir erzeigt' ein wenig Lieb und Ehre.
Ich meine nämlich so ein wohlgestalter,
Ehrbarer Greis, etwa von meinem Alter.
Ich meine, um mich ganz zu offenbaren,
Ein altes Männlein so von vierzehn Jahren.

I no longer eat my bread dry,
I have a thorn stuck in my foot.
In vain I look around to left and
    right
And find no one who wants to love me.
If there were only a little old man
Who loved and honoured me a little.
I mean, in other words, a well-proportioned,
Honourable old man of about my age.
I mean, to be entirely frank,
A little old man of about fourteen.

25

26 March 1896
El mio moroso m'a invitato a cena FROM DALMEDICO

Mein Liebster hat zu Tische mich geladen
Und hatte doch kein Haus mich zu empfangen,
Nicht Holz noch Herd zum Kochen und zum
    Braten,
Der Hafen auch war längst entzwei gegangen.
An einem Fäßchen Wein gebrach es auch,
Und Gläser hat er gar nicht im Gebrauch;

My sweetheart invited me to dinner,
Yet had no house to receive me,
No wood nor stove for boiling or roasting,
And the cooking pot had long since broken
    in two.
There was not even a small cask of wine,
And he simply didn't use glasses;

Der Tisch war schmal, das Tafeltuch nicht besser,	The table was tiny, the table-cloth no better,
Das Brot steinhart und völlig stumpf das Messer.	The bread rock hard and the knife quite blunt.

26

28 March 1896

Me xe stà dito, e me xe stà contà FROM DALMEDICO

Ich ließ mir sagen und mir ward erzählt,	I inquired and have been informed
Der schöne Toni hungre sich zu Tode;	That handsome Toni's starving himself to death;
Seit ihn so überaus die Liebe quält,	Ever since love's tormented him so cruelly,
Nimmt er auf einen Backzahn sieben Brote.	He eats seven loaves to a molar.
Nach Tisch, damit er die Verdauung stählt,	After meals, to steel his digestion,
Verspeist er eine Wurst und sieben Brote,	He devours a sausage and seven loaves,
Und lindert nicht Tonina seine Pein,	And if Tonina doesn't ease his pain,
Bricht nächstens Hungersnot und Teurung ein.	There'll soon be an outbreak of famine and rising prices.

27

29 March 1896

E m'ero spolto per andare a letto FROM TIGRI

Schon streckt' ich aus im Bett die müden Glieder,	I'd already stretched my tired limbs out in bed,
Da tritt dein Bildnis vor mich hin, du Traute.	When you appeared to me in a vision, my love.
Gleich spring' ich auf, fahr' in die Schuhe wieder	I jump straight up, get into my shoes again
Und wandre durch die Stadt mit meiner Laute.	And walk through the town with my lute.
Ich sing' und spiele, daß die Straße schallt;	The streets resound with my singing and playing;
So manche lauscht – vorüber bin ich bald.	Many a girl listens – I have soon passed by.
So manches Mädchen hat mein Lied gerührt,	Many a girl is moved by my song,
Indes der Wind schon Sang und Klang ent-führt.	While my singing and playing is wafted away on the wind.

28

30 March 1896

Tu vai dicendo ch'io non son regina FROM TOMMASEO

Du sagst mir, daß ich keine Fürstin sei;	You tell me that I'm no princess;
Auch du bist nicht auf Spaniens Thron entsprossen.	But you're not Spanish royalty either.
Nein, Bester, stehst du auf bei Hahnenschrei,	No, my dear, when you get up at cock-crow,
Fährst du aufs Feld und nicht in Staatskarossen.	You go to the fields, and don't ride in state carriages.
Du spottest mein um meine Niedrigkeit,	You mock at my lowly station,
Doch Armut tut dem Adel nichts zuleid.	But poverty doesn't hurt the noble soul.
Du spottest, daß mir Krone fehlt und Wappen,	You mock me for having no crown or crest,
Und fährst doch selber nur mit Schusters Rappen.	But Shanks's pony is all you ride yourself.

30–31 March 1896

Lassatela passar che fa la brava FROM TOMMASEO

Laß sie nur gehn, die so die Stolze spielt,	Let her go, then, if she acts so proud,
Das Wunderkräutlein aus dem Blumenfeld.	The magic herb in a field of flowers.
Man sieht, wohin ihr blankes Auge zielt,	You can see what her bright eyes are after,
Da Tag um Tag ein andrer ihr gefällt.	For day after day she fancies a different man.
Sie treibt es grade wie Toscanas Fluß,	She carries on just like Tuscany's river
Dem jedes Berggewässer folgen muß.	Which every mountain stream must follow.
Sie treibt es wie der Arno, will mir scheinen:	She carries on just like the Arno, it seems to me:
Bald hat sie viel Bewerber, bald nicht einen.	Now wooed by many, now by none.

37

2 April 1896

E quanto tempo ho perso per amarte! FROM TOMMASEO

Wie viele Zeit verlor ich, dich zu lieben!	How much time I've lost in loving you!
Hätt' ich doch Gott geliebt in all der Zeit,	If only I'd have loved God in all that time,
Ein Platz im Paradies wär' mir verschrieben,	I should now be allotted a place in Paradise,
Ein Heilger säße dann an meiner Seit'.	A saint would be seated at my side.
Und weil ich dich geliebt, schön frisch Gesicht,	And because I've loved you, fair and fresh of face,
Verscherzt' ich mir des Paradieses Licht,	I have forfeited the light of Paradise,
Und weil ich dich geliebt, schön Veigelein,	And because I've loved you, fair violet,
Komm' ich nun nicht ins Paradies hinein.	I shall never now gain Paradise.

34

3–4 April 1896

E la mattina quando vi levate FROM TOMMASEO

Und steht Ihr früh am Morgen auf vom Bette,	And when you rise from your bed at dawn,
Scheucht Ihr vom Himmel alle Wolken fort,	You chase all clouds from the sky,
Die Sonne lockt Ihr auf die Berge dort,	You lure the sun onto those hills
Und Engelein erscheinen um die Wette	And angels compete to appear
Und bringen Schuh und Kleider Euch sofort.	And bring at once your shoes and clothes.
Dann, wenn Ihr ausgeht in die heil'ge Mette,	Then, when you go out to Holy Mass,
So zieht Ihr alle Menschen mit Euch fort,	You draw everyone along with you,
Und wenn Ihr naht der benedeiten Stätte,	And when you draw near the sacred place,
So zündet Euer Blick die Lampen an.	Your glance lights up the lamps.
Weihwasser nehmt Ihr, macht des Kreuzes Zeichen	You take holy water, make the sign of the cross,
Und netzet Eure weiße Stirn sodann	And moisten then your white brow,
Und neiget Euch und beugt die Knie ingleichen –	And bow down and bend the knee –
O wie holdselig steht Euch alles an!	Ah, how beautifully it all becomes you!
Wie hold und selig hat Euch Gott begabt,	What blessed grace has God bestowed on you,
Die Ihr der Schönheit Kron' empfangen habt!	Who have been given the crown of beauty!

Wie hold und selig wandelt Ihr im Leben;
Der Schönheit Palme ward an Euch
gegeben.

How graciously, how blessedly you walk
    through life;
The palm of beauty was bestowed on you.

29
9 April 1896
Conosco il vostro stato, fior gentile FROM TIGRI

Wohl kenn' ich Euren Stand, der nicht gering.
Ihr brauchtet nicht so tief herabzusteigen,
Zu lieben solch ein arm und niedrig Ding,
Da sich vor Euch die Allerschönsten neigen.
Die schönsten Männer leicht besiegtet Ihr,
Drum weiß ich wohl, Ihr treibt nur Spiel mit
    mir.
Ihr spottet mein, man hat mich warnen wollen,
Doch ach, Ihr seid so schön! Wer kann Euch
    grollen?

Your station is no mean one, I'm well aware.
You had no need to stoop so far
And love so poor and humble creature as me,
When even the fairest bow before you.
You easily conquered the handsomest of men,
So I know full well you're just toying with
    me.
You're mocking me, they tried to warn me,
But ah! you're so handsome! Who could be
    angry with you?

40
12 April 1896
Vorría che la tua casa tralucesse FROM TIGRI

O wär' dein Haus durchsichtig wie ein Glas,
Mein Holder, wenn ich mich vorüberstehle!
Dann säh' ich drinnen dich ohn' Unterlaß,
Wie blickt' ich dann nach dir mit ganzer Seele!
Wie viele Blicke schickte dir mein Herz,
Mehr als da Tropfen hat der Fluß im März!
Wie viele Blicke schickt' ich dir entgegen,
Mehr als da Tropfen niedersprühn im Regen!

If only your house were transparent like glass,
My love, when I steal past!
Then I would always see you within,
How I would gaze at you with all my soul!
How many looks my heart would send you,
More than the river in March has drops!
How many looks I would send you,
More than the drops that shower down in rain!

31
12 April 1896
E come vuoi ch'io faccia a stare allegra FROM TOMMASEO

Wie soll ich fröhlich sein und lachen gar,
Da du mir immer zürnest unverhohlen?
Du kommst nur einmal alle hundert Jahr,
Und dann, als hätte man dir's anbefohlen.
Was kommst du, wenn's die Deinen ungern
    sehn?
Gib frei mein Herz, dann magst du weitergehn.
Daheim mit deinen Leuten leb', in Frieden,
Denn was der Himmel will, geschieht hie-
    nieden.
Halt Frieden mit den Deinigen zu Haus,
Denn was der Himmel will, das bleibt nicht
    aus.

How can I be happy and laugh indeed,
When you always rage at me so openly?
You only visit me once in a hundred years,
And then as though it were by order.
Why do you come if your family's against it?
Set free my heart, then go on your way.
Live in peace with your own folk at home,
Since what heaven ordains, happens here on
    earth.
Keep the peace with your family at home,
Since what heaven ordains will come to
    pass.

33
13 April 1896

Se moro, ricopritemi di fiori FROM TOMMASEO

Sterb' ich, so hüllt in Blumen meine Glieder;	If I should die, then shroud my limbs in flowers;
Ich wünsche nicht, daß ihr ein Grab mir grabt.	I do not wish you to dig me a grave.
Genüber jenen Mauern legt mich nieder,	Lay me down to face those walls
Wo ihr so manchmal mich gesehen habt.	Where you have so often seen me.
Dort legt mich hin, in Regen oder Wind;	Lay me down there in wind or rain;
Gern sterb' ich, ist's um dich, geliebtes Kind.	I'll gladly die if it's for you, dear child.
Dort legt mich hin in Sonnenschein und Regen;	Lay me down there in sunshine and rain;
Ich sterbe lieblich, sterb' ich deinetwegen.	I'll die happy if I die for your sake.

39
13 April 1896

Sia benedeto 'l verde e chi lo porta FROM DALMEDICO

Gesegnet sei das Grün und wer es trägt!	Blessed be green and whoever wears it!
Ein grünes Kleid will ich mir machen lassen.	I shall have a green dress made.
Ein grünes Kleid trägt auch die Frühlingsaue,	The meadow in spring wears a green dress too.
Grün kleidet sich der Liebling meiner Augen.	And the darling of my eyes wears green.
In Grün sich kleiden ist der Jäger Brauch,	Huntsmen are wont to dress in green,
Ein grünes Kleid trägt mein Geliebter auch;	My sweetheart too is clad in green;
Das Grün steht allen Dingen lieblich an,	All things look lovely in green,
Aus Grün wächst jede schöne Frucht heran.	Every lovely fruit grows from green.

38
19 April 1896

Quando incontri i miei occhi, e fai un riso FROM TOMMASEO

Wenn du mich mit den Augen streifst und lachst,	When you glance at me fleetingly and laugh,
Sie senkst und neigst das Kinn zum Busen dann,	Then look down and sink your chin on your breast,
Bitt ich, daß du mir erst ein Zeichen machst,	I implore you to give me first a sign,
Damit ich doch mein Herz auch bänd'gen kann,	So that I might restrain my heart.
Daß ich mein Herz mag bänd'gen, zahm und still,	That I might restrain and tame my heart,
Wenn es vor großer Liebe springen will,	When it would leap up for great love,
Daß ich mein Herz mag halten in der Brust,	That I might keep my heart in my breast,
Wenn es ausbrechen will vor großer Lust.	When it would break out for great joy.

32

20 April 1896
Caro amor mio, non mi far l'adirato FROM TOMMASEO

Was soll der Zorn, mein Schatz, der dich erhitzt,	Why this anger, my love, that inflames you so?
Ich bin mir keiner Sünde ja bewußt.	For I am not conscious of any wrong-doing.
Ach, lieber nimm ein Messer wohlgespitzt	Ah, I'd rather you take a well-sharpened knife
Und tritt zu mir, durchbohre mir die Brust.	And come to me and pierce my breast.
Und taugt ein Messer nicht, so nimm ein Schwert,	And if a knife won't do, then take a sword
Daß meines Blutes Quell gen Himmel fährt.	And let my blood stream up to the sky.
Und taugt ein Schwert nicht, nimm des Dolches Stahl	And if a sword won't do, a steel dagger
Und wasch' in meinem Blut all meine Qual.	And wash away all my torment in my blood.

35

21 April 1896
Benedetta sia la madre FROM AN UNKNOWN SOURCE

Benedeit die sel'ge Mutter	Blessed be your mother in heaven,
Die so lieblich dich geboren,	Who bore you to be so gracious,
So an Schönheit auserkoren,	You the paragon of beauty –
Meine Sehnsucht fliegt dir zu!	My yearning wings its way to you!
Du so lieblich von Gebärden,	You, so gracious of gesture,
Du die Holdeste der Erden,	You, the fairest on earth,
Du mein Kleinod, meine Wonne,	You, my jewel, my rapture,
Süße, benedeit bist du!	A blessing on you, my sweet!
Wenn ich aus der Ferne schmachte	When I languish from afar
Und betrachte deine Schöne,	And behold your beauty,
Siehe wie ich beb' und stöhne,	See how I tremble and groan,
Daß ich kaum es bergen kann!	That I can hardly hide it!
Und in meiner Brust gewaltsam	And powerfully in my breast
Fühl ich Flammen sich empören,	I feel the flames rise up
Die den Frieden mir zerstören,	That destroy my peace,
Ach, der Wahnsinn faßt mich an!	Ah, madness takes hold of me!

42

23 April 1896
Non posso più cantar, che tira vento FROM TOMMASEO AND TIGRI

Nicht länger kann ich singen, denn der Wind	I can sing no more, for the wind
Weht stark und macht dem Atem was zu schaffen.	Blows fiercely and makes breathing hard.
Auch fürcht' ich, daß die Zeit umsonst verrinnt.	I fear too that time slips by in vain.
Ja wär' ich sicher, ging' ich jetzt nicht schlafen.	If I were sure, I should not now go to bed.

Ja wüßt' ich was, würd ich nicht heimspazieren	If I really knew, I should not walk home
Und einsam diese schöne Zeit verlieren.	And waste this lovely time in solitude.

43
23 April 1896
Stattene zitta, brutta cicalina FROM TIGRI

Schweig' einmal still, du garst'ger Schwätzer dort!	Shut up out there, you odious ranter!
Zum Ekel ist mir dein verwünschtes Singen.	Your cursed singing makes me sick.
Und triebst du es bis morgen früh so fort,	And even if you kept it up till morning,
Doch würde dir kein schmuckes Lied gelingen.	You'd still not manage a decent song.
Schweig' einmal still und lege dich aufs Ohr!	Shut up for once and go to bed!
Das Ständchen eines Esels zög' ich vor.	I'd sooner hear a donkey's serenade.

36
24 April 1896
Quando, bellino, al cielo salirai FROM TIGRI

Wenn du, mein Liebster, steigst zum Himmel auf,	When you, my love, ascend to heaven,
Trag' ich mein Herz dir in der Hand entgegen.	I'll come to you with my heart in hand.
So liebevoll umarmst du mich darauf,	And then you will embrace me so lovingly
Dann woll'n wir uns dem Herrn zu Füßen legen.	And we shall fall at the Lord's feet.
Und sieht der Herrgott uns're Liebesschmerzen,	And when the Lord sees the anguish of our love,
Macht er ein Herz aus zwei verliebten Herzen,	He'll make one heart of two loving hearts,
Zu einem Herzen fügt er zwei zusammen,	He'll fashion two hearts into one,
Im Paradies, umglänzt von Himmelsflammen.	In Paradise, ringed by heavenly radiance.

46
25 April 1896
Ce l'ho un amante alla città di Penna FROM TIGRI

Ich hab' in Penna einen Liebsten wohnen,	I have one lover living in Penna,
In der Maremmeneb'ne* einen andern,	Another in the plain of Maremma,
Einen im schönen Hafen von Ancona,	One in the beautiful port of Ancona,
Zum vierten muß ich nach Viterbo wandern;	For the fourth I must go to Viterbo;
Ein andrer wohnt in Casentino dort,	Another lives over in Casentino,
Der nächste lebt mit mir am selben Ort,	The next with me in my own town,
Und wieder einen hab' ich in Magione,	And I've yet another in Magione,
Vier in La Fratta, zehn in Castiglione.	Four in La Fratta, ten in Castiglione.

* Maremma in the nineteenth century was a marshy region in the south part of Tuscany; it was drained and made habitable under Mussolini's regime. The men of Maremma were proverbially short – see also 'Mein Liebster ist so klein', p. 680.

41

25 April 1896

Stanotte a mezzanotte mi levai FROM TOMMASEO

Heut' nacht erhob ich mich um Mitternacht,
Da war mein Herz mir heimlich fort-
  geschlichen.
Ich frug: Herz, wohin stürmst du so mit
  Macht?
Es sprach: Nur Euch zu sehn, sei es entwichen.
Nun sieh, wie muß es um mein Lieben stehn:
Mein Herz entweicht der Brust, um dich zu
  sehn!

Tonight I rose at midnight,
And found my heart had secretly slipped
  away.
I asked: Heart, where are you pounding to so
  fast?
It said it had only stolen away to see you.
Now you can see the force of my love:
My heart steals from my breast to see
  you!

44

26 April 1896

Se ti savessi, o falsa renegada FROM DALMEDICO

O wüßtest du, wie viel ich deinetwegen,
Du falsche Renegatin, litt zur Nacht,
Indes du im verschloßnen Haus gelegen
Und ich die Zeit im Freien zugebracht.
Als Rosenwasser diente mir der Regen,
Der Blitz hat Liebesbotschaft mir gebracht;
Ich habe Würfel mit dem Sturm gespielt,
Als unter deinem Dach ich Wache hielt.
Mein Bett war unter deinem Dach bereitet,
Der Himmel lag als Decke drauf gebreitet,
Die Schwelle deiner Tür, das war mein Kissen –
Ich Ärmster, ach, was hab' ich ausstehn müssen!

Ah, if only you knew how much for you,
False traitress, I have suffered tonight,
While you lay in your locked house
And I spent the time outside.
The rain served me for rose-water,
The lightning brought tidings of love;
I played dice with the storm,
While keeping watch beneath your eaves.
My bed was laid beneath your eaves,
With the sky spread out as my blanket,
The threshold of your door was my pillow –
How much I've had to suffer, poor wretch!

45

29 April 1896

La casa del mi' amor vada in profondo FROM TOMMASEO

Verschling' der Abgrund meines Liebsten
  Hütte,
An ihrer Stelle schäum' ein See zur Stunde.
Bleikugeln soll der Himmel drüber schütten,
Und eine Schlange hause dort im Grunde.
Drin hause eine Schlange gift'ger Art,
Die ihn vergifte, der mir untreu ward.
Drin hause eine Schlange, giftgeschwollen,
Und bring' ihm Tod, der mich verraten
  wollen!

May a chasm engulf my lover's cottage,
Let a foaming lake appear promptly in its
  place,
Let heaven rain leaden bullets on it,
And a serpent dwell in its foundations.
Let a poisonous serpent dwell there
And poison him who was unfaithful to me.
Let a snake dwell there bloated with poison
And bring death to him who tried to betray
  me!

23

30 April 1896

Non so quale canzona mi cantare FROM TOMMASEO

Was für ein Lied soll dir gesungen werden,	What kind of song shall be sung to you
Das deiner würdig sei? Wo find ich's nur?	That does you justice? Wherever can I find it?
Am liebsten grüb ich es tief aus der Erden,	I'd prefer to dig it from deep in the earth,
Gesungen noch von keiner Kreatur.	As yet unsung by any creature.
Ein Lied, das weder Mann noch Weib bis heute	A song that till now no man nor woman
Hört oder sang, selbst nicht die ältsten Leute.	Has ever heard or sung, however old they be.

Carl Friedrich Zelter (1758–1832)

Zelter's father was a stonemason, involved in the construction of Sans Souci, Frederick the Great's palace in Potsdam, and he insisted, despite Zelter's talent for music, that his son pursue a career as a mason. Zelter obliged and it was not until the 1790s, when he was over thirty, that he devoted himself to music. He became Director of the Berlin Singakademie, where he promoted the music of Bach when it was far from fashionable. Despite Zelter's revolutionary ardour in reviving Bach's music, his own compositions – vocal, for the most part – were essentially conservative. In 1796 he published his first collection of Lieder, which included settings of poems by Goethe (of Zelters's three hundred or so songs, over a hundred are to Goethe's poetry). When the great man of German letters wrote to congratulate him, an intimate friendship began to blossom, and also a voluminous correspondence that is peppered with references to Lieder and word-setting. In a letter, dated 2 May 1820, Goethe expounds his belief that the accompaniment should not seek to illustrate the imagery of a poem (see SCHUBERT p. 298); and in many other letters he stresses that in Lieder the accompaniment should be subservient to the poem. And yet he expected the composer to render the nuances of the poem, which is precisely what Zelter achieves in 'Um Mitternacht', where he employs a single basic melody but varies it in each verse to bring out 'die verschiedenste Bedeutung der einzelnen Strophen' ('the most contrasting meanings of the different verses') [Goethe 1801]. Goethe had sent him the poem in manuscript on 16 February 1818, expressing the hope that Zelter should set it to music. The composer responded immediately and sent Goethe the song on 1 March 1818. The poet was delighted; it remained one of his favourite songs, and even as late as 1827 he confided to Eckermann: „Es ist von mir noch ein lebendiger Teil und lebt in mir fort." ('It's still a living part of me and continues to live in my heart.')

Johann Wolfgang von Goethe (1749–1832)

See Beethoven, Brahms, Hensel, Loewe, Mendelssohn, Reichardt, Schubert, Strauss, Tomášek, Wolf

'Um Mitternacht' is the 120th and last Goethe poem to appear in *The Book of Lieder*, and like most of the others it is, at least partially, a love poem. Goethe confided to Eckermann in March 1828 that men of genius (amongst whom he numbered himself) experienced 'eine wiederholte Pubertät' – 'a repeated puberty' – that allowed them to live a life of undiminished intensity. Like Picasso, he felt his life to be a series of rebirths which continued into old age; like Picasso, he expressed himself by using new forms and styles; and like Picasso he was always falling in love. Among the many women of his youth were Friederike Brion

('Mailied', 'Willkommen und Abschied') and Lili Schönemann ('Neue Liebe, neues Leben'). In Weimar he became infatuated – perhaps platonically – with the older Charlotte von Stein ('Wandrers Nachtlied', 'Ein gleiches' and 'An den Mond'). After his return from Italy in 1788 he started a relationship with Christiane Vulpius ('Gefunden'), a young woman working at an artificial flower factory in Weimar; to the moral outrage of Weimar society he took her into his house, where she lived with him as his mistress and bore him five children, only one of whom survived infancy. Goethe eventually married her in 1806, and she died a decade later. In 1807, he developed a passion for the eighteen-year-old Wilhelmine Herzlieb ('Die Liebende schreibt') whom he loved 'mehr wie billig' ('more than was proper'), as he confided to Zelter on 15 January 1813. Approaching his sixty-fifth birthday, he fell in love with the thirty-year-old Marianne Jung ('Suleika I and II'), shortly before her marriage to his friend and benefactor Geheimrat von Willemer; nine years later, aged seventy-four, he was swept off his feet by the extraordinarily beautiful Ulrike von Levetzow, then aged seventeen. Goethe's love poetry was almost always joyous and life-affirming – it was only within the framework of fiction (*Faust*, *Wilhelm Meister*, *Egmont* . . .) that he seemed capable of writing tortured and unrequited poems. Exceptions such as the *Marienbader Elegie* and 'Wonne der Wehmut' merely prove the rule.

1818 Um Mitternacht / At midnight

Um Mitternacht ging ich, nicht eben gerne,
Klein kleiner Knabe, jenen Kirchhof hin
Zu Vaters Haus, des Pfarrers; Stern am Sterne,
Sie leuchteten doch alle gar zu schön;
    Um Mitternacht.

At midnight, as a very little boy, I would walk,
Far from willingly, past that churchyard
To father's vicarage; star on star,
How beautifully they all shone;
    At midnight.

Wenn ich dann ferner in des Lebens Weite
Zur Liebsten mußte, mußte, weil sie zog,
Gestirn und Nordschein über mir im Streite,
Ich gehend, kommend Seligkeiten sog;
    Um Mitternacht.

When further on in life I had to go
To my beloved, had to because she drew me on,
I saw the stars and Northern Lights compete;
I came, I went, drinking in her bliss;
    At midnight.

Bis dann zuletzt des vollen Mondes Helle
So klar und deutlich mir ins Finstere drang,
Auch der Gedanke willig, sinnig, schnelle
Sich ums Vergangne wie ums Künftige schlang;
    Um Mitternacht.

Until at last the full moon's radiance
Pierced my darkness so clearly and brightly,
That also my thoughts, willingly, meaningfully, swiftl
Embraced the past and the future;
    At midnight.

(*Britten, Pepping*)

Alexander von Zemlinsky (1871–1942)

Zemlinsky composed some 120 Lieder which, musically, suffered the misfortune of falling between two stools: considered too modern by conservatives and too tonal by the avant-garde, they were for a long time neglected. Increasingly, however, they are becoming part of the standard repertoire. As a young composer he favoured the verse of established poets such as Eichendorff, Heine and Heyse, but gradually turned to lesser-known contemporary poets such as Bierbaum, Morgenstern, George, Werfel and Maeterlinck, whose *Sechs Gesänge*, Op. 13 (translations by Oppeln-Bronikowski of 6 of Maeterlinck's *Quinze Chansons*) remain Zemlinsky's most frequently performed vocal work. Equally fine are the *Sechs Lieder* Op. 22, composed in 1934 in Vienna, soon after Zemlinsky had left Berlin, following the Nazis' rise to power. Op. 22 ends with 'Das bucklichte Männlein', a poem from *Des Knaben Wunderhorn* about a little hunchbacked man – a scarcely veiled reference to Zemlinsky's own diminutive stature. The art song was for Zemlinsky the most intimate form of musical expression, and he often chose texts that spoke to his condition or mirrored his own experiences. Both 'Irmelin Rose' and 'Entbietung' from Op. 7, for example, open with the '*Tristan* chord' – a clandestine reference to his passion for Alma Schindler, who soon became Mahler's wife, to whom the songs of Op. 7 are dedicated. Similarly laden with significance is 'Es war ein alter König' to a poem by Heine from *Vier Lieder* (1903–05), which was only published posthumously, possibly because it commented obliquely on Alma's marriage to Mahler in March 1902.

Stylistically, Zemlinsky's Lieder develop from the melodic vocal line of the early songs, through a period in which the influence of Wagner is paramount, especially in the Dehmel and Maeterlinck Lieder, to the less tuneful late songs. Although Zemlinsky shied away from twelve-note music, there is an austerity and a dissolution of tonality in many of his songs which was certainly appreciated by Anton Webern who, on 24 November 1922 wrote to Zemlinsky: „Noch bin ich ganz erfüllt von dem tiefen, erschütternden Eindruck Ihrer Lieder. Ich habe sie [. . .] einstudiert und mich dabei ununterbrochen in Extase befunden." ('I am still quite overwhelmed by the profound moving impression your songs have on me. While studying them, I found myself in a continuous state of ecstasy.')

Anonymous

1934 Das bucklichte Männlein / The little hunchbacked man Op. 22, no. 6
FROM *Des Knaben Wunderhorn*, EDITED BY ACHIM VON ARNIM AND CLEMENS BRENIANO

Will ich in mein Gärtlein gehn,	When I go into my little garden
Will ich meine Zwiebeln gießen,	To water my little onions,

Steht ein bucklicht Männlein da,	A little hunchback's standing there,
Fängt als an zu niesen.	And starts at once to sneeze.
Will ich in mein Küchel gehn,	When I go into my little kitchen
Will mein Süpplein kochen,	To heat my little soup,
Steht ein bucklicht Männlein da,	A little hunchback's standing there,
Hat mein Töpflein brochen.	Who's smashed my little bowl.
Will ich in mein Stüblein gehn,	When I go into my little room
Will mein Müslein essen,	To eat my little porridge
Steht ein bucklicht Männlein da,	A little hunchback's standing there,
Hat schon halber gessen.	Who's eaten half of it.
Setz ich mich ans Rädlein hin,	When I sit down at my little wheel
Will mein Fädlein drehen,	To weave my little thread,
Steht ein bucklicht Männlein da,	A little hunchback's standing there,
Läßt mirs Rad nicht laufen.	And stops my wheel from spinning.
Geh ich in mein Kämmerlein,	When I go into my little chamber
Will mein Bettlein machen,	To make my little bed,
Steht ein bucklicht Männlein da,	A little hunchback's standing there,
Fängt als an zu lachen.	And starts at once to laugh.
Wenn ich an mein Bänklein knie,	When I kneel down at my little pew
Will ein wenig beten,	To pray a little while,
Steht ein bucklicht Männlein da,	A little hunchback's standing there,
Fängt als an zu reden:	And starts at once to speak:
„Liebes Kindlein, ach, ich bitt,	'Dear little child, please, ah do,
Bet' für's bucklicht Männlein mit!"	Pray for the little hunchback too.'

Richard Dehmel (1863–1920)

See Schoenberg

?1900 Entbietung / Summons Op. 7, no. 2

Schmück dir das Haar mit wildem Mohn,	Deck your hair with wild poppies,
die Nacht ist da,	night is here,
all ihre Sterne glühen schon.	all its stars gleam.
All ihre Sterne glühn heut Dir!	All of them gleam tonight for you!
du weißt es ja:	You know well:
all ihre Sterne glühn in mir!	all its stars gleam inside me!
Dein Haar ist schwarz, dein Haar ist wild	Your hair is black, your hair is wild
und knistert unter meiner Glut;	and crackles beneath my passion;
und wenn sie schwillt,	and when my passion surges,
jagt sie mit Macht	it chases the red blooms and your
die roten Blüten und dein Blut	blood
hoch in die höchste Mitternacht.	high into the highest midnight.

In deinen Augen glimmt ein Licht,
so grau in grün,
wie dort die Nacht den Stern umflicht.
Wann kommst du?! – Meine Fackeln loh'n!
laß glühn, laß glühn!
Schmück mir dein Haar mit wildem Mohn!

In your eyes a light gleams,
a sort of green-encircled grey,
like night enveloping that star.
When will you come?! – My torches blaze!
let them burn, let them burn!
Deck your hair for me with wild poppies!

Heinrich Heine (1797–1856)

See Mendelssohn, Robert Schumann, Wolf

1903 Es war ein alter König / There was an aged monarch Op. posth.

Es war ein alter König,
Sein Herz war schwer, sein Haupt war grau;
Der arme alte König,
Er nahm eine junge Frau.

There was an aged monarch,
His heart was sore, his head was grey;
The poor and aged monarch,
He took a youthful wife.

Es war ein junger Page,
Blond war sein Haupt, leicht war sein Sinn;
Er trug die seidne Schleppe
Der jungen Königin.

There was a handsome page-boy,
His head was blond, his heart was light;
He carried the silken train
Behind the youthful queen.

Kennst du das alte Liedchen?
Es klingt so süß, es klingt so trüb!
Sie mußten beide sterben,
Sie hatten sich viel zu lieb.
(*Cornelius, Grieg, Rubinstein, Vesque von
Püttlingen, Wolf*)

Do you know the age-old story?
It sounds so sweet, it sounds so sad!
Both of them had to die,
They loved each other too much.

Johann Rudolf Zumsteeg (1760–1802)

Zumsteeg composed some three hundred Lieder and ballads which, though rarely heard today, were once highly prized and much performed. Their rhapsodic form, pianistic depiction of mood and extensive use of recitative, greatly influenced the early ballads of Franz Schubert, six of whose songs are directly modelled on Zumsteeg's settings of the same texts: *Hagars Klage*, *Lied der Liebe*, *Nachtgesang*, *Ritter Toggenburg*, *Die Erwartung* and *Skolie*. According to Josef von Spaun in *Aufzeichnungen über meinen Verkehr mit Franz Schubert* (1858), Schubert admired Zumsteeg's Lieder:

> Er hatte mehrere Päcke Zumsteegscher Lieder vor sich und sagte mir, daß ihn diese Lieder auf das tiefste ergreifen. „Hören Sie", sagte er, „einmal das Lied, das ich hier habe", und da sang er mit schon halb brechender Stimme 'Colma', dann zeigte er mir 'Die Erwartung' (die 'Maria Stuart')*, den 'Ritter Toggenburg' etc. Er sagte, er könne tagelang in diesen Liedern schwelgen. Dieser Vorliebe in seiner Jugend verdanken wir wohl die Richtung, die Schubert genommen.

> He had several piles of Zumsteeg Lieder before him and told me that these songs moved him most profoundly. 'Listen to this song', he said, 'that I have here', and he proceeded to sing 'Colma' in a faltering voice – after which he showed me 'Die Erwartung' (the 'Maria Stuart' song)* and 'Ritter Toggenburg' etc. He said he could revel in these songs for days on end. It was his youthful predilection for them that caused Schubert's development to take the course it did.

Zumsteeg taught music at the Carlsschule in Stuttgart, where in 1791 he assumed responsibility for German music at the Court theatre. He enjoyed a close friendship with Schiller and wrote music for the songs in *Die Räuber*, which Schiller published in the second edition of the play, adding 'daß man den Text bei der Musik vergessen wird' ('that the poems will be forgotten, once the music is heard'). Zumsteeg's compositions include twelve stage-works and a number of choral and instrumental pieces, but it is his ballads and Lieder that have lasted best. Two of his most successful songs are *Maria Stuart*, mentioned by Spaun above, and a delightful setting of Gleim's *Ob ich dich liebe*. The text of the first is taken from Schiller's play at the beginning of Act 3 where Mary Stuart, talking to her confidante, longs in vain for freedom.

---

* Spaun's memory seems defective here – 'Die Erwartung' (also set by Schubert) and 'Maria Stuart' are two different songs.

Johann Wilhelm Ludwig Gleim (1719–1803)

See Beethoven

Ob ich dich liebe / Whether I love you

Ob ich dich liebe, weiß ich nicht.
Seh ich nur einmal dein Gesicht,
Seh dir ins Auge nur einmal,
Frei wird mein Herz von aller Qual.
Gott weiß, wie mir so wohl geschicht!
Ob ich dich liebe, weiß ich nicht.

Whether I love you, I do not know.
I only have to see your face,
I only have to gaze into your eyes,
And my heart is freed from all torment.
God knows how I feel such joy!
Whether I love you, I do not know.

Friedrich Schiller (1759–1805)

See Schubert

Maria Stuart / Maria Stuart

O Dank, Dank diesen freundlich grünen
  Bäumen,
Die meines Kerkers Mauern mir verstecken!
Ich will mich frei und glücklich träumen,
Warum aus meinem süßen Wahn mich wecken?
Umfängt mich nicht der weite Himmelsschoß?
Die Blicke, frei und fessellos,
Ergehen sich in ungemeßnen Räumen.
Dort, wo die grauen Nebelberge ragen,
Fängt meines Reiches Grenze an,
Und diese Wolken, die nach Mittag jagen,
Sie suchen Frankreichs fernen Ozean.

Eilende Wolken! Segler der Lüfte!
Wer mit euch wanderte, mit euch schiffte!
Grüßet mir freundlich mein Jugendland!
Ich bin gefangen, ich bin in Banden,
Ach, ich hab keinen andern Gesandten!
Frei in Lüften ist eure Bahn,
Ihr seid nicht dieser Königin untertan.

Dort legt ein Fischer den Nachen an!
Dieses elende Werkzeug könnte mich retten,
Brächte mich schnell zu befreundeten Städten.
Spärlich nährt es den dürftigen Mann.
Beladen wollt ich ihn reich mit Schätzen,
Einen Zug sollt er tun, wie er keinen getan,
Das Glück sollt er finden in seinen Netzen,
Nähm er mich ein in den rettenden Kahn.

I give thanks to these friendly green trees
That hide from me my dungeon walls!
I wish to dream I am happy and free,
Why wake me from my sweet illusion?
Am I not embraced by the vast vault of heaven?
My gaze, free and unfettered,
Revels in the boundless spaces.
There, where the grey misty mountains loom,
Is where my empire's boundaries begin,
And these clouds, scudding South,
Seek the distant ocean of France's shore.

Fleeting clouds! Birds of the air!
O to meander, to set sail with you!
Give friendly greetings to the land of my
  youth!
I am imprisoned, I am in chains,
Alas, I have no other envoy!
Free through the skies you pursue your path,
You are not subject to this Queen.

Over there a fisherman anchors his boat!
This wretched vessel could rescue me,
Could bring me swiftly to friendly towns.
It barely earns the poor wretch a living.
I would shower him with such treasures,
He would make a catch like never before,
He would find fortune in his nets,
If he would rescue me in his boat.

Index of poets and translators

Allmers, Hermann (1821–1902): 34–5
Andersen, Hans Christian (1805–75): 433–5, 525
Arnim, Ludwig Achim von (1781–1831): 539,

Baumberg, Gabriele von (1768–1839): 240
Beer, Michael (1800–33): 237
Bethge, Hans (1876–1946): 211–215
Bierbaum, Otto Julius (1865–1910): 540–1
Bodenstedt, Friedrich von (1819–92): 119
Boelitz, Martin (1874–1918): 262–3
Brecht, Bertolt (1898–1956): 105–6
Brentano, Clemens (1778–1842): 35–6, 542–4
Bruchmann, Franz von (1798–1867): 290–2
Bürger, Gottfried August (1747–94): 3–4, 544–5
Burns, Robert (1759–96): 506, 508, 510–11, 513–15
Byron, George Gordon (1788–1824): 225–6, 511–12

Campe, Johann Heinrich (1746–1818): 241
Candidus, Karl (1817–72): 36–7
Carpani, Giuseppe (1752–1825): 5
Chamisso, Adelbert von (1781–1838): 164–5, 248–9, 435–43
Claudius, Matthias (1740–1815): 292–94, 427–8
Collin, Matthäus von (1779–1824): 294–5
Conrat, Hugo (dates unknown): 37–9
Cornelius, Peter (1824–74): 97–103
Craigher, Jacob Nicolaus de Jachelutta (1797–1855): 295–8

Dach, Simon (1605–59): 531–2
Dahn, Felix (1834–1912): 545–6
Daumer, Georg (1800–75): 39–44,
Dehmel, Richard (1863–1920): 144–5, 249, 280–2, 547–8, 696–7
Des Knaben Wunderhorn: 187–201, 524, 527, 538, 695–6
Diepenbrock, Melchior von (1798–1853): 527–8
Dreves, Leberecht Blücher (1816–70): 444
Droysen, J. G. (1808–84): 236

Eichendorff, Joseph von (1788–1857): 126–7, 226–7, 249–56, 269–70, 444–53, 563, 579–89

Falke, Gustav (1853–1916): 548
Fanshawe, Catherine Maria (1765–1834): 511–12
Feuchtersleben, Ernst Freiherr von (1806–49): 227
Flem[m]ing, Paul (1609–40): 44–5
Fontane, Theodor (1819–98): 166–9
Freiligrath, Ferdinand von (1810–76): 113, 158–9, 512–13

Geibel, Emanuel (1815–84): 45, 228, 453–8, 520, 534–5, 652–7, 659–60, 662, 664–6, 668, 670–1, 672–3, 674–5
Gellert, Christian Fürchtegott (1715–69): 5–7
Gerhard, Wilhelm (1780–1858): 506, 508, 510–11, 513–15
George, Stefan (1868–1933): 282–6, 575–7
Gilm, Hermann von (1812–64): 549–51
Gleim, Johann Wilhelm Ludwig (1719–1803): 7–8, 122, 699
Goeble, Heinrich (dates unknown): 8

Goethe, Johann Wolfgang von (1749–1832): 9–15, 45–7, 93–6, 119, 127, 169–177, 222–3, 228–9, 241–2, 264–6, 270, 298–322, 505, 506–8, 526, 530, 551, 564, 589–611, 693–4,
Grillparzer, Franz (1791–1872): 128–9
Groth, Klaus (1819–99): 47–50
Gruppe, Otto (1804–76): 50–1
Gubitz, Friedrich Wilhelm (1786–1870): 570–4

Hafiz (c.1327–90): 40–2,
Hagedorn, Friedrich von (1709–54): 242–3
Halm, Friedrich (1806–71): 51–2,
Hart, Heinrich (1855–1906): 552
Hartleben, Otto Erich (1864–1905): 30
Haschka, Lorenz Leopold (1749–1827): 122–3
Haugwitz, Paul von (1791–1856): 15
Hauptmann, Carl (1858–1921): 28
Hebbel, Friedrich (1813–63): 25–6, 159, 525
Heine, Heinrich (1797–1856): 52–4, 114, 153–7, 159–60, 229–31, 322–4, 458–76, 507, 514–15, 532, 552–3, 611–13, 697
Henckell, Karl (1864–1929): 553–4
Herder, Johann Gottfried (1744–1803): 177–180
Herrosee, Karl Friedrich (1754–1821): 15–16
Herwegh, Georg (1817–75): 160–1
Hesse, Hermann (1877–1962): 271–2, 562–3
Heyse, Paul (1830–1914): 54–5, 220–1, 651–73, 675–92
Hiemer, Franz Karl: 574
Hoffmann von Fallersleben (1798–1874): 55–7, 516–19, 522, 524, 526–7, 535
Hofmannsthal, Hugo von (1874–1929): 216–19
Hohenberg, Paul (dates unknown): 30
Hölderlin, Friedrich (1770–1843): 89–92, 106–9, 110–12
Hölty, Ludwig (1748–76): 57–9, 231–2, 325–9
Honold, Elisabeth (dates unknown): 145

Jacobi, Johann Georg (1740–1814): 243–4, 329–40,
Jeitteles, Alois (1794–1858): 16–19

Kalbeck, Max (1850–1921): 59–60
Kaltneker, Hans (1895–1919): 146
Kannegiesser, Karl (1781–1861): 511–12
Kapper, Siegfried (1821–79): 34
Keller, Gottfried (1819–90): 256–7, 272–4, 286–7, 613–16
Kerner, Justinus (1786–1862): 476–83, 616–17
Kerr, Alfred (1867–1904): 146–7
Kletke, Hermann (1813–86): 523
Klingemann, Karl (1798–1862): 232–3, 233–5
Klopstock, Friedrich Gottlieb (1724–1803): 115–16, 330–1
Koch, Ernst (1808–58): 535–6
Körner, Julius (1783–1873): 511
Körner, Theodor (1791–1813): 331–2
Kosegarten, Ludwig Theobul (1758–1818): 332–3
Kugler, Franz (1808–58): 60
Kuh, Emil (1828–76): 161

Lappe, Karl (1773–1843): 333–4

701

Index of titles and first lines

Songs with titles are indexed by title, others by their opening words. Cycles are shown in italics.